Contents

REPAIRS & OVERHAUL

Introduced in March 1993, the Ford Mondeo models are available in four-door Saloon, five-door Hatchback and five-door Estate configurations. All feature a high standard of equipment, with driver/passenger safety in accidents being a particularly high design priority; all models are fitted with features such as side impact bars in all doors, 'anti-submarine' seats combined with seat belt pre-tensioners, and an airbag fitted to the steering wheel. Vehicle security is enhanced, with an in-built alarm system and engine immobiliser being fitted as standard, as well as double-locking doors with shielded locks, and security-coded audio equipment.

The Zetec 16-valve four-cylinder petrol engine is a new design, available in 1.6, 1.8 and 2.0 litre capacities. It is controlled by a sophisticated engine management system, which combines multi-point sequential fuel injection and distributorless ignition systems with evaporative emissions control, exhaust gas recirculation and a three-way regulated catalytic converter (with a pulse-air system for rapid warm-up) to ensure that the vehicle complies with the most stringent of the emissions control standards currently in force, and yet provides the levels of performance and fuel economy expected.

In September 1994, the petrol engine range was completed, with the introduction of the 2.5 litre Duratec V6 engine. Designed and built in the USA, where it is fitted to the parallel Ford Contour range, this 24-valve transverse design is particularly light and compact.

The range received a major facelift in October 1996, with heavily-modified front and rear styling reflecting the 'edge' design philosophy pioneered by the Ka. The already-acclaimed suspension and steering were further improved, and the latest EEC-V engine management system was fitted to all models

The transversely-mounted engine drives the front roadwheels through either a five-speed manual transmission with a cable- or hydraulically-operated clutch, or through an electronically-controlled four-speed automatic transmission.

The fully-independent suspension is by MacPherson strut on all four roadwheels, located by transverse lower arms at the front, and by transverse and trailing arms at the rear; anti-roll bars are fitted at the front and rear. The Estate rear suspension is of a different design, to give maximum loadspace inside the vehicle, with self-levelling suspension units available as an option. On some models, the suspension is electronically-controlled through an Adaptive Damping System.

The steering is power-assisted, the pump being belt-driven from the engine, and the rack-and-pinion steering gear mounted behind the engine.

1997 Mondeo V6 Ghia Saloon

The vacuum servo-assisted brakes are disc at the front, with drums at the rear on most models; disc rear brakes and an electronically-controlled Anti-lock Braking System (ABS) are available on some models, with a Traction Control System (TCS) available as a further option where ABS is fitted.

1993 Mondeo 1.8 GLX Estate

Provided that regular servicing is carried out in accordance with the manufacturer's recommendations, the Mondeo should prove a reliable and economical car. The engine compartment is well-designed, and most of the items needing frequent attention are easily accessible.

Your Ford Mondeo manual

The aim of this manual is to help you get the best value from your vehicle. It can do so in several ways. It can help you decide what work must be done (even should you choose to get it done by a garage). It will also provide information on routine maintenance and servicing, and give a logical course of action and diagnosis when random faults occur. However, it is hoped that you will use the manual by tackling the work yourself. On simpler jobs it may even be quicker than booking the car into a garage and going there twice, to leave and collect it. Perhaps most important, a lot of money can be saved by avoiding the costs a garage must charge to cover its labour and overheads.

The manual has drawings and descriptions to show the function of the various components so that their layout can be understood. Tasks are described and photographed in a clear step-by-step sequence. The illustrations are numbered by the Section number and paragraph number to which they relate - if there is more than one illustration per paragraph, the sequence is denoted alphabetically.

References to the 'left' or 'right' of the vehicle are in the sense of a person in the driver's seat, facing forwards.

Acknowledgements

Thanks are due to Champion Spark Plug, who supplied the illustrations showing spark plug conditions, and to Duckhams Oils, who provided lubrication data. Thanks are also due to Draper Tools Limited, who provided some of the workshop tools, and to all those people at Sparkford who helped in the production of this manual.

Working on your car can be dangerous. This page shows just some of the potential risks and hazards, with the aim of creating a safety-conscious attitude.

General hazards

Scalding

• Don't remove the radiator or expansion tank cap while the engine is hot.
• Engine oil, automatic transmission fluid or power steering fluid may also be dangerously hot if the engine has recently been running.

Burning

• Beware of burns from the exhaust system and from any part of the engine. Brake discs and drums can also be extremely hot immediately after use.

Crushing

• When working under or near a raised vehicle, always supplement the jack with axle stands, or use drive-on ramps. ***Never venture under a car which is only supported by a jack.***
• Take care if loosening or tightening high-torque nuts when the vehicle is on stands. Initial loosening and final tightening should be done with the wheels on the ground.

Fire

• Fuel is highly flammable; fuel vapour is explosive.
• Don't let fuel spill onto a hot engine.
• Do not smoke or allow naked lights (including pilot lights) anywhere near a vehicle being worked on. Also beware of creating sparks (electrically or by use of tools).
• Fuel vapour is heavier than air, so don't work on the fuel system with the vehicle over an inspection pit.
• Another cause of fire is an electrical overload or short-circuit. Take care when repairing or modifying the vehicle wiring.
• Keep a fire extinguisher handy, of a type suitable for use on fuel and electrical fires.

Electric shock

• Ignition HT voltage can be dangerous, especially to people with heart problems or a pacemaker. Don't work on or near the ignition system with the engine running or the ignition switched on.
• Mains voltage is also dangerous. Make sure that any mains-operated equipment is correctly earthed. Mains power points should be protected by a residual current device (RCD) circuit breaker.

Fume or gas intoxication

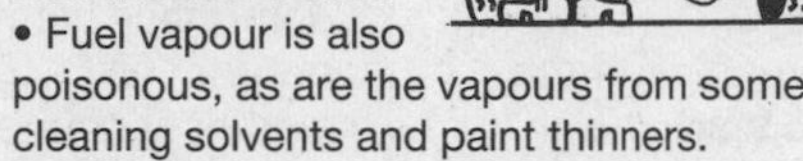

• Exhaust fumes are poisonous; they often contain carbon monoxide, which is rapidly fatal if inhaled. Never run the engine in a confined space such as a garage with the doors shut.
• Fuel vapour is also poisonous, as are the vapours from some cleaning solvents and paint thinners.

Poisonous or irritant substances

• Avoid skin contact with battery acid and with any fuel, fluid or lubricant, especially antifreeze, brake hydraulic fluid and Diesel fuel. Don't syphon them by mouth. If such a substance is swallowed or gets into the eyes, seek medical advice.
• Prolonged contact with used engine oil can cause skin cancer. Wear gloves or use a barrier cream if necessary. Change out of oil-soaked clothes and do not keep oily rags in your pocket.
• Air conditioning refrigerant forms a poisonous gas if exposed to a naked flame (including a cigarette). It can also cause skin burns on contact.

Asbestos

• Asbestos dust can cause cancer if inhaled or swallowed. Asbestos may be found in gaskets and in brake and clutch linings. When dealing with such components it is safest to assume that they contain asbestos.

Special hazards

Hydrofluoric acid

• This extremely corrosive acid is formed when certain types of synthetic rubber, found in some O-rings, oil seals, fuel hoses etc, are exposed to temperatures above 400°C. The rubber changes into a charred or sticky substance containing the acid. *Once formed, the acid remains dangerous for years. If it gets onto the skin, it may be necessary to amputate the limb concerned.*
• When dealing with a vehicle which has suffered a fire, or with components salvaged from such a vehicle, wear protective gloves and discard them after use.

The battery

• Batteries contain sulphuric acid, which attacks clothing, eyes and skin. Take care when topping-up or carrying the battery.
• The hydrogen gas given off by the battery is highly explosive. Never cause a spark or allow a naked light nearby. Be careful when connecting and disconnecting battery chargers or jump leads.

Air bags

• Air bags can cause injury if they go off accidentally. Take care when removing the steering wheel and/or facia. Special storage instructions may apply.

Diesel injection equipment

• Diesel injection pumps supply fuel at very high pressure. Take care when working on the fuel injectors and fuel pipes.

Warning: Never expose the hands, face or any other part of the body to injector spray; the fuel can penetrate the skin with potentially fatal results.

Remember...

DO

• Do use eye protection when using power tools, and when working under the vehicle.

• Do wear gloves or use barrier cream to protect your hands when necessary.

• Do get someone to check periodically that all is well when working alone on the vehicle.

• Do keep loose clothing and long hair well out of the way of moving mechanical parts.

• Do remove rings, wristwatch etc, before working on the vehicle – especially the electrical system.

• Do ensure that any lifting or jacking equipment has a safe working load rating adequate for the job.

DON'T

• Don't attempt to lift a heavy component which may be beyond your capability – get assistance.

• Don't rush to finish a job, or take unverified short cuts.

• Don't use ill-fitting tools which may slip and cause injury.

• Don't leave tools or parts lying around where someone can trip over them. Mop up oil and fuel spills at once.

• Don't allow children or pets to play in or near a vehicle being worked on.

The following pages are intended to help in dealing with common roadside emergencies and breakdowns. You will find more detailed fault finding information at the back of the manual, and repair information in the main chapters.

If your car won't start and the starter motor doesn't turn

- ☐ If it's a model with automatic transmission, make sure the selector is in 'P' or 'N'.
- ☐ Open the bonnet and make sure that the battery terminals are clean and tight.
- ☐ Switch on the headlights and try to start the engine. If the headlights go very dim when you're trying to start, the battery is probably flat. Get out of trouble by jump starting (see next page) using a friend's car.

If your car won't start even though the starter motor turns as normal

- ☐ Is there fuel in the tank?
- ☐ Is there moisture on electrical components under the bonnet? Switch off the ignition, then wipe off any obvious dampness with a dry cloth. Spray a water-repellent aerosol product (WD-40 or equivalent) on ignition and fuel system electrical connectors like those shown in the photos. Pay special attention to the ignition coil wiring connector and HT leads.

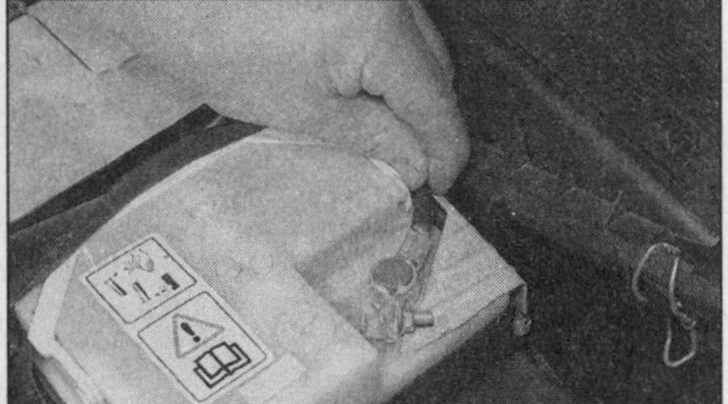

A Check the security and condition of the battery connections.

B Check the wiring plug connections to the ignition coil.

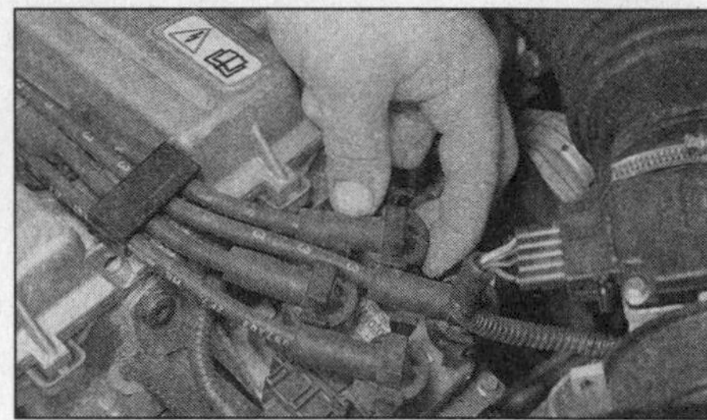

C Check the HT lead connections at the ignition coil.

Check that electrical connections are secure (with the ignition switched off). Spray the connector plugs with a water-dispersant spray like WD40 if you suspect a problem due to damp.

D Check that the HT leads are securely connected to the spark plugs (where possible).

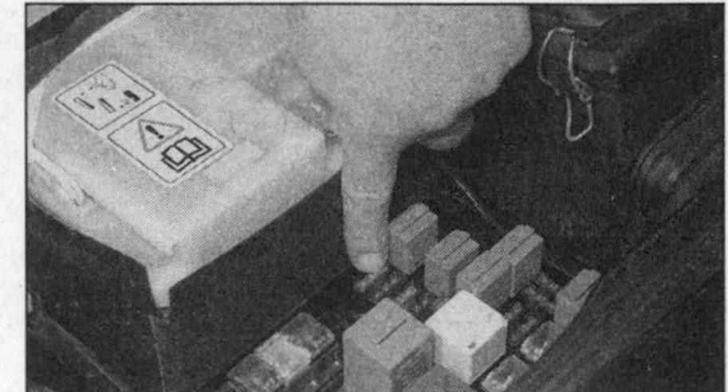

E Check that none of the engine compartment fuses have blown.

Jump starting

HAYNES HiNT *Jump starting will get you out of trouble, but you must correct whatever made the battery go flat in the first place. There are three possibilities:*

***1** The battery has been drained by repeated attempts to start, or by leaving the lights on.*

***2** The charging system is not working properly (alternator drivebelt slack or broken, alternator wiring fault or alternator itself faulty).*

***3** The battery itself is at fault (electrolyte low, or battery worn out).*

When jump-starting a car using a booster battery, observe the following precautions:

✔ Before connecting the booster battery, make sure that the ignition is switched off.

✔ Ensure that all electrical equipment (lights, heater, wipers, etc) is switched off.

✔ Take note of any special precautions printed on the battery case.

✔ Make sure that the booster battery is the same voltage as the discharged one in the vehicle.

✔ If the battery is being jump-started from the battery in another vehicle, the two vehicles MUST NOT TOUCH each other.

✔ Make sure that the transmission is in neutral (or PARK, in the case of automatic transmission).

1 Connect one end of the red jump lead to the positive (+) terminal of the flat battery

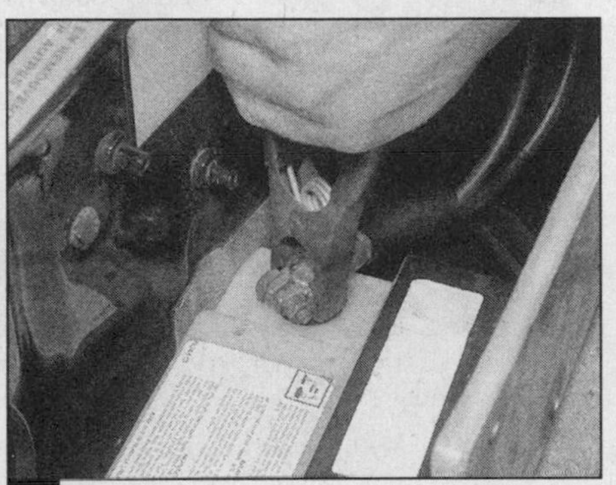

2 Connect the other end of the red lead to the positive (+) terminal of the booster battery.

3 Connect one end of the black jump lead to the negative (-) terminal of the booster battery

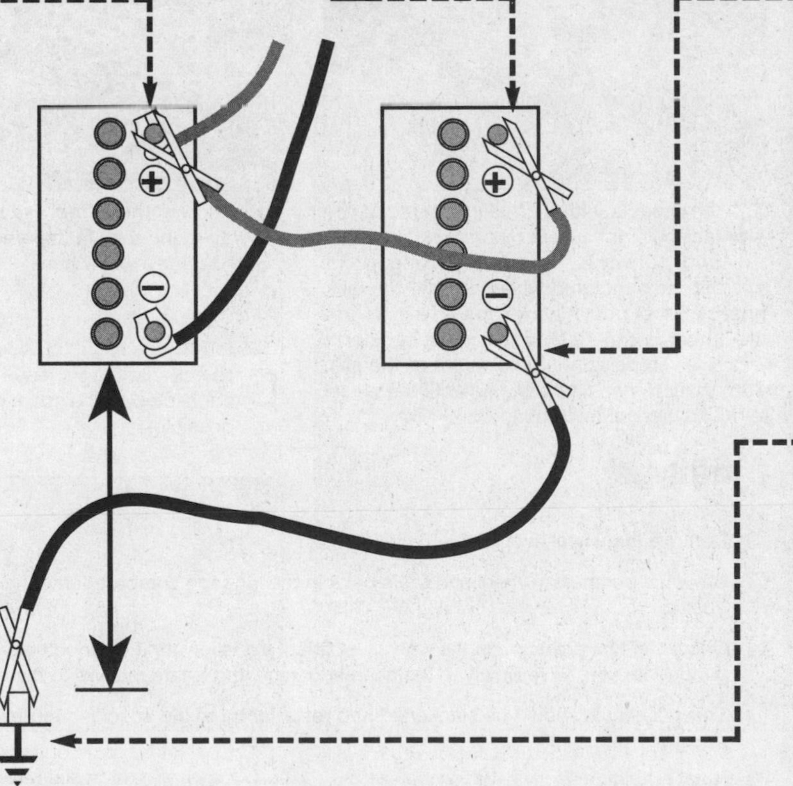

4 Connect the other end of the black jump lead to a bolt or bracket on the engine block, well away from the battery, on the vehicle to be started.

5 Make sure that the jump leads will not come into contact with the fan, drive-belts or other moving parts of the engine.

6 Start the engine using the booster battery and run it at idle speed. Switch on the lights, rear window demister and heater blower motor, then disconnect the jump leads in the reverse order of connection. Turn off the lights etc.

Wheel changing

Warning: Do not change a wheel in a situation where you risk being hit by another vehicle. On busy roads, try to stop in a lay-by or a gateway. Be wary of passing traffic while changing the wheel - it is easy to become distracted by the job in hand.

Preparation

- ☐ When a puncture occurs, stop as soon as it is safe to do so.
- ☐ Park on firm level ground, if possible, and well out of the way of other traffic.
- ☐ Use hazard warning lights if necessary.
- ☐ If you have one, use a warning triangle to alert other drivers of your presence.
- ☐ Apply the handbrake and engage first or reverse gear (or Park on models with automatic transmission.
- ☐ Chock the wheel diagonally opposite the one being removed – a couple of large stones will do for this.
- ☐ If the ground is soft, use a flat piece of wood to spread the load under the jack.

Changing the wheel

1 The spare wheel and tools are stored in the luggage compartment. Fold back the floor covering and lift up the cover panel.

2 Unscrew the retainer, and lift the spare wheel out.

3 Unscrew the retainer, and lift the jack and wheel brace out of the wheel well. The screw-in towing eye is also provided in the wheel well.

4 Where applicable, using the flat end of the wheelbrace, prise off the centre cover or wheel trim for access to the wheel nuts. Slacken each wheel nut by a half turn, using the wheelbrace. If the bolts are too tight, DON'T stand on the wheelbrace to undo them - call for assistance from one of the motoring organisations.

5 On models with side skirts, remove the jacking point covers by pressing upwards and outwards. Use the jacking point nearest the punctured wheel. Locate the jack head at the point in the lower sill flange indicated by the indentation in the sill (don't jack the vehicle at any other point of the sill). Turn the jack handle clockwise until the wheel is raised clear of the ground.

6 Unscrew the wheel nuts, noting which way round they fit (tapered side inwards), and remove the wheel.

7 Fit the spare wheel, and screw on the nuts. Lightly tighten the nuts with the wheel-brace, then lower the vehicle to the ground. Securely tighten the wheel nuts, then refit the wheel trim or centre cover, as applicable.

Finally...

- ☐ Remove the wheel chocks.
- ☐ Stow the punctured wheel and tools back in the luggage compartment, and secure them in position.
- ☐ Check the tyre pressure on the wheel just fitted. If it is low, or if you don't have a pressure gauge with you, drive slowly to the nearest garage and inflate the tyre to the right pressure.
- ☐ The wheel nuts should be slackened and retightened to the specified torque at the earliest possible opportunity.
- ☐ Have the punctured wheel repaired at the earliest opportunity, or another puncture will leave you stranded.

Identifying leaks

Puddles on the garage floor or drive, or obvious wetness under the bonnet or underneath the car, suggest a leak that needs investigating. It can sometimes be difficult to decide where the leak is coming from, especially if the engine bay is very dirty already. Leaking oil or fluid can also be blown rearwards by the passage of air under the car, giving a false impression of where the problem lies.

Warning: Most automotive oils and fluids are poisonous. Wash them off skin, and change out of contaminated clothing, without delay.

The smell of a fluid leaking from the car may provide a clue to what's leaking. Some fluids are distictively coloured. It may help to clean the car carefully and to park it over some clean paper overnight as an aid to locating the source of the leak. Remember that some leaks may only occur while the engine is running.

Sump oil

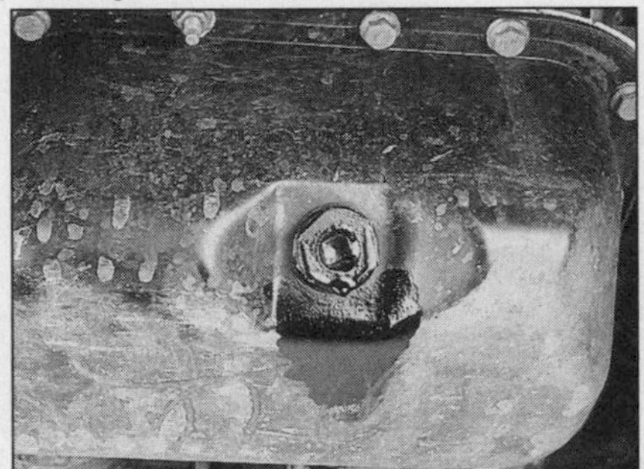

Engine oil may leak from the drain plug...

Oil from filter

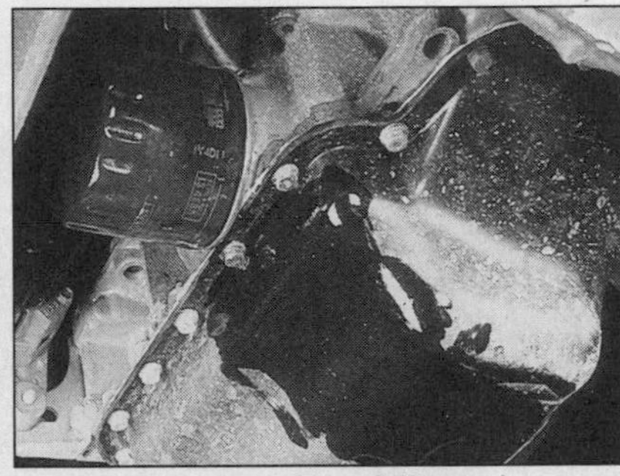

...or from the base of the oil filter.

Gearbox oil

Gearbox oil can leak from the seals at the inboard ends of the driveshafts.

Antifreeze

Leaking antifreeze often leaves a crystalline deposit like this.

Brake fluid

A leak occurring at a wheel is almost certainly brake fluid.

Power steering fluid

Power steering fluid may leak from the pipe connectors on the steering rack.

Towing

When all else fails, you may find yourself having to get a tow home - or of course you may be helping somebody else. Long-distance recovery should only be done by a garage or breakdown service. For shorter distances, DIY towing using another car is easy enough, but observe the following points:

☐ Use a proper tow-rope - they are not expensive. The vehicle being towed must display an 'ON TOW' sign in its rear window.

☐ Always turn the ignition key to the 'on' position when the vehicle is being towed, so that the steering lock is released, and that the direction indicator and brake lights will work.

☐ On early models, the front towing eye is below or behind a cover in the front bumper. The rear towing eye is located below the rear bumper, on all early models and later Estates.

☐ On later models, the front towing eye is of the screw-in type, and is found in the spare wheel well. The towing eye screws into the threaded hole below the right-hand headlight, accessible after prising out a cover in the bumper, and has a left-hand thread - ie it screws in anti-clockwise (see illustration). On later Saloons and Hatchbacks, a similar arrangement is used for the rear towing eye.

☐ Before being towed, release the handbrake and make sure the transmission is in neutral.

☐ Note that greater-than-usual pedal pressure will be required to operate the brakes, since the vacuum servo unit is only operational with the engine running.

☐ The driver of the car being towed must keep the tow-rope taut at all times to avoid snatching.

☐ Make sure that both drivers know the route before setting off.

☐ Only drive at moderate speeds, and keep the distance towed to a minimum. Drive smoothly, and allow plenty of time for slowing down at junctions.

☐ On models with automatic transmission, special precautions apply. If in doubt, do not tow, or transmission damage may result.

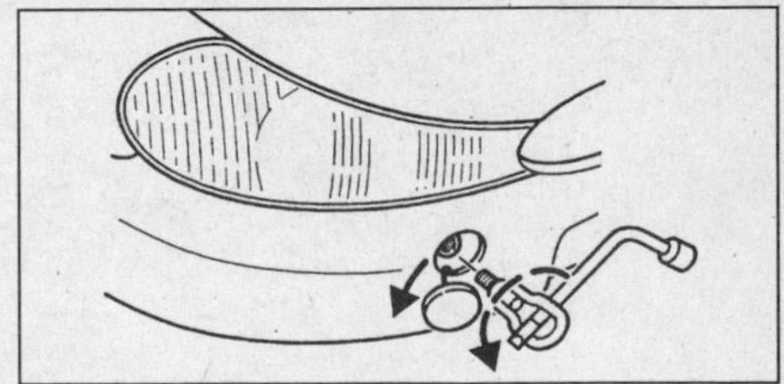

Front towing eye

Introduction

There are some very simple checks which need only take a few minutes to carry out, but which could save you a lot of inconvenience and expense.

These "Weekly checks" require no great skill or special tools, and the small amount of time they take to perform could prove to be very well spent, for example;

☐ Keeping an eye on tyre condition and pressures, will not only help to stop them wearing out prematurely, but could also save your life.

☐ Many breakdowns are caused by electrical problems. Battery-related faults are particularly common, and a quick check on a regular basis will often prevent the majority of these.

☐ If your car develops a brake fluid leak, the first time you might know about it is when your brakes don't work properly. Checking the level regularly will give advance warning of this kind of problem.

☐ If the oil or coolant levels run low, the cost of repairing any engine damage will be far greater than fixing the leak, for example.

Underbonnet check points

◀ **Four-cylinder engine**

A *Engine oil level dipstick*
B *Engine oil filler cap*
C *Coolant expansion tank*
D *Brake (and clutch) fluid reservoir*
E *Power steering fluid reservoir*
F *Screen washer fluid reservoir*
G *Battery*

◀ **V6 engine**

A *Engine oil level dipstick*
B *Engine oil filler cap*
C *Coolant expansion tank*
D *Brake (and clutch) fluid reservoir*
E *Power steering fluid reservoir*
F *Screen washer fluid reservoir*
G *Battery*

Engine oil level

Before you start

✔ Make sure that your car is on level ground.
✔ Check the oil level before the car is driven, or at least 5 minutes after the engine has been switched off.

If the oil is checked immediately after driving the vehicle, some of the oil will remain in the upper engine components, resulting in an inaccurate reading on the dipstick!

The correct oil

Modern engines place great demands on their oil. It is very important that the correct oil for your car is used (See "Lubricants, fluids and tyre pressures" on page 0•16).

Car Care

● If you have to add oil frequently, you should check whether you have any oil leaks. Place some clean paper under the car overnight, and check for stains in the morning. If there are no leaks, the engine may be burning oil *(see "Fault Finding").*

● Always maintain the level between the upper and lower dipstick marks (see photo 2). If the level is too low severe engine damage may occur. Oil seal failure may result if the engine is overfilled by adding too much oil.

1 The dipstick top is brightly coloured for easy identification (see *'Underbonnet check points'* on page 0•10 for exact location). Withdraw the dipstick. Using a clean rag or paper towel, remove all oil from the dipstick.

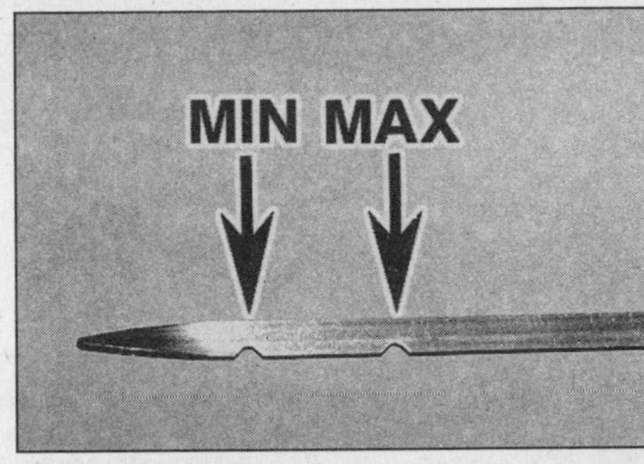

2 Insert the clean dipstick into the tube as far as it will go, then withdraw it again. Note the oil level on the end of the dipstick, which should be between the 'MAX' and 'MIN' marks. If the oil level is only just above, or below, the 'MIN' mark, topping-up is required.

3 Oil is added through the filler cap. Lift off or unscrew the cap . . .

4 . . . and top-up the level; a funnel may be useful in reducing spillage. Add the oil slowly, checking the level on the dipstick often, and allowing time for the oil to fall to the sump. Add oil until the level is just up to the 'MAX' mark on the dipstick - don't overfill (see '*Car care*' left).

Power steering fluid level

Before you start:

✔ Park the vehicle on level ground.
✔ Set the steering wheel straight-ahead.
✔ The engine should be turned off.

For the check to be accurate, the steering must not be turned once the engine has been stopped.

Safety First!

● The need for frequent topping-up indicates a leak, which should be investigated immediately.

1 The reservoir is located at the right-hand rear corner of the engine compartment. The fluid level is visible through the reservoir body; when the system is at operating temperature, the level should be up to the 'MAX' mark on the side of the reservoir.

2 If topping-up is required, wipe clean the area around the reservoir filler neck and unscrew the filler cap from the reservoir.

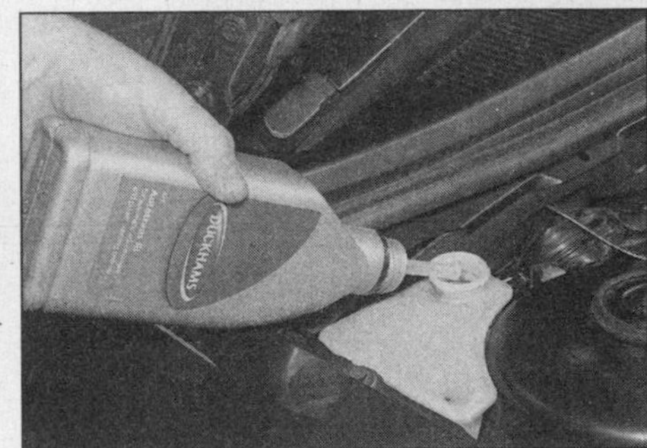

3 When topping-up, use the specified type of fluid and do not overfill the reservoir. When the level is correct, securely refit the cap.

Brake (and clutch*) fluid level

***On models with a hydraulically-operated clutch, this information is also applicable to the clutch fluid level**

Warning:

● Brake fluid can harm your eyes and damage painted surfaces, so use extreme caution when handling and pouring it.

● Do not use fluid that has been standing open for some time, as it absorbs moisture from the air, which can cause a dangerous loss of braking effectiveness.

• Make sure that your car is on level ground.

• The fluid level in the reservoir will drop slightly as the brake pads wear down, but the fluid level must never be allowed to drop below the "MIN" mark.

Safety First!

● If the reservoir requires repeated topping-up this is an indication of a fluid leak somewhere in the system, which should be investigated immediately.

● If a leak is suspected, the car should not be driven until the braking system has been checked. Never take any risks where brakes are concerned.

1 The brake fluid reservoir is located on the left-hand side of the engine compartment.

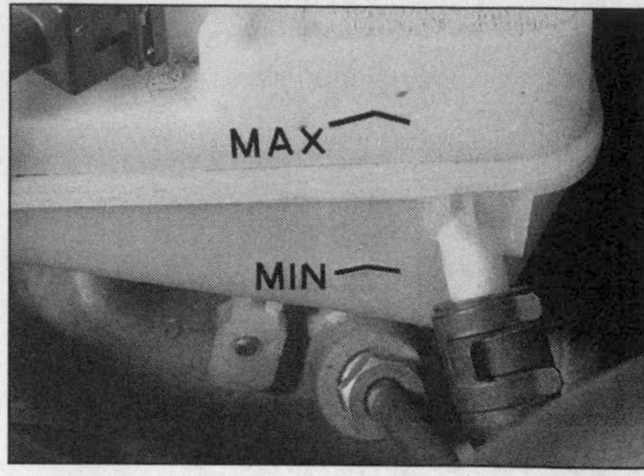

2 The 'MAX' and 'MIN' marks are indicated on the side of the reservoir. The fluid level must be kept between the marks at all times.

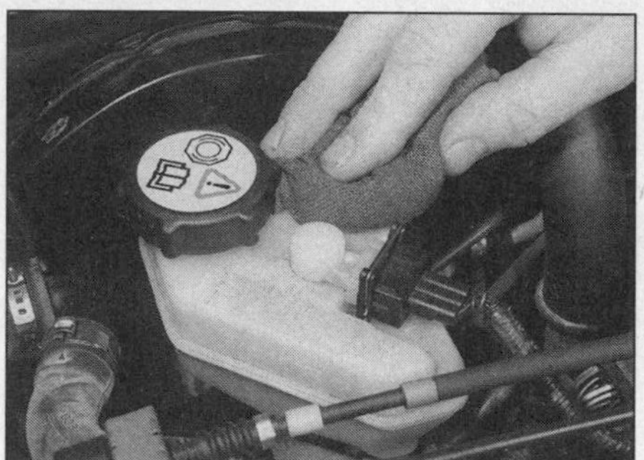

3 If topping-up is necessary, first wipe clean the area around the filler cap to prevent dirt entering the hydraulic system, then unscrew and remove the reservoir cap. Inspect the reservoir; if the fluid is dirty, the hydraulic system should be drained and refilled (see Chapter 1).

4 Carefully add fluid, taking care not to spill it onto the surrounding components. Use only the specified fluid; mixing different types can cause damage to the system. After topping-up to the correct level, securely refit the cap and wipe off any spilt fluid.

Screen washer fluid level*

***** The underbonnet reservoir also serves the tailgate washer, and the headlight washers, where fitted.***

Screenwash additives not only keep the winscreen clean during foul weather, they also prevent the washer system freezing in cold weather - which is when you are likely to need it most. Don't top up using plain water as the screenwash will become too diluted, and will freeze during cold weather. ***On no account use coolant antifreeze in the washer system - this could discolour or damage paintwork.***

1 The screen washer fluid reservoir filler neck is located in the right-hand front corner of the engine compartment, behind the headlight.

2 The screen washer level cannot easily be seen. Remove the filler cap, and look down the filler neck - if fluid is not visible, topping-up may be required.

3 When topping-up the reservoir, add a screenwash additive in the quantities recommended on the bottle.

Coolant level

Warning: DO NOT attempt to remove the expansion tank pressure cap when the engine is hot, as there is a very great risk of scalding. Do not leave open containers of coolant about, as it is poisonous.

Car Care

- With a sealed-type cooling system, adding coolant should not be necessary on a regular basis. If frequent topping-up is required, it is likely there is a leak. Check the radiator, all hoses and joint faces for signs of staining or wetness, and rectify as necessary.

- It is important that antifreeze is used in the cooling system all year round, not just during the winter months. Don't top-up with water alone, as the antifreeze will become too diluted.

1 The coolant level varies with the temperature of the engine, and is visible through the expansion tank. When the engine is cold, the coolant level should be between the 'MAX' mark on the side . . .

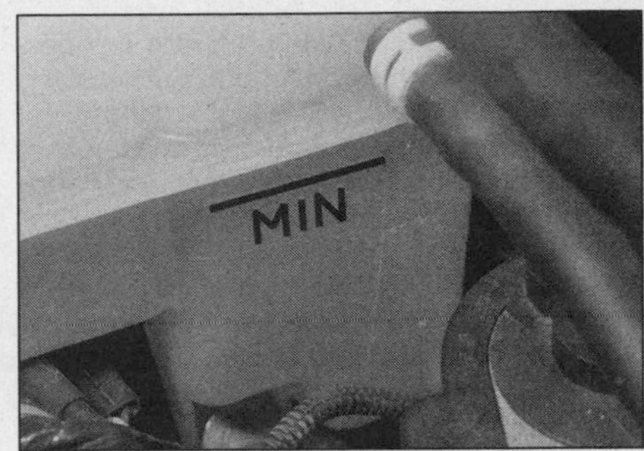

2 . . . and the 'MIN' mark on the front of the reservoir. When the engine is hot, the level may rise slightly above the 'MAX' mark.

3 If topping up is necessary, **wait until the engine is cold**. Slowly unscrew the expansion tank cap, to release any pressure present in the cooling system, and remove it.

4 Add a mixture of water and antifreeze to the expansion tank until the coolant level is halfway between the level marks. Refit the cap and tighten it securely.

Wiper blades

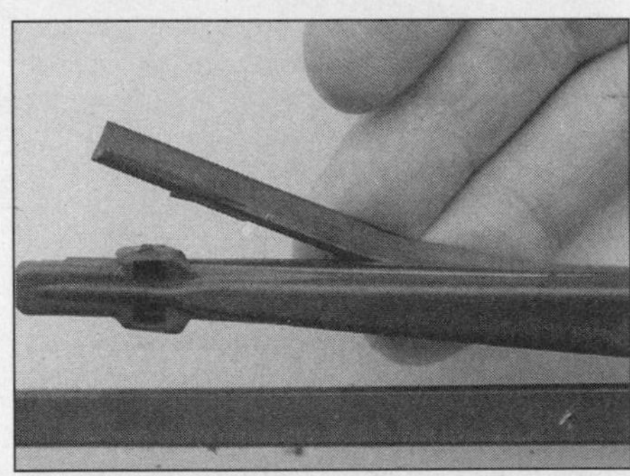

1 Check the condition of the wiper blades; if they are cracked or show any signs of deterioration, or if the glass swept area is smeared, renew them. Wiper blades should be renewed annually, regardless of their apparent condition.

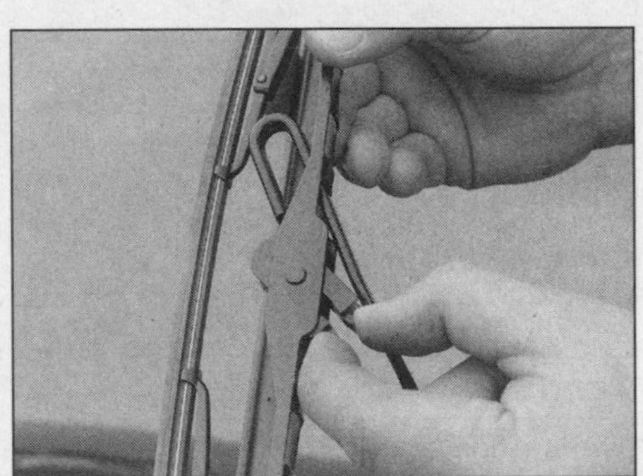

2 To remove a windscreen wiper blade, pull the arm fully away from the screen until it locks. Swivel the blade through 90°, press the locking tab with your fingers and slide the blade out of the arm's hooked end.

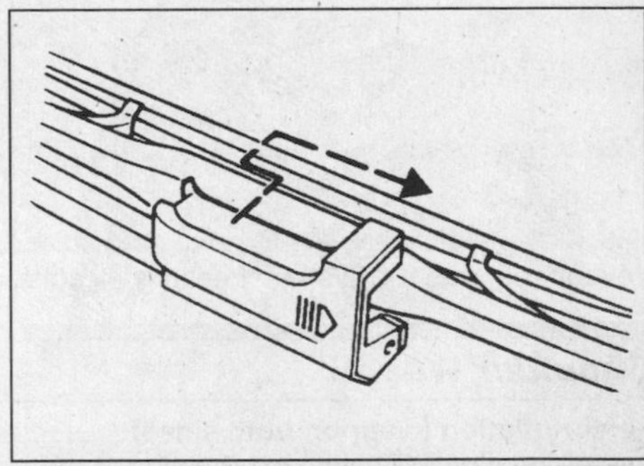

3 Don't forget to check the tailgate wiper blade as well (where applicable). Remove the blade using a similar technique to the windscreen wiper blades.

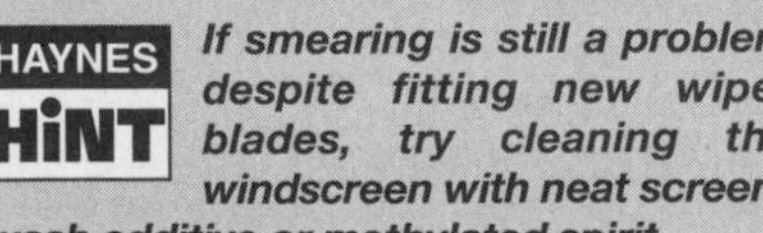

If smearing is still a problem despite fitting new wiper blades, try cleaning the windscreen with neat screen-wash additive or methylated spirit.

Tyre condition and pressure

It is very important that tyres are in good condition, and at the correct pressure - having a tyre failure at any speed is highly dangerous. Tyre wear is influenced by driving style - harsh braking and acceleration, or fast cornering, will all produce more rapid tyre wear. As a general rule, the front tyres wear out faster than the rears. Interchanging the tyres from front to rear ("rotating" the tyres) may result in more even wear. However, if this is completely effective, you may have the expense of replacing all four tyres at once!

Remove any nails or stones embedded in the tread before they penetrate the tyre to cause deflation. If removal of a nail does reveal that the tyre has been punctured, refit the nail so that its point of penetration is marked. Then immediately change the wheel, and have the tyre repaired by a tyre dealer.

Regularly check the tyres for damage in the form of cuts or bulges, especially in the sidewalls. Periodically remove the wheels, and clean any dirt or mud from the inside and outside surfaces. Examine the wheel rims for signs of rusting, corrosion or other damage. Light alloy wheels are easily damaged by "kerbing" whilst parking; steel wheels may also become dented or buckled. A new wheel is very often the only way to overcome severe damage.

New tyres should be balanced when they are fitted, but it may become necessary to re-balance them as they wear, or if the balance weights fitted to the wheel rim should fall off. Unbalanced tyres will wear more quickly, as will the steering and suspension components. Wheel imbalance is normally signified by vibration, particularly at a certain speed (typically around 50 mph). If this vibration is felt only through the steering, then it is likely that just the front wheels need balancing. If, however, the vibration is felt through the whole car, the rear wheels could be out of balance. Wheel balancing should be carried out by a tyre dealer or garage.

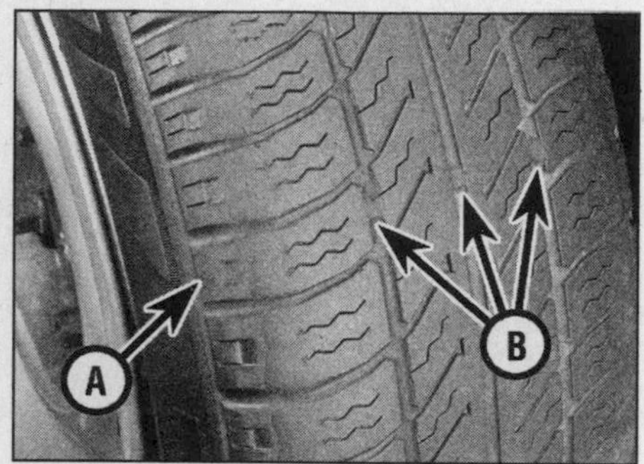

1 ***Tread Depth - visual check***
The original tyres have tread wear safety bands (B), which will appear when the tread depth reaches approximately 1.6 mm. The band positions are indicated by a triangular mark on the tyre sidewall (A).

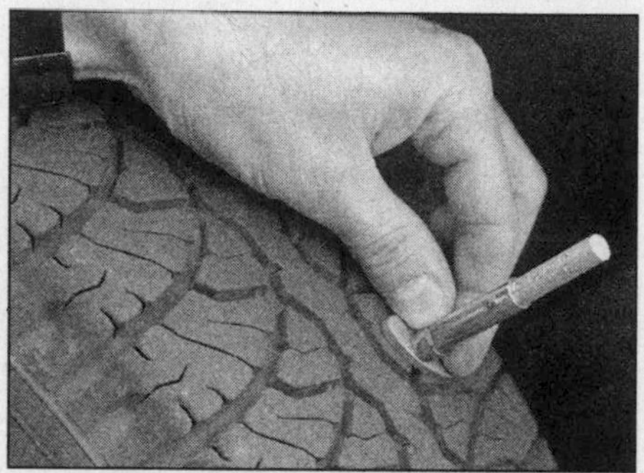

2 ***Tread Depth - manual check***
Alternatively, tread wear can be monitored with a simple, inexpensive device known as a tread depth indicator gauge.

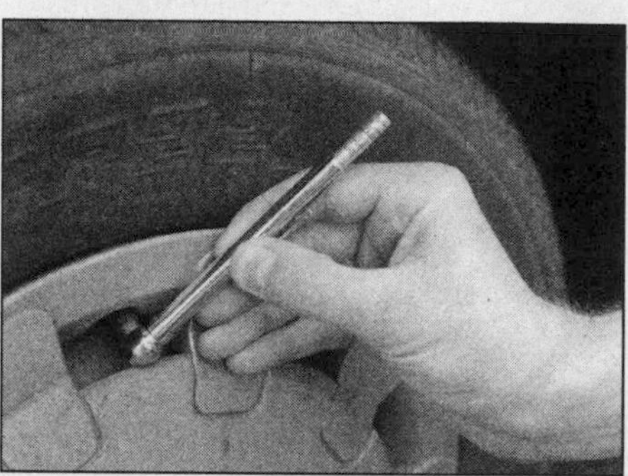

3 ***Tyre Pressure Check***
Check the tyre pressures regularly with the tyres cold. Do not adjust the tyre pressures immediately after the vehicle has been used, or an inaccurate setting will result. Tyre pressures are shown on page 0•16.

Tyre tread wear patterns

Shoulder Wear

Underinflation (wear on both sides)
Under-inflation will cause overheating of the tyre, because the tyre will flex too much, and the tread will not sit correctly on the road surface. This will cause a loss of grip and excessive wear, not to mention the danger of sudden tyre failure due to heat build-up.
Check and adjust pressures
Incorrect wheel camber (wear on one side)
Repair or renew suspension parts
Hard cornering
Reduce speed!

Centre Wear

Overinflation
Over-inflation will cause rapid wear of the centre part of the tyre tread, coupled with reduced grip, harsher ride, and the danger of shock damage occurring in the tyre casing.
Check and adjust pressures

If you sometimes have to inflate your car's tyres to the higher pressures specified for maximum load or sustained high speed, don't forget to reduce the pressures to normal afterwards.

Uneven Wear

Front tyres may wear unevenly as a result of wheel misalignment. Most tyre dealers and garages can check and adjust the wheel alignment (or "tracking") for a modest charge.
Incorrect camber or castor
Repair or renew suspension parts
Malfunctioning suspension
Repair or renew suspension parts
Unbalanced wheel
Balance tyres
Incorrect toe setting
Adjust front wheel alignment
Note: *The feathered edge of the tread which typifies toe wear is best checked by feel.*

Battery

***Caution:** Before carrying out any work on the vehicle battery, read the precautions given in "Safety first" at the start of this manual.*

✔ Make sure that the battery tray is in good condition, and that the clamp is tight. Corrosion on the tray, retaining clamp and the battery itself can be removed with a solution of water and baking soda. Thoroughly rinse all cleaned areas with water. Any metal parts damaged by corrosion should be covered with a zinc-based primer, then painted.

✔ Periodically (approximately every three months), check the charge condition of the battery as described in Chapter 5A.

✔ If the battery is flat, and you need to jump start your vehicle, see **Roadside Repairs**.

Battery corrosion can be kept to a minimum by applying a layer of petroleum jelly to the clamps and terminals after they are reconnected.

1 The battery is located in the left-hand front corner of the engine compartment. The exterior of the battery should be inspected periodically for damage such as a cracked case or cover.

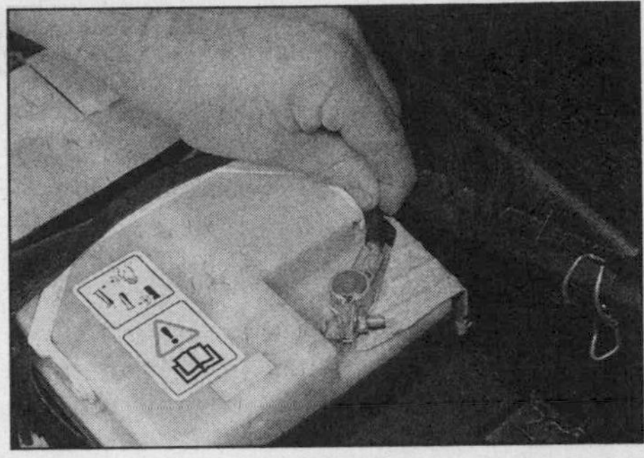

2 Check the tightness of battery clamps to ensure good electrical connections. You should not be able to move them. Also check each cable for cracks and frayed conductors.

3 If corrosion (white, fluffy deposits) is evident, remove the cables from the battery terminals, clean them with a small wire brush, then refit them. Automotive stores sell a useful tool for cleaning the battery post . . .

4 . . . as well as the battery cable clamps

Bulbs and fuses

✔ Check all external lights and the horn. Refer to the appropriate Sections of Chapter 12 for details if any of the circuits are found to be inoperative.

✔ Visually check all accessible wiring connectors, harnesses and retaining clips for security, and for signs of chafing or damage.

If you need to check your brake lights and indicators unaided, back up to a wall or garage door and operate the lights. The reflected light should show if they are working properly.

1 If a single indicator light, stop-light or headlight has failed, it is likely that a bulb has blown and will need to be replaced. Refer to Chapter 12 for details. If both stop-lights have failed, it is possible that the switch has failed (see Chapter 9).

2 If more than one indicator light or tail light has failed, it is likely that either a fuse has blown or that there is a fault in the circuit (see Chapter 12). The main fusebox is located below the facia panel on the passenger's side, and is accessed by a lever behind the glovebox. The auxiliary fusebox is located next to the battery - unclip and remove the cover for access.

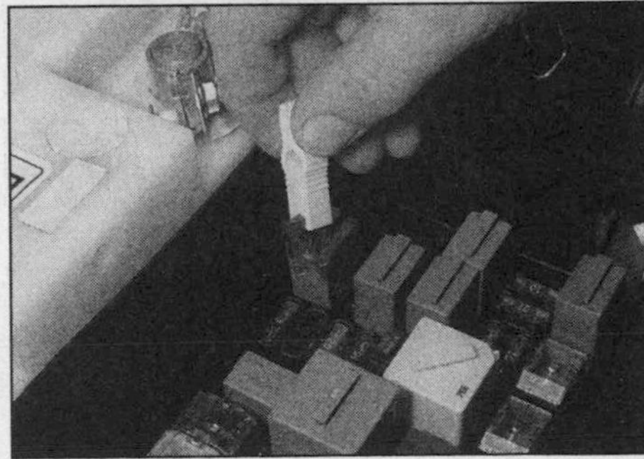

3 To replace a blown fuse, simply pull it out and fit a new fuse of the correct rating (see Chapter 12). If the fuse blows again, it is important that you find out why - a complete checking procedure is given in Chapter 12.

Lubricants and fluids

Engine	Multigrade engine oil, viscosity SAE 5W/30, 5W/40, 10W/30 or 10W/40*, to Ford specification WSS-M2C912-A1, API SH or ACEA A1-96 *(Duckhams QXR Premium Petrol Engine Oil)*
Cooling system	Motorcraft Super Plus 4 antifreeze to Ford specification ESD-M97B49-A, or Motorcraft Super Plus 2000 antifreeze to Ford specification WSS-M97B44-D *(Duckhams Antifreeze and Summer Coolant)*
Manual transmission	Gear oil to Ford specification WSD-M2C200B
Automatic transmission	Automatic transmission fluid to Ford specification ESP-M2C 166-H *(Duckhams ATF Autotrans III)*
Brake (and clutch) hydraulic system	Hydraulic fluid to Ford specification ESDM 6C57-A, Super DOT 4 *(Duckhams Universal Brake & Clutch Fluid)*
Power steering	Automatic transmission fluid to Ford specification ESP-M2C 166-H *(Duckhams ATF Autotrans III)*

***Note:** *Do not use engine oils of higher viscosity, eg 15W/40, 15W/50 or 20W/50, as doing so may lead to engine running problems. Certain oil additives may increase effective oil viscosity, and are not recommended in these engines.*

Choosing your engine oil

Engines need oil, not only to lubricate moving parts and minimise wear, but also to maximise power output and to improve fuel economy. By introducing a simplified and improved range of engine oils, Duckhams has taken away the confusion and made it easier for you to choose the right oil for your engine.

HOW ENGINE OIL WORKS

• *Beating friction*

Without oil, the moving surfaces inside your engine will rub together, heat up and melt, quickly causing the engine to seize. Engine oil creates a film which separates these moving parts, preventing wear and heat build-up.

• *Cooling hot-spots*

Temperatures inside the engine can exceed 1000° C. The engine oil circulates and acts as a coolant, transferring heat from the hot-spots to the sump.

• *Cleaning the engine internally*

Good quality engine oils clean the inside of your engine, collecting and dispersing combustion deposits and controlling them until they are trapped by the oil filter or flushed out at oil change.

OIL CARE - FOLLOW THE CODE

To handle and dispose of used engine oil safely, always:

- ***Avoid skin contact with used engine oil. Repeated or prolonged contact can be harmful.***
- ***Dispose of used oil and empty packs in a responsible manner in an authorised disposal site. Call 0800 663366 to find the one nearest to you. Never tip oil down drains or onto the ground.***

Tyre pressures

Tyre pressures (tyres cold):	**Front**	**Rear**
Normally-laden (up to 3 people)	2.1 bar (31 psi)	2.1 bar (31 psi)
Fully-laden	2.4 bar (35 psi)	2.8 bar (41 psi)

Note 1: *Pressures apply to original-equipment tyres, and may vary if any other make of tyre is fitted; check with the tyre manufacturer or supplier for the correct pressures if necessary.*

Note 2: *For sustained high speeds above 100 mph (160 km/h), increased pressures are necessary. Consult the driver's handbook supplied with the vehicle.*

Chapter 1
Routine maintenance and servicing

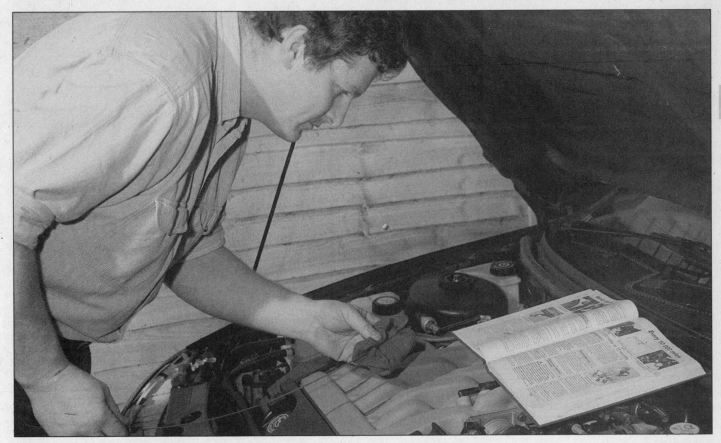

Contents

1

Degrees of difficulty

Easy, suitable for novice with little experience 

Fairly easy, suitable for beginner with some experience 

Fairly difficult, suitable for competent DIY mechanic 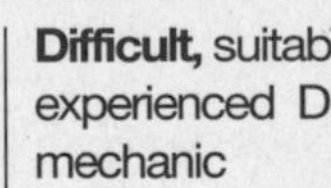

Difficult, suitable for experienced DIY mechanic 

Very difficult, suitable for expert DIY or professional 

Lubricants and fluids — Refer to the end of *'Weekly checks'*.

Capacities

Engine oil:	
At oil and filter change:	
Four-cylinder engines	4.25 litres
V6 engine	5.5 litres
Difference between dipstick minimum and maximum marks	0.5 to 1.0 litre
Cooling system:	
Manual transmission models:	
Four-cylinder engines	6.6 litres
V6 engine	9.5 litres
Automatic transmission models:	
Four-cylinder engines	7.1 litres
V6 engine	9.7 litres
Fuel tank	61.5 litres
Manual transmission	2.6 litres
Automatic transmission:	
Four-cylinder engines:	
Total, including fluid cooler	9.0 litres
Drain and refill	5.5 litres
V6 engines:	
Total, including fluid cooler	10.3 litres
Drain and refill	6.5 litres

Engine

Oil filter	Champion C148

Cooling system

Coolant protection at 40% antifreeze/water mixture ratio:	
Slush point	-25°C (-13°F)
Solidifying point	-30°C (-22°F)

Fuel system

Air filter element	Champion U632
Fuel filter	Champion L218

Ignition system

Firing order:	
Four-cylinder engines	1-3-4-2
V6 engine	1-4-2-5-3-6
No 1 cylinder position:	
Four-cylinder engines	Timing belt end of engine
V6 engine	Timing chain end, rear (in car)
Spark plugs:*	
Type / Electrode gap:	
Four-cylinder engines	Champion RE7PYC5 / 1.3 mm
V6 engine	Champion RS9YCC / 0.9 mm

** Information on spark plug types and electrode gaps is as recommended by Champion. Where alternative types are used, refer to their manufacturer's recommendations.*

Braking system

Note: *No minimum lining thicknesses are given by Ford - the following is given as a general recommendation. If the pad wear warning light comes on before the front brake pad linings reach the minimum thickness, the pads should nevertheless be renewed immediately.*

Minimum front or rear brake pad lining thickness	1.5 mm
Minimum rear brake shoe lining thickness	1.0 mm

Torque wrench settings

	Nm	lbf ft
Automatic transmission fluid drain plug	27	20
Engine oil drain plug:		
Four-cylinder engines	25	18
V6 engine	26	19
Manual transmission filler/level plug	35	26
Roadwheel nuts	85	63
Seat belt mounting bolts	38	28
Spark plugs:		
Four-cylinder engines	15	11
V6 engine	14	10

The manufacturer's recommended maintenance schedule for these vehicles is as described below - note that the schedule starts from the vehicle's date of registration. These are the minimum maintenance intervals recommended by the factory for Mondeos driven daily, but subjected only to 'normal' use. If you wish to keep your vehicle in peak condition at all times, you may wish to perform some of these procedures even more often. Because frequent maintenance enhances the efficiency, performance and resale value of your vehicle, we encourage you to do so. If your usage is not 'normal', shorter intervals are also recommended - the most important examples of these are noted in the schedule. These shorter intervals apply particularly if you drive in dusty areas, tow a caravan or trailer, sit with the engine idling or drive at low speeds for extended periods (ie, in heavy traffic), or drive for short distances (less than four miles) in below-freezing temperatures.

When your vehicle is new, it should be serviced by a Ford dealer service department to protect the factory warranty. In many cases, the initial maintenance check is done at no cost to the owner. Note that this first free service (carried out by the selling dealer 1500 miles or 3 months after delivery), although an important check for a new vehicle, is not part of the regular maintenance schedule, and is therefore not mentioned here.

Every 250 miles (400 km) or weekly

- ☐ Refer to *'Weekly checks'*

Every 10 000 miles or 12 months, whichever occurs first

Note: *If the vehicle is used regularly for very short (less than 10 miles), stop/go journeys, the oil and filter should be renewed between services (ie, every 5000 miles/6 months). Seek the advice of a local Ford dealer if in doubt on this point.*

- ☐ Change the engine oil and filter (Section 3)
- ☐ Check the battery (Section 4)
- ☐ Check the auxiliary drivebelt(s) (Section 5)
- ☐ Check the automatic transmission fluid level (Section 6)
- ☐ Check the electrical system (Section 7)
- ☐ Check under the bonnet for fluid leaks and hose condition (Section 8)
- ☐ Check the condition of all engine compartment wiring (Section 9)
- ☐ Check the condition of all air conditioning system components (Section 10)
- ☐ Check the manual transmission oil level (Section 11)
- ☐ Check the seat belts (Section 12)
- ☐ Check the adjustment of the clutch pedal (Section 13)
- ☐ Lubricate the automatic transmission linkage (Section 14)
- ☐ Check the steering, suspension and roadwheels (Section 15)
- ☐ Check the driveshaft rubber gaiters and CV joints (Section 16)
- ☐ Check the exhaust system (Section 17)
- ☐ Check the underbody, and all fuel/brake lines (Section 18)
- ☐ Check the braking system (Section 19)
- ☐ Check the doors and bonnet, and lubricate their hinges and locks (Section 20)
- ☐ Check the security of all roadwheel nuts (Section 21)
- ☐ Road test (Section 22)

Every 20 000 miles or 2 years, whichever occurs first

In addition to the relevant items listed in the previous services, carry out the following:

- ☐ Renew the ventilation system pollen filter (Section 23)

Every 30 000 miles or 3 years, whichever occurs first

In addition to the relevant items listed in the previous services, carry out the following:

- ☐ Renew the air filter element (Section 24). Note that this task must be carried out at more frequent intervals if the vehicle is used in dusty or polluted conditions
- ☐ Check the Positive Crankcase Ventilation (PCV) system, and clean the filter (Section 25)
- ☐ Renew the automatic transmission fluid (Section 26)

Every 3 years (regardless of mileage)

- ☐ Renew the brake fluid (Section 27)
- ☐ Renew the coolant (Section 28)

Every 40 000 miles

In addition to the relevant items listed in the previous services, carry out the following:

- ☐ Renew the spark plugs - four-cylinder engines (Section 29)

Every 4 years (regardless of mileage)

- ☐ Check the condition of the expansion tank pressure cap seal (Section 30)

Every 60 000 miles

In addition to the relevant items listed in the previous services, carry out the following:

- ☐ Renew the fuel filter (Section 31)
- ☐ Renew the spark plugs - V6 engine (Section 32)

Every 80 000 miles or 5 years, whichever occurs first

In addition to the relevant items listed in the previous services, carry out the following:

- ☐ Renew the timing belt - four-cylinder engines only (Section 33)

Note: *It is strongly recommended that the timing belt renewal interval is reduced to 30 000 miles or 3 years on vehicles which are subjected to intensive use, ie. mainly short journeys or a lot of stop-start driving. The actual belt renewal interval is therefore very much up to the individual owner, but bear in mind that severe engine damage will result if the belt breaks.*

Underbonnet view of a 4-cylinder engine model

1. *Coolant expansion tank filler cap*
2. *Front suspension strut mounting nut*
3. *Power steering fluid reservoir*
4. *Accelerator cable*
5. *Spark plugs and HT leads*
6. *Intake plenum chamber*
7. *Ignition coil*
8. *Brake (and clutch) fluid reservoir*
9. *Airflow meter*
10. *Air cleaner*
11. *Battery*
12. *Fusebox*
13. *Engine oil filler cap*
14. *Engine oil level dipstick*
15. *Washer fluid reservoir*

Underbonnet view of a V6 engine model

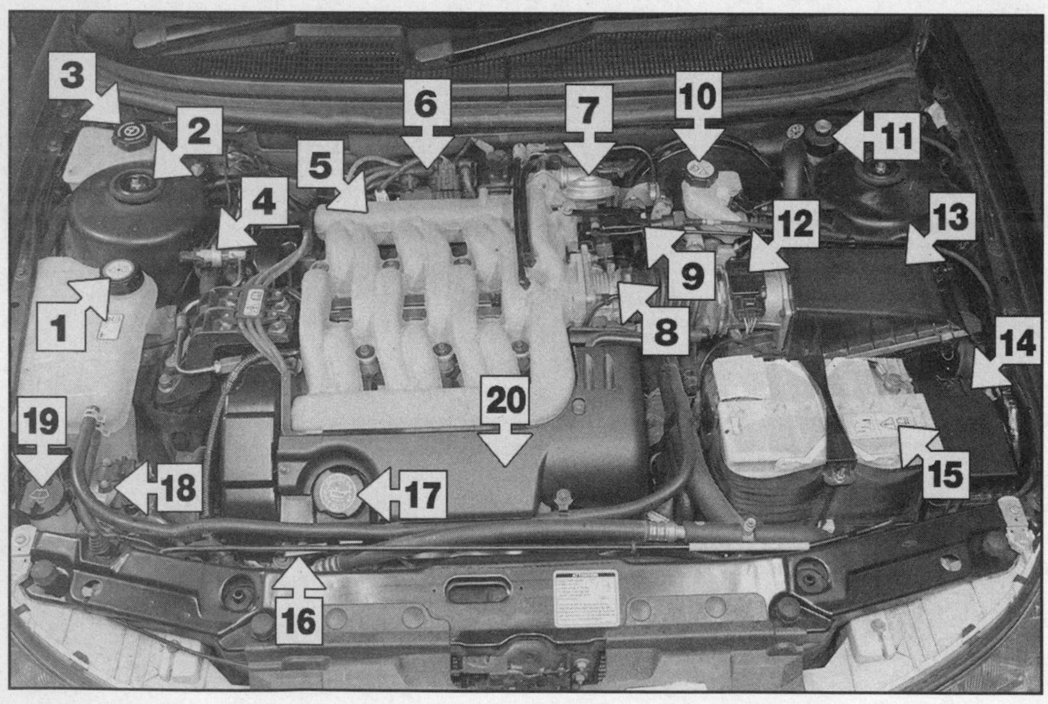

1. *Coolant expansion tank filler cap*
2. *Front suspension strut mounting nut*
3. *Power steering fluid reservoir*
4. *Power steering fluid pressure switch*
5. *Upper inlet manifold*
6. *Ignition coil*
7. *Exhaust gas recirculation (EGR) valve*
8. *Throttle housing*
9. *Accelerator and traction control cables*
10. *Brake (and clutch) fluid reservoir*
11. *EGR vacuum regulator*
12. *Airflow meter*
13. *Air cleaner*
14. *Fusebox*
15. *Battery*
16. *Engine oil level dipstick*
17. *Engine oil filler cap*
18. *Traction control actuator*
19. *Washer fluid reservoir*
20. *Water pump drivebelt cover*

Front underbody view of a 4-cylinder engine model

1. *Front disc brake*
2. *Front suspension lower arm*
3. *Front exhaust pipe*
4. *Air conditioning compressor*
5. *Sump oil drain plug*
6. *Front roll restrictor (engine mounting)*
7. *Manual transmission oil filler/level plug*
8. *Front subframe*
9. *Left-hand driveshaft*
10. *Steering track rod*
11. *Rear roll restrictor (engine mounting)*

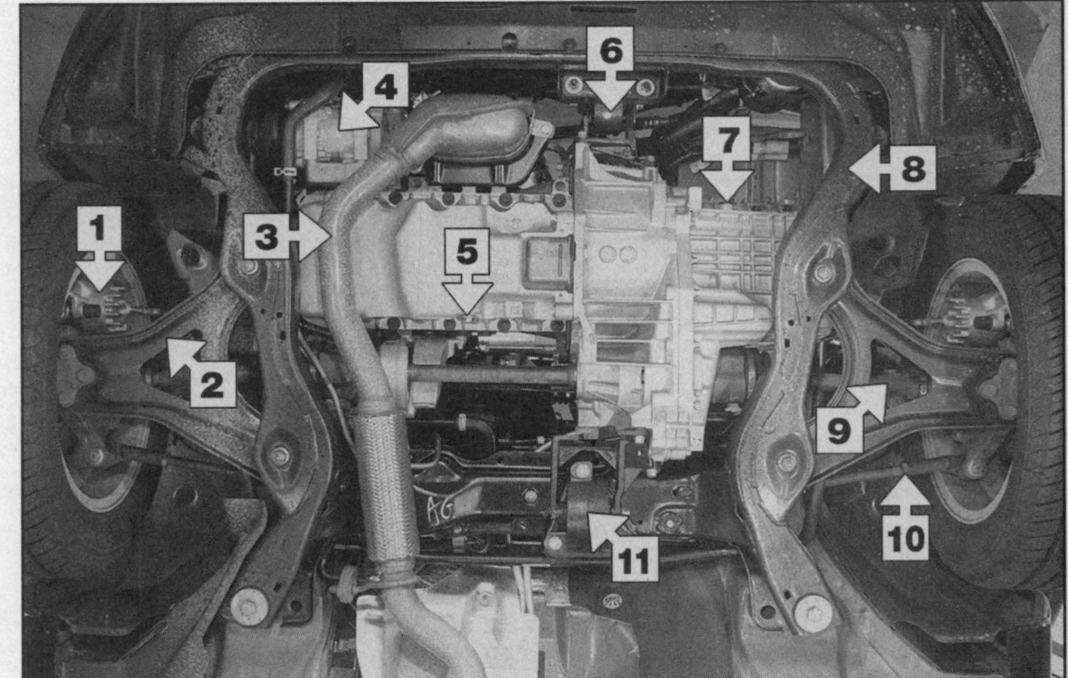

Front underbody view of a V6 engine model

1. *Front disc brake*
2. *Front suspension lower arm*
3. *Exhaust system Y-piece*
4. *Alternator*
5. *Oil filter*
6. *Sump oil drain plug*
7. *Front exhaust manifold and catalytic converter*
8. *Front roll restrictor (engine mounting)*
9. *Transmission*
10. *Front subframe*
11. *Left-hand driveshaft*
12. *Steering track rod*
13. *Rear roll restrictor (engine mounting)*
14. *Exhaust system front silencer*

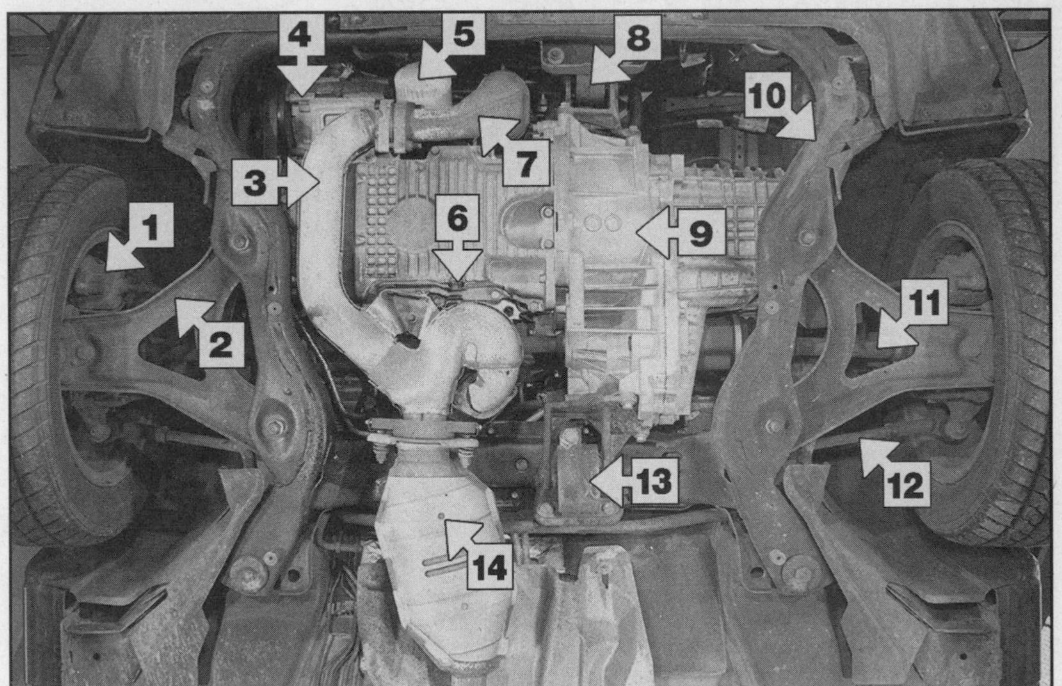

Rear underbody view - Saloon and Hatchback models

1. Silencers
2. Rear brakes
3. Exhaust system rubber mounting
4. Handbrake cables
5. Suspension struts and springs
6. Fuel tank filler neck
7. Fuel filter

Rear underbody view - Estate models

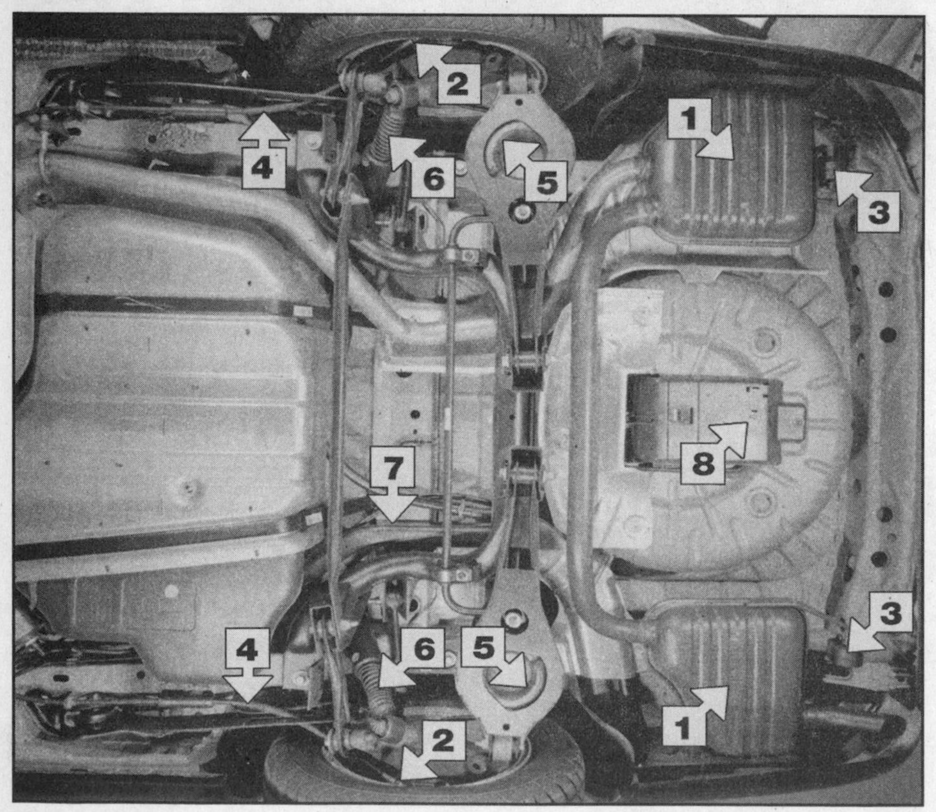

1. Silencers
2. Rear brakes
3. Exhaust system rubber mounting
4. Handbrake cables
5. Suspension springs
6. Suspension shock absorbers
7. Fuel tank filler neck
8. Evaporative emissions control system charcoal canister

1 Introduction

General information

This Chapter is designed to help the home mechanic maintain his/her vehicle for safety, economy, long life and peak performance.

The Chapter contains a master maintenance schedule, followed by Sections dealing specifically with each task in the schedule. Visual checks, adjustments, component renewal and other helpful items are included. Refer to the accompanying illustrations of the engine compartment and the underside of the vehicle for the locations of the various components.

Servicing your vehicle in accordance with the mileage/time maintenance schedule and the following Sections will provide a planned maintenance programme, which should result in a long and reliable service life. This is a comprehensive plan, so maintaining some items but not others at the specified service intervals, will not produce the same results.

As you service your vehicle, you will discover that many of the procedures can - and should - be grouped together, because of the particular procedure being performed, or because of the proximity of two otherwise unrelated components to one another. For example, if the vehicle is raised for any reason, the exhaust can be inspected at the same time as the suspension and steering components.

The first step in this maintenance programme is to prepare yourself before the actual work begins. Read through all the Sections relevant to the work to be carried out, then make a list and gather all the parts and tools required. If a problem is encountered, seek advice from a parts specialist, or a dealer service department.

Service interval display

The auxiliary warning system fitted to all models also includes a service interval reminder warning light, which is illuminated if the specified mileage (or time) since the last service has been reached.

The light should not necessarily be used as a definitive guide to the servicing needs of your Mondeo, but it is useful as a reminder, to ensure that servicing is not accidentally overlooked. Owners of older cars, or those covering a small annual mileage, may feel inclined to service their car more often, in which case the service interval reminder is perhaps less relevant.

The light should be reset whenever a service is carried out, as follows:

a) *On models up to 1996, a switch inside the glovebox must be depressed for a minimum of 4 seconds with the ignition switched on.*
b) *On 1997 and later models, the switch is behind the arrow-shaped symbol in the display panel, and is depressed using a thin probe, again for 4 seconds with the ignition switched on* ***(see illustration)****.*

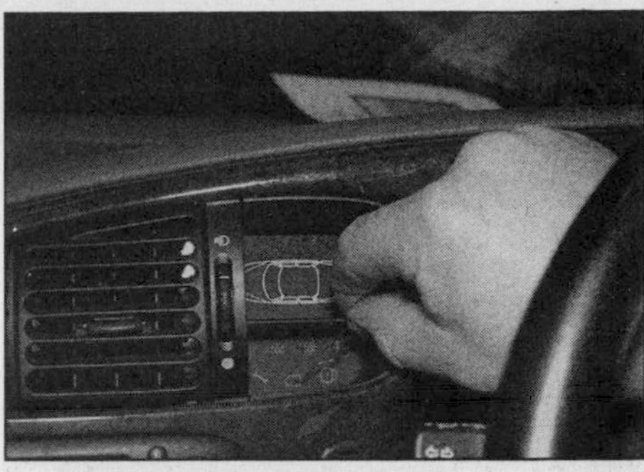

1.8 On later models, use a thin wire to reset the service interval reminder switch

2 Intensive maintenance

1 If, from the time the vehicle is new, the routine maintenance schedule is followed closely, and frequent checks are made of fluid levels and high-wear items, as suggested throughout this manual, the engine will be kept in relatively good running condition, and the need for additional work will be minimised.

2 It is possible that there will be times when the engine is running poorly due to the lack of regular maintenance. This is even more likely if a used vehicle, which has not received regular and frequent maintenance checks, is purchased. In such cases, additional work may need to be carried out, outside of the regular maintenance intervals.

3 If engine wear is suspected, a compression test (refer to the relevant Part of Chapter 2) will provide valuable information regarding the overall performance of the main internal components. Such a test can be used as a basis to decide on the extent of the work to be carried out. If, for example, a compression test indicates serious internal engine wear, conventional maintenance as described in this Chapter will not greatly improve the performance of the engine, and may prove a waste of time and money, unless extensive overhaul work is carried out first.

4 The following series of operations are those most often required to improve the performance of a generally poor-running engine:

Primary operations

a) *Clean, inspect and test the battery (See 'Weekly checks' and Section 4, where applicable).*
b) *Check all the engine-related fluids (See 'Weekly checks').*
c) *Check the condition and tension of the auxiliary drivebelt(s) (Section 5).*
d) *Renew the spark plugs (Section 29 or 32, as applicable).*
e) *Check the condition of the air filter, and renew if necessary (Section 24).*
f) *Check the fuel filter (Section 31).*
g) *Check the condition of all hoses, and check for fluid leaks (Sections 8 and 18).*

5 If the above operations do not prove fully effective, carry out the following secondary operations:

Secondary operations

All items listed under 'Primary operations', plus the following:

a) *Check the charging system (Chapter 5A).*
b) *Check the ignition system (Chapter 5B).*
c) *Check the fuel system (see Chapter 4A).*
d) *Renew the ignition HT leads (see Chapter 5B).*

1

Every 10 000 miles or 12 months

3 Engine oil and filter renewal

HAYNES HiNT ***Frequent oil changes are the best preventive maintenance the home mechanic can give the engine, because ageing oil becomes diluted and contaminated, which leads to premature engine wear.***

1 Make sure that you have all the necessary tools before you begin this procedure. You should also have plenty of rags or newspapers handy, for mopping up any spills.

2 To avoid any possibility of scalding, and to protect yourself from possible skin irritants and other harmful contaminants in used engine oils, it is advisable to wear gloves when carrying out this work.

3 Access to the underside of the vehicle is greatly improved if the vehicle can be lifted on a hoist, driven onto ramps, or supported by axle stands.

Warning: Do not work under a vehicle which is supported only by a hydraulic or scissors-type jack, or by bricks, blocks of wood, etc.

4 If this is your first oil change, get under the vehicle and familiarise yourself with the position of the engine oil drain plug, which is located at the rear of the sump. The engine and exhaust components will be warm during the actual work, so try to anticipate any potential problems while the engine and accessories are cool.

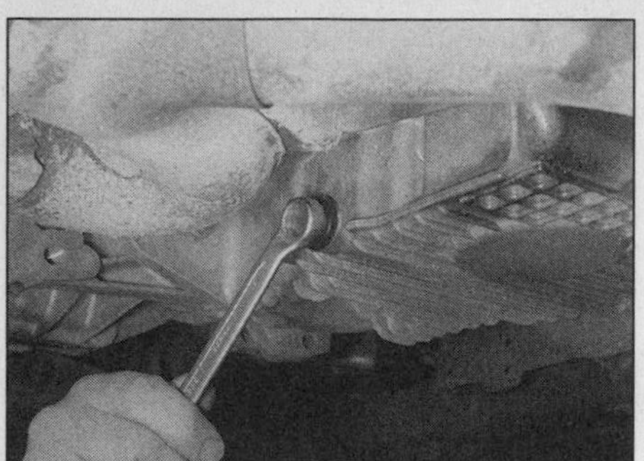

3.10 Use the correct-size spanner or socket to remove the oil drain plug and avoid rounding it off

5 The oil should preferably be changed when the engine is still fully warmed-up to normal operating temperature, just after a run (the needle on the temperature gauge should be in the 'Normal' sector of the gauge); warm oil and sludge will flow out more easily.

6 Park the vehicle on firm, level ground, and switch off the engine. Apply the handbrake firmly, then select 1st or reverse gear (manual transmission) or the 'P' position (automatic transmission). Open the bonnet and remove the engine oil filler cap from the cylinder head cover, then remove the oil level dipstick from its tube.

7 Raise the front of the vehicle, and support it securely on axle stands.

8 On four-cylinder engines, remove the front right-hand roadwheel to provide access to the oil filter; if the additional working clearance is required, remove also the auxiliary drivebelt cover (two fasteners).

9 On models with the V6 engine, access to the oil filter (at the front of the engine) can be improved by removing the radiator under-shield, but even this is not strictly necessary.

10 Being careful not to touch the hot exhaust components, place the drain pan under the drain plug, and unscrew the plug **(see illustration)** and **(Haynes Hint)**.

11 Allow the oil to drain into the drain pan, and check the condition of the plug's sealing washer; renew it if worn or damaged.

12 Allow some time for the old oil to drain, noting that it may be necessary to reposition the pan as the oil flow slows to a trickle; when the oil has completely drained, wipe clean the drain plug and its threads in the sump and refit the plug, tightening it to the specified torque wrench setting.

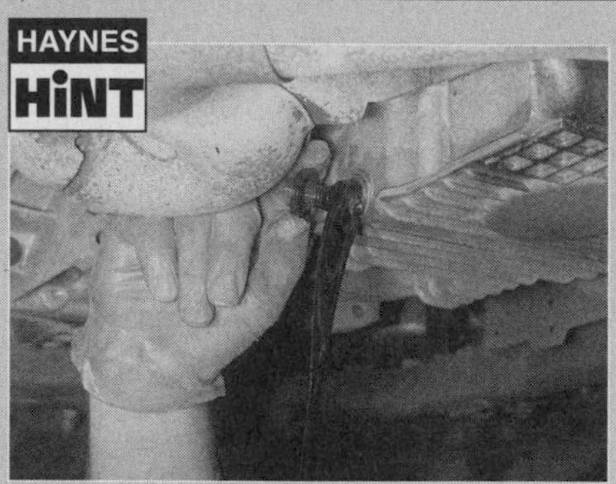

Keep the plug pressed into the sump while unscrewing it by hand the last couple of turns. As the plug releases from the threads, move it away sharply, so the stream of oil issuing from the sump runs into the pan, not up your sleeve!

13 Move the drain pan into position below the oil filter. On four-cylinder engine models, the filter is on the right-hand rear face of the cylinder block; on the V6 engine, the oil filter is on the front of the block.

14 Using a suitable filter removal tool if necessary, unscrew the oil filter from the cylinder block; be prepared for some oil spillage **(see illustration)**. Check the old filter to make sure that the rubber sealing ring hasn't stuck to the engine; if it has, carefully remove it. Withdraw the filter, quickly turning it so that its open end is uppermost, in order to spill as little oil as possible.

15 Using a clean, lint-free rag, wipe clean the cylinder block around the filter mounting. Unless there are any specific instructions supplied with it, fit the new oil filter as follows.

16 Apply a light coating of clean engine oil to the filter's sealing ring **(see illustration)**.

17 Screw the filter into position on the engine until it seats, then tighten it through a further half- to three-quarters of a turn *only*. Tighten the filter by hand only - do not use any tools.

18 Remove the old oil and all tools from under the vehicle. Refit any components removed for access, then lower the vehicle to the ground. On four-cylinder engine models, tighten the right-hand roadwheel nuts to the specified torque.

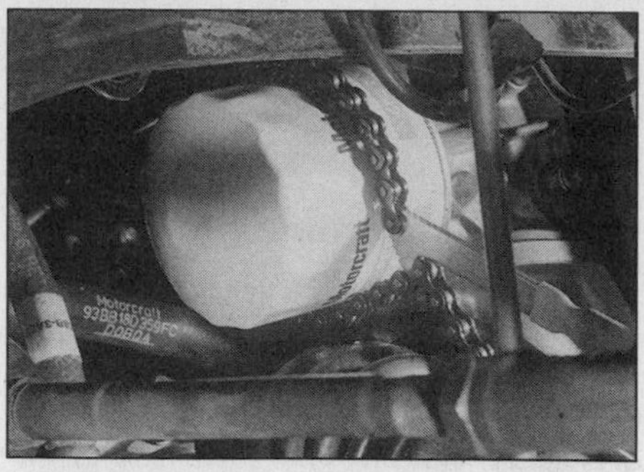

3.14 Using a chain-type wrench to remove the oil filter (4-cylinder engine shown)

19 Refill the engine with the correct grade and type of oil, as specified at the end of the *'Weekly checks'* section **(see illustration)**. Pour in half the specified quantity of oil first, then wait a few minutes for the oil to fall to the sump. Continue adding oil a small quantity at a time, until the level is up to the lower notch on the dipstick. Adding approximately 0.5 to 1.0 litre will raise the level to the dipstick's upper notch.

20 Start the engine. The oil pressure warning light will take a few seconds to go out while the new filter fills with oil; do not race the engine while the light is on. Run the engine for a few minutes, while checking for leaks around the oil filter seal and the drain plug.

21 Switch off the engine, and wait a few minutes for the oil to settle in the sump once more. With the new oil circulated and the filter now completely full, recheck the level on the dipstick, and add more oil as necessary.

22 Dispose of the used engine oil safely, with reference to *'General repair procedures'*.

OIL BANK LINE
0800 66 33 66

Note: It is antisocial and illegal to dump oil down the drain. To find the location of your local oil recycling bank, call this number free.

3.16 Lubricate the filter's sealing ring with clean engine oil before installing the filter on the engine

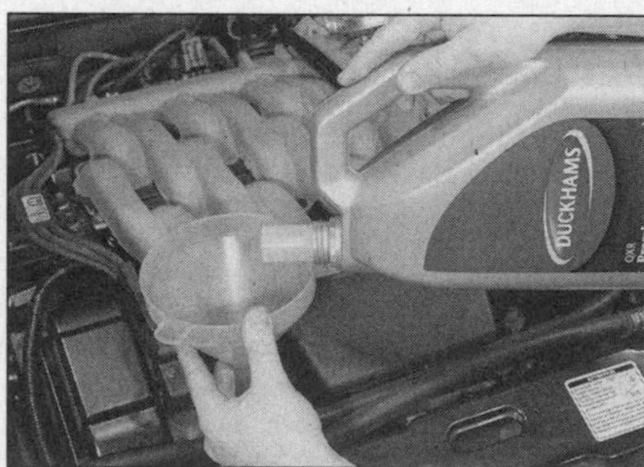

3.19 Refilling the engine with oil - note the use of a funnel

4 Battery maintenance and charging

Warning: Certain precautions must be followed when checking and servicing the battery. Hydrogen gas, which is highly flammable, is always present in the battery cells, so keep lighted tobacco and all other open flames and sparks away from the battery. The electrolyte inside the battery is actually dilute sulphuric acid, which will

cause injury if splashed on your skin or in your eyes. It will also ruin clothes and painted surfaces. When disconnecting the battery, always detach the negative (earth) lead first and connect it last!

Note: *Before disconnecting the battery, refer to Section 1 of Chapter 5A.*

General

1 A routine preventive maintenance programme for the battery in your vehicle is the only way to ensure quick and reliable starts. For general maintenance, refer to '*Weekly checks*' at the start of this manual. Also at the front of the manual is information on jump starting. For details of removing and installing the battery, refer to Chapter 5A.

Battery electrolyte level

2 On models not equipped with a sealed or 'maintenance-free' battery, check the electrolyte level of all six battery cells.

3 The level must be approximately 10 mm above the plates; this may be shown by maximum and minimum level lines marked on the battery's casing.

4 If the level is low, use a coin or screwdriver to release the filler/vent cap, and add distilled water **(see illustrations)**. To improve access to the centre caps, it may be helpful to remove the battery hold-down clamp.

5 Install and securely retighten the cap, then wipe up any spillage.

Caution: Overfilling the cells may cause electrolyte to spill over during periods of heavy charging, causing corrosion or damage.

Charging

Warning: When batteries are being charged, hydrogen gas, which is very explosive and flammable, is produced. Do not smoke, or allow open flames, near a charging or a recently-charged battery. Wear eye protection when near the battery during charging. Also, make sure the charger is unplugged before connecting or disconnecting the battery from the charger.

6 Slow-rate charging is the best way to restore a battery that's discharged to the point where it will not start the engine. It's also a good way to maintain the battery charge in a vehicle that's only driven a few miles between starts. Maintaining the battery charge is particularly important in winter, when the battery must work harder to start the engine, and electrical accessories that drain the battery are in greater use.

7 Check the battery case for any instructions regarding charging the battery. Some maintenance-free batteries may require a particularly low charge rate or other special conditions, if they are not to be damaged.

8 It's best to use a one- or two-amp battery charger (sometimes called a 'trickle' charger). They are the safest, and put the least strain on the battery. They are also the least expensive.

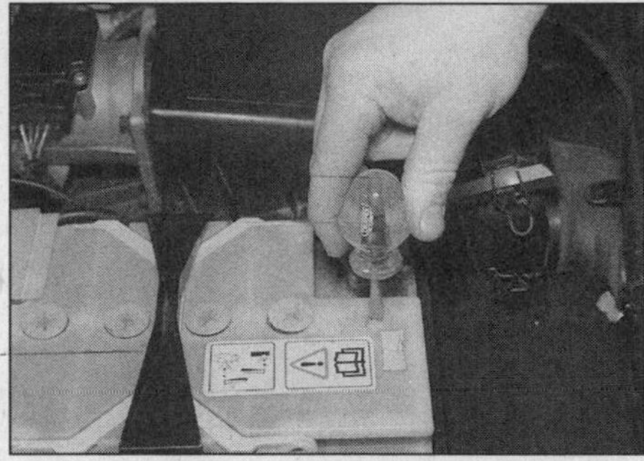

4.4a Unscrew the filler/vent cap . . .

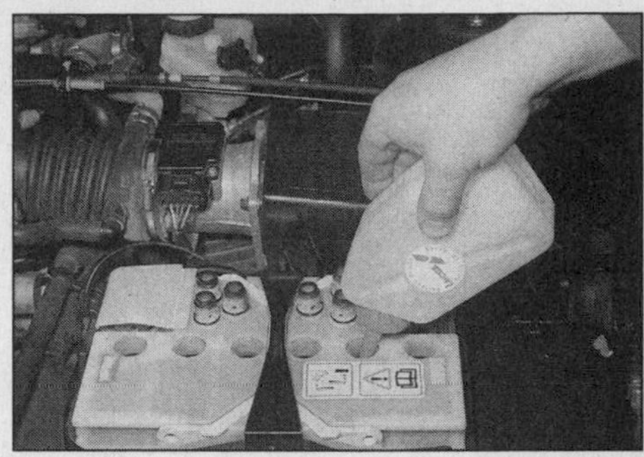

4.4b . . . and top-up each cell with distilled water

For a faster charge, you can use a higher-amperage charger, but don't use one rated more than 1/10th the amp/hour rating of the battery (ie no more than 5 amps, typically). Rapid boost charges that claim to restore the power of the battery in one to two hours are hardest on the battery, and can damage batteries not in good condition. This type of charging should only be used in emergency situations.

9 The average time necessary to charge a battery should be listed in the instructions that come with the charger. As a general rule, a trickle charger will charge a battery in 12 to 16 hours.

5 Auxiliary drivebelt(s) check and renewal

General

1 The main auxiliary drivebelt is of the flat, multi-ribbed (or 'polyvee') type, and is located on the right-hand end of the engine. It drives the alternator, water pump (on four-cylinder engine models), power steering pump and (when fitted) the air conditioning compressor from the engine's crankshaft pulley **(see illustrations)**.

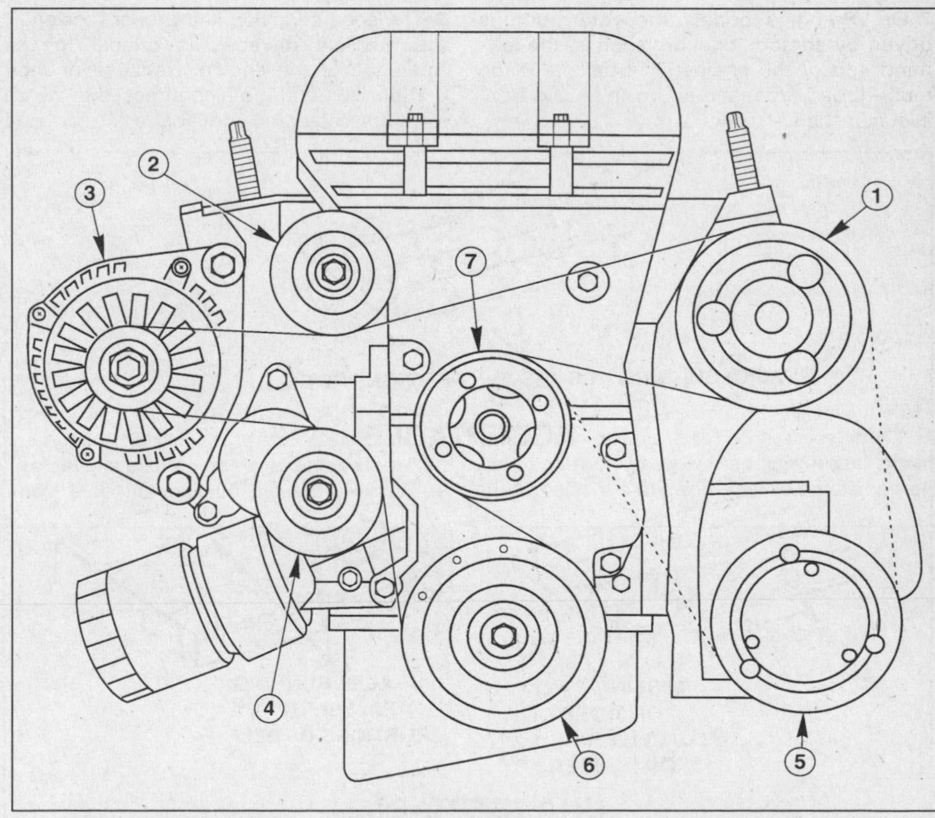

5.1a Auxiliary drivebelt routing on four-cylinder engine models up to June 1998

1 Power steering pump
2 Idler pulley
3 Alternator
4 Automatic tensioner
5 Air conditioning compressor (when fitted)
6 Crankshaft pulley
7 Water pump pulley

1

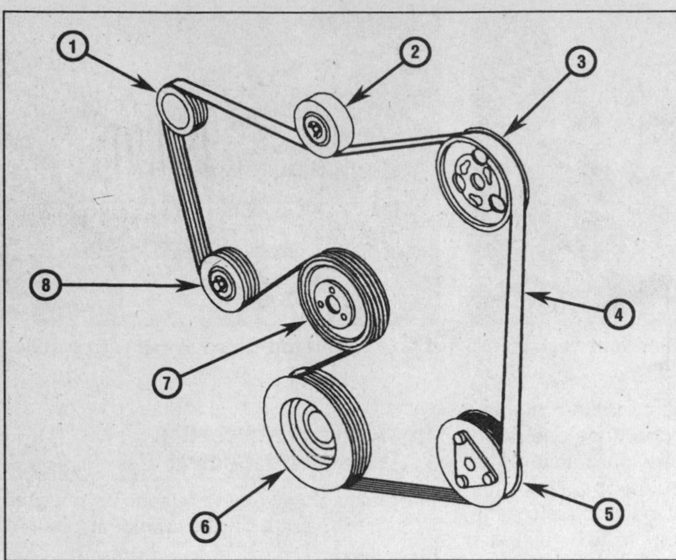

5.1b Auxiliary drivebelt routing for June 1998-on four-cylinder engine models with air conditioning - on models without air conditioning, the routing is the same with the air conditioning compressor pulley deleted

1 *Alternator*
2 *Idler pulley*
3 *Power steering pump*
4 *Drivebelt*
5 *Air conditioning compressor*
6 *Crankshaft pulley*
7 *Water pump*
8 *Drivebelt tensioner*

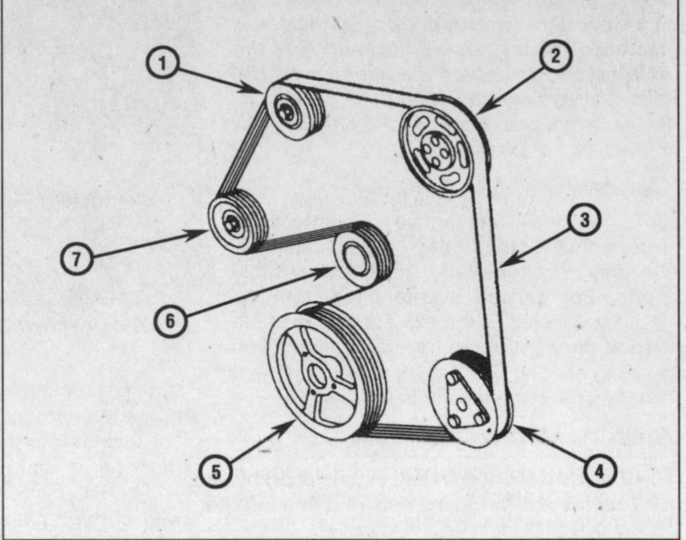

5.1c Auxiliary drivebelt routing on V6 engine models with air conditioning - on models without air conditioning, the routing is the same with the air conditioning compressor pulley deleted

1 *Idler pulley*
2 *Power steering pump*
3 *Drivebelt*
4 *Air conditioning compressor*
5 *Crankshaft pulley*
6 *Drivebelt tensioner*
7 *Alternator*

2 On V6 engine models, the water pump is driven by an additional drivebelt at the left-hand end of the engine. The belt is of the multi-ribbed type, and is driven by the front inlet camshaft.

3 The good condition and proper tension of the auxiliary drivebelt is critical to the operation of the engine. Because of their composition and the high stresses to which they are subjected, drivebelts stretch and deteriorate as they get older. They must, therefore, be regularly inspected.

Check

4 With the engine switched off, open and support the bonnet. For improved access to the right-hand end of the engine, first loosen the right-hand front wheel nuts, then jack up the front right-hand side of the vehicle and support it securely on an axle stand. Remove the roadwheel, then remove the auxiliary drivebelt cover (two fasteners) from inside the wheel arch. If necessary, also remove the rear section of the inner wheel arch liner, which is secured by two further bolts.

5 Using an inspection light or a small electric torch, and rotating the engine when necessary with a spanner applied to the crankshaft pulley bolt, check the whole length of the drivebelt for cracks, separation of the rubber, and torn or worn ribs **(see illustration)**. Also check for fraying and glazing, which gives the drivebelt a shiny appearance.

6 Both sides of the drivebelt should be inspected, which means you will have to twist the drivebelt to check the underside. Use your fingers to feel the drivebelt where you can't see it. If you are in any doubt as to the condition of the drivebelt, renew it as described below.

7 On models with the V6 engine, remove the water pump drivebelt cover from the top and front of the engine. Inspect the drivebelt as described in paragraphs 5 and 6.

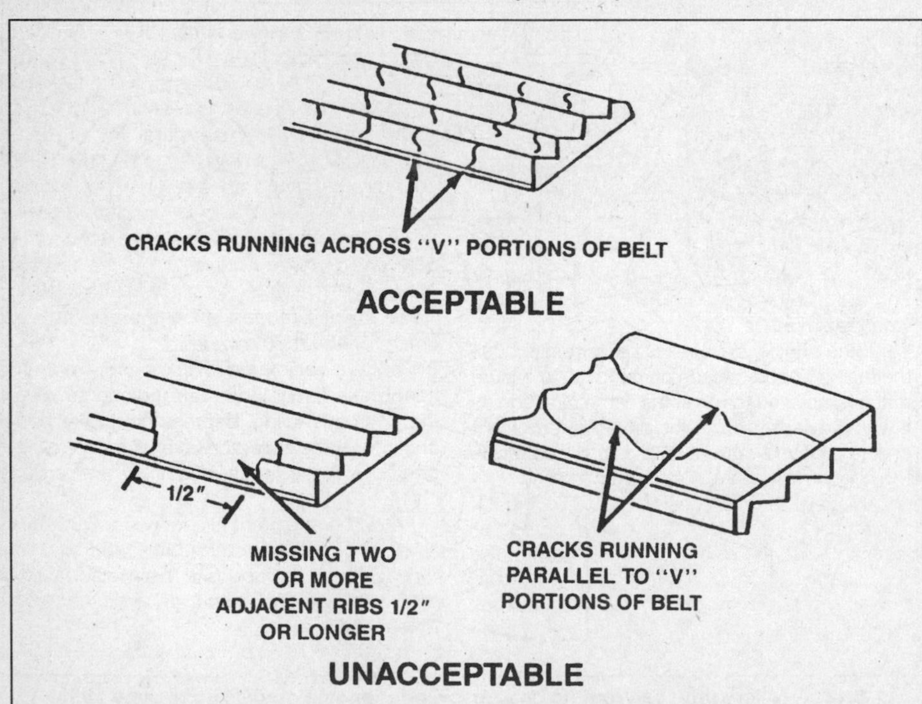

5.5 Check the auxiliary drivebelt for signs of wear like these. Very small cracks across the drivebelt ribs are acceptable. If the cracks are deep, or if the drivebelt looks worn or damaged in any other way, renew it

5.10 The auxiliary drivebelt is tensioned by an automatic tensioner; Torx screws (arrowed) secure it to alternator mounting bracket

5.13 Rotate the tensioner pulley clockwise to release its pressure on the drivebelt, then slip the drivebelt off the crankshaft pulley

Drivebelt tension

8 The auxiliary drivebelt is tensioned by an automatic tensioner; regular checks are not required, and manual 'adjustment' is not possible.

9 If you suspect that the drivebelt is slipping and/or running slack, or that the tensioner is otherwise faulty, it must be renewed. To do this, first remove the drivebelt as described below.

10 Unbolt the tensioner, which is secured by two Torx-type screws **(see illustration)**. On fitting the new tensioner, ensure it is aligned correctly on its mountings, and tighten the screws securely.

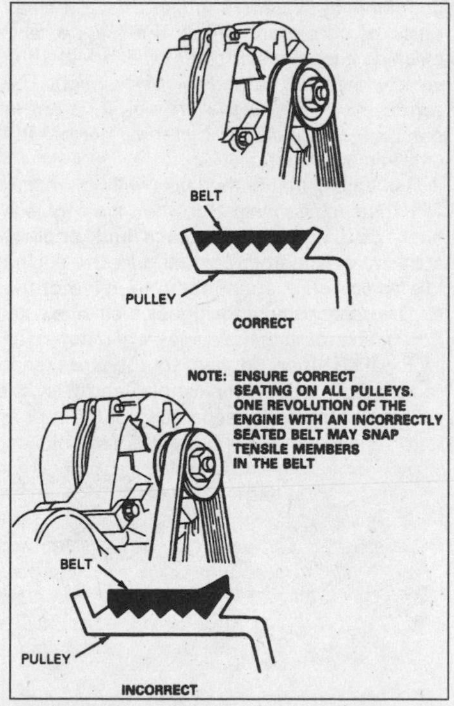

5.16 When installing the auxiliary drivebelt, make sure that it is centred - it must not overlap either edge of the grooved pulleys

Drivebelt renewal

11 Gain access to the drivebelt as described in paragraph 4 or 7, as applicable.

12 If the existing drivebelt is to be refitted, mark it, or note the maker's markings on its flat surface, so that it can be installed the same way round.

13 Rotate the tensioner pulley clockwise to release its pressure on the drivebelt **(see illustration)**. Depending on model and equipment, the tensioner will either have a hex fitting for a spanner or socket, or a square hole into which a ratchet handle from a socket set can be fitted.

14 Slip the drivebelt off the drive pulley, and release the tensioner again. Working from the wheel arch or engine compartment as necessary, and noting its routing, slip the drivebelt off the remaining pulleys and withdraw it.

15 Check all the pulleys, ensuring that their grooves are clean, and removing all traces of oil and grease. Check that the tensioner works properly, with strong spring pressure being felt when its pulley is rotated clockwise, and a smooth return to the limit of its travel when released.

16 If the original drivebelt is being refitted, use the marks or notes made on removal, to ensure that it is installed to run in the same direction as it was previously. To fit the drivebelt, arrange it on the grooved pulleys so that it is centred in their grooves **(see illustration)**, and not overlapping their raised sides (note that the flat surface of the drivebelt is engaged on one or more pulleys) and routed correctly. Start at the top, and work down to finish at the bottom pulley; rotate the tensioner pulley clockwise, slip the drivebelt onto the bottom pulley, then release the tensioner again.

17 Using a spanner applied to the crankshaft pulley bolt, rotate the crankshaft through at least two full turns clockwise to settle the drivebelt on the pulleys, then check that the drivebelt is properly installed.

18 Refit the components removed for access, then (where applicable) lower the vehicle to the ground. If the right-hand roadwheel was removed, tighten the wheel nuts to the specified torque.

6 Automatic transmission fluid level check

1 The level of the automatic transmission fluid should be carefully maintained. Low fluid level can lead to slipping or loss of drive, while overfilling can cause foaming, loss of fluid and transmission damage.

2 The transmission fluid level should only be checked when the transmission is hot (at its normal operating temperature). If the vehicle has just been driven over 10 miles (15 miles in cold weather), the transmission is hot. **Note:** *If the vehicle has just been driven for a long time at high speed or in city traffic in hot weather, or if it has been pulling a trailer, an accurate fluid level reading cannot be obtained. In these circumstances, allow the fluid to cool down for about 30 minutes.*

3 Park the vehicle on level ground, apply the handbrake firmly, and start the engine. While the engine is idling, depress the brake pedal and move the selector lever through all the positions three times, beginning and ending in 'P'.

4 Allow the engine to idle for one minute, then (with the engine still idling) remove the dipstick from its tube **(see illustration)**. Note the condition and colour of the fluid on the dipstick.

5 Wipe the fluid from the dipstick with a clean rag, and re-insert it into the filler tube until the cap seats.

6 Pull the dipstick out again, and note the fluid level. The level should be between the 'MIN' and 'MAX' marks **(see illustration)**.

6.4 Removing the automatic transmission dipstick from its tube

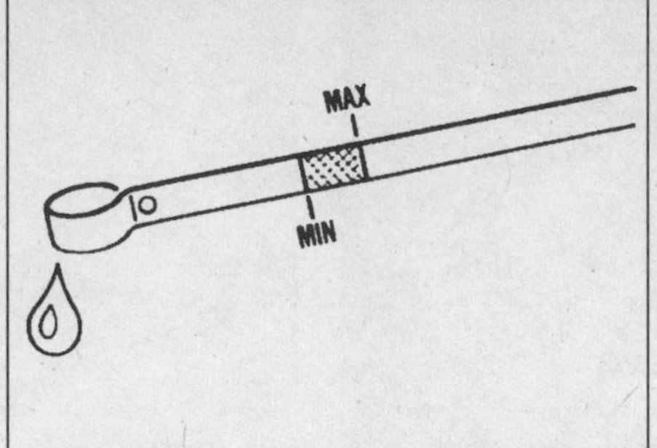

6.6 Transmission fluid dipstick 'MIN' and 'MAX' marks

6.7 Adding automatic transmission fluid through the dipstick tube

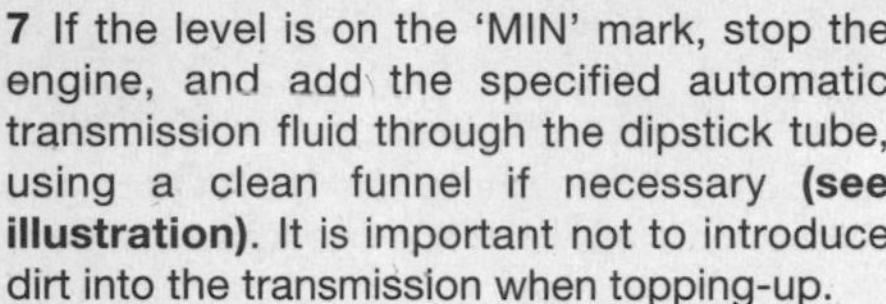

7 If the level is on the 'MIN' mark, stop the engine, and add the specified automatic transmission fluid through the dipstick tube, using a clean funnel if necessary **(see illustration)**. It is important not to introduce dirt into the transmission when topping-up.

8 Add the fluid a little at a time, and keep checking the level as previously described until it is correct.

9 The need for regular topping-up of the transmission fluid indicates a leak, which should be found and rectified without delay.

10 The condition of the fluid should also be checked along with the level. If the fluid at the end of the dipstick is black or a dark reddish-brown colour, or if it has a burned smell, the fluid should be changed. If you are in doubt about the condition of the fluid, purchase some new fluid, and compare the two for colour and smell.

8.2 Check the condition of all coolant hoses

8.3 The clips securing the air hoses should be checked regularly

7 Electrical system check

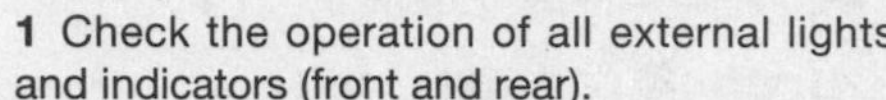

1 Check the operation of all external lights and indicators (front and rear).

2 Check for satisfactory operation of the instrument panel, its illumination and warning lights, the switches and their function lights.

3 Check the horn(s) for satisfactory operation.

4 Check all other electrical equipment for satisfactory operation.

8 Underbonnet check for fluid leaks and hose condition

Caution: Renewal of air conditioning hoses must be left to a dealer service department or air conditioning specialist who has the equipment to depressurise the system safely. Never remove air conditioning components or hoses until the system has been depressurised.

General

1 High temperatures in the engine compartment can cause the deterioration of the rubber and plastic hoses used for engine, accessory and emission systems operation. Periodic inspection should be made for cracks, loose clamps, material hardening and leaks.

2 Carefully check the large top and bottom radiator hoses, along with the other smaller-diameter cooling system hoses and metal pipes; do not forget the heater hoses/pipes which run from the engine to the bulkhead, and those to the engine oil cooler (where fitted). Inspect each hose along its entire length, replacing any that is cracked, swollen or shows signs of deterioration. Cracks may become more apparent if the hose is squeezed, and may often be apparent at the hose ends **(see illustration)**.

3 Make sure that all hose connections are tight. If the large-diameter air hoses from the air cleaner are loose, they will leak air, and upset the engine idle quality **(see illustration)**. If the spring clamps that are used to secure many of the hoses appear to be slackening, they should be replaced with worm-drive clips to prevent the possibility of leaks.

4 Some other hoses are secured to their fittings with clamps. Where clamps are used, check to be sure they haven't lost their tension, allowing the hose to leak. If clamps aren't used, make sure the hose has not expanded and/or hardened where it slips over the fitting, allowing it to leak **(see Haynes Hint)**.

5 Check all fluid reservoirs, filler caps, drain plugs and fittings etc, looking for any signs of leakage of oil, transmission and/or brake hydraulic fluid, coolant and power steering fluid.

6 If the vehicle is regularly parked in the same place, close inspection of the ground underneath it will soon show any leaks; ignore the puddle of water which will be left if the air conditioning system is in use. Place a clean piece of cardboard below the engine, and examine it for signs of contamination after the vehicle has been parked over it overnight - be aware, however, of the fire risk inherent in placing combustible material below the catalytic converter.

7 Remember that some leaks will only occur with the engine running, or when the engine is hot or cold. With the handbrake firmly applied, start the engine from cold, and let the engine idle while you examine the underside of the engine compartment for signs of leakage.

A leak in the cooling system will usually show up as white- or rust-coloured deposits on the area adjoining the leak

8 If an unusual smell is noticed inside or around the car, especially when the engine is thoroughly hot, this may point to the presence of a leak.

9 As soon as a leak is detected, its source must be traced and rectified. Where oil has been leaking for some time, it is usually necessary to use a steam cleaner, pressure washer or similar, to clean away the accumulated dirt, so that the exact source of the leak can be identified.

Vacuum hoses

10 It's quite common for vacuum hoses, especially those in the emissions system, to be colour-coded, or to be identified by coloured stripes moulded into them. Various systems require hoses with different wall thicknesses, collapse resistance and temperature resistance. When renewing hoses, be sure the new ones are made of the same material.

11 Often the only effective way to check a hose is to remove it completely from the vehicle. If more than one hose is removed, be sure to label the hoses and fittings to ensure correct installation.

12 When checking vacuum hoses, be sure to include any plastic T-fittings in the check. Inspect the fittings for cracks, and check the hose where it fits over the fitting for distortion, which could cause leakage.

13 A small piece of vacuum hose (quarter-inch inside diameter) can be used as a stethoscope to detect vacuum leaks. Hold one end of the hose to your ear, and probe around vacuum hoses and fittings, listening for the 'hissing' sound characteristic of a vacuum leak.

Warning: When probing with the vacuum hose stethoscope, be very careful not to come into contact with moving engine components such as the auxiliary drivebelt, radiator electric cooling fan, etc.

Fuel hoses

Warning: There are certain precautions which must be taken when inspecting or servicing fuel system components. Work in a well-ventilated area, and do not allow open flames (cigarettes, appliance pilot lights, etc.) or bare light bulbs near the work area. Mop up any spills immediately, and do not store fuel-soaked rags where they could ignite.

14 Check all fuel hoses for deterioration and chafing. Check especially for cracks in areas where the hose bends, and also just before fittings, such as where a hose attaches to the fuel filter.

15 High-quality fuel line, usually identified by the word 'Fluoroelastomer' printed on the hose, should be used for fuel line renewal. Never, under any circumstances, use unreinforced vacuum line, clear plastic tubing or water hose as a substitute for fuel lines.

16 Spring-type clamps are commonly used on fuel lines. These clamps often lose their tension over a period of time, and can be 'sprung' during removal. Replace all spring-type clamps with screw clamps whenever a hose is replaced.

Metal lines

17 Sections of metal piping are often used for fuel line between the fuel filter and the engine. Check carefully to be sure the piping has not been bent or crimped, and that cracks have not started in the line.

18 If a section of metal fuel line must be renewed, only seamless steel piping should be used, since copper and aluminium piping don't have the strength necessary to withstand normal engine vibration.

19 Check the metal lines where they enter the brake master cylinder, ABS hydraulic unit or clutch master/slave cylinders (as applicable) for cracks in the lines or loose fittings. Any sign of brake fluid leakage calls for an immediate and thorough inspection.

9 Engine compartment wiring check

1 With the vehicle parked on level ground, apply the handbrake firmly and open the bonnet. Using an inspection light or a small electric torch, check all visible wiring within and beneath the engine compartment.

2 What you are looking for is wiring that is obviously damaged by chafing against sharp edges, or against moving suspension/transmission components and/or the auxiliary drivebelt, by being trapped or crushed between carelessly-refitted components, or melted by being forced into contact with the hot engine castings, coolant pipes, etc. In almost all cases, damage of this sort is caused in the first instance by incorrect routing on reassembly after previous work has been carried out.

3 Depending on the extent of the problem, damaged wiring may be repaired by rejoining the break or splicing-in a new length of wire, using solder to ensure a good connection, and remaking the insulation with adhesive insulating tape or heat-shrink tubing, as appropriate. If the damage is extensive, given the implications for the vehicle's future reliability, the best long-term answer may well be to renew that entire section of the loom, however expensive this may appear.

4 When the actual damage has been repaired, ensure that the wiring loom is re-routed correctly, so that it is clear of other components, and not stretched or kinked, and is secured out of harm's way using the plastic clips, guides and ties provided.

5 Check all electrical connectors, ensuring that they are clean, securely fastened, and that each is locked by its plastic tabs or wire clip, as appropriate **(see illustration)**. If any connector shows external signs of corrosion (accumulations of white or green deposits, or streaks of 'rust'), or if any is thought to be dirty, it must be unplugged and cleaned using electrical contact cleaner. If the connector pins are severely corroded, the connector must be renewed; note that this may mean the renewal of that entire section of the loom - see your local Ford dealer for details.

6 If the cleaner completely removes the corrosion to leave the connector in a satisfactory condition, it would be wise to pack the connector with a suitable material which will exclude dirt and moisture, preventing the corrosion from occurring again; a Ford dealer may be able to recommend a suitable product.

7 Check the condition of the battery connections - remake the connections or renew the leads if a fault is found (see Chapter 5A). Use the same techniques to ensure that all earth points in the engine compartment provide good electrical contact through clean, metal-to-metal joints, and that all are securely fastened.

8 Refer to Sections 29 and 32 for details of spark plug (HT) lead checks.

10 Air conditioning system check

1

Warning: The air conditioning system is under high pressure. Do not loosen any fittings or remove any components until after the system has been discharged. Air conditioning refrigerant must be properly discharged into an approved type of container, at a dealer service department or an automotive air conditioning repair facility capable of handling R134a refrigerant. Always wear eye protection when disconnecting air conditioning system fittings.

1 The following maintenance checks should be performed on a regular basis, to ensure that the air conditioner continues to operate at peak efficiency:

a) Check the auxiliary drivebelt. If it's worn or deteriorated, renew it (see Section 5).

9.5 Check the condition of all visible electrical connectors and their wiring

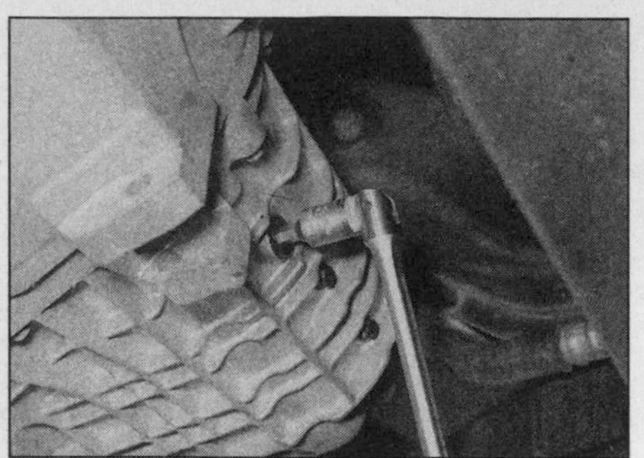
11.3a Using a suitable Allen key or socket, unscrew . . .

11.3b . . . and remove the transmission oil filler/level plug

b) Check the system hoses. Look for cracks, bubbles, hard spots and deterioration. Inspect the hoses and all fittings for oil bubbles and seepage. If there's any evidence of wear, damage or leaks, renew the hose(s).

c) Inspect the condenser fins for leaves, insects and other debris. Use a 'fin comb' or compressed air to clean the condenser.

d) Check that the drain tube from the front of the evaporator is clear - note that it is normal to have clear fluid (water) dripping from this while the system is in operation, to the extent that quite a large puddle can be left under the vehicle when it is parked.

Warning: Wear eye protection when using compressed air!

2 It's a good idea to operate the system for about 30 minutes at least once a month, particularly during the winter. Long term non-use can cause hardening, and subsequent failure, of the seals.
3 Because of the complexity of the air conditioning system and the special equipment necessary to service it, in-depth fault diagnosis and repairs are not included in this manual.
4 The most common cause of poor cooling is simply a low system refrigerant charge. If a noticeable drop in cool air output occurs, the following quick check will help you determine if the refrigerant level is low.
5 Warm the engine up to normal operating temperature.
6 Place the air conditioning temperature selector at the coldest setting, and put the blower at the highest setting. Open the doors - to make sure the air conditioning system doesn't cycle off as soon as it cools the passenger compartment.
7 With the compressor engaged - the clutch will make an audible click, and the centre of the clutch will rotate - feel the inlet and outlet pipes at the compressor. One side should be cold, and one hot. If there's no perceptible difference between the two pipes, there's something wrong with the compressor or the system. It might be a low charge - it might be something else. Take the vehicle to a dealer service department or an automotive air conditioning specialist.

11 Manual transmission oil level check

1 The manual transmission does not have a dipstick. To check the oil level, raise the vehicle and support it securely on axle stands, making sure that the vehicle is level.
2 Remove the engine undershields as necessary for access to the front of the transmission.
3 On the lower front side of the transmission housing, you will see the filler/level plug. Using a suitable Allen key or socket, unscrew and remove it - take care, as it will probably be very tight **(see illustrations)**.
4 If the lubricant level is correct, the oil should be up to the lower edge of the hole.
5 If the transmission needs more lubricant (if the oil level is not up to the hole), use a syringe, or a plastic bottle and tube, to add more **(see illustration)**.
6 Stop filling the transmission when the lubricant begins to run out of the hole, then wait until the flow of oil ceases.
7 Refit the filler/level plug, and tighten it to the specified torque wrench setting. Drive the vehicle a short distance, then check for leaks.
8 A need for regular topping-up can only be due to a leak, which should be found and rectified without delay.

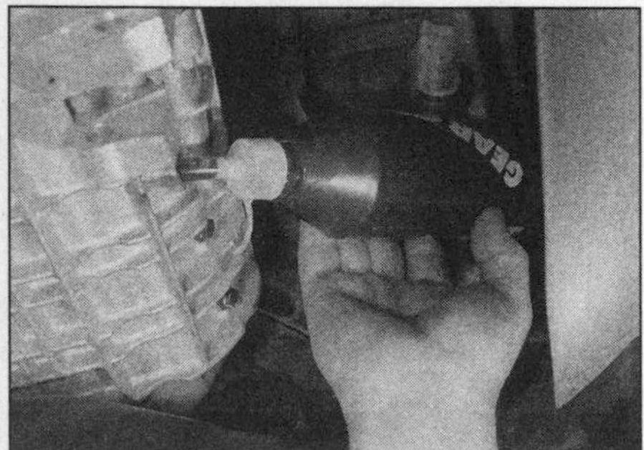

11.5 Topping-up the manual transmission oil

15.2a Check the condition of the track rod balljoint dust cover (arrowed)

12 Seat belt check

1 Check the seat belts for satisfactory operation and condition. Inspect the webbing for fraying and cuts. Check that they retract smoothly and without binding into their reels.
2 Check that the seat belt mounting bolts are tight, and if necessary tighten them to the specified torque wrench setting.

13 Clutch pedal adjustment

The procedure is described in Chapter 6, Section 3.

14 Automatic transmission linkage lubrication

1 Apply the handbrake, then loosen the left-hand front wheel nuts. Jack up the front of the vehicle and support on axle stands. Remove the left-hand front wheel.
2 Apply a little oil to the cable end fitting on the selector lever on the left-hand side of the transmission (refer to the information in Chapter 7B if necessary).
3 Refit the wheel, and lower the vehicle to the ground. Tighten the wheel nuts to the specified torque.

15 Steering, suspension and roadwheel check

Front suspension and steering check

1 Apply the handbrake, then raise the front of the vehicle and support it on axle stands.
2 Visually inspect the balljoint dust covers and the steering gear gaiters for splits, chafing or deterioration **(see illustrations)**. Any wear of these components will cause loss of lubricant, together with dirt and water entry, resulting in rapid deterioration of the balljoints or steering gear.

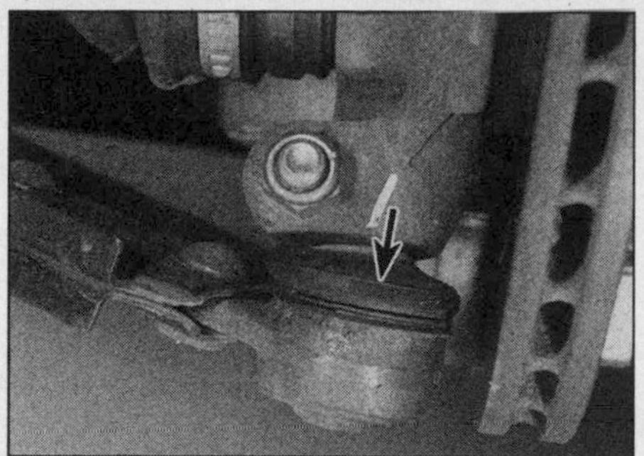
15.2b Check the condition of the lower arm balljoint dust cover (arrowed)

15.2c Check the condition of the steering rack gaiters

15.4 Checking for wear in the front suspension and hub bearings

3 Check the power-assisted steering fluid hoses for chafing or deterioration, and the pipe and hose unions for fluid leaks. Also check for signs of fluid leakage under pressure from the steering gear rubber gaiters, which would indicate failed fluid seals within the steering gear.

4 Grasp the roadwheel at the 12 o'clock and 6 o'clock positions, and try to rock it **(see illustration)**. Very slight free play may be felt, but if the movement is appreciable, further investigation is necessary to determine the source. Continue rocking the wheel while an assistant depresses the footbrake. If the movement is now eliminated or significantly reduced, it is likely that the hub bearings are at fault. If the free play is still evident with the footbrake depressed, then there is wear in the suspension joints or mountings.

5 Now grasp the wheel at the 9 o'clock and 3 o'clock positions, and try to rock it as before. Any movement felt now may again be caused by wear in the hub bearings or the steering track rod balljoints. If the outer track rod balljoint is worn, the visual movement will be obvious. If the inner joint is suspect, it can be felt by placing a hand over the rack-and-pinion rubber gaiter, and gripping the track rod. If the wheel is now rocked, movement will be felt at the inner joint if wear has taken place.

6 Using a large screwdriver or flat bar, check for wear in the suspension mounting and subframe bushes by levering between the relevant suspension component and its attachment point. Some movement is to be expected as the mountings are made of rubber, but excessive wear should be obvious. Also check the condition of any visible rubber bushes, looking for splits, cracks or contamination of the rubber.

7 With the vehicle standing on its wheels, have an assistant turn the steering wheel back-and-forth, about an eighth of a turn each way. There should be very little, if any, lost movement between the steering wheel and roadwheels. If this is not the case, closely observe the joints and mountings previously described, but in addition, check the steering column joints for wear, and also check the rack-and-pinion steering gear itself.

Rear suspension check

8 Chock the front wheels, then raise the rear of the vehicle and support it on axle stands.

9 Check the rear hub bearings for wear, using the method described for the front hub bearings (paragraph 4).

10 Using a large screwdriver or flat bar, check for wear in the suspension mounting bushes by levering between the relevant suspension component and its attachment point. Some movement is to be expected as the mountings are made of rubber, but excessive wear should be obvious.

Roadwheel check and balancing

11 Periodically remove the roadwheels, and clean any dirt or mud from the inside and outside surfaces. Examine the wheel rims for signs of rusting, corrosion or other damage. Light alloy wheels are easily damaged by 'kerbing' whilst parking, and similarly, steel wheels may become dented or buckled. Renewal of the wheel is very often the only course of remedial action possible.

12 The balance of each wheel and tyre assembly should be maintained, not only to avoid excessive tyre wear, but also to avoid wear in the steering and suspension components. Wheel imbalance is normally signified by vibration through the vehicle's bodyshell, although in many cases it is particularly noticeable through the steering wheel. Conversely, it should be noted that wear or damage in suspension or steering components may cause excessive tyre wear.

16.2 Check the driveshaft gaiters by hand for cracks and/or leaking grease

Out-of-round or out-of-true tyres, damaged wheels and wheel bearing wear/maladjustment also fall into this category. Balancing will not usually cure vibration caused by such wear.

13 Wheel balancing may be carried out with the wheel either on or off the vehicle. If balanced on the vehicle, ensure that the wheel-to-hub relationship is marked in some way prior to subsequent wheel removal, so that it may be refitted in its original position.

16 Driveshaft rubber gaiter and CV joint check

1

1 The driveshaft rubber gaiters are very important, because they prevent dirt, water and foreign material from entering and damaging the constant velocity (CV) joints. External contamination can cause the gaiter material to deteriorate prematurely, so it's a good idea to wash the gaiters with soap and water occasionally.

2 With the vehicle raised and securely supported on axle stands, turn the steering onto full-lock, then slowly rotate each front wheel in turn. Inspect the condition of the outer constant velocity (CV) joint rubber gaiters, squeezing the gaiters to open out the folds **(see illustration)**. Check for signs of cracking, splits, or deterioration of the rubber, which may allow the escape of grease, and lead to the ingress of water and grit into the joint. Also check the security and condition of the retaining clips. Repeat these checks on the inner CV joints. If any damage or deterioration is found, the gaiters should be renewed as described in Chapter 8.

3 At the same time, check the general condition of the outer CV joints themselves, by first holding the driveshaft and attempting to rotate the wheels. Repeat this check on the inner joints, by holding the inner joint yoke and attempting to rotate the driveshaft.

4 Any appreciable movement in the CV joint indicates wear in the joint, wear in the driveshaft splines, or a loose driveshaft retaining nut.

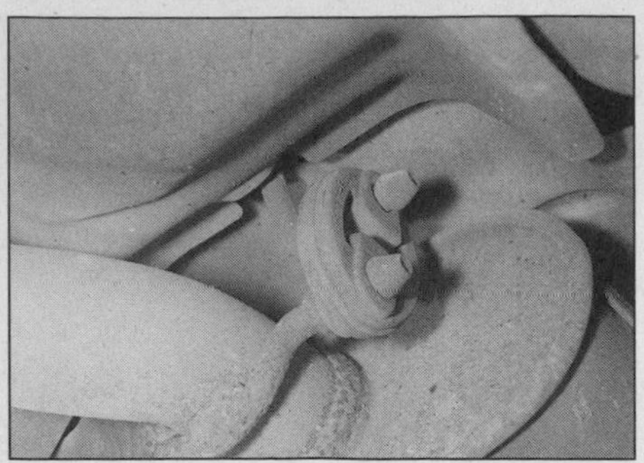

17.2 Check the condition of the exhaust system rubber mountings

17.3 Look for signs of leakage at the exhaust joints

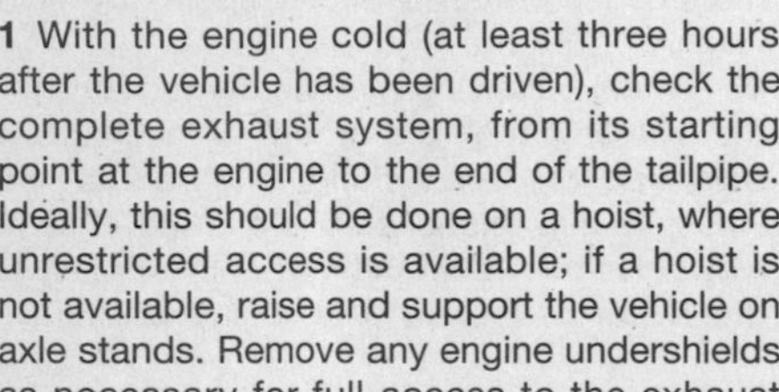

17 Exhaust system check

1 With the engine cold (at least three hours after the vehicle has been driven), check the complete exhaust system, from its starting point at the engine to the end of the tailpipe. Ideally, this should be done on a hoist, where unrestricted access is available; if a hoist is not available, raise and support the vehicle on axle stands. Remove any engine undershields as necessary for full access to the exhaust system.

2 Make sure that all brackets and rubber mountings are in good condition, and tight; if any of the mountings are to be renewed, ensure that the replacements are of the correct type **(see illustration)**. If any of the exhaust system rubber mountings are to be renewed, ensure that the replacements are of the correct type - their colour is a good guide. Those nearest to the catalytic converter are more heat-resistant than the others.

3 Check the pipes and connections for evidence of leaks, severe corrosion, or damage **(see illustration)**. Leakage at any of the joints or in other parts of the system will usually show up as a black sooty stain in the vicinity of the leak. **Note:** *Exhaust sealants should not be used on any part of the exhaust system upstream of the catalytic converter - even if the sealant does not contain additives harmful to the converter, pieces of it may break off and foul the element, causing local overheating.*

4 At the same time, inspect the underside of the body for holes, corrosion, open seams, etc. which may allow exhaust gases to enter the passenger compartment. Seal all body openings with silicone or body putty.

5 Rattles and other noises can often be traced to the exhaust system, especially the rubber mountings. Try to move the system, silencer(s) and catalytic converter. If any components can touch the body or suspension parts, secure the exhaust system with new mountings.

6 Check the running condition of the engine by inspecting inside the end of the tailpipe; the exhaust deposits here are an indication of the engine's state of tune. The inside of the tailpipe should be dry, and should vary in colour from dark grey to light grey/brown; if it is black and sooty, or coated with white deposits, the engine is in need of a thorough fuel system inspection.

18 Underbody and fuel/brake line check

1 With the vehicle raised and supported on axle stands or over an inspection pit, thoroughly inspect the underbody and wheel arches for signs of damage and corrosion. In particular, examine the bottom of the side sills, and any concealed areas where mud can collect.

2 Where corrosion and rust is evident, press and tap firmly on the panel with a screwdriver, and check for any serious corrosion which would necessitate repairs.

3 If the panel is not seriously corroded, clean away the rust, and apply a new coating of underseal. Refer to Chapter 11 for more details of body repairs.

4 At the same time, inspect the PVC-coated lower body panels for stone damage and general condition.

5 Inspect all of the fuel and brake lines on the underbody for damage, rust, corrosion and leakage. Also make sure that they are correctly supported in their clips. Where applicable, check the PVC coating on the lines for damage.

19 Braking system check

1 The work described in this Section should be carried out at the specified intervals, or whenever a defect is suspected in the braking system. Any of the following symptoms could indicate a potential brake system defect:

a) The vehicle pulls to one side when the brake pedal is depressed.
b) The brakes make squealing, scraping or dragging noises when applied.
c) Brake pedal travel is excessive, or pedal feel is poor.
d) The brake fluid requires repeated topping-up. Note that, on models with a hydraulic clutch (see Chapter 6), this problem could be due to a leak in the clutch system.

Front disc brakes

2 Apply the handbrake, then loosen the front wheel nuts. Jack up the front of the vehicle, and support it on axle stands.

3 For better access to the brake calipers, remove the wheels.

4 Look through the inspection window in the caliper, and check that the thickness of the friction lining material on each of the pads is not less than the recommended minimum thickness given in the Specifications **(see illustration)**. **Note:** *Bear in mind that the lining material is normally bonded to a metal backing plate.*

5 If it is difficult to determine the exact thickness of the pad linings, or if you are at all concerned about the condition of the pads, then remove them from the calipers for further inspection (refer to Chapter 9).

6 Check the other caliper in the same way.

7 If any one of the brake pads has worn down to, or below, the specified limit, *all four* pads at that end of the car must be renewed as a set.

8 Measure the thickness of the discs with a micrometer, if available, to make sure that they still have service life remaining **(see illustration)**. If any disc is thinner than the specified minimum thickness, renew it (refer to Chapter 9). In any case, check the general condition of the discs. Look for excessive

19.4 Check the thickness of the pad friction material through the caliper inspection window

19.8 Check the disc thickness with a micrometer, if available

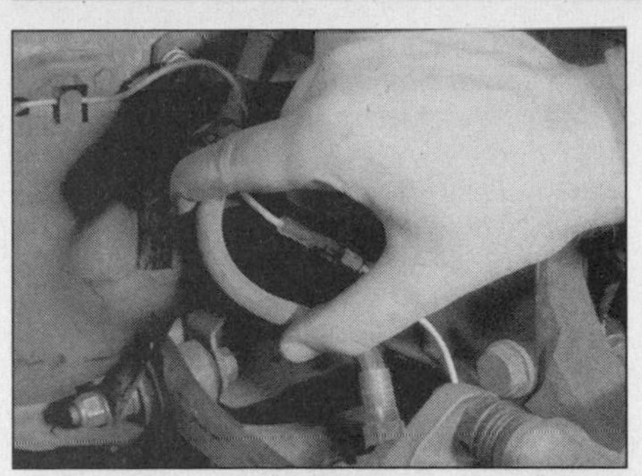

19.9 Checking the condition of a flexible brake hose

scoring and discolouration caused by overheating. If these conditions exist, remove the relevant disc and have it resurfaced or renewed (refer to Chapter 9).

9 Before refitting the wheels, check all brake lines and hoses (refer to Chapter 9). In particular, check the flexible hoses in the vicinity of the calipers, where they are subjected to most movement. Bend them between the fingers (but do not actually bend them double, or the casing may be damaged) and check that this does not reveal previously-hidden cracks, cuts or splits **(see illustration)**.

10 On completion, refit the wheels and lower the car to the ground. Tighten the wheel nuts to the specified torque.

Rear disc brakes

11 Loosen the rear wheel nuts, then chock the front wheels. Jack up the rear of the car, and support it on axle stands. Remove the rear wheels.

12 The procedure for checking the rear brakes is much the same as described in paragraphs 2 to 10 above.

Rear drum brakes

13 Loosen the rear wheel nuts, then chock the front wheels. Jack up the rear of the car, and support on axle stands. Remove the rear wheels.

14 To check the brake shoe lining thickness without removing the brake drums, prise the rubber plugs from the backplates, and use an electric torch to inspect the linings of the leading brake shoes **(see illustration)**. Check that the thickness of the lining material on the brake shoes is not less than the recommendation given in the Specifications.

15 If it is difficult to determine the exact thickness of the brake shoe linings, or if you are at all concerned about the condition of the shoes, then remove the rear drums for a more comprehensive inspection (refer to Chapter 9).

16 With the drum removed, check the shoe return and hold-down springs for correct installation, and check the wheel cylinders for leakage of brake fluid. Check the friction surface of the brake drums for scoring and discoloration. If excessive, the drum should be resurfaced or renewed.

17 Before refitting the wheels, check all brake lines and hoses (refer to Chapter 9). On completion, apply the handbrake and check that the rear wheels are locked. The handbrake is self-adjusting, and no manual adjustment is possible.

18 On completion, refit the wheels and lower the car to the ground. Tighten the wheel nuts to the specified torque.

20 Door and bonnet check and lubrication

1 Check that the doors, bonnet and tailgate/boot lid close securely. Check that the bonnet safety catch operates correctly. Check the operation of the door check straps.

2 Lubricate the hinges, door check straps, the striker plates and the bonnet catch sparingly with a little oil or grease.

21 Roadwheel nut tightness check

1 Checking the tightness of the wheel nuts is more relevant than you might think. Apart from the obvious safety aspect of ensuring they are sufficiently tight, this check will reveal whether they have been over-tightened, as may have happened the last time new tyres were fitted, for example. If the car suffers a puncture, you may find that the wheel nuts cannot be loosened with the wheelbrace.

2 Apply the handbrake, chock the wheels, and engage 1st gear (or 'P').

3 Remove the wheel cover (or wheel centre cover), using the flat end of the wheelbrace supplied in the tool kit.

4 Loosen the first wheel nut, using the wheelbrace if possible. If the nut proves stubborn, use a close-fitting socket and a long extension bar.

Warning: Do not use makeshift means to loosen the wheel nuts if the proper tools are not available. If extra force is required, make sure that the tools fit properly, and are of good quality. Even so, consider the consequences of the tool slipping or breaking, and take precautions - wearing stout gloves is advisable to protect your hands. Do not be tempted to stand on the tools used - they are not designed for this, and there is a high risk of personal injury if the tool slips or breaks. If the wheel nuts are simply too tight, take the car to a garage equipped with suitable power tools.

5 Once the nut has been loosened, remove it and check that the wheel stud threads are clean. Use a small wire brush to clean any rust or dirt from the threads, if necessary.

6 Refit the nut, with the tapered side facing inwards. Tighten it fully, using the wheelbrace alone - no other tools. This will ensure that the wheel nuts can be loosened using the

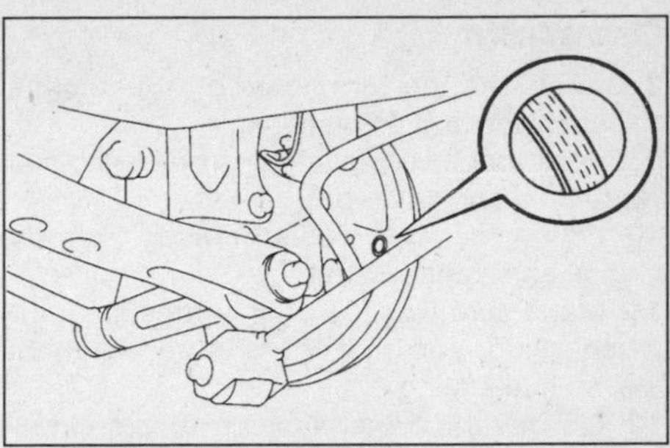

19.14 Prise the rubber plugs from the backplates to inspect the leading brake shoe linings

wheelbrace if a puncture occurs. However, if a torque wrench is available, tighten the nut to the specified torque wrench setting.

7 Repeat the procedure for the remaining three nuts, then refit the wheel cover or centre cover, as applicable.

8 Work around the car, checking and re-tightening the nuts for all four wheels.

22 Road test

Braking system

1 Make sure that the vehicle does not pull to one side when braking, and that the wheels do not lock prematurely when braking hard.

2 Check that there is no vibration through the steering when braking. On models equipped with ABS brakes, if vibration is felt through the pedal under heavy braking, this is a normal characteristic of the system operation, and is not a cause for concern.

3 Check that the handbrake operates correctly, without excessive movement of the lever, and that it holds the vehicle stationary on a slope, in both directions (facing up or down a slope).

4 With the engine switched off, test the operation of the brake servo unit as follows. Depress the footbrake four or five times to exhaust the vacuum, then start the engine. As the engine starts, there should be a noticeable 'give' in the brake pedal as vacuum builds up. Allow the engine to run for at least two minutes, and then switch it off. If the brake pedal is now depressed again, it should be possible to detect a hiss from the servo as the pedal is depressed. After about four or five applications, no further hissing should be heard, and the pedal should feel considerably harder.

Steering and suspension

5 Check for any abnormalities in the steering, suspension, handling or road 'feel'.

6 Drive the vehicle, and check that there are no unusual vibrations or noises.

7 Check that the steering feels positive, with no excessive sloppiness or roughness, and check for any suspension noises when cornering and driving over bumps.

Drivetrain

8 Check the performance of the engine, transmission and driveshafts.

9 Check that the engine starts correctly, both when cold and when hot.

10 Listen for any unusual noises from the engine and transmission.

11 Make sure that the engine runs smoothly when idling, and that there is no hesitation when accelerating.

12 On manual transmission models, check that all gears can be engaged smoothly without noise, and that the gear lever action is not abnormally vague or 'notchy'.

13 On automatic transmission models, make sure that all gearchanges occur smoothly without snatching, and without an increase in engine speed between changes. Check that all the gear positions can be selected with the vehicle at rest. If any problems are found, they should be referred to a Ford dealer.

14 Listen for a metallic clicking sound from the front of the vehicle as the vehicle is driven slowly in a circle with the steering on full-lock. Carry out this check in both directions. If a clicking noise is heard, this indicates wear in a driveshaft joint, in which case renew the joint if necessary.

Clutch

15 Check that the clutch pedal moves smoothly and easily through its full travel, and that the clutch itself functions correctly, with no trace of slip or drag.

16 On models with a cable-operated clutch, if the movement is uneven or stiff in places, check that the cable is routed correctly, with no sharp turns. Inspect both ends of the clutch inner cable, both at the gearbox end and inside the car, for signs of wear and fraying.

17 On models with a hydraulically-operated clutch, if the clutch is slow to release, it is possible that the system requires bleeding (see Chapter 6). Also check the fluid pipes under the bonnet for signs of leakage.

18 Check the clutch adjustment as described in Chapter 6.

Instruments and electrical equipment

19 Check the operation of all instruments and electrical equipment.

20 Make sure that all instruments read correctly, and switch on all electrical equipment in turn, to check that it functions properly.

Every 20 000 miles or 2 years

23 Ventilation system pollen filter renewal

1 The air entering the vehicle's ventilation system is passed through a very fine pleated-paper air filter element, which removes particles of pollen, dust and other airborne foreign matter. To ensure its continued effectiveness, this filter's element must be renewed at regular intervals. Failure to renew the element will also result in greatly-reduced airflow into the passenger compartment, reducing demisting and ventilation.

2 Where necessary, remove the left-hand side windscreen wiper arm (see Chapter 12).

3 Prise off their trim caps, then unscrew the two screws securing the windscreen edge of the cowl grille panel; remove the clips beneath the screws. Open the bonnet and remove the remaining Torx screws **(see illustrations)**.

4 Peel back the rubber seal and withdraw the cowl grille panel, unclipping it where it joins the top of the wing **(see illustrations)**.

5 Releasing the clip at each end, lift out the pollen filter housing, and withdraw the element **(see illustrations)**.

6 Wipe out the ventilation system intake and the filter housing, removing any leaves, dead insects etc.

7 If carrying out a routine service, the element must be renewed regardless of its apparent condition. If you are checking the element for any other reason, inspect its front surface; if it is very dirty, renew the element. If it is only moderately dusty, it can be re-used by blowing it clean from the rear to the front surface with compressed air.

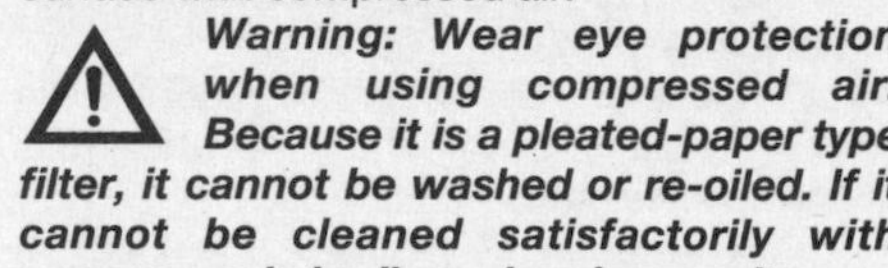

Warning: Wear eye protection when using compressed air! Because it is a pleated-paper type filter, it cannot be washed or re-oiled. If it cannot be cleaned satisfactorily with compressed air, discard and renew it.

8 Refitting is the reverse of the removal procedure; ensure that the element and housing are securely seated, so that unfiltered air cannot enter the passenger compartment.

23.3a Remove cowl grille panel screws (arrowed) - on some models, only two lower (Torx) screws are fitted . . .

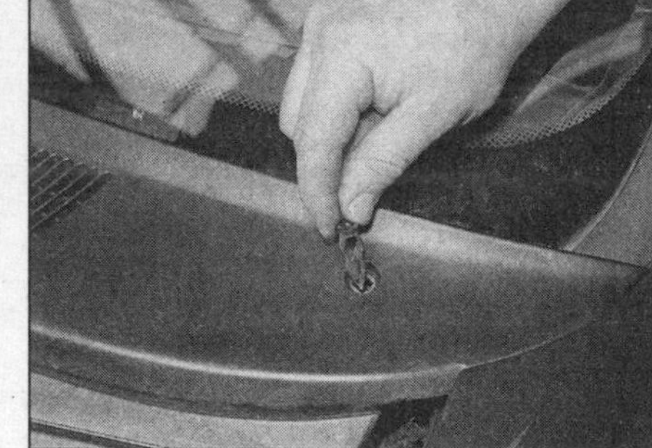

23.3b . . . and remove the clips beneath the upper screws

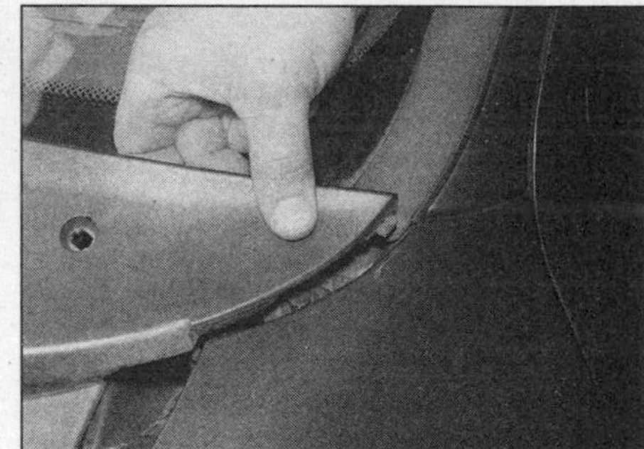

23.4a Unclip the end of the grille panel from the wing . . .

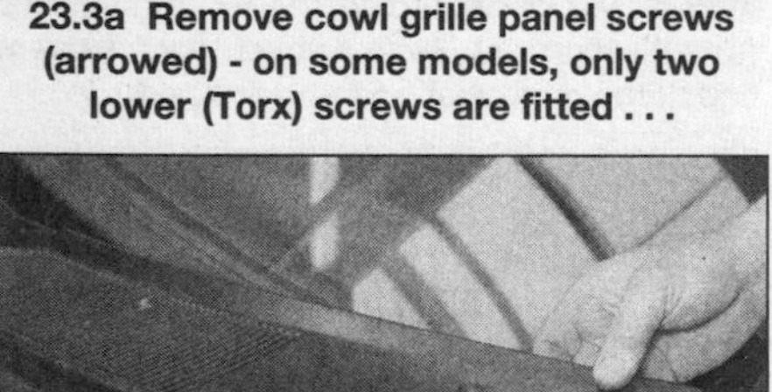

23.4b . . . and remove the grille panel

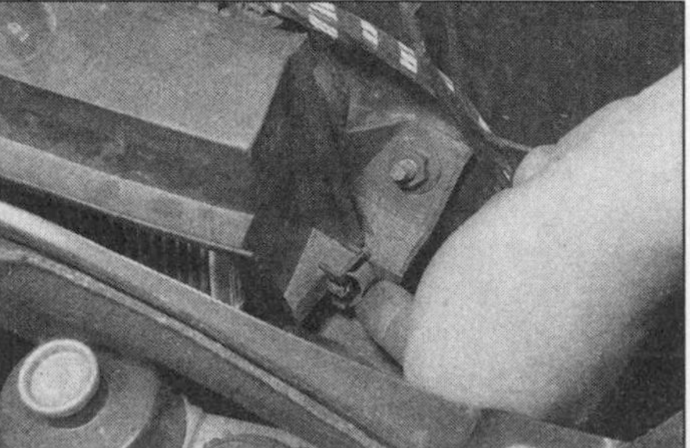

23.5a . . . release clips to lift out pollen filter housing . . .

23.5b . . . then withdraw pollen filter element from its housing

24.1a Release the wire clips to detach the cover from the air cleaner assembly . . .

24.1b . . . on four-cylinder engines, note the long clip normally hidden by the battery

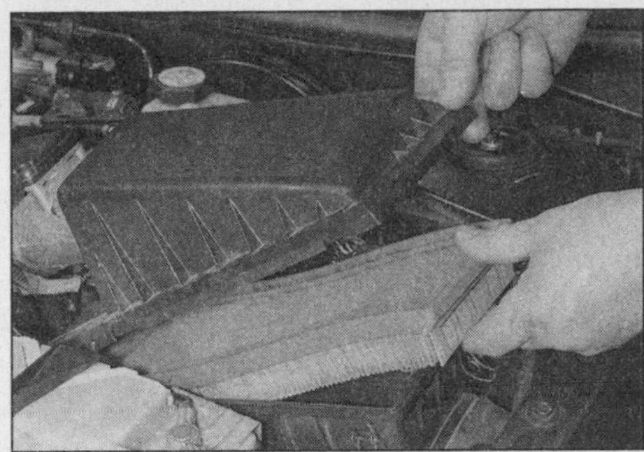

24.3 Lift the element out of the housing, noting its direction of fitting

Every 30 000 miles or 3 years

24 Air filter element renewal

Caution: Never drive the vehicle with the air cleaner filter element removed. Excessive engine wear could result, and backfiring could even cause a fire under the bonnet.

1 The air filter element is located in the air cleaner assembly on the left-hand side of the engine compartment. Release the over-centre wire clips, and lift up the air cleaner cover **(see illustrations)**.

2 If additional working clearance is required, remove the cover completely; on four-cylinder models, unclip the cover from the air mass meter, while on the V6 engine, slacken the air inlet hose clip and detach it from the air mass meter.

3 Lift out the element, noting its direction of fitting, and wipe out the housing **(see illustration)**. Check that no foreign matter is visible, either in the air intake or in the air mass meter.

4 If carrying out a routine service, the element must be renewed regardless of its apparent condition.

5 On four-cylinder engine models, note that the small foam filter in the rear right-hand corner of the air cleaner housing must be cleaned whenever the air filter element is renewed (see Section 25).

6 If you are checking the element for any other reason, inspect its lower surface; if it is oily or very dirty, renew the element. If it is only moderately dusty, it can be re-used by blowing it clean from the upper to the lower surface with compressed air.

Warning: Wear eye protection when using compressed air! Because it is a pleated-paper type filter, it cannot be washed or re-oiled. If it cannot be cleaned satisfactorily with compressed air, discard and renew it.

7 Refitting is the reverse of the removal procedure, noting the following points:

a) Make sure that the filter is fitted the correct way up (observe any direction-of-fitting markings).

b) Ensure that the element and cover are securely seated, so that unfiltered air cannot enter the engine.

c) Secure the cover with all the over-centre wire clips. If the cover was removed, reconnect the cover or hose to the air mass meter.

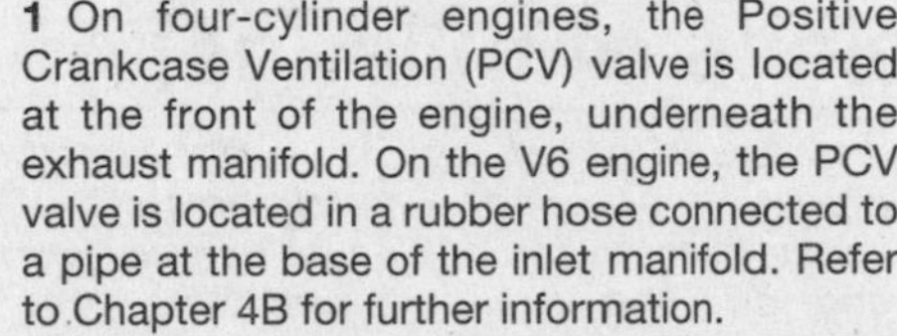

25 Positive Crankcase Ventilation (PCV) system check and filter cleaning

1 On four-cylinder engines, the Positive Crankcase Ventilation (PCV) valve is located at the front of the engine, underneath the exhaust manifold. On the V6 engine, the PCV valve is located in a rubber hose connected to a pipe at the base of the inlet manifold. Refer to Chapter 4B for further information.

2 Check that all components of the system are securely fastened, correctly routed (with no kinks or sharp bends to restrict flow) and in sound condition; renew any worn or damaged components.

3 The PCV valve is designed to allow gases to flow out of the crankcase only, so that a depression is created in the crankcase under most operating conditions, particularly at idle. Therefore, if either the oil separator or the PCV valve are thought to be blocked, they must be renewed (see Chapter 4B). In such a case, however, there is nothing to be lost by attempting to flush out the blockage using a suitable solvent. The PCV valve should rattle when shaken.

4 If oil leakage is noted, disconnect the various hoses and pipes, and check that all are clear and unblocked.

Four-cylinder engines

5 Remove the air cleaner assembly cover, air mass meter and resonator (where applicable), then check that the hose from the cylinder head cover to the air cleaner housing is clear and undamaged.

6 Disconnect the rubber T-piece both from the union on the inlet manifold left-hand end, and from the metal crankcase breather pipe under the ignition coil. Connect a spare, clean, length of hose to the breather pipe. Suck on the end of the hose, then blow through it - little or no restriction to airflow should be felt in either direction.

7 A similar test can be applied to check that the inlet manifold passages are clear - air should be heard hissing out of the plenum chamber mouth as you blow.

8 While the air filter element is removed (see Section 24), wipe out the housing, and withdraw the small foam filter from its location in the rear right-hand corner of the housing **(see illustration)**. If the foam is badly clogged with dirt or oil, it must be cleaned by soaking it in a suitable solvent, and allowed to dry before being refitted.

V6 engine

9 Unplug the two breather hoses from the air inlet hose connected to the air mass meter **(see illustration)**. Blow through each hose to check that it is clear and undamaged.

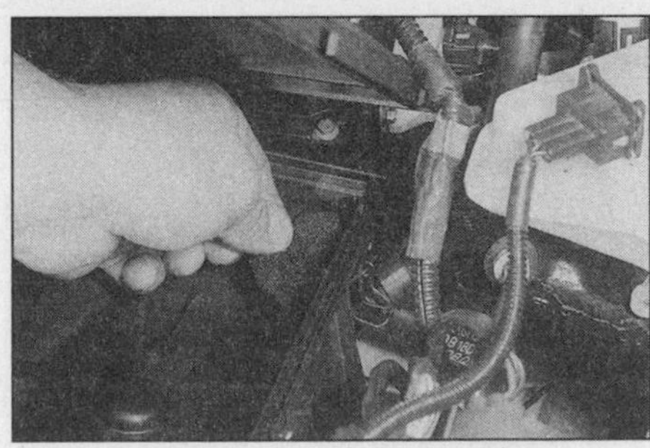

25.8 Removing the PCV system filter from the air cleaner assembly

25.9 Check that the breather hoses are clear

10 Disconnect the short piece of rubber hose from the metal pipe at the base of the inlet manifold, and check that the pipe and hose are clear.

11 Disconnect the hose from the rear of the PCV valve - the hose is normally encased in plastic insulation - and check that it is clear.

All models

12 On completion, ensure that all connections which were disturbed are securely remade, so that there are no air (or oil) leaks.

26 Automatic transmission fluid renewal

1 Park the car on level ground, and switch off the engine. Apply the handbrake, and engage 'P'. Jack up the front of the car and support on axle stands. Remove the transmission fluid dipstick.

2 Depending on model, it may be necessary to remove the engine undershield for access to the transmission drain plug. The plug is fitted on the base of the transmission housing, and may be identified by its recessed square fitting.

3 Taking adequate precautions against burning or scalding if the engine and transmission are hot (wear gloves), position a suitable container below the transmission drain plug.

4 Using a suitable adaptor, or possibly the drive end of a socket handle, loosen and remove the drain plug **(see illustration)**, and allow the fluid to drain into the container.

5 Clean the drain plug thoroughly, then when the flow of fluid has ceased, refit the plug and tighten it to the specified torque.

6 Remove the fluid container from under the car. Refit the engine undershield (where removed), then lower the car to the ground.

7 The transmission is filled via the dipstick tube, making it a long and potentially messy job. Use a narrow funnel, and take great care to avoid introducing any kind of dirt into the transmission as it is filled.

8 After about half the specified 'drain and refill' quantity of fluid has been added, start checking the fluid level with the dipstick. Once the fluid level is up to the 'MIN' mark, refit the dipstick. Refer to Section 6 for details of dipstick location and markings.

9 Start the engine, and let it idle. Depress the brake pedal and move the selector lever through all the positions three times, beginning and ending in 'P'.

10 Allow the engine to idle for one minute, then (with the engine still idling) remove the dipstick from its tube.

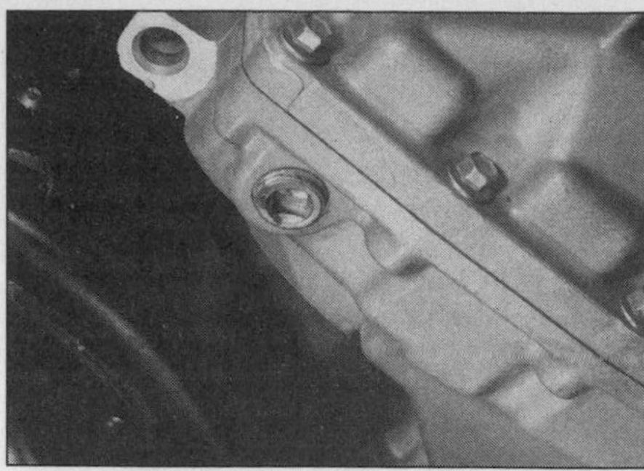

26.4 Automatic transmission fluid drain plug

11 Wipe the fluid from the dipstick with a clean rag, and re-insert it into the filler tube until the cap seats.

12 Pull the dipstick out again, and note the fluid level. The level should be between the 'MIN' and 'MAX' marks. If the level is on or below the 'MIN' mark, stop the engine, and add more fluid through the dipstick tube.

13 Repeat the checking and topping-up procedure until the level is correct. On completion, refit the dipstick, ensuring it is properly seated.

Every 3 years (regardless of mileage)

27 Brake fluid renewal

The procedure is similar to that for the bleeding of the hydraulic system as described in Chapter 9, except that the brake fluid reservoir should be emptied by siphoning, and allowance should be made for the old fluid to be removed from the circuit when bleeding a section of the circuit.

28 Coolant renewal

Note: *If the antifreeze used is Ford's own, or of similar quality, Ford state that the coolant need not be renewed for the life of the vehicle. If the vehicle's history is unknown, if antifreeze of lesser quality is known to be in the system, or simply if you prefer to follow conventional servicing intervals, the coolant should be changed periodically (typically, every 3 years) as described here.*

Warning: Do not allow antifreeze to come in contact with your skin or painted surfaces of the vehicle. Flush contaminated areas immediately with plenty of water. Don't store new coolant, or leave old coolant lying around, where it's accessible to children or pets - they're attracted by its sweet smell. Ingestion of even a small amount of coolant can be fatal! Wipe up garage-floor and drip-pan spills immediately. Keep antifreeze containers covered, and repair cooling system leaks as soon as they're noticed.

Warning: Never remove the expansion tank filler cap when the engine is running, or has just been switched off, as the cooling system will be hot, and the consequent escaping steam and scalding coolant could cause serious injury.

Coolant draining

Warning: Wait until the engine is cold before starting this procedure.

1 To drain the system, first remove the expansion tank filler cap (see Section 30).

2 If the additional working clearance is required, raise the front of the vehicle and support it securely on axle stands.

3 Remove the radiator undershield (eight or nine screws), then place a large drain tray underneath, and unscrew the radiator drain plug; direct as much of the escaping coolant as possible into the tray **(see illustrations)**.

System flushing

4 With time, the cooling system may gradually lose its efficiency, as the radiator core becomes choked with rust, scale deposits from the water, and other sediment. To minimise this, as well as using only good-quality antifreeze and clean soft water, the system should be flushed as follows

28.3a Remove the screws (arrowed) and withdraw the radiator undershield . . .

28.3b . . . then unscrew the radiator drain plug (arrowed) and empty the cooling system

whenever any part of it is disturbed, and/or when the coolant is renewed.

5 With the coolant drained, refit the drain plug and refill the system with fresh water. Refit the expansion tank filler cap, start the engine and warm it up to normal operating temperature, then stop it and (after allowing it to cool down completely) drain the system again. Repeat as necessary until only clean water can be seen to emerge, then refill finally with the specified coolant mixture.

6 If only clean, soft water and good-quality antifreeze (even if not to Ford's specification) has been used, and the coolant has been renewed at the suggested intervals, the above procedure will be sufficient to keep clean the system for a considerable length of time. If, however, the system has been neglected, a more thorough operation will be required, as follows.

7 First drain the coolant, then disconnect the radiator top and bottom hoses. Insert a garden hose into the radiator top hose connection, and allow water to circulate through the radiator until it runs clean from the bottom outlet.

8 To flush the engine, insert the garden hose into the bottom hose, wrap a piece of rag around the garden hose to seal the connection, and allow water to circulate until it runs clear. Try the effect of repeating this procedure in the top hose, although this may not be effective, since the thermostat will probably close and prevent the flow of water.

9 If, after a reasonable period, the water still does not run clear, the radiator should be flushed with a good proprietary cleaning agent.

10 In severe cases of contamination, reverse-flushing of the radiator may be necessary. This may be achieved by inserting the garden hose into the bottom outlet, wrapping a piece of rag around the hose to seal the connection, then flushing the radiator until clear water emerges from the top hose outlet.

11 If the radiator is suspected of being severely choked, remove the radiator (Chapter 3), turn it upside-down, and repeat the procedure described in paragraph 10.

12 Flushing the heater matrix can be achieved using a similar procedure to that described in paragraph 10, once the heater inlet and outlet hoses have been identified. These two hoses will be of the same diameter, and pass through the engine compartment bulkhead (refer to the heater matrix removal procedure in Chapter 3 for more details).

13 The use of chemical cleaners is not recommended, and should be necessary only as a last resort. Normally, regular renewal of the coolant will prevent excessive contamination of the system.

Coolant filling

14 With the cooling system drained and flushed, ensure that all disturbed hose unions are correctly secured, and that the radiator drain plug is securely tightened. Refit the radiator undershield, noting that it is located by three clips at its front edge; tighten the retaining screws securely **(see illustration)**. If it was raised, lower the vehicle to the ground.

15 Prepare a sufficient quantity of the specified coolant mixture (see below); allow for a surplus, so as to have a reserve supply for topping-up.

16 Slowly fill the system through the expansion tank **(see illustration)**. Since the tank is the highest point in the system, all the air in the system should be displaced into the tank by the rising liquid. Slow pouring reduces the possibility of air being trapped and forming air-locks.

17 Continue filling until the coolant level reaches the expansion tank 'MAX' level line, then cover the filler opening to prevent coolant splashing out.

18 Start the engine and run it at idle speed, until it has warmed-up to normal operating temperature and the radiator electric cooling fan has cut in; watch the temperature gauge to check for signs of overheating. If the level in the expansion tank drops significantly, top-up to the 'MAX' level line, to minimise the amount of air circulating in the system.

19 Stop the engine, allow it to cool down *completely* (overnight, if possible), then uncover the expansion tank filler opening and top-up the tank to the 'MAX' level line. Refit the filler cap, tightening it securely, and wash off any spilt coolant from the engine compartment and bodywork.

20 After refilling, always check carefully all components of the system (but especially any unions disturbed during draining and flushing) for signs of coolant leaks. Fresh antifreeze has a searching action, which will rapidly expose any weak points in the system.

21 **Note:** *If, after draining and refilling the system, symptoms of overheating are found which did not occur previously, then the fault is almost certainly due to trapped air at some point in the system, causing an air-lock and restricting the flow of coolant; usually, the air is trapped because the system was refilled too quickly. In some cases, air-locks can be released by tapping or squeezing the various hoses. If the problem persists, stop the engine and allow it to cool down completely, before unscrewing the expansion tank filler cap or disconnecting hoses to bleed out the trapped air.*

Antifreeze type and mixture

22 Ford state that, if the only antifreeze used is the type with which the system was first filled at the factory (antifreeze to specification ESD-M97B-49-A, or more recently, specification WSS-M97B44-D) it will last the lifetime of the vehicle. This is subject to it being used in the recommended concentration, unmixed with any other type of antifreeze or additive, and topped-up when necessary using only that antifreeze mixed 50/50 with clean water. If any other type of antifreeze is added, the lifetime guarantee no longer applies; to restore the lifetime protection, the system must be drained and thoroughly reverse-flushed before fresh coolant mixture is poured in.

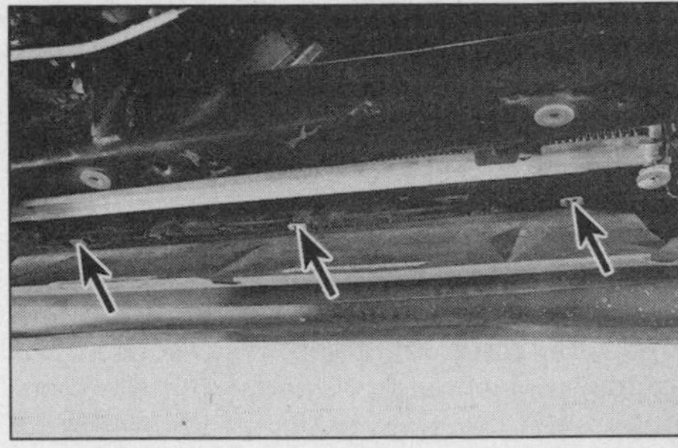

28.14 Ensure the radiator undershield is located securely in three clips at front edge (arrowed) when refitting

23 If the vehicle's history (and therefore the quality of the antifreeze in it) is unknown, owners who wish to follow Ford's recommendations are advised to drain and thoroughly reverse-flush the system, before refilling with fresh coolant mixture. If the appropriate quality of antifreeze is used, the coolant can then be left for the life of the vehicle.

24 If any antifreeze other than Ford's is to be used, the coolant must be renewed at regular intervals to provide an equivalent degree of protection; the conventional recommendation is to renew the coolant every three years.

25 If the antifreeze used is to Ford's specification, the levels of protection it affords are indicated in the Specifications Section of this Chapter. To give the recommended *standard* mixture ratio for this antifreeze, 40% (by volume) of antifreeze must be mixed with 60% of clean, soft water; if you are using any other type of antifreeze, follow its manufacturer's instructions to achieve the correct ratio.

26 It is best to make up slightly more than the system's specified capacity, so that a supply is available for subsequent topping-up. However, note that you are unlikely to fully drain the system at any one time (unless the engine is being completely stripped), and the capacities quoted are therefore slightly academic for routine coolant renewal.

28.16 Filling the cooling system

27 Before adding antifreeze, the cooling system should be completely drained, preferably flushed, and all hoses checked for condition and security. As noted earlier, fresh antifreeze will rapidly find any weaknesses in the system.

28 After filling with antifreeze, a label should be attached to the expansion tank, stating the type and concentration of antifreeze used, and the date installed. Any subsequent topping-up should be made with the same type and concentration of antifreeze. If topping-up using antifreeze to Ford's specification, note that a 50/50 mixture is permissible, purely for convenience.

29 Do not use engine antifreeze in the windscreen/tailgate washer system, as it will damage the vehicle's paintwork. A screen wash additive should be added to the washer system in its maker's recommended quantities.

General cooling system checks

30 The engine should be cold for the cooling system checks, so perform the following procedure before driving the vehicle, or after it has been shut off for at least three hours.

31 Remove the expansion tank filler cap (also see Section 30), and clean it thoroughly inside and out with a rag. Also clean the filler neck on the expansion tank. The presence of rust or corrosion in the filler neck indicates that the coolant should be changed. The coolant inside the expansion tank should be relatively clean and transparent. If it is rust-coloured, drain and flush the system, and refill with a fresh coolant mixture.

32 Carefully check the radiator hoses and heater hoses along their entire length; renew any hose which is cracked, swollen or deteriorated (see Section 8).

33 Inspect all other cooling system components (joint faces, etc.) for leaks. A leak in the cooling system will usually show up as white- or rust-coloured deposits on the area adjoining the leak. Where any problems of this nature are found on system components, renew the component or gasket with reference to Chapter 3.

34 Clean the front of the radiator with a soft brush to remove all insects, leaves, etc, embedded in the radiator fins. Be careful not to damage the radiator fins, or cut your fingers on them. To do a more thorough job, remove the radiator grille as described in Chapter 11.

Every 40 000 miles

29 Spark plug renewal - four-cylinder engines

Spark plug check and renewal

1 It is vital for the correct running, full performance and proper economy of the engine that the spark plugs perform with maximum efficiency. The most important factor in ensuring this is that the plugs fitted are appropriate for the engine.

2 The spark plug type is given in the Specifications Section at the beginning of this Chapter, on the Vehicle Emissions Control Information (VECI) label located on the underside of the bonnet (only on models sold in some areas) or in the vehicle's handbook. If these sources specify different plugs, purchase the spark plug type specified on the VECI label (where appropriate), as that information is provided specifically for your engine.

3 If the correct plugs are used and the engine is in good condition, the spark plugs should not need attention between scheduled renewal intervals. Spark plug cleaning is rarely necessary, and should not be attempted unless specialised equipment is available, as damage can easily be caused to the firing ends.

4 Spark plug removal and refitting requires a spark plug socket, with an extension which can be turned by a ratchet handle or similar. This socket is lined with a rubber sleeve, to protect the porcelain insulator of the spark plug, and to hold the plug while you insert it into the spark plug hole. You will also need feeler blades, to check and adjust the spark plug electrode gap, and (ideally) a torque wrench to tighten the new plugs to the specified torque.

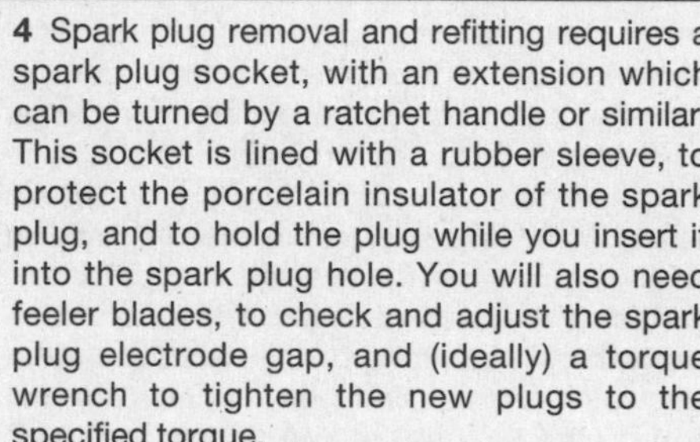

5 To remove the spark plugs, first open the bonnet; the plugs are easily reached at the top of the engine. Note how the spark plug (HT) leads are routed and secured by clips along the channel in the cylinder head cover. To prevent the possibility of mixing up spark plug (HT) leads, it is a good idea to try to work on one spark plug at a time.

6 If the marks on the original-equipment spark plug (HT) leads cannot be seen, mark the leads 1 to 4, to correspond to the cylinder the lead serves (No 1 cylinder is at the timing belt end of the engine). Pull the leads from the plugs by gripping the rubber boot sealing the cylinder head cover opening, not the lead, otherwise the lead connection may be fractured **(see illustration)**.

7 It is advisable to soak up any water in the spark plug recesses with a rag, and to remove any dirt from them using a clean brush, vacuum cleaner or compressed air before removing the plugs, to prevent any dirt or water from dropping into the cylinders.

Warning: Wear eye protection when using compressed air!

8 Unscrew the spark plugs, ensuring that the socket is kept in alignment with each plug - if the socket is forcibly moved to either side, the porcelain top of the plug may be broken off. Remove the plug from the engine **(see illustrations)**.

9 If any undue difficulty is encountered when unscrewing any of the spark plugs, carefully check the cylinder head threads and tapered sealing surfaces for signs of wear, excessive corrosion or damage; if any of these conditions is found, seek the advice of a Ford dealer as to the best method of repair.

10 As each plug is removed, examine it as follows - this will give a good indication of the condition of the engine:

a) *If the insulator nose of the spark plug is clean and white, with no deposits, this is indicative of a weak mixture.*
b) *If the tip and insulator nose are covered with hard black-looking deposits, then this is indicative that the mixture is too rich.*
c) *Should the plug be black and oily, then it is likely that the engine is fairly worn, as well as the mixture being too rich.*

29.6 Pull off the HT leads from the spark plugs

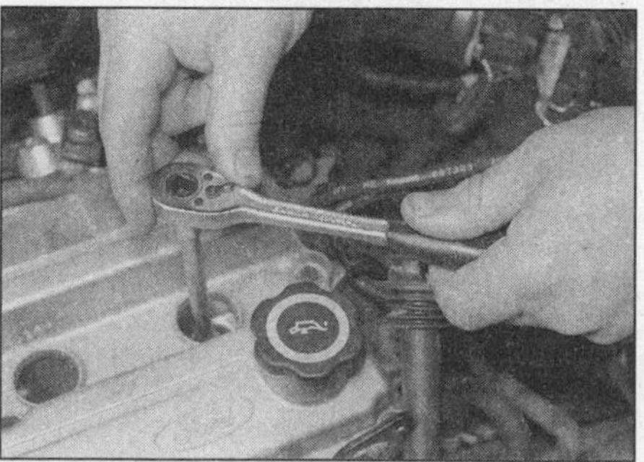

29.8a Using a suitable plug socket and handle, unscrew . . .

29.8b . . . and remove the plugs from the engine

29.13 Spark plug manufacturers recommend using a wire-type gauge when checking the gap

d) If the insulator nose is covered with light tan to greyish-brown deposits, then the mixture is correct, and it is likely that the engine is in good condition.

11 If you are renewing the spark plugs, purchase the new plugs, then check each of them first for faults such as cracked insulators or damaged threads. Note also that, whenever the spark plugs are renewed as a routine service operation, the spark plug (HT) leads should be checked as described below.

12 The spark plug electrode gap is of considerable importance as, if it is too large or too small, the size of the spark and its efficiency will be seriously impaired. The gap should be set to the value given in the Specifications Section of this Chapter. New plugs will not necessarily be set to the correct gap, so they should always be checked before fitting.

13 Special spark plug electrode gap adjusting tools are available from most motor accessory shops **(see illustration)**.

14 To set the electrode gap, measure the gap with a feeler gauge, and then bend open, or closed, the outer plug electrode until the correct gap is achieved **(see illustration)**. The centre electrode should never be bent, as this may crack the insulation and cause plug failure, if nothing worse. If the outer electrode is not exactly over the centre electrode, bend it gently to align them.

15 Before fitting the spark plugs, check that the threaded connector sleeves at the top of the plugs are tight, and that the plug exterior surfaces and threads are clean. Brown staining on the porcelain, immediately above the metal body, is quite normal, and does not necessarily indicate a leak between the body and insulator.

16 On installing the spark plugs, first check that the cylinder head thread and sealing surface are as clean as possible; use a clean rag wrapped around a paintbrush to wipe clean the sealing surface. Apply a smear of copper-based grease or anti-seize compound to the threads of each plug, and screw them in by hand where possible. Take extra care to enter the plug threads correctly, as the cylinder head is made of aluminium alloy - it's often difficult to insert spark plugs into their holes without cross-threading them **(see Haynes Hint)**.

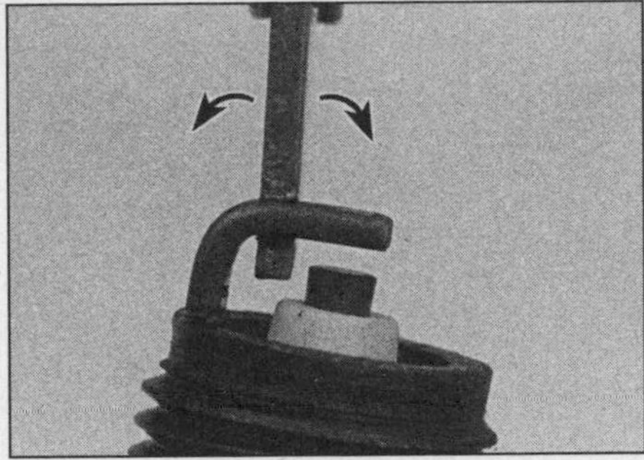

29.14 To change the gap, bend the outer electrode only, as indicated by the arrows

17 When each spark plug is started correctly on its threads, screw it down until it just seats lightly, then tighten it to the specified torque wrench setting. If a torque wrench is not available - and this is one case where the use of a torque wrench is strongly recommended - tighten each spark plug through *no more than* 1/16th of a turn. *Do not* exceed the specified torque setting, and *NEVER* overtighten these spark plugs - their tapered seats mean they are almost impossible to remove if abused.

18 Reconnect the spark plug (HT) leads in their correct order, using a twisting motion on the boot until it is firmly seated on the end of the spark plug and on the cylinder head cover.

Spark plug (HT) lead check

19 The spark plug (HT) leads should be checked whenever the plugs themselves are renewed. Start by making a visual check of the leads while the engine is running. In a darkened garage (make sure there is ventilation) start the engine and observe each lead. Be careful not to come into contact with any moving engine parts. If there is a break in the lead, you will see arcing or a small spark at the damaged area.

20 The spark plug (HT) leads should be inspected one at a time, to prevent mixing up the firing order, which is essential for proper engine operation. Each original lead should be numbered to identify its cylinder. If the number is illegible, a piece of tape can be marked with the correct number, and wrapped around the lead (the leads should be numbered 1 to 4, with No 1 lead nearest the timing belt end of the engine). The lead can then be disconnected.

21 Check inside the boot for corrosion, which will look like a white crusty powder. Clean this off as much as possible; if it is excessive, or if cleaning leaves the metal connector too badly corroded to be fit for further use, the lead must be renewed. Push the lead and boot back onto the end of the spark plug. The boot should fit tightly onto the end of the plug - if it doesn't, remove the lead and use pliers carefully to crimp the metal connector inside the boot until the fit is snug.

22 Using a clean rag, wipe the entire length of the lead to remove built-up dirt and grease. Once the lead is clean, check for burns, cracks and other damage. Do not bend the lead sharply, because the conductor might break.

To avoid the possibility of cross-threading a spark plug, fit a short piece of hose over the end of the plug. The flexible hose acts as a universal joint, to help align the plug with the plug hole. Should the plug begin to cross-thread, the hose will slip on the spark plug, preventing thread damage.

23 Disconnect the lead from the ignition coil by pressing together the plastic retaining catches and pulling the end fitting off the coil terminal. Check for corrosion and for a tight fit.

24 If a meter with the correct measuring range is available, measure the resistance of the disconnected lead from its coil connector to its spark plug connector **(see illustration)**. If the resistance recorded for any of the leads greatly exceeds 30 000 ohms per metre length, all the leads should be renewed as a set.

25 Refit the lead to the coil, noting that each coil terminal is marked with its respective cylinder number, so that there is no risk of mixing up the leads and upsetting the firing order.

26 Inspect the remaining spark plug (HT) leads, ensuring that each is securely fastened at the ignition coil and spark plug when the check is complete. If any sign of arcing, severe connector corrosion, burns, cracks or other damage is noticed, obtain new spark plug (HT) leads, renewing them as a set. If new spark plug leads are to be fitted, remove and refit them one at a time, to avoid mix-ups in the firing order.

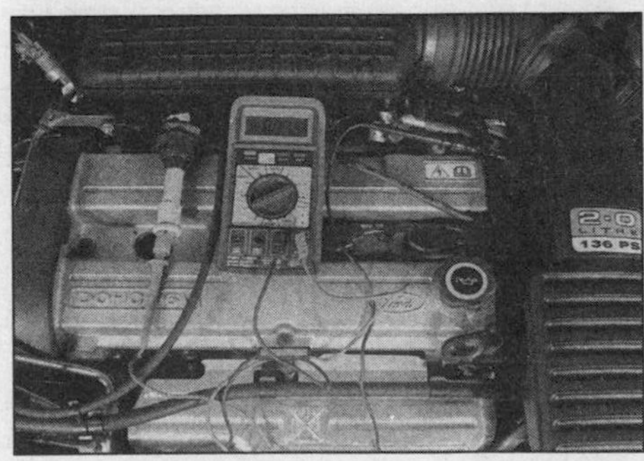

29.24 Measure the resistance of the spark plug leads using a suitable multi-meter

Every 4 years (regardless of mileage)

30 Expansion tank pressure cap check

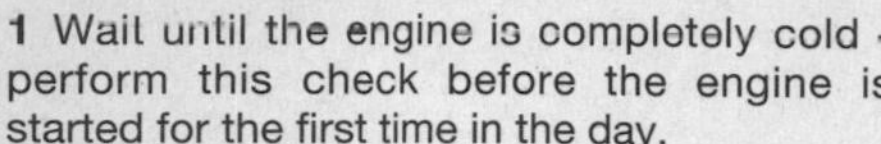

1 Wait until the engine is completely cold - perform this check before the engine is started for the first time in the day.

2 Place a wad of cloth over the expansion tank cap, then unscrew it slowly and remove it.

3 Examine the condition of the rubber seal on the underside of the cap. If the rubber appears to have hardened, or cracks are visible in the seal edges, a new cap should be fitted.

4 If the car is several years old, or has covered a large mileage, consider renewing the cap regardless of its apparent condition - they are not expensive. If the pressure relief valve built into the cap fails, excess pressure in the system will lead to puzzling failures of hoses and other cooling system components.

Every 60 000 miles

31 Fuel filter renewal

Warning: Petrol is extremely flammable, so extra precautions must be taken when working on any part of the fuel system. Do not smoke, or allow open flames or bare light bulbs, near the work area. Also, do not work in a garage if a natural gas-type appliance with a pilot light is present. While performing any work on the fuel system, wear safety glasses, and have a suitable (Class B) fire extinguisher on hand. If you spill any fuel on your skin, rinse it off immediately with soap and water.

1 The fuel filter is located at the front right-hand corner of the fuel tank, just forward of the vehicle's right-hand rear jacking point. The filter performs a vital role in keeping dirt and other foreign matter out of the fuel system, and so must be renewed at regular intervals, or whenever you have reason to suspect that it may be clogged.

2 It is always unpleasant working under a vehicle - pressure-washing or hosing clean the underbody in the filter's vicinity will make working conditions more tolerable, and will reduce the risk of getting dirt into the fuel system.

3 Before disturbing any fuel lines, which may contain fuel under pressure, any residual pressure in the system must be relieved as follows.

4 With the ignition switched off, open the engine compartment fusebox and remove the fuel pump fuse (No 14).

5 Start the engine, if possible - if the engine will not start, turn it over on the starter for a few seconds.

6 If the engine starts, allow it to idle until it dies. Turn the engine over once or twice on the starter, to ensure that all pressure is released, then switch off the ignition.

Warning: This procedure will merely relieve the increased pressure necessary for the engine to run - remember that fuel will still be present in the system components, and take precautions accordingly before disconnecting any of them.

7 Noting the comments made in Section 1 of Chapter 5A, disconnect the battery earth terminal.

8 Jack up the rear right-hand side of the vehicle, and support it securely on an axle stand.

9 Using rag to soak up any spilt fuel, release the fuel feed and outlet pipe unions from the filter, by squeezing together the protruding locking lugs on each union, and carefully pulling the union off the filter stub **(see illustration)**. Where the unions are colour-coded, the feed and outlet pipes cannot be confused; where both unions are the same colour, note carefully which pipe is connected to which filter stub, and ensure that they are correctly reconnected on refitting.

10 Noting the arrows and/or other markings on the filter showing the direction of fuel flow (towards the engine), slacken the filter clamp screw and withdraw the filter. Note that the filter will still contain fuel; care should be taken, to avoid spillage and to minimise the risk of fire.

11 On installation, slide the filter into its clamp so that the arrow marked on it faces the same direction as noted when removing the old filter **(see illustration)**.

12 Slide each pipe union onto its (correct) respective filter stub, and press it down until the locking lugs click into their groove **(see illustration)**. Tighten the clamp screw carefully, until the filter is just prevented from moving; do not overtighten the clamp screw, or the filter casing may be crushed.

13 Refit the fuel pump fuse and reconnect the battery earth terminal, then switch the ignition on and off five times, to pressurise the system. Check for any sign of fuel leakage around the filter unions before lowering the vehicle to the ground and starting the engine.

32 Spark plug renewal - V6 engine

Spark plug check and renewal

1 It is vital for the correct running, full performance and proper economy of the engine that the spark plugs perform with maximum efficiency. The most important factor in ensuring this is that the plugs fitted are appropriate for the engine.

31.9 Squeeze together the fuel filter pipe union locking lugs to release the unions

31.11 When installing the new filter, ensure the arrow showing direction of fuel flow points towards the engine

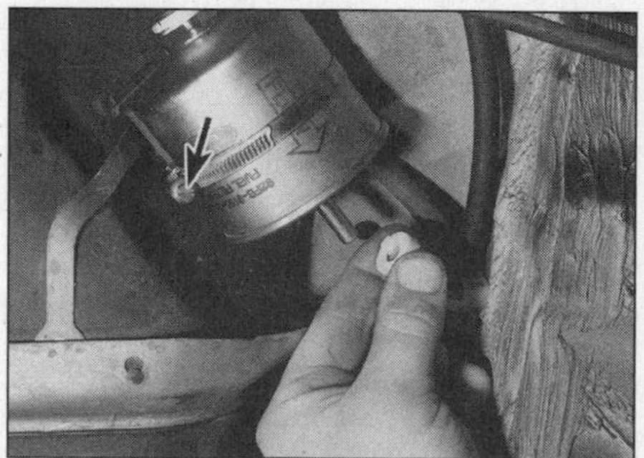

31.12 Secure the pipe unions as described - do not overtighten the clamp screw (arrowed)

32.7a Unscrew and remove the three bolts (arrowed) . . .

32.7b . . . and lift off the IMRC motor for access to the front plugs

32.9a Pull the HT leads from the spark plugs . . .

32.9b . . . and release the leads from their retaining clips (arrowed) as necessary

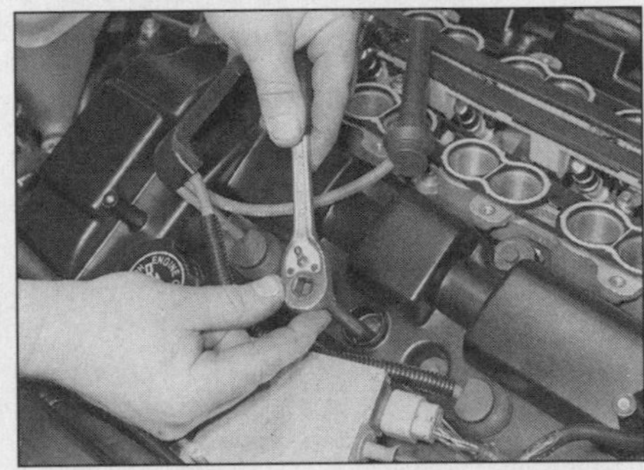
32.11a Using a spark plug socket and handle, unscrew . . .

32.11b . . . and remove the plugs from the engine

2 The spark plug type is given in the Specifications Section at the beginning of this Chapter, on the Vehicle Emissions Control Information (VECI) label located on the underside of the bonnet (only on models sold in some areas) or in the vehicle's handbook. If these sources specify different plugs, purchase the spark plug type specified on the VECI label (where appropriate), as that information is provided specifically for your engine.

3 If the correct plugs are used and the engine is in good condition, the spark plugs should not need attention between scheduled renewal intervals. Spark plug cleaning is rarely necessary, and should not be attempted unless specialised equipment is available, as damage can easily be caused to the firing ends.

4 Spark plug removal and refitting requires a spark plug socket, with an extension which can be turned by a ratchet handle or similar. This socket is lined with a rubber sleeve, to protect the porcelain insulator of the spark plug, and to hold the plug while you insert it into the spark plug hole. You will also need feeler blades, to check and adjust the spark plug electrode gap, and (ideally) a torque wrench to tighten the new plugs to the specified torque.

5 Remove the water pump drivebelt cover from the top and front of the engine - the cover is secured by three bolts.

6 Remove the upper section of the inlet manifold as described in Chapter 2B.

7 To gain access to the plugs on the front bank of cylinders, unscrew the retaining bolts from the Inlet Manifold Runner Control (IMRC) motor. Place the motor out of the way - there is no need to disconnect the wiring or operating cable **(see illustrations)**.

8 The spark plugs are numbered from the timing chain end of the engine - 1 to 3 along the rear bank, and 4 to 6 along the front.

9 If the marks on the original-equipment spark plug (HT) leads cannot be seen, mark the leads to correspond to the cylinder the lead serves. Pull the leads from the plugs by gripping the rubber boot sealing the cylinder head cover opening, not the lead, otherwise the lead connection may be fractured. Where necessary, release the HT leads from their retaining clips **(see illustrations)**.

10 It is advisable to soak up any water in the spark plug recesses with a rag, and to remove any dirt from them using a clean brush, vacuum cleaner or compressed air before removing the plugs, to prevent any dirt or water from dropping into the cylinders.

Warning: Wear eye protection when using compressed air!

11 Unscrew the spark plugs, ensuring that the socket is kept in alignment with each plug - if the socket is forcibly moved to either side, the porcelain top of the plug may be broken off. Remove the plug from the engine **(see illustrations)**.

12 The remainder of the procedure is as described for four-cylinder engines in Section 29, paragraphs 9 to 18. On completion, refit the IMRC motor, tightening the retaining screws securely. Refit the upper section of the inlet manifold as described in Chapter 2B.

Spark plug (HT) lead check

13 Refer to Section 29, paragraph 19 onwards, noting that the plug leads on the V6 engine are numbered as described in paragraph 8 above.

1

Every 80 000 miles or 5 years

33 Timing belt renewal - four-cylinder engines only

Refer to Chapter 2A.

Chapter 2 Part A:
4-cylinder (Zetec) engine in-car repair procedures

Contents

Degrees of difficulty

Easy, suitable for novice with little experience 

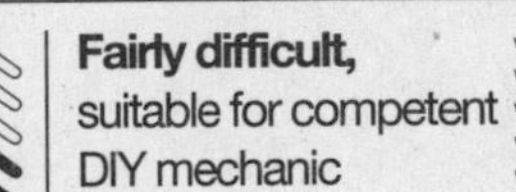

Fairly easy, suitable for beginner with some experience

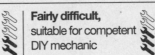

Fairly difficult, suitable for competent DIY mechanic

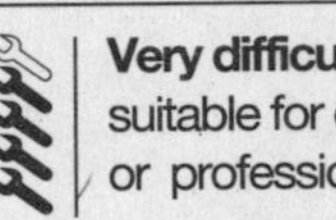

Difficult, suitable for experienced DIY mechanic

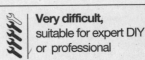

Very difficult, suitable for expert DIY or professional

Specifications

General

Engine type	Four-cylinder, in-line, double overhead camshafts
Engine code:	
1.6 litre models	L1F, L1J, L1L
1.8 litre models	RKA, RKB, RKF, RKJ
2.0 litre models	NGA, NGB
Capacity:	
1.6 litre models	1597 cc
1.8 litre models	1796 cc
2.0 litre models	1988 cc
Bore:	
1.6 litre models	76.0 mm
1.8 litre models	80.6 mm
2.0 litre models	84.8 mm
Stroke - all models	88.0 mm
Compression ratio:	
1.6 litre models	10.3:1
1.8 and 2.0 litre models	10.0:1
Power output:	
1.6 litre models	66 kW at 5250 rpm
1.8 litre models	85 kW at 5750 rpm
2.0 litre models:	
Pre 5/1998 models	96 kW at 5700 rpm
5/1998-on models	91 kW at 6000 rpm
Compression pressure	Not available
Firing order	1-3-4-2 (No 1 cylinder at timing belt end)
Direction of crankshaft rotation	Clockwise (seen from right-hand side of vehicle)

Cylinder head

Hydraulic tappet bore inside diameter	28.395 to 28.425 mm

Camshafts

Camshaft bearing journal diameter	25.960 to 25.980 mm
Camshaft bearing journal-to-cylinder head running clearance	0.020 to 0.070 mm
Camshaft endfloat	0.080 to 0.220 mm

Tappets

Hydraulic tappet diameter - models pre-5/1998	28.400 mm
Valve clearances (cold) - 5/1998-on:	
Checking:	
Inlet	0.11 to 0.18 mm
Exhaust	0.27 to 0.34 mm
Setting:	
Inlet	0.15 mm
Exhaust	0.30 mm

Lubrication

Engine oil type/specification	See end of "*Weekly checks*"
Engine oil capacity	See Chapter 1
Oil pressure	No information available at time of writing
Oil pump clearances	No information available at time of writing

Torque wrench settings

	Nm	lbf ft
Cylinder head cover bolts:		
Stage 1	2	1.5
Stage 2	7	5
Camshaft toothed pulley bolts	68	50
Camshaft bearing cap bolts:		
Stage 1	10	7
Stage 2	19	14
Cylinder head bolts:		
Models to 30/06/1998:		
Stage 1	25	18
Stage 2	45	33
Stage 3	Angle-tighten a further 105°	
Models from 01/07/1998 (build code WU):		
Stage 1	10	7
Stage 2	35	26
Stage 3	Angle-tighten a further 90°	
Stage 4	Angle-tighten a further 90°	
Timing belt cover fasteners:		
Upper-to-middle (outer) cover bolts	4	3
Cover-to-cylinder head or block bolts	7	5
Cover studs-to-cylinder head or block	9 to 11	6.5 to 8
Timing belt tensioner bolt	38	28
Timing belt tensioner backplate locating peg	8 to 11	6 to 8
Timing belt tensioner spring retaining pin	10	7
Timing belt guide pulley bolts	35 to 40	26 to 30
Water pump pulley bolts	10	7
Auxiliary drivebelt idler pulley	48	35
Inlet manifold nuts and bolts	18	13
Alternator mounting bracket-to-cylinder block bolts	47	35
Cylinder head support plates:		
Front plate Torx screws - to power steering pump/air conditioning compressor mounting bracket and cylinder head	47	35
Rear plate/engine lifting eye - to alternator mounting bracket and cylinder head bolts	47	35
Front engine lifting eye bolt	16	12
Inlet and exhaust manifold studs-to-cylinder head	10 maximum	7 maximum
Exhaust manifold heat shield bolts:		
Shield-to-cylinder head	7	5
Shield/dipstick tube	10	7
Shield/coolant pipe-to-manifold	23	17
Exhaust manifold nuts	16	12
Air conditioning refrigerant pipe-to-exhaust manifold bolts	10	7
Crankshaft pulley bolt	108 to 115	80 to 85
Oil pump-to-cylinder block bolts	10	7
Oil pick-up pipe-to-pump screws	10	7
Oil baffle/pump pick-up pipe nuts	19	14
Oil filter adaptor-to-pump	18 to 25	13 to 18
Oil pressure warning light switch	27	20
Oil level sensor	27	20

Torque wrench settings (continued)	Nm	lbf ft
Sump bolts:		
Models up to 10/1996	21 to 22	15 to 16
Models from 10/1996 up to 5/1998:		
Stage 1	12	9
Stage 2	22	16
Models 5/1998-on:		
Stage 1	24	18
Stage 2	11	8
Sump-to-transmission bolts (models from 10/1996 to 5/1998):		
Upper	10	7
Lower	40	30
Lower crankcase to cylinder block	30	22
Coolant pipe-to-sump bolt	10	7
Flywheel/driveplate bolts	112	83
Crankshaft left-hand oil seal carrier bolts	22	16
Transmission-to-engine bolts:		
Pre 5/1998 models	40	30
4/1998-on models	48	35
Torque converter to driveplate	36	26
Main bearing cap bolts and nuts	80	59
Big-end bearing cap bolts:		
Pre-5/1998 models:		
Stage 1	18	13
Stage 2	Angle-tighten a further 90°	
5/1998 models:		
Stage 1	35	26
Stage 2	Angle-tighten a further 90°	
Piston-cooling oil jet/blanking plug Torx screws	10	7
Cylinder block and head oil way blanking plugs:		
M6 x 10	8 to 11	6 to 8
M10 x 11.5 - in block	24	17
1/4 PTF plug - in block	25	18
Power steering pump/air conditioning compressor mounting bracket-to-cylinder block bolts	47	35
Exhaust manifold heat shield mounting bracket-to-cylinder block bolts	32	24
Crankcase breather system:		
Oil separator-to-cylinder block bolts	10	7
Pipe-to-cylinder head bolt	23	17
Driveshaft support bearing bracket-to-cylinder block bolts	48	35
Front suspension subframe bolts	130	96
Engine/transmission front mounting:		
Mounting bracket-to-transmission	Not available	
Mounting-to-subframe bolts/nuts - stage 1	10	7
Mounting-to-subframe bolts/nuts - stage 2	48	35
Mounting centre bolt	120	89
Engine/manual transmission rear mounting:		
Mounting bracket-to-transmission -12 mm fasteners	84	62
Mounting bracket-to-transmission -10 mm fasteners	48	35
Mounting-to-subframe bolts and nut - stage 1	10	7
Mounting-to-subframe bolts and nut - stage 2	48	35
Mounting centre bolt	120	89
Engine/automatic transmission rear mounting:		
Mounting bracket-to-transmission	48 to 49	35 to 36
Mounting-to-subframe bolts - stage 1	10	7
Mounting-to-subframe bolts - stage 2	48	35
Mounting centre bolt	120	89
Engine/transmission left-hand mounting:		
Bracket-to-transmission nuts	83	61
Mounting centre bolt	Not available	
Mounting-to-body bolts	Not available	
Engine/transmission right-hand mounting:		
Bracket-to-engine and mounting nuts	83 to 90	61 to 66
Mounting-to-body bolts	84	62

1 General information

How to use this Chapter

This Part of Chapter 2 is devoted to repair procedures possible while the engine is still installed in the vehicle, and includes only the Specifications relevant to those procedures. Since these procedures are based on the assumption that the engine is installed in the vehicle, if the engine has been removed from the vehicle and mounted on a stand, some of the preliminary dismantling steps outlined will not apply.

Information concerning engine/transmission removal and refitting, and engine overhaul, can be found in Part C of this Chapter, which also includes the Specifications relevant to those procedures.

General description - engine

The engine, known by Ford's internal code name "Zetec" (formerly "Zeta") or "Zetec-E", is of four-cylinder, in-line type, mounted transversely at the front of the vehicle, with the (clutch and) transmission on its left-hand end **(see illustrations)**.

Apart from the plastic timing belt covers and the cast-iron cylinder block/crankcase, all major engine castings are of aluminium alloy.

The crankshaft runs in five main bearings, the centre main bearing's upper half incorporating thrustwashers to control crankshaft endfloat. The connecting rods rotate on horizontally-split bearing shells at their big-ends. The pistons are attached to the connecting rods by gudgeon pins which are an interference fit in the connecting rod small-end eyes. The aluminium alloy pistons are

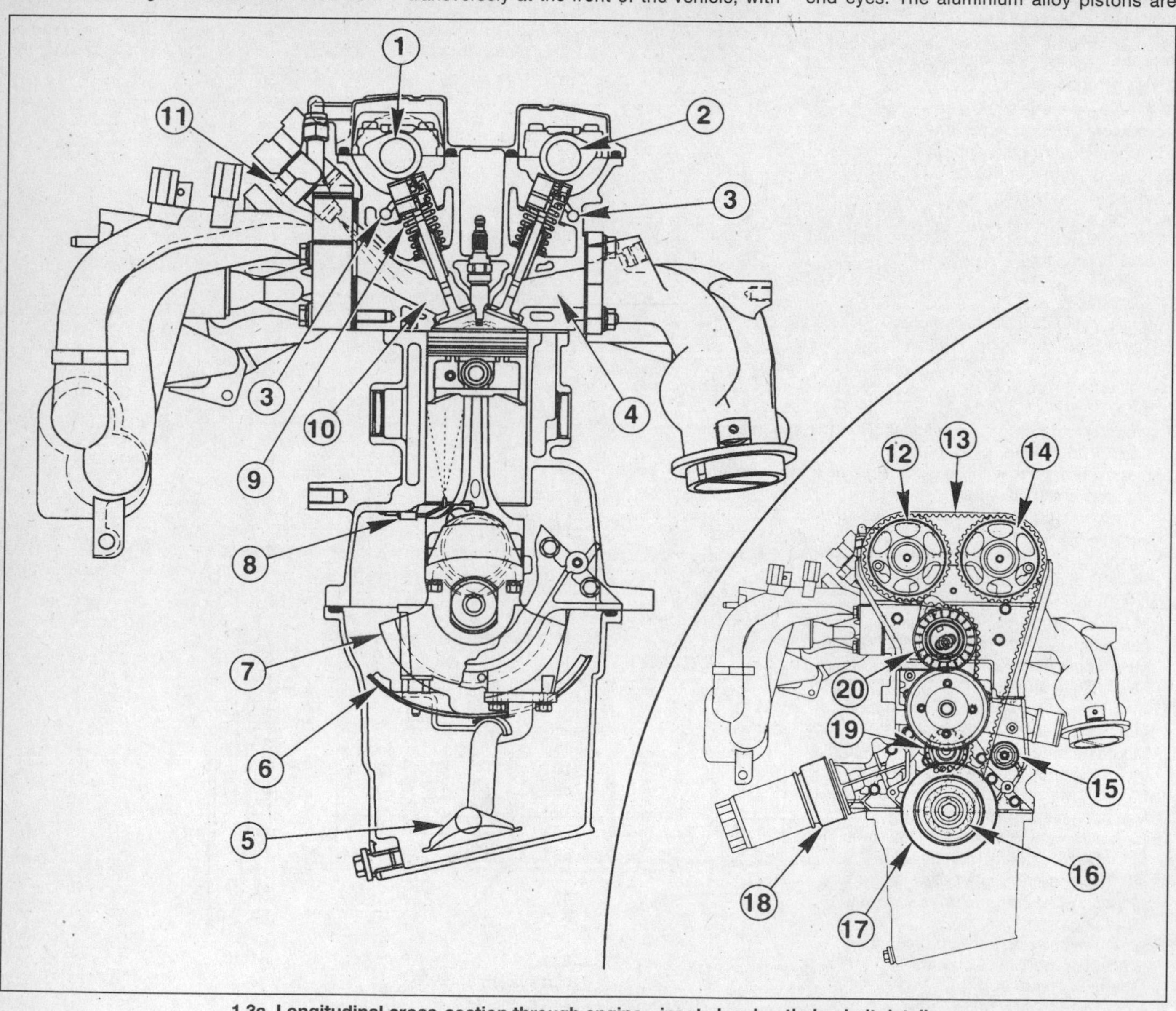

1.3a Longitudinal cross-section through engine - inset showing timing belt details

1 Inlet camshaft
2 Exhaust camshaft
3 Oil galleries
4 Exhaust port
5 Oil strainer and pick-up pipe
6 Oil baffle
7 Crankshaft
8 Piston-cooling oil jet (where fitted)
9 Inlet valve
10 Inlet port
11 Fuel injector
12 Inlet camshaft toothed pulley
13 Timing belt
14 Exhaust camshaft toothed pulley
15 Timing belt (front) guide pulley
16 Crankshaft toothed pulley - behind
17 Crankshaft pulley
18 Oil cooler (where fitted)
19 Timing belt (rear) guide pulley
20 Timing belt tensioner

fitted with three piston rings: two compression rings and an oil control ring. After manufacture, the cylinder bores and piston skirts are measured and classified into three grades, which must be carefully matched together, to ensure the correct piston/cylinder clearance; no oversizes are available to permit reboring.

The inlet and exhaust valves are each closed by coil springs; they operate in guides which are shrink-fitted into the cylinder head, as are the valve seat inserts.

Both camshafts are driven by the same toothed timing belt, each operating eight valves via self-adjusting hydraulic tappets on pre-5/1998 models, thus eliminating the need for routine checking and adjustment of the valve clearances. Models from 5/1998-on are fitted with conventional tappets with shims. Each camshaft rotates in five bearings that are line-bored directly in the cylinder head and the (bolted-on) bearing caps; this means that the bearing caps are not available separately from the cylinder head, and must not be interchanged with caps from another engine.

The water pump is bolted to the right-hand end of the cylinder block, inboard of the timing belt, and is driven with the power steering pump and alternator by a flat "polyvee" type auxiliary drivebelt from the crankshaft pulley.

When working on this engine, note that Torx-type (both male and female heads) and hexagon socket (Allen head) fasteners are widely used; a good selection of bits, with the necessary adaptors, will be required, so that these can be unscrewed without damage and, on reassembly, tightened to the torque wrench settings specified.

General description - lubrication system

Lubrication is by means of an eccentric-rotor trochoidal pump, which is mounted on the crankshaft right-hand end, and draws oil through a strainer located in the sump. The pump forces oil through an externally-mounted full-flow cartridge-type filter - on some versions of the engine, an oil cooler is fitted to the oil filter mounting, so that clean oil entering the engine's galleries is cooled by the

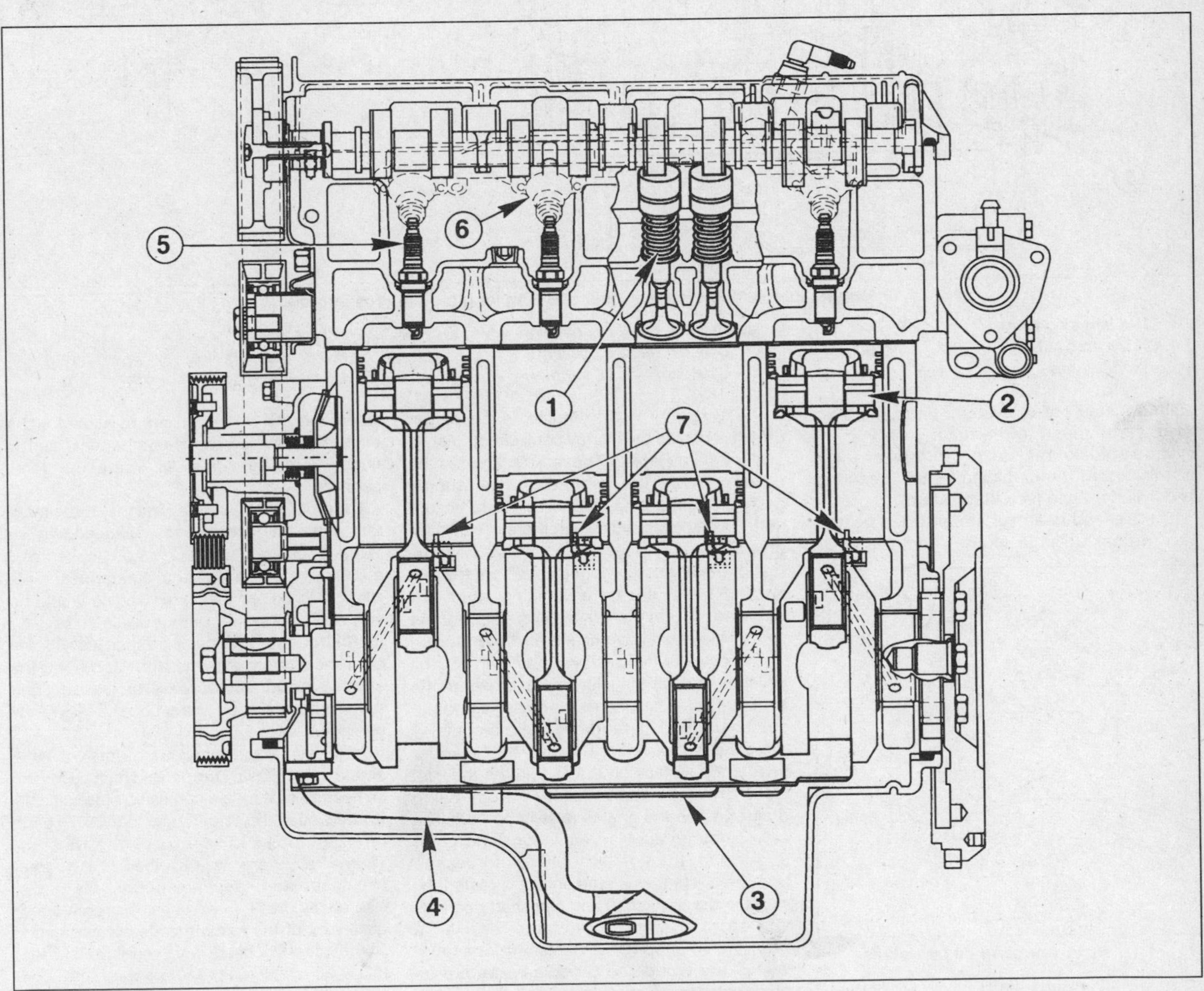

1.3b Lateral cross-section through engine

1 *Exhaust valve*
2 *Piston*
3 *Oil baffle*
4 *Oil strainer and pick-up pipe*
5 *Spark plug*
6 *Fuel injector*
7 *Piston-cooling oil jets (where fitted)*

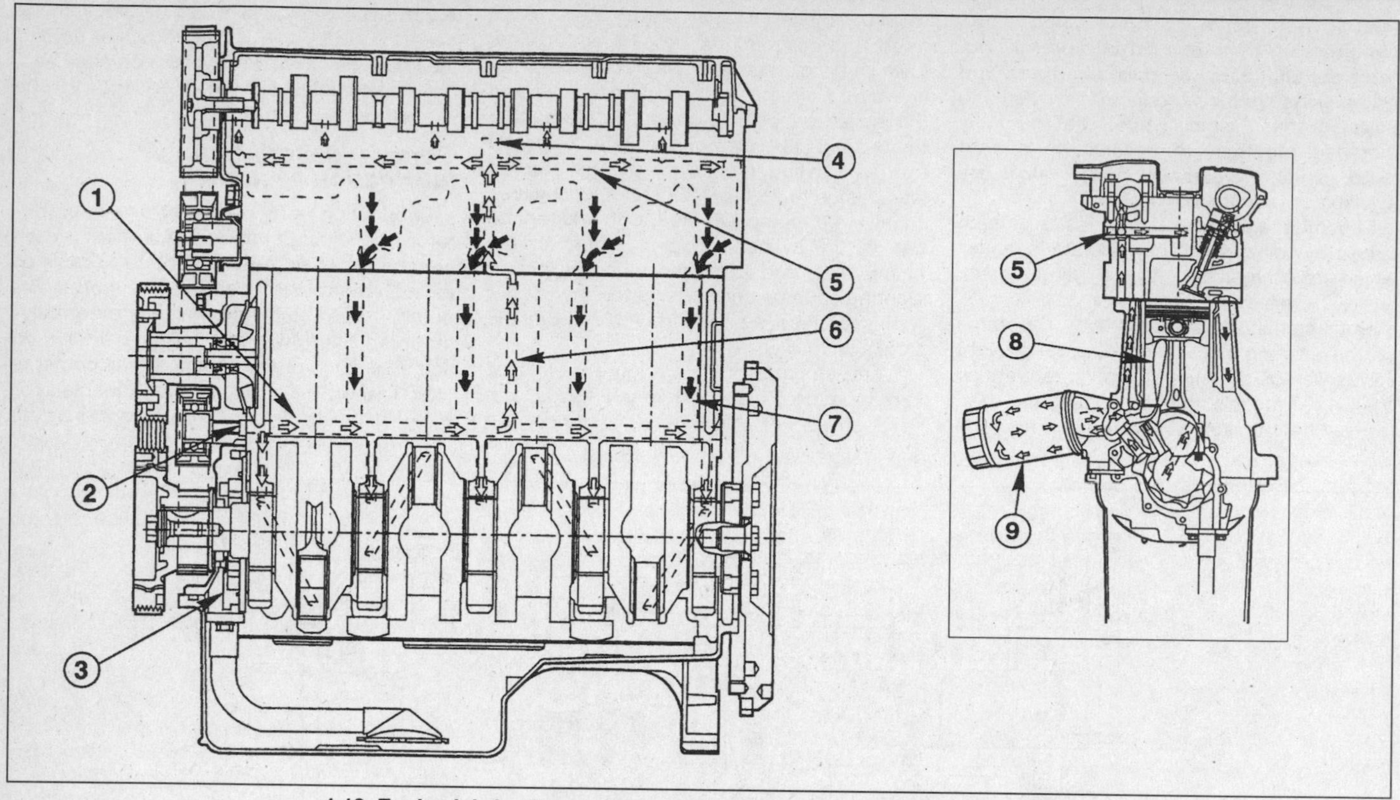

1.10 Engine lubrication system - inset showing longitudinal cross-section

1 Main oil gallery
2 From oil filter
3 Oil pump
4 Cylinder head oil-retaining valve
5 Cylinder head oil gallery
6 Cylinder head oil supply
7 Oil return
8 Piston-cooling oil spray (where fitted)
9 Oil filter - oil cooler not shown here

main engine cooling system. From the filter, the oil is pumped into a main gallery in the cylinder block/crankcase, from where it is distributed to the crankshaft (main bearings) and cylinder head **(see illustration).**

The big-end bearings are supplied with oil via internal drillings in the crankshaft. On some versions of the engine, each piston crown is cooled by a spray of oil directed at its underside by a jet. These jets are fed by passages off the crankshaft oil supply galleries, with spring-loaded valves to ensure that the jets open only when there is sufficient pressure to guarantee a good oil supply to the rest of the engine components; where the jets are not fitted, separate blanking plugs are provided, so that the passages are sealed, but can be cleaned at overhaul **(see illustration).**

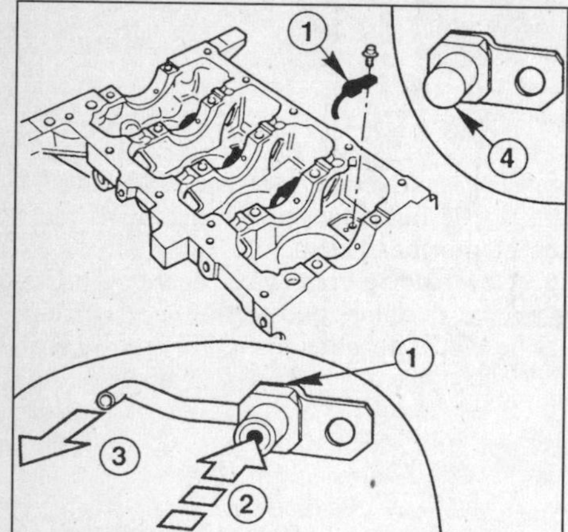

1.11 Piston-cooling oil jet details

1 Oil jets (when fitted)
2 Oil flow - only when valve opens at set pressure
3 Oil spray
4 Blanking plug (when fitted)

The cylinder head is provided with two oil galleries, one on the inlet side and one on the exhaust, to ensure constant oil supply to the camshaft bearings and hydraulic tappets. A retaining valve (inserted into the cylinder head's top surface, in the middle, on the inlet side) prevents these galleries from being drained when the engine is switched off. The valve incorporates a ventilation hole in its upper end, to allow air bubbles to escape from the system when the engine is restarted.

While the crankshaft and camshaft bearings and the hydraulic tappets receive a pressurised supply, the camshaft lobes and valves are lubricated by splash, as are all other engine components.

Valve clearances - general

It is necessary for a clearance to exist between the tip of each valve stem and the valve operating mechanism, to allow for the expansion of the various components as the engine reaches normal operating temperature.

On most older engine designs, this meant that the valve clearances (also known as "tappet" clearances) had to be checked and adjusted regularly. If the clearances were allowed to be too slack, the engine would be very noisy, its power output would suffer, and its fuel consumption would increase. If the clearances were allowed to be too tight, the engine's power output would be reduced, and the valves and their seats could be severely damaged.

Engines manufactured before 5/1998 employ hydraulic tappets which use the lubricating system's oil pressure automatically to take up the clearance between each camshaft lobe and its respective valve stem. Therefore, there is no need for regular checking and adjustment of the valve clearances, but it is essential that only good-quality oil of the recommended viscosity and specification is used in the engine, and that this oil is always changed at the recommended intervals. If this advice is not followed, the oilways and tappets may become clogged with particles of dirt, or deposits of burnt (inferior) engine oil, so that the system cannot work properly; ultimately, one or more of the tappets may fail, and expensive repairs may be required. As from 5/1998, the hydraulic tappets were discontinued in favour of conventional tappets and shims.

On starting the engine from cold, there will be a slight delay while full oil pressure builds up in all parts of the engine, especially in the tappets; the valve components, therefore, may well "rattle" for about 10 seconds or so, and then quieten. This is a normal state of affairs, and is nothing to worry about, provided that all tappets quieten quickly and stay quiet.

After the vehicle has been standing for several days, the valve components may "rattle" for longer than usual, as nearly all the oil will have drained away from the engine's top end components and bearing surfaces. While this is only to be expected, care must be taken not to damage the engine under these circumstances - avoid high speed running until all the tappets are refilled with oil and operating normally. With the vehicle stationary, hold the engine at no more than a fast idle speed (maximum 2000 to 2500 rpm) for 10 to 15 seconds, or until the noise ceases. *Do not run the engine at more than 3000 rpm until the tappets are fully recharged with oil and the noise has ceased.*

If the valve components are thought to be noisy, or if a light rattle persists from the top end after the engine has warmed up to normal operating temperature, take the vehicle to a Ford dealer for expert advice. Depending on the mileage covered and the usage to which each vehicle has been put, some vehicles may be noisier than others; only a good mechanic experienced in these engines can tell if the noise level is typical for the vehicle's mileage, or if a genuine fault exists. If any tappet's operation is faulty, it must be renewed (Section 13).

2 Repair operations possible with the engine in the vehicle

The following major repair operations can be accomplished without removing the engine from the vehicle. However, owners should note that any operation involving the removal of the sump requires careful forethought, depending on the level of skill and the tools and facilities available; refer to the relevant text for details.

a) Compression pressure - testing.
b) Cylinder head cover - removal and refitting.
c) Timing belt covers - removal and refitting.
d) Timing belt - renewal.
e) Timing belt tensioner and toothed pulleys - removal and refitting.
f) Camshaft oil seals - renewal.
g) Camshafts and hydraulic tappets - removal and refitting.
h) Cylinder head - removal, overhaul and refitting.
i) Cylinder head and pistons - decarbonising.
j) Sump - removal and refitting.
k) Crankshaft oil seals - renewal.
l) Oil pump - removal and refitting.
m) Piston/connecting rod assemblies - removal and refitting but see note below).
n) Flywheel/driveplate - removal and refitting.
o) Engine/transmission mountings - removal and refitting.

Clean the engine compartment and the exterior of the engine with some type of degreaser before any work is done. It will make the job easier, and will help to keep dirt out of the internal areas of the engine.

Depending on the components involved, it may be helpful to remove the bonnet, to improve access to the engine as repairs are performed (refer to Chapter 11 if necessary). Cover the wings to prevent damage to the paint; special covers are available, but an old bedspread or blanket will also work.

If vacuum, exhaust, oil or coolant leaks develop, indicating a need for component/gasket or seal replacement, the repairs can generally be made with the engine in the vehicle. The intake and exhaust manifold gaskets, sump gasket, crankshaft oil seals and cylinder head gasket are all accessible with the engine in place.

Exterior components such as the intake and exhaust manifolds, the sump, the oil pump, the water pump, the starter motor, the alternator and the fuel system components can be removed for repair with the engine in place.

Since the cylinder head can be removed without lifting out the engine, camshaft and valve component servicing can also be accomplished with the engine in the vehicle, as can renewal of the timing belt and toothed pulleys.

In extreme cases caused by a lack of necessary equipment, repair or renewal of piston rings, pistons, connecting rods and big-end bearings is possible with the engine in the vehicle. However, this practice is not recommended, because of the cleaning and preparation work that must be done to the components involved, and because of the amount of preliminary dismantling work required - these operations are therefore covered in Part B of this Chapter.

3 Compression test - description and interpretation

1 When engine performance is down, or if misfiring occurs which cannot be attributed to the ignition or fuel systems, a compression test can provide diagnostic clues as to the engine's condition. If the test is performed regularly, it can give warning of trouble before any other symptoms become apparent.

2 The engine must be fully warmed-up to normal operating temperature, the oil level must be correct, the battery must be fully charged, and the spark plugs must be removed. The aid of an assistant will be required also.

3 Disable the ignition system by unplugging the ignition coil's electrical connector, and remove fuse 14 to disconnect the fuel pump.

4 Fit a compression tester to the No 1 cylinder spark plug hole - the type of tester which screws into the plug thread is to be preferred.

5 Have the assistant hold the throttle wide open and crank the engine on the starter motor; after one or two revolutions, the compression pressure should build up to a maximum figure, and then stabilise. Record the highest reading obtained.

6 Repeat the test on the remaining cylinders, recording the pressure developed in each.

7 At the time of writing, no compression specifications were available from Ford, but a typical reading would be in excess of 12 bars. All cylinders should produce very similar pressures; any difference greater than 10% indicates the existence of a fault. Note that the compression should build up quickly in a healthy engine; low compression on the first stroke, followed by gradually-increasing pressure on successive strokes, indicates worn piston rings. A low compression reading on the first stroke, which does not build up during successive strokes, indicates leaking valves or a blown head gasket (a cracked head could also be the cause). Deposits on the undersides of the valve heads can also cause low compression.

8 If the pressure in any cylinder is considerably lower than the others, introduce a teaspoonful of clean oil into that cylinder through its spark plug hole, and repeat the test.

9 If the addition of oil temporarily improves the compression pressure, this indicates that bore or piston wear is responsible for the pressure loss. No improvement suggests that leaking or burnt valves, or a blown head gasket, may be to blame.

10 A low reading from two adjacent cylinders is almost certainly due to the head gasket having blown between them; the presence of coolant in the engine oil will confirm this.

11 If one cylinder is about 20 percent lower than the others and the engine has a slightly rough idle, a worn camshaft lobe or faulty hydraulic tappet could be the cause.

12 If the compression is unusually high, the combustion chambers are probably coated with carbon deposits. If this is the case, the cylinder head should be removed and decarbonised.

13 On completion of the test, refit the spark plugs, then reconnect the ignition system and fuel pump.

4 Top Dead Centre (TDC) for No 1 piston - locating

General

1 Top Dead Centre (TDC) is the highest point in its travel up-and-down its cylinder bore that each piston reaches as the crankshaft rotates. While each piston reaches TDC both at the top of the compression stroke and again at the top of the exhaust stroke, for the purpose of timing the engine, TDC refers to the No 1 piston position at the top of its compression stroke.

2 It is useful for several servicing procedures to be able to position the engine at TDC.

3 No 1 piston and cylinder are at the right-hand (timing belt) end of the engine (right- and left-hand are always quoted as seen from the driver's seat). Note that the crankshaft rotates clockwise when viewed from the right-hand side of the vehicle.

Locating TDC

4 Remove all the spark plugs (Chapter 1).

5 Disconnect the battery negative (earth) lead (see Chapter 5A) unless the starter motor is to be used to turn the engine.

4.7 Cover retaining bolts under the right-hand wheel arch

6 Apply the handbrake, then jack up the front of the vehicle and support it on axle stands (see "Jacking and Vehicle Support"). Remove the right-hand front roadwheel.

7 Remove the cover from under the right-hand front wheel arch to expose the crankshaft pulley and timing marks **(see illustration)**.

8 It is best to rotate the crankshaft using a spanner applied to the crankshaft pulley bolt; however, it is possible also to use the starter motor (switched on either by an assistant using the ignition key, or by using a remote starter switch) to bring the engine close to TDC, then finish with a spanner. If the starter is used, be sure to disconnect the battery leads immediately it is no longer required.

9 Note the notches in the outer rim (and inner rim on pre 5/1998 models) of the crankshaft pulley. In the normal direction of crankshaft rotation (clockwise, seen from the right-hand side of the vehicle) the first notch is irrelevant to the vehicles covered in this manual, while the second notch indicates TDC when aligned with the rear edge of the raised mark on the sump. Rotate the crankshaft clockwise until the second notch aligns with the edge of the sump mark; use a straight edge extended out from the sump if greater accuracy is required **(see illustrations)**.

10 On 5/1998-on models a TDC timing hole is provided on the front of the cylinder block to position the crankshaft at TDC **(see illustration)**. With the second notch on the crankshaft pulley aligned with the timing mark on the lower crankcase frame, unscrew the timing hole plug and insert a timing peg (obtainable from Ford dealers or a tool supplier) **(see illustration)**. It may be

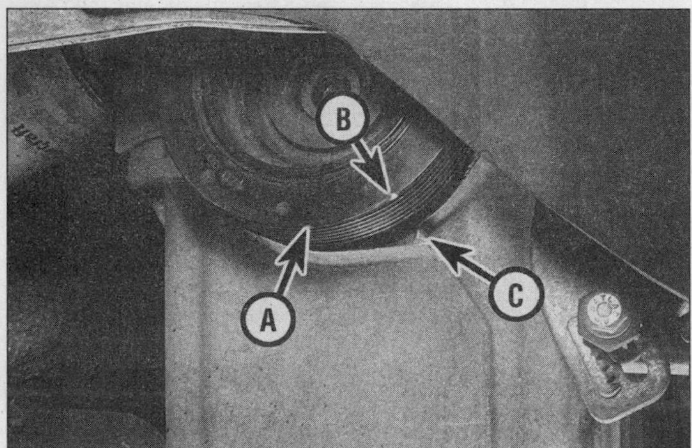

4.9a Do not use crankshaft pulley's first pair of notches "A" - align second pair of notches "B" with raised rib on sump "C" . . .

4.9b . . . using a straight edge extended out from the sump (arrowed) if greater accuracy is required

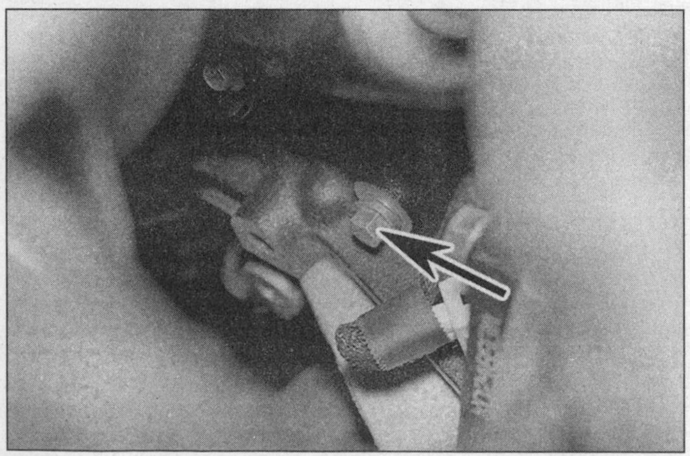

4.10a TDC timing hole plug on 5/1998-on models

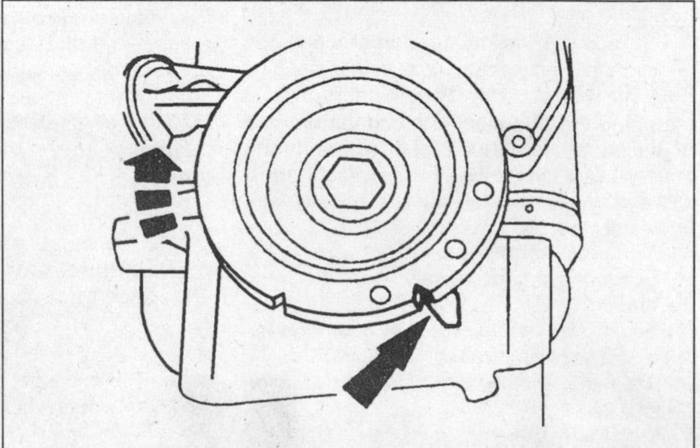

4.10b TDC notch on the crankshaft pulley on 5/1998-on models

necessary to slightly turn the crankshaft either way in order to insert the timing peg fully.

11 Nos 1 and 4 cylinders are now at TDC, one of them on the compression stroke. Remove the oil filler cap; if No 4 cylinder exhaust cam lobe is pointing to the rear of the vehicle and slightly downwards, it is No 1 cylinder that is correctly positioned. If the lobe is pointing horizontally forwards, rotate the crankshaft one full turn (360°) clockwise until the pulley notches align again, and the lobe is pointing to the rear and slightly down. No 1 cylinder will then be at TDC on the compression stroke.

12 Once No 1 cylinder has been positioned at TDC on the compression stroke, TDC for any of the other cylinders can then be located by rotating the crankshaft clockwise 180° at a time and following the firing order (see Specifications).

13 An alternative method of locating TDC is to remove the cylinder head cover (see Section 5) and to rotate the crankshaft (clockwise, as described in paragraph 8 above) until the inlet valves for the cylinder concerned have opened and just closed again. Insert a length of wooden dowel (approximately 150 mm/6 in long) or similar into the spark plug hole until it rests on the piston crown, and slowly further rotate the crankshaft (taking care not to allow the dowel to be trapped in the cylinder) until the dowel stops rising - the piston is now at the top of its compression stroke, and the dowel can be removed.

14 There is a "dead" area around TDC (as the piston stops rising, pauses and then begins to descend) which makes difficult the exact location of TDC by this method; if accuracy is required, either establish carefully the exact mid-point of the dead area, or refer to the timing marks (paragraph 9 above).

15 Before turning the engine again, make sure that the timing peg is removed on 5/1998-on models.

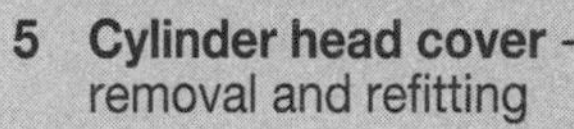

5 Cylinder head cover - removal and refitting

Removal

1 Unplug the two electrical connectors and disconnect the vacuum hose (where fitted), then remove the air cleaner assembly cover with the air mass meter, the resonator (where fitted) and the plenum chamber (see Chapter 4A).

2 Disconnect the accelerator cable from the throttle linkage as described in Chapter 4A. Where fitted, also disconnect the cruise control actuator cable (see Chapter 12).

3 Remove the timing belt upper cover (see Section 9).

4 Disconnect the crankcase breather hose from the cylinder head cover union **(see illustration)**.

5.4 Disconnecting crankcase breather hose from cylinder head cover union

5 Unplug the HT leads from the spark plugs and withdraw them, unclipping the leads from the cover.

6 Working progressively, unscrew the cylinder head cover retaining bolts, noting the spacer sleeve and rubber seal at each, then withdraw the cover **(see illustration)**.

7 Discard the cover gasket; this must be renewed whenever it is disturbed. Check that the sealing faces are undamaged, and that the rubber seal at each retaining bolt is serviceable; renew any worn or damaged seals.

Refitting

8 On refitting, clean the cover and cylinder head gasket faces carefully, then fit a new gasket to the cover, ensuring that it locates correctly in the cover grooves **(see illustration)**.

9 Refit the cover to the cylinder head, then insert the rubber seal and spacer sleeve at each bolt location **(see illustration)**. Start all bolts finger-tight, ensuring that the gasket remains seated in its groove.

10 Working in a diagonal sequence from the centre outwards, and in two stages (see Specifications), tighten the cover bolts to the specified torque wrench setting.

11 Refit the HT leads, clipping them into place so that they are correctly routed; each is numbered, and can also be identified by the numbering on its respective coil terminal.

12 Reconnect the crankcase breather hose, and refit the timing belt upper cover. Reconnect and adjust the accelerator cable, then refit the air cleaner assembly cover with the air mass meter, the resonator and the plenum chamber (see Chapter 4A).

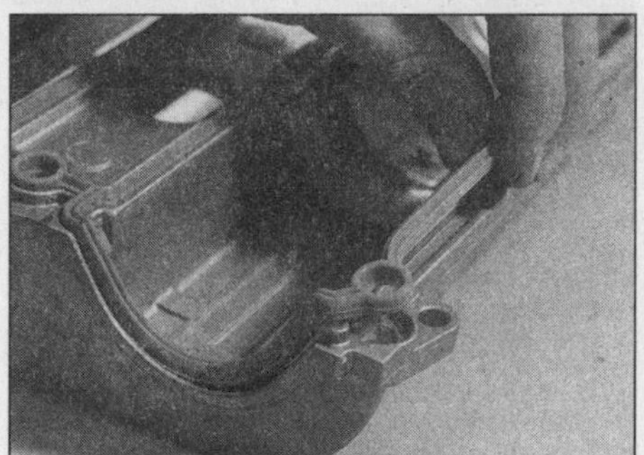

5.8 Ensure gasket is located correctly in cover groove

5.6 Removing cylinder head cover

6 Inlet manifold - removal and refitting

Warning: Petrol is extremely flammable, so take extra precautions when disconnecting any part of the fuel system. Don't smoke, or allow naked flames or bare light bulbs in or near the work area. Don't work in a garage where a natural gas appliance (such as a clothes dryer or water heater) is installed. If you spill petrol on your skin, rinse it off immediately. Have a fire extinguisher rated for petrol fires handy, and know how to use it.

Removal

1 Park the vehicle on firm, level ground, apply the handbrake firmly, and slacken the nuts securing the right-hand front roadwheel.

2 Relieve the fuel system pressure (see Chapter 4A).

3 Disconnect the battery negative (earth) lead - see Chapter 5A, Section 1.

4 Unplugging the two electrical connectors and disconnecting the vacuum hose (where fitted), remove the air cleaner assembly cover with the air mass meter, the resonator and the plenum chamber (see Chapter 4A).

5 Disconnect the accelerator cable from the throttle linkage as described in Chapter 4A - where fitted, disconnect also the cruise control actuator cable (see Chapter 12).

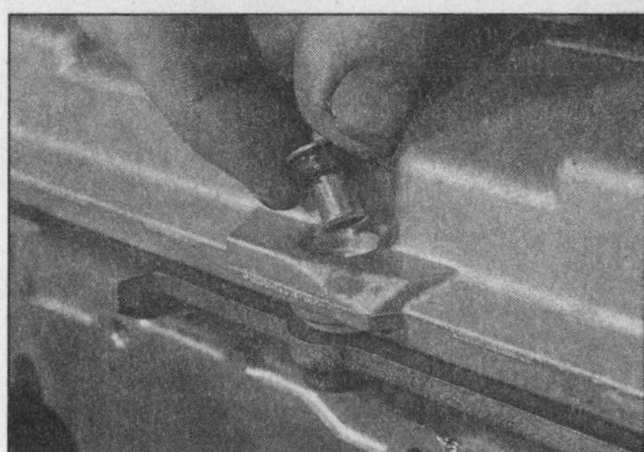

5.9 Ensure rubber seal is fitted to each cover bolt spacer, as shown

6.15 Alternator mounting bracket must be unbolted from rear of cylinder block to permit access to inlet manifold nut

6.16 Withdrawing the inlet manifold

6 Disconnect the crankcase breather hose from the cylinder head cover union.

7 Unbolt the upper part of the exhaust manifold heat shield; unclip the coolant hose to allow it to be withdrawn. Slacken the sleeve nut securing the EGR pipe to the manifold, remove the two screws securing the pipe to the ignition coil bracket, then unscrew the sleeve nut securing the pipe to the EGR valve - see Chapter 4B for full details if required.

8 Remove the two screws securing the wiring "rail" to the top of the manifold - this is simply so that it can be moved as required to reach the manifold bolts. Unplug their electrical connectors to disconnect the camshaft position sensor and the coolant temperature sensor, then unclip the wiring from the ignition coil bracket, and secure it to the manifold.

9 Remove the three screws securing the wiring "rail" to the rear of the manifold. Releasing its wire clip, unplug the large electrical connector (next to the fuel pressure regulator) to disconnect the wiring of the manifold components from the engine wiring loom.

10 Marking or labelling them as they are unplugged, disconnect the vacuum hoses as follows:

a) *One from the rear of the throttle housing (only the one hose - there is no need to disconnect the second hose running to the fuel pressure regulator).*
b) *One from the union on the manifold's left-hand end.*
c) *The braking system vacuum servo unit hose (see Chapter 9 for details).*
d) *One from the Exhaust Gas Recirculation (EGR) valve.*

11 Equalise the pressure in the fuel tank by removing the filler cap, then undo the fuel feed and return lines connecting the engine to the chassis (see Chapter 4A). Plug or cap all open fittings.

12 Unbolt the power steering high-pressure pipe and the earth lead from the cylinder head rear support plate/engine lifting eye, then unscrew the bolt securing the support plate/lifting eye to the alternator mounting bracket.

13 Unscrew the six nuts securing the engine/transmission right-hand mounting bracket, then withdraw the bracket.

14 Remove the alternator (see Chapter 5A).

15 Unbolt the alternator mounting bracket from the rear of the cylinder block and withdraw it, together with the cylinder head rear support plate/engine lifting eye **(see illustration)**.

16 Unscrew the bolts and nuts securing the manifold to the cylinder head and withdraw it **(see illustration)**. Take care not to damage vulnerable components such as the EGR pipe and valve as the manifold assembly is manoeuvred out of the engine compartment.

Refitting

17 Refitting is the reverse of the removal procedure, noting the following points:

a) *When using a scraper and solvent to remove all traces of old gasket material and sealant from the manifold and cylinder head, be careful to ensure that you do not scratch or damage the material of either; the cylinder head is of aluminium alloy, while the manifold is a plastics moulding - any solvents used must be suitable for this application. If the gasket was leaking, have the mating surfaces checked for warpage at an automotive machine shop. While it may be possible to have the cylinder head gasket surface skimmed if necessary, to remove any distortion, the manifold must be renewed if it is found to be warped, cracked - check with special care around the mounting points for components such as the idle speed control valve and EGR pipe - or otherwise faulty.*
b) *Provided the relevant mating surfaces are clean and flat, a new gasket will be sufficient to ensure the joint is gas-tight.* ***Do not*** *use any kind of silicone-based sealant on any part of the fuel system or inlet manifold.*
c) *Fit a new gasket, then locate the manifold on the head and install the nuts and bolts* ***(see illustration)****.*
d) *Tighten the nuts/bolts in three or four equal steps to the torque listed in this Chapter's Specifications. Work from the centre outwards, to avoid warping the manifold.*
e) *Refit the remaining parts in the reverse order of removal - tighten all fasteners to the torque wrench settings specified.*
f) *When reassembling the engine/transmission right-hand mounting, renew the self-locking nuts, and do not allow the mounting to twist as the middle two of the bracket's six nuts are tightened.*
g) *Before starting the engine, check the accelerator cable for correct adjustment and the throttle linkage for smooth operation.*
h) *When the engine is fully warmed up, check for signs of fuel, intake and/or vacuum leaks* ***(see illustration)****.*
i) *Road test the vehicle, and check for proper operation of all disturbed components.*

6.17a Always renew inlet manifold gasket - do not rely on sealants

6.17b Check all disturbed components - braking system vacuum servo unit hose (arrowed) shown here - for leaks on reassembly

7 Exhaust manifold - removal, inspection and refitting

Warning: The engine must be completely cool before beginning this procedure.

Note: *In addition to the new gasket and any other parts, tools or facilities needed to carry out this operation, a new plastic guide sleeve will be required on reassembly.*

Removal

1 Disconnect the battery negative (earth) lead (see Chapter 5A).

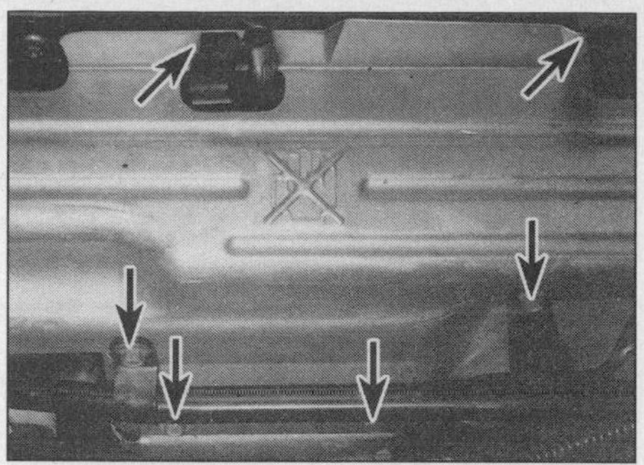
7.5 Exhaust manifold heat shield upper part securing bolts (arrowed)

7.7 Pulse-air system (sleeve nuts arrowed) need not be removed unless required - assembly can be withdrawn with exhaust manifold

2 Unbolt the resonator support bracket from the engine compartment front crossmember, slacken the two clamp screws securing the resonator to the air mass meter and plenum chamber hoses, then swing the resonator up clear of the thermostat housing (see Chapter 4A).

3 Drain the cooling system (see Chapter 1).

4 Disconnect the coolant hose and the coolant pipe/hose from the thermostat housing; secure them clear of the working area.

5 Unbolt the exhaust manifold heat shield, and withdraw both parts of the shield **(see illustration)**. Apply penetrating oil to the EGR pipe sleeve nut, and to the exhaust manifold mounting nuts (also to the pulse-air system sleeve nuts, if they are to be unscrewed).

6 Unscrew the sleeve nut securing the EGR pipe to the manifold, remove the two screws securing the pipe to the ignition coil bracket, then slacken the sleeve nut securing the pipe to the EGR valve - see Chapter 4B for full details if required.

7 While the manifold can be removed with the pulse-air system components attached - unbolt the filter housing and disconnect its vacuum hose if this is to be done - it is easier to remove the pulse-air assembly first, as described in Chapter 4B **(see illustration)**.

8 Unplugging the oxygen sensor electrical connector to avoid straining its wiring, unscrew the nuts to disconnect the exhaust system front downpipe from the manifold (see Chapter 4A).

9 Remove the nuts and detach the manifold and gasket **(see illustration)**. Take care not to damage vulnerable components such as the EGR pipe as the manifold assembly is manoeuvred out of the engine compartment. When removing the manifold with the engine in the vehicle, additional clearance can be obtained by unscrewing the studs from the cylinder head; a female Torx-type socket will be required **(see illustration)**.

10 Always fit a new gasket on reassembly, to carefully-cleaned components (see below). Do not attempt to re-use the original gasket.

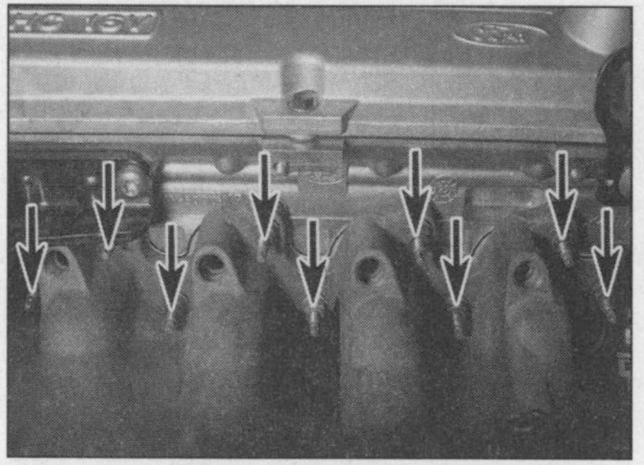
7.9a Unscrew nuts (arrowed) to remove exhaust manifold . . .

7.9b . . . studs can be unscrewed also, if required, to provide additional working space

Inspection

11 Use a scraper to remove all traces of old gasket material and carbon deposits from the manifold and cylinder head mating surfaces. If the gasket was leaking, have the manifold checked for warpage at an automotive machine shop, and have it resurfaced if necessary.

Caution: When scraping, be very careful not to gouge or scratch the delicate aluminium alloy cylinder head.

12 Provided both mating surfaces are clean and flat, a new gasket will be sufficient to ensure the joint is gas-tight. Do not use any kind of exhaust sealant upstream of the catalytic converter.

13 Note that the downpipe is secured to the manifold by two bolts, with a coil spring, spring seat and self-locking nut on each. On refitting, tighten the nuts until they stop on the bolt shoulders; the pressure of the springs will then suffice to make a leakproof joint **(see illustrations)**.

14 Do not overtighten the nuts to cure a leak - the bolts will shear; renew the gasket and the springs if a leak is found. The bolts themselves are secured by spring clips to the manifold, and can be renewed easily if damaged **(see illustration)**.

Refitting

15 Refitting is the reverse of the removal procedure, noting the following points:

a) Position a new gasket over the cylinder head studs, and fit a new plastic guide sleeve to the stud nearest to the

2A

7.13a Showing exhaust downpipe-to-manifold securing bolts - note coil spring and shoulder on bolt

7.13b Renew exhaust system downpipe-to-manifold gasket to prevent leaks

7.14 Release spring clip to extract securing bolt from manifold, when required

7.15 Fit plastic guide sleeve to stud arrowed when refitting exhaust manifold

8.4a Unscrew pulley bolt to release crankshaft pulley

8.4b Ensure pulley is located on crankshaft Woodruff key on reassembly

thermostat housing, so that the manifold will be correctly located ***(see illustration)****.* ***Do not*** *refit the manifold without this sleeve.*

b) Refit the manifold, and finger-tighten the mounting nuts.

c) Working from the centre out, and in three or four equal steps, tighten the nuts to the torque wrench setting given in the Specifications Section of this Chapter.

d) Refit the remaining parts in the reverse order of removal. Tighten all fasteners to the specified torque wrench settings.

e) Refill the cooling system (see Chapter 1).

f) Run the engine, and check for exhaust leaks. Check the coolant level when fully warmed-up to normal operating temperature.

8 Crankshaft pulley - removal and refitting

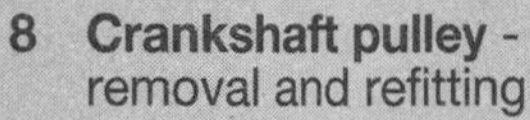

Removal

1 Remove the auxiliary drivebelt - either remove the drivebelt completely, or just secure it clear of the crankshaft pulley, depending on the work to be carried out (see Chapter 1).

2 If necessary, rotate the crankshaft until the timing marks align (see Section 4).

3 The crankshaft must now be locked to prevent its rotation while the pulley bolt is unscrewed. Proceed as follows:

a) If the engine/transmission is still installed in the vehicle:

1) If the vehicle is fitted with manual transmission, select top gear, and have an assistant apply the brakes hard.

2) If the vehicle is fitted with automatic transmission, unbolt the small metal cover plate from the sump, and use a large screwdriver or similar to lock the driveplate ring gear teeth while an assistant slackens the pulley bolt; take care not to damage the teeth or the surrounding castings when using this method.

b) If the engine/transmission has been removed but not yet separated:

1) If the vehicle is fitted with manual transmission, remove the starter motor (see Chapter 5A) and lock the flywheel using the method outlined in (2) above.

2) If the vehicle is fitted with automatic transmission, see (2) above.

c) If the engine/transmission has been removed and separated, use the method shown in illustrations) 21.11.

4 Unscrew the pulley bolt and remove the pulley **(see illustrations)**.

Refitting

5 Refitting is the reverse of the removal procedure; ensure that the pulley's keyway is aligned with the crankshaft's locating key, and tighten the pulley bolt to the specified torque wrench setting.

9 Timing belt covers - removal and refitting

Upper cover

Removal

1 Unscrew the mounting bolts and withdraw the upper cover **(see illustration)**. On 5/1998-on models, it is necessary to support the engine with a trolley jack and block of wood beneath the sump, then remove the right-hand engine mounting and studs before the timing cover can be removed **(see illustrations)**.

Refitting

2 Refitting is the reverse of the removal procedure; ensure the cover edges engage correctly with each other, and note the torque wrench setting specified for the bolts.

Middle cover

Removal

3 Support the engine using a trolley jack and block of wood beneath the sump, then unscrew the nuts/bolts securing the engine/transmission right-hand mounting bracket and withdraw the bracket.

4 Slacken the water pump pulley bolts.

5 Remove the timing belt upper cover (see paragraph 1 above).

6 Remove the auxiliary drivebelt (see Chapter 1).

9.1a Remove bolts (arrowed) to release timing belt upper cover

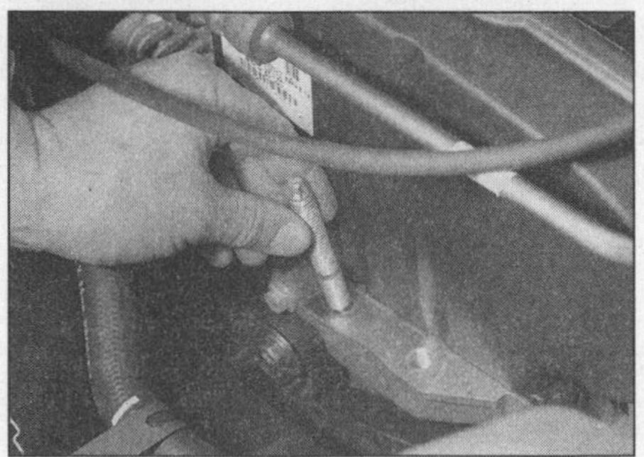

9.1b On 5/1998-on models, unscrew and remove the engine mounting studs . . .

9.1c . . . and remove the upper cover

9.7 Slacken water pump pulley bolts and remove pulley

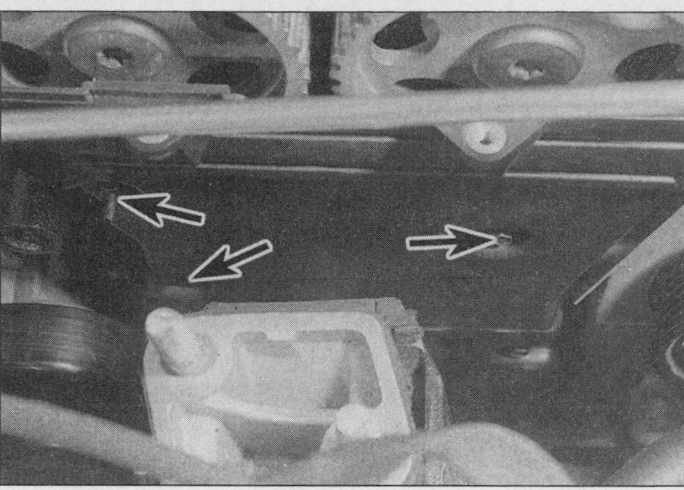
9.8 Remove fasteners (arrowed) to release timing belt middle cover

7 Unbolt and remove the water pump pulley **(see illustration)**.
8 Unscrew the middle cover nuts/bolts and withdraw the cover **(see illustration)**. Note on 5/1998-on models the middle cover is manufactured of aluminium alloy.

Refitting

9 Refitting is the reverse of the removal procedure. Ensure the cover edges engage correctly with each other, and note the torque wrench settings specified for the various fasteners. On early models, when reassembling the engine/transmission right-hand mounting, renew the self-locking nuts, and do not allow the mounting to twist as the middle two of the bracket's six nuts are tightened.

Lower cover

Removal

10 Remove the crankshaft pulley (see Section 8).
11 Unscrew the cover's three securing bolts and withdraw it **(see illustration)**.

Refitting

12 Refitting is the reverse of the removal procedure; ensure the cover edges engage correctly with each other, and note the torque wrench settings specified for the various fasteners.

Inner shield

Removal

13 Remove the timing belt, its tensioner components and the camshaft toothed pulleys (see Sections 10 and 11).
14 The shield is secured to the cylinder head by two bolts at the top, and by two studs lower down; unscrew these and withdraw the shield **(see illustration)**.

Refitting

15 Refitting is the reverse of the removal procedure; note the torque wrench settings specified for the various fasteners.

10 Timing belt - removal, refitting and adjustment

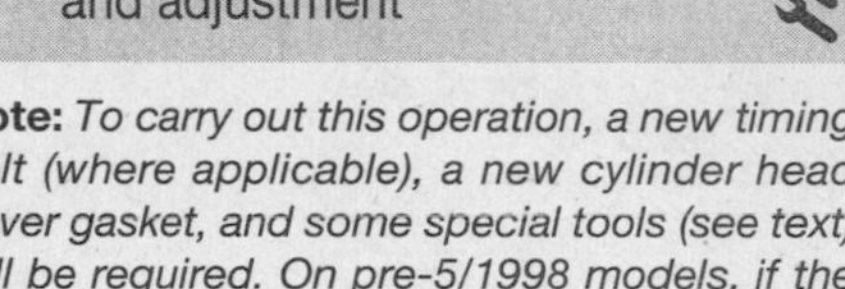

Note: *To carry out this operation, a new timing belt (where applicable), a new cylinder head cover gasket, and some special tools (see text) will be required. On pre-5/1998 models, if the timing belt is being removed for the first time since the vehicle left the factory, a tensioner spring and retaining pin must be obtained for fitting on reassembly.*

Removal

2A

1 Disconnect the battery negative (earth) lead (see Chapter 5A, Section 1). Apply the handbrake, then jack up the front of the vehicle and support it on axle stands (see "*Jacking and Vehicle Support*"). Remove the right-hand wheel arch liner with reference to Chapter 11 **(see illustration)**.
2 Unbolt the power steering high-pressure

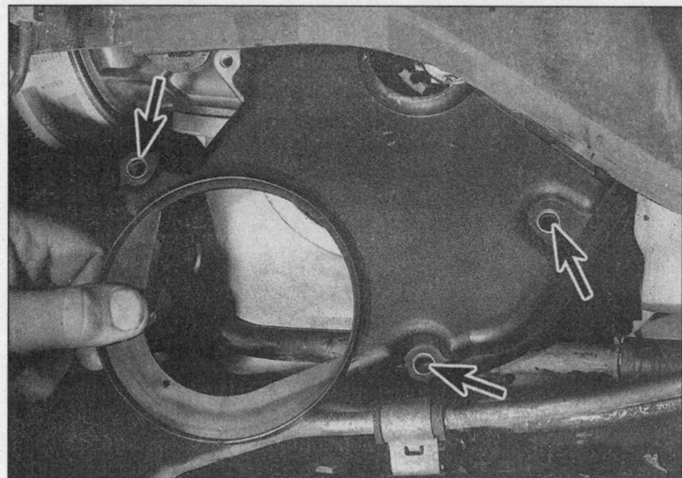
9.11 Removing timing belt lower cover - bolt locations arrowed

9.14 Timing belt inner shield fasteners (arrowed)

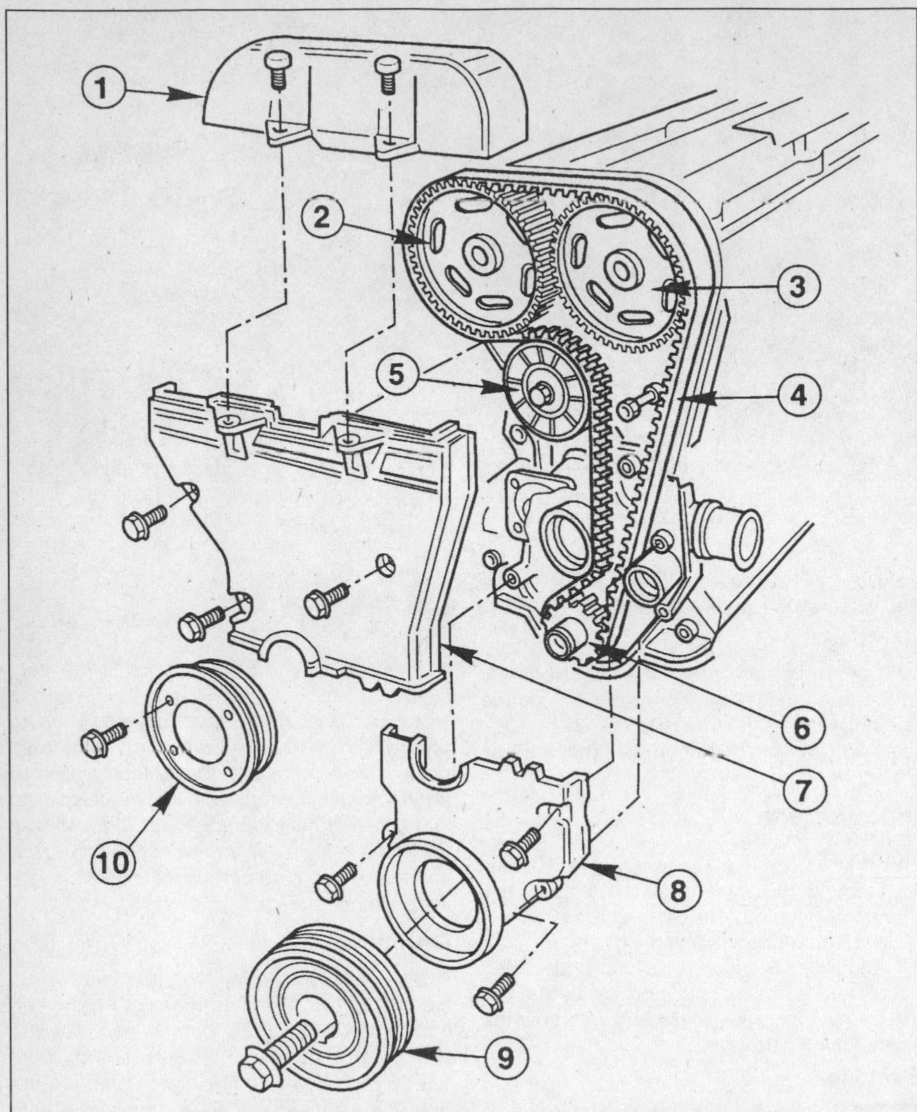

10.1 Timing belt and cover details (pre-5/1998 models)

1 Timing belt upper cover
2 Inlet camshaft toothed pulley
3 Exhaust camshaft toothed pulley
4 Timing belt
5 Timing belt tensioner
6 Crankshaft toothed pulley
7 Timing belt middle cover
8 Timing belt lower cover
9 Crankshaft pulley
10 Water pump pulley

pipe from the cylinder head rear support plate/engine lifting eye, and from the front support plate/pump bracket.

3 Support the engine with a trolley jack and block of wood beneath the sump, then mark the position of the right-hand engine mounting bracket, unscrew the nuts/bolts, and withdraw the bracket. Note on later models it will be necessary to unbolt the coolant expansion tank and position it to one side without disconnecting the hoses. One of the engine mounting bolts also secures a hose support bracket **(see illustrations).**

4 Slacken the water pump pulley bolts.

5 Remove the cylinder head cover (see Section 5) **(see illustration).**

6 Remove the spark plugs, covering their holes with clean rag, to prevent dirt or other foreign bodies from dropping in (see Chapter 1).

7 Remove the auxiliary drivebelt (see Chapter 1).

8 Rotate the crankshaft clockwise until the second pair of notches (or notch) in the pulley rim align with the edge of the sump mark (or mark on the lower crankcase frame on later models), so that Nos 1 and 4 cylinders are at TDC (see Section 4).

9 Unbolt and remove the water pump pulley and the auxiliary drivebelt idler pulley.

10 Obtain Ford service tool 21-162B, or fabricate a substitute from a strip of metal 5 mm thick (while the strip's thickness is critical, its length and width are not, but should be approximately 180 to 230 mm by 20 to 30 mm). Check that Nos 1 and 4 cylinders are at Top Dead Centre (TDC) - No 1 on the compression stroke - by resting this tool on the cylinder head mating surface, and sliding it into the slot in the left-hand end of both camshafts **(see illustration)**. The tool should slip snugly into both slots while resting on the cylinder head mating surface; if one camshaft is only slightly out of alignment, it is permissible to use an open-ended spanner to rotate the camshaft gently and carefully until the tool will fit.

11 If both camshaft slots (they are machined significantly off-centre) are below the level of the cylinder head mating surface, rotate the crankshaft through one full turn clockwise and

10.3a On later models unbolt the coolant expansion tank and position it to one side . . .

10.3b . . . then remove the engine mounting, noting the location of the hose support bracket

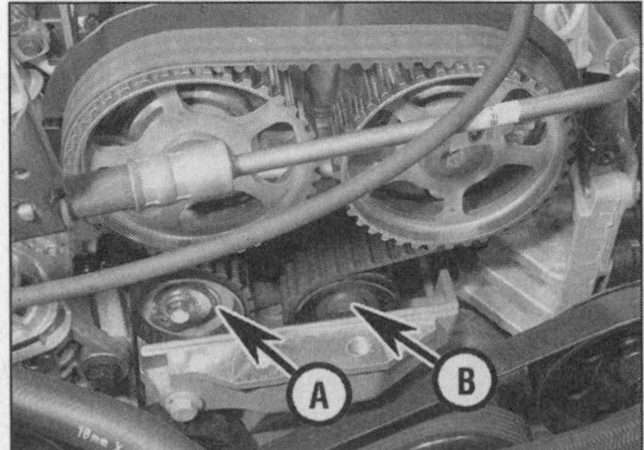

10.5 View of the upper timing belt on 5/1998-on models, showing tensioner (A) and idler (B)

10.10 Fit camshaft aligning tool to ensure engine is locked with Nos 1 and 4 cylinders at TDC

10.14a Slacken tensioner bolt, and use Allen key to rotate tensioner away from timing belt

10.14b On 5/1998-on models, unhook the tensioner from the backplate

fit the tool again; it should now fit as described in the previous paragraph.

12 With the camshaft aligning tool remaining in place, remove the crankshaft pulley. Do not use the locked camshafts to prevent the crankshaft from rotating - use only the locking methods described in Section 8.

13 Remove the timing belt lower and middle covers (see Section 9).

14 With the camshaft aligning tool still in place, slacken the tensioner bolt, and use an Allen key inserted into its centre to rotate the tensioner clockwise (models up to 10/1996) or anticlockwise (models from 10/1996 to 5/1998) as far as possible away from the belt; retighten the bolt to secure the tensioner clear of the timing belt **(see illustration)**. On 5/1998-on models, unscrew the tensioner bolt 4 turns and unhook the tensioner from the backplate **(see illustration)**.

15 If the timing belt is to be re-used, use white paint or similar to mark its direction of rotation, and note from the manufacturer's markings which way round it is fitted. Withdraw the belt **(see illustration)**. Do not rotate the crankshaft until the timing belt is refitted.

10.15 Removing the timing belt

16 If the belt is being removed for reasons other than routine renewal, check it carefully for any signs of uneven wear, splitting, cracks (especially at the roots of the belt teeth) or contamination with oil or coolant. Renew the belt if there is the slightest doubt about its condition. As a safety measure, the belt must be renewed as a matter of course at the intervals given in Chapter 1; if its history is unknown, the belt should be renewed irrespective of its apparent condition whenever the engine is overhauled. Similarly, check the tensioner spring (where fitted), renewing it if there is any doubt about its condition. Check also the toothed pulleys for signs of wear or damage, and ensure that the tensioner and guide pulleys rotate smoothly on their bearings; renew any worn or damaged components. If signs of oil or coolant contamination are found, trace the source of the leak and rectify it, then wash down the engine timing belt area and related components, to remove all traces of oil or coolant.

Refitting and adjustment

17 On reassembly, temporarily refit the crankshaft pulley, to check that the pulley notches and sump rib are aligned as described above, then ensure that both camshafts are aligned at TDC by the special tool. If the engine is being reassembled after major dismantling, both camshaft toothed pulleys should be free to rotate on their respective camshafts; if the timing belt alone is being renewed, both pulleys should still be securely fastened.

18 A holding tool will be required to prevent the camshaft toothed pulleys from rotating while their bolts are slackened and retightened; either obtain Ford service tool 15-030A, or fabricate a substitute as follows. Find two lengths of steel strip, one approximately 600 mm long and the other about 200 mm, and three bolts with nuts and washers; one nut and bolt forming the pivot of a forked tool, with the remaining nuts and bolts at the tips of the "forks", to engage with the pulley spokes as shown in the accompanying illustrations)s. Note: Do not use the camshaft aligning tool (whether genuine Ford or not) to prevent rotation while the camshaft toothed pulley bolts are slackened or tightened; the risk of damage to the camshaft concerned and to the cylinder head is far too great. Use only a forked holding tool applied directly to the pulleys, as described.

19 If it is being fitted for the first time on pre-5/1998 models, screw the timing belt tensioner spring retaining pin into the cylinder head, tightening it to the specified torque wrench setting. Unbolt the tensioner, hook the spring on to the pin and the tensioner backplate, then refit the tensioner, engaging its backplate on the locating peg. In all cases, slacken the tensioner bolt (if necessary), and use an Allen key inserted into its centre to rotate the tensioner clockwise as far as possible against spring tension, then retighten the bolt to secure the tensioner **(see illustrations)**.

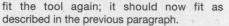

2A

10.19a Fitting tensioner spring retaining pin

10.19b Hook spring onto tensioner and refit as shown - engage tensioner backplate on locating peg (arrowed) . . .

10.19c . . . then use Allen key to position tensioner so that timing belt can be refitted

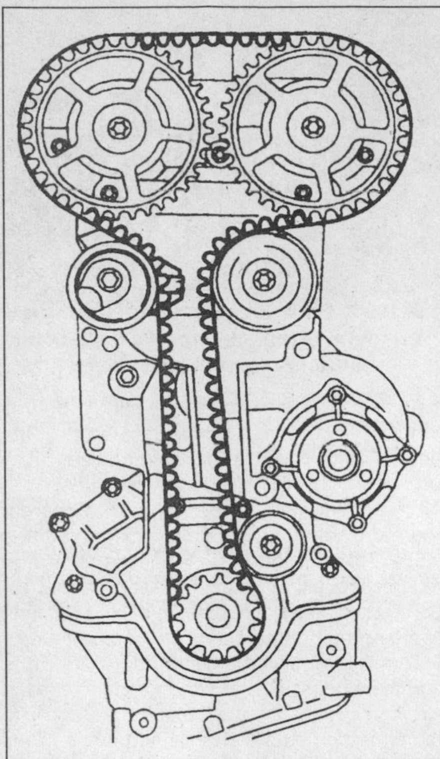

10.20 Timing belt configuration on models from 5/1998-on

20 On 5/1998-on models, the timing belt tensioner and idlers are different to earlier models and the tensioner spring mentioned in the previous paragraph is not required **(see illustration)**. When fitting the belt, the tensioner bracket must not be hooked into the backplate until after the belt is fully positioned around the pulleys and idlers.

21 Fit the timing belt; if the original is being refitted, ensure that the marks and notes made on removal are followed, so that the belt is refitted the same way round, and to run in the same direction. Starting at the crankshaft toothed pulley, work anti-clockwise around the pulleys and tensioner. The front run must be kept taut, without altering the position either of the crankshaft or of the camshafts - if necessary, the position of the camshaft toothed pulleys can be altered by rotating each on its camshaft (which remains fixed by the aligning tool). Where the pulley is still fastened, use the holding tool to prevent the pulley from rotating while its retaining bolt is slackened - the pulley can then be rotated on the camshaft until the belt will slip into place; retighten the pulley bolt.

10.22a Slacken tensioner bolt to give initial belt tension

10.22b On 5/1998-on models, turn the tensioner (2) anticlockwise until the arrow is aligned with the mark on the bracket (1)

22 On pre-5/1998 models, slacken the tensioner bolt gently until the spring pulls the tensioner against the belt; the tensioner should be retained correctly against the timing belt inner shield and cylinder head, but must be just free to respond to changes in belt tension. On 5/1998-on models, hook the tensioner into the backplate and insert the bolt loosely (approximately loosened 4 turns). Using the key, turn the tensioner anticlockwise until the arrow is aligned with the mark or square hole on the bracket, then tighten the centre bolt **(see illustrations)**.

23 Tighten both camshaft toothed pulley bolts (or check that they are tight, as applicable) and remove the camshaft aligning tool. Temporarily refit the crankshaft pulley, and rotate the crankshaft through two full turns clockwise to settle and tension the timing belt, returning the crankshaft (pulley notches) to the position described in paragraph 8 above. Refit the camshaft aligning tool; it should slip into place as described in paragraph 10. If all is well, proceed to paragraph 26 below.

24 If one camshaft is only just out of line, fit the forked holding tool to its toothed pulley, adjust its position as required, and check that any slack created has been taken up by the tensioner; rotate the crankshaft through two further turns clockwise, and refit the camshaft aligning tool to check that it now fits as it should. If all is well, proceed to paragraph 26 below.

25 If either camshaft is significantly out of line, use the holding tool described in paragraph 18 above to prevent its pulley from rotating while its retaining bolt is slackened - the camshaft can then be rotated (gently and carefully, using an open-ended spanner) until the camshaft aligning tool will slip into place; take care not to disturb the relationship of the pulley to the timing belt. Without disturbing the pulley's new position on the camshaft, tighten the pulley bolt to its specified torque wrench setting **(see illustration)**. Remove the camshaft aligning tool, rotate the crankshaft through two further turns clockwise and refit the tool to check that it now fits as it should.

26 When the timing belt has been settled at its correct tension, and the camshaft aligning tool fits correctly when the crankshaft pulley notches are exactly aligned, tighten the tensioner bolt to its specified torque wrench setting **(see illustration)**. Fitting the forked holding tool to the spokes of each pulley in turn, check that the pulley bolts are tightened to their specified torque wrench setting. Remove the camshaft aligning tool, rotate the crankshaft through two further turns clockwise, and refit the tool to make a final check that it fits as it should.

27 On 5/1998-on models, note that the timing belt tensioner automatically adjusts the tension constantly by internal spring forces, and it is not possible to check the tension once set, for instance by depressing or twisting the timing belt.

28 The remainder of the reassembly procedure is the reverse of removal, noting the following points:

a) Tighten all fasteners to the torque wrench settings specified.

b) When reassembling the engine/transmission right-hand mounting, renew the self-locking nuts, and do not allow the mounting to twist as the middle two of the bracket's six nuts are tightened.

10.25 Using forked holding tool while camshaft toothed pulley bolt is tightened

10.26 When setting is correct, tighten tensioner bolt to specified torque wrench setting

11.3 Removing timing belt tensioner

11.8 Note "FRONT" marking on outside face of crankshaft toothed pulley

11.13 Tighten timing belt guide pulley bolts to specified torque settings on refitting

11 Timing belt tensioner and toothed pulleys - removal and refitting

Tensioner

Note: *On pre-5/1998 models, if the tensioner is being removed for the first time since the vehicle left the factory, a tensioner spring and retaining pin must be obtained for fitting on reassembly. This is not necessary on later models.*

Removal

1 While it is possible to reach the tensioner once the timing belt upper and middle covers only have been removed (see Section 9), the whole procedure outlined below must be followed, to ensure that the valve timing is correctly reset once the belt's tension has been disturbed.

2 Release the tension from the timing belt as described in Section 10.

3 Unscrew the tensioner bolt and withdraw the tensioner, unhooking the spring, if fitted **(see illustration)**. Check the tensioner and spring as described in Section 10.

Refitting

4 On reassembly on pre-5/1998 models, if it is being fitted for the first time, screw the timing belt tensioner spring retaining pin into the cylinder head, tightening it to the specified torque wrench setting. Hook the spring onto the pin and the tensioner backplate, then refit the tensioner, engaging its backplate on the locating peg. Use an Allen key inserted into its centre to rotate the tensioner clockwise as far as possible against spring tension, then tighten the bolt to secure the tensioner.

5 On 5/1998-on models, hook the tensioner on the metal cover and insert the bolt.

6 Check the camshaft alignment (valve timing) and set the timing belt tension, as described in Section 10.

Camshaft and crankshaft toothed pulleys

Removal

7 While it may be possible to remove any of these pulleys once their respective covers have been removed, the complete timing belt removal/refitting procedure (see Section 10) must be followed, to ensure that the valve timing is correctly reset once the belt's tension has been disturbed.

8 With the timing belt removed, the camshaft toothed pulleys can be detached once their retaining bolts have been unscrewed as described in Section 10. The crankshaft toothed pulley can be pulled off the end of the crankshaft once the crankshaft (grooved) pulley and the timing belt have been removed. Note the "FRONT" marking identifying the pulley's outboard face, and the thrustwasher behind it; note which way round the thrustwasher is fitted **(see illustration)**. Note the pulley-locating Woodruff key; if this is loose, it should be removed for safe storage with the pulley.

9 Check the pulleys as described in Section 10.

Refitting

10 Refitting is the reverse of the removal procedure.

Timing belt guide pulleys

Removal

11 Remove the timing belt covers (see Section 9).

12 Unbolt and withdraw the pulley(s); check their condition as described in Section 10.

Refitting

13 Refitting is the reverse of the removal procedure; tighten the pulley bolts to the specified torque wrench setting **(see illustration)**.

12 Camshaft oil seals - renewal

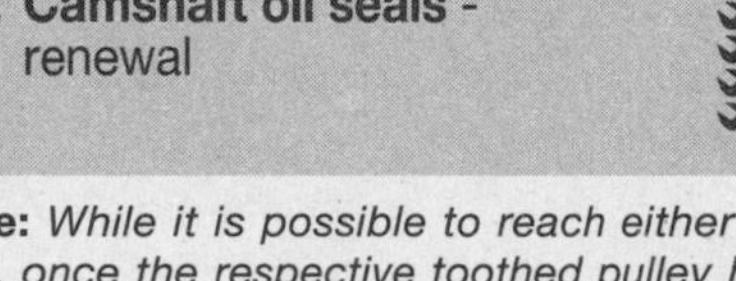

Note: *While it is possible to reach either oil seal, once the respective toothed pulley has been removed (see Section 11) to allow the seal to be prised out, this procedure is not recommended. Not only are the seals very soft, making this difficult to do without risk of damage to the seal housing, but it would be very difficult to ensure that the valve timing and the timing belt's tension, once disturbed, are correctly reset. Owners are advised to follow the whole procedure outlined below.*

1 Release the tension from the timing belt as described in Section 10, paragraphs 1 to 14. **Note:** *If the timing belt is found to be contaminated by oil, remove it completely as described, then renew the oil seal (see below). Wash down the engine timing belt area and all related components, to remove all traces of oil. Fit a new belt on reassembly.*

2 If the timing belt is still clean, slip it off the toothed pulley, taking care not to twist it too sharply; use the fingers only to handle the belt. Do not rotate the crankshaft until the timing belt is refitted. Cover the belt, and secure it so that it is clear of the working area and cannot slip off the remaining toothed pulley.

3 Unfasten the pulley bolt and withdraw the pulley (see Section 11).

4 Unbolt the camshaft right-hand bearing cap, and withdraw the defective oil seal. Clean the seal housing, and polish off any burrs or raised edges, which may have caused the seal to fail in the first place.

5 To fit a new seal, Ford recommend the use of their service tool 21-009B, with a bolt (10 mm thread size, 70 mm long) and a washer, to draw the seal into place when the camshaft bearing cap is bolted down; a substitute can be made using a suitable socket **(see illustration)**. Grease the seal lips and periphery to ease installation, and draw the seal into place until it is flush with the housing/bearing cap outer edge. Refit the bearing cap, using sealant and tightening the cap bolts as described in Section 13.

12.5 Using socket and toothed pulley bolt to install camshaft oil seal

2A

12.6 Alternatively, seal can be inserted when camshaft bearing cap is unbolted

6 For most owners, the simplest answer will be to grease the seal lips, and to slide it on to the camshaft (until it is flush with the housing's outer edge). Refit the bearing cap, using sealant and tightening the cap bolts as described in Section 13 **(see illustration)**. Take care to ensure that the seal remains absolutely square in its housing, and is not distorted as the cap is tightened down.

7 Refit the pulley to the camshaft, tightening the retaining bolt loosely, then slip the timing belt back onto the pulley (refer to paragraphs 18 and 21 of Section 10) and tighten the bolt securely.

8 The remainder of the reassembly procedure, including checking the camshaft alignment (valve timing) and setting the timing belt tension, is as described in Section 10.

13.3 Using forked holding tool while camshaft toothed pulley bolt is slackened

13 Camshafts and tappets - removal, inspection and refitting

Removal

1 Release the tension from the timing belt as described in Section 10.

2 Either remove the timing belt completely (see Section 10) or slip it off the camshaft toothed pulleys, taking care not to twist it too sharply; use the fingers only to handle the belt. Cover the belt, and secure it so that it is clear of the working area. Do not rotate the crankshaft until the timing belt is refitted.

3 Unfasten the pulley bolts as described in Section 10, paragraphs 18 and 21, and withdraw the pulleys; while both are the same and could be interchanged, it is good working practice to mark them so that each is refitted only to its original location **(see illustration)**.

4 Working in the sequence shown, slacken the camshaft bearing cap bolts progressively by half a turn at a time **(see illustrations)**. Work only as described, to release gradually and evenly the pressure of the valve springs on the caps.

5 Withdraw the caps, noting their markings and the presence of the locating dowels, then remove the camshafts and withdraw their oil seals. The inlet camshaft can be identified by the reference lobe for the camshaft position sensor; therefore, there is no need to mark the camshafts **(see illustrations)**.

6 Obtain sixteen small, clean containers, and number them 1 to 16. On 5/1998-on models make sure the shims remain with their corresponding tappets to ensure correct refitting. On earlier models, the hydraulic tappets must be remain immersed in clean engine oil while they are removed to ensure the oil does not drain from them. Using a rubber sucker, withdraw each tappet in turn and place them in the containers **(see illustrations)**. Do not interchange the tappets, or the rate of wear will be much increased. Do not allow the hydraulic tappets to lose oil, or they will take a long time to refill on restarting the engine. Note: As from February 1997, the exhaust valve hydraulic tappets are different to the inlet valve hydraulic tappets.

Inspection

7 With the camshafts and tappets removed, check each for signs of obvious wear (scoring, pitting etc) and for ovality, and renew if necessary.

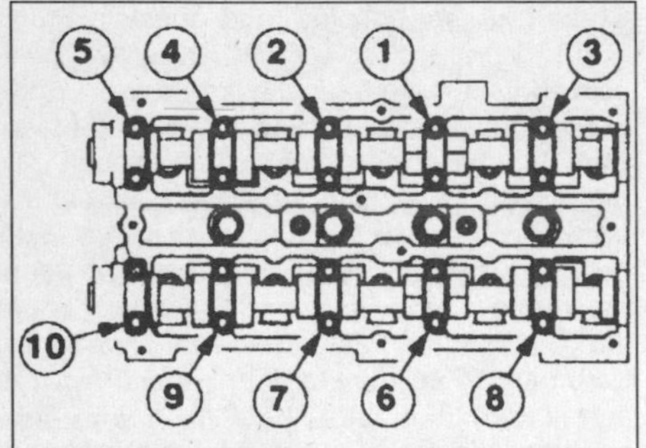

13.4a Camshaft bearing cap loosening sequence for pre 5/1998 models

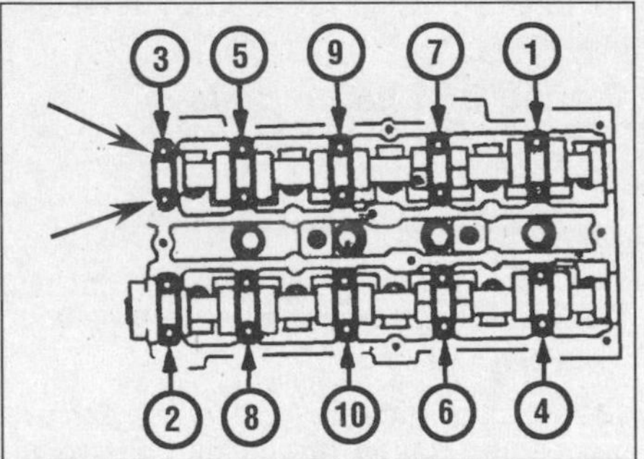

13.4b Camshaft bearing cap loosening sequence for 5/1998-on models

13.5a Note locating dowels when removing camshaft bearing caps

13.5b Inlet camshaft has lobe for camshaft position sensor

13.6a Removing hydraulic tappets

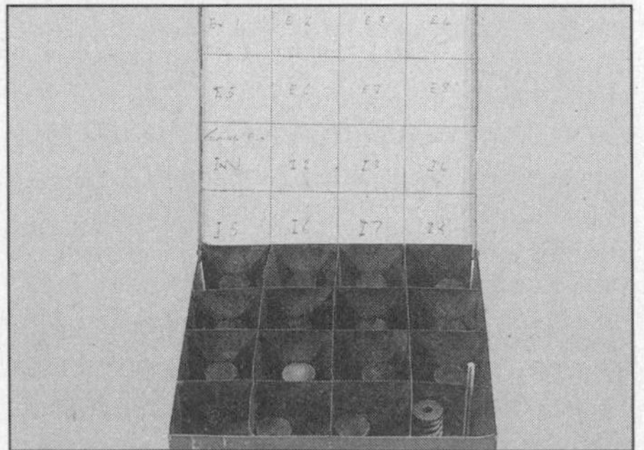

13.6b Hydraulic tappets must be stored as described in text

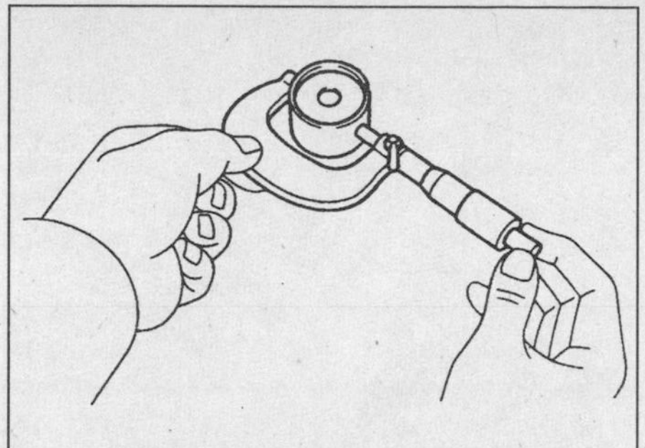
13.8 Use a micrometer to measure diameter of hydraulic tappets

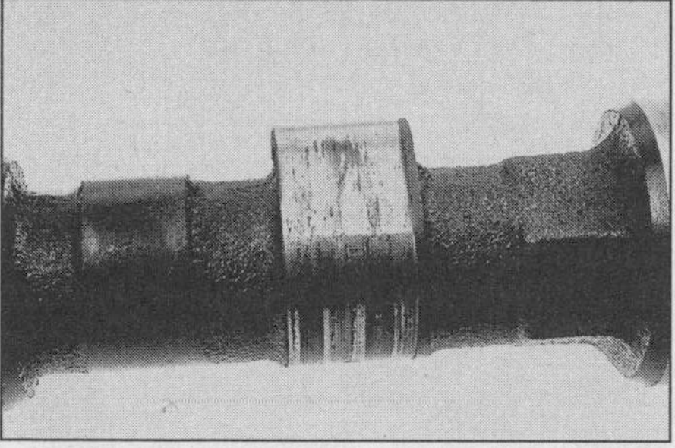
13.10 Check the cam lobes for pitting, wear and score marks - if scoring is excessive, as is the case here, renew the camshaft

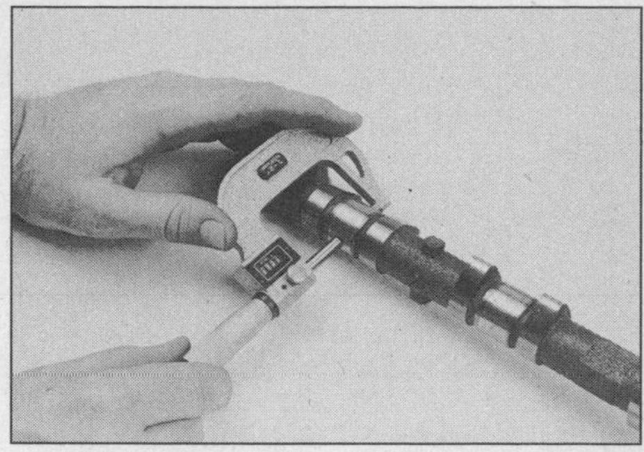
13.12 Measure each journal diameter with a micrometer

8 Measure the outside diameter of each tappet **(see illustration)** - take measurements at the top and bottom of each tappet, then a second set at right-angles to the first; if any measurement is significantly different from the others, the tappet is tapered or oval (as applicable) and must be renewed. If the necessary equipment is available, measure the inside diameter of the corresponding cylinder head bore. Compare the measurements obtained to those given in the Specifications Section of this Chapter; if the tappets or the cylinder head bores are excessively worn, new tappets and/or a new cylinder head will be required.

9 If the engine's valve components have sounded noisy, particularly if the noise persists after initial start-up from cold, there is reason to suspect a faulty hydraulic tappet or incorrect shim thickness. Only a good mechanic experienced in these engines can tell whether the noise level is typical, or if renewal of one or more of the hydraulic tappets is warranted. If faulty tappets are diagnosed, and the engine's service history is unknown, it is always worth trying the effect of renewing the engine oil and filter (see Chapter 1), using only good-quality engine oil of the recommended viscosity and specification, before going to the expense of renewing any of the tappets - refer also to the advice in Section 1 of this Chapter.

10 Visually examine the camshaft lobes for score marks, pitting, galling (wear due to rubbing) and evidence of overheating (blue, discoloured areas). Look for flaking away of the hardened surface layer of each lobe **(see illustration)**. If any such signs are evident, renew the component concerned.

11 Examine the camshaft bearing journals and the cylinder head bearing surfaces for signs of obvious wear or pitting. If any such signs are evident, renew the component concerned.

12 Using a micrometer, measure the diameter of each journal at several points **(see illustration)**. If the diameter of any one journal is less than the specified value, renew the camshaft.

13 To check the bearing journal running clearance, remove the tappets, use a suitable solvent and a clean lint-free rag to clean carefully all bearing surfaces, then refit the camshafts and bearing caps with a strand of Plastigage across each journal **(see illustration)**. Tighten the bearing cap bolts to the specified torque wrench setting (do not rotate the camshafts), then remove the bearing caps and use the scale provided to measure the width of the compressed strands **(see illustration)**. Scrape off the Plastigage with your fingernail or the edge of a credit card - don't scratch or nick the journals or bearing caps.

14 If the running clearance of any bearing is found to be worn to beyond the specified service limits, fit a new camshaft and repeat the check; if the clearance is still excessive, the cylinder head must be renewed.

15 To check camshaft endfloat, remove the tappets, clean the bearing surfaces carefully, and refit the camshafts and bearing caps. Tighten the bearing cap bolts to the specified torque wrench setting, then measure the endfloat using a DTI (Dial Test Indicator, or dial gauge) mounted on the cylinder head so that its tip bears on the camshaft right-hand end.

16 Tap the camshaft fully towards the gauge, zero the gauge, then tap the camshaft fully away from the gauge, and note the gauge reading. If the endfloat measured is found to be at or beyond the specified service limit, fit a new camshaft and repeat the check; if the clearance is still excessive, the cylinder head must be renewed.

Refitting

17 On reassembly, liberally oil the cylinder head tappet bores and the tappets **(see illustration)**. Note that if new hydraulic tappets are being fitted, they must be charged with clean engine oil before installation. Carefully refit the tappets to the cylinder head, ensuring that each tappet is refitted to its original bore, and is the correct way up. Some care will be required to enter the tappets squarely into their bores. On 5/1998-on models locate the shims in their previously noted positions.

18 Liberally oil the camshaft bearings and lobes **(see illustration)**. Ensuring that each camshaft is in its original location, refit the camshafts, locating each so that the slot in its left-hand end is approximately parallel to, and just above, the cylinder head mating surface **(see illustration)**.

19 Ensure that the locating dowels are

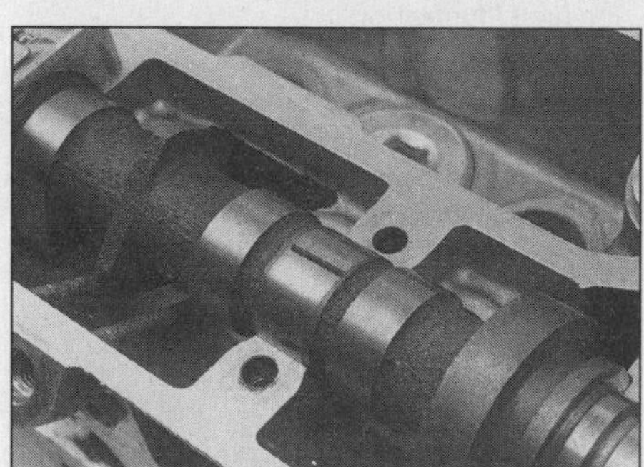
13.13a Lay a strip of Plastigage on each camshaft journal

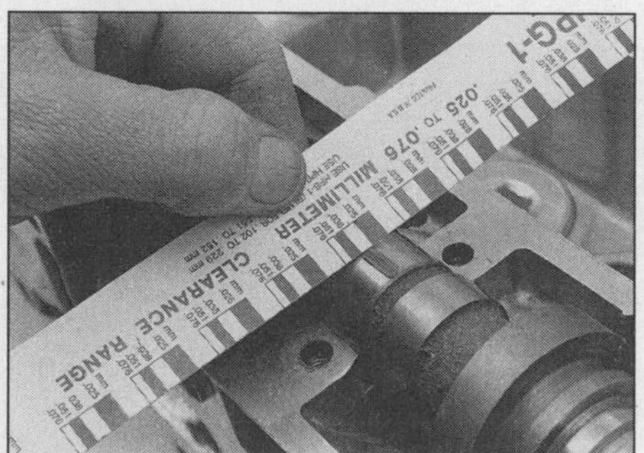

13.13b Compare the width of the crushed Plastigage to the scale on the envelope to determine the running clearance

13.17 Oil liberally when refitting hydraulic tappets

13.18a Apply engine assembly lubricant or molybdenum disulphide-based grease to the cam lobes and journals before refitting a camshaft

pressed firmly into their recesses, and check that all mating surfaces are completely clean, unmarked and free from oil. Apply a thin film of suitable sealant (Ford recommend Loctite 518) to the mating surfaces of each camshaft's right-hand bearing cap **(see illustration)**. Referring to paragraph 6 of Section 12, some owners may wish to fit the new camshaft oil seals at this stage.

20 All camshaft bearing caps have a single-digit identifying number etched on them **(see illustration)**. The exhaust camshaft's bearing caps are numbered in sequence 0 (right-hand cap) to 4 (left-hand cap), the inlet's 5 (right-hand cap) to 9 (left-hand cap). Each cap is to be fitted so that its numbered side faces outwards, to the front (exhaust) or to the rear (inlet).

21 Ensuring that each cap is kept square to the cylinder head as it is tightened down, and working in the sequence shown, tighten the camshaft bearing cap bolts slowly and by one turn at a time, until each cap touches the cylinder head **(see illustrations)**. Next, go round again in the same sequence, tightening the bolts to the first stage torque wrench setting specified, then once more, tightening them to the second stage setting. Work only as described, to impose gradually and evenly the pressure of the valve springs on the caps. Fit the camshaft aligning tool; it should slip into place as described in Section 10 **(see illustration)**.

22 Wipe off all surplus sealant, so that none is left to find its way into any oilways. Follow the sealant manufacturer's instructions as to the time needed for curing; usually, at least an hour must be allowed between application of the sealant and starting the engine.

13.20 Etched marks on camshaft bearing caps must be arranged as shown, and face outwards

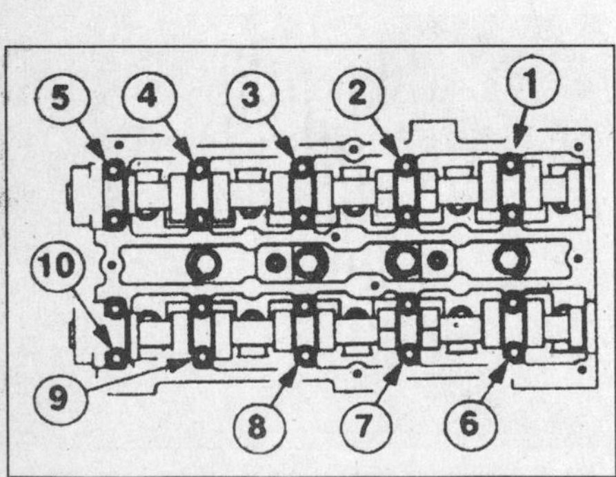

13.21b Camshaft bearing cap tightening sequence

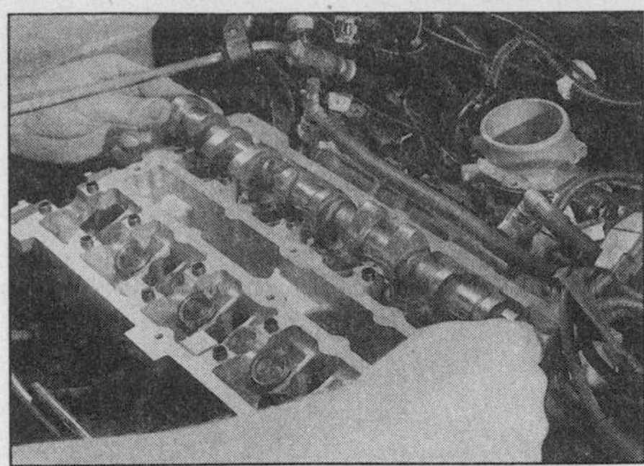

13.18b Use camshaft position sensor lobe to identify inlet camshaft on refitting - locate camshafts as described in text

13.21a Keep caps square to cylinder head at all times when tightening down

13.21c Fit camshaft aligning tool to set TDC position . . .

13.19 Apply sealant to mating surface of camshaft right-hand bearing caps

23 If using Ford's recommended procedure, fit new oil seals to the camshafts as described in paragraph 5 of Section 12.

24 Using the marks and notes made on dismantling to ensure that each is refitted to its original camshaft, refit the toothed pulleys to the camshafts, tightening the retaining bolts loosely **(see illustration)**. Slip the timing belt back onto the pulleys (refer to paragraph 21 of Section 10) and tighten the bolts securely - use the forked holding tool described in Section 10.

25 The remainder of the reassembly procedure, including valve timing and setting the timing belt tension, is as described in Section 10. On models manufactured from 5/1998-on, check and adjust the valve clearances as described in Section 14.

14 Valve clearances - checking and adjustment

Note: *This procedure applies to models manufactured from 5/1998-on. Before this date, the Zetec engine is fitted with automatic hydraulic tappets.*

Checking

1 Disconnect the battery negative (earth) lead (see Chapter 5A). Also undo the screw and disconnect the earth cable and power steering fluid pipe support bracket from the rear engine lifting eye. Move the pipe to one side **(see illustration)**.

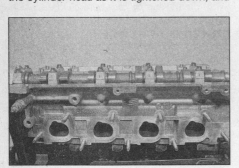

13.24 . . . while camshaft toothed pulleys are refitted

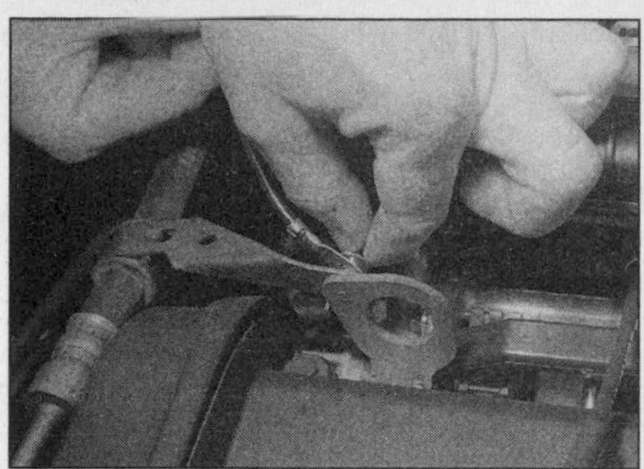

14.1 Disconnecting the earth cable and power steering fluid support bracket

14.2 Removing the upper timing cover securing screws

14.3 Disconnecting the spark plug HT leads

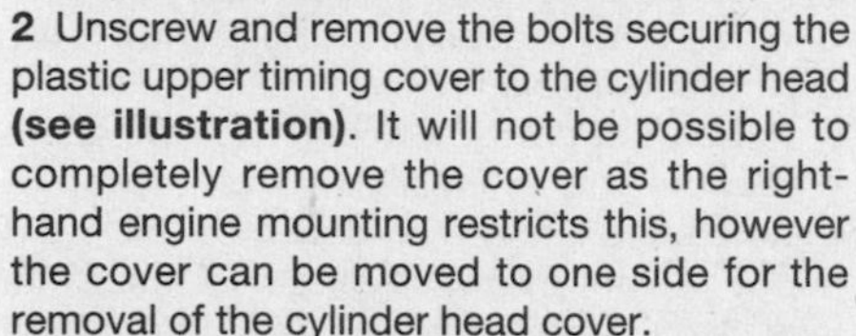

2 Unscrew and remove the bolts securing the plastic upper timing cover to the cylinder head **(see illustration)**. It will not be possible to completely remove the cover as the right-hand engine mounting restricts this, however the cover can be moved to one side for the removal of the cylinder head cover.

3 Disconnect the HT leads from the spark plugs and move them to one side **(see illustration)**.

4 Release the clip and disconnect the positive crankcase ventilation (PCV) hose from the cylinder head cover **(see illustration)**.

5 Progressively unscrew the bolts, then lift the cover from the cylinder head. Recover the gasket **(see illustrations)**.

6 Set the engine to TDC on cylinder No 1 as described in Section 4. The inlet and exhaust cam lobes of No 1 cylinder will be pointing upwards (though not vertical) and the valve clearances can be checked.

7 Working on each valve, measure the clearance between the base of the cam lobe and the shim using feeler blades **(see illustration)**. Record the thickness of the blade required to give a firm sliding fit on all the valves of No 1 cylinder. The desired clearances are given in the Specifications. Note that the clearances for inlet and exhaust valves are different. The inlet camshaft is at the rear of the engine and the exhaust camshaft at the front. Record all four clearances.

8 Now turn the crankshaft clockwise through 180° so that the valves of cylinder No 3 are pointing upwards. Check and record the valve clearances for cylinder No 3. The clearances for cylinders 4 and 2 can be checked after turning the crankshaft through 180° each time.

Adjustment

9 If adjustment is required, the shim thicknesses must be changed by depressing the tappets and removing the old shim, then fitting the new one.

10 Before changing a shim, the piston for the relevant cylinder needs to be lowered from its TDC position by turning the crankshaft approximately 90° clockwise. If this is not done, the piston will prevent the tappet from being depressed, and damage may result.

11 Ford technicians use a special tool to depress the tappets. The tool consists of a bar bolted to the top of the cylinder head, with a lever and extension which is used to depress the edge of the tappet. It is highly recommended that this tool is used rather than the use of other means, since the design of the surrounding housing makes it impossible to use a screwdriver or similar tool without the risk of damage.

12 With the tappet depressed, remove the shim with a small screwdriver or magnetic probe.

13 If the valve clearance was too small, a thinner shim must be fitted. If the clearance was too large, a thicker shim must be fitted. The thickness of the shim (in mm) is engraved on the side facing away from the camshaft. If the marking is missing or illegible, a micrometer will be needed to establish shim thickness.

14 When the shim thickness and the valve clearance are known, the required thickness of the new shim can be calculated as follows:

14.4 Disconnecting the PCV hose from the cylinder head cover

14.5a Progressively unscrew the bolts . . .

14.5b . . . then lift off the cylinder head cover . . .

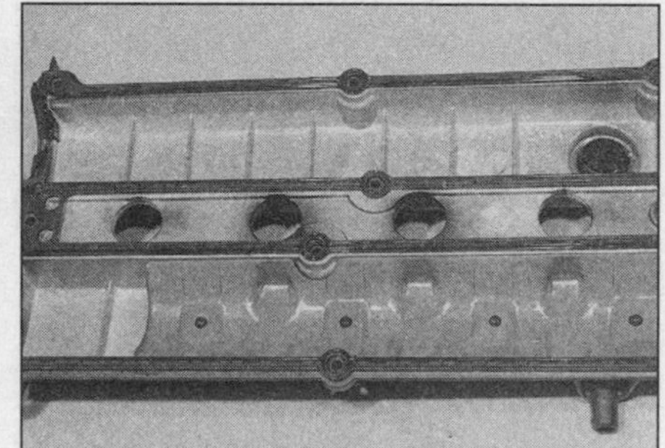

14.5c . . . and remove the gasket

14.7 Measure the clearance between the base of the cam lobe and the shim using feeler blades

15.8a Release wire clip to unplug engine wiring loom connector from inlet manifold

Sample calculation - clearance too small

Desired clearance (A)	*= 0.15 mm*
Measured clearance (B)	*= 0.09 mm*
Shim thickness found (C)	*= 2.55 mm*
Thickness required (D)	*= C + B - A = 2.49 mm*

Sample calculation - clearance too large

Desired clearance (A)	*= 0.30 mm*
Measured clearance (B)	*= 0.36 mm*
Shim thickness found (C)	*= 2.19 mm*
Thickness required (D)	*= C + B - A = 2.25 mm*

15 With the correct shim fitted, release the tappet depressing tool. Turn the engine back so that the cam lobes are again pointing upwards and check that the clearance is now correct.

16 Repeat the process for the remaining valves, turning the engine each time to bring the relevant cam lobes upwards.

17 It will be helpful for future adjustment if a record is kept of the thickness of shim fitted at each position. The shims required can be purchased in advance once the clearances and the existing shim thicknesses are known.

18 It is permissible to interchange shims between tappets to achieve the correct clearances but it is not advisable to turn the camshaft with any shims removed.

19 When all the clearances are correct, remove the tool then refit the cylinder head cover using a new gasket if necessary. Reconnect the PCV hose and the spark plug leads. Refit the timing cover and tighten the bolts. Reconnect the battery negative (earth) lead (see Chapter 5A, Section 1).

15.8b Unplug connectors (arrowed) to disconnect ignition coil wiring

15 Cylinder head - removal and refitting

Removal

Models manufactured up to 10/1996

Note: *The following text assumes that the cylinder head will be removed with both inlet and exhaust manifolds attached; this simplifies the procedure, but makes it a bulky and heavy assembly to handle - an engine hoist will be required, to prevent the risk of injury, and to prevent damage to any delicate components as the assembly is removed and refitted. If it is wished first to remove the manifolds, proceed as described in Sections 6 and 7 of this Chapter; amend the following procedure accordingly.*

1 Depressurise the fuel system (see Chapter 4A).

2 With the vehicle parked on firm level ground, open the bonnet and disconnect the battery negative (earth) lead (see Chapter 5A).

3 Whenever you disconnect any vacuum lines, coolant and emissions hoses, wiring loom connectors, earth straps and fuel lines as part of the following procedure, always label them clearly, so that they can be correctly reassembled.

Masking tape and/or a touch-up paint applicator work well for marking items. Take instant photos, or sketch the locations of components and brackets.

4 Unplugging the two electrical connectors, disconnecting the vacuum hose (where fitted) and disconnecting the crankcase breather hose from the cylinder head cover, remove the complete air cleaner assembly with the air mass meter, the resonator and the plenum chamber (see Chapter 4A).

5 Equalise the pressure in the fuel tank by removing the filler cap, then undo the fuel feed and return lines connecting the engine to the chassis (see Chapter 4A). Plug or cap all open fittings.

6 Disconnect the accelerator cable from the throttle linkage as described in Chapter 4A - where fitted, disconnect also the cruise control actuator cable (see Chapter 12). Secure the cable(s) clear of the engine/transmission.

7 Unbolt the power steering high-pressure pipe from the cylinder head rear support plate/engine lifting eye, and from the front support plate/pump bracket. Releasing its wire clip, unplug the power steering pressure switch electrical connector, then unbolt the earth lead from the cylinder head rear support plate/engine lifting eye.

8 Remove the three screws securing the wiring "rail" to the rear of the manifold. Releasing its wire clip, unplug the large electrical connector (next to the fuel pressure regulator) to disconnect the engine wiring from the main loom **(see illustration)**. Unplug the electrical connectors on each side of the ignition coil, and the single connector from beneath the front of the thermostat housing, to disconnect the coil and coolant temperature gauge sender wiring **(see illustration)**.

9 Marking or labelling them as they are unplugged, disconnect the vacuum hoses as follows:

a) One from the rear of the throttle housing (only the one hose - there is no need to disconnect the second hose running to the fuel pressure regulator).
*b) One from the union on the inlet manifold's left-hand end **(see illustration)**.*
c) The braking system vacuum servo unit hose (see Chapter 9 for details).
d) Disconnect all vacuum hoses from the Exhaust Gas Recirculation system components - one from the EGR valve and two from the EGR pipe. (Note that these last two are of different sizes, as are their pipe stubs, so that they can only be connected the correct way round.)

10 Unbolt both parts of the exhaust manifold heat shield; unclip the coolant hose to allow the upper part to be withdrawn. Either remove the dipstick and tube, or swing them out of the way.

11 Unscrew the single bolt securing the pulse-air filter housing to the engine/transmission front mounting bracket, then disconnect its vacuum hose.

12 Drain the cooling system (see Chapter 1).

13 Disconnect all coolant hoses from the thermostat housing **(see illustration)**.

15.9 Disconnect vacuum hoses (arrowed) as described in text

15.13 Disconnect all coolant hoses (arrowed) from thermostat housing

15.17 Unbolt auxiliary drivebelt idler pulley

15.18a Remove cylinder head front . . .

15.18b . . . and rear support plates

14 Unscrew the two nuts to disconnect the exhaust system front downpipe from the manifold (see Chapter 4A); disconnect the oxygen sensor wiring, so that it is not strained by the weight of the exhaust system.

15 Remove the auxiliary drivebelt (see Chapter 1).

16 Support the weight of the engine/transmission using a trolley jack, with a wooden spacer to prevent damage to the sump.

17 Unscrew the six nuts securing the engine/transmission right-hand mounting bracket, then withdraw the bracket. Unbolt the auxiliary drivebelt idler pulley **(see illustration)**.

18 Unbolt the cylinder head front and rear support plates **(see illustrations)**.

19 Remove the timing belt and both camshafts (see Sections 10 and 13); if the cylinder head is to be dismantled, withdraw the hydraulic tappets.

20 Remove the timing belt inner shield (see Section 9).

21 Working in the reverse of the sequence shown (see illustration 15.72c), slacken the ten cylinder head bolts progressively and by one turn at a time; a Torx key (TX 55 size) will be required. Remove each bolt in turn, and ensure that new replacements are obtained for reassembly; these bolts are subjected to severe stresses and so must be renewed, regardless of their apparent condition, whenever they are disturbed.

22 Lift the cylinder head away; use assistance if possible, as it is a heavy assembly **(see illustration)**. Remove the gasket, noting the two dowels, and discard it.

Models manufactured from 10/1996-on

23 Disconnect the battery negative (earth) lead (see Chapter 5A, Section 1), and depressurise the fuel system (see Chapter 4A).

24 Apply the handbrake, then jack up the front of the vehicle and support it on axle stands (see "*Jacking and Vehicle Support*"). Remove the right-hand front wheel.

25 Remove the engine undershield and radiator lower cover. Also on 5/1998-on models, unbolt and remove the cover from over the auxiliary drivebelt.

26 Position a container beneath the radiator, then where applicable, loosen the drain plug and drain the coolant. On 5/1998-on models disconnect the coolant hose below the right-hand end of the engine. Refer to Chapter 1 if necessary.

27 Remove the right-hand wheel arch liner.

28 Remove the auxiliary drivebelt with reference to Chapter 1.

29 On 5/1998-on models, unbolt and remove the water pump pulley and idler pulley. Also remove the crankshaft pulley and lower timing cover (see Section 9).

30 On 1.6 and 1.8 litre models, remove the catalytic converter with reference to Chapter 4A.

31 Disconnect the engine wiring harness and brake servo vacuum hose from the inlet manifold. Also disconnect the PCV hose from the manifold.

32 Disconnect the oil pressure switch wiring.

33 Loosen the rear roll restrictor centre bolt, then unbolt the roll restrictor from the subframe.

34 Unscrew and remove the front roll restrictor centre bolt, then unscrew the nuts securing the restrictor to the subframe. Note that it is not possible to remove the restrictor at this stage.

35 Remove the plenum chamber, inlet ducting and air cleaner cover with reference to Chapter 4A.

36 Disconnect the accelerator cable from the throttle housing segment, then pull up the plastic clip and disconnect the cable from the support bracket. Position the cable to one side.

37 Note their positions, then disconnect all the vacuum hoses from the inlet manifold.

38 Disconnect the wiring harness from the inlet manifold, noting its routing and location. On 5/1998-on models, detach the wiring conduit from the inlet manifold.

39 Identify the vacuum hoses on the EGR valve, then disconnect them.

40 Disconnect the wiring from the ignition coil, radio interference suppressor, and engine coolant temperature sensor.

41 Disconnect the wiring from the power steering pressure switch, and unbolt the earth lead from the engine lifting eye. Unbolt the PAS pipe support bracket. On 5/1998-on models, unbolt the oil dipstick tube from the cylinder head.

42 On 2.0 litre models, unbolt the air conditioning pipe support.

43 Unbolt the heatshield from the exhaust manifold and remove the engine oil level dipstick.

44 Unscrew the bolts and detach the EGR valve from the inlet manifold, the EGR pipe from the engine lifting eye, and the EGR pipe from the ignition coil.

45 On 2.0 litre models, unscrew the nuts and detach the catalytic converter from the exhaust manifold, then unscrew the union nuts and detach the pulse air system pipes.

46 Loosen the clips and disconnect the coolant hoses from the thermostat housing.

47 Disconnect the wiring from the coolant temperature gauge sender switch.

48 On 2.0 litre models, disconnect the crankshaft position sensor wiring, then unbolt and remove the pulse air system filter.

49 Mark the position of the right-hand engine mounting, then support the weight of the engine using a trolley jack and block of wood beneath the sump. Unbolt and remove the right-hand engine mounting bracket.

50 Unscrew the nuts and bolts and remove the power steering pump bracket from the cylinder head. On 5/1998-on models, unbolt the coolant expansion tank and position it to one side.

51 Unbolt and remove the alternator bracket from the cylinder head.

52 Release the fuel pressure as described in Chapter 4A.

53 Disconnect the quick release connectors on the fuel feed and return hoses.

15.22 Using an engine hoist to lift off the cylinder head complete with manifolds

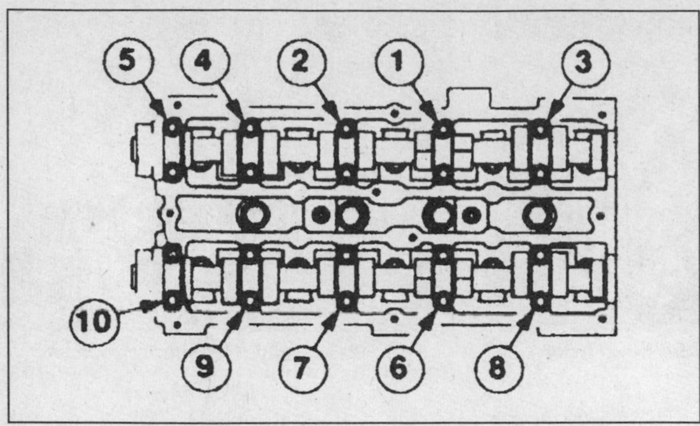

15.59 **Camshaft bearing cap bolt loosening sequence**

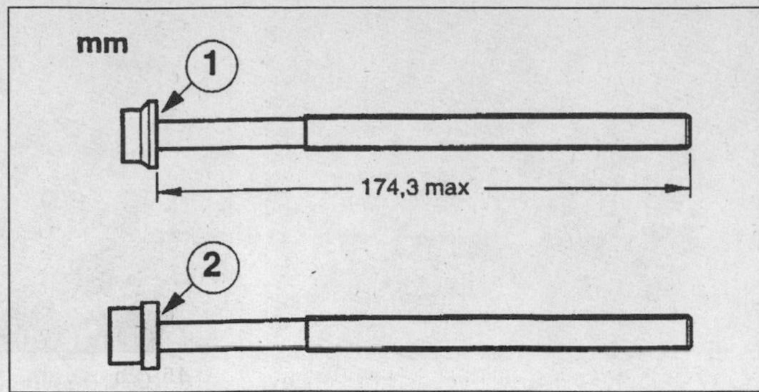

15.61 On models manufactured after 30/06/1998 the cylinder head bolts need only be renewed if they are longer than 174.3 mm

1 New cylinder head bolt with integral washer
2 Old cylinder head bolt with separate washer

54 Unbolt the auxiliary drivebelt idler, then remove the upper timing belt cover followed by the middle cover.
55 Disconnect the HT leads from the spark plugs, then unscrew the bolts and remove the cylinder head cover.
56 Unscrew and remove the spark plugs. Also remove the engine oil level dipstick.
57 Mark the timing belt to indicate its running direction, then loosen the tensioner nut and turn the tensioner pulley clockwise using an Allen key. Secure the tensioner in its new position by tightening the nut again. Remove the timing belt.
58 Remove the camshaft sprockets with reference to Section 13.
59 Loosen the camshaft bearing cap bolts progressively in the sequence shown **(see illustration)**. With all the bolts loose, remove the bearing caps, camshafts, and oil seals.
60 Remove the tappets and place them in a compartmentalised container so that they are identified for position. Where hydraulic tappets are fitted, they should be covered with clean engine oil.
61 Working in the reverse of the sequence shown (see illustration 15.72c), slacken the ten cylinder head bolts progressively and by one turn at a time; a Torx key (TX 55 size) will be required. Remove each bolt and check it for damage. It is recommended that the head bolts are renewed as a matter of course, however, on models manufactured after 30/06/1998, they need only be renewed if they are longer than 174.3 mm **(see illustration)**.
62 Lift the cylinder head away; use assistance if possible, as it is a heavy assembly. Remove the gasket, noting the two dowels, and discard it.

Refitting

63 The mating faces of the cylinder head and cylinder block must be perfectly clean before refitting the head. Use a hard plastic or wood scraper to remove all traces of gasket and carbon; also clean the piston crowns. Take particular care, as the soft aluminium alloy is easily damaged. Also, make sure that the carbon is not allowed to enter the oil and water passages - this is particularly important for the lubrication system, as carbon could block the oil supply to any of the engine's components. Using adhesive tape and paper, seal the water, oil and bolt holes in the cylinder block. Clean all the pistons in the same way.

To prevent carbon entering the gap between the pistons and bores, smear a little grease in the gap. After cleaning each piston, use a small brush to remove all traces of grease and carbon from the gap, then wipe away the remainder with a clean rag.

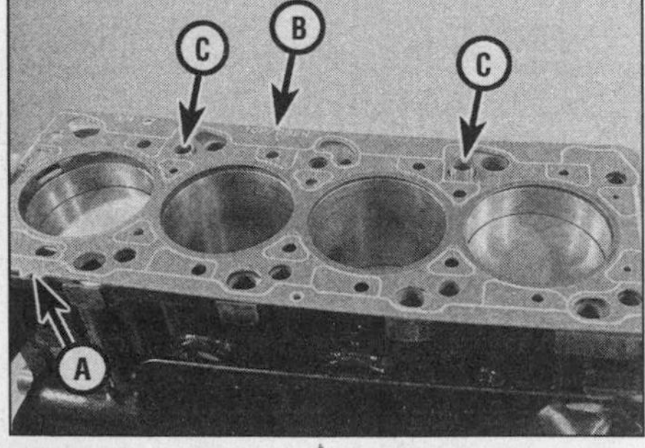

15.67 Ensuring protruding tooth (or teeth) "A" are at front and marking "B" is upwards, locate new cylinder head gasket on dowels "C"

64 Check the mating surfaces of the cylinder block and the cylinder head for nicks, deep scratches and other damage. If slight, they may be removed carefully with a file, but if excessive, machining may be the only alternative to renewal.
65 If warpage of the cylinder head gasket surface is suspected, use a straight edge to check it for distortion. Refer to Part C of this Chapter, if necessary.
66 Wipe clean the mating surfaces of the cylinder head and cylinder block. Check that the two locating dowels are in position in the cylinder block, and that all cylinder head bolt holes are free from oil.
67 Position a new gasket over the dowels on the cylinder block surface, so that the "TOP/OBEN" mark is uppermost, and the tooth (or teeth, according to engine size) protruding from one edge point to the front of the vehicle **(see illustration)**.
68 Temporarily refit the crankshaft pulley, and rotate the crankshaft anti-clockwise so that No 1 cylinder's piston is lowered to approximately 20 mm before TDC, thus avoiding any risk of valve/piston contact and damage during reassembly.
69 As the cylinder head is such a heavy and awkward assembly to refit with manifolds, it is helpful to make up a pair of guide studs from two 10 mm (thread size) studs approximately 90 mm long, with a screwdriver slot cut in one end - two old cylinder head bolts with their heads cut off would make a good starting point. Screw these guide studs, screwdriver slot upwards to permit removal, into the bolt holes at diagonally-opposite corners of the cylinder block surface (or into those where the locating dowels are fitted, as shown); ensure that approximately 70 mm of stud protrudes above the gasket.
70 Refit the cylinder head, sliding it down the guide studs (if used) and locating it on the dowels **(see illustration)**. Unscrew the guide studs (if used) when the head is in place.
71 Fit the new cylinder head bolts dry (do not oil their threads); carefully enter each into its hole and screw it in, by hand only, until finger-tight.

15.70 Refitting cylinder head - note fabricated guide studs (arrowed)

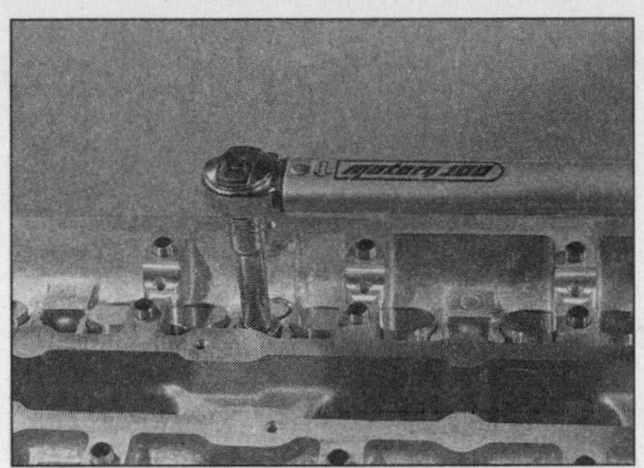

15.72a Tightening cylinder head bolts using torque wrench . . .

15.72b . . . and using angle gauge

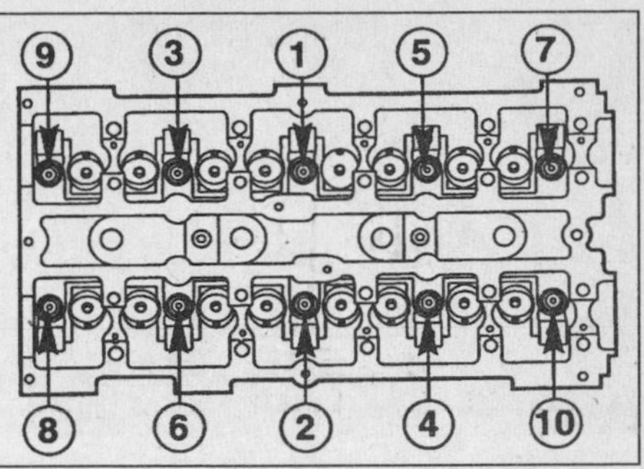

15.72c Cylinder head bolt tightening sequence for models manufactured up to 30/06/1998

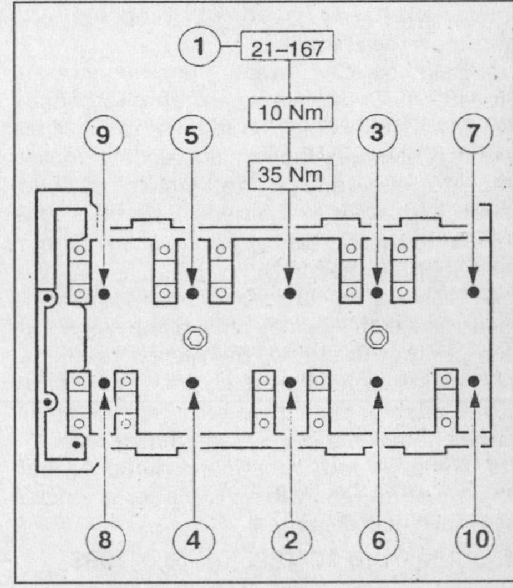

15.72d Cylinder head bolt tightening sequence for models manufactured from 01/07/1998-on

72 Working progressively and in the sequence shown, use first a torque wrench, then an ordinary socket extension bar and an angle gauge, to tighten the cylinder head bolts in the stages given in the Specifications Section of this Chapter **(see illustrations)**.

Note: *Once tightened correctly, following this procedure, the cylinder head bolts do not require check-tightening, and must not be re-torqued.*

73 Refit the tappets, the camshafts, and their oil seals and pulleys. Temporarily refit the crankshaft pulley, and rotate the crankshaft clockwise to return the pulley notches to the position described in Section 10.

74 Refit the timing belt and covers, checking the camshaft alignment (valve timing) and setting the timing belt tension, as described in Section 10.

75 The remainder of reassembly is the reverse of the removal procedure, noting the following points:

a) *Tighten all nuts and bolts to the torque wrench settings specified.*
b) *When reassembling the engine/transmission right-hand mounting, renew the self-locking nuts, and do not allow the mounting to twist as the middle two of the bracket's six nuts are tightened.*
c) *Refill the cooling system, and top-up the engine oil.*
d) *Check all disturbed joints for signs of oil or coolant leakage, once the engine has been restarted and warmed-up to normal operating temperature.*

16 Sump - removal and refitting

Removal

Note: *To carry out this task with the engine/transmission installed in the vehicle on models manufactured up to 5/1998 requires the assistance of at least one person, plus the equipment necessary to raise and support the front of the vehicle (high enough that the sump can be withdrawn from underneath), and to lift and support the complete engine/transmission unit 2 to 3 inches from its mountings while the vehicle is raised. Precise details of the procedure will depend on the equipment available - the following is typical. It is not necessary to support the engine on models manufactured from 5/1998-on.*

1 Apply the handbrake, then jack up the front of the vehicle and support it on axle stands (see "Jacking and Vehicle Support").

2 Drain the engine oil, then clean and refit the engine oil drain plug, tightening it to the specified torque wrench setting. Although not strictly necessary as part of the dismantling procedure, owners are advised to remove and discard the oil filter, so that it can be renewed with the oil (see Chapter 1).

Models up to 10/1996

3 Disconnect the battery negative (earth) lead (see Chapter 5A, Section 1).

4 Drain the cooling system (see Chapter 1).

5 Disconnect the radiator bottom hose from the radiator union and from the (heater) coolant pipe. Unbolt the coolant pipe from the sump; if they will prevent sump removal, disconnect or release the coolant hoses from the oil cooler unions (where fitted).

6 Unscrew the two bolts securing the power steering system pipes to the right-hand side of the subframe.

7 Unplug the electrical connector(s) to disconnect the oxygen sensor and, where fitted, the oil level sensor wiring - unclip the connectors to release the wiring where necessary.

8 Where the vehicle is fitted with automatic transmission, trace the fluid cooler lines from the transmission to the radiator, and release them from any clips etc, so that they have as much movement as possible.

9 Remove the auxiliary drivebelt cover (see Chapter 1).

10 Unscrew the nuts to disconnect the exhaust system front downpipe from the manifold, then either unhook all the system's rubber mountings and withdraw the complete exhaust system from under the vehicle, or remove only the downpipe/catalytic converter (see Chapter 4A for details).

11 Unscrew the sump-to-transmission bolts, also any securing the engine/transmission lower adaptor plate.

12 Unplugging the two electrical connectors, disconnecting the vacuum hose (where fitted) and disconnecting the crankcase breather hose from the cylinder head cover, remove the complete air cleaner assembly with the air mass meter, the resonator and the plenum chamber (see Chapter 4A).

13 Take the weight of the engine/transmission unit using the lifting eyes provided on the cylinder head; bolt on additional lifting eyes where required **(see illustration)**. Remove completely the engine/transmission front mounting, unscrew the rear mounting's centre bolt, and unbolt the left-hand mounting

16.13 Equipment must be available to raise and support engine/transmission unit while vehicle is raised, to allow sump removal

16.33 Sump retaining bolts on a 5/1998-on model - note the lower crankcase frame bolted to the bottom of the crankcase

16.35 Ensure gasket is located correctly in sump groove

16.36 Engine/transmission lower adaptor plate (arrowed) must be refitted with sump

from the body. Unscrew the six nuts securing the right-hand mounting bracket, and withdraw the bracket.

14 Being careful to watch the wiring, coolant hoses, fluid cooler pipes or gearchange linkage and transmission support rods (where appropriate), and the radiator electric cooling fan, to ensure that nothing is trapped, stretched or damaged, lift the engine/transmission approximately 75 mm and support it securely.

15 Progressively unscrew the sump retaining bolts. Break the joint by striking the sump with the palm of the hand, then lower the sump and withdraw it with the engine/transmission lower adaptor plate; note the presence of any shims between the sump and transmission.

16 Remove and discard the sump gasket; this must be renewed as a matter of course whenever it is disturbed.

Models from 10/1996 up to 5/1998

17 Remove the engine oil level dipstick.

18 On 2.0 litre models, release the coolant hose from the supports on the exhaust manifold heatshield.

19 Unscrew the upper and lower bolts and remove the heatshield from over the exhaust manifold.

20 Trace the wiring back from the oxygen sensor on the exhaust manifold, and disconnect the wiring at the plug.

21 Unscrew the nuts and detach the catalytic converter from the exhaust manifold. Support the converter on an axle stand.

22 Attach a suitable hoist to the engine and take its weight.

23 Loosen the right-hand suspension top mounting nut by five turns while holding the piston rod stationary with an Allen key.

24 Remove the undershield from under the engine compartment.

25 Unscrew the flange bolts and disconnect the catalytic converter from the exhaust intermediate section. Release the catalytic converter from the rubber mountings and withdraw from under the car.

26 With reference to Chapter 8, remove the right-hand driveshaft.

27 Unscrew and remove the centre bolt from the front and rear engine roll restrictors.

28 Undo the bolt and detach the coolant pipe bracket from the sump.

29 Mark the position of the right-hand engine mounting, then unbolt and remove the bracket.

30 Raise the engine approximately 75 mm. Make sure it is supported adequately.

31 Progressively unscrew the sump retaining bolts. Break the joint by striking the sump with the palm of the hand, then lower the sump and withdraw it with the engine/transmission lower adaptor plate; note the presence of any shims between the sump and transmission.

32 Remove and discard the sump gasket; this must be renewed as a matter of course whenever it is disturbed.

Models from 5/1998

33 With the front of the car raised, progressively unscrew the sump retaining bolts **(see illustration)**. Break the joint by striking the sump with the palm of the hand, then turn the sump through 90° and lower it from the lower crankcase frame. There is no gasket fitted to the sump.

Refitting

34 On reassembly, thoroughly clean and degrease the mating surfaces of the cylinder block/crankcase and sump, then use a clean rag to wipe out the sump and the engine's interior.

Models up to 10/1996

35 Fit the new gasket to the sump so that the gasket fits into the groove **(see illustration)**.

36 If the sump is being refitted with the engine/transmission still connected and in the vehicle, proceed as follows:

a) Check that the mating surfaces of the sump, the cylinder block/crankcase and the transmission are absolutely clean and flat. Any shims found on removal of the sump must be refitted in their original locations.

*b) Apply a thin film of suitable sealant (Ford recommend Hylosil 102) to the junctions of the cylinder block/crankcase with the oil pump and the crankshaft left-hand oil seal carrier. Without delay - the sump bolts must be fully tightened within 10 to 20 minutes of applying the sealant - offer up the sump and engine/transmission lower adaptor plate, and refit the bolts, tightening them lightly at first **(see illustration)**.*

c) Ensuring that the engine/transmission lower adaptor plate is correctly located, firmly press the sump against the transmission, and tighten the transmission-to-sump (ie, engine) bolts to the specified torque wrench setting.

d) Without disturbing the position of the sump, and working in a diagonal sequence from the centre outwards, tighten the sump bolts to the specified torque wrench setting.

e) Proceed to paragraph 38.

37 If the sump is being refitted with the engine and transmission separated (in or out of the vehicle), proceed as follows:

*a) Apply a thin film of suitable sealant (Ford recommend Hylosil 102) to the junctions of the cylinder block/crankcase with the oil pump and the crankshaft left-hand oil seal carrier **(see illustration)**. Without delay -*

16.37a Apply sealant (arrowed) as directed when refitting sump

16.37b Checking alignment of sump with cylinder block/crankcase

the sump bolts must be fully tightened within 10 to 20 minutes of applying the sealant - offer up the sump to the cylinder block/crankcase, and insert the sump bolts, tightening them lightly at first.

b) *Using a suitable straight edge to check alignment across the flat-machined faces of each, move the sump as necessary so that its left-hand face - including any shims found on removal - is flush with that of the cylinder block/crankcase* ***(see illustration)****. Without disturbing the position of the sump, and working in a diagonal sequence from the centre outwards, tighten the sump bolts to the specified torque wrench setting.*

c) *Check again that both faces are flush before proceeding; if necessary, unbolt the sump again, clean the mating surfaces, and repeat the full procedure to ensure that the sump is correctly aligned.*

d) *If it is not possible to achieve exact alignment by moving the sump, shims are available in thicknesses of 0.25 mm (colour-coded yellow) or 0.50 mm (colour-coded black) to eliminate the discrepancy* ***(see illustration)****.*

38 The remainder of reassembly is the reverse of the removal procedure, noting the following points.

a) *Tighten all fasteners to the torque wrench settings specified.*

b) *Always renew any self-locking nuts disturbed on removal.*

c) *Lower the engine/transmission unit into place, and reassemble the rear, left-hand and right-hand mountings. Do not yet release the hoist; the weight of the engine/transmission unit must not be taken by the mountings until all are correctly aligned.*

d) *Fitting the Ford service tool in place of the front mounting, tighten the engine/transmission mounting fasteners to their specified torque wrench settings, and in the sequence described in Part C of this Chapter.*

e) *Refill the cooling system (see Chapter 1).*

f) *Refill the engine with oil, remembering that you are advised to fit a new filter (see Chapter 1).*

g) *Check for signs of oil or coolant leaks once the engine has been restarted and warmed-up to normal operating temperature.*

Models from 10/1996 up to 5/1998

39 Apply a little silicone sealant to the joints between the oil pump and block and between the rear oil seal housing and block.

40 Place the new gasket on the sump and offer them onto the block. Insert the sump-to-block bolts and tighten them progressively to the Stage 1 torque.

41 Refit the intermediate plate, then press the sump firmly against the transmission clutch housing. Insert the sump-to-transmission bolts and tighten to the specified torque.

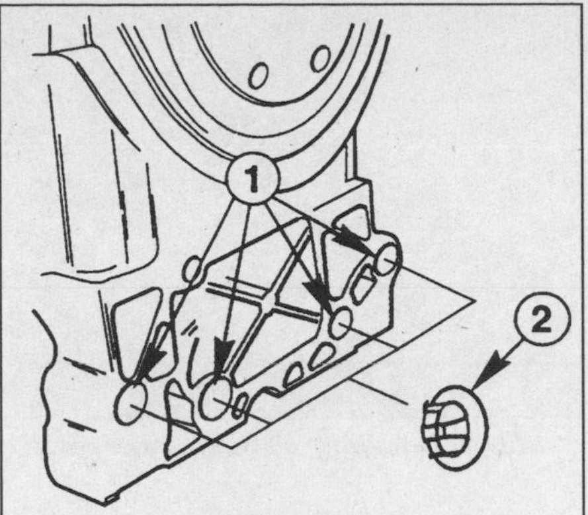

16.37c Sump-to-cylinder block/crankcase alignment shims

1 Fitting points on sump
2 Shim

42 Progressively tighten the sump-to-block bolts to the Stage 2 torque.

43 Lower the engine and refit the right-hand engine mounting in its previously noted position. Tighten the nuts and bolts to the specified torque.

44 Refit the coolant pipe bracket and tighten the bolt.

45 Refit and tighten the roll restrictor bolts. If necessary, check and realign the restrictors with reference to Section 23.

46 Refit the right-hand driveshaft (see Chapter 8).

47 Refit the catalytic converter with reference to Chapter 4A.

48 Refit the undershield.

49 Tighten the right-hand suspension top mounting nut to the correct torque, as given in Chapter 10.

50 Remove the hoist.

51 Reconnect the oxygen sensor wiring.

52 Refit the exhaust manifold heat shield and tighten the bolts.

53 On 2.0 litre models, locate the coolant hose in the supports on the exhaust manifold heatshield.

54 Refit the engine oil level dipstick, then lower the car to the ground and refill the engine with oil with reference to Chapter 1.

Models from 5/1998

55 Apply a 3.0 mm bead of sealant to the sump flange so that the bead is approximately 5.0 mm from the outside edge of the flange. Make sure the bead is around the inside edge of the bolt holes. **Note:** *The sump must be refitted within 10 minutes of applying the sealant.*

56 Insert the bolts and progressively tighten them to the specified torque in the sequence shown **(see illustration)**.

57 Lower the car to the ground and refill the engine with oil with reference to Chapter 1.

17 Oil pump - removal, inspection and refitting

Removal

Note 1: *While this task is theoretically possible when the engine is in place in the vehicle, in practice, it requires so much preliminary dismantling, and is so difficult to carry out due to the restricted access, that owners are advised to remove the engine from the vehicle first. Note, however, that the oil pump pressure relief valve can be removed with the engine in situ - see paragraph 8.*

Note 2: *In addition to the new pump gasket and other replacement parts required, read through Section 15, and ensure that the necessary tools and facilities are available.*

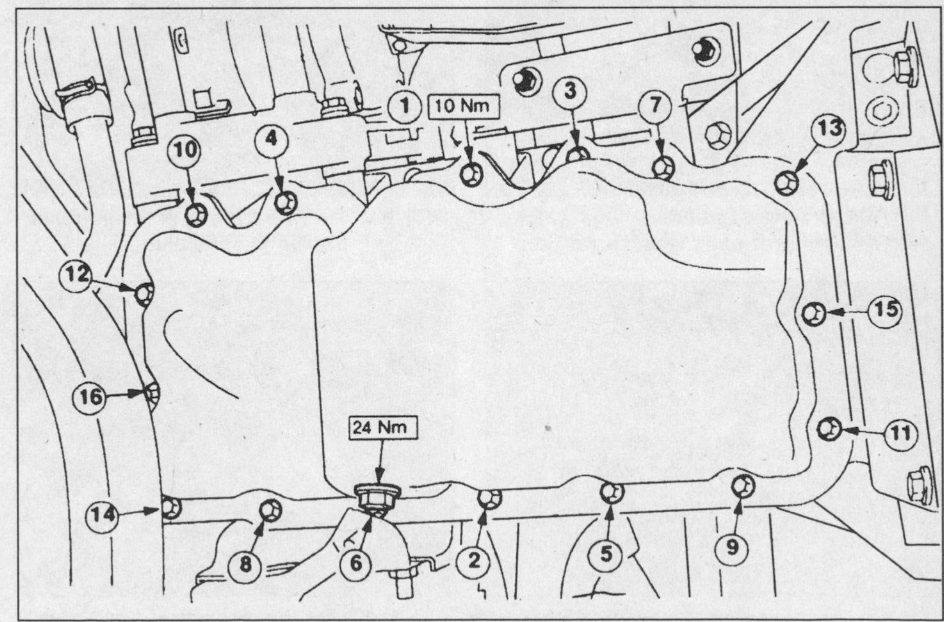

16.56 Sump bolt tightening sequence for models from 5/1998 on

17.5 Unscrew bolts (arrowed) to remove oil pump

17.6 Withdrawing oil pump inner rotor

1 Remove the timing belt (see Section 10).
2 Withdraw the crankshaft toothed pulley and the thrustwasher behind it, noting which way round the thrustwasher is fitted (see Section 11).
3 Remove the sump (see Section 16).
4 Undo the screws securing the oil pump pick-up/strainer pipe to the pump, then unscrew the nut and withdraw the oil pump pick-up/strainer pipe. Discard the gasket.
5 Unbolt the pump from the cylinder block/crankcase **(see illustration)**. Withdraw and discard the gasket, and remove the crankshaft right-hand oil seal. Thoroughly clean and degrease all components, particularly the mating surfaces of the pump, the sump, and the cylinder block/crankcase.

Inspection

6 Unscrew the Torx screws, and remove the pump cover plate; noting any identification marks on the rotors, withdraw the rotors **(see illustration)**.
7 Inspect the rotors for obvious signs of wear or damage, and renew if necessary; if either rotor, the pump body, or its cover plate are scored or damaged, the complete oil pump assembly must be renewed.
8 The oil pressure relief valve can be dismantled, if required, without disturbing the pump. With the vehicle parked on firm level ground, apply the handbrake securely and raise its front end, supporting it securely on axle stands. Remove the front right-hand roadwheel and auxiliary drivebelt cover (see Chapter 1) to provide access to the valve.
9 Unscrew the threaded plug, and recover the valve spring and plunger **(see illustrations)**. If the plug's sealing O-ring is worn or damaged, a new one must be obtained, to be fitted on reassembly.
10 Reassembly is the reverse of the dismantling procedure; ensure the spring and valve are refitted the correct way round, and tighten the threaded plug securely.

Refitting

11 The oil pump must be primed on installation, by pouring clean engine oil into it, and rotating its inner rotor a few turns.
12 Using grease to stick the new gasket in place on the cylinder block/crankcase, and rotating the pump's inner rotor to align with the flats on the crankshaft, refit the pump and insert the bolts, tightening them lightly at first **(see illustration)**.
13 Using a suitable straight edge and feeler gauges, check that the pump is both centred exactly around the crankshaft, and aligned squarely so that its (sump) mating surface is exactly the same amount - between 0.3 and 0.8 mm - below that of the cylinder block/crankcase on each side of the crankshaft. Being careful not to disturb the gasket, move the pump into the correct position, and tighten its bolts to the specified torque wrench setting **(see illustration)**.
14 Check that the pump is correctly located; if necessary, unbolt it again, and repeat the full procedure to ensure that the pump is correctly aligned.
15 Fit a new crankshaft right-hand oil seal (see Section 21).
16 Using grease to stick the gasket in place on the pump, refit the pick-up/strainer pipe, tightening its screws and nut to their specified torque wrench settings **(see illustration)**.
17 The remainder of reassembly is the reverse of the removal procedure, referring to the relevant text for details where required.

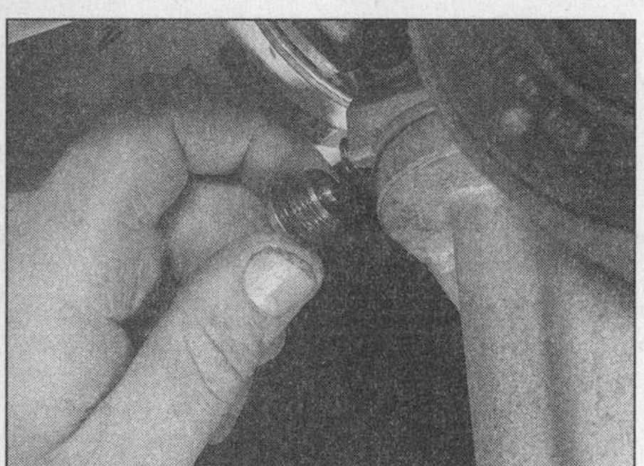

17.9a Unscrew threaded plug - seen through right-hand wheel arch . . .

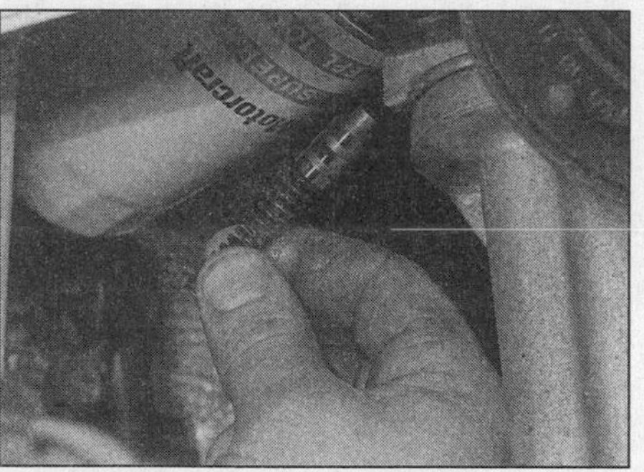

17.9b . . . to withdraw oil pressure relief valve spring and plunger

18 Oil cooler - removal and refitting

1 Drain the cooling system (see Chapter 1). Disconnect the coolant hoses from the oil cooler.
2 Unscrew the oil filter (see Chapter 1) - catch any escaping oil in a drip tray.
3 Unscrew the filter adaptor from the oil pump, and withdraw the oil cooler; note how its unions are aligned, and be prepared for oil loss from the cooler.

17.12 Use new gasket when refitting oil pump

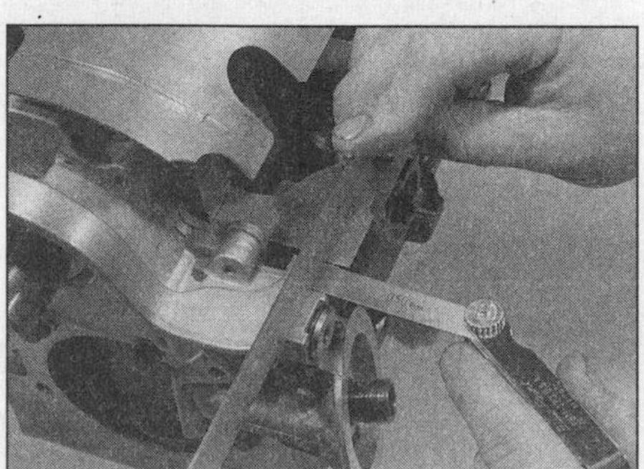

17.13 Check the oil pump is positioned correctly

17.16 Use new gasket when refitting oil pick-up pipe to pump

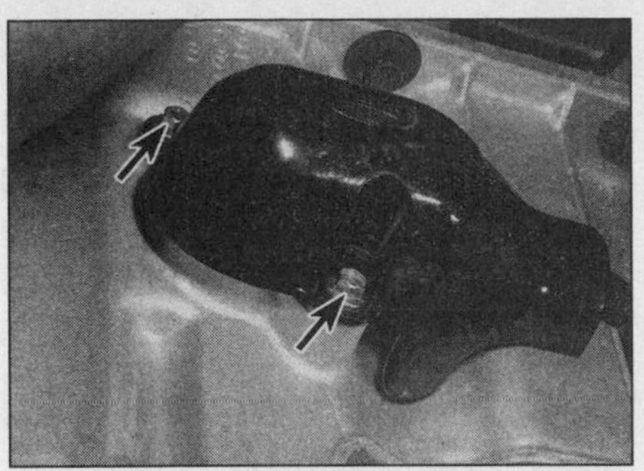

19.3 Remove screws (arrowed) to remove oil level sensor cover . . .

4 Refitting is the reverse of the removal procedure, noting the following points:

a) Renew all O-rings and seals disturbed on removal.

b) Align the cooler's unions as noted on removal, and tighten the adaptor to the specified torque wrench setting.

c) Refill the cooling system (see Chapter 1).

d) Refit the oil filter, then check the engine oil level, and top-up as necessary (see "Weekly checks")

e) Check for signs of oil or coolant leaks once the engine has been restarted and warmed-up to normal operating temperature.

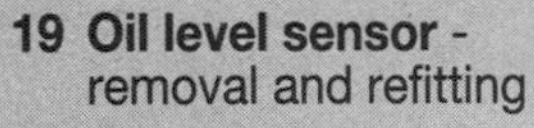

19 Oil level sensor - removal and refitting

Removal

1 With the vehicle parked on firm level ground, open the bonnet and disconnect the battery negative (earth) lead - see Chapter 5A, Section 1.

2 Raise the front of the vehicle, and support it securely on axle stands.

3 Undo the two screws, and remove the sensor's cover from the front of the sump **(see illustration)**.

4 Unplug the wiring from the sensor **(see illustration)**. Where necessary, unplug the electrical connector to disconnect the sensor wiring, and unclip the connector to release the wiring from the vehicle.

19.4 . . . disconnecting wiring from sensor

5 Unscrew the sensor, and quickly plug the sump aperture to minimise oil loss; note the sensor's seal.

Refitting

6 Refitting is the reverse of the removal procedure; renew the sensor's seal if it is worn or damaged, and tighten the sensor to the specified torque wrench setting. Check the engine oil level, and top-up as necessary (see "*Weekly checks*") - check for signs of oil leaks once the engine has been restarted and warmed-up to normal operating temperature.

20 Oil pressure warning light switch - removal and refitting

Removal

1 The switch is screwed into the rear of the cylinder block, above the right-hand driveshaft's support bearing **(see illustration)**.

2 With the vehicle parked on firm level ground, open the bonnet and disconnect the battery negative (earth) lead - see Chapter 5A, Section 1.

3 Raise the front of the vehicle, and support it securely on axle stands.

4 Unplug the wiring from the switch, and unscrew it; be prepared for some oil loss.

Refitting

5 Refitting is the reverse of the removal procedure; apply a thin smear of suitable sealant to the switch threads, and tighten it to the specified torque wrench setting. Check the engine oil level, and top-up as necessary (see "Weekly checks"). Check for signs of oil leaks once the engine has been restarted and warmed-up to normal operating temperature.

21 Crankshaft oil seals - renewal

Note: *Don't try to prise these seals out without removing the oil pump or seal carrier - the seals are too soft, and the amount of space available is too small, for this to be possible without considerable risk of damage to the seal housing and/or the crankshaft journal. Follow exactly the procedure given below.*

Right-hand seal

1 Remove the oil pump (see Section 17).

2 Drive the oil seal out of the pump from behind **(see illustration)**.

3 Clean the seal housing and crankshaft, polishing off any burrs or raised edges, which may have caused the seal to fail in the first place.

4 Refit the oil pump (see Section 17). Grease the lips and periphery of the new seal, to ease installation.

5 To fit a new seal, Ford recommend the use of their service tool 21-093A, with the crankshaft pulley bolt, to draw the seal into place; an alternative can be arranged using a socket of suitable size, with a washer to match the crankshaft pulley bolt **(see illustration)**.

6 If such tools are not available, press the seal squarely into place by hand; tap it in until it is flush with the pump housing, using a soft-faced mallet and a socket with an outside diameter only slightly smaller than the seal's **(see illustration)**. This approach requires great care, to ensure that the seal is fitted squarely, without distortion or damage.

2A

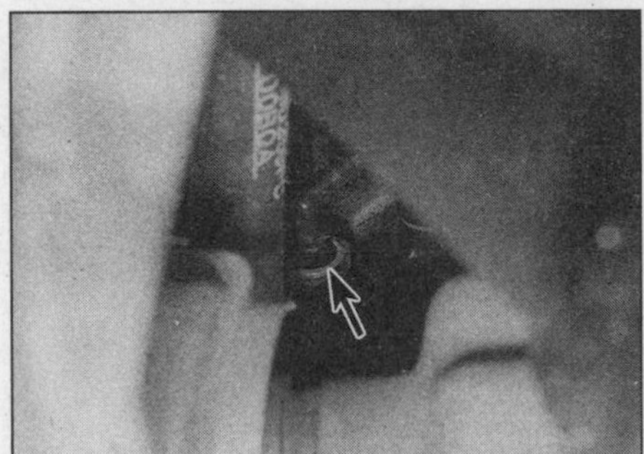

20.1 Oil pressure warning light switch (arrowed) is screwed into rear of cylinder block, above right-hand driveshaft support bearing

21.2 Driving out crankshaft right-hand oil seal

21.5 Socket of correct size can be used to replace Ford service tool, drawing new seal into place as described

21.6 If seal is tapped into place as shown, exercise great care to prevent seal from being damaged or distorted

21.12 Unscrew bolts (arrowed) to remove crankshaft left-hand oil seal carrier . . .

21.13 . . . and ensure that carrier is properly supported when driving out used oil seal - note notches provided in carrier for drift

7 Wash off any traces of oil. The remainder of reassembly is the reverse of the removal procedure, referring to the relevant text for details where required. Check for signs of oil leakage when the engine is restarted.

Left-hand seal

8 Remove the transmission (see the relevant Part of Chapter 7).

9 Where appropriate, remove the clutch (see Chapter 8).

10 Unbolt the flywheel/driveplate (see Section 22).

11 Remove the sump (see Section 16).

12 Unbolt the oil seal carrier **(see illustration)**. Remove and discard its gasket.

13 Supporting the carrier evenly on wooden blocks, drive the oil seal out of the carrier from behind **(see illustration)**.

14 Clean the seal housing and crankshaft, polishing off any burrs or raised edges, which may have caused the seal to fail in the first place. Clean also the mating surfaces of the cylinder block/crankcase and carrier, using a scraper to remove all traces of the old gasket - be careful not to scratch or damage the material of either - then use a suitable solvent to degrease them.

15 Use grease to stick the new gasket in place on the cylinder block/crankcase, then offer up the carrier **(see illustration)**.

16 Using a suitable straight edge and feeler gauges, check that the carrier is both centred exactly around the crankshaft, and aligned squarely so that its (sump) mating surface is exactly the same amount - between 0.3 and 0.8 mm - below that of the cylinder block/crankcase on each side of the crankshaft. Being careful not to disturb the gasket, move the carrier into the correct position, and tighten its bolts to the specified torque wrench setting **(see illustration)**.

17 Check that the carrier is correctly located; if necessary, unbolt it again, and repeat the full procedure to ensure that the carrier is correctly aligned.

18 Ford's recommended method of seal fitting is to use service tool 21-141, with two flywheel bolts to draw the seal into place. If this is not available, make up a guide from a thin sheet of plastic or similar, lubricate the lips of the new seal and the crankshaft shoulder with grease, then offer up the seal, with the guide feeding the seal's lips over the crankshaft shoulder **(see illustration)**. Press the seal evenly into its housing by hand only, and use a soft-faced mallet gently to tap it into place until it is flush with the surrounding housing.

19 Wipe off any surplus oil or grease; the remainder of the reassembly procedure is the reverse of dismantling, referring to the relevant text for details where required. Check for signs of oil leakage when the engine is restarted.

22 Flywheel/driveplate - removal, inspection and refitting

Removal

1 Remove the transmission (see the relevant Part of Chapter 7). Now is a good time to check components such as oil seals and renew them if necessary.

2 Where appropriate, remove the clutch (Chapter 6). Now is a good time to check or renew the clutch components and pilot bearing.

3 Use a centre-punch or paint to make alignment marks on the flywheel/driveplate and crankshaft, to ensure correct alignment during refitting.

4 Prevent the flywheel/driveplate from turning by locking the ring gear teeth, or by bolting a strap between the flywheel/driveplate and the cylinder block/crankcase. Slacken the bolts evenly until all are free.

5 Remove each bolt in turn, and ensure that new replacements are obtained for reassembly; these bolts are subjected to severe stresses, and so must be renewed, regardless of their apparent condition, whenever they are disturbed.

6 Noting the reinforcing plate (automatic transmission-equipped models only), withdraw the flywheel/driveplate; do not drop it - it is very heavy.

21.15 Use new gasket when refitting left-hand oil seal carrier

21.16 Check the oil seal carrier is correctly positioned

21.18 Using guide made from thin sheet of plastic to slide oil seal lips over crankshaft shoulder

Inspection

7 Clean the flywheel/driveplate to remove grease and oil. Inspect the surface for cracks, rivet grooves, burned areas and score marks. Light scoring can be removed with emery cloth. Check for cracked and broken ring gear teeth. Lay the flywheel/driveplate on a flat surface, and use a straight edge to check for warpage.

8 Clean and inspect the mating surfaces of the flywheel/driveplate and the crankshaft. If the crankshaft left-hand seal is leaking, renew it (see Section 21) before refitting the flywheel/driveplate.

9 While the flywheel/driveplate is removed, clean carefully its inboard (right-hand) face, particularly the recesses which serve as the reference points for the crankshaft speed/position sensor. Clean the sensor's tip, and check that the sensor is securely fastened. Thoroughly clean the threaded bolt holes in the crankshaft, and also clean the threads of the bolts - this is important, since if old sealer remains in the threads, the bolts will settle over a period and will not retain their correct torque wrench settings.

Refitting

10 On refitting, ensure that the engine/transmission adaptor plate is in place (where necessary), then fit the flywheel/driveplate to the crankshaft so that all bolt holes align - it will fit only one way - check this using the marks made on removal. Do not forget the reinforcing plate (where fitted). Apply suitable sealer to the threads of the bolts then insert them.

11 Lock the flywheel/driveplate by the method used on dismantling. Working in a diagonal sequence to tighten them evenly, and increasing to the final amount in two or three stages, tighten the new bolts to the specified torque wrench setting **(see illustration)**.

12 The remainder of reassembly is the reverse of the removal procedure, referring to the relevant text for details where required.

23 Engine/transmission mountings - inspection and renewal

General

1 The engine/transmission mountings seldom require attention, but broken or deteriorated mountings should be renewed immediately, or the added strain placed on the driveline components may cause damage or wear.

2 While separate mountings may be removed and refitted individually, if more than one is disturbed at a time - such as if the engine/transmission unit is removed from its mountings - they must be reassembled and their fasteners tightened in a strict sequence.

3 On reassembly, the weight of the engine/transmission unit must not be taken by the mountings until all are correctly aligned. Fitting the Ford service tool in place of the front mounting, tighten the engine/transmission mounting fasteners to their specified torque wrench settings, and in the sequence described in Part C of this Chapter, Section 4, paragraphs 49 and 50.

Inspection

4 During the check, the engine/transmission unit must be raised slightly, to remove its weight from the mountings.

5 Raise the front of the vehicle, and support it securely on axle stands. Position a jack under the sump, with a large block of wood between the jack head and the sump, then carefully raise the engine/transmission just enough to take the weight off the mountings.

Warning: DO NOT place any part of your body under the engine when it is supported only by a jack!

6 Check the mountings to see if the rubber is cracked, hardened or separated from the metal components. Sometimes the rubber will split right down the centre.

22.11 Note method used to lock flywheel/driveplate while (new) bolts are tightened

7 Check for relative movement between each mounting's brackets and the engine/transmission or body (use a large screwdriver or lever to attempt to move the mountings). If movement is noted, lower the engine and check-tighten the mounting fasteners.

Renewal

Note: *The following paragraphs assume the engine is supported beneath the sump as described earlier.*

Front mounting (roll restrictor)

8 Unbolt the resonator support bracket from the engine compartment front crossmember, slacken the two clamp screws securing the resonator to the air mass meter and plenum chamber hoses, then swing the resonator up clear of the thermostat housing (see Chapter 4A). Unbolt the pulse-air filter housing from the mounting bracket, then unfasten the bolts/nuts securing the mounting to the subframe, unscrew the centre bolt and withdraw the mounting; note the location of the wiring connector bracket. The mounting's bracket can be unbolted from the transmission if required **(see illustration)**.

9 On refitting, ensure that the mounting-to-transmission bolts are securely tightened,

2A

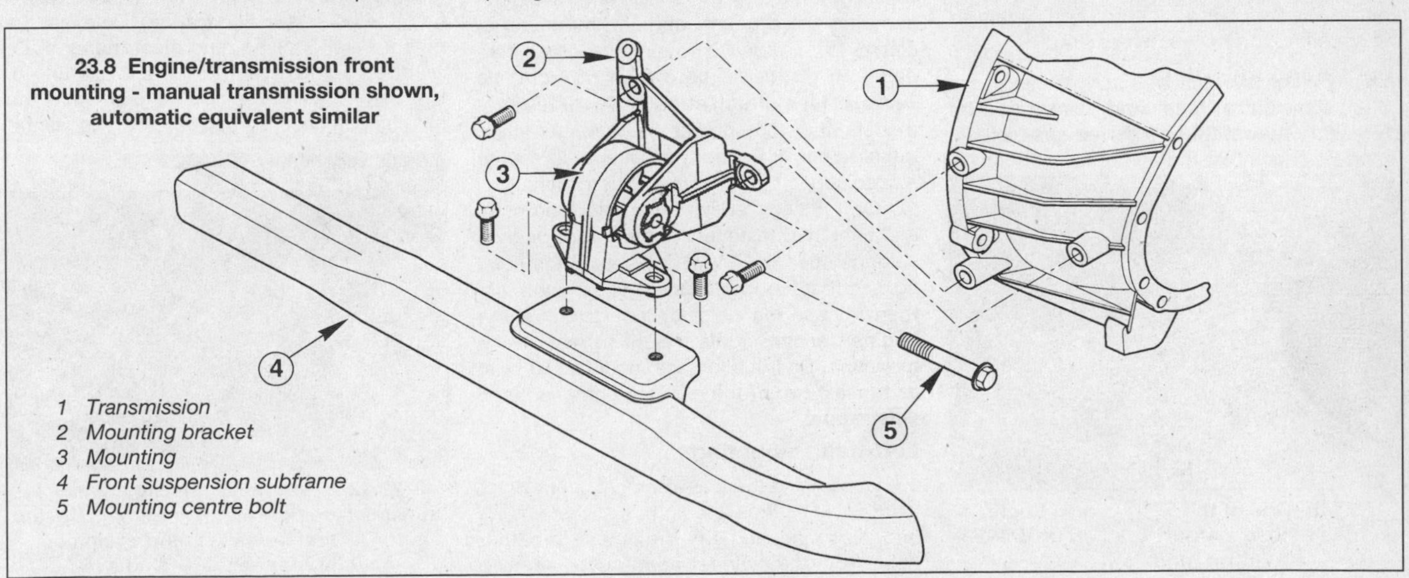

23.8 Engine/transmission front mounting - manual transmission shown, automatic equivalent similar

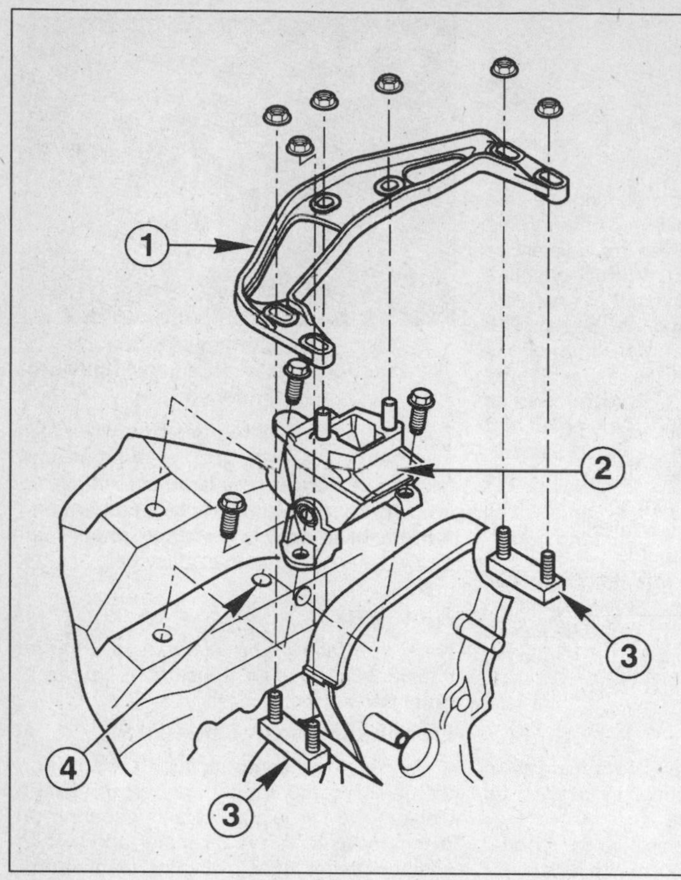

23.10 Engine/transmission right-hand mounting - standard type

1 *Bracket*
2 *Mounting*
3 *Brackets bolted to cylinder block/crankcase*
4 *Vehicle body*

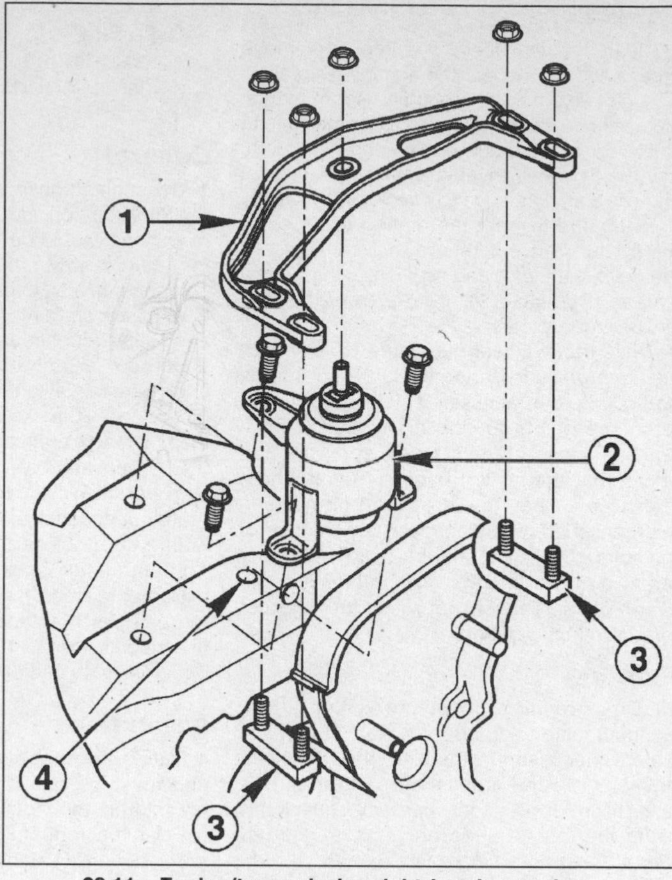

23.11a Engine/transmission right-hand mounting - hydraulic type (where fitted)

1 *Bracket*
2 *Hydraulic mounting*
3 *Brackets bolted to cylinder block/crankcase*
4 *Vehicle body*

then refit the mounting and wiring connector bracket. Tighten first the mounting-to-subframe bolts/nuts, noting that these are to be tightened in two stages to the final specified torque wrench setting. Finally tighten the mounting's centre bolt, again to the specified torque wrench setting.

Right-hand mounting

10 Unscrew the nuts and withdraw the bracket; note that these nuts are self-locking, and must therefore be renewed whenever they are disturbed. Unbolt the mounting from the body **(see illustration)**.

11 Where hydraulic-type mountings are fitted to early models - there are only five nuts securing the bracket, and the mounting is clearly identifiable from its shape - take care never to tilt these more than 5° from the vertical **(see illustration)**. On 5/1998-on models, the cross bracket is no longer fitted, but note one of the body bracket bolts secure a hose support bracket **(see illustration)**.

12 On refitting, renew the self-locking nuts, and tighten all fasteners to the torque wrench settings specified. When tightening the nuts, tighten first the four bracket-to-engine nuts, then release the hoist or jack to allow the engine/transmission's weight to rest on the mounting. Do not allow the mounting to twist as the last two of the nuts are tightened **(see illustration)**.

Left-hand mounting

13 Unplugging the two electrical connectors, disconnecting the vacuum hose (where fitted) and disconnecting the crankcase breather hose from the cylinder head cover, remove the complete air cleaner assembly with the air mass meter, the resonator and the plenum chamber (see Chapter 4A).

14 Unscrew the three nuts to release the mounting from the transmission, then unbolt it from the body **(see illustration)**. Note that the nuts are self-locking, and must therefore be renewed whenever they are disturbed. Unscrew the centre bolt to dismantle the mounting, if necessary to renew components.

23.11b One of the body bracket bolts secures a hose support bracket on 5/1998-on models

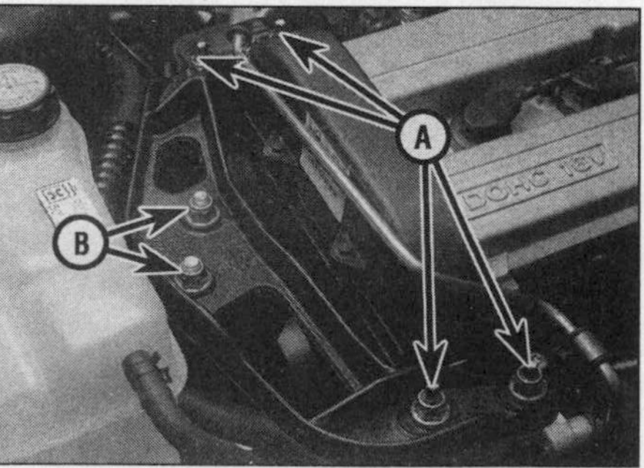

23.12 When reassembling engine/transmission right-hand mounting, tighten nuts "A" first, release lifting equipment, then tighten remaining nuts "B"

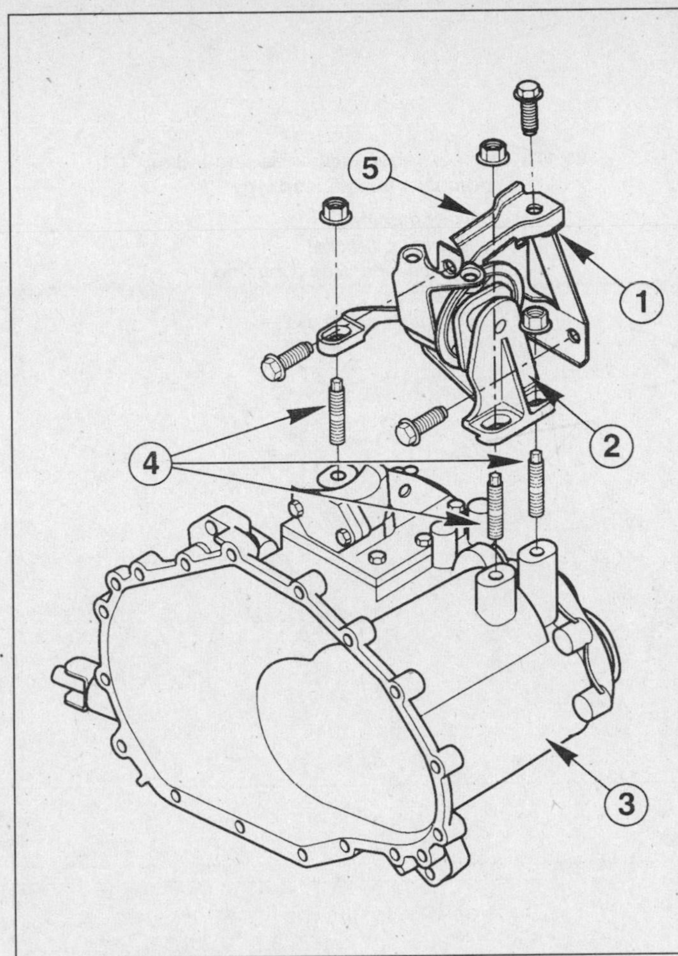

23.14 Engine/transmission left-hand mounting - manual transmission shown, automatic equivalent similar

1 Mounting bracket
2 Mounting
3 Transmission
4 Studs
5 Fastening plate - where fitted

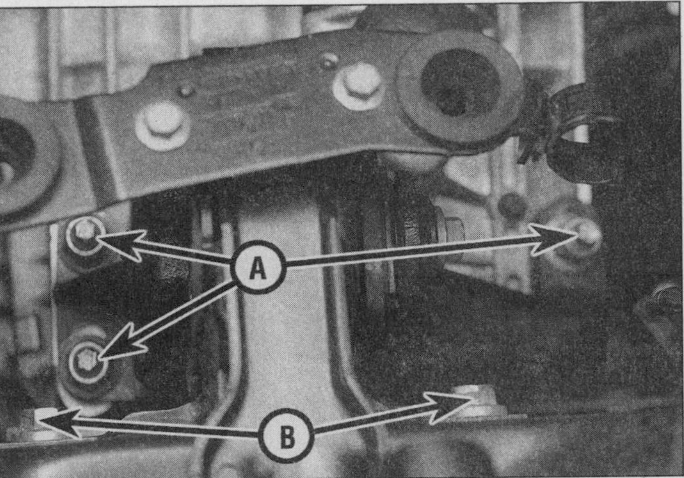

23.15 Engine/transmission left-hand mounting is secured by self-locking nuts "A" to transmission, by bolts "B" to body

23.16 On automatic transmission models, additional damper may be fastened to underside of engine/transmission rear mounting

15 On refitting, renew the self-locking nuts, and do not allow the mounting to twist as the nuts are tightened **(see illustration)**. Tighten all fasteners to the specified torque wrench settings.

Rear mounting (roll restrictor)

16 Where the vehicle is fitted with automatic transmission, a separate damper may be fitted beneath the subframe, which must be unbolted to reach the mounting's fasteners **(see illustration)**.

17 Unbolt the mounting from the subframe, then unscrew the mounting's centre bolt. If required, unbolt the mounting's bracket from the transmission **(see illustrations overleaf)**.

18 On refitting, ensure that the mounting-to-transmission bolts are securely tightened, then refit the mounting. Tighten first the mounting-to-subframe bolts, noting that these are to be tightened in two stages to the final specified torque wrench setting. Finally tighten the mounting's centre bolt, again to the specified torque wrench setting.

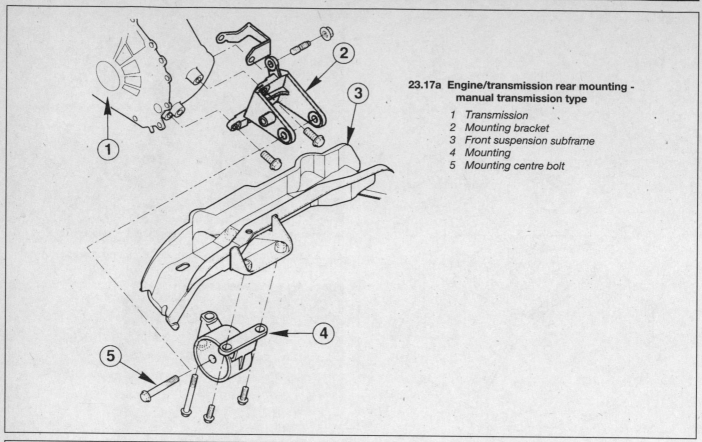

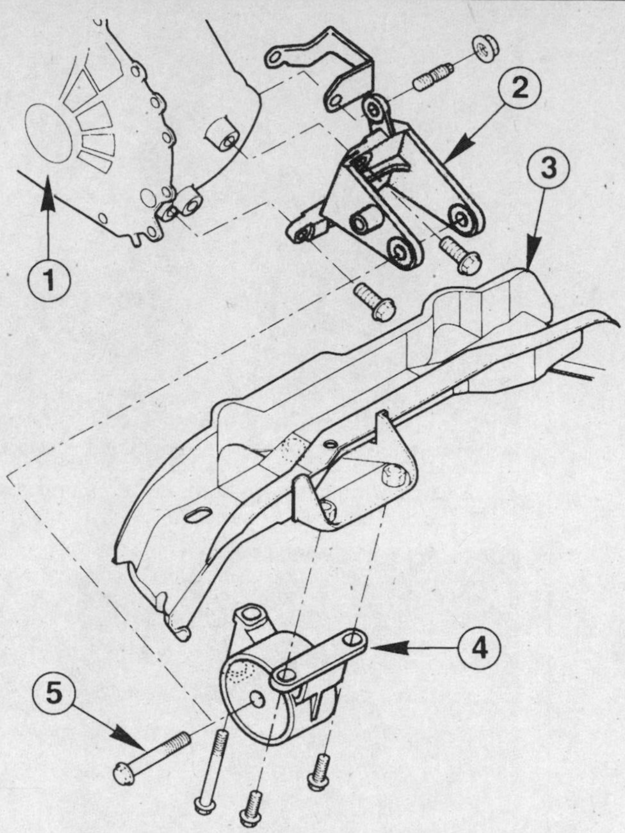

23.17a Engine/transmission rear mounting - manual transmission type

1 *Transmission*
2 *Mounting bracket*
3 *Front suspension subframe*
4 *Mounting*
5 *Mounting centre bolt*

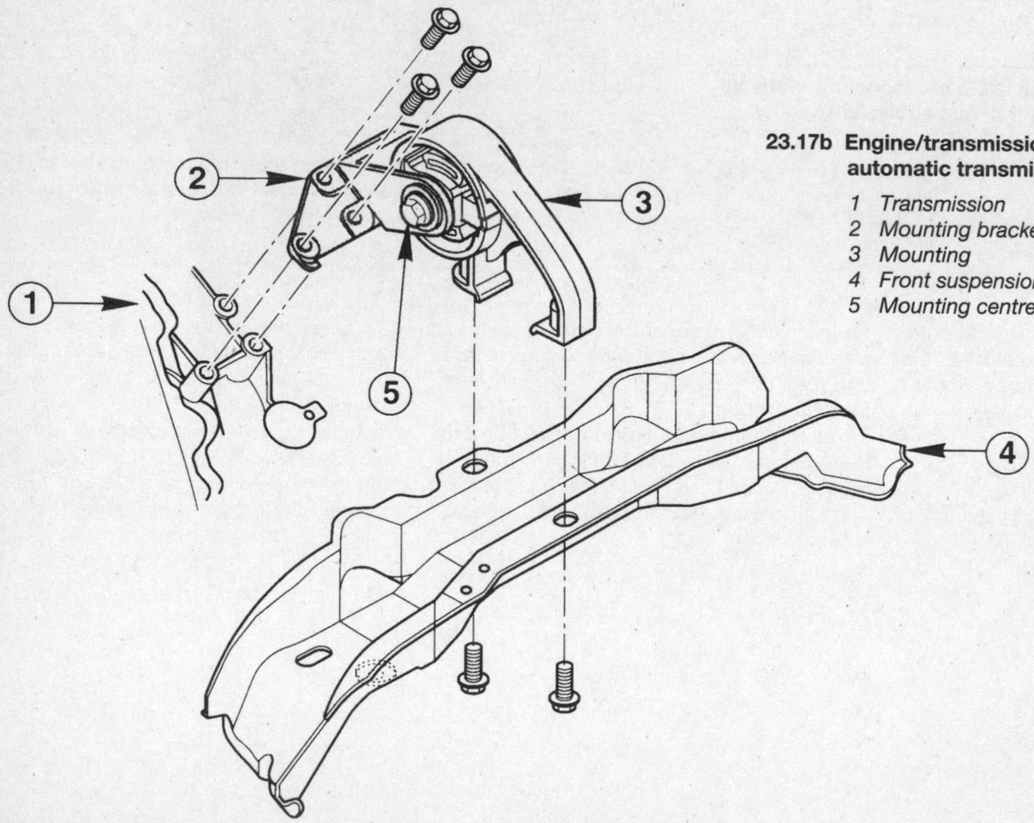

23.17b Engine/transmission rear mounting - automatic transmission type

1 *Transmission*
2 *Mounting bracket*
3 *Mounting*
4 *Front suspension subframe*
5 *Mounting centre bolt*

Chapter 2 Part B:
V6 (Duratec) engine in-car repair procedures

Contents

Degrees of difficulty

Easy, suitable for novice with little experience 

Fairly easy, suitable for beginner with some experience 

Fairly difficult, suitable for competent DIY mechanic

Difficult, suitable for experienced DIY mechanic 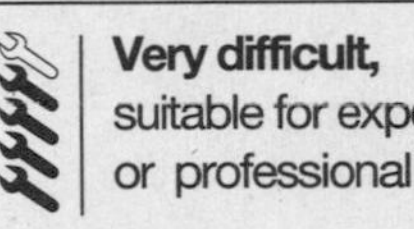

Very difficult, suitable for expert DIY or professional

Specifications

General

Engine type	Six-cylinder, V6 24-valve, in two banks of three cylinders, double overhead camshafts on each bank (4 camshafts in total)
Engine code	SEA
Capacity	2544 cc
Bore	82.4 mm
Stroke	79.5 mm
Compression ratio	9.7 : 1
Power output	125 kW at 6250 rpm
Compression pressure at starter speed	9.0 to 15.0 bars
Firing order	1-4-2-5-3-6 (No 1 cylinder at timing chain end)
Direction of crankshaft rotation	Clockwise (seen from right-hand side of vehicle)

Cylinder head

Camshaft bearing diameter	26.987 to 27.012 mm
Hydraulic tappet bore diameter	16.018 to 16.057 mm
Cylinder head gasket thickness	1.0 mm
Cylinder head warp (maximum)	0.08 mm

Camshafts

Camshaft bearing journal diameter	26.936 to 26.942 mm
Camshaft bearing journal-to-cylinder head running clearance	0.0125 to 0.038 mm
Camshaft endfloat	0.025 to 0.165 mm

Lubrication

Engine oil type/specification	See *"Lubricants and Fluids"*
Engine oil capacity	See Chapter 1
Oil pressure:	
At idle speed	0.5 bars
At 1500 rpm	1.38 to 3.10 bars
At 3000 rpm	3.0 to 3.5 bars
Oil pump clearances (inner to outer rotor max.)	0.18 mm

Torque wrench settings

	Nm	lbf ft
Cylinder head bolts:		
Stage 1	40	30
Stage 2	Angle-tighten 90°	
Stage 3	Loosen 360°	
Stage 4	40	30
Stage 5	Angle-tighten 90°	
Stage 6	Angle-tighten 90°	
Right-hand engine mounting	83	61
Left-hand engine mounting (automatic transmission models)	48	35
Left-hand engine mounting (manual transmission models)	83	61
Rear engine roll restrictor to subframe	48	35
Centre bolt to rear engine roll restrictor	120	88
Front engine roll restrictor to subframe	48	35
Centre bolt to front engine roll restrictor	120	88
Engine mounting bracket to cylinder block	47	35
Fixed timing chain guide to cylinder block	25	18
Timing chain tensioner to cylinder block	25	18
Timing cover to cylinder block	25	18
Crankshaft position sensor to timing cover	10	7
Crankshaft pulley/vibration damper centre bolt:		
Stage 1	120	88
Stage 2	Loosen 360°	
Stage 3	50	37
Stage 4	Angle-tighten 90°	
Torque converter to driveplate	36	27
Flywheel/driveplate to crankshaft	80	59
Camshaft bearing cap	10	7
Camshaft oil seal housing to front cylinder head	10	7
Camshaft position sensor	10	7
Cylinder head cover	10	7
Engine lifting eye to cylinder head	82	60
Exhaust manifold	25	18
Oil pump cover	10	7
Oil pump to cylinder block	11	8
Oil baffle to crankcase	10	7
Oil pump intake pipe to crankcase:		
M6	10	7
M8	25	18
Oil separator to cylinder block	10	7
Oil cooler pipe to transmission	23	17
Oil baffle to sump	10	7
Sump oil drain plug	25	18
Sump	25	18
Oil cooler to cylinder block	57	42
Oil pressure switch	14	10
Lower inlet manifold	10	7
Upper inlet manifold	10	7
Coolant pipe to cylinder head	10	7
Coolant transfer pipe to cylinder head	6	4
Oil dipstick tube to transfer pipe	10	7
Transmission-to-engine bolts	40	30
Subframe to body	130	96
Gearshift linkage to body	44	32
Front suspension strut to body	46	34
Exhaust front pipe	40	30
Big-end bolts:		
Stage 1	23	17
Stage 2	43	32
Stage 3	Angle-tighten 90°	
Lower crankcase to block:		
Note: *Bolts 1 to 16 are torque-to-yield bolts and must be renewed whenever removed.*		
Stage 1 (bolts 1 to 8)	25	18
Stage 2 (bolts 9 to 16)	40	30
Stage 3 (bolts 1 to 16)	90	66
Stage 4 (bolts 17 to 22)	25	18
Wheel nuts	85	63

1 General information

How to use this Chapter

This Part of Chapter 2 is devoted to in-car repair procedures for the engine. All procedures concerning engine removal and refitting, and engine block/cylinder head overhaul can be found in Chapter 2C.

The operations included in this Part are based on the assumption that the engine is still installed in the car. Therefore, if this information is being used during a complete engine overhaul, with the engine already removed, many of the steps included here will not apply.

General description - engine

The engine, also known by Ford's internal code name "Duratec" (DURAble TEChnique), is of V6 type, mounted transversely at the front of the vehicle, with the transmission on its left-hand end. The engine is of all-aluminium construction, incorporating two banks of three cylinders each. Each cylinder has four valves, two inlet and two exhaust, making a total of 24 valves. The inlet manifold includes a vacuum operated switching system to optimise the torque and power output - below 3200 rpm the engine effectively operates as a 12-valve engine, however at higher speeds it operates as a 24-valve engine.

The crankshaft runs in four main bearings, the bearing at the flywheel/driveplate end incorporates thrustwashers at each side of the bearing shell to control crankshaft endfloat. The connecting rods rotate on horizontally-split bearing shells at their big-ends. The pistons are attached to the connecting rods by fully-floating gudgeon pins which are retained by circlips in the pistons. The aluminium alloy pistons are fitted with three piston rings: two compression rings and an oil control ring. After manufacture, the cylinder bores and piston skirts are measured and classified into three grades, which must be carefully matched together, to ensure the correct piston/cylinder clearance; no oversizes are available to permit reboring.

The inlet and exhaust valves are closed by coil springs; they operate in guides which are shrink-fitted into the cylinder heads, as are the valve seat inserts.

The camshafts on each bank are driven by a twin-row timing chain (one to the front bank and another to the rear bank), each operating the twelve valves on each bank via self-adjusting hydraulic tappets, thus eliminating the need for routine checking and adjustment of the valve clearances. Except for the front bank inlet camshaft which rotates in five bearings, the remaining camshafts rotate in four bearings which are line-bored directly in the cylinder head and bearing caps; the bearing caps are not available separately from the cylinder head, and must not be interchanged with caps from another engine.

The water pump is bolted to the left-hand end of the cylinder block, and is driven by drivebelt from a pulley attached to the left-hand end of the front bank inlet camshaft.

Lubrication is by means of an eccentric-rotor trochoidal pump, which is mounted on the crankshaft right-hand end, and draws oil through a strainer located in the sump. The pump forces oil through an externally-mounted full-flow cartridge-type filter - on some versions of the engine, an oil cooler is fitted to the oil filter mounting, so that clean oil entering the engine's galleries is cooled by the main engine cooling system. From the filter, the oil is pumped into a main gallery in the cylinder block/crankcase, from where it is distributed to the crankshaft (main bearings) and cylinder head.

The V6 engine covered in this Chapter, employs hydraulic tappets which use the lubricating system's oil pressure to take up the clearance between each rocker tip and its respective valve stem. Therefore, there is no need for regular checking and adjustment of the valve clearances, but it is essential that only good-quality oil of the recommended viscosity and specification is used in the engine, and that this oil is always changed at the recommended intervals. On starting the engine from cold, there will be a slight delay while full oil pressure builds up in all parts of the engine, especially in the tappets; the valve components, therefore, may well "rattle" for about 10 seconds or so, and then quieten. This is a normal state of affairs, and is nothing to worry about, provided that all tappets quieten quickly and stay quiet.

After the vehicle has been standing for several days, the valve components may "rattle" for longer than usual, as nearly all the oil will have drained away from the engine's top end components and bearing surfaces. While this is only to be expected, care must be taken not to damage the engine under these circumstances - avoid high speed running until all the tappets are refilled with oil and operating normally. With the vehicle stationary, hold the engine at no more than a fast idle speed (maximum 2000 to 2500 rpm) for 10 to 15 seconds, or until the noise ceases. *Do not run the engine at more than 3000 rpm until the tappets are fully recharged with oil and the noise has ceased.*

2 Repair operations possible with the engine in the vehicle

1 The following repair operations can be accomplished without removing the engine from the vehicle.

a) Inlet and exhaust manifolds
b) Timing chains, tensioners and guides
c) Camshafts and hydraulic tappets
d) Cylinder heads
e) Sump
f) Oil pump
g) Crankshaft oil seals
h) Flywheel/driveplate
i) Engine/transmission mountings
j) Pistons and connecting rods

2 Although it is possible to remove the pistons and connecting rods with the engine installed in the car after removal of the sump, it is better for the engine to be removed, in the interests of cleanliness and improved access. For this reason, the procedure is described in Chapter 2C.

3 Compression test - description and interpretation

1 When engine performance is down, or if misfiring occurs which cannot be attributed to the ignition or fuel systems, a compression test can provide diagnostic clues as to the engine's condition. If the test is performed regularly, it can give warning of trouble before any other symptoms become apparent.

2 The engine must be fully warmed-up to normal operating temperature, the oil level must be correct, the battery must be fully charged, and the spark plugs must be removed. The aid of an assistant will be required also.

3 Disable the ignition system by unplugging the ignition coil or DIS unit electrical connector, and remove fuse 14 to disconnect the fuel pump.

4 Fit a compression tester to the No 1 cylinder spark plug hole - the type of tester which screws into the plug thread is to be preferred.

5 Have the assistant hold the throttle wide open and crank the engine on the starter motor; after one or two revolutions, the compression pressure should build up to a maximum figure, and then stabilise. Record the highest reading obtained.

6 Repeat the test on the remaining cylinders, recording the pressure developed in each.

7 All cylinders should produce very similar pressures which should be within the range given in the Specifications. Note that the compression should build up quickly in a healthy engine; low compression on the first stroke, followed by gradually-increasing pressure on successive strokes, indicates worn piston rings. A low compression reading on the first stroke, which does not build up during successive strokes, indicates leaking valves or a blown head gasket (a cracked head could also be the cause).

8 If the pressure in any cylinder is considerably lower than the others, introduce a teaspoonful of clean oil into that cylinder through its spark plug hole, and repeat the test. If the addition of oil temporarily improves the compression pressure, this indicates that bore or piston wear is responsible for the pressure loss. No improvement suggests that leaking or burnt valves, or a blown head gasket, may be to blame.

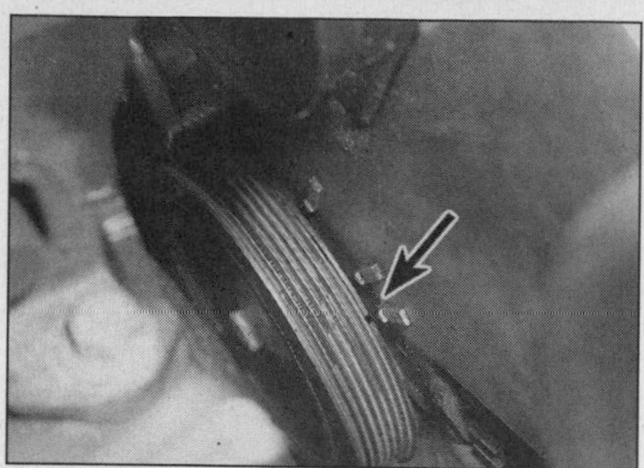
4.6a TDC mark on the timing cover

9 A low reading from two adjacent cylinders is almost certainly due to the head gasket having blown between them; the presence of coolant in the engine oil will confirm this.
10 On completion of the test, refit the spark plugs, then reconnect the ignition system and fuel pump.

4 Top Dead Centre (TDC) for No 1 piston - locating

1 Top Dead Centre (TDC) is the highest point in the cylinder that each piston reaches as it travels up-and-down when the crankshaft rotates. Each piston reaches TDC on the compression stroke and again on the exhaust stroke, but TDC generally refers to piston position on the compression stroke. The timing marks on the vibration damper fitted to the front of the crankshaft refer to the number one piston at TDC on the compression stroke.
2 No 1 piston is at the right-hand end of the rear bank, with pistons 2 and 3 on the same bank. No 4 piston is at the right-hand end of the front bank, with pistons 5 and 6 on the same bank.
3 Remove all the spark plugs (Chapter 1). This will make turning the engine easier. For better access to the crankshaft pulley, the front wheel and wheel arch liner can be removed if preferred.
4 The engine may be turned using a socket on the crankshaft pulley centre bolt. Alternatively on a manual transmission model, it may be turned by jacking up the right-hand side of the car so that the wheel is just clear of the ground, and turning the wheel with 4th gear engaged.
5 Turn the engine clockwise and feel for compression from the No 1 spark plug hole. To do this, temporarily insert a suitable plug (such as the handle of a screwdriver) over the spark plug hole. It is important that compression is felt, otherwise the following procedure will position the No 1 piston at TDC on the exhaust stroke instead of the compression stroke.
6 Continue to turn the engine until the crankshaft pulley keyway on the crankshaft is at the 11 o'clock position. The timing mark on the edge of the pulley must be exactly in line with the TDC arrow on the timing cover. Note that there are two other timing marks on the timing cover indicating 10° and 30° advance **(see illustrations)**.
7 If necessary, for a further check, the cylinder head covers may be removed (see Section 5) and the position of the timing marks on the rear of the camshaft sprockets checked. With No 1 piston at TDC on compression, the marks must point to each other **(see illustration)**.
8 Once the engine has been positioned at TDC for No 1 piston, TDC for any of the remaining cylinders can be located by turning the crankshaft 120° and following the firing order (refer to the Specifications). Mark the crankshaft pulley at 120° intervals past the TDC notch. Turning the engine to the first mark past the No 1 TDC position, will locate No 4 piston at TDC. Another 120° will locate No 2 piston at TDC.

5 Cylinder head cover - removal and refitting

Front cylinder head cover

Removal

1 Disconnect the battery negative (earth) lead (see Chapter 5A, Section 1).
2 Undo the bolts securing the plastic cover to the top of the front cylinder bank. Lift the cover and release the coolant hose.
3 Disconnect the crankcase ventilation hoses from each side of the air inlet duct leading from the air cleaner to the throttle body.
4 Loosen the clip and disconnect the vacuum hose.
5 Loosen the two clips and disconnect the air inlet duct from the throttle body and air cleaner. Remove the duct.
6 Disconnect the two brake vacuum servo hoses from the upper inlet manifold.
7 Remove the throttle cable bracket and the EGR (exhaust gas recirculation) valve as follows. Release the safety retainer, and disconnect the wiring. Disconnect the wiring from the IAC valve and throttle position sensor. Disconnect the vacuum hose from the EGR valve, then unscrew the mounting bolts and remove the EGR valve. Recover the gasket.
8 Disconnect the PCV hose and disconnect the wiring and vacuum hose from the electronic vacuum regulator.
9 Unscrew the retaining bolts in the reverse order to the sequence shown (see illustration 5.20) and lift off the upper inlet manifold. Recover the gaskets.
10 Unscrew the bolts securing the inlet manifold runner control actuator (IMRC) to the front cylinder head cover and unclip the wiring and cable and position to one side. Disconnect the wiring if necessary **(see illustrations)**.

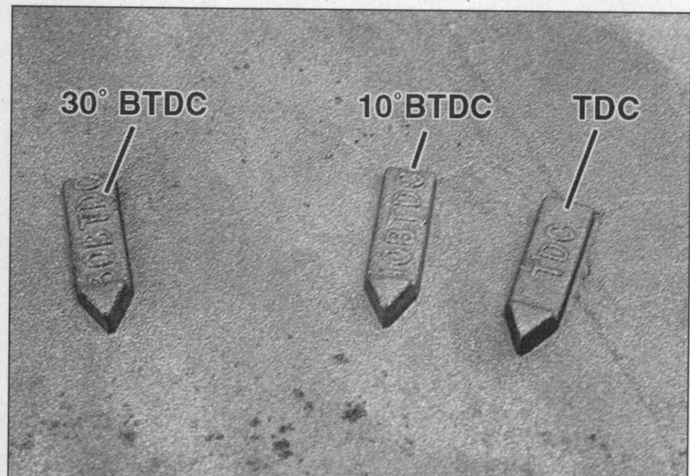

4.6b Timing marks on the timing cover

4.7 With No 1 piston at TDC on compression, these marks must point to each other

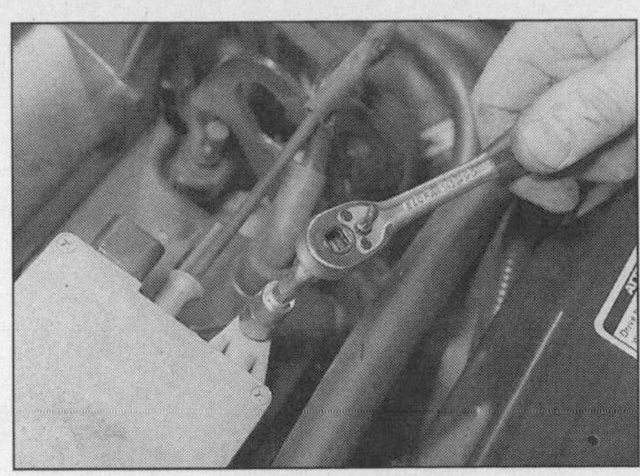
5.10a Unscrew the bolts . . .

5.10b . . . and remove the IMRC actuator from the valve cover . . .

5.10c . . . then release the cable from the clips near the water pump pulley . . .

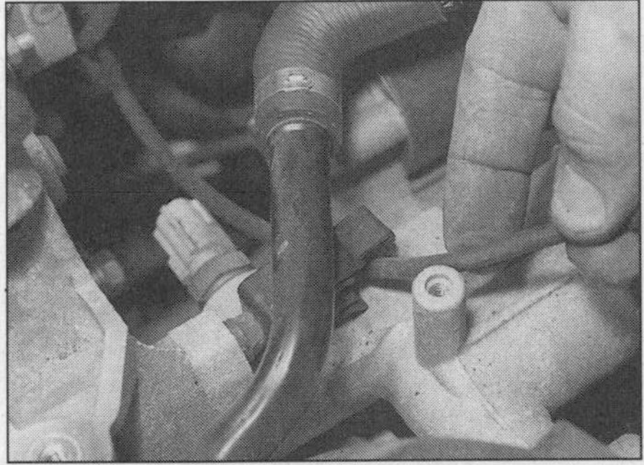
5.10d . . . and coolant connecting housing

5.10e If necessary disconnect the wiring from the IMRC actuator

5.11a Disconnect the HT leads from the spark plugs . . .

11 Note the location of the HT leads and if necessary identify them. Disconnect the HT leads from the spark plugs and remove the lead support from the right-hand engine mounting **(see illustrations)**.

12 Release the coolant hose from the clip and pull off the bracket, then disconnect the crankcase ventilation hose from the top of the valve cover **(see illustration)**.

13 Unclip the wiring loom from the cylinder head cover.

14 Using the reverse of the sequence shown (see illustration 5.16C), progressively unscrew the cylinder head cover bolts. With all the bolts removed, lift off the cover and remove the gaskets **(see illustrations)**.

5.11b . . . and remove the lead support from the top of the right-hand engine mounting

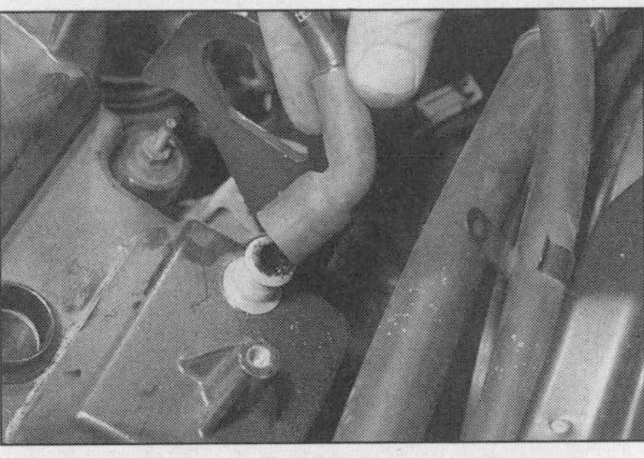
5.12 Disconnecting the crankcase ventilation hose from the top of the valve cover

Refitting

15 Make sure the mating faces of the cover and cylinder head are perfectly clean. Apply an 8 mm diameter bead of suitable sealer to the joints between the timing cover and cylinder head. Observe the instructions with the sealer, as normally the fitting procedure must be completed within a few minutes of applying the sealer.

16 Locate new spark plug hole gaskets in the cylinder head cover, then fit the outer gasket in the groove **(see illustrations)**. Fit the cylinder head cover and tighten the mounting bolts to the specified torque in the sequence

5.14a Removing the front valve cover . . .

5.14b . . . and gasket

5.16a Locate new spark plug hole gaskets in the cylinder head cover . . .

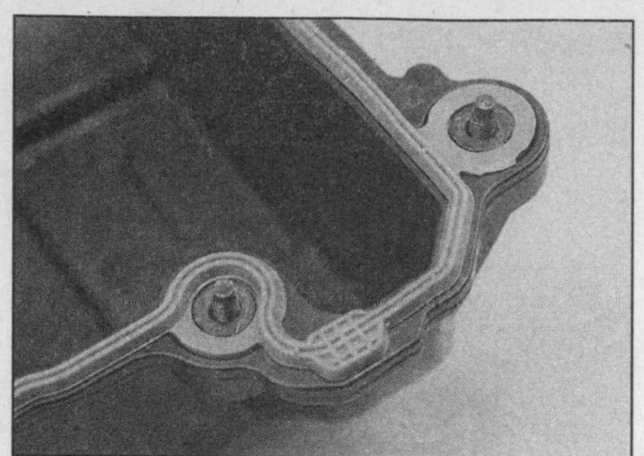
5.16b . . . then fit the outer gasket in the groove

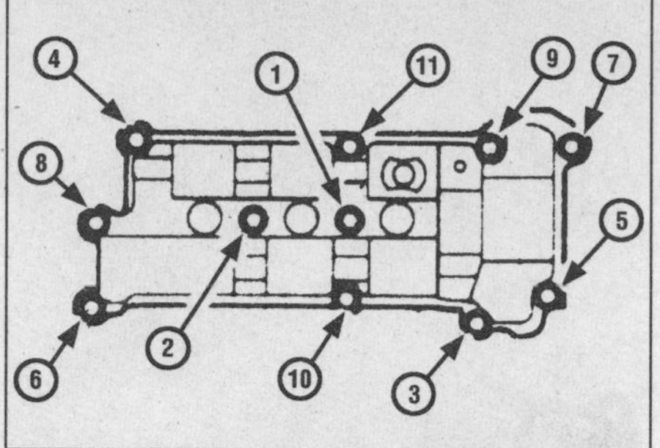

5.16c Tightening sequence for the front cylinder head cover bolts

5.19a Refit the inlet manifold runner control actuator (IMRC) . . .

shown **(see illustration)**. Make sure the O-ring seals are correctly fitted to the bolts.

17 Clip the wiring loom to the cylinder head cover. Refit the bracket and locate the coolant hose in the clip.

18 Reconnect the HT leads to the spark plugs and to the lead support on the right-hand engine mounting.

19 Refit the inlet manifold runner control actuator (IMRC) wiring and support **(see illustrations)**.

20 Refit the upper inlet manifold together with new gaskets and tighten the retaining bolts in the sequence shown **(see illustration)**.

21 Reconnect the PCV hose. Also reconnect the wiring and vacuum hose to the electronic vacuum regulator.

22 Refit the EGR valve together with a new gasket and tighten the bolts. Reconnect the vacuum hose. Reconnect the wiring to the IAC valve and throttle position sensor, and refit the safety retainer. Refit the cable bracket.

5.19b . . . and reconnect the wiring

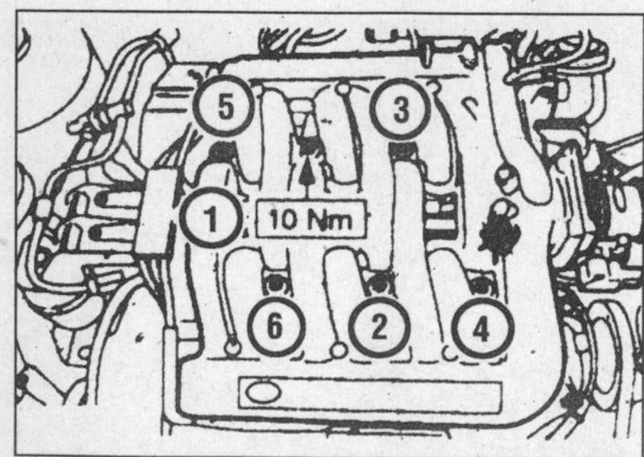

5.20 Tightening sequence for the upper inlet manifold bolts

23 Reconnect the two brake vacuum servo hoses to the upper inlet manifold.

24 Reconnect the air inlet duct to the throttle body and air cleaner and tighten the clips.

25 Reconnect the vacuum hose and tighten the clip.

26 Reconnect the crankcase ventilation hoses to each side of the air inlet duct leading from the air cleaner to the throttle body.

27 Refit the plastic cover to the top of the front cylinder bank and refit the coolant hose. Insert and tighten the retaining bolts.

28 Reconnect the battery negative (earth) lead (see Chapter 5A, Section 1). **Note:** *After the battery has been disconnected, the engine management system requires approximately 10 miles of driving to relearn its optimum settings. During this period, the engine may not perform normally.*

Rear cylinder head cover

Removal

29 Disconnect the battery negative (earth) lead (see Chapter 5A, Section 1).

30 Undo the bolts securing the plastic water pump pulley cover to the top of the front cylinder bank. Lift the cover and release the coolant hose.

31 Disconnect the crankcase ventilation hoses from each side of the air inlet duct leading from the air cleaner to the throttle body.

32 Loosen the clip and disconnect the vacuum hose.

33 Loosen the two clips and disconnect the air inlet duct from the throttle body and air cleaner. Remove the duct.

34 Disconnect the two vacuum servo hoses from the upper inlet manifold.

35 Remove the throttle cable bracket and the EGR (exhaust gas recirculation) valve as follows. Release the safety retainer, and disconnect the wiring. Disconnect the wiring from the IAC valve and throttle position sensor. Disconnect the vacuum hose from the EGR valve, then unscrew the mounting bolts and remove the EGR valve. Recover the gasket.

36 Disconnect the PCV hose and disconnect the wiring and vacuum hose from the EGR vacuum regulator. Also disconnect the crankcase ventilation hose from the top of the cover **(see illustration)**.

37 Unscrew the retaining bolts in the reverse order to the sequence shown (see illustration 5.20) and lift off the upper inlet manifold. Recover the gaskets.

38 Note the location of the HT leads and if necessary identify them. Disconnect the HT leads from the spark plugs and from the lead support on the right-hand engine mounting.

39 Unscrew the mounting bolts, and remove the injector wiring rail.

40 Unscrew the bolts and remove the ignition coil assembly. Disconnect the wiring and unclip it from the support. Also remove the earth cable and suppressor.

41 Unscrew the bolt and remove the front wiring harness bracket from the front cylinder head cover, then similarly remove the rear wiring bracket from the rear cylinder head cover **(see illustration)**.

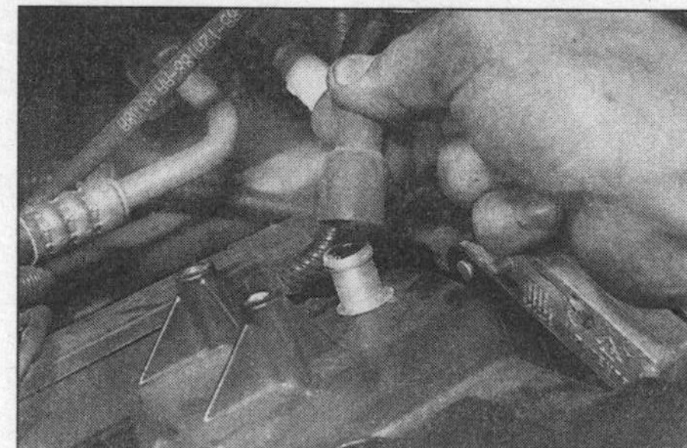
5.36 Disconnecting the crankcase ventilation hose from the rear cylinder head cover

5.41 Remove the wiring harness bracket from the rear cylinder head cover

5.42 Removing the wiring harness support bracket from the right-hand side of the rear cylinder head cover

42 Disconnect the wiring then unbolt the wiring harness bracket from the rear cylinder head cover **(see illustration)**.

43 Using the reverse of the sequence shown (see illustration 5.45a), progressively unscrew the cylinder head cover bolts. With all the bolts removed, lift off the cover and remove the gasket **(see illustrations)**.

Refitting

44 Make sure the mating faces of the cover and cylinder head are perfectly clean. Apply an 8 mm diameter bead of suitable sealer to the joints between the timing cover and cylinder head. Observe the instructions with the sealer, as normally the fitting procedure must be completed within a few minutes of applying the sealer.

45 Locate new spark plug hole gaskets in the cylinder head cover, then fit the outer gasket in the groove. Fit the cylinder head cover and tighten the mounting bolts to the specified torque in the sequence shown **(see illustration)**. Make sure the O-ring seals are correctly fitted to the mounting bolts **(see illustration)**.

46 Refit the wiring harness rail to the rear cylinder head cover and tighten the bolt.

47 Refit the front wiring harness bracket to the front cylinder head cover and tighten the bolt. Also refit the rear wiring bracket to the rear cylinder head cover.

48 Refit the ignition coil assembly and tighten the bolts. Reconnect the wiring to the support and refit the earth cable.

49 Refit the injector wiring rail and tighten the bolts.

50 Reconnect the HT leads to the spark plugs and to the lead support on the right-hand engine mounting.

51 Refit the upper inlet manifold together with new gaskets and tighten the retaining bolts in the sequence shown (see illustration 5.20).

52 Reconnect the PCV hose. Also reconnect the wiring and vacuum hose to the electronic vacuum regulator.

53 Refit the EGR valve together with a new gasket and tighten the bolts. Reconnect the vacuum hose. Reconnect the wiring to the IAC valve and throttle position sensor, and

5.43a Unscrew the bolts . . .

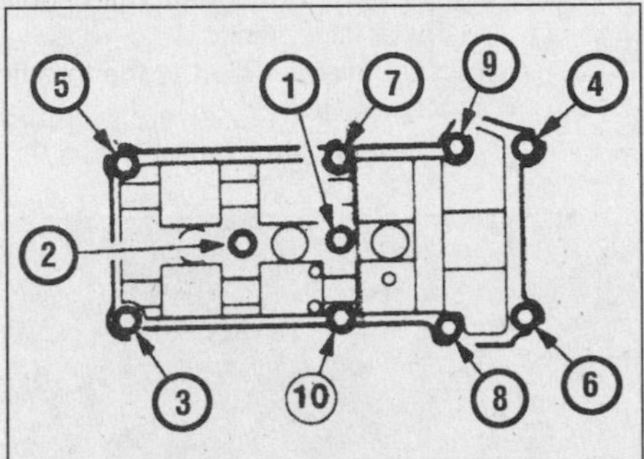

5.45a Tightening sequence for the rear cylinder head cover bolts

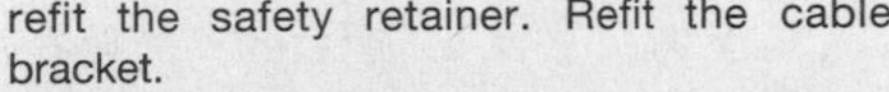

refit the safety retainer. Refit the cable bracket.

54 Reconnect the two brake vacuum servo hoses to the upper inlet manifold.

55 Reconnect the air inlet duct to the throttle body and air cleaner and tighten the clips.

56 Reconnect the vacuum hose and tighten the clip.

57 Reconnect the crankcase ventilation hoses to each side of the air inlet duct leading from the air cleaner to the throttle body.

58 Refit the plastic cover to the top of the front cylinder bank and refit the coolant hose. Insert and tighten the retaining bolts.

59 Reconnect the battery negative (earth) lead (see Chapter 5A, Section 1). **Note:** *After the battery has been disconnected, the engine management system requires approximately 10 miles of driving to relearn its optimum settings. During this period, the engine may not perform normally.*

6.2a One of the cover bolts secures a coolant hose clip

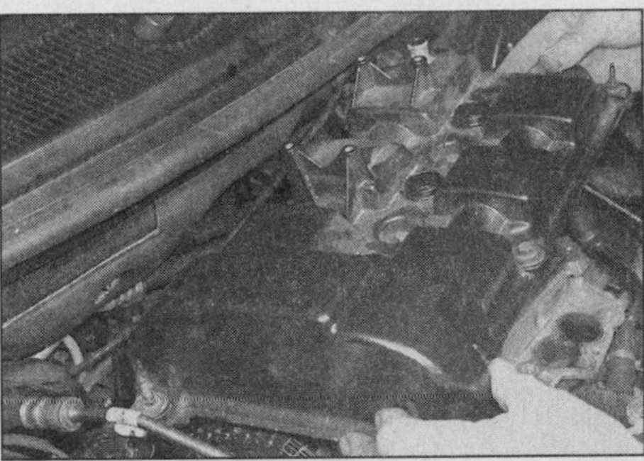

5.43b . . . and lift off the rear cylinder head cover

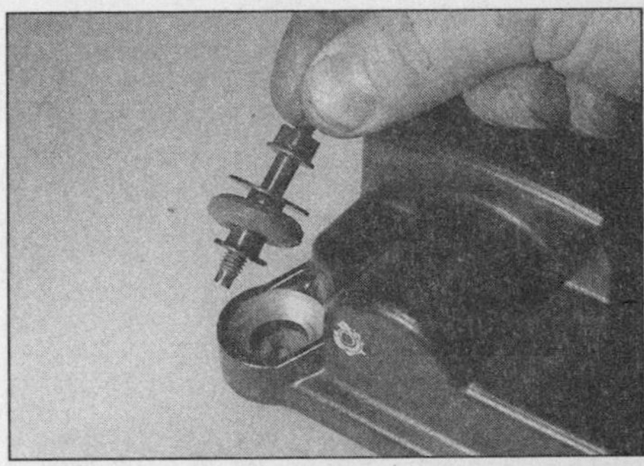

5.45b Note the O-ring seals on the cover mounting bolts

6 Inlet manifolds - removal and refitting

Upper manifold

Removal

1 Disconnect the battery negative (earth) lead (see Chapter 5A, Section 1).

2 Undo the bolts securing the plastic cover to the top of the front cylinder bank. Note that one of the bolts secures the coolant hose. Lift the cover from the engine **(see illustrations)**.

3 Disconnect the crankcase ventilation hoses from the air inlet duct and EGR valve **(see illustrations)**.

4 Prise out the vacuum hose from the upper manifold **(see illustration)**.

5 Loosen the two clips and disconnect the air

6.2b Lifting the plastic cover from the top of the front cylinder bank

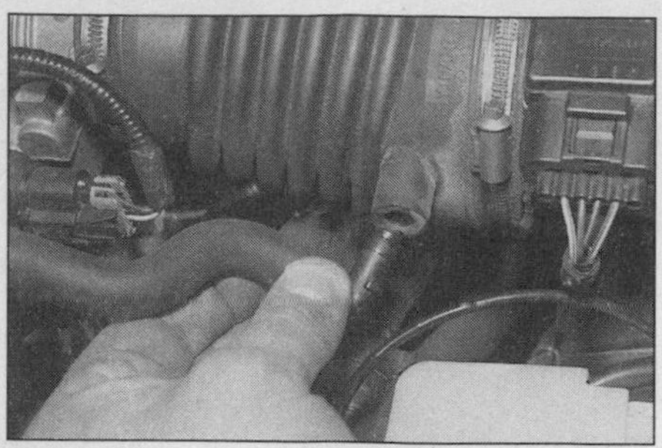

6.3a Disconnecting the crankcase ventilation hose from the front of the air duct . . .

6.3b . . . the EGR valve . . .

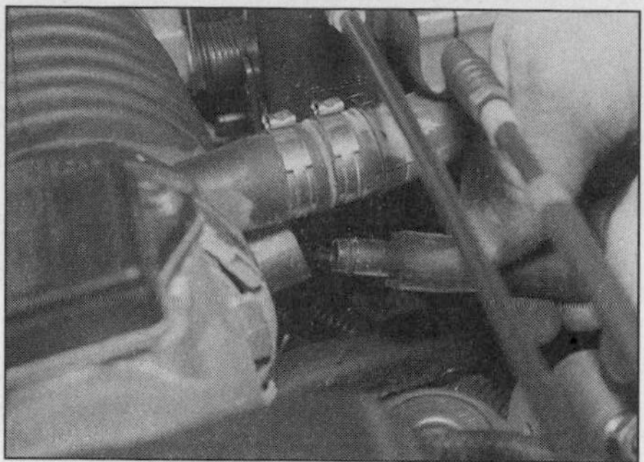

6.3c . . . and the rear of the air duct

inlet duct from the throttle body and airflow meter. Remove the duct **(see illustrations)**.

6 Prise out the brake vacuum servo hose from the upper inlet manifold **(see illustration)**.

7 Use a screwdriver to prise off the retaining clip, then disconnect the throttle and speed control cables from the mounting bracket **(see illustration)**.

8 Unbolt and remove the throttle cable mounting bracket **(see illustration)**.

9 Disconnect the wiring from the idle air control valve and throttle position sensor **(see illustrations)**.

10 Disconnect the vacuum hose from the EGR valve, then unscrew the valve mounting bolts

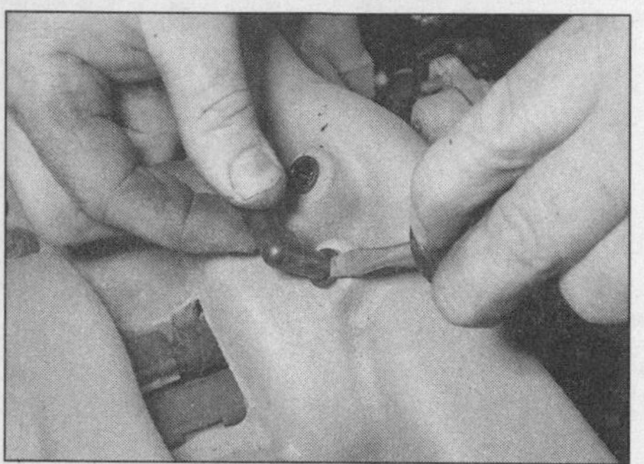

6.4 Disconnecting the vacuum hose from the upper manifold

6.5a Loosen the clips . . .

6.5b . . . and remove the air inlet duct

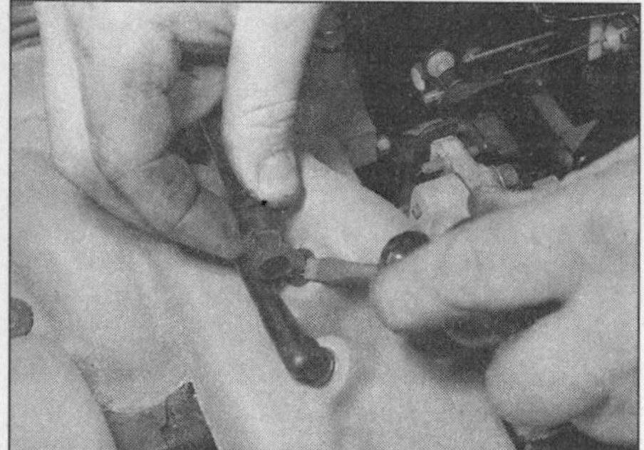

6.6 Prise out the brake vacuum hose from the manifold

6.7 Disconnecting the speed control cable

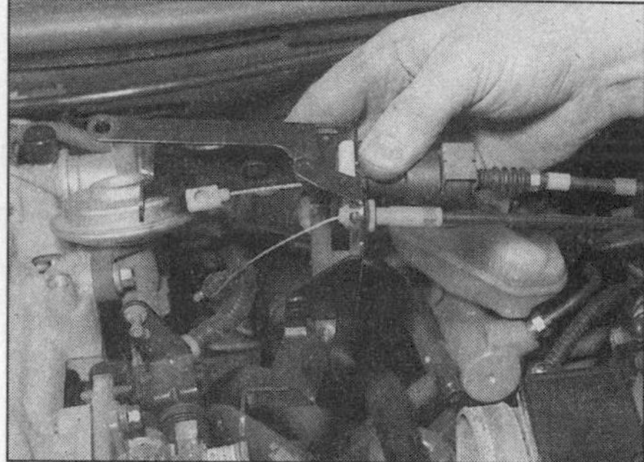

6.8 Removing the throttle cable mounting bracket complete with cables

6.9a Disconnecting the wiring from the idle air control valve . . .

6.9b . . . and throttle position sensor

6.10a Disconnecting the vacuum hose from the EGR valve

6.10b Unscrew the bolts . . .

6.10c . . . and recover the gasket from the EGR valve

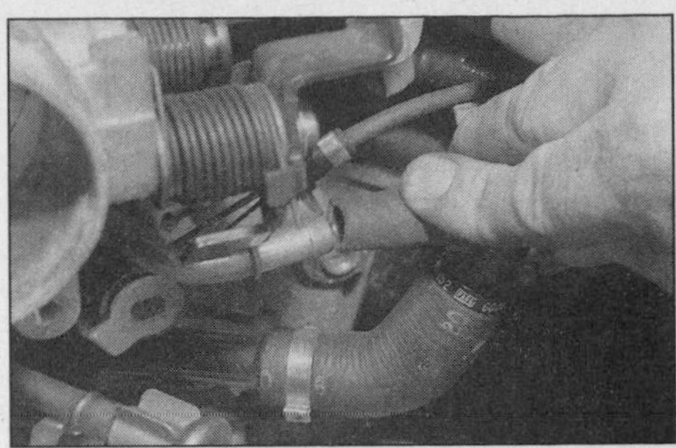
6.11 Disconnecting the positive crankcase ventilation (PCV) hose from the upper inlet manifold

and recover the gasket. If necessary, remove the valve from the tube **(see illustrations)**.

11 Disconnect the positive crankcase ventilation (PCV) hose from the inlet manifold stub **(see illustration)**.

6.12a Disconnect the wiring . . .

12 Disconnect the wiring and vacuum hoses from the EGR vacuum regulator **(see illustrations)**.

13 Progressively unscrew the upper inlet manifold mounting bolts in the reverse order to that shown (see illustration 5.20) , then remove the upper manifold. Recover the gaskets from the lower inlet manifold. Recover the rubber insulators from the mounting bolts and inspect them - if they are not serviceable, renew them **(see illustrations)**.

Refitting

14 Clean the mating surfaces of the upper and lower inlet manifolds.

15 Locate new gaskets on the lower manifold, then refit the upper manifold. Insert the bolts **(see illustration)** and tighten to the specified torque in the sequence shown (see illustration 5.20).

16 Reconnect the vacuum hose and wiring to the EGR vacuum regulator.

17 Reconnect the PCV hose to the inlet manifold stub.

18 Refit the EGR valve together with a new gasket and tighten the bolts. Reconnect the vacuum hose.

19 Reconnect the wiring to the throttle position sensor and air inlet temperature control valve.

20 Refit the throttle cable mounting bracket and tighten the bolts.

21 Reconnect the throttle and speed control cables to the mounting bracket and retain with the clip.

22 Reconnect the two brake vacuum servo hoses to the upper inlet manifold.

23 Refit the air inlet duct and tighten the clips.

24 Reconnect the vacuum hose.

25 Reconnect the crankcase ventilation hoses each side of the air inlet duct.

6.12b . . . and vacuum hoses from the EGR vacuum regulator

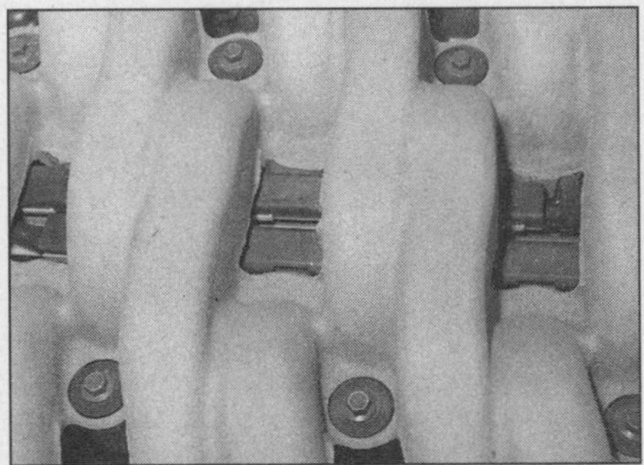
6.13a Upper inlet manifold mounting bolts

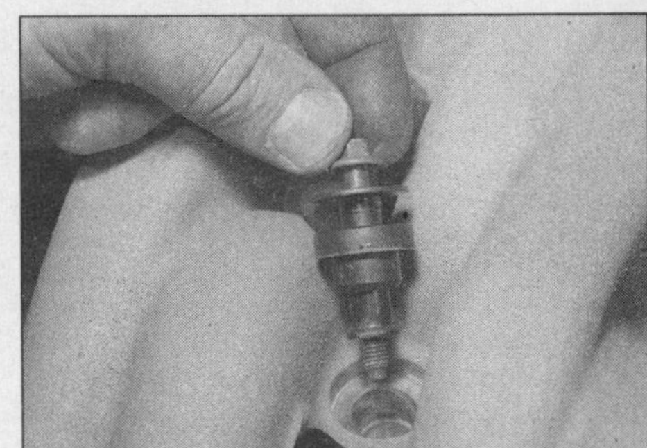
6.13b Mounting bolts and rubber insulators

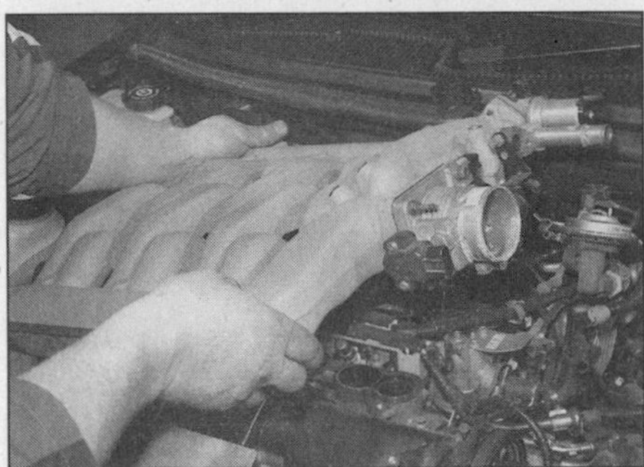
6.13c Removing the upper inlet manifold . . .

6.13d . . . and gaskets

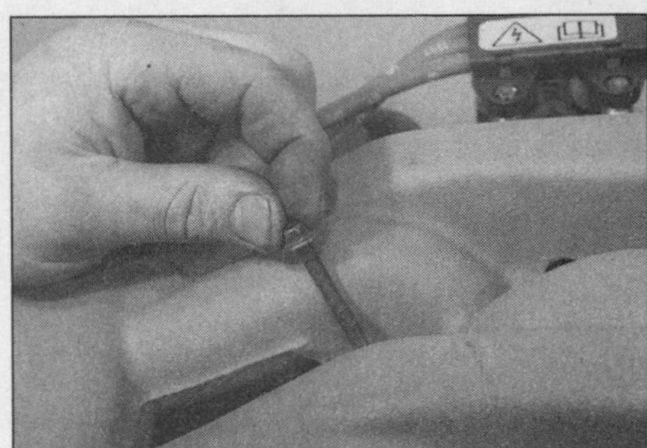
6.15 Inserting the upper manifold bolts

6.36a Unscrew and remove the bolts . . .

6.36b . . . then remove the lower inlet manifold from the cylinder heads . . .

6.36c . . . and recover the gaskets

26 Refit the plastic cover and tighten the bolts. Locate the coolant hose in the clips.

27 Reconnect the battery negative (earth) lead (see Chapter 5A, Section 1). **Note:** *After the battery has been disconnected, the engine management system requires approximately 10 miles of driving to relearn its optimum settings. During this period, the engine may not perform normally.*

Lower manifold

Removal

28 Depressurise the fuel system as described in Chapter 4A.

29 Disconnect the battery negative (earth) lead (see Chapter 5A, Section 1).

30 Remove the upper inlet manifold as described earlier in this Section.

31 Disconnect the fuel feed and return lines. The lines have fittings that require a special tool to release them, however it is possible to use a home-made tool made from a coil of thin plastic about 15 mm wide. Insert the coil into the open end of the fitting so that the internal coiled spring is lifted over the retaining lip, then separate the lines.

32 Disconnect the wiring from the coolant temperature sensor (located above the starter motor) and from the EGR back pressure transducer at the left-hand rear of the engine, then disconnect the wiring from the injectors.

33 Disconnect the vacuum hose from the fuel pressure regulator.

34 Disconnect the intake manifold runner control (IMRC) actuator rod or cable from the stud and bracket on the front cylinder head cover, and disconnect the vacuum hose from the IMRC vacuum solenoid.

35 Progressively unscrew the lower inlet manifold mounting bolts in the reverse sequence to that shown (see illustration 6.40).

36 With all the bolts removed, lift the lower inlet manifold from the cylinder heads and recover the gaskets **(see illustrations)**.

37 Clean the mating surfaces of the manifold and cylinder head taking care not to damage the aluminium surfaces.

Refitting

38 Place the new gaskets on the cylinder head, making sure that the locating pins are pointing downwards.

39 Carefully position the lower inlet manifold on the gaskets making sure that the gaskets are not displaced.

40 Insert the bolts and progressively tighten them to the specified torque in the sequence shown **(see illustration)**.

41 Reconnect the IMRC vacuum hose or actuator rod.

42 Reconnect the vacuum hose to the fuel pressure regulator.

43 Reconnect the wiring to the injectors, EGR back pressure transducer and coolant temperature sensor.

44 Reconnect the fuel line.

45 Reconnect the battery negative (earth) lead (see Chapter 5A, Section 1). **Note:** *After the battery has been disconnected, the engine management system requires approximately 10 miles of driving to relearn its optimum settings. During this period, the engine may not perform normally.*

7 Exhaust manifold - removal and refitting

Warning: The engine must be completely cold before starting this procedure.

Front exhaust manifold

Removal

1 Disconnect the battery negative (earth) lead (see Chapter 5A, Section 1).

2 Disconnect the wiring from the oxygen sensor located on the exhaust manifold.

3 Unscrew the union nuts and remove the exhaust gas recirculation (EGR) transfer pipe from the exhaust and inlet manifolds.

4 If necessary for additional working room, drain the cooling system and remove the radiator bottom hose.

5 Unbolt the exhaust front pipe from the exhaust manifold.

6 Unscrew the mounting nuts and withdraw the exhaust manifold from the studs on the cylinder head. Remove the gasket and discard it **(see illustrations)**.

7 If necessary, unscrew the oxygen sensor with reference to Chapter 4B.

8 Clean the mating surfaces of the exhaust manifold and cylinder head.

Refitting

9 If removed, refit the oxygen sensor and tighten to the specified torque with reference to Chapter 4B.

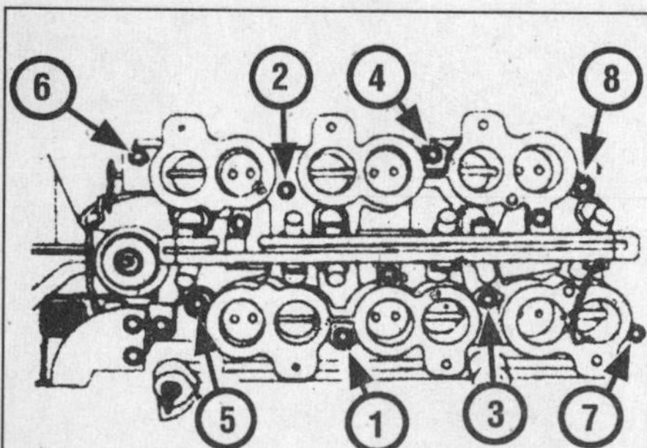

6.40 Tightening sequence for the lower inlet manifold bolts

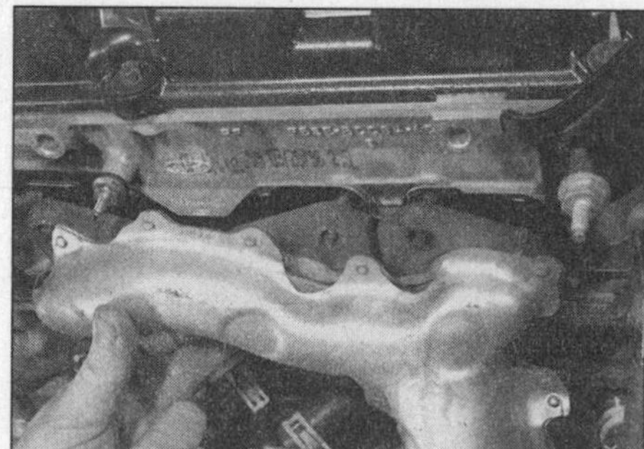

7.6a Remove the front exhaust manifold . . .

7.6b . . . and remove the gasket

7.24a Remove the rear exhaust manifold . . .

7.24b . . . and remove the gasket

10 Position a new gasket on the cylinder head studs.
11 Refit the exhaust manifold and progressively tighten the mounting nuts to the specified torque.
12 Reconnect the exhaust front pipe to the exhaust manifold and tighten the bolts to the specified torque.
13 Where removed, reconnect the radiator bottom hose and tighten the clip. Refill the cooling system with reference to Chapter 1.
14 Refit the EGR transfer pipe to the exhaust and inlet manifold, and tighten the union nuts to the specified torque.
15 Reconnect the oxygen sensor wiring.
16 Reconnect the battery negative (earth) lead (see Chapter 5A, Section 1). **Note:** *After the battery has been disconnected, the engine management system requires approximately 10 miles of driving to relearn its optimum settings. During this period, the engine may not perform normally.*

Rear exhaust manifold

Removal

17 Disconnect the battery negative (earth) lead (see Chapter 5A, Section 1).
18 Apply the handbrake, then jack up the front of the vehicle and support it on axle stands (see "*Jacking and vehicle support*"). Remove the right-hand front wheel.
19 Remove the alternator as described in Chapter 5A. Also unbolt and remove the alternator mounting bracket from the cylinder block.
20 With reference to Chapter 4A, remove the catalytic converter from the exhaust system. Also remove the exhaust front pipe from the bottom of the exhaust manifold.
21 Unscrew and remove the oxygen sensor from the manifold with reference to Chapter 4B.
22 Unbolt the right-hand driveshaft support bearing from the rear of the cylinder block.
23 Unscrew the union nut and disconnect the EGR transfer tube from the exhaust manifold.
24 Unscrew the mounting nuts and withdraw the exhaust manifold from the studs on the cylinder head. Remove the gasket and discard it **(see illustrations)**.
25 Clean the mating surfaces of the exhaust manifold and cylinder head.

Refitting

26 Position a new gasket on the cylinder head studs.
27 Refit the exhaust manifold and progressively tighten the mounting nuts to the specified torque.
28 Reconnect the EGR transfer tube and tighten the union nut.
29 Refit the right-hand driveshaft support bearing to the cylinder block and tighten the bolts to the specified torque.
30 Refit the oxygen sensor to the manifold with reference to Chapter 4B.
31 Refit the exhaust front pipe and catalytic converter with reference to Chapter 4A.
32 Refit the alternator mounting bracket and tighten the bolts, then refit the alternator with reference to Chapter 5A.
33 Refit the right-hand wheel and lower the car to the ground.
34 Reconnect the battery negative (earth)

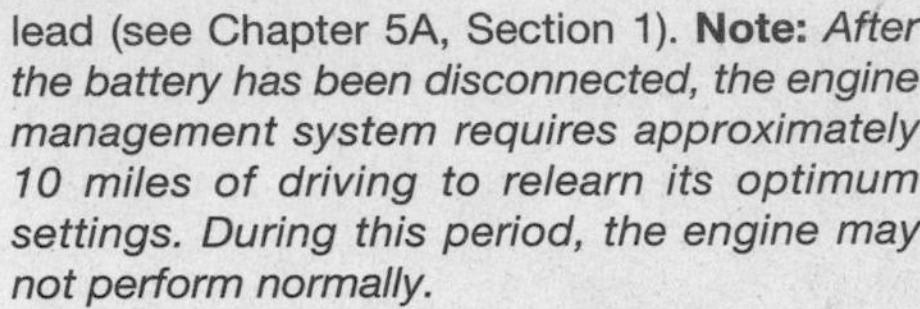

lead (see Chapter 5A, Section 1). **Note:** *After the battery has been disconnected, the engine management system requires approximately 10 miles of driving to relearn its optimum settings. During this period, the engine may not perform normally.*

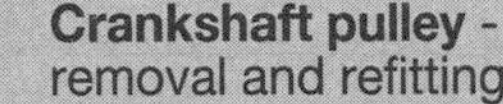

8 Crankshaft pulley - removal and refitting

Removal

1 Apply the handbrake, then jack up the front of the vehicle and support it on axle stands (see "*Jacking and vehicle support*"). Remove the right-hand wheel.
2 Remove the right-hand wheel arch liner with reference to Chapter 11.
3 Using a socket in the square provided, turn the main auxiliary drivebelt tensioner clockwise and slip the belt from the pulleys on the right-hand end of the engine. Carefully release the tensioner.
4 The crankshaft pulley must now be held stationary while the bolt is loosened. On manual transmission models have an assistant engage 4th gear and firmly depress the footbrake pedal. On automatic transmission models, remove the cover from the transmission bellhousing and have an assistant engage a wide-blade screwdriver with the teeth of the starter ring gear. Alternatively, the pulley can be held stationary by bolting a length of metal bar to it using the threaded holes provided, or by using a scissor bar **(see illustration)**.
5 Loosen the bolt then unscrew it completely and remove the washer **(see illustration)**. When fitted, the bolt is torqued-to-yield, and a new bolt must therefore be used on refitting.
6 Using a suitable puller, draw the crankshaft pulley from the end of the crankshaft. If the Woodruff key is loose, remove it from the groove in the crankshaft and keep it in a safe place **(see illustrations)**.
7 Clean the crankshaft pulley and the end of the crankshaft.

Refitting

8 Apply suitable sealer to the key groove on

8.4 Hold the crankshaft stationary using a scissor bar while the pulley bolt is loosened

8.5 Removing the crankshaft pulley bolt and washer

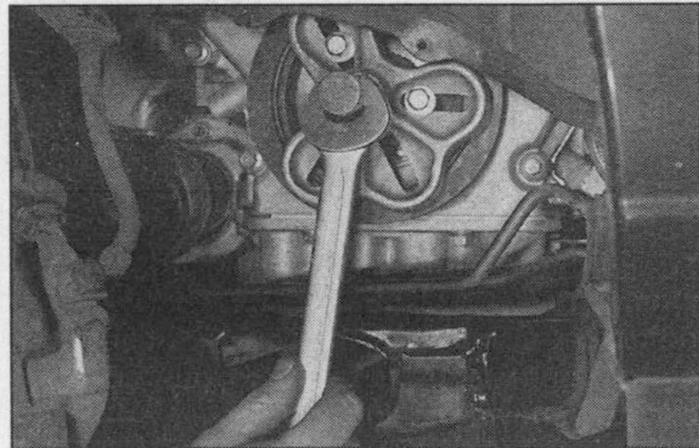

8.6a Using a puller to remove the crankshaft pulley from the end of the crankshaft

8.6b Removing the crankshaft pulley

8.10a Using a torque wrench to tighten the crankshaft pulley bolt

8.10b Using an angle disc to tighten the crankshaft pulley bolt to the specified angle

the inside of the pulley. If removed, locate the Woodruff key in the crankshaft groove, making sure that it is parallel with the surface of the crankshaft.

9 Locate the pulley on the crankshaft and engage it with the key. Use the old pulley bolt and washer to draw the pulley fully onto the crankshaft. Unscrew the old bolt and discard it.

10 Insert the new bolt together with the washer, and tighten it to the specified torque and angle while holding the crankshaft stationary using the method described in paragraph 4. Note that the bolt is tightened in four stages as described in the Specifications **(see illustrations)**.

11 Remove the holding tool, and on automatic transmission models refit the cover to the transmission bellhousing.

12 Refit the main auxiliary drivebelt to the right-hand end of the engine with reference to Chapter 1.

13 Refit the right-hand wheel arch liner with reference to Chapter 11.

14 Refit the right-hand wheel and lower the car to the ground.

9 Timing cover - removal and refitting

Removal

1 Disconnect the battery negative (earth) lead (see Chapter 5A, Section 1). Apply the handbrake, then jack up the front of the vehicle and support it on axle stands (see "*Jacking and vehicle support*"). Remove the right-hand wheel.

2 Drain the engine oil (see Chapter 1).

3 Remove both cylinder head covers as described in Section 5.

4 Remove the alternator as described in Chapter 5A. Also unbolt the alternator mounting bracket from the cylinder block and timing cover.

5 Remove the crankshaft pulley as described in Section 8.

6 Support the weight of the engine with a hoist or engine support bar. If the timing cover is being removed in order to remove the cylinder heads, the hoist must be attached to the right-hand mounting bracket on the cylinder block **(see illustration)**.

7 Disconnect the wiring from the low coolant warning switch, then undo the coolant expansion tank mounting screws and position the tank to one side. If the timing cover is being removed in order to remove the cylinder heads, drain the cooling system and remove the expansion tank completely after disconnecting the hoses **(see illustrations)**.

8 Mark the position of the right-hand engine mounting, then unscrew the nuts and bolts and remove the mounting and bracket, noting the location of the earth cable.

9 Loosen only the bolts securing the pulley to the power steering pump.

10 Using a socket in the square provided, turn the main auxiliary drivebelt tensioner clockwise and slip the belt from the pulleys. Carefully release the tensioner.

11 Fully unscrew the bolts and remove the pulley from the power steering pump, then remove the pump with reference to Chapter 10 but do not disconnect the hydraulic fluid hoses. Position the pump together with the hydraulic lines on the bulkhead **(see illustrations)**.

9.6 Engine support bar attached to the right-hand mounting bracket on the cylinder block

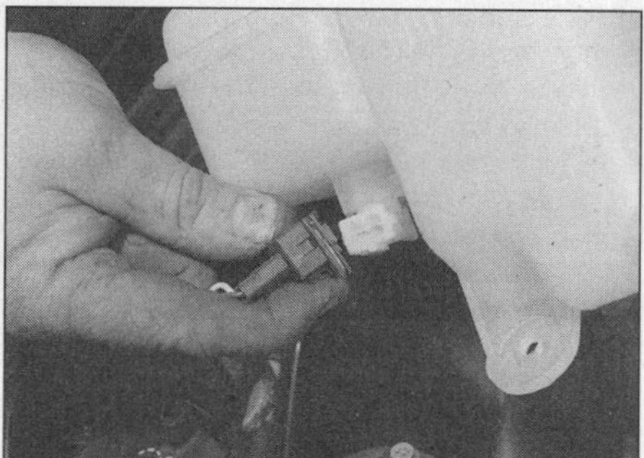
9.7a Disconnecting the low coolant warning switch wiring

9.7b Coolant hoses on the expansion tank

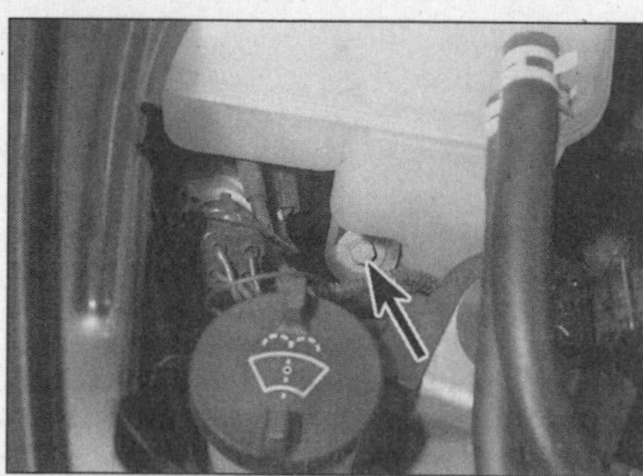
9.7c Expansion tank front mounting bolt

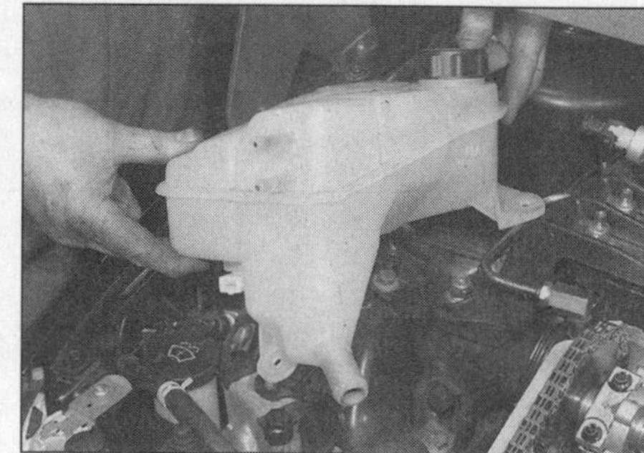
9.7d Removing the expansion tank

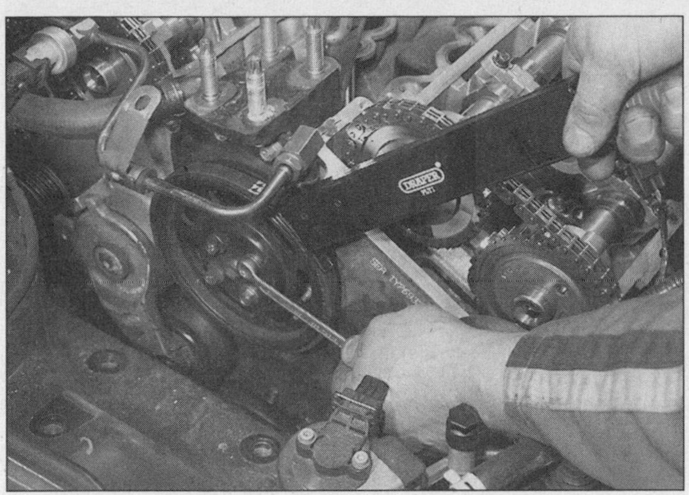

9.11a Using a strap wrench to hold the pulley while the bolts are unscrewed

9.11b Removing the power steering pump pulley

12 Remove the sump with reference to Section 14.

13 Disconnect the wiring from the camshaft position sensor on the timing cover. If necessary, the sensor can be removed at this stage.

14 Disconnect the wiring from the crankshaft position sensor on the timing cover. If necessary, the sensor can be removed at this stage.

15 If necessary for improved working room, unbolt the air conditioning compressor and position it to one side. Do not disconnect the refrigerant lines from the compressor.

16 Note the location of the bolts and stud bolts on the timing cover to ensure correct refitting. If necessary, make a drawing of the bolt positions **(see illustration)**.

17 Progressively unscrew the bolts from the timing cover in the reverse sequence to that shown (see illustration 9.23) **(see illustration)**.

18 Remove the timing cover from the location dowels on the engine and withdraw it over the nose of the crankshaft. Carefully remove the cover from the engine compartment, taking care not to damage it as there is very little room to manœuvre it between the engine and inner wing panel. Remove the three gaskets from the cover **(see illustration)**.

19 Clean the contact surfaces of the timing cover, cylinder block and head, taking care not to damage the aluminium faces.

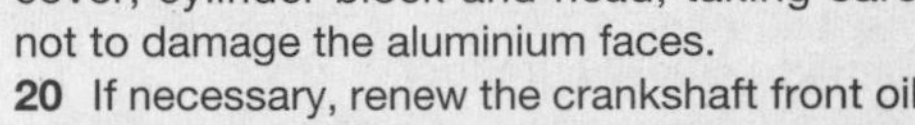

20 If necessary, renew the crankshaft front oil seal as described in Section 18. Alternatively, it can be fitted after the timing cover is in position **(see illustration)**. Also if necessary, remove the auxiliary drivebelt tensioner and idler from the timing cover.

Refitting

21 Apply suitable sealer as beads, 6.0 mm long, at the joints between the cylinder head and block, and between the main bearing ladder and cylinder block **(see illustration)**.

2B

9.11c Withdrawing the power steering pump with the hydraulic lines still connected

9.16 Stud bolts at the top of the timing cover (power steering pump mounting)

9.17 Removing the timing cover bolts

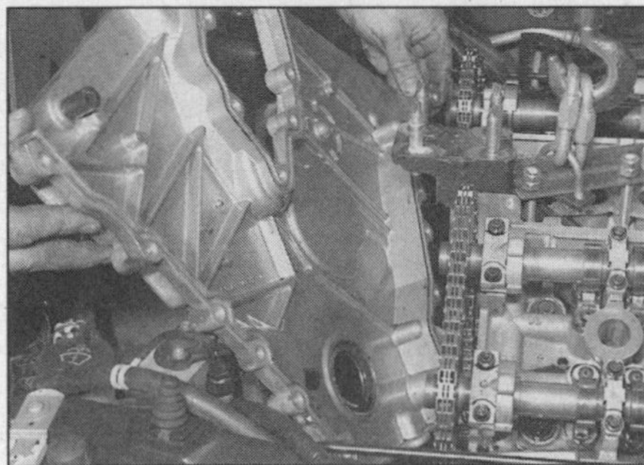

9.18 Removing the timing cover from the engine

9.20 Fitting a new crankshaft front oil seal with the timing cover on the bench

9.21 Apply sealer at the joints between the main bearing ladder and block

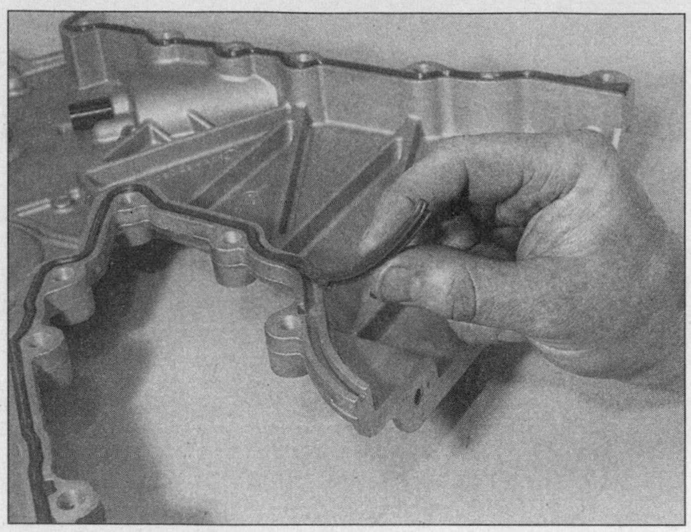

9.22 Locate a new gasket in the timing cover grooves

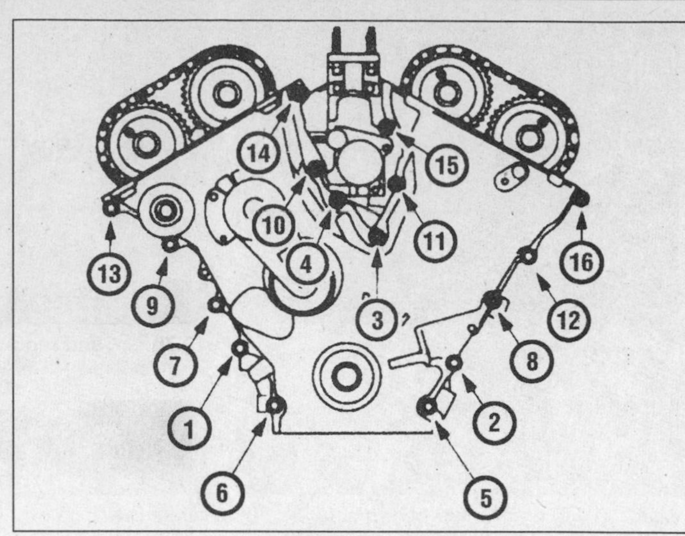

9.23 Tightening sequence for the timing cover bolts/studs

22 Locate new gaskets in the timing cover grooves **(see illustration)**.

23 Refit the timing cover with gaskets, making sure that it locates correctly on the dowels. Insert the bolts and stud bolts in their original positions, and first tighten them by hand only. Finally, progressively tighten the bolts to the specified torque in the sequence shown **(see illustration)**.

24 If removed, refit the auxiliary drivebelt tensioner and idler to the timing cover **(see illustrations)**.

25 If removed, refit the air conditioning compressor with reference to Chapter 3 and tighten the bolts.

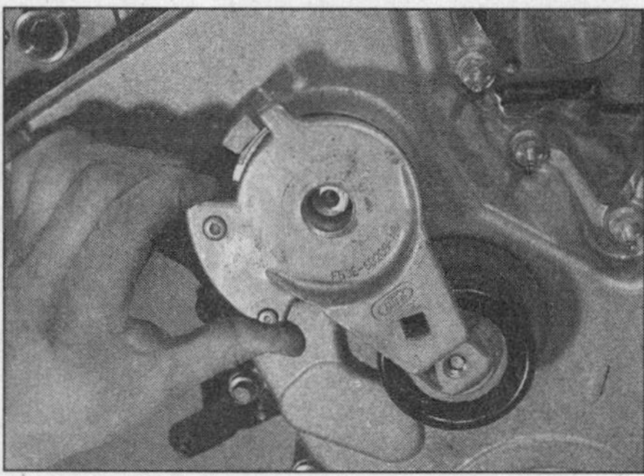

9.24a Refit the auxiliary drivebelt tensioner . . .

26 Refit the sump with reference to Section 14.

27 Refit the crankshaft position sensor and the camshaft position sensor, and reconnect the wiring.

28 Refit the power steering pump with reference to Chapter 10 and tighten the bolts to the specified torque. Refit the pulley and tighten the bolts.

29 Locate the main auxiliary drivebelt on its pulleys and release the tensioner with reference to Chapter 1.

30 Refit the right-hand engine mounting and bracket in their previously noted positions and tighten the nuts and bolts to the specified torque. Make sure the earth cable is fitted to the bracket. Refit the expansion tank and tighten the mounting screws.

31 Remove the engine lifting hoist.

32 Refit the crankshaft pulley with reference to Section 8.

33 Refit the alternator bracket and alternator with reference to Chapter 5A.

34 Refit the cylinder head covers with reference to Section 5.

35 Reconnect the battery negative (earth) lead (see Chapter 5A, Section 1). **Note:** *After the battery has been disconnected, the engine management system requires approximately 10 miles of driving to relearn its optimum settings. During this period, the engine may not perform normally.*

36 Refit the right-hand wheel and lower the car to the ground.

37 Refill the engine with oil (see Chapter 1).

10 Timing chains, tensioners and guides - removal, inspection and refitting

Removal

1 Set the engine to TDC on No 1 cylinder as described in Section 4.

2 Remove the timing cover as described in Section 9.

3 Slide the crankshaft position sensor pulse ring from the front of the crankshaft noting which way round it is fitted. Mark the sensor to ensure it is refitted correctly **(see illustration)**.

4 Temporarily screw the crankshaft pulley bolt in the end of the crankshaft so the crankshaft can be turned with a socket.

5 Note that the timing chain for a particular bank must be removed with the crankshaft at the relevant removal position for that bank.

9.24b . . . and secure with the special bolt

9.24c Refitting the auxiliary drivebelt idler

10.3 Slide the crankshaft position sensor pulse ring from the front of the crankshaft

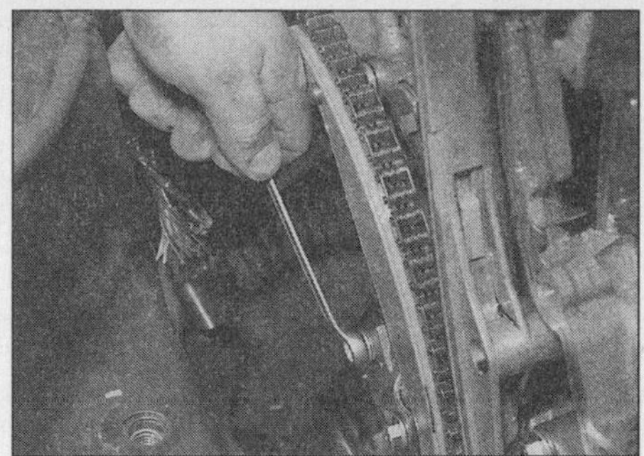
10.7a Unscrew the bolts . . .

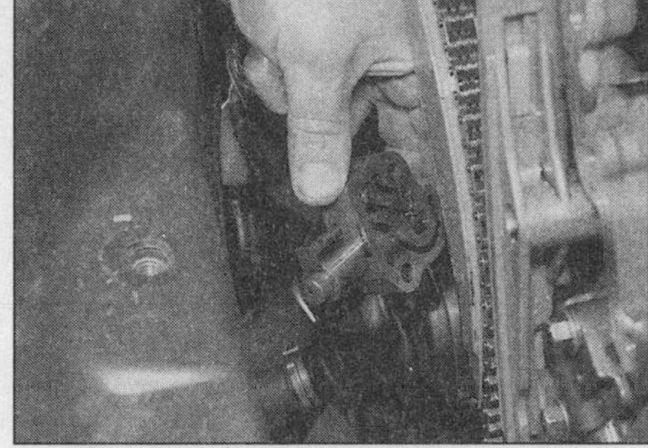
10.7b . . . and remove the rear timing chain tensioner

10.7c Removing the rear timing chain tensioner guide

10.8a Disconnecting the rear timing chain from the crankshaft sprocket . . .

10.8b . . . and camshaft sprockets

10.9 Removing the fixed timing chain guide for the rear timing chain

This ensures the camshafts have even valve spring pressure along their lengths. To remove the rear timing chain, turn the crankshaft until the crankshaft pulley keyway is at the 3 o'clock position. The position mark on the outer faces of the rear bank exhaust camshaft sprocket should be at the 12 o'clock position, and the mark on the outer faces of the rear bank inlet camshaft sprocket should be at the 3 o'clock position in relation to the upper edge of the cylinder head.

10.10 Removing the rear crankshaft sprocket

6 If there are no markings on the timing chains, mark them in relation to the sprocket timing marks with dabs of paint as an aid to refitting. If there are markings on the chains, it is unlikely that they will be aligned with the sprocket marks, however they may be used when refitting the chains. The original marks may be in the form of copper links or white painted dots.

7 Unbolt the rear timing chain tensioner, then remove the tensioner guide from its pivot **(see illustrations)**. **Note:** *On early models an adapter plate may be fitted between the tensioner and block.*

8 Disengage the rear timing chain from the crankshaft and camshaft sprockets and remove from the engine **(see illustrations)**. If it is to be reused, make sure it is identified for fitted position.

9 Unbolt the fixed timing chain guide for the rear timing chain **(see illustration)**.

10 Slide the rear timing chain sprocket from the crankshaft, noting which way round it is fitted. Mark the sprocket to ensure it is refitted the same way round **(see illustration)**.

11 To remove the front timing chain, first turn the crankshaft back until the crankshaft pulley keyway is at the 11 o'clock position. The position mark on the outer faces of the front bank inlet camshaft sprocket should be at the 9 o'clock position, and the mark on the outer faces of the front bank exhaust camshaft sprocket should be at the 12 o'clock position.

12 Unbolt the front timing chain tensioner, then remove the tensioner guide from its pivot **(see illustrations)**. **Note:** *On early models, an adapter plate may be fitted between the tensioner and block.*

10.12a Unscrew the bolt . . .

10.12b . . . and remove the front timing chain tensioner . . .

10.12c . . . and tensioner guide

10.13a Disengage the front timing chain from the crankshaft sprocket . . .

10.13b . . . and camshaft sprocket

10.14 Fixed timing chain guide for the front timing chain

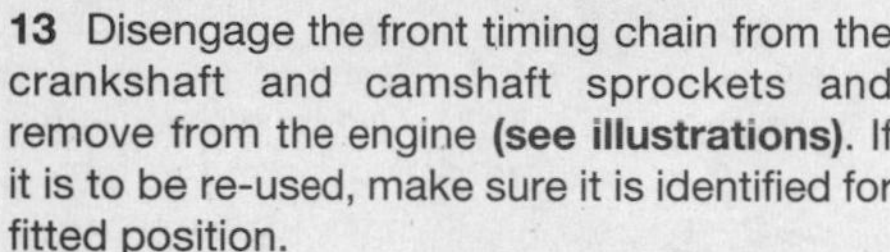

13 Disengage the front timing chain from the crankshaft and camshaft sprockets and remove from the engine **(see illustrations)**. If it is to be re-used, make sure it is identified for fitted position.

14 Unbolt the fixed timing chain guide for the front timing chain **(see illustration)**.

15 Slide the front timing chain sprocket from the crankshaft, noting which way round it is fitted. Mark the sprocket to ensure it is refitted the same way round **(see illustration)**.

Inspection

Note: *Keep all components identified for position to ensure correct refitting.*

16 Clean all components thoroughly and wipe dry.

17 Examine the chain tensioners and tensioner guides for excessive wear or other damage. Check the guides for deep grooves made by the timing chains.

18 Examine the timing chains for excessive wear. Hold them horizontally and check how much movement exists in the chain links. If there is any doubt, compare them to new chains. Renew as necessary.

19 Examine the teeth of the camshaft and crankshaft sprockets for excessive wear and damage. Note that the sprockets are integral with the camshafts, and if worn excessively, the complete camshaft must be renewed.

20 Before refitting the timing chain tensioners, their pistons must be compressed and locked until refitted. To do this, insert a small screwdriver into the access hole in the tensioner and release the pawl mechanism. Now lightly clamp the tensioner in a soft-jawed vice and slowly compress the piston. Do not apply excessive force and make sure that the piston remains aligned with its cylinder. When completely compressed, insert a paper clip or similar 1.5 mm diameter wire rod into the special hole to lock the piston in its compressed position.

Refitting

21 If necessary, turn the crankshaft so that the crankshaft pulley keyway is in the 11 o'clock position. This is the position for refitting the front timing chain.

22 Check that the markings on the outer faces of the front bank camshaft sprockets are positioned as follows. The inlet sprocket mark must be at the 9 o'clock position and the exhaust sprocket mark must be at the 12 o'clock position in relation to the upper edge of the cylinder head.

23 Refit the fixed timing chain guide for the front timing chain and tighten the mounting bolts.

10.15 Slide the front timing chain sprocket from the crankshaft

24 Engage the front timing chain with the camshaft sprockets, making sure that the chain marks are aligned with the marks on the outside of the sprockets **(see illustration)**.

25 Locate the crankshaft sprocket in the timing chain making sure that the timing marks are correctly aligned, then fit the sprocket onto the crankshaft and engage it with the key **(see illustration)**. The front run of the chain must be against the fixed guide, but the rear run will be loose at this stage.

26 Refit the tensioner guide on its pivot, then refit the tensioner (and adapter plate if fitted) and tighten the mounting bolts to the

10.24 Engage the front timing chain with the camshaft sprockets, making sure that the timing marks are correctly aligned

10.25 Locate the sprocket on the front of the crankshaft, making sure that the timing marks are correctly aligned

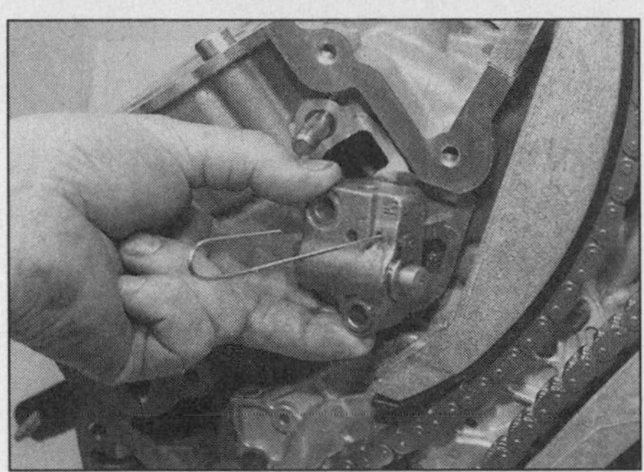

10.26a Locate the timing chain tensioner on the block. Note the welding rod holding the tensioner plunger

10.26b Tightening the tensioner mounting bolts

10.26c Hold the chain guide against the spring tension when removing the locking wire rod

specified torque. Check that the position marks are still aligned, then remove the wire rod to release the tensioner. The internal spring is very strong, and it is preferable to hold the chain guide against the tension and release it slowly **(see illustrations)**.

27 Turn the crankshaft so that the crankshaft pulley key groove is in the 3 o'clock position. This is the position for refitting the rear timing chain.

28 Slide the rear timing chain sprocket onto the crankshaft.

29 Check that the markings on the outer faces of the rear bank camshaft sprockets are positioned as follows. The exhaust sprocket mark must be at the 12 o'clock position and the inlet sprocket mark must be at the 3 o'clock position in relation to the upper edge of the cylinder head.

30 Refit the fixed timing chain guide for the rear timing chain and tighten the mounting bolts.

31 Engage the rear timing chain with the camshaft and crankshaft sprockets, making sure that the copper links are aligned with the marks on the outside of the sprockets. The front run of the chain must be against the fixed guide, but the rear run will be loose at this stage.

32 Refit the tensioner guide on its pivot, then refit the tensioner (and adapter plate if fitted) and tighten the mounting bolts to the specified torque. Check that the timing marks are still aligned then remove the wire to release the tensioner.

33 Slide the crankshaft position sensor pulse ring onto the front of the crankshaft making sure that the key groove with the blue painted mark is engaged with the key. The ring may be marked '2.5L' and 'FRONT' **(see illustration)**.

34 Temporarily refit the crankshaft pulley bolt, and rotate the engine clockwise two complete turns so that the crankshaft key is located at the 11 o'clock position. **Note:** *After turning the engine, the timing chain timing marks will no longer align with the marks on the sprockets, but the timing marks on the rear of the camshaft sprockets must face each other.*

35 Refit the timing cover with reference to Section 9.

11 Camshaft oil seal - renewal

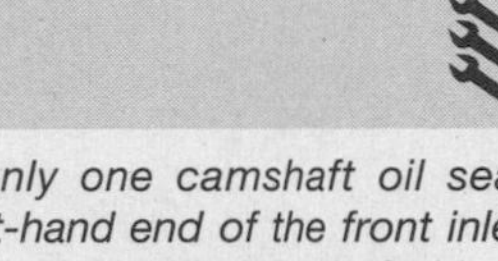

Note: *There is only one camshaft oil seal located on the left-hand end of the front inlet camshaft. This is because this camshaft drives the water pump by means of a drivebelt. Note that on later models the seal is supplied together with the housing, and it is not possible to obtain the seal separately. The sprockets at the timing end of the camshafts are enclosed within the timing cover.*

1 Disconnect the battery negative (earth) lead (see Chapter 5A, Section 1).

2 Unclip the coolant hose from the plastic top cover on the front of the engine, then unscrew the bolts and remove the cover.

3 Remove the water pump drivebelt by moving the tensioner towards the camshaft. Remove the drivebelt from the pulleys, then carefully release the tensioner.

4 The pulley must now be removed from the camshaft. To do this, use a suitable puller.

5 On early models (see note), use a screwdriver to carefully prise the oil seal from its bore, taking care not to damage the camshaft or bore.

6 On later models, the oil seal is supplied together with the housing and it is necessary to unbolt the housing from the cylinder head and remove the gasket.

7 Wipe clean the camshaft and bore, or cylinder head.

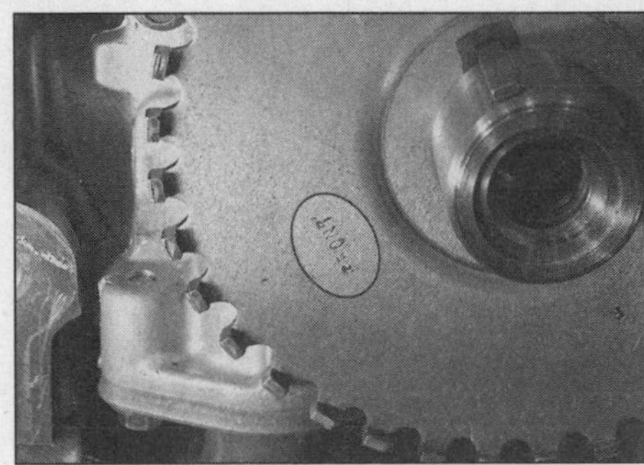

10.33 The crankshaft position sensor pulse ring has a 'FRONT' mark on it

8 On early models, smear clean engine oil on the new oil seal outer periphery and sealing lip, then use a suitable socket or metal tube to drive the oil seal into its bore, making sure it is kept square. Wipe clean any surplus engine oil.

9 On later models, fit a new gasket to the oil seal housing, then smear clean engine oil on the sealing lip of the oil seal. Fit the housing to the cylinder head while guiding the oil seal onto the end of the camshaft, then insert and tighten the bolts to the specified torque.

10 Press the pulley onto the camshaft using a bolt screwed into the centre hole, together with a nut and washers. The pulley outer face must be flush with the end of the camshaft to ensure correct alignment with the water pump pulley and tensioner. If the pulley is very tight, pre-heat it with a heat gun before fitting it.

11 Move the tensioner towards the camshaft and refit the water pump drivebelt on the pulleys. Release the tensioner and make sure that the drivebelt is correctly engaged with the pulleys.

12 Refit the plastic top cover and tighten the bolts. Locate the coolant hose in the clips.

13 Reconnect the battery negative (earth) lead (see Chapter 5A, Section 1). **Note:** *After the battery has been disconnected, the engine management system requires approximately 10 miles of driving to relearn its optimum settings. During this period, the engine may not perform normally.*

12 Camshafts, hydraulic tappets and rocker arms - removal, inspection and refitting

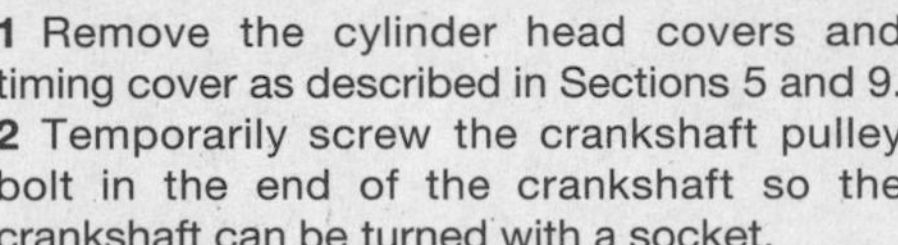

Removal

1 Remove the cylinder head covers and timing cover as described in Sections 5 and 9.

2 Temporarily screw the crankshaft pulley bolt in the end of the crankshaft so the crankshaft can be turned with a socket.

3 Remove the timing chains as described in Section 10. Note that the camshafts for a particular bank must be removed with the crankshaft at the relevant removal position for that bank. This ensures the camshafts have even valve spring pressure along their lengths.

12.4a Removing the water pump pulley drivebelt

12.4b Unbolt the housing from the left-hand end of the front cylinder head

12.4c Use a puller to pull off the water pump pulley . . .

12.4d . . . then unbolt the housing

12.5a The camshaft bearing caps are numbered from the timing chain end of the engine . . .

12.5b . . . with corresponding numbers on the cylinder head

If the procedure described in Section 10 is followed correctly, then the camshafts will be at the correct positions.

4 If removing the front bank inlet camshaft, move the water pump drivebelt tensioner towards the camshaft and remove the drivebelt. Also unscrew and remove the bolts securing the housing to the left-hand end of the front cylinder head - the water pump pulley may remain in position **(see illustrations)**. Alternatively, pull the water pump pulley from the camshaft, then unbolt the housing **(see illustrations)**.

5 Check that the camshaft bearing caps are marked to indicate their positions. The numbers have the letter 'R' or 'L' to indicate the bank they are fitted to. The 'right-hand' bank is the rear bank, and the 'left-hand' bank is the front bank **(see illustrations)**.

12.6 Removing a camshaft bearing cap

6 Working on one bank at a time, remove the thrust bearing caps first - they are numbered 1L and 5L (or 1R and 5R). These caps must be completely removed before loosening the remaining cap bolts. Unscrew the bolts and remove the thrust bearing caps **(see illustration)**.

7 Using the sequence given progressively unscrew the bolts securing the camshaft bearing caps to the cylinder head. With all the bolts loose, remove the bearing caps. If they are tight, tap them lightly with a soft-faced mallet **(see illustrations)**.

8 Identify the camshafts (inlet and exhaust) and lift them directly from the cylinder head **(see illustrations)**.

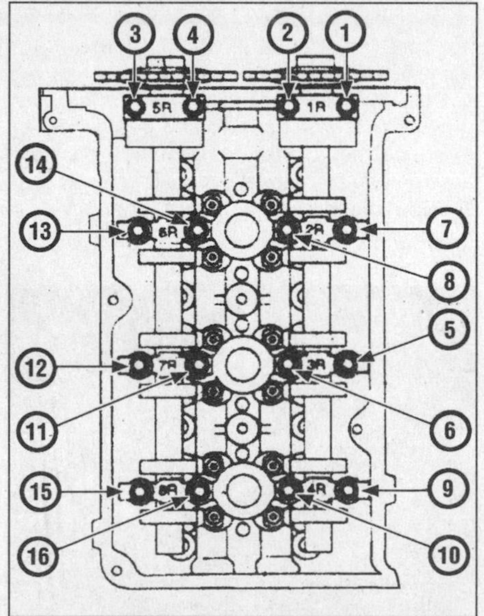

12.7a Loosening sequence for the rear (right-hand) camshaft bearing cap bolts

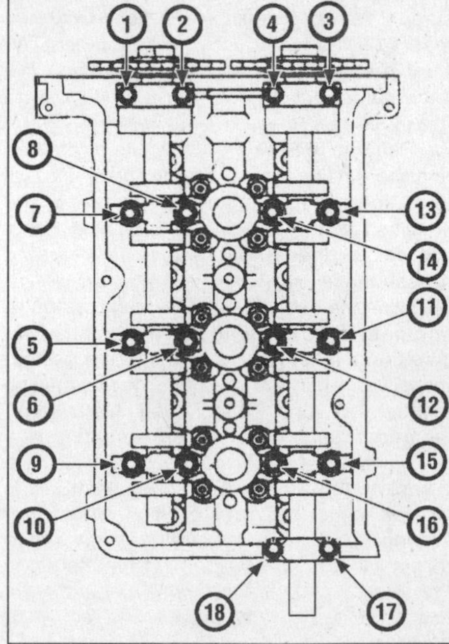

12.7b Loosening sequence for the front (left-hand) camshaft bearing cap bolts

12.7c Unscrewing the camshaft bearing cap bolts

12.8a Front exhaust camshaft sprocket marking

12.8b Rear inlet camshaft sprocket marking

12.8c Removing the front inlet camshaft . . .

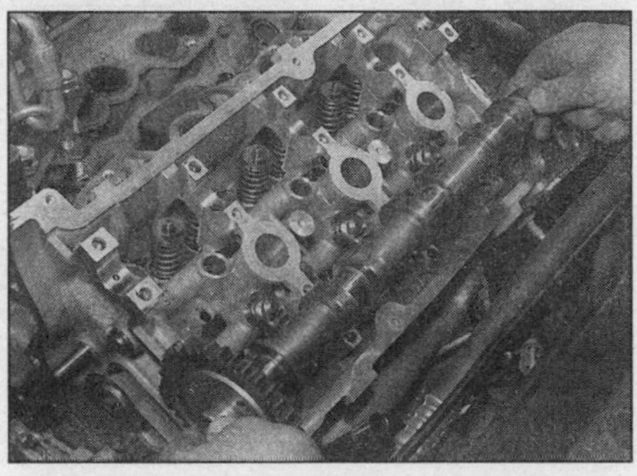
12.8d . . . and front exhaust camshaft

12.9 Removing the rocker arms

9 Note the fitted positions of the rocker arms. Remove the rocker arms from the head, keeping them identified for position by placing them in a container marked with their locations **(see illustration)**.

10 Remove the hydraulic tappets from their bores in the cylinder head, and place them in a container marked with their locations **(see illustration)**.

Inspection

11 With the camshafts and hydraulic tappets removed, check each for obvious wear (scoring, pitting and out-of-round). Renew if necessary.

12 Using a micrometer, measure the outside diameter of each tappet - take measurements at the top and bottom of each tappet, then a second set at right-angles to the first. If any measurement is significantly different from the others, the tappet is tapered or out-of-round and must be renewed. If the necessary equipment is available, measure the inside diameter of the corresponding cylinder head bore. Compare the measurements obtained to those given in the Specifications. If the tappets or the cylinder head bores are excessively worn, new tappets and/or a new cylinder head will be required.

13 If a top-end noise is evident, particularly if the noise persists after initial start-up from cold, there is reason to suspect a faulty hydraulic tappet. However, this is best checked with the engine running.

14 Visually examine the camshaft lobes for score marks, pitting, and evidence of overheating. Look for flaking away of the hardened surface layer of each lobe. If necessary renew the camshaft.

15 Examine the camshaft bearing journals and the cylinder head bearing surfaces for obvious wear or pitting. If excessive wear is evident, it may be necessary to obtain a new or reconditioned cylinder head.

16 Using a micrometer, measure the diameter of each journal at several points. If the diameter of any one journal is less than the specified amount, renew the camshaft. If an internal micrometer is available, measure the internal diameters of the bores in the cylinder head and caps.

17 The camshaft endplay can be checked using a dial gauge in contact with the end of the camshaft. Move the camshaft fully one way and zero the gauge, then move it fully the other way and check the endplay. If excessive, new thrust caps must be fitted to the relevant camshaft.

Refitting

18 Working on the front bank, lubricate the hydraulic tappets and locate them in their relevant bores in the cylinder head.

19 Lubricate the rocker arms and locate them in their relevant positions in the cylinder head.

20 Lubricate the journals of the inlet and exhaust camshafts, then locate the camshafts in the cylinder head in their relevant positions. The outer mark on the inlet camshaft sprocket must be at the 9 o'clock position. The outer mark on the exhaust camshaft sprocket must be at the 12 o'clock position in relation to the upper edge of the cylinder head **(see illustrations)**.

21 Locate the bearing caps in their correct positions on the cylinder head. Insert the bolts and progressively hand-tighten them initially,

12.10 Removing the hydraulic tappets

12.20a Locating the front exhaust camshaft in the cylinder head

2B

12.20b Position the camshafts as shown

12.21a Refitting the camshaft bearing caps

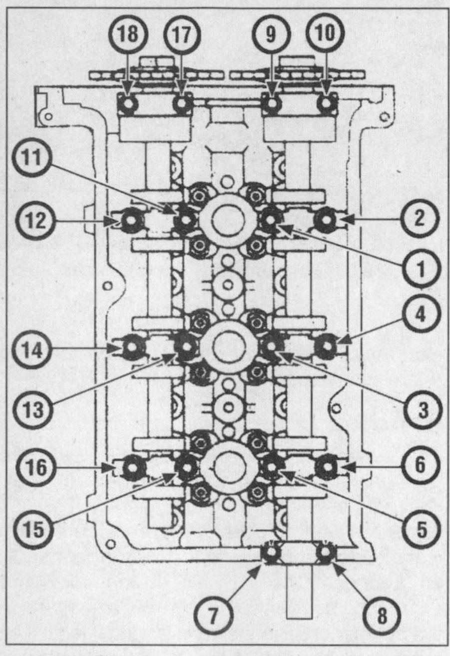

12.21b Tightening sequence for the front (left-hand) camshaft bearing cap bolts

until they are fully seated, using the sequence shown. Finally, tighten all the bearing cap bolts to the specified torque in the sequence given (**see illustrations**).

22 Refit the front timing chain as described in Section 10.

23 Working on the rear bank, lubricate the hydraulic tappets and locate them in their relevant bores in the cylinder head.

24 Lubricate the rocker arms and locate them in their relevant positions in the cylinder head.

25 Lubricate the journals of the inlet and exhaust camshafts, then locate the camshafts in the cylinder head in their relevant positions. The outer mark on the inlet camshaft sprocket must be at the 3 o'clock position. The outer mark on the exhaust camshaft sprocket must be at the 12 o'clock position in relation to the upper edge of the cylinder head (**see illustrations**).

26 Locate the bearing caps in their correct positions on the cylinder head. Insert the bolts and progressively hand-tighten them initially, until they are fully seated, using the sequence shown (**see illustration**). Finally, tighten all the bearing cap bolts to the specified torque in the sequence given.

27 Refit the rear timing chain as described in Section 10.

28 Refit the timing cover and cylinder head covers as described in Sections 9 and 5.

29 If removed, refit the housing to the front inlet camshaft together with a new gasket, then press on the water pump pulley (**see illustrations**).

13 Cylinder heads - removal and refitting

Removal

1 Disconnect the battery negative (earth) lead (see Chapter 5A, Section 1). To provide additional working room, remove the battery and the air cleaner assembly.

2 Drain the cooling system as described in Chapter 1.

3 Remove the upper and lower inlet manifolds as described in Section 6.

4 Drain the engine oil (see Chapter 1).

5 Remove the timing chains as described in Section 10. **Note:** *If only the rear cylinder head is to be removed, it is only necessary to remove the rear timing chain. If the front*

12.25a The outer mark on the exhaust camshaft sprocket must be at the 12 o'clock position when locating the camshaft in the cylinder head

12.25b The outer mark on the inlet camshaft sprocket must be at the 3 o'clock position when locating the camshaft in the cylinder head

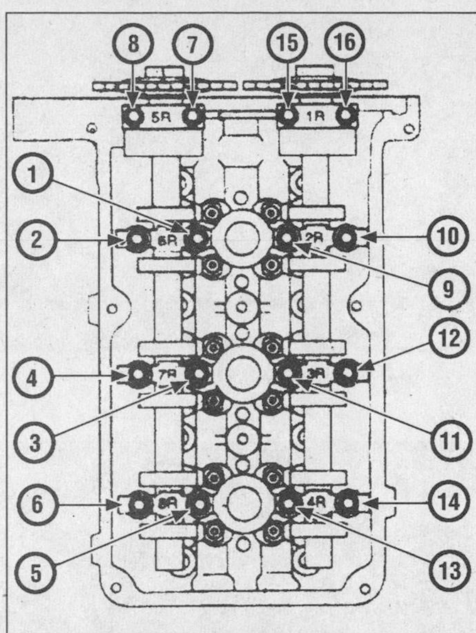

12.26 Tightening sequence for the rear (right-hand) camshaft cap bolts

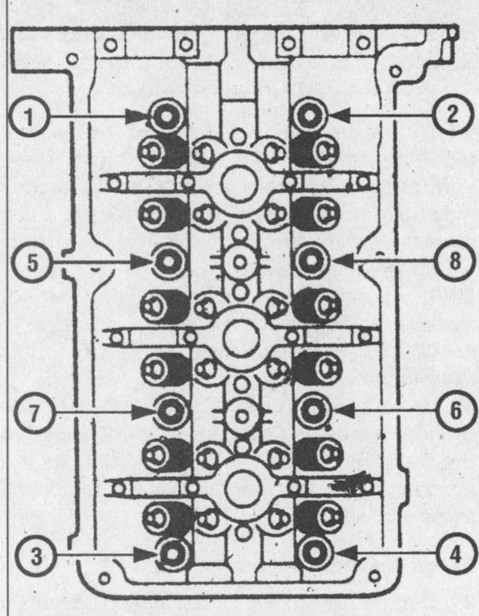

13.15 Loosening sequence for the rear cylinder head bolts

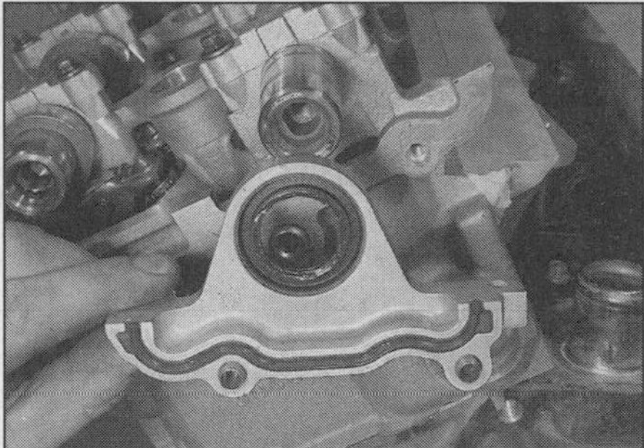

12.29a Refitting the housing and new gasket to the front inlet camshaft

cylinder head is to be removed, it is still necessary to remove the rear timing chain.

6 Temporarily refit the right-hand engine mounting (removed in paragraph 5), and remove the hoist.

7 Remove the camshafts, hydraulic tappets and rocker arms as described in Section 12.

Rear cylinder head

8 Unscrew and remove the oxygen sensor from the rear exhaust manifold (refer to Chapter 4B). Also unbolt the rear engine lifting eye and exhaust gas pressure sensor and bracket from the cylinder head **(see illustration)**.

9 Disconnect the EGR valve back pressure transducer hoses from the EGR valve-to-exhaust manifold tube.

10 Disconnect the wiring from the EGR valve back pressure transducer and from the EGR unit.

11 Unscrew the union nut and detach the EGR valve tube from the rear exhaust manifold.

12 Loosen the clips and disconnect the hoses from the coolant connecting pipe at the left-hand end of the cylinder heads. Also disconnect the wiring from the temperature sensors on the pipe.

13 Unscrew the bolts and remove the coolant connecting pipe from the rear cylinder head. Withdraw the pipe from the front cylinder head and recover the O-rings. Note that the upper bolt has a stud extension.

14 The rear exhaust manifold can be removed at this stage, or alternatively it can be removed together with the rear cylinder head and separated on the bench (see Section 7).

12.29b Using a threaded rod and nut to press on the water pump pulley

13.8 Removing the exhaust gas pressure sensor and bracket from the rear cylinder head

15 Loosen each cylinder head bolt, one turn at a time, following the order shown **(see illustration)**. With all the head bolts loose, remove them together with their washers. It is recommended that the head bolts are renewed as a matter of course.

16 Carefully lift the rear cylinder head from the cylinder block and place it on the bench. Recover the gasket from the block.

17 Unbolt the exhaust manifold from the cylinder head and recover the gasket.

Front cylinder head

18 Remove the water pump with reference to Chapter 3. If necessary, also remove the thermostat housing and hoses **(see illustrations)**.

19 Loosen the clips and disconnect the hoses from the coolant connecting pipe at the left-hand end of the cylinder heads. Also disconnect the wiring from the temperature sensors on the pipe **(see illustration)**.

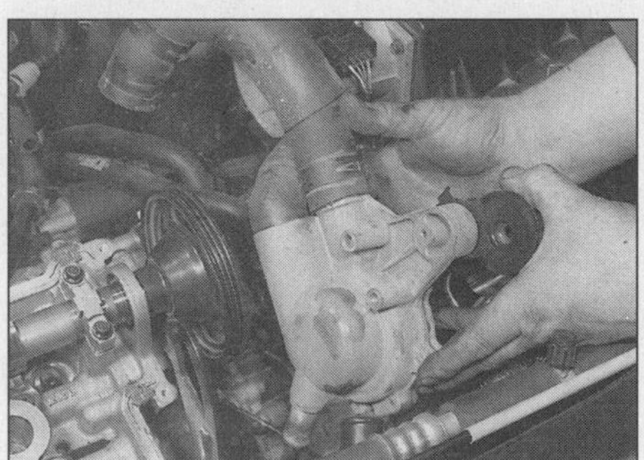

13.18a Removing the water pump

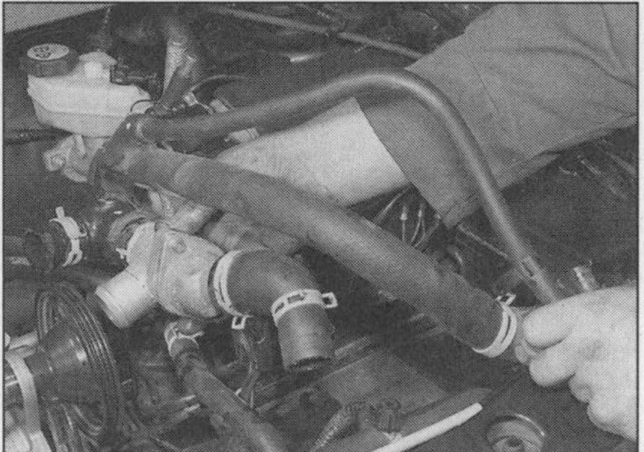

13.18b Removing the thermostat housing and hoses

13.19 Disconnecting the hoses from the coolant connecting pipe

13.20 Removing the coolant connecting pipe

20 Unscrew the bolts and remove the coolant connecting pipe from the rear cylinder head. Withdraw the pipe from the front cylinder head and recover the O-rings. Note that the upper bolt has a stud extension **(see illustration)**.

21 Loosen the clip and disconnect the radiator bottom hose from the elbow on the front cylinder head, then unbolt the elbow.

22 Pull out the engine oil level dipstick tube.

23 The front exhaust manifold can be removed at this stage, or alternatively it can be removed together with the front cylinder head and separated on the bench (see Section 7). If it is decided to remove the head together with the manifold, unbolt the air conditioning compressor from the engine block and place it on the front crossmember, and also remove the oil filter. This will provide additional room for the exhaust downpipe to be lifted from the engine compartment.

24 Loosen each cylinder head bolt, one turn at a time, following the order shown **(see illustration)**. With all the head bolts loose, remove them together with their washers and check them for damage **(see illustrations)**. It is recommended that the head bolts are renewed as a matter of course.

25 Carefully lift the front cylinder head from the cylinder block and place it on the bench. Recover the gasket from the block **(see illustrations)**.

26 Unbolt the exhaust manifold from the cylinder head and recover the gasket.

Refitting

27 The mating faces of the cylinder heads and cylinder blocks must be perfectly clean before refitting the heads. Use a hard plastic or wood scraper to remove all traces of gasket and carbon; also clean the piston crowns. Take particular care, as the soft aluminium alloy is easily damaged. Also, make sure that the carbon is not allowed to enter the oil and water passages - this is particularly important for the lubrication system, as carbon could block the oil supply to any of the engine's components. Using adhesive tape and paper, seal the water, oil and bolt holes in the cylinder block. Clean all the pistons in the same way.

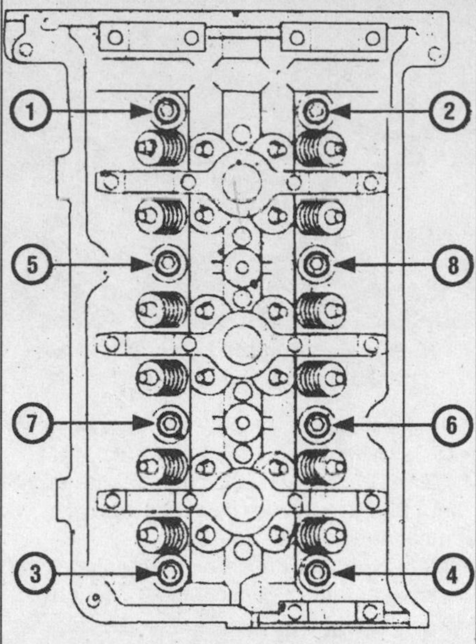

13.24a Loosening sequence for the front cylinder head bolts

To prevent carbon entering the gap between the pistons and bores, smear a little grease in the gap. After cleaning each piston, use a small brush to remove all traces of grease and carbon from the gap, then wipe away the remainder with a clean rag.

13.24b Unscrew the cylinder head bolts . . .

13.24c . . . and remove them together with their washers

28 Check the mating surfaces of the cylinder block and the cylinder head for nicks, deep scratches and other damage. If slight, they may be removed carefully with a fine file, but if excessive, machining may be the only alternative to renewal.

29 If warpage of the cylinder head gasket surface is suspected, use a straight edge to check it for distortion. Refer to Part C of this Chapter if necessary.

30 Wipe clean the mating surfaces of the cylinder heads and cylinder block. Check that the locating dowels are in position in the cylinder block, and that all cylinder head bolt holes are free from oil.

Front cylinder head

31 Locate the front cylinder head gasket on the cylinder block **(see illustration)**.

32 Clean the surfaces of the exhaust manifold and cylinder head, then refit the

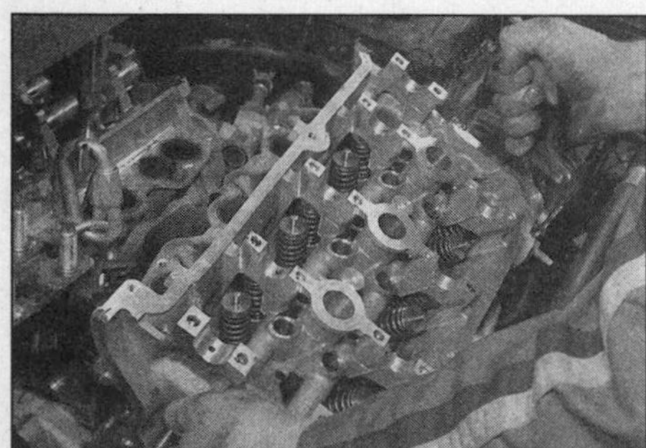

13.25a Lifting the front cylinder head from the cylinder block

13.25b Engine with the front cylinder head and gasket removed

13.31 Locating the front cylinder head gasket on the cylinder block

13.33 Carefully lower the front cylinder head onto the gasket

manifold together with a new gasket and tighten the bolts (see Section 7). Alternatively, the exhaust manifold can be refitted after refitting the cylinder head on the cylinder block.

33 Carefully lower the front cylinder head onto the gasket, making sure that it is aligned with the locating dowels **(see illustration)**.

34 Insert the head bolts together with washers, and initially hand-tighten them.

35 Using a torque wrench, tighten the head bolts to the Stage 1 torque in the sequence shown **(see illustrations)**.

36 Tighten the bolts in the remaining stages given in the Specifications. For the angle-tightening, use an angle disc socket attachment to ensure the correct angle **(see illustration)**.

37 If applicable, refit the exhaust manifold together with a new gasket.

38 Insert the engine oil level dipstick.

39 Refit the elbow to the front cylinder head together with a new gasket, and tighten the bolts. Reconnect the radiator bottom hose and tighten the clip.

40 Refit the coolant connecting pipe together with a new gasket and O-rings, and tighten the bolts. Reconnect the hoses and tighten the clips. Reconnect the wiring to the temperature sensors, then refit the water pump with reference to Chapter 3.

Rear cylinder head

41 Note: *If this procedure is being used during an engine overhaul, make sure that the right-hand engine mounting bracket is bolted in position on the cylinder block before refitting the rear cylinder head, as it will be impossible to fit the bracket between the front and rear cylinder heads with them already fitted* ***(see illustration)***.

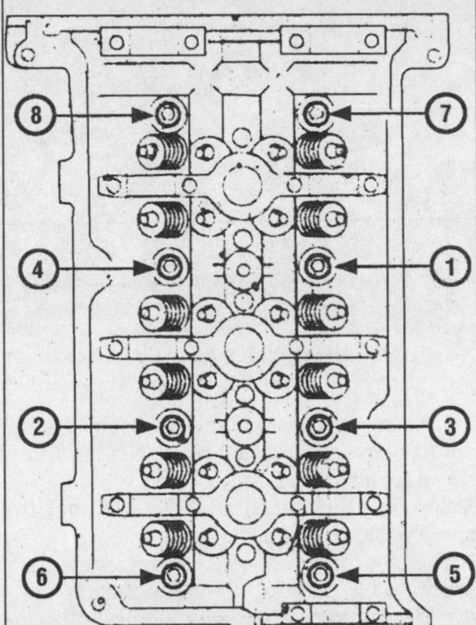

13.35a Tightening sequence for the cylinder head bolts (front shown, rear similar)

42 Locate the rear cylinder head gasket on the cylinder block **(see illustration)**.

43 Clean the surfaces of the exhaust manifold and cylinder head, then refit the manifold together with a new gasket and tighten the bolts (see Section 7). Alternatively, the exhaust manifold can be refitted after refitting the cylinder head on the cylinder block.

44 Carefully lower the rear cylinder head onto the gasket, making sure that it is aligned with the locating dowels.

45 Insert the head bolts together with washers, and initially hand-tighten them.

46 Using a torque wrench, tighten the head bolts to the Stage 1 torque in the sequence shown (see illustration 13.35a).

47 Tighten the bolts in the remaining stages given in the Specifications. For the angle-tightening, use an angle disc socket attachment to ensure the correct angle.

13.35b Tightening the head bolts with a torque wrench

48 If applicable, refit the exhaust manifold together with a new gasket.

49 Refit the coolant connecting pipe together with a new gasket and O-rings, and tighten the bolts. Reconnect the hoses and tighten the clips. Reconnect the wiring to the temperature sensors.

50 Refit the EGR valve tube to the rear exhaust manifold and tighten the union nut.

51 Reconnect the wiring to the EGR valve back pressure transducer.

52 Reconnect the EGR valve back pressure transducer hoses to the EGR valve-to-exhaust manifold tube.

53 Refit the oxygen sensor to the rear exhaust manifold (refer to Chapter 4B).

Front and rear cylinder heads

54 Refit the camshafts, hydraulic tappets and rocker arms as described in Section 12.

56 Support the weight of the engine with the hoist, then remove the right-hand engine mounting in order to refit the timing chains and timing cover.

57 Refit the timing chains and cover as described in Section 10, then refit the engine mounting and remove the hoist.

58 Refit the upper and lower inlet manifolds as described in Section 6.

59 If removed, refit the battery and air cleaner. Reconnect the battery negative (earth) lead (see Chapter 5A). **Note:** *After the battery has been disconnected, the engine management system requires approximately 10 miles of driving to relearn its optimum settings. During this period, the engine may not perform normally.*

13.36 Using an angle disc socket attachment to angle-tighten the cylinder head bolts

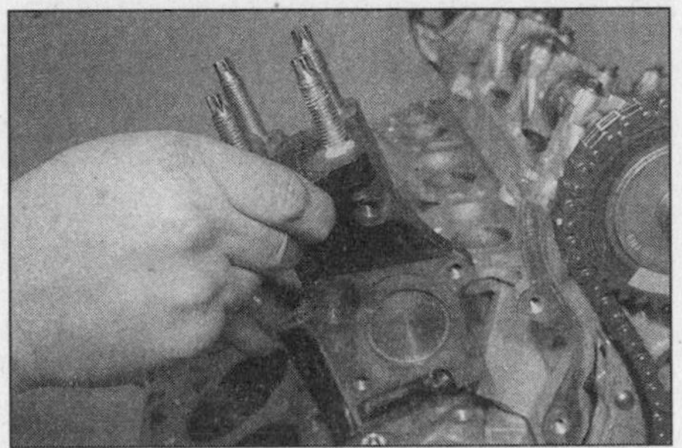

13.41 The right-hand engine mounting bracket must be fitted before fitting the rear cylinder head

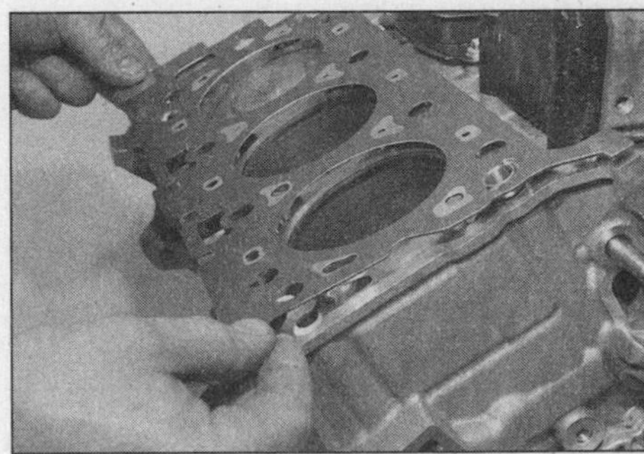

13.42 Locating the rear cylinder head gasket on the cylinder block

60 Refill the engine with oil with reference to Chapter 1.

61 Refill the cooling system with reference to Chapter 1.

62 Start the engine and run to normal operating temperature. Check for coolant and oil leaks. **Note:** *After the battery has been disconnected, the engine management system requires approximately 10 miles of driving to relearn its optimum settings. During this period, the engine may not perform normally.*

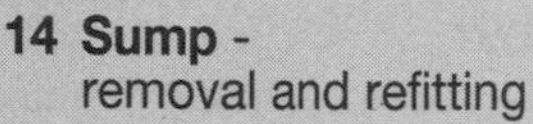

14 Sump - removal and refitting

Removal

1 Apply the handbrake, then jack up the front of the vehicle and support it on axle stands (see "*Jacking and vehicle support*").

2 Drain the engine oil as described in Chapter 1. On completion, clean the drain plug and threaded hole, then refit the plug and tighten to the specified torque. If necessary, renew the sealing washer.

3 Unbolt the plastic cover above the water pump from the front cylinder head.

4 Unscrew the nuts and bolts and remove the exhaust Y-pipe from the bottom of the front downpipes and intermediate exhaust section. Also unbolt the exhaust support bracket from the studs on the rear of the sump **(see illustrations)**.

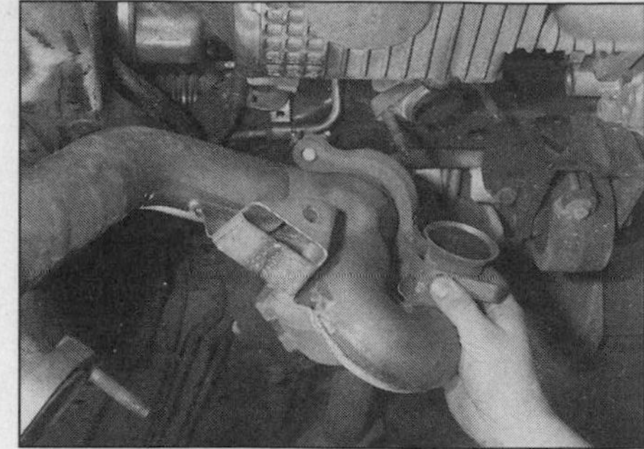

14.4a Removing the exhaust Y-piece from under the sump

14.4b Exhaust support bracket on the rear of the sump

5 Unscrew the nuts and remove the air conditioning compressor heat shield from the sump **(see illustration)**.

14.5 Air conditioning compressor heat shield attached to the sump

6 Unbolt the access cover from the transmission bellhousing.

7 Unscrew and remove the lower flange bolts securing the sump to the transmission. Note the location of the different length bolts (the longer through-bolts are at the front).

8 Attach a suitable hoist to the engine and take its weight.

9 Mark the position of the right-hand engine mounting bracket, then unscrew the nuts and remove the bracket. Note the location of the earth cable on the bracket.

10 Raise the engine slightly to provide room to remove the sump. Do not strain the front and rear engine mounting roll restrictors. Make sure the engine is supported adequately.

11 Note the location of the stud bolts on the sump, then unscrew and remove the bolts, leaving two opposite ones in place. Finally support the sump, and remove the last two bolts. Lower the sump from the engine. Remove the gasket and discard it **(see illustrations)**.

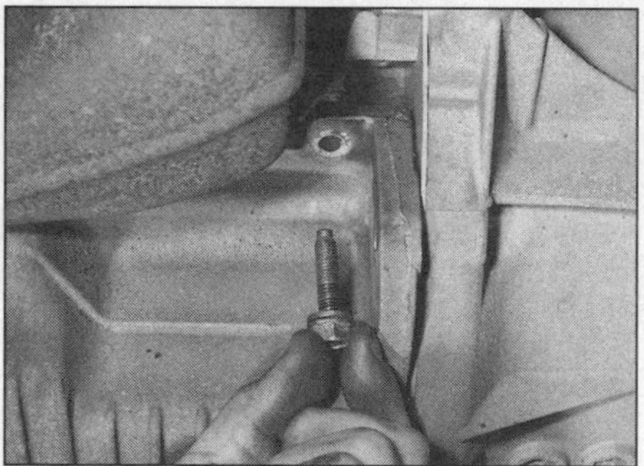

14.11a Unscrew the bolts . . .

14.11b . . . and lower the sump from the cylinder block

Refitting

12 Thoroughly clean the contact surfaces of the sump and cylinder block. Also clean the inside of the sump. If necessary, unbolt and remove the baffle plate **(see illustration)**. After cleaning, refit the baffle plate and tighten the bolts.

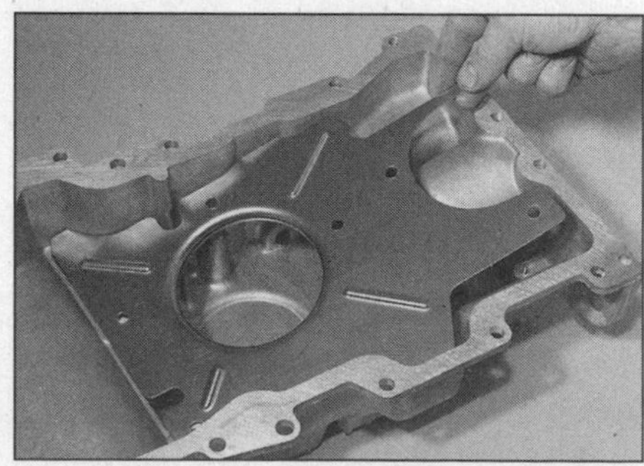

14.12 Removing the baffle plate from the sump

13 Apply a bead of sealant to the joints between the timing cover and cylinder block, on the bottom of the block.

14 Locate a new gasket on the sump **(see illustration)**. Retain it with a little grease if necessary.

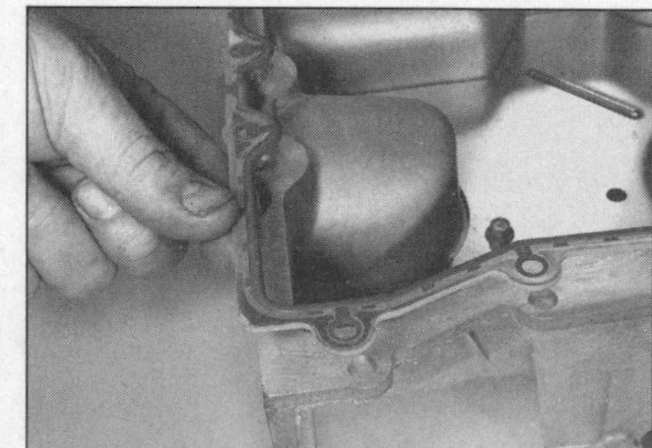

14.14 Locating a new gasket on the sump

15 Raise the sump and gasket onto the bottom of the cylinder block and insert several bolts to hold it in position. Make sure the gasket remains in position. Insert the remaining bolts then hand-tighten all the bolts.

16 Tighten the bolts to the specified torque, starting at the front right-hand corner and working in a clockwise direction around the sump **(see illustration)**.

17 Lower the engine and refit the right-hand engine mounting bracket in its previously noted position. Tighten the nuts to the specified torque. Refit the earth cable and tighten the bolt. Remove the hoist.

18 Insert and tighten the lower flange bolts securing the sump to the transmission.

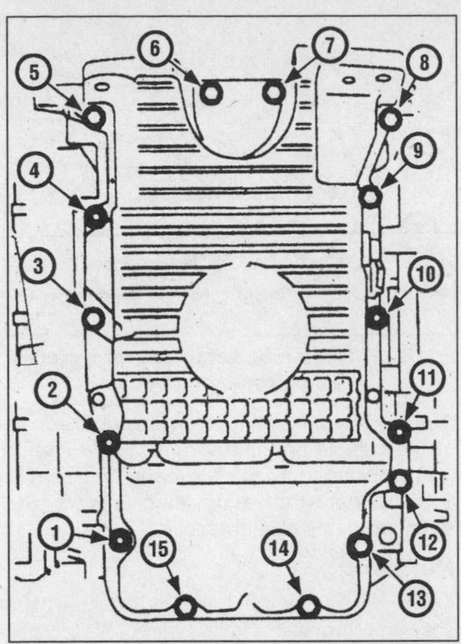

14.16 Tightening sequence for the sump bolts

19 Refit the access cover to the transmission bellhousing and tighten the bolts.
20 Refit the air conditioning compressor heat shield to the sump and tighten the nuts.
21 Refit the exhaust Y-pipe to the bottom of the front downpipes and intermediate exhaust section and tighten the nuts and bolts. Also refit the exhaust support bracket to the rear of the sump and tighten the bolts **(see illustration)**.

14.21 Refitting the exhaust support bracket

22 Refit the plastic cover above the water pump and tighten the bolts.
23 Lower the vehicle to the ground, then fill the engine with fresh oil as described in Chapter 1.

15 Oil pump - removal, inspection and refitting

Removal

1 Remove the timing chains and sprockets as described in Section 10. This procedure includes the removal of the sump as described in Section 14.
2 Unscrew the flange bolts and support nut, and remove the oil pump pick-up tube and filter. Recover the O-ring from the pump.
3 Although not essential at this stage, undo the screws and remove the oil baffle from the crankcase.

15.4a Unscrew the bolts . . .

4 Progressively loosen the mounting bolts one at a time in the reverse sequence to that shown (see illustration 15.11). With all of the bolts removed, withdraw the oil pump from the cylinder block **(see illustrations)**.

Inspection

5 Using a Torx key, undo the screws and remove the cover from the oil pump **(see illustration)**.
6 Note the location of the identification marks on the inner and outer rotors, then remove the rotors. The dot on the outer rotor faces the cover, but the dot on the inner rotor faces the body **(see illustrations)**.
7 Unscrew the plug and remove the pressure relief valve, spring and plunger **(see illustration)**.

15.4b . . . and withdraw the oil pump from the cylinder block

15.5 Removing the cover from the oil pump

15.6a Oil pump and rotors with the cover removed

15.6b Removing the inner rotor . . .

15.6c . . . and outer rotor

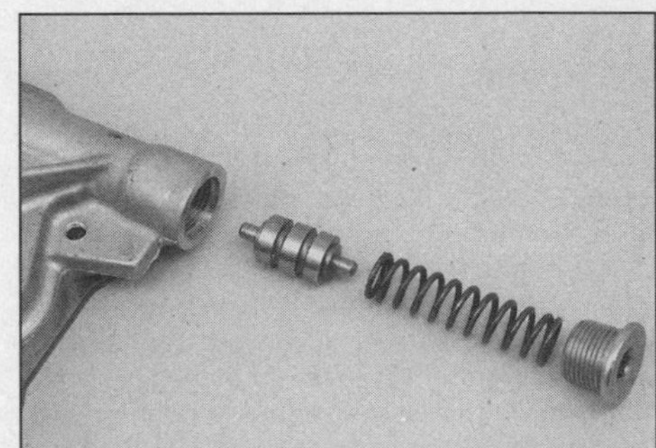
15.7 Pressure relief valve components

15.8 Lubricate the rotors with clean engine oil before fitting the cover

8 Clean all the components and examine them for wear and damage. If the rotors or body are excessively scored or damaged, the complete oil pump must be renewed. If the components are still serviceable, first refit the pressure relief valve components and tighten the plug. Lubricate the rotors with fresh engine oil and insert them in the body making sure that the identification marks are position as noted on removal **(see illustration)**.

9 Refit the pump cover and tighten the screws to the specified torque **(see illustration)**.

10 Before refitting the oil pump, prime it by pouring fresh engine oil into the pick-up tube flange port. Turn the rotors by hand so that the oil enters the internal cavities.

Refitting

11 Position the inner rotor so that it will align with the flat on the crankshaft, then locate the oil pump on the cylinder block. Insert the bolts and tighten to the specified torque in the sequence shown **(see illustration)**.

12 If removed, refit the baffle to the crankcase and tighten the bolts.

13 Locate the oil pump pick-up tube and filter in the oil pump together with a new O-ring, then insert the flange bolts and tighten to the specified torque. Refit and tighten the support nut.

14 Refit the timing chains and sprockets as described in Section 10.

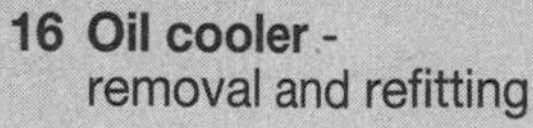

16 Oil cooler - removal and refitting

Removal

1 The oil cooler is located on the front of the cylinder block between the oil filter and cylinder block. First drain the cooling system as described in Chapter 1.

2 Apply the handbrake, then jack up the front of the vehicle and support it on axle stands (see "*Jacking and vehicle support*"). Remove the splash shield from the bottom of the radiator.

3 Loosen the clips and disconnect the coolant hoses from the oil cooler.

4 Position a container beneath the oil filter, then unscrew and remove the oil filter. Keep the oil filter upright to prevent oil spillage.

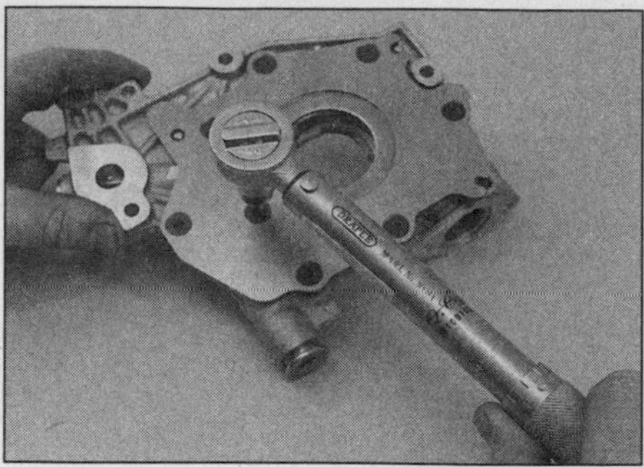

15.9 Tightening the oil pump cover screws

5 Note the position of the oil cooler stubs, then unscrew the nut and withdraw the oil cooler from the mounting stud. Recover the O-ring **(see illustration)**. Be prepared for loss of oil and coolant.

Refitting

6 Wipe clean the cylinder block and contact surfaces of the oil cooler and oil filter.

7 Locate the oil cooler onto the mounting stub together with a new O-ring. Position the coolant stubs as noted on removal, then tighten the nut to the specified torque.

8 Smear some fresh engine oil onto the sealing ring of the oil filter, then screw it onto the stud and tighten firmly using only the hands. Wipe clean the oil filter and cooler.

9 Reconnect the hoses and tighten the clips.

10 Refit the splash shield to the bottom of the radiator, and lower the vehicle to the ground.

11 Refill the cooling system with reference to Chapter 1.

12 Check and if necessary top up the engine oil level with reference to "*Weekly checks*".

17 Oil pressure warning light switch - removal and refitting

Removal

1 The oil pressure warning light switch is located on the front of the cylinder block next to the oil filter.

16.5 Removing the oil cooler and O-ring

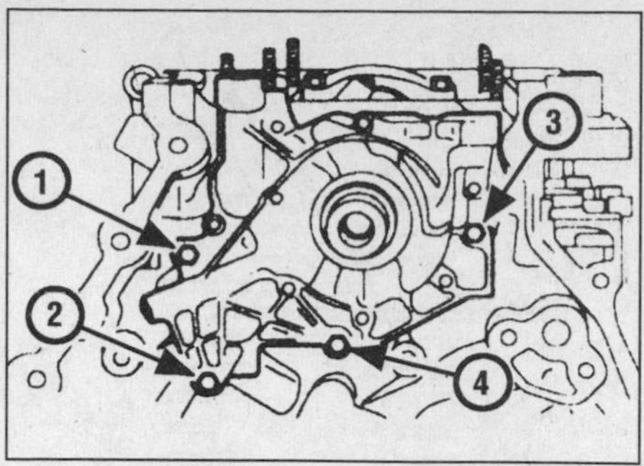

15.11 Tightening sequence for the oil pump mounting bolts

2 Apply the handbrake, then jack up the front of the vehicle and support it on axle stands (see "*Jacking and vehicle support*").

3 Disconnect the wiring, then unscrew the switch from the cylinder block.

Refitting

4 Insert the switch and tighten to the specified torque.

5 Reconnect the wiring.

6 Check and if necessary top up the engine oil level as described in "*Weekly checks*".

18 Crankshaft oil seals - renewal

Right-hand (timing end) oil seal

1 Disconnect the battery negative (earth) lead (see Chapter 5A, Section 1).

2 Apply the handbrake, then jack up the front of the vehicle and support it on axle stands (see "*Jacking and vehicle support*"). Remove the right-hand wheel.

3 Remove the right-hand wheel arch liner with reference to Chapter 11.

4 Using a socket in the square provided, turn the main auxiliary drivebelt tensioner clockwise and slip the belt from the pulleys. Carefully release the tensioner.

5 The engine must now be held stationary while the crankshaft pulley bolt is loosened. To do this on manual transmission models, have an assistant engage 4th gear and depress the footbrake pedal. On automatic transmission models, unbolt the bottom cover from the transmission bellhousing and have an assistant engage a wide-bladed screwdriver with the starter ring gear. Alternatively, a holding tool can be fabricated out of flat metal bar and bolted to the crankshaft pulley to hold it stationary.

6 With the bolt loosened, unscrew and remove it and remove the washer. When fitted, the bolt is torqued-to-yield, and a new bolt must therefore be used on refitting.

7 Using a suitable puller, draw the crankshaft pulley from the end of the crankshaft. If the Woodruff key is loose, remove it from the groove in the crankshaft and keep it in a safe place.

8 Using a screwdriver, prise the old oil seal from the timing cover. Take care not to damage the surface of the timing cover and crankshaft. If the oil seal is tight, carefully drill two holes diagonally opposite each other in the oil seal, then insert self-tapping screws and use a pair of pliers to pull out the oil seal.
9 Wipe clean the seating in the timing cover and the nose of the crankshaft.
10 Smear clean engine oil on the outer periphery and sealing lips of the new oil seal, then start it into the timing cover by pressing it in squarely. Using a large socket or metal tubing, drive in the oil seal until flush with the outer surface of the timing cover. Make sure the oil seal remains square as it is being inserted. Wipe off any excess oil.
11 Apply suitable sealer to the key groove on the inside of the pulley. If removed, locate the Woodruff key in the crankshaft groove, making sure that it is parallel with the surface of the crankshaft.
12 Locate the pulley on the crankshaft and engage it with the key. Use the old pulley bolt and washer to draw the pulley fully onto the crankshaft. Unscrew the old bolt and discard it.
13 Insert the new bolt together with the washer, and tighten it to the specified torque while holding the crankshaft stationary using the method described in paragraph 5. Note that the bolt is tightened in four stages as described in the Specifications.
14 Remove the holding tool, and on automatic transmission models refit the cover to the transmission bellhousing.
15 Refit the main auxiliary drivebelt to the right-hand end of the engine with reference to Chapter 1.
16 Refit the right-hand wheel arch liner with reference to Chapter 11.
17 Refit the right-hand wheel and lower the car to the ground.

Left-hand (transmission end) oil seal

18 Remove the transmission as described in Chapter 7A or 7B.
19 Remove the flywheel or driveplate (as applicable) as described in Section 19.
20 Remove the adapter plate from the engine.
21 Using a screwdriver, prise the old oil seal from the cylinder block. Take care not to damage the surface of the oil seal seating and crankshaft. If the oil seal is tight, carefully drill two holes diagonally opposite each other in the oil seal, then insert self-tapping screws and use a pair of pliers to pull out the oil seal.
22 Wipe clean the seating in the block and the crankshaft.
23 Smear clean engine oil on the outer periphery and sealing lips of the new oil seal, then start it into the cylinder block by pressing it in squarely. Using a large socket or metal tubing, drive in the oil seal until flush with the outer surface of the cylinder block. Make sure the oil seal remains square as it is being inserted. Wipe off any excess oil.

19.4 Remove the flywheel bolts . . .

19.5 . . . then lift the flywheel from the crankshaft

24 Locate the adapter plate on the dowels in the cylinder block.
25 Refit the flywheel or driveplate (as applicable) with reference to Section 19.
26 Refit the transmission as described in Chapter 7A or 7B.

19 Flywheel/driveplate - removal, inspection and refitting

Removal

1 Remove the transmission as described in Chapter 7A or 7B. Now is a good time to check components such as oil seals and renew them if necessary.
2 On manual transmission models, remove the clutch as described in Chapter 6. Now is a good time to check or renew the clutch components.
3 Make alignment marks on the flywheel/driveplate and crankshaft as an aid to refitting.
4 Prevent the flywheel/driveplate from turning by locking the ring gear teeth, or by bolting a strap between the flywheel/driveplate and the cylinder block/crankcase. Unscrew and remove the bolts **(see illustration)**.
5 Withdraw the flywheel/driveplate from the crankshaft, taking care not to drop it - it is very heavy **(see illustration)**.
6 If necessary, remove the adapter plate from the dowels on the cylinder block **(see illustration)**.

Inspection

7 Clean the flywheel/driveplate to remove grease and oil. Inspect the surface for cracks, rivet grooves, burned areas and score marks. Light scoring can be removed with emery cloth. Check for cracked and broken ring gear teeth. Lay the flywheel/driveplate on a flat surface, and use a straight edge to check for warpage.
8 Clean and inspect the mating surfaces of the flywheel/driveplate and the crankshaft. If the crankshaft left-hand oil seal is leaking, renew it (see Section 18) before refitting the flywheel/driveplate.
9 While the flywheel/driveplate is removed, clean carefully its inner face. Thoroughly clean the threaded bolt holes in the crankshaft, and also clean the threads of the bolts - this is important, since if old sealer remains in the threads, the bolts will settle over a period and will not retain their correct torque wrench settings.

Refitting

10 Locate the adapter plate on the cylinder block dowels.
11 Refit the flywheel/driveplate on the crankshaft and align the previously made marks (the bolt holes are arranged so that the flywheel/driveplate will only fit in one position). Apply suitable sealer to the threads of the bolts then insert them and progressively tighten to the specified torque while holding the flywheel/driveplate stationary using the method described in paragraph 4.
12 On manual transmission models, refit the clutch with reference to Chapter 6.
13 Refit the transmission with reference to Chapter 7A or 7B (as applicable).

2B

20 Engine/transmission mountings - inspection and renewal

1 The engine/transmission mountings seldom require attention, but broken or deteriorated mountings should be renewed immediately, otherwise the added strain placed on the transmission components may cause damage or wear.

19.6 Removing the adapter plate

20.10a Unscrew the right-hand engine mounting bracket nuts and bolts . . .

20.10b . . . noting the location of the earth cable

20.10c Removing the right-hand engine mounting brackets

2 While separate mountings may be removed and refitted individually, if more than one is disturbed at a time - such as if the engine/transmission unit is removed - they must be reassembled and tightened in the sequence described in Chapter 2C for engine refitting.

Inspection

3 For access to the right-hand engine mounting, undo the screws securing the coolant expansion tank to the right-hand inner wing panel and temporarily position the tank to one side. For access to the left-hand engine mounting, remove the battery (Chapter 5A) and air cleaner (Chapter 4A). For access to the front and rear engine roll restrictors, apply the handbrake, then jack up the front of the vehicle and support it on axle stands (see "*Jacking and vehicle support*"). The use of a mirror will help to view the engine mounting from all angles.

4 Check the mounting rubber to see if it is cracked, hardened or separated from the metal at any point; renew the mounting if any such damage or deterioration is evident.

5 Check that all the mounting nuts/bolts are securely tightened; use a torque wrench to check if possible.

6 Using a large screwdriver or lever, check for wear in the mounting by carefully levering against it to check for free play; where this is not possible, enlist the aid of an assistant to move the engine/transmission unit back and forth, or from side-to-side, while you watch the mounting. While some free play is to be expected even from new components, excessive wear should be obvious. If excessive free play is found, check first that the nuts/bolts are correctly tightened, then renew any worn components as described below.

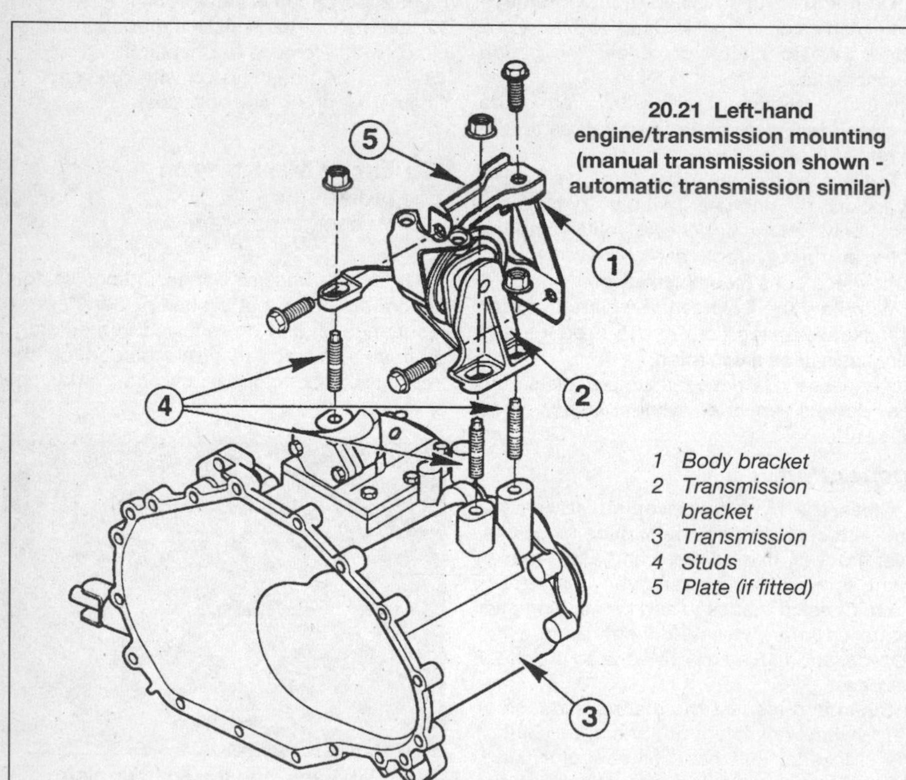

20.21 Left-hand engine/transmission mounting (manual transmission shown - automatic transmission similar)

1 *Body bracket*
2 *Transmission bracket*
3 *Transmission*
4 *Studs*
5 *Plate (if fitted)*

Renewal

Right-hand engine mounting

7 Unbolt the water pump pulley cover from the top of the engine.

8 Undo the screws and position the coolant expansion tank to one side.

9 Support the weight of the engine using a suitable hoist. Alternatively, if only the right-hand engine mounting is to be renewed, it is acceptable to carefully support the weight of the engine using a trolley jack and piece of wood beneath the engine sump.

10 Mark the position of the engine mounting bracket for correct refitting, then unscrew the nuts and remove the bracket. Note the position of the earth cable **(see illustrations)**. **Note:** *The nuts are self-locking and must be renewed.*

11 Unbolt the mounting from the body panel.

12 Fit the new mounting to the body panel and tighten the bolts to the specified torque.

13 Locate the bracket on the mounting and engine and position it as noted before removal. Fit the new nuts and tighten to the specified torque. Make sure the earth cable is refitted in its correct position.

14 Lower the engine and remove the hoist.

15 Refit the coolant expansion tank and tighten the screws.

16 Refit the water pump pulley cover to the top of the engine.

Left-hand engine mounting

17 Remove the battery as described in Chapter 5A.

18 Remove the air filter and housing as described in Chapter 4A.

19 Unbolt the water pump pulley cover from the top of the engine.

20 Support the weight of the transmission using a suitable hoist. Alternatively, if only the left-hand engine mounting is to be renewed, it is acceptable to carefully support the weight of the transmission using a trolley jack and piece of wood.

21 Mark the position of the engine mounting bracket for correct refitting, then unscrew the nuts securing the mounting to the studs on the transmission **(see illustration)**. **Note:** *The nuts are self-locking and must be renewed.*

20.22 Left-hand engine mounting body bracket bolt

22 Unscrew the bolts and remove the mounting from the body panel **(see illustration)**.

23 Fit the new mounting to the body panel and tighten the bolts to the specified torque.

24 Locate the bracket on the mounting and transmission and position it as noted before removal. Fit the new nuts and tighten to the specified torque.

25 Lower the transmission and remove the hoist.

26 Refit the water pump pulley cover to the top of the engine.

27 Refit the air filter and housing with reference to Chapter 4A.

28 Refit the battery with reference to Chapter 5A. **Note:** *After the battery has been disconnected, the engine management system requires approximately 10 miles of driving to relearn its optimum settings. During this period, the engine may not perform normally.*

Front roll restrictor

29 Apply the handbrake, then jack up the front of the vehicle and support it on axle stands (see "*Jacking and vehicle support*").

30 Unscrew the bolts securing the front roll restrictor to the subframe, and also unscrew the centre bolt. Remove the roll restrictor **(see illustration)**.

31 If necessary, unbolt the bracket from the transmission.

32 Refit the bracket to the transmission and tighten the bolts to the specified torque.

33 Locate the new front roll restrictor in the bracket and insert the centre bolt.

34 Insert the bolts securing the front roll restrictor to the subframe, and tighten to the specified torque.

35 Tighten the centre bolt to the specified torque.

36 Lower the vehicle to the ground.

Rear roll restrictor

37 Apply the handbrake, then jack up the front of the vehicle and support it on axle stands (see "*Jacking and vehicle support*").

38 Unscrew the nuts/bolts and centre bolt, and remove the rear roll restrictor from its bracket **(see illustrations)**. If necessary, use a trolley jack and block of wood to slightly raise the transmission. Note on certain automatic transmission models, an additional rubber damper is fitted in a bracket below the subframe.

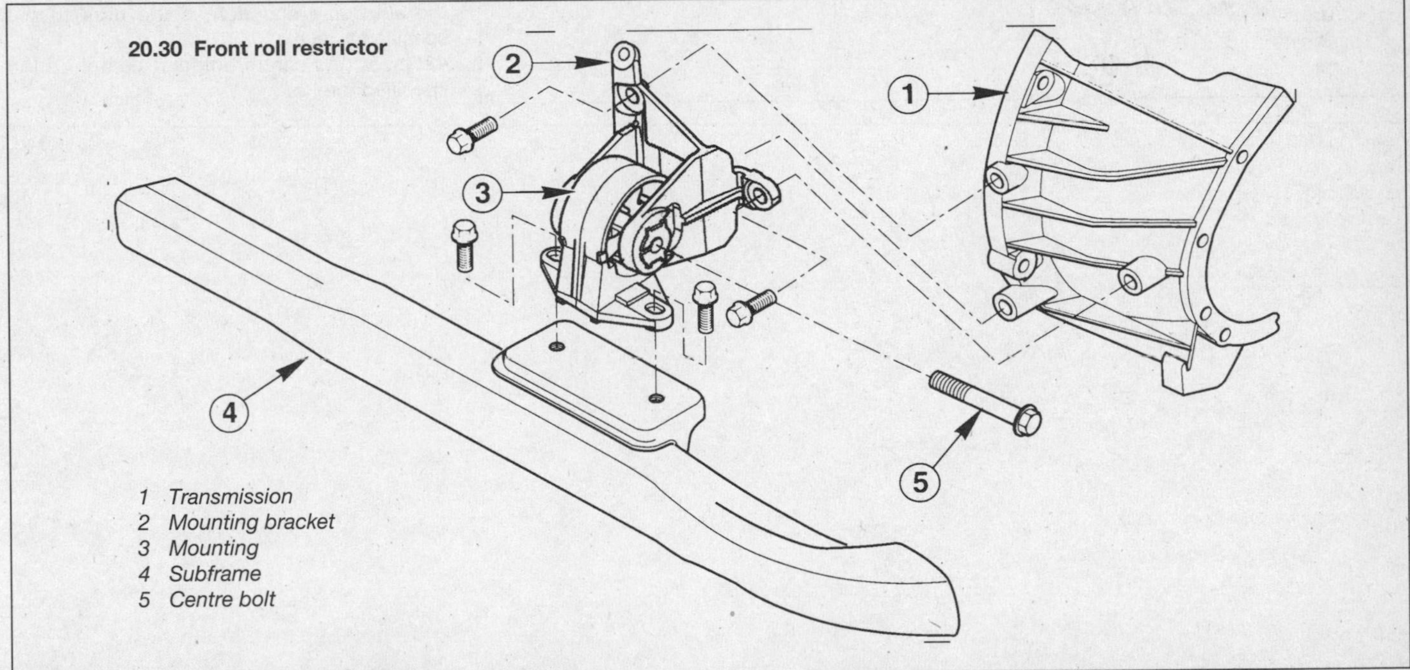

20.30 Front roll restrictor

20.38a Rear roll restrictor viewed from under the car

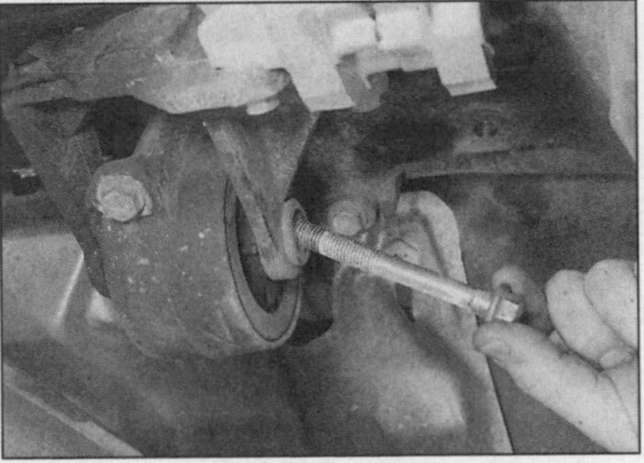

20.38b Removing the rear roll restrictor centre bolt

20.38c Removing the rear roll restrictor

2B

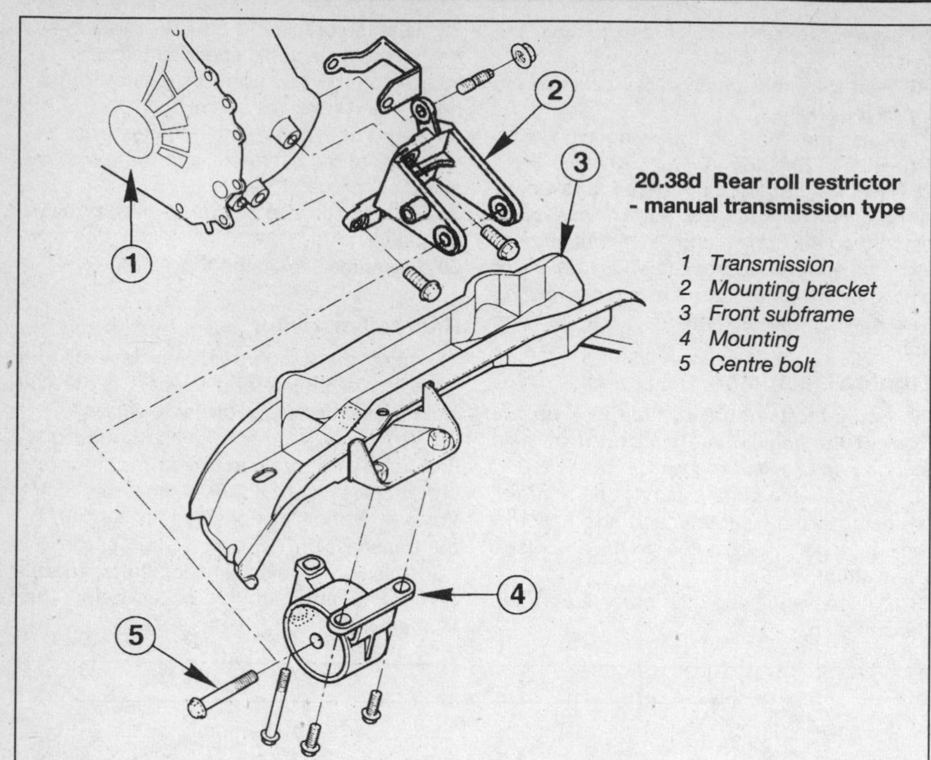

20.38d Rear roll restrictor - manual transmission type

1 *Transmission*
2 *Mounting bracket*
3 *Front subframe*
4 *Mounting*
5 *Centre bolt*

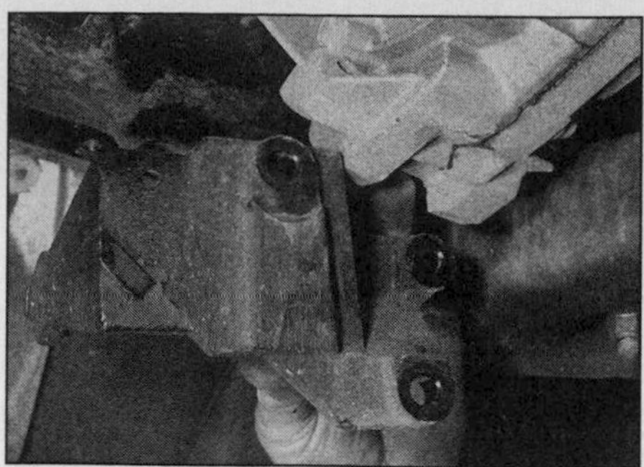

20.39 Removing the rear roll restrictor bracket from the transmission

39 If necessary, unbolt the bracket from the transmission **(see illustration)**.

40 Refit the bracket to the transmission and tighten the bolts to the specified torque.

41 Locate the rear roll restrictor in its bracket and tighten the nuts/bolts to the specified torque. On automatic transmission models, locate a new rubber damper to the bracket on the subframe and tighten the nuts to the specified torque.

42 Insert the centre bolt and tighten to the specified torque.

Chapter 2 Part C: Engine removal and overhaul procedures

Contents

Degrees of difficulty

Easy, suitable for novice with little experience 

Fairly easy, suitable for beginner with some experience 

Fairly difficult, suitable for competent DIY mechanic

Difficult, suitable for experienced DIY mechanic 

Very difficult, suitable for expert DIY or professional

Specifications

2C

4-cylinder engines

Cylinder head

Maximum permissible gasket surface distortion	0.10 mm
Valve guide bore	6.060 to 6.091 mm
Valve seat included angle	90°
Valve seat width	1.4 to 1.7 mm

Valves - general

	Inlet	Exhaust
Valve lift	7.500 to 7.685 mm	7.610 to 7.765 mm
Valve length	96.870 to 97.330 mm	96.470 to 96.930 mm
Valve head diameter:		
1.6 litre engine	26.0 mm	24.5 mm
1.8 and 2.0 litre engines	32.0 mm	28.0 mm
Valve stem diameter	6.028 to 6.043 mm	6.010 to 6.025 mm
Valve stem-to-guide clearance:		
Except 2.0 litre (5/1998-on)	0.017 to 0.064 mm	0.035 to 0.081 mm
2.0 litre (5/1998-on)	0.017 to 0.064 mm	0.017 to 0.064 mm

Cylinder block

Cylinder bore diameter - 1.6 litre engine:	
Class 1	76.000 to 76.010 mm
Class 2	76.010 to 76.020 mm
Class 3	76.020 to 76.030 mm
Cylinder bore diameter - 1.8 litre engine:	
Class 1	80.600 to 80.610 mm
Class 2	80.610 to 80.620 mm
Class 3	80.620 to 80.630 mm
Cylinder bore diameter - 2.0 litre engine:	
Class 1	84.800 to 84.810 mm
Class 2	84.810 to 84.820 mm
Class 3	84.820 to 84.830 mm

Pistons and piston rings

Piston diameter - 1.6 litre engine:	
Class 1	75.975 to 75.985 mm
Class 2	75.985 to 75.995 mm
Class 3	75.995 to 76.005 mm
Piston diameter - 1.8 litre engine:	
Class 1	80.570 to 80.580 mm
Class 2	80.580 to 80.590 mm
Class 3	80.590 to 80.600 mm
Piston diameter - 2.0 litre engine (pre 5/1998):	
Class 1	84.770 to 84.780 mm
Class 2	84.780 to 84.790 mm
Class 3	84.790 to 84.800 mm
Piston diameter - 2.0 litre engine (5/1998-on):	
Class 1	84.750 to 84.760 mm
Class 2	84.760 to 84.770 mm
Class 3	84.770 to 84.780 mm
Oversizes - all engines	None available
Piston-to-cylinder bore clearance	No information available at time of writing
Piston ring end gaps - installed:	
Top compression ring - 1.6 and 1.8 litre engines	0.30 to 0.50 mm
Top compression ring - 2.0 litre engine	0.26 to 0.50 mm
Second compression ring	0.30 to 0.50 mm
Oil control ring - 1.6 litre engine	0.25 to 1.00 mm
Oil control ring - 1.8 litre engine	0.38 to 1.14 mm
Oil control ring - 2.0 litre engine	0.40 to 1.40 mm

Gudgeon pin

Diameter:	
White colour code/piston crown marked "A"	20.622 to 20.625 mm
Red colour code/piston crown marked "B"	20.625 to 20.628 mm
Blue colour code/piston crown marked "C"	20.628 to 20.631 mm
Clearance in piston:	
Except 2.0 litre 5/1998-on	0.010 to 0.016 mm
2.0 litre 5/1998-on	0.016 to 0.049 mm
Connecting rod small-end eye internal diameter	20.589 to 20.609 mm
Interference fit in connecting rod	0.011 to 0.042 mm

Crankshaft and bearings

Big-end bearing shell standard inside diameter - installed	46.926 to 46.960 mm
Big-end bearing shell undersizes available	0.02 mm, 0.25 mm
Crankpin (big-end) bearing journal standard diameter	46.890 to 46.910 mm
Crankpin (big-end) bearing journal-to-shell running clearance	0.016 to 0.070 mm
Crankshaft endfloat	0.090 to 0.310 mm
Main bearing journal standard diameter	57.980 to 58.000 mm
Main bearing journal-to-shell running clearance	0.011 to 0.058 mm
Main bearing shell standard inside diameter - installed	58.011 to 58.038 mm
Main bearing shell undersizes available	0.02 mm, 0.25 mm

Torque wrench settings

Refer to Chapter 2A Specifications

V6 engine

Cylinder head

Hydraulic tappet bore diameter	16.018 to 16.057 mm
Hydraulic tappet clearance in bore	0.018 0.069 mm
Hydraulic tappet diameter	15.988 to 16.000 mm
Maximum permissible gasket surface distortion	0.10 mm
Valve seat angle	45.5°
Valve seat included angle	90°
Valve seat width, inlet	1.1 to 1.4 mm
Valve seat width, exhaust	1.4 to 1.7 mm

Valves

	Inlet	Exhaust
Valve head diameter	32.0 mm	26.0 mm
Valve stem diameter	5.975 to 5.995 mm	5.950 to 5.970 mm
Valve stem-to-guide clearance	0.020 to 0.069 mm	0.045 to 0.094 mm
Valve spring free length	46.8 mm	46.8 mm

Cylinder block

Number of main bearings	4
Cylinder bore diameter:	
Class 1	82.400 to 82.410 mm
Class 2	82.410 to 82.420 mm
Class 3	82.420 to 82.430 mm

Pistons and piston rings

Piston diameter:	
Class 1:	
Coated	82.390 to 82.410 mm
Uncoated	82.370 to 82.380 mm
Class 2:	
Coated	82.398 to 82.422 mm
Uncoated	82.378 to 82392 mm
Class 3:	
Coated	82.410 to 82.430 mm
Uncoated	82.390 to 82.400 mm
Oversizes	None available
Piston protrusion at TDC	0.415 to 0.115 mm
Piston clearance in bore:	
Coated	0.012 to 0.022 mm
Uncoated	0.018 to 0.042 mm
Piston ring clearance in grooves:	
Top compression ring	0.04 to 0.75 mm
Second compression ring	0.04 to 0.85 mm
Oil control ring	Snug fit
Piston ring end gaps - installed:	
Top compression ring	0.10 to 0.25 mm
Second compression ring	0.27 to 0.42 mm
Oil control ring	0.15 to 0.65 mm

Gudgeon pin

Connecting rod endfloat	0.10 to 0.30 mm
Gudgeon pin bore diameter	21.008 to 21.012 mm
Gudgeon pin clearance in piston	0.005 to 0.001 mm
Gudgeon pin clearance in connecting rod	0.004 to 0.020 mm

Crankshaft and bearings

Crankpin (big-end) bearing journal standard diameter	49.970 to 49.990 mm
Crankpin (big-end) bearing running clearance	0.028 to 0.066 mm
Crankshaft endfloat	0.110 to 0.232 mm
Main bearing journal standard diameter	62.968 to 62.992 mm
Main bearing journal-to-shell running clearance	0.025 to 0.045 mm
Main bearing shell undersizes available	62.718 to 62.742 mm

Camshafts

Camshaft endfloat	0.025 to 0.165 mm
Camshaft bearing running clearance	0.0125 to 0.038 mm

Torque wrench settings

Refer to Chapter 2B Specifications

2C

1 General information and precautions

How to use this Chapter

This Part of Chapter 2 is devoted to engine/transmission removal and refitting, to those repair procedures requiring the removal of the engine/transmission from the vehicle, and to the overhaul of engine components. It includes only the Specifications relevant to those procedures. Refer to Part A for additional Specifications and for all torque wrench settings.

General information

The information ranges from advice concerning preparation for an overhaul and the purchase of replacement parts, to detailed step-by-step procedures covering removal and installation of internal engine components and the inspection of parts.

The following Sections have been written based on the assumption that the engine has been removed from the vehicle. For information concerning in-vehicle engine repair, as well as removal and installation of the external components necessary for the overhaul, see Part A or Part B of this Chapter.

When overhauling the engine, it is essential to establish first exactly what replacement parts are available. At the time of writing, very few under- or oversized components are available for engine reconditioning. In many cases, it would appear that the easiest and most economically-sensible course of action is to replace a worn or damaged engine with an exchange unit.

Precautions

Caution: Although it is possible to remove the pistons and crankshaft on the V6 engine, at the time of writing it is not possible to obtain genuine Ford replacement parts. In addition, Ford say that the cylinder bores cannot be rebored

or honed, the crankshaft cannot be reground, the main bearings cannot be renewed, and the lower crankcase cannot be reused once removed.

2 Engine overhaul - general information

It's not always easy to determine when, or if, an engine should be completely overhauled, as a number of factors must be considered.

High mileage is not necessarily an indication that an overhaul is needed, while low mileage doesn't preclude the need for an overhaul. Frequency of servicing is probably the most important consideration. An engine that's had regular and frequent oil and filter changes, as well as other required maintenance, will most likely give many thousands of miles of reliable service. Conversely, a neglected engine may require an overhaul very early in its life.

Excessive oil consumption is an indication that piston rings, valve seals and/or valve guides are in need of attention. Make sure that oil leaks aren't responsible before deciding that the rings and/or guides are worn. Perform a cylinder compression check (Part A or B of this Chapter) to determine the extent of the work required.

Loss of power, rough running, knocking or metallic engine noises, excessive valve train noise and high fuel consumption rates may also point to the need for an overhaul, especially if they're all present at the same time. If a full service doesn't remedy the situation, major mechanical work is the only solution.

An engine overhaul involves restoring all internal parts to the specification of a new engine. **Note:** *Always check first what replacement parts are available before planning any overhaul operation; refer to Section 1 of this Part. Ford dealers, or a good engine reconditioning specialist/automotive parts supplier may be able to suggest alternatives which will enable you to overcome the lack of replacement parts.*

During an overhaul, it is usual to renew the piston rings, and to rebore and/or hone the cylinder bores; where the rebore is done by an automotive machine shop, new oversize pistons and rings will also be installed - all these operations, of course, assume the availability of suitable replacement parts. The main and big-end bearings are generally renewed and, if necessary, the crankshaft may be reground to restore the journals. **Note:** *For V6 engines, the manufacturers state that the cylinder bores cannot be rebored or honed, the crankshaft cannot be reground, the lower crankcase cannot be re-used once removed, and the main bearings cannot be renewed.*

Generally, the valves are serviced as well during an overhaul, since they're usually in less-than-perfect condition at this point. While the engine is being overhauled, other components, such as the starter and alternator, can be renewed as well, or rebuilt, if the necessary parts can be found. The end result should be an as-new engine that will give many trouble-free miles. **Note:** *Critical cooling system components such as the hoses, drivebelt, thermostat and water pump MUST be replaced with new parts when an engine is overhauled. The radiator should be checked carefully, to ensure that it isn't clogged or leaking (see Chapter 3). Also, as a general rule, the oil pump should be renewed when an engine is rebuilt.*

Before beginning the engine overhaul, read through the entire procedure to familiarise yourself with the scope and requirements of the job. Overhauling an engine isn't difficult, but it is time-consuming. Plan on the vehicle being off the road for a minimum of two weeks, especially if parts must be taken to an automotive machine shop for repair or reconditioning. Check on availability of parts, and make sure that any necessary special tools and equipment are obtained in advance. Most work can be done with typical hand tools, although a number of precision measuring tools are required, for inspecting parts to determine if they must be replaced. Often, an automotive machine shop will handle the inspection of parts, and will offer advice concerning reconditioning and replacement. **Note:** *Always wait until the engine has been completely dismantled, and all components, especially the cylinder block/crankcase, have been inspected, before deciding what service and repair operations must be performed by an automotive machine shop. Since the block's condition will be the major factor to consider when determining whether to overhaul the original engine or buy a rebuilt one, never purchase parts or have machine work done on other components until the cylinder block/crankcase has been thoroughly inspected.* As a general rule, time is the primary cost of an overhaul, so it doesn't pay to install worn or sub-standard parts.

As a final note, to ensure maximum life and minimum trouble from a rebuilt engine, everything must be assembled with care, in a spotlessly-clean environment.

3 Engine/transmission removal - methods and precautions

If you've decided that an engine must be removed for overhaul or major repair work, several preliminary steps should be taken.

Locating a suitable place to work is extremely important. Adequate work space, along with storage space for the vehicle, will be needed. If a workshop or garage isn't available, at the very least, a flat, level, clean work surface made of concrete or asphalt is required.

Cleaning the engine compartment and engine/transmission before beginning the removal procedure will help keep tools clean and organised.

The engine can only be withdrawn by removing it complete with the transmission; the vehicle's body must be raised and supported securely, sufficiently high that the engine/transmission can be unbolted as a single unit and lowered to the ground; the engine/transmission unit can then be withdrawn from under the vehicle and separated. An engine hoist or A-frame will therefore be necessary. Make sure the equipment is rated in excess of the combined weight of the engine and transmission. Safety is of primary Importance, considering the potential hazards involved in removing the engine/transmission from the vehicle.

If this is the first time you have removed an engine, a helper should ideally be available. Advice and aid from someone more experienced would also be helpful. There are many instances when one person cannot simultaneously perform all of the operations required when removing the engine/transmission from the vehicle.

Plan the operation ahead of time. Arrange for, or obtain, all of the tools and equipment you'll need prior to beginning the job. Some of the equipment necessary to perform engine/transmission removal and installation safely and with relative ease, and which may have to be hired or borrowed, includes (in addition to the engine hoist) a heavy-duty trolley jack, a strong pair of axle stands, some wooden blocks, and an engine dolly (a low, wheeled platform capable of taking the weight of the engine/transmission, so that it can be moved easily when on the ground). A complete set of spanners and sockets (as described in the front of this manual) will obviously be needed, together with plenty of rags and cleaning solvent for mopping-up spilled oil, coolant and fuel. If the hoist is to be hired, make sure that you arrange for it in advance, and perform all of the operations possible without it beforehand. This will save you money and time.

Plan for the vehicle to be out of use for quite a while. A machine shop will be required to perform some of the work which the do-it-yourselfer can't accomplish without special equipment. These establishments often have a busy schedule, so it would be a good idea to consult them before removing the engine, to accurately estimate the amount of time required to rebuild or repair components that may need work.

Always be extremely careful when removing and installing the engine/transmission. Serious injury can result from careless actions. By planning ahead and taking your time, the job (although a major task) can be accomplished successfully.

4.7 Note colour-coding of unions when disconnecting fuel feed and return lines

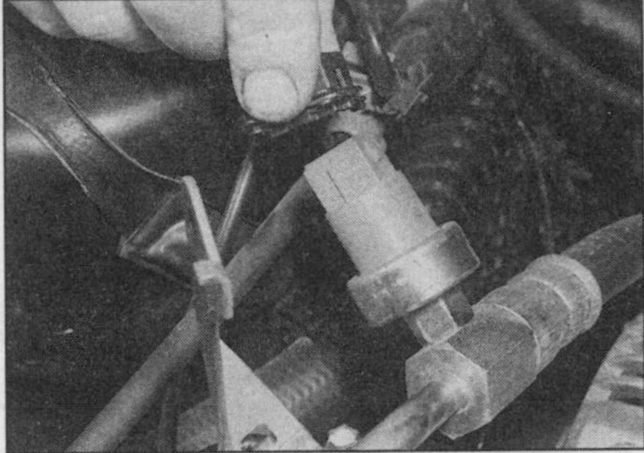

4.9a Unplug the power steering pressure switch electrical connector . . .

4.9b . . . unbolt the power steering high-pressure pipe . . .

4 Engine/transmission (4-cylinder models) - removal, separation and refitting

Warning: Petrol is extremely flammable, so take extra precautions when disconnecting any part of the fuel system. Don't smoke, or allow naked flames or bare light bulbs in or near the work area, and don't work in a garage where a natural gas appliance (such as a clothes dryer or water heater) is installed. If you spill petrol on your skin, rinse it off immediately. Have a fire extinguisher rated for petrol fires handy, and know how to use it.

Note: *Read through the entire Section, as well as reading the advice in the preceding Section, before beginning this procedure. The engine and transmission are removed as a unit, lowered to the ground and removed from underneath, then separated outside the vehicle.*

4-cylinder engine (pre 05/1998)

Removal

1 Park the vehicle on firm, level ground, apply the handbrake firmly, and slacken the nuts securing both front roadwheels.

2 Relieve the fuel system pressure (see Chapter 4A).

3 Disconnect the battery negative (earth) lead (see Chapter 5A, Section 1). For better access, the battery may be removed completely (see Chapter 5A).

4 Place protective covers on the wings and engine compartment front crossmember, then remove the bonnet (see Chapter 11).

5 Whenever you disconnect any vacuum lines, coolant and emissions hoses, wiring loom connectors, earth straps and fuel lines as part of the following procedure, always label them clearly, so that they can be correctly reassembled.

HAYNES HiNT ***Whenever any wiring is disconnected, mark or label it as shown, to ensure correct reconnection . . . vacuum hoses and pipes should be similarly marked.***

Masking tape and/or a touch-up paint applicator work well for marking items. Take instant photos, or sketch the locations of components and brackets.

6 Unplug the two electrical connectors, disconnect the vacuum hose (where fitted) and disconnect the crankcase breather hose from the cylinder head cover, then remove the complete air cleaner assembly, with the air mass meter, the resonator and the plenum chamber (see Chapter 4A).

7 Equalise the pressure in the fuel tank by removing the filler cap, then undo the fuel feed and return lines connecting the engine to the chassis (see Chapter 4A). Plug or cap all open fittings **(see illustration)**.

8 Disconnect the accelerator cable from the throttle linkage as described in Chapter 4A - where fitted, also disconnect the cruise control actuator cable (see Chapter 12). Secure the cable(s) clear of the engine/transmission.

9 Releasing its wire clip, unplug the power steering pressure switch electrical connector, then unbolt the power steering high-pressure pipe and the earth lead from the cylinder head rear support plate/engine lifting eye **(see illustrations)**.

10 Marking or labelling all components as they are disconnected (see paragraph 5 above), disconnect the vacuum hoses as follows:

a) One from the rear of the throttle housing (only the one hose - there is no need to disconnect the second hose running to the fuel pressure regulator) ***(see illustration)****.*

b) One from the union on the inlet manifold's left-hand end ***(see illustration)****.*

c) The braking system vacuum servo unit hose - from the inlet manifold (see Chapter 9 for details).

d) Also disconnect the vacuum hoses from the Exhaust Gas Recirculation system components - one from the EGR valve, two from the EGR pipe (note that these last two are of different sizes, as are their pipe stubs, so that they can only be connected the correct way round).

e) While you are there, trace the vacuum line from the pulse-air filter housing over the top of the transmission, and disconnect it by pulling the plastic pipe out of the

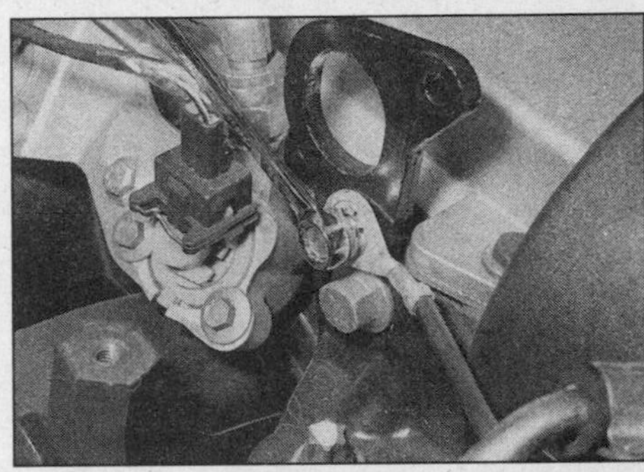

4.9c . . . and the earth lead from the cylinder head rear support plate/engine lifting eye

4.10a Disconnect vacuum hose shown from rear of throttle housing . . .

4.10b . . . vacuum hose (arrowed) from union on left-hand end on inlet manifold . . .

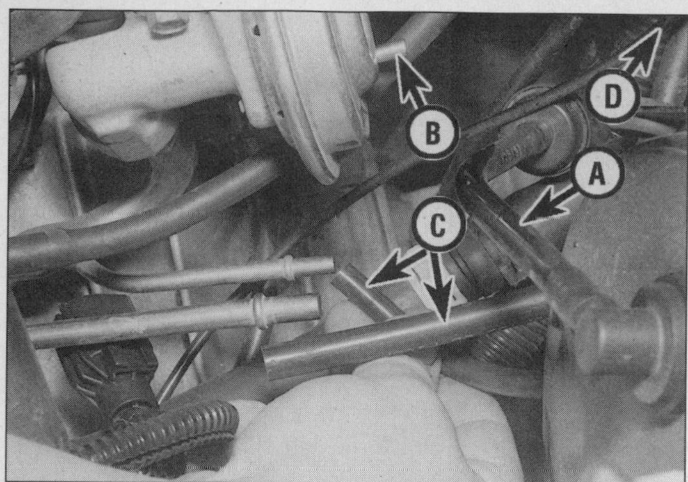

4.10c . . . also brake servo hose (A), EGR valve hose (B), EGR pipe hoses (C) and pulse-air filter vacuum line (D)

4.11 Unbolt the engine/transmission-to-body earth lead (hidden behind wiring loom guide) from the transmission's top surface (arrowed)

*rubber hose just beneath the bulkhead-mounted pulse-air solenoid valve **(see illustration)**.*

f) Secure all these hoses so that they won't get damaged as the engine/transmission is removed.

11 Unbolt the engine/transmission-to-body earth lead from the transmission's top surface **(see illustration)**. Disconnect the speedometer drive cable or electronic sender.

12 Where the vehicle is fitted with manual transmission, disconnect the clutch cable (see Chapter 6). Where automatic transmission is fitted, disconnect the selector cable (see Chapter 7B). Secure the cable clear of the engine/transmission.

13 Marking or labelling all components as they are disconnected, disconnect the engine wiring loom from the body as follows:

*a) Starting at the left-hand side of the engine compartment, release and unplug the three large electrical connectors clipped to the suspension mounting - note the wire clips fitted to some connectors **(see illustration)**.*

b) Disconnect and/or release the battery-to-starter motor wiring, noting the single connector which must be unplugged.

c) Unplug the electrical connector(s) to disconnect the vehicle speed sensor, oxygen sensor and, where fitted, the oil level sensor wiring - unclip the connectors to release the wiring where necessary.

*d) Work along the loom to the bulkhead, unclipping the loom and unplugging the various bulkhead-mounted components connected into it, until you reach the right-hand side of the engine compartment **(see illustration)**.*

*e) Carefully prise the power steering fluid reservoir upwards out of its clip on the suspension mounting, then unscrew the ECU connector's retaining bolt and unplug the connector **(see illustration)**.*

f) Unbolt the earth lead from the right-hand inner wing panel, release the engine wiring loom and refit the power steering fluid reservoir.

g) Secure the engine wiring loom neatly to the engine/transmission so that it cannot be damaged as the unit is removed from the vehicle.

14 Unbolt both parts of the exhaust manifold heat shield; unclip the coolant hose to allow the upper part to be withdrawn.

15 Remove the auxiliary drivebelt (see Chapter 1).

16 Unbolt the power steering pump (see Chapter 10); secure it as far as possible (without disconnecting the system's hoses) clear of the engine/transmission.

17 Raise the vehicle and support it securely on axle stands, then remove the front roadwheels. Drain the cooling system and (if the engine is to be dismantled) drain the engine oil and remove the oil filter (see Chapter 1). Also drain the transmission as described in the relevant Part of Chapter 7.

18 Withdraw the lower part of the exhaust manifold heat shield.

19 Unscrew the nuts to disconnect the exhaust system front downpipe from the manifold, then unhook all the system's rubber mountings and withdraw the complete exhaust system from under the vehicle (see Chapter 4A for details).

20 Where the vehicle is fitted with manual transmission, mark their positions, then disconnect the gearchange linkage and transmission support rods from the rear of the transmission. Unscrew the retaining nuts, and withdraw the gear linkage heat shield from the underbody. Unbolt the rear end of the linkage from the underbody, swivel the linkage around to the rear, and tie it to the underbody (see Chapter 7A for details).

21 Disconnect both anti-roll bar links from

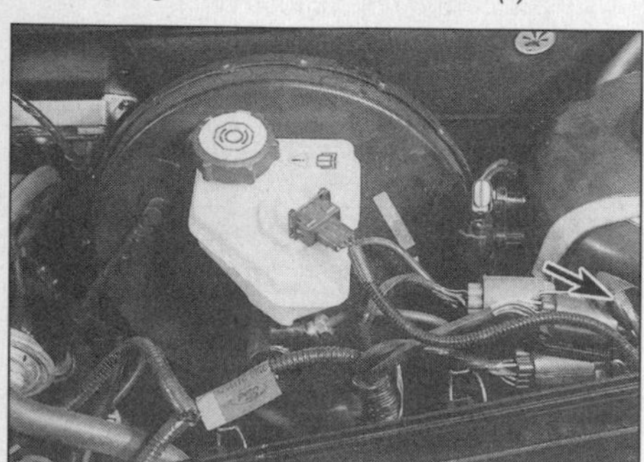
4.13a Unplug three large electrical connectors (arrowed) . . .

4.13b . . . unplug engine wiring loom from battery wiring and bulkhead components (arrowed) . . .

4.13c . . . and disconnect ECU wiring and earth lead (arrowed) to release engine wiring loom from vehicle body

their respective suspension strut - note the flexible brake hose bracket attached to each link stud - and both track rod ends from their steering knuckles. Unfasten the clamp bolt securing each front suspension lower arm balljoint to its steering knuckle (see Chapter 10 for details). Check that both balljoints can be released from the knuckle assemblies when required, but leave them in place for the time being, secured by the clamp bolts if necessary.

22 Where the vehicle is fitted with air conditioning, unbolt the accumulator/dehydrator from the subframe; secure it as far as possible (without disconnecting the system's hoses) clear of the engine/transmission.

Warning: Do not disconnect the refrigerant hoses.

23 Unbolt the steering gear from the subframe; if the bolts are not accessible from above, a Ford service tool will be required to reach them from underneath the vehicle (see Chapter 10 for details).

24 Unscrew the two bolts securing the power steering system pipes to the right-hand side of the subframe.

25 Hold the radiator in its raised position, by inserting split pins through the holes in the rear of the engine compartment front crossmember and into the radiator's upper mounting extensions. Unbolt the radiator mounting brackets from the subframe; note that they are handed, and are marked to ensure correct refitting **(see illustrations)**. Collect and store the bottom mounting rubbers for safekeeping, noting which way up they are fitted.

26 Unbolt the engine/transmission rear mounting from the subframe - where the vehicle is fitted with automatic transmission, a separate damper may be fitted beneath the subframe, which must be unbolted to reach the mounting's fasteners. Where the vehicle is fitted with manual transmission, also unscrew the mounting centre bolt, and unbolt the mounting bracket from the transmission.

27 Unscrew the engine/transmission front mounting centre bolt, and unbolt the mounting from the subframe, noting the location of the wiring connector bracket.

28 Use white paint or similar (do not use a sharp-pointed scriber, which might break the underbody protective coating and cause rusting) to mark the exact relationship of the subframe to the underbody. Unscrew the four mounting bolts from the subframe (note their different-sized washers) and allow the subframe to hang down on the suspension lower arm balljoints. Disconnect the balljoints one at a time from the steering knuckle assemblies (see Chapter 10) and lower the subframe to the ground; withdraw the subframe from under the vehicle.

29 Marking or labelling all components as they are disconnected (see paragraph 5 above) and catching as much as possible of the escaping coolant in the drain tray, disconnect the cooling system hoses and pipes as follows - refer to Chapter 3 for further details, if required:

a) Remove the radiator top hose.
b) Remove the (heater) hose running from the thermostat to the engine compartment bulkhead union.
c) Disconnect from the thermostat the hose running to the expansion tank - secure the hose clear of the working area.
d) Disconnect from the thermostat the coolant hose/pipe which runs to the radiator bottom hose.
e) Disconnect the radiator bottom hose from the radiator union, from the (sump) heater coolant pipe and from the water pump union - secure the hose clear of the working area.
f) Unbolt the (heater) coolant pipe from the sump, trace the pipe/hose round to the engine compartment bulkhead union, disconnecting (where fitted) the oil cooler hoses from the cooler unions, then remove it.
g) Unless the vehicle has air conditioning fitted, secure the radiator as far forwards as possible while it is in its raised position; if air conditioning is fitted, remove the radiator completely (see Chapter 3).

30 Where the vehicle is fitted with air conditioning, unplug the compressor's electrical connector, and unbolt the compressor from the engine **(see illustration)**. Secure it as far as possible (without disconnecting the system's hoses) clear of the engine/transmission.

Warning: Do not disconnect the refrigerant hoses.

4.25a Use split pins as shown to secure radiator in its raised position . . .

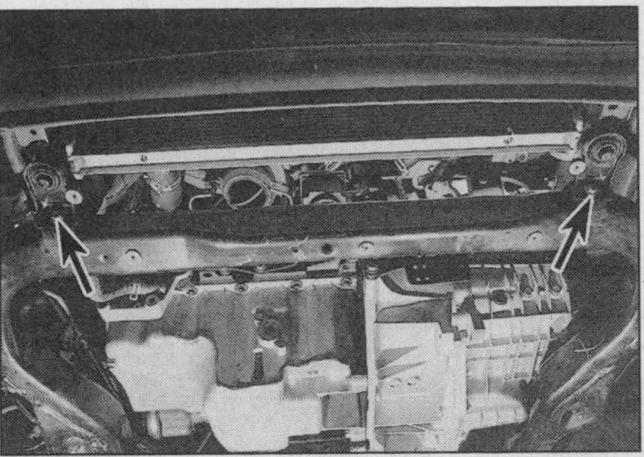

4.25b . . . while you unbolt the bottom mountings (arrowed)

4.30 Unscrew bolts (arrowed) to release air conditioning compressor from engine

31 Where the vehicle is fitted with manual transmission, disconnect the driveshafts from the transmission as follows, referring to Chapter 8 for further details when required:

a) Unscrew the nuts securing the right-hand driveshaft support bearing, and withdraw the heat shield.
b) Pull the right-hand driveshaft out of the transmission; be prepared to catch any spilt oil.
c) Secure the driveshaft clear of the engine/transmission - remember that the unit is to be lowered out of the vehicle - and ensure that the inner joint is not turned through more than 18°.
d) Prise the left-hand driveshaft out of the transmission - again, be prepared for oil spillage. Secure the driveshaft clear of the engine/transmission, and ensure that its inner joint is not turned through more than 18°.

32 Where the vehicle is fitted with automatic transmission, proceed as follows, referring to Chapter 7B and to Chapter 8 for further details when required:

a) Unscrew its centre bolt, then unbolt the engine/transmission rear mounting bracket from the transmission.
b) Disconnect the fluid cooler pipe from the rear of the transmission, and secure it clear of the unit.
c) Prise the left-hand driveshaft out of the transmission; be prepared to catch any spilt oil.
d) Secure the driveshaft clear of the engine/transmission - remember that the unit is to be lowered out of the vehicle - and ensure that the inner joint is not turned through more than 18°.
e) Unscrew the nuts securing the right-hand driveshaft support bearing, and withdraw the heat shield.
f) Pull the right-hand driveshaft out of the transmission - again, be prepared for oil spillage. Secure the driveshaft clear of the engine/transmission, and ensure that its inner joint is not turned through more than 18°.
g) Disconnect the fluid cooler pipe from the front of the transmission, and secure it clear of the unit.

33 The engine/transmission unit should now be hanging on the right- and left-hand

4.35 Lowering the engine/transmission unit out of the vehicle

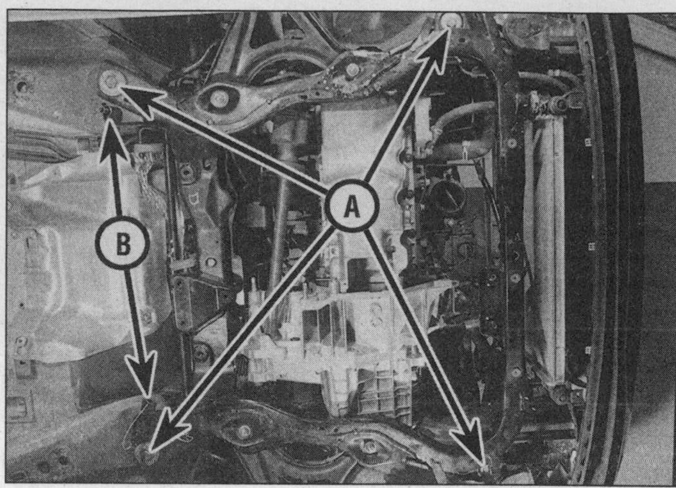

4.47a Tighten subframe mounting bolts (A) while ensuring that alignment remains correct - Ford service tools (B) shown in use here . . .

mountings only, with all components which connect it to the rest of the vehicle disconnected or removed and secured well clear of the unit. Make a final check that this is the case, then ensure that the body is securely supported, high enough to permit the withdrawal of the engine/transmission unit from underneath; allow for the height of the engine dolly, if used.

34 Take the weight of the engine/transmission unit, using the lifting eyes provided on the cylinder head. Unscrew the six nuts securing the right-hand mounting bracket, then the three nuts securing the left-hand bracket.

35 Lower the engine/transmission to the ground, and withdraw it from under the vehicle **(see illustration)**.

Separation

36 Referring to the relevant Part of Chapter 7, separate the transmission from the engine.

37 While the engine/transmission is removed, check the mountings; renew them if they are worn or damaged. Similarly, check the condition of all coolant and vacuum hoses and pipes (see Chapter 1); components that are normally hidden can now be checked properly, and should be renewed if there is any doubt at all about their condition. Where the vehicle is fitted with manual transmission, take the opportunity to overhaul the clutch components (see Chapter 6). It is regarded by many as good working practice to renew the clutch assembly as a matter of course, whenever major engine overhaul work is carried out. Check also the condition of all components (such as the transmission oil seals) disturbed on removal, and renew any that are damaged or worn.

Refitting

38 Refitting is the reverse of the removal procedure, noting the following points. Tighten all fasteners to the torque wrench settings given; where settings are not quoted in the Specifications Sections of the two Parts of this Chapter, refer to the Specifications Section of the relevant Chapter of this manual.

39 In addition to the points noted in paragraph 37 above, always renew any circlips and self-locking nuts disturbed on removal.

40 Where wiring, etc, was secured by cable ties which had to be cut on removal, ensure that it is secured with new ties on refitting.

41 With all overhaul operations completed, refit the transmission to the engine as described in Chapter 7A or 7B.

42 Manoeuvre the engine/transmission unit under the vehicle, attach the hoist, and lift the unit into position until the right- and left-hand mountings can be reassembled; tighten the (new) nuts only lightly at this stage. Do not yet release the hoist; the weight of the engine/transmission unit must not be taken by the mountings until all are correctly aligned.

43 Using new circlips, and ensuring that the inner joints are not twisted through too great an angle (see Chapter 8), refit the driveshafts. Where the vehicle is fitted with manual transmission, the procedure is the reverse of that outlined in paragraph 31 above. Where the vehicle is fitted with automatic transmission, proceed as follows, referring to Chapter 7B and to Chapter 8 for further details when required:

a) *Refit the left-hand driveshaft.*
b) *Using the clips provided to ensure that they are correctly routed, and tightening the couplings to the specified torque wrench setting where possible, reconnect the fluid cooler pipes, first to the rear, then to the front, of the transmission.*
c) *Refit the right-hand driveshaft to the transmission, refit the heat shield, and tighten the support bearing nuts to the specified torque wrench setting.*
d) *Refit the engine/transmission rear mounting bracket to the transmission, tightening the bolts to the torque wrench setting specified, then refit the mounting, tightening the centre bolt only lightly at this stage.*

44 Where the vehicle is fitted with air conditioning, do not forget to refit the compressor; tighten the bolts to the specified torque wrench setting, and plug in its electrical connector.

45 Using the marks and notes made on removal, refit the cooling system hoses. Where they are left disconnected or unclipped for the time being, do not forget to secure them at the appropriate moment during the reassembly procedure. Refit the radiator (if removed), using split pins to secure it in the raised position.

46 Offer up the subframe one side at a time, and hold it by securing the suspension lower arm balljoints to the steering knuckle assemblies. Refit the subframe bolts, ensuring that the washers are refitted correctly, and tightening the bolts only lightly at this stage.

47 The subframe must now be aligned on the underbody. Ford specify the use of service tool 15-097, which is a pair of tapered guides, with attachments to hold them in the subframe as it is refitted. However, since the working diameter of these tools is 20.4 mm, and since the corresponding aligning holes in the subframe and underbody are respectively 21 mm and 22 mm in diameter, there is a significant in-built tolerance possible in the subframe's alignment, even if the correct tools are used. If these tools are not available, you can align the subframe by eye, centring the subframe aligning holes on those of the underbody, and using the marks made on removal for assistance. Alternatively, you can align the subframe using a tapered drift (such as a clutch-aligning tool), or even a deep socket spanner of suitable size **(see illustrations)**.

48 Once the subframe is aligned as precisely as possible, tighten its bolts to the specified torque wrench setting without disturbing its

4.47b . . . but alternative methods using ordinary hand tools can achieve acceptable alignment, with care

4.49 Special tool required to hold engine/transmission unit precisely, so that mountings can be tightened into correct position

4.50a Do not allow the left-hand mounting to twist as its nuts (arrowed) are tightened

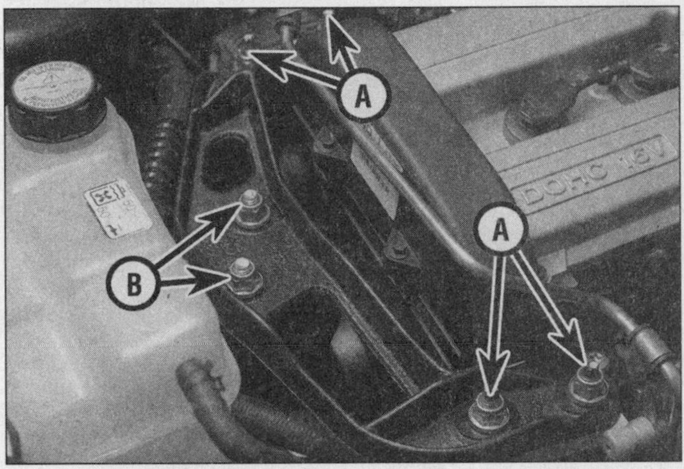

4.50b Tighten the right-hand mounting's four bracket-to-engine nuts (A), release the hoist, then tighten the two bracket-to-mounting nuts (B)

4.50c Unbolt special tool . . .

position. Recheck the alignment once all the bolts are securely tightened.

49 With the subframe aligned and securely fastened, the engine/transmission unit must now be positioned precisely, before the mountings can be reassembled. Ford specify the use of service tool 21-172; this is a fixture bolted to the subframe in place of the engine/transmission front mounting, so that when the mounting's centre bolt is refitted, it is held 60 mm above the subframe's top surface, and offset 20 mm to the rear of the mounting's subframe bolt holes (centres). DIY mechanics are advised to obtain the Ford tool; the only alternative is to have a copy fabricated **(see illustration)**.

50 Fasten the tool to the subframe in place of the engine/transmission front mounting, and lightly tighten the mounting's centre bolt. Refit the engine/transmission mountings in the following sequence:

- *a) Tighten the left-hand mounting's nuts to the specified torque wrench setting - do not allow the mounting to twist as it is tightened* ***(see illustration)****.*
- *b) Tighten the right-hand mounting's four bracket-to-engine nuts to the specified torque wrench setting.*
- *c) Slowly release the hoist so that the weight of the engine/transmission unit is taken by the mountings.*
- *d) Tighten the right-hand mounting's two bracket-to-mounting nuts to the specified torque wrench setting - do not allow the mounting to twist as it is tightened* ***(see illustration)****.*
- *e) Reassemble the engine/transmission rear mounting, tightening the fasteners to the specified torque wrench settings; tighten the centre bolt last.*
- *f) Refit the steering gear to the subframe; if the Ford service tool is used to tighten the bolts from underneath the vehicle (see Chapter 10 for details), note that a torque wrench which can tighten in an anti-clockwise direction will be required.*
- *g) Unbolt the special tool from the front mounting, refit the mounting - do not forget the wiring connector bracket - and tighten first the mounting's bolts/nuts, then its centre bolt, to their respective specified torque wrench settings* ***(see illustrations)****.*

51 Refit the bottom mounting rubbers to the radiator - ensure that both are the correct way up - then refit the radiator mounting brackets to the subframe, ensuring that each is returned to its correct (marked) location, and tightening the bolts to the torque wrench setting specified. Remove the split pins, and secure the coolant hose connections (where necessary).

52 Refit the air conditioning accumulator/dehydrator (where appropriate) to the subframe.

53 Tighten the two bolts securing the power steering system pipes to the right-hand side of the subframe.

4.50d . . . then refit front mounting - tighten the mounting's nuts first, then its centre bolt

54 Fasten each front suspension lower arm balljoint and track rod end to their respective steering knuckles, and both anti-roll bar links to their respective suspension strut. Note the flexible brake hose bracket attached to each link stud (see Chapter 10 for details).
55 Where the vehicle is fitted with manual transmission, swivel the linkage around to the front, tighten its rear fasteners, then refit the gear linkage heat shield. Reconnect the gearchange linkage and transmission support rods to the transmission, adjusting the linkage using the marks made on removal (see Chapter 7A).
56 Re-install the remaining components and fasteners in the reverse order of removal.
57 Add coolant, engine oil and transmission fluids as needed (see "*Weekly checks*" and Chapter 1).
58 Run the engine, and check for proper operation and the absence of leaks. Shut off the engine, and recheck the fluid levels.
59 Remember that, since the front suspension subframe and steering gear have been disturbed, the wheel alignment and steering angles must be checked fully and carefully as soon as possible, with any necessary adjustments being made. This operation is best carried out by an experienced mechanic, using proper checking equipment; the vehicle should therefore be taken to a Ford dealer or similarly-qualified person for attention.

4-cylinder engine (05/1998-on)

Note: *The following procedure is for manual transmission models. The engine and automatic transmission assembly is removed from under the car as described earlier in this Section for pre 05/1998 models.*

Removal

60 Remove the battery (see Chapter 5A). Engage neutral (manual transmission) or Park (automatic transmission).
61 Remove the bonnet (see Chapter 11).
62 Working on each side in turn, unscrew the front suspension top mounting nuts about 5 turns each while holding the shock absorber centre rods with a key.
63 Apply the handbrake, then jack up the front of the vehicle and support it on axle stands (see "*Jacking and vehicle support*"). Remove both front wheels.
64 Remove the radiator lower cover, then drain the cooling system as described in Chapter 1.
65 Disconnect the wiring from the mass air flow meter and air temperature sensor.
66 Remove the air cleaner assembly (Chapter 4A) then unbolt and remove the plenum chamber.
67 Disconnect the battery wiring (including the earth wire) from the battery support panel.
68 At the right-hand front corner of the engine compartment, unbolt the wiring junction box and place it to one side.
69 Unbolt and remove the battery support, noting the location of the wiring.
70 At the right-hand rear corner of the engine compartment, lift the power steering fluid reservoir from its mounting and place it to one side. Unbolt the PCM (powertrain control module) cable support, and disconnect the two earth cables, then disconnect the wiring connector from the PCM.
71 Disconnect the earth cable from the engine lifting eye.
72 Disconnect the wiring from the power steering pressure sensor, and release the wiring from the cable ties on the fluid pipe.
73 On the left-hand side of the engine compartment, disconnect the main engine wiring plug, and where fitted the automatic transmission earth cable. Release the wiring from the cable ties.
74 On models with cruise control, disconnect the wiring from the throttle housing then disconnect and remove the cruise control cable. Refer to Chapter 12 if necessary.
75 Disconnect and remove the accelerator cable from the throttle housing. Refer to Chapter 4A if necessary.
76 Disconnect the vacuum hoses from the inlet manifold, noting their location for correct refitting.
77 At the front of the engine, pull out the engine oil level dipstick then unbolt and remove the exhaust manifold heatshield. At the same time remove the coolant pipe bracket.
78 Remove the coolant pipe and disconnect the hose from the coolant pipe and water pump.
79 Unscrew the nuts securing the catalytic converter to the exhaust manifold, and position the converter to one side.
80 On models with air conditioning, disconnect the plug from the compressor on the right-hand side of the engine.
81 Disconnect the wiring from the engine coolant temperature sensor located near the engine lifting eye.
82 At the front of the engine, detach the cable from the engine compartment front crossmember.
83 Loosen the clips and disconnect the coolant hoses from the radiator and thermostat housing.
84 Disconnect the wiring from the electric cooling fan motor.
85 Disconnect the hoses from the expansion tank located in the right-hand front corner of the engine compartment.
86 Unbolt and remove the upper drivebelt cover from the right-hand end of the engine.
87 Position a container beneath the clutch slave cylinder, then pull out the clip and disconnect the hydraulic pipe (refer to Chapter 6 if necessary). Remove the pipe from the transmission and tie it to one side.
88 Detach the earth cable from the transmission.
89 Unbolt and remove the right-hand front wheel arch liner.
90 Turn the auxiliary drivebelt tensioner clockwise and remove the drivebelt.
91 Undo the quick release coupling and disconnect the brake servo vacuum pipe from the inlet manifold.
92 Trace the oxygen sensor wiring to the bottom of the front valance, and disconnect it. Also release the cable tie.
93 Unscrew the bolts securing the front exhaust pipe flange to the intermediate section. Unhook the rubber mounting, then remove the pipe and recover the gasket.
94 Unscrew and remove the clamp bolts from the front suspension lower balljoints and pull the lower arms from the hub carriers. Refer to Chapter 10 if necessary. Also remove the ABS wiring brackets from the struts. Take care not to damage the balljoint rubber boots or the ABS sensor ring.
95 Remove both driveshafts with reference to Chapter 8.
96 Unbolt and remove the rear engine mounting roll restrictor. Also unbolt the mounting bracket from the transmission.
97 Using a trolley jack, slightly raise the transmission then unscrew the front engine mounting roll restrictor nuts and centre bolt and remove the restrictor.
98 Unscrew the clamp bolt and remove the catalytic converter.
99 On models fitted with air conditioning, detach the dehydrator and tie it to one side.
100 Loosen the clips and disconnect the lower coolant hoses.
101 Loosen the clip and disconnect the heater hose from the bulkhead.
102 On models fitted with air conditioning, unbolt the compressor and tie it to one side of the engine compartment. Do not disconnect the hydraulic lines from the compressor.
103 Disconnect the gearchange cable from the lever on the transmission. Turn the bracket anticlockwise to pre-tension it then remove the cable. Disconnect the remaining cable from the lever on the transmission. Turn the remaining bracket anticlockwise to pre-tension it then remove the cable. Press in the adjustment mechanism to release it.
104 Depressurise the fuel system with reference to Chapter 4A.
105 Disconnect the fuel feed and return hoses.
106 Unscrew the coolant expansion tank mounting bolts, and position the tank to one side. If fitted, disconnect the cruise control cable from the tank.
107 Attach a suitable hoist to the engine and transmission and take its weight.
108 Using a marker pen or scribe, mark the position of the right-hand engine mounting. Unscrew the nuts from the mounting and loosen the bolts by two turns only.
109 Using the marker pen or scribe, mark the position of the left-hand engine mounting, then unscrew and remove the nuts and bolts.
110 With the help of an assistant, carefully raise the engine and transmission until the power steering pump is visible. Unbolt the

power steering pump from the engine and tie it to one side.

111 Carefully lift the engine and transmission from the engine compartment, taking care not to damage the surrounding components. Lower the assembly to the floor.

Separation

112 Disconnect the wiring from the reversing light switch and vehicle speed sensor.

113 Disconnect the wiring from the starter motor main terminal and solenoid terminal.

114 Unscrew and remove the starter motor upper mounting bolts and the transmission to engine upper mounting bolts.

115 Unbolt the earth cable from the transmission.

116 Unscrew the lower bolt and remove the starter motor. Also remove the wiring harness.

117 Unscrew and remove the remaining flange bolts.

118 With the help of an assistant withdraw the transmission direct from the engine making sure that the transmission is kept level with the engine until the input shaft is clear of the clutch.

Refitting

119 On automatic transmission models, check that the torque converter is fully engaged with the pump on the transmission output shaft by measuring the distance from the flange to the spigot on the torque converter with a straight-edge. This should be at least 12.0 mm indicating that the torque converter is fully engaged with the transmission pump. Move the selector lever on the transmission to the 'D' position. Smear a little high temperature grease on the spigot.

120 With the help of an assistant, locate the transmission on the engine making sure that the location studs enter the holes in the driveplate. On automatic transmission models align the torque converter with the driveplate.

121 Insert the flange bolts and progressively tighten them to the specified torque.

122 On automatic transmission models, turn the engine as necessary, then tighten the torque converter mounting nuts to the specified torque.

123 The remaining refitting procedure is a reversal of removal, but note the following points.

a) Position the engine mountings as noted on removal.
b) Tighten all nuts and bolts to the specified torque wrench settings where given.
c) Bleed the clutch hydraulic system with reference to Chapter 6.
d) Adjust the accelerator cable with reference to Chapter 4A, and the cruise control cable with reference to Chapter 12.
e) Refill and bleed the cooling system as described in Chapter 1.

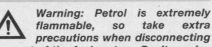

5 Engine/transmission (V6 models) - removal, separation and refitting

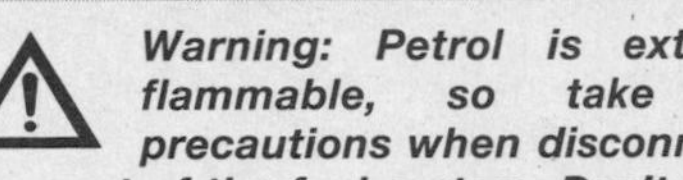

Warning: Petrol is extremely flammable, so take extra precautions when disconnecting any part of the fuel system. Don't smoke, or allow naked flames or bare light bulbs in or near the work area, and don't work in a garage where a natural gas appliance (such as a clothes dryer or water heater) is installed. If you spill petrol on your skin, rinse it off immediately. Have a fire extinguisher rated for petrol fires handy, and know how to use it.

Note: *Read through the entire Section, as well as reading the advice in the preceding Section, before beginning this procedure. The engine and transmission are removed as a unit, lowered to the ground and removed from underneath, then separated outside the vehicle.*

V6 (Duratec) engine

Removal

Note: *Ford technicians use a special tool to align the engine/transmission assembly with the subframe. Before removing the assembly mark the engine mountings and roll restrictors to ensure they are refitted in exactly the same position.*

1 Park the vehicle on firm, level ground and apply the handbrake firmly.

2 Disconnect and remove the battery as described in Chapter 5A.

3 Insert welding rods, split pins or similar rods through the radiator upper mounting extensions on the crossmember, to prevent the radiator dropping when the lower mountings are disconnected.

4 Unbolt and remove the engine top cover. At the same time, release the coolant hose from the clip.

5 Jack up the front of the vehicle and support it on axle stands (see "*Jacking and vehicle support*"). Make sure that there is sufficient height to allow the engine and transmission assembly to be removed from under the car. Remove both front wheels.

6 Working beneath the front of the car, undo the screws and remove the radiator bottom cover.

7 Drain the cooling system as described in Chapter 1.

8 Position a container beneath the transmission then unscrew the drain plug and drain the transmission oil (manual transmission) or fluid (automatic transmission) as applicable. Refer to Chapter 7A or 7B if necessary. On completion, clean the refit the drain plug, tightening it securely.

Warning: Make sure the engine is cold before draining the fluid, since it may be very hot!

9 Disconnect the accelerator cable from the throttle body with reference to Chapter 4A. Position the cable to one side.

10 Disconnect the cruise control cable from the throttle body with reference to Chapter 12. Position the cable to one side.

11 Loosen the clips and disconnect the PCV (positive crankcase ventilation) hoses from each side of the inlet duct between the air cleaner and throttle housing.

12 Loosen the clips and disconnect the inlet duct from the air cleaner and throttle body.

13 Loosen the clip and disconnect the vacuum hose from the EGR valve on the left-hand side of the rear cylinder head.

14 Disconnect the wiring from the sensor on top of the airflow meter, and also disconnect the wiring from the intake air temperature sensor located on the rear of the air cleaner cover.

15 Remove the air cleaner assembly as described in Chapter 4A.

16 Loosen the clip and disconnect the brake servo vacuum hose from the upper inlet manifold.

17 Wrap some cloth around the fuel line pressure relief valve, then unscrew the cap and use a screwdriver to depress the centre pin to depressurise the fuel system. When released, refit the cap.

18 Disconnect the fuel supply and return lines on the left-hand side of the engine, and place them to one side. The connectors have special quick release fittings requiring a specific removal tool (refer to Chapter 4A).

19 Loosen the clips and disconnect the hoses from the coolant distribution pipe on the left-hand side of the cylinder heads. Also disconnect the top hose from the radiator and thermostat housing.

20 Unbolt the earth cables from the transmission. Also unscrew the bolt and disconnect the main wiring loom plug in the left-hand side of the engine compartment and detach the wires from the battery support bracket.

21 On manual transmission models, disconnect the gearchange selector rods or cables (as applicable) from the transmission with reference to Chapter 7A. Also disconnect the clutch hydraulic line from the top of the transmission with reference to Chapter 6 - to prevent loss of fluid, fit a hose clamp to the line just below the brake hydraulic fluid reservoir.

22 On automatic transmission models, unbolt the selector cable support bracket from the side of the transmission, and disconnect the end of the cable from the lever with reference to Chapter 7B.

23 Disconnect the wiring from the starter motor with reference to Chapter 5A. Where necessary, prise apart the plastic cover for access to the terminals.

24 Disconnect the two plugs for the cooling fan located on the left-hand side of the radiator and unclip the wiring loom.

25 At the right-hand rear corner of the engine compartment, pull up the power steering fluid reservoir from its mounting and position it upright to one side. Make sure the reservoir remains upright.

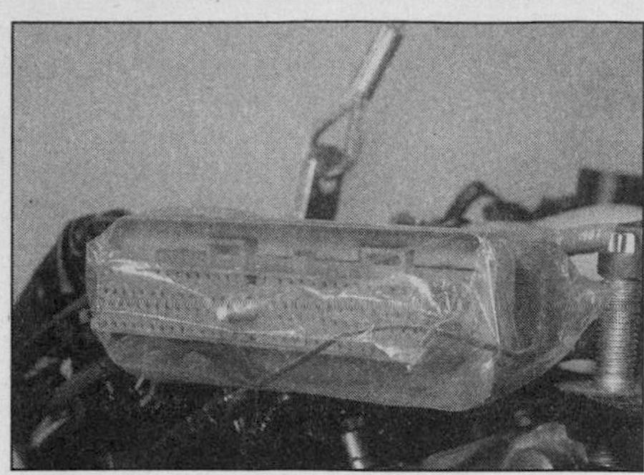

5.26 Protect the ECU by placing it in a polythene bag

26 Unbolt the engine wiring harness earth cable from the left-hand inner wing panel, behind the headlight. The engine wiring harness must now be disconnected from the powertrain control module (PCM). On later models it will be necessary to drill out the rivets in order to lift the cover from the module. Unscrew the bolt and disconnect the multiplug. To prevent entry of dust and dirt, cover the multiplug and ECU with polythene sheeting or place it in a polythene bag **(see illustration)**. Withdraw the wiring harness onto the engine.

27 Identify the hoses for location, then loosen the clips and disconnect the three hoses from the cooling system expansion tank located in the right-hand front corner of the engine compartment. Undo the screws, and lift the expansion tank from the inner wing.

28 Disconnect the heater vacuum hoses at the rear of the engine.

29 At the left-hand rear of the rear cylinder head, disconnect the evaporation control system hose from the throttle body.

30 Release the cable tie and disconnect the oxygen sensor wiring at the rear of the engine.

31 Unbolt and remove the exhaust front 'Y' section and rear catalytic converter from the exhaust manifolds and intermediate section with reference to Chapter 4A. Recover the gaskets.

32 Working under the wheel arches, undo the screws and remove the lower wheel arch liners from each side.

33 Remove both driveshafts as described in Chapter 8. This includes removing the clamp bolts and detaching the front suspension lower arm balljoints from the hub knuckle assemblies. Tie the suspension struts to one side to prevent damage to the balljoint rubber boots.

34 Unbolt and remove the heat shield from over the steering gear.

35 Unscrew the steering gear mounting bolts and tie the steering gear to the bulkhead using wire, string or cable ties. If available, use the special U-shaped spanner described in Chapter 10, however, if the tool is not available the bolts can be unscrewed after lowering the subframe to the extent of the subframe mounting bolts as described later. Note that the steering gear pinion remains attached to the bottom of the column.

36 Unscrew the nuts/bolts and centre bolt, and remove the rear roll restrictor complete with bracket. If necessary, use a trolley jack and block of wood to slightly raise the transmission. Also unbolt the restrictor from the transmission.

37 Unscrew the bolts securing the front roll restrictor to the subframe, and also unscrew the centre bolt. Remove the roll restrictor.

38 On models equipped with air conditioning, unbolt the dehydrator from the left-hand side of the subframe, and tie it to one side. Do not disconnect the refrigerant lines.

39 On later models, unbolt the short struts from each side of the subframe.

40 On automatic transmission models, unbolt the transmission fluid pipe support bracket from the front of the subframe.

41 Unbolt the power steering fluid pipe bracket from the right-hand side of the subframe.

42 Before removing the subframe, mark it for position to ensure correct refitting. Note that Ford technicians use special tools to centralise the subframe when refitting it.

43 Support the weight of the subframe using a strong length of wood and a trolley jack. Unscrew the mounting bolts then carefully lower the subframe from the engine compartment. If necessary, unscrew the steering gear mounting bolts when the subframe has been lowered to the extent of the subframe mounting bolts. As the subframe is lowered, make sure that the radiator is released from its lower rubber guides. If preferred, the radiator lower mounting rubbers and brackets can be unbolted from the subframe **(see illustration)**.

5.43 Radiator lower mounting brackets on the subframe

5.46 Turn the tensioner clockwise to release the tension on the auxiliary drivebelt

44 Disconnect the wiring from the vehicle speed sensor on the rear of the transmission.

45 On models with air conditioning, disconnect the wiring from the compressor and dehydrator, and place the wiring on the engine.

46 Remove the auxiliary drivebelt using a 3/8' square drive socket bar to turn the tensioner clockwise **(see illustration)**. However, before removing the belt, check the position of the cast lug in relation to the stops on the bracket. If the lug is touching the right-hand stop, the drivebelt is stretched beyond it serviceable life and must be renewed.

47 On models with air conditioning, unbolt the heatshield from the compressor.

48 Loosen the clip and disconnect the bottom hose from the radiator.

49 Unscrew the union nut and disconnect the oil cooler pipe from the radiator. Be prepared for some loss of fluid.

50 On automatic transmission models, unscrew the union nuts and disconnect the fluid cooler feed and return pipes from the transmission. Plug the ends of the pipes and the apertures, then unbolt the return pipe from the transmission.

51 On models with air conditioning, unbolt the condenser from the radiator and tie it up to the crossmember using string or cable ties. Unbolt the compressor from the cylinder block and lift it onto the engine compartment front crossmember. Tie it securely in this position using string or cable ties. Also unbolt the refrigerant pipe support bracket from the coolant pipe. Do not disconnect the refrigerant lines.

52 Extract the split pins inserted earlier, then lower the radiator and withdraw from the front of the car. If necessary, remove the upper mounting rubbers from the crossmember. The radiator is a tight fit and care must be taken to prevent damage to the cooling fins.

53 To provide additional working room, remove the electric cooling fans and shroud before removing the radiator - refer to Chapter 3.

54 Attach a hoist to the engine and transmission assembly and take its weight. Lifting eyes are provided at the front left-hand side and rear right-hand side.

55 Unscrew the nuts from the right-hand engine mounting and remove the mounting upper bracket. Unbolt and remove the mounting lower bracket from the right-hand inner wing panel.

56 Unbolt the power steering pump pulley **(see illustration)**. Hold the pulley stationary using an oil filter strap wrench. Unscrew the nuts/bolts and withdraw the power steering pump from the right-hand engine mounting bracket on the engine. Position the pump

5.56 Remove the power steering pump pulley

together with hydraulic lines on the bulkhead and tie it to the windscreen wiper spindle using string or cable ties.

57 Unscrew the nuts securing the left-hand engine mounting bracket to the transmission. If necessary, the left-hand engine mounting bracket can be unbolted from the inner wing panel.

58 Carefully lower the engine and transmission assembly to the ground, taking care to avoid the components on the side of the engine compartment. If available, lower the assembly onto a wheeled platform so that it can be withdrawn from under the car.

Separation

59 Unbolt and remove the starter motor support bracket, then unbolt the starter motor from the transmission casing.

60 Disconnect and unclip the following wiring:

a) Speed sensor
b) Control plug (automatic transmission)
c) Engine coolant temperature sensor
d) Transmission range sensor (automatic transmission)

61 On automatic transmission models, prise out the plastic cover and unscrew the nuts securing the torque converter to the driveplate. It will be necessary to turn the engine so that the nuts are visible through the aperture in the transmission housing.

62 Unscrew the flange bolts securing the transmission to the engine. Note that some of the bolts are located on the right-hand side of the transmission housing.

63 With the help of an assistant, carefully withdraw the transmission from the engine **(see illustration)**. On manual transmission models, make sure that the weight of the transmission is not allowed to hang on the clutch centre plate. On automatic transmission models, make sure that the torque converter remains fully engaged with the pump on the transmission output shaft.

Refitting

64 Make sure that the adapter plate is fitted onto the location dowels.

65 On automatic transmission models, check that the torque converter is fully engaged with the pump on the transmission output shaft by measuring the distance from the flange to the spigot on the torque converter with a straight-edge. This should be at least 12.0 mm indicating that the torque converter is fully engaged with the transmission pump **(see illustration)**. Move the selector lever on the transmission to the 'D' position. Smear a little high temperature grease on the spigot.

5.63 Withdrawing the transmission from the engine

66 With the help of an assistant, locate the transmission on the engine. On automatic transmission models, make sure that the location studs enter the holes in the driveplate.

67 Insert the flange bolts and progressively tighten them to the specified torque.

68 On automatic transmission models, turn the engine as necessary, then tighten the torque converter mounting nuts to the specified torque.

69 The remaining refitting procedure is a reversal of removal, but note the following points.

a) When refitting the subframe, it must be centralised using Ford tools 15-079A (or pattern tool) before tightening the mounting bolts ***(see illustration)****. If the tools are not available, align it to the previously made marks.*
b) Position the engine mountings as noted on removal. Ford technicians use a dummy front roll restrictor tool to align the engine onto the subframe while the remaining mountings are fitted. If this tool is available, fit it to the subframe in place of the front roll restrictor, making sure the arrow on it points to the front. If not available, reposition the mountings as noted during removal.

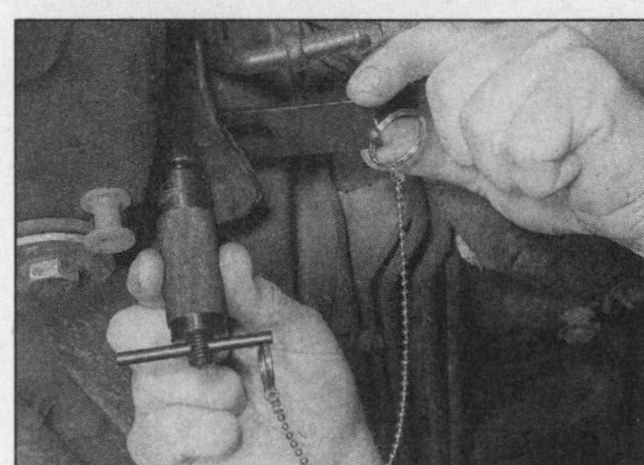
5.69 Using a special tool to centralise the subframe

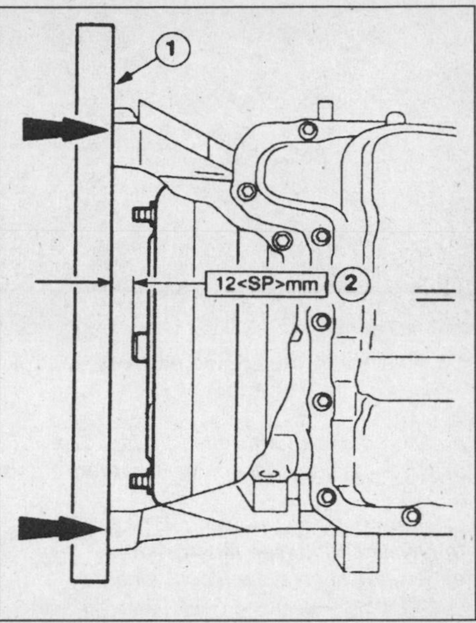

5.65 The distance from the flange (1) to the torque converter spigot (2) must be at least 12.0 mm

c) Tighten all nuts and bolts to the specified torque wrench settings where given.
d) Bleed the clutch hydraulic system with reference to Chapter 6.
e) Adjust the accelerator cable with reference to Chapter 4A, and the cruise control cable with reference to Chapter 12.
f) Refill and bleed the cooling system as described in Chapter 1.

6 Engine overhaul - dismantling sequence

1 It is much easier to dismantle and work on the engine if it is mounted on a portable engine stand. These stands can often be hired from a tool hire shop. Before the engine is mounted on a stand, the flywheel/driveplate should be removed (Part A or B of this Chapter) so that the stand bolts can be tightened into the end of the cylinder block/crankcase.

2 If a stand is not available, it is possible to dismantle the engine with it mounted on blocks, on a sturdy workbench or on the floor. Be extra-careful not to tip or drop the engine when working without a stand.

3 If you are going to obtain a reconditioned engine, all external components must be removed first, to be transferred to the replacement engine (just as they will if you are doing a complete engine overhaul yourself). **Note:** *When removing the external components from the engine, pay close attention to details that may be helpful or important during refitting. Note the fitted position of gaskets, seals, spacers, pins, washers, bolts and other small items. These external components include the following:*

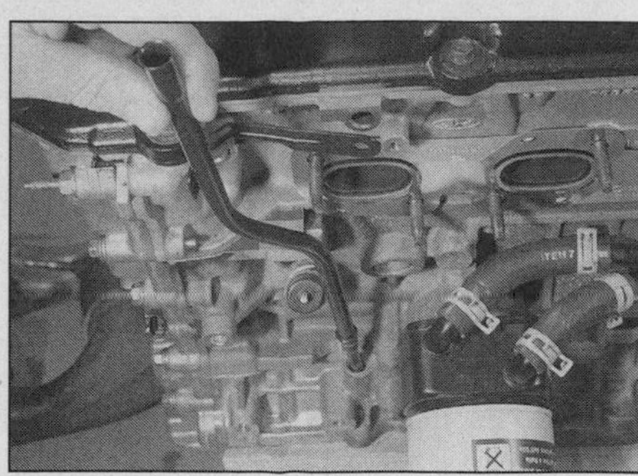

6.3 Removing the engine oil level dipstick tube

a) Alternator and brackets (Chapter 5A).
b) HT leads and spark plugs (Chapters 1 and 5B).
c) Thermostat and housing (Chapter 3).
d) Dipstick tube ***(see illustration).***
e) Fuel injection system components (Chapter 4A).
f) All electrical switches and sensors.
g) Inlet and exhaust manifolds (Part A or B of this Chapter).
h) Oil filter (Chapter 1).
i) Engine/transmission mounting brackets (Part A or B of this Chapter).
j) Flywheel/driveplate (Part A or B of this Chapter).

4 If you are obtaining a "short" engine (which consists of the engine cylinder block/crankcase, crankshaft, pistons and connecting rods all assembled), then the cylinder head, sump, oil pump and timing belt (4-cylinder) or chains (V6) will have to be removed also.

5 If you are planning a complete overhaul, the engine can be dismantled and the internal components removed in the following order.

a) Inlet and exhaust manifolds (Part A or B of this Chapter).
b) Timing belt (4-cylinder) or timing chains (V6) and toothed pulleys (Part A or B of this Chapter).
c) Cylinder head(s) (Part A or B of this Chapter).
d) Flywheel/driveplate (Part A or B of this Chapter).
e) Sump (Part A or B of this Chapter).
f) Oil pump (Part A or B of this Chapter).
g) Piston/connecting rod assemblies (Section 13).
h) Crankshaft (Section 11).

6 Before beginning the dismantling and overhaul procedures, make sure that you have all of the correct tools necessary. Refer to the introductory pages at the beginning of this manual for further information.

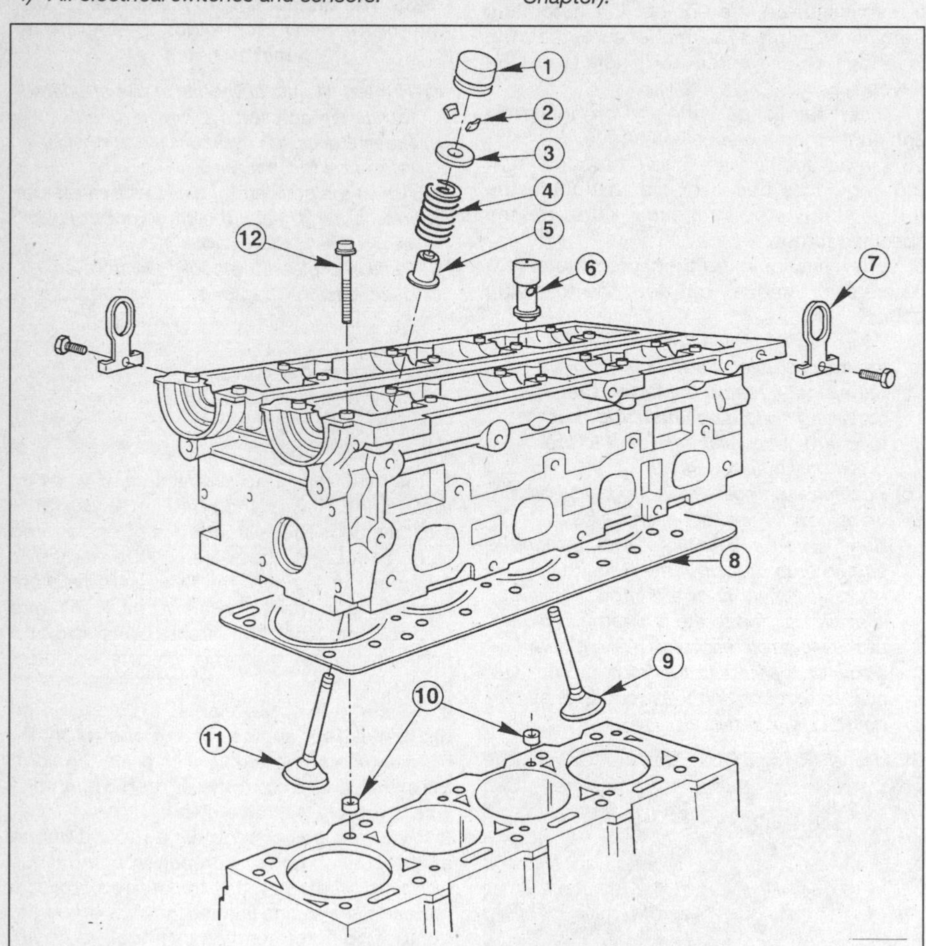

7.1 Cylinder head components (early 4-cylinder models)

1 Hydraulic tappet
2 Valve collets
3 Valve spring upper seat
4 Valve spring
5 Valve spring lower seat/stem oil seal
6 Oil-retaining valve
7 Engine lifting eye
8 Cylinder head gasket
9 Inlet valve
10 Locating dowels
11 Exhaust valve
12 Cylinder head bolt

7 Cylinder head - dismantling

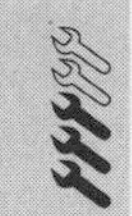

Note: *New and reconditioned cylinder heads are available from the manufacturers, and from engine overhaul specialists. Due to the fact that some specialist tools are required for the dismantling and inspection procedures, and new components may not be readily available (refer to Section 1), it may be more practical and economical for the home mechanic to purchase a reconditioned head, rather than to dismantle, inspect and recondition the original head.*

1 Remove the camshafts and tappets (Part A or B of this Chapter) **(see illustration).**

2 Remove the cylinder head(s) (Part A or B of this Chapter).

3 Using a valve spring compressor, compress each valve spring in turn until the split collets can be removed. A special valve spring compressor will be required, to reach into the deep wells in the cylinder head without risk of damaging the hydraulic tappet bores; such compressors are now widely available from most good motor accessory shops. Release the compressor, and lift off the spring upper seat and spring **(see illustrations).**

4 If, when the valve spring compressor is screwed down, the spring upper seat refuses to free and expose the split collets, gently tap the top of the tool, directly over the upper seat, with a light hammer. This will free the seat.

5 Withdraw the valve through the combustion chamber. If it binds in the guide (won't pull through), push it back in, and de-burr the area around the collet groove with a fine file or

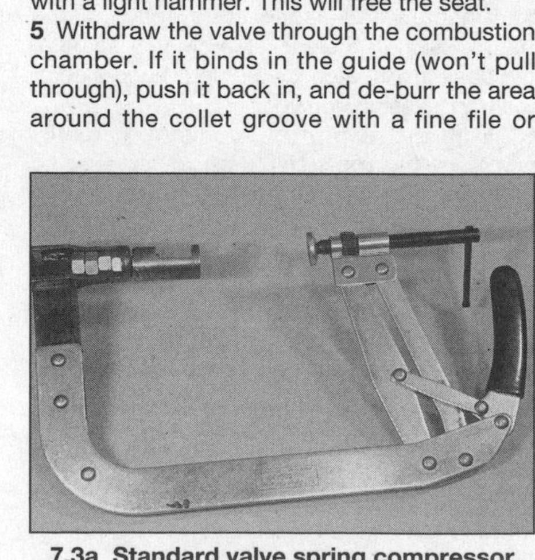

7.3a Standard valve spring compressor modified as shown . . .

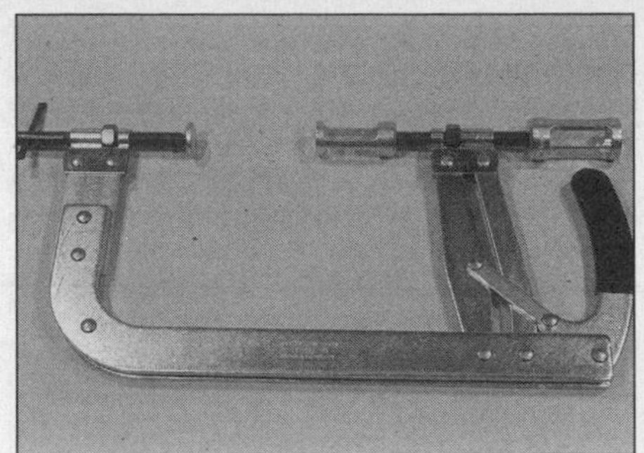

7.3b . . . or purpose-built special version, is required to compress valve springs without damaging cylinder head . . .

7.3c . . . so that both valve split collets can be removed from the valve's stem - small magnetic pick-up tool prevents loss of small metal components on removal and refitting

7.6a Ford service tool in use to remove valve spring lower seat/stem oil seals . . .

7.6b . . . can be replaced by home-made tool if suitable spring can be found

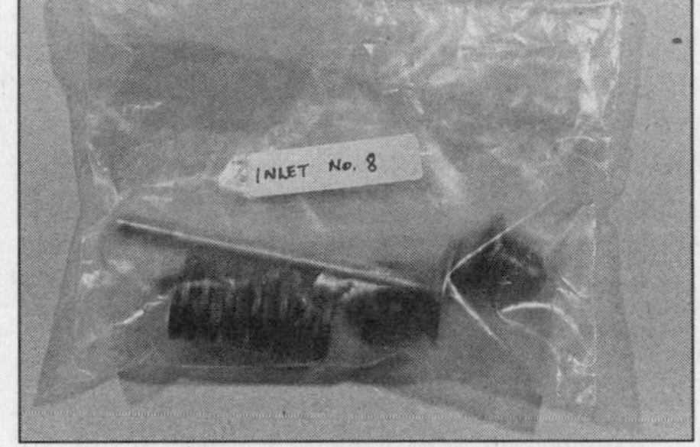

7.7 Use clearly-marked containers to identify components and to keep matched assemblies together

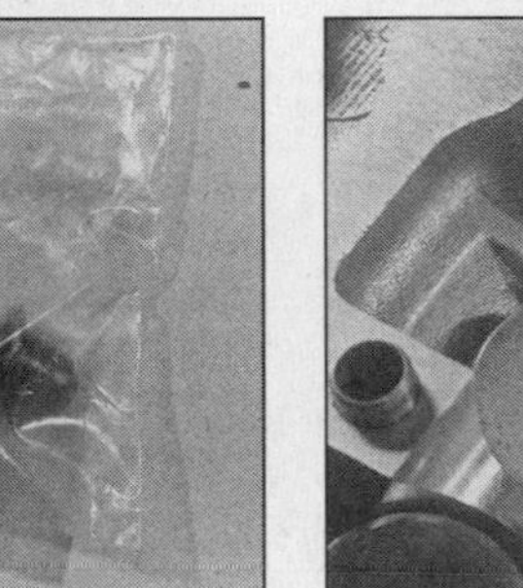

7.8 Cylinder head oil-retaining valve (arrowed)

whetstone; take care not to mark the hydraulic tappet bores.

6 Ford recommend the use of their service tool 21-160 to extract the valve spring lower seat/stem oil seals; while this is almost indispensable if the seals are to be removed without risk of (extremely expensive) damage to the cylinder head, we found that a serviceable substitute can be made from a strong spring of suitable size. Screw on the tool or spring so that it bites into the seal, then draw the seal off the valve guide **(see illustrations)**.

7 It is essential that the valves are kept together with their collets, spring seats and springs, and in their correct sequence (unless they are so badly worn that they are to be renewed). If they are going to be kept and used again, place them in a labelled polythene bag or similar small container **(see illustration)**. Note that No 1 valve is nearest to the timing belt end of the engine.

8 If the oil-retaining valve is to be removed (to flush out the cylinder head oil galleries thoroughly), seek the advice of a Ford dealer as to how it can be extracted; it may be that the only course of action involves destroying the valve as follows. Screw a self-tapping screw into its ventilation hole, and use the screw to provide purchase with which the valve can be drawn out; a new valve must be purchased and pressed into place on reassembly **(see illustration)**.

8 Cylinder head and valve components - cleaning and inspection

1 Thorough cleaning of the cylinder head and valve components, followed by a detailed inspection, will enable you to decide how much valve service work must be carried out during the engine overhaul. **Note:** *If the engine has been severely overheated, it is best to assume that the cylinder head is warped, and to check carefully for signs of this.*

Cleaning

2 Scrape away all traces of old gasket material and sealing compound from the cylinder head.

3 Scrape away the carbon from the combustion chambers and ports, then wash the cylinder head thoroughly with paraffin or a suitable solvent.

4 Scrape off any heavy carbon deposits that may have formed on the valves, then use a power-operated wire brush to remove deposits from the valve heads and stems.

Inspection

Note: *Be sure to perform all the following inspection procedures before concluding that the services of a machine shop or engine overhaul specialist are required. Make a list of all items that require attention.*

Cylinder head

5 Inspect the head very carefully for cracks, evidence of coolant leakage, and other damage. If cracks are found, a new cylinder head should be obtained.

6 Use a straight edge and feeler blade to check that the cylinder head gasket surface is not distorted **(see illustration)**. If it is, it may be possible to re-surface it.

7 Examine the valve seats in each of the combustion chambers. If they are severely pitted, cracked or burned, then they will need to be renewed or re-cut by an engine overhaul specialist. If they are only slightly pitted, this

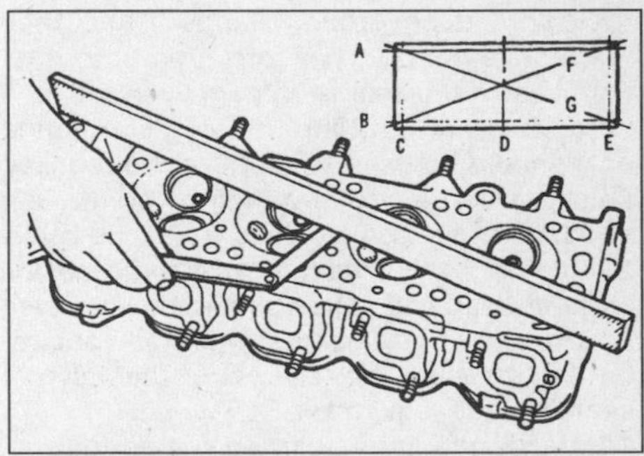

8.6 Check the cylinder head gasket surfaces for warpage, in the planes indicated (A to G). Try to slip a feeler blade under the precision straight edge (see Specifications for maximum distortion allowed and use a blade of that thickness)

2C

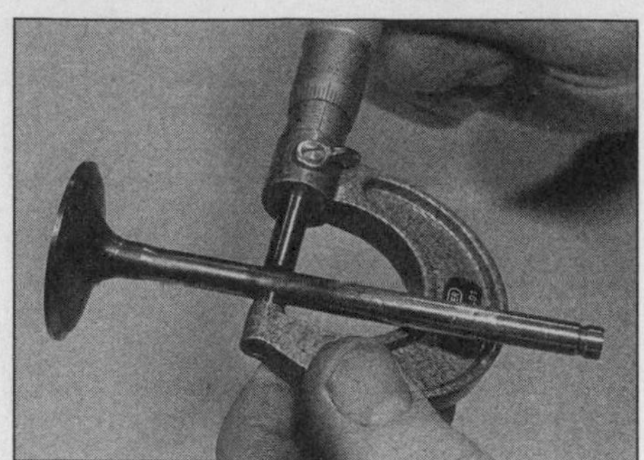

8.12 Measuring the diameter of a valve stem

8.15 Grinding-in a valve seat - do not grind in the valves any more than absolutely necessary or their seats will be prematurely sunk into the cylinder head

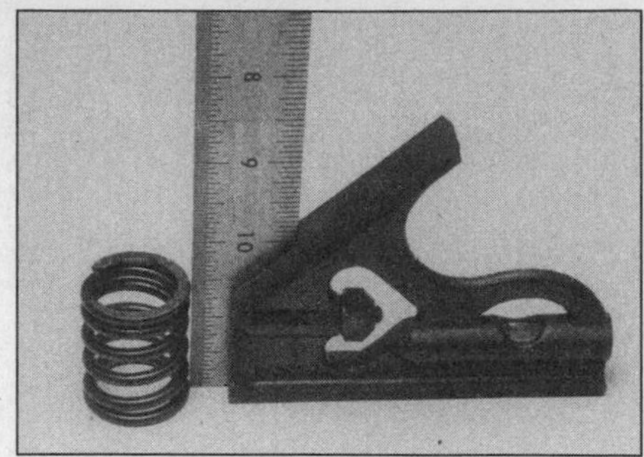

8.19 Check each valve spring for squareness

can be removed by grinding-in the valve heads and seats with fine valve-grinding compound, as described below.

8 If the valve guides are worn, indicated by a side-to-side motion of the valve, new guides must be fitted. Measure the diameter of the existing valve stems (see below) and the bore of the guides, then calculate the clearance, and compare the result with the specified value; if the clearance is excessive, renew the valves or guides as necessary.

9 The renewal of valve guides is best carried out by an engine overhaul specialist.

10 If the valve seats are to be re-cut, this must be done only after the guides have been renewed.

Valves

11 Examine the head of each valve for pitting, burning, cracks and general wear, and check the valve stem for scoring and wear ridges. Rotate the valve, and check for any obvious indication that it is bent. Look for pits and excessive wear on the tip of each valve stem. Renew any valve that shows any such signs of wear or damage.

12 If the valve appears satisfactory at this stage, measure the valve stem diameter at several points, using a micrometer **(see illustration)**. Any significant difference in the readings obtained indicates wear of the valve stem. Should any of these conditions be apparent, the valve(s) must be renewed.

13 If the valves are in satisfactory condition, they should be ground (lapped) into their respective seats, to ensure a smooth gas-tight seal. If the seat is only lightly pitted, or if it has been re-cut, fine grinding compound only should be used to produce the required finish. Coarse valve-grinding compound should not be used unless a seat is badly burned or deeply pitted; if this is the case, the cylinder head and valves should be inspected by an expert, to decide whether seat re-cutting, or even the renewal of the valve or seat insert, is required.

14 Valve grinding is carried out as follows. Place the cylinder head upside-down on a bench, with a block of wood at each end to give clearance for the valve stems.

15 Smear a trace of (the appropriate grade of) valve-grinding compound on the seat face, and press a suction grinding tool onto the valve head. With a semi-rotary action, grind the valve head to its seat, lifting the valve occasionally to redistribute the grinding compound **(see illustration)**. A light spring placed under the valve head will greatly ease this operation.

16 If coarse grinding compound is being used, work only until a dull, matt even surface is produced on both the valve seat and the valve, then wipe off the used compound, and repeat the process with fine compound. When a smooth unbroken ring of light grey matt finish is produced on both the valve and seat, the grinding operation is complete. Do not grind in the valves any further than absolutely necessary, or the seat will be prematurely sunk into the cylinder head.

17 When all the valves have been ground-in, carefully wash off all traces of grinding compound, using paraffin or a suitable solvent, before reassembly of the cylinder head.

Valve components

18 Examine the valve springs for signs of damage and discolouration, and also measure their free length by comparing each of the existing springs with a new component.

19 Stand each spring on a flat surface, and check it for squareness **(see illustration)**. If any of the springs are damaged, distorted, or have lost their tension, obtain a complete set of new springs.

20 Check the spring upper seats and collets for obvious wear and cracks. Any questionable parts should be renewed, as extensive damage will occur if they fail during engine operation. Any damaged or excessively-worn parts must be renewed; the valve spring lower seat/stem oil seals must be renewed as a matter of course whenever they are disturbed.

21 Check the tappets (hydraulic or conventional) as described in Part A or B of this Chapter.

9 Cylinder head - reassembly

1 Regardless of whether or not the head was sent away for repair work of any sort, make sure that it is clean before beginning reassembly. Be sure to remove any metal particles and abrasive grit that may still be present from operations such as valve grinding or head resurfacing. Use compressed air, if available, to blow out all the oil holes and passages.

2 Beginning at one end of the head, lubricate and install the first valve. Apply molybdenum disulphide-based grease or clean engine oil to the valve stem, and refit the valve **(see illustration)**. Where the original valves are being re-used, ensure that each is refitted in its original guide. If new valves are being fitted, insert them into the locations to which they have been ground.

3 Fit the plastic protector supplied with new valve spring lower seat/stem oil seals to the end of the valve stem, then put the new seal squarely on top of the guide, and leave it there; the action of refitting the valve spring presses the lower seat/stem oil seal into place **(see illustration)**.

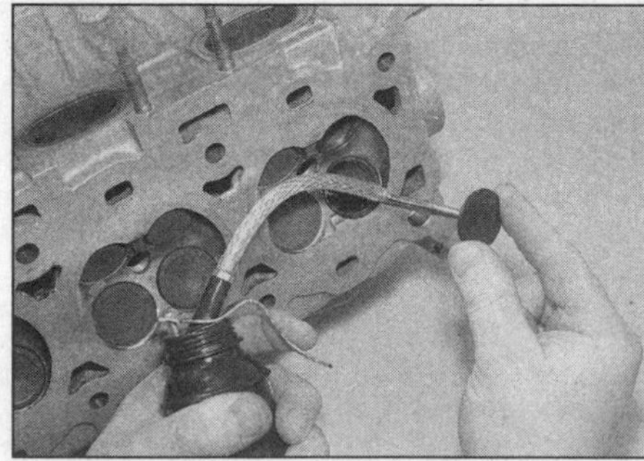

9.2 Oil the valve stems before refitting them (V6 shown)

9.3 Valve spring pressure is sufficient to seat lower seat/stem oil seals on reassembly

9.4a Refitting the valve spring . . .

9.4b . . . and upper seat (V6 shown)

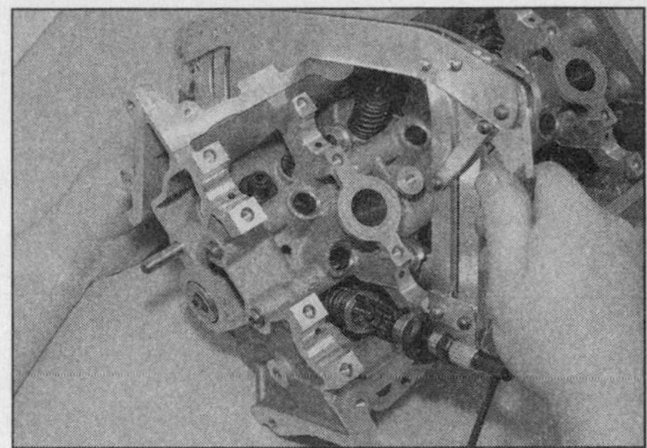
9.5a Using a valve spring compressor (V6 shown)

4 Refit the valve spring and upper seat **(see illustrations)**.
5 Compress the spring with a valve spring compressor, and carefully install the collets in the stem groove. Apply a small dab of grease to each collet to hold it in place if necessary. Slowly release the compressor, and make sure the collets seat properly **(see illustrations)**.
6 When the valve is installed, place the cylinder head flat on the bench and, using a hammer and interposed block of wood, tap the end of the valve stem gently, to settle the components.
7 Repeat the procedure for the remaining valves. Be sure to return the components to their original locations - don't mix them up!
8 Refit the tappets (Part A or B of this Chapter).

10 Piston/connecting rod assemblies - removal

Note: *While this task is theoretically possible when the engine is in place in the vehicle, in practice, it requires so much preliminary dismantling, and is so difficult to carry out due to the restricted access, that owners are advised to remove the engine from the vehicle first. The following paragraphs assume the engine is removed from the car.*
1 Remove the cylinder head(s) with reference to Part A or B of this Chapter.
2 Remove the sump with reference to Part A or B of this Chapter.
3 Unbolt the oil pump pick-up tube and filter, and recover the O-ring from the pump. On V6 engines, undo the nuts and remove the oil baffle from the crankcase **(see illustrations)**. On 4-cylinder engines from 5/1998-on, unbolt and remove the crankcase lower frame.
4 On 4-cylinder engines manufactured from 5/1998-on the connecting rods and caps are of 'cracked' design. During production, the connecting rod and cap are forged as one piece, then the cap is broken apart from the rod using a special technique. Because of this design, the mating surfaces of each cap and rod is unique and, therefore, nearly impossible to mix up.
5 Temporarily refit the crankshaft pulley, so that the crankshaft can be rotated. Note that each piston/connecting rod assembly can be identified by its cylinder number (counting from the timing belt/chain end of the engine)

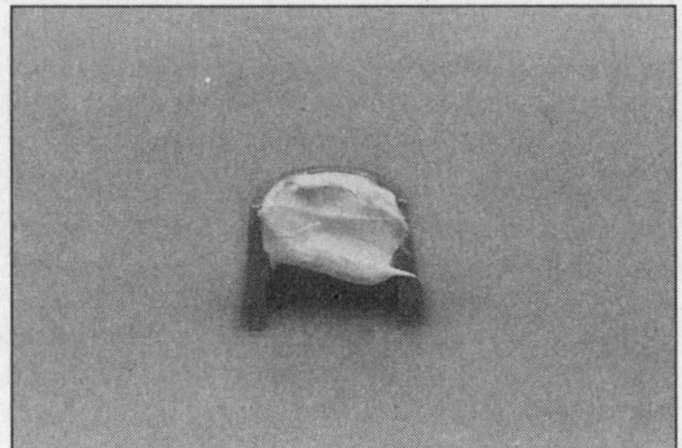
9.5b Apply a small dab of grease to each collet to hold them in place on the valve stem until the spring is released

10.3a On the V6 engine, unscrew the flange bolts . . .

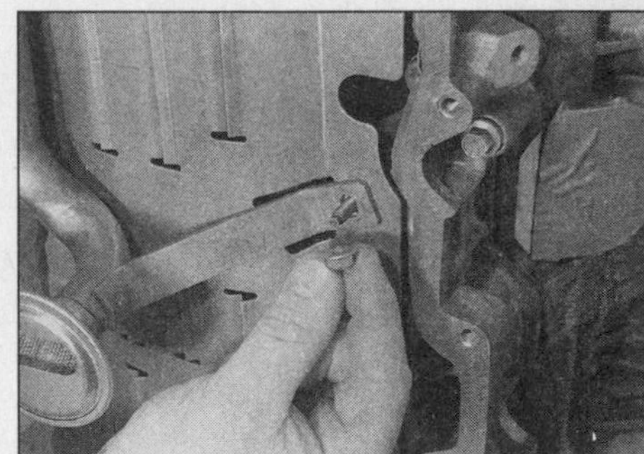
10.3b . . . and support nuts . . .

10.3c . . . remove the oil pump pick-up tube and filter . . .

10.3d . . . recover the flange O-ring . . .

10.3e . . . then unscrew the nuts and remove the oil baffle

10.5a Each connecting rod and big-end bearing cap will have a flat-machined surface visible from the front (exhaust) side of the engine, with the cylinder number etched in it

etched into the flat-machined surface of both the connecting rod and its cap. Furthermore, each piston has an arrow stamped into its crown, pointing towards the timing belt/chain end of the engine. If no marks can be seen, make your own before disturbing any of the components, so that you can be certain of refitting each piston/connecting rod assembly the right way round, to its correct (original) bore, with the cap also the right way round **(see illustrations)**.

6 Use your fingernail to feel if a ridge has formed at the upper limit of ring travel (about 6 mm down from the top of each cylinder). If carbon deposits or cylinder wear have produced ridges, they must be completely removed with a special tool called a ridge reamer **(see illustration)**. Follow the manufacturer's instructions provided with the tool.

Caution: Failure to remove the ridges before attempting to remove the piston/connecting rod assemblies may result in piston ring breakage.

7 On 5/1998-on 4-cylinder models, unscrew the bolts securing the lower crankcase to the cylinder block. Loosen the bolts gradually and evenly, then separate the lower crankcase from the cylinder block.

8 Slacken each of the big-end bearing cap bolts half a turn at a time, until they can be removed by hand. Remove the No 1 cap and bearing shell. Don't drop the shell out of the cap.

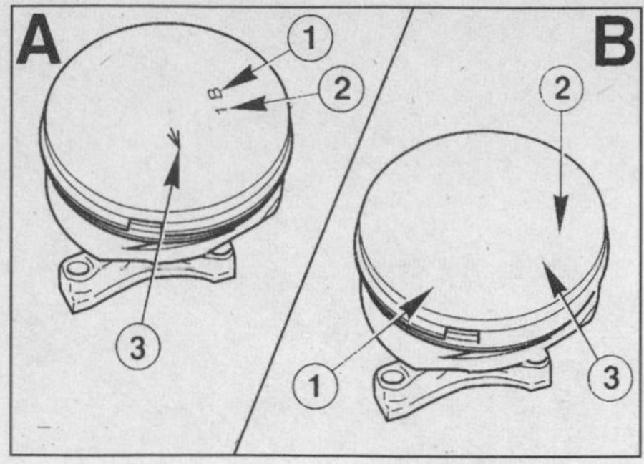

10.5b Piston crown markings

A 1.6 and 1.8 litre engines
B 2.0 litre engines
1 Gudgeon pin diameter grade - when used
2 Piston skirt diameter grade
3 Arrow mark - pointing to timing belt end of engine

9 Remove the upper bearing shell, and push the connecting rod/piston assembly out through the top of the engine. Use a wooden hammer handle to push on the connecting rod's bearing recess. If resistance is felt, double-check that all of the ridge was removed from the cylinder.

10 Repeat the procedure for the remaining cylinders.

11 After removal, reassemble the big-end bearing caps and shells on their respective connecting rods, and refit the bolts finger-tight. Leaving the old shells in place until reassembly will help prevent the bearing recesses from being accidentally nicked or gouged. New shells should be used on reassembly.

12 Don't attempt to separate the pistons from the connecting rods.

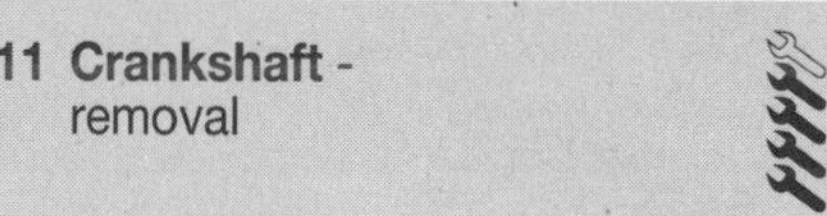

11 Crankshaft - removal

Caution: Refer to the Caution and Note in Sections 1 and 2 on models fitted with the V6 engine.

Note: *The crankshaft can be removed only after the engine/transmission has been removed from the vehicle. It is assumed that the transmission and flywheel/driveplate, timing belt, lower crankcase on 5/1998-on 4-cylinder models, cylinder head, sump, oil pump pick-up/strainer pipe and oil baffle, oil pump, and piston/connecting rod assemblies, have already been removed. The crankshaft left-hand oil seal carrier must be unbolted from the cylinder block/crankcase before proceeding with crankshaft removal.*

10.6 A ridge reamer may be required, to remove the ridge from the top of each cylinder

1 Before the crankshaft is removed, check the endfloat. Mount a DTI (Dial Test Indicator, or dial gauge) with the probe in line with the crankshaft and just touching the crankshaft **(see illustration)**.

2 Push the crankshaft fully away from the gauge, and zero it. Next, lever the crankshaft towards the gauge as far as possible, and check the reading obtained. The distance that the crankshaft moved is its endfloat; if it is greater than specified, check the crankshaft thrust surfaces for wear. If no wear is evident, new thrustwashers should correct the endfloat. On 4-cylinder models, the thrust control bearing is part of the No 3 (centre) main bearing **(see illustration)**. On V6 models, the thrust control bearing consists of the No 4 (rear) lower main bearing half and a washer that fits into the cylinder block.

3 If a dial gauge is not available, feeler gauges can be used. Gently lever or push the crankshaft all the way towards the right-hand end of the engine. Slip feeler gauges between the crankshaft and the right-hand face of the No 3 (centre) main bearing to determine the clearance **(see illustration)**.

11.1 Checking crankshaft endfloat with a dial gauge

11.2 Thrustwashers integral with No 3 (centre) main bearing upper shell control crankshaft endfloat

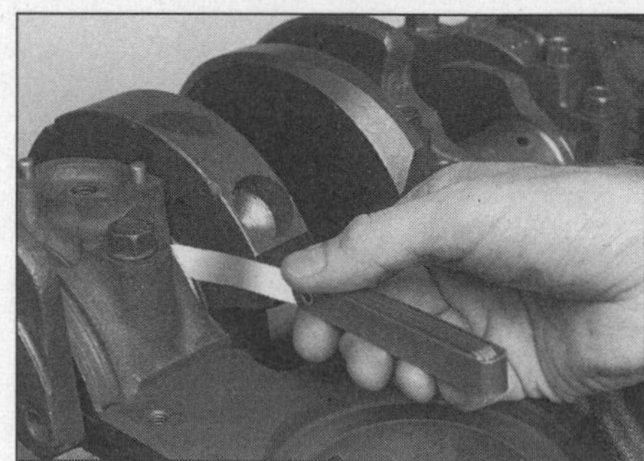

11.3 Checking crankshaft endfloat with a feeler gauge

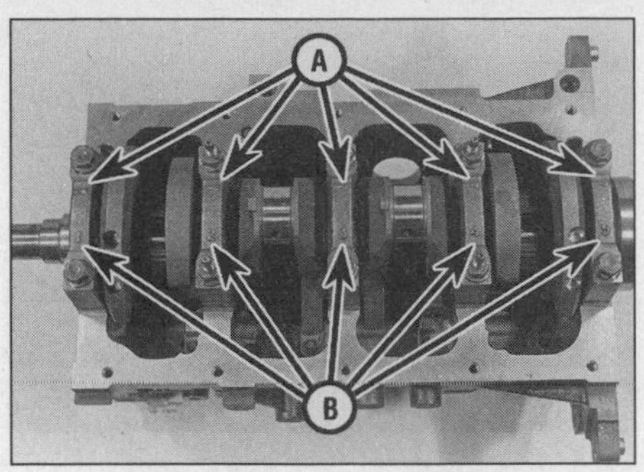

11.4 Before unbolting crankshaft main bearing caps, note arrows pointing to timing belt end of engine (A) and bearing numbers (B) consecutive from timing belt end

4 On 4-cylinder models, check the main bearing caps, to see if they are marked to indicate their locations **(see illustration)**. They should be numbered consecutively from the timing belt end of the engine - if not, mark them with number-stamping dies or a centre-punch. The caps will also have an embossed arrow pointing to the timing belt end of the engine. Noting the different fasteners (for the oil baffle nuts) used on caps 2 and 4, slacken the cap bolts a quarter-turn at a time each, starting with the left- and right-hand end caps and working toward the centre, until they can be removed by hand.

5 On V6 models, the lower crankcase holds the lower main bearing halves and the crankshaft in the cylinder block. Conventional main bearing caps are not used on V6 models. In addition, the interior lower

12.1a Remove water pump . . .

crankcase bolts are the torque-to-yield design and must be renewed during reassembly. Progressively loosen the lower crankcase bolts, then remove them and separate the lower crankcase from the block. Note the position of the lower main bearing halves for reassembly reference.

6 On 4-cylinder models, gently tap the caps with a soft-faced hammer, then separate them from the cylinder block/crankcase. If necessary, use the bolts as levers to remove the caps. Try not to drop the bearing shells if they come out with the caps.

7 Carefully lift the crankshaft out of the engine. It may be a good idea to have an assistant available, since the crankshaft is quite heavy. With the bearing shells in place in the cylinder block/crankcase and main bearing caps (4-cylinder engine) or lower crankcase (V6 engine), return the caps to their respective locations on the block, or refit the lower crankcase, and tighten the bolts finger-tight. Leaving the old shells in place until reassembly will help prevent the bearing recesses from being accidentally nicked or gouged. New shells should be used on reassembly.

12 Cylinder block/crankcase - cleaning and inspection

Cleaning

1 For complete cleaning, remove the water pump, all external components, and all electrical switches/sensors. Unbolt the piston-cooling oil jets or blanking plugs (as applicable). Note that Ford states that the piston-cooling oil jets (where fitted) must be renewed whenever the engine is dismantled for full overhaul **(see illustrations)**.

2 Remove the main bearing caps or lower crankcase, and separate the bearing shells from the caps/lower crankcase and the cylinder block. Mark or label the shells, indicating which bearing they were removed from, and whether they were in the cap or the block (4-cylinder engine) or lower crankcase (V6 engine), then set them aside **(see illustration)**. Wipe clean the block and cap bearing recesses, and inspect them for nicks, gouges and scratches.

2C

12.1b . . . crankcase breather pipe and PCV valve . . .

12.1c . . . unbolt crankcase ventilation system oil separator . . .

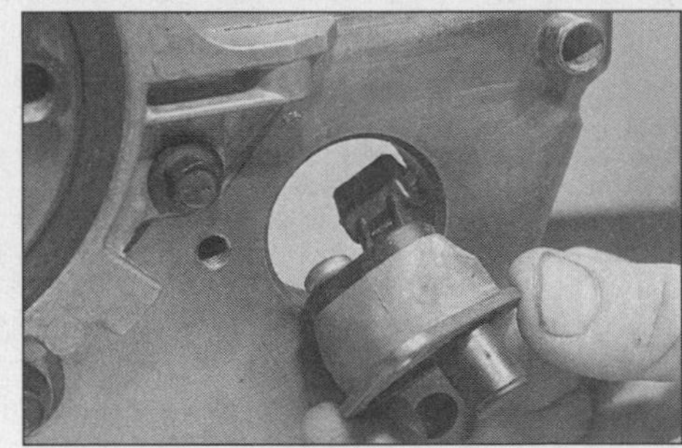
12.1d . . . remove electrical switches/sensors such as crankshaft speed/position sensor . . .

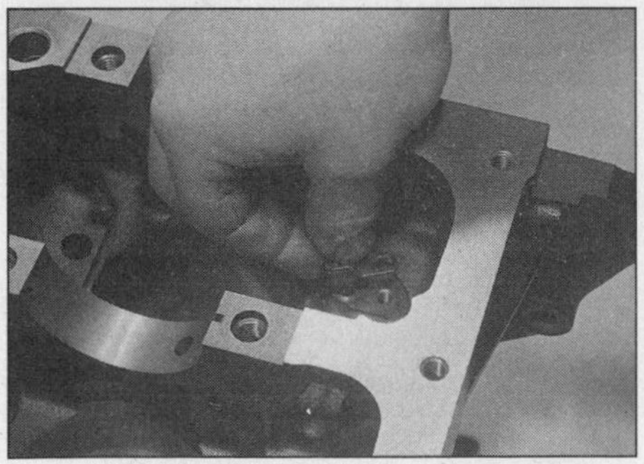
12.1e . . . unbolt blanking plugs (where fitted) to clean out oilways . . .

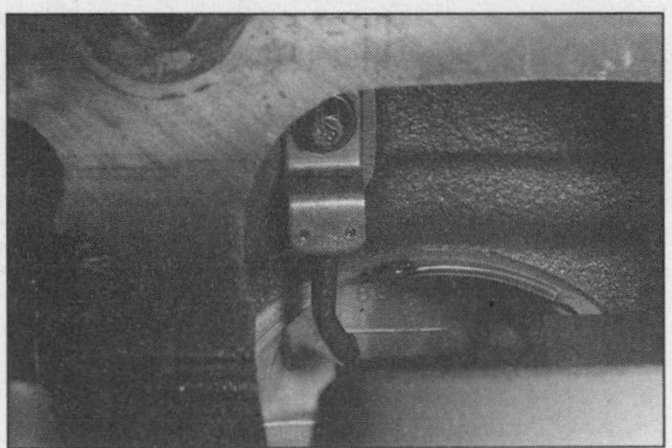
12.1f . . . piston-cooling oil jets (where fitted) must be renewed as a matter of course whenever engine is overhauled

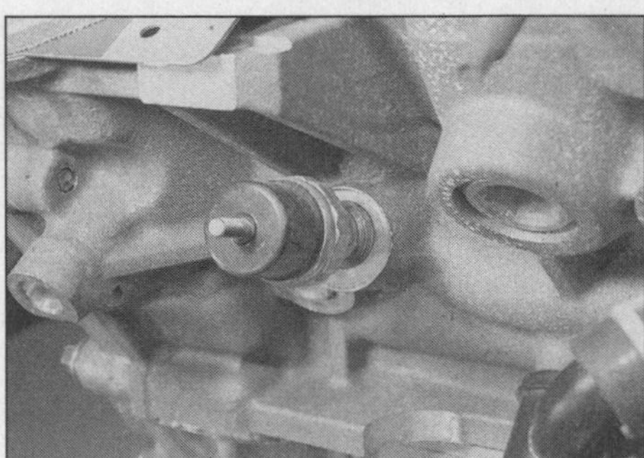
12.1g Oil pressure sender in the cylinder block

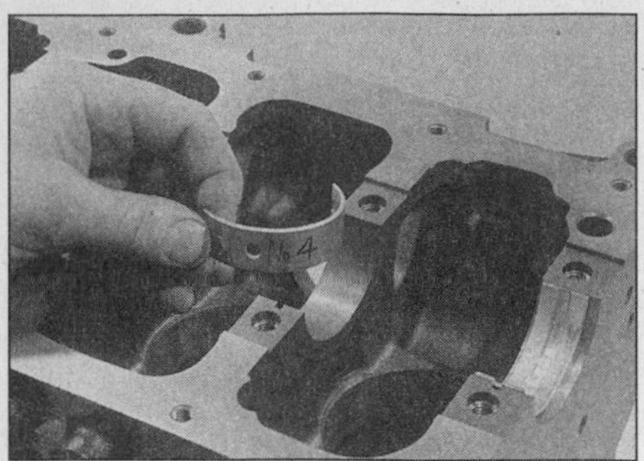

12.2 Felt marker pens can be used as shown to identify bearing shells without damaging them

12.4 The core plugs should be removed with a puller - if they're driven into the block, they may be impossible to retrieve

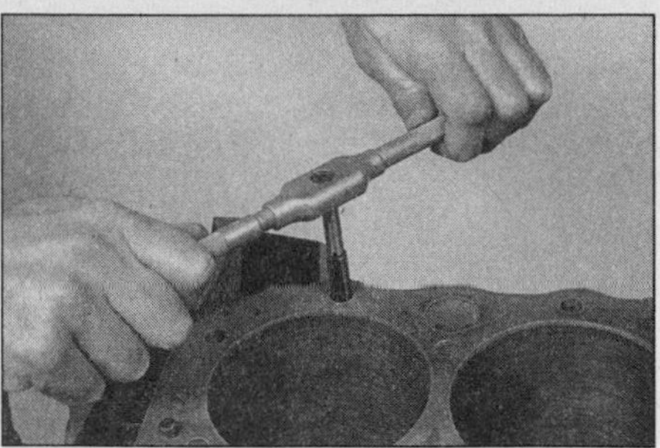

12.8 All bolt holes in the block - particularly the main bearing cap and head bolt holes - should be cleaned and restored with a tap

3 Scrape all traces of gasket from the cylinder block/lower crankcase, taking care not to damage the sealing surfaces.

4 Remove all oil gallery plugs (where fitted). The plugs are usually very tight - they may have to be drilled out and the holes re-tapped. Use new plugs when the engine is reassembled. Remove the core plugs by knocking them sideways in their bores with a hammer and a punch, then grasping them with large pliers and pulling them back through their holes. Alternatively, drill a small hose in the centre of each core plug, and pull them out with a car bodywork dent puller **(see illustration)**.

Caution: The core plugs (also known as freeze or soft plugs) may be difficult or impossible to retrieve if they are driven into the block coolant passages.

5 If any of the castings are extremely dirty, they should be steam-cleaned.

6 After the castings are returned from steam-cleaning, clean all oil holes and oil galleries one more time. Flush all internal passages with warm water until the water runs clear, then dry thoroughly, and apply a light film of oil to all machined surfaces, to prevent rusting. If you have access to compressed air, use it to speed the drying process, and to blow out all the oil holes and galleries.

7 If the castings are not very dirty, you can do an adequate cleaning job with hot soapy water (as hot as you can stand!) and a stiff brush. Take plenty of time, and do a thorough job. Regardless of the cleaning method used, be sure to clean all oil holes and galleries very thoroughly, and to dry all components completely; protect the machined surfaces as described above, to prevent rusting.

8 All threaded holes must be clean and dry, to ensure accurate torque readings during reassembly; now is also a good time to clean and check the threads of all principal bolts - however, note that some, such as the cylinder head, flywheel/driveplate bolts and lower crankcase inner bolts on V6 engines, must be renewed as a matter of course whenever they are disturbed. Run the proper-size tap into each of the holes, to remove rust, corrosion, thread sealant or sludge, and to restore damaged threads **(see illustration)**. If possible, use compressed air to clear the holes of debris produced by this operation.

9 When all inspection and repair procedures are complete (see below) and the block is ready for reassembly, apply suitable sealant to the new oil gallery plugs, and insert them into the holes in the block. Tighten them securely. After coating the sealing surfaces of the new core plugs with suitable sealant, install them in the cylinder block/crankcase **(see illustration)**. Make sure they are driven in straight and seated properly, or leakage could result. Special tools are available for this purpose, but a large socket with an outside diameter that will just slip into the core plug, used with an extension and hammer, will work just as well.

10 Refit the blanking plugs or (new) piston-cooling oil jets (as applicable), tightening their Torx screws to the torque wrench setting specified **(see illustration)**. Also refit all other external components removed, referring to the relevant Chapter of this manual for further details where required. Refit the main bearing caps (4-cylinder engine) or lower crankcase (V6 engine), and tighten the bolts finger-tight.

11 If the engine is not going to be reassembled right away, cover it with a large plastic bag to keep it clean. Apply a thin coat of engine oil to all machined surfaces to prevent rust.

Inspection

12 Visually check the castings for cracks and corrosion. Look for stripped threads in the threaded holes. If there has been any history of internal coolant leakage, it may be

12.9 A large socket on an extension can be used to drive the new core plugs into their bores

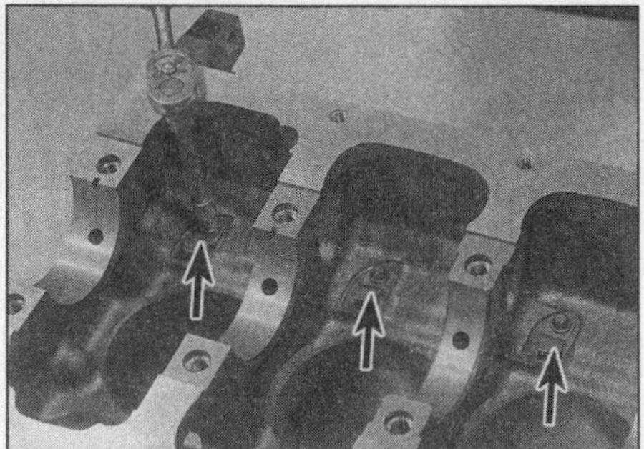

12.10 Oilway blanking plugs (three of four arrowed)

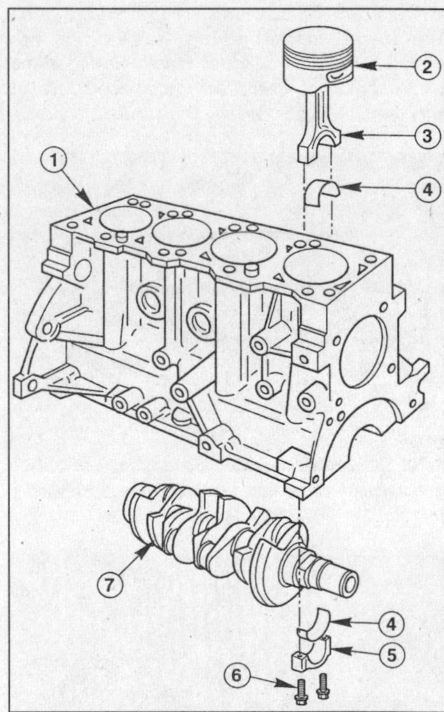

12.12 Cylinder block, piston/connecting rod and crankshaft details (4-cylinder models)

1 Cylinder block/crankcase
2 Piston
3 Connecting rod
4 Big-end bearing shell
5 Big-end bearing cap
6 Big-end bearing cap bolts
7 Crankshaft

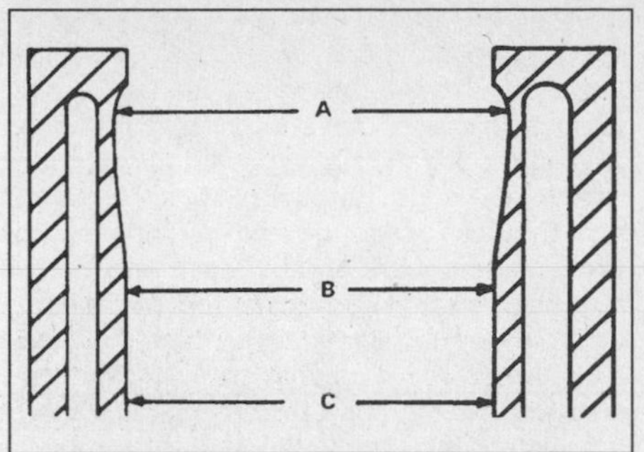

12.14a Measure the diameter of each cylinder just under the wear ridge (A), at the centre (b) and at the bottom (C)

worthwhile having an engine overhaul specialist check the cylinder block/crankcase for cracks with special equipment. If defects are found, have them repaired, if possible, or renew the assembly **(see illustration)**.

13 Check each cylinder bore for scuffing and scoring.

14 Noting that the cylinder bores must be measured with all the crankshaft main bearing caps (4-cylinder models) or lower crankcase (V6 models) bolted in place (without the crankshaft and bearing shells), to the specified torque wrench settings, measure the diameter of each cylinder at the top (just under the ridge area), centre and bottom of the cylinder bore, parallel to the crankshaft axis. Next, measure each cylinder's diameter at the same three locations across the crankshaft axis **(see illustrations)**. Note the measurements obtained.

15 Measure the piston diameter at right-angles to the gudgeon pin axis, just above the bottom of the skirt; again, note the results **(see illustration)**.

16 If it is wished to obtain the piston-to-bore clearance, measure the bore and piston skirt as described above, and subtract the skirt diameter from the bore measurement. If the precision measuring tools shown are not available, the condition of the pistons and bores can be assessed, though not quite as accurately, by using feeler gauges as follows. Select a feeler gauge of thickness equal to the specified piston-to-bore clearance, and slip it into the cylinder along with the matching piston. The piston must be positioned exactly

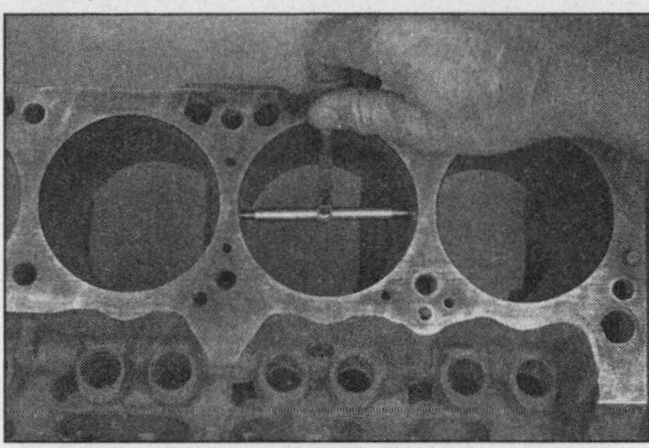
12.14b The ability to "feel" when the telescoping gauge is at the correct point will be developed over time, so work slowly and repeat the check until you're satisfied that the bore measurement is accurate

as it normally would be. The feeler gauge must be between the piston and cylinder on one of the thrust faces (at right-angles to the gudgeon pin bore). The piston should slip through the cylinder (with the feeler gauge in place) with moderate pressure; if it falls through or slides through easily, the clearance is excessive, and a new piston will be required. If the piston binds at the lower end of the cylinder, and is loose toward the top, the cylinder is tapered. If tight spots are encountered as the piston/feeler gauge is rotated in the cylinder, the cylinder is out-of-round (oval).

17 Repeat these procedures for the remaining pistons and cylinder bores.

18 Compare the results with the Specifications at the beginning of this Chapter; if any measurement is beyond the dimensions specified for that class (check the piston crown marking to establish the class of piston fitted), or if any bore measurement is significantly different from the others (indicating that the bore is tapered or out-of-round), the piston or bore is excessively-worn.

19 Worn pistons must be renewed. Check for availability with a Ford dealer or engine reconditioning specialist.

20 If any of the cylinder bores are badly scuffed or scored, or if they are excessively-worn, out-of-round or tapered, the usual course of action would be to have the cylinder block/crankcase rebored, and to fit new, oversized, pistons on reassembly. See a Ford

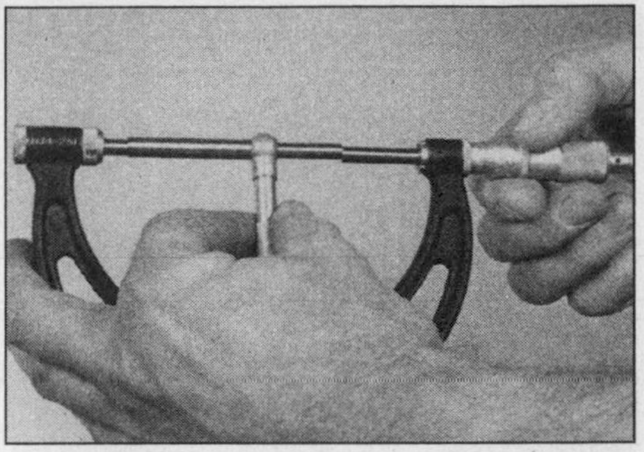
12.14c The gauge is then measured with a micrometer to determine the bore size

dealer or engine reconditioning specialist for advice.

21 If the bores are in reasonably good condition and not excessively-worn, then it may only be necessary to renew the piston rings.

22 If this is the case, the bores should be honed, to allow the new rings to bed in correctly and provide the best possible seal. Before honing the bores, refit the main bearing caps (4-cylinder models) or lower crankcase (V6 models) without the bearing shells, and tighten the bolts to the specified torque wrench setting. **Note:** *If you don't have the tools, or don't want to tackle the honing operation, most engine reconditioning specialists will do it for a reasonable fee.*

23 Two types of cylinder hones are commonly available - the flex hone or "bottle-brush" type, and the more traditional surfacing hone with spring-loaded stones. Both will do the job and are used with a power drill, but for the less-experienced mechanic, the "bottle-brush" hone will probably be easier to use. You will also need some paraffin or honing oil, and rags. Proceed as follows:

*a) Mount the hone in the drill, compress the stones, and slip it into the first bore **(see illustration)**. Be sure to wear safety goggles or a face shield!*

*b) Lubricate the bore with plenty of honing oil, switch on the drill, and move the hone up and down the bore, at a pace that will produce a fine cross-hatch pattern on the cylinder walls. Ideally, the cross-hatch lines should intersect at approximately a 60° angle **(see illustration)**. Be sure to*

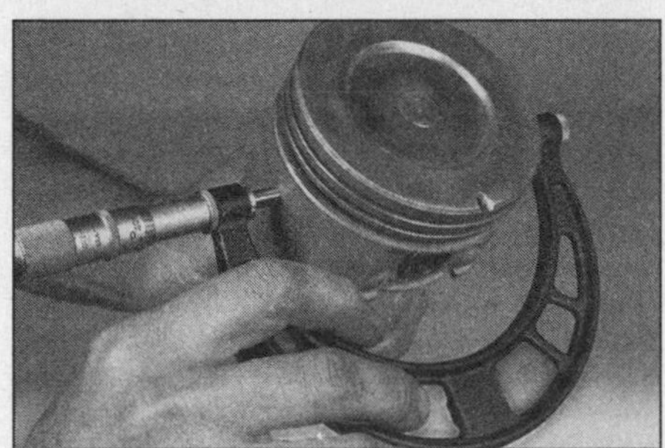
12.15 Measure the piston skirt diameter at right-angles to the gudgeon pin axis, just above the base of the skirt

12.23a A "bottle-brush" hone will produce better results if you have never honed cylinders before

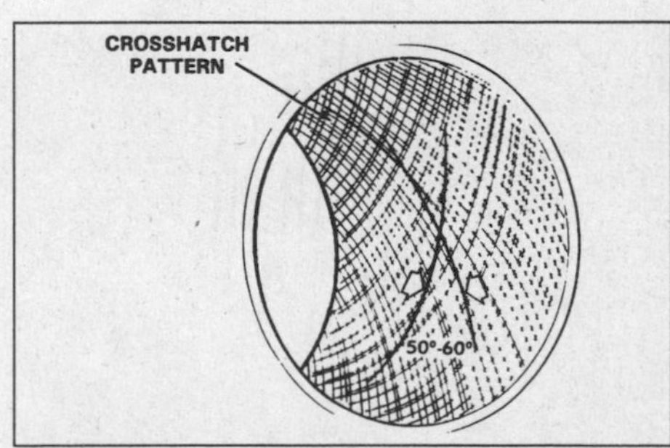

12.23b The cylinder hone should leave a smooth, cross-hatch pattern with the lines intersecting at approximately a 60° angle

2C

TOOL TIP

If a piston ring removal tool is not available, the rings can be removed by hand, expanding them over the top of the pistons. The use of two or three old feeler blades will be helpful in preventing the rings dropping into empty grooves.

use plenty of lubricant, and don't take off any more material than is absolutely necessary to produce the desired finish. **Note:** *Piston ring manufacturers may specify a different crosshatch angle - read and follow any instructions included with the new rings.*

c) Don't withdraw the hone from the bore while it's running. Instead, switch off the drill, and continue moving the hone up and down the bore until it comes to a complete stop, then compress the stones and withdraw the hone. If you're using a "bottle-brush" hone, switch off the drill, then turn the chuck in the normal direction of rotation while withdrawing the hone from the bore.

d) Wipe the oil out of the bore, and repeat the procedure for the remaining cylinders.

e) When all the cylinder bores are honed, chamfer the top edges of the bores with a small file, so the rings won't catch when the pistons are installed. Be very careful not to nick the cylinder walls with the end of the file.

f) The entire cylinder block/crankcase must be washed very thoroughly with warm, soapy water, to remove all traces of the abrasive grit produced during the honing operation. **Note:** *The bores can be considered clean when a lint-free white cloth - dampened with clean engine oil - used to wipe them out doesn't pick up any more honing residue, which will show up as grey areas on the cloth. Be sure to run a brush through all oil holes and galleries, and flush them with running water.*

g) When the cylinder block/crankcase is completely clean, rinse it thoroughly and dry it, then lightly oil all exposed machined surfaces, to prevent rusting.

24 The cylinder block/crankcase should now be completely clean and dry, with all components checked for wear or damage, and repaired or overhauled as necessary. Refit as many ancillary components as possible, for safekeeping. If reassembly is not to start immediately, cover the block with a large plastic bag to keep it clean, and protect the machined surfaces as described above to prevent rusting.

13 Piston/connecting rod assemblies - inspection

1 Before the inspection process can be carried out, the piston/connecting rod assemblies must be cleaned, and the original piston rings removed from the pistons. The rings should have smooth, polished working surfaces, with no dull or carbon-coated sections (showing that the ring is not sealing correctly against the bore wall, so allowing combustion gases to blow by) and no traces of wear on their top and bottom surfaces. The end gaps should be clear of carbon, but not polished (indicating a too-small end gap), and all the rings (including the elements of the oil control ring) should be free to rotate in their grooves, but without excessive up-and-down movement. If the rings appear to be in good condition, they are probably fit for further use; check the end gaps (in an unworn part of the bore) as described in Section 17. If any of the rings appears to be worn or damaged, or has an end gap significantly different from the specified value, the usual course of action is to renew all of them as a set. **Note:** *While it is usual to renew piston rings when an engine is overhauled, they may be re-used if in acceptable condition. If re-using the rings, make sure that each ring is marked during removal to ensure that it is refitted correctly.*

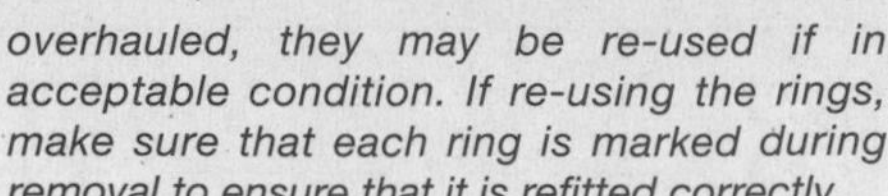

2 Using a piston ring removal tool, carefully remove the rings from the pistons. Be careful not to nick or gouge the pistons in the process, and mark or label each ring as it is removed, so that its original top surface can be identified on reassembly, and so that it can be returned to its original groove. Take care also with your hands - piston rings are sharp! If a piston ring removal tool is not available, the rings can be removed by hand, expanding them over the top of the pistons. The use of two or three old feeler blades will be helpful in preventing the rings dropping into empty grooves (see **Tool Tip**).

3 Scrape all traces of carbon from the top of the piston. A hand-held wire brush or a piece of fine emery cloth can be used, once the majority of the deposits have been scraped away. Do not, under any circumstances, use a wire brush mounted in a drill motor to remove deposits from the pistons - the piston material is soft, and may be eroded away by the wire brush.

4 Use a piston ring groove-cleaning tool to remove carbon deposits from the ring grooves. If a tool isn't available, but replacement rings have been found, a piece broken off the old ring will do the job. Be very careful to remove only the carbon deposits - don't remove any metal, and do not nick or scratch the sides of the ring grooves **(see illustrations)**. Protect your fingers - piston rings are sharp!

5 Once the deposits have been removed, clean the piston/rod assemblies with solvent, and dry them with compressed air (if available). Make sure the oil return holes in the back sides of the ring grooves, and the oil hole in the lower end of each rod, are clear.

6 If the pistons and cylinder walls aren't damaged or worn excessively and if the cylinder block/crankcase is not rebored, new pistons won't be necessary. Normal piston wear appears as even vertical wear on the piston thrust surfaces, and slight looseness of the top ring in its groove.

7 Carefully inspect each piston for cracks around the skirt, at the pin bosses, and at the ring lands (between the ring grooves).

8 Look for scoring and scuffing on the thrust faces of the skirt, holes in the piston crown, and burned areas at the edge of the crown. If the skirt is scored or scuffed, the engine may have been suffering from overheating and/or abnormal combustion, which caused excessively-high operating temperatures. The cooling and lubrication systems should be checked thoroughly. A hole in the piston crown is an indication that abnormal combustion (pre-ignition) was occurring. Burned areas at the edge of the piston crown are usually evidence of spark knock (detonation). If any of the above problems exist, the causes must be corrected, or the

13.4a The piston ring grooves can be cleaned with a special tool, as shown here . . .

13.4b . . . or a section of a broken ring, if available

damage will occur again. The causes may include intake air leaks, incorrect fuel/air mixture, incorrect ignition timing, or EGR system malfunctions.

9 Corrosion of the piston, in the form of small pits, indicates that coolant is leaking into the combustion chamber and/or the crankcase. Again, the cause must be corrected, or the problem may persist in the rebuilt engine.

10 Check the piston-to-rod clearance by twisting the piston and rod in opposite directions. Any noticeable play indicates excessive wear, which must be corrected. The piston/connecting rod assemblies should be taken to a Ford dealer or engine reconditioning specialist to have the pistons, gudgeon pins and rods checked, and new components fitted as required.

11 Don't attempt to separate the pistons from the connecting rods. This is a task for a Ford dealer or similar engine reconditioning specialist, due to the special heating equipment, press, mandrels and supports required to do the job. If the piston/connecting rod assemblies do require this sort of work, have the connecting rods checked for bend and twist, since only such engine repair specialists will have the facilities for this purpose.

12 Check the connecting rods for cracks and other damage. Temporarily remove the big-end bearing caps and the old bearing shells, wipe clean the rod and cap bearing recesses, and inspect them for nicks, gouges and scratches. After checking the rods, replace the old shells, slip the caps into place, and tighten the bolts finger-tight.

14 Crankshaft - inspection

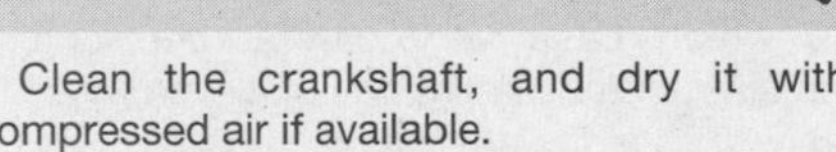

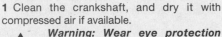

1 Clean the crankshaft, and dry it with compressed air if available.

Warning: Wear eye protection when using compressed air! Be sure to clean the oil holes with a pipe cleaner or similar probe.

2 Check the main and crankpin (big-end) bearing journals for uneven wear, scoring, pitting and cracking.

3 Rub a penny across each journal several times **(see illustration)**. If a journal picks up copper from the penny, it is too rough and should be reground.

4 Remove all burrs from the crankshaft oil holes with a stone, file or scraper.

5 Using a micrometer, measure the diameter of the main bearing and crankpin (big-end) journals, and compare the results with the Specifications at the beginning of this Chapter **(see illustration)**.

6 By measuring the diameter at a number of points around each journal's circumference, you will be able to determine whether or not the journal is out-of-round. Take the measurement at each end of the journal, near the webs, to determine if the journal is tapered.

14.3 Rubbing a penny lengthwise along each journal will reveal its condition

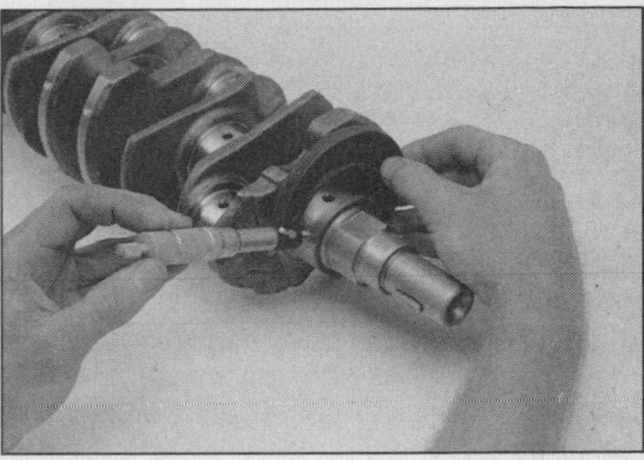

14.5 Measure the diameter of each crankshaft journal at several points, to detect taper and out-of-round conditions

7 If the crankshaft journals are damaged, tapered, out-of-round, or worn beyond the limits specified in this Chapter, the crankshaft must be taken to an engine overhaul specialist, who will regrind it, and who can supply the necessary undersize bearing shells.

8 Check the oil seal journals at each end of the crankshaft for wear and damage. If either seal has worn an excessive groove in its journal, consult an engine overhaul specialist, who will be able to advise whether a repair is possible, or whether a new crankshaft is necessary.

15 Main and big-end bearings - inspection

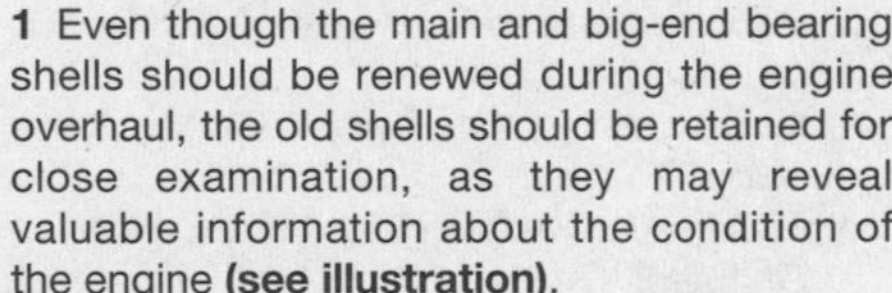

1 Even though the main and big-end bearing shells should be renewed during the engine overhaul, the old shells should be retained for close examination, as they may reveal valuable information about the condition of the engine **(see illustration)**.

2 Bearing failure occurs because of lack of lubrication, the presence of dirt or other foreign particles, overloading the engine, and corrosion. Regardless of the cause of bearing failure, it must be corrected before the engine is reassembled, to prevent it from happening again.

3 When examining the bearing shells, remove them from the cylinder block/crankcase and main bearing caps (4-cylinder models) or lower crankcase (V6 models), and from the connecting rods and the big-end bearing caps, then lay them out on a clean surface in the same general position as their location in the engine. This will enable you to match any bearing problems with the corresponding crankshaft journal. Do not touch any shell's bearing surface with your fingers while checking it, or the delicate surface may be scratched.

4 Dirt or other foreign matter gets into the engine in a variety of ways. It may be left in the engine during assembly, or it may pass through filters or the crankcase ventilation system. It may get into the oil, and from there into the bearings. Metal chips from machining operations and normal engine wear are often present. Abrasives are sometimes left in engine components after reconditioning, especially when parts are not thoroughly cleaned using the proper cleaning methods. Whatever the source, these foreign objects often end up embedded in the soft bearing material, and are easily recognized. Large particles will not embed in the material, and will score or gouge the shell and journal. The best prevention for this cause of bearing failure is to clean all parts thoroughly, and to keep everything spotlessly-clean during engine assembly. Frequent and regular engine oil and filter changes are also recommended.

5 Lack of lubrication (or lubrication breakdown) has a number of inter-related causes. Excessive heat (which thins the oil), overloading (which squeezes the oil from the bearing face) and oil leakage (from excessive bearing clearances, worn oil pump or high engine speeds) all contribute to lubrication

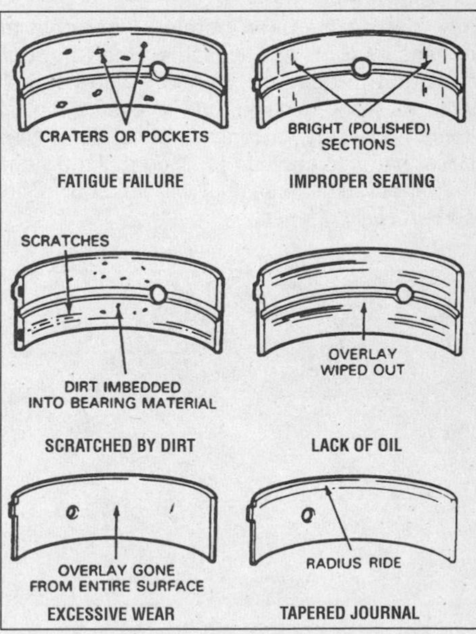

15.1 When inspecting the main and big-end bearings, look for these problems

breakdown. Blocked oil passages, which usually are the result of misaligned oil holes in a bearing shell, will also starve a bearing of oil, and destroy it. When lack of lubrication is the cause of bearing failure, the bearing material is wiped or extruded from the shell's steel backing. Temperatures may increase to the point where the steel backing turns blue from overheating.

6 Driving habits can have a definite effect on bearing life. Full-throttle, low-speed operation (labouring the engine) puts very high loads on bearings, which tends to squeeze out the oil film. These loads cause the shells to flex, which produces fine cracks in the bearing face (fatigue failure). Eventually, the bearing material will loosen in pieces, and tear away from the steel backing. Short-distance driving leads to corrosion of bearings, because insufficient engine heat is produced to drive off condensed water and corrosive gases. These products collect in the engine oil, forming acid and sludge. As the oil is carried to the engine bearings, the acid attacks and corrodes the bearing material.

7 Incorrect shell refitting during engine assembly will lead to bearing failure as well. Tight-fitting shells leave insufficient bearing running clearance, and will result in oil starvation. Dirt or foreign particles trapped behind a bearing shell result in high spots on the bearing, which lead to failure. Do not touch any shell's bearing surface with your fingers during reassembly; there is a risk of scratching the delicate surface, or of depositing particles of dirt on it.

16 Engine overhaul - reassembly sequence

1 Before reassembly begins, ensure that all new parts have been obtained, and that all necessary tools are available. Read through the entire procedure, to familiarise yourself with the work involved, and to ensure that all items necessary for reassembly of the engine are at hand. In addition to all normal tools and materials, suitable sealant will be required for certain seal surfaces.

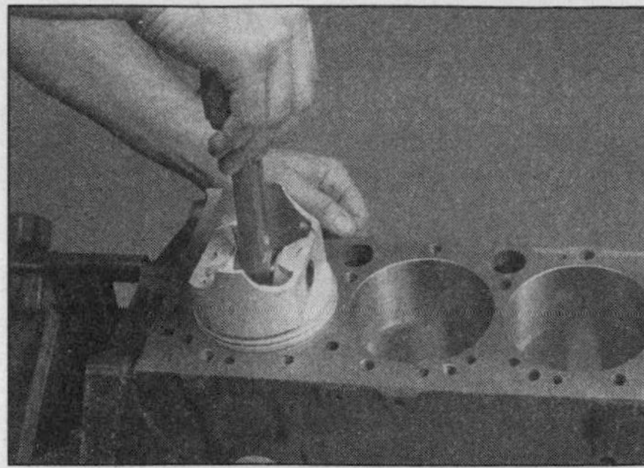

17.2 When checking piston ring end gap, the ring must be square in the cylinder bore: push the ring down with the top of a piston, as shown

Caution: Certain types of high-volatility RTV can foul the oxygen sensor and cause it to fail. Be sure that any RTV used is a low-volatility type and meets Ford specifications for use on engines equipped with an oxygen sensor.

Ford recommend Hylosil 102 for the cylinder block/crankcase-to-sump/oil pump/oil seal carrier joints, and Loctite 518 for the camshaft right-hand bearing caps. In all other cases, provided the relevant mating surfaces are clean and flat, new gaskets will be sufficient to ensure joints are oil-tight. *Do not* use any kind of silicone-based sealant on any part of the fuel system or inlet manifold, and *never* use exhaust sealants upstream of the catalytic converter.

2 In order to save time and avoid problems, engine reassembly can be carried out in the following order:

a) Crankshaft (Section 18).
b) Piston/connecting rod assemblies (Section 19).
c) Oil pump (Part A or B of this Chapter).
d) Sump (Part A or B of this Chapter).
e) Flywheel/driveplate (Part A or B of this Chapter).
f) Cylinder head(s) (Part A or B of this Chapter).
g) Timing belt/timing chains, tensioner(s) and toothed pulleys (Part A or B of this Chapter).
h) Engine external components.

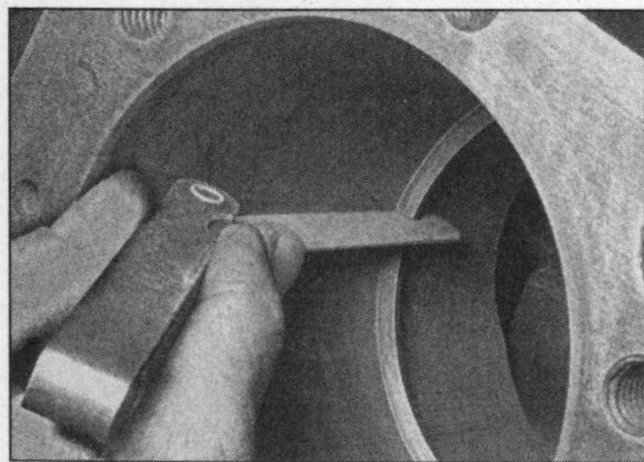

17.3 With the ring square in the bore, measure the end gap with a feeler gauge

17.6 Look for etched markings ("STD" - indicating a standard-sized ring - shown here) identifying piston ring top surface

3 At this stage, all engine components should be absolutely clean and dry, with all faults repaired. All components should be neatly arranged on a completely clean work surface or in individual containers.

17 Piston rings - refitting

1 Before installing new piston rings, check the end gaps. Lay out each piston set with a piston/connecting rod assembly, and keep them together as a matched set from now on.

2 Insert the top compression ring into the first cylinder, and square it up with the cylinder walls by pushing it in with the top of the piston **(see illustration)**. The ring should be near the bottom of the cylinder, at the lower limit of ring travel.

3 To measure the end gap, slip feeler gauges between the ends of the ring, until a gauge equal to the gap width is found **(see illustration)**. The feeler gauge should slide between the ring ends with a slight amount of drag. Compare the measurement to the value given in the Specifications Section of this Chapter; if the gap is larger or smaller than specified, double-check to make sure you have the correct rings before proceeding. If you are assessing the condition of used rings, have the cylinder bores checked and measured by a Ford dealer or similar engine reconditioning specialist, so that you can be sure of exactly which component is worn, and seek advice as to the best course of action to take.

4 If the end gap is still too small, it must be opened up by careful filing of the ring ends using a fine file. If it is too large, this is not as serious, unless the specified limit is exceeded, in which case very careful checking is required of the dimensions of all components, as well as of the new parts.

5 Repeat the procedure for each ring that will be installed in the first cylinder, and for each ring in the remaining cylinders. Remember to keep rings, pistons and cylinders matched up.

6 Refit the piston rings as follows. Where the original rings are being refitted, use the marks or notes made on removal, to ensure that each ring is refitted to its original groove and the same way up. New rings generally have their top surfaces identified by markings (often an indication of size, such as "STD", or the word "TOP") - the rings must be fitted with such markings uppermost **(see illustration)**. **Note:** *Always follow the instructions printed on the ring package or box - different manufacturers may require different approaches. Do not mix up the top and second compression rings, as they usually have different cross-sections.*

7 The oil control ring (lowest one on the piston) is usually installed first. It is composed of three separate elements. Slip the spacer/expander into the groove **(see**

illustration). Next, install the lower side rail. Don't use a piston ring installation tool on the oil ring side rails, as they may be damaged. Instead, place one end of the side rail into the groove between the spacer/expander and the ring land, hold it firmly in place, and slide a finger around the piston while pushing the rail into the groove **(see illustration)**. Next, install the upper side rail in the same manner.

8 After the three oil ring components have been installed, check that both the upper and lower side rails can be turned smoothly in the ring groove.

9 The second compression (middle) ring is installed next, followed by the top compression ring - ensure their marks are uppermost. Don't expand either ring any more than necessary to slide it over the top of the piston.

10 With all the rings in position, space the ring gaps (including the elements of the oil control ring) uniformly around the piston at 120° intervals. Repeat the procedure for the remaining pistons and rings.

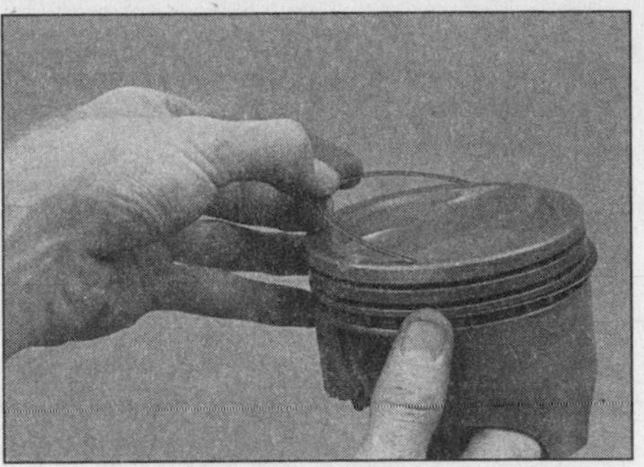

17.7a Installing the spacer/expander in the oil control ring groove

17.7b DO NOT use a piston ring installation tool when installing the oil ring side rails

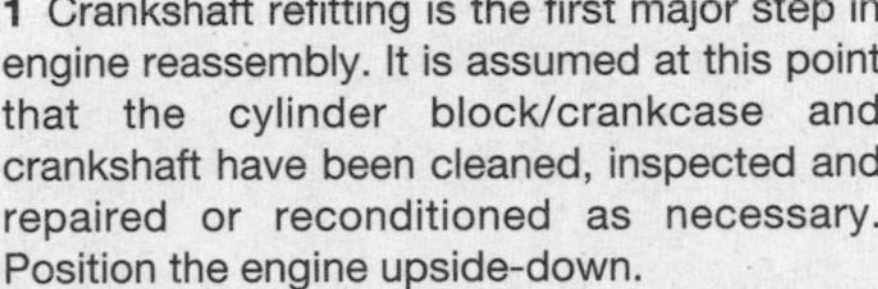

18 Crankshaft - refitting and main bearing running clearance check

1 Crankshaft refitting is the first major step in engine reassembly. It is assumed at this point that the cylinder block/crankcase and crankshaft have been cleaned, inspected and repaired or reconditioned as necessary. Position the engine upside-down.

2 On 4-cylinder models, remove the main bearing cap bolts, and lift out the caps. Lay the caps out in the proper order, to ensure correct installation. On V6 models, remove the lower crankcase from the cylinder block.

3 If they're still in place, remove the old bearing shells from the block and the main bearing caps (or lower crankcase on the V6 engine). Wipe the bearing recesses with a clean, lint-free cloth. They must be kept spotlessly-clean!

Main bearing running clearance check

4 Clean the backs of the new main bearing shells. Fit the shells with an oil groove in each main bearing location in the block. On 4-cylinder models, note the thrustwashers integral with the No 3 (centre) upper main bearing shell. On V6 models, note the semi-circle shaped thrustwasher located adjacent to the No 4 (transmission end) upper main bearing. Fit the other shell from each bearing set in the corresponding main bearing cap (4-cylinder models) or lower crankcase (V6 models). Make sure the tab on each bearing shell fits into the notch in the block or cap/lower crankcase. Also, the oil holes in the block must line up with the oil holes in the bearing shell **(see illustration)**. Don't hammer the shells into place, and don't nick or gouge the bearing faces. No lubrication should be used at this time.

5 Clean the bearing surfaces of the shells in the block and the crankshaft main bearing journals with a clean, lint-free cloth. Check or clean the oil holes in the crankshaft, as any dirt here will go straight through the new bearings.

6 Once you're certain the crankshaft is clean, carefully lay it in position in the main bearings. Trim several pieces of the appropriate-size Plastigage (they must be slightly shorter than the width of the main bearings), and place one piece on each crankshaft main bearing journal, parallel with the crankshaft centre-line **(see illustration)**.

7 Clean the bearing surfaces of the bearings in the caps (4-cylinder models) or lower crankcase (V6 models). On 4-cylinder models, install the caps in their respective positions (don't mix them up) with the arrows pointing to the timing belt end of the engine. Don't disturb the Plastigage **(see illustration)**. On V6 models, refit the lower crankcase.

8 On 4-cylinder models, working on one cap at a time, from the centre main bearing outwards (and ensuring that each cap is tightened down squarely and evenly onto the block), tighten the main bearing cap bolts to the specified torque wrench setting. **Note:** *On V6 models, the interior bolts securing the lower crankcase to the cylinder block are the torque-to-yield type and must be renewed during final assembly. It is acceptable, however, to perform the main bearing oil clearance check using the original bolts. On V6 models, tighten the lower crankcase bolts as described later in this Section. Don't rotate the crankshaft at any time during this operation!*

9 Remove the bolts, and carefully lift off the main bearing caps (4-cylinder models) or lower crankcase (V6 models). Don't disturb the Plastigage or rotate the crankshaft. If any of the main bearing caps are difficult to remove, tap them gently from side-to-side with a soft-faced mallet to loosen them.

10 Compare the width of the crushed Plastigage on each journal with the scale printed on the Plastigage envelope to obtain the main bearing running clearance **(see illustration)**. Check the Specifications to make sure that the clearance is correct.

11 If the clearance is not as specified, seek

2C

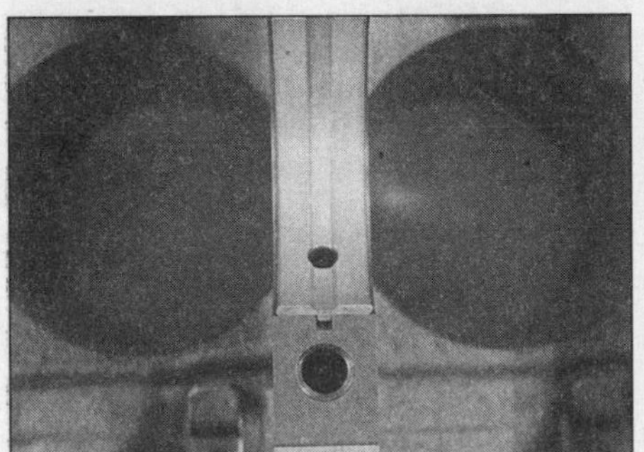

18.4 Tab on each bearing shell must engage with notch in block or cap, and oil holes in upper shells must align with block oilways

18.6 Lay the Plastigage strips (arrowed) on the main bearing journals, parallel to the crankshaft centre-line

18.7 Refit the main bearing caps and tighten the bolts as specified

18.10 Compare the width of the crushed Plastigage to the scale on the envelope to determine the main bearing clearance (always take the measurement at the widest point of the Plastigage)

the advice of a Ford dealer or similar engine reconditioning specialist - if the crankshaft journals are in good condition, it may be possible simply to renew the shells to achieve the correct clearance. If this is not possible, the crankshaft must be reground by a specialist who can supply the necessary undersized shells. First though, make sure that no dirt or oil was between the bearing shells and the caps or block when the clearance was measured. If the Plastigage is noticeably wider at one end than the other, the journal may be tapered.

12 Carefully scrape all traces of the Plastigage material off the main bearing journals and the bearing surfaces. Be very careful not to scratch the bearing - use your fingernail or the edge of a credit card.

Final refitting

13 Carefully lift the crankshaft out of the engine. Clean the bearing surfaces of the shells in the block, then apply a thin, uniform layer of clean molybdenum disulphide-based grease, engine assembly lubricant, or clean engine oil to each surface **(see illustration)**. Coat the thrustwasher surfaces as well.

14 Lubricate the crankshaft oil seal journals with molybdenum disulphide-based grease, engine assembly lubricant, or clean engine oil.

15 Make sure the crankshaft journals are

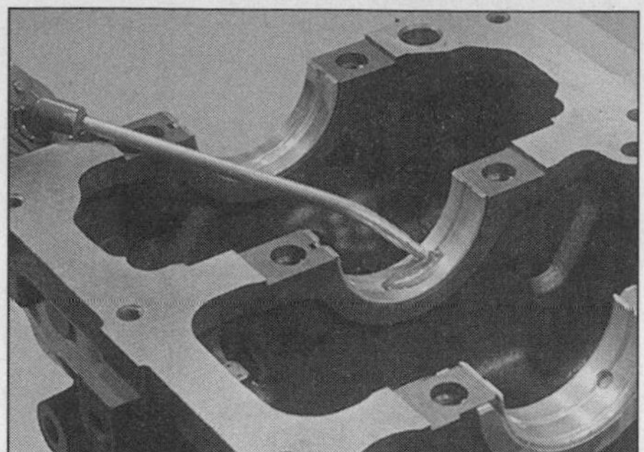

18.13 Ensure bearing shells are absolutely clean, lubricate liberally . . .

clean, then lay the crankshaft back in place in the block **(see illustration)**.

16 On 4-cylinder models, refit and tighten the main bearing caps as follows:

a) Clean the bearing surfaces of the shells in the caps, then lubricate them. Refit the caps in their respective positions, with the arrows pointing to the timing belt end of the engine.

b) Working on one cap at a time, from the centre main bearing outwards (and ensuring that each cap is tightened down squarely and evenly onto the block), tighten the main bearing cap bolts to the specified torque wrench setting.

17 On V6 models, clean the bearing surfaces of the bearings in the lower crankcase. Lubricate the bearings. Note that the No 4 bearing (transmission end) is also the thrust control bearing.

a) Apply a 3.0 mm bead of RTV sealant to the cylinder block in the positions indicated in the accompanying illustration ***(see illustration). Do not*** *apply the sealant within 6.0 mm of the rear oil seal seating.*

b) Apply a 1.0 mm bead of RTV sealant to the cylinder block in the positions indicated in the accompanying illustration ***(see illustration). Do not*** *apply the sealant within 6.0 mm of the rear oil seal seating.*

c) Insert the lower crankcase bolts. Make sure new interior bolts are fitted. Tighten the bolts in the sequence and stages given in Specifications.

18.15 . . . and refit the crankshaft

18 Rotate the crankshaft a number of times by hand, to check for any obvious binding.

19 Check the crankshaft endfloat (see Section 11). It should be correct if the crankshaft thrust faces aren't worn or damaged, and if the thrust control bearing(s) has been renewed.

20 On 4-cylinder models, refit the crankshaft left-hand oil seal carrier, and install a new seal (see Part A of this Chapter).

21 On V6 models, fit a new rear oil seal (see Part B of this Chapter).

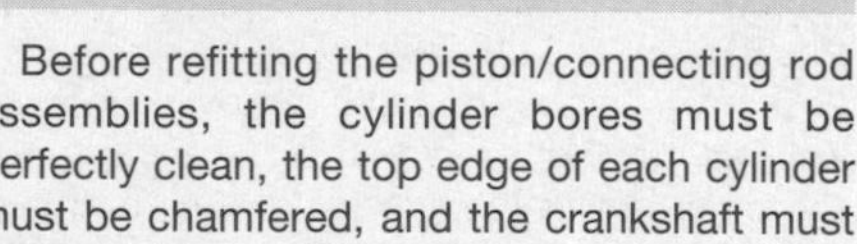

19 Piston/connecting rod assemblies - refitting and big-end bearing running clearance check

1 Before refitting the piston/connecting rod assemblies, the cylinder bores must be perfectly clean, the top edge of each cylinder must be chamfered, and the crankshaft must be in place.

2 Remove the big-end bearing cap from No 1 cylinder connecting rod (refer to the marks noted or made on removal). Remove the original bearing shells, and wipe the bearing recesses of the connecting rod and cap with a clean, lint-free cloth. They must be kept spotlessly-clean!

Big-end bearing running clearance check

3 Clean the back of the new upper bearing shell, fit it to the connecting rod, then fit the other shell of the bearing set to the big-end bearing cap. Make sure the tab on each shell fits into the notch in the rod or cap recess **(see illustration)**.

Caution: Don't hammer the shells into place, and don't nick or gouge the bearing face. Don't lubricate the bearing at this time.

4 It's critically important that all mating surfaces of the bearing components are perfectly clean and oil-free when they're assembled.

5 Position the piston ring gaps as described in Section 17, lubricate the piston and rings with clean engine oil, and attach a piston ring

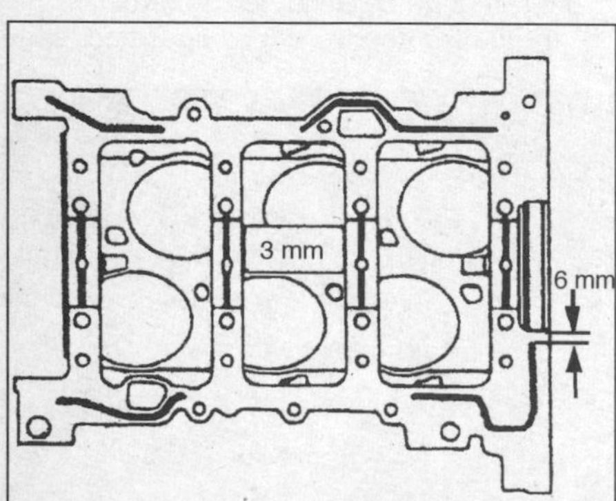

18.17a Before refitting the lower crankcase, apply a 3.0 mm bead of RTV sealant as shown on the cylinder block . . .

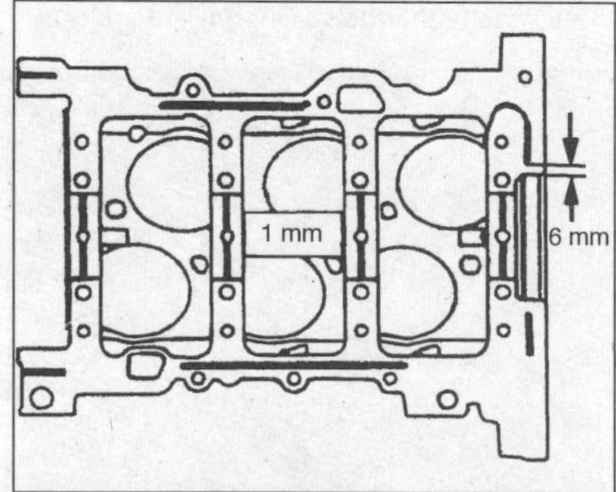

18.17b . . . then apply a 1.0 mm bead of RTV sealant as shown on the cylinder block

19.3 Tab on each big-end bearing shell must engage with notch in connecting rod or cap

compressor to the piston. Leave the skirt protruding about a quarter-inch, to guide the piston into the cylinder bore. The rings must be compressed until they're flush with the piston.

6 Rotate the crankshaft until No 1 crankpin (big-end) journal is at BDC (Bottom Dead Centre), and apply a coat of engine oil to the cylinder walls.

7 Arrange the No 1 piston/connecting rod assembly so that the arrow on the piston crown points to the timing belt (4-cylinder models) or timing chain (V6 models) end of the engine. Gently insert the assembly into the No 1 cylinder bore, and rest the bottom edge of the ring compressor on the engine block.

8 Tap the top edge of the ring compressor to make sure it's contacting the block around its entire circumference.

9 Gently tap on the top of the piston with the end of a wooden hammer handle **(see illustration)**, while guiding the connecting rod's big-end onto the crankpin. The piston rings may try to pop out of the ring compressor just before entering the cylinder bore, so keep some pressure on the ring compressor. Work slowly, and if any resistance is felt as the piston enters the cylinder, stop immediately. Find out what's binding, and fix it before proceeding. Do not, for any reason, force the piston into the cylinder - you might break a ring and/or the piston.

10 To check the big-end bearing running clearance, cut a piece of the appropriate-size Plastigage slightly shorter than the width of the connecting rod bearing, and lay it in place on the No 1 crankpin (big-end) journal, parallel with the crankshaft centre-line.

11 Clean the connecting rod-to-cap mating surfaces, and refit the big-end bearing cap. Make sure the etched number on the cap is on the same side as that on the rod **(see illustration)**. **Note:** *On V6 models, the big-end bolts are torque-to-yield bolts. During final assembly, the original bolts must be discarded and new ones fitted. It is acceptable, however, to use the original bolts during the oil clearance check. Tighten the cap bolts evenly. First use a torque wrench to tighten the bolts to the specified torque stage(s), then use an ordinary socket extension bar and an angle gauge to tighten the bolts further through the specified angle. Use a thin-walled socket, to avoid erroneous torque readings that can result if the socket is wedged between the cap and nut/bolt. If the socket tends to wedge itself between the nut/bolt and the cap, lift it up slightly until it no longer contacts the cap. Don't rotate the crankshaft at any time during this operation!*

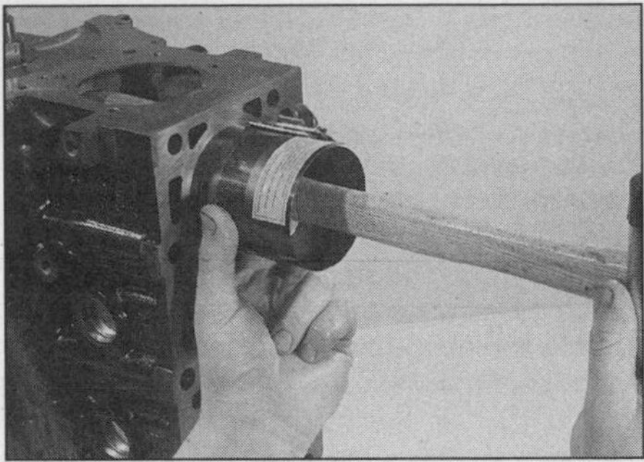

19.9 The piston can be driven gently into the cylinder bore with the end of a wooden or plastic hammer handle

12 Unscrew the bolts and detach the cap, being very careful not to disturb the Plastigage.

13 Compare the width of the crushed Plastigage to the scale printed on the Plastigage envelope, to obtain the running clearance. Compare it to the Specifications, to make sure the clearance is correct.

14 If the clearance is not as specified, seek the advice of a Ford dealer or similar engine reconditioning specialist - if the crankshaft journals are in good condition, it may be possible simply to renew the shells to achieve the correct clearance. If this is not possible, the crankshaft must be reground by a specialist, who can also supply the necessary undersized shells. First though, make sure that no dirt or oil was trapped between the bearing shells and the connecting rod or cap when the clearance was measured. Also, recheck the crankpin diameter. If the Plastigage was wider at one end than the other, the crankpin journal may be tapered.

15 Carefully scrape all traces of the Plastigage material off the journal and the bearing surface. Be very careful not to scratch the bearing - use your fingernail or the edge of a credit card.

Final piston/connecting rod refitting

16 Make sure the bearing surfaces are perfectly clean, then apply a uniform layer of clean molybdenum disulphide-based grease, engine assembly lubricant, or clean engine oil, to both of them. You'll have to push the piston into the cylinder to expose the bearing surface of the shell in the connecting rod.

17 Slide the connecting rod back into place on the crankpin (big-end) journal, refit the big-end bearing cap, and then tighten the bolts in stages described above.

19.11 The connecting rod and big-end bearing cap of each assembly must share the same etched cylinder number, visible from the same (front/exhaust) side of the engine

18 Repeat the entire procedure for the remaining piston/connecting rod assemblies.

19 The important points to remember are:

a) Keep the backs of the bearing shells and the recesses of the connecting rods and caps perfectly clean when assembling them.

b) Make sure you have the correct piston/rod assembly for each cylinder - use the etched cylinder numbers to identify the front-facing side of both the rod and its cap.

c) The arrow on the piston crown must face the timing belt (4-cylinder engine) or timing chain (V6 engine) end of the engine ***(see illustration)****.*

d) Lubricate the cylinder bores with clean engine oil.

e) Lubricate the bearing surfaces when refitting the big-end bearing caps after the running clearance has been checked.

20 After all the piston/connecting rod assemblies have been properly installed, rotate the crankshaft a number of times by hand, to check for any obvious binding.

21 On 5/1998-on 4-cylinder models, apply sealant to the joints between the cylinder block and oil pump/oil seal carrier, then refit the new lower crankcase-to-cylinder block gasket. Refit the lower crankcase to the cylinder block, insert the bolts and hand-tighten. Place a straight-edge across the transmission mating surface of the cylinder

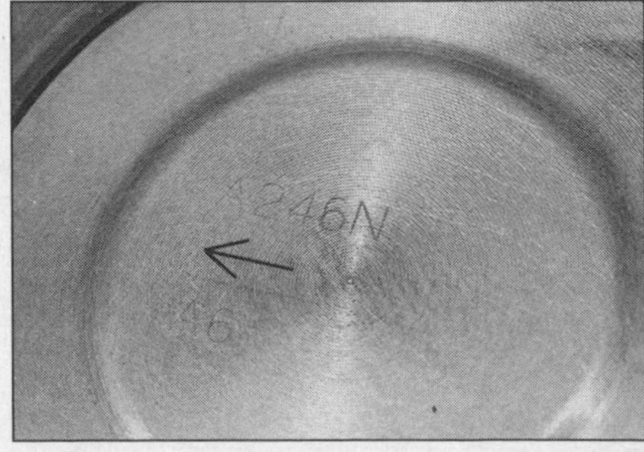

19.19 The arrow on the piston crown must point to the timing belt/chain end of the engine

block and the lower crankcase to check the lower crankcase-to-cylinder block alignment. The lower crankcase should be flush with the cylinder block. If not flush, the alignment should be within:

a) *A 0.10 mm overlap to a 0.25 mm gap on models equipped with a manual transmission.*
b) *No overlap to a 0.25 mm gap on models equipped with an automatic transmission.*

If necessary, fit shims to the lower crankcase.

22 Once the alignment is within specifications, tighten the lower crankcase bolts to the specified torque.

20 Engine - initial start-up after overhaul

1 With the engine refitted in the vehicle, double-check the engine oil and coolant levels. Make a final check that everything has been reconnected, and that there are no tools or rags left in the engine compartment.

2 With the spark plugs removed and the ignition system disabled by unplugging the ignition coil's electrical connector, remove fuse 14 to disconnect the fuel pump. Turn the engine on the starter until the oil pressure warning light goes out.

3 Refit the spark plugs, and connect all the spark plug (HT) leads (Chapter 1). Reconnect the ignition coil wiring, refit the fuel pump fuse, then switch on the ignition and listen for the fuel pump; it will run for a little longer than usual, due to the lack of pressure in the system.

4 Start the engine, noting that this also may take a little longer than usual, due to the fuel system components being empty.

5 While the engine is idling, check for fuel, coolant and oil leaks. Don't be alarmed if there are some odd smells and smoke from parts getting hot and burning off oil deposits. If the hydraulic tappets have been disturbed, some valve gear noise may be heard at first; this should disappear as the oil circulates fully around the engine, and normal pressure is restored in the tappets.

6 Keep the engine idling until hot water is felt circulating through the top hose, check that it idles reasonably smoothly and at the usual speed, then switch it off.

7 After a few minutes, recheck the oil and coolant levels, and top-up as necessary ("*Weekly checks*").

8 If they were tightened as described, there is no need to re-tighten the cylinder head bolts once the engine has first run after reassembly - in fact, Ford state that the bolts must not be re-tightened.

9 If new components such as pistons, rings or crankshaft bearings have been fitted, the engine must be run-in for the first 500 miles (800 km). Do not operate the engine at full-throttle, or allow it to labour in any gear during this period. It is recommended that the oil and filter be changed at the end of this period.

Chapter 3
Cooling, heating & air conditioning systems

Contents

Degrees of difficulty

Easy, suitable for novice with little experience 

Fairly easy, suitable for beginner with some experience 

Fairly difficult, suitable for competent DIY mechanic

Difficult, suitable for experienced DIY mechanic

Very difficult, suitable for expert DIY or professional 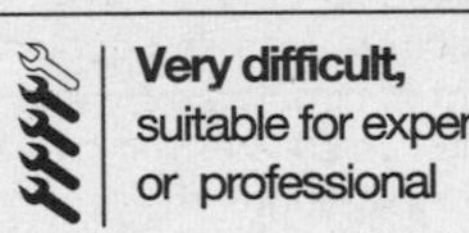

3

Specifications

Coolant

Mixture type	See *"Lubricants and fluids"*
Cooling system capacity	See Chapter 1

System pressure

Pressure test	1.2 bars - should hold this pressure for at least 10 seconds

Expansion tank filler cap

Pressure rating	1.2 bars approximately - see cap for actual value

Thermostat

Starts to open	92°C
Fully-open	106°C

Radiator electric cooling fan

Switches on at:	
Single-speed fans, two-speed fans - first stage	100°C
Two-speed fans - second stage	103°C
Switches off at:	
Single-speed fans, two-speed fans - first stage	93°C
Two-speed fans - second stage	100°C

Coolant temperature sensor

Resistance:	
At -40°C	860.0 to 900.0 kilohms
At 20°C	35.0 to 40.0 kilohms
At 100°C	1.9 to 2.5 kilohms
At 120°C	1.0 to 1.3 kilohms

Air conditioning system

Refrigerant	R134a

Torque wrench settings

	Nm	lbf ft
Air conditioning compressor mounting bolts	25	18
Air conditioning dehydrator to subframe	11	8
Coolant temperature gauge sender	8	6
Coolant temperature sensor	23	17
Fluid cooler pipe unions - automatic transmission	27	20
Radiator support bracket bolts	10	7
Thermostat cover/housing bolts:		
Four-cylinder engines	9	7
V6 engine	18	13
Water outlet-to-thermostat housing bolts	8 to 11	6 to 8
Water pump bolts:		
Four-cylinder engines	20	15
V6 engine:		
Water pump housing-to-cylinder head bolts (three):		
Stage 1	10	7
Stage 2	Angle-tighten a further 90°	
Water pump-to-housing bolts (five)	18	13
Water pump pulley bolts (four-cylinder engines)	12	9

1 General information

Engine cooling system

All vehicles covered by this manual employ a pressurised engine cooling system with thermostatically-controlled coolant circulation. The coolant is circulated by an impeller-type water pump, which is driven by the crankshaft pulley on four-cylinder engines, or by a pulley attached to the front inlet camshaft on the V6 engine. In both cases, an auxiliary drivebelt is used to drive the water pump. The coolant flows through the cylinder block around each cylinder; in the cylinder head(s), cast-in coolant passages direct coolant around the inlet and exhaust ports, near the spark plug areas and close to the exhaust valve guides.

A wax pellet type thermostat is located in a housing at the transmission end of the engine. During warm-up, the closed thermostat prevents coolant from circulating through the radiator. Instead, it returns through the coolant metal pipe running across the front of the engine to the radiator bottom hose. The supply to the heater is made from the rear of the thermostat housing. As the engine nears normal operating temperature, the thermostat opens and allows hot coolant to travel through the radiator, where it is cooled before returning to the engine.

The radiator is of aluminium construction, and has plastic end tanks. On models with automatic transmission, the fluid cooler is incorporated in the left-hand end tank.

The cooling system is sealed by a pressure-type filler cap in the expansion tank. The pressure in the system raises the boiling point of the coolant, and increases the cooling efficiency of the radiator. When the engine is at normal operating temperature, the coolant expands, and the surplus is displaced into the expansion tank. When the system cools, the surplus coolant is automatically drawn back from the tank into the radiator.

Warning: DO NOT attempt to remove the expansion tank filler cap, or to disturb any part of the cooling system, while it or the engine is hot, as there is a very great risk of scalding. If the expansion tank filler cap must be removed before the engine and radiator have fully cooled down (even though this is not recommended) the pressure in the cooling system must first be released. Cover the cap with a thick layer of cloth, to avoid scalding, and slowly unscrew the filler cap until a hissing sound can be heard. When the hissing has stopped, showing that pressure is released, slowly unscrew the filler cap further until it can be removed; if more hissing sounds are heard, wait until they have stopped before unscrewing the cap completely. At all times, keep well away from the filler opening.

Warning: Do not allow antifreeze to come in contact with your skin, or with the painted surfaces of the vehicle. Rinse off spills immediately with plenty of water. Never leave antifreeze lying around in an open container, or in a puddle in the driveway or on the garage floor. Children and pets are attracted by its sweet smell, but antifreeze is fatal if ingested.

Warning: If the engine is hot, the electric cooling fan may start rotating even if the engine is not running, so be careful to keep hands, hair and loose clothing well clear when working in the engine compartment.

Heating/ventilation system

The heating system consists of a blower fan and heater matrix (radiator) located in the heater unit, with hoses connecting the heater matrix to the engine cooling system. Hot engine coolant is circulated through the heater matrix. When the heater temperature control on the facia is operated, a flap door opens to expose the heater box to the passenger compartment. When the blower control is operated, the blower fan forces air through the unit according to the setting selected. On models without air conditioning, the heater control is linked to the flap door by a Bowden cable.

Incoming fresh air for the ventilation system passes through a pollen filter mounted below the windscreen cowl panel (see Chapter 1) - this ensures that most particules will be removed before the air enters the cabin. However, it is vital that the pollen filter is changed regularly, since a blocked filter will significantly reduce airflow to the cabin, leading to reduced demisting.

The ventilation system air distribution is controlled by a number of vacuum-operated flap doors on the heater housing. Vacuum supply is taken from the engine, through a one-way valve, to a vacuum reservoir. From there, the vacuum is taken through a vacuum distribution block to the three vacuum units on the heater housing. The vacuum hoses are colour-coded as follows:

a) Black - main vacuum supply
b) White - supply to recirculation flap
c) Grey and blue - supply/return to floor level flap
d) Red and yellow - supply/return to demister flap

Air conditioning system

See Section 11.

2 Antifreeze - general information

The cooling system should be filled with a water/ethylene glycol-based antifreeze solution, of a strength which will prevent freezing down to at least -25°C, or lower if the local climate requires it. Antifreeze also provides protection against corrosion, and increases the coolant boiling point.

The cooling system should be maintained according to the schedule described in Chapter 1. If antifreeze is used that is not to Ford's specification, old or contaminated coolant mixtures are likely to cause damage, and encourage the formation of corrosion and scale in the system. Use distilled water with the antifreeze, if available - if not, be sure to use only soft water. Clean rainwater is suitable.

Before adding antifreeze, check all hoses and hose connections, because antifreeze tends to leak through very small openings. Engines don't normally consume coolant, so if the level goes down, find the cause and correct it.

The exact mixture of antifreeze-to-water which you should use depends on the relative weather conditions. The mixture should contain at least 40% antifreeze, but not more than 70%. Consult the mixture ratio chart on the antifreeze container before adding coolant. Hydrometers are available at most automotive accessory shops to test the coolant. Use antifreeze which meets the vehicle manufacturer's specifications.

3 Cooling system hoses - disconnection and renewal

Note: *Refer to the warnings given in Section 1 of this Chapter before starting work.*

1 If the checks described in Chapter 1 reveal a faulty hose, it must be renewed as follows.

2 First drain the cooling system (see Chapter 1); if the antifreeze is not due for renewal, the drained coolant may be re-used, if it is collected in a clean container.

3 To disconnect any hose, use a pair of pliers to release the spring clamps (or a screwdriver to slacken screw-type clamps), then move them along the hose clear of the union. Carefully work the hose off its stubs. The hoses can be removed with relative ease when new - on an older car, they may have stuck.

4 If a hose proves stubborn, try to release it by rotating it on its unions before attempting to work it off. Gently prise the end of the hose with a blunt instrument (such as a flat-bladed screwdriver), but do not apply too much force, and take care not to damage the pipe stubs or hoses. Note in particular that the radiator hose unions are fragile; do not use excessive force

4.5 Unbolt the cover and withdraw the thermostat

when attempting to remove the hoses. If all else fails, cut the hose with a sharp knife, then slit it so that it can be peeled off in two pieces. While expensive, this is preferable to buying a new radiator. Check first, however, that a new hose is readily available.

5 When refitting a hose, first slide the clamps onto the hose, then work the hose onto its unions. If the hose is stiff, use soap (or washing-up liquid) as a lubricant, or soften it by soaking it in boiling water, but take care to prevent scalding.

6 Work each hose end fully onto its union, then check that the hose is settled correctly and is properly routed. Slide each clip along the hose until it is behind the union flared end, before tightening it securely.

7 Refill the system with coolant (see Chapter 1).

8 Check carefully for leaks as soon as possible after disturbing any part of the cooling system.

4 Thermostat - removal, testing and refitting

Note: *Refer to the warnings given in Section 1 of this Chapter before starting work.*

Removal

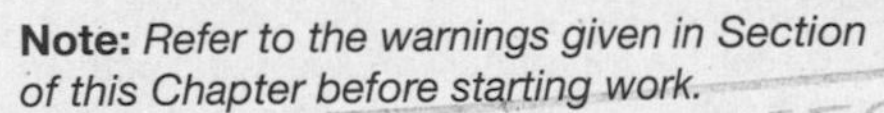

1 Disconnect the battery negative (earth) lead (see Chapter 5A, Section 1).

2 Drain the cooling system (see Chapter 1). If the coolant is relatively new or in good condition, drain it into a clean container and re-use it.

4.8a Unscrew the two thermostat housing bolts . . .

Four-cylinder engines

3 Where applicable, unbolt the resonator support bracket from the engine compartment front crossmember. Slacken the two clamp screws securing the resonator to the air mass meter and plenum chamber hoses, then swing the resonator up clear of the thermostat housing (see Chapter 4A, Section 4).

4 Disconnect the expansion tank coolant hose and the radiator top hose from the thermostat housing's water outlet.

5 Unbolt the thermostat cover and withdraw the thermostat **(see illustration)**. Note the position of the air bleed valve, and how the thermostat is installed (which end is facing outwards).

V6 engine

6 Loosen and remove the retaining screws, and remove the water pump drivebelt cover.

7 Remove the battery as described in Chapter 5A, and disconnect the air cleaner inlet hose with reference to Chapter 4A.

8 Separate the halves of the housing by unscrewing the two bolts, and remove the O-ring seal **(see illustrations)**. Discard the O-ring seal - a new one must be used on reassembly. 3

9 Extract the thermostat, noting its direction of fitting **(see illustration)**.

Testing

General check

10 Before assuming the thermostat is to blame for a cooling system problem, check the coolant level (see "*Weekly checks*"), the

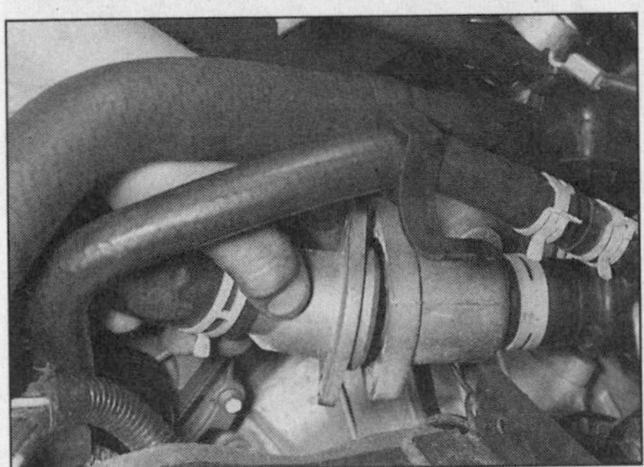

4.8b . . . separate the two halves of the housing . . .

4.8c . . . and remove the O-ring seal

4.9 Removing the thermostat

auxiliary drivebelt tension and condition (see Chapter 1) and the temperature gauge operation.

11 If the engine seems to be taking a long time to warm up (based on heater output or temperature gauge operation), the thermostat is probably stuck open. Renew the thermostat.

12 Equally, a lengthy warm-up period might suggest that the thermostat is missing - it may have been removed or inadvertently omitted by a previous owner or mechanic. Don't drive the vehicle without a thermostat - the engine management system's ECU will then stay in warm-up mode for longer than necessary, causing emissions and fuel economy to suffer.

13 If the engine runs hot, use your hand to check the temperature of the radiator top hose. If the hose isn't hot, but the engine is, the thermostat is probably stuck closed, preventing the coolant inside the engine from escaping to the radiator - renew the thermostat.

14 If the radiator top hose is hot, it means that the coolant is flowing and the thermostat is open. Consult the "*Fault finding*" Section at the end of this manual to assist in tracing possible cooling system faults.

Thermostat test

15 If the thermostat remains in the open position at room temperature, it is faulty, and must be renewed as a matter of course.

16 To test it fully, suspend the (closed) thermostat on a length of string in a container of cold water, with a thermometer beside it; ensure that neither touches the side of the container.

17 Heat the water, and check the temperature at which the thermostat begins to open; compare this value with that specified. Checking the fully-open temperature is not possible in an open container, as it is higher than the boiling point of water at atmospheric pressure. Remove the thermostat and allow it to cool down; check that it closes fully.

18 If the thermostat does not open and close as described, if it sticks in either position, or if it does not open at the specified temperature, it must be renewed.

Refitting

19 Refitting is the reverse of the removal procedure, noting the following points:

a) *Clean the mating surfaces carefully, and renew the thermostat's sealing ring.*
b) *Fit the thermostat in the same position as noted on removal - on four-cylinder models, the air bleed valve should be uppermost* **(see illustration)**.
c) *Tighten the thermostat cover/housing bolts to the specified torque wrench setting.*
d) *Remake all the coolant hose connections, then refill the cooling system as described in Chapter 1.*
e) *Start the engine and allow it to reach normal operating temperature, then check for leaks and proper thermostat operation.*

4.19 On four-cylinder models, ensure the thermostat is refitted as shown

5 Radiator electric cooling fan(s) - testing, removal and refitting

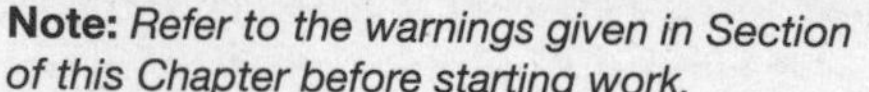

Note: *Refer to the warnings given in Section 1 of this Chapter before starting work.*

Testing

1 The radiator cooling fan is controlled by the engine management system's ECU, acting on the information received from the coolant temperature sensor. Where twin fans or two-speed fans are fitted, control is through a resistor assembly, secured to the bottom left-hand corner of the fan shroud - this can be renewed separately if faulty.

2 First, check the relevant fuses and relays (see Chapter 12).

3 To test the fan motor, unplug the electrical connector, and use fused jumper wires to connect the fan directly to the battery. If the fan still does not work, renew the motor.

4 If the motor proved sound, the fault lies in the coolant temperature sensor (see Section 6 for testing details), in the wiring loom (see Chapter 12 for testing details) or in the engine management system (see Chapter 4A).

Removal

Four-cylinder engine models

5 Disconnect the battery negative (earth) lead (see Chapter 5A, Section 1).

6 Where applicable, unbolt the resonator support bracket from the engine compartment front crossmember. Slacken the two clamp screws securing the resonator to the air mass meter and plenum chamber hoses, then swing the resonator up clear of the thermostat housing (see Chapter 4A, Section 4).

7 Drain the cooling system (see Chapter 1).

8 Remove the radiator top hose completely. Disconnect the metal coolant pipe/hose from the thermostat, and unbolt the coolant pipe from the exhaust manifold heat shield.

9 Unplug the cooling fan electrical connector(s), then release all wiring and hoses from the fan shroud.

10 Unscrew the two nuts securing the fan shroud, then lift the assembly to disengage it from its bottom mountings and from the radiator top edge **(see illustrations)**.

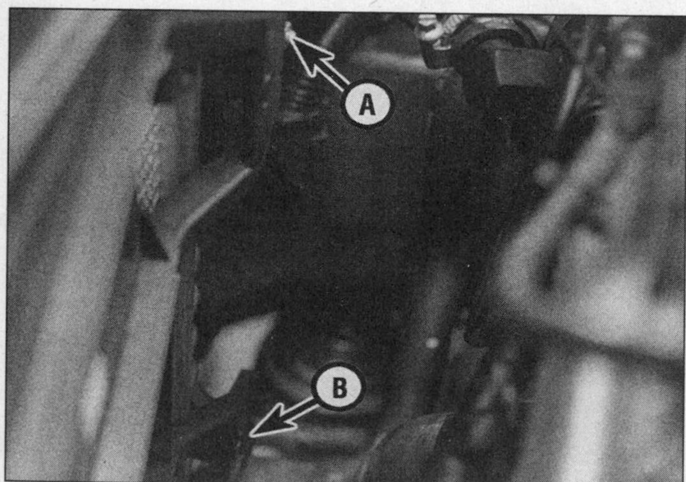

5.10a Fan shroud is secured at top by mounting nut (A), at bottom by clip (B) . . .

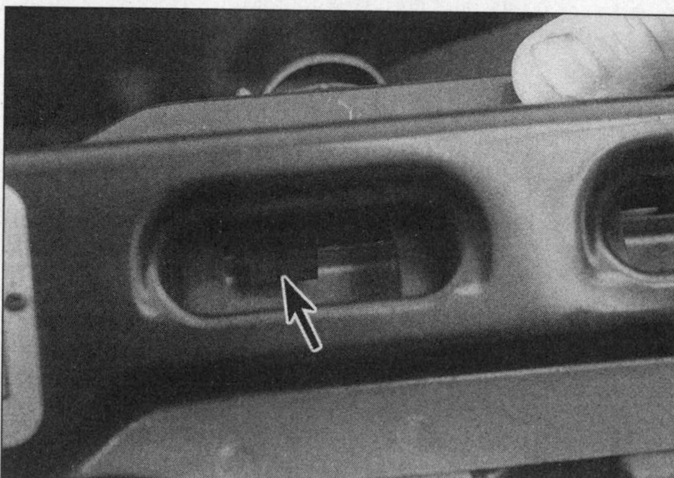

5.10b . . . and is hooked over radiator top edge (one point arrowed)

5.11 Removing the radiator electric cooling fan and shroud assembly

11 Withdraw the fan and shroud as an assembly **(see illustration)**.

V6 engine models

12 Disconnect the battery negative (earth) lead (see Chapter 5A, Section 1).

13 Drain the cooling system (see Chapter 1).

14 Unplug the cooling fan electrical connector(s), then release all wiring and hoses from the fan shroud. On models with air conditioning, move the air conditioning hoses as necessary for access, but do not disconnect any of them.

15 Unscrew the two nuts securing the fan shroud, then lift the assembly to disengage it from its bottom mountings and from the radiator top edge.

16 Move the assembly as far to the rear as possible - if preferred, tie it back to the engine, out of the way.

17 Owing to the extremely limited access at the front of the engine compartment, we found that the radiator must be removed to allow the cooling fan assembly to be withdrawn. Refer to the procedure in Section 7.

18 With the radiator removed, the cooling fan assembly can be lowered out of the engine compartment, and removed.

All models

19 At the time of writing, the fan, motor and shroud are available only as a complete assembly, and must be renewed together if faulty.

Refitting

20 Refitting is the reverse of the removal procedure, noting the following points:

a) *On V6 engine models, lift the fan assembly into position before refitting the radiator as described in Section 7. If the radiator is fitted first, there will not be enough room to refit the fan assembly.*
b) *Ensure that the shroud is settled correctly at all four mounting points before refitting and tightening the nuts.*
c) *Refill the cooling system as described in Chapter 1.*

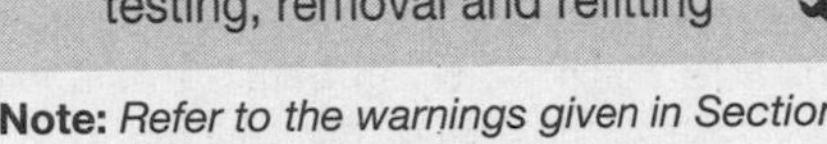

6 Cooling system electrical switches and sensors - testing, removal and refitting

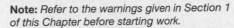

Note: *Refer to the warnings given in Section 1 of this Chapter before starting work.*

Coolant temperature gauge sender

1 The sender is screwed into the left-hand end of the cylinder head on four-cylinder models **(see illustration)**.

2 On models with the V6 engine, the sender is at the front of the bypass housing on the left-hand end of the engine **(see illustration)**.

Testing

3 If the coolant temperature gauge is inoperative, check the fuses first (see Chapter 12).

4 If the gauge indicates hot at any time, consult the "*Fault finding*" Section at the end of this manual, to assist in tracing possible cooling system faults.

5 If the gauge indicates hot shortly after the engine is started from cold, unplug the coolant temperature sender's electrical connector. If the gauge reading now drops, renew the sender. If the reading remains high, the wire to the gauge may be shorted to earth, or the gauge is faulty.

6 If the gauge fails to indicate after the engine has been warmed up (approximately 10 minutes) and the fuses are known to be sound, switch off the engine. Unplug the sender's electrical connector, and use a jumper wire to connect the white/red wire to a clean earth point (bare metal) on the engine. Switch on the ignition without starting the engine. If the gauge now indicates hot, renew the sender.

7 If the gauge still does not work, the circuit may be open, or the gauge may be faulty. See Chapter 12 for additional information.

Removal

8 Drain the cooling system (see Chapter 1).

9 Where applicable on four-cylinder models, unbolt the resonator support bracket from the engine compartment front cross-member. Slacken the two clamp screws securing the resonator to the air mass meter and plenum chamber hoses, then swing the resonator up clear of the thermostat housing (see Chapter 4A, Section 4).

10 On V6 engine models, to improve access, remove the water pump drivebelt cover. Refer to Chapter 4A and disconnect the air inlet hose from the air cleaner housing. Access will be made easier if the battery is also removed (see Chapter 5A).

11 On four-cylinder models, disconnect the expansion tank coolant hose and the radiator top hose from the thermostat housing's water outlet, then disconnect the metal coolant pipe/hose from the thermostat.

12 Unplug the electrical connector from the sender **(see illustration)**.

13 Unscrew the sender and withdraw it.

Refitting

14 Clean any traces of old sealant from the sender location, then apply a light coat of sealant to the sender's threads. Screw in the sender and tighten it securely, and plug in its electrical connector.

15 Reconnect and refit any hoses and components removed for access. Refill the cooling system as described in Chapter 1 and run the engine. Check for leaks and proper gauge operation.

3

6.1 Location (arrowed) of the coolant temperature gauge sender - four-cylinder models

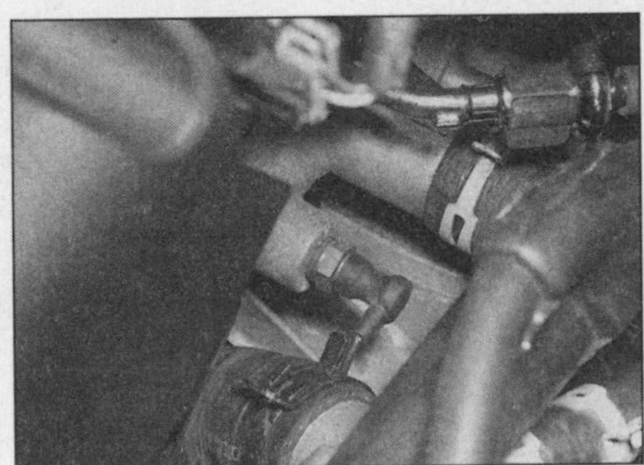

6.2 Coolant temperature sender on V6 engine models

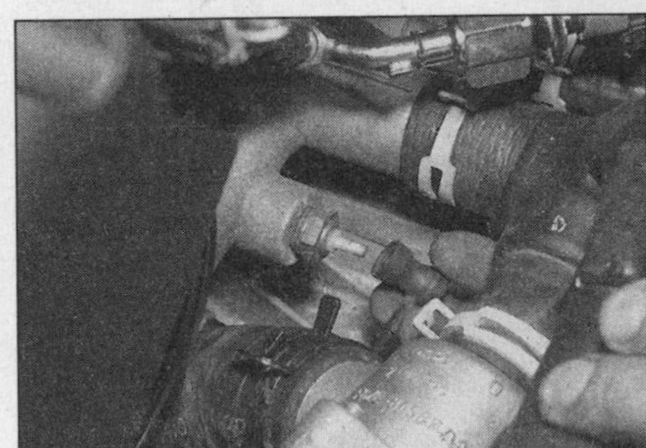

6.12 Disconnecting the wiring plug from the sender - V6 engine shown

6.17 Location (arrowed) of coolant temperature sensor - early four-cylinder engine models

6.18 Coolant temperature sensor (arrowed) on V6 engine models

Coolant temperature sensor

16 The temperature sensor is distinct from the gauge sender, in that it provides the engine management system with coolant temperature information. This information is also used to determine the point at which the radiator cooling fan is switched on.

17 On four-cylinder models, the sensor is screwed into the top of the thermostat housing **(see illustration)**.

18 On V6 engine models, the sensor is fitted into the rear of the bypass housing at the left-hand end of the engine **(see illustration)**.

Testing

19 Disconnect the battery negative (earth) lead (see Chapter 5A, Section 1).

20 Where applicable on four-cylinder models, unbolt the resonator support bracket from the engine compartment front crossmember. Slacken the two clamp screws securing the resonator to the air mass meter and plenum chamber hoses, then swing the resonator up clear of the thermostat housing (see Chapter 4A, Section 4).

21 On V6 engine models, access to the sensor is poor. Matters can be improved by removing the air inlet hose from the air cleaner - if preferred, remove the air cleaner housing completely, as described in Chapter 4A. Move the wiring harness around the sensor out of the way as far as possible.

22 Unplug the electrical connector from the sensor.

23 Using an ohmmeter, measure the resistance between the sensor terminals. Depending on the temperature of the sensor tip, the resistance measured will vary, but should be within the broad limits given in the Specifications Section of this Chapter. If the sensor's temperature is varied - by removing it (see below) and placing it in a freezer for a while, or by warming it gently - its resistance should alter accordingly.

24 Provided the sensor resistance falls significantly as the temperature rises, the sensor is likely to be performing well enough. However, if the results obtained show the sensor to be faulty, renew it.

25 On completion, plug in the connector and refit the components removed for access.

Removal

26 Disconnect the battery negative (earth) lead (see Chapter 5A, Section 1).

27 Where applicable on four-cylinder models, it is not absolutely essential to drain the cooling system, providing the system is completely cool. Remove the expansion tank filler cap to release any pressure, then refit the cap. Provided you work swiftly and plug the opening as soon as the sensor is unscrewed, coolant loss will be minimised.

28 On V6 engine models, drain the cooling system as described in Chapter 1.

29 Gain access to the sensor as described in the "*Testing*" Section above.

30 Unscrew the sensor and withdraw it. On four-cylinder models, if the cooling system has not been drained, plug the opening as quickly as possible.

Refitting

31 Clean any traces of old sealant from the sensor location, then apply a light coat of sealant to the sensor's threads. Remove the material used to plug the sensor hole (where applicable), and quickly install the sensor to prevent coolant loss. Tighten the sensor securely, and plug in its electrical connector.

32 Refit the components removed for access, then refill or top-up the cooling system (see Chapter 1 or "*Weekly checks*"). Run the engine, checking for leaks.

Coolant low level switch

Testing

33 The switch is a reed-type unit mounted in the bottom of the cooling system expansion tank, activated by a magnetic float. If the coolant level falls to the 'MIN' level or less, the appropriate bulb lights in the warning display.

34 If the bulb fails to light during the 5-second bulb test when the ignition is switched on, check the bulb, and renew if necessary as described in Chapter 12.

35 To check the switch itself, unplug its electrical connector, and use an ohmmeter to measure the resistance across the switch terminals. With the float up, a resistance of 90 ohms should be measured; when it is down, the resistance should increase to approximately 150 kilohms.

36 If the results obtained from the check are significantly different from those expected, the switch is faulty, and must be renewed.

37 If the switch and bulb are proven to be sound, the fault must be in the wiring or in the auxiliary warning control assembly (see Chapter 12).

Removal

38 Disconnect the battery negative (earth) lead (see Chapter 5A, Section 1).

39 Remove the expansion tank (see Section 7). The tank need not be drained, if preferred - we found that the switch could be removed without risk of spillage.

40 Unplug the switch electrical connector **(see illustration)**.

41 Release the switch by twisting it anti-clockwise, then withdraw it **(see illustrations)**.

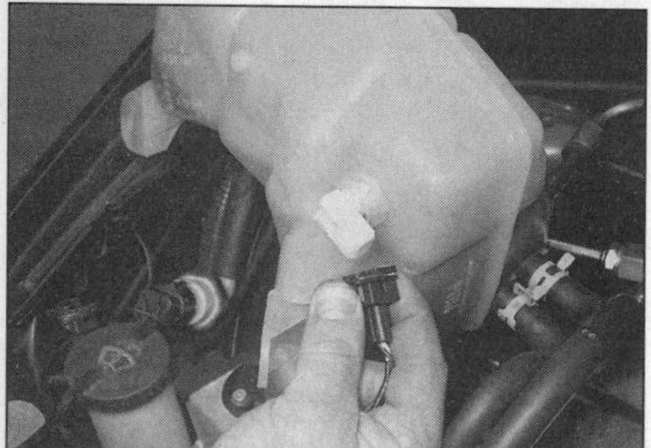
6.40 Disconnect the wiring connector . . .

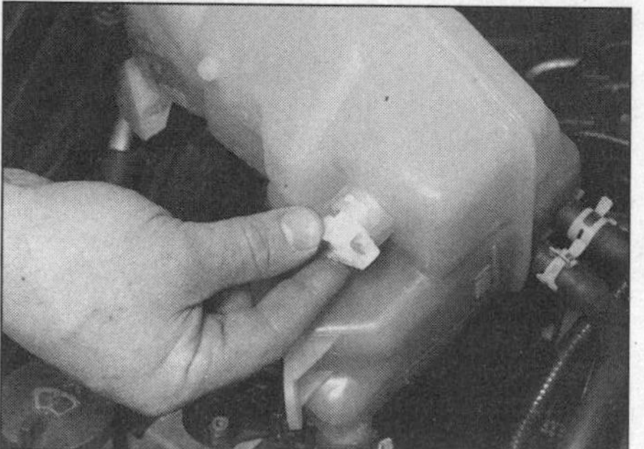
6.41a . . . then twist the level switch anti-clockwise . . .

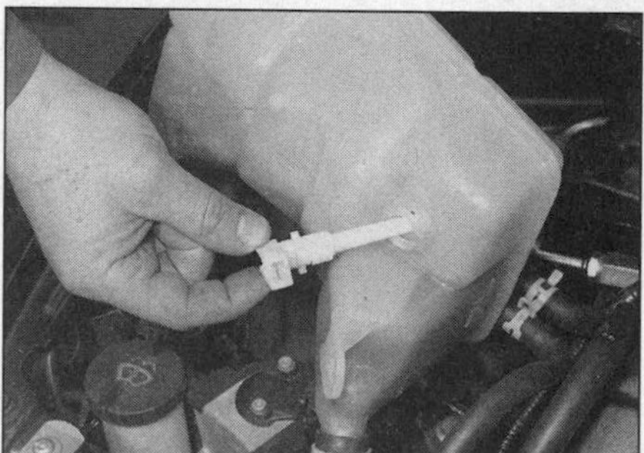
6.41b . . . and withdraw it from the expansion tank

7.6a Radiator mounting bracket-to-subframe bolts (A), air conditioning system condenser mounting bolt (B)

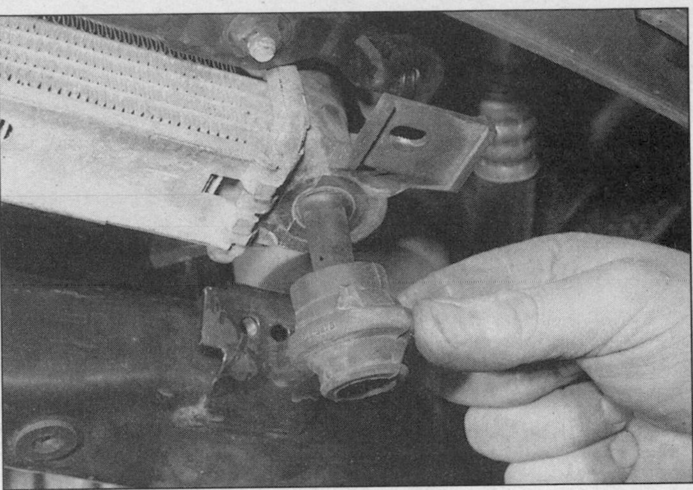
7.6b Remove the radiator bottom mounting rubbers, noting their fitted direction

Refitting

42 Refitting is the reverse of the removal procedure. If it was drained, refill the cooling system (see Chapter 1). Start the engine, and check for coolant leaks when it is fully warmed-up.

7 Radiator and expansion tank - removal, inspection and refitting

Note: *Refer to the warnings given in Section 1 of this Chapter before starting work.*

Radiator

Removal

Note: *If leakage is the reason for removing the radiator, bear in mind that minor leaks can often be cured using a radiator sealant added to the coolant with the radiator in situ.*

1 On four-cylinder engines, remove the radiator fan and shroud assembly (see Section 5). On models with the V6 engine, using the information in Section 5, detach the fan assembly from the radiator, and move it rearwards as far as possible.

2 To provide greater clearance for the radiator to be lowered and removed, ensure that the handbrake is firmly applied, then raise and support the front of the car on axle stands (see "*Jacking and vehicle support*"). Remove the radiator lower cover.

3 Disconnect the bottom hose from the radiator, and the top hose, if not already done.

4 On automatic transmission models, disconnect the fluid cooler lines, and plug the lines and fittings.

5 If the vehicle has air conditioning, unscrew the condenser mounting nuts or bolts, detach the condenser from the radiator, and tie it to the engine compartment front crossmember. Disconnect the wiring from the air conditioning compressor, and from the low pressure switch.

Warning: Do not disconnect any of the refrigerant hoses.

6 Unbolt the radiator mounting brackets from the subframe; note that they are handed, and are marked to ensure correct refitting. Collect the bottom mounting rubbers, noting which way up they are fitted, and store them carefully **(see illustrations)**.

7 Carefully lower the radiator from the car, and withdraw it **(see illustration)**.

Inspection

8 With the radiator removed, it can be inspected for leaks and damage. If it needs repair, have a radiator specialist or dealer service department perform the work, as special techniques are required.

9 Insects and dirt can be removed from the radiator with a garden hose or a soft brush. Don't bend the cooling fins as this is done.

Refitting

10 Refitting is the reverse of the removal procedure, noting the following points:

a) *On models with the V6 engine, raise the cooling fan assembly into position first, moving it back as close to the engine as possible. The radiator can then be lifted into position, and the fan assembly refitted as described in Section 5.*

b) *Be sure the mounting rubbers are seated properly at the base of the radiator.*

c) *After refitting, refill the cooling system with the proper mixture of antifreeze and water (see Chapter 1).*

d) *Start the engine, and check for leaks. Allow the engine to reach normal operating temperature, indicated by the radiator top hose becoming hot. Once the engine has cooled (ideally, leave overnight), recheck the coolant level, and add more if required.*

e) *On automatic transmission models, check and add transmission fluid as needed (see Chapter 1).*

Expansion tank

11 With the engine completely cool, remove the expansion tank filler cap to release any pressure, then refit the cap.

12 Disconnect the hoses from the tank, upper hose first. As each hose is disconnected, drain the tank's contents into a clean container. If the antifreeze is not due for renewal, the drained coolant may be re-used, if it is kept clean.

13 Unscrew the tank's two mounting bolts and withdraw it, unplugging the coolant low level switch electrical connector (where fitted) **(see illustrations)**.

7.7 Lower the radiator out of the car

7.13a Unscrew the expansion tank mounting bolts . . .

7.13b . . . and disconnect the level switch wiring plug

14 Wash out the tank, and inspect it for cracks and chafing - renew it if damaged.

15 Refitting is the reverse of the removal procedure. Refill the cooling system with the proper mixture of antifreeze and water (see Chapter 1), then start the engine and allow it to reach normal operating temperature, indicated by the radiator top hose becoming hot. Recheck the coolant level and add more if required, then check for leaks.

8 Water pump - checking, removal and refitting

Note: *Refer to the warnings given in Section 1 of this Chapter before starting work.*

Checking

1 A failure in the water pump can cause serious engine damage due to overheating.

2 There are three ways to check the operation of the water pump while it's installed on the engine. If the pump is defective, it should be replaced with a new or rebuilt unit.

3 With the engine running at normal operating temperature, squeeze the radiator top hose. If the water pump is working properly, a pressure surge should be felt as the hose is released.

Warning: Keep your hands away from the radiator electric cooling fan blades!

4 Water pumps are equipped with weep or vent holes. If a failure occurs in the pump seal, coolant will leak from the hole. In most cases you'll need a torch to find the hole on the water pump from underneath to check for leaks.

5 The water pump is at the timing belt end of the engine on four-cylinder models - to check for a leak, it may be helpful to remove the timing belt covers, as described in Chapter 2A.

6 On V6 engine models, the water pump is at the transmission end of the engine. If the water pump is leaking, it is likely there will be evidence of this when the pump drivebelt cover is removed - also examine the drivebelt itself for signs of coolant.

7 If the water pump shaft bearings fail, there may be a howling sound at the drivebelt end of the engine while it's running. Shaft wear can be felt if the water pump pulley is rocked up and down. Don't mistake drivebelt slippage, which causes a squealing sound, for water pump bearing failure.

Removal

Note: *The design of the four-cylinder engine water pump was changed in June 1998. The removal procedure is much the same for each type, but take care to order the correct part, if a new pump is being fitted.*

Four-cylinder engines up to June 1998

8 Drain the cooling system (see Chapter 1).

9 Remove the engine oil dipstick, and unclip the coolant hose from the exhaust system heat shield. Remove the upper and lower retaining bolts, noting the fitted positions of the coolant hose clips, and remove the heat shield from the front of the engine.

10 Remove the timing belt and tensioner as described in Chapter 2A. If the belt is fouled with coolant, it must be renewed as a matter of course.

11 The engine must now be supported, as the engine front mounting is disconnected. Support the engine from above with a hoist or engine support bar, if available. If the engine is supported from below with a trolley jack, use a wide block of wood between the jack head and the sump, to spread the load.

12 Remove the three bolts securing the engine front mounting to the subframe, then lift the engine up by approximately 20 mm.

13 Disconnect the radiator bottom hose from the pump union **(see illustration)**. Particularly on models with air conditioning, it is easier to reach this union if the power steering pump is unbolted and moved aside as described in Chapter 10. There is no need to disconnect any of the power steering system hoses.

14 Unbolt and remove the water pump, and recover the gasket **(see illustrations)**. If the pump is to be renewed, unbolt the timing belt guide pulleys, and transfer them to the new pump.

Four-cylinder engines from June 1998 onwards

15 Drain the cooling system (see Chapter 1).

16 Slacken the water pump pulley bolts.

17 Remove the auxiliary drivebelt as described in Chapter 1, then remove the water pump pulley.

18 Remove the timing belt and upper idler pulley as described in Chapter 2A. If the belt is fouled with coolant, it must be renewed as a matter of course.

19 Apply the handbrake, then raise and support the front of the vehicle on axle stands.

20 Working from below, disconnect the coolant hose from the water pump.

21 Loosen and remove the two pump retaining bolts, and manoeuvre the water pump out of the engine compartment. Recover the gasket.

V6 engine

22 Remove the battery as described in Chapter 5A.

23 Drain the cooling system as described in Chapter 1.

24 Unscrew the fasteners and remove the water pump drivebelt cover from the top and front of the engine **(see illustrations)**.

25 Rotate the water pump drivebelt tensioner clockwise to relieve the belt tension, and slip the drivebelt off the pulleys **(see illustration)**. If the belt is to be re-used, mark its direction of fitting.

26 Taking care to note their fitted locations, disconnect the coolant hoses as necessary for access to the water pump housing. Release the wiring harness from its retaining clips around the pump, and move it aside.

8.13 Power steering system pump should be removed to reach water pump hose union (arrowed)

8.14a Unscrew the bolts (arrowed) . . .

8.14b . . . to remove the water pump - always renew the gasket and clean all mating surfaces carefully

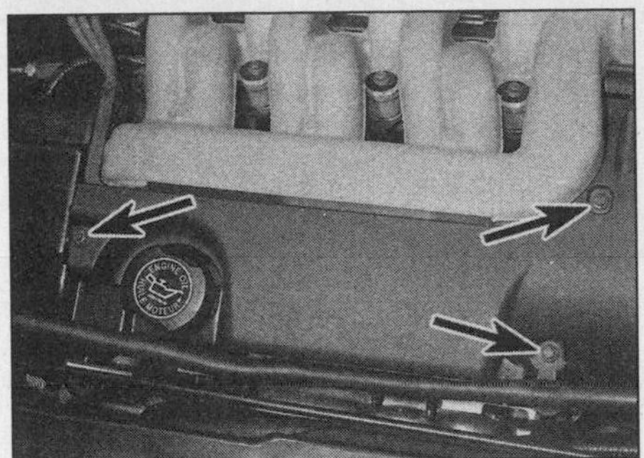
8.24a Remove the three screws (arrowed) . . .

8.24b . . . and lift off the water pump drivebelt cover

8.25 Slip the water pump drivebelt off the pulleys

8.27a Identify and loosen the pump housing bolts . . .

8.27b . . . remove the bolts (arrowed) . . .

8.27c . . . and withdraw the pump housing

27 Remove the three bolts (out of the total of eight visible) which secure the pump housing in position, and withdraw it from the engine **(see illustrations)**.

28 The water pump impeller is secured to the housing by the remaining five bolts **(see illustration)**. At the time of writing, the impeller is not available separately (neither is its gasket), and if the pump is leaking or noisy, the complete housing must be renewed. It would be worth checking with your Ford dealer or parts supplier, however, as this situation may change in the future.

Refitting

29 If the impeller has been removed from the pump housing, clean the pump mating surfaces carefully; the gasket must be renewed whenever it is disturbed. Use a little grease to stick the new gasket in place, refit the impeller to the pump housing, and tighten the five bolts to the specified torque wrench setting.

30 Refitting the pump housing is the reverse of dismantling, noting the following points:

a) *Tighten the three pump housing bolts to the specified torque wrench setting, then through the specified angle.*
b) *Refill the system with coolant as described in Chapter 1.*

9 Heater/ventilation components - removal and refitting

Heater blower motor

Removal

1 Disconnect the battery negative (earth) lead (see Chapter 5A, Section 1).

2 Release the four clips (by pulling them out) securing the passenger side footwell upper trim panel, then withdraw the panel.

3 Unplug the motor's electrical connector.

4 Lift the motor's retaining lug slightly, twist the motor anti-clockwise (seen from beneath) through approximately 30°, then withdraw the assembly.

5 The motor's control resistor can be removed by sliding a slim screwdriver into the slot provided in one end. Press the screwdriver in approximately 5 mm against spring pressure, and prise the resistor out **(see illustration)**.

Refitting

6 Refitting is the reverse of the removal procedure. Refit the motor, and twist it clockwise until the retaining lug engages securely **(see illustration)**.

3

8.28 Water pump impeller-to-housing bolts (arrowed)

9.5 Heater blower motor control resistor can be prised out of heater unit

9.6 Ensure the blower motor retaining lug (arrowed) engages securely in the heater unit on reassembly

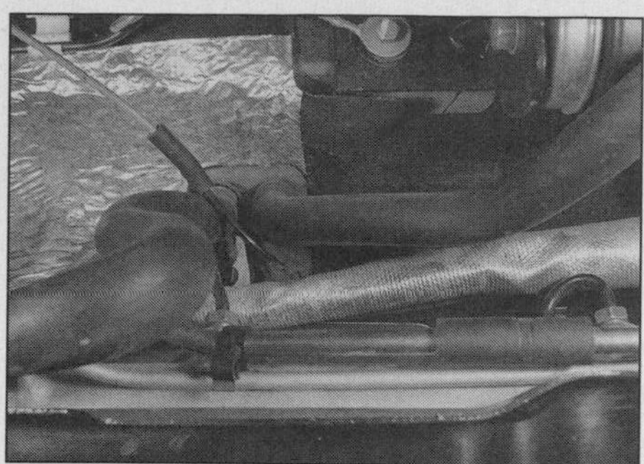
9.9a Coolant pipes to the heater matrix must be disconnected . . .

9.9b . . . but can be reached best from below (arrowed)

9.11 Remove the screw to release the air duct in the base of the heater unit . . .

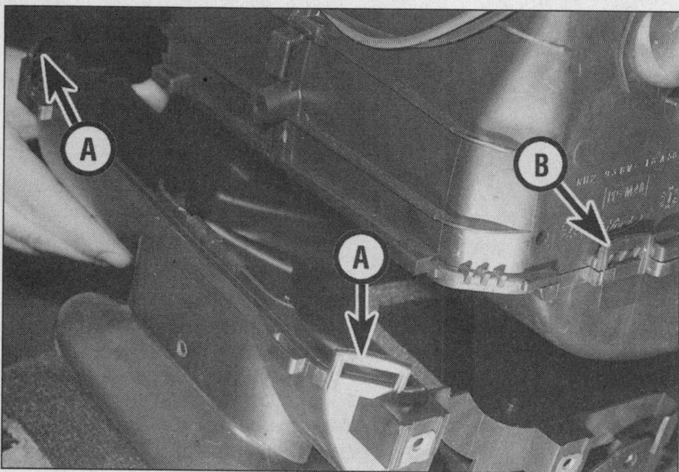

9.12 . . . release the clips (A) to free the air distributor from the heater unit - note the clips (B) securing . . .

9.13 . . . heater unit's bottom cover, complete with matrix

Heater matrix

Removal

7 Disconnect the battery negative (earth) lead (see Chapter 5A, Section 1).

8 Apply the handbrake, then raise and support the front of the car on axle stands. Drain the cooling system (see Chapter 1).

9 Disconnect the coolant hoses from the heater matrix unions protruding through the engine compartment bulkhead - this is most easily done from underneath **(see illustrations)**.

10 Working inside the passenger compartment, remove the trim panels from each footwell, just in front of the centre console. Each panel is secured by two screws. If additional clearance is required, the centre console can be removed as well (see Chapter 11), but this is not essential.

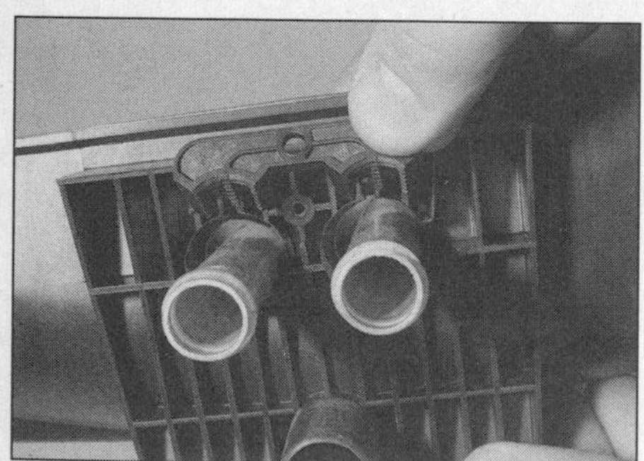
9.14 Remove the clamp (one screw) to separate the matrix from heater unit's bottom cover

11 Remove the single screw to release the air duct in the base of the heater unit **(see illustration)**.

12 Remove the three Torx-type screws (size T20) securing the air distributor to the heater unit bottom cover, then release the clips. There is a single plastic clip on each side, and additional metal clips may be found. Push the duct up to retract it, and withdraw the air distributor **(see illustration)**.

13 Release the clips - there are two plastic clips on each side, and additional metal clips may be found - then withdraw the heater unit's bottom cover, complete with the matrix **(see illustration)**.

14 Undo the screw and withdraw the clamp to separate the matrix from the bottom cover **(see illustration)**.

Refitting

15 Refitting is the reverse of the removal procedure. Additional metal clips may be required to secure the heater unit's bottom cover and the air distributor. Ensure that the duct is lowered from the air distributor and secured with its screw.

16 Refill the cooling system with the proper mixture of antifreeze and water (see Chapter 1). Start the engine and allow it to reach normal operating temperature, indicated by the radiator top hose becoming hot. Recheck the coolant level and add more if required, then check for leaks. Check the operation of the heater.

Pollen filter

17 Refer to Chapter 1.

Facia vents

Driver's side and centre vents

18 The driver's side and centre vents are removed complete with the instrument panel surround. Refer to Chapter 12.

Passenger side vent

19 Remove the glovebox as described in Chapter 11.

20 Using a suitable screwdriver, and a pad to protect the facia, prise out the vent from the end of the facia panel.

21 Working through the glovebox aperture, detach the ventilation duct from the base of the vent, and remove the vent.

22 Refitting is a reversal of removal.

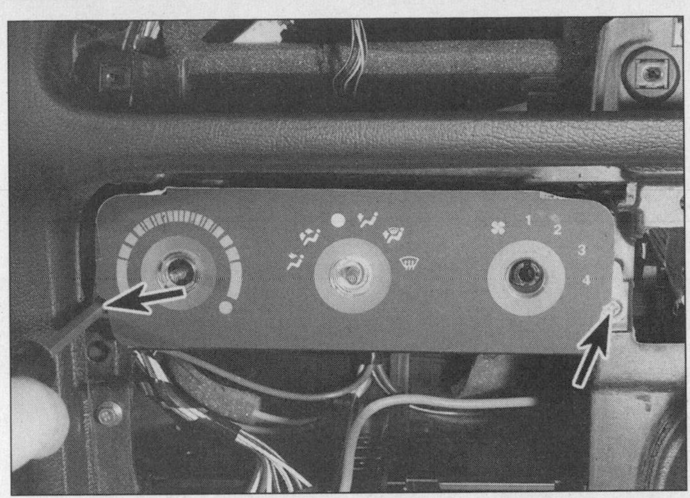

10.6 Remove the screws (arrowed) securing each end of the heater control unit

10.7a Disconnect the wiring and vacuum connections from the rear of the control panel

10 Heater/air conditioning controls - removal and refitting

Heater control panel

1 Disconnect the battery negative (earth) lead (see Chapter 5A, Section 1).

2 Remove the ashtray, and prise off the cigar lighter bezel. Referring to the relevant Sections of Chapter 11, remove all the centre console securing screws, and slide the console to the rear.

10.7b Unhook the operating cable from the temperature control - note retaining screw (arrowed)

3 Remove the radio/cassette player as described in Chapter 12.

Models up to 1996

4 Pull out the cassette storage compartment below the radio/cassette player.

5 Pull the heater control/radio bezel out of the three clips securing its top edge, and pull it forwards.

6 Pull off the heater control knobs, and remove the screw securing each end of the heater control unit **(see illustration)**. Pull the control unit out of the facia.

7 Taking careful note of all their locations, disconnect the various wiring and vacuum connections from the rear of the panel. On vehicles without air conditioning, unhook the operating cable from the temperature control **(see illustrations)**.

10.9 Remove the two screws inside the radio/cassette aperture

8 Make sure that nothing remains attached to the panel, then withdraw it from the facia.

1997 models onwards

9 Remove the two screws (one each side) inside the radio/cassette aperture **(see illustration)**.

10 Pull the heater control/radio bezel out of the three clips securing its top edge, and pull it forwards.

11 Taking careful note of all their locations, disconnect the various wiring and vacuum connections from the rear of the panel **(see illustrations)**. On vehicles without air conditioning, unhook the operating cable from the temperature control.

12 Make sure that nothing remains attached to the panel, then withdraw it from the facia.

Blower/air conditioning control and temperature control

13 Remove the heater control panel as described above.

14 If not already done, pull off the control knob. Remove the retaining screw and withdraw the control, twisting it to release it from the panel **(see illustrations)**.

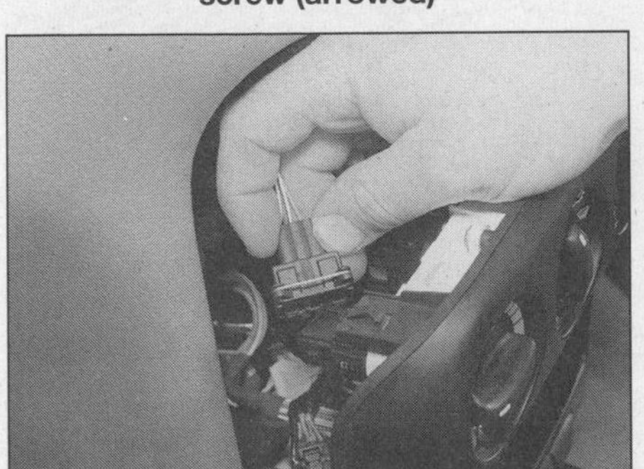

10.11a Disconnect the wiring . . .

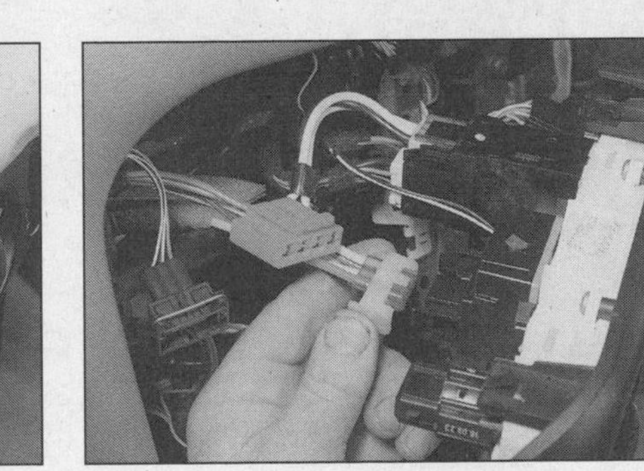

10.11b . . . and vacuum connections from the control panel

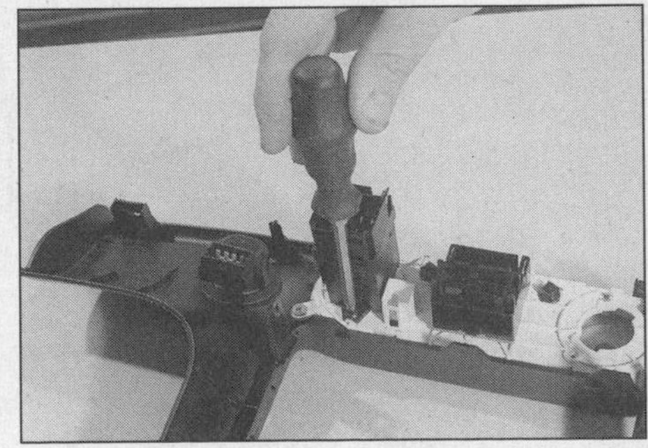

10.14a Remove the retaining screw . . .

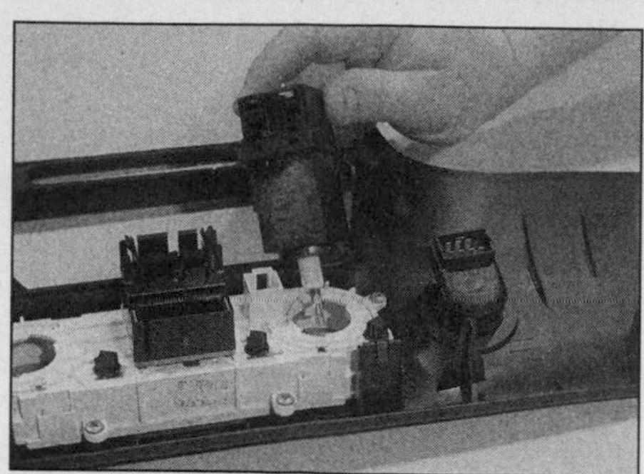

10.14b . . . and remove the control from the bayonet fitting

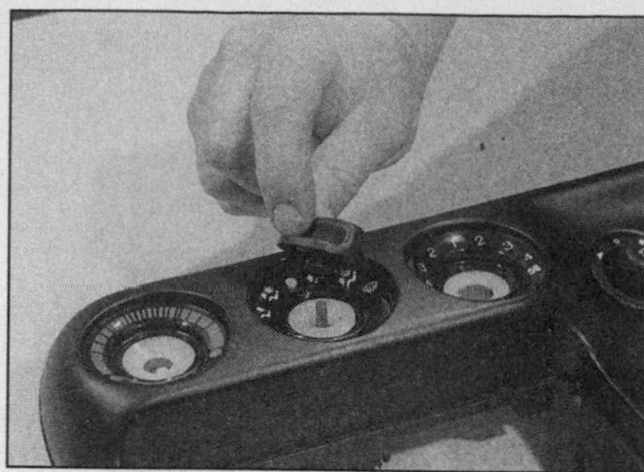

10.17a Pull off the control knob (1997-on model shown) . . .

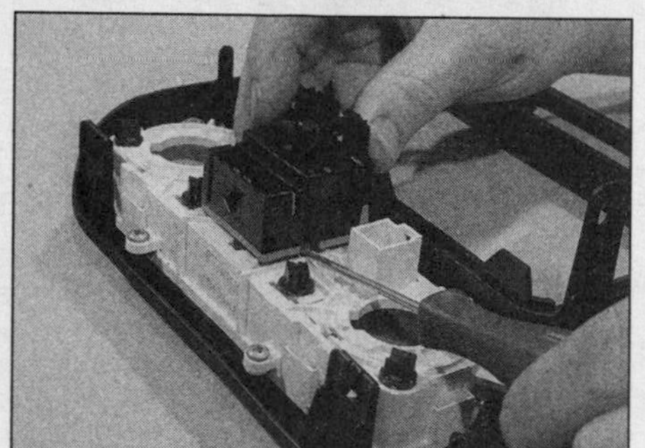

10.17b . . . release the clips using a small screwdriver . . .

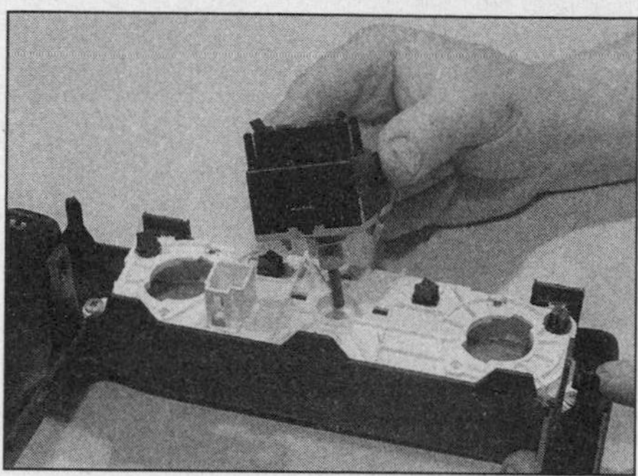

10.17c . . . and remove the air distribution control

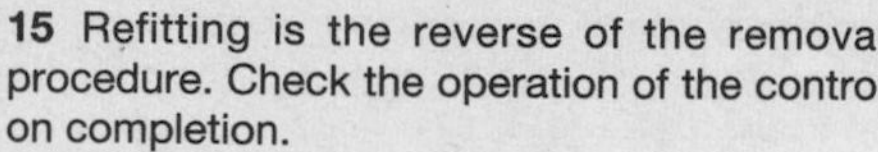

15 Refitting is the reverse of the removal procedure. Check the operation of the control on completion.

Air distribution control

16 Remove the heater control panel as described above.

17 If not already done, pull off the control knob. Use a pair of slim screwdrivers to release the clips on each side of the control, then withdraw the control from the unit **(see illustrations)**.

18 Refitting is the reverse of the removal procedure. Check the operation of the controls on completion.

11 Air conditioning system - general information and precautions

General information

The air conditioning system consists of a condenser mounted in front of the radiator, an evaporator mounted adjacent to the heater matrix, a compressor driven by an auxiliary drivebelt, an accumulator/dehydrator, and the plumbing connecting all of the above components - this contains a choke (or 'venturi') mounted in the inlet to the evaporator, which creates the drop in pressure required to produce the cooling effect **(see illustration)**.

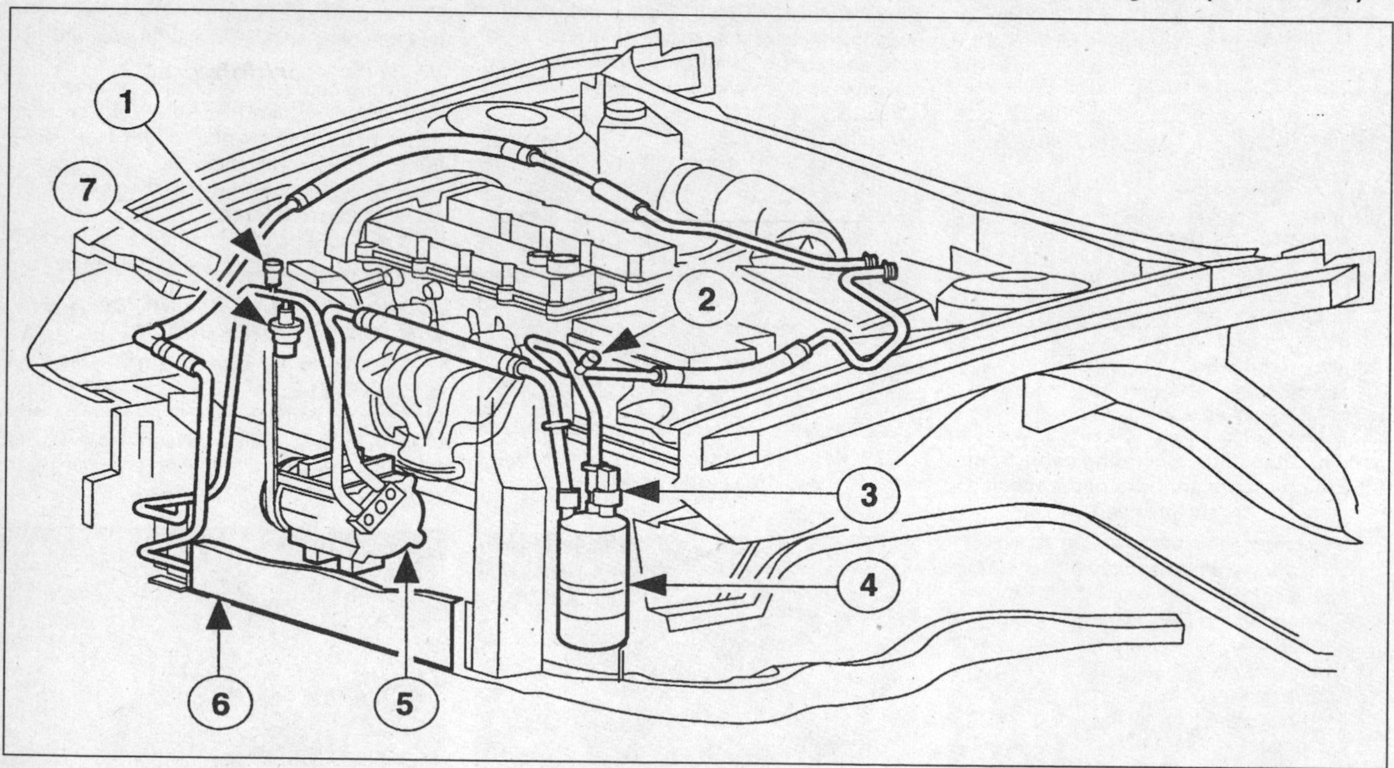

11.1 Air conditioning system components

1 *Quick-release Schrader valve-type coupling - high-pressure side*
2 *Quick-release Schrader valve-type coupling - low-pressure side*
3 *Pressure-cycling switch - low-pressure side*
4 *Accumulator/dehydrator*
5 *Compressor*
6 *Condenser*
7 *Pressure-regulating switch - high-pressure side*

A blower fan forces the warmer air of the passenger compartment through the evaporator core (rather like a radiator in reverse), transferring the heat from the air to the refrigerant. The liquid refrigerant boils off into low-pressure vapour, taking the heat with it when it leaves the evaporator.

Precautions

Warning: The air conditioning system is under high pressure. Do not loosen any fittings or remove any components until after the system has been discharged. Air conditioning refrigerant should be properly discharged into an approved type of container, at a dealer service department or an automotive air conditioning repair facility capable of handling R134a refrigerant. Always wear eye protection when disconnecting air conditioning system fittings.

When an air conditioning system is fitted, it is necessary to observe the following special precautions whenever dealing with any part of the system, its associated components, and any items which necessitate disconnection of the system:

a) *While the refrigerant used - R134a - is less damaging to the environment than the previously-used R12, it is still a very dangerous substance. It must not be allowed into contact with the skin or eyes, or there is a risk of frostbite. It must also not be discharged in an enclosed space - while it is not toxic, there is a risk of suffocation. The refrigerant is heavier than air, and so must never be discharged over a pit.*

b) *The refrigerant must not be allowed to come in contact with a naked flame, otherwise a poisonous gas will be created - under certain circumstances, this can form an explosive mixture with air. For similar reasons, smoking in the presence of refrigerant is highly dangerous, particularly if the vapour is inhaled through a lighted cigarette.*

c) *Never discharge the system to the atmosphere - R134a is not an ozone-depleting ChloroFluoroCarbon (CFC) as is R12, but is instead a hydrofluorocarbon, which causes environmental damage by contributing to the "greenhouse effect" if released into the atmosphere.*

d) *R134a refrigerant must not be mixed with R12; the system uses different seals (now green-coloured, previously black) and has different fittings requiring different tools, so that there is no chance of the two types of refrigerant becoming mixed accidentally.*

e) *If for any reason the system must be disconnected, entrust this task to your Ford dealer or a refrigeration engineer.*

f) *It is essential that the system be professionally discharged prior to using any form of heat - welding, soldering, brazing, etc - in the vicinity of the system, before having the vehicle oven-dried at a temperature exceeding 70°C after repainting, and before disconnecting any part of the system.*

12 Air conditioning system components - removal and refitting

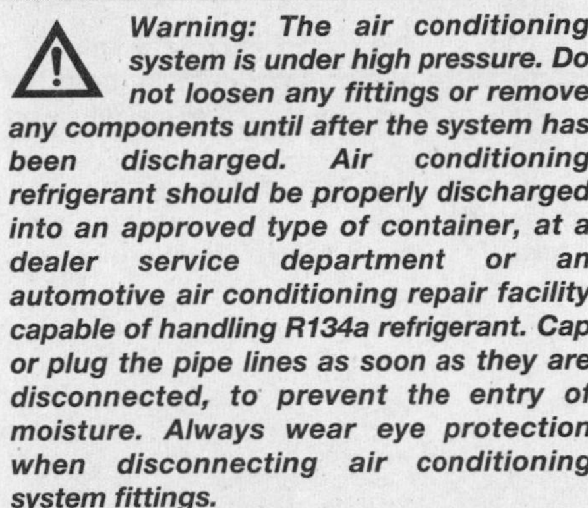

Warning: The air conditioning system is under high pressure. Do not loosen any fittings or remove any components until after the system has been discharged. Air conditioning refrigerant should be properly discharged into an approved type of container, at a dealer service department or an automotive air conditioning repair facility capable of handling R134a refrigerant. Cap or plug the pipe lines as soon as they are disconnected, to prevent the entry of moisture. Always wear eye protection when disconnecting air conditioning system fittings.

Note: *This Section refers to the components of the air conditioning system itself - refer to Sections 9 and 10 for details of components common to the heating/ventilation system.*

Condenser

1 Have the refrigerant discharged at a dealer service department or an automotive air conditioning repair facility.

2 Disconnect the battery negative (earth) lead (see Chapter 5A, Section 1).

3 Remove the radiator undershield (see Chapter 1, Section 28).

4 Using the Ford service tool 34-001, disconnect the refrigerant lines from the condenser. Immediately cap the open fittings, to prevent the entry of dirt and moisture.

5 Remove the radiator as described in Section 7. Alternatively, just remove the radiator support brackets (note that the condenser is also mounted on the brackets), and have a jack or pair of axle stands ready to support the weight.

6 Disengage the condenser upper mountings, then push it rearwards and remove it from below. Store it upright, to prevent oil loss.

7 Refitting is the reverse of removal. If a new condenser was installed, add 20 cc of refrigerant oil to the system.

8 Have the system evacuated, charged and leak-tested by the specialist who discharged it.

Evaporator

9 The evaporator is mounted with the heater matrix. Apart from the need to have the refrigerant discharged, and to use Ford service tools 34-001 and 34-003 to disconnect the lines, the procedure is as described in Section 9 of this Chapter.

10 On reassembly, if a new evaporator was installed, add 20 cc of refrigerant oil to the system.

11 Have the system evacuated, charged and leak-tested by the specialist who discharged it.

Compressor

12 Have the refrigerant discharged at a dealer service department or an automotive air conditioning repair facility.

13 Disconnect the battery negative (earth) lead (see Chapter 5A, Section 1).

14 Remove the radiator undershield and the auxiliary drivebelt as described in Chapter 1, Sections 28 and 5 respectively.

15 Unbolt the compressor from the cylinder block/crankcase, press it to one side, and unscrew the clamping bolt to disconnect the refrigerant lines.

16 Plug the line connections, swing the compressor upright, unplug its electrical connector, then withdraw the compressor from the vehicle. **Note:** *Keep the compressor level during handling and storage. If the compressor has seized, or if you find metal particles in the refrigerant lines, the system must be flushed out by an air conditioning technician, and the accumulator/dehydrator must be renewed.*

17 Prior to installation, turn the compressor clutch centre six times, to disperse any oil that has collected in the head.

18 Refit the compressor in the reverse order of removal; renew all seals disturbed.

19 If you are installing a new compressor, refer to the compressor manufacturer's instructions for adding refrigerant oil to the system.

20 Have the system evacuated, charged and leak-tested by the specialist that discharged it.

Accumulator/dehydrator

21 Have the refrigerant discharged at a dealer service department or an automotive air conditioning repair facility.

22 Disconnect the battery negative (earth) lead (see Chapter 5A, Section 1).

23 The accumulator/dehydrator, which acts as a reservoir and filter for the refrigerant, is located in the left-hand front corner of the engine compartment. Using the Ford service tool 34-003, disconnect the refrigerant line next to the accumulator/dehydrator from the compressor. Immediately cap the open fittings, to prevent the entry of dirt and moisture, then unplug the pressure-cycling switch electrical connector **(see illustration)**.

12.23 Unplug the pressure-cycling switch electrical connector (arrowed)

12.33 Unplug the pressure-regulating switch electrical connector (arrowed)

24 Remove the radiator undershield (see Chapter 1, Section 28).

25 Unbolt the accumulator/dehydrator from the front suspension subframe.

26 Using the Ford service tool 34-003, disconnect the lower refrigerant line from the accumulator/dehydrator. It may be necessary to unscrew the pressure-cycling switch to allow the use of the tool. Immediately cap the open fittings, to prevent the entry of dirt and moisture.

27 Withdraw the accumulator/dehydrator.

28 Refit the accumulator/dehydrator in the reverse order of removal; renew all seals disturbed.

29 If you are installing a new accumulator/ dehydrator, refer to the manufacturer's instructions for adding refrigerant oil to the system.

30 Have the system evacuated, charged and leak-tested by the specialist that discharged it.

Pressure-cycling and pressure-regulating switches

31 Have the refrigerant discharged at a dealer service department or an automotive air conditioning repair facility.

32 Disconnect the battery negative (earth) lead (see Chapter 5A, Section 1).

33 Unplug the switch electrical connector, and unscrew it **(see illustration)**.

34 Refitting is the reverse of the removal procedure; there is no need to top-up the refrigerant oil.

35 Have the system evacuated, charged and leak-tested by the specialist that discharged it.

Chapter 4 Part A:
Fuel and exhaust systems

Contents

Degrees of difficulty

Easy, suitable for novice with little experience	**Fairly easy,** suitable for beginner with some experience	**Fairly difficult,** suitable for competent DIY mechanic	**Difficult,** suitable for experienced DIY mechanic	**Very difficult,** suitable for expert DIY or professional

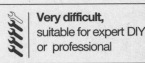

Specifications

General

System type	Sequential Electronic Fuel injection (SEFi)
Recommended fuel (Minimum octane rating)	95 RON unleaded
Idle speed:	
4-cylinder (Zetec) engine:	
Regulated - nominal (± 50 rpm):	
Manual transmission models	880 rpm*
Automatic transmission models	710 rpm*
Unregulated - base (to 7/1996 only)	1500 rpm*
V6 (Duratec) engine:	
Regulated - nominal (± 50 rpm)	725 rpm*
Idle mixture (CO level):	
4-cylinder (Zetec) engine	0.5% maximum*
V6 (Duratec) engine	0.5% maximum*

** Given for reference only - not adjustable.*

Rev limiter operation

Fuel injectors shut off at:	
Automatic transmission, position "N" selected	4100 rpm
Automatic transmission, any other position selected	6800 rpm (approximately)
Manual transmission	6800 to 7100 rpm

Fuel pressure

Regulated fuel pressure - engine running at idle speed:	
Pressure regulator vacuum hose connected	2.1 ± 0.2 bars
Pressure regulator vacuum hose disconnected	2.7 ± 0.2 bars

Note: *When the ignition is switched off, the system should hold 1.8 bars for 5 minutes. If the engine is hot, the pressure may rise to maximum of 2.7 bars during this check. Pressure regulator (when reconnected) should prevent any higher pressure being reached.*

Fuel injectors

Resistance	13.7 to 15.2 ohms

Idle speed control valve

Resistance	6 to 14 ohms

Idle increase solenoid valve

Resistance	50 to 120 ohms

Crankshaft speed/position sensor

Resistance	200 to 450 ohms

Camshaft position sensor

Resistance	200 to 900 ohms

Intake air temperature sensor

Resistance:	
At -40°C	860 to 900 k ohms
At 20°C	35 to 40 k ohms
At 100°C	1.9 to 2.5 k ohms
At 120°C	1.0 to 1.3 k ohms

Throttle potentiometer

Resistance - see text	400 to 6000 ohms

Power steering pressure switch

Operating pressure - green switch body:	
Contacts open - infinite resistance	31.5 ± 3.5 bars
Contacts close - 0 to 2.5 ohms resistance	Between 13.5 and 24.0 bars

Torque wrench settings

	Nm	lbf ft
Plenum chamber-to-inlet manifold fasteners	4	3
Throttle housing-to-inlet manifold screws	10	7
Idle speed control valve bolts	6	4
Fuel pressure regulator bolts:		
4-cylinder engine:		
To mid 1997	6	4
From mid 1997	10	7
V6 engine	6	4
Fuel pressure relief valve (V6)	8	6
Fuel injector bolts	6	4
Fuel rail-to-inlet manifold bolts	10	7
Fuel feed and return line threaded couplings at fuel rail	27	20
Inlet air temperature sensor	23	17
All exhaust system nuts and bolts	40	30
Camshaft position sensor screw	21	16
Crankshaft speed/position sensor:		
Sensor-to-bracket screw	8	6
Bracket-to-cylinder block crankcase screw	21	15

1 General information and precautions

The fuel system consists of a plastic tank (mounted under the body, beneath the rear seats), fuel hoses and metal lines, an electric fuel pump mounted in the fuel tank, and an electronic fuel injection system.

The exhaust system consists of an exhaust manifold (or two on the V6 engine), front downpipe, catalytic converter and a rear section incorporating two or three silencers. The service replacement exhaust system consists of three or four sections. The system is suspended throughout its entire length by rubber mountings.

Extreme caution should be exercised when dealing with either the fuel or exhaust systems. Fuel is a primary element for combustion. Be very careful! The exhaust system is an area for exercising caution, as it operates at very high temperatures. Serious burns can result from even momentary contact with any part of the exhaust system, and the fire risk is ever-present. The catalytic converter in particular runs at very high temperatures.

When removing the fuel injection electronic control unit (ECU), do not touch the terminals as there is a chance that static electricity may damage the internal electronic components.

Warning: Many of the procedures in this Chapter require the removal of fuel lines and connections, which may result in some fuel spillage. Before carrying out any operation on the fuel system, refer to the precautions given in "Safety first!" at the beginning of this manual, and follow them implicitly. Petrol is a highly-dangerous and volatile liquid, and the precautions necessary when handling it cannot be overstressed.

2.3 Fuel pressure relief valve cap on the fuel rail (V6 engine)

2 Fuel system - depressurisation

Warning: Refer to the warning note in Section 1 before proceeding.

1 The fuel system referred to in this Chapter is defined as the fuel tank and tank-mounted fuel pump/fuel gauge sender unit, the fuel filter, the fuel injectors and the pressure regulator in the injector rail, and the metal pipes and flexible hoses of the fuel lines between these components. All these contain fuel, which will be under pressure while the engine is running and/or while the ignition is switched on.

2 The pressure will remain for some time after the ignition has been switched off, and must be relieved before any of these components is disturbed for servicing work.

3 The Ford method of depressurisation is to use service tool 23-033 fitted to the fuel rail pressure test/release fitting. The fitting consists of a Schrader-type valve with a plastic cap located on the fuel rail **(see illustration)**, and the tool acts as a tap by depressing the valve core. On 1997-on models it will be necessary to remove the air inlet duct from between the air cleaner and airflow meter.

4 To release the pressure without using the service tool, use a suitable container and rag wrapped around the fitting to catch the fuel. Do not simply depress the valve core without wrapping rag around it, as fuel will spray out, with the consequent risk of fire, and personal injury.

5 An alternative method is simply to disconnect the fuel pump's electrical supply while the engine is running, by removing the fuel pump fuse (number 14), and to allow the engine to idle until it dies through lack of fuel. Turn the engine over once or twice on the starter to ensure that all pressure is released, then switch off the ignition. Do not forget to refit the fuse when work is complete.

6 Note that, once the fuel system has been depressurised, it may take longer to restart the engine - perhaps several seconds of cranking - before the system is refilled and pressure restored.

3 Fuel lines and fittings - general information

Warning: Refer to the warning note in Section 1 before proceeding.

1 Quick-release couplings are employed at all unions in the fuel feed and return lines.

2 Before disconnecting any fuel system component, relieve the pressure in the system as described in Section 2, and equalise tank pressure by removing the fuel filler cap.

3 On early models, release the protruding locking lugs on each fuel line union, by squeezing them together and carefully pulling the coupling apart. On later models, Ford technicians use a special tool to release the quick release fittings - the tool expands the internal coil spring so that the two sections of the fitting can be disconnected. A home-made tool can be made out of a coiled piece of plastic which may be inserted beneath the coil spring. Use rag to soak up any spilt fuel. Where the unions are colour-coded, the pipes cannot be confused. Where both unions are the same colour, note carefully which pipe is connected to which, and ensure that they are correctly reconnected on refitting **(see illustration)**.

4 To reconnect one of these couplings, press them together until they are locked. Switch the ignition on to pressurise the system, and check for any sign of fuel leakage around the disturbed coupling before attempting to start the engine.

5 Checking procedures for the fuel lines are included in Chapter 1.

6 Always use genuine fuel lines and hoses when renewing sections of the fuel system. Do not fit substitutes constructed from inferior or inappropriate material, or you could cause a fuel leak or a fire.

7 Before disconnecting any part of the fuel system, note the routing of all hoses and pipes, and the orientation of all clamps and clips to ensure correct refitting.

4 Air cleaner assembly and ducts - removal and refitting

Air cleaner assembly (4-cylinder Zetec engine)

Removal

1 Disconnect the battery negative (earth) lead (see Chapter 5A).

2 Unclip the air mass meter from the air cleaner cover (see Section 14).

3 Release the rubber band where fitted **(see illustration)** from the left-hand side of the air cleaner.

4 Disconnect the crankcase breather hose, either from the air cleaner housing or from the cylinder head cover union **(see illustration)**.

5 Withdraw the air cleaner assembly, lifting it upwards out of its grommets, and releasing it from the air inlet duct in the inner wing panel.

Refitting

6 Refitting is the reverse of the removal procedure. Ensure that the housing pegs seat correctly in their grommets, and that the intake mouth is fully engaged inside the connector sleeve **(see illustration)**.

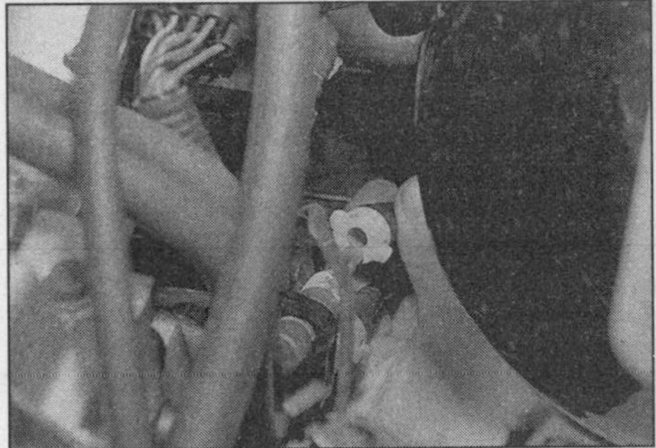

3.3 Disconnect fuel line quick-release couplings by squeezing together protruding locking lugs and pulling coupling apart

Air cleaner assembly (V6 Duratec engine)

Removal

7 Disconnect the battery negative (earth) lead (see Chapter 5A).

8 Disconnect the wiring from the air mass meter.

9 Disconnect the wiring from the air temperature sensor on the side of the air cleaner.

10 Loosen the clip and disconnect the air outlet hose from the air cleaner.

11 On early models, release the rubber band from the left-hand side of the air cleaner. **Note:** *Later models do not have the rubber band fitted.*

12 Lift the air cleaner from its location grommets, and at the same time disconnect the inlet pipe from the left-hand side.

13 Check the location grommets and if necessary renew them.

Refitting

14 Make sure the location grommets are correctly fitted to the bracket.

15 Locate the air cleaner pegs in the grommets and at the same time reconnect the side inlet pipe.

16 Where fitted, hook the rubber band onto the left-hand side of the air cleaner.

17 Reconnect the air outlet hose and tighten the clip. **Note:** *Make sure the alignment tab is correctly positioned.*

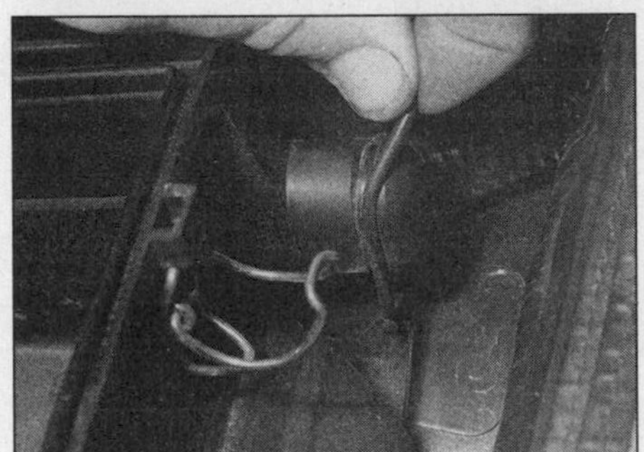

4.3 Remove rubber retaining band to withdraw air cleaner assembly

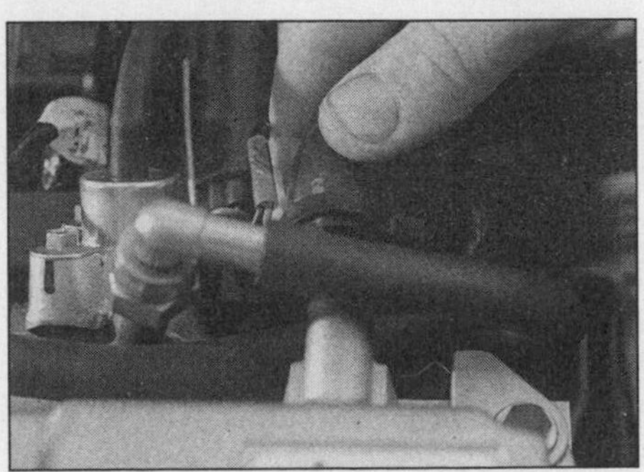

4.4 Disconnecting the crankcase breather hose from the cylinder head union

4.6 Ensure air filter housing intake mouth is fully engaged inside connector sleeve

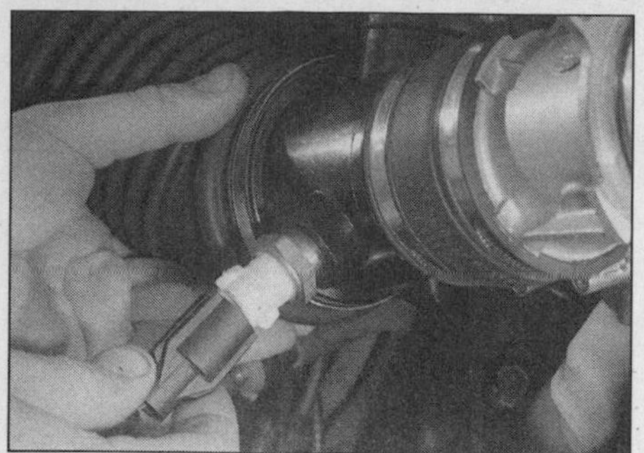
4.21 Unplugging intake air temperature sensor's electrical connector

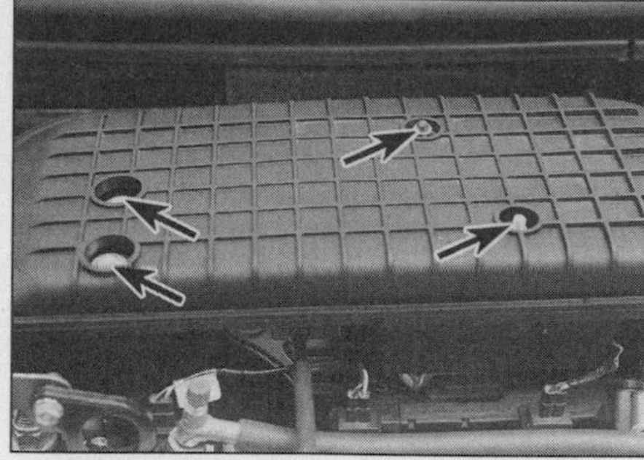
4.23a Plenum chamber fasteners (arrowed) - four shown here, some vehicles may only have three

4.23b Unscrew the nuts . . .

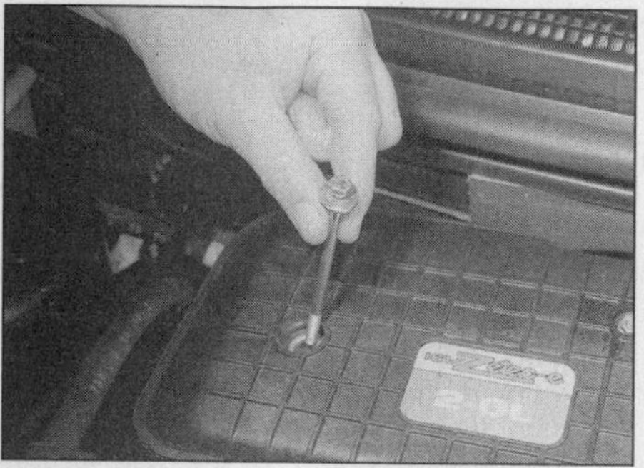

4.23c . . . and bolt securing the plenum

4.24a Lift plenum chamber and (where fitted) disconnect the vacuum hose - note the two rubber spacers (arrowed) . . .

4.24b . . . and the sealing O-ring (arrowed) in the chamber's mouth

18 Reconnect the wiring to the air temperature sensor.
19 Reconnect the wiring to the air mass meter.
20 Reconnect the battery negative (earth) lead (see Chapter 5A).

Air intake resonator (early 4-cylinder Zetec engine)

Removal

21 Unbolt the resonator support bracket from the engine compartment front crossmember. Slacken the two clamp screws securing the resonator to the air mass meter and plenum hoses. Swing the resonator clear of the thermostat housing, and unplug the intake air temperature sensor's electrical connector **(see illustration)**. Withdraw the resonator.

Refitting

22 Refitting is the reverse of the removal procedure.

Plenum chamber (4-cylinder Zetec engine)

Removal

23 Prising out the rubber plugs covering them, undo the plenum's fasteners. Slacken the clamp screw securing the plenum to the resonator or hose. Alternatively, the airflow meter may be unclipped from the air cleaner **(see illustrations)**.
24 Lift the plenum and (where fitted) disconnect the vacuum hose from its underside. Withdraw the plenum - note the two rubber spacers (one on each throttle housing stud) and the sealing O-ring in the plenum's mouth **(see illustrations)**.

Refitting

25 Refitting is the reverse of the removal procedure. Ensure that the O-ring and spacers are correctly seated.

Underwing components

Removal

26 Remove the left-hand wheel arch liner (see Chapter 11).
27 Unbolt and withdraw the air intake tube and both resonators as required.

Refitting

28 Refitting is the reverse of the removal procedure.

5 Accelerator cable - removal, refitting and adjustment

Models with 4-cylinder Zetec engine (without traction control)

Removal

1 Disconnect the battery negative (earth) lead (see Chapter 5A).
2 Remove the plenum chamber (see Section 4).
3 Remove the clip securing the cable to the throttle housing bracket. Disconnect the cable end nipple from the throttle linkage, and release the cable from any securing clips or ties **(see illustrations)**.

4.24c On later models, recover the spacers from the top of the plenum . . .

4.24d . . . then remove the plenum from the throttle housing

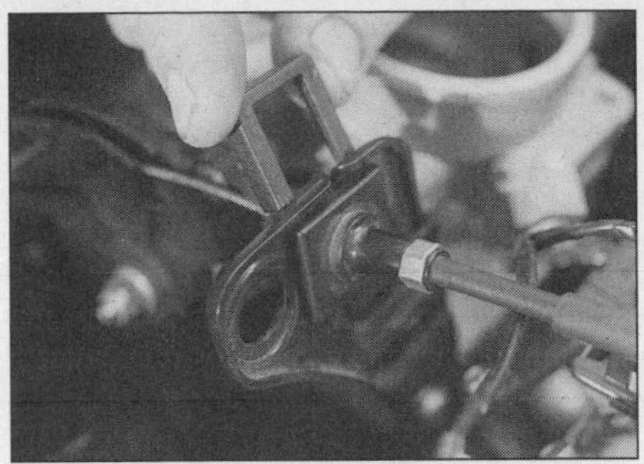
5.3a Removing clip securing accelerator cable to throttle housing bracket

5.3b Accelerator cable on 5/1998-on models

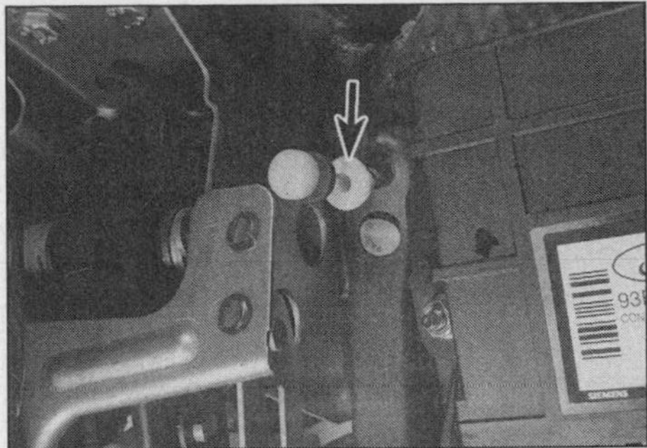
5.4 Pull the accelerator cable end fitting (arrowed) out of the pedal

4 Working in the passenger compartment, reach up to the top of the accelerator pedal. Pull the end fitting and collar out of the pedal, then release the cable inner wire through the slot in the pedal **(see illustration)**. Tie a length of string to the end of the cable.

5 Returning to the engine compartment, pull the cable through the bulkhead until the string can be untied and the cable removed.

Refitting

6 Refitting is the reverse of the removal procedure; use the string to draw the cable through the bulkhead.

7 Adjust the cable as described below.

Adjustment

8 Remove the plenum chamber (see Section 4).

9 Find the cable adjuster - this is either at the throttle housing bracket, or two-thirds along the length of the cable, clipped to the front suspension right-hand mounting **(see illustration)**. Remove the metal clip and lubricate the adjuster's grommet with soapy water.

10 Remove any slack by pulling the cable outer as far as possible out of the adjuster. Have an assistant depress the accelerator pedal fully - the cable outer will move back into the adjuster - and hold it there while the clip is refitted.

11 Check that the throttle valve moves smoothly and easily from the fully-closed to the fully-open position and back again, as the assistant depresses and releases the accelerator pedal. Re-adjust the cable if required.

12 When the setting is correct, refit the plenum chamber (see Section 4).

Models with 4-cylinder Zetec engine (with traction control)

Note: *While the following procedure deals with the complete cable, the pedal-to-actuator and actuator-to-throttle housing sections of the cable are available separately, and can be removed and refitted individually. If doing this, modify the procedure as required.*

Removal

13 Disconnect the battery negative (earth) lead (see Chapter 5A).

14 Remove the plenum chamber (see Section 4).

15 Remove the clip securing the cable to the throttle housing bracket, then pull the cable's grommet out of the bracket. Disconnect the cable end nipple from the throttle linkage, and release the cable from any securing clips or ties.

16 Unplug the TCS throttle actuator's electrical connector, and prise off its cover **(see illustration)**.

17 Noting which cable section is connected to which pulley, disconnect the first cable end nipple from the throttle actuator's upper pulley, then slide the cable outer upwards out of the actuator housing. Disconnect the second cable in the same way from the actuator's lower pulley.

18 Working in the passenger compartment, reach up to the top of the accelerator pedal. Pull the end fitting and collar out of the pedal, then release the cable inner wire through the slot in the pedal. Tie a length of string to the end of the cable.

19 Returning to the engine compartment, pull the cable through the bulkhead until the string can be untied and the pedal-to-actuator cable removed.

Refitting

20 Refitting is the reverse of the removal procedure. Use the string to draw the pedal-to-actuator cable through the bulkhead. Ensure that each cable end is connected to the correct actuator pulley.

21 Adjust both cables as described below.

Adjustment

Note: *Both sections of the cable must be adjusted together, even if only one has been disturbed.*

22 Remove the plenum chamber (see Section 4).

4A

5.9 Location of accelerator cable adjuster - remove metal clip (arrowed) to enable adjustment to be made

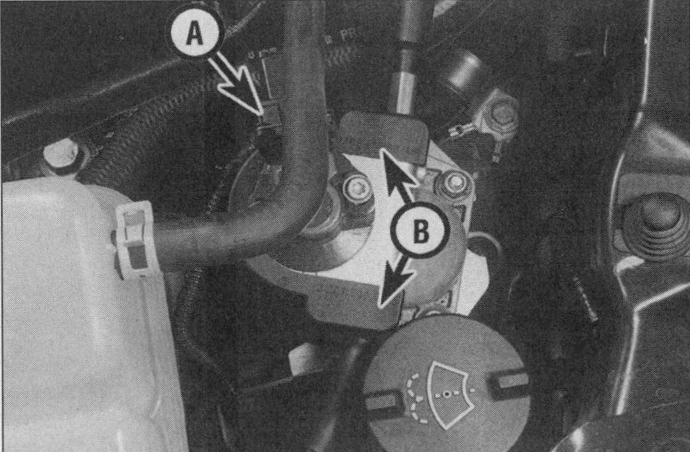

5.16 Unplug TCS throttle actuator's electrical connector (A) and prise off its cover at two points (B)

5.23 Location of TCS throttle actuator-to-throttle housing cable adjuster (arrowed)

23 Remove the metal clip from the adjuster of each cable section **(see illustration)**, and lubricate the adjusters' grommets with soapy water.

24 Remove any slack by pulling both outer cables as far as possible out of their respective adjusters.

25 Unplug the TCS throttle actuator's electrical connector, and prise off its cover. Lock both pulleys together by pushing a locking pin (a pin punch or a similar tool of suitable size) into their alignment holes. Disconnect the actuator-to-throttle housing cable's end nipple from the throttle linkage.

26 Have an assistant depress the accelerator pedal fully. The pedal-to-actuator cable outer will move back into the adjuster; hold it there, and refit the clip.

27 Connect the actuator-to-throttle housing cable end nipple to the throttle linkage, and check that the outer cable grommet is correctly secured in the housing bracket.

28 Again have the assistant depress the accelerator pedal fully. The actuator-to-throttle housing cable outer will move back into the adjuster; hold it there, and refit the clip.

29 Remove the locking pin from the pulleys. Check that the throttle valve moves smoothly and easily from the fully-closed to the fully-open position and back again, as the assistant depresses and releases the accelerator pedal. Re-adjust the cable(s) if required.

30 When the setting is correct, refit the TCS throttle actuator's cover and electrical connector, then refit the plenum chamber (see Section 4).

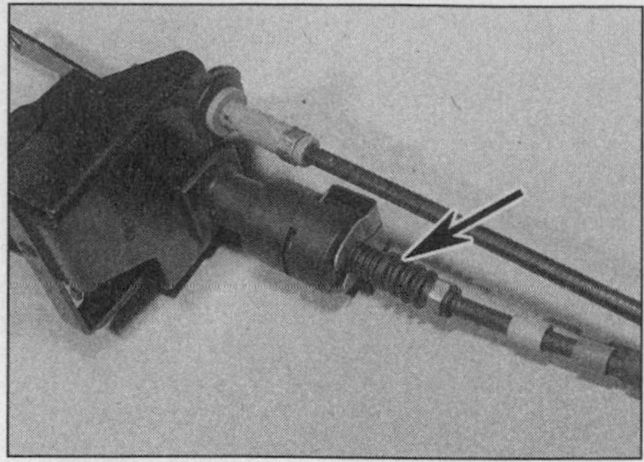

5.32 Outer cable and adjustment ferrule

Models with V6 Duratec engine (with traction control)

Note: *While the following procedure deals with the complete cable, the pedal-to-actuator and actuator-to-throttle housing sections of the cable are available separately, and can be removed and refitted individually. If doing this, modify the procedure as required.*

Removal

31 The accelerator cable consists of a primary and secondary cable. The primary cable is attached to the accelerator pedal and traction control unit actuator located in the right-hand front corner of the engine compartment. The secondary cable is attached to the traction control unit actuator and throttle housing quadrant.

32 Pull out the clip and lift the secondary outer cable from the support bracket **(see illustration)**.

33 Disconnect the inner cable from the quadrant or lever on the throttle housing. Where necessary, prise off the spring clip first **(see illustrations)**.

34 On models manufactured up to 1/1997, detach the secondary cable from the clip on the left-hand inner wing panel.

35 Unhook the secondary cable from the front support clip.

36 Disconnect the wiring from the traction control motor.

37 Carefully remove the cover from the traction control motor (see Chapter 9, Section 24).

38 Disconnect the secondary inner cable from the motor upper quadrant, then detach the secondary cable from the bracket on the motor.

39 Release the cable tie, and disconnect the primary inner cable from the motor lower quadrant. Detach the primary cable from the bracket on the motor.

40 Inside the car, disconnect the primary inner cable from the accelerator pedal. Tie a length of string to the end of the cable.

41 Returning to the engine compartment, pull the cable through the bulkhead until the string can be untied and the pedal-to-actuator cable removed.

Refitting and adjustment

42 Refitting is the reverse of the removal procedure. Use the string to draw the pedal-to-actuator cable through the bulkhead. Ensure that each cable end is connected to the correct actuator quadrant.

43 Adjust both cables as described in paragraphs 23 to 30.

6 Accelerator pedal - removal and refitting

Removal

1 Working in the driver's footwell, reach up to the top of the accelerator pedal. Pull the end fitting and collar out of the pedal, then release the inner cable from the slot in the pedal.

2 Undo the retaining nuts and bolt, then withdraw the pedal assembly **(see illustration)**.

Refitting

3 Refitting is a reversal of removal. Check and if necessary adjust the cable(s) as described in Section 5.

7 Fuel pump/fuel pressure - check

Warning: Refer to the warning note in Section 1 before proceeding.

Fuel pump operation check

1 Switch on the ignition and listen for the fuel pump (the sound of an electric motor running, audible from beneath the rear seats).

5.33a Prise off the spring clip . . .

5.33b . . . and disconnect the inner cable from the lever

6.2 Removing the accelerator pedal assembly

7.4 Use a gauge, equipped with an adaptor to suit the Schrader-type valve on the fuel rail pressure test/release fitting to check fuel pressure

8.4 Unplugging the fuel pump/fuel gauge sender unit electrical connector (arrowed)

Assuming there is sufficient fuel in the tank, the pump should start and run for several seconds, then stop. **Note:** *If the pump runs continuously all the time the ignition is switched on, the electronic control system is running in the backup (or "limp-home") mode referred to by Ford as "Limited Operation Strategy" (LOS). This almost certainly indicates a fault in the ECU itself, and the vehicle should therefore be taken to a Ford dealer for a full test of the complete system, using the correct diagnostic equipment; do not waste time trying to test the system without such facilities.*

2 Listen for fuel return noises from the fuel pressure regulator. It should be possible to feel the fuel pulsing in the regulator and in the feed hose from the fuel filter. If the pump does not run at all, check the fuse, relay and wiring (see Chapter 12).

Fuel pressure check

3 A fuel pressure gauge, equipped with an adaptor to suit the Schrader-type valve on the fuel rail pressure test/release fitting (identifiable by its blue plastic cap, and located on the union of the fuel feed line and the fuel rail) is required for the following procedure. If the Ford special tool 23-033 is available (see Section 2), the tool can be attached to the valve, and a conventional-type pressure gauge attached to the tool.

4 If using the service tool, ensure that its tap is turned fully anti-clockwise, then attach it to the valve. Connect the pressure gauge to the service tool. If using a fuel pressure gauge with its own adaptor, connect it in accordance with its maker's instructions **(see illustration)**.

5 Start the engine and allow it to idle. Note the gauge reading as soon as the pressure stabilises, and compare it with the pressure listed in this Chapter's Specifications.

a) If the pressure is high, check for a restricted fuel return line. If the line is clear, renew the pressure regulator.

b) If the pressure is low, pinch the fuel return line. If the pressure now goes up, renew the fuel pressure regulator. If the pressure does not increase, check the fuel feed line, the fuel pump and the fuel filter.

6 Detach the vacuum hose from the fuel pressure regulator; the pressure shown on the gauge should increase. Note the increase in pressure, and compare it with that listed in this Chapter's Specifications. If the pressure increase is not as specified, check the vacuum hose and pressure regulator.

7 Reconnect the regulator vacuum hose, and switch off the engine. Verify that the fuel pressure stays at the specified level for five minutes after the engine is turned off.

8 Carefully disconnect the fuel pressure gauge. Be sure to cover the fitting with a rag before slackening it. Mop up any spilt petrol.

9 Run the engine, and check that there are no fuel leaks.

8 Fuel pump/fuel gauge sender unit - removal and refitting

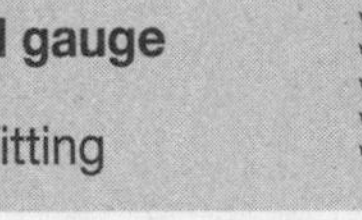

Warning: Refer to the warning note in Section 1 before proceeding.

Removal

Note: *Ford specify the use of their service tool 23-038 (a large box spanner with projecting teeth to engage the fuel pump/sender unit retaining ring's slots) for this task. While alternatives are possible, as shown below, in view of the difficulty experienced in removing and refitting the pump/sender unit, owners are strongly advised to obtain this tool before starting work. The help of an assistant will be required.*

1 Depressurise the fuel system (see Section 2), and equalise the tank pressure by removing the fuel filler cap.

2 Make sure the ignition is switched off.

3 Unbolt or fold forwards (as appropriate) the rear seat base cushion (see Chapter 11). Withdraw from the vehicle's floor the grommet covering the fuel pump/sender unit. Wash off any dirt from the tank's top surface, and dry it; use a vacuum cleaner to clean the immediate surroundings of the vehicle's interior, to reduce the risk of introducing water, dirt and dust into the tank while it is open.

4 Unplug the fuel pump/sender unit's electrical connector **(see illustration)**.

5 To disconnect the fuel feed and return pipes from the unit, release each pipe's coupling, by squeezing together the protruding locking lugs on each union and carefully pulling the coupling apart. Use rag to soak up any spilt fuel. Where the couplings are difficult to separate, use a pair of pliers and a block of wood as shown, to lever the pipe out of the union. Considerable force may be required, but be as careful as possible to avoid damaging any of the components **(see illustration)**.

6 Release the fuel pump/sender unit's retaining ring by turning it anti-clockwise. As noted above, Ford recommend the use of

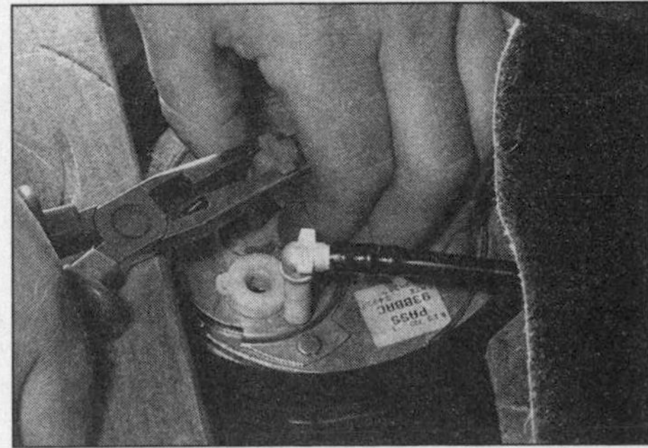

8.5 If fuel couplings are difficult to release, use pliers and a block of wood as shown to prise pipe end out of union

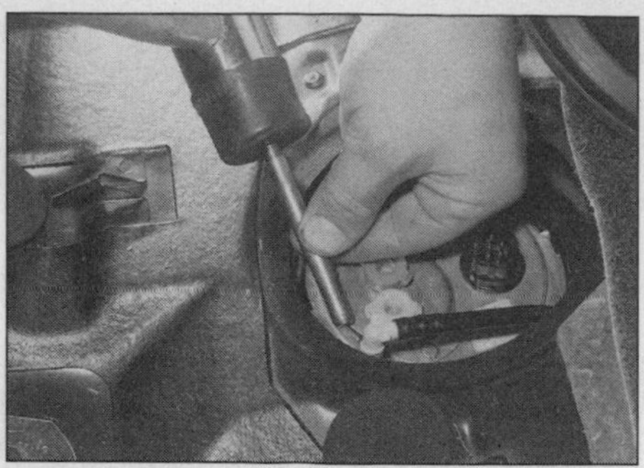

8.6 Fuel pump/sender unit's retaining ring can be released using ordinary tools as shown

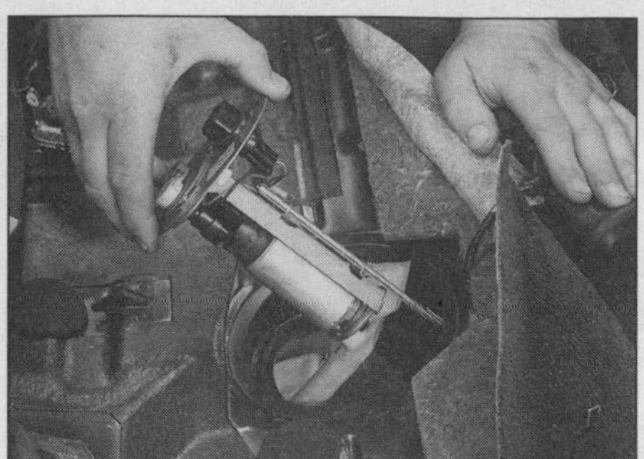

8.7a Removing fuel pump/sender unit - take care not to bend float arm, and note how it is fitted on spring-loaded extension

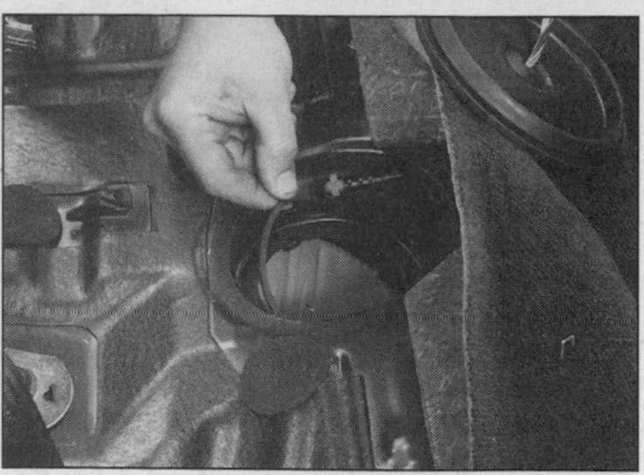

8.7b Fuel pump/sender unit's sealing ring must be renewed whenever it is disturbed

service tool 23-038. For those without access to such equipment, a hammer and drift, or a pair of slip-jointed pliers, will serve as an adequate substitute **(see illustration)**.

7 Withdraw the fuel pump/fuel gauge sender unit, taking care not to bend the float arm. The float arm is mounted on a spring-loaded extension, to hold it closely against the bottom of the tank. Note the sealing ring; this must be renewed whenever it is disturbed **(see illustrations)**.

Refitting

8 On refitting, use a new sealing ring, and ensure that the gauze filter over the base of the pump pick-up is clean.

9 Align the pump/sender unit with the tank opening, and refit it, ensuring that the float arm is not bent. Insert the unit so that the float arm slides correctly up the extension, until the unit's top mounting plate can be aligned with the tank opening and pressed onto the sealing ring. This may require a considerable amount of pressure; if so, be careful to avoid damaging any of the components. The Ford service tool provides the best way of holding the ring square to the tank and turning it at the same time.

10 Maintain the pressure while an assistant refits and engages the retaining ring. When the ring is engaged in the tank lugs, turn it clockwise to tighten it until it is secured.

11 The remainder of the refitting procedure is the reverse of removal. Observe the colour-coding to ensure that the fuel pipes are reconnected to the correct unions.

9 Fuel tank - removal, inspection and refitting

Warning: Refer to the warning note in Section 1 before proceeding.

Removal

1 A fuel tank drain plug is not provided, therefore it is preferable to carry out the removal operation when the tank is nearly empty **(see illustration)**. First depressurise the fuel system as described in Section 2.

2 Syphon or hand-pump the remaining fuel from the tank. Alternatively, position a clean container beneath the fuel filter, then disconnect the feed pipe and connect a length of hose from the filter to the container. Switch on the ignition and allow the fuel pump to empty the tank into the container. Be sure to take all necessary precautions to prevent the risk of fire. Reconnect the hose after draining the tank.

3 Make sure the ignition is switched off.

4 Unbolt or fold forwards (as appropriate) the rear seat base cushion (see Chapter 11). Prise the grommet from the floor for access to the fuel pump/sender unit.

5 Disconnect the wiring from the fuel pump/sender unit, and also disconnect the fuel return pipe (coded red) from the unit.

6 Chock the front wheels, then jack up the rear of the vehicle and support on axle stands (see "*Jacking and Vehicle Support*").

7 Either remove the fuel filter, or disconnect its outlet pipe (see Chapter 1).

8 Unhook the exhaust system rubber mountings. Lower the system onto a suitable support, so that the front downpipe-to-exhaust manifold joint is not strained, or remove it completely (see Chapter 4A).

9 Unbolt the rear suspension anti-roll bar mounting clamps **(see illustration)**. Swing the bar down as far as possible - if preferred, remove the bar completely (see Chapter 10).

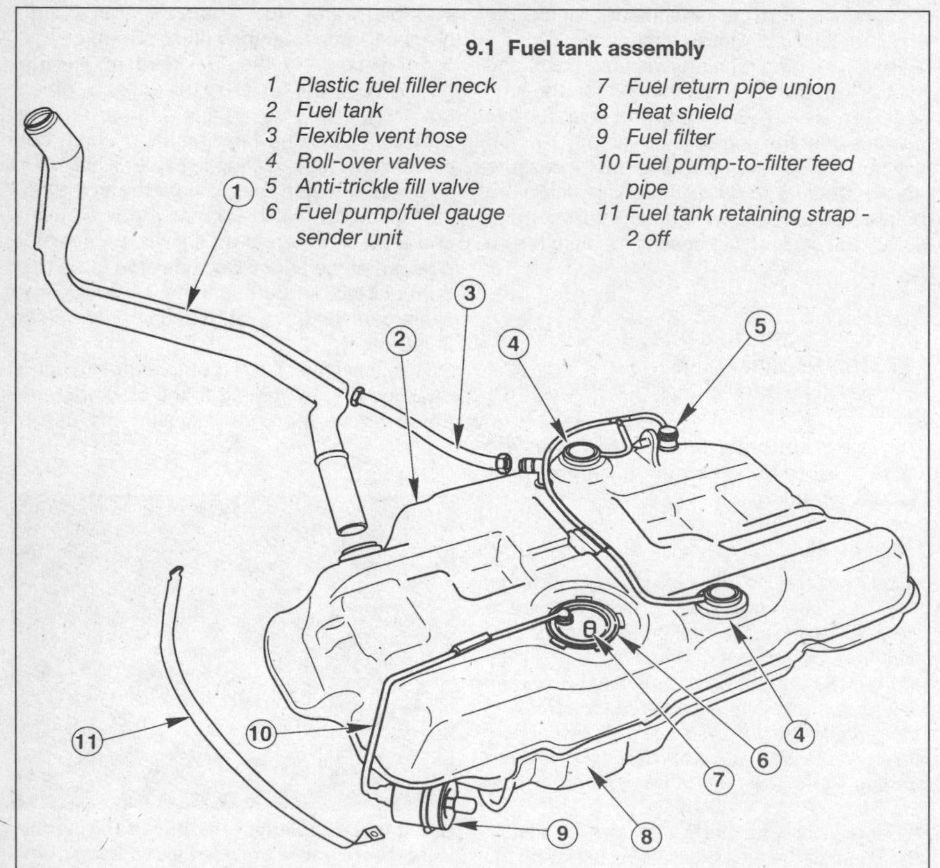

9.9 Unbolt rear anti-roll bar mounting clamps (one arrowed) when preparing to remove the fuel tank

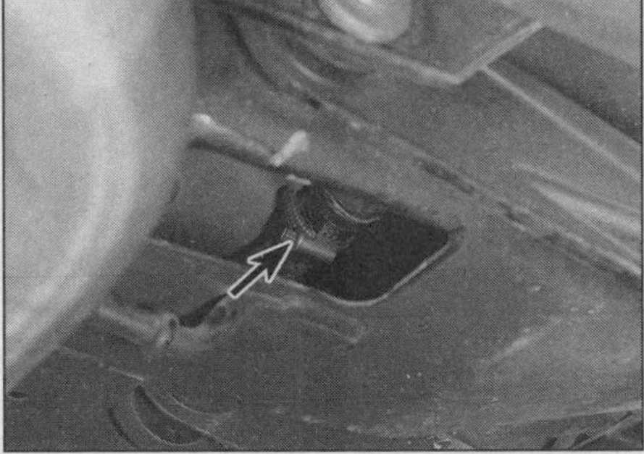

9.10a Fuel filler vent hose clamp (arrowed) accessible through right-hand side aperture in rear suspension crossmember on Saloon and Hatchback models . . .

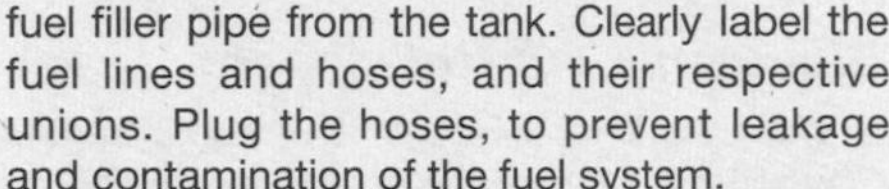

9.10b . . . on Estate models, it is immediately above rear suspension anti-roll bar

10 On models manufactured up to 1/1997, disconnect the flexible vent hose from the fuel tank as follows:

a) *On Saloon and Hatchback models, reach up into the right-hand side aperture in the rear suspension crossmember, loosen the clamp, and remove the hose* ***(see illustration)****.*

b) *On Estate models, loosen the clamp immediately above the rear anti-roll bar, and remove the hose* ***(see illustration)****.*

11 Unscrew the six retaining nuts, and withdraw the exhaust system's rear heat shield from the underbody **(see illustration)**.

12 Support the tank with a trolley jack and block of wood.

13 Unscrew the bolt at the front of each retaining strap, and pivot them down until they are hanging out of the way. Note the earth lead under the left-hand strap's bolt - clean the mating surfaces before the tank is refitted, so that clean, metal-to-metal contact is ensured.

14 Lower the tank enough to unclip the fuel return pipe (coded red) from its top surface, then disconnect the charcoal canister's vapour hose from the union at the top rear of the tank **(see illustration)**. On models manufactured from 1/1997-on, disconnect the fuel filler pipe from the tank. Clearly label the fuel lines and hoses, and their respective unions. Plug the hoses, to prevent leakage and contamination of the fuel system.

15 Remove the tank from the vehicle, releasing it from the filler neck stub. While the tank is removed, unhook the retaining straps (twist them through 90° to do so), and check that they and their locations in the underbody are in good condition.

16 With the fuel tank removed, the filler neck can be withdrawn. It is secured by a single screw in the filler opening, and by two bolts to the underbody.

Inspection

17 Check the fuel tank for damage. Any sediment inside the tank should be removed, either by swilling out with clean fuel or by steam cleaning.

18 Any repairs to the fuel tank or filler neck should be carried out by a professional who has experience in this critical and potentially-dangerous work. Even after cleaning and flushing of the fuel system, explosive fumes can remain and ignite during repair of the tank.

Refitting

19 Refitting is a reversal of removal.

10 Roll-over valves - removal and refitting

Warning: Refer to the warning note in Section 1 before proceeding.

Removal

1 Remove the fuel tank (see Section 9).

2 Prise the two valves out of the tank, and remove the anti-trickle fill valve from its mounting. Take care not to damage the valves or the tank. Prise out the rubber seals from the tank openings, and renew then if they are worn, distorted, or if either has been leaking.

3 If either valve is thought to be faulty, seek the advice of a Ford dealer as to whether they can be renewed individually. If not, the complete valve and pipe assembly must be renewed.

Refitting

4 Refitting is the reverse of the removal procedure. Ensure that both roll-over valves are pressed securely into their seals, so that there can be no fuel leaks.

9.11 Exhaust system must be lowered and heat shield removed to enable fuel tank removal - retaining strap front bolts arrowed

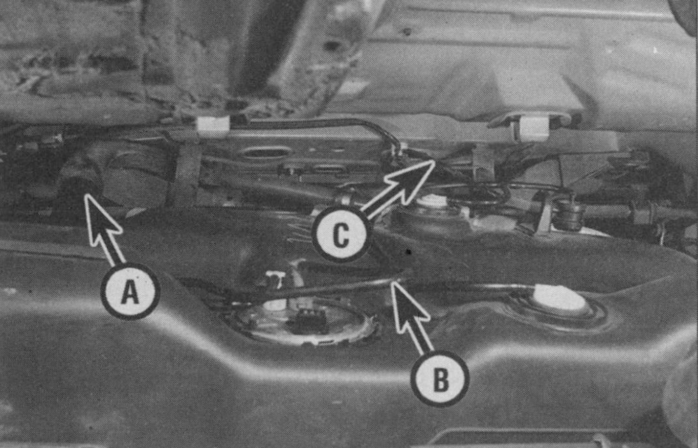

9.14 Lower fuel tank - do not distort filler neck stub (A) - and unclip (red-coded) fuel return pipe (B), then disconnect charcoal canister's vapour hose (C)

11 Fuel cut-off switch - removal and refitting

Removal

1 Disconnect the battery negative (earth) lead (see Chapter 5A).
2 Remove the trim panel from the left-hand footwell.
3 Peel back the sound-insulating material from the switch, and undo the two retaining screws **(see illustration)**.
4 Disconnect the wiring, and withdraw the switch.

Refitting

5 Refitting is the reverse of the removal procedure. Ensure that the switch is reset by depressing its red button.

12 Fuel injection system - general description

1 All petrol models are equipped with a Sequential Electronically-controlled Fuel Injection (SEFi) system.

Fuel supply and air induction systems

2 An electric fuel pump located inside the fuel tank supplies fuel under pressure to the fuel rail, which distributes fuel to the injectors. A filter between the fuel pump and the fuel rail protects the components of the system. A pressure regulator controls the system pressure in relation to inlet depression. From the fuel rail, fuel is injected into the inlet ports, just above the inlet valves, by four fuel injectors.
3 The amount of fuel supplied by the injectors is precisely controlled by an Electronic Control Unit (ECU). The ECU uses the signals from the engine speed/crankshaft position sensor and the camshaft position sensor, to trigger each injector separately in cylinder firing order (sequential injection).
4 The air induction system consists of an air filter housing, an air mass meter, intake ducting, and a throttle housing. The air mass meter is an information-gathering device for the ECU; it uses a "hot-wire" system to send the ECU a constantly-varying (analogue) voltage signal corresponding to the volume of air passing into the engine. Another sensor in the air mass meter measures intake air temperature. The ECU uses these signals to calculate the mass of air entering the engine.
5 The throttle valve inside the throttle housing is controlled by the driver, through the accelerator pedal. As the valve opens, the quantity of air entering the engine increases. The throttle potentiometer is attached to the throttle valve and informs the ECU of the throttle position. The ECU calculates the

11.3 Fuel cut-off switch retaining screws (arrowed)

relevant period of injection, and controls the injector opening times.

Electronic control system

6 The EEC-IV and EEC-V (Electronic Engine Control) engine management systems control fuel injection by means of a microcomputer known as the ECU (Electronic Control Unit) **(see illustrations)**. The ECU receives signals from a number of sensors, which monitor the intake air mass and temperature, coolant temperature, engine speed and crankshaft position, acceleration/deceleration, and exhaust gas oxygen content. The signals are processed by the ECU to determine the injection duration necessary for the optimum air/fuel ratio. The sensors and associated ECU-controlled relays are located throughout the engine compartment.
7 In the event of a sensor malfunction, a back-up circuit will take over, to provide driveability until the problem is identified and fixed. The following paragraphs describe the components of the electronic control system.

ECU (Electronic Control Unit)

8 This component is the heart of the entire engine management system, controlling the fuel injection, ignition and emissions control systems. It also controls sub-systems such as the radiator cooling fan, air conditioning and automatic transmission, where appropriate.

Air mass meter

9 This uses a "hot-wire" system, sending the ECU a constantly-varying (analogue) voltage signal corresponding to the mass of air passing into the engine. Since air mass varies with temperature (cold air being denser than warm), measuring air mass provides the ECU with a very accurate means of determining the correct amount of fuel required to achieve the ideal air/fuel mixture ratio.

Crankshaft speed/position sensor

10 This is an inductive pulse generator bolted to the cylinder block/crankcase (4-cylinder) or timing cover (V6). On 4-cylinder engines it scans ridges between 36 holes machined in the inboard (right-hand) face of the flywheel/driveplate; as each ridge passes the sensor tip, a signal is generated, which is used by the ECU to determine engine speed. On V6 engines, the sensor scans similar cut-outs machined on a timing disc located on the timing end of the crankshaft.
11 The ridge between the 35th and 36th holes (corresponding to 90° BTDC) is missing - this step in the incoming signals is used by the ECU to determine crankshaft (ie, piston) position.

Camshaft position sensor

12 On 4-cylinder models the camshaft position sensor is bolted to the rear left-hand end of the cylinder head, and is triggered by a high-point on the inlet camshaft. On V6 models, the camshaft position sensor is mounted on the right-hand side of the front cylinder head and is triggered by a high-point on the front inlet camshaft. The sensor functions in the same way as the crankshaft speed/position sensor, producing a series of pulses (corresponding to No 1 cylinder at 46° ATDC). This gives the ECU a reference point, to enable it to determine the firing order, and operate the injectors in the appropriate sequence.

Coolant temperature sensor

13 This component, which is screwed into the top of the thermostat housing on 4-cylinder models or into the coolant crossover on V6 models, is an NTC (Negative Temperature Coefficient) thermistor - that is, a semi-conductor whose electrical resistance decreases as its temperature increases. It provides the ECU with a constantly-varying (analogue) voltage signal, corresponding to the temperature of the engine coolant. This is used to refine the calculations made by the ECU, when determining the correct amount of fuel required to achieve the ideal air/fuel mixture ratio.

Intake air temperature sensor

14 On 4-cylinder models manufactured up to 1997, this component is screwed into the underside of the air intake resonator. On 1998-on models it is located in the air inlet duct. On V6 models it is located in the air cleaner cover. The sensor is an NTC thermistor - see the previous paragraph - providing the ECU with a signal corresponding to the temperature of air passing into the engine. This is used to refine the calculations made by the ECU, when determining the correct amount of fuel required to achieve the ideal air/fuel mixture ratio.

Throttle potentiometer

15 This is mounted on the end of the throttle valve spindle, to provide the ECU with a constantly-varying (analogue) voltage signal corresponding to the throttle opening. This allows the ECU to register the driver's input when determining the amount of fuel required by the engine.

Vehicle speed sensor

16 This component is a Hall-effect generator, mounted on the transmission's speedometer drive. It supplies the ECU with a series of pulses corresponding to the vehicle's road

speed, enabling the ECU to control features such as the fuel shut-off on the overrun, and to provide information for the trip computer, adaptive damping and cruise control systems (where fitted).

Power steering pressure switch

17 This is a pressure-operated switch, screwed into the power steering system's high-pressure pipe. Its contacts are normally closed, opening when the system reaches the specified pressure - on receiving this signal, the ECU increases the idle speed, to compensate for the additional load on the engine.

Air conditioning system

18 Two pressure-operated switches and the compressor clutch solenoid are connected to the ECU, to enable it to determine how the system is operating. The ECU can increase idle speed or switch off the system, as necessary, so that normal vehicle operation and driveability are not impaired. See Chapter 3 for further details, but note that diagnosis and repair should be left to a dealer service department or air conditioning specialist.

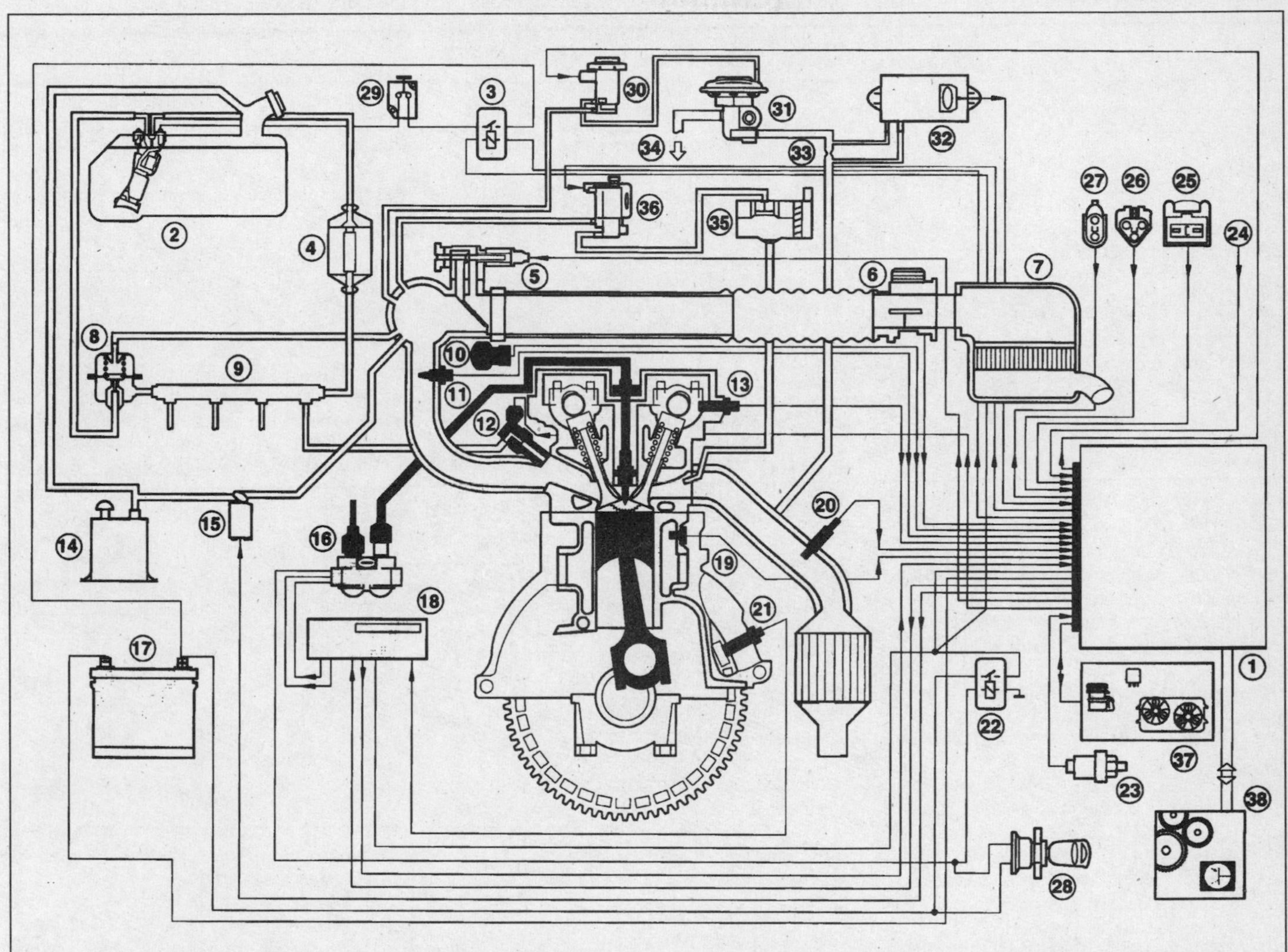

12.6a Engine management system, showing fuel injection, ignition and emissions control sub-systems

1 ECU (Electronic Control Unit)
2 Fuel pump/fuel gauge sender unit
3 Fuel pump relay
4 Fuel filter
5 Idle speed control valve
6 Air mass meter
7 Air cleaner assembly
8 Fuel pressure regulator
9 Fuel rail
10 Throttle potentiometer
11 Intake air temperature sensor
12 Fuel injector
13 Camshaft position sensor
14 Charcoal canister
15 Charcoal canister-purge solenoid valve
16 Ignition coil
17 Battery
18 Ignition module - only separate (from ECU) on vehicles with automatic transmission
19 Coolant temperature sensor
20 Oxygen sensor
21 Crankshaft speed/position sensor
22 Power supply relay
23 Power steering pressure switch
24 Air conditioning compressor clutch solenoid
25 Service connector - for octane adjustment
26 Self-test connector - for Ford STAR tester diagnostic equipment
27 Diagnosis connector - for Ford diagnostic equipment FDS 2000
28 Ignition switch
29 Fuel cut-off switch
30 Exhaust Gas Recirculation (EGR) solenoid valve
31 Exhaust Gas Recirculation (EGR) valve
32 Exhaust Gas Recirculation (EGR) exhaust gas pressure differential sensor
33 Exhaust Gas Recirculation (EGR) pressure differential measuring point
34 To inlet manifold
35 Pulse-air filter housing
36 Pulse-air solenoid valve
37 Air conditioning/radiator electric cooling fan control
38 Automatic transmission control system - where applicable

Idle speed control valve

19 The idle speed control valve maintains a stable idle speed by varying the quantity of air entering the engine through an auxiliary air passage. The valve is activated by a signal from the ECU.

Automatic transmission sensors

20 In addition to the driver's controls, the transmission has a speed sensor, a fluid temperature sensor (built into the solenoid valve unit), and a selector lever position sensor. All of these are connected to the ECU, to enable it to control the transmission through the solenoid valve unit. See Chapter 7B for further details.

Exhaust gas oxygen sensor

21 The oxygen sensor in the exhaust system provides the ECU with constant feedback - "closed-loop" control - which enables it to adjust the mixture to provide the best possible conditions for the catalytic converter to operate. Refer to Chapter 4B for more information.

Heated front windscreen solenoid

22 When the heated front windscreen is switched on, the solenoid admits additional air to the inlet manifold in order to counteract the extra load on the alternator.

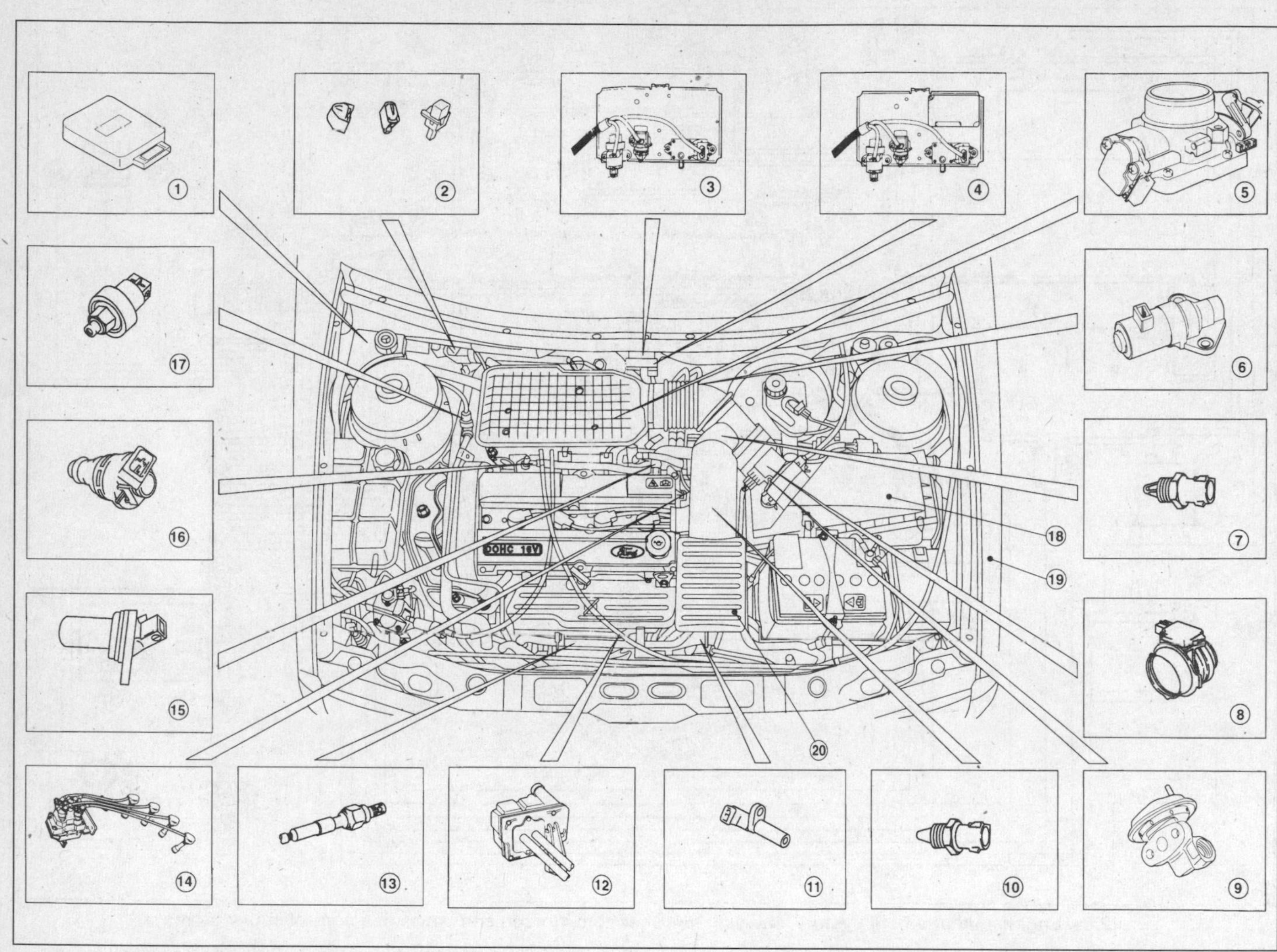

12.6b Location of principal fuel injection, ignition and emissions control system components on 4-cylinder models

1 ECU (Electronic Control Unit)
2 Self-test, diagnosis and service connectors (left to right)
3 Bulkhead component mounting bracket - manual transmission - showing from left to right, (EGR) solenoid valve, pulse-air solenoid valve and (EGR) exhaust gas pressure differential sensor
4 Bulkhead component mounting bracket - automatic transmission - showing from left to right, (EGR) solenoid valve, pulse-air solenoid valve and (EGR) exhaust gas pressure differential sensor, with separate ignition module above
5 Throttle housing, including potentiometer
6 Idle speed control valve
7 Intake air temperature sensor
8 Air mass meter
9 Exhaust Gas Recirculation (EGR) valve
10 Coolant temperature sensor
11 Crankshaft speed/position sensor
12 Pulse-air filter housing
13 Oxygen sensor
14 Ignition coil and spark plug (HT) leads
15 Camshaft position sensor
16 Fuel injector(s)
17 Power steering pressure switch
18 Air cleaner assembly
19 Air intake tube and resonators - under left-hand front wing
20 Resonator

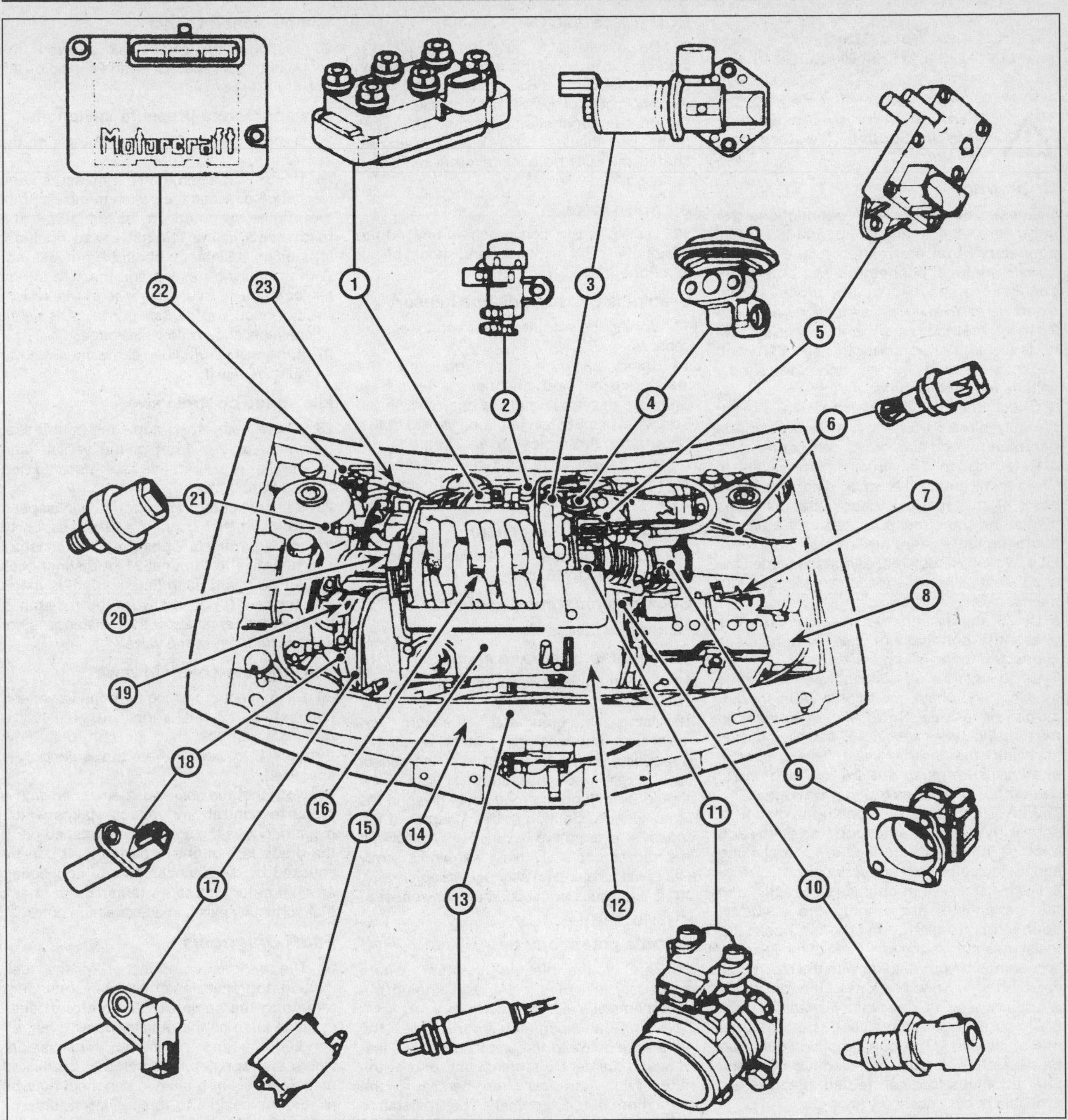

12.6c Location of principal fuel injection, ignition and emissions control system components on V6 models

1 *Ignition coil*
2 *Electronic vacuum regulator*
3 *Idle air control valve (IAC)*
4 *Exhaust Gas Recirculation (EGR) valve*
5 *Electronic differential pressure sensor (DPFE)*
6 *Intake air temperature sensor (IAT)*
7 *Air cleaner*
8 *Battery junction box*
9 *Mass air flow sensor (MAF)*
10 *Coolant temperature sensor (ECT)*
11 *Throttle housing and throttle position sensor (TP)*
12 *Water pump drivebelt cover*
13 *Heated oxygen sensor (HO2S)*
14 *Front catalytic converter (rear on rear exhaust manifold)*
15 *Inlet manifold runner control (IMRC)*
16 *Upper inlet manifold*
17 *Camshaft position sensor (CMP)*
18 *Crankshaft position sensor (CKP)*
19 *Hydraulic engine mounting*
20 *Right-hand engine mounting*
21 *Power steering pressure switch (PSPS)*
22 *Power train control module (PCM) or Electronic control unit (ECU)*
23 *Service plug (octane adjustment)*

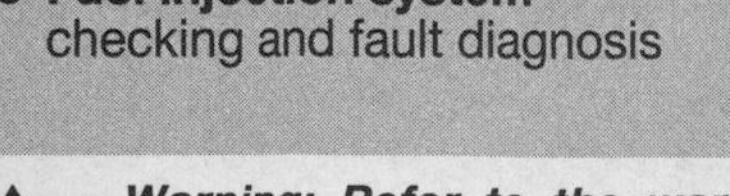

13 Fuel injection system - checking and fault diagnosis

Warning: Refer to the warning note in Section 1 before proceeding.

Checking

1 Check all earth wire connections for tightness. Check all wiring and electrical connectors that are related to the system. Loose electrical connectors and poor earth connections can cause many problems that resemble more serious malfunctions.

2 Check that the battery is fully-charged and its leads tightened correctly. The ECU and sensors depend on an accurate supply voltage to properly meter the fuel.

3 Check the air filter element - a dirty or partially-blocked filter will severely impede performance and economy (see Chapter 1).

4 Referring to the information given in Chapter 12 and in the wiring diagrams at the back of this manual, check that all fuses protecting the circuits related to the engine management system are in good condition. Fit new fuses if required, and at the same time check that all relays are securely plugged into their sockets.

5 Check the air intake ducts for leaks. Also check the condition of the vacuum hoses connected to the inlet manifold.

6 Disconnect the air ducting from the throttle housing, and check the throttle valve for dirt, carbon or residue. **Note:** *A warning label on the housing states specifically that the housing bore and the throttle valve have a special coating, and must not be cleaned using carburettor cleaner, as this may damage it.*

7 With the engine running, place a screwdriver or a stethoscope against each injector, one at a time. Listen for a clicking sound, indicating correct operation.

8 If an injector is not operating correctly, turn off the engine, and unplug the electrical connector from the injector. Check the resistance across the terminals of the injector, and compare your reading with the resistance value listed in Specifications. If the resistance is not as specified, renew the injector.

9 A rough idle, diminished performance and/or increased fuel consumption could also be caused by clogged or fouled fuel injectors. Fuel additives to clean fouled injectors are available at car accessory shops.

10 If these checks fail to reveal the cause of the problem, the vehicle should be taken to a suitably-equipped Ford dealer for testing. A wiring block connector is incorporated in the engine management circuit, into which a special electronic diagnostic tester can be plugged. The tester will locate the fault quickly and simply, alleviating the need to test all the system components individually, which is a time-consuming operation that also carries a risk of damaging the ECU.

ECU (Electronic Control Unit)

11 Do not attempt to "test" the ECU with any kind of equipment. If it is thought to be faulty, take the vehicle to a Ford dealer for the entire electronic control system to be checked using the proper diagnostic equipment. Only if all other possibilities have been eliminated should the ECU be considered at fault, and replaced.

Air mass meter

12 Testing of this component is beyond the scope of the DIY mechanic, and should be left to a Ford dealer.

Crankshaft speed/position sensor

13 Unplug the electrical connector from the sensor.

14 Using an ohmmeter, measure the resistance between the sensor terminals. Compare this reading to the one listed in the Specifications Section at the beginning of this Chapter. If the indicated resistance is not within the specified range, renew the sensor.

15 Plug in the sensor's electrical connector on completion.

Camshaft position sensor

16 The procedure is as described in paragraphs 13 to 15 above.

Coolant temperature sensor

17 Refer to Chapter 3.

Intake air temperature sensor

18 Unplug the electrical connector from the sensor.

19 Using an ohmmeter, measure the resistance between the sensor terminals. Depending on the temperature of the sensor tip, the resistance measured will vary, but it should be within the broad limits given in the Specifications Section of this Chapter. If the sensor's temperature is varied - by placing it in a freezer for a while, or by warming it gently - its resistance should alter accordingly.

20 If the results obtained show the sensor to be faulty, renew it.

Throttle potentiometer

21 Remove the plenum chamber, where necessary (see Section 4) and unplug the potentiometer's electrical connector.

22 Using an ohmmeter, measure the resistance between the unit's terminals - first between the centre terminal and one of the outer two, then from the centre to the remaining outer terminal. The resistance should be within the limits given in the Specifications Section of this Chapter, and should alter smoothly as the throttle valve is moved from the fully-closed (idle speed) position to fully open and back again.

23 If the resistance measured is significantly different from the specified value, if there are any breaks in continuity, or if the reading fluctuates erratically as the throttle is operated, the potentiometer is faulty, and must be renewed.

Vehicle speed sensor

24 Testing of this component is beyond the scope of the DIY mechanic, and should be left to a Ford dealer.

Power steering pressure switch

25 Unplug the electrical connector from the sensor.

26 Using an ohmmeter, measure the resistance between the switch terminals. With the engine switched off, or idling with the roadwheels in the straight-ahead position, little or no resistance should be measured. With the engine running and the steering on full-lock, the pressure increase in the system should open the switch contacts, so that infinite resistance is now measured.

27 If the results obtained show the switch to be faulty, renew it.

Idle speed control valve

28 Where necessary, apply the handbrake, then jack up the front of the vehicle and support it on axle stands (see "*Jacking and Vehicle Support*").

29 Disconnect the wiring from the idle speed control valve, then connect a 12-volt supply to the valve terminals - positive to terminal 37 and negative to terminal 21. A distinct click should be heard each time contact is made and broken. If not, measure the resistance between the terminals. If the resistance is not as specified, renew the valve.

Idle increase solenoid valve

30 Disconnect the wiring from the valve, and connect a 12-volt supply to the valve terminals. Check that air can only flow through the valve when the solenoid is energised.

31 Note that the solenoid is equipped with a diode to control any voltage spikes which might occur as the solenoid is switched off. If the diode is thought to be faulty, it can be checked by disconnecting it and connecting an ohmmeter across its terminals to check that continuity exists in one direction only.

Fault diagnosis

32 The various components of the fuel, ignition and emissions control systems (not forgetting the same ECU's control of sub-systems such as the radiator cooling fan, air conditioning and automatic transmission, where appropriate) are so closely interlinked that diagnosis of a faulty component may be almost impossible to trace using traditional methods.

33 To quickly and accurately find faults, the ECU is provided with a built-in self-diagnosis facility, which detects malfunctions in the system's components. When a fault occurs, the ECU identifies the fault and stores it in its memory, and (in most cases) runs the system using back-up values pre-programmed ("mapped") into its memory. Good driveability is thus maintained, to enable the vehicle to be driven to a garage for attention.

13.40a Vacuum hose routing schematic diagram

- A Exhaust Gas Recirculation (EGR) solenoid valve
- B Pulse-air solenoid valve
- C Exhaust Gas Recirculation (EGR) exhaust gas pressure differential sensor
- D Exhaust Gas Recirculation (EGR) valve
- E Charcoal canister-purge solenoid valve
- F Restrictor
- G Idle-increase solenoid valve - where fitted
- H Connection to plenum chamber
- J Connection to inlet manifold
- K Fuel pressure regulator
- L Connection to Positive Crankcase Ventilation (PCV) valve
- M Pulse-air filter housing
- N Connection to heating/air conditioning system controls
- P Charcoal canister

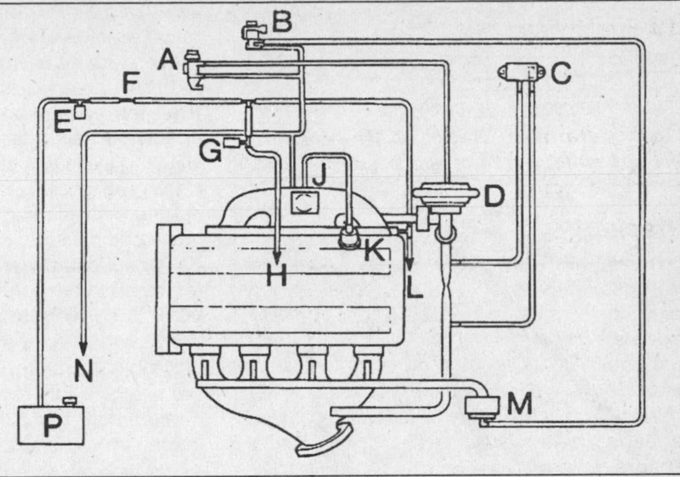

34 Any faults that may have occurred are indicated in the form of three-digit codes (EEC-IV) or a description (EEC-V) when the system is connected (via the built-in diagnosis or self-test connectors, as appropriate) to special diagnostic equipment - this points the user in the direction of the faulty circuit, so that further tests can pinpoint the exact location of the fault.

35 Given below is the procedure that would be followed by a Ford technician to trace a fault from scratch. Should your vehicle's engine management system develop a fault, read through the procedure and decide how much you can attempt, depending on your skill and experience and the equipment available to you, or whether it would be simpler to have the vehicle attended to by your local Ford dealer.

- *a) Preliminary checks*
- *b) Fault code or description read-out **
- *c) Check ignition timing and base idle speed. Recheck fault codes to establish whether fault has been cured or not **
- *d) Carry out basic check of ignition system components. Recheck fault codes to establish whether fault has been cured or not **
- *e) Carry out basic check of fuel system components. Recheck fault codes to establish whether fault has been cured or not **
- *f) If fault is still not located, carry out system test **

**Operations marked with an asterisk require special test equipment.*

Preliminary checks

Note: *When carrying out these checks to trace a fault, remember that if the fault has appeared only a short time after any part of the vehicle has been serviced or overhauled, the first place to check is where that work was carried out, however unrelated it may appear, to ensure that no carelessly-refitted components are causing the problem.*

36 If you are tracing the cause of a "partial" engine fault, such as lack of performance, in addition to the checks outlined below, check the compression pressures (see the relevant Part of Chapter 2) and bear in mind the possibility that one of the hydraulic tappets might be faulty, producing an incorrect valve clearance. Check also that the fuel filter has been renewed at the recommended intervals.

37 If the system appears to be completely dead, remember the possibility that the alarm/inhibitor system may be responsible.

38 The first check for anyone without special test equipment is to switch on the ignition, and to listen for the fuel pump (the sound of an electric motor running, audible from beneath the rear seats); assuming there is sufficient fuel in the tank, the pump should start and run for approximately one or two seconds, then stop. If the pump runs continuously all the time the ignition is switched on, the electronic control system is running in the back-up (or "limp-home") mode referred to by Ford as "Limited Operation Strategy" (LOS). This almost certainly indicates a fault in the ECU itself, and the vehicle should therefore be taken to a Ford dealer for a full test of the complete system using the correct diagnostic equipment; do not waste time trying to test the system without such facilities.

39 After checking the fuel pump, a considerable amount of fault diagnosis is still possible without special test equipment. Refer to the information given at the beginning of this Section.

40 Following the accompanying schematic diagram, and working methodically around the engine compartment, check carefully that all vacuum hoses and pipes are securely fastened and correctly routed, with no signs of cracks, splits or deterioration to cause air leaks, or of hoses that are trapped, kinked, or bent sharply enough to restrict air flow **(see illustrations)**. Check all connections and sharp bends, and renew any damaged or deformed lengths of hose.

41 Working from the fuel tank, via the filter, to the fuel rail (and including the feed and return), check the fuel lines, and renew any that are found to be leaking, trapped or kinked.

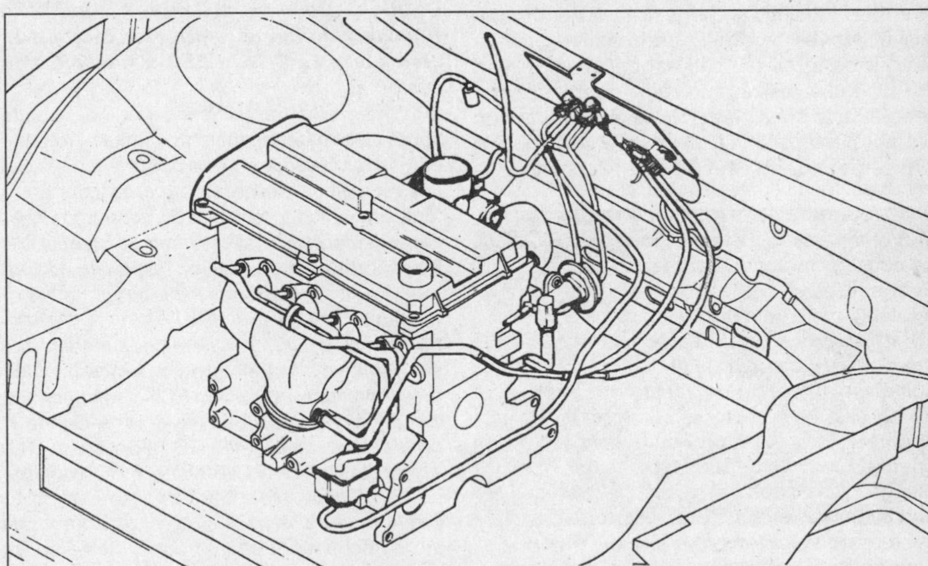

13.40b Installation of vacuum hoses in engine compartment

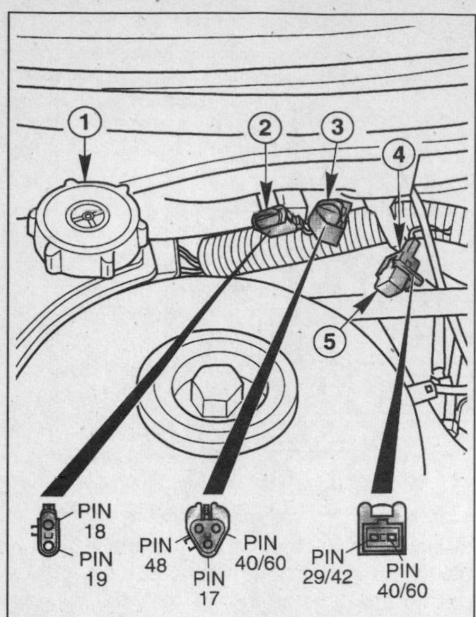

13.53a Location and terminal identification of engine management system self-test, diagnosis and service connectors on pre-8/1996 models

1 *Power steering fluid reservoir*
2 *Diagnosis connector - for Ford diagnostic equipment FDS 2000*
3 *Self-test connector - for fault code read-out - pin 17 is output terminal, pin 48 is input terminal, pin 40/60 is earth*
4 *Service connector - for octane adjustment*
5 *Plug-in bridge - to suit 95 RON fuel*

42 Check that the accelerator cable is correctly secured and adjusted; renew the cable if there is any doubt about its condition, or if it appears to be stiff or jerky in operation. Refer to the Section 5 for further information, if required.

43 If there is any doubt about the operation of the throttle, remove the air ducting from the throttle housing, and check that the throttle valve moves smoothly and easily from the fully-closed to the fully-open position and back again, as an assistant depresses the accelerator pedal. If the valve shows any sign of stiffness, sticking or otherwise-inhibited movement (and the accelerator cable is known to be in good condition), spray the throttle linkage with penetrating lubricant, allow time for it to work, and repeat the check.

13.53b For 8/1996-on models, the test socket is located beneath the steering column, behind a hinged plastic cover

44 Run the engine at idle speed. Working from the air intake at the inner wing panel, check the air inlet ducting for air leaks. Usually, these will be revealed by sucking or hissing noises. If a leak is found at any point, tighten the fastening clamp and/or renew the faulty components, as applicable.

45 Check the exhaust system for leaks with reference to Section 15.

46 It is possible to make a further check of the electrical connections by wiggling each electrical connector of the system in turn as the engine is idling; a faulty connector will be immediately evident from the engine's response as contact is broken and remade.

47 Switch off the engine. If the fault is not yet identified, the next step is to check the ignition voltages, using an engine analyser with an oscilloscope - without such equipment, the only tests possible are to remove and check each spark plug in turn, to check the spark plug (HT) lead connections and resistances, and to check the connections and resistances of the ignition coil. Refer to the relevant Sections of Chapters 1 and 5B.

48 The final step in these preliminary checks would be to use an exhaust gas analyser to measure the CO level at the exhaust tailpipe. This check cannot be made without special test equipment - see your local Ford dealer for details.

Fault code read-out

Note: *The remainder of this section is primarily for models fitted with the EEC-IV fuel injection system on models up to 8/1996. For later models with EEC-IV and EEC-V fuel injection systems, the Ford FDS 2000 tester must be used. This tester will display the fault without reference to a fault code.*

Caution: Do not attempt to use the following analogue voltmeter method to check later EEC-IV or EEC-V fuel injection systems.

49 The preliminary checks outlined above should eliminate the majority of faults from the engine management system. If the fault is not yet identified, the next step is to connect a fault code reader to the ECU, so that its self-diagnosis facility can be used to identify the faulty part of the system; further tests can then be made to identify the exact cause of the fault.

50 In their basic form, fault code readers are simply hand-held electronic devices, which take data stored within an ECU's memory and display it when required (as a three-digit fault code, in the case of the EEC-IV system). The more sophisticated versions now available can also control sensors and actuators, to provide more effective testing; some can store information, so that a road test can be carried out, and any faults encountered during the test can be displayed afterwards.

51 Ford's STAR (Self-Test Automatic Readout) tester can be used to check the EEC-IV fuel injection system. Most Ford dealers should have such equipment, and the trained staff to use it. The Ford FDS 2000 diagnostic tester can also be used on later models, however this uses model-specific software only available to Ford dealers. The only alternatives to using the Ford equipment are as follows:

a) *To obtain a proprietary reader which can interpret EEC-IV three-digit codes.*
b) *To use an analogue voltmeter, whereby the stored codes are displayed as sweeps of the voltmeter needle. This option limits the operator to a read-out of any codes stored - ie, there is no control of sensors and/or actuators - but can still be useful in pinpointing the faulty part of the engine management system. The display is interpreted as follows. Each code (whether fault code or command/separator) is marked by a three-to-four second pause - code "538" would therefore be shown as long (3 to 4 seconds) pause, five fast sweeps of the needle, slight (1 second) pause, three fast sweeps, slight pause, eight fast sweeps, long pause.*
c) *Owners without access to such equipment must take the vehicle to a Ford dealer, or to an expert who has similar equipment and the skill to use it.*

52 Because of the variations in the design of fault code readers, it is not possible to give exact details of the sequence of tests; the manufacturer's instructions must be followed, in conjunction with the codes given below. The following ten paragraphs outline the procedure to be followed using a version of the Ford STAR tester, to illustrate the general principles, as well as notes to guide the owner using only a voltmeter.

53 The vehicle must be prepared by applying the handbrake, switching off the air conditioning (where fitted) and any other electrical loads (lights, heated rear window, etc), then selecting neutral (manual transmission) or the "P" position (automatic transmission). Where the engine is required to be running, it must be fully warmed-up to normal operating temperature before the test is started. Using any adapters required, connect the fault code reader to the system. On pre-8/1996 models a triangular, three-pin self-test connector is located on the right-hand end of the engine compartment bulkhead. On later models, the test socket is located beneath the steering column, behind a hinged plastic cover **(see illustrations)**.

Caution: Do not use the STAR tester on later models - only use the FDS2000 tester.

If a voltmeter is being used, connect the positive lead to the battery positive terminal, and its negative lead to the self-test connector's output terminal, pin 17. Have a pen and paper ready to write down the codes displayed.

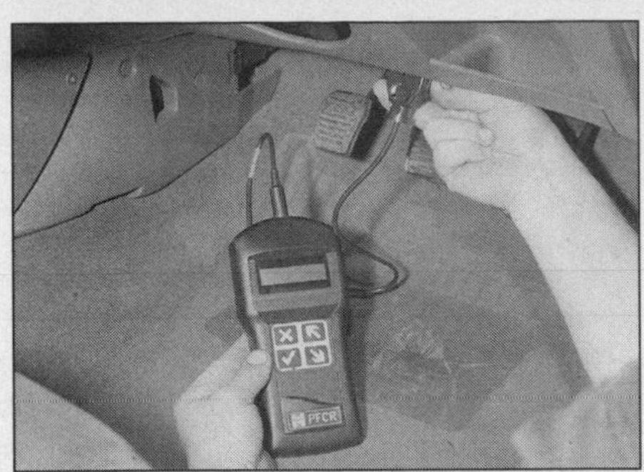

13.53c Connecting a fault code reader to the test socket on a 1997 model

54 Set the tester in operation. For the Ford STAR tester, a display check will be carried out and the test mode requirements must be entered. If a voltmeter is being used, connect a spare length of wire to earth the self-test connector's input terminal, pin 48. Be very careful to ensure that you earth the correct terminal - the one with the white/green wire. The first part of the test starts with the ignition switched on, but with the engine off. On pressing the "Mem/test" button, the tester displays "TEST" and the ready code "000", followed by a command code "010" - the accelerator pedal must be fully depressed within 10 seconds of the command code appearing, or fault codes "576" or "577" will appear when they are called up later. If a voltmeter is being used, code "000" will not appear (except perhaps as a flicker of the needle) and "010" will appear as a single sweep - to ensure correct interpretation of the display, watch carefully for the interval between the end of one code and the beginning of the next, otherwise you will become confused and misinterpret the read-out.

55 The tester will then display the codes for any faults in the system at the time of the test. Each code is repeated once; if no faults are present, code "111" will be displayed. If a voltmeter is being used, the pause between repetitions will vary according to the equipment in use and the number of faults in the system, but was found to be approximately 3 to 4 seconds - it may be necessary to start again, and to repeat the read-out until you are familiar with what you are seeing.

56 Next the tester will display code "010" (now acting as a separator), followed by the codes for any faults stored in the ECU's memory; if no faults were stored, code "111" will be displayed.

57 When prompted by the tester, the operator must next depress the accelerator pedal fully; the tester then checks several actuators. Further test modes include a "wiggle test" facility, whereby the operator can check the various connectors as described previously (in this case, any fault will be logged and the appropriate code will be displayed), a facility for recalling codes displayed, and a means for clearing the ECU's memory at the end of the test procedure when any faults have been rectified.

58 The next step when using the Ford STAR tester is to conduct a test with the engine running. With the tester set in operation (see paragraph 53 above) the engine is started and allowed to idle. On pressing the "Mem/test" button, the tester displays "TEST", followed by one of two codes, as follows.

59 If warning code "998" appears, followed by the appropriate fault code, switch off and check as indicated the coolant temperature sensor, the intake air temperature sensor, the air mass meter, the throttle potentiometer and/or their related circuits, then restart the test procedure.

60 If command code "020" appears, carry out the following procedure within ten seconds:

a) *Depress the brake pedal fully.*
b) *Turn the steering to full-lock (either way) and centre it again, to produce a signal from the power steering pressure switch - if no signal is sent, fault code "521" will be displayed.*
c) *If automatic transmission is fitted, switch the overdrive cancel button on and off, then do the same for the "Economy/Sport" mode switch.*
d) *Wait for separator code "010" to be displayed, then within 10 seconds, depress the accelerator pedal fully, increasing engine speed rapidly above 3000 rpm - release the pedal.*

61 Any faults found in the system will be logged and displayed. Each code is repeated once; if no faults are present, code "111" will be displayed.

62 When the codes have been displayed for all faults logged, the ECU enters its "Service Adjustment Programme", as follows:

a) *The programme lasts for 2 minutes.*
b) *The idle speed control valve is deactivated, and the idle speed is set to its pre-programmed (unregulated) value. If the appropriate equipment is connected, the base idle speed can be checked (note, however, that it is not adjustable).*
c) *The ignition timing can be checked if a timing light is connected (note, however, that it is not adjustable).*
d) *Pressing the accelerator pedal fully at any time during this period will execute a cylinder balance test. Each injector in turn is switched off, and the corresponding decrease in engine speed is logged - code "090" will be displayed if the test is successful.*
e) *At the end of the 2 minutes, the completion of the programme is shown by the engine speed briefly rising, then returning to normal idling speed as the idle speed control valve is reactivated.*

63 As with the engine-off test, further test modes include a "wiggle test" facility, whereby the operator can check the various connectors as described in paragraph 53 above (in this case, any fault will be logged and the appropriate code will be displayed), a facility for recalling codes displayed, and a means for clearing the ECU's memory at the end of the test procedure when any faults have been rectified. If equipment other than the Ford STAR tester is used, the ECU's memory can be cleared by disconnecting the battery - if this is not done, the code will reappear with any other codes in the event of subsequent trouble, but remember that other systems with memory (such as the clock and audio equipment) will also be affected. Should it become necessary to disconnect the battery during work on any other part of the vehicle, first check to see if any fault codes have been logged.

64 Starting below are the possible codes, their meanings, and where relevant, the action to be taken as a result of a code being displayed.

Code	Meaning	Action
000	Ready for test	-
010	Command/separator code	Depress accelerator pedal fully, then release
020	Command code	Depress brake pedal fully, then release
10	Cylinder No 1 low	During cylinder balance test
20	Cylinder No 2 low	During cylinder balance test
30	Cylinder No 3 low	During cylinder balance test
40	Cylinder No 4 low	During cylinder balance test
90	Cylinder balance test successful	-
111	No faults found	-
112 to 114	Intake air temperature sensor	Check component (see above)
116 to 118	Coolant temperature sensor - normal operating temperature not reached	If fault still exists on reaching normal operating temperature, check component (Chapter 3)
121 to 125	Throttle potentiometer	Check component (see above)
129	Incorrect response from air mass meter while conducting test	Repeat test
136, 137	Oxygen sensor	Check component (Chapter 4B)

4A

Code	Meaning	Action
139	Oxygen sensor	Check component (Chapter 4B)
144	Oxygen sensor	Check component (Chapter 4B)
157 to 159	Air mass meter	Check component (see above)
167	Incorrect response from throttle potentiometer while conducting test	Repeat test
171	Oxygen sensor	Check component (Chapter 4B)
172	Oxygen sensor - mixture too weak	Check component (Chapter 4B)
173	Oxygen sensor - mixture too rich	Check component (Chapter 4B)
174, 175	Oxygen sensor	Check component (Chapter 4B)
176	Oxygen sensor - mixture too weak	Check component (Chapter 4B)
177	Oxygen sensor - mixture too rich	Check component (Chapter 4B)
178	Oxygen sensor	Check component (Chapter 4B)
179	Fuel system - mixture too weak	Check EGR valve (Chapter 4B)
181	Fuel system - mixture too rich	Check EGR valve (Chapter 4B)
182	Idle mixture too weak	Check idle speed control valve (see above)
183	Idle mixture too rich	If mixture OK, check fuel system (see below)
184, 185	Air mass meter	Check component (see above)
186	Injector opening time (pulse width) too long	Carry out system test (see below)
187	Injector opening time (pulse width) too short	Carry out system test (see below)
188	Oxygen sensor - mixture too weak	Check component (Chapter 4B)
189	Oxygen sensor - mixture too rich	Check component (Chapter 4B)
191	Idle mixture too weak	Check EGR valve (Chapter 4B) and idle speed control valve (see above)
192	Idle mixture too rich	Check EGR valve (Chapter 4B) and idle speed control valve (see above)
194, 195	Oxygen sensor	Check component (Chapter 4B)
211	No ignition signal to ECU	Carry out system test (see below)
212	Tachometer circuit	Carry out system test (see below)
213	No ignition signal from ECU	Carry out system test (see below)
214	Camshaft position sensor	Check component (see above)
215 to 217	Ignition coil	Carry out system test (see below)
218, 222	Tachometer circuit	Carry out system test (see below)
226	ECU/ignition module pulse	Carry out system test (see below)
227	Crankshaft speed/position sensor	Check component (see above)
228	Ignition module/ignition coil winding 1	Carry out system test (see below)
229	Ignition module/ignition coil winding 2	Carry out system test (see below)
231	Ignition module/ignition coil winding 3	Carry out system test (see below)
232	Ignition coil primary windings	Carry out system test (see below)
233	Ignition module	Carry out system test (see below)
234 to 237	Ignition coil primary windings	Carry out system test (see below)
238	Ignition module/ignition coil primary windings	Carry out system test (see below)
239	No ignition signal to ECU on cranking	Carry out system test (see below)
241	Incorrect response from ECU and/or ignition module while conducting test	Repeat test
243	Ignition coil failure	Carry out system test (see below)
311 to 316	Pulse-air system	Carry out system test (see below)
326	EGR system exhaust gas pressure differential sensor	Check component (Chapter 4B)
327	EGR system exhaust gas pressure differential sensor or solenoid valve	Check components (Chapter 4B)
328	EGR system solenoid valve	Check component (Chapter 4B)
332	EGR valve not opening	Check component (Chapter 4B)
334	EGR system solenoid valve	Check component (Chapter 4B)
335	EGR system exhaust gas pressure differential sensor	Check component (Chapter 4B)
336	Exhaust gas pressure too high	Check system (Chapter 4B)
337	EGR system exhaust gas pressure differential sensor or solenoid valve	Check components (Chapter 4B)
338, 339	Coolant temperature sensor	Carry out system test (see below)
341	Service connector earthed	Unplug connector and repeat test - reconnect on completion
411	Engine speed too low during test	Check for air leaks, then repeat test
412	Engine speed too high during test	Check for air leaks, then repeat test
413 to 416	Idle speed control valve	Check component (see above)
452	Vehicle speed sensor	Check component (see above)
511, 512	ECU memory	Check whether battery was disconnected, then check fuse 11 - if fault still exists, renew ECU (Section 14)
513	ECU reference voltage	Carry out system test (see below)
519, 521	Power steering pressure switch not operated during test	Check component is fitted and connected, then repeat test - if fault still exists, carry out system test (see below)

Code	Meaning	Action
522, 523	Selector lever position sensor	Check component (Chapter 7B)
536	Brake on/off switch not activated during test	Repeat test
538	Operator error during test	Repeat test
539	Air conditioning switched on during test	Switch off and repeat test
542, 543	Fuel pump circuit	Carry out system test (see below)
551	Idle speed control valve circuit	Carry out system test (see below)
552	Pulse-air system circuit	Carry out system test (see below)
556	Fuel pump circuit	Check fuel pump relay - if fault still exists, carry out system test (see below)
558	EGR system solenoid valve circuit	Carry out system test (see below)
563	Radiator (high-speed) electric cooling fan relay and/or circuit	Carry out system test (see below)
564	Radiator electric cooling fan relay and/or circuit	Carry out system test (see below)
565	Charcoal canister-purge solenoid valve	Check component (Chapter 4B)
573	Radiator electric cooling fan relay and/or circuit	Carry out system test (see below)
574	Radiator (high-speed) electric cooling fan relay and/or circuit	Carry out system test (see below)
575	Fuel pump and/or fuel cut-off switch circuits	Carry out system test (see below)
576, 577	Accelerator pedal not depressed fully during test procedure - automatic transmission kickdown not activated	Repeat test
621	Automatic transmission shift solenoid 1 circuit	Refer to Chapter 7B
622	Automatic transmission shift solenoid 2 circuit	Refer to Chapter 7B
624	Automatic transmission electronic pressure control solenoid	Refer to Chapter 7B
625	Automatic transmission electronic pressure control solenoid circuit	Refer to Chapter 7B
629	Automatic transmission torque converter clutch solenoid	Refer to Chapter 7B
634	Selector lever position sensor circuit	Check component (Chapter 7B)
635, 637	Automatic transmission fluid temperature sensor	Refer to Chapter 7B
639	Automatic transmission speed sensor	Refer to Chapter 7B
645	Automatic transmission 1st speed	Refer to Chapter 7B
646	Automatic transmission 2nd speed	Refer to Chapter 7B
647	Automatic transmission 3rd speed	Refer to Chapter 7B
648	Automatic transmission 4th speed	Refer to Chapter 7B
653	Automatic transmission overdrive cancel button and "Economy/Sport" mode switch not operated during test	Repeat test
998	Warning code	Check fault(s) indicated by subsequent code(s)

Ignition timing and base idle speed check

Note: *The following procedure is a check only, essentially of the ECU on the EEC-IV fuel injection system. Both the ignition timing and the base idle speed are controlled by the ECU. The ignition timing is not adjustable at all; the base idle speed is set in production, and should not be altered.*

65 If the fault code read-out (with any checks resulting from it) has not eliminated the fault, the next step is to check the ECU's control of the ignition timing and the base idle speed. This task requires the use of a Ford STAR tester (a proprietary fault code reader can be used only if it is capable of inducing the ECU to enter its "Service Adjustment Programme"), coupled with an accurate tachometer and a good-quality timing light. Without this equipment, the task is not possible; the vehicle must be taken to a Ford dealer for attention.

66 To make the check, apply the handbrake, switch off the air conditioning (where fitted) and any other electrical loads (lights, heated rear window, etc), then select neutral (manual transmission) or the "P" position (automatic transmission). Start the engine, and warm it up to normal operating temperature. The radiator electric cooling fan must be running continuously while the check is made; this should be activated by the ECU, when prompted by the tester. Switch off the engine, and connect the test equipment as directed by the manufacturer.

67 Raise and support the front of the vehicle securely, and remove the auxiliary drivebelt cover (see Chapter 1). Highlight the two pairs of notches in the inner and outer rims of the crankshaft pulley, using white paint. Note that an ignition timing reference mark is not provided on the pulley - in the normal direction of crankshaft rotation (clockwise, seen from the right-hand side of the vehicle) the first pair of notches are irrelevant to the vehicles covered in this manual, while the second pair indicate Top Dead Centre (TDC) when aligned with the rear edge of the raised mark on the sump; when checking the ignition timing, therefore, the (rear edge of the) sump mark should appear just before the TDC notches.

68 Start the engine and allow it to idle. Work through the engine-running test procedure until the ECU enters its "Service Adjustment Programme".

69 Use the timing light to check that the timing marks appear approximately as outlined above at idle speed. Do not spend too much time on this check; if the timing appears to be incorrect, the system may have a fault, and a full system test must be carried out (see below) to establish its cause.

70 Using the tachometer, check that the base idle speed is as given in the Specifications.

71 If the recorded speed differs significantly from the specified value, check for air leaks, as described in the preliminary checks above, or any other faults which might cause the discrepancy.

72 The base idle speed is set in production by means of an air bypass screw (located in the front right-hand corner of the throttle housing) which controls the amount of air that is allowed to pass through a bypass passage, past the throttle valve when it is fully closed in the idle position; the screw is then sealed with a white tamperproof plug **(see illustration)**.

13.72 Throttle housing air bypass screw is sealed on production with a white tamperproof plug (arrowed)

In service, the idle speed is controlled by the ECU, which has the ability to compensate for engine wear, build-up of dirt in the throttle housing, and other factors which might require changes in idle speed. The air bypass screw setting should not, therefore, be altered. If any alterations are made, a blue tamperproof plug must be fitted, and the engine should be allowed to idle for at least five minutes on completion, so that the ECU can re-learn its idle values.

73 When both checks have been made and the "Service Adjustment Programme" is completed, follow the tester instructions to return to the fault code read-out, and establish whether the fault has been cured or not.

Basic check of ignition system

74 If the checks so far have not eliminated the fault, the next step is to carry out a basic check of the ignition system components, using an engine analyser with an oscilloscope - without such equipment, the only tests possible are to remove and check each spark plug in turn, to check the spark plug (HT) lead connections and resistances, and to check the connections and resistances of the ignition coil. Refer to the relevant Sections of Chapters 1 and 5B.

Basic check of fuel system

75 If the checks so far have not eliminated the fault, the next step is to carry out a basic check of the fuel system components.

76 Assuming that the preliminary checks have established that the fuel pump is operating correctly, that the fuel filter is unlikely to be blocked, and also that there are no leaks in the system, the next step is to check the fuel pressure (see Section 7). If this is correct, check the injectors (see beginning of this Section) and the Positive Crankcase Ventilation system (see Chapter 1).

System test

77 The final element of the Ford testing procedure is to carry out a system test, using a break-out box - this is a device that is connected between the ECU and its electrical connector, so that the individual circuits indicated by the fault code read-out can be tested while connected to the system, if necessary with the engine running. In the case of many of the system's components, this enables their output voltages to be measured - a more accurate means of testing.

78 In addition to the break-out box and the adapters required to connect it, several items of specialist equipment are needed to complete these tests. This puts them quite beyond the scope of many smaller dealers, let alone the DIY owner, therefore the vehicle should be taken to a Ford dealer for attention.

Idle speed and mixture

79 Both the idle speed and mixture are under the control of the ECU, and cannot be adjusted. The settings can only be checked using special diagnostic equipment.

80 If the idle speed and mixture are thought to be incorrect, take the vehicle to a Ford dealer for the complete system to be tested.

81 On models equipped with a heated windscreen, an idle-increase solenoid valve is fitted, which raises the idle speed to compensate for the increased load on the engine when the heated windscreen is switched on. When the valve is open, air from the plenum chamber bypasses the throttle housing and idle speed control valve, passing directly into the inlet manifold through the union on its left-hand end. The system is active only for the four minutes when the heated windscreen circuit is live, and is supplementary to the main (ECU-controlled) idle speed regulation.

14 Fuel injection system components - removal and refitting

Warning: Refer to the warning note in Section 1 before proceeding.

ECU (Electronic Control Unit)

Caution: The ECU is fragile. Take care not to drop it or subject it to any other kind of impact, and do not subject it to extremes of temperature, or allow it to get wet. Do not touch the ECU terminals as there is a chance that static electricity may damage the internal electronic components.

Note: *If renewing an EEC-V fuel injection system ECU, note that it must be re-programmed for the specific model by a Ford dealer using the FDS 2000 diagnostic equipment. Failure to do so will result in the ECU assuming its limited operating strategy (LOS) settings giving poor performance and economy.*

Removal

1 Disconnect the battery negative (earth) lead (see Chapter 5A).

2 Carefully lift the power steering fluid reservoir upwards out of its clip on the suspension mounting. The ECU connector is secured with a bolt, however on later models a cover is riveted over the ECU and it will be necessary to drill out the rivets to remove the cover. Additionally on later models, unbolt the earth cable from the inner wing panel. Unscrew the retaining bolt, and unplug the connector - to prevent dust and dirt entering the multiplug, cover it with a polythene bag **(see illustrations)**.

14.2a Unclip and lift power steering fluid reservoir - take care not to spill fluid . . .

14.2b . . . unscrew bolt (arrowed) to release ECU's electrical connector

14.2c On later models, drill out the rivets to remove the ECU cover

14.2d Carefully disconnect the multiplug from the ECU

14.2e ECU multiplug earth cable bolted to the inner wing panel

14.2f Wrap the ECU multiplug in a polythene bag to prevent entry of dust and dirt

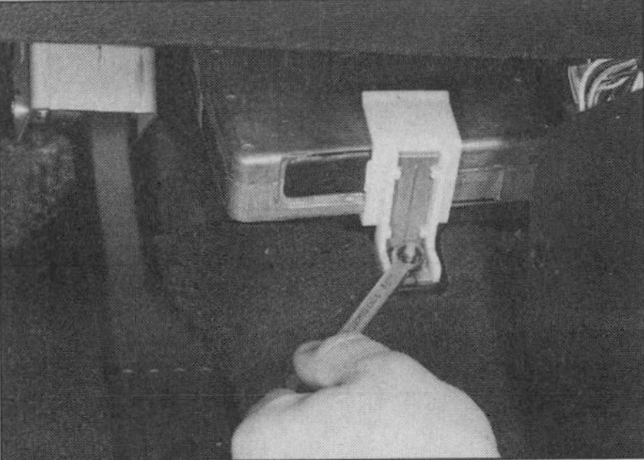
14.3 Unscrew retaining bolt and withdraw ECU's mounting bracket . . .

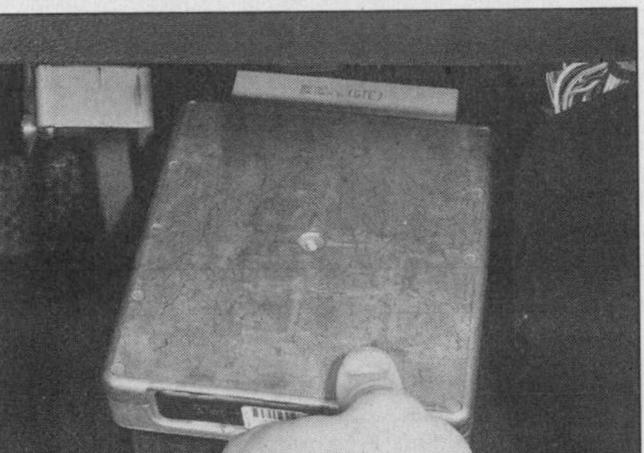
14.4 . . . then lift ECU to disengage it, and withdraw it

3 Working inside the car, unscrew the retaining bolt and withdraw the mounting bracket **(see illustration)**.

4 Lift the ECU to release it from the bulkhead carrier bracket, then withdraw the unit **(see illustration)**.

Refitting

5 Refitting is the reverse of the removal procedure. Whenever the ECU (or battery) is disconnected, the information relating to idle speed control and other operating values will be lost from its memory until the unit has re-programmed itself; until then, there may be surging, hesitation, erratic idle and a generally-inferior level of performance. To allow the ECU to re-learn these values, start the engine and run it as close to idle speed as possible until it reaches its normal operating temperature, then run it for approximately two minutes at 1200 rpm. Next, drive the vehicle as far as necessary - approximately 5 miles of varied driving conditions is usually sufficient - to complete the re-learning process. Refer to the note at the beginning of this Section for models fitted with the EEC-V fuel injection system.

Air mass meter

Removal

6 Disconnect the battery negative (earth) lead (see Chapter 5A).

7 On 4-cylinder (Zetec) engines, release the wire clip, and unplug the meter's electrical connector. Release the clips and lift the air cleaner cover, then release the two smaller clips and detach the meter from the cover. Slacken the clamp securing the meter to the resonator hose, and withdraw the meter **(see illustrations)**.

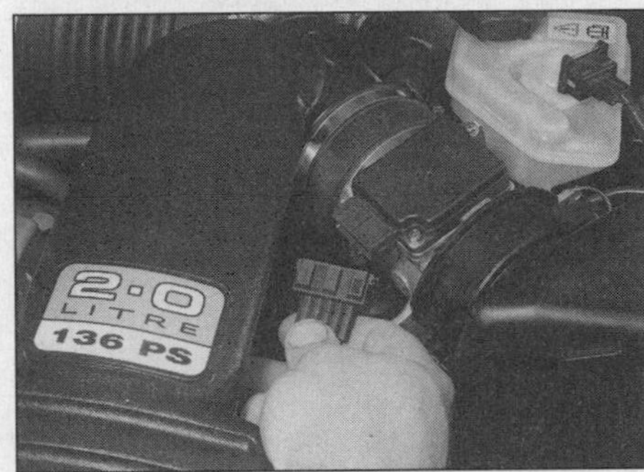

14.7a Unplugging the air mass meter's electrical connector . . .

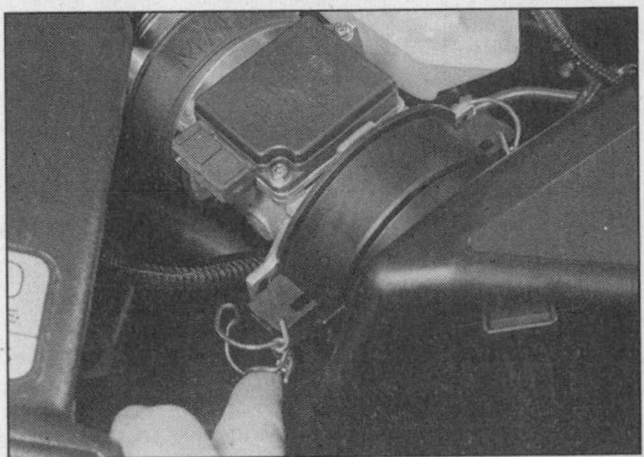
14.7b . . . release clips to separate meter from air cleaner cover

8 On V6 (Duretec) engines, remove the air cleaner assembly as described in Section 4. Unscrew and remove the meter mounting bolts and withdraw the meter from the air cleaner cover.

Refitting

9 Refitting is the reverse of the removal procedure. Ensure that the meter and air cleaner cover are seated correctly and securely fastened, so that there are no air leaks.

Crankshaft speed/position sensor

Removal

10 Disconnect the battery negative (earth) lead (see Chapter 5A).

11 Apply the handbrake, then jack up the front of the vehicle and support it on axle stands (see "*Jacking and Vehicle Support*").

12 On 4-cylinder models remove the left-hand wheel arch liner. On V6 models, remove the right-hand wheel arch liner.

13 Disconnect the wiring from the sensor **(see illustrations)**.

14 Undo the retaining screw and withdraw the sensor.

Refitting

15 Refitting is the reverse of the removal procedure.

4A

Camshaft position sensor

Removal

16 On 4-cylinder models, the camshaft sensor is located at the left-hand rear of the cylinder head. On V6 models, the sensor is located on the right-hand end of the timing cover **(see illustration)**.

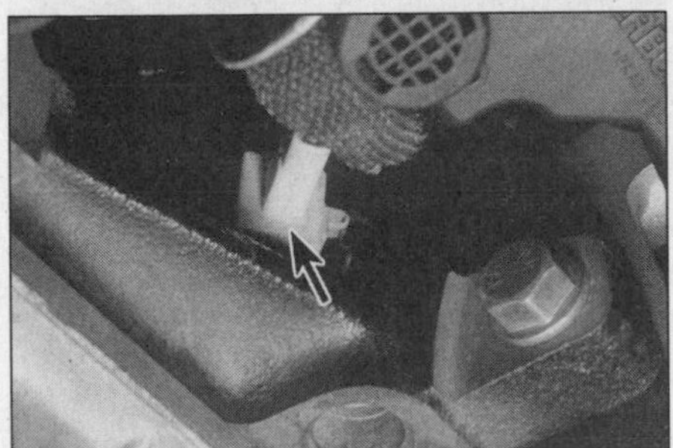
14.13a On 4-cylinder models, the crankshaft speed/position sensor is located on the front of the cylinder block/crankcase

14.13b On V6 models, the crankshaft speed/position sensor is located on the timing cover

14.16 Camshaft position sensor on V6 models

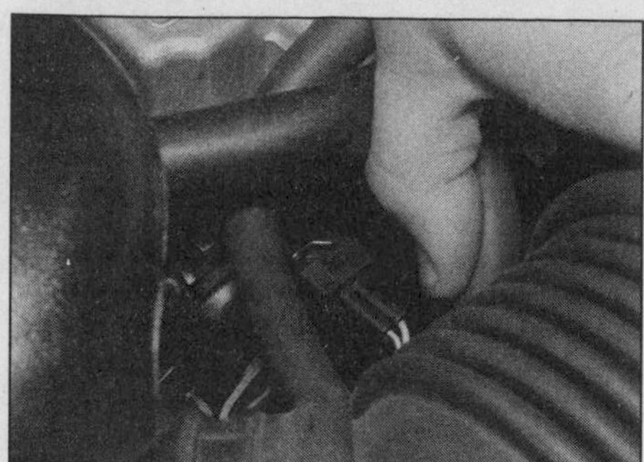
14.17 Camshaft position sensor is located at left-hand rear end of cylinder head

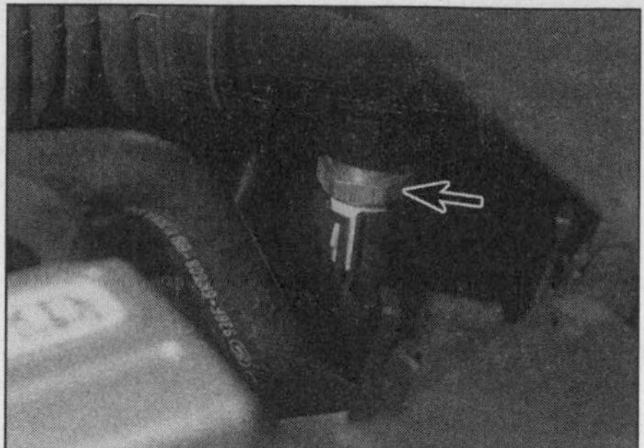
14.21 Intake air temperature sensor (arrowed) is screwed into underside of air intake resonator

14.25a Throttle potentiometer is secured by two screws (4-cylinder engine shown)

17 Remove the air mass meter and on 4-cylinder models the resonator to gain access to the sensor **(see illustration)**. Release the fuel feed and return hoses from their clips.

18 Release the wire clip and disconnect the sensor's electrical connector. Remove the retaining screw, and withdraw the sensor from the cylinder head; be prepared for slight oil loss.

Refitting

19 Refitting is the reverse of the removal procedure, noting the following points:

a) *Apply petroleum jelly or clean engine oil to the sensor's sealing O-ring.*
b) *Locate the sensor fully in the cylinder head, and wipe off any surplus lubricant before securing it.*
c) *Tighten the screw to the specified torque wrench setting.*

Coolant temperature sensor

20 Refer to Chapter 3.

Intake air temperature sensor

Removal

21 Remove the air mass meter (and resonator on 4-cylinder models) to gain access to the sensor **(see illustration)**.

22 Releasing its clip, unplug the sensor's electrical connector, then unscrew the sensor from the resonator, air inlet duct or air cleaner housing.

Refitting

23 Refitting is the reverse of the removal procedure. Tighten the sensor to the specified torque wrench setting. If it is over-tightened, its tapered thread may crack the resonator, duct or air cleaner housing.

Throttle position sensor (potentiometer)

Removal

24 On 4-cylinder models, remove the plenum chamber (see Section 4). On V6 models, remove the water pump pulley shield. If necessary, remove the PCV hose from the air inlet duct.

25 Disconnect the wiring plug. Remove the retaining screws, and withdraw the unit from the throttle housing **(see illustrations)**. Do not force the sensor's centre to rotate past its normal operating sweep, otherwise the unit will be seriously damaged.

Refitting

26 Refitting is the reverse of the removal procedure, noting the following points:

a) *Ensure that the sensor is correctly orientated, by locating its centre on the D-shaped throttle shaft (throttle closed), and aligning the sensor body so that the bolts pass easily into the throttle housing.*
b) *Tighten the screws to the Specified torque (but do not overtighten them, or the sensor body will be cracked).*

Vehicle speed sensor

27 On models manufactured up to 1997, the sensor is mounted at the base of the speedometer drive cable, and is removed with the speedometer drive pinion **(see illustration)**. On later models it is located in the same position, however the cable is not fitted as the speedometer is operated electronically. Refer to the relevant Section of Chapter 7A or 7B, as applicable.

Power steering pressure switch

Removal

28 Disconnect the wiring from the switch **(see illustration)**.

29 Position a cloth rag beneath the switch then unscrew it from the pipe. Where fitted, recover the sealing washer.

Refitting

30 Refitting is the reverse of the removal procedure; tighten the switch securely, then top-up the fluid reservoir (see "*Weekly checks*") to replace any fluid lost from the system, and bleed out any trapped air (see Chapter 10).

Throttle housing (4-cylinder models)

Removal

31 Disconnect the battery negative (earth) lead (see Chapter 5A).

32 Remove the plenum chamber (see Section 4).

33 Disconnect the accelerator cable from the throttle linkage. Where fitted, also disconnect the cruise control actuator cable.

14.25b Disconnecting the wiring from the throttle potentiometer (V6 engine shown)

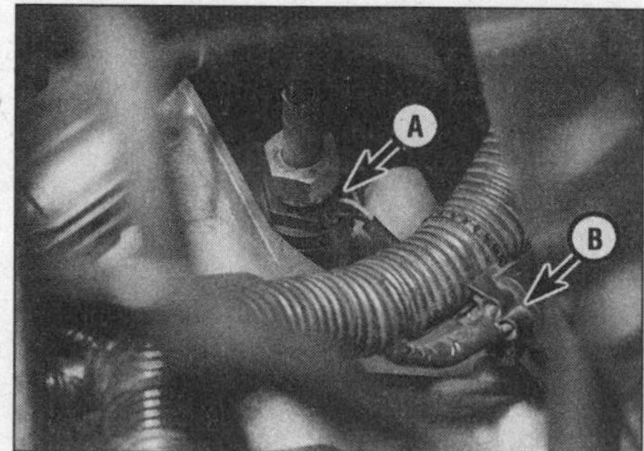

14.27 Vehicle speed sensor "A", with its electrical connector "B"

14.28 Power steering pressure switch is screwed into pipe at right-hand rear end of engine

14.36 Undo screws (arrowed) to remove throttle housing

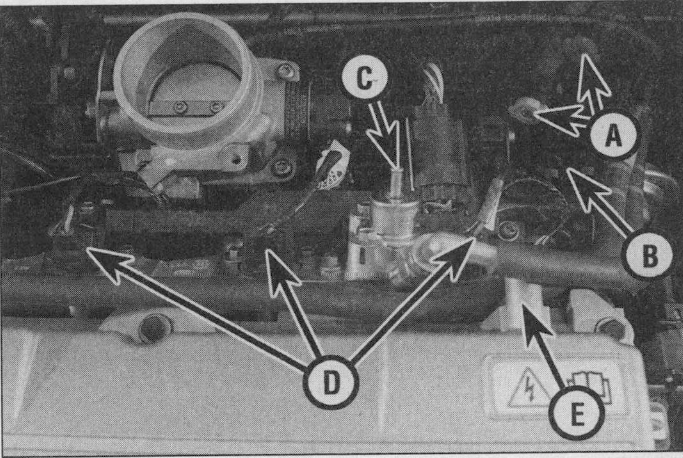

14.51 Injector removal - disconnect fuel lines at quick-release couplings (A), unclip hoses (B), disconnect vacuum hose from regulator (C), unplug electrical connectors (D) - three of four shown - and disconnect breather hose from union (E)

34 Disconnect the wiring from the large connector next to the fuel pressure regulator. Similarly release and unplug the throttle position sensor's electrical connector.

35 Clearly label, then detach, all vacuum hoses from the throttle housing.

36 Remove the throttle housing mounting screws **(see illustration)**, then detach the throttle housing and gasket from the inlet manifold. Discard the gasket - this must be renewed whenever it is disturbed.

37 Using a soft brush and a suitable liquid cleaner, thoroughly clean the exterior of the throttle housing, then blow out all passages with compressed air.

Caution: Do not clean the throttle housing's bore, the throttle valve, or the throttle position sensor, either by scraping or with a solvent. Just wipe them over carefully with a clean soft cloth.

Refitting

38 Refitting is the reverse of the removal procedure. Fit a new gasket, and tighten the housing screws to the specified torque.

Throttle housing (V6 models)

Removal

39 Disconnect the battery negative (earth) lead (see Chapter 5A).

40 Remove the air cleaner and air inlet duct (see Section 4). Also remove the water pump pulley shield.

41 Disconnect the wiring from the throttle position sensor and detach the wiring from the stud. Position the wiring to one side.

42 Disconnect the accelerator cable and speed control cable (if fitted) from the throttle housing.

43 Unscrew the mounting bolts and nut, and withdraw the throttle housing from the upper inlet manifold. Recover the gasket.

44 Using a soft brush and a suitable liquid cleaner, thoroughly clean the exterior of the throttle housing, then blow out all passages with compressed air.

Caution: Do not clean the throttle housing's bore, the throttle valve, or the throttle position sensor, either by scraping or with a solvent. Just wipe them over carefully with a clean soft cloth.

Refitting

45 Refitting is the reverse of the removal procedure. Fit a new gasket, and tighten the housing bolts and nut to the specified torque.

Fuel rail and injectors (4-cylinder models)

Removal

Note: *The following procedure describes the removal of the fuel rail assembly, complete with the injectors and pressure regulator, to enable the injectors to be serviced individually on a clean work surface. It is possible to remove and refit an individual injector once the fuel system has been depressurised and the battery has been disconnected.*

46 Depressurise the fuel system as described in Section 2. Also equalise tank pressure by removing the fuel filler cap.

47 Disconnect the battery negative (earth) lead (see Chapter 5A).

48 Remove the plenum chamber (Section 4).

49 If the additional clearance is required, disconnect the accelerator cable from the throttle linkage. Where fitted, also disconnect the cruise control actuator cable.

50 Disconnect the wiring from the four fuel injector electrical connectors. On mid 1997-on models the wiring is contained in a holder.

51 Disconnect the fuel feed and return lines at the quick-release couplings next to the braking system vacuum servo unit, then unclip the fuel hoses from the inlet manifold; use rag to soak up any spilt fuel **(see illustration)**. **Note:** *Do not disturb the threaded couplings at the fuel rail unions unless absolutely necessary; these are sealed at the factory. The quick-release couplings will suffice for all normal service operations.*

52 Disconnect the crankcase breather hose from the cylinder head cover union (pre mid 1997 models), and the vacuum hose from the fuel pressure regulator.

53 Unscrew the bolts securing the fuel rail, and withdraw the rail, carefully prising it out of the inlet manifold, and draining any remaining fuel into a suitable clean container **(see illustrations)**. Note that mid 1997-on models are fitted with a different fuel rail, and the injectors locate directly in the inlet manifold.

14.53a Unscrew bolts (arrowed) . . .

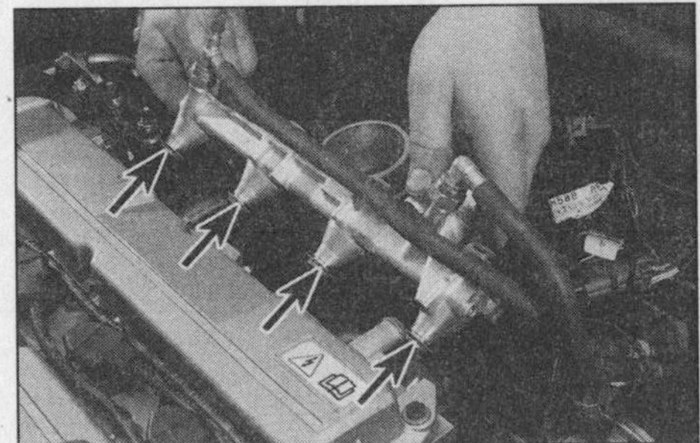

14.53b . . . and withdraw fuel rail with injectors and pressure regulator - renew nose seals (arrowed) whenever rail is disturbed

14.54a Fuel injectors can be unbolted (arrowed) . . .

14.54b . . . and removed individually if required, but it is better to remove them with the fuel rail, if servicing is necessary. O-ring seals (arrowed) must be renewed whenever injector is removed

Recover the seals from the manifold and obtain new ones.

54 Clamp the rail carefully in a vice fitted with soft jaws. On pre mid 1997 models, unscrew the two bolts securing each injector, and withdraw the injectors. On later models, pull the clips apart and withdraw the injectors from the fuel rail, then remove the injectors from the clips. Place the injectors in a clean storage container **(see illustrations)**.

55 Discard the nose seals/O-rings and obtain new ones.

56 Further testing of the injectors is beyond the scope of the home mechanic. If you are in doubt as to the status of any injector, it can be tested at a dealer service department.

14.61a Using a screwdriver to release the spring clip and disconnect the wiring from the injectors

Refitting

57 Refitting is the reverse of the removal procedure, noting the following points:

a) Lubricate each (new) seal/O-ring with clean engine oil before refitting.

b) On pre mid 1997 models, locate each injector carefully in the fuel rail recess, ensuring that the locating tab on the injector head fits into the slot provided in the rail. Tighten the bolts to the specified torque.

c) Tighten the fuel rail bolts to the torque wrench setting specified.

d) Fasten the fuel feed and return quick-release couplings as described in Section 3.

e) Ensure that the breather hose, vacuum hose and wiring are routed correctly, and secured on reconnection by any clips or ties provided.

f) On completion, switch the ignition on to activate the fuel pump and pressurise the system, without cranking the engine. Check for signs of fuel leaks around all disturbed unions and joints before attempting to start the engine.

Fuel rail and injectors (V6 models)

Removal

58 Depressurise the fuel system as described in Section 2. Also equalise tank pressure by removing the fuel filler cap.

59 Disconnect the battery negative (earth) lead (see Chapter 5A).

60 Remove the upper inlet manifold as described in Chapter 2B.

61 Disconnect the wiring harnesses from the injectors, and position to one side **(see illustrations)**.

Pre-1997 models

62 The injectors can be removed at this stage by unscrewing the clamp bolts, removing the clamps and removing the injectors from the fuel rail. Place them in a clean container. Alternatively, the injectors can be removed together with the fuel rail.

63 To remove the fuel rail, loosen the clips and disconnect the fuel hoses from the fuel rail, and also disconnect the vacuum hose from the regulator, then unscrew the fuel rail mounting bolts and remove the rail from the lower inlet manifold.

1997-on models

64 Disconnect the vacuum hose from the pressure regulator **(see illustration)**.

65 Disconnect the inlet manifold runner control (IMRC) actuator rod, by disconnecting the cable and cable end **(see illustrations)**.

66 Disconnect the fuel feed and return lines by first releasing the clips. The lines have fittings that require a special tool to release

14.61b Positioning the injector wiring to one side

14.64 Disconnecting the vacuum hose from the fuel pressure regulator

14.65a Disconnecting the IMRC outer cable . . .

14.65b . . . and inner cable

14.66a Pull off the clip . . .

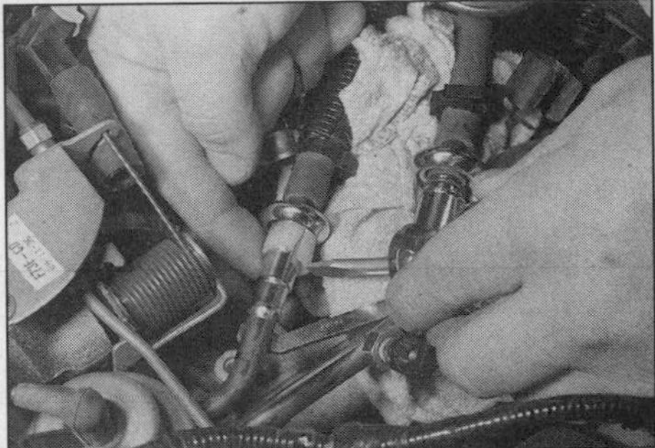
14.66b . . . then insert a coil of thin plastic . . .

14.66c . . . and separate the quick-release fuel feed and return lines

14.67a Unscrew the mounting bolts . . .

14.67b . . . and remove the fuel rail

them, however it is possible to use a home-made tool made from a coil of thin plastic about 15 mm wide. Insert the coil into the open end of the fitting so that the internal coiled spring is lifted over the retaining lip, then separate the lines **(see illustrations)**.

67 Unscrew the mounting bolts and remove the fuel rail from the lower inlet manifold **(see illustrations)**. The injectors may come away with the rail or they may remain in the inlet manifold.

68 Carefully ease the injectors from the lower inlet manifold or fuel rail and place them in a clean container.

All models

69 Remove and discard all O-ring seals. Further testing of the injectors is beyond the scope of the home mechanic. If you are in doubt as to the status of any injector, it can be tested at a dealer service department.

Refitting

70 Refitting is the reverse of the removal procedure, noting the following points:

a) *Lubricate each (new) O-ring seal with clean engine oil before refitting, and refit the injectors in the lower inlet manifold before fitting the fuel rail to them* ***(see illustration)****.*

b) *Tighten the fuel rail bolts to the specified torque.*

c) *On completion, switch the ignition on to activate the fuel pump and pressurise the system, without cranking the engine. Check for signs of fuel leaks around the unions and joints before attempting to start the engine.*

Fuel pressure regulator

Removal

71 Depressurise the fuel system as described in Section 2. Also equalise tank pressure by removing the fuel filler cap.

72 Disconnect the battery negative (earth) lead (see Chapter 5A).

73 On 4-cylinder models, remove the plenum chamber as described in Section 4, then disconnect the vacuum hose from the regulator. Unscrew the two regulator mounting screws and remove the regulator **(see illustration)**. On mid 1997-on models it will also be necessary to disconnect the fuel return hose and release it from the clip. Recover the O-ring seal. Soak up spilled fuel using a clean rag.

74 On pre mid 1997 V6 models, remove the fuel rail as described earlier. On later models, remove the upper inlet manifold. Disconnect the vacuum hose from the regulator. Remove the two regulator screws and remove the regulator. Recover the O-ring seal. Soak up spilled fuel using a clean rag.

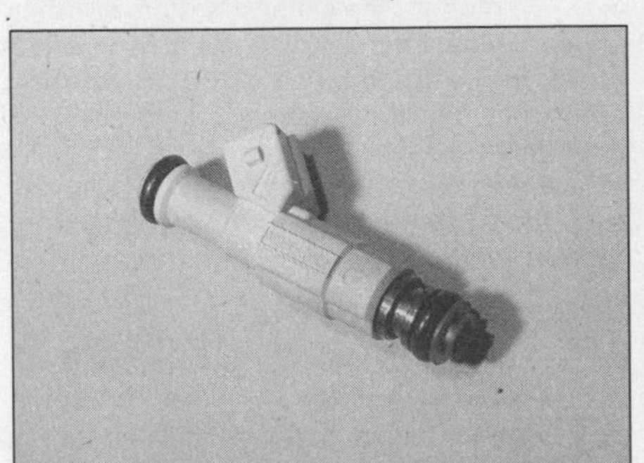
14.67c A fuel injector removed from the rail and inlet manifold

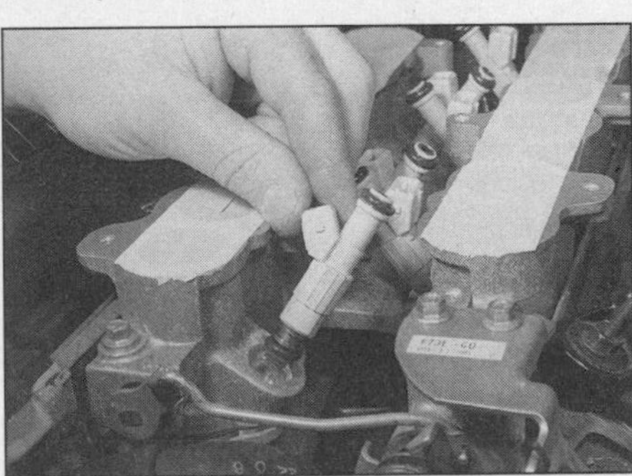
14.70 Inserting the injectors in the lower inlet manifold

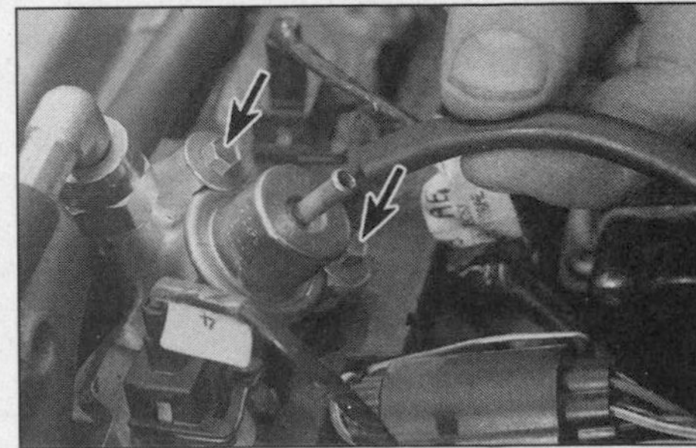
14.73 Disconnect vacuum hose and unscrew bolts (arrowed) to withdraw fuel pressure regulator

14.77 Access to idle speed control valve is from underneath vehicle - unplug electrical connector (arrowed) to check valve

14.78 Disconnecting the wiring from the idle speed control valve (V6 engine shown)

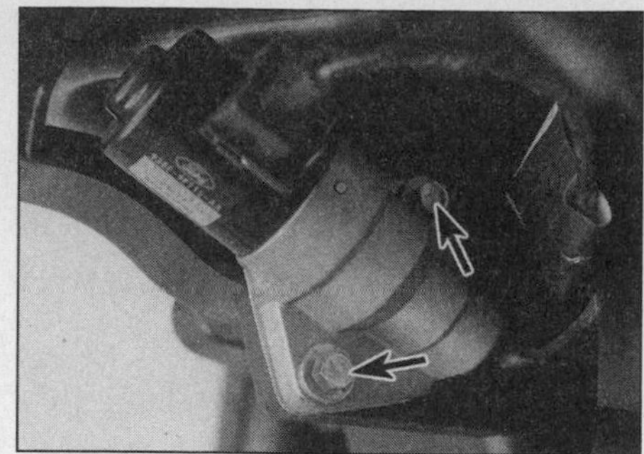
14.79 Unscrew bolts (arrowed) to remove idle speed control valve

Refitting

75 Refitting is the reverse of the removal procedure, noting the following points:

a) Renew the regulator sealing O-ring whenever the regulator is disturbed. Lubricate the new O-ring with clean engine oil on installation.

b) Locate the regulator carefully in the fuel rail recess, and tighten the bolts to the specified torque wrench setting.

c) On completion, switch the ignition on and off five times, to activate the fuel pump and pressurise the system, without cranking the engine. Check for signs of fuel leaks around all disturbed unions and joints before attempting to start the engine.

Idle speed control valve

Removal

76 Disconnect the battery negative (earth) lead (see Chapter 5A).

77 On 4-cylinder models, apply the handbrake, then jack up the front of the vehicle and support it on axle stands (see "*Jacking and Vehicle Support*") **(see illustration)**.

78 Disconnect the wiring from the idle speed control valve **(see illustration)**.

79 Unscrew the two retaining bolts (4-cylinder) or nuts (V6), and withdraw the valve from the inlet manifold **(see illustration)**. Recover the gasket.

80 Since the valve's individual components are not available separately, and the complete assembly must be renewed if it is thought to be faulty, there is nothing to be lost by attempting to flush out the passages, using carburettor cleaner or similar solvent. This won't take much time or effort, and may well cure the fault.

Refitting

81 Refitting is the reverse of the removal procedure, noting the following points:

a) Clean the mating surfaces carefully, and always fit a new gasket whenever the valve is disturbed.

b) Tighten the bolts evenly and to the specified torque wrench setting.

c) Once the wiring and battery are reconnected, start the engine and allow it to idle. When it has reached normal operating temperature, check that the idle speed is stable, and that no induction (air) leaks are evident. Switch on all electrical loads (headlights, heated rear window, etc), and check that the idle speed is still correct.

Idle-increase solenoid valve

Removal

82 If better access is required, remove the plenum chamber (see Section 4).

83 Disconnect the battery negative (earth) lead (see Chapter 5A).

84 Unplug the valve's electrical connector. Unclip the valve from the bulkhead, then disconnect the vacuum hoses and withdraw it **(see illustration)**.

Refitting

85 Refitting is the reverse of the removal procedure.

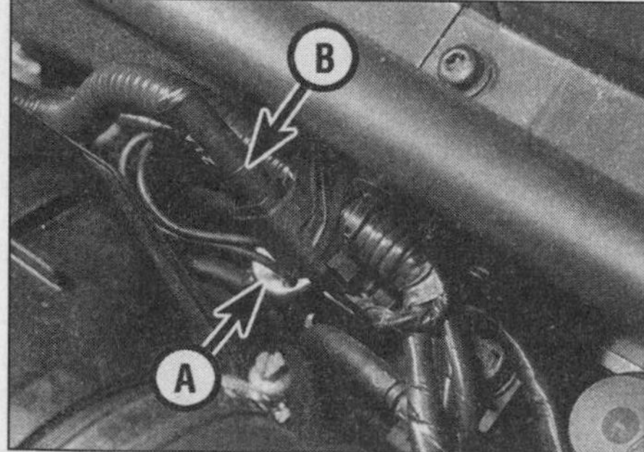

14.84 Location of idle-increase solenoid valve (A) and diode (B)

15.2 Front exhaust pipe and support bracket on a 5/1998-on model

15 Exhaust system - general description and component renewal

Warning: Inspection and repair of exhaust system components should be done only after the system has cooled completely. This applies particularly to the catalytic converter, which runs at very high temperatures.

General description

1 On 4-cylinder models manufactured up until 1/1998, the exhaust system consists of an exhaust manifold, front downpipe and catalytic converter, and a rear section incorporating two silencers (three on some versions) and the tailpipe assembly. The service replacement exhaust system consists of three or four sections: the front downpipe/catalytic converter, the intermediate pipe and front silencer, and the tailpipe and rear silencer. On some versions, the tailpipe is in two pieces, with two rear silencers.

2 4-cylinder models manufactured from 1/1998-on are fitted with an exhaust system consisting of a downpipe, catalytic converter, and a rear section incorporating two silencers **(see illustration)**.

3 On V6 models, the exhaust system consists of two exhaust manifolds (one from each bank) with a connecting Y-piece, catalytic converter, and a rear section incorporating three silencers **(see illustrations)**.

4 The exhaust system on all models is suspended throughout its entire length by rubber mounting rings **(see illustration)**.

Component renewal

5 If any section of the exhaust is damaged or deteriorated, excessive noise and vibration will occur.

6 Carry out regular inspections of the exhaust system, to check security and condition. Look for any damaged or bent parts, open seams,

15.3a Exhaust Y-piece to front downpipe connection

15.3b Exhaust Y-piece to rear manifold connection

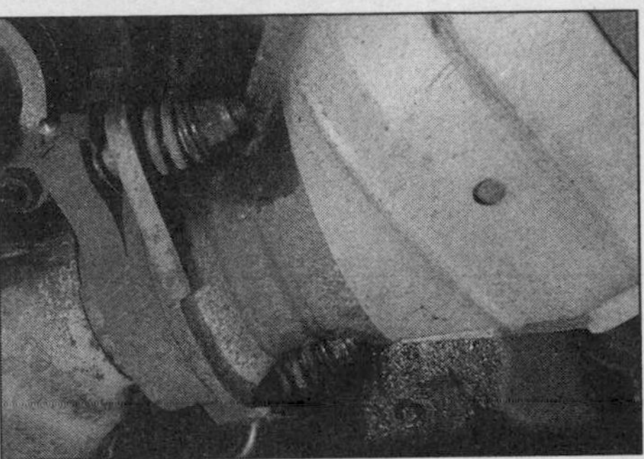
15.3c Exhaust Y-piece to catalytic converter connection

holes, loose connections, excessive corrosion, or other defects which could allow exhaust fumes to enter the vehicle. Deteriorated sections of the exhaust system should be renewed.

7 If the exhaust system components are extremely corroded or rusted together, it may not be possible to separate them. In this case, simply cut off the old components with a hacksaw, and remove any remaining corroded pipe with a cold chisel. Be sure to wear safety glasses to protect your eyes, and wear gloves to protect your hands. If the factory-new system is still fitted, it must be cut at the points shown **(see illustrations)** for the service-replacement system sections to fit.

8 Here are some simple guidelines to follow when repairing the exhaust system:

a) *Work from the back to the front when removing exhaust system components.*
b) *Apply penetrating fluid to the flange nuts before unscrewing them.*
c) *Use new gaskets and rubber mountings when installing exhaust system components.*
d) *Apply anti-seize compound to the threads of all exhaust system studs during reassembly.*

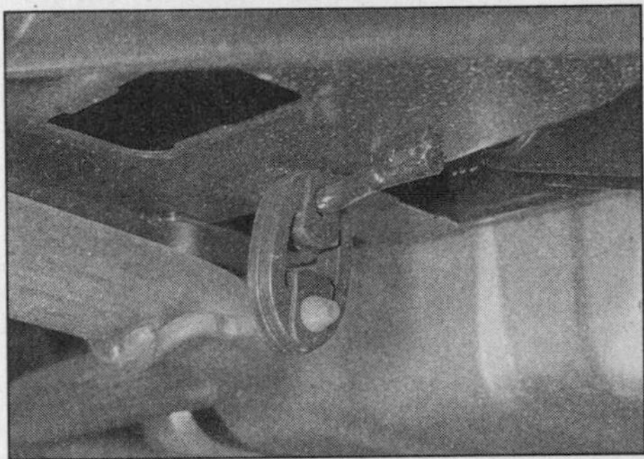
15.4 Rubber exhaust mounting beneath the rear of the car

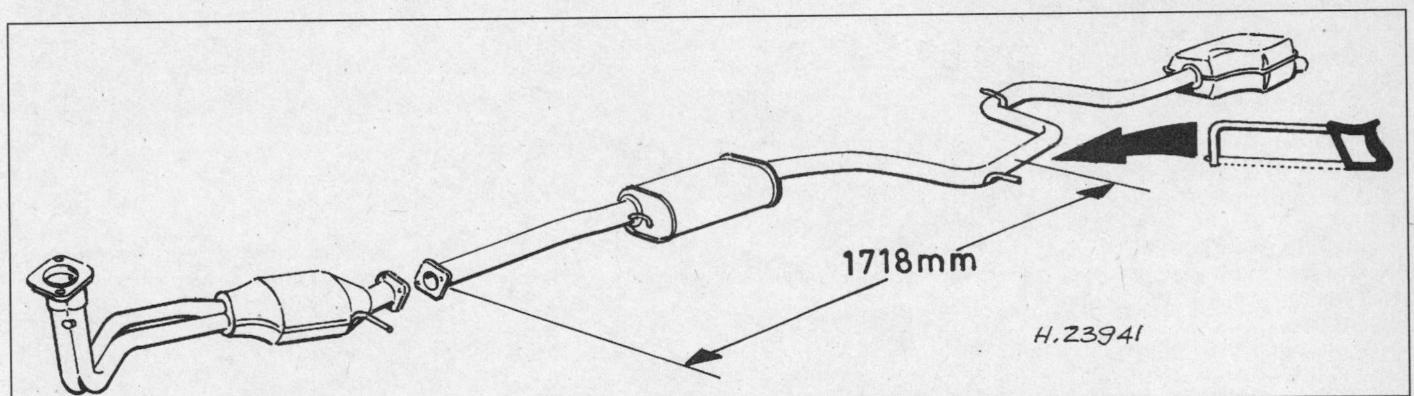

15.7a Cutting point for renewal of production-fit exhaust system - 1.6 and 1.8 models

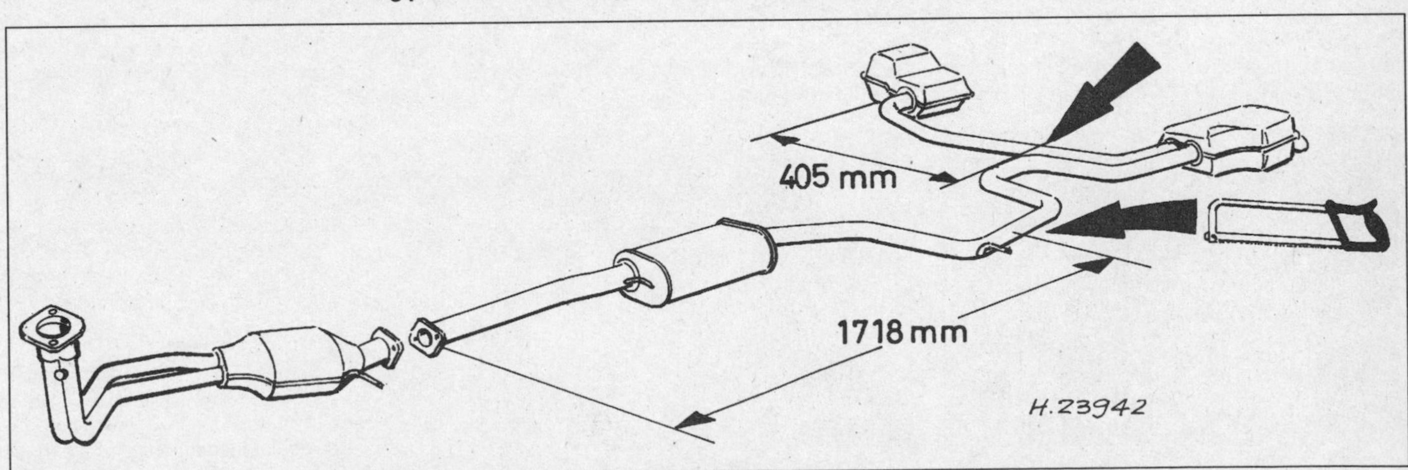

15.7b Cutting points for renewal of production-fit exhaust system - 2.0 models

15.8 Tighten exhaust system front downpipe-to-manifold nuts as described - do not overtighten them

*e) Note that on some models, the downpipe is secured to the manifold by two coil springs, spring seats and a self-locking nut on each **(see illustration)**. Where fitted, tighten the nuts until they stop on the bolt shoulders; the pressure of the springs will then be sufficient to make a leakproof connection. Do not overtighten the nuts to cure a leak - the studs will shear. Renew the gasket and the springs if a leak is found.*

f) Be sure to allow sufficient clearance between newly-installed parts and all points on the underbody, to avoid overheating the floorpan, and possibly damaging the interior carpet and insulation. Pay particularly close attention to the catalytic converter and its heat shield.

Chapter 4 Part B:
Emission control systems

Contents

Degrees of difficulty

Easy, suitable for novice with little experience 	**Fairly easy,** suitable for beginner with some experience 	**Fairly difficult,** suitable for competent DIY mechanic	**Difficult,** suitable for experienced DIY mechanic 	**Very difficult,** suitable for expert DIY or professional

Specifications

Charcoal canister-purge solenoid valve

Resistance	50 to 120 ohms

Pulse-air solenoid valve

Resistance	50 to 120 ohms

Torque wrench settings

	Nm	lbf ft
Oxygen sensor	60	44
Exhaust Gas Recirculation (EGR) system components:		
Valve-to-inlet manifold bolts	9	6
Pipe-to-ignition coil screws	10	7
Pulse-air system components:		
Filter housing mounting bolt	47	35
Piping-to-exhaust manifold sleeve nuts	32	24

1 General information

1 To minimise pollution of the atmosphere from incompletely-burned and evaporating gases, and to maintain good driveability and fuel economy, a number of emission control systems are fitted. They include the following:

a) Positive Crankcase Ventilation (PCV) system.
b) Evaporative Emissions Control (EVAP) system.
c) Exhaust Gas Recirculation (EGR) system.
d) Pulse-air system.
e) Catalytic converter and oxygen sensor.

2 The Sections of this Chapter include general descriptions, checking procedures within the scope of the home mechanic, and component renewal procedures (when possible) for each of the systems listed above.

3 Before assuming an emissions control system is malfunctioning, check the fuel and ignition systems carefully (see Chapters 4A and 5B). The diagnosis of some emission control devices requires specialised tools, equipment and training. If checking and servicing become too difficult, or if a procedure is beyond the scope of your skills, consult your dealer service department or other specialist.

4 This doesn't mean, however, that emission control systems are particularly difficult to maintain and repair. You can quickly and easily perform many checks, and do most of the regular maintenance, at home with common tune-up and hand tools. **Note:** *The most frequent cause of emissions problems is simply a loose or broken electrical connector or vacuum hose, so always check the electrical connectors and vacuum hoses first.*

5 Vehicles sold in some countries carry a Vehicle Emissions Control Information (VECI) label, and a vacuum hose diagram located in the engine compartment. These contain important specifications and setting procedures for the various emissions control systems, with the vacuum hose diagram identifying emissions control components. When servicing the engine or emissions systems, the VECI label should always be checked for up-to-date information.

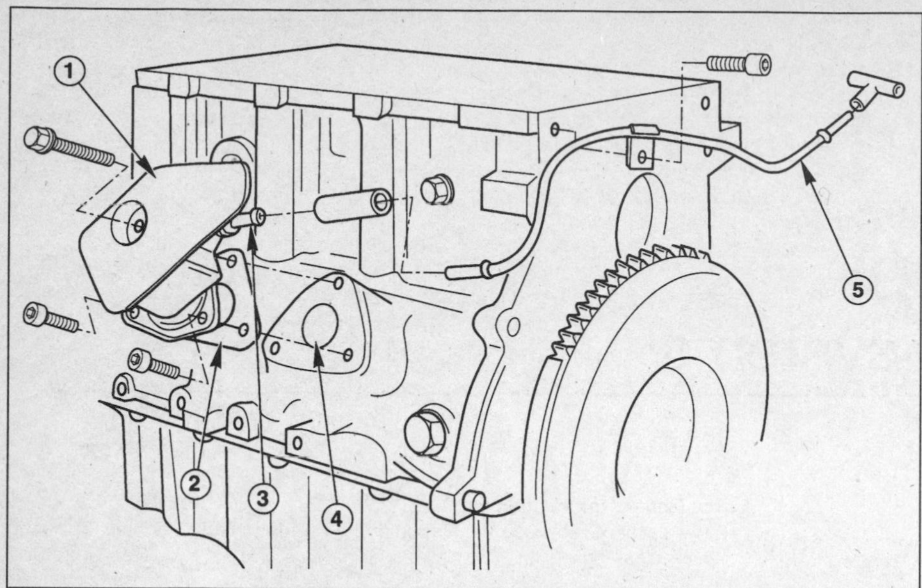

2.1a Positive Crankcase Ventilation system

1 Oil separator
2 Gasket
3 Positive Crankcase Ventilation (PCV) valve
4 Cylinder block/crankcase opening
5 Crankcase breather pipe and flexible hoses

2 Emission control systems - description

Positive Crankcase Ventilation (PCV) system

1 On 4-cylinder models, the crankcase ventilation system main components are the oil separator mounted on the front (radiator) side of the cylinder block/crankcase, and the Positive Crankcase Ventilation (PCV) valve set in a rubber grommet in the separator's left-hand upper end. The associated pipework consists of a crankcase breather pipe and two flexible hoses connecting the PCV valve to a union on the left-hand end of the inlet manifold, and a crankcase breather hose connecting the cylinder head cover to the air cleaner assembly **(see illustration)**. On V6 models, the system is similar but the oil separator is located on top of the cylinder block between the cylinder heads **(see illustration)**. A small foam filter in the air cleaner prevents dirt from being drawn directly into the engine.

2 The function of these components is to reduce the emission of unburned hydrocarbons from the crankcase, and to minimise the formation of oil sludge. By ensuring that a depression is created in the crankcase under most operating conditions, particularly at idle, and by positively inducing fresh air into the system, the oil vapours and "blow-by" gases collected in the crankcase are drawn from the crankcase, through the oil separator, into the inlet tract, to be burned by the engine during normal combustion.

Evaporative Emissions Control (EVAP) system

3 This system is fitted to minimise the escape of unburned hydrocarbons into the atmosphere. The fuel tank filler cap is sealed, and a charcoal canister is mounted either above the fuel tank on Saloon and Hatchback models, or beneath the spare wheel location on Estate models. The canister stores petrol vapours generated in the tank when the vehicle is parked. When the engine is running, the vapours are cleared from the canister under the control of the ECU via the canister-purge solenoid valve located on the bulkhead in the engine compartment. The vapours are drawn into the inlet manifold, to be burned by the engine during normal combustion.

4 To ensure that the engine runs correctly when it is cold and/or idling, and to protect the catalytic converter from the effects of an over-rich mixture, the canister-purge solenoid valve is not opened by the ECU until the engine is fully warmed-up and running under part-load. The solenoid valve is then switched on and off, to allow the stored vapour to pass into the inlet manifold.

2.1b Oil separator on V6 models

2.6 EGR vacuum regulator on V6 models

Exhaust Gas Recirculation (EGR) system

5 To reduce oxides of nitrogen (NO_x) emissions, some of the exhaust gases are recirculated through the EGR valve to the inlet manifold. This has the effect of lowering combustion temperatures.

6 The system consists of the EGR valve, the EGR exhaust gas pressure differential sensor, the EGR solenoid valve, the ECU, and various sensors. The ECU is programmed to produce the ideal EGR valve lift for all operating conditions. On V6 models, an EGR vacuum regulator is located on the bulkhead **(see illustration)**.

Pulse-air system

7 This system consists of the pulse-air solenoid valve, the pulse-air valve itself, contained in the filter housing, and the piping. It passes filtered air directly into the exhaust ports, using the pressure variations in the exhaust gases to draw air through from the filter housing. Air flows into the exhaust only when its pressure is below atmospheric. The pulse-air valve allows gases to flow only one way, so there is no risk of hot exhaust gases flowing back into the filter.

8 The system's primary function is to supply fresh air into the exhaust system during the warm-up period, in order to allow more efficient burning of the exhaust gases. The system reduces emission of unburned hydrocarbon particles (HC) and carbon monoxide (CO), and only operates until the oxygen sensor has reached its normal temperature.

9 To ensure the system does not upset the smooth running of the engine under normal driving conditions, it is linked by the pulse-air solenoid valve to the ECU, so that it only functions during engine warm-up, when the oxygen sensor is not influencing the fuel/air mixture ratio.

Catalytic converter

10 The exhaust gases of any petrol engine (however efficient or well-tuned) consist largely (approximately 99 %) of nitrogen (N_2), carbon dioxide (CO_2), oxygen (O_2), other inert gases and water vapour (H_2O). The remaining 1% is made up of the noxious materials (CO_2 apart) which are currently seen as the major polluters of the environment. These are carbon monoxide (CO), unburned hydrocarbons (HC), oxides of nitrogen (NO_x) and some solid matter, including a small lead content.

11 Left to themselves, most of these pollutants are thought eventually to break down naturally (CO and NO_x, for example, break down in the upper atmosphere to release CO_2) having first caused ground-level environmental problems. The massive increase world-wide in the use of motor vehicles, and the current popular concern for the environment has caused the introduction in most countries of legislation, in varying degrees of severity, to combat the problem.

12 The device most commonly used to clean up vehicle exhausts is the catalytic converter. It is fitted into the vehicle's exhaust system, and uses precious metals (platinum and palladium or rhodium) as catalysts to speed up the reaction between the pollutants and the oxygen in the vehicle's exhaust gases, CO and HC being oxidised to form H_2O and CO_2 and (in the three-way type of catalytic converter) NO_x being reduced to N_2. **Note:** *The catalytic converter is not a filter in the physical sense. Its function is to promote a chemical reaction, but it is not itself affected by that reaction.*

13 The converter consists of an element (or "substrate") of ceramic honeycomb, coated with a combination of precious metals in such a way as to produce a vast surface area over which the exhaust gases must flow, the whole being mounted in a stainless-steel box. A simple "oxidation" (or "two-way") catalytic converter can deal with CO and HC only, while a "reduction" (or "three-way") catalytic converter can deal with CO, HC and NO_x. Three-way catalytic converters are further sub-divided into "open-loop" (or "uncontrolled") converters which can remove 50 to 70% of pollutants and "closed-loop" (also known as "controlled" or "regulated") converters which can remove over 90% of pollutants.

14 The catalytic converter fitted to the Mondeo models covered in this manual is of the three-way closed-loop type.

Oxygen sensor

15 The oxygen sensor in the exhaust system provides the ECU with constant feedback - "closed-loop" control - which enables it to adjust the mixture to provide the best possible conditions for the catalytic converter to operate.

16 The sensor has a built-in heating element which is controlled by the ECU, in order to bring the sensor's tip to an efficient operating temperature as rapidly as possible. The sensor's tip is sensitive to oxygen, and sends the ECU a varying voltage depending on the amount of oxygen in the exhaust gases. If the intake air/fuel mixture is too rich, the exhaust gases are low in oxygen, so the sensor sends a low-voltage signal, the voltage rising as the mixture weakens and the amount of oxygen in the exhaust gases rises. Peak conversion efficiency of all major pollutants occurs if the intake air/fuel mixture is maintained at the chemically-correct ratio for the complete combustion of petrol, of 14.7 parts (by weight) of air to 1 part of fuel (the "stoichiometric" ratio). The sensor output voltage alters sharply around this point, the ECU using the signal change as a reference point, and correcting the air/fuel mixture by altering the fuel injector pulse width.

Exhaust gas pressure differential sensor

17 This component measures the difference in pressure of the exhaust gases across a venturi (restriction) in the Exhaust Gas Recirculation (EGR) system's pipe, and sends the ECU a voltage signal corresponding to the pressure difference.

3 Emission control systems - testing and component renewal

Positive Crankcase Ventilation (PCV) system

Testing

1 Checking procedures for the system components are included in Chapter 1.

Component renewal

Cylinder head cover-to-air cleaner hose

2 Disconnect the hose from the cylinder head cover and air cleaner, then fit the new hose using a reversal of removal.

Positive Crankcase Ventilation (PCV) valve

3 The valve is plugged into the oil separator. Depending on the tools available, access is possible once the pulse-air assembly has been removed and the valve may then be removed. Alternatively, remove the exhaust manifold (see relevant Part of Chapter 2). The Positive Crankcase Ventilation (PCV) valve can now be pulled out and flushed, or renewed, as required, as described in Chapter 1.

Oil separator

4 Remove the exhaust manifold (see relevant Part of Chapter 2).

5 Unbolt the oil separator from the cylinder block/crankcase, and withdraw it. Remove and discard the gasket.

6 Flush out or renew the oil separator, as required.

7 On reassembly, fit a new gasket, and tighten the bolts securely.

8 The remainder of the refitting procedure is the reverse of removal. If the bottom hose was disconnected from the radiator for the exhaust manifold removal, refill the cooling system as described in Chapter 1. Run the engine, check for exhaust leaks, and check the coolant level when it is fully warmed-up.

Evaporative Emissions Control (EVAP) system

Testing

9 Poor idle, stalling and poor driveability can be caused by an inoperative canister-purge solenoid valve, a damaged canister, split or cracked hoses, or hoses connected to the wrong fittings. Check the fuel filler cap for a damaged or deformed gasket.

10 Fuel loss or fuel odour can be caused by liquid fuel leaking from fuel lines, a cracked or damaged canister, an inoperative canister-purge solenoid valve, and disconnected, incorrectly routed, kinked or damaged vapour or control hoses.

11 Inspect each hose attached to the canister for kinks, leaks and cracks along its entire length. Repair or renew as necessary.

12 Inspect the canister. If it is cracked or damaged, renew it. Look for fuel leaking from the bottom of the canister. If fuel is leaking, renew the canister, and check the hoses and hose routing.

13 If the canister-purge solenoid valve is thought to be faulty, unplug its electrical connector and disconnect its vacuum hoses. Connect a 12-volt battery directly across the valve terminals. Check that air can flow through the valve passages when the solenoid is energised, and that nothing can pass when the solenoid is not energised. Alternatively, connect an ohmmeter to measure the resistance across the solenoid terminals, and compare this reading to the one listed in Specifications. Renew the solenoid valve if it is faulty.

14 Further testing should be left to a dealer service department.

Component renewal

Charcoal canister-purge solenoid valve

15 Disconnect the battery negative (earth) lead (see Chapter 5A). If better access is required on 4-cylinder models, remove the plenum chamber as described in Chapter 4A. On V6 models, remove the ignition coil as described in Chapter 5B.

16 Disconnect the valve's electrical connector **(see illustration)**. Unclip the valve from the bulkhead, then disconnect the vacuum hoses and withdraw it.

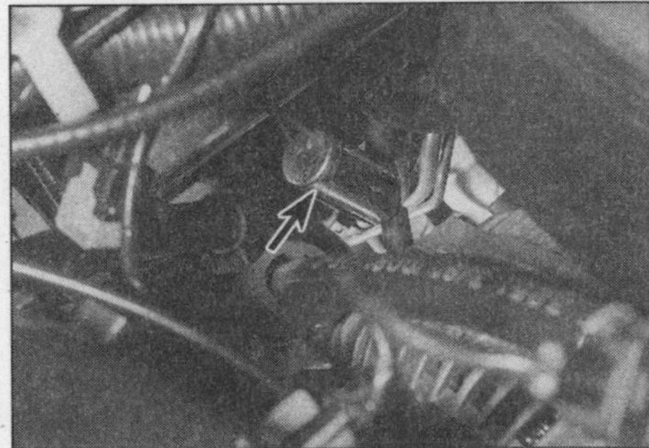

3.16 Charcoal canister-purge solenoid valve (arrowed) is clipped to bulkhead behind engine

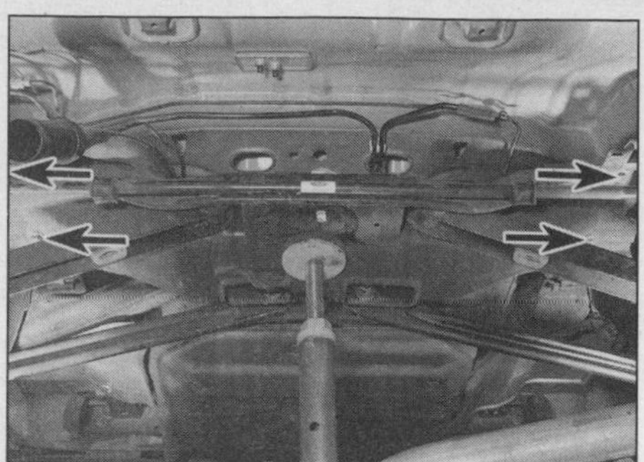
3.20 Support rear suspension crossmember on jack, and remove mounting bolts (arrowed) . . .

3.21 . . . lower crossmember by 3 inches, and unscrew charcoal canister assembly rear retaining bolts (arrowed) . . .

3.22 . . . unplug hoses (arrowed) from canister assembly . . .

17 Refitting is the reverse of the removal procedure.

Charcoal canister - Saloon and Hatchback models

Note: *Read through this procedure carefully before starting work, and ensure that the equipment is available that is required to carry it out safely and with minimum risk of damage, and to align the crossmember with sufficient accuracy on reassembly.*

18 Remove the fuel tank (see Chapter 4A).

19 Ensure that the rear of the vehicle's body is supported securely on axle stands, then support the rear suspension crossmember with a jack. Remove the roadwheels and unscrew the rear suspension strut top mounting bolts (two per side - see Chapter 10).

20 Use white paint or similar (do not use a sharp-pointed scriber, which might break the underbody protective coating and cause rusting) to mark the exact relationship of the crossmember to the underbody. Unscrew the four mounting bolts **(see illustration)**. Lower the crossmember approximately 75 mm on the jack, and support it securely.

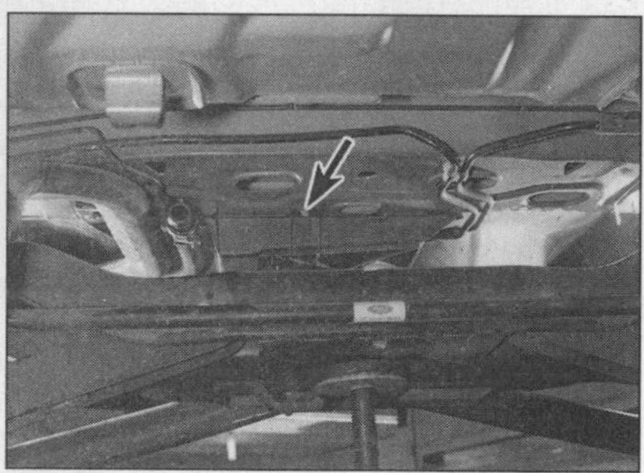
3.23 . . . and remove front retaining bolt (arrowed) to release canister assembly - Saloon and Hatchback models

21 Unscrew the two rearmost canister assembly retaining bolts **(see illustration)**.

22 Unplug the two hoses from the canister assembly, noting which way round they are fitted **(see illustration)**.

23 Unscrew the canister assembly's front retaining bolt **(see illustration)**. Withdraw the canister assembly.

24 Release the clip, and drive out the pin to separate the canister from its bracket **(see illustration)**.

25 On reassembly, refit the canister to its bracket and refit the assembly to the vehicle, tightening the retaining bolts securely, and ensuring that the two hoses are securely reconnected to their original unions.

26 Offer up the crossmember and refit the crossmember bolts, tightening them only lightly at this stage.

27 The crossmember must now be aligned on the underbody. Ford specify the use of service tool 15-097, which is a pair of tapered guides, with attachments to hold them in the crossmember as it is refitted **(see illustration)**. However, since the working diameter of these tools is 20.4 mm, and since the corresponding aligning holes in the crossmember and underbody are 21 mm and 22 mm in diameter, there is a significant in-built tolerance possible in the crossmember's alignment, even if the correct tools are used. If these tools are not available, align the crossmember by eye, centring the crossmember aligning holes on those of the underbody, and using the marks made on removal for assistance. Alternatively, use a tapered drift such as a clutch-aligning tool, or a deep socket spanner of suitable size.

28 Once the crossmember is aligned as precisely as possible, tighten its bolts to the specified torque (see Chapter 10 Specifications) without disturbing its position **(see illustration)**. Recheck the alignment once all the bolts are securely tightened.

29 The remainder of the refitting procedure is the reverse of removal.

30 Remember that, since the rear suspension crossmember has been disturbed, the wheel alignment and steering angles must be checked fully and carefully as soon as possible, with any necessary adjustments being made. This operation is best carried out by an experienced mechanic using proper checking equipment; the vehicle should therefore be taken to a Ford dealer or similar for attention.

Charcoal canister - Estate models

31 Disconnect the battery negative (earth) lead (see Chapter 5A).

32 Chock the front wheels, then jack up the rear of the vehicle and support on axle stands (see *"Jacking and Vehicle Support"*).

33 Disconnect the two hoses from the canister assembly, noting which way round they are fitted.

3.24 Release clip and drive out pin to separate canister from mounting bracket

3.27 Refitting rear suspension crossmember with Ford service tools (arrowed) in place to align it with underbody . . .

3.28 . . . ensure aligned crossmember does not move - Ford tools used here - while mounting bolts are tightened

3.35 Charcoal canister assembly - Estate models - showing plastic cover (arrowed) and pin securing canister to mounting bracket

34 Unscrew the canister assembly retaining bolt and withdraw the assembly, unclipping it from the front mounting.

35 Remove the plastic cover, and drive out the pin to separate the canister from its bracket **(see illustration)**.

36 On refitting, secure the canister to its bracket, and refit the assembly to the vehicle. Tighten the retaining bolt securely, and ensure that the two hoses are securely reconnected to their original unions.

Exhaust Gas Recirculation (EGR) system

Testing

EGR valve

37 Start the engine and allow it to idle.

3.44 Check end fitting of EGR pipe into inlet manifold whenever manifold is removed, but do not disturb

3.43a Disconnecting vacuum hose from EGR valve . . .

38 Detach the vacuum hose from the EGR valve, and attach a hand vacuum pump in its place.

39 Apply vacuum to the EGR valve. Vacuum should remain steady, and the engine should run poorly or stall.

a) *If the vacuum doesn't remain steady and the engine doesn't run poorly, renew the EGR valve and recheck it.*
b) *If the vacuum remains steady but the engine doesn't run poorly, remove the EGR valve, and check the valve and the inlet manifold for blockage. Clean or renew parts as necessary, and recheck.*

EGR system

40 Any further checking of the system requires special tools and test equipment. Take the vehicle to a dealer service department for checking.

Component renewal

Note: *These components will be very hot when the engine is running. Always allow the engine to cool down fully before starting work, to prevent the possibility of burns.*

EGR valve

41 Disconnect the battery negative (earth) lead (see Chapter 5A).

42 Remove the air mass meter and, where necessary on 4-cylinder models, the resonator. On V6 models, remove the idle air control valve.

43 Detach the vacuum hose, unscrew the sleeve nut securing the EGR pipe to the valve, remove the two valve mounting bolts, and withdraw the valve from the inlet manifold **(see illustrations)**. Ensure that the end of the pipe is not damaged or distorted as the valve is withdrawn, and note the valve's gasket; this must be renewed whenever the valve is disturbed.

3.43b . . . unscrew EGR pipe sleeve nut and remove bolts (arrowed) to release valve from inlet manifold

44 Note that the metal pipe from the valve to the manifold itself should not be disturbed - it is not available separately from the manifold. However, check whenever the manifold is removed that the pipe's end fitting is securely fastened **(see illustration)**.

45 Check the valve for sticking and heavy carbon deposits. If such is found, clean the valve or renew it.

46 Refitting is the reverse of the removal procedure. Apply a smear of anti-seize compound to the sleeve nut threads, fit a new gasket, and tighten the valve bolts to the specified torque wrench setting **(see illustration)**.

EGR pipe - 4-cylinder models

47 Disconnect the battery negative (earth) lead (see Chapter 5A).

48 Remove the air mass meter and where necessary the resonator.

49 Unbolt the exhaust manifold heat shield and remove both parts, or move them aside as required to reach the end of the EGR pipe. Unscrew the sleeve nut securing the pipe to the exhaust manifold **(see illustration)**.

50 Undo the two screws securing the pipe to the ignition coil bracket, then disconnect the two vacuum hoses - note that these are of different sizes, to ensure that they cannot be mixed up on reconnection. Unscrew the sleeve nut securing the EGR pipe to the valve **(see illustration)**. Withdraw the pipe.

3.46 Refitting the EGR valve together with a new gasket

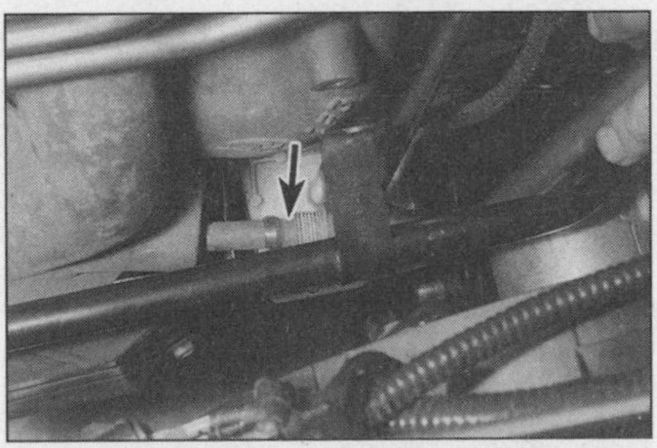

3.49 Unbolt exhaust manifold heat shield and unscrew sleeve nut (arrowed) securing EGR pipe to exhaust manifold . . .

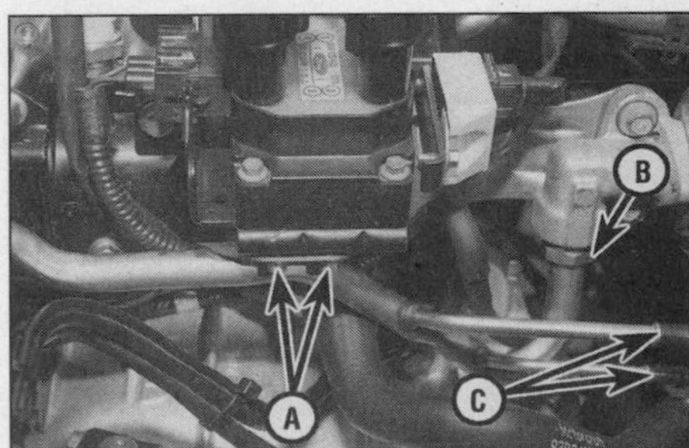

3.50 . . . undo screws "A" and sleeve nut "B", then disconnect hoses "C" - note different sizes - to release EGR pipe

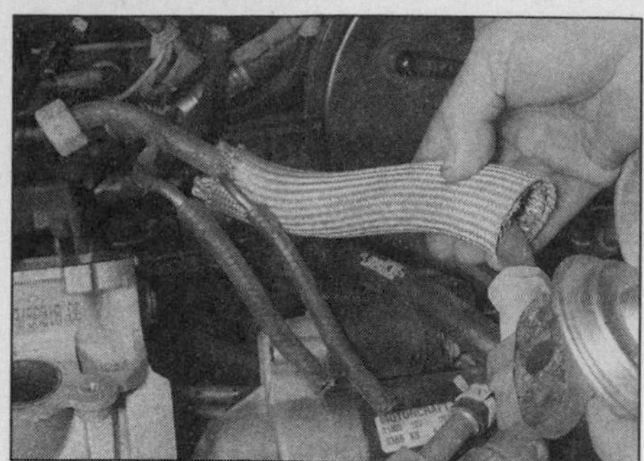

3.56 Removing the EGR tube on V6 models

51 Check the condition of both hoses, and renew them if necessary. Note that if the exhaust gases have been backfiring excessively - eg, due to a blockage - both hoses must be renewed, and their connections on the pipe must be cleaned thoroughly.

52 Refitting is the reverse of the removal procedure; ensure that the hoses are securely connected to the correct unions. Apply a smear of anti-seize compound to the sleeve nut threads, tighten the nuts securely, and tighten the two screws to their specified torque wrench setting.

EGR pipe - V6 models

53 Disconnect the idle air control valve tube from the air cleaner and upper inlet manifold.

54 Unscrew the EGR tube sleeve nut from the EGR valve and disconnect the tube.

55 Chock the front wheels, then jack up the rear of the vehicle and support on axle stands (see "*Jacking and Vehicle Support*"). Remove the front left-hand wheel and the wheel arch liner.

56 Remove the EGR tube nut from the rear exhaust manifold and remove the tube **(see illustration)**.

57 Refitting is a reversal of removal. Apply anti-seize compound to the nuts on both ends of the tube.

EGR solenoid valve

Note: *This component can be identified by its larger top and its two fastening screws. Do not confuse it with the adjacent pulse-air solenoid valve, especially when reconnecting vacuum hoses.*

3.59 EGR solenoid valve "A" and EGR exhaust gas pressure differential sensor "B", located on bulkhead mounting bracket

58 Disconnect the battery negative (earth) lead (see Chapter 5A).

59 Remove the air mass meter and, where necessary on 4-cylinder models, the resonator. If better access is required, remove the plenum chamber also **(see illustration)**.

60 Release the wire clip and unplug the electrical connector from the valve. Remove the two retaining screws, and withdraw the valve from the bulkhead mounting bracket, then label and disconnect the two vacuum hoses.

61 Refitting is the reverse of the removal procedure, but ensure that the hoses are correctly reconnected.

EGR exhaust gas pressure differential system

Testing

EGR exhaust gas pressure differential sensor

62 Testing of this component is beyond the scope of the DIY mechanic, and should be left to a Ford dealer.

Component renewal

EGR exhaust gas pressure differential sensor

63 On 4-cylinder models, if better access is required, remove the resonator where fitted.

64 Disconnect the sensor's electrical connector. Remove the two retaining screws, withdraw the unit from the bulkhead mounting bracket on 4-cylinder models, or the left-hand rear cylinder head on V6 models, then disconnect the two vacuum hoses. Note that the hoses are of different sizes to ensure that they cannot be mixed up on reconnection **(see illustrations)**.

65 Check the condition of both hoses and renew them if necessary.

66 Refitting is a reversal of removal. Ensure that the hoses are securely connected to the correct fittings.

Pulse-air injection system

Testing

67 Poor idle, stalling, backfiring and poor driveability can be caused by a fault in the system.

68 Inspect the vacuum pipe/hose connected between the filter housing and the solenoid valve for kinks, leaks and cracks along its entire length. Repair or renew as necessary.

69 Inspect the filter housing and piping. If either is cracked or damaged, renew it.

70 If the pulse-air solenoid valve is thought to be faulty, unplug its electrical connector and disconnect its vacuum hoses. Connect a battery directly across the valve terminals, and check that air can flow through the valve passages when the solenoid is thus energised, and that nothing can pass when the solenoid is not energised. Alternatively, connect an ohmmeter to measure the resistance across the valve terminals, and compare this reading to the one listed in the Specifications Section at the beginning of this Chapter. Renew the solenoid valve if it is faulty.

71 Further testing should be left to a dealer service department.

Component renewal

Pulse-air solenoid valve

Note: *This component can be identified by its smaller top and its clip fastening. Do not confuse it with the adjacent EGR solenoid valve, especially when reconnecting vacuum hoses.*

72 Disconnect the battery negative (earth) lead (see Chapter 5A).

73 Remove the air mass meter and resonator as described in Chapter 4A. If better access is required, remove the plenum chamber also.

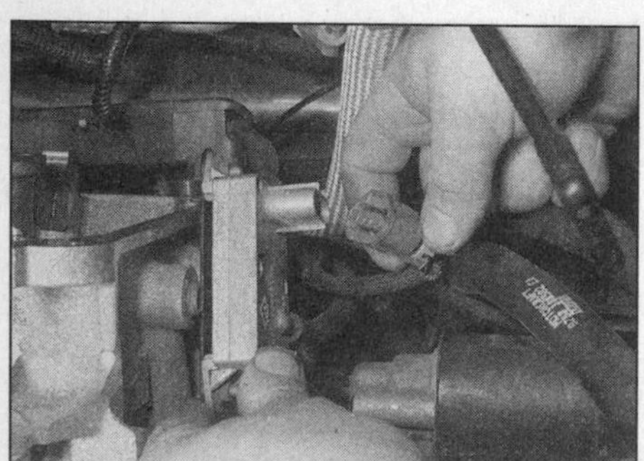

3.64a Disconnect the wiring plug . . .

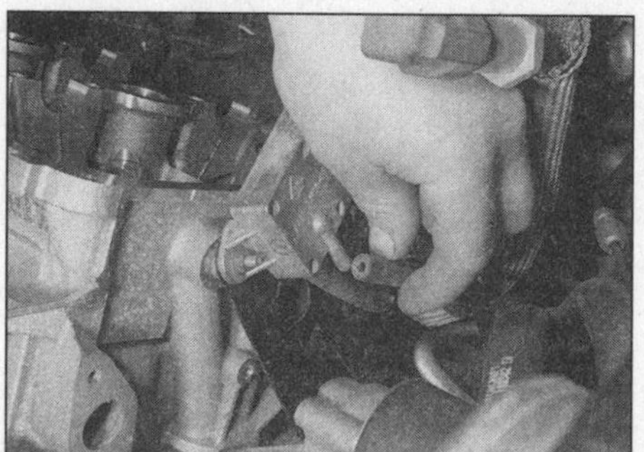

3.64b . . . and vacuum hoses from the exhaust gas pressure differential sensor

3.64c Exhaust gas pressure differential sensor (4-cylinder 2.0 litre model)

3.74 Pulse-air solenoid valve (arrowed) located on bulkhead mounting bracket

3.77 Disconnect vacuum hose from base of pulse-air filter housing . . .

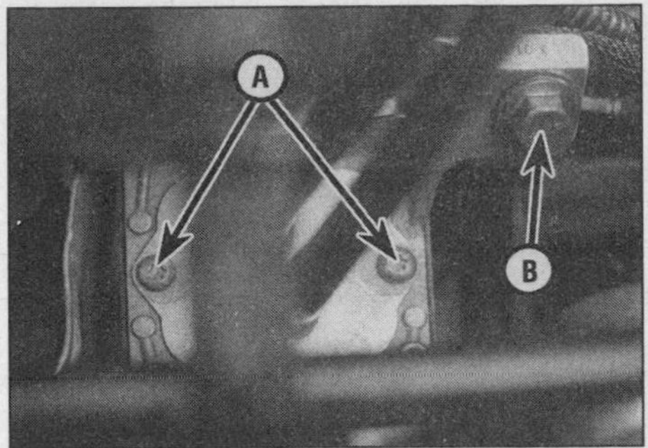

3.80 . . . undo screws "A" to disconnect piping from housing, and mounting bolt "B" to release housing

74 Release the wire clip from the valve, then disconnect the electrical connector and use a small screwdriver to release the clip securing the valve to the bulkhead mounting bracket **(see illustration)**.

75 Withdraw the valve, then label and disconnect the two vacuum hoses.

76 Refitting is the reverse of the removal procedure, but ensure that the hoses are correctly reconnected.

Pulse-air filter housing

Note: *This component, and those around it, will be very hot when the engine is running. Always allow the engine to cool down fully before starting work, to prevent the possibility of burns.*

77 Raise the front of the vehicle, and support it securely on axle stands. Disconnect the vacuum hose from the base of the filter housing **(see illustration)**.

78 Disconnect the battery negative (earth) lead (see Chapter 5A).

79 Unbolt the resonator support bracket from the engine compartment front crossmember, slacken the two clamp screws securing the resonator to the air mass meter and plenum chamber hoses, then swing the resonator up clear of the thermostat housing (see Chapter 4A).

80 Remove the screws securing the filter housing to the piping, unscrew the mounting bolt, then withdraw the housing **(see illustration)**.

81 To dismantle the filter housing, undo the four screws and separate the top from the base of the housing, then extract the foam filter and clean it in a suitable solvent **(see illustrations)**. If any of the housing's components are worn or damaged, the assembly must be renewed.

82 Refitting is the reverse of the removal procedure.

Pulse-air piping

Note: *This component, and those around it, will be very hot when the engine is running. Always allow the engine to cool down fully before starting work, to prevent the possibility of burns.*

83 Disconnect the battery negative (earth) lead (see Chapter 5A).

84 Remove the air mass meter and resonator as described in Chapter 4A.

85 Unbolt the exhaust manifold heat shield and unclip the coolant hose to allow the upper part to be withdrawn. Apply penetrating oil to the EGR pipe sleeve nut, and to the pulse-air system sleeve nuts.

86 Remove the EGR pipe as described earlier.

87 Remove the screws securing the filter housing to the piping. Unscrew the four sleeve nuts securing the pipes into the exhaust manifold, and remove the piping as an assembly, taking care not to distort it **(see illustration)**.

88 Carefully clean the piping, particularly its threads and those of the manifold, removing all traces of corrosion, which might prevent them seating properly, causing air leaks when the engine is restarted.

89 On refitting, insert the piping carefully into the cylinder head ports, taking care not to bend or distort it. Apply anti-seize compound to the threads, and tighten the retaining sleeve nuts while holding each pipe firmly in its port; if a suitable spanner is available, tighten the sleeve nuts to the specified torque wrench setting.

90 The remainder of the refitting procedure is the reverse of removal.

Pulse-air filter housing and piping assembly

Note: *These components, and those around them, will be very hot when the engine is running. Always allow the engine to cool down fully before starting work, to prevent the possibility of burns.*

91 Disconnect the battery negative (earth) lead (see Chapter 5A). Unbolt the resonator support bracket from the engine compartment front crossmember. Slacken the two clamp screws securing the resonator to the air mass meter and plenum chamber hoses, then swing the resonator up clear of the thermostat housing.

92 Drain the cooling system (see Chapter 1) and disconnect the coolant hose and the coolant pipe/hose from the thermostat housing.

93 Unbolt the exhaust manifold heat shield. Apply penetrating oil to the EGR pipe sleeve nut, and to the pulse-air system sleeve nuts.

94 Remove the EGR pipe as described earlier.

95 Unscrew the filter housing mounting bolt.

3.81a Remove four screws to release filter housing top from base . . .

3.81b . . . and withdraw foam filter for cleaning, if required - note valve in base of housing

3.87 Removing pulse-air piping - take care not to bend or distort it

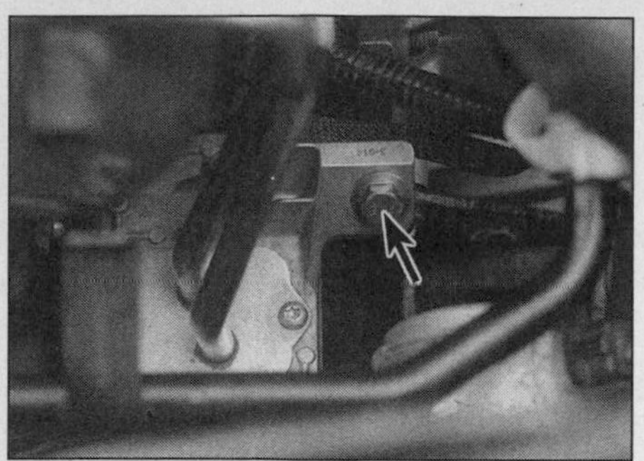
3.95 Remove mounting bolt (arrowed) to remove complete pulse-air assembly - again, take care not to bend or distort piping

Unscrew the four sleeve nuts securing the pipes into the exhaust manifold and remove the assembly, taking care not to distort it **(see illustration)**.

96 Clean the piping, particularly the threads and those of the manifold, removing all traces of corrosion, which might prevent them seating properly or causing air leaks when the engine is restarted.

97 On refitting, insert the piping carefully into the cylinder head ports, taking care not to bend or distort it. Apply anti-seize compound to the threads, and tighten the retaining sleeve nuts while holding each pipe firmly in its port. If a suitable spanner is available, tighten the sleeve nuts to the specified torque wrench setting.

98 The remainder of the refitting procedure is the reverse of removal. Refill the cooling system (see Chapter 1). Run the engine, check for exhaust leaks, and check the coolant level when it is fully warmed-up.

Catalytic converter

Testing

99 Checking the operation of a catalytic converter requires expensive and sophisticated diagnostic equipment, starting with a high-quality exhaust gas analyser. If the level of CO in the exhaust gases is too high, a full check of the engine management system must be carried out to eliminate all other possibilities before the converter is suspected of being faulty. The vehicle should be taken to

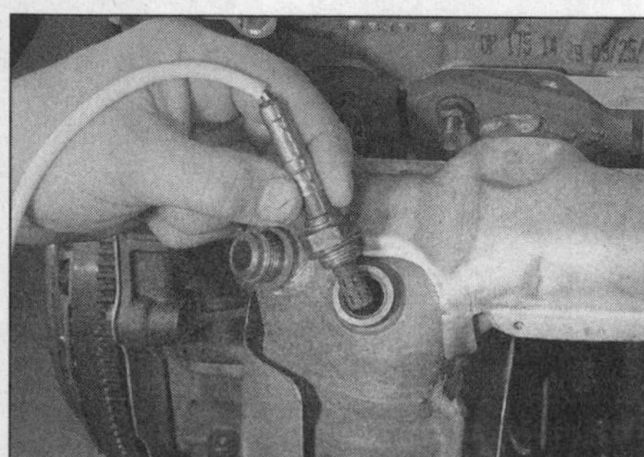
3.103 Removing the oxygen sensor from the exhaust manifold on V6 models

3.102 On 4-cylinder models, the oxygen sensor is screwed into the exhaust system front downpipe

a Ford dealer for this work to be carried out using the correct diagnostic equipment. Do not waste time trying to test the system without such facilities.

Component renewal

100 On 4-cylinder models, the catalytic converter is part of the exhaust system front downpipe. On V6 models, the catalytic converters are part of the exhaust manifolds. Refer to Chapter 4A for details of removal and refitting.

Oxygen sensor

Testing

101 Testing the oxygen sensor is only possible by connecting special diagnostic equipment to the sensor wiring, and checking that the voltage varies from low to high values when the engine is running. **Do not** attempt to "test" any part of the system with anything other than the correct test equipment. This is beyond the scope of the DIY mechanic, and should be left to a Ford dealer.

Component renewal

Note: *The sensor is delicate, and will not work if it is dropped or knocked, or if any cleaning materials are used on it.*

102 Disconnect the sensor wiring at the plug **(see illustration)**.

103 Raise and support the front of the vehicle if required to remove the sensor from underneath. Unscrew the sensor from the exhaust system front downpipe on 4-cylinder models or from each exhaust manifold on V6 models **(see illustration)**. Recover the gasket (where fitted).

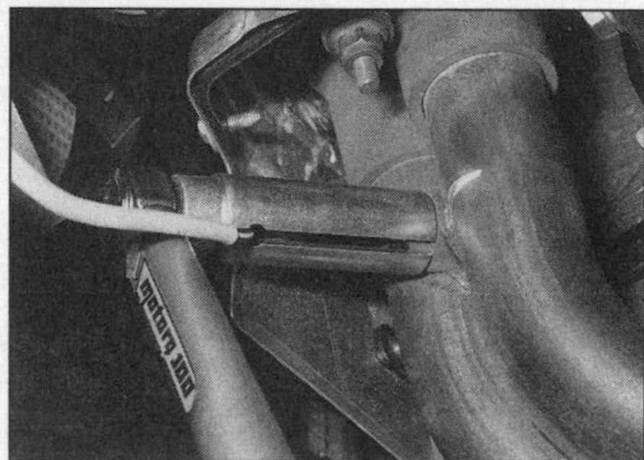
3.104 A slotted socket will be required to tighten the sensor with a torque wrench

104 On refitting, clean the sealing gasket (where fitted) and renew it if damaged. Apply a smear of anti-seize compound to the sensor's threads. Fit the new sensor, and tighten it to the specified torque wrench setting. A slotted socket will be required to do this **(see illustration)**. Reconnect the wiring plug.

4 Catalytic converter - precautions

1 The catalytic converter is a reliable and simple device, which needs no maintenance in itself, but there are some facts of which an owner should be aware if the converter is to function properly for its full service life.

a) *DO NOT use leaded petrol in a car equipped with a catalytic converter - the lead will coat the precious metals, reducing their converting efficiency and will eventually destroy the converter.*
b) *Always keep the ignition and fuel systems well-maintained in accordance with the manufacturer's schedule.*
c) *If the engine develops a misfire, do not drive the car at all (or at least as little as possible) until the fault is cured.*
d) *DO NOT push- or tow-start the car - this will soak the catalytic converter in unburned fuel, causing it to overheat when the engine does start.*
e) *DO NOT switch off the ignition at high engine speeds.*
f) *DO NOT use fuel or engine oil additives - these may contain substances harmful to the catalytic converter.*
g) *DO NOT continue to use the car if the engine burns oil to the extent of leaving a visible trail of blue smoke.*
h) *Remember that the catalytic converter operates at very high temperatures. DO NOT, therefore, park the car in dry undergrowth, over long grass or piles of dead leaves after a long run.*
i) *Remember that the catalytic converter is FRAGILE - do not strike it with tools during servicing work.*
j) *In some cases a sulphurous smell (like that of rotten eggs) may be noticed from the exhaust. This is common to many catalytic converter-equipped cars and once the car has covered a few thousand miles the problem should disappear.*
k) *The catalytic converter, used on a well-maintained and well-driven car, should last for between 50 000 and 100 000 miles - if the converter is no longer effective it must be renewed.*

Chapter 5 Part A:
Starting and charging systems

Contents

Degrees of difficulty

Easy, suitable for novice with little experience 

Fairly easy, suitable for beginner with some experience 

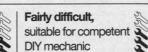

Fairly difficult, suitable for competent DIY mechanic

Difficult, suitable for experienced DIY mechanic 

Very difficult, suitable for expert DIY or professional

Specifications

Battery

Type	Lead-acid
Rating - Cold cranking/Reserve capacity	500 A/75 RC, 590 A/95 RC, or 650 A/130 RC

Alternator

Type:	**Model**	**Rated output**
Bosch unit	NC 14V 60-90A	90A
Mitsubishi unit	A004T	90A
Minimum brush length - all types	5.0 mm	
Regulated voltage at 4000 rpm and 3 to 7 amp load - all types	13.5 to 14.6 volts	

Starter motor

Type:	**Model**	**Rated output**
Bosch unit	DW	1.1 or 1.4 kW
Lucas/Magneti Marelli unit	M79	1.0 kW
Minimum brush length - all types	8.0 mm	
Commutator minimum diameter:		
Bosch units	32.8 mm	
Lucas/Magneti Marelli unit	Not available	
Armature endfloat:		
Bosch units	0.30 mm	
Lucas/Magneti Marelli unit	0.25 mm	

Torque wrench settings	**Nm**	**lbf ft**
Alternator mounting bolts:		
4-cylinder models:		
Pre 1/1997 models	45	33
1/1997 models on	25	19
V6 models	45	33
Starter motor mounting bolts	35	26

5A

1.2 Always disconnect battery - negative (earth) lead first - to prevent the possibility of short-circuits

1 General information, precautions and battery disconnection

General information

The engine electrical systems include all ignition, charging and starting components. Because of their engine-related functions, these components are discussed separately from body electrical devices such as the lights, the instruments, etc (which are included in Chapter 12).

Precautions

Always observe the following precautions when working on the electrical system:

a) Be extremely careful when servicing engine electrical components. They are easily damaged if checked, connected or handled improperly.

b) Never leave the ignition switched on for long periods of time when the engine is not running.

c) Don't disconnect the battery leads while the engine is running.

d) Maintain correct polarity when connecting a battery lead from another vehicle during jump starting - see the "Booster battery (jump) starting" Section at the front of this manual.

e) Always disconnect the negative lead first, and reconnect it last, or the battery may be shorted by the tool being used to loosen the lead clamps **(see illustration).**

It's also a good idea to review the safety-related information regarding the engine electrical systems located in the *"Safety first!"* section at the front of this manual, before beginning any operation included in this Chapter.

Battery disconnection

Several systems fitted to the vehicle require battery power to be available at all times, either to ensure their continued operation (such as the clock) or to maintain control unit memories (such as that in the engine management system's ECU) which would be wiped if the battery were to be disconnected. Whenever the battery is to be disconnected therefore, first note the following, to ensure that there are no unforeseen consequences of this action:

a) First, on any vehicle with central locking, it is a wise precaution to remove the key from the ignition, and to keep it with you, so that it does not get locked in if the central locking should engage accidentally when the battery is reconnected!

b) The engine management system's ECU will lose the information stored in its memory - referred to by Ford as the "KAM" (Keep-Alive Memory) - when the battery is disconnected. This includes idling and operating values, and any fault codes detected - in the case of the fault codes, if it is thought likely that the system has developed a fault for which the corresponding code has been logged, the vehicle must be taken to a Ford dealer for the codes to be read, using the special diagnostic equipment necessary for this (see Chapter 4A). Whenever the battery is disconnected, the information relating to idle speed control and other operating values will have to be re-programmed into the unit's memory. The ECU does this by itself, but until then, there may be surging, hesitation, erratic idle and a generally inferior level of performance. To allow the ECU to relearn these values, start the engine and run it as close to idle speed as possible until it reaches its normal operating temperature, then run it for approximately two minutes at 1200 rpm. Next, drive the vehicle as far as necessary - approximately 5 miles of varied driving conditions is usually sufficient - to complete the relearning process.

c) If the battery is disconnected while the alarm system is armed or activated, the alarm will remain in the same state when the battery is reconnected. The same applies to the engine immobiliser system (where fitted).

d) If a trip computer is in use, any information stored in memory will be lost.

e) If a Ford "Keycode" audio unit is fitted, and the unit and/or the battery is disconnected, the unit will not function again on reconnection until the correct security code is entered. Details of this procedure, which varies according to the unit and model year, are given in the "Ford Audio Systems Operating Guide" supplied with the vehicle when new, with the code itself being given in a "Radio Passport" and/or a "Keycode Label" at the same time. Ensure you have the correct code before you disconnect the battery. For obvious security reasons, the procedure is not given in this manual. If you do not have the code or details of the correct procedure, but can supply proof of ownership and a legitimate reason for wanting this information, the vehicle's selling dealer may be able to help.

Devices known as "memory-savers" (or "code-savers") can be used to avoid some of the above problems. Precise details vary according to the device used. Typically, it is plugged into the cigarette lighter, and is connected by its own wires to a spare battery; the vehicle's own battery is then disconnected from the electrical system, leaving the "memory-saver" to pass sufficient current to maintain audio unit security codes and ECU memory values, and also to run permanently-live circuits such as the clock, all the while isolating the battery in the event of a short-circuit occurring while work is carried out.

Warning: Some of these devices allow a considerable amount of current to pass, which can mean that many of the vehicle's systems are still operational when the main battery is disconnected. If a "memory-saver" is used, ensure that the circuit concerned is actually "dead" before carrying out any work on it!

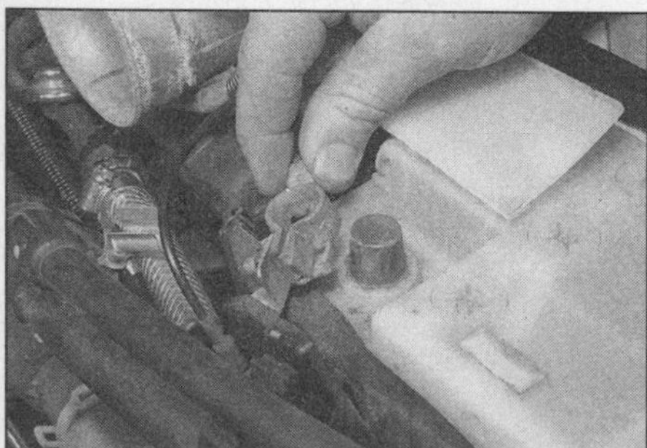
2.1 Disconnecting the battery positive cable

2.2a Unscrew hold-down nuts (one of two arrowed) . . .

2 Battery - removal and refitting

Note: *See also the relevant Sections of Chapter 1.*

Removal

1 Disconnect the battery leads, negative (earth) lead first - see Section 1 **(see illustration).**

2 Remove the battery hold-down clamp **(see illustrations).**

2.2b . . . and withdraw hold-down clamp to release battery

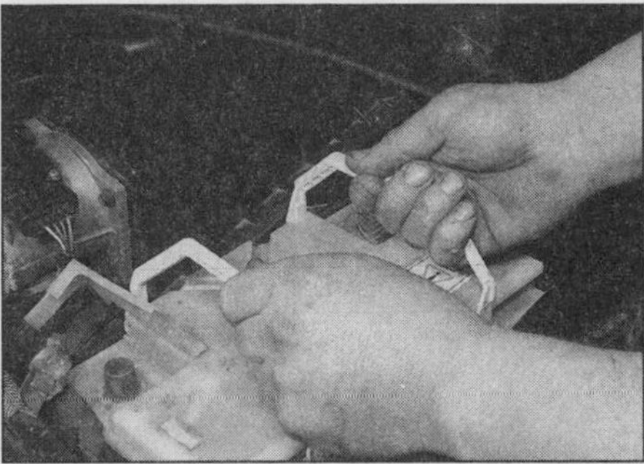

2.3 On V6 models, the battery has lifting handles

3 Lift out the battery **(see illustration)**.
Caution: Be careful! the battery is heavy

4 While the battery is out, inspect the tray for corrosion (see "*Weekly checks*").

5 If you are renewing the battery, make sure that you get one that's identical, with the same dimensions, amperage rating, cold cranking rating, etc. Dispose of the old battery in a responsible fashion. Most local authorities have facilities for the collection and disposal of such items - batteries contain sulphuric acid and lead, and should not be simply thrown out with the household rubbish!

Refitting

6 Refitting is the reverse of the removal procedure. **Note:** *After the battery has been disconnected, the engine management system requires approximately 10 miles of driving to relearn its optimum settings. During this period, the engine may not perform normally.*

3 Charging system - general information and precautions

General information

The charging system includes the alternator, an internal voltage regulator, a no-charge (or "ignition") warning light, the battery, and the wiring between all the components. The charging system supplies electrical power for the ignition system, the lights, the radio, etc. The alternator is driven by the auxiliary drivebelt at the front (right-hand end) of the engine.

The purpose of the voltage regulator is to limit the alternator's voltage to a preset value. This prevents power surges, circuit overloads, etc., during peak voltage output.

The charging system doesn't ordinarily require periodic maintenance. However, the drivebelt, battery and wires and connections should be inspected at the intervals outlined in Chapter 1.

The dashboard warning light should come on when the ignition key is turned to positions "II" or "III", then should go off immediately the engine starts. If it remains on, or if it comes on while the engine is running, there is a malfunction in the charging system. If the light does not come on when the ignition key is turned, and the bulb is sound (see Chapter 12), there is a fault in the alternator.

Precautions

Be very careful when making electrical circuit connections to a vehicle equipped with an alternator, and note the following:

a) When reconnecting wires to the alternator from the battery, be sure to note the polarity.
b) Before using arc-welding equipment to repair any part of the vehicle, disconnect the wires from the alternator and the battery terminals.
c) Never start the engine with a battery charger connected.
d) Always disconnect both battery leads before using a battery charger.
e) The alternator is driven by an engine drivebelt which could cause serious injury if your hand, hair or clothes become entangled in it with the engine running.
f) Because the alternator is connected directly to the battery, it could arc or cause a fire if overloaded or shorted-out.
g) Wrap a plastic bag over the alternator, and secure it with rubber bands, before steam-cleaning or pressure-washing the engine.
h) Never disconnect the alternator terminals while the engine is running.

4 Charging system - testing

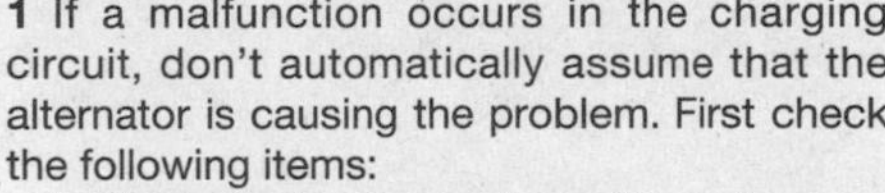

1 If a malfunction occurs in the charging circuit, don't automatically assume that the alternator is causing the problem. First check the following items:

a) Check the tension and condition of the auxiliary drivebelt - renew it if it is worn or deteriorated (see Chapter 1).
b) Ensure the alternator mounting bolts and nuts are tight.
c) Inspect the alternator wiring harness and the electrical connections at the alternator; they must be in good condition, and tight.
d) Check the large main fuses in the engine compartment (see Chapter 12). If any is blown, determine the cause, repair the circuit and renew the fuse (the vehicle won't start and/or the accessories won't work if the fuse is blown).
e) Start the engine and check the alternator for abnormal noises - for example, a shrieking or squealing sound may indicate a badly-worn bearing or brush.
f) Make sure that the battery is fully-charged - one bad cell in a battery can cause overcharging by the alternator.
g) Disconnect the battery leads (negative first, then positive). Inspect the battery posts and the lead clamps for corrosion. Clean them thoroughly if necessary (see "Weekly checks"). Reconnect the lead to the negative terminal.
h) With the ignition and all accessories switched off, insert a test light between the battery negative post and the disconnected negative lead clamp:
1) If the test light does not come on, re-attach the clamp and proceed to the next step.
2) If the test light comes on, there is a short in the electrical system of the vehicle. The short must be repaired before the charging system can be checked.
3) To find the short, disconnect the alternator wiring harness:
a) If the light goes out, the alternator is at fault.
b) If the light stays on, remove each fuse until it goes out - this will tell you which component is short-circuited.

2 Using a voltmeter, check the battery voltage with the engine off. It should be approximately 12 volts.

3 Start the engine and check the battery voltage again. Increase engine speed until the voltmeter reading remains steady; it should now be approximately 13.5 to 14.6 volts.

4 Switch on as many electrical accessories (eg the headlights, heated rear window and heater blower) as possible, and check that the alternator maintains the regulated voltage at around 13 to 14 volts. The voltage may drop and then come back up; it may also be necessary to increase engine speed slightly, even if the charging system is working properly.

5 If the voltage reading is greater than the specified charging voltage, renew the voltage regulator.

6 If the voltmeter reading is less than that specified, the fault may be due to worn brushes, weak brush springs, a faulty voltage regulator, a faulty diode, a severed phase winding, or worn or damaged slip rings. The brushes and slip rings may be checked, but if the fault persists, the alternator should be renewed or taken to an auto-electrician for testing and repair.

5.3 Disconnecting the alternator wiring on 4-cylinder models

5.6 Withdrawing the alternator through the right-hand front wheel arch

5.15 Removing the right-hand front wheel arch lower liners

5 Alternator - removal and refitting

4-cylinder models

Removal

1 Disconnect the battery negative (earth) lead (see Section 1).

2 Remove the plenum chamber (see Chapter 4A).

Models up to 1/1997

3 Unscrew the nuts to disconnect the wiring from the alternator **(see illustration)**. Also unbolt the earth cable. If additional working clearance is required, undo the right-hand of the three screws securing the wiring "rail" to the rear of the inlet manifold.

4 Apply the handbrake, then jack up the front of the vehicle and support it on axle stands (see *"Jacking and Vehicle Support"*). Remove the radiator undershield and the right-hand front wheel arch liner. If necessary for additional working room, remove the oil filter, oil cooler (where fitted), and disconnect the right-hand track rod end.

5 Remove the auxiliary drivebelt as described in Chapter 1.

6 Remove the mounting bolts and nuts (one at the top, two at the bottom) **(see illustration)**.

7 Turn the alternator so that the pulley is uppermost, then carefully lift the alternator upwards from the engine taking care not to damage the surrounding components, and finally disconnect the remaining wiring. Note that there is little room to manoeuvre the alternator.

Models from 1/1997

8 Remove the auxiliary drivebelt as described in Chapter 1.

9 Disconnect the wiring from the alternator.

10 Unscrew the alternator mounting bolts, and carefully lift it upwards from the engine.

All models

11 If you are renewing the alternator, take the old one with you when purchasing a replacement unit. Make sure that the new or rebuilt unit is identical to the old alternator. Look at the terminals - they should be the same in number, size and location as the terminals on the old alternator. Finally, look at the identification markings - they will be stamped in the housing, or printed on a tag or plaque affixed to the housing. Make sure that these numbers are the same on both alternators.

12 Many new/rebuilt alternators do not have a pulley installed, so you may have to switch the pulley from the old unit to the new/rebuilt one. When buying an alternator, ask about the installation of pulleys - some auto-electrical specialists will perform this service free of charge.

Refitting

13 Refitting is the reverse of the removal procedure, referring where necessary to the relevant Chapters of this manual. Tighten all nuts and bolts to the specified torque wrench settings.

V6 models

Removal

14 Apply the handbrake, then jack up the front of the vehicle and support it on axle stands (see *"Jacking and Vehicle Support"*). Remove the right-hand front wheel.

15 Unbolt and remove the right-hand front wheel arch lower liners **(see illustration)**.

16 Remove the auxiliary drivebelt as described in Chapter 1.

17 Disconnect the battery negative (earth) lead (see Section 1).

18 Working under the car, use a long extension bar with a universal joint and a socket to unscrew the nut and disconnect the main wire from the rear of the alternator **(see illustration)**. The extension bar should be inserted next to the exhaust pipes at the rear of the engine. If preferred, unscrew the nut later when the alternator is being removed.

19 Using a screwdriver, disconnect the remaining charge indicator wire plug. Again, this is a difficult task as there is very little room, and if necessary the plug can be disconnected later when the alternator is removed.

20 Disconnect the right-hand track rod end from the hub carrier with reference to Chapter 10 **(see illustration)**.

21 Unbolt and remove the alternator rear support bracket. Access to the bolts is possible by inserting the extension bar between the exhaust pipe and cylinder block.

22 Using the extension bar and socket, unscrew and remove the alternator upper mounting bolt **(see illustration)**. It will be

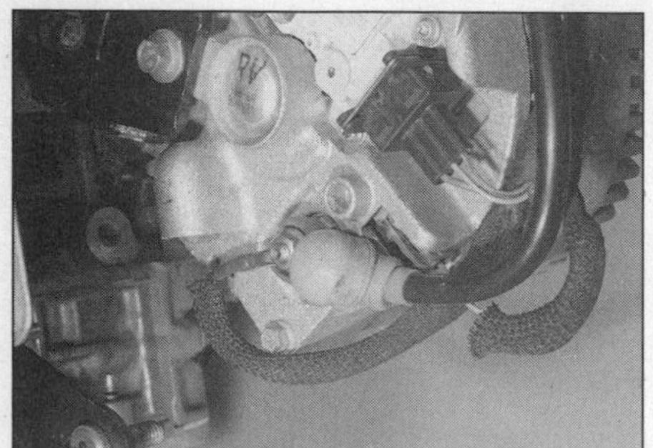

5.18 Wiring on the rear of the alternator

5.20 Disconnecting the right-hand track rod end using a separator tool

5.22 Removing the alternator upper mounting bolt

necessary to locate the bar between the gearchange rods and the body.

23 Unscrew and remove the lower mounting bolt using an extension bar located between the sump and front exhaust pipe.

24 Carefully withdraw the alternator through the right-hand wheel arch. Disconnect the wiring if not already done **(see illustrations)**.

25 If necessary, unbolt the bracket from the cylinder block **(see illustration)**.

Refitting

26 Refitting is a reversal of the removal procedure, referring where necessary to the relevant Chapters of this manual **(see illustration)**. Tighten all nuts and bolts to the specified torque wrench settings.

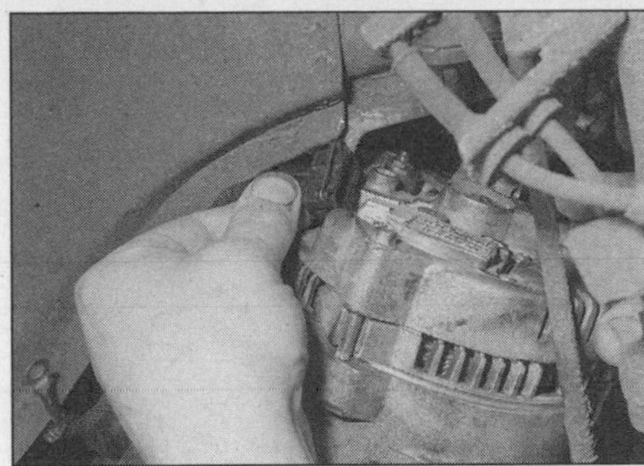

5.24a Removing the alternator through the right-hand wheel arch

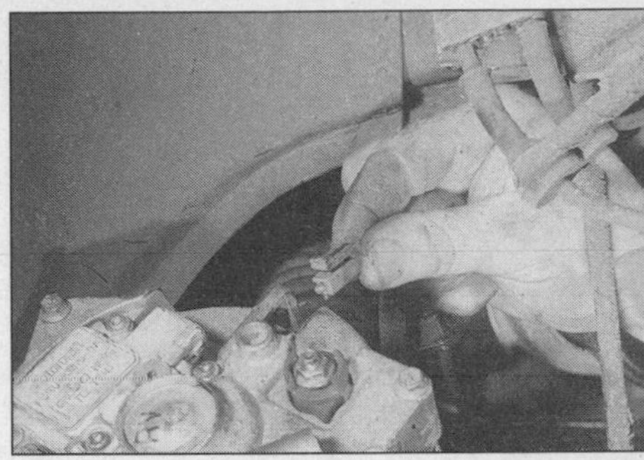

5.24b Disconnecting the wiring from the alternator

5.25 Removing the alternator mounting bracket

5.26 Refitting the alternator to the mounting bracket

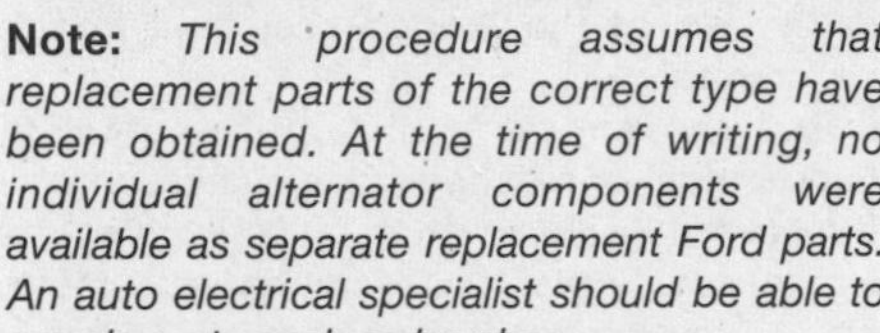

6 Alternator brushes and voltage regulator - renewal

Note: *This procedure assumes that replacement parts of the correct type have been obtained. At the time of writing, no individual alternator components were available as separate replacement Ford parts. An auto electrical specialist should be able to supply parts such as brushes.*

1 Remove the alternator from the vehicle (see Section 5) and place it on a clean workbench.

Bosch alternator

2 Remove the three screws, and withdraw the plastic end cover **(see illustration)**.

3 Remove the two voltage regulator/brush holder mounting screws.

4 Remove the regulator/brush holder from the end frame **(see illustration)**.

Motorcraft alternator

5 Using a Torx key, undo the screws and remove the regulator/brush holder from the rear of the alternator **(see illustration)**.

All makes

6 Measure the exposed length of each brush, and compare it to the minimum length listed in this Chapter's Specifications. If the length of either brush is less than the specified minimum, renew the assembly.

7 Make sure that each brush moves smoothly in the brush holder.

8 Check that the slip rings - the ring of copper on which each brush bears - are clean **(see illustration)**. Wipe them with a solvent-moistened cloth; if either appears scored or blackened, take the alternator to a repair specialist for advice.

Bosch alternator

9 Fit the voltage regulator/brush holder, ensuring that the brushes bear correctly on the slip rings, and that they compress into their holders. Tighten the screws securely.

10 Install the rear cover, and tighten the screws securely.

Motorcraft alternator

11 Carefully press the brushes into the holder and retain them by inserting a suitable rod (eg welding rod) through the hole provided **(see illustration)**.

6.2 Renewing voltage regulator/brush holder - Bosch alternator. Remove three screws and withdraw end cover . . .

6.4 . . . then remove regulator/brush holder assembly (secured by two screws)

6.5 Regulator/brush holder retaining screws

6.8 Check that the slip rings are clean

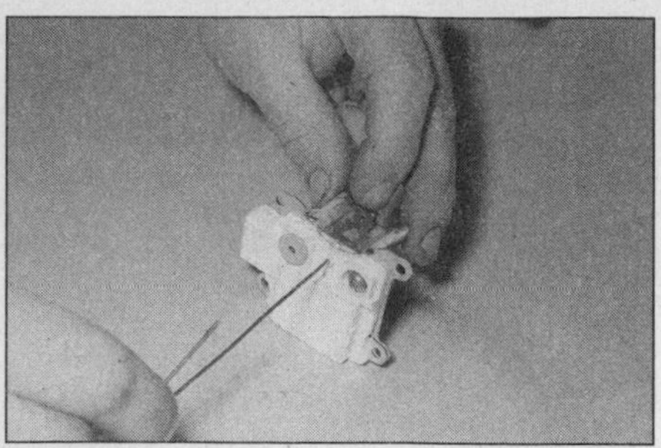

6.11 Insert a rod through the special hole to retain the brushes in their retracted position

12 Fit the regulator/brush holder to the alternator, then insert and tighten the retaining screws **(see illustration)**.

All makes

13 Refit the alternator (see Section 5).

7 Starting system - general information and precautions

General information

The sole function of the starting system is to turn over the engine quickly enough to allow it to start.

The starting system consists of the battery, the starter motor, the starter solenoid, and the wires connecting them. The solenoid is mounted directly on the starter motor.

The solenoid/starter motor assembly is installed on the rear upper part of the engine, next to the transmission bellhousing.

When the ignition key is turned to position "III", the starter solenoid is actuated through the starter control circuit. The starter solenoid then connects the battery to the starter. The battery supplies the electrical energy to the starter motor, which does the actual work of cranking the engine.

The starter motor on a vehicle equipped with automatic transmission can be operated only when the selector lever is in Park or Neutral ("P" or "N").

If the alarm system is armed or activated, the starter motor cannot be operated. The same applies with the engine immobiliser system (where fitted).

Precautions

Always observe the following precautions when working on the starting system:

a) Excessive cranking of the starter motor can overheat it, and cause serious damage. Never operate the starter motor for more than 15 seconds at a time without pausing to allow it to cool for at least two minutes. Excessive starter operation will also risk unburned fuel collecting in the catalytic converter's element, causing it to overheat when the engine does start.

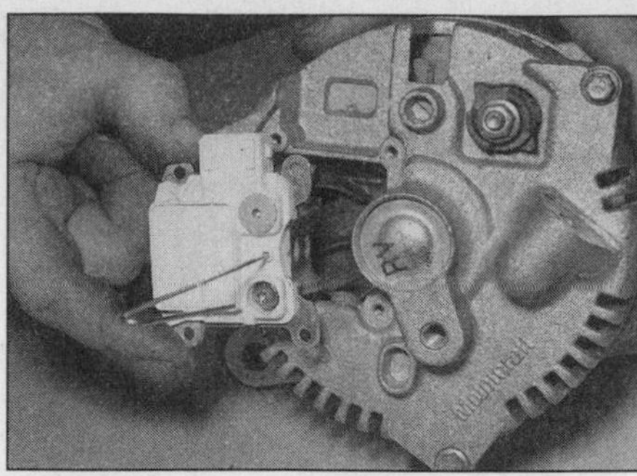

6.12 Fitting the regulator/brush holder to the rear of the alternator

b) The starter is connected directly to the battery, and could arc or cause a fire if mishandled, overloaded or shorted-out.

c) Always detach the lead from the negative terminal of the battery before working on the starting system (see Section 1).

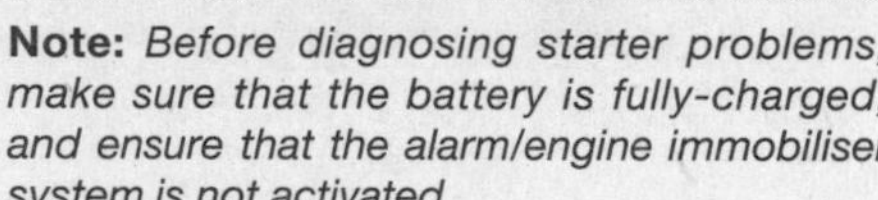

8 Starting system - testing

Note: *Before diagnosing starter problems, make sure that the battery is fully-charged, and ensure that the alarm/engine immobiliser system is not activated.*

1 If the starter motor does not turn at all when the switch is operated, make sure that, on automatic transmission models, the selector lever is in Park or Neutral ("P" or "N").

2 Make sure that the battery is fully-charged, and that all leads, both at the battery and starter solenoid terminals, are clean and secure.

3 If the starter motor spins but the engine is not cranking, the overrunning clutch or (when applicable) the reduction gears in the starter motor may be slipping, in which case the starter motor must be overhauled or renewed. (Other possibilities are that the starter motor mounting bolts are very loose, or that teeth are missing from the flywheel/driveplate ring gear.)

4 If, when the switch is actuated, the starter motor does not operate at all but the solenoid clicks, then the problem lies with either the battery, the main solenoid contacts, or the starter motor itself (or the engine is seized).

5 If the solenoid plunger cannot be heard to click when the switch is actuated, the battery is faulty, there is a fault in the circuit, or the solenoid itself is defective.

6 To check the solenoid, connect a fused jumper lead between the battery (+) and the ignition switch terminal (the small terminal) on the solenoid. If the starter motor now operates, the solenoid is OK, and the problem is in the ignition switch, selector lever position sensor (automatic transmission) or in the wiring.

7 If the starter motor still does not operate, remove it. The brushes and commutator may be checked, but if the fault persists, the motor should be renewed, or taken to an auto-electrician for testing and repair.

8 If the starter motor cranks the engine at an abnormally-slow speed, first make sure that the battery is charged, and that all terminal connections are tight. If the engine is partially seized, or has the wrong viscosity oil in it, it will crank slowly.

9 Run the engine until normal operating temperature is reached, then switch off and disable the ignition system by unplugging the ignition coil's electrical connector; remove fuse 14 to disconnect the fuel pump.

10 Connect a voltmeter positive lead to the battery positive terminal, and connect the negative lead to the negative terminal.

11 Crank the engine, and take the voltmeter readings as soon as a steady figure is indicated. Do not allow the starter motor to turn for more than 15 seconds at a time. A reading of 10.5 volts or more, with the starter motor turning at normal cranking speed, is normal. If the reading is 10.5 volts or more but the cranking speed is slow, the solenoid contacts are burned, the motor is faulty, or there is a bad connection. If the reading is less than 10.5 volts and the cranking speed is slow, the starter motor is faulty or there is a problem with the battery.

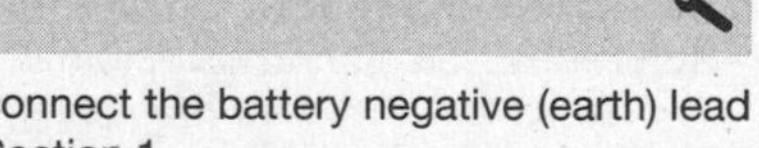

9 Starter motor - removal and refitting

1 Disconnect the battery negative (earth) lead - see Section 1.

4-cylinder models

Removal

2 Remove the air mass meter and resonator as described in Chapter 4A.

3 Unscrew the upper two starter motor mounting bolts, noting that one also secures an engine/transmission earth lead **(see illustration)**.

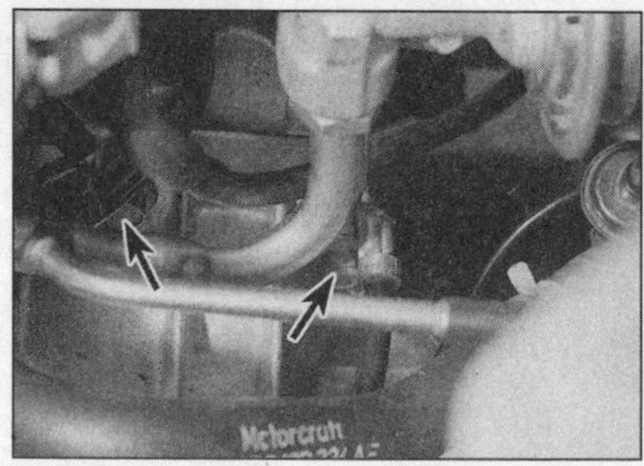

9.3 Unscrew the upper two starter motor mounting bolts (arrowed) from above

4 Apply the handbrake, then jack up the front of the vehicle and support it on axle stands (see *"Jacking and Vehicle Support"*).

5 Unscrew the nuts to disconnect the wiring from the starter/solenoid terminals.

9.6 Disconnect the wiring (A), then unscrew the remaining mounting bolt (B), and remove the starter motor from beneath

9.10 Disconnecting the wiring and support bracket from the starter motor

6 Remove the remaining starter motor mounting bolt **(see illustration)**. Remove the starter.

Refitting

7 Refitting is the reverse of the removal procedure. Tighten the bolts to the specified torque wrench settings.

V6 models

Removal

8 Remove the air cleaner and air cleaner mounting bracket.

9 Apply the handbrake, then jack up the front of the vehicle and support it on axle stands (see *"Jacking and Vehicle Support"*).

10 Disconnect the wiring from the starter motor. Also remove the two nuts and bolt securing the support bracket to the starter motor and transmission housing. Remove the bracket **(see illustration)**.

11 On automatic transmission models, remove the shift cable bracket from the transmission housing, and disconnect the cable from the transmission.

12 Remove the fuel lines from the fuel line support bracket located on the accelerator cable mounting bracket. Remove the fuel line support bracket.

13 Unscrew the mounting bolts from the starter motor, then release the starter motor from the dowels on the transmission housing and withdraw from the engine compartment **(see illustrations)**.

Refitting

14 Refitting is a reversal of removal. Tighten the bolts to the specified torque wrench settings.

10 Starter motor - brush and solenoid renewal

Note: *This procedure assumes that replacement brushes of the correct type have been obtained - at the time of writing, no individual starter motor components were available as separate replacement Ford parts. An auto electrical specialist should be able to supply parts such as brushes.*

Note: *The following procedures are for the Lucas/Magneti Marelli unit fitted to the project vehicle - the procedure is essentially the same for the Bosch unit that may be found on other models.*

1 Remove the starter motor from the vehicle (Section 9) **(see illustration)**.

Brush renewal

2 Remove the brushes as shown **(see illustrations overleaf)**.

3 In some cases, the brushes will have wear limit marks, in the form of a groove etched along one face of each brush; when the brushes are worn down to these marks, they must be renewed. If no marks are provided, measure the length of each brush, and compare it with the minimum length given in the Specifications Section of this Chapter. If any brush is worn below this limit, renew the brushes as a set. If the brushes are still serviceable, clean them with a petrol-moistened cloth. Check that the spring pressure is equal for all brushes, and holds the brushes securely against the commutator.

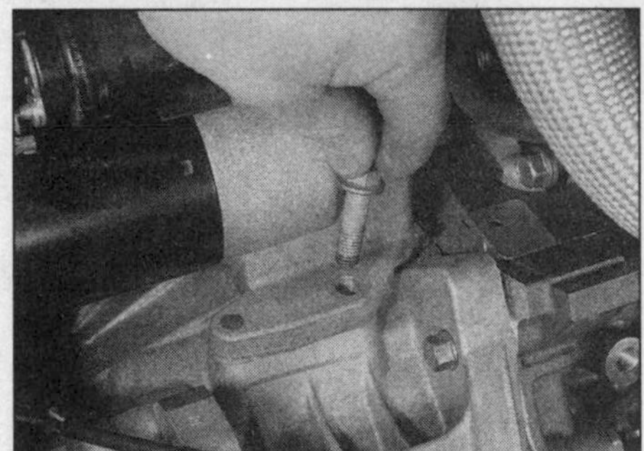
9.13a Unscrew the mounting bolts . . .

9.13b . . . and withdraw the starter motor from the transmission

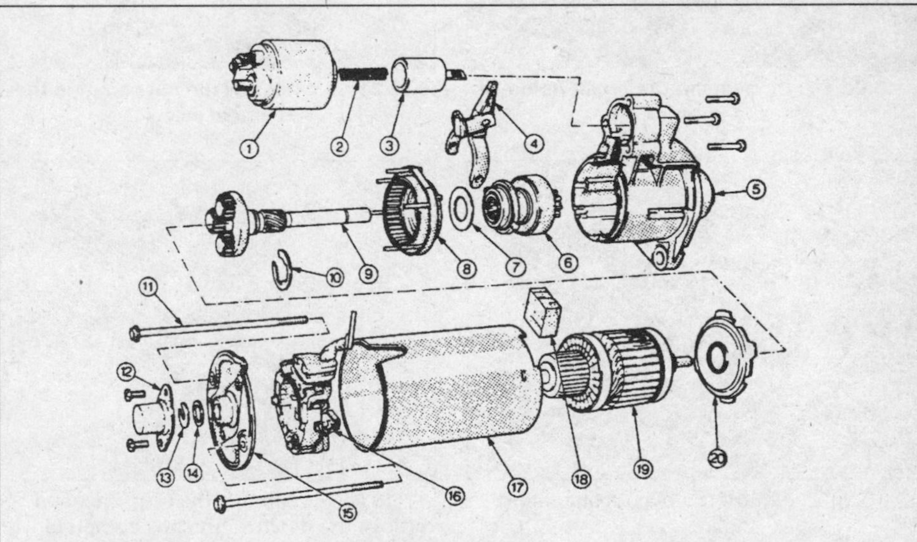

10.1 Exploded view of the Bosch DW starter motor (4-cylinder models)

1 Solenoid
2 Spring
3 Plunger
4 Engaging lever
5 Drive end housing
6 Drive pinion and clutch
7 Spacer
8 Ring gear and carrier
9 Output shaft and planet gear unit
10 Circlip
11 Screw
12 End cap
13 C-clip
14 Shim
15 Commutator end housing
16 Brushplate
17 Yoke
18 Rubber block
19 Armature
20 Retaining plate

10.2a Remove the two screws to release the end cap. Withdraw the gasket and prise out the C-clip, noting any shims fitted to control armature endfloat . . .

10.2b . . . unscrew the two screws . . .

10.2c . . . and withdraw the end housing . . .

If in doubt about the condition of the brushes and springs, compare them with new components.

4 Clean the commutator with a petrol-moistened cloth, then check for signs of scoring, burning, excessive wear or severe pitting. If worn or damaged, the commutator should be attended to by an auto-electrician.

5 Refitting is the reverse of the removal procedure.

Solenoid renewal

6 Unscrew the nut, noting the lockwasher(s), and disconnect the motor link from the solenoid terminal.

7 Unscrew the two bolts securing the solenoid to the motor drive end housing.

8 Release the solenoid plunger from the starter engaging lever, then withdraw the solenoid, noting the spring.

9 Refitting is the reverse of the removal procedure. Clean the solenoid, its plunger and the motor/solenoid mating surfaces carefully, and lubricate the plunger/starter engaging lever surfaces with a smear of grease.

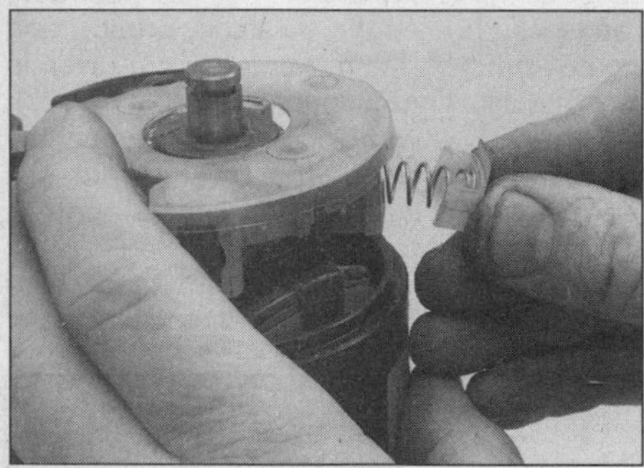

10.2d . . . then unclip the brush holders and springs . . .

10.2e . . . unscrew the nut securing the solenoid link . . .

10.2f . . . withdraw the negative brushes . . .

10.2g . . . lift off the plastic insulating plate . . .

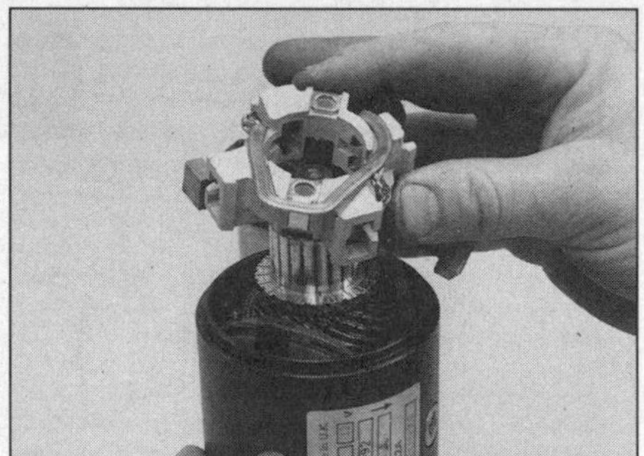

10.2h . . . remove the brushbox and remove the positive brushes complete with the bus bar . . .

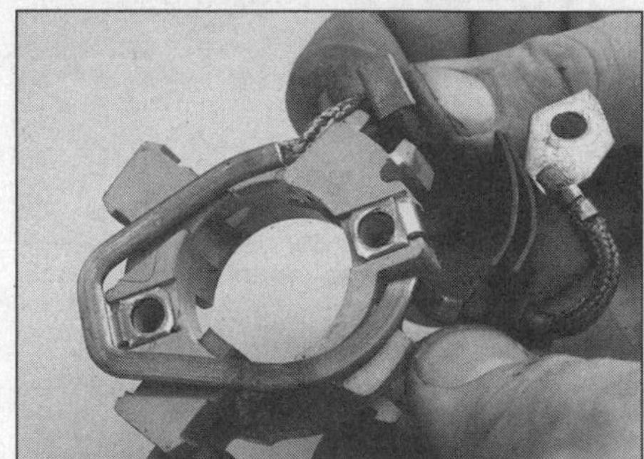

10.2i . . . note how the bus bar is engaged on the brushbox before removing it

Chapter 5 Part B: Ignition system

Contents

Degrees of difficulty

Easy, suitable for novice with little experience 	**Fairly easy,** suitable for beginner with some experience 	**Fairly difficult,** suitable for competent DIY mechanic 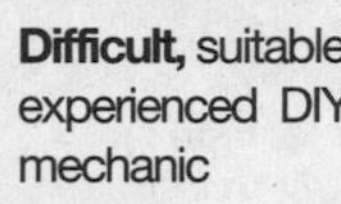	**Difficult,** suitable for experienced DIY mechanic 	**Very difficult,** suitable for expert DIY or professional

Specifications

Ignition timing

Nominal	10° ± 2° BTDC

Note: *Ignition timing is under control of ECU - it may vary constantly at idle speed, and is not adjustable.*

Ignition coil

Output	37.0 kilovolts (minimum)
Primary resistances - measured at coil connector terminal pins	0.50 ± 0.05 ohms

Torque wrench setting

Torque wrench setting	Nm	lbf ft
Ignition coil bracket-to-cylinder head screws (4-cylinder models)	21	15

1 Ignition system - general information and precautions

General information

The ignition system includes the ignition switch, the battery, the crankshaft speed/position sensor, the coil, the primary (low tension/LT) and secondary (high tension/HT) wiring circuits, and the spark plugs. On models with automatic transmission, a separate ignition module is also fitted, its functions being incorporated in the ECU on models with manual transmission. The ignition system is controlled by the engine management system's Electronic Control Unit (ECU). Using data provided by information sensors which monitor various engine functions (such as engine speed and piston position, intake air mass and temperature, engine coolant temperature, etc.), the ECU ensures a perfectly-timed spark under all conditions (see Chapter 4A). **Note:** *The ignition timing is under the full control of the ECU, and cannot be adjusted - see Chapter 4A for further details.*

Precautions

When working on the ignition system, take the following precautions:

a) Do not keep the ignition switch on for more than 10 seconds if the engine will not start.

b) If a separate tachometer is ever required for servicing work, consult a dealer service department before buying a tachometer for use with this vehicle - some tachometers may be incompatible with this ignition system - and always connect it in accordance with the equipment manufacturer's instructions.

c) Never connect the ignition coil terminals to earth. This could result in damage to the coil and/or the ECU or ignition module (whichever is fitted).

d) Do not disconnect the battery when the engine is running.

e) Make sure that the ignition module (where fitted) is properly earthed.

f) Refer to the warning at the beginning of the next Section concerning HT voltage.

2 Ignition system - testing

Warning: Because of the high voltage generated by the ignition system, extreme care should be taken whenever an operation is performed involving ignition components. This not only includes the ignition module/ECU, coil and spark plug (HT) leads, but related components such as electrical connectors, tachometer and other test equipment also.

Note: *This is an initial check of the "ignition part" of the main engine management system, to be carried out as part of the preliminary checks of the complete engine management system (see Chapter 4A).*

1 If the engine turns over but won't start, disconnect the (HT) lead from any spark plug, and attach it to a calibrated tester (available at most automotive accessory shops). Connect the clip on the tester to a good earth - a bolt or metal bracket on the engine. If you're unable to obtain a calibrated ignition tester, have the check carried out by a Ford dealer service department or similar. Any other form of testing (such as jumping a spark from the end of an HT lead to earth) is not recommended, because of the risk of personal injury, or of damage to the ECU/ignition module (see notes above and in Section 1).

2 Crank the engine and watch the end of the tester to see if bright blue, well-defined sparks occur.

3 If sparks occur, sufficient voltage is reaching the plug to fire it. Repeat the check at the remaining plugs, to ensure that all leads are sound and that the coil is serviceable.

3.8 HT leads on the ignition coil (5/1998-on 2.0 litre 4-cylinder engine)

3.9 Unplug the coil wiring (A), suppressor connector (B), and spark plug/HT leads (C), then remove screws (D), and undo Torx-type screws (E) to release ignition coil assembly

However, the plugs themselves may be fouled or faulty, so remove and check them as described in Chapter 1.

4 If no sparks or intermittent sparks occur, the spark plug lead(s) may be defective - check them as described in Chapter 1.

5 If there's still no spark, check the coil's electrical connector, to make sure it's clean and tight. Check for full battery voltage to the coil at the connector's centre terminal. The coil is earthed through the ECU - do not attempt to check this. Check the coil itself (see Section 3). Make any necessary repairs, then repeat the check again.

6 The remainder of the system checks should be left to a dealer service department or other qualified repair facility, as there is a chance that the ECU may be damaged if tests are not performed properly.

3 Ignition coil - check, removal and refitting

Warning: Because of the high voltage generated by the ignition system, extreme care should be taken whenever an operation is performed involving ignition components. This not only includes the ignition module/ECU, coil and spark plug (HT) leads, but related components such as electrical connectors, tachometer and other test equipment also.

Check

1 Having checked that full battery voltage is available at the centre terminal of the coil's electrical connector (see Section 2), disconnect the battery negative (earth) lead - see Chapter 5A.

2 Unplug the coil's electrical connector, if not already disconnected.

3 Using an ohmmeter, measure the resistance of the coil's primary windings, connecting the meter between the coil's terminal pins as follows. Measure first from one outer pin to the centre pin, then from the other outer pin to the centre. Compare your readings with the coil primary resistance listed in the Specifications Section at the beginning of this Chapter.

4 Disconnect the spark plug (HT) leads - note their connections or label them carefully, as described in Chapter 1. Use the meter to check that there is continuity (ie, a resistance corresponding to that of the coil secondary winding) between each pair of (HT) lead terminals. On 4-cylinder models, coil terminals 1 and 2 are connected by their secondary windings as are terminals 3 and 4. On V6 models, terminals 1 and 5 are connected, terminals 3 and 4 are connected and terminals 2 and 6 are connected. Now switch to the highest resistance scale, and check that there is no continuity between either pair of terminals and the other - ie, there should be infinite resistance between terminals 1 and 2, or 4 and 3 - and between any terminal and earth.

5 If either of the above tests yield resistance values outside the specified amount, or results other than those described, renew the coil. Any further testing should be left to a dealer service department or other qualified repair facility.

3.13a Disconnecting the wiring from the suppressor . . .

Removal and refitting

4-cylinder models

Note: *On 4-cylinder models, the ignition coil is mounted on a bracket located at the rear of the cylinder head.*

6 Disconnect the battery negative (earth) lead (see Chapter 5A).

7 Remove the air mass meter and resonator - refer to Chapter 4A.

8 Unplug the electrical connector from each side of the coil, then disconnect the spark plug (HT) leads - note their connections or label them carefully, as described in Chapter 1 **(see illustration)**.

9 On pre-1998 models, undo the two screws securing the EGR pipe to the coil bracket, then remove the coil mounting (Torx-type) screws. Withdraw the coil assembly from the cylinder head **(see illustration)**.

10 The suppressor can be unbolted from the mounting bracket, if required; note that the coil and bracket are only available as a single unit.

11 Refitting is the reverse of the removal procedure. Ensure that the spark plug (HT) leads are correctly reconnected, and tighten the coil screws securely.

V6 models

Note: *On V6 models, the ignition coil is mounted on the rear valve cover.*

12 Disconnect the battery negative (earth) lead (see Chapter 5A).

13 Disconnect and unclip the wiring from the ignition coil and suppressor **(see illustrations)**. If necessary, remove the EGR valve vacuum regulator solenoid from the upper inlet manifold.

14 Note their location, then disconnect the spark plug (HT) leads from the ignition coil. Squeeze the locking tabs, and carefully twist and lift the wires off the coil **(see illustration)**.

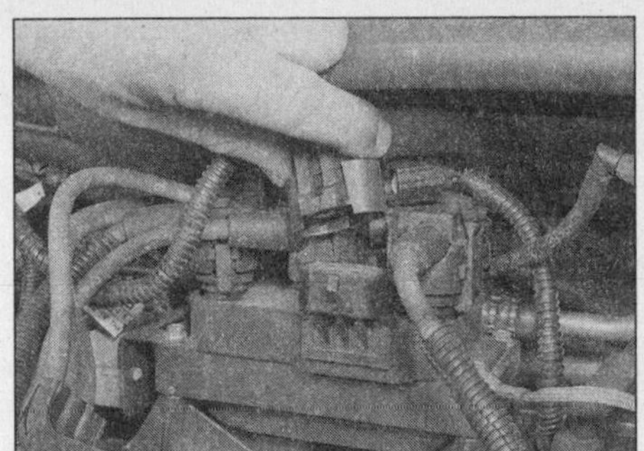

3.13b . . . and ignition coil

3.14a Spark plug leads on the ignition coil

3.14b Each HT lead is marked with its corresponding cylinder number

3.15a An earth wire is attached to one of the ignition coil mounting bolts

Label the wires for location to ensure correct refitting. Each lead is marked with its corresponding cylinder number **(see illustration)**.

15 Unscrew the mounting screws and remove the coil, noting that an earth wire is attached to one of the mounting bolts and the suppressor is attached to two of the bolts **(see illustrations)**.

16 Refitting is a reversal of removal. Make sure the earth wire is attached to one of the coil mounting screws. Also, ensure that the spark plug (HT) leads are connected correctly.

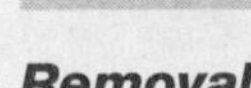

3.15b Removing the suppressor

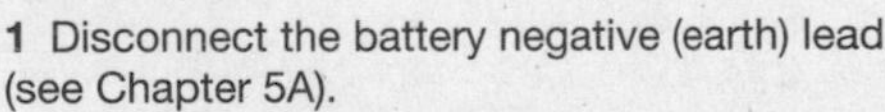

4 Ignition module (automatic transmission models only) - removal and refitting

Removal

1 Disconnect the battery negative (earth) lead (see Chapter 5A).

2 If better access is required, remove the resonator (see Chapter 4A).

3 Unplug the electrical connector from the module **(see illustration)**.

4 Remove the retaining screws, and detach the module from the bulkhead mounting bracket.

Refitting

5 Refitting is a reversal of removal.

5 Ignition timing - checking

1 The ignition timing is controlled entirely by the ECU (acting with the ignition module, on models with automatic transmission), and cannot be adjusted. The value quoted in the Specifications Section of this Chapter is for reference only, and may vary significantly if "checked" by simply connecting a timing light to the system and running the engine at idle speed.

2 Not only can the ignition timing not be adjusted, it cannot be checked either, except with the use of special diagnostic equipment - this makes it a task for a Ford dealer service department.

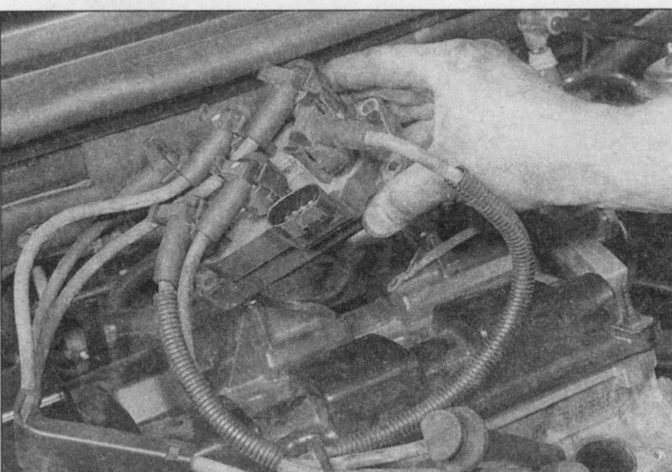

3.15c Removing the ignition coil (note inlet manifold already removed)

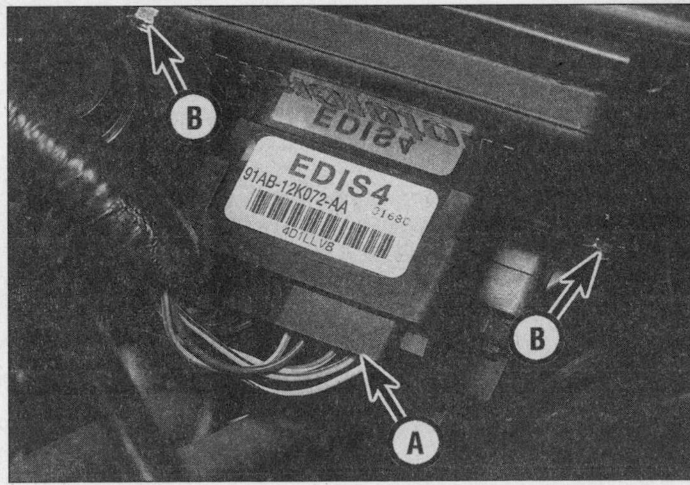

4.3 Separate ignition module is fitted to automatic transmission models only - note electrical connector (A) and retaining screws (B)

5.3 Service connector (A) mounted on engine compartment bulkhead is fitted with "plug-in bridge" (B) to set engine to use (unleaded) petrol of 95 RON octane rating

3 Owners who are taking their vehicles abroad should note that the ignition system is set for the engine to use petrol of 95 RON octane rating by fitting a "plug-in bridge" to the service connector on the engine compartment bulkhead **(see illustration)**. Removing the "plug-in bridge" retards the ignition timing - by an unspecified value - to allow the engine to run on 91 RON fuel. This grade of fuel is the "Regular" or "Normal" widely used abroad, but not at present available in the UK. If you are taking the vehicle abroad, seek the advice of a Ford dealer (or of one of the motoring organisations). This will ensure that you are familiar with the grades of fuel you are likely to find (and the sometimes confusing names for those grades), and that the vehicle is set correctly at all times for the fuel used. **Note:** *The octane ratings mentioned above are both, of course, for* ***unleaded*** *petrol. Do not use leaded petrol at any time in a vehicle equipped with a catalytic converter.*

Chapter 6
Clutch

Contents

Degrees of difficulty

Easy, suitable for novice with little experience 

Fairly easy, suitable for beginner with some experience 

Fairly difficult, suitable for competent DIY mechanic

Difficult, suitable for experienced DIY mechanic

Very difficult, suitable for expert DIY or professional

Specifications

Clutch

Type	Single dry plate. Cable-operated on early models, hydraulically-operated from approximately 1994 onwards
Disc diameter:	
1.6 and 1.8 litre engine	210 mm
2.0 litre engine	228 mm
V6 engine	240 mm
Lining thickness (new):	
Cable clutch	8.8 mm
Hydraulic clutch	7.3 mm
Pedal stroke:	
Cable-operated clutch:	
Right-hand-drive models	155 ± 5.0 mm
Left-hand-drive models	145 ± 5.0 mm
Hydraulically-operated clutch	135 ± 5.0 mm

Torque wrench settings	Nm	lbf ft
Clutch master/slave cylinder mounting nuts/bolts	10	7
Clutch pressure plate to flywheel	29	21
Clutch release lever clamp bolt	25	18

1 General information

Vehicles with manual transmission are fitted with a pedal-operated single dry plate clutch system. When the clutch pedal is depressed, effort is transmitted to the clutch release mechanism either mechanically, by means of a cable, or hydraulically, via a master cylinder. The release mechanism transfers effort to the pressure plate diaphragm spring, which withdraws from the flywheel and releases the driven plate.

The flywheel is mounted on the crankshaft, with the pressure plate bolted to it. Removal of the flywheel is described in Chapter 2A or 2B.

Since many of the procedures covered in this Chapter involve working under the vehicle, make sure that it is securely supported on axle stands placed on a firm, level floor (see "*Jacking and vehicle support*").

Warning: On models with a hydraulic clutch, the fluid used in the system is brake fluid, which is poisonous. Take care to keep it off bare skin, and in particular not to get splashes in your eyes. The fluid also attacks paintwork, and may discolour carpets, etc - keep spillages to a minimum, and wash any off immediately with cold water. Finally, brake fluid is highly inflammable, and should be handled with the same care as petrol.

6

2 Clutch - description and checking

Description

1 All manual transmission models are equipped with a single dry plate diaphragm spring clutch assembly. The cover assembly consists of a steel cover (dowelled and bolted to the rear face of the flywheel), the pressure plate, and a diaphragm spring.

2 The clutch disc is free to slide along the splines of the gearbox input shaft, and is held in position between the flywheel and the pressure plate by the pressure of the diaphragm spring. Friction lining material is riveted to the clutch disc (driven plate), which has a spring-cushioned hub, to absorb transmission shocks and help ensure a smooth take-up of the drive.

3 The clutch release bearing contacts the fingers of the diaphragm spring. Depressing the clutch pedal pushes the release bearing against the diaphragm fingers, so moving the centre of the diaphragm spring inwards. As the centre of the spring is pushed inwards, the outside of the spring pivots outwards, so moving the pressure plate backwards and disengaging its grip on the clutch disc.

4 When the pedal is released, the diaphragm spring forces the pressure plate back into contact with the friction linings on the clutch disc. The disc is now firmly held between the pressure plate and the flywheel, thus transmitting engine power to the gearbox.

5 On early Mondeos, the clutch is actuated by a cable. The cable runs from the pedal to a release arm, mounted on the transmission housing. Depressing the clutch pedal actuates the release arm, and the arm pushes the release bearing against the diaphragm fingers.

6 Unlike some other models in the Ford range, the cable clutch is not of the self-adjusting type, although it uses the same serrated quadrant fitted to models with a self-adjusting pedal. The normal self-adjusting spring-tensioned pawl is not fitted to the quadrant, although the pedal moves the quadrant when it contacts the end stops. This arrangement means that pedal adjustment must be carried out manually.

7 Later Mondeos (from approximately 1994 onwards) have a hydraulically-operated clutch. A master cylinder is mounted below the clutch pedal, and takes its hydraulic fluid supply from a separate chamber in the brake fluid reservoir. Depressing the clutch pedal operates the master cylinder pushrod, and the fluid pressure is transferred along the fluid lines to a slave cylinder mounted inside the bellhousing. The slave cylinder is incorporated into the release bearing - when the slave cylinder operates, the release bearing moves against the diaphragm spring fingers and disengages the clutch.

8 The hydraulic clutch offers several advantages over the cable type previously used - it is self-adjusting, requires less pedal effort, and is less subject to wear problems.

Checking

9 The following checks may be performed to diagnose a clutch problem:

a) *On models with a cable clutch, first check the entire length of the clutch cable in the engine compartment for obvious damage. Check also that it is located correctly, without any sharp turns.*

b) *Similarly, on models with a hydraulic clutch, check the fluid lines from the clutch master cylinder into the bellhousing for damage, signs of leakage, or for kinks or dents which might restrict fluid flow.*

c) *To check "clutch spin down time", run the engine at normal idle speed with the transmission in neutral (clutch pedal up). Disengage the clutch (pedal down), wait several seconds, then engage reverse. No grinding noise should be heard. A grinding noise would most likely indicate a problem in the pressure plate or the clutch disc. Remember, however, that the transmission reverse gear has synchromesh fitted to it, so the probable symptom of a clutch fault would be a slight rearwards movement (or attempted movement) of the vehicle. If the check is made on level ground with the handbrake released, the movement would be more noticeable.*

d) *To check for complete clutch release, run the engine at idle, and hold the clutch pedal approximately half an inch from the floor. Shift between 1st gear and reverse several times. If the shift is not smooth, or if the vehicle attempts to move forwards or backwards, component failure is indicated. Check the pedal adjustment as described in Section 3.*

e) *On models with a hydraulic clutch, slow or poor operation may be due to air being present in the fluid. The system can be bled of air as described in Section 10.*

f) *Check the clutch pedal for excessive wear of the bushes, and for any obstructions which may restrict the pedal movement.*

3.4 Clutch pedal stroke (A)

3 Clutch adjustment - check

Cable-operated clutch

1 If this check is being made after fitting a new clutch cable, the pedal should be depressed fully 10 times first.

2 Fully depress and hold down the clutch pedal, then place a steel rule against the bulkhead, and measure and record the distance to the middle of the rubber pad (dimension "C").

3 Release the pedal, and measure the distance from the bulkhead to the middle of the rubber pad again (dimension "B"). Do not lift the pedal when making the measurement.

4 Subtract dimension "C" from dimension "B" to determine the clutch pedal stroke - dimension "A" **(see illustration)**:

"A" (stroke) = "B" (released dimension) minus "C" (depressed dimension)

5 Check that the dimension is within the tolerance given in the Specifications. If adjustment is required, proceed as follows.

6 Remove the air cleaner assembly as described in Chapter 4A.

7 Loosen the locknut on the clutch cable adjuster sleeve near the release arm on the transmission **(see illustration)**. Turn the sleeve until the correct clutch pedal stroke is obtained. On completion, tighten the locknut. Refit the air cleaner assembly as described in Chapter 4A.

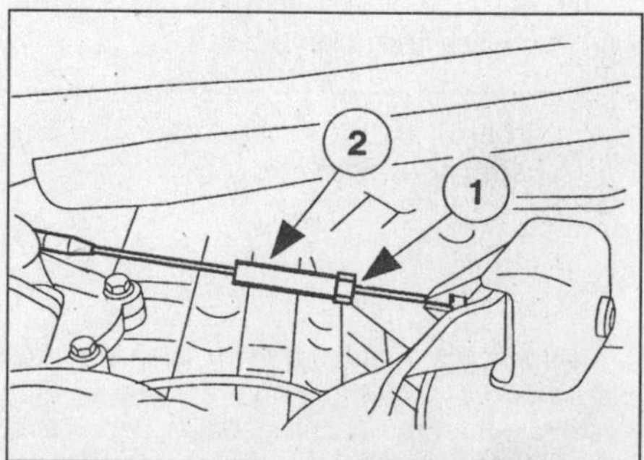

3.7 Locknut (1) and adjustment sleeve (2) for the clutch pedal stroke adjustment

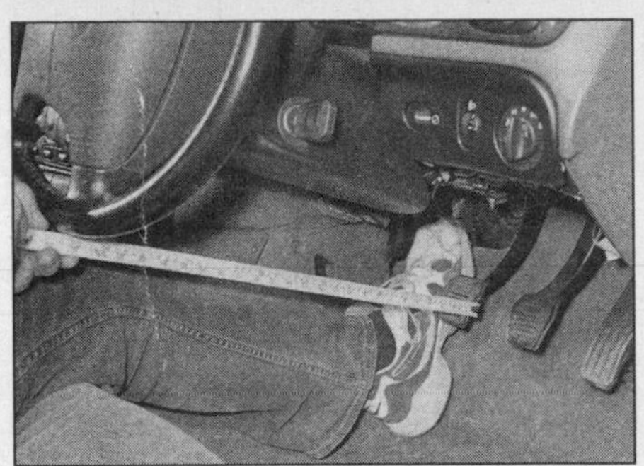

3.10 To obtain the pedal stroke, measure from steering wheel to pedal with the pedal released . . .

3.11 . . . and with it fully depressed

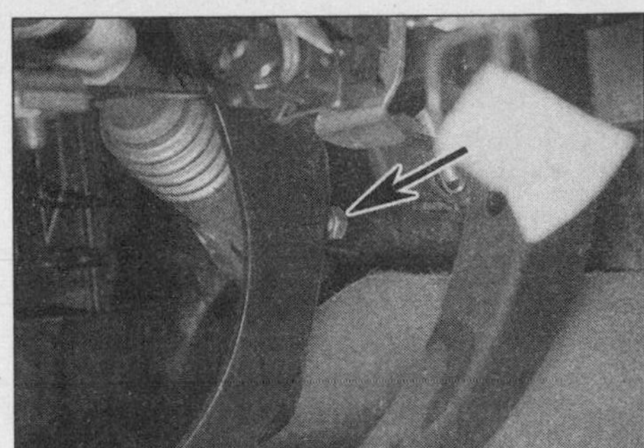

3.14a Clutch pedal stop bolt (arrowed)

Hydraulically-operated clutch

8 Turn the steering wheel (from the straight-ahead position) to the left by about 30°.

9 Using tape or a cable-tie, attach the end lip of a measuring tape to the clutch pedal rubber. Alternatively, have an assistant hold the measuring tape in place - either way, make sure that the end of the tape does not move from one measurement to the next.

10 Without touching the pedal, read off and record the distance measured from the pedal to the front of the steering wheel rim (dimension "C") **(see illustration)**.

11 Now press the pedal down to its stop, and record the new distance (dimension "B") **(see illustration)**. Make sure that the pedal action is not hindered by the carpets or floormats, or by incorrect fitting of the master cylinder.

12 The pedal stroke "A" is obtained by subtracting dimension "C" from dimension "B":

"A" (stroke) = "B" (depressed dimension) minus "C" (released dimension)

13 Check that the dimension is within the tolerance given in the Specifications. If adjustment is required, proceed as follows.

14 Loosen the locknut on the clutch pedal stop bolt (on the master cylinder mounting bracket). Turn the stop bolt in or out to alter the pedal stroke as required **(see illustrations)**. On completion, tighten the locknut securely.

3.14b Adjusting the clutch pedal stroke

4.3 Rubber cushion (arrowed) on the end of the outer cable

4 Clutch cable - removal and refitting

Removal

1 Remove the air cleaner assembly as described in Chapter 4A.

2 Disengage the clutch cable from the release arm, by gripping the inner cable with pliers and pulling it forwards to disengage the cable nipple from the release arm. Take care not to damage the cable, if it is to be re-used.

3 Disengage the outer cable from the support lug on top of the gearbox bellhousing. Note the rubber cushion on the end of the outer cable **(see illustration)**.

4 Working inside the vehicle, remove the facia lower trim panel from beneath the steering column for access to the clutch pedal. Refer to Chapter 11, Section 29 if necessary.

5 Disconnect the clutch pedal return spring from the pedal and bracket. Note where the spring is attached to the bracket, as the small hole is not easy to see.

6 Unhook the inner cable from the pedal quadrant **(see illustration)**.

7 Pull the cable through the aperture in the bulkhead. Detach the cable from the support stay near the brake servo unit, and withdraw it from the engine compartment **(see illustration)**.

Refitting

8 To refit the cable, thread it through the bulkhead from the engine compartment side. Fit the inner cable over the quadrant, engaging the end stop to secure it **(see illustration)**.

9 Reconnect the pedal return spring, making sure that it is correctly fitted in the small hole.

10 Reconnect the cable at the transmission end, passing it through the support lug on the

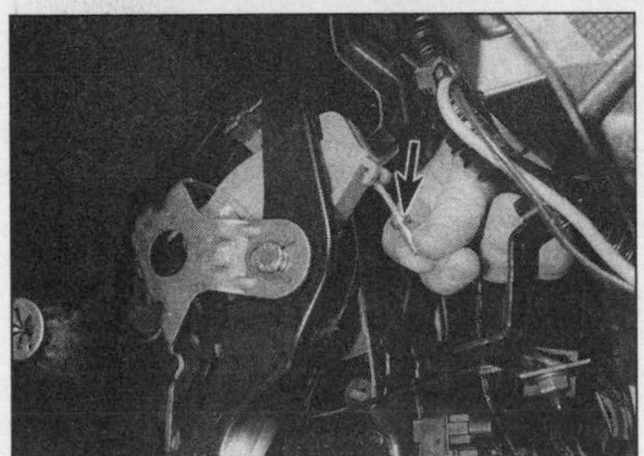

4.6 Unhooking the clutch inner cable (arrowed) from the pedal segment

4.7 Clutch cable support stay (arrowed) located next to the brake servo unit

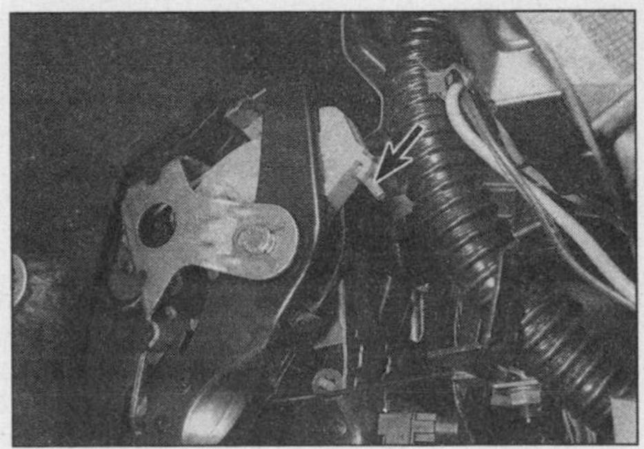

4.8 Inner cable (arrowed) fitted to the pedal segment

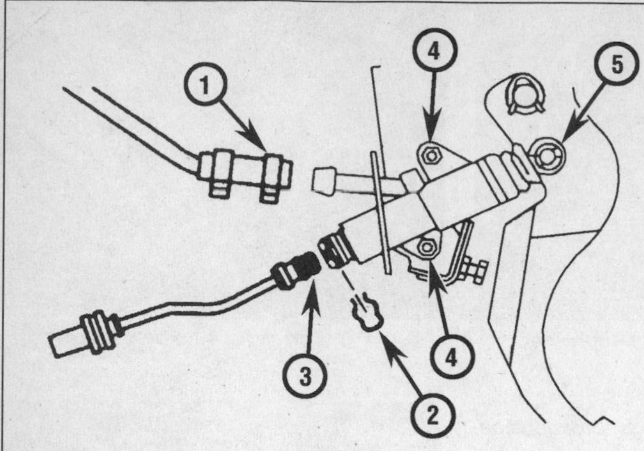

5.6 Clutch master cylinder and related fittings

1 *Fluid supply (low-pressure) hose*
2 *Hose retaining clip*
3 *High-pressure fluid pipe*
4 *Master cylinder mounting nuts*
5 *Master cylinder-to-pedal circlip*

top of the transmission, and engaging it with the release arm.

11 Locate the rubber grommet in the clutch cable support stay. Renew the grommet if necessary.

12 Adjust the pedal stroke as described in Section 3.

13 Check the operation of the clutch.

14 Refit the trim panel under the steering column.

15 Refit the air cleaner assembly as described in Chapter 4A.

5 Clutch master cylinder - removal and refitting

Note: *Refer to the warning in Section 1 concerning the dangers of hydraulic fluid before proceeding.*

Removal

1 Disconnect the battery negative lead, and position the lead away from the terminal.

2 Working inside the vehicle, move the driver's seat fully to the rear, to allow maximum working area. Remove the fasteners securing the driver's side lower facia trim panel, and remove the panel from the car.

3 Before proceeding, anticipate some spillage of hydraulic (brake) fluid - most will occur on the engine compartment side. However, if sufficient fluid comes into contact with the carpet, it may be discoloured or worse. Place a good quantity of clean rags below the clutch pedal, and have a container ready in the engine compartment.

4 Remove the brake fluid reservoir cap, and then tighten it down over a piece of polythene or cling film, to obtain an airtight seal. This may help to reduce the spillage of fluid when the lines are disconnected.

5 To gain access to the fluid connections where they pass through the engine compartment bulkhead, move any wiring and hoses to one side as necessary. On four-cylinder models, remove the air cleaner inlet hose and plenum chamber as described in Chapter 4A. On V6 models, it may be necessary to remove the upper section of the inlet manifold as described in Chapter 2B.

6 Working in the engine compartment, release the hose clips and disconnect the (upper) fluid supply hose from the clutch master cylinder **(see illustration)**. Plug or clamp the hose end if possible, to reduce fluid loss and to prevent dirt entry.

7 To remove the (lower) fluid pipe, pull out the spring clip to the side, then pull the pipe fitting out of the base of the cylinder. Again, plug or tape over the pipe end, to avoid losing fluid, and to prevent dirt entry.

8 Returning to the driver's footwell, prise off the circlip which secures the top of the master cylinder to the clutch pedal.

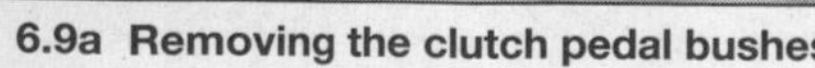

6.9a Removing the clutch pedal bushes

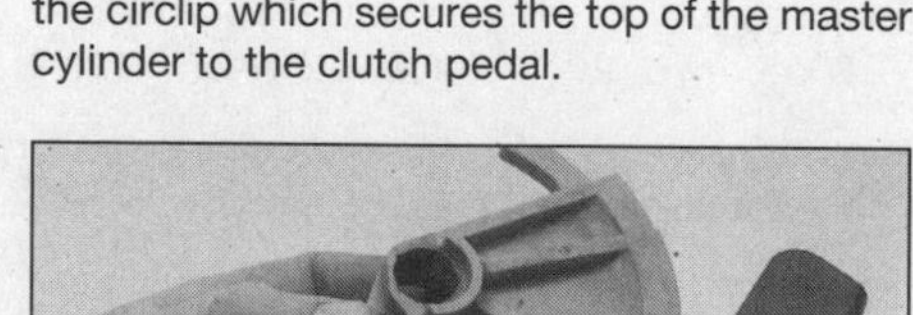

6.9b Removing the cable quadrant from the clutch pedal

9 Remove the two master cylinder mounting nuts, and withdraw the master cylinder through the bulkhead and from the footwell, taking care to avoid spilling any remaining fluid onto the interior fittings.

Refitting

10 Refitting is a reversal of removal, noting the following points:

a) Tighten the mounting nuts to the specified torque.
b) Use new clips when refitting the fluid feed hose.
c) Refit any components removed for access.
d) Remove the polythene from under the fluid reservoir cap, and top-up the fluid level (see "Weekly checks").
e) Refer to Section 10 and bleed the clutch hydraulic system.
f) If the fluid level in the reservoir fell sufficiently, it may be necessary to bleed the braking system also - refer to Chapter 9.

6 Clutch pedal - removal and refitting

Removal

1 Remove the brake pedal (see Chapter 9).

2 Remove the blue nylon spacer from the pedal pivot shaft.

3 Unhook and remove the clutch pedal return spring.

Cable-operated clutch

4 Remove the air cleaner assembly as described in Chapter 4A.

5 Disconnect the clutch cable from the release arm as described in Section 4.

6 Working inside the vehicle, release the inner cable from the pedal quadrant on the clutch pedal.

Hydraulically-operated clutch

7 Prise off the circlip which secures the top of the clutch master cylinder to the clutch pedal.

All models

8 Withdraw the pedal pivot shaft through the mounting bracket, and remove the pedal together with the blue nylon spacer. Note that this spacer is additional to the spacer located next to the brake pedal.

9 With the pedal removed, prise out the bushes from each side. Also remove the rubber pad. On models with the cable-operated clutch, remove the cable quadrant **(see illustrations)**. Renew the components as necessary.

Refitting

10 Prior to refitting the pedal, apply a little grease to the pivot shaft and pedal bushes.

11 Refitting is a reversal of the removal procedure, making sure that the bushes and spacers are correctly located.

12 Adjust the clutch pedal stroke as described in Section 3.

7 Clutch components - removal, inspection and refitting

Warning: Dust created by clutch wear and deposited on the clutch components may contain asbestos, which is a health hazard. DO NOT blow it out with compressed air, and do not inhale any of it. DO NOT use petrol or petroleum-based solvents to clean off the dust. Brake system cleaner or methylated spirit should be used to flush the dust into a suitable receptacle. After the clutch components are wiped clean with rags, dispose of the contaminated rags and cleaner in a sealed, marked container.

Removal

1 Access to the clutch may be gained in one of two ways. The engine/transmission unit can be removed, as described in Chapter 2C, and the transmission separated from the engine on the bench. Alternatively, the engine may be left in the vehicle and the transmission removed independently, as described in Chapter 7A or 7B. If the latter course of action is taken, note that the transmission need only be moved to the left of the engine compartment - it is not necessary to remove it completely **(see illustration)**.

2 Having separated the transmission from the engine, check if there are any marks identifying the relation of the clutch cover to the flywheel. If not, make your own marks using a dab of paint or a scriber **(see illustration)**. These marks will be used if the original cover is refitted, and will help to maintain the balance of the unit. A new cover may be fitted in any position allowed by the locating dowels.

3 Unscrew and remove the six clutch cover retaining bolts, working in a diagonal sequence, and slackening the bolts only a turn at a time **(see illustration)**. If necessary, the flywheel may be held stationary using a wide-bladed screwdriver, inserted in the teeth of the starter ring gear and resting against part of the cylinder block.

4 Ease the clutch cover off its locating dowels. Be prepared to catch the clutch disc, which will drop out as the cover is removed **(see illustration)**. Note which way round the disc is fitted.

7.1 Clutch is accessible with the transmission moved to one side, on four-cylinder models

Inspection

5 The most common problem which occurs in the clutch is wear of the clutch disc (driven plate). However, all the clutch components should be inspected at this time, particularly if the engine has covered a high mileage. Unless the clutch components are known to be virtually new, it is worth renewing them all as a set (disc, pressure plate and release bearing). Renewing a worn clutch disc by itself is not always satisfactory, especially if the old disc was slipping and causing the pressure plate to overheat.

6 Examine the linings of the clutch disc for wear and loose rivets, and the disc hub and rim for distortion, cracks, broken torsion springs, and worn splines. The surface of the friction linings may be highly glazed, but as long as the friction material pattern can be clearly seen, and the rivet heads are at least 1 mm below the lining surface, this is satisfactory. The disc must be renewed if the lining thickness has worn down to, or just above, the level of the rivet heads.

7 If there is any sign of oil contamination, indicated by shiny black discoloration, the disc must be renewed, and the source of the contamination traced and rectified. This will be a leaking crankshaft oil seal or gearbox input shaft oil seal. The renewal procedure for the former is given in the relevant Part of Chapter 2. Renewal of the gearbox input shaft oil seal should be entrusted to a Ford dealer, as it involves dismantling the gearbox, and (where applicable) the renewal of the clutch release bearing guide tube, using a press.

8 Check the machined faces of the flywheel and pressure plate. If either is grooved, or heavily scored, renewal is necessary. The pressure plate must also be renewed if any cracks are apparent, or if the diaphragm spring is damaged or its pressure suspect. Pay particular attention to the tips of the spring fingers, where the release bearing acts upon them.

9 With the gearbox removed, it is also advisable to check the condition of the release bearing, as described in Section 8. Having got this far, it is almost certainly worth renewing it.

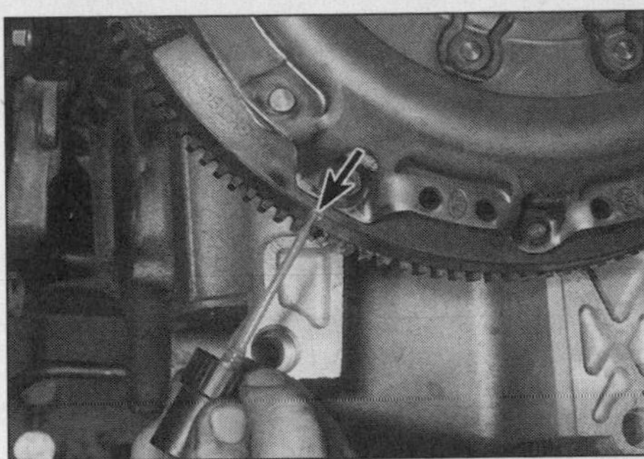

7.2 Marking the clutch cover and flywheel with a dab of paint (arrowed)

Refitting

10 It is important that no oil or grease is allowed to come into contact with the friction material of the clutch disc or the pressure plate and flywheel faces. To ensure this, it is advisable to refit the clutch assembly with clean hands, and to wipe down the pressure plate and flywheel faces with a clean dry rag before assembly begins.

11 Ford technicians use a special tool for centralising the clutch disc at this stage. The tool holds the disc centrally on the pressure plate, and locates in the middle of the diaphragm spring fingers. If the tool is not available, it will be necessary to centralise the disc after assembling the cover loosely on the flywheel, as described in the following paragraphs.

12 Place the clutch disc against the flywheel, ensuring that it is the right way round. It should be marked "FLYWHEEL SIDE", but if not, position it so that the raised hub with the cushion springs is facing away from the flywheel **(see illustration)**.

7.3 Unscrewing the clutch cover bolts

7.4 Removing the clutch cover and disc

7.12 "FLYWHEEL-SIDE" marking on the clutch disc

7.16 Using a clutch-aligning tool to centralise the clutch disc

13 Place the clutch cover over the dowels. Refit the retaining bolts, and tighten them finger-tight so that the clutch disc is gripped lightly, but can still be moved.

14 The clutch disc must now be centralised so that, when the engine and transmission are mated, the splines of the gearbox input shaft will pass through the splines in the centre of the clutch disc hub.

15 Centralisation can be carried out by inserting a round bar through the hole in the centre of the clutch disc, so that the end of the bar rests in the hole in the rear end of the crankshaft. Move the bar sideways or up and down, to move the clutch disc in whichever direction is necessary to achieve centralisation. Centralisation can then be checked by removing the bar and viewing the clutch disc hub in relation to the diaphragm spring fingers, or by viewing through the side apertures of the cover, and checking that the disc is central in relation to the outer edge of the pressure plate.

16 An alternative and more accurate method of centralisation is to use a commercially-available clutch-aligning tool, obtainable from most accessory shops **(see illustration)**.

17 Once the clutch is centralised, progressively tighten the cover bolts in a diagonal sequence to the torque setting given in the Specifications.

18 Ensure that the input shaft splines, clutch disc splines and release bearing guide sleeve are clean. Apply a thin smear of high melting-point grease to the input shaft splines and the release bearing guide sleeve.

19 Refit the transmission to the engine.

8 Clutch release bearing (and slave cylinder) - removal, inspection and refitting

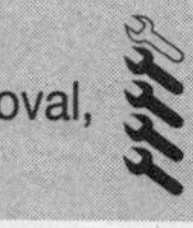

Removal

1 Separate the engine and transmission as described in the previous Section.

Cable-operated clutch

2 Withdraw the release bearing from its guide sleeve by turning the release arm **(see illustrations)**.

Hydraulically-operated clutch

3 The release bearing and slave cylinder are combined into one unit.

4 If not already done, remove the retaining clip and disconnect the quick-release fitting on the slave cylinder high-pressure fluid pipe **(see illustrations)**. Tape over or plug the open connections, to reduce fluid loss and to prevent dirt entry.

5 Remove the bleed screw dust cap, and prise out the grommet from the top of the transmission housing **(see illustrations)**.

8.2a Clutch release bearing in place on the guide sleeve

8.2b Release bearing removed from the transmission

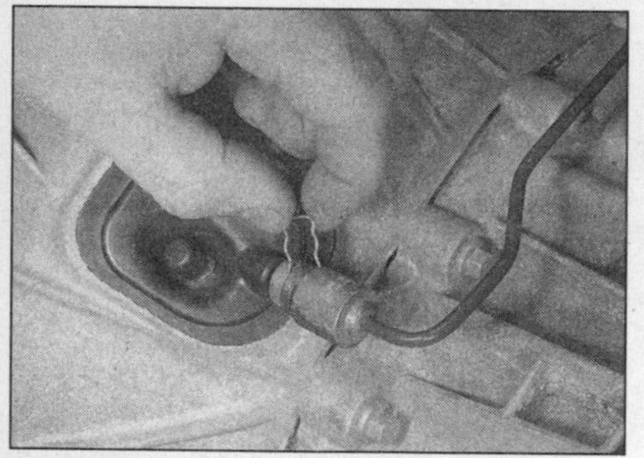

8.4a Remove the retaining clip . . .

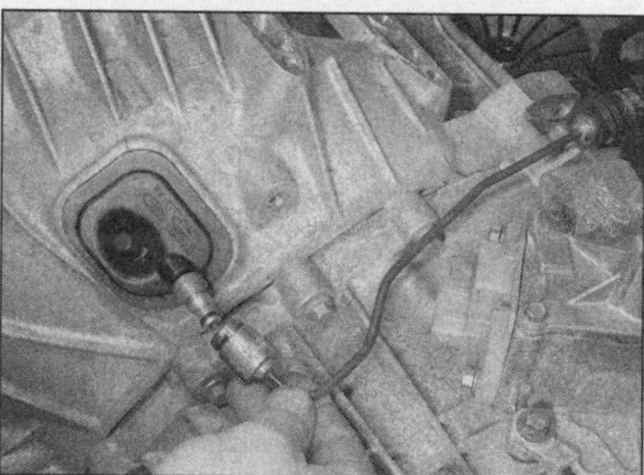

8.4b . . . and disconnect the high-pressure pipe from the slave cylinder

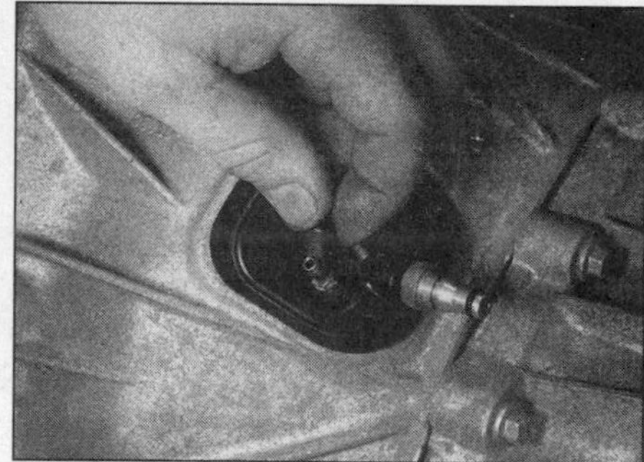

8.5a Take off the bleed screw cap . . .

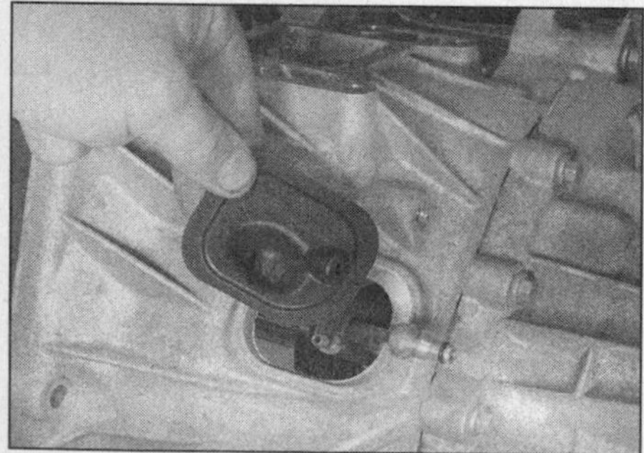

8.5b . . . then prise out the grommet from the transmission housing

8.6a Remove the three mounting bolts (arrowed) . . .

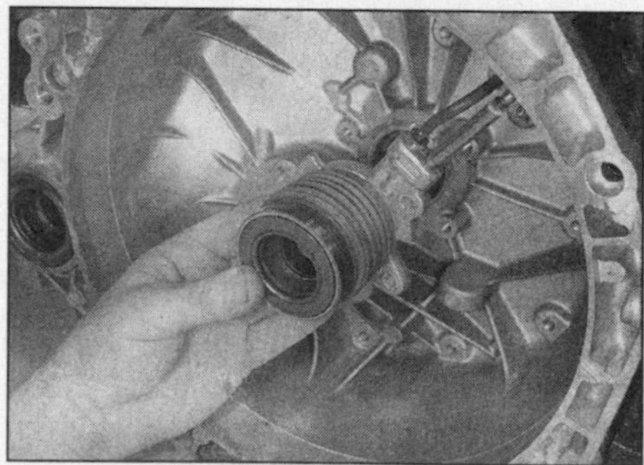

8.6b . . . and withdraw the slave cylinder/release bearing assembly

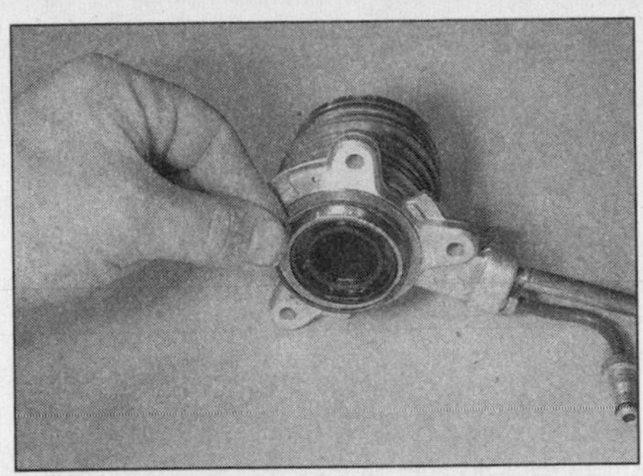

8.9a Check the condition of the large O-ring on the slave cylinder . . .

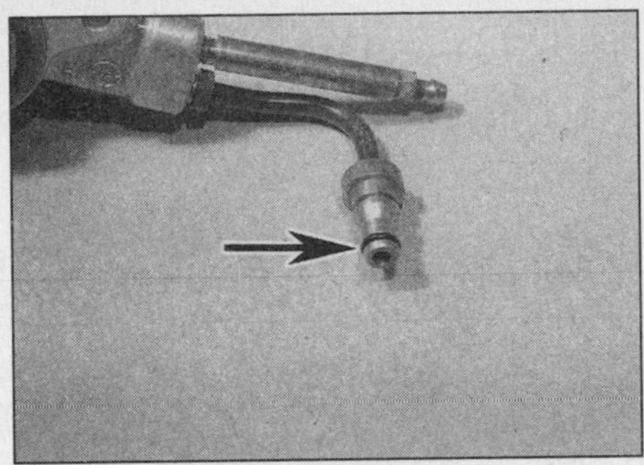

8.9b . . . and of the smaller pipe connection O-rings

6 Remove the three mounting bolts, and withdraw the slave cylinder and release bearing **(see illustrations)**.

Inspection

7 Check the bearing for smoothness of operation, and renew it if there is any sign of harshness or roughness as the bearing is spun. Do not attempt to dismantle, clean or lubricate the bearing.

8 As mentioned earlier, it is worth renewing the release bearing as a matter of course, unless it is known to be in perfect condition.

9 On models with the hydraulic clutch, check the condition of all O-ring seals, and renew if necessary **(see illustrations)**. Considering the difficulty in gaining access to some of the seals if they fail, it would be wise to renew these as a precaution.

Refitting

10 Refitting of the clutch release bearing is a reversal of the removal procedure, noting the following points:

a) On cable clutch models, make sure that the bearing is correctly located on the release arm fork. It is helpful to slightly lift the release arm while locating the bearing on its guide sleeve. Keep the fork in contact with the plastic shoulders on the bearing as the bearing is being located.

b) On hydraulically-operated clutch models, tighten the mounting bolts to the specified torque. Reconnect the fluid pipe, and bleed the system on completion.

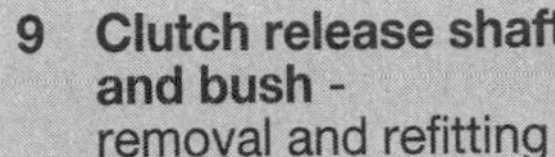

9 Clutch release shaft and bush - removal and refitting

Note: *This Section does not apply to models with the hydraulic clutch.*

Removal

1 Remove the clutch release bearing as described in the previous Section.

2 Unscrew the clamp bolt securing the release arm to the shaft. Mark the relative position of the shaft to the arm, then withdraw the arm from the shaft. The shaft has a master spline, to ensure that the arm is fitted correctly **(see illustrations)**.

3 Remove the protective cap from around the top of the release shaft splines, to allow access to the bush.

4 Extract the bush by gently levering it from the housing, using grips or a pair of screwdrivers **(see illustration)**, then lift it out over the splines of the shaft.

5 With the bush removed, the release shaft can be removed by lifting it from its lower bearing bore, manoeuvring it sideways and withdrawing it **(see illustration)**.

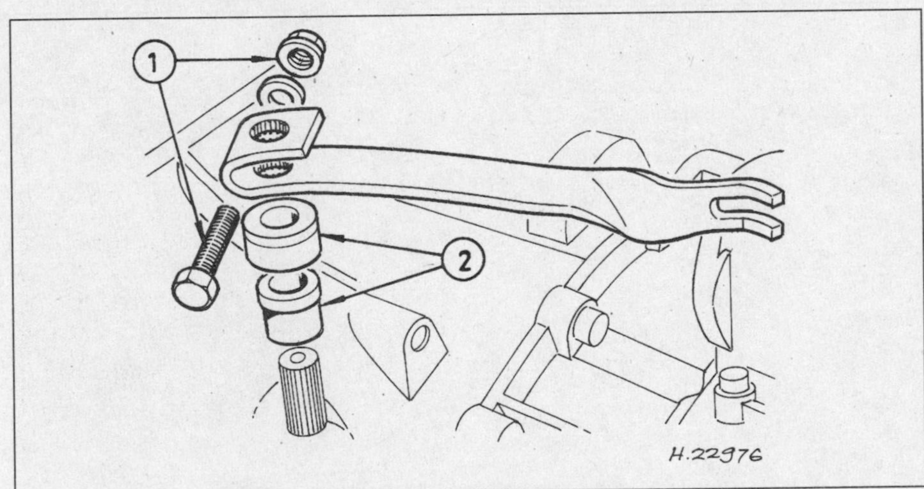

9.2a Clutch release arm removal

1 *Clamp bolt*
2 *Protective cap and bearing bush*

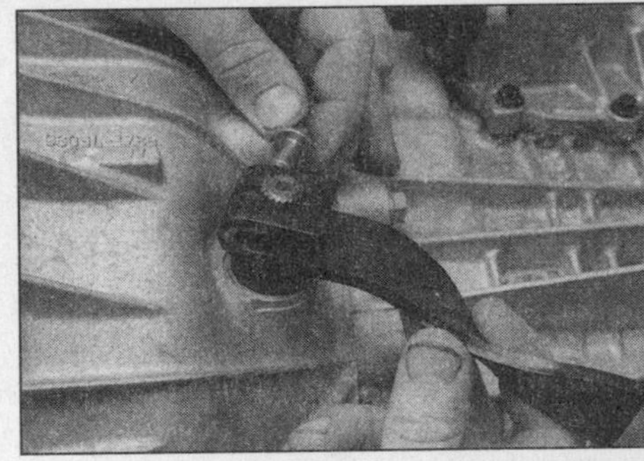

9.2b Removing the clamp bolt

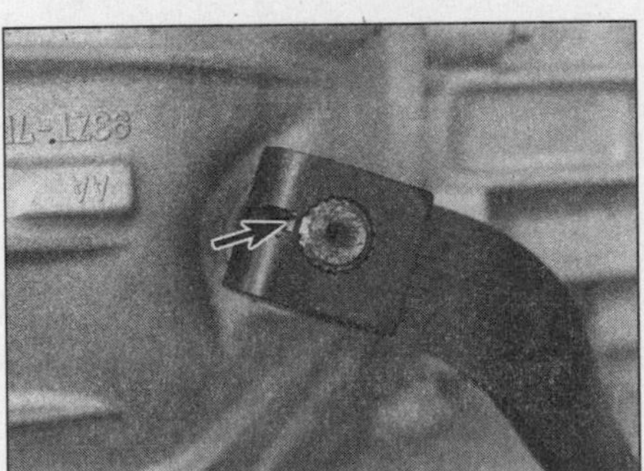

9.2c Master spline (arrowed) on the shaft

9.4 Removing the bush using grips

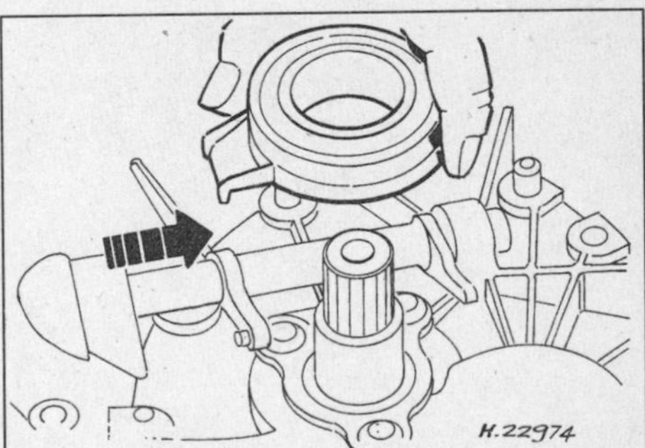

9.5 Removing the clutch release arm shaft

6

Refitting

6 Refitting is a reversal of the removal procedure. Apply a little grease to the bearing surfaces, both in the transmission and in the bush.

10 Clutch hydraulic system - bleeding

1 The clutch hydraulic system will not normally require bleeding, and this task should only be necessary when the system has been opened for repair work. However, as with the brake pedal, if the clutch pedal feels at all soggy or unresponsive in operation, this may indicate the need for bleeding.

2 The system bleed screw is located on top of the transmission bellhousing.

3 Remove the battery as described in Chapter 5A, and the air cleaner as described in Chapter 4A. Move the pipework and wiring harness to one side as necessary to reach the access cover.

4 Remove the bleed screw cap (refer to illustration 8.5a).

5 Bleeding the clutch is much the same as bleeding the brakes - refer to Chapter 9 for the various methods which may be used. Ensure that the level in the brake fluid reservoir is maintained well above the 'MIN' mark at all times, otherwise the clutch and brake hydraulic systems will both need bleeding.

6 On completion, tighten the bleed screw securely, and top-up the brake fluid level to the 'MAX' mark. If possible, test the operation of the clutch before refitting all the components removed for access.

7 Failure to bleed correctly may point to a leak in the system, or to a worn master or slave cylinder. At the time of writing, it appears that the master and slave cylinders are only available as complete assemblies - overhaul is not possible.

Chapter 7 Part A:
Manual transmission

Contents

Degrees of difficulty

Easy, suitable for novice with little experience 

Fairly easy, suitable for beginner with some experience 

Fairly difficult, suitable for competent DIY mechanic

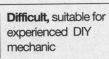

Difficult, suitable for experienced DIY mechanic 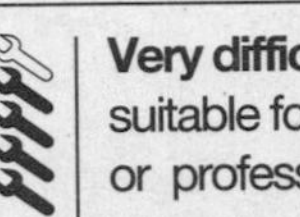

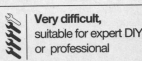

Very difficult, suitable for expert DIY or professional

Specifications

Manufacturer's code

Manual transmission	MTX-75

Gear ratios

	Gear set A	Gear set B	Gear set B1	Gear set D
1st	3.417:1	3.231:1	3.417:1	3.666:1
2nd	2.136:1	2.136:1	2.136:1	2.047:1
3rd	1.448:1	1.483:1	1.483:1	1.258:1
4th	1.028:1	1.114:1	1.114:1	0.864:1
5th	0.767:1	0.854:1	0.854:1	0.674:1
Reverse	3.46:1	3.46:1	3.46:1	3.46:1

Gear set application

1.6, 1.8, 2.0 and V6 models	A
Early 2.0 models	B
2.0 models for Italy and France, and all sports variants in the UK	B1
1.6 models for France	D

Final drive ratios

1.6 models with gear set A	4.06:1
1.6 models with gear set D	3.84:1
1.8 models with gear set A:	
Except France	3.84:1
France	3.41:1
2.0 models with gear set A	3.84:1
2.0 models with gear set B1	3.84:1
V6 models:	
Except France	3.82:1
France	3.41:1

Torque wrench settings

	Nm	lbf ft
Transmission to engine	40	30
Pre 1997 models		
Gearchange support rod	55	41
Gearchange linkage clamp bolt	16	12
Gearchange assembly rear mounting	44	32
Gearchange linkage to selector shaft	23	17
1997-on models		
Selector and shift cable bush	9	7
Gear lever assembly to floor	10	7
Bearing housing	10	7

1 General information

The vehicles covered by this manual are equipped with either a 5-speed manual or a 4-speed automatic transmission. This Part of Chapter 7 contains information on the manual transmission. Service procedures for the automatic transmission are contained in Part B.

The manual transmission is a compact, two-piece, lightweight aluminium alloy housing, containing both the transmission and differential assemblies. The manual transmission code name is MTX-75, MT standing for *M*anual *T*ransmission, X for transa*X*le (front-wheel-drive), and 75 being the distance between the input and output shafts in mm.

Note that as from model year 1997, the rod gearchange has been superseded by a cable gearchange.

Because of the complexity, possible unavailability of replacement parts and special tools necessary, internal repair procedures for the manual transmission are not recommended for the home mechanic. For readers who wish to tackle a transmission rebuild, exploded views and brief notes on overhaul are provided. The bulk of the information in this Chapter is devoted to removal and refitting procedures.

2 Gearchange linkage - adjustment

Rod gearchange (pre 1997 models)

Note: *The special Ford tool 16-073-01 will be required in order to carry out the following adjustment. This tool is simply a slotted ring which locks the gear lever in the neutral position during adjustment. If the tool is not available, adjustment is still possible by proceeding on a trial-and-error basis, preferably with the help of an assistant to hold the gear lever in the neutral position.*

1 Remove the centre console as described in Chapter 11.

2 Apply the handbrake, jack up the front of the vehicle and support it on axle stands. Move the gear lever to the neutral position.

3 Working beneath the vehicle, loosen the clamp bolt on the gearchange linkage located behind the transmission.

4 With the gear lever still in neutral, fit the special Ford tool 16-073-01 over the gear lever, and locate it in the recess in the lever retaining housing on top of the transmission. Twist the tool clockwise to lock the lever in the neutral position. Take care during the adjustment not to move the gear lever or displace the adjustment tool.

5 Check that the front part of the gearchange linkage from the transmission is in neutral. It will be necessary to move the linkage slightly forwards and backwards to determine that it is in the correct position.

2.11 Release the cable adjusters by depressing the tabs on the sides of the red plastic locking sliders

6 Recheck that the adjustment tool is still correctly fitted to the gear lever, then tighten the clamp bolt on the gearchange linkage.

7 Remove the adjustment tool from the gear lever.

8 Lower the vehicle to the ground, then refit the centre console with reference to Chapter 11.

Cable gearchange (1997-on models)

Note: *The special Ford tool 16-088 will be required in order to carry out the following adjustment. This tool locks the gear lever in the neutral position during adjustment. If the tool is not available, adjustment is still possible by proceeding on a trial-and-error basis, preferably with the help of an assistant to hold the gear lever in the neutral position.*

9 Disconnect the battery negative (earth) lead (see Chapter 5A), then select neutral.

10 Remove the air cleaner assembly as described in Chapter 4A.

11 On the transmission, release the adjusters on the cables by depressing the tabs on the sides of the red plastic locking sliders **(see illustration)**.

12 Inside the car, release the gaiter from the gearchange lever and pull it up onto the knob.

13 Lock the gear lever in neutral using the special tool 16-088 **(see illustration)**.

14 With the levers on the transmission in neutral, lock the red plastic locking sliders by pressing them in.

15 Remove the special tool, and refit the gaiter to the gearchange lever.

2.13 Ford special tool 16-088 used to lock the gear lever in neutral

16 Refit the air cleaner assembly with reference to Chapter 4A.

17 Reconnect the battery negative (earth) lead (see Chapter 5A).

3 Gearchange linkage and gear lever - removal and refitting

Rod gearchange (pre 1997 models)

Removal

1 Remove the centre console as described in Chapter 11 **(see illustration)**.

2 Apply the handbrake, jack up the front of the vehicle and support it on axle stands. Move the gear lever to its neutral position.

3 Working beneath the vehicle, unscrew the bolt and disconnect the gearchange linkage from the selector shaft on the rear of the transmission.

4 Mark the position of the gearchange linkage front and rear sections in relation to each other. Loosen the clamp bolt and remove the front section.

5 Unscrew the bolt securing the gearchange support rod to the bracket on the rear of the transmission.

6 Remove the heat shield. Support the weight of the gearchange linkage assembly, unscrew the nuts from the rear mounting bracket, and lower the assembly from the underbody **(see illustration)**.

7 Remove the insulator rubber from the rear of the assembly.

3.1 View of the top of the gearchange assembly with the centre console removed

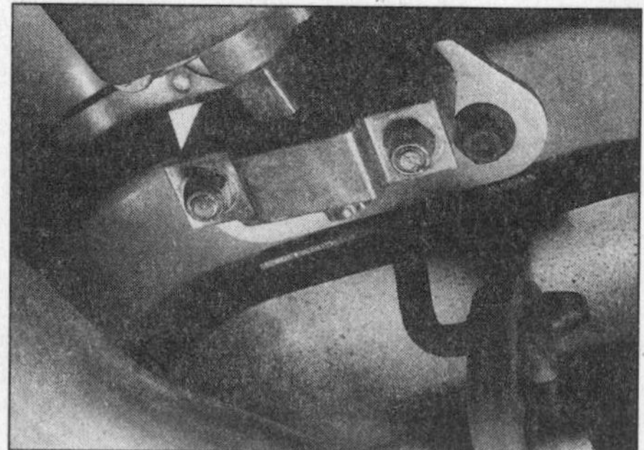

3.6 Gearchange linkage assembly rear mounting

8 Examine the insulator rubber and the stabiliser bar mounting rubber for wear and deterioration, and if necessary obtain new ones.

Refitting

9 Refitting is a reversal of the removal procedure, but adjust the linkage as described in Section 2.

Cable gearchange (1997-on models)

Removal

10 Disconnect the battery negative (earth) lead (see Chapter 5A).

11 Apply the handbrake, then jack up the front of the vehicle and support it on axle stands (see *"Jacking and Vehicle Support"*). Remove both wheels.

12 Remove the engine undershield and left-hand wheel arch liner.

13 At the transmission, remove the cables from the support brackets by twisting the spring-loaded knurled collars anticlockwise from each other (ie in different directions). Prise off the retaining clips and release the cables from the transmission levers - note their fitted locations. Withdraw the cables downwards from the engine compartment **(see illustrations).**

14 Make sure that the levers on the transmission are both vertical (ie in neutral).

15 Remove the air cleaner as described in Chapter 4A.

16 Remove the gear lever knob. On early models the knob is pressed on, but on later models it is screwed on.

17 Unclip and remove the gaiter up from the gear lever.

18 Remove the centre console as described in Chapter 11.

19 Prise the cable end fittings from the gear lever stubs, then detach the cable ferrules from the bracket by turning the serrated collars anticlockwise to each other.

20 Unscrew the bolt and lift the air duct up from the centre channel.

21 Cut the carpet if necessary, and fold it away from the area over the cable adapter.

22 Unscrew the nuts and release the adapter from the floor, then withdraw the cables through the bulkhead and into the car.

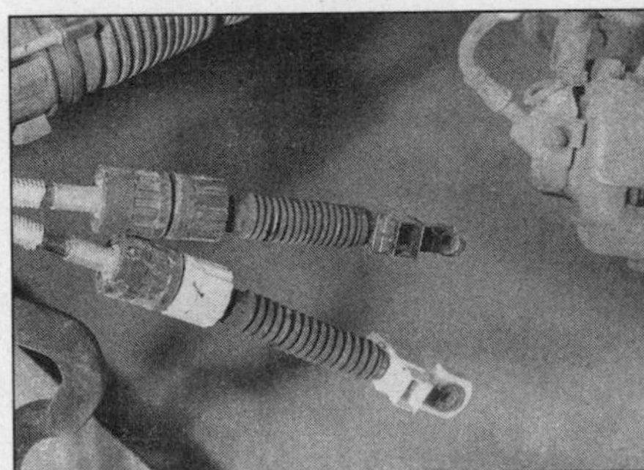

3.13b The cable ends disconnected from the transmission and mounting bracket

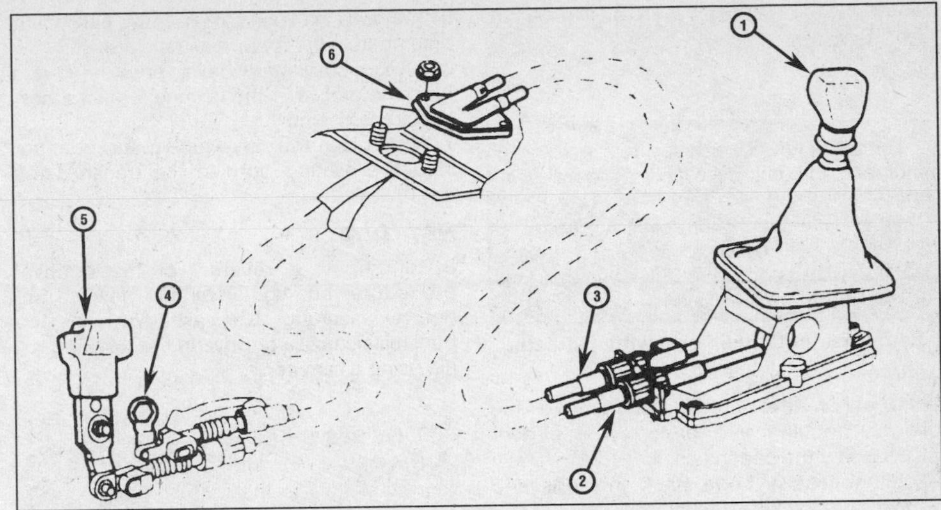

3.13a Cable gearchange components fitted from 1997 models

1 *Gear lever*
2 *Shift cable*
3 *Selector cable*
4 *Selector lever on the transmission*
5 *Shift lever on the transmission*
6 *Bulkhead adapter*

23 To remove the gear lever assembly, extract the circlip from the end of the bearing bolt and remove the spacer, spring and lever **(see illustration).**

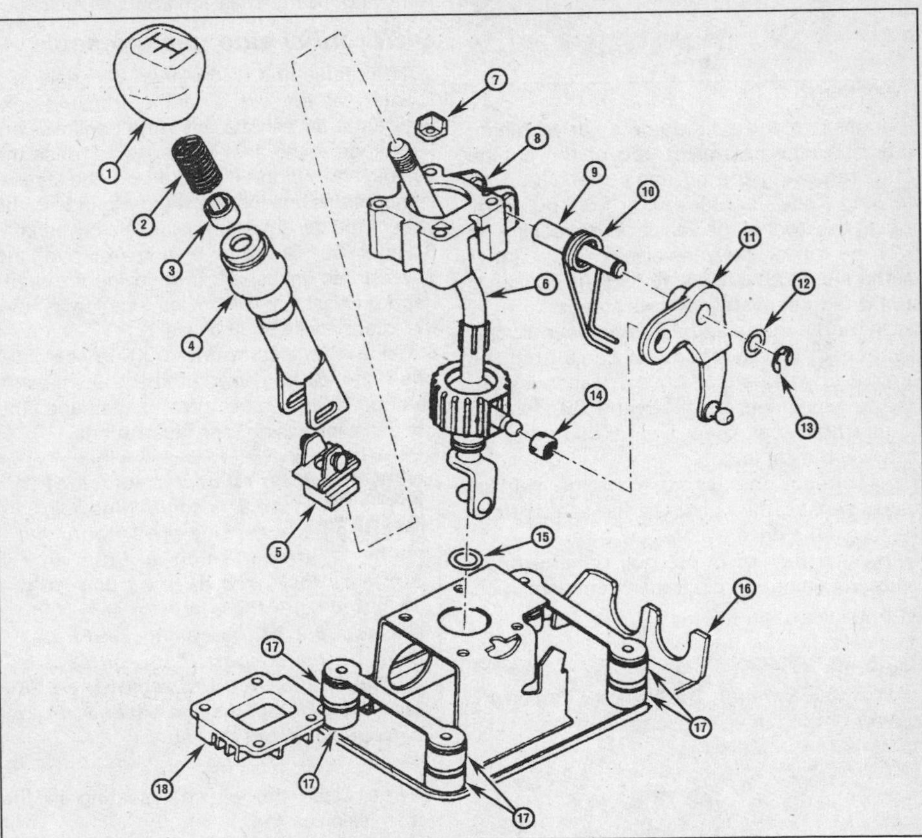

3.23 Gear lever assembly components

1 *Knob*
2 *Spring*
3 *Damping sleeve*
4 *Reverse gear release*
5 *Stop sleeve*
6 *Gear lever*
7 *Reverse gear lockout*
8 *Bearing housing*
9 *Bearing bolt*
10 *Spring*
11 *Lever*
12 *Spacer*
13 *Circlip*
14 *Bearing shell*
15 *O-ring*
16 *Housing bracket*
17 *Damping rings*
18 *Plate*

5.4a Prise out the oil seal with a suitable lever

24 Unscrew the bolts and remove the bearing housing and plate, reverse gear lockout, and the bearing shell.
25 If necessary, bend back the lugs and remove the brackets and studs.

Refitting

26 Refitting is a reversal of removal, but adjust the cables as described in Section 2.

4 Speedometer drive pinion - removal and refitting

Removal

1 Access to the speedometer drive pinion may be gained from the top of the engine (after removing the air mass meter and air trunking - see Chapter 4A), or from below by raising the front of the vehicle and reaching up over the top of the transmission. If the latter method is used, make sure that the vehicle is supported adequately on axle stands.
2 On early models, unscrew the nut and disconnect the speedometer cable from the vehicle speed sensor on the transmission. Use two spanners to loosen the nut - one to counterhold the sensor, and the other to unscrew the cable nut.
3 Disconnect the wiring from the vehicle speed sensor, then unscrew the sensor from the top of the drive pinion.
4 Using a pair of grips, pull out the drive pinion retaining roll pin from the transmission casing.

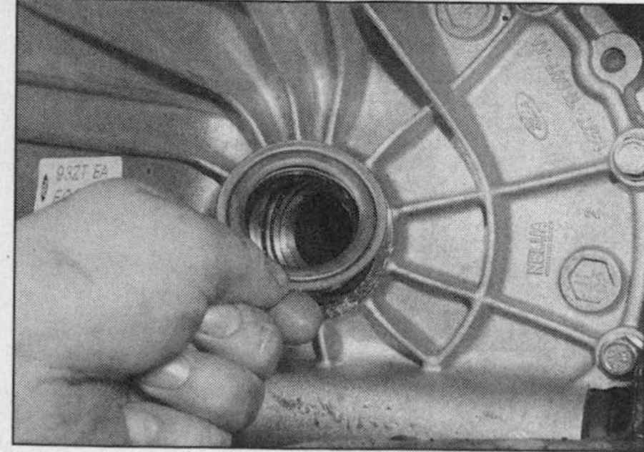

5.4b Removing the oil seal from the transmission casing

5 Withdraw the speedometer drive pinion and bearing from the top of the transmission.
6 Using a small screwdriver, prise the O-ring from the groove in the bearing; obtain a new one for reassembly.
7 Wipe clean the drive pinion and bearing, also the seating bore in the transmission casing.

Refitting

8 Refitting is a reversal of the removal procedure, but lightly oil the new O-ring before inserting the assembly in the transmission casing. Drive in the retaining roll pin using a hammer.

5 Oil seals - renewal

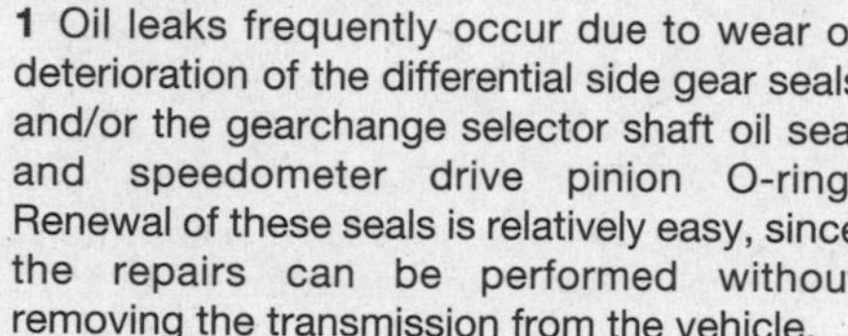

1 Oil leaks frequently occur due to wear or deterioration of the differential side gear seals and/or the gearchange selector shaft oil seal and speedometer drive pinion O-ring. Renewal of these seals is relatively easy, since the repairs can be performed without removing the transmission from the vehicle.

Differential side gear oil seals

2 The differential side gear oil seals are located at the sides of the transmission, where the driveshafts enter the transmission. If leakage at the seal is suspected, raise the vehicle and support it securely on axle stands. If the seal is leaking, oil will be found on the side of the transmission below the driveshaft.
3 Refer to Chapter 8 and remove the appropriate driveshaft. If removing the right-hand driveshaft, it will be necessary to remove the intermediate shaft as well.
4 Using a large screwdriver or lever, carefully prise the oil seal out of the transmission casing, taking care not to damage the transmission casing **(see illustrations)**.

If an oil seal is reluctant to move, it is sometimes helpful to carefully drive it into the transmission a little way, applying the force at one point only. This will have the effect of swivelling the seal out of the casing, and it can then be pulled out. If the oil seal is particularly difficult to remove, an oil seal removal tool may be obtained from a garage or accessory shop.

5 Wipe clean the oil seal seating in the transmission casing.
6 Dip the new oil seal in clean oil, then press it a little way into the casing by hand, making sure that it is square to its seating.
7 Using suitable tubing or a large socket, carefully drive the oil seal fully into the casing until it contacts the seating.
8 Refit the driveshaft with reference to Chapter 8.

Gearchange selector shaft oil seal

9 Apply the handbrake, jack up the front of the vehicle and support it on axle stands.
10 Unscrew the bolt securing the gearchange linkage to the shaft on the rear of the transmission. Pull off the linkage and remove the rubber boot.
11 Using a suitable tool or grips, pull the oil seal out of the transmission casing. Ford technicians use a slide hammer, with an end fitting which locates over the oil seal extension. In the absence of this tool, if the oil seal is particularly tight, drill one or two small holes in the oil seal, and screw in self-tapping screws. The oil seal can then be removed from the casing by pulling on the screws.
12 Wipe clean the oil seal seating in the transmission.
13 Dip the new oil seal in clean oil, then press it a little way into the casing by hand, making sure that it is square to its seating.
14 Using suitable tubing or a large socket, carefully drive the oil seal fully into the casing.
15 Locate the rubber boot over the selector shaft.
16 Refit the gearchange linkage to the shaft on the rear of the transmission, and tighten the bolt.
17 If necessary, adjust the gearchange linkage as described in Section 2.

Speedometer drive pinion oil seal

18 The procedure is covered in Section 4.

6 Reversing light switch - removal and refitting

Removal

1 Remove the air cleaner and the air mass meter as described in Chapter 4A.
2 Disconnect the wiring leading to the reversing light switch on the top of the transmission.
3 Unscrew the mounting bolts, and remove the reversing light switch from the cover housing on the transmission.

Refitting

4 Refitting is a reversal of the removal procedure.

7 Manual transmission - removal and refitting

Note: *Read through this procedure before starting work to see what is involved, particularly in terms of lifting equipment. Depending on the facilities available, the home mechanic may prefer to remove the engine and transmission together, then separate them on the bench, as described in Chapter 2C.*

7.3 Use split pins to hold the radiator in its raised position

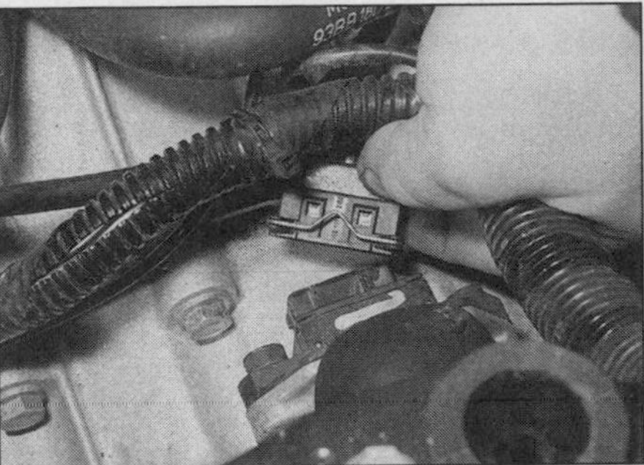

7.6 Disconnecting the wiring multi-plug from the reversing light switch

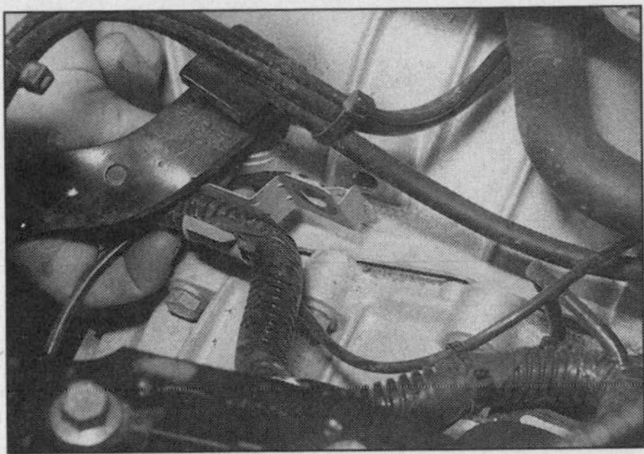

7.7 Removing the wiring loom bracket from the top of the transmission

Removal

1 Disconnect the battery negative (earth) lead (see Chapter 5A). For better access, the battery may be removed completely.

2 If necessary, the bonnet may be removed as described in Chapter 11 for better access, and for fitting the engine lifting hoist.

3 Hold the radiator in its raised position by inserting split pins through the holes in the upper mounting extensions **(see illustration)**. This is necessary to retain the radiator when the subframe is removed.

4 Remove the air mass meter and air inlet duct with reference to Chapter 4A. On V6 models, remove the water pump pulley cover.

5 Remove the air cleaner assembly as described in Chapter 4A.

6 Disconnect the wiring from the reversing light switch on the transmission **(see illustration)**.

7 Unscrew the bolt, and remove the wiring loom bracket from the top of the transmission **(see illustration)**.

8 Detach the earth cable located between the transmission and the body. On V6 models, disconnect the accelerator and speed control cables. Also on V6 models, disconnect the wiring from the power steering pressure switch wiring, then remove the power steering line from the clamp at the right-hand engine support bracket and position the steering line to one side.

9 Disconnect the clutch cable or hydraulic line from the transmission, with reference to Chapter 6.

10 Unscrew and remove the three upper bolts securing the transmission to the engine. Also unscrew the mounting bolt with the earth lead, located beneath the exhaust manifold **(see illustration)**.

11 On 4-cylinder models, unscrew and remove the starter motor upper mounting bolt, noting that an earth cable is attached to it **(see illustration)**. On V6 models, remove the starter motor as described in Chapter 5A.

12 Apply the handbrake, jack up the front of the vehicle and support it on axle stands. Remove the front wheels.

13 Remove the front lower cover from under the radiator by prising out the side clips and un-screwing the retaining bolts **(see illustration)**.

14 Remove the wheel arch liner from the right-hand side of the vehicle as described in Chapter 11.

15 Unscrew the bolts and remove the auxiliary drivebelt cover.

16 Working on each side of the vehicle in turn, unscrew the nut and disconnect the anti-roll bar link from the strut, noting that the flexible brake hose bracket is attached to the link stud.

17 Extract the split pins (where fitted), then unscrew the nuts securing the track rod ends to the steering knuckles on each side. Release the balljoints from the steering knuckle arms, using a balljoint separator tool.

18 Working on each side in turn, note which way round the front suspension lower arm balljoint clamp bolt is fitted, then unscrew and remove it from the knuckle assembly. Lever

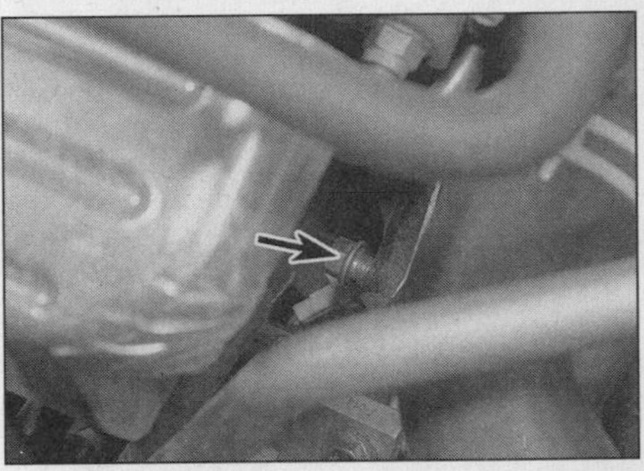

7.10 Mounting bolt with earth lead located beneath the exhaust manifold

the balljoint down from the knuckle - if it is tight, prise the joint open carefully using a large flat-bladed tool. Take care not to damage the balljoint seal during the separation procedure.

19 Disconnect the cooling fan multi-plug on the subframe behind the radiator, and unclip the plug from the bracket.

20 Disconnect the multi-plug from the wiring leading to the oxygen sensor, then unclip the wiring from the engine rear mounting.

21 Disconnect the vacuum hose from the pulse-air system filter (where fitted).

22 Remove the complete exhaust system as described in Chapter 4A.

Early models with rod gearchange (pre 1997)

23 Unscrew the bolt securing the gearchange linkage rod to the selector shaft on the rear of the transmission **(see illustration)**.

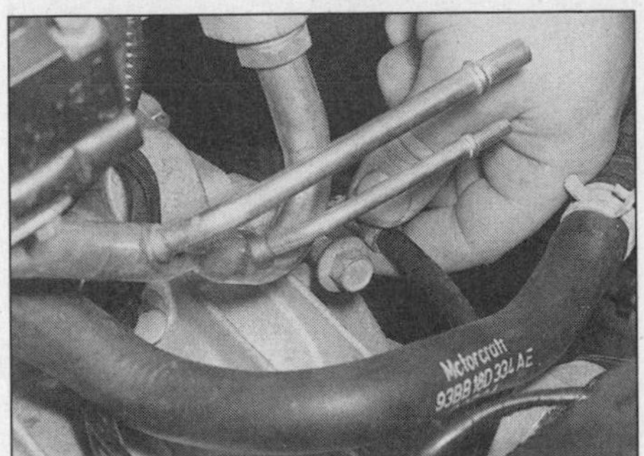

7.11 Removing the starter motor bolt with the earth cable (4-cylinder models)

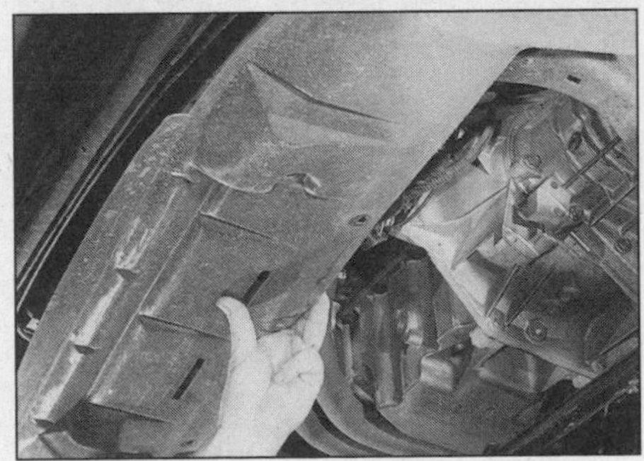

7.13 Radiator front lower cover removal

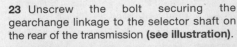

7.23 Unscrew the bolt securing the gearchange linkage rod to the shaft on the rear of the transmission

7.24 Removing the gearchange linkage front section (early models)

7.25 Unscrewing the bolt securing the gearchange support rod to the bracket on the rear of the transmission (early models)

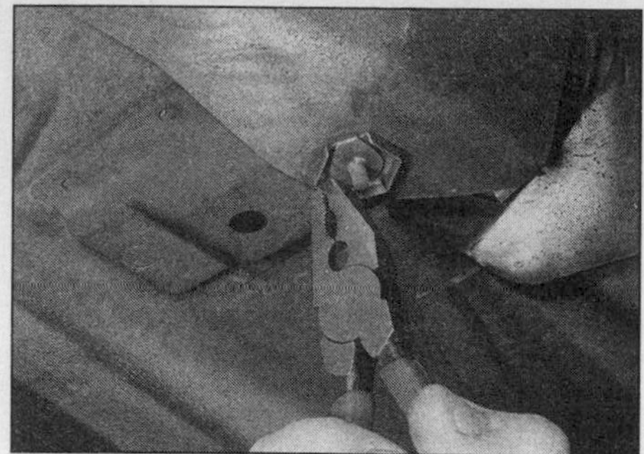

7.26a Removing the gear linkage heat shield (early models)

24 Mark the position of the gearchange linkage front and rear sections, then unscrew the clamp bolt. Disconnect the linkage from the selector shaft on the rear of the transmission, and separate the front and rear sections of the linkage **(see illustration)**.

25 Unscrew the mounting bolt, and disconnect the gearchange support rod from the bracket on the rear of the transmission **(see illustration)**.

26 Remove the gear linkage heat shield from the underbody by unscrewing the nuts. Unscrew and remove the gear linkage rear mounting bolts, swivel the linkage around to the rear, and tie it to the underbody **(see illustrations)**.

Later models with cable gearchange (1997-on)

27 Disconnect the two gearchange cables from the transmission with reference to Section 3.

All models

28 On models fitted with air conditioning, unscrew and remove the mounting bolts securing the dehydrator to the left-hand side of the subframe, and tie it to one side.

29 Unscrew and remove the bolts securing the steering gear to the subframe. The bolts are difficult to reach using normal spanners; if possible, the special cranked Ford tool should be obtained (see Chapter 10).

30 Unscrew and remove the centre bolt from the engine/transmission rear mounting (roll restrictor), then unbolt the mounting from the subframe **(see illustrations)**. To ensure correct refitting, note the fitted position of the mounting before removing it.

31 On rod-gearchange models, unscrew the nut and bolt, and remove the support rod bracket from the rear of the transmission **(see illustrations)**.

32 Unscrew the nuts and bolts, and remove the engine/transmission rear mounting (roll restrictor) bracket from the transmission **(see illustrations)**. To ensure correct refitting, note the fitted position of the mounting before removing it.

7.26b Unscrew the gear linkage rear mounting bolts (arrowed) (early models) . . .

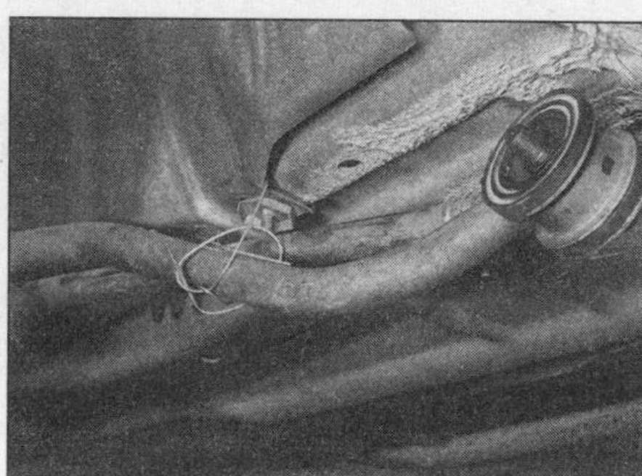

7.26c . . . swivel the linkage around, and tie it to the underbody (early models)

7.30a Remove the centre bolt (arrowed) from the rear mounting . . .

7.30b . . . then unbolt the mounting from the subframe and remove it

7.31a Unscrew the nut and bolt (arrowed) . . .

7.31b . . . and remove the transmission support rod bracket (rod-gearchange models)

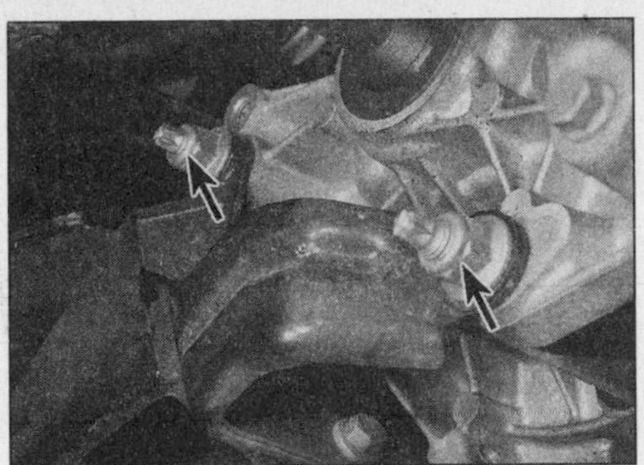
7.32a Nuts securing the rear mounting bracket to the transmission

7.32b Removing the rear mounting bracket

7.33 Removing the bolt from the engine front mounting bracket

33 Where applicable, unscrew and remove the centre bolt from the engine front mounting, and detach the pulse-air filter from the bracket on the mounting **(see illustration)**.

34 With the help of an assistant, support the weight of the subframe, using trolley jacks if possible. Unscrew the bolts securing the power steering fluid cooler pipes to the subframe, then unscrew the subframe mounting bolts, and lower the subframe to the ground **(see illustrations)**.

35 Position a suitable container beneath the transmission, then unscrew the drain plug and drain the oil **(see illustration)**. Refit and tighten the plug on completion.

36 Unscrew the bolts securing the right-hand driveshaft centre bearing to the cylinder block. Remove the heat shield, then pull out the right-hand strut so that the intermediate shaft is removed from the transmission differential gears. Be prepared for oil spillage.

37 Support the right-hand driveshaft on axle stands, making sure that the inner tripod joint is not turned through more than 18° (damage may occur if the joint is turned through too great an angle).

38 Insert a suitable lever between the left-hand driveshaft inner joint and the transmission case (with a thin piece of wood against the case), then prise free the joint from the differential. If it proves reluctant to move, strike the lever firmly with the palm of the hand. Be careful not to damage the adjacent components, and be prepared for oil spillage. As the right-hand driveshaft has already been removed, it is possible to release the left-hand driveshaft by inserting a forked drift from the right-hand side, but care must be taken to prevent damage to the differential gears.

39 Support the left-hand driveshaft on axle stands, making sure that the inner tripod joint is not turned through more than 18° (damage may occur if the joint is turned through too great an angle).

40 Disconnect the multi-plug from the wiring leading to the vehicle speed sensor.

41 On early models with a speedometer cable, unscrew the cable nut, and disconnect the speedometer cable from the top of the vehicle speed sensor. Hold the sensor with a spanner while the cable nut is loosened. Disconnect the wiring from the speed sensor.

42 If necessary, the vehicle may be lowered to the ground at this stage, in order to connect an engine hoist. If an engine support bar which locates over the engine compartment is to be used, then the vehicle may be left in its raised position.

43 Attach the hoist to diagonally-opposite positions on the engine, and take the weight of the engine and transmission **(see illustration)**.

44 Unscrew the nuts from the engine right-hand mounting bracket. Note that, where a hydraulic mounting is fitted, the mounting must never be tilted by more than 5°. To ensure correct refitting, note the fitted position of the mounting before removing it.

45 Unscrew the retaining nuts, and remove the engine/transmission left-hand mounting from the transmission. To ensure correct refitting, note the fitted position of the mounting before removing it.

7.34a Removing the power steering fluid cooler pipes from the subframe

7.34b Unscrewing the subframe front . . .

7.34c . . . and rear mounting bolts

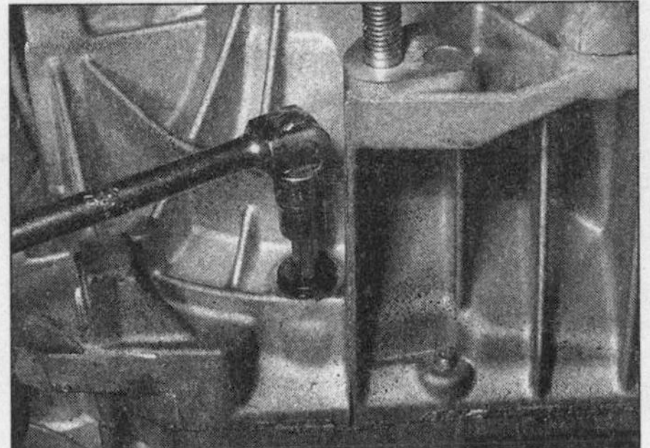
7.35 Unscrewing the transmission oil drain plug

7.43 Supporting the engine with a hoist

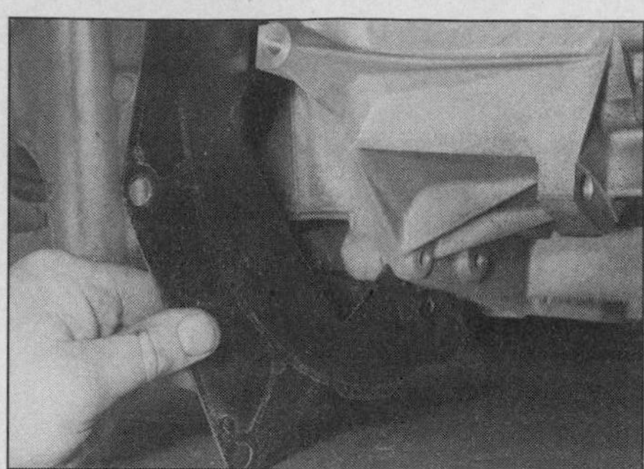

7.51 Removing the lower cover plate (4-cylinder models)

46 On models fitted with air conditioning, lower the engine until the compressor is below the right-hand side member.
47 On models without air conditioning, lower the transmission until it is opposite the aperture on the left-hand side of the engine compartment.
48 Support the weight of the transmission on a trolley jack. Use safety chains or a cradle to steady the transmission on the jack.
49 On 4-cylinder models, remove the remaining starter motor mounting bolts.
50 Unscrew and remove the lower bolts securing the transmission to the engine. Also unscrew the bolts securing the lower cover plate to the transmission.
51 With the help of an assistant, withdraw the transmission squarely from the engine, taking care not to allow its weight to hang on the clutch friction disc. As the transmission is being withdrawn, remove the lower cover plate sandwiched between the transmission and engine **(see illustration)**. Lower the transmission to the ground.
52 The clutch components can now be inspected with reference to Chapter 6, and renewed if necessary. (Unless they are virtually new, it is worth renewing the clutch components as a matter of course, even if the transmission has been removed for some other reason).

Refitting

53 If removed, refit the clutch components (see Chapter 6).
54 With the transmission secured to the trolley jack as on removal, raise it into position, and then carefully slide it onto the rear of the engine, at the same time engaging the input shaft with the clutch friction disc splines. Do not use excessive force to refit the transmission - if the input shaft does not slide into place easily, readjust the angle of the transmission so that it is level, and/or turn the input shaft so that the splines engage properly with the disc. If problems are still experienced, check that the clutch friction disc is correctly centred (Chapter 6).
55 Refit the lower bolts securing the transmission to the engine, and tighten moderately at this stage.
56 On 4-cylinder models, insert and tighten the starter mounting bolts, noting that an earth cable is attached to one of them. On V6 models, refit the starter motor as described in Chapter 5A.
57 Raise the transmission to its normal position.
58 Refit the engine/transmission left-hand mounting, and tighten the nuts. Align the mounting as noted during removal.
59 Refit the engine right-hand mounting bracket, and tighten the nuts. Align the mounting as noted during removal.
60 If previously lowered, raise the front of the vehicle, and support on axle stands.
61 Refit the speedometer cable to the vehicle speed sensor, and tighten the cable nut.
62 Reconnect the wiring to the speed sensor.
63 Insert the left-hand driveshaft into the transmission, making sure that it is fully engaged with the internal circlip.
64 Refit the right-hand driveshaft and intermediate shaft, and tighten the bolts.
65 Refit and align the subframe, with reference to Chapter 2C, Section 4. Tighten the mounting bolts to the specified torque.
66 Refit the pulse-air filter. Tighten the centre bolt in the engine front mounting.
67 Refit the engine rear mounting bracket, and tighten the bolts.
68 Where fitted, refit the transmission support rod and bracket, and tighten the bolts and nut.
69 Refit the engine rear mounting to the subframe, and tighten the bolts.
70 Refit the steering gear to the subframe, and tighten the mounting bolts.
71 On models with air conditioning, refit the dehydrator to the subframe, and tighten the mounting bolts.
72 Refit the gear linkage and heat shield.
73 Refit the transmission gearchange support rod to the rear of the transmission, and tighten the bolt. Adjust the gearchange linkage if necessary, with reference to Section 2.
74 Refit the exhaust system, with reference to Chapter 4A.
75 Reconnect the vacuum hose to the pulse-air system filter (where fitted).
76 Reconnect the oxygen sensor wiring.
77 Reconnect and secure the cooling fan multi-plug.
78 Refit the front suspension lower arm balljoints to the knuckle assemblies, with reference to Chapter 10.
79 Refit the track rod ends to the steering knuckles on each side, with reference to Chapter 10.
80 Refit the anti-roll bar links to the struts, and tighten the nuts.
81 Refit the auxiliary drivebelt cover and the wheel arch liner.
82 Refit the front lower cover beneath the radiator.
83 Refit the wheels, and lower the vehicle to the ground.
84 Insert the upper bolts securing the transmission to the engine.
85 Reconnect the clutch cable or hydraulic line with reference to Chapter 6. Reconnect the power steering line on V6 models. Make sure that the steering line is securely clamped in position on the right-hand engine support bracket. Note that the earth wire is also located under one of the nuts on the support bracket. Reconnect the power steering pressure switch electrical connector.
86 Refit the earth cable between the transmission and the body.
87 Refit the wiring loom bracket to the top of the transmission.
88 Reconnect the wiring to the reversing light switch.
89 Tighten all transmission mounting bolts fully.
90 Refit the air cleaner assembly, air mass meter and air inlet duct, with reference to Chapter 4A.
91 Remove the split pins holding the radiator in its raised position.
92 If removed, refit the bonnet.
93 If removed, refit the battery and reconnect the leads.
94 Fill the transmission with oil, and check the level as described in Chapter 1.
95 Make a final check that all connections have been made, and all bolts tightened fully.
96 Road test the vehicle to check for proper transmission operation, then check the transmission visually for leakage of oil.

8 Manual transmission mounting - checking and renewal

This procedure is covered in Chapter 2A or 2B.

9 Manual transmission overhaul - general

1 Overhauling a manual transmission is a difficult job for the do-it-yourselfer. It involves the dismantling and reassembly of many small parts. Numerous clearances must be precisely measured and, if necessary, changed with selected spacers and circlips. As a result, if transmission problems arise, while the unit can be removed and refitted by a competent do-it-yourselfer, overhaul should be left to a transmission specialist. Rebuilt transmissions may be available - check with your dealer parts department, motor factors, or transmission specialists. At any rate, the time and money involved in an overhaul is almost sure to exceed the cost of a rebuilt unit.
2 Nevertheless, it's not impossible for an inexperienced mechanic to rebuild a transmission, providing the special tools are available, and the job is done in a deliberate step-by-step manner so nothing is overlooked.

3 The tools necessary for an overhaul include: internal and external circlip pliers, a bearing puller, a slide hammer, a set of pin punches, a dial test indicator, and possibly a hydraulic press. In addition, a large, sturdy workbench and a vice or transmission stand will be required.

4 During dismantling of the transmission, make careful notes of how each part comes off, where it fits in relation to other parts, and what holds it in place. Exploded views are included **(see illustrations)** to show where the parts go - but actually noting how they are fitted when you remove the parts will make it much easier to get the transmission back together.

5 Before taking the transmission apart for repair, it will help if you have some idea what area of the transmission is malfunctioning. Certain problems can be closely tied to specific areas in the transmission, which can make component examination and replacement easier. Refer to the *"Fault finding"* Section at the end of this manual for information regarding possible sources of trouble.

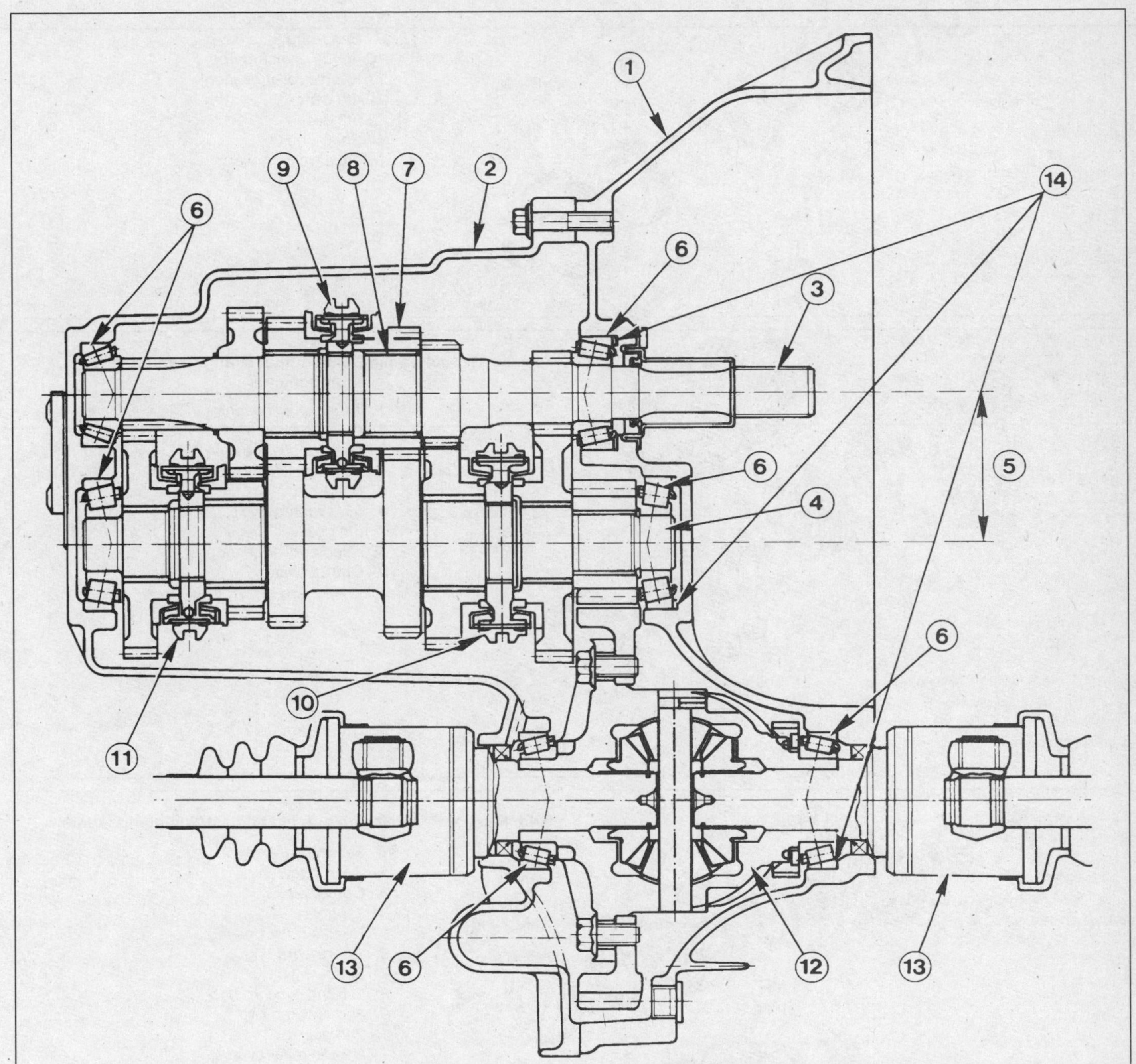

9.4a Sectional diagram of the manual transmission

1 Clutch housing
2 Transmission housing
3 Input shaft
4 Output shaft
5 Distance between shaft centres = 75 mm
6 Taper roller bearings
7 4th gear
8 Needle roller bearing
9 3rd/4th synchro
10 1st/2nd synchro
11 5th/reverse synchro
12 Differential
13 Driveshafts
14 Shims

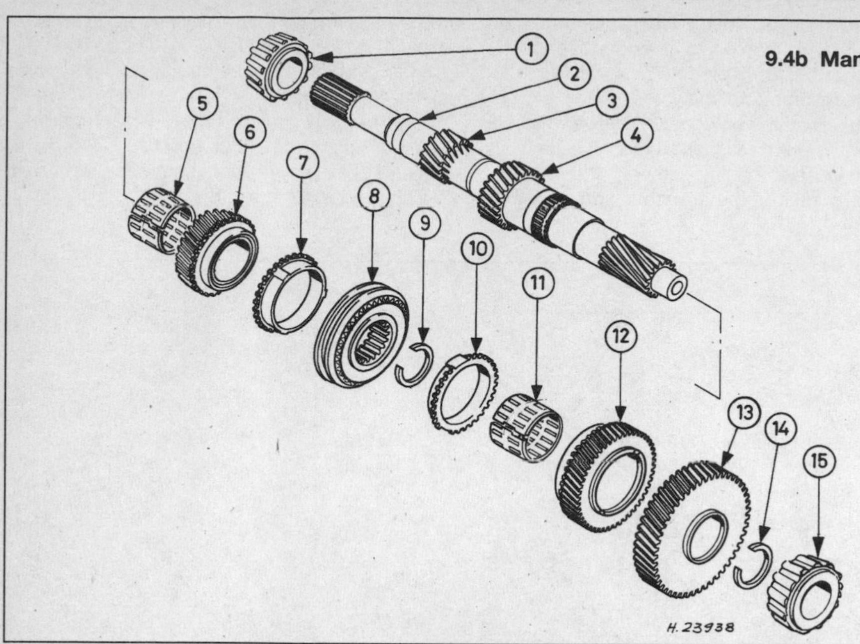

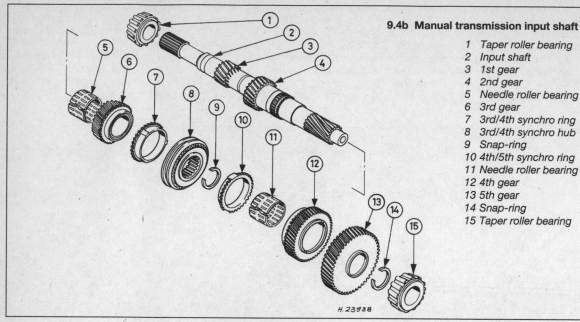

9.4b Manual transmission input shaft components

1 Taper roller bearing
2 Input shaft
3 1st gear
4 2nd gear
5 Needle roller bearing
6 3rd gear
7 3rd/4th synchro ring
8 3rd/4th synchro hub
9 Snap-ring
10 4th/5th synchro ring
11 Needle roller bearing
12 4th gear
13 5th gear
14 Snap-ring
15 Taper roller bearing

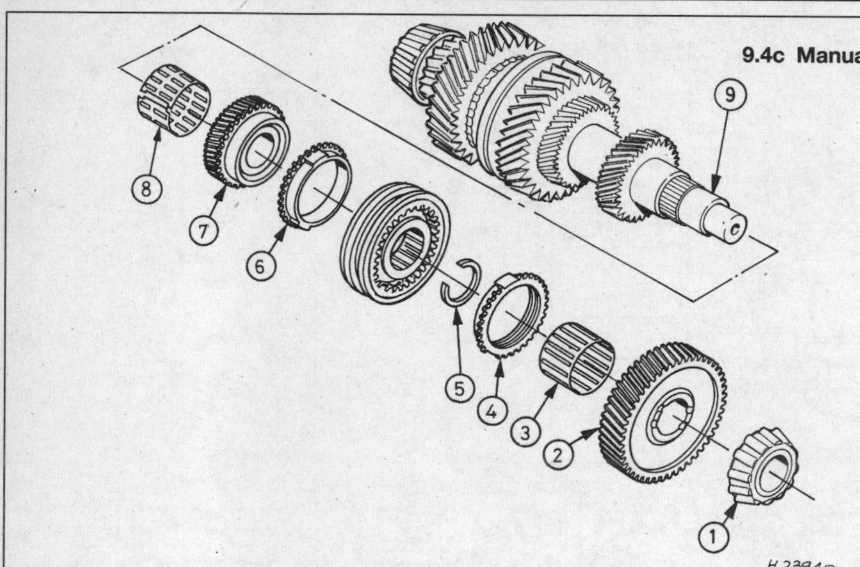

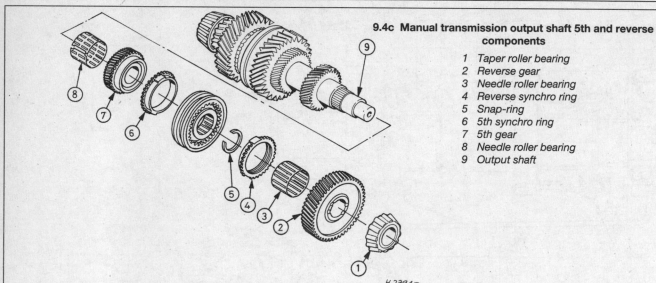

9.4c Manual transmission output shaft 5th and reverse components

1 Taper roller bearing
2 Reverse gear
3 Needle roller bearing
4 Reverse synchro ring
5 Snap-ring
6 5th synchro ring
7 5th gear
8 Needle roller bearing
9 Output shaft

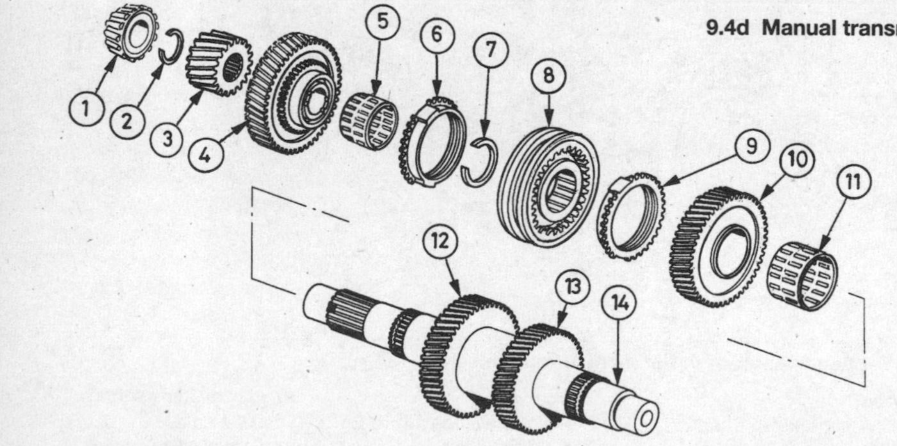

9.4d Manual transmission output shaft 1st/2nd components

1 Taper roller bearing
2 Snap-ring
3 Output pinion
4 1st gear
5 Needle roller bearing
6 1st synchro ring
7 Snap-ring
8 1st/2nd synchro hub
9 2nd synchro ring
10 2nd gear
11 Needle roller bearing
12 4th gear
13 3rd gear
14 Output shaft

Chapter 7 Part B: Automatic transmission

Contents

Degrees of difficulty

Easy, suitable for novice with little experience 	**Fairly easy,** suitable for beginner with some experience 	**Fairly difficult,** suitable for competent DIY mechanic 	**Difficult,** suitable for experienced DIY mechanic 	**Very difficult,** suitable for expert DIY or professional

Specifications

Torque wrench settings	**Nm**	**lbf ft**
Automatic transmission to engine	40	30
Driveplate to crankshaft	112	83
Oil cooler pipes	23	17
Selector cable support bracket	19	14
Selector lever position sensor	10	7
Selector lever to floor	9	7
Speed sensor	5	4
Torque converter to driveplate	36	27
Transmission drain plug	21	15

1 General information

The CD4E automatic transmission is controlled electronically by the engine management electronic control unit. There are two operational modes (Economy and Sport), and a driver-operated overdrive inhibit switch prevents the 4th gear from operating when required during certain conditions. With the Economy mode selected, gear changes occur at low engine speeds, whereas with the Sport mode selected, the changes occur at high engine speeds.

The transmission incorporates a chain drive between the planetary gearsets and the final drive. The transmission fluid is cooled by a cooler located within the radiator.

There is no kickdown switch, as kickdown is controlled by the throttle position sensor in the engine management system.

The electronic control system has a failsafe mode, which gives the transmission limited operation in order to drive the vehicle home or to a repair garage.

The gear selection includes the normal P, R, N, D, 2, and 1 positions. As a safety measure, it is necessary for the ignition to be switched on and for the brake pedal to be depressed in order to move the selector from position P. If the vehicle battery is discharged, the selector lever release solenoid will not function; if it is required to move the vehicle in this state, insert a pen or a similar small instrument into the aperture on the left-hand side of the centre console. Push the locking lever rearwards to allow the selector lever to be moved.

2 Fault finding - general

In the event of a fault occurring on the transmission, first check that the fluid level is correct (see Chapter 1). If there has been a loss of fluid, check the oil seals as described in Section 7. Also check the hoses to the fluid cooler in the radiator for leaks. The only other checks possible for the home mechanic are the adjustment of the selector cable (Section 3) and the selector lever position sensor (Section 6).

If the fault still persists, it is necessary to determine whether it is of an electrical, mechanical or hydraulic nature; to do this, special test equipment is required. It is therefore essential to have the work carried out by an automatic transmission specialist or Ford dealer if a transmission fault is suspected.

Do not remove the transmission from the vehicle for possible repair before professional fault diagnosis has been carried out, since most tests require the transmission to be in the vehicle.

3.6 Selector lever (arrowed) on the side of the transmission

3.7 Cable support bracket bolts (arrowed)

3 Selector cable - removal, refitting and adjustment

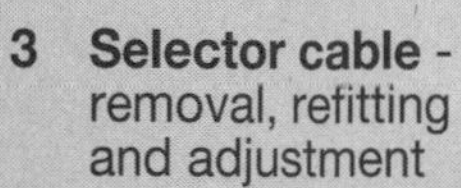

Removal

1 Apply the handbrake, jack up the front of the vehicle and support it on axle stands. Remove the left-hand front wheel.

2 Remove the air mass meter and trunking (Chapter 4A) in order to gain access to the selector cable, which is located on the left-hand side of the transmission.

3 Working beneath the vehicle, remove the heat shield for access to the bottom of the selector lever assembly.

4 Disconnect the inner cable from the bottom of the selector lever assembly.

5 Turn the outer cable locking ring anti-clockwise by 90° to unlock it from the selector lever plate on the bottom of the selector lever assembly. Hold the collar while turning the locking ring.

6 Working in the engine compartment, pull the inner cable end fitting outwards from the lever on the side of the transmission **(see illustration)**.

7 Unbolt the cable support bracket from the transmission **(see illustration)**.

8 Detach the remaining cable supports, and withdraw the cable assembly from the vehicle.

Refitting and adjustment

9 Refitting is a reversal of the removal procedure, but adjust the cable as follows.

10 Inside the vehicle, move the selector lever to position "D".

11 With the inner cable disconnected from the lever on the side of the transmission, check that the lever is in the "D" position. To do this, it will be necessary to move the lever slightly up and down until it is positioned correctly. A further check can be made by observing that the "D" mark on the selector lever position sensor is correctly aligned **(see illustration)**.

12 Check that the cable locking ring beneath the vehicle is still unlocked (ie turned anti-clockwise by 90°).

13 With both the selector levers inside the vehicle and on the side of the transmission in position "D", refit the cable end fitting to the transmission lever, then turn the locking ring 90° clockwise to lock it.

14 Refit the heat shield to the underbody.

15 Refit the air mass meter and trunking.

16 Refit the left-hand front wheel, then lower the vehicle to the ground. Tighten the wheel nuts to the specified torque.

17 Road test the vehicle to check the operation of the transmission.

4 Selector assembly - removal and refitting

Removal

1 Remove the centre console as described in Chapter 11.

2 Apply the handbrake, then jack up the front of the vehicle and support on axle stands.

3 Working beneath the vehicle, remove the heat shield, then disconnect the selector cable end fitting from the bottom of the selector lever assembly.

4 Unscrew the mounting nuts securing the selector cable plate to the bottom of the lever assembly.

5 Disconnect the wiring multi-plugs, then withdraw the selector lever assembly from inside the vehicle. Recover the gasket.

6 If necessary, the selector lever and position indicator may be unbolted from the top of the assembly.

Refitting

7 Refitting is a reversal of the removal procedure, but adjust the selector cable as described in Section 3.

5 Speedometer drive pinion - removal and refitting

Removal

1 The speedometer drive pinion is located on the rear right-hand side of the transmission. First apply the handbrake, then jack up the front of the vehicle and support it on axle stands.

2 On early models, unscrew the nut and disconnect the speedometer cable from the vehicle speed sensor on the transmission. Use two spanners to loosen the nut - one to counterhold the sensor, and the other to unscrew the cable nut.

3 Disconnect the wiring from the vehicle speed sensor.

4 Unscrew the clamp bolt, and remove the clamp plate securing the drive pinion and vehicle speed sensor in the transmission.

5 Pull out the speedometer drive pinion and bearing assembly, together with the vehicle speed sensor.

6 Unscrew the vehicle speed sensor from the drive pinion bearing.

7 Remove the pinion from the bearing.

8 Using a small screwdriver, prise the rubber O-ring from the groove in the bearing; obtain a new one for reassembly.

9 Wipe clean the drive pinion and bearing, also the seating bore in the transmission casing.

Refitting

10 Refitting is a reversal of the removal procedure. Lightly oil the new O-ring before inserting the assembly in the transmission casing. Tighten the clamp bolt.

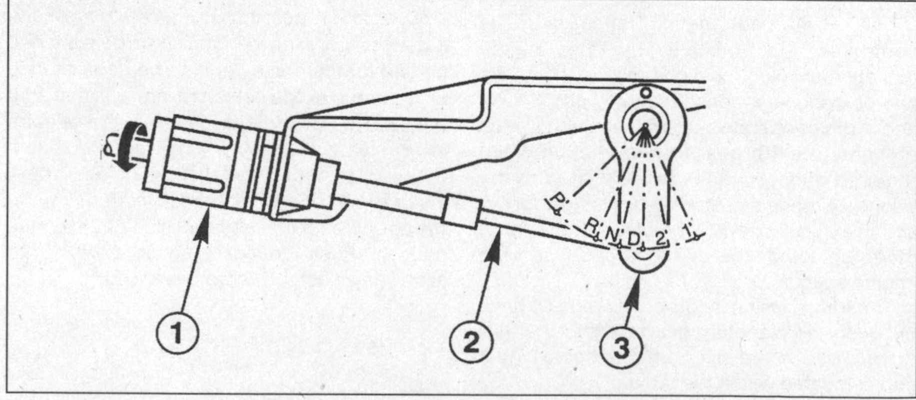

3.11 Selecting position "D" at the transmission

1 Locking ring *2 Cable* *3 Transmission lever*

6.2 Multi-plug (arrowed) for the selector lever position sensor

6.6 Alignment tool for the selector lever position sensor (selector in position "N")

1 Sensor
2 Alignment tool (pegs arrowed)

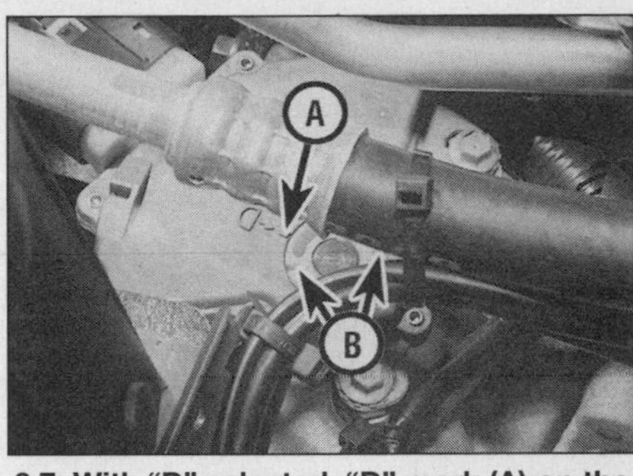

6.7 With "D" selected, "D" mark (A) on the selector lever position sensor should align with cut-outs (B) in shaft's plastic insert (shown here with "P" selected)

6 Selector lever position sensor - removal, refitting and adjustment

Removal

1 Remove the air mass meter and trunking (Chapter 4A) in order to gain access to the selector lever position sensor, which is located on top of the transmission.
2 Disconnect the wiring multi-plug **(see illustration)**.
3 Unscrew the mounting bolts, and remove the sensor.

Refitting and adjustment

4 Refitting is a reversal of the removal procedure, but check the alignment of the sensor as follows before fully tightening the mounting bolts.
5 Move the selector lever to position "N".
6 The Ford tool for aligning the sensor consists of a metal plate, with pegs to engage with the cut-outs in the sensor and shaft **(see illustration)**. A similar tool may be made up, or alternatively, a straight edge may be used to check the alignment.
7 Twist the sensor on the shaft until the slots in the sensor housing and the plastic insert in the shaft are correctly aligned. With the sensor correctly aligned, tighten the bolts, then remove the alignment tool. As a further check, move the selector lever to position "D", and check that the "D" mark on the sensor is aligned with the slots in the shaft's plastic insert **(see illustration)**.

7 Oil seals - renewal

Differential side gear oil seals

1 The procedure is the same as that for the manual transmission (refer to Chapter 7A).

Speedometer drive pinion oil seal

2 The procedure is covered in Section 5.

8 Automatic transmission - removal and refitting

Note: *Read through this procedure before starting work, to see what is involved, particularly in terms of lifting equipment. Depending on the facilities available, the home mechanic may prefer to remove the engine and transmission together, then separate them on the bench, as described in Chapter 2C.*

Removal

1 Disconnect the battery negative (earth) lead (see Chapter 5A). For better access, the battery may be removed completely.
2 If necessary, remove the bonnet (Chapter 11) for better access, and for fitting the engine lifting hoist.
3 Raise the radiator, and hold it in the raised position by inserting split pins through the holes in the upper mounting extensions. This is necessary to retain the radiator when the subframe is removed.
4 Remove the air mass meter and trunking (Chapter 4A).
5 Remove the air cleaner assembly (Chapter 4A).
6 Detach the battery earth lead from the transmission **(see illustration)**.
7 Disconnect the wiring multi-plugs from the inhibitor switch, control unit and transmission speed sensor **(see illustrations)**.
8 Pull the selector cable end fitting from the lever on the side of the transmission, then unbolt the support bracket.
9 Apply the handbrake, jack up the front of the vehicle and support it on axle stands. Remove the front wheels.
10 Remove the wheel arch liner from the right-hand side of the vehicle (Chapter 11).
11 Remove the auxiliary drivebelt cover (see Chapter 1).
12 Working on each side of the vehicle in turn, unscrew the nut and disconnect the anti-roll bar link from the strut, noting that the flexible brake hose bracket is attached to the link stud.
13 Extract the split pins, then unscrew the nuts securing the track rod ends to the

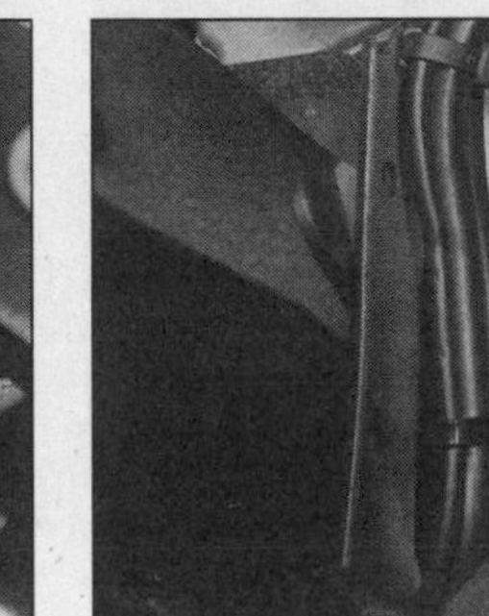

8.6 Earth lead attachment (arrowed) on the transmission

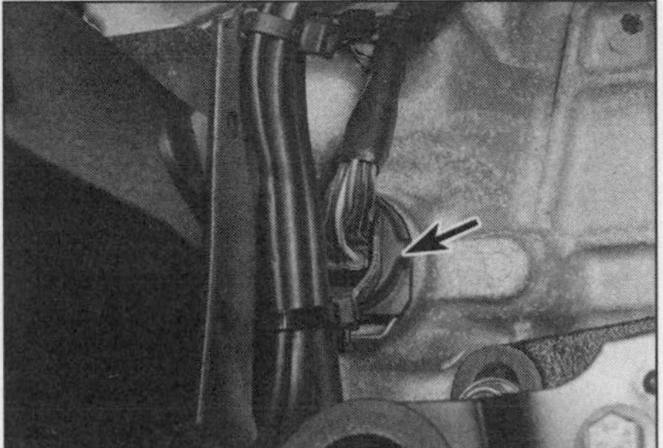

8.7a Inhibitor switch multi-plug (arrowed) on the top of the transmission

8.7b Transmission speed sensor multi-plug on the side of the transmission

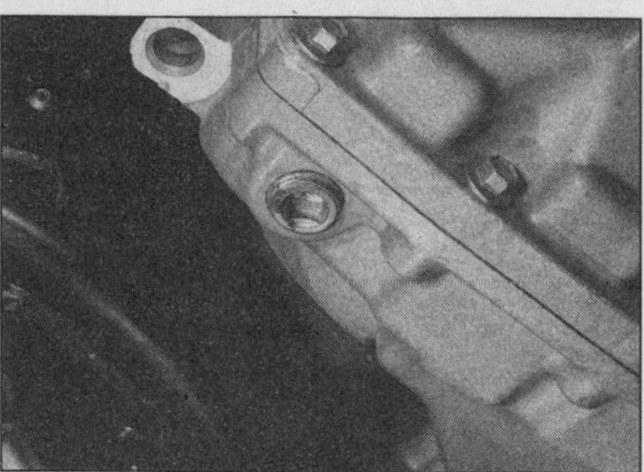

8.28 Automatic transmission fluid drain plug

steering knuckles on each side. Release the balljoints from the steering knuckle arms, using a balljoint separator tool.

14 Working on each side in turn, note which way round the front suspension lower arm balljoint clamp bolt is fitted, then unscrew and remove it from the knuckle assembly. Lever the balljoint down from the knuckle - if it is tight, prise the joint open carefully using a large flat-bladed tool. Take care not to damage the balljoint seal during the separation procedure.

15 Remove the front lower cover from under the radiator, by prising out the side clips and unscrewing the retaining bolts.

16 Drain the cooling system as described in Chapter 1.

17 Disconnect the multi-plug from the wiring leading to the oxygen sensor, then unclip the wiring from the engine rear mounting.

18 Where fitted, disconnect the vacuum hose from the pulse-air system filter.

19 Remove the complete exhaust system (Chapter 4A).

20 On models fitted with air conditioning, unscrew and remove the mounting bolts securing the dehydrator to the subframe, and tie it to one side.

21 Unscrew and remove the bolts securing the steering gear to the subframe. The bolts are difficult to reach using normal spanners, and if possible the special cranked Ford tool should be obtained (see Chapter 10).

22 Unbolt the engine/transmission rear mounting from the subframe.

23 Unscrew and remove the centre bolt from the engine front mounting, and where necessary detach the pulse-air filter from the bracket on the mounting.

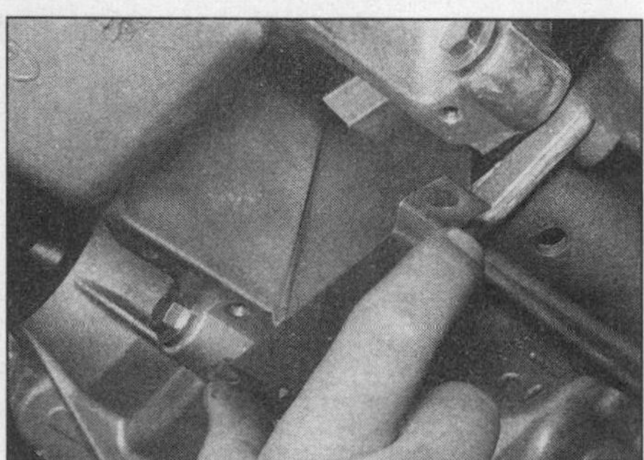

8.34 Removing the cover plate from the bottom of the transmission

24 Unbolt the radiator bracket from the subframe.

25 With the help of an assistant, support the weight of the subframe, using trolley jacks if possible. Unscrew the bolts securing the power steering fluid cooler pipes to the subframe, then unscrew and remove the subframe mounting bolts, and lower the subframe to the ground.

26 Unscrew and remove the centre bolt from the engine/transmission rear mounting, then unbolt the mounting from the transmission.

27 Unscrew the union nut securing the automatic transmission fluid cooler pipe to the left-hand side of the transmission. Unclip the pipe, and move it to one side. Plug the end of the pipe, to prevent dust and dirt entering the hydraulic system.

28 Position a suitable container beneath the transmission, then unscrew the drain plug and drain the fluid **(see illustration)**. Refit and tighten the plug on completion.

29 Insert a lever between the left-hand driveshaft inner joint and the transmission case (with a thin piece of wood against the case), then prise free the joint from the differential. If it proves reluctant to move, strike the lever firmly with the palm of the hand. Be careful not to damage the adjacent components, and be prepared for fluid spillage.

30 Support the left-hand driveshaft on axle stands, making sure that the inner joint is not turned through more than 18° (damage may occur if the joint is turned through too great an angle).

31 Unscrew the bolts securing the right-hand driveshaft centre bearing to the cylinder block, remove the heat shield, then pull out the right-hand strut so that the intermediate shaft is removed from the transmission differential gears. Be prepared for fluid spillage.

32 Support the right-hand driveshaft on axle stands, again making sure that the inner joint is not turned through more than 18° (damage may occur if the joint is turned through too great an angle).

33 At the front of the transmission, unscrew the union nut and disconnect the fluid cooler pipe. Plug the end of the pipe, to prevent dust and dirt entering the hydraulic system.

34 Unscrew the bolts and remove the cover plate from the bottom of the transmission, for access to the torque converter retaining bolts **(see illustration)**.

35 Unscrew and remove the torque converter retaining bolts. It will be necessary to turn the engine, using the crankshaft pulley bolt, so that each of the four bolts can be unscrewed through the aperture.

36 If necessary, the vehicle may be lowered to the ground at this stage, in order to connect an engine support hoist. If an engine support bar which locates over the engine compartment is to be used, then the vehicle may be left in its raised position.

37 Attach the hoist or engine support bar to diagonally-opposite positions on the engine, and take the weight of the engine and transmission.

38 At the top of the engine, disconnect the two wiring multi-plugs from the thermostat housing.

39 Disconnect the radiator hoses from the thermostat housing.

40 Unscrew the mounting bolts, and remove the thermostat housing.

41 Unscrew and remove the upper mounting bolts securing the automatic transmission to the engine.

42 Unscrew the nuts from the engine right-hand mounting bracket. Note that, where a hydraulic mounting is fitted, the mounting must never be tilted by more than 5°.

43 Unscrew the retaining nuts, and remove the engine/transmission left-hand mounting from the transmission.

44 On models fitted with air conditioning, lower the engine until the compressor is below the right-hand side member.

45 On models without air conditioning, lower the transmission until it is opposite the aperture on the left-hand side of the engine compartment.

46 Support the weight of the transmission on a trolley jack. Use safety chains or make up a cradle to steady the transmission on the jack.

47 Unscrew and remove the starter motor mounting bolts.

48 Unscrew and remove the lower bolts securing the transmission to the engine.

49 With the help of an assistant, withdraw the transmission squarely from the engine, making sure that the torque converter comes away with the transmission, and does not stay in contact with the driveplate. If this precaution is not taken, there is a risk of the torque converter falling out and being damaged.

50 Lower the transmission to the ground.

Refitting

51 Clean the contact surfaces of the driveplate and torque converter.

52 Check that the torque converter is fully entered in the transmission. To do this, place a straight-edge on the transmission flange, and check that the torque converter spigot is at least 10 mm below the straight-edge **(see illustration)**.

Caution: This procedure is important, to ensure that the torque converter is engaged with the fluid pump. If it is not fully engaged, serious damage will occur.

53 With the help of an assistant, raise the transmission, and locate it on the rear of the driveplate. The torque converter must remain in full engagement during the fitting procedure.

54 Refit and tighten the transmission-to-engine bolts.

55 Refit and tighten the starter motor mounting bolts.

56 Remove the trolley jack.

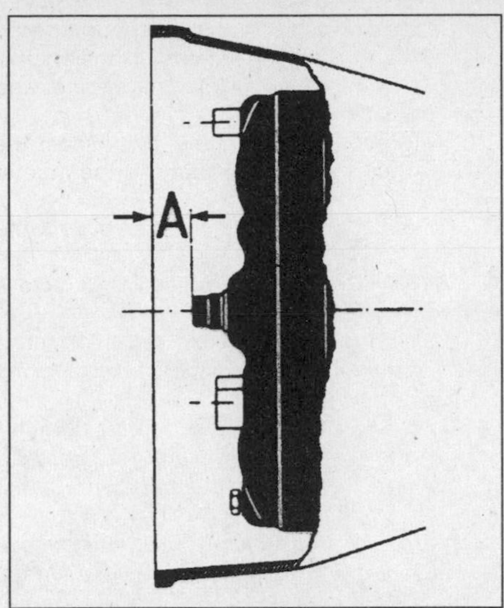

8.52 Torque converter spigot must be at least 10 mm below the transmission flange (dimension A)

57 Refit the engine/transmission left-hand and right-hand mountings, but do not fully tighten them at this stage.
58 Refit the thermostat housing, and tighten the bolts.
59 Reconnect the radiator hoses to the thermostat housing.
60 Reconnect the two wiring multi-plugs to the thermostat housing.
61 Insert and tighten all of the torque converter retaining bolts to the specified torque. Turn the engine as required to bring each of the bolts into view. **Note:** *Insert all of the bolts before tightening any of them.*
62 Refit the cover plate to the bottom of the transmission, and tighten the bolts.
63 Refit the fluid cooler pipe to the front of the transmission, and tighten the union nut.
64 Refit the right-hand driveshaft and intermediate shaft, together with the heat shield (refer to Chapter 8 if necessary).
65 Refit the left-hand driveshaft (refer to Chapter 8 if necessary).
66 Refit the fluid cooler pipe to the left-hand side of the transmission, making sure that it engages with the clips correctly. Tighten the union nut.
67 Refit the engine/transmission rear mounting to the transmission, but do not fully tighten the centre bolt at this stage.
68 Refit the subframe, and align it as described in Chapter 2B, Section 4. Tighten the mounting bolts to the specified torque.
69 Refit the power steering fluid cooler pipes to the subframe, and tighten the bolts.
70 Refit the radiator bracket to the subframe, and tighten the bolts.
71 Insert the centre bolt in the engine front mounting, and hand-tighten it.
72 Where fitted, refit the pulse-air filter to the engine front mounting bracket.
73 Secure the engine/transmission rear mounting to the subframe.
74 Remove the hoist from the engine.
75 Align and tighten the engine mounting bolts, with reference to Chapter 2A.
76 Refit the steering gear to the subframe, and tighten the bolts.
77 On models fitted with air conditioning, refit the dehydrator to the subframe, and tighten the bolts.
78 Refit the complete exhaust system, with reference to Chapter 4A.
79 Reconnect the vacuum hose to the pulse-air system filter where applicable.
80 Reconnect the oxygen sensor multi-plug, then clip the wiring to the engine rear mounting.
81 Refit the front lower cover under the radiator.
82 Refit both of the front suspension lower arm balljoints, and tighten the clamp bolts. Refer to Chapter 10 if necessary.
83 Refit the track rod ends to the steering knuckles on both sides. Refer to Chapter 10 if necessary.
84 Refit the anti-roll bar links to the struts on both sides.
85 Refit the auxiliary drivebelt cover and the right-hand side wheel arch liner.
86 Refit the front wheels, and lower the vehicle to the ground. Tighten the wheel nuts.
87 Refit the selector cable and bracket, and tighten the bolts.
88 Reconnect the wiring multi-plugs for the inhibitor switch and control switch.
89 Refit the battery earth lead to the transmission, and tighten the bolt.
90 Refit the air cleaner assembly as described in Chapter 4A.
91 Refit the air mass meter and air inlet duct, with reference to Chapter 4A.
92 Remove the split pins holding the radiator in its raised position.
93 If removed, refit the bonnet with reference to Chapter 11.
94 Reconnect the battery negative (earth) lead (see Chapter 5A).
95 Adjust the selector cable as described in Section 3.
96 Adjust the selector lever position sensor as described in Section 6.
97 Fill the transmission with the correct quantity of fluid, through the dipstick/filler tube (see Chapter 1).
98 Refill the cooling system with reference to Chapter 1.
99 After running the engine, recheck the transmission fluid level, and top-up if necessary (refer to Chapter 1).
100 Road test the vehicle to check the transmission for correct operation.

9 Automatic transmission mountings - checking and renewal

This procedure is covered in Chapter 2A.

10 Automatic transmission overhaul - general information

Overhaul of the automatic transmission should be left to an automatic transmission specialist or a Ford dealer. Refer to the information given in Section 2 before removing the unit.

Note that, if the vehicle is still within the warranty period, in the event of a fault it is important to take it to a Ford dealer, who will carry out a comprehensive diagnosis procedure using specialist equipment. Failure to do this will invalidate the warranty.

Chapter 8
Driveshafts

Contents

Degrees of difficulty

Easy, suitable for novice with little experience 	**Fairly easy,** suitable for beginner with some experience 	**Fairly difficult,** suitable for competent DIY mechanic 	**Difficult,** suitable for experienced DIY mechanic 	**Very difficult,** suitable for expert DIY or professional

Specifications

Torque wrench settings	**Nm**	**lbf ft**
Anti-roll bar link to suspension strut	47	35
Driveshaft support bearing bracket-to-cylinder block bolts	48	35
Driveshaft/hub retaining nut	340	251
Lower arm balljoint clamp bolt/nut	83	61
Right-hand intermediate shaft bearing and heat shield bolts	27	20
Roadwheel nuts	85	63
Suspension strut upper mounting nut	46	34
Track rod end balljoint nut	28	21

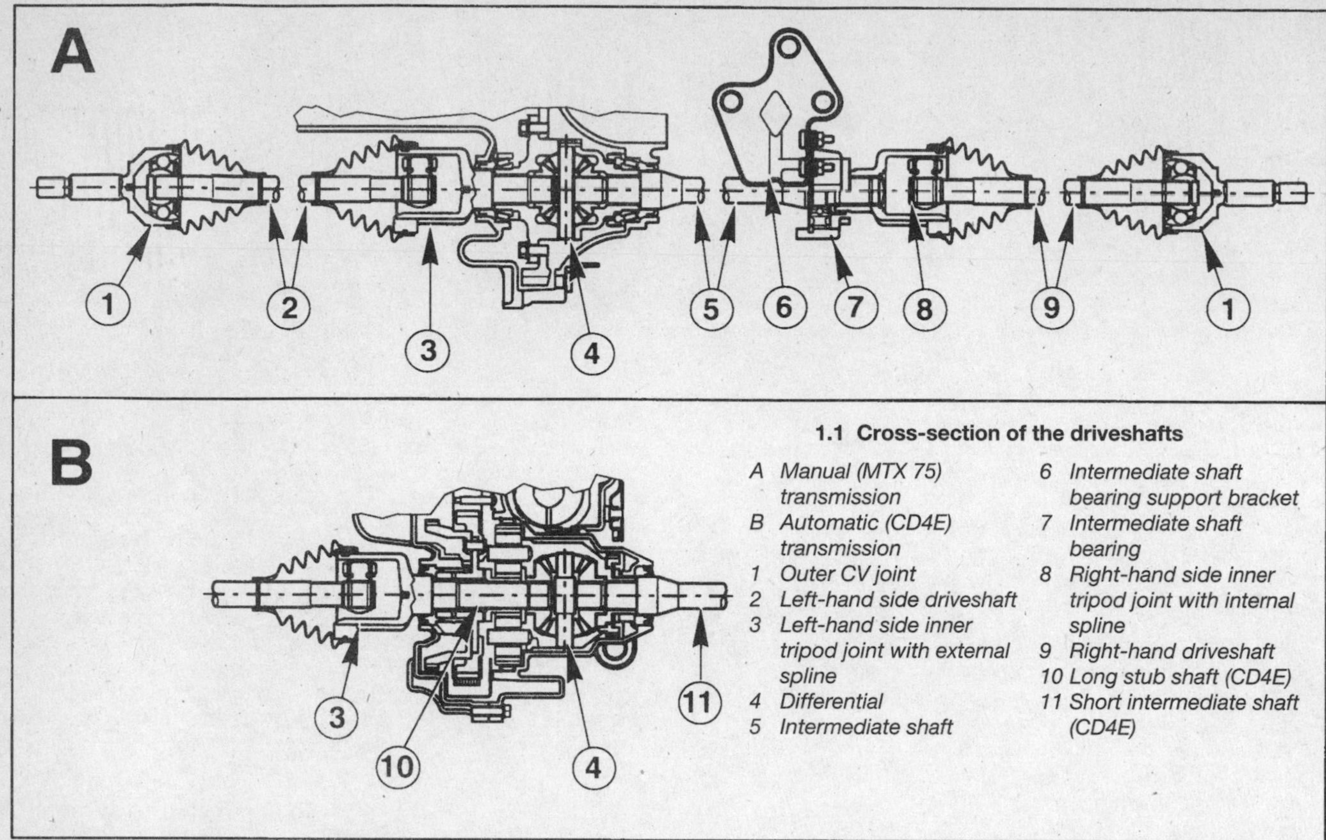

1.1 Cross-section of the driveshafts

A Manual (MTX 75) transmission
B Automatic (CD4E) transmission
1 Outer CV joint
2 Left-hand side driveshaft
3 Left-hand side inner tripod joint with external spline
4 Differential
5 Intermediate shaft
6 Intermediate shaft bearing support bracket
7 Intermediate shaft bearing
8 Right-hand side inner tripod joint with internal spline
9 Right-hand driveshaft
10 Long stub shaft (CD4E)
11 Short intermediate shaft (CD4E)

1 General information

Drive is transmitted from the transmission differential to the front wheels by means of two driveshafts. The right-hand driveshaft is in two sections, and incorporates a support bearing **(see illustration)**.

Each driveshaft consists of three main components: the sliding (tripod type) inner joint, the actual driveshaft, and the outer CV (constant velocity) joint. The inner (male) end of the left-hand tripod joint is secured in the differential side gear by the engagement of a circlip. The inner (female) end of the right-hand driveshaft is held on the intermediate shaft by the engagement of a circlip. The intermediate shaft is held in the transmission by the support bearing, which in turn is supported by a bracket bolted to the rear of the cylinder block. The outer CV joint on both driveshafts is of ball-bearing type, and is secured in the front hub by the hub nut.

2.1 Loosen the driveshaft nut with the wheel on the ground

2 Driveshafts - removal and refitting

Removal

1 Remove the wheel cover (or centre cover) from the wheel, apply the handbrake, and engage 1st gear or 'P'. Loosen the hub nut about half a turn **(see illustration)**. This nut is very tight - use only high-quality, close-fitting tools, and take adequate precautions against personal injury when loosening the hub nut.

2 Loosen the front wheel retaining nuts. Apply the handbrake, jack up the front of the vehicle and support it on axle stands. Remove the wheel.

3 To avoid spillage when the driveshafts are separated from the transmission, drain the transmission oil or fluid as described in Chapter 1.

4 Remove the front brake disc as described in Chapter 9.

5 Completely unscrew and remove the hub/driveshaft retaining nut. Note that the nut is of special laminated design, and should only be re-used a maximum of 5 times. (It is a good idea to file a small notch in the nut every time it is removed.) Obtain a new nut if necessary.

6 Retain the suspension strut piston with an Allen key, then loosen the strut upper mounting nut and unscrew it by five complete turns. It is not necessary to remove the nut at this stage, but note that a new one will be required on refitting. Where necessary, detach the ABS wiring from the strut.

7 Unscrew the nut securing the anti-roll bar link to the front suspension strut, and position the link to one side.

8 Extract the split pin from the track rod end balljoint nut. Unscrew the nut, and detach the rod from the arm on the steering knuckle using a conventional balljoint removal tool. Take care not to damage the balljoint seal.

9 Note which way round the front suspension lower arm balljoint clamp bolt is fitted, then unscrew and remove it from the knuckle assembly. Lever the balljoint down from the knuckle; if it is tight, carefully prise the clamp open using a large flat-bladed tool. Take care not to damage the balljoint seal during the separation procedure.

2.10a Using a puller on the hub flange . . .

2.10b . . . to press the driveshaft out of the front hub and steering knuckle

2.11 Removing the left-hand driveshaft from the transmission

10 Using a universal puller located on the hub flange, press the driveshaft through the front hub and steering knuckle by pulling the knuckle outwards **(see illustrations)**. When the driveshaft is free, support it on an axle stand, making sure that the inner tripod joint is not turned through more than 18° (damage may occur if the joint is turned through too great an angle).

Left-hand side

11 Insert a lever between the inner driveshaft joint and the transmission case, with a thin piece of wood against the case. Prise free the inner joint from the differential **(see illustration)**. If it proves reluctant to move, strike the lever firmly with the palm of the hand.

12 Be careful not to damage the adjacent components, and in particular, make sure that the driveshaft oil seal in the differential is not damaged. Especially if the transmission was not drained, be prepared for oil spillage.

13 On manual transmissions only, note that if the right-hand driveshaft has already been removed, it is possible to release the left-hand driveshaft by inserting a forked drift from the right-hand side. However, care must be taken to prevent damage to the differential gears, particularly if the special Ford tool is not used.

14 Withdraw the driveshaft from under the vehicle.

15 Extract the circlip from the groove on the inner end of the driveshaft, and obtain a new one.

Right-hand side

16 The right-hand driveshaft may either be removed complete with the intermediate shaft from the transmission, or it may be disconnected from the outer end of the intermediate shaft. If the latter course of action is taken, use a soft-faced mallet to sharply tap the inner CV joint housing from the intermediate shaft. The internal circlip will be released, and the driveshaft may be withdrawn from the splines.

17 Extract the circlip from the groove on the outer end of the intermediate shaft. Obtain a new circlip for use when refitting.

18 If the complete driveshaft is to be removed, proceed as follows. Unscrew the bolts securing the driveshaft support bearing bracket to the rear of the cylinder block, and remove the heat shield **(see illustration)**.

19 Withdraw the complete driveshaft from the transmission and from the bearing bracket, and remove it from under the vehicle **(see illustration)**. Especially if the transmission was not drained, be prepared for oil spillage.

Both sides

20 Check the condition of the differential oil seals, and if necessary renew them as described in Chapter 7A (manual transmission) or Chapter 7B (automatic transmission). Check the support bearing, and if necessary renew it as described in Section 5.

Refitting

Right-hand side

21 If the intermediate shaft has not been removed, proceed to paragraph 24. Otherwise, proceed as follows.

22 Carefully refit the complete driveshaft in the support bearing and into the transmission, taking care not to damage the oil seal. Turn the driveshaft until it engages the splines on the differential gears.

23 Tighten the bolts securing the support bearing to the bracket on the cylinder block to the specified torque. Proceed to paragraph 29.

24 Locate the new circlip in the groove on the outer end of the intermediate shaft, then smear a little grease over the entire circumference of the intermediate shaft splines.

25 Locate the right-hand driveshaft on the intermediate shaft splines, and push it on until the internal circlip is heard to engage with the groove in the shaft.

Left-hand side

26 Locate the new circlip in the groove on the inner end of the driveshaft.

27 On automatic transmissions, Ford technicians use a special sleeve to protect the differential oil seal as the driveshaft is inserted. If the sleeve is not used, take great care to avoid damaging the seal.

28 Insert the driveshaft into the transmission, making sure that the circlip is fully engaged.

Both sides

29 Pull the knuckle outwards, and insert the outer end of the driveshaft through the hub. Turn the driveshaft to engage the splines in the hub, and fully push on the hub. Ford use a special tool to draw the driveshaft into the hub, but it is unlikely that the splines will be tight. However, if they are, it will be necessary to obtain the tool, or to use a similar home-made tool.

30 Screw on the hub nut finger-tight.

31 Locate the front suspension lower arm balljoint stub in the bottom of the knuckle. Insert the clamp bolt in the previously-noted position, screw on the nut, and tighten it to the specified torque.

32 Refit the track rod end balljoint to the steering knuckle, and screw on the nut. Tighten the nut to the specified torque.

33 Check that the balljoint nut split pin holes are aligned. If not, re-position the nut, but make

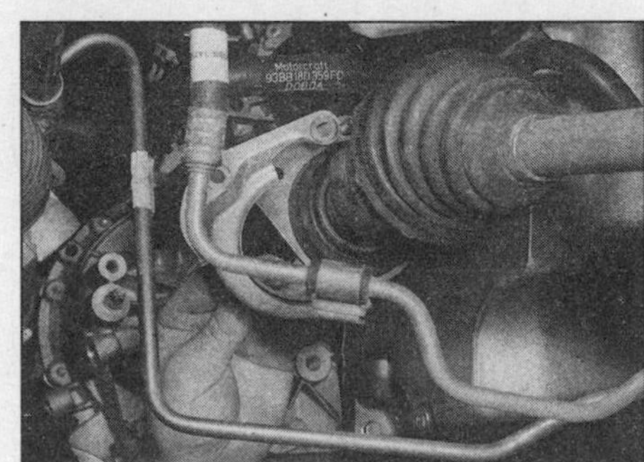

2.18 Removing the heat shield from the right-hand driveshaft support bearing

2.19 Removing the complete right-hand driveshaft

2.39 Torque-tightening the hub nut

sure that it is still tightened within the tolerance of the torque wrench setting. Insert a new split pin, and bend its legs back to secure it.
34 Locate the anti-roll bar link on the front suspension strut, and tighten the nut to the specified torque.
35 Remove the suspension strut upper mounting nut and fit the new nut, tightening it to the specified torque. Where necessary, refit the ABS wiring to the strut bracket.
36 Refit the front brake disc with reference to Chapter 9.
37 Fill the transmission with oil or fluid, and check the level as described in Chapter 1.
38 Refit the wheel, and lower the vehicle to the ground. Tighten the wheel retaining nuts to the specified torque.
39 Fully tighten the hub nut to the specified torque **(see illustration)**. Finally, refit the wheel cover (or centre cover).

3 Driveshaft inner CV joint gaiter - renewal

1 The inner CV joint gaiter is renewed by disconnecting the driveshaft from the inner CV joint housing at the transmission (left-hand side) or intermediate shaft (right-hand side). The work can be carried out either with the driveshaft removed from the vehicle, or with it in situ. If it is wished to fully remove the driveshaft, refer to Section 2 first. Note that if both the inner and outer gaiters are being renewed at the same time, the outer gaiter can be removed from the inner end of the driveshaft.

Renewal without removing the driveshaft

2 Loosen the front wheel nuts on the appropriate side. Apply the handbrake, jack up the front of the vehicle and support it on axle stands. Remove the wheel.
3 Unscrew the nut securing the anti-roll bar link to the front suspension strut, and position the link to one side.
4 Extract the split pin from the track rod end balljoint nut. Unscrew the nut, and detach the rod from the arm on the steering knuckle using a conventional balljoint removal tool. Take care not to damage the balljoint seal.
5 Note which way round the front suspension lower arm balljoint clamp bolt is fitted, then unscrew and remove it from the knuckle assembly. Lever the balljoint down from the knuckle; if it is tight, prise the clamp open carefully using a large flat-bladed tool. Take care not to damage the balljoint seal during the separation procedure.
6 Mark the driveshaft in relation to the joint housing, to ensure correct refitting.
7 Note the fitted location of both of the inner joint gaiter retaining clips. Release the clips from the gaiter, and slide the gaiter back along the driveshaft (away from the transmission) a little way.
8 Pull the front suspension strut outwards, while guiding the tripod joint out of the joint housing. As the joint tripod is being withdrawn from the housing, be prepared for some of the bearing rollers to fall out. Identify them for position with a dab of paint. Support the inner end of the driveshaft on an axle stand.
9 Remove the support ring from the joint housing.
10 Remove the remaining bearing rollers from the tripod, and identify them for position with a dab of paint.
11 Check that the inner end of the driveshaft is marked in relation to the splined tripod hub. If not, carefully centre-punch the two items, to ensure correct refitting. Alternatively, use dabs of paint on the driveshaft and one end of the tripod.
12 Extract the circlip retaining the tripod on the driveshaft.
13 Using a suitable puller, remove the tripod from the end of the driveshaft, and slide off the gaiter.
14 If the outer gaiter is also to be renewed, remove it with reference to Section 4.
15 Clean the driveshaft, and obtain a new tripod retaining circlip. The gaiter retaining clips and the steering track rod end split pin must also be renewed.
16 Slide the new gaiter on the driveshaft, together with new clips. Also locate the support ring on the joint housing.
17 Refit the tripod on the driveshaft splines, if necessary using a soft-faced mallet to drive it fully onto the splines. It must be fitted with the chamfered edge leading (towards the driveshaft), and with the previously-made marks aligned. Secure it in position using the new circlip. Ensure that the circlip is fully engaged in its groove.
18 Locate the bearing rollers on the tripod in their previously-noted positions, using grease to hold them in place.
19 With the front suspension strut pulled outwards, guide the tripod joint into the joint housing, making sure that the previously-made marks are aligned. Pack the joint with 180 grams of CV joint grease.
20 Slide the gaiter along the driveshaft, and locate it on the support ring located on the joint housing. The small-diameter end of the gaiter must be located in the groove on the driveshaft.
21 Ensure that the gaiter is not twisted or distorted, then insert a small screwdriver under the lip of the gaiter at the housing end. This will allow trapped air to escape during the next step.
22 Push the tripod fully into the housing, then pull it out by 20 mm. Remove the screwdriver, then fit the retaining clips and tighten them.
23 Reconnect the front suspension lower arm balljoint to the knuckle assembly. Refit and tighten the clamp nut and bolt.
24 Reconnect the track rod end balljoint to the steering knuckle, and tighten the nut to the specified torque. Check that the split pin holes are correctly aligned; if necessary, reposition the nut, making sure that it is still tightened within the torque tolerance. Insert a new split pin, and bend its legs back to secure it.
25 Refit the anti-roll bar link to the front suspension strut, and tighten the nut to the specified torque.
26 Refit the wheel, and lower the vehicle to the ground. Tighten the wheel nuts.

Renewal with the driveshaft on the bench

27 Mount the driveshaft in a vice.
28 Mark the driveshaft in relation to the joint housing, to ensure correct refitting.
29 Note the fitted location of both of the inner joint gaiter retaining clips, then release the clips from the gaiter, and slide the gaiter back along the driveshaft a little way **(see illustration)**.
30 Remove the inner joint housing from the tripod. As the housing is being removed, be prepared for some of the bearing rollers to fall out. Identify them for position with a dab of paint.
31 Remove the support ring from the joint housing **(see illustration)**.

3.29 Removing the gaiter from the inner joint housing

3.31 Removing the support ring from the joint housing

3.32 Removing the bearing rollers

3.34 Circlip (arrowed) retaining the tripod on the driveshaft

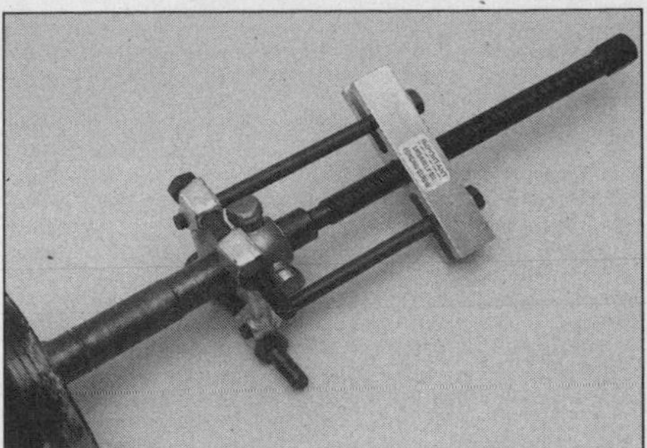

3.35 Using a puller to remove the tripod

3.38 Slide the gaiter and clips onto the driveshaft

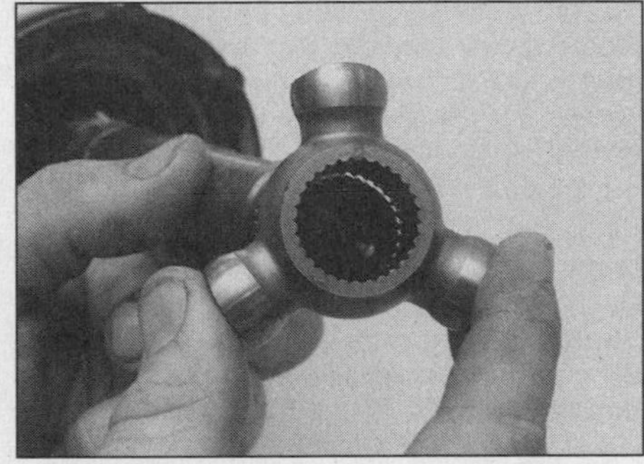

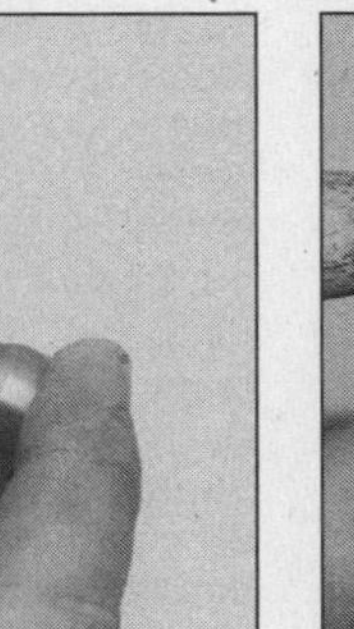

3.40a Locate the tripod on the splines . . .

3.40b . . . and drive it fully onto the driveshaft

32 Remove the remaining bearing rollers from the tripod, and identify them for position with a dab of paint **(see illustration)**.

33 Check that the inner end of the driveshaft is marked in relation to the splined tripod hub. If not, carefully centre-punch the two items, to ensure correct refitting. Alternatively, use dabs of paint on the driveshaft and one end of the tripod.

34 Extract the circlip retaining the tripod on the driveshaft **(see illustration)**.

35 Using a puller, remove the tripod from the end of the driveshaft, and slide off the gaiter **(see illustration)**.

36 If the outer gaiter is also to be renewed, remove it with reference to Section 4.

37 Clean the driveshaft, and obtain a new joint retaining circlip. The gaiter retaining clips must also be renewed.

38 Slide the new gaiter on the driveshaft, together with new clips **(see illustration)**.

3.45 Using pincers to tighten the retaining clips

39 Locate the support ring on the CV joint housing.

40 Refit the tripod on the driveshaft splines, if necessary using a soft-faced mallet and a suitable socket to drive it fully onto the splines **(see illustrations)**. It must be fitted with the chamfered edge leading (towards the driveshaft), and with the previously-made marks aligned. Secure it in position using a new circlip. Ensure that the circlip is fully engaged in its groove.

41 Locate the bearing rollers on the tripod in their previously-noted positions, using grease to hold them in place.

42 Guide the joint housing onto the tripod joint, making sure that the previously-made marks are aligned. Scoop out all of the old grease, then pack the joint with 180 grams of new CV joint grease.

43 Slide the gaiter along the driveshaft, and locate it on the support ring on the CV joint housing. The small-diameter end of the gaiter must be located in the groove on the driveshaft.

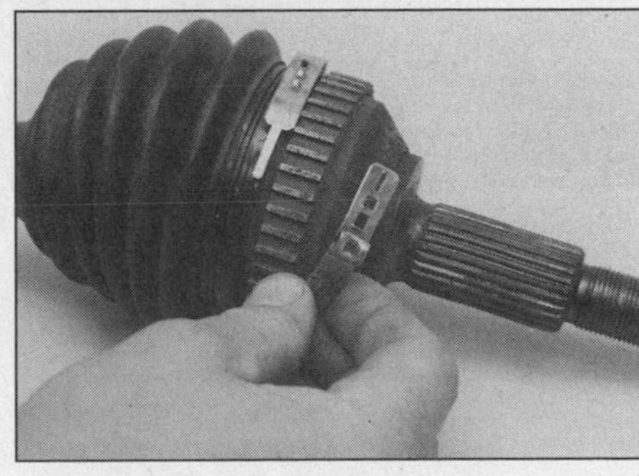

4.4a Release the clips . . .

44 Ensure that the gaiter is not twisted or distorted, then insert a small screwdriver under the lip of the gaiter at the housing end. This will allow trapped air to escape during the next step.

45 Push the housing fully on the tripod, then pull it out by 20 mm. Remove the screwdriver, then fit the retaining clips and tighten them **(see illustration)**.

4 Driveshaft outer CV joint gaiter - renewal

1 The outer CV joint gaiter can be renewed by removing the inner gaiter first as described in Section 3, or after removing the driveshaft complete as described in Section 2. If the driveshaft is removed, then the inner gaiter need not necessarily be removed. It is impractical to renew the outer gaiter by dismantling the outer joint with the driveshaft in position in the vehicle. The following paragraphs describe renewal of the gaiter on the bench.

2 Mount the driveshaft in a vice.

3 Mark the driveshaft in relation to the CV joint housing, to ensure correct refitting.

4 Note the fitted location of both of the outer joint gaiter retaining clips, then release the clips from the gaiter, and slide the gaiter back along the driveshaft a little way **(see illustrations)**.

4.4b . . . and remove the gaiter

4.5a Drive off the outer CV joint hub . . .

4.5b . . . and remove the joint from the driveshaft

5 Using a brass drift or a copper mallet, carefully drive the outer CV joint hub from the splines on the driveshaft **(see illustrations)**. Initial resistance will be felt until the internal circlips are released. Take care not to damage the bearing cage.

6 Extract the outer circlip from the end of the driveshaft **(see illustration)**.

7 Slide the gaiter over the remaining circlip, and remove it together with the clips.

8 Clean the driveshaft, and obtain new joint retaining circlips. The gaiter retaining clips must also be renewed.

9 Slide the new gaiter (together with new clips) onto the driveshaft and over the inner circlip **(see illustration)**.

10 Fit a new outer circlip to the groove in the driveshaft.

11 Scoop out all of the old grease, then pack the joint with 100 grams of new CV joint grease **(see illustration)**. If no new grease is supplied with the gaiter, use a good-quality molybdenum disulphide grease (such as Duckhams LBM 10). Take care that the fresh grease does not become contaminated with dirt or grit as it is being applied.

12 Locate the CV joint on the driveshaft so that the splines are aligned, then push the joint until the internal circlips are fully engaged.

13 Move the gaiter along the driveshaft, and locate it over the joint and onto the outer CV joint housing. The small-diameter end of the gaiter must be located in the groove on the driveshaft.

14 Ensure that the gaiter is not twisted or distorted, then insert a small screwdriver under the lip of the gaiter at the housing end, to allow any trapped air to escape.

15 Remove the screwdriver, fit the retaining clips in their previously-noted positions, and tighten them.

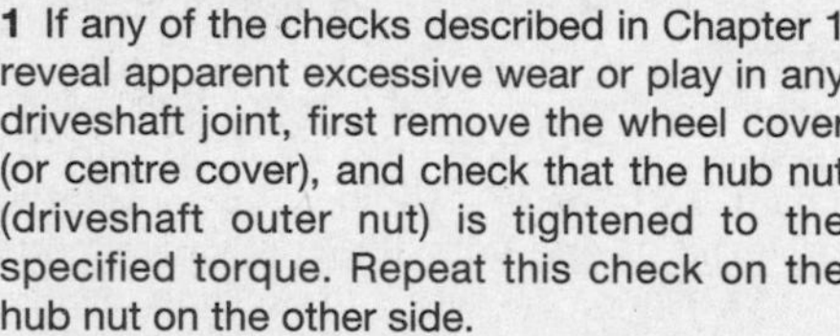

5 Driveshafts - inspection and joint renewal

1 If any of the checks described in Chapter 1 reveal apparent excessive wear or play in any driveshaft joint, first remove the wheel cover (or centre cover), and check that the hub nut (driveshaft outer nut) is tightened to the specified torque. Repeat this check on the hub nut on the other side.

2 Road test the vehicle, and listen for a metallic clicking from the front, as the vehicle is driven slowly in a circle on full-lock. If a clicking noise is heard, this indicates wear in the outer constant velocity joint, which means that the joint must be renewed; reconditioning is not possible.

3 To renew an outer CV joint, remove the driveshaft as described in Section 2, then separate the joint from the driveshaft with reference to Section 4. In principle, the gaiter can be left on the driveshaft, provided that it is in good condition; in practice, it makes sense to renew the gaiter in any case, having got this far.

4 If vibration, consistent with road speed, is felt through the car when accelerating, there is a possibility of wear in the inner tripod joints.

5 To renew an inner joint, remove the driveshaft as described in Section 2, then separate the joint from the driveshaft with reference to Section 3.

6 Continual noise from the right-hand driveshaft, increasing with road speed, may indicate wear in the support bearing. To renew this bearing, the driveshaft and intermediate shaft must be removed, and the bearing extracted using a puller.

7 Remove the bearing dust cover, and obtain a new one.

8 Drive or press on the new bearing, applying the pressure to the inner race only. Similarly drive or press on the new dust cover.

4.6 Circlips fitted on the outer end of the driveshaft

4.9 Fitting the new gaiter and clips on the driveshaft

4.11 Packing the outer CV joint with new grease

Chapter 9
Braking system

Contents

Degrees of difficulty

Easy, suitable for novice with little experience 	**Fairly easy,** suitable for beginner with some experience 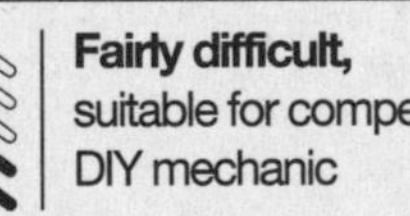	**Fairly difficult,** suitable for competent DIY mechanic	**Difficult,** suitable for experienced DIY mechanic	**Very difficult,** suitable for expert DIY or professional

Specifications

Front brakes

Type	Ventilated disc, with single-piston floating caliper
Disc diameter:	
Four-cylinder engine models	260.0 mm
V6 engine models	278.0 mm
Disc thickness:	
New	24.15 mm
Minimum	22.20 mm
Maximum disc run-out (fitted)	0.15 mm
Maximum disc thickness variation	0.015 mm
Front hub face maximum run-out	0.05 mm

Rear drum brakes

Type	Leading and trailing shoes, with automatic adjusters
Drum diameter:	
New:	
1.6 litre Saloon/Hatchback	203.0 mm
1.8 and 2.0 litre Saloon/Hatchback	228.6 mm
Estate	228.6 mm
Maximum diameter:	
1.6 litre Saloon/Hatchback	204.2 mm
1.8 and 2.0 litre Saloon/Hatchback	229.6 mm
Estate	229.6 mm

Rear disc brakes

Type	Solid disc, with single-piston floating caliper
Disc diameter	252.0 mm
Disc thickness:	
New	20.0 mm
Minimum	18.0 mm
Maximum disc run-out (fitted)	0.15 mm
Maximum disc thickness variation	0.015 mm
Rear hub face maximum run-out	0.05 mm

Torque wrench settings

Torque wrench settings	Nm	lbf ft
ABS hydraulic unit to bracket	20	15
Automatic transmission selector cable support bracket bolts	24	18
Brake pipe unions	13	10
Front caliper bracket	120	89
Front caliper guide bolts	28	21
Handbrake lever mountings	23	17
Master cylinder mountings	25	18
Rear caliper bracket	59	44
Rear caliper guide bolts	41	30
Rear drum brake backplate	50	37
Roadwheel nuts	85	63
Splash shield bolts	90	66
Vacuum servo unit	40	30

1 General information

The braking system is of diagonally-split, dual-circuit design, with ventilated discs at the front, and drum or disc brakes (according to model) at the rear. The front calipers are of floating single-piston design, using asbestos-free pads. The rear drum brakes are of the leading and trailing shoe type. They are self-adjusting during footbrake operation. The rear brake shoe linings are of different thicknesses, in order to allow for the different proportional rates of wear.

Pressure-control relief (PCR) valves are fitted to the rear brakes, to prevent rear wheel lock-up under hard braking. The valves are sometimes referred to as pressure-conscious reducing valves. On non-ABS models, they are fitted in the master cylinder rear brake outlet ports; on ABS models, they are located on the ABS unit.

When rear disc brakes are fitted, the rear brake caliper is located on the front of the knuckle on Saloon and Hatchback models, and on the rear of the knuckle on Estate models.

The handbrake is cable-operated, and acts on the rear brakes. On rear drum brake models, the cables operate on the rear trailing brake shoe operating levers, and on rear disc brake models, they operate on levers on the rear calipers. The handbrake lever incorporates an automatic adjuster, which removes any slack from the cables when the lever is disengaged. Handbrake lever movement remains consistent at all times, and no adjustment is necessary or possible.

Where fitted, the anti-lock braking system (ABS) is of the four-channel low-pressure type. It uses the basic conventional brake system, together with an ABS hydraulic unit fitted between the master cylinder and the four wheel brakes. The hydraulic unit consists of a hydraulic actuator, an ABS brake pressure pump, an ABS module with built-in relay box, and two pressure-control relief valves. Braking at each of the four wheels is controlled by separate solenoid valves in the hydraulic actuator. If wheel lock-up is detected on a wheel when the vehicle speed is above 3 mph, the valve opens, releasing pressure to the relevant brake, until the wheel regains a rotational speed corresponding to the speed of the vehicle. The cycle can be repeated many times a second. In the event of a fault in the ABS system, the conventional braking system is not affected. Diagnosis of a fault in the ABS system requires the use of special equipment, and this work should therefore be left to a Ford dealer. Diagnostic connectors are located on the side of the left-hand front suspension turret.

The traction control system (TCS) is fitted as an option to some models, and uses the basic ABS system, with an additional pump and valves fitted to the hydraulic actuator. If wheelspin is detected at a speed below 30 mph, one of the valves opens, to allow the pump to pressurise the relevant brake, until the spinning wheel slows to a rotational speed corresponding to the speed of the vehicle. This has the effect of transferring torque to the wheel with most traction. At the same time, the throttle plate is closed slightly, to reduce the torque from the engine. At speeds above 30 mph, the TCS operates by throttle plate adjustment only.

Note: *When servicing any part of the system, work carefully and methodically; also observe scrupulous cleanliness when overhauling any part of the hydraulic system. Always renew components (in axle sets, where applicable) if in doubt about their condition, and use only genuine Ford replacement parts, or at least those of known good quality. Note the warnings given in "Safety first!" and at relevant points in this Chapter concerning the dangers of asbestos dust and hydraulic fluid.*

2 Front brake pads - renewal

Warning: Disc brake pads must be renewed on BOTH front wheels at the same time - never renew the pads on only one wheel, as uneven braking may result. Although genuine Ford linings are asbestos-free, the dust created by wear of non-genuine pads may contain asbestos, which is a health hazard. Never blow it out with compressed air, and don't inhale any of it. DO NOT use petroleum-based solvents to clean brake parts; use brake cleaner or methylated spirit only. DO NOT allow any brake fluid, oil or grease to contact the brake pads or disc. Also refer to the warning at the start of Section 11 concerning brake fluid.

1 Apply the handbrake. Loosen the front wheel nuts, then jack up the front of the vehicle and support it on axle stands. Remove the front wheels. Work on one brake assembly at a time, using the assembled brake for reference if necessary.

2 Disconnect the brake pad wear warning light wiring plug, and release the wiring from the clip on the brake caliper, noting its routing **(see illustrations)**. Only the inner pad is fitted with a wear warning light wire.

3 Using a suitable screwdriver, prise the pad retaining clip from the caliper. Hold the clip with a pair of pliers as this is done, to avoid personal injury **(see illustration)**.

2.2a Disconnect the pad wear warning light wiring plug . . .

2.2b . . . and detach the wiring plug from the clip on the caliper

2.3 Prising the pad retaining clip from the caliper - note the use of pliers

2.4a Prise the plastic covers from the guide pins . . .

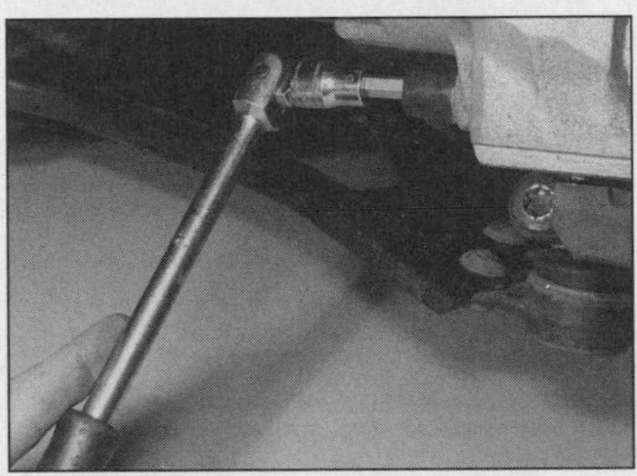
2.4b . . . using a 7 mm Allen key, unscrew . . .

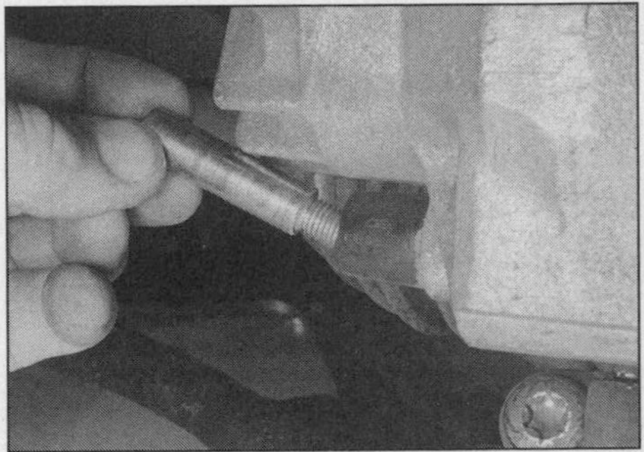
2.4c . . . and remove the caliper guide bolts

4 Prise the plastic covers from the ends of the two guide pins, then using a 7 mm Allen key, unscrew and remove the guide bolts securing the caliper to the carrier bracket **(see illustrations)**.

5 Withdraw the caliper from the disc, and support it on an axle stand to avoid straining the hydraulic hose. The outer pad will normally remain in position against the disc, but the inner pad will stay attached to the piston in the caliper **(see illustration)**.

6 Pull the inner pad from the piston in the caliper, then remove the outer pad from the carrier bracket, noting their fitted positions **(see illustrations)**.

7 Brush all dust and dirt from the caliper, pads and disc, but do not inhale it, as it may be harmful to health. Scrape any corrosion from the edge of the disc, taking care not to damage the friction surface.

8 Inspect the front brake disc for scoring and cracks. If a detailed inspection is necessary, refer to Section 4.

9 The piston must be pushed back into the caliper bore, to provide room for the new brake pads. A C-clamp can be used to accomplish this. As the piston is depressed to the bottom of the caliper bore, the fluid in the master cylinder will rise slightly. Make sure that there is sufficient space in the brake fluid reservoir to accept the displaced fluid, and if necessary, syphon some off first.

10 Fit the new pads using a reversal of the removal procedure, but tighten the guide bolts to the torque wrench setting given in the Specifications at the beginning of this Chapter.

11 On completion, firmly depress the brake pedal a few times, to bring the pads to their normal working position. Check the level of the brake fluid in the reservoir, and top-up if necessary.

12 Give the vehicle a short road test, to make sure that the brakes are functioning correctly, and to bed-in the new linings to the contours of the disc. New linings will not provide maximum braking efficiency until they have bedded-in; avoid heavy braking as far as possible for the first hundred miles or so.

3 Front brake caliper - removal, overhaul and refitting

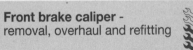

Note: *Refer to the warning at the beginning of the previous Section before proceeding.*

Removal

1 Apply the handbrake. Loosen the front wheel nuts, then jack up the front of the vehicle and support it on axle stands. Remove the appropriate front wheel.

2.5 Withdrawing the caliper and inner pad

2.6a Pull the inner pad out of the caliper piston . . .

2.6b . . . then remove the outer pad from the carrier bracket

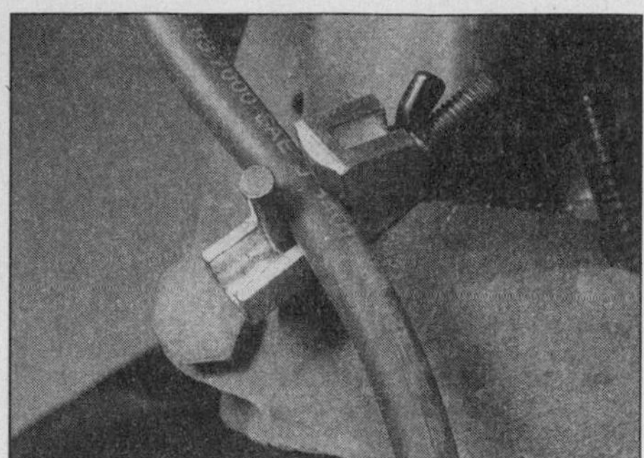
3.2 Brake hose clamp fitted to the front flexible brake hose

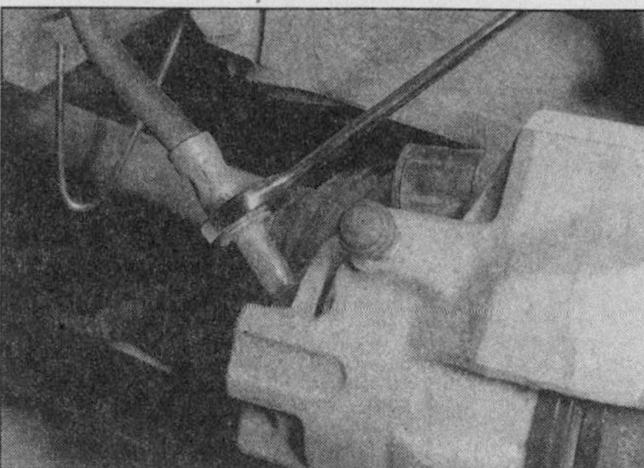
3.3 Loosening the flexible brake hose at the caliper

3.6 Removing the caliper carrier bracket

2 Fit a brake hose clamp to the flexible hose leading to the front brake caliper. This will minimise brake fluid loss during subsequent operations **(see illustration)**.
3 Loosen the union on the caliper end of the flexible brake hose **(see illustration)**. Once loosened, do not try to unscrew the hose at this stage.
4 Remove the front brake pads as described in Section 2.
5 Support the caliper in one hand, and prevent the hydraulic hose from turning with the other hand. Unscrew the caliper from the hose, making sure that the hose is not twisted unduly or strained. Once the caliper is detached, plug the open hydraulic unions in the caliper and hose, to keep out dust and dirt.
6 If required, the caliper carrier bracket can be unbolted and removed from the steering knuckle **(see illustration)**.

Overhaul

7 With the caliper on the bench, brush away all traces of dust and dirt, but take care not to inhale any dust, as it may be injurious to health.
8 Pull the dust-excluding rubber seal from the end of the piston.
9 Apply low air pressure to the fluid inlet union, and eject the piston. Only low air pressure is required for this, such as is produced by a foot-operated tyre pump.
Caution: The piston may be ejected with some force. Position a thin piece of wood between the piston and the caliper body, to prevent damage to the end face of the piston, in the event of it being ejected suddenly.

4.4a Using a micrometer to measure the thickness of the front brake disc

10 Using a suitable blunt instrument (for instance a knitting needle or a crochet hook), prise the piston seal from the groove in the cylinder bore. Take care not to scratch the surface of the bore.
11 Clean the piston and caliper body with methylated spirit, and allow to dry. Examine the surfaces of the piston and cylinder bore for wear, damage and corrosion. If the piston alone is unserviceable, a new piston must be obtained, along with seals. If the cylinder bore is unserviceable, the complete caliper must be renewed. The seals must be renewed, regardless of the condition of the other components.
12 Coat the piston and seals with clean brake fluid, then manipulate the piston seal into the groove in the cylinder bore.
13 Push the piston squarely into its bore.
14 Fit the dust-excluding rubber seal onto the piston and caliper, then depress the piston fully.

Refitting

15 Refit the caliper, and where applicable the carrier bracket, by reversing the removal operations. Make sure that the flexible brake hose is not twisted. Tighten the mounting bolts and wheel nuts to the specified torque **(see illustration)**.
16 Bleed the brake circuit according to the procedure given in Section 15, remembering to remove the brake hose clamp from the flexible hose. Make sure there are no leaks from the hose connections. Test the brakes carefully before returning the vehicle to normal service.

4.4b Disc minimum thickness marking

3.15 Tightening the carrier bracket mounting bolts

4 Front brake disc - inspection, removal and refitting

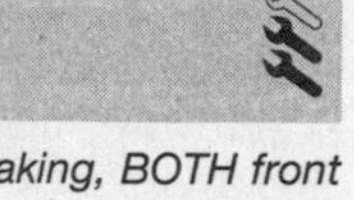

Note: *To prevent uneven braking, BOTH front brake discs should be renewed or reground at the same time.*

Inspection

1 Apply the handbrake. Loosen the relevant wheel nuts, jack up the front of the vehicle and support it on axle stands. Remove the appropriate front wheel.
2 Remove the front brake caliper and carrier bracket with reference to Section 3, but do not disconnect the flexible hose. Support the caliper on an axle stand, or suspend it out of the way with a piece of wire, taking care to avoid straining the flexible hose.
3 Temporarily refit two of the wheel nuts to diagonally-opposite studs, with the flat sides of the nuts against the disc. Tighten the nuts progressively, to hold the disc firmly.
4 Scrape any corrosion from the disc. Rotate the disc, and examine it for deep scoring, grooving or cracks. Using a micrometer, measure the thickness of the disc in several places. The minimum thickness is stamped on the disc hub **(see illustrations)**. Light wear and scoring is normal, but if excessive, the disc should be removed, and either reground by a specialist, or renewed. If regrinding is undertaken, the minimum thickness must be maintained. Obviously, if the disc is cracked, it must be renewed.

4.5 Measuring the disc run-out with a dial gauge

5 Using a dial gauge or a flat metal block and feeler gauges, check that the disc run-out 10 mm from the outer edge does not exceed the limit given in the Specifications. To do this, fix the measuring equipment, and rotate the disc, noting the variation in measurement as the disc is rotated **(see illustration)**. The difference between the minimum and maximum measurements recorded is the disc run-out.

6 If the run-out is greater than the specified amount, check for variations of the disc thickness as follows. Mark the disc at eight positions 45° apart, then using a micrometer, measure the disc thickness at the eight positions, 15 mm in from the outer edge. If the variation between the minimum and maximum readings is greater than the specified amount, the disc should be renewed.

7 The hub face run-out can also be checked in a similar way. First remove the disc as described later in this Section, fix the measuring equipment, then slowly rotate the hub, and check that the run-out does not exceed the amount given in the Specifications. If the hub face run-out is excessive, this should be corrected (by renewing the hub bearings - see Chapter 10) before rechecking the disc run-out.

Removal

8 With the wheel and caliper removed, remove the wheel nuts which were temporarily refitted in paragraph 3.

9 Mark the disc in relation to the hub, if it is to be refitted.

10 Remove the two special washers (where fitted), and withdraw the disc over the wheel studs **(see illustrations)**.

Refitting

11 Make sure that the disc and hub mating surfaces are clean, then locate the disc on the wheel studs. Align the previously-made marks if the original disc is being refitted.

12 Refit the two special washers, where fitted.

13 Refit the brake caliper and carrier bracket with reference to Section 3.

14 Refit the wheel, and lower the vehicle to the ground.

15 Test the brakes carefully before returning the vehicle to normal service.

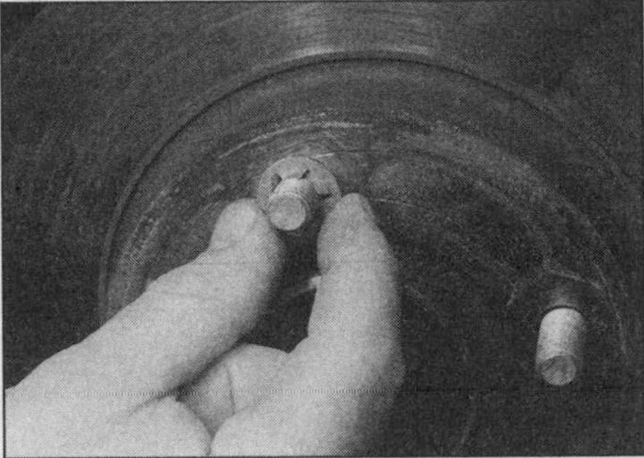

4.10a Remove the special washers . . .

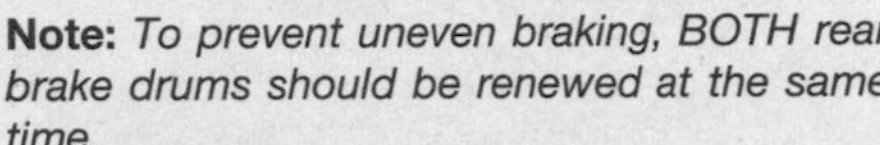

5 Rear brake drum - removal, inspection and refitting

Note: *To prevent uneven braking, BOTH rear brake drums should be renewed at the same time.*

Removal

1 Chock the front wheels, release the handbrake and engage 1st gear (or 'P'). Loosen the relevant wheel nuts, jack up the rear of the vehicle and support it on axle stands. Remove the appropriate rear wheel.

2 Remove the two special clips (where fitted), and withdraw the brake drum over the wheel studs. If the drum will not pass over the shoes, it is possible to release the automatic adjuster mechanism by prising out the small rubber grommet near the centre of the backplate, and inserting a screwdriver through the small hole **(see illustrations)**. The self-adjusting ratchet can then be rotated, so that the brake shoes move to their lowest setting. Refit the rubber grommet before proceeding.

3 With the brake drum removed, clean the dust from the drum, brake shoes, wheel cylinder and backplate, using brake cleaner or methylated spirit. Take care not to inhale the dust, as it may contain asbestos.

Inspection

4 Clean the inside surfaces of the brake drum, then examine the internal friction surface for signs of scoring or cracks. If it is cracked, deeply scored, or has worn to a diameter greater than the maximum given in the Specifications, then it should be renewed, together with the drum on the other side.

5 Regrinding of the brake drum is not recommended.

Refitting

6 Locate the brake drum over the wheel studs, and (where fitted) refit the special clips. Make sure that the drum contacts the hub flange.

7 Refit the wheel, then check the remaining rear drum.

8 Lower the vehicle to the ground, and tighten the wheel nuts to the specified torque. Depress the brake pedal several times, in order to operate the self-adjusting mechanism and set the shoes at their normal operating position.

9 Test the brakes carefully before returning the vehicle to normal service.

5.2a Releasing the automatic adjuster mechanism with a screwdriver inserted through the small hole in the backplate

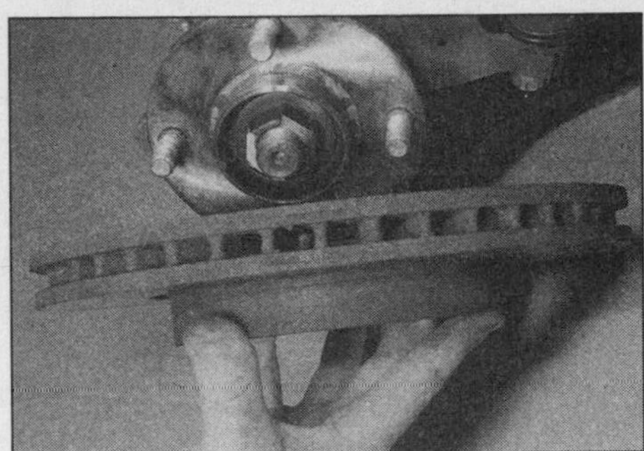

4.10b . . . and withdraw the disc

6 Rear brake shoes - renewal

Warning: Drum brake shoes must be renewed on BOTH rear wheels at the same time - never renew the shoes on only one wheel, as uneven braking may result. Also, the dust created by wear of the shoes may contain asbestos, which is a health hazard. Never blow it out with compressed air, and don't inhale any of it. An approved filtering mask

5.2b Removing a rear brake drum

6.2 Note the fitted position of all components

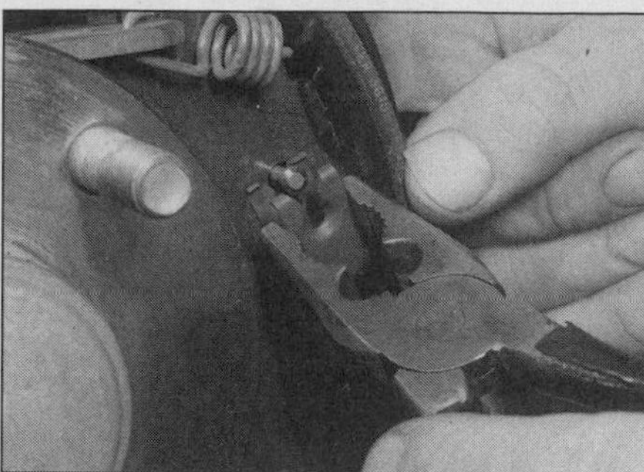
6.3a Using pliers to remove the two shoe hold-down springs

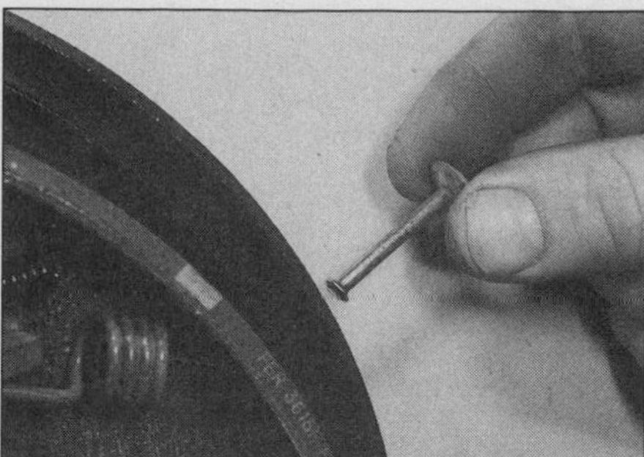
6.3b Removing the hold-down pins from the rear of the backplate

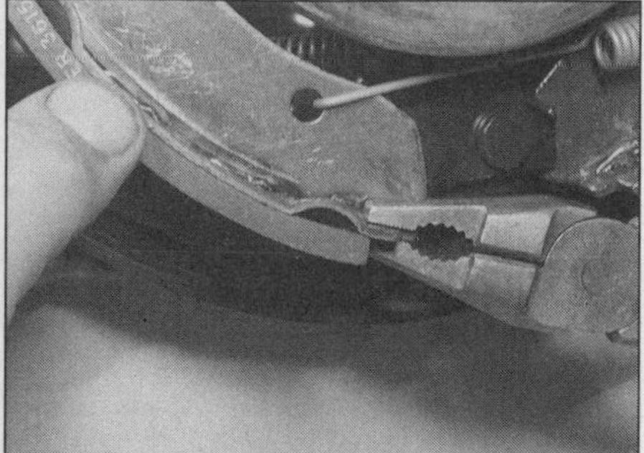
6.4 Using pliers, pull the bottom end of the leading brake shoe from the bottom anchor

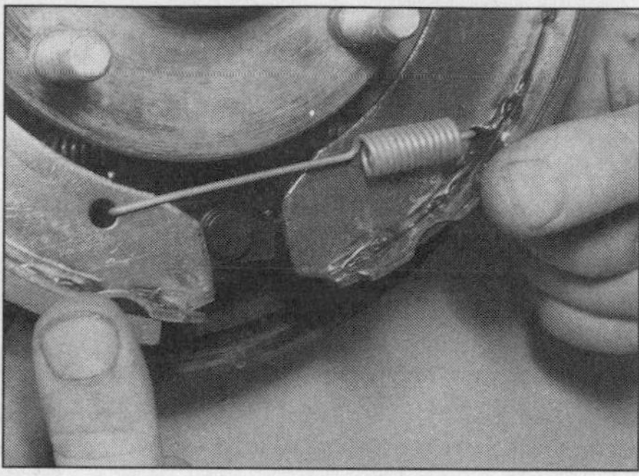
6.5a Release the trailing brake shoe from the anchor, then move the shoes together . . .

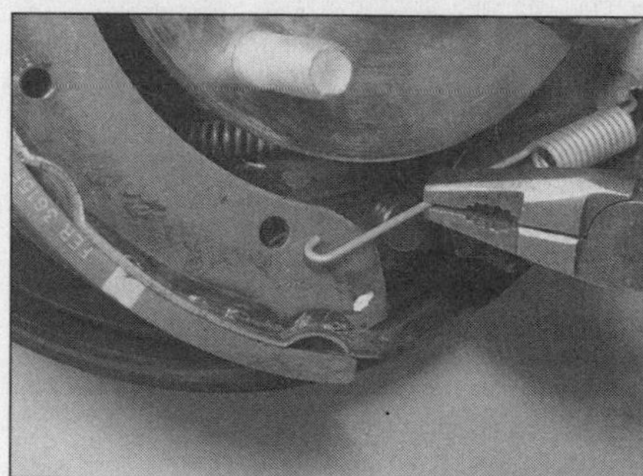
6.5b . . . so that the lower return spring can be unhooked

should be worn when working on the brakes. DO NOT use petroleum-based solvents to clean brake parts; use brake cleaner or methylated spirit only.

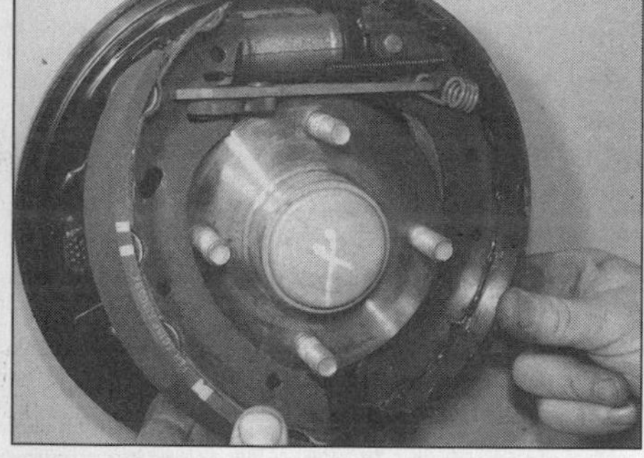
6.6 Disconnect the shoes from the wheel cylinder, taking care not to damage the rubber boots

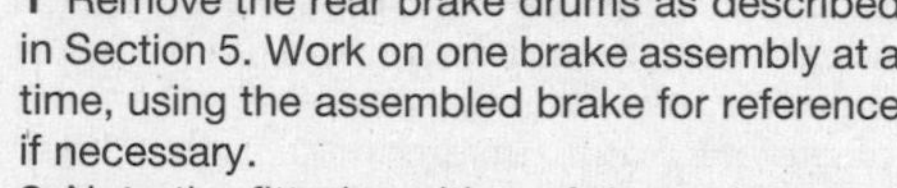
1 Remove the rear brake drums as described in Section 5. Work on one brake assembly at a time, using the assembled brake for reference if necessary.

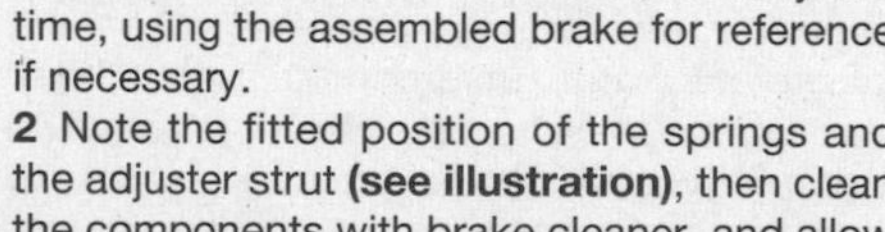
2 Note the fitted position of the springs and the adjuster strut **(see illustration)**, then clean the components with brake cleaner, and allow to dry. Position a tray beneath the backplate, to catch the fluid and residue.

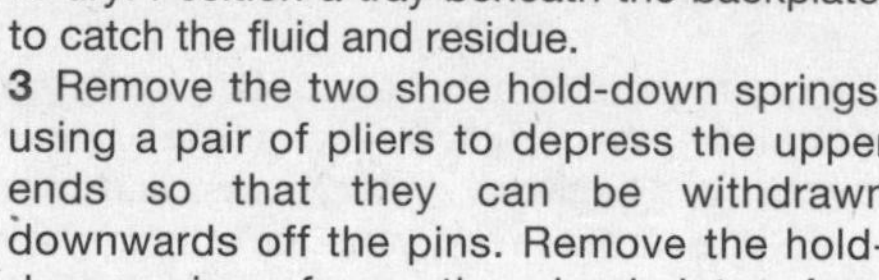
3 Remove the two shoe hold-down springs, using a pair of pliers to depress the upper ends so that they can be withdrawn downwards off the pins. Remove the hold-down pins from the backplate **(see illustrations)**.

4 Pull the bottom end of the leading (front) brake shoe from the bottom anchor (use pliers or an adjustable spanner over the edge of the shoe to lever it away) **(see illustration)**.

5 Release the trailing (rear) brake shoe from the anchor, then move the bottom ends of both shoes towards each other. Unhook the lower return spring from the shoes, noting the location holes **(see illustrations)**.

6 Move the bottom ends of the brake shoes together, and disconnect the top ends of the shoes from the wheel cylinder, taking care not to damage the rubber boots **(see illustration)**.

7 Unhook the upper return spring from the shoes, and withdraw the leading shoe from the backplate **(see illustrations)**.

8 To prevent the wheel cylinder pistons from being accidentally ejected, fit a suitable elastic band or wire lengthways over the cylinder/pistons **(see illustration)**. Don't press the brake pedal while the shoes are removed.

9 Pull the handbrake cable spring back from the operating lever on the rear of the trailing

6.7a Unhook the upper return spring . . .

6.7b . . . and withdraw the leading shoe

6.8 Elastic band fitted over the wheel cylinder, to prevent ejection of the pistons

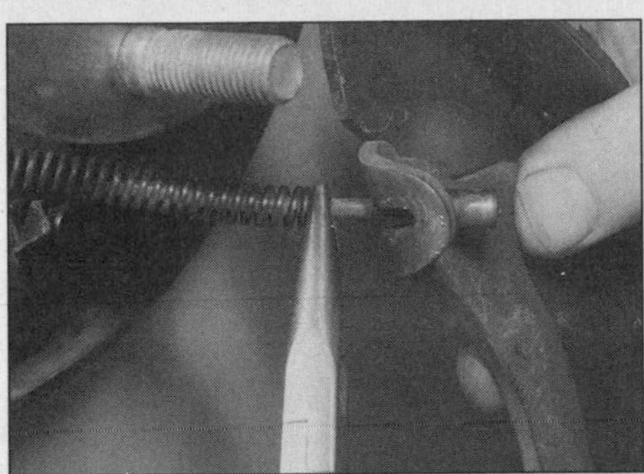

6.9 Using thin-nosed pliers, pull the handbrake cable spring and unhook the cable

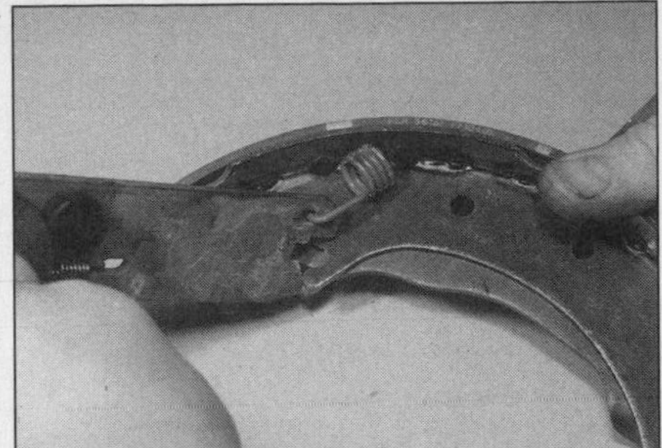

6.10a Unhook the automatic adjustment strut . . .

6.10b . . . and remove the small spring

shoe **(see illustration)**. Unhook the cable end from the cut-out in the lever, and remove the shoe.

10 Unhook the automatic adjustment strut from the trailing brake shoe, and remove the small spring **(see illustrations)**.

11 If the wheel cylinder shows signs of fluid leakage, or if there is any reason to suspect it of being defective, inspect it now, as described in the next Section.

12 Clean the backplate, and apply small amounts of high-melting-point brake grease to the brake shoe contact points **(see illustration)**. Be careful not to get grease on any friction surfaces.

13 Lubricate the sliding components of the automatic adjuster with a little high-melting-point brake grease, but leave the serrations on the eccentric cam clean **(see illustration)**.

14 Fit the new brake shoes using a reversal of the removal procedure, but set the eccentric cam at its lowest position before assembling it to the trailing shoe.

15 Before refitting the brake drum, it should be checked as described in Section 5.

16 With the drum in position, refit the wheel, then carry out the renewal procedure on the remaining rear brake.

17 Lower the vehicle to the ground, and tighten the wheel nuts to the specified torque.

18 Depress the brake pedal several times, in order to operate the self-adjusting mechanism and set the shoes at their normal operating position.

19 Make several forward and reverse stops, and operate the handbrake fully two or three times. Give the vehicle a road test, to make sure that the brakes are functioning correctly, and to bed-in the new shoes to the contours of the drum. Remember that the new shoes will not give full braking efficiency until they have bedded-in.

7 Rear wheel cylinder - removal, overhaul and refitting

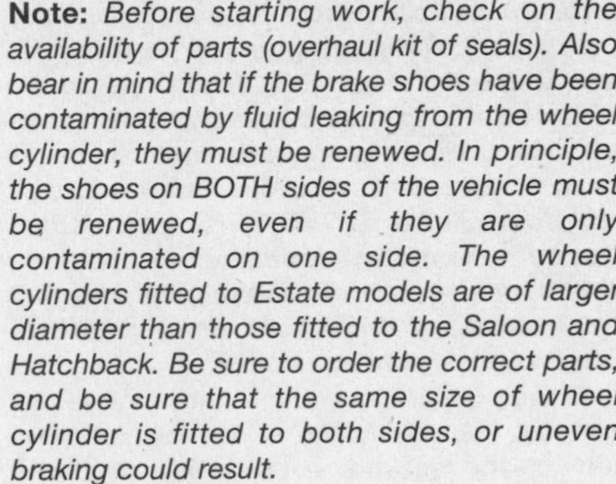

Note: *Before starting work, check on the availability of parts (overhaul kit of seals). Also bear in mind that if the brake shoes have been contaminated by fluid leaking from the wheel cylinder, they must be renewed. In principle, the shoes on BOTH sides of the vehicle must be renewed, even if they are only contaminated on one side. The wheel cylinders fitted to Estate models are of larger diameter than those fitted to the Saloon and Hatchback. Be sure to order the correct parts, and be sure that the same size of wheel cylinder is fitted to both sides, or uneven braking could result.*

Removal

1 Remove the brake drum as described in Section 5.

2 Minimise fluid loss either by removing the master cylinder reservoir cap, and then tightening it down onto a piece of polythene to obtain an airtight seal, or by using a brake hose clamp, a G-clamp, or similar tool, to clamp the flexible hose at the nearest convenient point to the wheel cylinder.

3 Pull the brake shoes apart at their top ends, so that they are just clear of the wheel cylinder. The automatic adjuster will hold the shoes in this position, so that the cylinder can be withdrawn.

4 Wipe away all traces of dirt around the hydraulic union at the rear of the wheel cylinder, then undo the union nut.

5 Unscrew the two bolts securing the wheel cylinder to the backplate **(see illustration)**.

6 Withdraw the wheel cylinder from the backplate so that it is clear of the brake shoes. Plug the open hydraulic unions, to prevent the entry of dirt, and to minimise further fluid loss whilst the cylinder is detached.

Overhaul

7 Clean the external surfaces of the cylinder, and unscrew the bleed screw.

8 Carefully prise off the dust cover from each end of the cylinder.

9 Tap the wheel cylinder on a block of wood to eject the pistons and seals, keeping them identified for location. Finally remove the spring.

10 Clean the pistons and the cylinder by washing in methylated spirit or fresh hydraulic fluid. Do not use petrol, paraffin or any other mineral-based fluid. Remove and discard the old seals, noting which way round they are fitted.

11 Examine the surfaces of the pistons and the cylinder bores, and look for any signs of rust or scoring. If such damage is evident, the complete wheel cylinder must be renewed.

12 Reassemble by lubricating the first piston in clean hydraulic fluid, then manipulating a

6.12 Apply a little high-melting-point brake grease to the brake shoe contact points

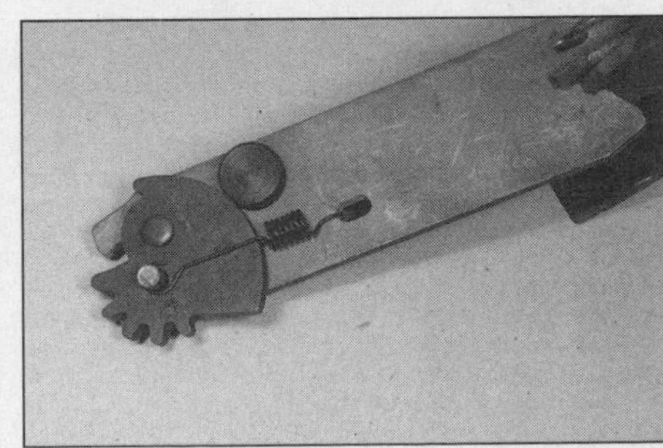

6.13 Lubricate the automatic adjuster, but leave the eccentric cam serrations shown here clean

7.5 Bolts securing the wheel cylinder to the backplate. Hydraulic union nut and bleed screw cover are also visible

8.3a Disconnect the pad wear warning light wiring plug . . .

8.3b . . . and detach the wiring plug from the clip on the caliper

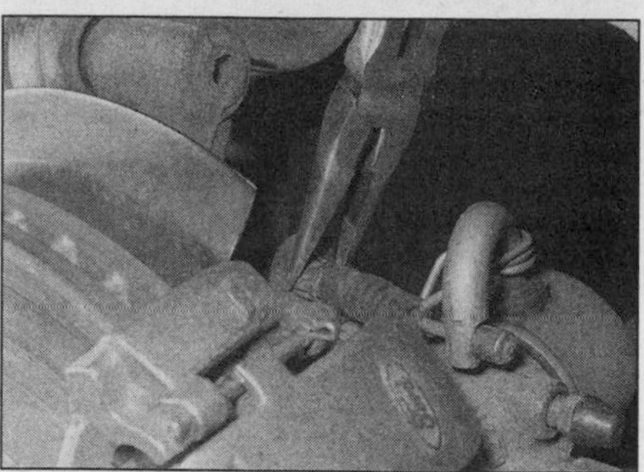
8.4a Compress the retaining clip tangs to release the outer cable . . .

new seal into position, so that its raised lip faces away from the brake shoe bearing face of the piston.

13 Insert the piston into the cylinder. As the seal enters the bore, twist the piston back and forth so that the seal lip is not trapped.

14 Insert the spring, then refit the remaining piston and seal, again making sure that the seal lip is not trapped as it enters the bore.

15 Fit new dust covers to the grooves in the pistons and wheel cylinder body.

16 Refit the bleed screw.

Refitting

17 Wipe clean the backplate, and remove the plug from the end of the hydraulic pipe. Fit the cylinder onto the backplate, and screw in the hydraulic union nut by hand, being careful not to cross-thread it.

18 Tighten the mounting bolts, then fully tighten the hydraulic union nut.

19 Retract the automatic brake adjuster mechanism, so that the brake shoes engage with the pistons of the wheel cylinder. To do this, prise the shoes apart slightly, turn the automatic adjuster to its minimum position, and release the shoes.

20 Remove the clamp from the flexible brake hose, or the polythene from the master cylinder (as applicable).

21 Refit the brake drum with reference to Section 5.

22 Bleed the brake hydraulic system as described in Section 15. Providing suitable precautions were taken to minimise loss of fluid, it should only be necessary to bleed the relevant rear brake.

23 Test the brakes carefully before returning the vehicle to normal service.

8 Rear brake pads - renewal

Warning: Disc brake pads must be renewed on BOTH rear wheels at the same time - never renew the pads on only one wheel, as uneven braking may result. Although genuine Ford linings are asbestos-free, the dust created by wear of non-genuine pads may contain asbestos, which is a health hazard. Never blow it out with compressed air, and don't inhale any of it. DO NOT use petroleum-based solvents to clean brake parts; use brake cleaner or methylated spirit only. DO NOT allow any brake fluid, oil or grease to contact the brake pads or disc.

1 Chock the front wheels, and engage 1st gear (or 'P'). Loosen the rear wheel nuts, then jack up the rear of the vehicle and support it on axle stands. Remove the rear wheels, and release the handbrake.

2 Work on one brake assembly at a time, using the assembled brake for reference if necessary.

3 Disconnect the brake pad wear warning light wiring plug, and release the wiring from the clip on the brake caliper, noting its routing **(see illustrations)**. Only the inner pad is fitted with a wear warning light wire.

4 On Estate models only, to enable the caliper to pivot rearwards to allow pad removal, the handbrake cable must be disconnected from the caliper. Using pliers, compress the tangs on the outer cable retaining clip, and release the outer cable from the caliper bracket. Ensure that the handbrake is released, then swivel the caliper handbrake arm to obtain some slack in the cable, and use a pair of pliers to pull out and disconnect the inner cable from the arm **(see illustrations)**. Once the cable has been disconnected, don't operate the handbrake arm excessively, as this will make refitting the cable more difficult.

5 Extract the spring clip, and pull out the retaining pin securing the caliper to the carrier bracket **(see illustrations)**. Note that on Saloon and Hatchback models, the pin is at the bottom of the caliper, whereas on Estate models, it is at the top.

6 Swivel the caliper away from the carrier bracket, to expose the brake pads **(see illustrations)**.

7 On Saloon and Hatchback models, unbolt the brake hose bracket from the rear suspension strut, to avoid straining the flexible hose.

8 On Estate models, the flexible hose cannot be readily detached to avoid straining it. To relieve the strain on the hose, place a jack below the suspension arm, and carefully compress the suspension a little.

9 If necessary, the caliper may be completely removed by prising off the cap and unscrewing the pivot guide bolt. Support the caliper on an axle stand, or tie it to one side with wire. Do not allow it to hang down unsupported, as this will strain the brake hose.

8.4b . . . then disconnect the inner cable end fitting from the handbrake arm

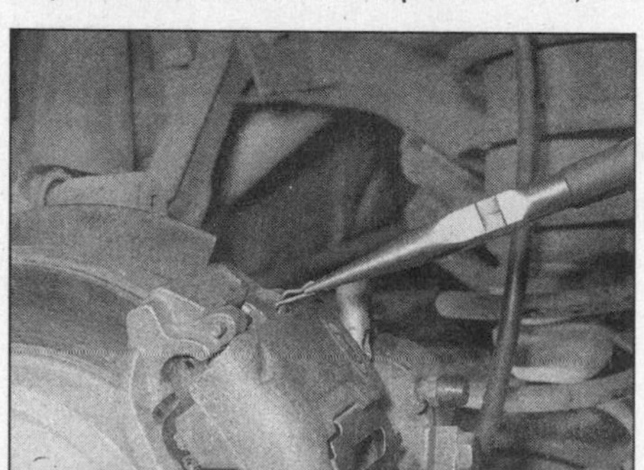
8.5a Extract the spring clip . . .

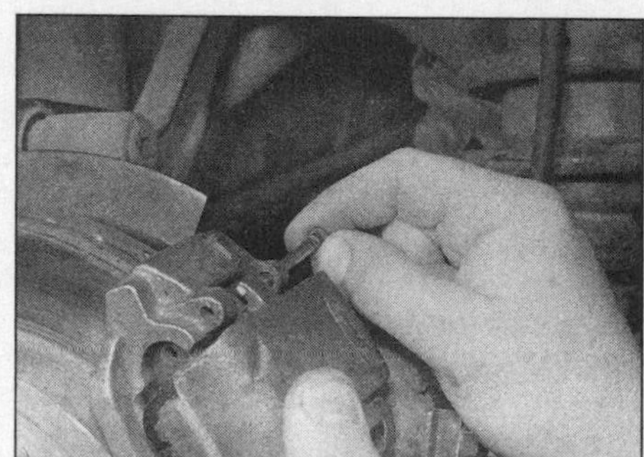
8.5b . . . and withdraw the caliper retaining pin

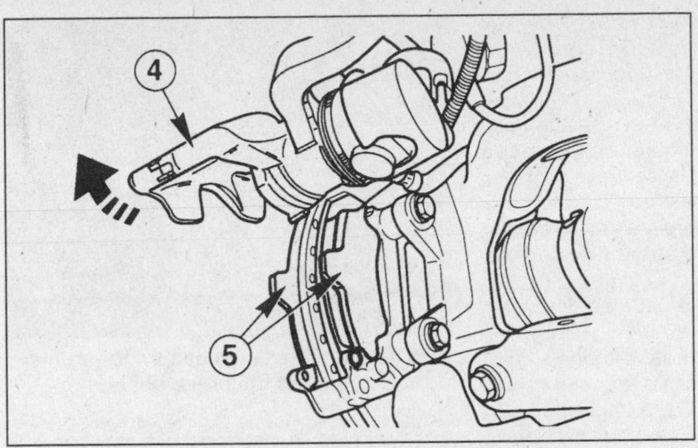

8.6a Rear brake pad removal on Saloon and Hatchback models

4 Brake caliper *5 Brake pads*

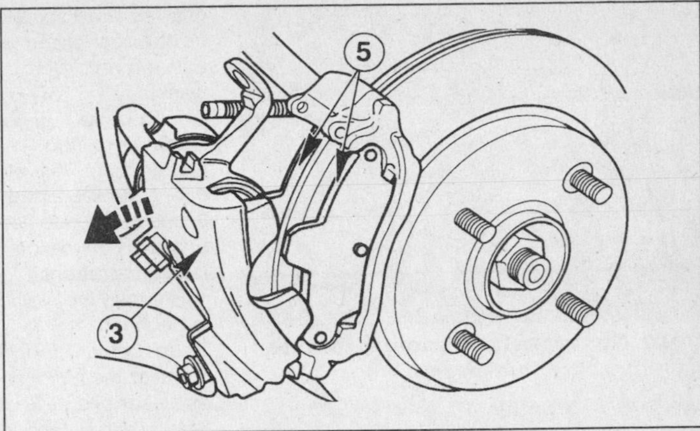

8.6b Rear brake pad removal on Estate models

3 Brake caliper *5 Brake pads*

10 Remove the pads from the carrier bracket, noting their fitted positions (the inner pad is fitted with the wear warning light wire). Brush all dust and dirt from the caliper, pads and disc, but do not inhale it, as it may be harmful to health. Scrape any corrosion from the edge of the disc.

11 Inspect the rear brake disc as described in Section 10.

12 Before fitting the new pads, screw the caliper piston fully into its bore, at the same time pressing the piston fully to the bottom of the bore **(see illustration)**. Proprietary tools are available for this operation - at a pinch, it may be possible to use long-nosed pliers engaged with the cut-outs in the piston. Brake fluid will be displaced into the master cylinder reservoir, so check first that there is enough space to accept the fluid. If necessary, syphon off some of the fluid.

13 The caliper piston must be rotated so that one of the cut-outs is positioned to engage with the lug on the back of the inner pad, with the piston's round orientation drilling uppermost **(see illustration)**.

14 Fit the new pads, noting that the inner pad has the wear warning light wire. Apply a little copper-based brake grease to the contact areas on the pad backing plates, taking care not to get any on the friction material **(see illustrations)**.

15 Swivel the caliper back into position **(see illustration)**, engaging the piston cut-out with the lug on the back of the inner pad, and secure with the retaining pin and spring clip. Do not depress the brake pedal until the handbrake cable has been reconnected, since the extra pad-to-disc clearance makes reconnecting the cable easier.

16 Reconnect the cable to the caliper operating arm, noting the points made in Section 27.

17 Refit the brake hose bracket, or lower the jack under the suspension arm, as applicable.

18 Reconnect the brake pad wear warning light connector plug, and clip the plug onto the caliper. The wiring should not be under any strain - check the wire routing on the other rear brake if in doubt.

19 Firmly depress the brake pedal a few times, to bring the pads to their normal working position. Check the level of the brake fluid in the reservoir, and top-up if necessary.

20 Give the vehicle a road test, to make sure that the brakes are functioning correctly, and to bed-in the new linings to the contours of the disc. Remember that full braking efficiency will not be obtained until the new linings have bedded-in.

8.12 Using a proprietary tool to screw the caliper piston back into the caliper

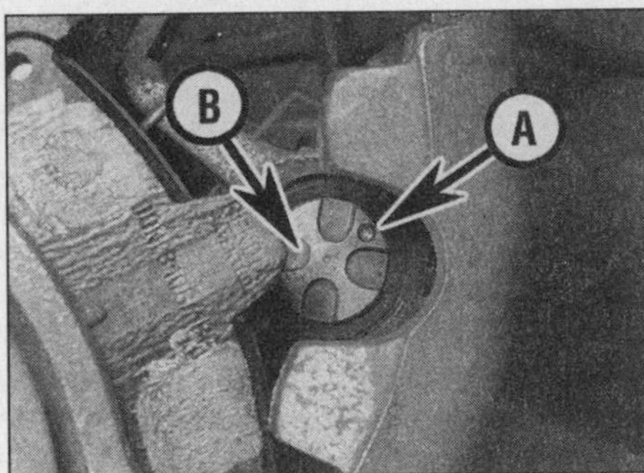

8.13 The piston must be aligned with drilling (A) uppermost, so that one of the cut-outs (B) will engage the lug on the back of the inner pad

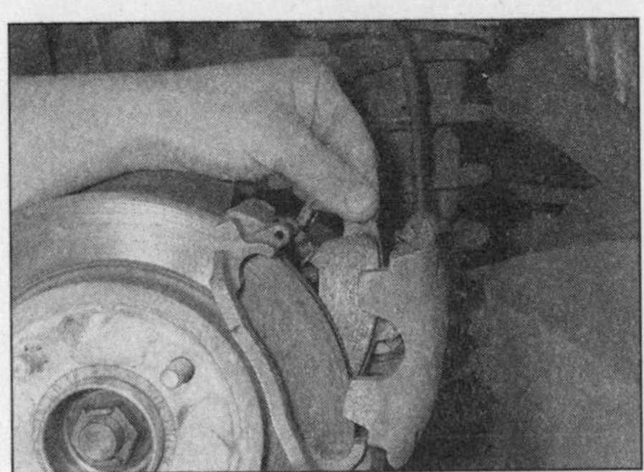

8.14a Fit the inner pad . . .

8.14b . . . and the outer pad - note the brake grease applied to the backing plate

8.15 Swivel the caliper back into position

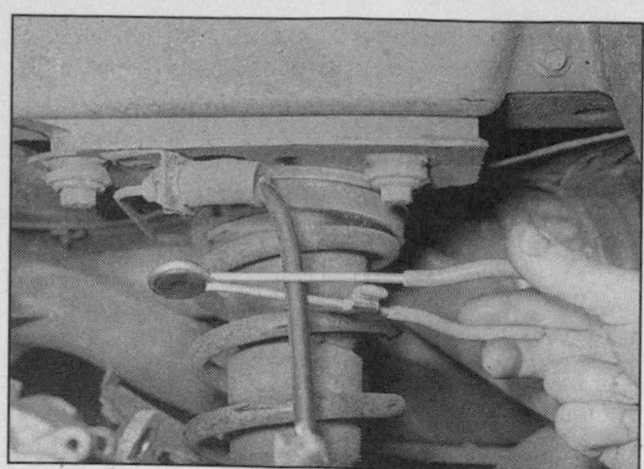
9.2 Fit a brake hose clamp to the rear brake hose

9 Rear brake caliper - removal, overhaul and refitting

Removal

1 Chock the front wheels, and engage 1st gear (or 'P'). Loosen the rear wheel nuts, jack up the rear of the vehicle and support it on axle stands. Remove the appropriate rear wheel.

2 Fit a brake hose clamp to the flexible hose leading to the rear brake caliper **(see illustration)**. This will minimise brake fluid loss during subsequent operations.

3 Loosen (but do not completely unscrew) the union on the caliper end of the flexible hose **(see illustration)**.

4 Remove the rear brake pads as described in Section 8.

5 On Saloon and Hatchback models, disconnect the handbrake cable from the caliper as described in Section 8, paragraph 4. On Saloon and Hatchback models, the handbrake lever faces away from the caliper, unlike on Estate models, where it faces towards the caliper **(see illustrations)**.

6 Prise off the cap, then unscrew and remove the pivot guide bolt. Remove the caliper, and support it on an axle stand, or tie it to one side with wire **(see illustrations)**. Do not allow it to hang down unsupported, as this will strain the brake hose.

9.3 Loosen the union bolt on the caliper end of the brake hose

7 Unscrew the caliper from the hydraulic hose, making sure that the hose is not twisted or strained unduly. Plug the open hydraulic unions to keep dust and dirt out.

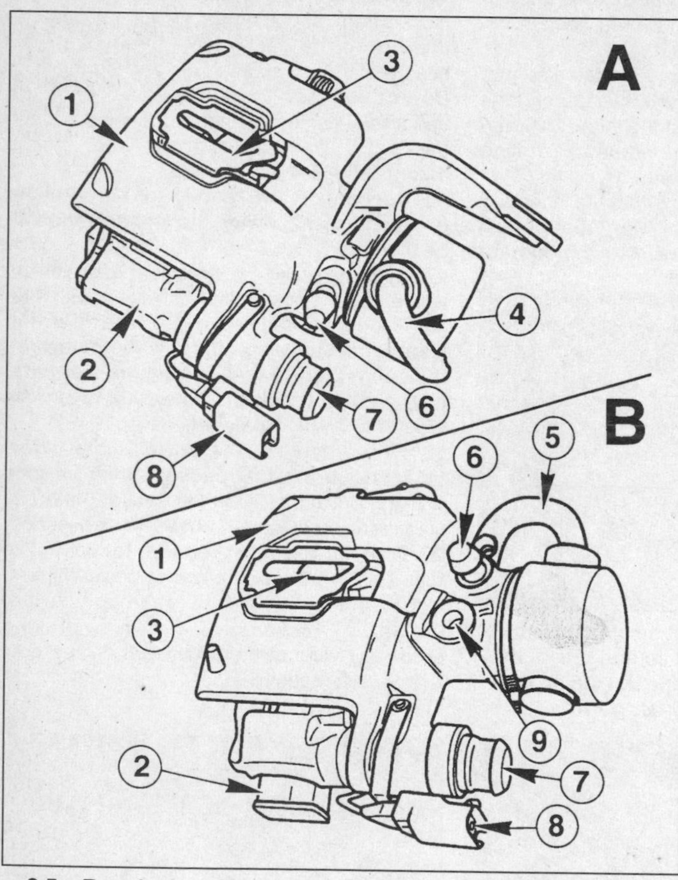

9.5a Rear brake caliper on Saloon/Hatchback models (A) and Estate models (B)

1 Caliper body
2 Frame
3 Brake pad spring clip
4 Handbrake cable lever facing away from caliper
5 Handbrake cable lever facing towards caliper
6 Bleed screw
7 Guide pin protective cap
8 Pad wear warning light connector
9 Flexible hydraulic hose connection

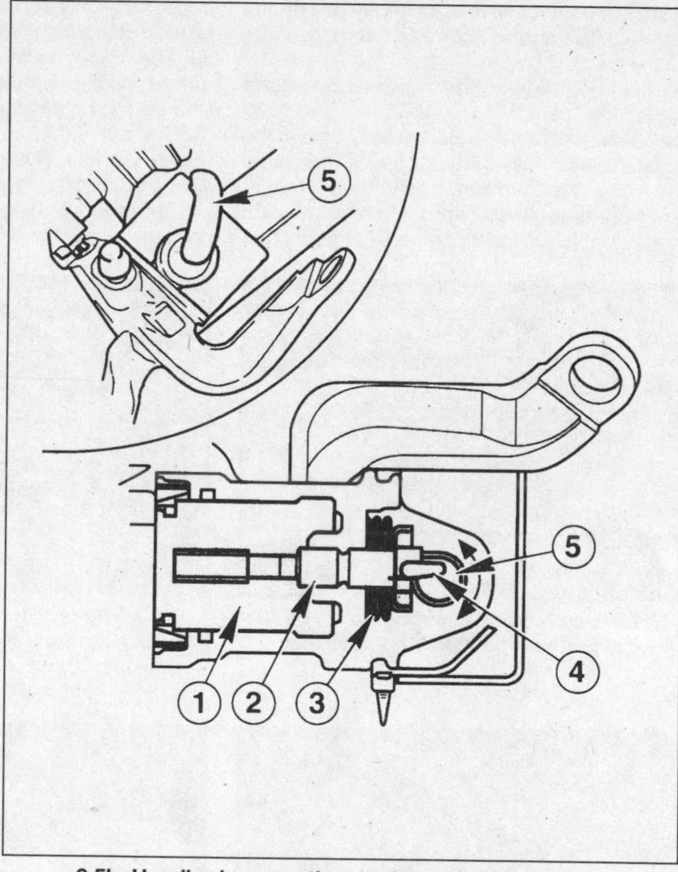

9.5b Handbrake operation on the rear brake caliper

1 Piston
2 Automatic adjusting screw
3 Spring washers
4 Cam
5 Handbrake cable lever

9.6a Prise off the bolt cap . . .

9.6b . . . unscrew and remove the guide bolt . . .

9.6c . . . and remove the caliper

8 If necessary, unbolt the carrier bracket from the knuckle.

Overhaul

9 No overhaul procedures were available at the time of writing, so check availability of spares before dismantling the caliper. In principle, the overhaul information given for the front brake caliper will apply, noting that it will be necessary to unscrew the piston from the handbrake mechanism (see Section 8, paragraph 10) before being able to expel the piston from the caliper. On reassembly, push the piston fully into the caliper, and screw it back onto the handbrake mechanism. Do not attempt to dismantle the handbrake mechanism; if the mechanism is faulty, the complete caliper assembly must be renewed.

Refitting

10 Refit the caliper, and where applicable the carrier bracket, by reversing the removal operations. Refer to the points made in Section 27 when reconnecting the handbrake cable. Tighten the mounting bolts and wheel nuts to the specified torque, and do not forget to remove the brake hose clamp from the flexible brake hose.

11 Bleed the brake circuit according to the procedure given in Section 15. Make sure there are no leaks from the hose connections. Test the brakes carefully before returning the vehicle to normal service.

10 Rear brake disc - inspection, removal and refitting

Refer to Section 4 (front disc inspection). Once the rear caliper is removed, the procedure is the same.

11 Master cylinder - removal and refitting

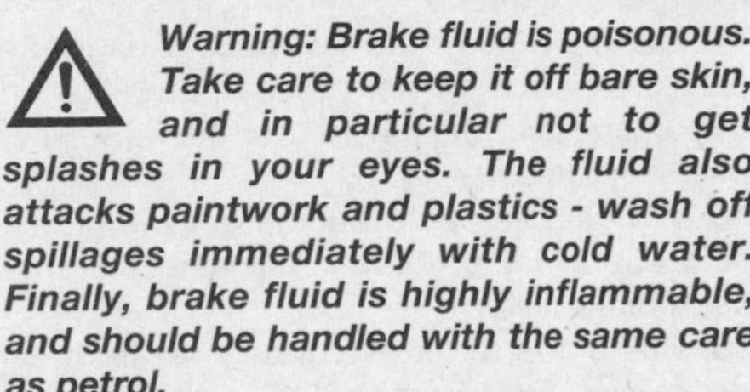

Warning: Brake fluid is poisonous. Take care to keep it off bare skin, and in particular not to get splashes in your eyes. The fluid also attacks paintwork and plastics - wash off spillages immediately with cold water. Finally, brake fluid is highly inflammable, and should be handled with the same care as petrol.

Removal

1 Exhaust the vacuum in the servo by pressing the brake pedal a few times, with the engine switched off.

2 On models with automatic transmission, withdraw the transmission fluid dipstick, to improve access.

3 Disconnect the low fluid level warning light multi-plug from the fluid reservoir **(see illustration)**. Unscrew and remove the cap.

4 Draw off the hydraulic fluid from the reservoir, using an old battery hydrometer or a poultry baster.

Warning: Do not syphon the fluid by mouth; it is poisonous. Any brake fluid spilt on paintwork should be washed off with clean water, without delay - brake fluid is also a highly-effective paint-stripper!

5 On models with a hydraulically-operated clutch, release the hose clip and disconnect the fluid supply hose from the rear of the brake fluid reservoir **(see illustration)**. Keeping the hose end uppermost, plug or cap the hose, to prevent fluid loss or dirt entry.

6 Identify the locations of each brake pipe on the master cylinder. On non-ABS models, there are four pipes; the two rear brake pipes are attached to PCR (pressure-conscious relief) valves on the master cylinder. On ABS models, there are only two pipes, which lead to the ABS hydraulic unit **(see illustration)**.

7 Place rags beneath the master cylinder to catch spilt hydraulic fluid.

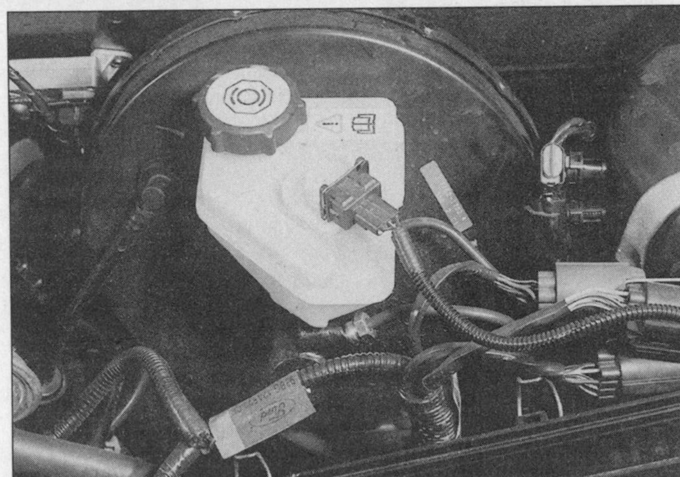

11.3 Brake fluid reservoir and low level warning light multi-plug

11.5 Disconnecting the clutch fluid supply hose from the rear of the fluid reservoir

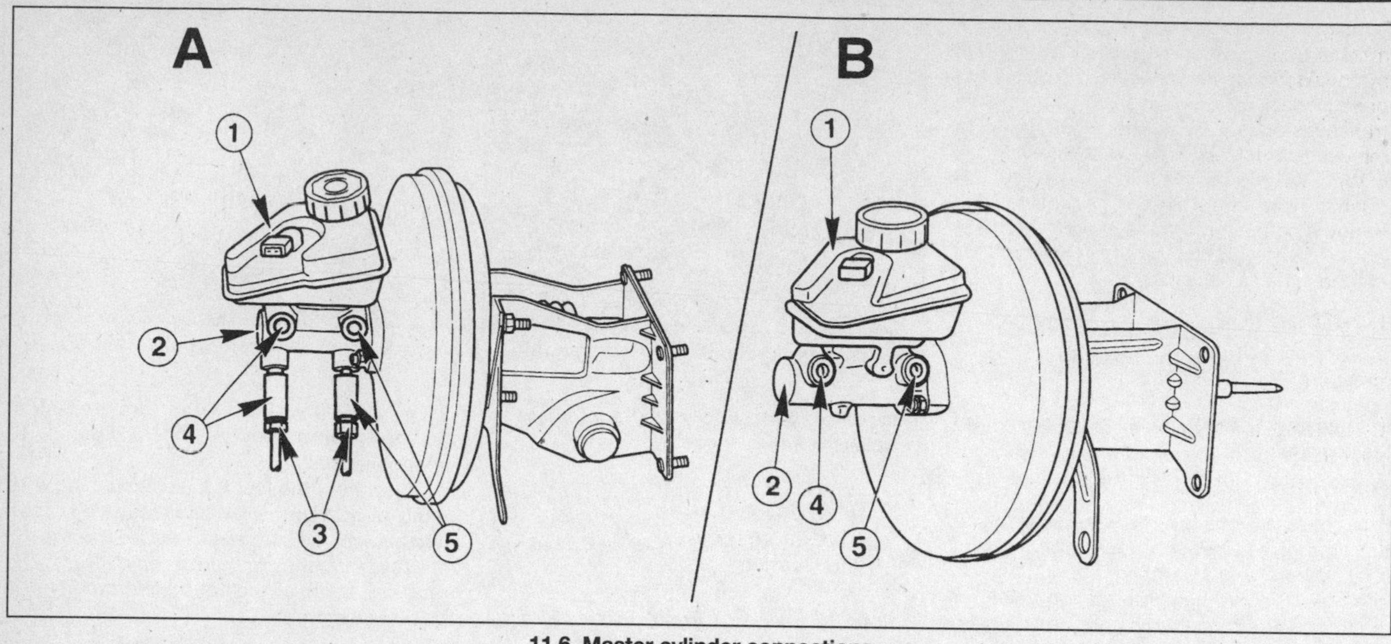

11.6 Master cylinder connections

A Non-ABS models
B ABS models
1 Brake fluid reservoir
2 Master cylinder
3 PCR valves for rear brakes
4 Primary brake hydraulic circuit (front right/rear left)
5 Secondary brake hydraulic circuit (front left/rear right)

8 Clean around the hydraulic union nuts. Unscrew the nuts, and disconnect the hydraulic lines from the master cylinder.

9 Unscrew the mounting nuts, and withdraw the master cylinder from the studs on the front of the servo unit. If the nuts are tight, a split ring spanner should be used in preference to an open-ended spanner. Plug or cap open unions, to keep dust and dirt out.

10 Recover the gasket from the master cylinder.

11 If the master cylinder is faulty, it must be renewed. At the time of writing, no overhaul kits were available.

Refitting

12 Clean the contact surfaces of the master cylinder and servo, and locate a new gasket on the master cylinder.

13 Position the master cylinder on the studs on the servo unit. Refit and tighten the nuts to the specified torque.

14 Carefully insert the hydraulic lines in the apertures in the master cylinder, then tighten the union nuts. Make sure that the nuts enter their threads correctly.

15 Where applicable, reconnect the clutch fluid supply hose, then fill the reservoir with fresh brake fluid.

16 Bleed the brake hydraulic system as described in Section 15, and where applicable, the clutch hydraulic system as described in Chapter 6.

17 Refit the reservoir filler cap, and reconnect the multi-plug for the low fluid level warning light.

18 On automatic transmission models, insert the transmission fluid dipstick.

19 Test the brakes carefully before returning the vehicle to normal service.

12 Brake pedal - removal and refitting

Removal

1 Working inside the vehicle, move the driver's seat fully to the rear, to allow maximum working area.

2 Unscrew the screws and remove the lower facia panel.

3 Prise the hairpin clip from the right-hand end of the pedal pivot shaft **(see illustration)**, and remove the washer.

4 Unscrew the nut securing the pedal trunnion to the pushrod. The nut is located near the top of the pedal **(see illustrations)**.

5 Press the pedal pivot shaft to the left, through the mounting bracket, just far enough

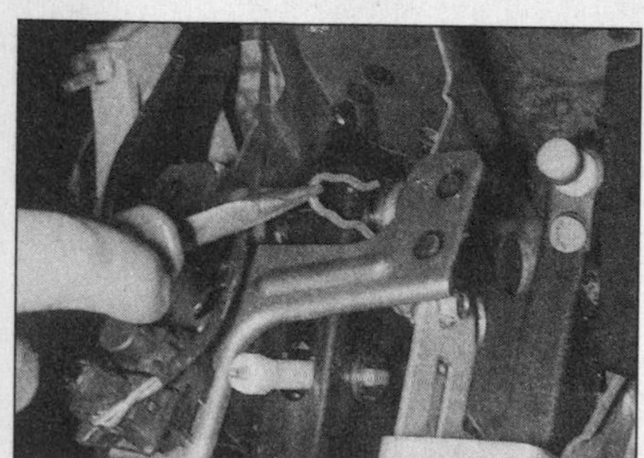

12.3 Removing the hairpin clip from the right-hand end of the brake pedal pivot shaft

12.4a Unscrew the nut securing the pedal trunnion to the pushrod . . .

12.4b . . . and remove the tube from the pushrod

to allow the pedal to be withdrawn. On manual transmission models, leave the blue nylon spacer (located between the clutch and brake pedals) on the pivot shaft. On automatic transmission models, the shaft can be removed completely **(see illustrations)**.

6 With the pedal removed, prise out the bushes from each side. If necessary, also remove the pushrod trunnion and the rubber pad **(see illustrations)**. Renew the components as necessary.

Refitting

7 Prior to refitting the pedal, apply a little grease to the pivot shaft, pedal bushes and trunnion.

8 Refitting is a reversal of the removal procedure, but make sure that the pedal bushes are correctly located, and that the pedal shaft 'D' section locates in the right-hand side of the pedal bracket. Also make sure that the hairpin clip is correctly located.

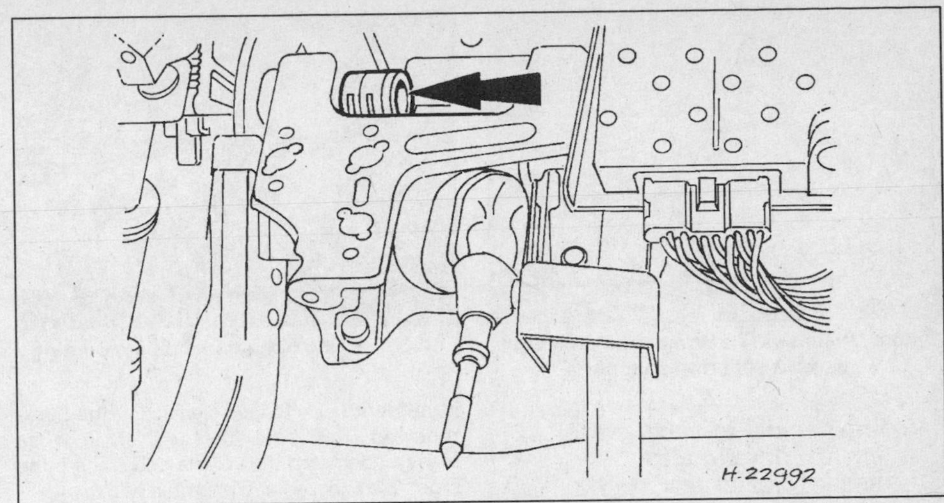

12.5a Leave the nylon spacer (arrowed) in position on the pivot shaft (left-hand drive shown, right-hand drive similar)

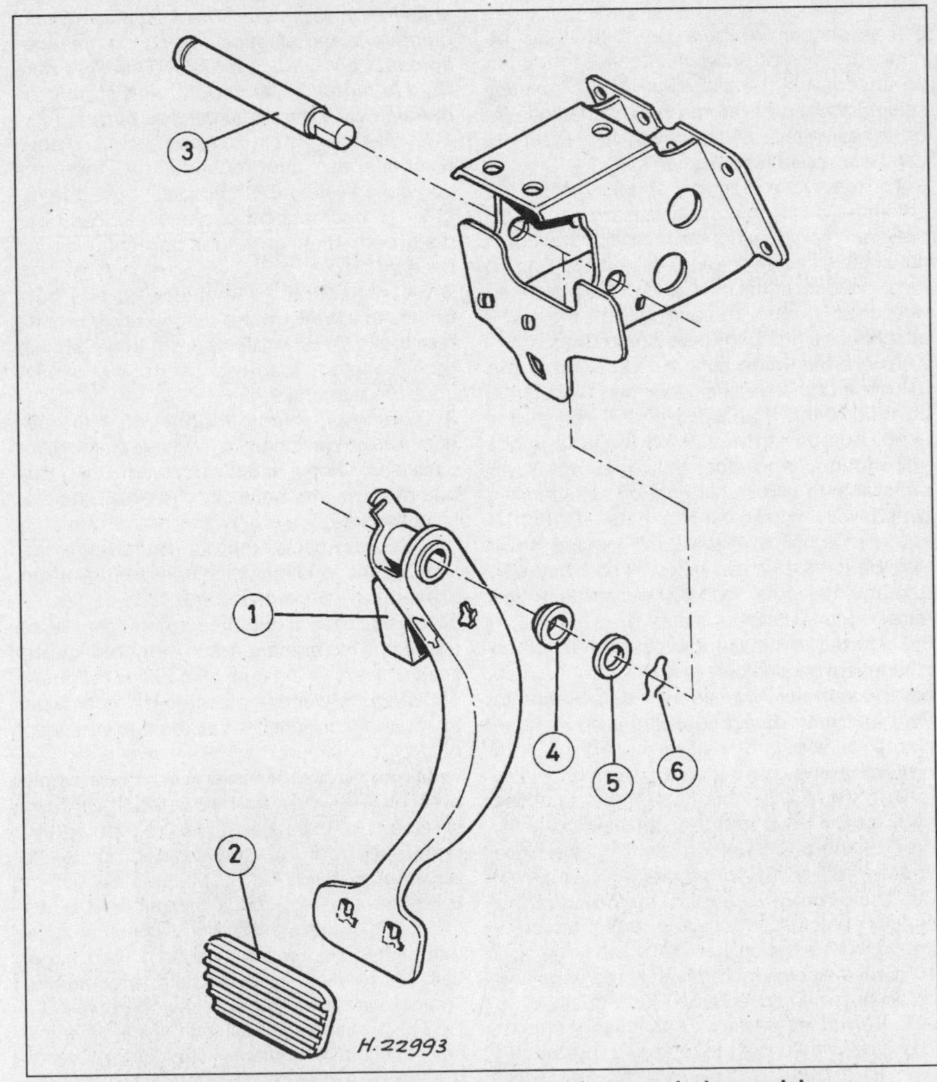

12.5b Brake pedal components - automatic transmission models

1 Pedal
2 Rubber pad
3 Pivot shaft
4 Bush
5 Washer
6 Hairpin clip

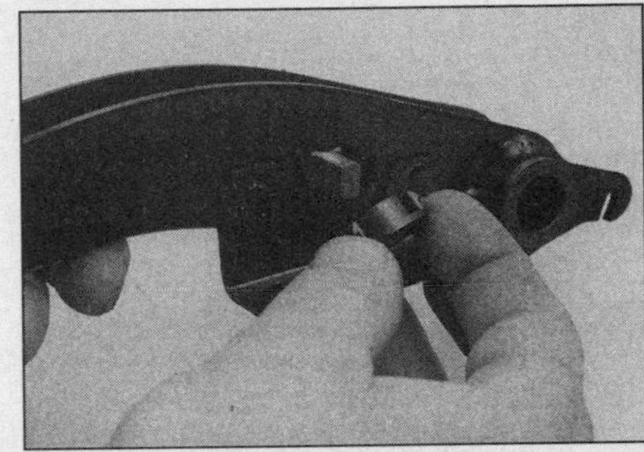

12.6a Prise out the bushes . . .

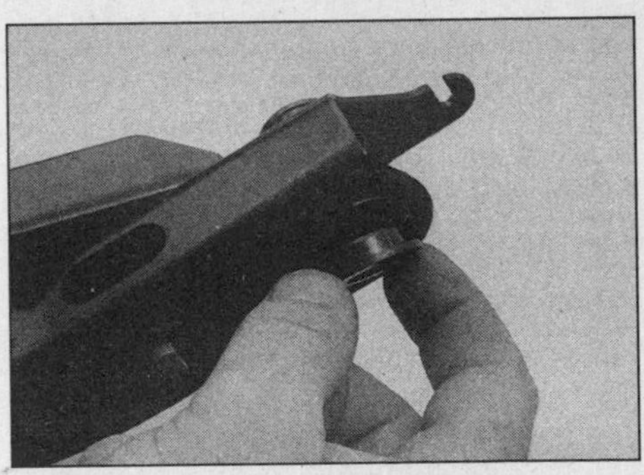

12.6b . . . from each side of the pedal . . .

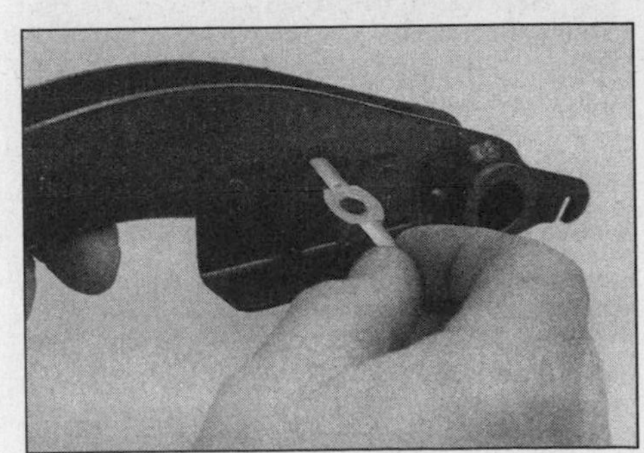

12.6c . . . and remove the pushrod trunnion

14.6a Unscrewing a brake pipe union nut using a split ring spanner

14.6b Pulling out a brake pipe mounting clip

13 Brake pedal-to-servo cross-link (RH drive models) - removal and refitting

Removal

1 Disconnect the battery negative (earth) lead (Chapter 5A, Section 1).

2 Remove the master cylinder and the vacuum servo unit as described in Sections 11 and 16. If preferred, the master cylinder may be left attached to the servo unit.

3 Working inside the passenger compartment, fold down the covering from the front of both front footwells.

4 Have an assistant support the cross-link assembly from inside the engine compartment.

5 Unscrew and remove the nuts and bolts on each side of the bulkhead, and remove the link assembly from inside the engine compartment. If necessary, have the assistant hold the bolt heads from inside the engine compartment while the nuts are being loosened.

6 Clean the cross-link components, and examine the bushes for wear. Renew the bushes if necessary.

Refitting

7 Refitting is a reversal of the removal procedure. Refer to Sections 11 and 16 when refitting the master cylinder and vacuum servo unit.

14 Hydraulic pipes and hoses - inspection, removal and refitting

Note: *Refer to the warning at the start of Section 15 concerning the dangers of brake fluid.*

Inspection

1 Jack up the front and rear of the vehicle, and support on axle stands.

2 Check for signs of leakage at the pipe unions, then examine the flexible hoses for signs of cracking, chafing and fraying.

3 The brake pipes should be examined carefully for signs of dents, corrosion or other damage. Corrosion should be scraped off, and if the depth of pitting is significant, the pipes renewed. This is particularly likely in those areas underneath the vehicle body where the pipes are exposed and unprotected.

4 Renew any defective brake pipes and/or hoses.

Removal

5 If a section of pipe or hose is to be removed, loss of brake fluid can be reduced by unscrewing the filler cap, and completely sealing the top of the reservoir with cling film or adhesive tape. Alternatively, the reservoir can be emptied (see Section 11).

6 To remove a section of pipe, hold the adjoining hose union nut with a spanner to prevent it from turning, then unscrew the union nut at the end of the pipe, and release it. Repeat the procedure at the other end of the pipe, then release the pipe by pulling out the clips attaching it to the body **(see illustrations)**.

7 Where the union nuts are exposed to the full force of the weather, they can sometimes be quite tight. If an open-ended spanner is used, burring of the flats on the nuts is not uncommon, and for this reason, it is preferable to use a split ring (brake) spanner, which will engage all the flats. If such a spanner is not available, self-locking grips may be used as a last resort; these may well damage the nuts, but if the pipe is to be renewed, this does not matter.

8 To further minimise the loss of fluid when disconnecting a flexible brake line from a rigid pipe, clamp the hose as near as possible to the pipe to be detached, using a brake hose clamp or a pair of self-locking grips with protected jaws.

9 To remove a flexible hose, first clean the ends of the hose and the surrounding area, then unscrew the union nuts from the hose ends. Recover the spring clip, and withdraw the hose from the serrated mounting in the support bracket. Where applicable, unscrew the hose from the caliper.

10 Brake pipes supplied with flared ends and union nuts can be obtained individually or in sets from Ford dealers or accessory shops. The pipe is then bent to shape, using the old pipe as a guide, and is ready for fitting. Be careful not to kink or crimp the pipe when bending it; ideally, a proper pipe-bending tool should be used.

Refitting

11 Refitting of the pipes and hoses is a reversal of removal. Make sure that all brake pipes are securely supported in their clips, and ensure that the hoses are not kinked. Check also that the hoses are clear of all suspension components and underbody fittings, and will remain clear during movement of the suspension and steering.

12 On completion, bleed the brake hydraulic system as described in Section 15, and where applicable, the clutch hydraulic system as described in Chapter 6.

15 Hydraulic system - bleeding

Warning: Brake fluid is poisonous. Take care to keep it off bare skin, and in particular not to get splashes in your eyes. The fluid also attacks paintwork and plastics - wash off spillages immediately with cold water. Finally, brake fluid is highly inflammable, and should be handled with the same care as petrol.

1 If the master cylinder has been disconnected and reconnected, then the complete system (both circuits) must be bled of air. If a component of one circuit has been disturbed, then only that particular circuit need be bled.

2 Bleeding should commence on one front brake, followed by the diagonally-opposite rear brake. The remaining front brake should then be bled, followed by its diagonally-opposite rear brake.

3 There are a variety of do-it-yourself 'one-man' brake bleeding kits available from motor accessory shops, and it is recommended that one of these kits be used wherever possible, as they greatly simplify the brake bleeding operation. Follow the kit manufacturer's instructions in conjunction with the following procedure. If a pressure-bleeding kit is obtained, then it will not be necessary to depress the brake pedal in the following procedure.

4 During the bleeding operation, do not allow the brake fluid level in the reservoir to drop below the minimum mark. If the level is allowed to fall so far that air is drawn in, the whole procedure will have to be started again from scratch. Only use new fluid for topping-up, preferably from a freshly-opened container. Never re-use fluid bled from the system.

5 Before starting, check that all rigid pipes and flexible hoses are in good condition, and that all hydraulic unions are tight. Take great care not to allow hydraulic fluid to come into contact with the vehicle paintwork, otherwise the finish will be seriously damaged. Wash off any spilt fluid immediately with cold water.

6 If a brake bleeding kit is not being used, gather together a clean jar, a length of plastic or rubber tubing which is a tight fit over the bleed screw, and a new container of the specified brake fluid (see "*Lubricants and fluids*"). The help of an assistant will also be required.

7 Clean the area around the bleed screw on the front brake unit to be bled (it is important that no dirt be allowed to enter the hydraulic system), and remove the dust cap. Connect one end of the tubing to the bleed screw, and immerse the other end in the jar, which should be filled with sufficient brake fluid to keep the end of the tube submerged **(see illustrations)**.

8 Open the bleed screw by one or two turns, and have the assistant depress the brake pedal to the floor. Tighten the bleed screw at the end of the downstroke, then have the assistant release the pedal. Continue this procedure until clean brake fluid, free from air bubbles, can be seen flowing into the jar. Finally tighten the bleed screw with the pedal in the fully-depressed position.

9 Remove the tube, and refit the dust cap. Top-up the master cylinder reservoir if necessary, then repeat the procedure on the diagonally-opposite rear brake.

10 Repeat the procedure on the remaining circuit, starting with the front brake, and followed by the diagonally-opposite rear brake.

11 Check the feel of the brake pedal - it should be firm. If it is spongy, there is still some air in the system, and the bleeding procedure should be repeated.

12 When bleeding is complete, top-up the master cylinder reservoir and refit the cap.

13 On models with a hydraulically-operated clutch, check the clutch operation on completion; it may be necessary to bleed the clutch hydraulic system as described in Chapter 6.

16 Vacuum servo unit - testing, removal and refitting

Testing

1 To test the operation of the servo unit, depress the footbrake four or five times to dissipate the vacuum, then start the engine while keeping the footbrake depressed. As the engine starts, there should be a noticeable 'give' in the brake pedal as vacuum builds up. Allow the engine to run for at least two minutes, and then switch it off. If the brake pedal is now depressed again, it should be possible to hear a hiss from the servo when the pedal is depressed. After four or five applications, no further hissing should be heard, and the pedal should feel harder.

2 Before assuming that a problem exists in the servo unit itself, inspect the non-return valve as described in the next Section.

Removal

3 Refer to Section 11 and remove the master cylinder.

4 Remove the air cleaner and air inlet trunking as described in Chapter 4A.

5 On models with air conditioning, unbolt the refrigerant pipe brackets in the vicinity of the servo unit, and move the brackets aside.

15.7a Remove the bleed screw dust cap . . .

15.7b . . . and connect up the bleeding equipment

6 Disconnect the vacuum hose adaptor at the servo unit by pulling it free from the rubber grommet. If it is reluctant to move, prise it free, using a screwdriver with its blade inserted under the flange.

7 Unscrew the four nuts securing the servo unit to the mounting brackets on the bulkhead in the engine compartment **(see illustration)**.

Right-hand-drive models

8 Withdraw the servo unit so that its studs are just clear of the brackets. Have an assistant hold the brake pedal depressed, then extract the spring clip and remove the clevis pin securing the servo unit pushrod to the pedal cross-link arm.

Left-hand-drive models

9 Disconnect the engine wiring harness multi-plug in front of the servo unit.

10 Inside the passenger compartment, remove the driver's side lower facia panel for access to the brake pedal.

11 Unscrew the nut securing the pedal trunnion to the servo unit pushrod. The nut is located near the top of the pedal, and is accessible through an access hole.

12 Again inside the passenger compartment, remove the four servo unit mounting bracket nuts above the pedals.

13 Remove the servo unit mounting bracket from inside the engine compartment.

V6 engine models

14 Refer to Chapter 4A and disconnect the accelerator cable and cruise control cable (where applicable) from the throttle housing.

15 On models with automatic transmission, unscrew the two bolts securing the support bracket for the transmission selector cable. Disconnect the cable end fitting, and move the cable to one side.

16 If not already done, disconnect the engine wiring harness multi-plug in front of the servo unit.

17 Refer to Chapter 4A and disconnect the fuel supply and return pipes from the fuel rail.

18 Disconnect the main starter motor supply cable with reference to Chapter 5A.

All models

19 Withdraw the servo unit from the bulkhead, and remove it from the engine compartment. On left-hand-drive models, take care not to damage the bulkhead rubber grommet as the pushrod passes through it.

20 Note that the servo unit cannot be dismantled for repair or overhaul and, if faulty, must be renewed.

Refitting

21 Refitting is a reversal of the removal procedure. Refer to Section 11 for details of refitting the master cylinder.

17 Vacuum servo unit vacuum hose and non-return valve - removal, testing and refitting

Removal

1 With the engine switched off, depress the brake pedal four or five times, to dissipate any remaining vacuum from the servo unit.

2 Disconnect the vacuum hose adaptor at the servo unit, by pulling it free from the rubber grommet **(see illustration)**. If it is reluctant to

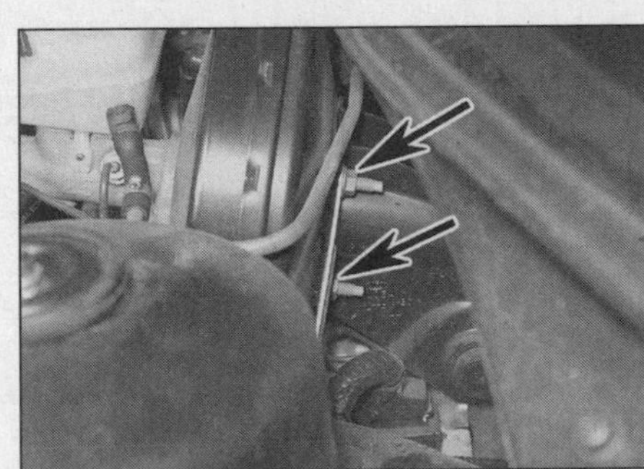

16.7 Two of the servo unit mounting nuts (arrowed)

17.2 Removing the plastic adaptor from the servo unit

move, prise it free, using a screwdriver with its blade inserted under the flange.

3 Detach the vacuum hose from the inlet manifold connection, pressing in the collar to disengage the tabs, then withdrawing the collar slowly.

4 If the hose or the fixings are damaged or in poor condition, they must be renewed.

Testing

5 Examine the non-return valve for damage and signs of deterioration, and renew it if necessary. The valve may be tested by blowing through its connecting hoses in both directions. It should only be possible to blow from the servo end towards the inlet manifold.

Refitting

6 Refitting is a reversal of the removal procedure. If fitting a new non-return valve, ensure that it is fitted the correct way round.

18 Pressure-control relief valve (non-ABS models) - removal and refitting

Note: *Refer to the warning at the start of Section 15 concerning the dangers of brake fluid.*

Removal

1 On non-ABS models, the two pressure-control relief valves (sometimes referred to as pressure-conscious reducing valves) are located on the master cylinder outlets to the rear brake line circuits.

2 Unscrew and remove the fluid reservoir filler cap, and draw off the fluid - see Section 11.

3 Position some rags beneath the master cylinder, to catch any spilled fluid.

4 Clean around the valve to be removed. Hold the PCR valve stationary with one spanner, and unscrew the hydraulic pipe union nut with another spanner. Pull out the pipe, and bend it slightly away from the valve.

5 Unscrew the PCR valve from the master cylinder.

6 Note that the primary and secondary PCR valves have different thread diameters, to prevent incorrect fitment. The primary valve has a 12 mm diameter thread, and the secondary valve has a 10 mm diameter thread **(see illustration)**.

Refitting

7 Refitting is a reversal of the removal procedure. On completion, bleed the hydraulic system as described in Section 15.

19 Pressure-control relief valve (early ABS models) - removal and refitting

Note 1: *The PCR valves are only removable on models with the early Mecatronic ABS unit (see Section 20). On later ABS units, the function of the PCR valves is built into the unit itself.*

Note 2: *Refer to the warning at the start of Section 15 concerning the dangers of brake fluid.*

Removal

1 The pressure-control relief valves are located on the ABS hydraulic unit **(see illustration)**.

2 Disconnect the battery negative (earth) lead (Chapter 5A, Section 1).

3 Remove the air cleaner assembly and air inlet duct as described in Chapter 4A. On four-cylinder engine models, also remove the plenum chamber.

4 Disconnect the low fluid level warning multi-plug from the brake fluid reservoir. Where applicable, detach the clutch fluid supply hose from its bracket, and move it aside, if possible without disconnecting the hose

5 Unscrew and remove the brake fluid reservoir filler cap, and completely seal the top of the reservoir using cling film or adhesive tape. This will reduce loss of fluid when the PCR valve is removed.

6 Unscrew the master cylinder mounting nuts, and carefully withdraw the cylinder from the servo unit, leaving the brake pipes still connected to it. Move the master cylinder over to the left-hand side of the engine compartment, to rest against the left-hand suspension turret. (Throughout this manual, left- and right-hand are as seen from the driver's seat.)

7 Unscrew the servo unit mounting nuts, and move the unit away from the bulkhead.

8 Position some rags beneath the ABS unit, to catch spilled fluid.

9 Clean around the valve to be removed. Hold the PCR valve stationary with one spanner, and unscrew the hydraulic pipe union nut with another spanner. Pull out the pipe, and bend it slightly away from the valve.

10 Unscrew the PCR valve from the ABS unit.

Refitting

11 Refitting is a reversal of the removal procedure. On completion, bleed the hydraulic system as described in Section 15.

20 ABS hydraulic unit - removal and refitting

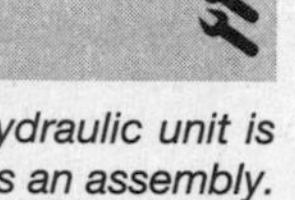

Note: *If any part of the ABS hydraulic unit is defective, it must be renewed as an assembly. Apart from the relay box (Section 22), individual spare parts are not available.*

1 Models up to December 1997 are equipped with a Mecatronic ABS unit, while models after this date have a Bosch 5.3 unit. There are also two 'generations' of Mecatronic unit

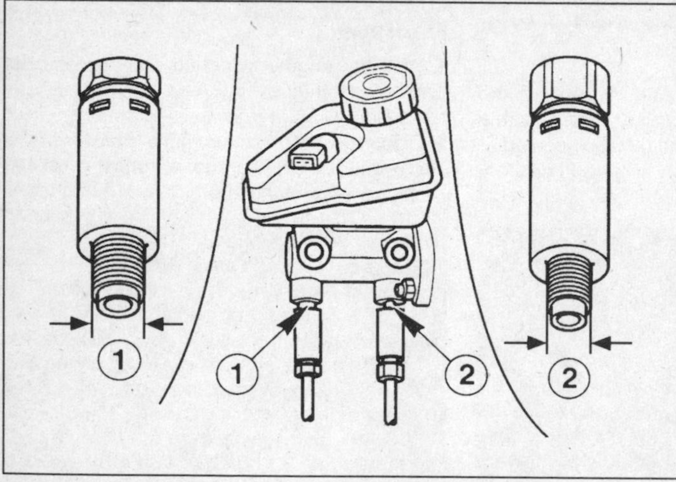

18.6 Pressure-control relief valve locations

1 Primary PCR valve (12 mm)
2 Secondary PCR valve (10 mm)

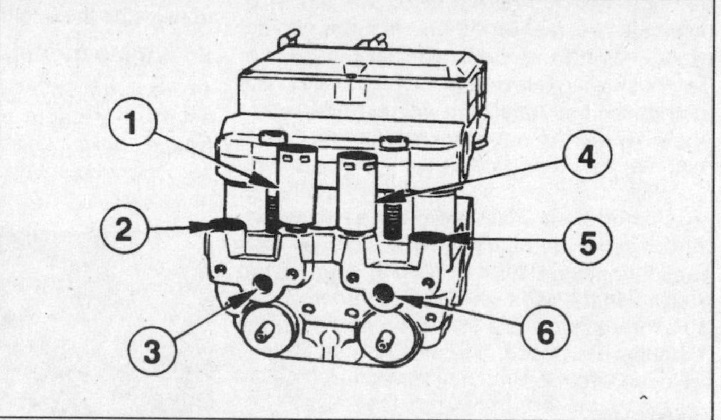

19.1 Pressure-control relief valve locations on the ABS hydraulic unit

1 PCR valve, rear right brake circuit
2 Outlet, front left brake circuit
3 Inlet, from brake master cylinder secondary circuit
4 PCR valve, rear left brake circuit
5 Outlet, front right brake circuit
6 Inlet, from brake master cylinder primary circuit

fitted, and it is unclear at the time of writing at what point the changeover was made from the early to the later type. Removal and refitting procedures for all units are broadly similar, at least in terms of the preliminary dismantling required. Refer to the relevant sub-section below.

Removal - early Mecatronic ABS unit

2 Remove both pressure-control relief valves as described in Section 19.

V6 engine models

3 Remove the driver's side facia lower trim panel, then working in the footwell, remove the nuts securing the pedal box assembly, and lower the pedals as far as possible.

4 On models with air conditioning, have the system discharged by a specialist. Disconnect the air conditioning pipework as necessary from the area around the ABS hydraulic unit.

> ⚠ ***Warning: Do not disconnect the air conditioning pipework if the system has not been discharged - see Chapter 3, Section 12.***

5 Unbolt and remove the servo unit mounting brackets from the engine compartment.

Right-hand drive models

6 Have an assistant hold the brake pedal depressed, then extract the spring clip and remove the clevis pin securing the servo unit pushrod to the pedal cross-link arm.

7 Remove the vacuum servo unit from the engine compartment.

Left-hand drive models

8 Unscrew the nut securing the pedal trunnion to the servo unit pushrod inside the passenger compartment. The nut is located near the top of the pedal, and is accessible through an access hole. For improved access, remove the lower facia panel first (see Chapter 11, Section 29).

9 Remove the vacuum servo unit, together with the pushrod, from the engine compartment. Take care not to damage the rubber grommet in the bulkhead.

All models

10 Identify the location of the remaining brake hydraulic pipes on the ABS hydraulic unit, then unscrew the union nuts and pull out the pipes. Carefully bend the pipes away from the hydraulic unit, to allow the unit to be removed.

11 Disconnect the multi-plugs from the hydraulic unit. To disconnect the main 22-pin multi-plug, push the locktab, then swivel the multi-plug outwards and unhook it.

12 Unscrew the pump mounting nut, and the unit retaining nuts, as applicable.

13 Raise the left-hand side of the ABS hydraulic unit, then swivel the unit out of the right-hand mounting. Take care not to lose the bracket studs and insulator ring.

Refitting - early Mecatronic ABS unit

14 Locate the insulator ring on the pump end, and fit the stud cap to the insulator ring.

15 Lower the ABS hydraulic unit into position, right-hand end first.

16 Fit the right-hand bracket studs onto the insulators.

17 Lower the left-hand end of the ABS hydraulic unit onto the bracket. Fit and tighten the pump mounting nut and the remaining unit mountings, as applicable.

Left-hand drive models

18 Locate the vacuum servo unit and pushrod on the bulkhead bracket, taking care not to damage the rubber grommet.

19 Insert the pushrod in the pedal trunnion, and tighten the nut.

20 Refit the lower facia panel if it was removed.

Right-hand drive models

21 Locate the vacuum servo unit and pushrod on the bulkhead bracket.

22 Refit the clevis pin and spring clip securing the servo unit pushrod to the pedal cross-link arm.

All models

23 The remainder of refitting is a reversal of removal. Ensure that the multi-plugs are securely connected, and that the brake pipe unions are tightened to the specified torque. Refit both pressure-control relief valves, with reference to Section 19. On V6 models, have the air conditioning system recharged after reconnecting the disturbed pipework.

Removal - later Mecatronic ABS unit

24 Disconnect the battery negative (earth) lead (Chapter 5A, Section 1).

25 Remove the air cleaner assembly and air inlet duct as described in Chapter 4A. On four-cylinder engine models, also remove the plenum chamber.

26 Disconnect the low fluid level warning multi-plug from the brake fluid reservoir. Detach the clutch fluid supply hose from its bracket, and move it aside, if possible without disconnecting the hose.

27 Unscrew and remove the brake fluid reservoir filler cap, and completely seal the top of the reservoir using cling film or adhesive tape. This will reduce loss of fluid when the hydraulic pipes are disconnected.

28 Unscrew the master cylinder mounting nuts, and carefully withdraw the cylinder from the servo unit, leaving the brake pipes still connected to it. Move the master cylinder over to the left-hand side of the engine compartment, to rest against the left-hand suspension turret. (Throughout this manual, left- and right-hand are as seen from the driver's seat.)

29 Unscrew the servo unit mounting nuts, and move the unit away from the bulkhead.

Right-hand drive models

30 Have an assistant hold the brake pedal depressed, then extract the spring clip and remove the clevis pin securing the servo unit pushrod to the pedal cross-link arm.

31 Remove the vacuum servo unit from the engine compartment.

Left-hand drive models

32 Unscrew the nut securing the pedal trunnion to the servo unit pushrod inside the passenger compartment. The nut is located near the top of the pedal, and is accessible through an access hole. For improved access, remove the lower facia panel first, disconnecting the diagnostic plug from the panel as it is removed.

33 Remove the vacuum servo unit, together with the pushrod, from the engine compartment. Take care not to damage the rubber grommet in the bulkhead.

All models

34 Disconnect the multi-plug from the hydraulic unit.

35 Position some rags beneath the ABS unit, to catch spilled fluid.

36 Identify the location of the brake hydraulic pipes on the ABS hydraulic unit, then unscrew the union nuts and pull out the pipes. Carefully bend the pipes away from the hydraulic unit, to allow the unit to be removed.

37 Remove the four mounting bracket bolts, and remove the hydraulic unit, complete with brackets, from the engine compartment.

Refitting - later Mecatronic ABS unit

38 Refitting is a reversal of removal. Ensure that the multi-plug is securely connected, and that the brake pipe unions are tightened to the specified torque.

Removal - Bosch ABS unit

39 Disconnect the battery negative (earth) lead (Chapter 5A, Section 1).

40 Remove the air cleaner assembly and air inlet duct as described in Chapter 4A. On four-cylinder engine models, also remove the plenum chamber. Remove the air cleaner support bracket

41 Disconnect the low fluid level warning multi-plug from the brake fluid reservoir. Detach the clutch fluid supply hose from its bracket, and move it aside, if possible without disconnecting the hose.

42 Unscrew and remove the brake fluid reservoir filler cap, and completely seal the top of the reservoir using cling film or adhesive tape. This will reduce loss of fluid when the hydraulic pipes are disconnected.

43 Unscrew the master cylinder mounting nuts, and carefully withdraw the cylinder from the servo unit, leaving the brake pipes still connected to it. Move the master cylinder over to the left-hand side of the engine compartment, to rest against the left-hand suspension turret. (Throughout this manual, left- and right-hand are as seen from the driver's seat.)

21.7 Unscrew the mounting bolt and remove the ABS sensor

44 Unscrew the servo unit mounting nuts, and move the unit away from the bulkhead.

Right-hand drive models

45 Have an assistant hold the brake pedal depressed, then extract the spring clip and remove the clevis pin securing the servo unit pushrod to the pedal cross-link arm.

46 Remove the vacuum servo unit from the engine compartment.

Left-hand drive models

47 Unscrew the nut securing the pedal trunnion to the servo unit pushrod inside the passenger compartment. The nut is located near the top of the pedal, and is accessible through an access hole. For improved access, remove the lower facia panel first, disconnecting the diagnostic plug from the panel as it is removed.

48 Remove the vacuum servo unit, together with the pushrod, from the engine compartment. Take care not to damage the rubber grommet in the bulkhead.

49 Remove the nuts around the base of the steering column securing the servo unit mounting bracket, and withdraw the mounting bracket from the bulkhead.

50 On models with air conditioning, move the air conditioning pipe bracket to one side.

51 Unbolt and remove the brake servo side support brackets.

All models

52 Disconnect the multi-plug from the hydraulic unit.

53 Position some rags beneath the ABS unit, to catch spilled fluid.

54 Identify the location of the brake hydraulic pipes on the ABS hydraulic unit, then unscrew the union nuts and pull out the pipes. Carefully bend the pipes away from the hydraulic unit, to allow the unit to be removed.

55 On V6 engine models, remove the four bolts securing the ABS unit mounting brackets, and move the unit and brackets forwards.

56 Remove the two mounting nuts, and slide the hydraulic unit off its locating peg and out of the mounting brackets.

Refitting - Bosch ABS unit

57 Refitting is a reversal of removal. Ensure that the multi-plug is securely connected, and that the brake pipe unions are tightened to the specified torque.

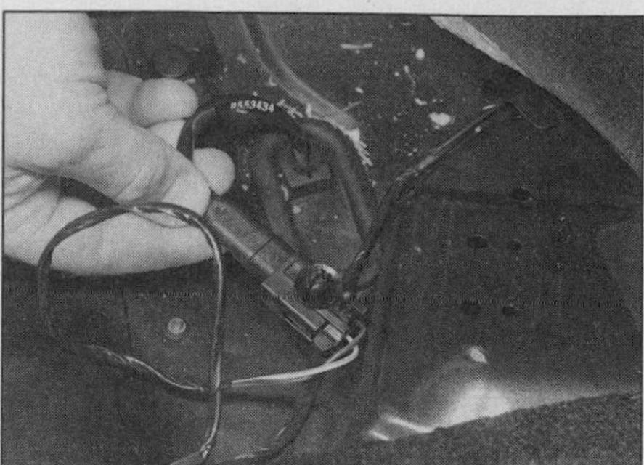

21.15 Rear ABS sensor wiring multi-plug located beneath the rear seat

21 ABS wheel sensor - testing, removal and refitting

Testing

1 Checking of the sensors is done before removal, connecting a voltmeter to the disconnected sensor multi-plug. Using an analogue (moving coil) meter is not practical, since the meter does not respond quickly enough. A digital meter having an AC facility may be used to check that the sensor is operating correctly.

2 To do this, raise the relevant wheel then disconnect the wiring to the ABS sensor and connect the meter to it.

3 Spin the wheel and check that the output voltage is between 1.5 and 2.0 volts, depending on how fast the wheel is spun.

4 Alternatively, an oscilloscope may be used to check the output of the sensor - an alternating current will be traced on the screen, of magnitude depending on the speed of the rotating wheel.

5 If the sensor output is low or zero, renew the sensor.

Removal

Front wheel sensor

6 Apply the handbrake and loosen the relevant front wheel nuts. Jack up the front of the vehicle and support it on axle stands. Remove the relevant wheel.

7 Unscrew the sensor mounting bolt located on the steering knuckle, and withdraw the sensor **(see illustration)**.

8 Remove the sensor wiring loom from the support brackets on the front suspension strut and wheel arch.

9 Prise out the stud clips, and remove the Torx screws and screw clips holding the wheel arch liner in position. Withdraw the liner.

10 Disconnect the multi-plug, and withdraw the sensor and wiring loom.

Rear wheel sensor

11 Chock the front wheels, and engage 1st gear (or 'P'). Jack up the rear of the vehicle and support it on axle stands. Remove the relevant wheel.

12 Unscrew the sensor mounting bolt, located on the brake backplate (drum brakes) or rear suspension knuckle (disc brakes), and withdraw the sensor.

13 On disc brake models, prise out the stud clips, and remove the Torx screws and screw clips holding the wheel arch liner in position. Withdraw the liner.

14 Disconnect the sensor wiring loom from the supports on the rear suspension strut (or knuckle) and wheel arch.

15 Working inside the vehicle, lift the rear seat cushion, then disconnect the multi-plug for the sensor wiring loom **(see illustration)**.

16 Withdraw the sensor and wiring loom through the rubber grommet in the rear floor.

Refitting

Front and rear wheel sensors

17 Refitting is a reversal of the removal procedure.

22 ABS relay box - removal and refitting

Note: *This Section only applies to the ABS unit fitted up to December 1997 (Mecatronic). On the Bosch unit fitted after this date, the system relays are integral with the unit.*

Removal

1 Disconnect the battery negative (earth) lead (see Chapter 5A, Section 1).

2 On four-cylinder models, detach the vacuum hose from the inlet manifold connection, pressing in the collar to disengage the tabs, then withdrawing the collar slowly.

3 To improve access, remove the air cleaner as described in Chapter 4A. Free the heater hose from its retaining clips, and position it clear of the relay box.

4 Disconnect the wiring connector(s) from the relay box and, where necessary, the speed sender unit.

5 Slacken and remove the four Torx retaining screws, and withdraw the relay box from the hydraulic unit **(see illustration)**.

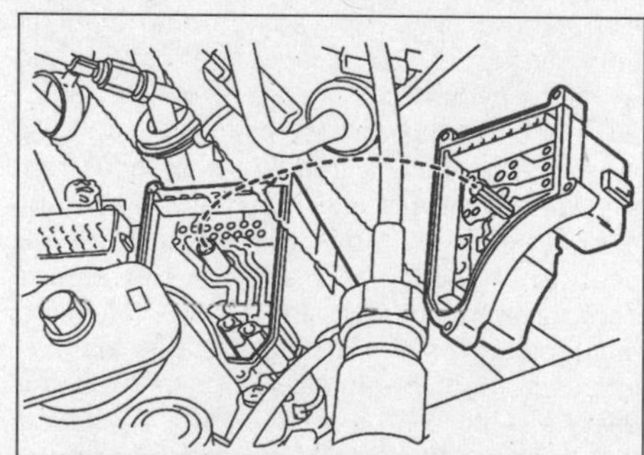

22.5 Removing the ABS relay box

24.3a Disconnect the TCS actuator upper . . .

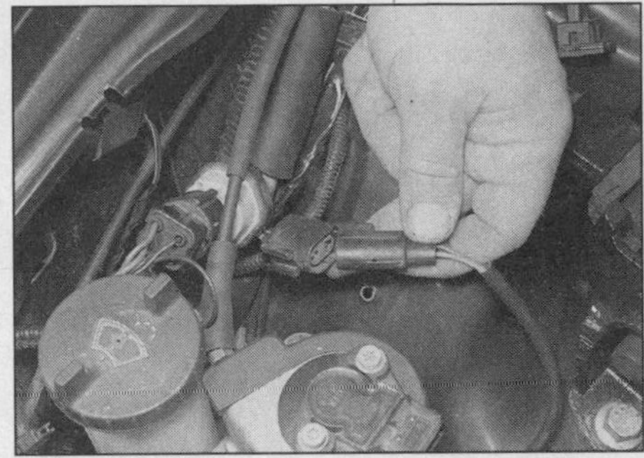

24.3b . . . and lower wiring plugs

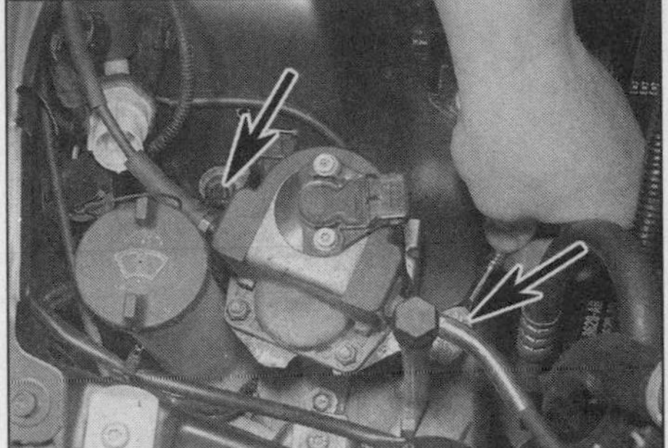

24.4a Remove the three mounting bolts (arrowed) . . .

Refitting

6 Refitting is a reversal of the removal procedure. Do not overtighten the relay box retaining screws, as the plastic is easily cracked.

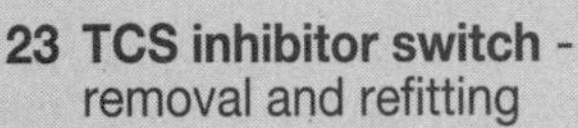

23 TCS inhibitor switch - removal and refitting

Refer to Chapter 12.

24 TCS throttle actuator - removal and refitting

Removal

1 The TCS throttle actuator is located in the front right-hand corner of the engine compartment. First disconnect the battery negative (earth) lead (Chapter 5A, Section 1).

2 To improve access to the actuator, unbolt the coolant expansion tank (refer to Chapter 3 if necessary), and carefully lift it on top of the engine, without disturbing any of the hoses. Ensure that the tank cap is securely fastened, to prevent leaks.

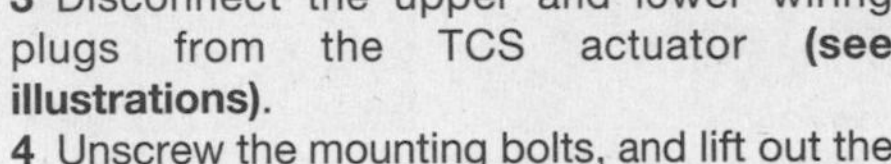

3 Disconnect the upper and lower wiring plugs from the TCS actuator **(see illustrations)**.

4 Unscrew the mounting bolts, and lift out the TCS throttle actuator **(see illustrations)**.

5 Unclip the motor cover **(see illustration)**.

6 Turn the upper throttle control segment, to provide some play in the accelerator cable from the accelerator pedal, then disconnect the cable by unhooking the end fitting **(see illustration)**.

7 Prise back the retaining catch, and slide the cable guide upwards from the motor housing **(see illustration)**.

8 Turn the lower accelerator control segment, to provide play in the accelerator cable leading to the throttle housing, then disconnect the cable by unhooking the end fitting. Release the cable from the motor housing as described in paragraph 6 **(see illustrations)**.

24.4b . . . and lift out the TCS actuator for cable removal

Refitting

9 Refitting is a reversal of the removal procedure. If necessary, check the accelerator cable adjustment as described in Chapter 4A.

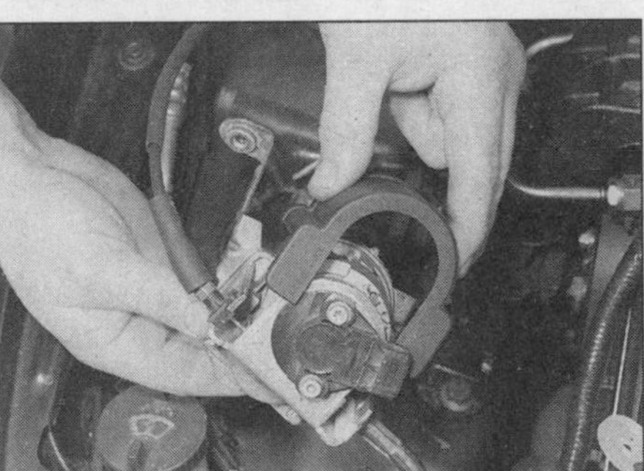

24.5 Unclip the actuator cover for access to the cables

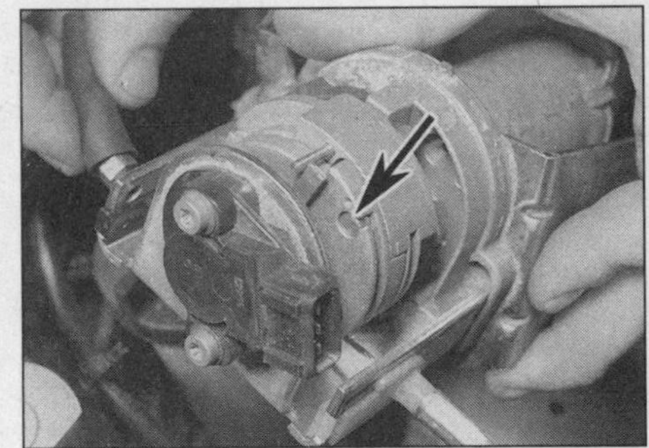

24.6 Unhook the inner cable end fitting (arrowed) . . .

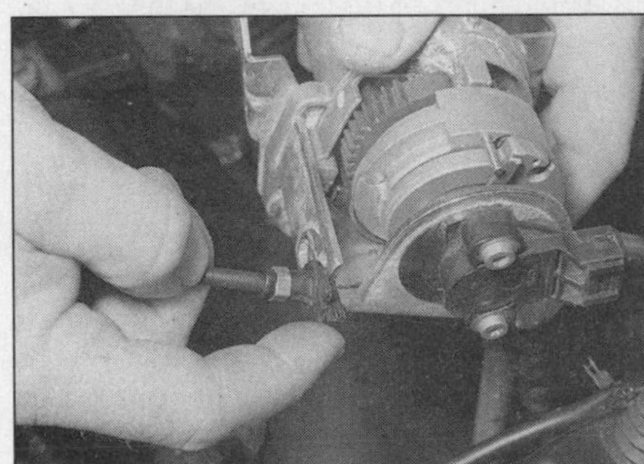

24.7 . . . then unclip the cable outer from the actuator housing

24.8a Unhook the inner cable end fitting . . .

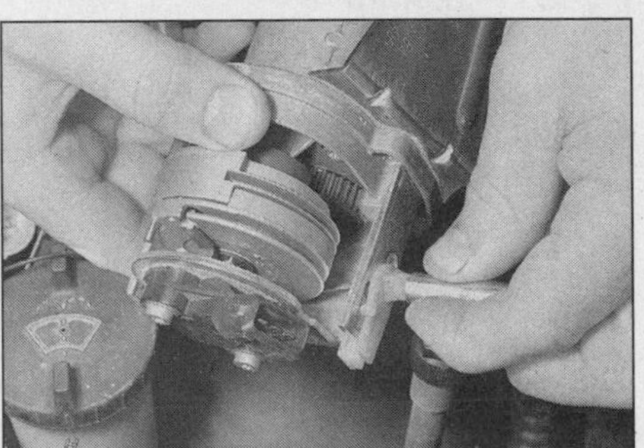

24.8b . . . and disconnect the cable outer guide

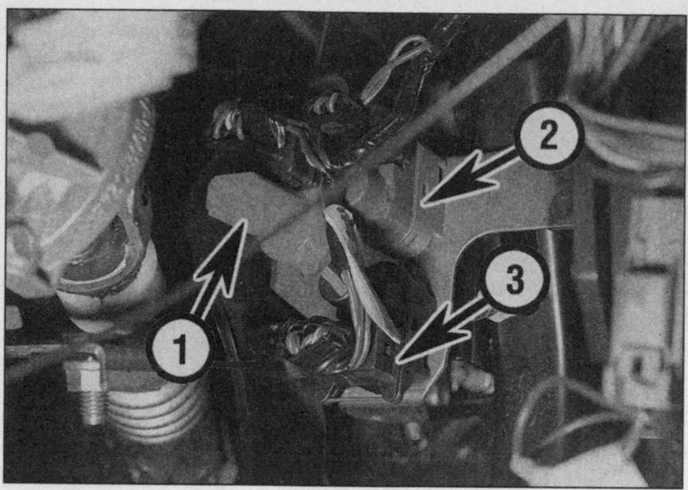

25.3 On models with cruise control, there are three switches on the pedal bracket

1 Clutch pedal position switch
2 Brake pedal de-activator switch
3 Stop-light switch

25.4 Removing the stop-light switch

25 Stop-light switch - removal, refitting and adjustment

Removal

1 Disconnect the battery negative (earth) lead (see Chapter 5A, Section 1).

2 Remove the lower facia panel, with reference to Chapter 11, Section 29.

3 Disconnect the wiring multi-plug from the switch. On models with cruise control, note that the stop-light switch is the lower of the two switches above the brake pedal **(see illustration)**.

4 On models without cruise control, rotate the switch anti-clockwise by a quarter-turn, and withdraw it from the pedal bracket **(see illustration)**. Where cruise control is fitted, the switch is rotated clockwise to remove it.

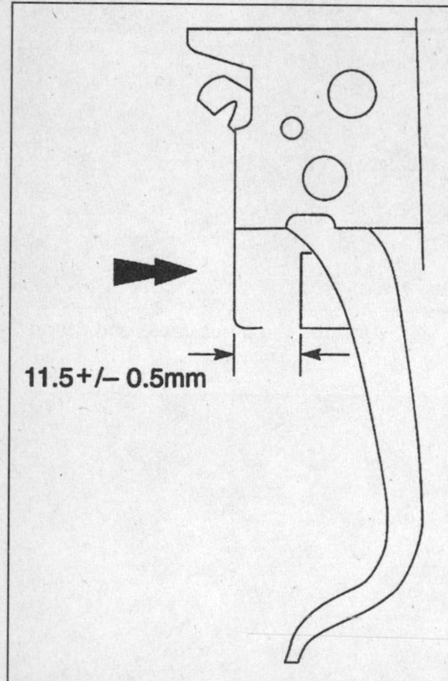

25.6 To ensure correct adjustment, position the brake pedal as shown prior to refitting the switch to its mounting bracket

Refitting and adjustment

5 With the switch removed, reset it by fully extending its plunger.

6 Depress the brake pedal until the distance between the pedal and mounting bracket is as shown **(see illustration)**.

7 Hold the pedal in this position, and refit the stop-light switch to the mounting bracket.

8 With the switch securely clipped in position, release the brake pedal, and gently pull it fully back to the at-rest position. This will automatically set the adjustment of the stop-light switch.

9 Reconnect the wiring connector and the battery, and check the operation of the switch prior to refitting the lower facia panel.

26 Handbrake lever - removal and refitting

Removal

1 Raise the front and rear of the vehicle, and support it on axle stands. Fully release the handbrake lever.

2 Remove the centre console as described in Chapter 11.

3 Working beneath the vehicle, release the exhaust system from the rubber mountings. Lower the exhaust system as far as possible, supporting it on blocks or more axle stands.

4 Detach the exhaust heat shield from the underbody.

5 Unhook the secondary (rear) handbrake cables from the equaliser bar **(see illustration)**.

6 Working inside the vehicle, unscrew and remove the two mounting bolts securing the handbrake lever to the floor **(see illustration)**.

7 Turn the handbrake lever upside-down, then disconnect the primary cable end from the segment.

8 Withdraw the handbrake from inside the vehicle.

Refitting

9 If a new lever is being fitted, the self-adjust mechanism is pre-set to the correct position. When refitting the old lever, it may be necessary to reset the mechanism, as follows.

10 Lift the lever to the fully-raised position, then sit down and grip the cable and equaliser bracket between your feet.

11 Release the pawl from the adjuster mechanism, lift the lever, and pull out approximately 40 mm of cable **(see illustration)**. Allow the pawl to engage the mechanism, and release the cable. The mechanism should now be in the correct position for refitting.

12 Make sure that the primary cable is correctly located in the segment.

13 Check the operation of the handbrake before returning the vehicle to normal service.

27 Handbrake cables - removal and refitting

Removal

Primary (front)

1 Remove the handbrake lever as described in Section 26.

2 Prise the grommet from the underbody, and withdraw the cable from beneath the vehicle.

26.5 Handbrake lever and associated components

1 *Handbrake lever*
2 *Clock spring*
3 *Handbrake cable*
4 *Toothed segment and pawl to lock the handbrake lever*
5 *Fine-toothed segment for the clock spring*
6 *Pawl for the clock spring*
7 *Underbody bracket, secondary cables and equaliser bar*

Secondary (rear)

3 Chock the front wheels, and engage 1st gear (or 'P'). Loosen the wheel nuts on the relevant rear wheel, then jack up the rear of the vehicle and support it on axle stands. Fully release the handbrake lever.

4 Remove the relevant rear wheel.

5 Working beneath the vehicle, release the exhaust system from the rubber mountings. Lower the exhaust system as far as possible, supporting it on blocks or more axle stands.

6 Unbolt the exhaust heat shield(s) from the underbody.

7 Unhook the relevant cable from the equaliser bar.

8 On drum brake models, remove the rear brake shoes on the relevant side as described in Section 6, then remove the outer cable from the backplate by compressing the three retaining lugs (use a suitable ring spanner) and pushing the cable through **(see illustration)**.

26.6 Handbrake lever mounting bolts

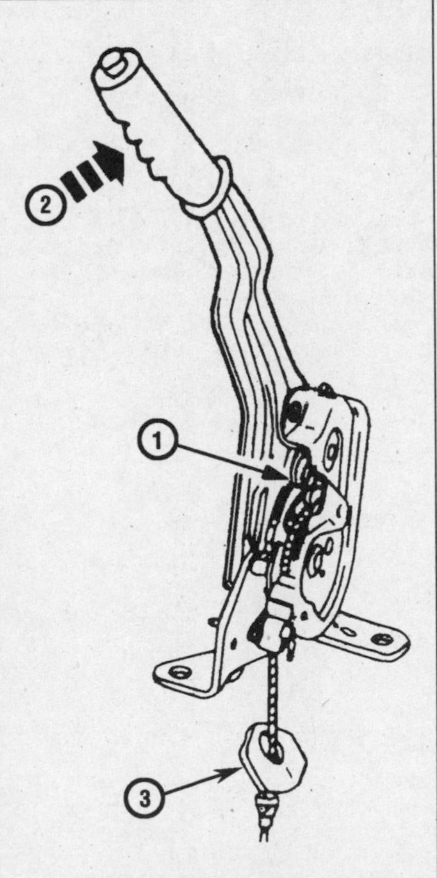

26.11 Release the pawl (1), lift the lever (2) and pull out the cable (3)

9 On disc brake models, swivel the caliper handbrake arm towards the front of the car, and unhook the end of the cable inner from the arm **(see illustration)**. Compress the tangs of the outer cable retaining clip, and release the cable from the caliper bracket.

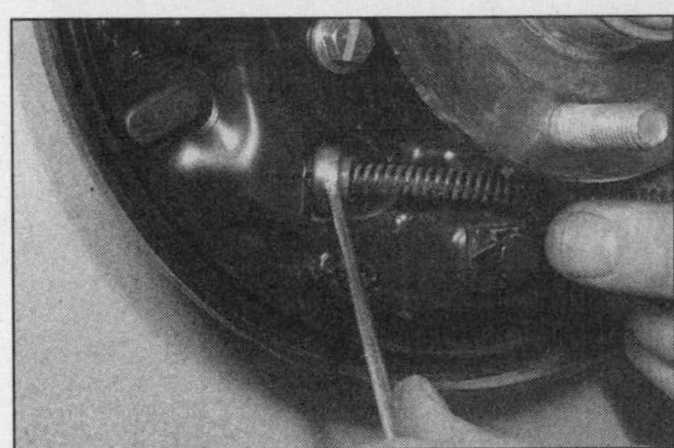

27.8 Using a ring spanner to compress the retaining lugs securing the outer cable to the backplate

27.9 Disconnect the inner cable from the caliper handbrake arm

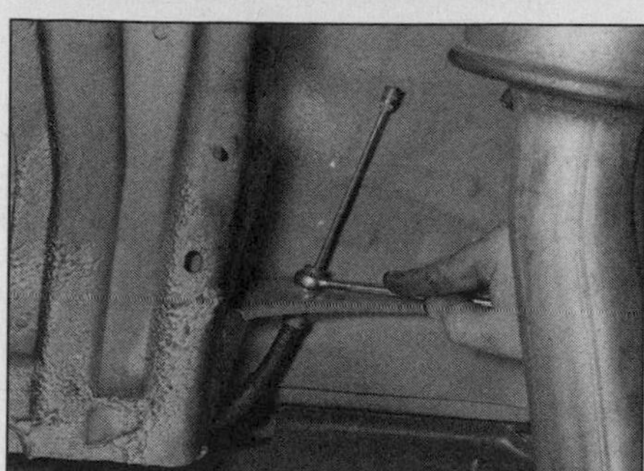

27.10a Release the lugs using a ring spanner . . .

27.10b . . . and remove the outer cable from the underbody brackets

10 Release the lugs securing the outer cable to the underbody brackets, then release the cable from the clips, and withdraw it from under the vehicle **(see illustrations)**.

Refitting

All cables

11 Refitting is a reversal of the removal procedure, noting the following points:

a) *The handbrake cables are self-adjusting, using a ratchet and pawl mechanism on the base of the handbrake lever. When reconnecting the cables to the rear brakes, don't be alarmed by any clicking noises heard.*

b) *Make sure that the cable end fittings are correctly located.*

c) *Check the operation of the handbrake. The cables will adjust themselves to the optimum setting once the handbrake has been applied and released a few times. Make sure that both wheels are locked, then free to turn, as the handbrake is operated.*

Chapter 10
Suspension and steering

Contents

Degrees of difficulty

Easy, suitable for novice with little experience 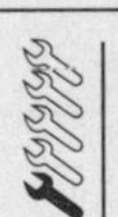

Fairly easy, suitable for beginner with some experience 

Fairly difficult, suitable for competent DIY mechanic

Difficult, suitable for experienced DIY mechanic 

Very difficult, suitable for expert DIY or professional

Specifications

Front wheel alignment

Toe setting:	
Tolerance allowed before resetting required	1.5 mm toe-in to 1.5 mm toe-out (0°15' to -0°15')
Adjustment setting (if required)	0 mm ± 1.0 mm (0°00' ± 0°10')

Rear wheel alignment

Toe setting:	
Tolerance allowed before resetting required:	
Saloon/Hatchback	3.9 mm toe-in to 0.1 mm toe-out (0°39' to -0°01')
Estate	2.7 mm toe-in to 1.3 mm toe-out (0°27' to -0°13')
Adjustment setting (if required):	
Saloon/Hatchback	1.9 mm toe-in ± 1.2 mm (0°18' ± 0°12')
Estate	0.7 mm toe-in ± 1.2 mm (0°07' ± 0°12')

Roadwheels and tyres

Wheel sizes:	
Steel	14x5.5, 15x5.5, or 15x6
Alloy*	14x5.5, 15x6, 16x6, or 16x6.5
Tyre sizes (depending on model)	185/65/14, 195/60/14, 195/60/15, 195/55/15, 195/50/16, 205/55/15, or 205/50/16
Tyre pressures	See end of *"Weekly checks"*

**On some models with alloy wheels, a steel spare wheel may be provided*

10

Torque wrench settings

	Nm	lbf ft
Front suspension		
Anti-roll bar clamp bolts	24	18
Anti-roll bar link	47	35
Driveshaft/hub retaining nut	340	251
Front subframe	130	96
Lower arm balljoint to lower arm (service replacement, bolted on)	58	43
Lower arm balljoint-to-steering knuckle clamp bolt	83	61
Lower arm to subframe:		
Stage 1	50	37
Stage 2	Tighten through further 90°	
Suspension strut thrust bearing retaining nut	59	44
Suspension strut upper mounting nut (renew)	46	34
Suspension strut-to-steering knuckle pinch-bolt	84	62
Rear suspension (Saloon/Hatchback)		
Anti-roll bar	25	18
Anti-roll bar link	35	26
Crossmember mounting bolts	120	89
Disc brake splash shield	90	66
Drum brake backplate	50	37
Front lower arm to knuckle and to crossmember	84	62
Hub nut	290	214
Rear lower arm to crossmember	84	62
Rear lower arm to knuckle	120	89
Suspension strut to knuckle	84	62
Suspension strut upper mounting bolts	27	20
Suspension strut upper nut	50	37
Tie-bar and tie-bar bracket	120	89
Rear suspension (Estate)		
Same as for Saloon/Hatchback, except for the following.		
Anti-roll bar	23	17
Front lower arm to knuckle and to crossmember	120	89
Hub assembly-to-knuckle retaining bolts	65	48
Shock absorber lower mounting bolt	120	89
Shock absorber upper mounting bolt	84	62
Tie-bar bracket to underbody	120	89
Tie-bar to bracket	120	89
Tie-bar to knuckle	84	62
Upper arm to crossmember	84	62
Upper arm to knuckle	120	89
Steering		
Flexible coupling-to-pinion shaft clamp bolt (renew)	28	21
Power steering pipe unions to valve body	31	23
Steering column mounting bolts	24	18
Steering column-to-flexible coupling clamp bolt (renew)	24	18
Steering gear cover plate bolts (V6 models)	50	37
Steering gear mounting bolts	137	101
Steering pump mounting bolts:		
Four-cylinder engine models	24	18
V6 engine models	48	35
Steering pump pressure line joint union (V6 models)	17	13
Steering pump pressure line-to-pump	65	48
Steering pump pulley bolts (V6 models)	25	18
Steering pump retaining plate bolts (V6 models)	25	18
Steering pump retaining plate nuts (V6 models)	10	7
Steering wheel bolt	50	37
Track rod end locknut	41	30
Track rod end to steering knuckle	28	21
Track rod locknuts	110	81
Roadwheel nuts	85	63

1 General information

The independent front suspension is of MacPherson strut type, incorporating coil springs, integral telescopic shock absorbers, and an anti-roll bar. The struts are attached to steering knuckles at their lower ends, and the knuckles are in turn attached to the lower suspension arm by balljoints. The anti-roll bar is bolted to the rear of the subframe, and is connected to the front suspension struts by links **(see illustration)**.

On Saloon/Hatchback models, the independent rear suspension is of 'Quadralink' type, having four mounting points on each side of the vehicle. The two lower arms are attached to the rear suspension knuckle at their outer ends, and to the rear crossmember at their inner ends. A tie-bar, located between the bottom of the knuckle and the floor, counteracts braking and acceleration forces on each side **(see illustration)**.

On Estate models, the independent rear suspension is of 'SLA' (Short and Long Arm) type. This allows a larger load area, since there are no suspension points projecting into the luggage area. There are three side arms on each side: one forged upper arm, and two pressed-steel lower side arms. A tie-bar on each side supports the rear suspension knuckles. The coil springs are separate from the shock absorbers **(see illustration)**.

A rear anti-roll bar is fitted to all models. On Si and some V6 engine models, the front and rear shock absorbers are gas-filled; on other models, they are filled with fluid. Self-levelling rear shock absorbers are available on Estate models.

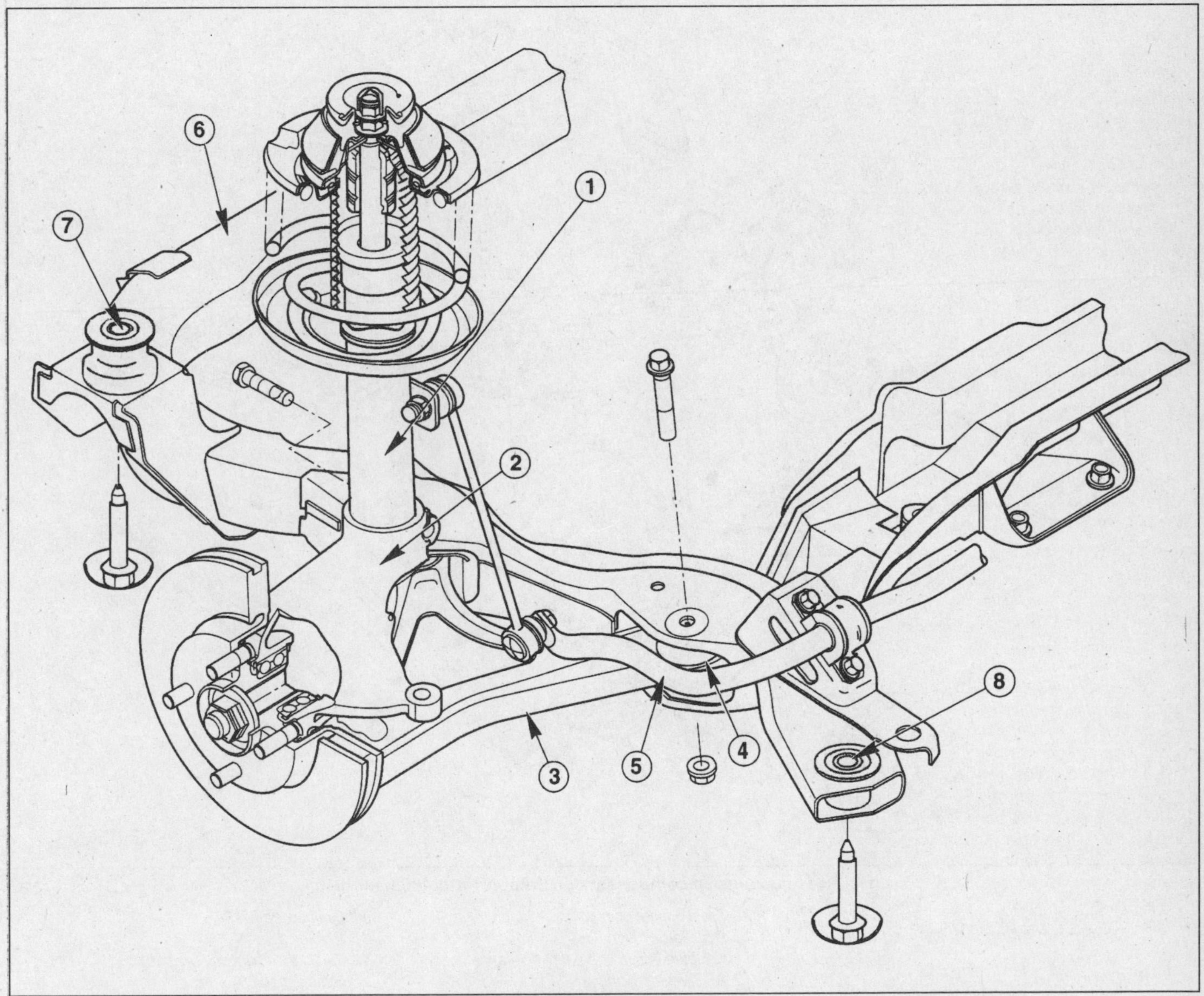

1.1 Front suspension components

1 MacPherson strut
2 Steering knuckle
3 Lower arm
4 Vertical silent bush on lower arm
5 Anti-roll bar
6 Front subframe
7 Front subframe rubber bush
8 Rear subframe rubber bush

A variable-ratio type rack-and-pinion steering gear is fitted, together with a conventional column and telescopic coupling, incorporating two universal joints. Power-assisted steering is fitted to all models. A power steering system fluid cooler is fitted, in front of the cooling system radiator on the crossmember (see Section 35). On models with adaptive damping, a steering position sensor with sensor disc is located above the upper universal joint.

An adaptive damping system was offered on certain early models. With this system, it is possible to select a hard or soft setting for the front and rear shock absorbers. The system is computer-controlled; a switch is provided near the handbrake lever for selection of 'Sport' or 'Normal' mode. With this system, a solenoid valve is fitted to each suspension strut. When the valve is open, the hydraulic oil inside the shock absorber is routed through a bypass channel, making the action 'softer'. When the solenoid valve is closed, the shock absorber action becomes 'harder'. The system takes into consideration the road speed of the vehicle; at high speeds, the shock absorbers are automatically set to 'hard'. The adaptive damping computer module is located in the luggage compartment, behind the rear seat, and incorporates a self-test function **(see illustrations)**. Adaptive damping is not available on Estate models.

When working on the suspension or steering, you may come across nuts or bolts which seem impossible to loosen. These nuts and bolts on the underside of the vehicle are

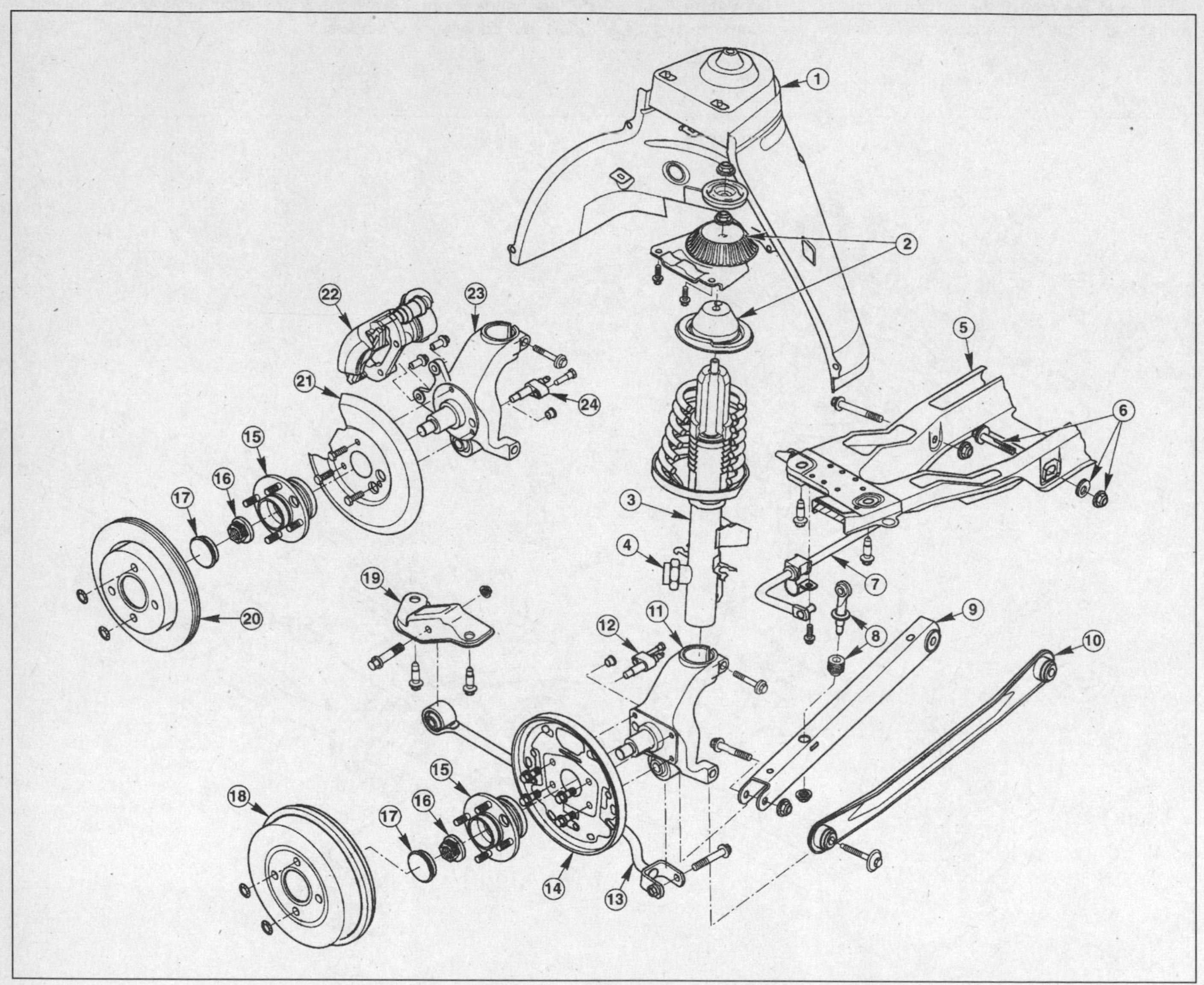

1.2 Rear suspension components on Saloon/Hatchback models

1 *Wheel housing*
2 *Upper mounting bracket and coil spring seat*
3 *Strut*
4 *Solenoid valve for adaptive damping*
5 *Rear suspension crossmember*
6 *Eccentric bolt for rear toe setting*
7 *Anti-roll bar*
8 *Link*
9 *Front lower arm*
10 *Rear lower arm*
11 *Knuckle (drum brake models)*
12 *ABS wheel sensor (drum brake models)*
13 *Tie-bar*
14 *Backplate*
15 *Hub and bearing assembly*
16 *Hub nut*
17 *Grease cap*
18 *Brake drum*
19 *Tie-bar mounting bracket*
20 *Brake disc*
21 *Splash shield (disc brake models)*
22 *Brake caliper (disc brake models)*
23 *Knuckle (disc brake models)*
24 *ABS wheel sensor (disc brake models)*

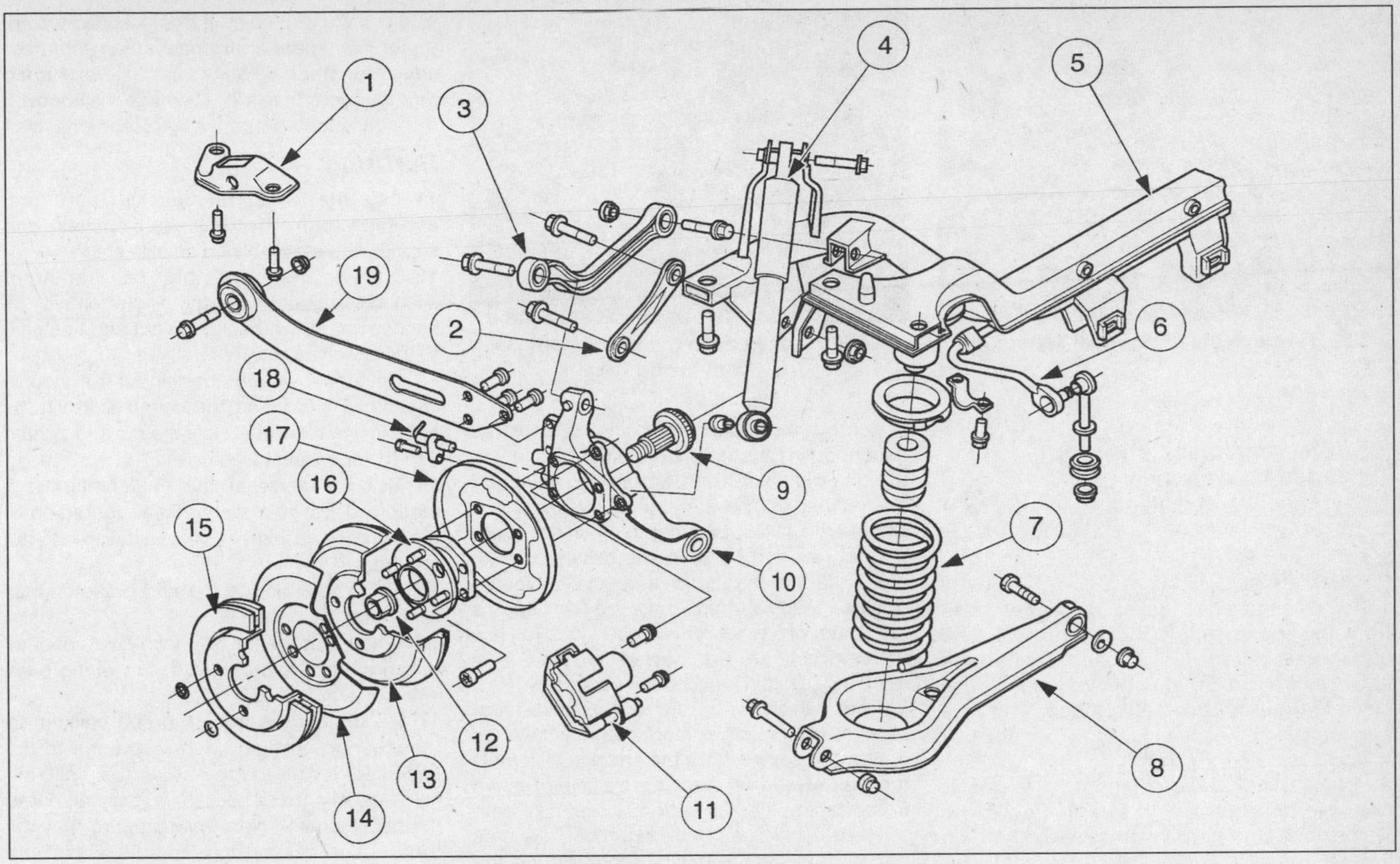

1.3 Rear suspension components on Estate models

1 *Tie-bar bracket*
2 *Short front lower arm*
3 *Long front upper arm*
4 *Shock absorber*
5 *Crossmember*
6 *Anti-roll bar*
7 *Coil spring*
8 *Rear lower arm*
9 *Stub axle (part of hub and bearing assembly)*
10 *Knuckle*
11 *Brake caliper (disc brake models)*
12 *Hub nut*
13 *Brake drum*
14 *Splash guard (disc brake models)*
15 *Brake disc*
16 *Hub and bearing assembly*
17 *Backplate (drum brake models)*
18 *ABS wheel sensor*
19 *Tie-bar*

continually subjected to water, road grime, mud, etc, and can become rusted or seized, making them extremely difficult to remove. In order to unscrew these stubborn nuts and bolts without damaging them (or other components), use lots of penetrating oil, and allow it to soak in for a while. Using a wire brush to clean exposed threads will also ease removal of the nut or bolt, and will help to prevent damage to the threads. Sometimes, a sharp blow with a hammer and punch will break the bond between a nut and bolt, but care must be taken to prevent the punch from slipping off and ruining the threads. Heating the nut or bolt and surrounding area with a blow lamp sometimes helps too, but this is not recommended, because of the obvious dangers associated with fire. Extension bars or pipes will increase leverage, but never use one on a ratchet, as the internal mechanism could be damaged. Actually *tightening* the nut or bolt first may help to break it loose. Nuts or bolts which have required drastic measures to remove them should always be renewed.

Since most of the procedures dealt with in this Chapter involve jacking up the vehicle and working underneath it, a good pair of axle stands will be needed. A hydraulic trolley jack is the preferred type of jack to lift the vehicle, and it can also be used to support certain components during removal and refitting operations.

Warning: Never, under any circumstances, rely on a jack alone to support the vehicle while working beneath it. When jacking up the vehicle, do not lift or support it beneath the front subframe or rear crossmember (see "Jacking and vehicle support").

1.6a Adaptive damping switch located near the handbrake lever

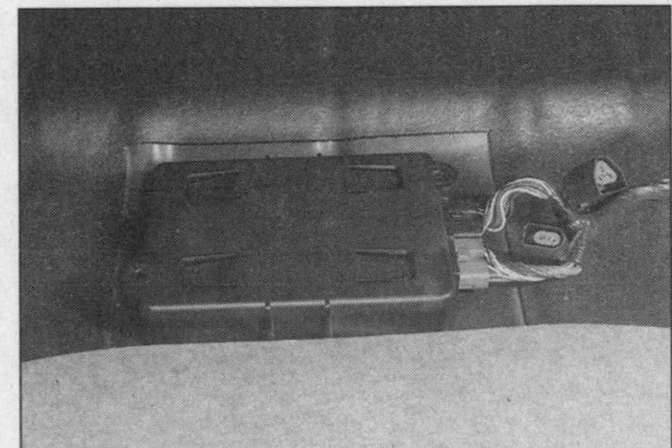

1.6b Adaptive damping computer module located in the luggage compartment

2.5a Remove the ABS wheel sensor . . .

2.5b . . . and unclip the wiring harness from the hub

2 Steering knuckle and hub assembly - removal and refitting

Removal

1 Remove the wheel cover (or centre cover) from the wheel, apply the handbrake, and engage 1st gear or 'P'. Loosen the hub nut about half a turn. This nut is very tight - use only high-quality, close-fitting tools, and take adequate precautions against personal injury when loosening the hub nut.

2 Working inside the engine compartment, remove the strut cap (if fitted). Retain the suspension strut piston with an Allen key, then loosen the strut upper mounting nut and unscrew it by five complete turns. Do not remove the nut completely at this stage, but note that, on completion, a new nut should be fitted.

3 Loosen the relevant front wheel nuts and chock the rear wheels. Jack up the front of the vehicle and support it on axle stands. Remove the front wheel.

4 Extract the split pin from the track rod end balljoint nut. Unscrew the nut, and detach the rod from the arm on the steering knuckle using a conventional balljoint removal tool. Take care not to damage the balljoint seal.

5 Remove the ABS sensor (when fitted) as described in Chapter 9; disconnect the wiring from the clip on the hub **(see illustrations)**.

6 Remove the brake caliper and brake disc as described in Chapter 9, but do not disconnect the flexible hose from the caliper. Suspend the caliper from a suitable point under the wheel arch, taking care not to strain the hose.

7 Unscrew and remove the driveshaft/hub nut. Note that the nut is of special laminated design, and should only be re-used a maximum of 5 times. (It is a good idea to file a small notch on the nut every time it is removed.) Obtain a new nut if necessary.

8 Note which way round the lower arm balljoint clamp bolt is fitted, then unscrew the nut and remove it from the knuckle assembly **(see illustrations)**. Lever the balljoint down from the knuckle; if it is tight, prise the clamp open using a large flat-bladed tool. Take care not to damage the balljoint seal during the separation procedure.

9 Unscrew and remove the pinch-bolt securing the steering knuckle assembly to the front suspension strut, noting which way round it is fitted **(see illustration)**. Prise open the clamp using a wedge-shaped tool, and release the knuckle from the strut. If necessary, tap the knuckle downwards with a soft-headed mallet to separate the two components. Support the knuckle on an axle stand.

10 Pull the steering knuckle and hub assembly from the driveshaft splines. If it is tight, connect a universal puller to the hub flange, and withdraw it from the driveshaft. When the driveshaft is free, support it on an axle stand, or suspend it from a suitable point under the wheel arch, making sure that the inner constant velocity joint is not turned through more than 18°. (Damage may occur if the joint is turned through too great an angle.)

Refitting

11 Lift the steering knuckle and hub assembly onto the driveshaft splines, and support the assembly on an axle stand.

12 Locate the assembly on the front suspension strut. Insert the pinch-bolt with its head facing forwards. Fit the nut and tighten it to the specified torque.

13 Refit the lower arm balljoint to the knuckle assembly, and insert the clamp bolt with its head facing forwards. Refit the nut and tighten it to the specified torque.

14 Refit the driveshaft/hub nut, and tighten it moderately at this stage. Final tightening of the nut is made with the vehicle lowered to the ground.

15 Refit the brake caliper and brake disc as described in Chapter 9.

16 Where applicable, refit the ABS sensor as described in Chapter 9. Clip the wiring back into place.

17 Reconnect the track rod end balljoint to the steering arm, and tighten the nut to the specified torque. Check that the split pin holes are aligned; if necessary, turn the nut to the nearest alignment, making sure that the torque wrench setting is still within the specified range. Insert a new split pin, and bend it back to secure.

18 Refit the front wheel, and lower the vehicle to the ground. Tighten the wheel nuts to the specified torque.

19 Tighten the driveshaft/hub nut to the specified torque, and refit the wheel cover.

20 Remove the suspension strut upper mounting nut, and fit a new one. Tighten the nut to the specified torque, while holding the piston rod with an 8 mm Allen key. If the adaptor needed to do this is not available, the nut can be tightened initially with a ring spanner while the piston rod is held. Final tightening can then be carried out using a torque wrench and a conventional socket.

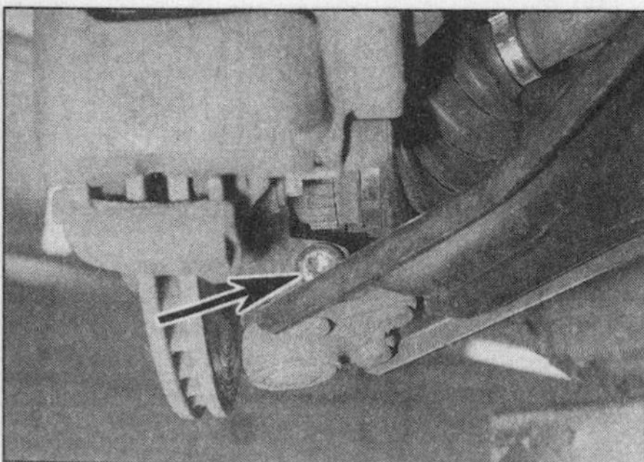

2.8a Lower arm balljoint clamp bolt (arrowed) . . .

2.8b . . . and nut - note direction of fitting before removal

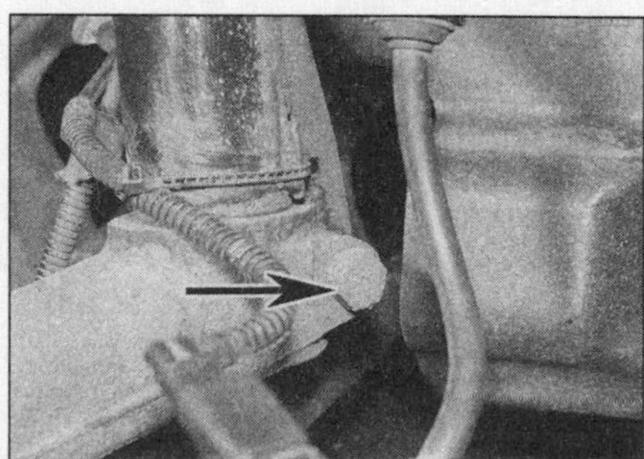

2.9 Steering knuckle-to-strut pinch-bolt (arrowed)

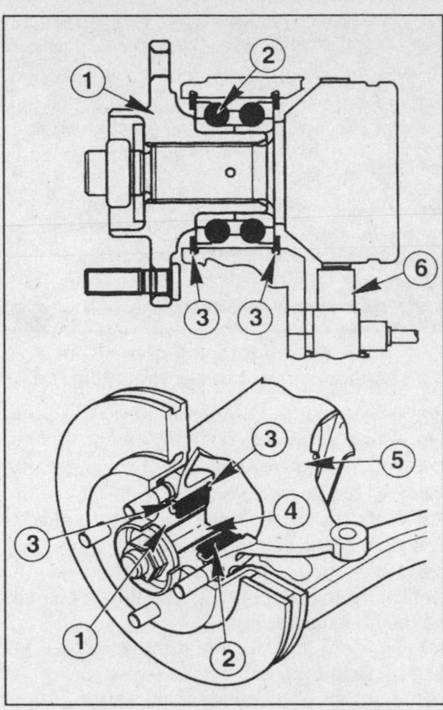

3.1 Front hub and bearing

1	*Hub*	4	*Stub axle*
2	*Double-row ball-bearing*	5	*Steering knuckle*
3	*Circlips*	6	*ABS sensor*

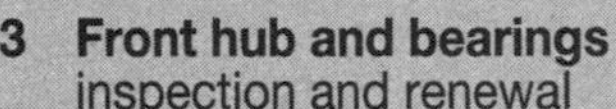

3 Front hub and bearings - inspection and renewal

Inspection

1 The front hub bearings are non-adjustable, and are supplied already greased **(see illustration)**.

2 To check the bearings for excessive wear, first chock the rear wheels and apply the handbrake. Jack up the front of the vehicle and support it on axle stands.

3 Grip the front wheel at top and bottom, and attempt to rock it. If excessive movement is noted, it may be that the hub bearings are worn. Do not confuse wear in the driveshaft outer joint or front suspension lower arm balljoint with wear in the bearings. Hub bearing wear will show up as roughness or vibration when the wheel is spun; it will also be noticeable as a rumbling or growling noise when driving.

Renewal

4 Remove the steering knuckle and hub assembly as described in Section 2.

5 The hub must now be removed from the bearing inner races. It is preferable to use a press to do this, but it is possible to drive out the hub using a length of metal tube of suitable diameter.

6 Part of the inner race will remain on the hub, and this should be removed using a puller.

7 Note that if this procedure is being used to renew the hub only (ie it is not intended to renew the bearings), then it is important to check the condition of the bearing balls and races, to see if they are fit for re-use. It is difficult to be sure that no damage has occurred, especially if makeshift methods have been used during removal; in practice, it is probably false economy not to renew the bearings in any case, having got this far.

8 Using circlip pliers, extract the inner and outer circlips securing the hub bearing in the steering knuckle **(see illustration)**.

9 Press or drive out the bearing, using a length of metal tubing of diameter slightly less than the bearing outer race.

10 Clean the bearing seating faces in the steering knuckle.

11 Locate one of the circlips in the outer groove of the knuckle.

12 Press or drive the new bearing into the knuckle until it contacts the circlip, using a length of metal tube of diameter slightly less than the outer race. Do not apply any pressure to the inner race.

13 Locate the remaining circlip in the inner groove of the knuckle.

14 Support the inner race on a length of metal tube, then press or drive the hub fully into the bearing.

15 Refit the steering knuckle and hub assembly as described in Section 2.

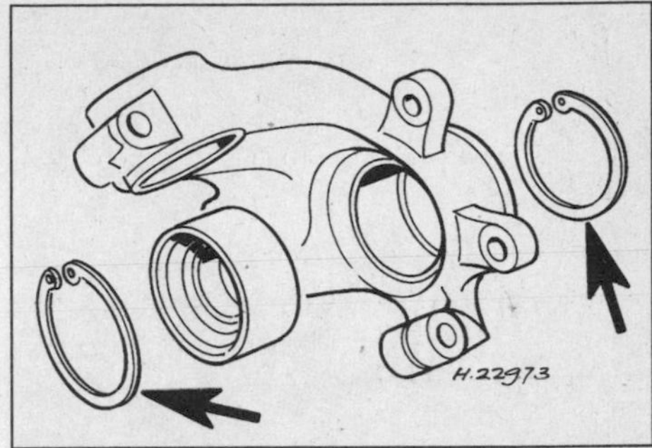

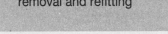

3.8 Front wheel bearing retaining circlips (arrowed)

4 Front suspension strut - removal and refitting

Removal

1 Remove the wheel cover (or centre cover) from the wheel, apply the handbrake, and engage 1st gear or 'P'. Loosen the hub nut about half a turn. This nut is very tight - use only high-quality, close-fitting tools, and take adequate precautions against personal injury when loosening the hub nut.

2 Working inside the engine compartment, remove the strut cap (if fitted). Retain the suspension strut piston with an Allen key, then loosen the strut upper mounting nut and unscrew it by five complete turns **(see illustration)**. Do not remove the nut completely at this stage, but note that, on completion, a new nut should be fitted.

3 Loosen the relevant front wheel nuts and chock the rear wheels. Jack up the front of the vehicle and support it on axle stands. Remove the front wheel.

4 Unbolt the brake hose support bracket from the front of the suspension strut. Alternatively, unclip the hose from the bracket **(see illustrations)**.

5 Remove the ABS sensor (when fitted) as described in Chapter 9.

6 Remove the nut and disconnect the anti-roll bar link from the strut. Note that the ABS

4.2 Front suspension strut upper mounting nut

4.4a Either unbolt the brake hose support bracket from the suspension strut . . .

4.4b . . . or unclip the brake hose from the bracket

4.6 Removing the anti-roll bar link and wiring bracket

4.12 Steering knuckle-to-strut pinch-bolt

4.28 Final tightening of the front suspension strut upper mounting nut

wheel sensor and pad wear warning light wiring support bracket is located beneath the nut **(see illustration)**.

7 Where applicable, disconnect the adaptive damping wiring multi-plug at the strut, and unclip the wire.

8 Remove the brake caliper and brake disc as described in Chapter 9, but do not disconnect the flexible hose from the caliper. Suspend the caliper from a suitable point under the wheel arch, taking care not to strain the hose.

9 Extract the split pin from the track rod end balljoint nut. Unscrew the nut, and detach the rod from the arm on the steering knuckle using a conventional balljoint removal tool. Take care not to damage the balljoint seal.

10 Unscrew and remove the driveshaft/hub nut. Note that the nut is of special laminated design, and should only be re-used a maximum of 5 times. (It is a good idea to file a small notch on the nut every time it is removed.) Obtain a new nut if necessary.

11 Note which way round the lower arm balljoint clamp bolt is fitted, then unscrew and remove it from the knuckle assembly. Lever the balljoint down from the knuckle; if it is tight, prise the clamp open using a large flat-bladed tool. Take care not to damage the balljoint seal during the separation procedure.

12 Unscrew and remove the pinch-bolt securing the steering knuckle assembly to the front suspension strut, noting which way round it is fitted **(see illustration)**. Prise open the clamp using a wedge-shaped tool, and release the knuckle from the strut. If necessary, tap the knuckle downwards with a soft-headed mallet to separate the two components. Support the knuckle on an axle stand.

13 Pull the steering knuckle and hub assembly from the driveshaft splines. If it is tight, connect a universal puller to the hub flange, and withdraw it from the driveshaft. When the driveshaft is free, support it on an axle stand, or suspend it from a suitable point under the wheel arch, making sure that the inner constant velocity joint is not turned through more than 18°. (Damage may occur if the joint is turned through too great an angle.)

14 Holding the suspension strut body with one hand, fully unscrew and remove the front suspension strut upper mounting nut. Lower the suspension strut out from under the wheel arch.

Refitting

15 Lift the suspension strut into position, feeding the threaded end of the piston rod up through the hole in the inner wing. Fit the new upper mounting nut, and tighten it by a few threads so that the weight of the strut is supported.

16 Lift the steering knuckle and hub assembly onto the driveshaft splines, and support the assembly on an axle stand.

17 Locate the assembly on the front suspension strut. Insert the pinch-bolt with its head facing forwards. Fit the nut and tighten it to the specified torque.

18 Refit the lower arm balljoint to the knuckle assembly, and insert the clamp bolt with its head facing forwards. Refit the nut and tighten it to the specified torque.

19 Refit the driveshaft/hub nut, and tighten it moderately at this stage. Final tightening of the nut is made with the vehicle lowered to the ground.

20 Reconnect the track rod end balljoint to the steering arm, and tighten the nut to the specified torque. Check that the split pin holes are aligned; if necessary, turn the nut to the nearest alignment, making sure that the torque wrench setting is still within the specified range. Insert a new split pin, and bend it back to secure.

21 Refit the brake caliper and brake disc as described in Chapter 9.

22 Reconnect the anti-roll bar link to the strut, and tighten the nut to the specified torque. Do not forget to locate the wiring support bracket beneath the nut.

5.3 Coil spring compressor tools fitted to the coil spring

23 Where applicable, refit the ABS sensor as described in Chapter 9.

24 Reconnect the adaptive damping multi-plug, where applicable.

25 Refit the brake hose support bracket to the front of the suspension strut.

26 Refit the front wheel, and lower the vehicle to the ground. Tighten the wheel nuts to the specified torque.

27 Tighten the driveshaft/hub nut to the specified torque, and refit the wheel cover.

28 Tighten the suspension strut upper mounting nut to the specified torque, while holding the piston rod with an 8 mm Allen key. If the adaptor needed to do this is not available, the nut can be tightened initially with a ring spanner while the piston rod is held. Final tightening can then be carried out using a torque wrench and a conventional socket **(see illustration)**.

5 Front suspension strut - overhaul

Warning: Before attempting to dismantle the front suspension strut, a tool to hold the coil spring in compression must be obtained. Do not attempt to use makeshift methods. Uncontrolled release of the spring could cause damage and personal injury. Use a high-quality spring compressor, and carefully follow the tool manufacturer's instructions provided with it. After removing the coil spring, store it with the compressor still fitted, in a safe area.

1 If the front suspension struts exhibit signs of wear (leaking fluid, loss of damping capability, sagging or cracked coil springs) then they should be dismantled and overhauled as necessary. The struts themselves cannot be serviced, and should be renewed if faulty, but the springs and related components can be renewed. To maintain balanced characteristics on both sides of the vehicle, the components on both sides should be renewed at the same time.

2 With the strut removed from the vehicle, clean away all external dirt, then mount it in a vice.

5.4 Unscrewing the nut from the top of the strut

3 Fit the coil spring compressor tools (ensuring that they are fully engaged), and compress the spring until all tension is relieved from the upper mounting **(see illustration)**.
4 Hold the strut piston with an Allen key, and unscrew the thrust bearing retaining nut with a ring spanner **(see illustration)**.
5 Withdraw the top mounting, thrust bearing, upper spring seat and spring, followed by the gaiter and the bump stop **(see illustrations)**.
6 If a new spring is to be fitted, the original spring must now be carefully released from the compressor. If it is to be re-used, the spring can be left in compression.
7 With the strut assembly now completely dismantled, examine all the components for wear and damage, and check the bearing for smoothness of operation. Renew components as necessary.
8 Examine the strut for signs of fluid leakage. Check the strut piston for signs of pitting along its entire length, and check the strut body for signs of damage.
9 Test the operation of the strut, while holding it in an upright position, by moving the piston through a full stroke, and then through short strokes of 50 to 100 mm. In both cases, the resistance felt should be smooth and continuous. If the resistance is jerky, uneven, or if there is any visible sign of wear or damage to the strut, renewal is necessary.
10 Reassembly is a reversal of dismantling, noting the following points:
a) Make sure that the coil spring ends are correctly located in the upper and lower seats before releasing the compressor.
b) Check that the bearing is correctly fitted to the piston rod seat.
c) Tighten the thrust bearing retaining nut to the specified torque.

5.5b Removing the top mounting from the strut

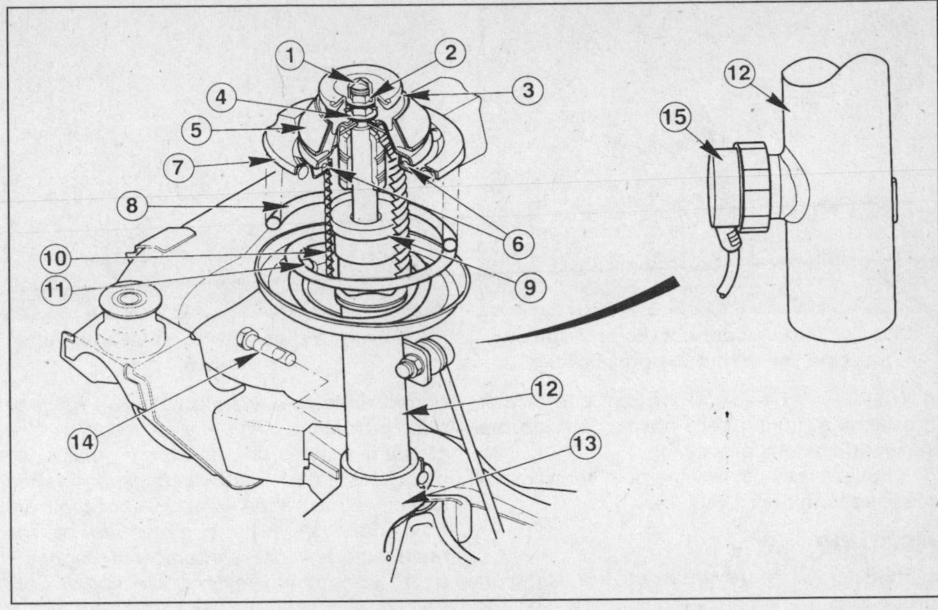

5.5a Front suspension strut components

1 Cap
2 Nut
3 Retainer
4 Nut
5 Top mounting
6 Thrust bearing
7 Upper spring seat
8 Spring
9 Bump stop
10 Gaiter
11 Lower spring seat
12 Strut
13 Steering knuckle
14 Clamp bolt
15 Solenoid valve for models with adaptive damping

6 Front anti-roll bar and links - removal and refitting

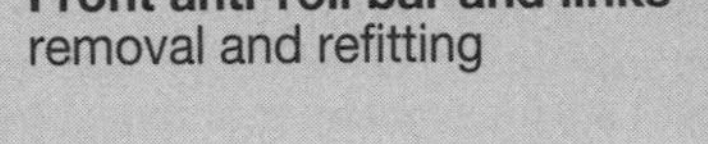

Removal

1 Apply the handbrake and chock the rear wheels. Loosen the front wheel nuts, then jack up the front of the vehicle and support it on axle stands. Remove the front wheels.
2 Unscrew the nuts, and disconnect the anti-roll bar links from the front suspension struts on both sides of the vehicle. Note the wiring support brackets located beneath the nuts **(see illustrations)**.
3 Unscrew and remove the anti-roll bar mounting bolts from the engine subframe on both sides of the vehicle **(see illustration)**.

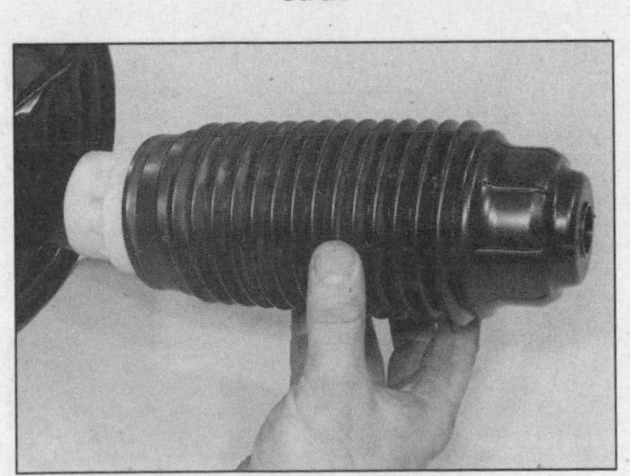

5.5c Removing the gaiter

5.5d Removing the bump stop

6.2a Unscrew the nut . . .

6.2b . . . and disconnect the anti-roll bar link and the wiring support bracket

4 Withdraw the anti-roll bar from one side of the vehicle, taking care not to damage the surrounding components.

5 If necessary, unscrew the nuts and remove the links from the anti-roll bar.

Refitting

6 Refitting is a reversal of the removal procedure.

7 Front suspension lower arm - removal, overhaul and refitting

Note: *Removal of the left-hand lower arm is hampered by the fact that the bolts are inserted from the top of the arm - this means that the bolts must be removed upwards. The proximity of the transmission housing means that, on the left-hand arm, the front of the two*

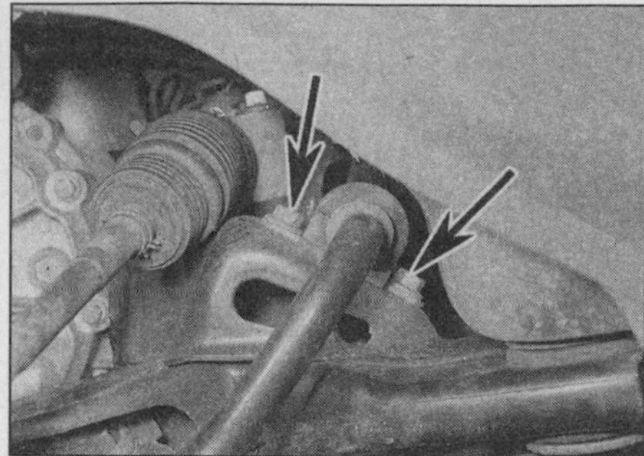

6.3 Front anti-roll bar-to-subframe bolts (arrowed)

bolts cannot be withdrawn upwards ***(see illustrations)****. As a result, the engine/transmission assembly must be disconnected from its mountings, and raised sufficiently to permit withdrawal of the front bolt. Although not recommended by the manufacturers, on reassembly it might be worth considering refitting the bolt(s) from below, and securing with the nut and a suitable washer on top, to make any subsequent removal much easier. Bear in mind, however, that this is potentially less safe - if the bolt were to work loose and fall out from below, this would be more dangerous than the nut falling off.*

Removal

Right-hand lower arm

1 Apply the handbrake and chock the rear wheels. Loosen the front wheel nuts, then jack up the front of the vehicle and support it on axle stands. Remove the front wheels.

2 Remove the auxiliary drivebelt cover where necessary.

3 Unscrew and remove the nuts and bolts securing the lower arm to the subframe **(see illustration)**.

4 Unscrew the nut and disconnect the anti-roll bar link from the anti-roll bar.

5 Extract the split pin from the track rod end balljoint nut. Unscrew the nut, and detach the rod from the arm on the steering knuckle using a conventional balljoint removal tool. Take care not to damage the balljoint seal.

6 Using the information in Chapter 8, disconnect the right-hand driveshaft from the transmission. Support the inner end of the driveshaft on an axle stand.

7 Note which way round the front suspension lower arm balljoint clamp bolt is fitted, then unscrew and remove it from the knuckle assembly. Lever the balljoint down from the knuckle; if it is tight, prise the joint open carefully using a large flat-bladed tool. Take care not to damage the balljoint seal during the separation procedure **(see illustrations)**.

8 Remove the lower arm from the subframe, and withdraw it from the vehicle.

Left-hand lower arm - manual transmission models

9 Working inside the engine compartment, remove the strut cap (if fitted). Retain the suspension strut piston with an Allen key, then loosen the strut upper mounting nut and unscrew it by five complete turns. Do not remove the nut completely at this stage, but note that, on completion, a new nut should be fitted.

10 Remove the air cleaner as described in Chapter 4A.

11 Apply the handbrake and chock the rear wheels. Loosen the front wheel nuts, then jack up the front of the vehicle and support it on axle stands. Remove the front wheels.

12 Disconnect the gearchange linkage and support rods from the transmission, as described in Chapter 7A.

13 Disconnect the left-hand driveshaft from the transmission, using the information in Chapter 8. Support the inner end of the driveshaft on an axle stand.

7.0a While the left-hand arm rear bolt (arrowed) can be withdrawn . . .

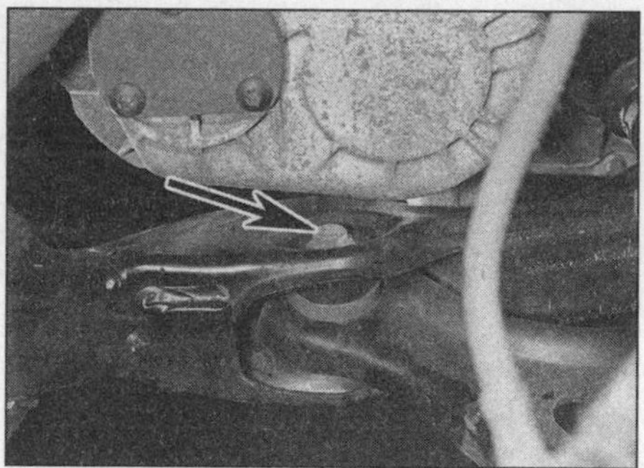

7.0b . . . the front bolt is prevented from doing so by the transmission

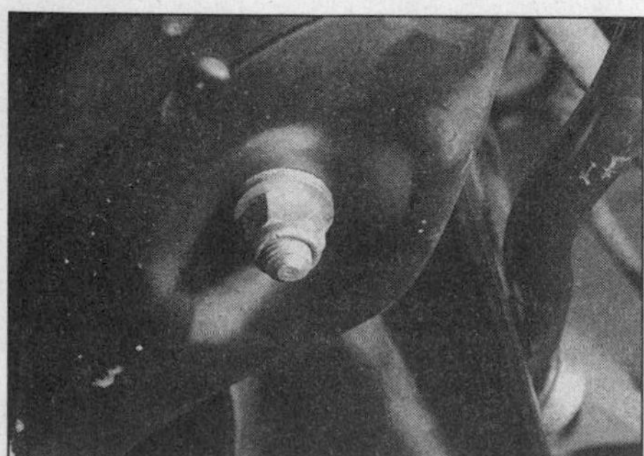

7.3 One of the nuts and bolts securing the lower arm to the subframe

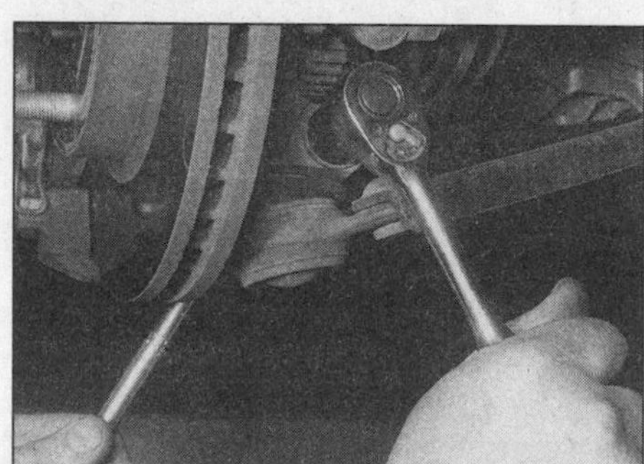

7.7a Unscrew the lower arm balljoint clamp bolt . . .

7.7b . . . and disconnect the balljoint from the knuckle

14 Note which way round the front suspension lower arm balljoint clamp bolt is fitted, then unscrew and remove it from the knuckle assembly. Lever the balljoint down from the knuckle; if it is tight, prise the joint open carefully using a large flat-bladed tool. Take care not to damage the balljoint seal during the separation procedure.
15 The weight of the engine and transmission must now be supported, as the engine mountings must be disconnected. Either use an engine crane or hoist, or if available, an engine support bar mounted on the inner wing flanges. Given that you will be working under the car, supporting from below is not recommended.
16 Unbolt and separate the front and rear engine mountings from the subframe, noting the fitted position of all components. Make accurate alignment marks for refitting the front mounting.
17 With the weight of the engine and transmission supported, unbolt and separate the engine right- and left-hand mountings.
18 Carefully raise the engine and transmission by approximately 50 mm, taking care that no pipes, cables or wiring are strained excessively as this is done.
19 Remove the lower arm-to-subframe nuts and bolts, and remove the lower arm **(see illustration)**.

Left-hand lower arm - automatic transmission models

20 Refer to Section 28 and disconnect the steering column shaft from the flexible coupling.
21 Apply the handbrake and chock the rear wheels. Loosen the front wheel nuts, then jack up the front of the vehicle and support it on axle stands. Remove the front wheels.
22 Refer to Chapter 4A and remove the exhaust downpipe.
23 Remove the radiator lower cover, and the left- and right-hand wheel arch liners, by unscrewing the screws and releasing the clips.
24 Detach the front bumper support brackets, and move them to one side.
25 Support the radiator in its raised position, by inserting split pins through the small holes in the radiator mounting extensions which protrude through the upper mountings.
26 Unbolt and remove the radiator lower mounting brackets.
27 Where applicable, unscrew the bolts securing the air conditioning accumulator to the subframe. Support the accumulator to avoid straining the pipework.
28 Unscrew the nuts and disconnect the anti-roll bar links from the anti-roll bar. Swivel the anti-roll bar upwards away from the lower arm.
29 Extract the split pins from the track rod end balljoint nuts. Unscrew the nuts, and detach the rods from the arms on the steering knuckles using a conventional balljoint removal tool. Take care not to damage the balljoint seals.
30 Note which way round the front suspension lower arm balljoint clamp bolts are fitted, then unscrew and remove them from the knuckle assembly each side. Lever the balljoint down from the knuckle; if it is tight, prise the joint open carefully using a large flat-bladed tool. Take care not to damage the balljoint seal during the separation procedure.
31 Detach the power steering fluid cooler pipes from the subframe.
32 Unbolt and separate the front and rear engine mountings from the subframe, noting the fitted position of all components. Make accurate alignment marks for refitting the front mounting in particular - see paragraph 34.
33 Loosen the lower arm-to-subframe nuts at this stage. Until the subframe is lowered, it will not be possible to withdraw both the bolts.
34 The subframe must now be lowered out of position. The alignment of the subframe is critical to maintaining the front suspension geometry, so take time to make suitable alignment markings for use on reassembly. Have ready a pair of axle stands or sturdy blocks to support the rear of the subframe when the bolts are removed.
35 Loosen and remove the subframe rear mounting bolts, and loosen the front mounting bolts by two turns. Lower the subframe for access to the power steering fluid pipe unions on top of the steering gear. Note that the front subframe mounting bolts are gold in colour - the rear ones are silver.
36 Position a suitable container beneath the steering gear, then unscrew the union nuts securing the power steering fluid supply, return, and cooler lines to the steering gear. Identify the lines for position, then unbolt the clamps, disconnect the lines, and allow the fluid to drain into the container. Cover the apertures in the steering gear and also the ends of the fluid pipes, to prevent the ingress of dust and dirt into the hydraulic circuit.

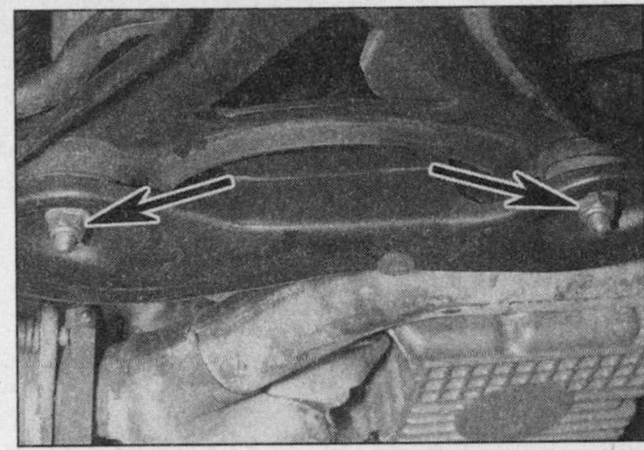

7.19 Remove the lower arm bolt nuts (arrowed) from below

37 Check to see that nothing else remains connected to the subframe which would prevent it being lowered.
38 Remove the subframe front mounting bolts, and lower the subframe sufficiently to remove the lower arm-to-subframe bolts, and remove the lower arm.

Overhaul

39 Examine the rubber bushes and the suspension lower balljoint for wear and damage. The balljoint may be renewed as described in Section 8. The rubber bushes may be removed using a press, or a length of metal tubing together with a long bolt, washers and nut.
40 Note that the front and rear bushes are different. The front one has a solid rubber bush with a cylindrical inner tube, whereas the rear one has a voided rubber bush with a barrel-shaped inner tube **(see illustration)**.

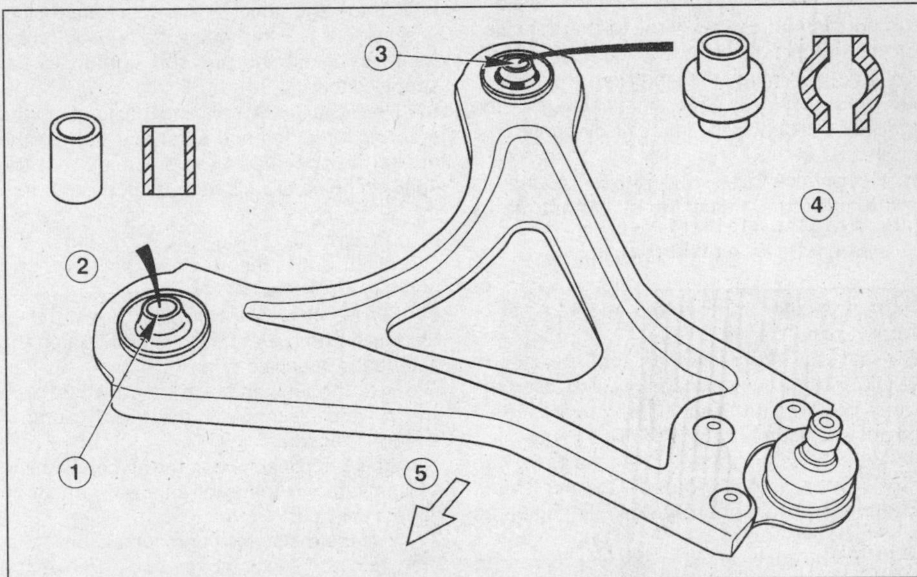

7.40 Front suspension lower arm bushes

1 *Front bush*
2 *Cylindrical inner tube*
3 *Rear bush*
4 *Barrel-shaped inner tube*
5 *Front of vehicle*

10

41 Press the new bushes into the lower arm, using the same method as used for removal. Note that, when fitting the rear bush, the voids must be in line with the front bush location. On later models, a pip on the rear bush must be aligned with a triangular alignment mark on the arm.

Refitting

Right-hand lower arm

42 Locate the lower arm on the subframe, and insert the mounting bolts. Fit the nuts and tighten them in stages, first to the specified torque and then through the angle specified.

43 Refit the inner end of the right-hand driveshaft as described in Chapter 8.

44 Refit the front suspension lower arm balljoint to the knuckle assembly, and insert the clamp bolt with its head facing forwards. Refit the nut and tighten to the specified torque.

45 Refit the track rod end balljoint to the steering knuckle, and tighten the nut to the specified torque. Check that the split pin holes are aligned; if necessary, turn the nut to align the holes, making sure that the torque wrench setting is still within the specified range. Insert a new split pin, and bend it back to secure.

46 Swivel the anti-roll bar down, then reconnect the link to the bar and tighten the nut to the specified torque.

47 Refit the auxiliary drivebelt cover where necessary.

48 Refit the wheel, and lower the vehicle to the ground. Tighten the wheel nuts to the specified torque.

Left-hand lower arm - manual transmission models

49 Locate the lower arm on the subframe, and insert the mounting bolts. Fit the nuts and tighten them in stages, first to the specified torque and then through the angle specified.

50 Carefully lower the engine/transmission back into position, and reconnect the left- and right-hand mountings. Do not fully tighten the mountings at this stage.

51 Reconnect the front and rear mountings to the subframe, using the alignment marks made on removal.

52 Tighten all the engine mountings to the specified torque (see the relevant Part of Chapter 2), then remove the engine hoist or support bar.

53 Refit the front suspension lower arm balljoint to the knuckle assembly, and insert the clamp bolt with its head facing forwards. Refit the nut and tighten to the specified torque.

54 Refit the left-hand driveshaft to the transmission as described in Chapter 8, and reconnect the gearchange linkage as described in Chapter 7A.

55 Refit the front wheel and lower the car to the ground. Tighten the wheel nuts to the specified torque.

56 Refit the air cleaner as described in Chapter 4A.

57 Remove the suspension strut upper mounting nut, and fit a new one. Tighten the nut to the specified torque, while holding the piston rod with an 8 mm Allen key. If the adaptor needed to do this is not available, the nut can be tightened initially with a ring spanner while the piston rod is held. Final tightening can then be carried out using a torque wrench and a conventional socket.

Left-hand lower arm - automatic transmission models

58 Refit the lower arm to the subframe, insert the bolts and tighten the nuts to the specified torque.

59 Raise the subframe into position, and loosely fit the mounting bolts so that the weight of the subframe is supported.

60 Reconnect the power steering fluid pipe unions with reference to Section 30.

61 Raise the subframe into position, making sure that the alignment holes are in line with the holes in the underbody. At the same time, make sure that the flexible coupling locates correctly on the steering column.

62 Use the alignment markings made on removal to refit the subframe in exactly the same position as before - Ford technicians use special aligning tools for this, but if the subframe is refitted accurately, these should not be necessary.

63 When the subframe is correctly aligned, progressively tighten the mounting bolts to the specified torque.

64 Bolt the front and rear engine mountings to the subframe, using the alignment markings made on removal, and tightening the bolts to the specified torque (see the relevant Part of Chapter 2).

65 Reattach the power steering fluid cooler pipes to the subframe.

66 Refit the front suspension lower arm balljoint to the knuckle assembly each side, and insert the clamp bolt with its head facing forwards. Refit the nut and tighten to the specified torque.

67 Refit the track rod end balljoint to the steering knuckle each side, and tighten the nut to the specified torque. Check that the split pin holes are aligned; if necessary, turn the nut to align the holes, making sure that the torque wrench setting is still within the specified range. Insert a new split pin, and bend it back to secure.

68 Swivel the anti-roll bar down, then reconnect the links to the bar and tighten the nuts to the specified torque.

69 Refit the left- and right-hand wheel arch liners, and reconnect the front bumper support brackets.

70 Where applicable, refit the air conditioning accumulator to the subframe, and securely tighten the bolts.

71 Refit the radiator lower mounting brackets, then refit the lower cover and remove the supporting pins from the radiator upper mountings.

72 Refit the exhaust downpipe with reference to Chapter 4A.

73 Refit the front wheels, then lower the car to the ground. Tighten the wheel nuts to the specified torque.

74 Reconnect the steering column shaft to the flexible coupling, with reference to Section 28.

75 Fill and bleed the power steering hydraulic system as described in Section 33.

76 If on completion, the car pulls to one side, or abnormal tyre wear is noted, have the subframe alignment (and front wheel alignment) checked by a Ford dealer.

8 Front suspension lower arm balljoint - renewal

Note: *If the lower arm balljoint is worn, it appears at the time of writing that the complete lower arm must be renewed (see Section 7), although the balljoint was apparently available separately at one time. Seek the advice of your Ford dealer or parts supplier to establish whether the balljoint is available separately. If the balljoint has already been renewed, it will be bolted in position; if the original balljoint is being renewed, then it will be riveted in position. This Section describes the renewal of a riveted balljoint.*

1 Remove the front suspension lower arm as described in Section 7. It is not recommended that the balljoint be replaced with the lower arm in position on the vehicle; the accurate drilling necessary may not be possible, and the holes in the arm may be enlarged.

2 With the lower arm on the bench, use a 3 mm drill to make a pilot hole through each of the three rivets **(see illustration)**. Now use a 9 mm drill to drill the rivets to a depth of 12 mm, then use a 7 or 8 mm drift to drive the rivets out of the arm.

3 Clean any rust or dirt from the rivet holes.

4 The new balljoint is supplied with a protective plastic cover over the rubber boot and stub, and it is recommended that this remains in position until it is time to connect the balljoint to the steering knuckle.

5 Locate the new balljoint on the lower arm, and use three new bolts to secure it, inserting the bolts from the top of the arm. Tighten the nuts to the specified torque. Make sure that

8.2 Original riveted front suspension lower arm balljoint

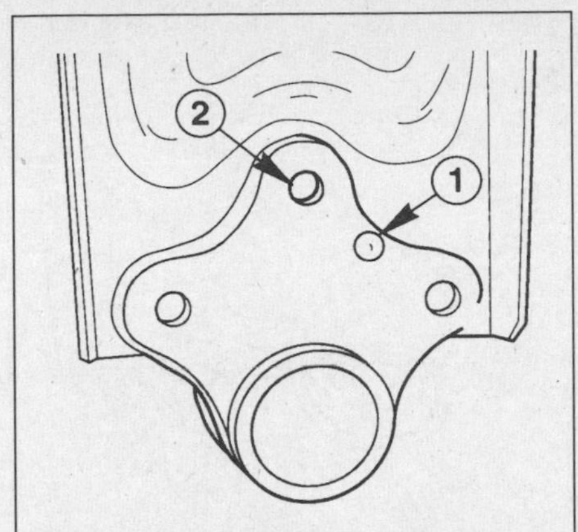

8.5 Location lug (1) and bolt hole (2) in the front suspension lower arm balljoint

the location lug on the balljoint engages the hole in the lower arm **(see illustration)**.

6 Refit the front suspension lower arm as described in Section 7.

9 Rear hub and bearings (Saloon/Hatchback models) - inspection and renewal

Note: *Removal of the rear hub damages the bearings, and renders them unserviceable for future use. The hub and bearing assembly must always be renewed if it is removed.*

Inspection

1 The rear hub bearings are non-adjustable, and are supplied complete with the hub. It is not possible to renew the bearings separately from the hub.

2 To check the bearings for excessive wear, chock the front wheels, then jack up the rear of the vehicle and support it on axle stands. Fully release the handbrake.

3 Grip the rear wheel at the top and bottom, and attempt to rock it **(see illustration)**. If excessive movement is noted, or if there is any roughness or vibration felt when the wheel is spun, it is indicative that the hub bearings are worn.

Renewal

4 Remove the rear wheel.

5 On models fitted with rear brake drums, remove the rear brake drum as described in Chapter 9.

6 On models fitted with rear brake discs, remove the rear brake disc as described in Chapter 9.

7 On all models, tap off the dust cap and unscrew the hub nut. Note that the nut is of special laminated design, and should only be re-used a maximum of 5 times. It is a good idea to mark the nut with a file every time it is removed. Obtain a new one if necessary.

8 Using a suitable puller, draw the hub and bearing assembly off the stub axle. Note that this procedure renders the bearings unserviceable for future use.

9 Locate the new rear hub and bearing assembly on the stub axle, then refit the hub nut and tighten it to the specified torque.

10 Tap the dust cap fully onto the hub.

11 Refit the rear brake disc or drum as applicable, as described in Chapter 9.

12 Refit the rear wheel, and lower the vehicle to the ground.

10 Rear suspension knuckle (Saloon/Hatchback models) - removal and refitting

Note: *Removal of the rear hub from the knuckle damages the bearings, and renders them unserviceable for future use. The hub and bearing assembly must always be renewed if it is removed.*

Removal

1 Chock the front wheels, engage 1st gear (or 'P'), and loosen the relevant rear wheel nuts. Jack up the rear of the vehicle and support it on axle stands. Remove the rear wheel.

2 When applicable, remove the ABS sensor from the knuckle as described in Chapter 9.

3 Remove the rear hub and bearing assembly as described in Section 9.

Drum brake models

4 Fit a brake hose clamp to the flexible brake hose, then release the clip and detach the flexible hose from the strut.

5 Unscrew the union nut, and detach the rigid brake pipe from the wheel cylinder. If preferred (to eliminate any bleeding procedure during refitting) the rigid brake pipe may remain attached to the wheel cylinder, provided that care is taken to prevent damage to both the rigid and flexible brake pipes.

6 Unbolt the backplate from the rear suspension knuckle, and support it to one side on an axle stand **(see illustration)**. The brake shoes and handbrake cable can remain attached.

Disc brake models

7 Unbolt the splash shield from the rear suspension knuckle.

All models

8 Unscrew and remove the bolt securing the tie-bar to the bottom of the knuckle, and move the tie-bar downwards.

9 Unscrew and remove the bolts securing the front and rear lower arms to the knuckle, and move the arms to one side.

10 Support the knuckle on an axle stand, then unscrew and remove the clamp bolt securing the knuckle to the strut.

11 Prise the top of the knuckle apart carefully using a large flat-bladed tool, and withdraw the knuckle downwards from the strut. Withdraw the knuckle from under the rear wheel arch.

9.3 Assessing rear wheel bearing play

Refitting

12 Locate the knuckle fully on the strut, then insert the clamp bolt and tighten to the specified torque.

13 Refit the front and rear lower arms to the knuckle, and insert the bolts finger-tight at this stage.

14 Refit the tie-bar to the bottom of the knuckle, and insert the bolt finger-tight at this stage.

15 Refit the backplate (or splash shield, as applicable) to the rear suspension knuckle, and tighten the bolts to the specified torque.

Drum brake models

16 Reconnect the rigid brake pipe to the wheel cylinder (if disconnected), and tighten the union nut.

17 Attach the flexible hose to the strut, refit the clip, and remove the hose clamp.

All models

18 Fit a new rear hub and bearing assembly as described in Section 9.

19 Where applicable, refit the ABS sensor as described in Chapter 9.

20 Refit the wheel, and lower the vehicle to the ground.

21 With the weight of the vehicle on the suspension, fully tighten the mounting bolts for the tie-bar and lower arms.

22 Where applicable, bleed the hydraulic brake circuit as described in Chapter 9.

10.6 Two of the bolts securing the brake backplate to the rear suspension knuckle

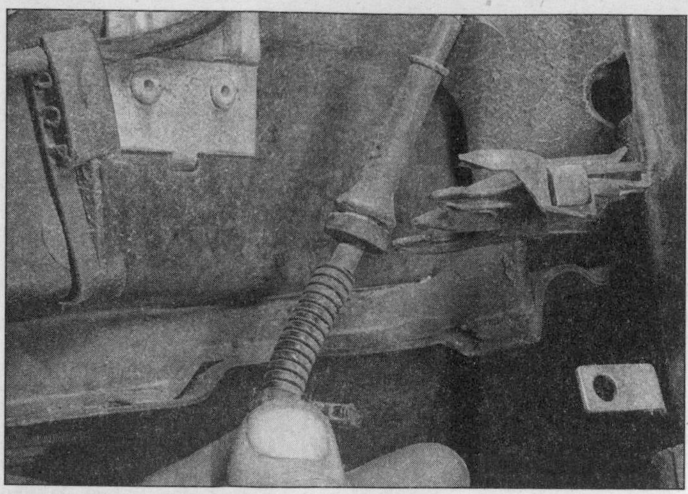
11.2 Unclipping the ABS sensor wiring from the strut

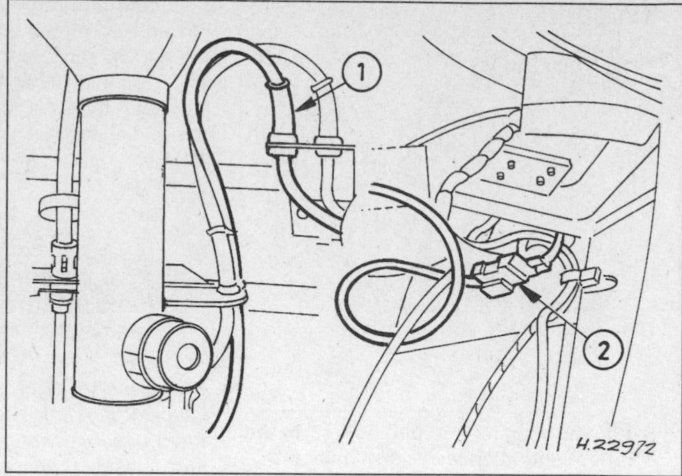

11.3 Location of the adaptive damping lead (1) and multi-plug (2)

11 Rear suspension strut (Saloon/Hatchback models) - removal and refitting

Removal

Note: *In order to remove the rear suspension strut, the coil spring must be temporarily compressed. This will enable the piston rod to be retracted into the strut, and will provide additional room for releasing the strut from the bump stop on top of the rear suspension crossmember.*

Warning: It is important to only use a high-quality spring compressor; carefully follow the tool manufacturer's instructions provided with it.

1 Chock the front wheels, engage 1st gear (or 'P'), and loosen the relevant rear wheel nuts. Jack up the rear of the vehicle and support it on axle stands. Remove the rear wheel.

2 Where fitted, unclip the ABS sensor wiring from the strut, and remove the sensor from the knuckle as described in Chapter 9 **(see illustration)**.

3 On models fitted with adaptive damping, unclip the wiring from the strut and disconnect the multi-plug **(see illustration)**.

4 On drum brake models, fit a brake hose clamp to the rear flexible brake hose, then unscrew the union nut securing the rigid brake pipe to the flexible hose on the strut. Extract the clip, and disconnect the flexible hose from the strut.

5 On models fitted with rear disc brakes, unbolt the caliper from the knuckle as described in Chapter 9, but leave the hydraulic hose attached. Support the caliper on an axle stand, making sure that the flexible hose is not strained.

6 Unscrew the nut securing the rear anti-roll bar link to the front lower arm on the appropriate side. Hold the actual link with an adjustable spanner or grips while unscrewing the nut, to prevent damage to the link joint.

7 Unscrew and remove the bolt securing the tie-bar to the bottom of the knuckle. Move the tie-bar downwards **(see illustrations)**.

8 Unscrew and remove the bolts securing the front and rear lower arms to the knuckle, and move the arms to one side **(see illustrations)**.

9 Support the knuckle on a trolley jack, then unscrew and remove the clamp bolt securing the knuckle to the strut **(see illustrations)**.

10 Prise the clamp on the knuckle apart using a large flat-bladed tool. Disconnect the

11.7a Tie-bar mounting bolt on knuckle

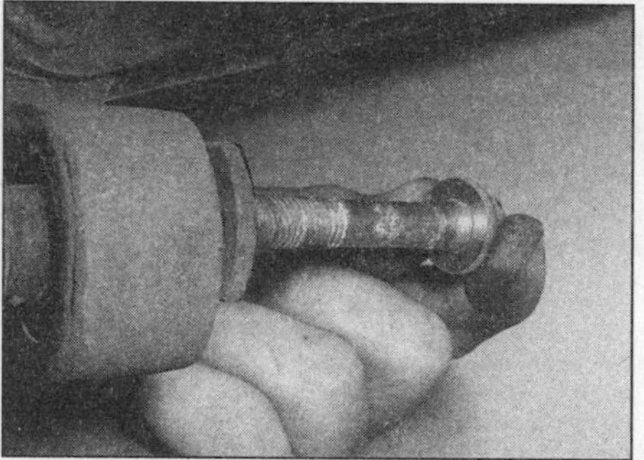
11.7b Remove the bolt . . .

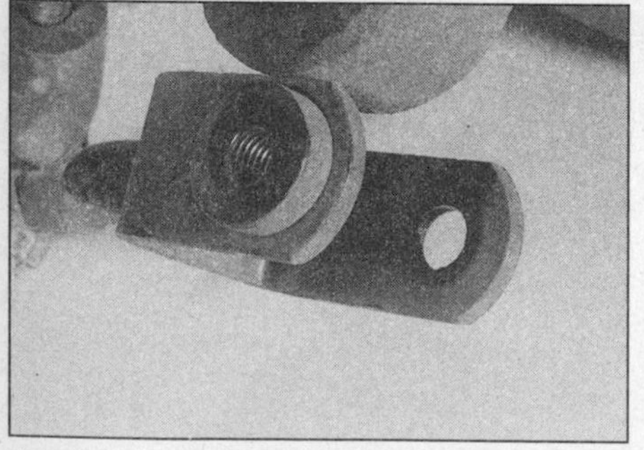
11.7c . . . and move the tie-bar downwards

11.8a Unscrew the bolt . . .

11.8b . . . and remove the rear lower arm from the knuckle

11.9a Support the knuckle on a trolley jack . . .

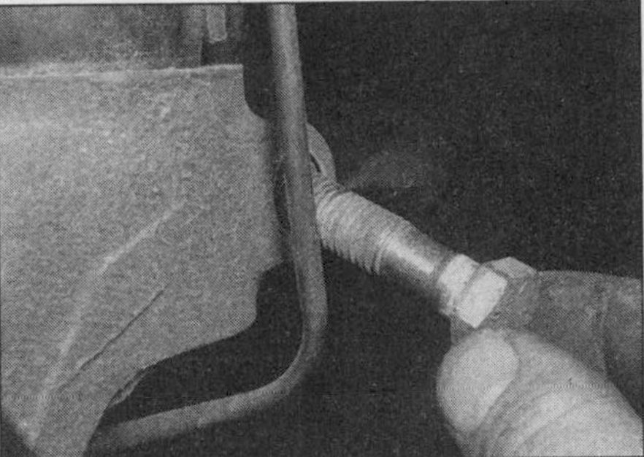

11.9b . . . and remove the knuckle-to-strut clamp bolt

11.10 Separating the knuckle from the strut

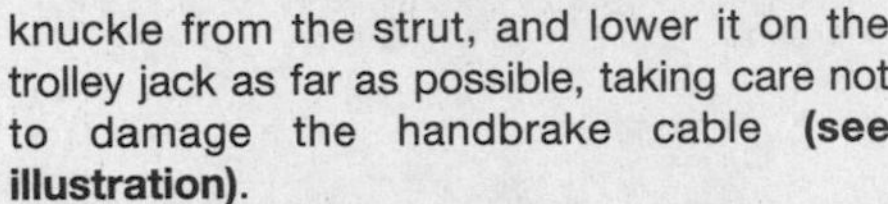

knuckle from the strut, and lower it on the trolley jack as far as possible, taking care not to damage the handbrake cable **(see illustration)**.

11 Fit the coil spring compressor tool (ensuring that it is fully engaged), and compress the coil spring until all tension is relieved from the upper and lower mountings **(see illustration)**. This will also release the bracket on the strut from the bump stop rubber on the top of the rear crossmember.

12 Support the strut, then reach up under the wheel arch, and unscrew the two bolts securing the upper mounting to the underbody **(see illustration)**.

13 Slightly lift the strut, to force the piston into the shock absorber and release the strut bracket from the bump stop on the crossmember. Lower the strut assembly and withdraw it from under the vehicle **(see illustration)**.

Refitting

14 Locate the strut assembly (together with the coil spring compressor tool) under the wheel arch, and locate the bracket on the bump stop on the rear suspension crossmember. Insert the two bolts securing the upper mounting to the underbody tower, and tighten them to the specified torque.

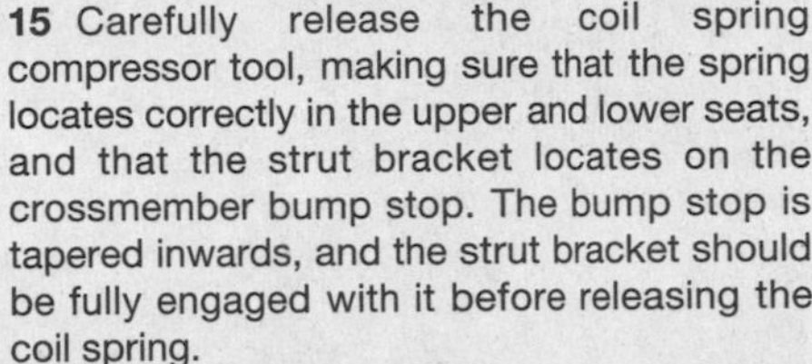

15 Carefully release the coil spring compressor tool, making sure that the spring locates correctly in the upper and lower seats, and that the strut bracket locates on the crossmember bump stop. The bump stop is tapered inwards, and the strut bracket should be fully engaged with it before releasing the coil spring.

16 Raise the knuckle and engage it with the strut, then insert the clamp bolt and tighten to the specified torque.

17 Reconnect the front and rear lower arms to the knuckle, and finger-tighten the bolts at this stage.

18 Reconnect the tie-bar to the bottom of the knuckle, and finger-tighten the bolt at this stage.

19 Refit the anti-roll bar link to the lower arm, and tighten the nut to the specified torque.

20 On disc brake models, refit the caliper bracket to the knuckle, and tighten the mounting bolts to the specified torque (see Chapter 9). Make sure that the flexible brake hose is not twisted.

21 On drum brake models, connect the flexible hose to the strut, insert the clip, then insert the rigid brake line and tighten the union nut. Remove the brake hose clamp, then bleed the hydraulic brake circuit as described in Chapter 9.

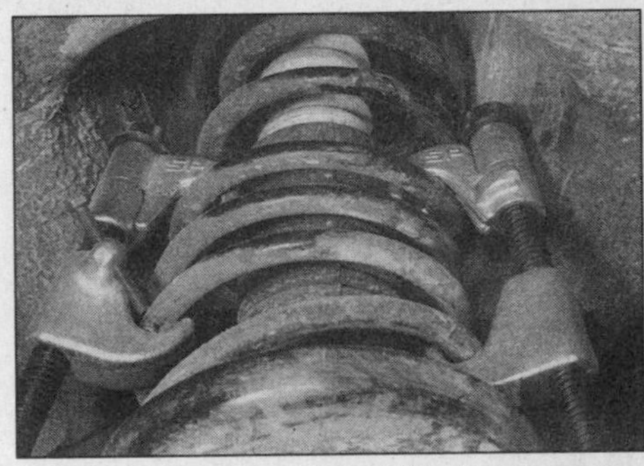

11.11 Compressor tools fitted to the rear coil spring

22 Where applicable, reconnect the wiring multi-plug for the adaptive damping, and clip the wiring to the strut.

23 Where applicable, refit the ABS sensor as described in Chapter 9, and clip the wiring to the strut.

24 Refit the wheel, and lower the vehicle to the ground.

25 With the weight of the vehicle on the rear suspension, fully tighten the lower arm and tie-bar mounting bolts.

11.12 Bolts (arrowed) securing the strut upper mounting to the underbody

11.13 Removing the rear suspension strut

12.1a Rear strut dismantling - unscrew the upper mounting nut . . .

12.1b . . . remove the cup . . .

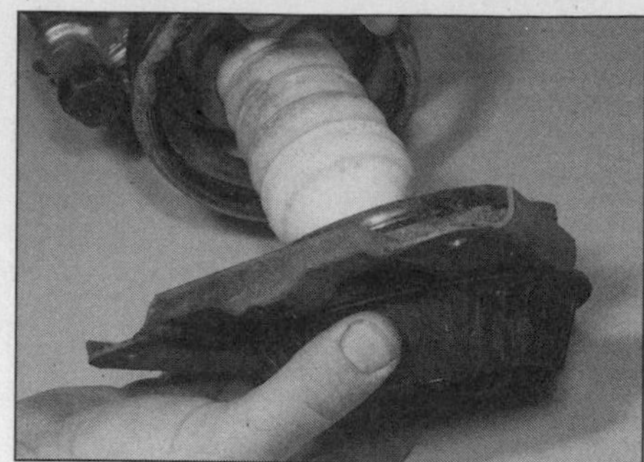

12.1c . . . upper mounting bracket and seat . . .

12 Rear suspension strut (Saloon/Hatchback models) - overhaul

1 The procedure is similar to that for the front suspension strut, and reference should be made to Section 5. Note that the spring compressor tools will already be in position on the coil spring following the removal operation. Refer also to the accompanying illustrations for details of the separate components **(see illustrations)**.

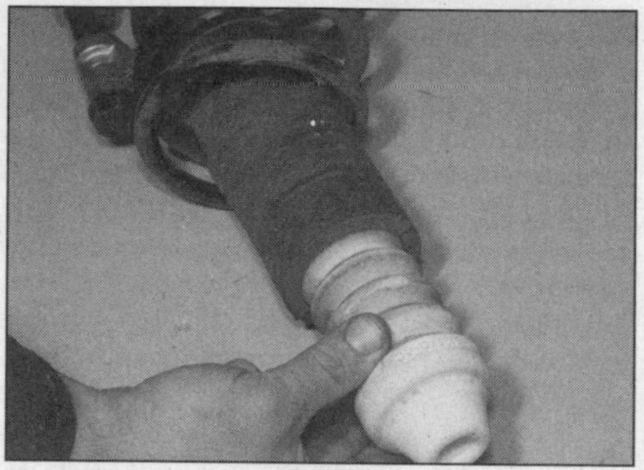

12.1d . . . gaiter and bump stop . . .

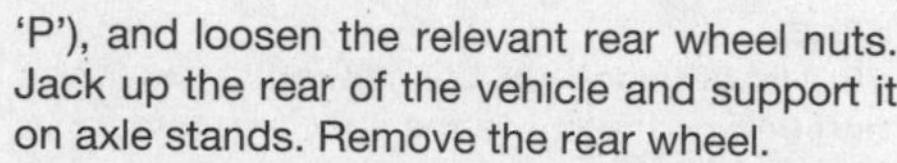

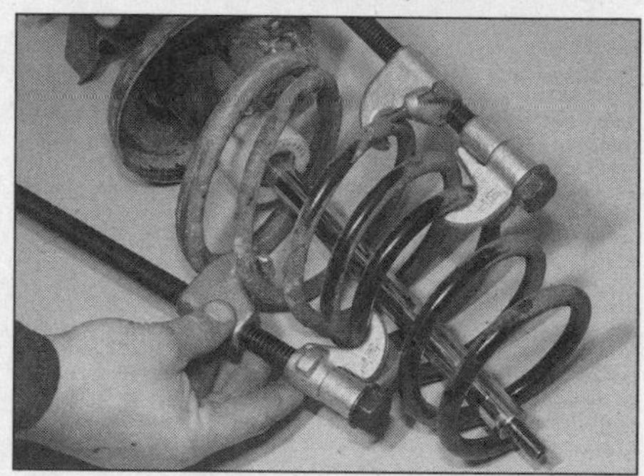

12.1e . . . and coil spring

13 Rear anti-roll bar and links (Saloon/Hatchback models) - removal and refitting

Removal

1 Chock the front wheels, engage 1st gear (or 'P'), and loosen the relevant rear wheel nuts. Jack up the rear of the vehicle and support it on axle stands. Remove the rear wheel.

13.2a Loosen the nut . . .

2 Unscrew the nuts securing the anti-roll bar links to the front lower arms on both sides. Hold the upper part of the links with a spanner while loosening the nuts. Recover the rubber bushes **(see illustrations)**.

3 Unscrew the bolts securing the anti-roll bar mounting clamps to the rear suspension crossmember **(see illustration)**, then unhook the clamps and withdraw the anti-roll bar from under the vehicle.

4 Examine the rubber bushes for the mounting clamps and links, and if necessary renew them. The links are available individually.

Refitting

5 Locate the anti-roll bar on the rear crossmember, hook the mounting clamps in position, and insert the bolts. Tighten the bolts to the specified torque.

6 Locate the anti-roll bar links in the front lower arms on both sides, making sure that the rubber bushes are in position. Refit the nuts and tighten them to the specified torque.

7 Refit the rear wheels, and lower the vehicle to the ground.

14 Rear suspension lower arms (Saloon/Hatchback models) - removal and refitting

Removal

1 Chock the front wheels, engage 1st gear (or 'P'), and loosen the relevant rear wheel nuts. Jack up the rear of the vehicle and support it on axle stands. Remove the rear wheel.

13.2b . . . remove the nut and rubber bush . . .

13.2c . . . and remove the anti-roll bar link from the lower arm

13.3 Rear anti-roll bar mounting clamp

Front lower arm

2 To remove the front lower arm, it is necessary to remove the fuel tank first. Refer to Chapter 4A for details.

3 Unscrew the nut and disconnect the anti-roll bar link from the lower arm. Hold the actual link with an adjustable spanner or grips while unscrewing the nut, to prevent damage to the link joint. Recover the rubber bush.

4 Unscrew and remove the bolt securing the front lower arm to the knuckle.

5 Unscrew and remove the bolt securing the front lower arm to the crossmember.

6 Withdraw the front lower arm from under the vehicle.

Rear lower arm

7 Unscrew and remove the bolt securing the rear lower arm to the knuckle.

8 The bolt securing the rear lower arm to the crossmember has an eccentric head and spacer, which are used to adjust the rear toe setting. Before removing this bolt, mark its position, using a scriber or similar sharp instrument through the aperture in the crossmember.

9 Unscrew and remove the bolt securing the rear lower arm to the crossmember **(see illustration)**. The bolt may be removed through the aperture in the crossmember. Recover the eccentric spacer.

10 Withdraw the rear lower arm from under the vehicle.

Refitting

11 Refitting is a reversal of the removal procedure, noting the following points:

a) The arm mounting bolts should be finger-tightened initially, and only fully tightened after the vehicle is lowered to the ground, so that its weight is on the rear suspension. Note that the rear lower arm is marked 'TOP' for correct refitting ***(see illustration)****.*

b) The rear toe setting should be checked, and if necessary adjusted, at the earliest opportunity.

14.9 Bolt securing the rear lower arm to the crossmember

14.11 'TOP' marking on the rear lower arm

15 Rear suspension tie-bar (Saloon/Hatchback models) - removal and refitting

Removal

1 Chock the front wheels, engage 1st gear (or 'P'), and loosen the relevant rear wheel nuts. Jack up the rear of the vehicle and support it on axle stands. Remove the rear wheel.

2 Disconnect the handbrake cable from the tie-bar bracket on the underbody.

3 Unscrew and remove the bolt securing the tie-bar bracket to the rear suspension knuckle.

4 Unscrew the bolts securing the tie-bar bracket to the underbody, and withdraw the bracket from the vehicle **(see illustration)**.

5 Mount the bracket in a vice, then unscrew and remove the bolt, and remove the tie-bar from the bracket.

6 It is not possible to renew the rubber bushes - if they are worn excessively, the tie-bar should be renewed complete.

Refitting

7 Refitting is a reversal of the removal procedure, noting the following points:

a) The bracket-to-underbody bolts should be fully tightened to the specified torque before lowering the vehicle.

b) The bolts securing the tie-bar to the bracket and knuckle should be finger-tightened initially, and only fully tightened after the vehicle is lowered to the ground, so that its weight is on the rear suspension.

16 Rear suspension crossmember (Saloon/Hatchback models) - removal and refitting

Note: *Before attempting to remove the rear suspension crossmember, tools to hold the coil springs in compression must be obtained. Careful use of conventional coil spring compressors will prove satisfactory.*

Removal

1 Chock the front wheels, engage 1st gear (or 'P'), and loosen the rear wheel nuts. Jack up the rear of the vehicle and support it on axle stands, making sure that the vehicle is supported high enough for the crossmember to be removed. Remove the rear wheels.

2 Remove the complete exhaust system as described in Chapter 4A.

3 Unscrew and remove the bolts securing the tie-bars to the rear suspension knuckles, and disconnect the tie-bars.

4 Unscrew the nuts securing the rear anti-roll bar links to the front lower arms. Hold the actual links stationary while the nuts are being unscrewed, to prevent damage to the joints. Swivel the anti-roll bar upwards, and recover the rubber bushes.

5 Where applicable, remove the ABS wheel sensor from the rear suspension knuckle as described in Chapter 9.

6 Unscrew and remove the bolts, and disconnect both lower arms from the rear suspension knuckle.

7 To allow the rear suspension struts to be released from the rubber stops on the top of the crossmember, it is necessary to fit coil spring compressor tools to both of the rear coil springs, and compress them until all tension is removed from the upper and lower mountings.

Warning: It is important to only use high-quality spring compressors, and to carefully follow the tool manufacturer's instructions provided with them. With the compressor tools fitted, support the struts to one side.

8 Make accurate alignment markings between the crossmember and the underbody, for use on refitting. Support the rear suspension crossmember on a trolley jack, then unscrew the four mounting bolts from the underbody **(see illustration)**.

9 Lower the crossmember to the ground.

15.4 Tie-bar bracket on the underbody

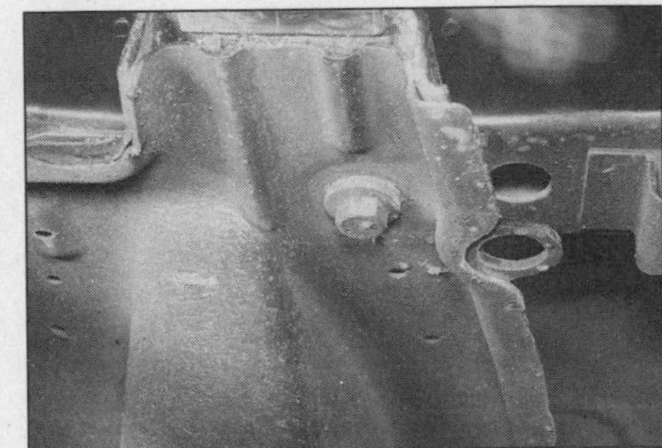

16.8 One of the rear suspension crossmember mounting bolts

10 Unscrew the bolts securing the anti-roll bar clamps to the crossmember, then remove the clamps and withdraw the anti-roll bar.

11 Remove the lower arms from the crossmember as described in Section 14.

Refitting

12 Refitting is a reversal of the removal procedure, noting the following points:

a) *Ford specify the use of a special tool (tool number 15-097) to accurately align the crossmember onto the underbody before tightening the mounting bolts. This tool should be obtained if possible, since inaccurate alignment would result in bad handling and excessive tyre wear. However, if the marks made on removal are accurately aligned, the crossmember should be refitted in exactly the same position as before.*

b) *The tie-bar and arm mounting bolts should be finger-tightened initially, and only fully tightened after the vehicle is lowered to the ground, so that its weight is on the rear suspension.*

c) *The rear toe setting should be checked, and if necessary adjusted, at the earliest opportunity.*

17 Rear hub and bearings (Estate models) - inspection and renewal

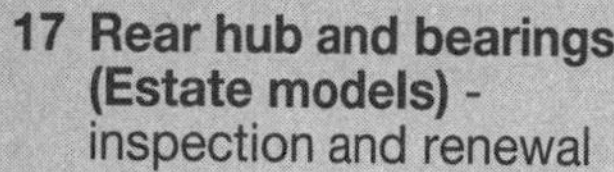

Inspection

1 The rear hub bearings are non-adjustable, and are supplied complete with the hub. It is not possible to renew the bearings separately from the hub.

2 To check the bearings for excessive wear, chock the front wheels, then jack up the rear of the vehicle and support it on axle stands. Fully release the handbrake.

3 Grip the rear wheel at the top and bottom, and attempt to rock it. If excessive movement is noted, or if there is any roughness or vibration felt when the wheel is spun, it is indicative that the hub bearings are worn.

Renewal

4 Remove the rear wheel.

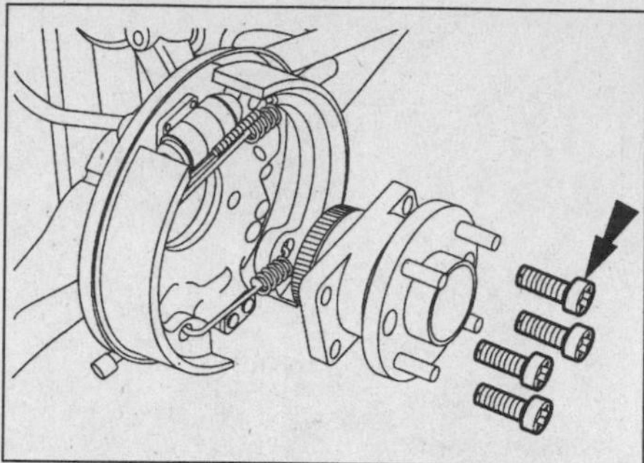

17.7 Mounting bolts (arrowed) for the rear hub on Estate models

5 On drum brake models, remove the rear brake drum as described in Chapter 9.

6 On disc brake models, remove the rear brake disc as described in Chapter 9.

7 Turning the hub as necessary, line up the hole in the flange with the each of the bolts securing the hub assembly to the rear suspension knuckle; unscrew and remove the bolts **(see illustration)**.

8 Withdraw the hub and bearing assembly. Refit two of the hub mounting bolts, to hold the backplate/splash shield in place.

9 If necessary, the stub shaft may be removed from the hub for inspection of the bearing, by unscrewing the hub nut. Note that the hub nut is of special laminated design, and may only be re-used a maximum of five times. (It is a good idea to file a small notch on the nut every time it is removed; obtain a new nut if necessary.) Tighten the nut on reassembly.

10 Fit the new hub and bearing assembly using a reversal of the removal procedure. Tighten all nuts and bolts to the specified torque.

18 Rear suspension knuckle (Estate models) - removal and refitting

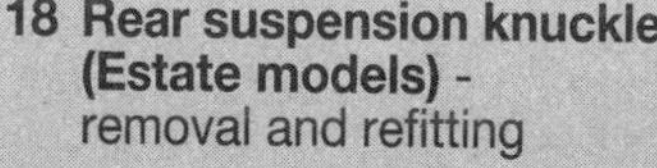

Removal

1 Chock the front wheels, engage 1st gear (or 'P'), and loosen the relevant rear wheel nuts. Jack up the rear of the vehicle and support it on axle stands. Remove the rear wheel, then release the handbrake.

2 Position a trolley jack or axle stand beneath the rear suspension lower arm, to keep the coil spring in compression.

3 Where applicable, remove the ABS sensor as described in Chapter 9.

Drum brake models

4 Remove the rear brake drum as described in Chapter 9.

5 Disconnect the flexible hydraulic brake hose at the bracket on the rear suspension crossmember as described in Chapter 9.

Disc brake models

6 Remove the rear brake disc as described in Chapter 9.

All models

7 Remove the rear hub as described in Section 17.

8 Remove the backplate or splash shield, as applicable. On drum brake models, support the backplate assembly on an axle stand, to prevent damage to the handbrake cable.

9 Unscrew and remove the shock absorber lower mounting bolt.

10 Unscrew and remove the three bolts securing the tie-bar to the knuckle.

11 Unscrew and remove the bolt securing the front lower arm to the knuckle **(see illustration)**.

12 Unscrew and remove the bolt securing the upper arm to the knuckle **(see illustration)**.

13 Support the knuckle, then unscrew and remove the bolt securing the rear lower arm to the knuckle **(see illustration)**, and withdraw the knuckle.

Refitting

14 Refitting is a reversal of the removal procedure, noting the following points:

a) *Delay fully tightening the rubber bush mounting bolts until the weight of the vehicle is on the suspension. Tighten all bolts to the specified torque.*

b) *Where the flexible rear brake hose was disconnected, bleed the hydraulic system as described in Chapter 9.*

c) *Finally check, and if necessary adjust, the rear wheel toe setting as described in Section 37.*

18.11 Front lower arm-to-knuckle bolt

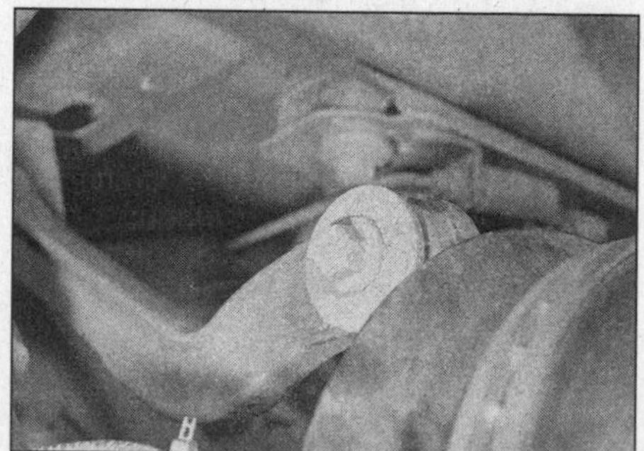

18.12 Upper arm-to-knuckle bolt

18.13 Rear lower arm-to-knuckle bolt

19.3 Rear shock absorber lower mounting bolt (Estate)

20.2a Mounting nut (arrowed) and rubber bush securing the rear anti-roll bar link to the rear lower arm

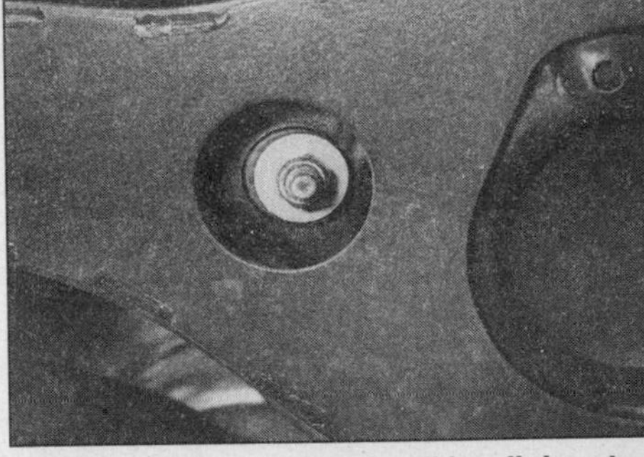

20.2b View of the anti-roll bar link nut through the rear lower arm

19 Rear shock absorber (Estate models) - removal, testing and refitting

Removal

1 Chock the front wheels, engage 1st gear (or 'P'), and loosen the relevant rear wheel nuts. Jack up the rear of the vehicle and support it on axle stands. Remove the rear wheel.

2 Position a trolley jack under the coil spring area of the rear lower suspension arm, to keep the coil spring in compression.

3 Unscrew and remove the shock absorber lower mounting bolt **(see illustration)**.

4 Unscrew and remove the upper mounting bolt, and withdraw the shock absorber from under the vehicle.

Testing

5 Check the mounting rubbers for damage and deterioration. If they are worn, they may be renewed separately from the shock absorber body.

6 Mount the shock absorber in a vice, gripping it by the lower mounting. Examine the shock absorber for signs of fluid leakage. Test the operation of the shock absorber by moving it through a full stroke, and then through short strokes of 50 to 100 mm. In both cases, the resistance felt should be smooth and continuous. If the resistance is jerky or uneven, the shock absorber should be renewed.

Refitting

7 Refitting is a reversal of the removal procedure, tightening the mounting bolts to the specified torque.

20 Rear anti-roll bar and links (Estate models) - removal and refitting

Removal

1 Chock the front wheels, engage 1st gear (or 'P'), and loosen the rear wheel nuts. Jack up the rear of the vehicle and support it on axle stands. Remove the rear wheels.

2 Unscrew the nuts, and remove the washers and bushes securing the anti-roll bar links to the rear lower arms **(see illustrations)**.

3 Using a Torx key, unscrew the bolts securing the anti-roll bar mounting clamps to the rear suspension crossmember **(see illustration)**; release the clamps, and withdraw the anti-roll bar from under the vehicle.

4 Examine the rubber bushes for the mounting clamps and links, and if necessary renew them. The links are available individually.

Refitting

5 Locate the anti-roll bar on the rear crossmember, then refit the clamps and tighten the bolts to the specified torque.

6 Refit the anti-roll bar links to the rear lower arms, together with the bushes and washers. Tighten the nuts to the specified torque, while holding the actual links stationary in their central position.

7 Refit the rear wheels, and lower the vehicle to the ground.

21 Rear coil spring (Estate models) - removal and refitting

Note: *Before attempting to remove the rear suspension coil spring, a tool to hold the coil spring in compression must be obtained. Careful use of conventional coil spring compressors will prove satisfactory.*

Removal

1 Chock the front wheels, engage 1st gear (or 'P'), and loosen the relevant rear wheel nuts. Jack up the rear of the vehicle and support it on axle stands. Remove the rear wheel.

2 Support the weight of the rear lower arm beneath the coil spring position with a trolley jack.

3 Fit the coil spring compressor tool (ensuring that it is fully engaged), and compress the coil spring until all tension is relieved from the upper mounting.

4 Unscrew the nut, and remove the washer and bush attaching the anti-roll bar link to the rear lower arm.

5 Unscrew and remove the bolt securing the rear lower arm to the knuckle **(see illustration)**.

6 Unscrew and remove the bolt securing the front lower arm to the knuckle **(see illustration)**.

20.3 Anti-roll bar mounting clamp on the rear suspension crossmember

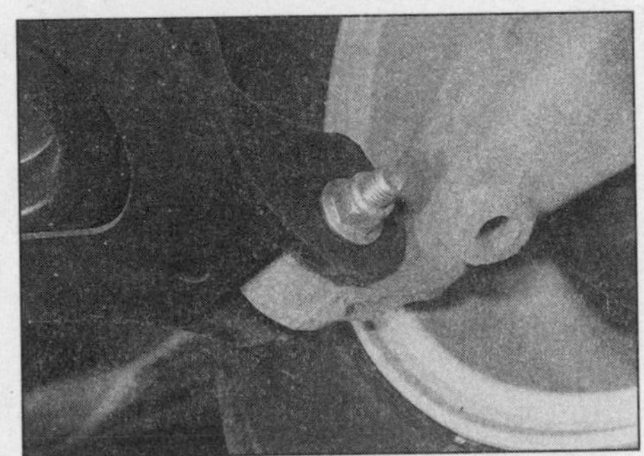

21.5 Rear lower arm-to-knuckle mounting bolt

21.6 Front lower arm-to-knuckle mounting bolt

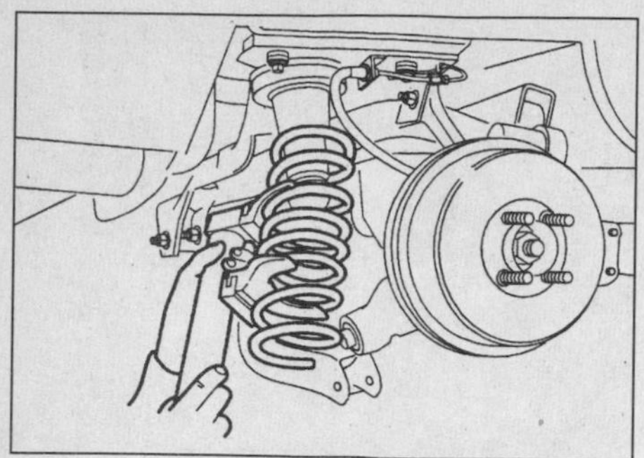

21.7 Removing the coil spring, with compressor tool attached, from under the vehicle

7 Lower the rear lower arm, and withdraw the coil spring from under the vehicle **(see illustration)**. Take care to keep the compressor tool in full engagement with the coil spring.

8 If a new coil spring is to be fitted, the original coil spring must be released from the compressor. If it is to be re-used, the coil spring can be left in compression.

Refitting

9 Refitting is a reversal of the removal procedure, noting the following points:

a) *Make sure that the coil spring is located correctly in the upper and lower seats* ***(see illustration)****.*

b) *Delay fully tightening the two lower arm mounting bolts until the weight of the vehicle is on the rear suspension.*

c) *Finally check, and if necessary adjust, the rear wheel toe setting as described in Section 37.*

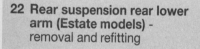

22 Rear suspension rear lower arm (Estate models) - removal and refitting

Removal

1 Remove the rear suspension coil spring as described in Section 21.

2 The bolt securing the rear lower arm to the crossmember has an eccentric head and spacer, which are used to adjust the rear toe setting. Before removing this bolt, mark its

23.2 Front lower arm-to-crossmember securing bolt

21.9 Correct location of the coil spring in the upper seat (arrowed)

position, using a scriber or similar sharp instrument through the aperture in the crossmember.

3 Unscrew and remove the bolt securing the rear lower arm to the crossmember. The bolt may be removed through the aperture in the crossmember. Recover the eccentric spacer **(see illustration)**.

4 Withdraw the rear lower arm from under the vehicle.

Refitting

5 Refitting is a reversal of the removal procedure, noting the following points:

a) *Delay fully tightening the lower arm mounting bolts until the weight of the vehicle is on the rear suspension.*

b) *Finally check, and if necessary adjust, the rear wheel toe setting as described in Section 37.*

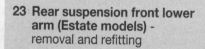

23 Rear suspension front lower arm (Estate models) - removal and refitting

Removal

1 Chock the front wheels, engage 1st gear (or 'P'), and loosen the relevant rear wheel nuts. Jack up the rear of the vehicle and support it on axle stands. Remove the rear wheel.

2 Unscrew and remove the bolt securing the front lower arm to the crossmember **(see illustration)**.

23.3 Front lower arm (arrowed)

22.3 Bolts securing the rear lower arms to the crossmember - note the eccentric spacers

3 Unscrew and remove the bolt securing the front lower arm to the knuckle, and withdraw the arm from under the vehicle **(see illustration)**.

Refitting

4 Refitting is a reversal of the removal procedure, but delay fully tightening the mounting bolts until the weight of the vehicle is on the rear suspension.

24 Rear suspension upper arm (Estate models) - removal and refitting

Removal

1 Chock the front wheels, engage 1st gear (or 'P'), and loosen the relevant rear wheel nuts. Jack up the rear of the vehicle and support it on axle stands. Remove the rear wheel.

2 Using a trolley jack, support the rear lower arm beneath the coil spring position.

3 Unscrew and remove the bolt securing the upper arm to the knuckle **(see illustration)**.

4 Unscrew and remove the bolt securing the upper arm to the crossmember, and withdraw the arm from under the vehicle.

Refitting

5 Refitting is a reversal of the removal procedure, but delay fully tightening the mounting bolts until the weight of the vehicle is on the rear suspension.

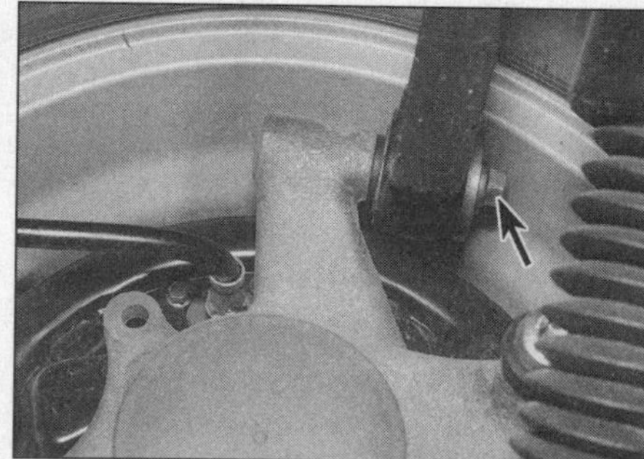

24.3 Bolt (arrowed) securing the upper arm to the knuckle

25.7 Bolts (arrowed) securing the rear suspension tie-bar to the knuckle

25.8a Tie-bar bracket front bolt (arrowed) on the underbody

25.8b Tie-bar bracket rear bolt (arrowed) on the underbody

25 Rear suspension tie-bar (Estate models) - removal and refitting

Removal

1 Chock the front wheels, engage 1st gear (or 'P'), and loosen the relevant rear wheel nuts. Jack up the rear of the vehicle and support it on axle stands. Remove the rear wheel.
2 Using a trolley jack, support the rear lower arm beneath the coil spring position.
3 Unscrew and remove the bolt securing the rear shock absorber to the knuckle.
4 Where applicable, release the ABS wheel sensor lead from the tie-bar.
5 Detach the handbrake cable from the tie-bar bracket.
6 Refer to Chapter 9, and disconnect the handbrake cable from the rear brake shoes or rear caliper, as applicable. Pass the cable through the hole in the tie-bar.
7 Unscrew and remove the three bolts securing the tie-bar to the knuckle **(see illustration)**.
8 Unbolt the tie-bar bracket from the underbody, and withdraw the assembly from under the vehicle **(see illustrations)**.
9 Mount the tie-bar in a vice, then unscrew the bolt, and separate the tie-bar from its bracket.
10 It is not possible to renew the rubber bush in the tie-bar, and if it is excessively worn, the complete tie-bar must be renewed.

Refitting

11 Refitting is a reversal of the removal procedure, noting the following points:

a) Delay fully tightening the bolt which secures the arm to the bracket until the weight of the vehicle is on the rear suspension.
b) On completion, check the operation of the handbrake.

26 Rear suspension crossmember (Estate models) - removal and refitting

Removal

1 Chock the front wheels, engage 1st gear (or 'P'), and loosen the rear wheel nuts. Jack up the rear of the vehicle and support it on axle stands, making sure that the vehicle is supported high enough for the crossmember to be removed. Remove the rear wheels.
2 Disconnect the handbrake rear cables from the front primary cable, as described in Chapter 9.
3 Where applicable, remove the ABS wheel sensors from the rear knuckles, and disconnect the wiring leads from the clips as described in Chapter 9.
4 Disconnect the flexible brake hoses from the brackets on both sides of the crossmember, as described in Chapter 9.
5 Working on each side of the vehicle, unbolt the tie-bar brackets from the underbody.
6 Support the rear suspension crossmember on a trolley jack.
7 Unscrew the mounting bolts, and lower the crossmember to the ground **(see illustrations)**.
8 If necessary, remove the suspension components from the crossmember as described in the appropriate Sections of this Chapter.

Refitting

9 Refitting is a reversal of the removal procedure, noting the following points:

a) When raising the crossmember, note that guide pins are provided to ensure correct alignment ***(see illustration).***
b) Delay fully tightening the suspension mounting bolts until the weight of the vehicle is on the rear suspension.
c) Tighten all bolts to the specified torque.
d) Bleed the brake hydraulic system as described in Chapter 9.
e) Check, and if necessary adjust, the rear wheel toe setting as described in Section 37.

27 Steering wheel - removal and refitting

Warning: All models are equipped with an air bag system. Make sure that the safety recommendations given in Chapter 12 are followed, to prevent personal injury.

26.7a Rear suspension crossmember rear mounting bolt

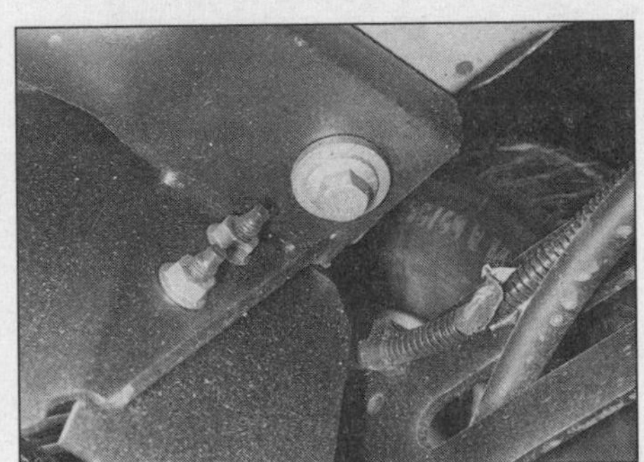
26.7b Rear suspension crossmember front mounting bolt

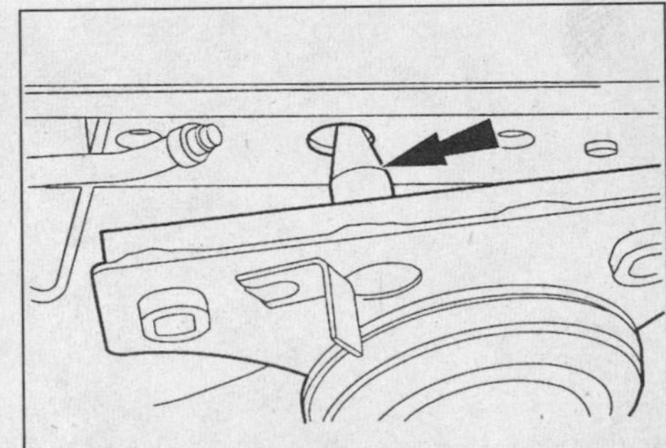
26.9 Guide pin (arrowed) for correct alignment of the rear crossmember

27.5 Removing the steering wheel retaining bolt

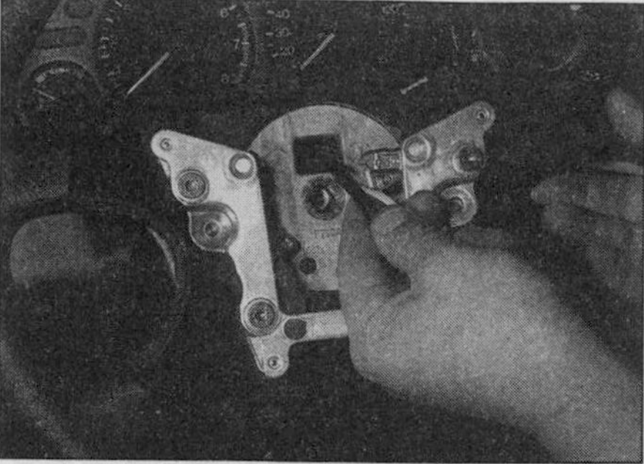
27.6 Feeding the horn and air bag wiring through the hole in the steering wheel hub

27.8 Tightening the steering wheel retaining bolt

Removal

1 Disconnect the battery negative (earth) lead (refer to Chapter 5A, Section 1).

⚠ ***Warning: Before proceeding, wait a minimum of 15 minutes, as a precaution against accidental firing of the air bag unit. This period ensures that any stored energy in the back-up capacitor is dissipated.***

2 Turn the steering wheel so that the front wheels are in the straight-ahead position.

3 Unscrew the screws (two above, three below), and remove the steering column upper and lower shrouds.

4 Remove the air bag unit from the steering wheel as described in Chapter 12.

⚠ ***Warning: Position the air bag module in a safe place, with the mechanism facing downwards as a precaution against accidental operation.***

5 Make sure that the steering lock is not engaged. Unscrew the retaining bolt from the centre of the steering wheel **(see illustration)**.

6 Remove the steering wheel from the top of the column, while feeding the horn and air bag wiring through the hole in the steering wheel hub **(see illustration)**.

Refitting

7 Make sure that the front wheels are still facing straight-ahead, then locate the steering wheel on the top of the steering column.

8 Refit the retaining bolt, and tighten it to the specified torque while holding the steering wheel **(see illustration)**. Do not tighten the bolt with the steering lock engaged, as this may damage the lock.

9 Reconnect the horn wiring connections and air bag multi-plug.

10 Locate the air bag module/horn contact on the steering wheel, then insert the mounting screws and tighten them.

11 Refit the steering column upper and lower shrouds, ensuring that the rubber ring around the lock barrel is fitted before offering the lower shroud into place, and that the column switch gaiters engage correctly.

12 Reconnect the battery negative lead.

28 Steering column - removal, inspection and refitting

⚠ ***Warning: All models are equipped with an air bag system. Make sure that the safety recommendations given in Chapter 12 are followed, to prevent personal injury.***

Removal

1 Disconnect the battery negative (earth) lead (refer to Chapter 5A, Section 1).

⚠ ***Warning: Before proceeding, wait a minimum of 15 minutes, as a precaution against accidental firing of the air bag unit. This period ensures that any stored energy in the back-up capacitor is dissipated.***

2 Turn the steering wheel so that the front wheels are in the straight-ahead position.

3 Remove the ignition key, then turn the steering wheel slightly as necessary until the steering lock engages.

4 Unscrew the screws (two above, three below), and remove the steering column lower and upper shrouds. As the lower shroud is being removed, it will be necessary to remove the rubber ring from the ignition switch/steering lock **(see illustrations)**.

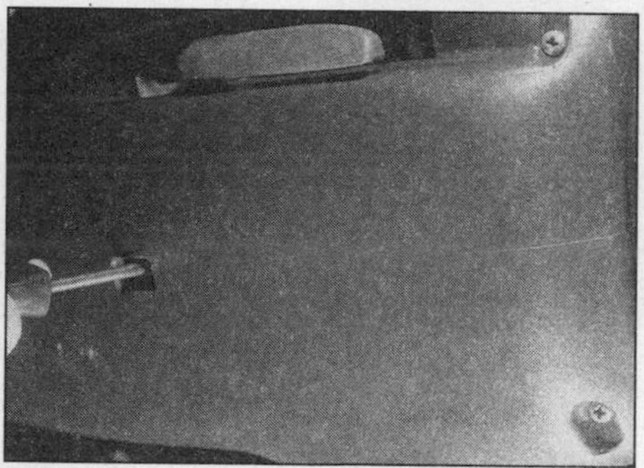
28.4a Unscrew the screws from the lower shroud . . .

28.4b . . . remove the rubber ring . . .

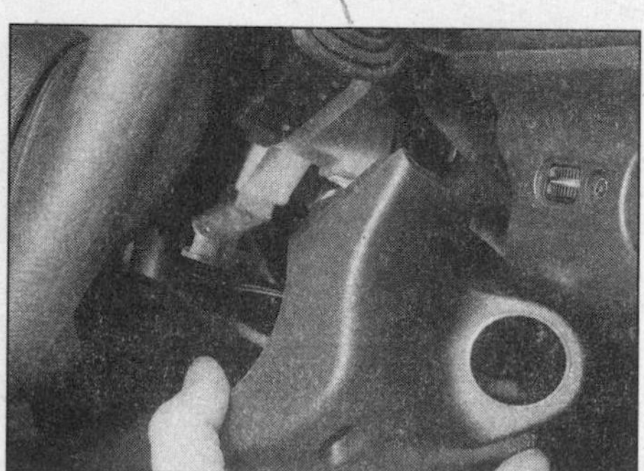
28.4c . . . and remove the lower shroud

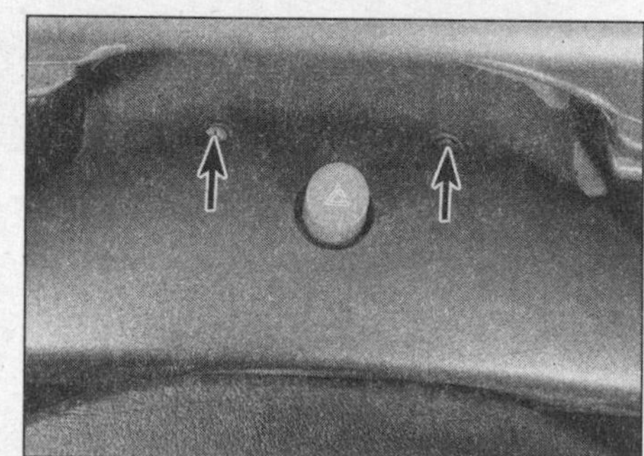
28.4d Upper shroud retaining screws (arrowed)

28.4e Removing the upper shroud

28.5a On models with the PATS immobiliser, disconnect the wiring plug . . .

5 On models with the PATS ('Safeguard') immobiliser, remove the immobiliser transceiver from the ignition switch by disconnecting the wiring plug and removing the mounting screw **(see illustrations)**.

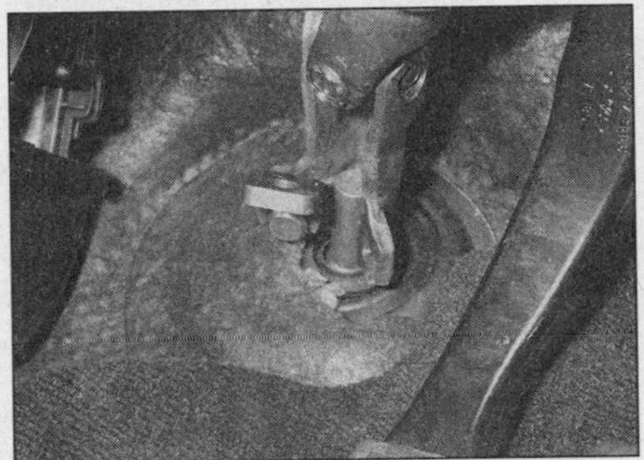

28.7b . . . and swivel the clamp plate around

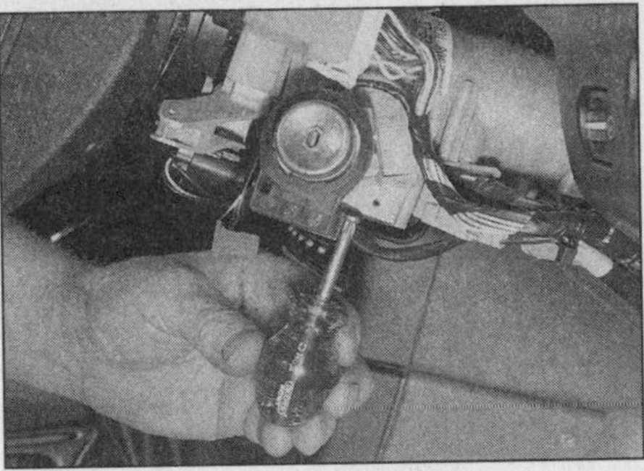

28.5b . . . then remove the mounting screw and remove the transceiver

6 Remove the driver's side lower facia panel (see Chapter 11, Section 29).

7 Unscrew the clamp plate bolt securing the steering column shaft to the flexible coupling. Swivel the clamp plate around, and disengage it from the flexible coupling stub **(see illustrations)**.

8 Release the cable-tie from the wiring loom at the steering column, and disconnect the multi-plugs from both sides of the column, noting their locations as necessary **(see illustrations)**.

9 Remove the mounting nut and detach the column lower support brace.

10 On left-hand-drive models, disconnect the airbag control module multi-plug, and release its wiring by cutting the cable-tie.

11 Unscrew and remove the steering column mounting bolts. Taking care not to damage the column switches, slide the column upwards to disengage the retaining tab from the groove in the cross-beam bracket, and withdraw it from inside the vehicle **(see illustrations)**.

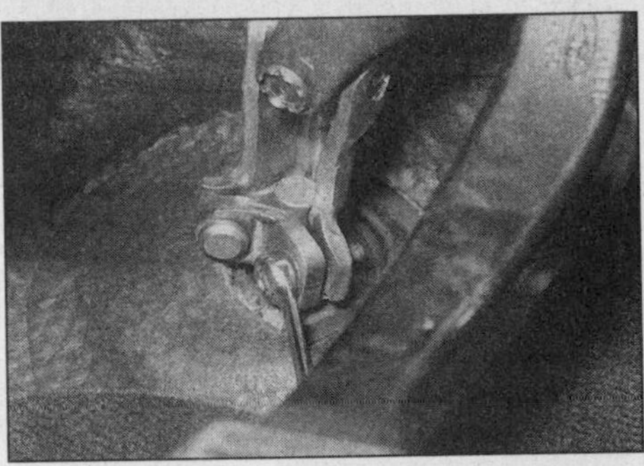

28.7a Unscrew the clamp plate bolt . . .

Inspection

12 With the steering column removed, check the universal joints for wear, and examine the column upper and lower shafts for any signs of damage or distortion **(see illustration)**. Where evident, the column should be renewed complete.

13 Examine the height adjustment lever mechanism for wear and damage **(see illustration)**.

14 With the steering lock disengaged, turn the inner column, and check the upper and lower bearings for smooth operation. The bearings are obtainable separately, and should be renewed if necessary. Dismantling and reassembly of the column assembly is a relatively easy operation.

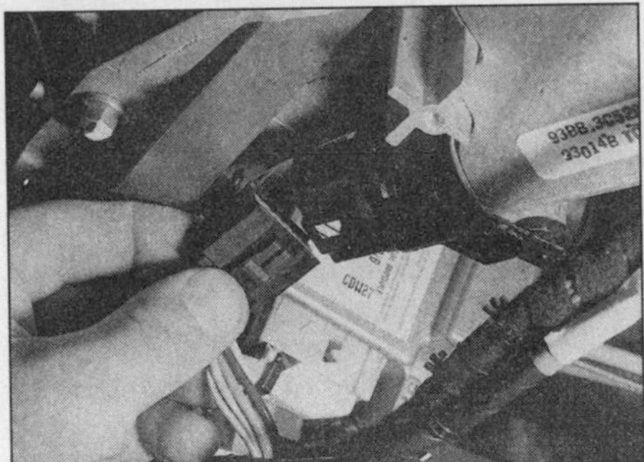

28.8a Disconnecting the multi-plug from the ignition switch

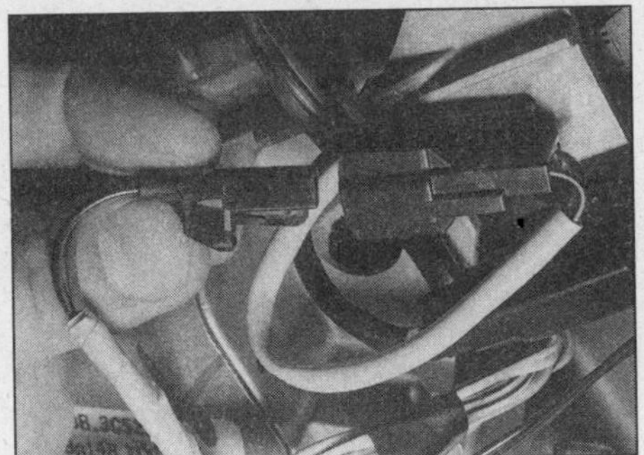

28.8b Disconnecting the small multi-plug . . .

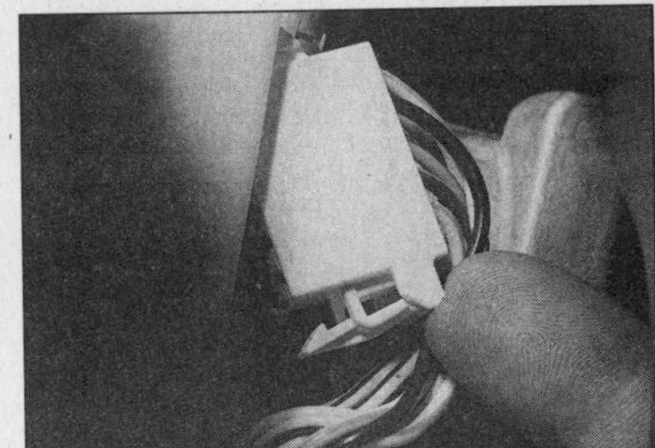

28.8c . . . and main multi-plug from the steering column

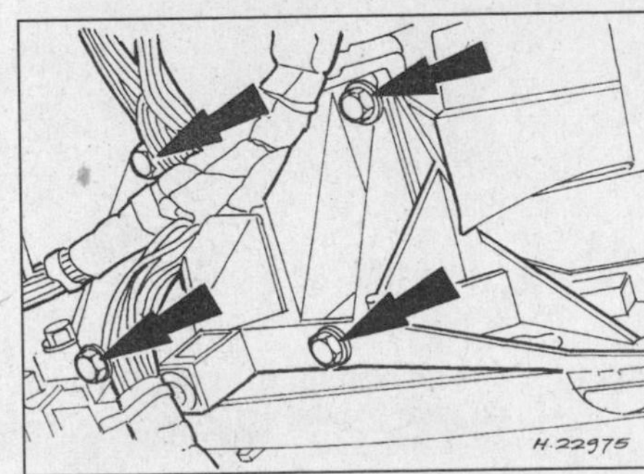

28.11a Steering column mounting bolt locations (arrowed)

28.11b Removing the steering column

28.12 Steering column and universal joint

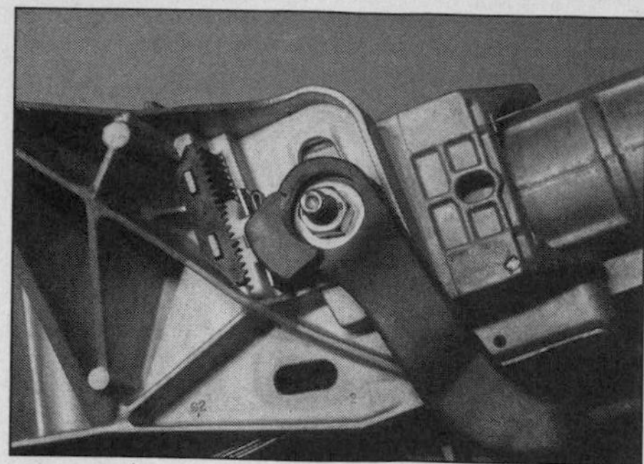

28.13 Height adjustment lever mechanism

Refitting

15 Locate the steering column on its bracket, making sure that the tab slides down into the groove correctly.
16 Insert the mounting bolts and tighten to the specified torque **(see illustration)**.
17 Reconnect the column lower support brace, and tighten the mounting nut.
18 On left-hand-drive models, reconnect the airbag control module multi-plug, and secure the wiring with a new cable-tie.
19 Reconnect the various multi-plugs to their correct locations, and secure the wiring loom with a cable-tie.
20 Locate the steering column shaft on the flexible coupling, swivel the clamp plate round, then insert a new bolt and tighten to the specified torque.
21 Refit the driver's side lower trim panel.
22 Where applicable, refit the PATS transceiver to the ignition switch.
23 Refit the steering column upper and lower shrouds, ensuring that the rubber ring around the lock barrel is fitted before offering the lower shroud into place, and that the column switch gaiters engage correctly.
24 Reconnect the battery negative lead.

29 Steering column flexible coupling - removal and refitting

Removal

1 Disconnect the battery negative (earth) lead (refer to Chapter 5A, Section 1).
2 Turn the steering wheel so that the front wheels are in the straight-ahead position. Remove the ignition key, then turn the steering wheel slightly as necessary until the steering lock engages.
3 Unscrew the clamp plate bolt securing the steering column shaft to the flexible coupling. Swivel the clamp plate around, and disengage it from the flexible coupling stub.
4 Carefully prise the rubber boot from the bulkhead, and withdraw it into the passenger compartment. Take care not to damage the sealing lip of the boot.
5 Using an Allen key, unscrew the clamp bolt securing the flexible coupling to the pinion shaft on the steering gear, and withdraw the coupling from inside the vehicle.

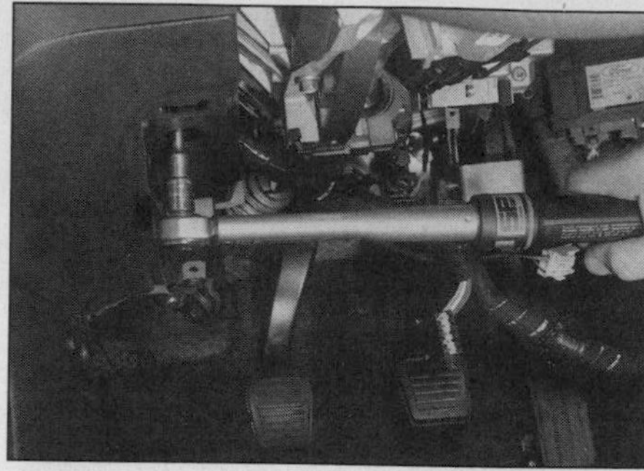

28.16 Tightening the steering column mounting bolts

Refitting

6 Refitting is a reversal of the removal procedure, noting the following points:

a) *Use new clamp bolts, tightened to the specified torque.*
b) *Make sure that the rubber boot engages correctly in the bulkhead and on the flexible coupling.*

30 Steering gear (four-cylinder and RHD models with ABS) - removal and refitting

Removal

1 Remove the steering column flexible coupling as described in Section 29.
2 Apply the handbrake, then loosen the front wheel nuts. Jack up the front of the vehicle and support it on axle stands. Remove both front wheels.
3 Working beneath the vehicle, unbolt the front and rear engine mountings from the subframe. Make accurate alignment markings for refitting the front mounting in particular.
4 Although not essential, to improve access, remove the exhaust downpipe complete as described in Chapter 4A.
5 Extract the split pins from the track rod end balljoint nuts, then unscrew the nuts, and detach the rods from the arms on the steering knuckles using a conventional balljoint removal tool. Take care not to damage the balljoint seals.
6 Release the securing clips and screws, and remove the auxiliary drivebelt cover from the right-hand wheel arch.
7 Position a suitable container beneath the steering gear, then unscrew the union nuts securing the power steering fluid supply, return, and cooler lines to the steering gear. Identify the lines for position, then unbolt the clamps, disconnect the lines, and allow the fluid to drain into the container. Cover the apertures in the steering gear and also the ends of the fluid pipes, to prevent the ingress of dust and dirt into the hydraulic circuit.
8 Where applicable, remove the steering gear cover plate, then unscrew and remove the mounting bolts. The bolts are located on top of the steering gear, and are difficult to reach. Ideally, the special U-shaped Ford spanner should be used, but it is just possible to reach them with a normal spanner **(see illustration)**.
9 Withdraw the steering gear through the wheel arch. Take care that the pressure check valve does not fall out of its port as the gear is removed.

30.8 U-shaped Ford spanner for unscrewing the steering gear mounting bolts

Refitting

10 If the steering gear is being replaced with a new one, the new unit will be supplied together with union nuts already fitted. The new nuts must only be used with new feed and return lines - otherwise, they must be removed and discarded.
11 If the original lines and union nuts are being used, the Teflon rings on the union nuts must be renewed. To do this, the rings must be expanded individually onto a fitting adaptor, then located in the grooves of the union nuts **(see illustration)**.
12 Locate the steering gear on the subframe, and insert the two mounting bolts. Tighten the bolts to the specified torque. Note that, if the special Ford tool is being used, the bottom of the tool must be turned anti-clockwise in order to tighten the mounting bolts **(see illustration)**.

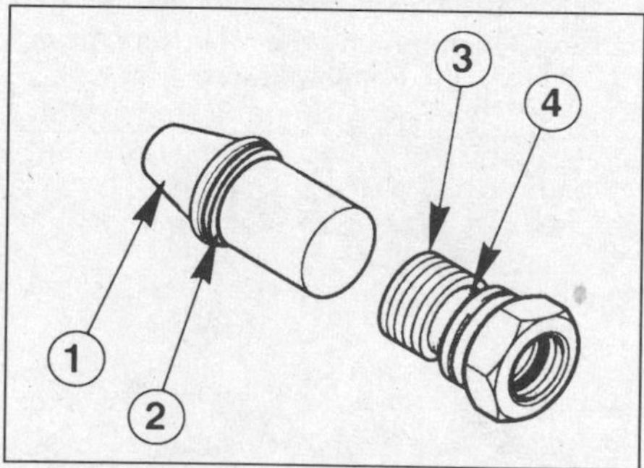

30.11 Using an adaptor to fit the Teflon rings to the union nuts

1 Adaptor
2 Teflon ring
3 Union nut
4 Groove location for the Teflon ring

13 Reconnect the fluid lines and tighten the union nuts to the specified torque. Refit the clamps and tighten the bolts. Where applicable, refit the steering gear cover, and tighten the five bolts to the specified torque.
14 Refit the engine front and rear mountings to the subframe, aligning the marks made on removal and tightening the bolts to the specified torque (see the relevant Part of Chapter 2).
15 Refit the exhaust downpipe with reference to Chapter 4A.
16 Refit the auxiliary drivebelt cover.
17 Refit the track rod end balljoints to the steering knuckles, and tighten the nuts to the specified torque. Check that the split pin holes are aligned; if necessary, turn the nuts to the nearest alignment, making sure that the torque wrench setting is still within the specified range. Insert new split pins, and bend them back to secure.
18 Refit the front wheels, and lower the vehicle to the ground. Tighten the wheel nuts to the specified torque.
19 Refit the steering column flexible coupling with reference to Section 29.
20 Fill and bleed the power steering hydraulic system as described in Section 33.
21 Have the front wheel alignment checked, and if necessary adjusted, at the earliest opportunity (refer to Section 37).

31 Steering gear (V6 and LHD models with ABS) - removal and refitting

Removal

1 Disconnect the battery negative (earth) lead (refer to Chapter 5A, Section 1).
2 Working inside the vehicle, unscrew the clamp plate bolt securing the steering column shaft to the flexible coupling. Swivel the clamp plate around, and disengage it from the flexible coupling stub.
3 Apply the handbrake, then loosen the front wheel nuts. Jack up the front of the vehicle and support it on axle stands. Remove both front wheels.
4 On manual transmission models, disconnect the gearchange linkage and support rods from the transmission, as described in Chapter 7A.
5 Remove the exhaust downpipe complete, as described in Chapter 4A.
6 Remove the radiator lower cover, and the left- and right-hand wheel arch liners, by unscrewing the screws and releasing the clips.
7 Detach the front bumper support brackets, and move them to one side.
8 Support the radiator in its raised position, by inserting split pins through the small holes in the radiator mounting extensions which protrude through the upper mountings **(see illustration)**.

30.12 Tightening the steering gear mounting bolts using the U-shaped spanner

9 Unbolt and remove the radiator lower mounting brackets.
10 Where applicable, unscrew the bolts securing the air conditioning accumulator to the subframe.
11 Working beneath the vehicle, remove the through-bolts from the engine front and rear mountings. On models with automatic transmission, it will be necessary to remove the rear mounting completely.
12 Detach the power steering fluid cooler pipes from the subframe.
13 Extract the split pins from the track rod end balljoint nuts, then unscrew the nuts, and detach the rods from the arms on the steering knuckles using a conventional balljoint removal tool. Take care not to damage the balljoint seals.
14 Working on each side in turn, unscrew the mounting nuts, and remove the anti-roll bar links from the front suspension struts. Note that, on models fitted with ABS, the ABS sensor wiring support brackets are located beneath the nuts.
15 Working on each side in turn, note which way round the front suspension lower arm balljoint clamp bolt is fitted, then unscrew and remove it from the knuckle assembly. Lever the balljoint down from the knuckle - if it is tight, prise the joint open carefully using a large flat-bladed tool. Take care not to damage the balljoint seal during the separation procedure.
16 The subframe must now be lowered out of position. The alignment of the subframe is critical to maintaining the front suspension geometry, so take time to make suitable alignment markings for use on reassembly.
17 Support the weight of the front subframe assembly on two trolley jacks (or two scissor jacks).
18 Loosen and remove the subframe rear mounting bolts, and loosen the front mounting bolts by two turns. Lower the subframe for access to the power steering fluid pipe unions on top of the steering gear. Note that the front subframe mounting bolts are gold in colour - the rear ones are silver.
19 Position a suitable container beneath the steering gear, then unscrew the union nuts securing the power steering fluid supply, return, and cooler lines to the steering gear. Identify the lines for position, then unbolt the clamps, disconnect the lines, and allow the fluid to drain into the container. Cover the apertures in the steering gear and also the ends of the fluid pipes, to prevent the ingress of dust and dirt into the hydraulic circuit.
20 Check to see that nothing else remains connected to the subframe which would prevent it being lowered.
21 Remove the subframe front mounting bolts, and lower the subframe, together with the power steering gear, to the ground.
22 Where applicable, remove the steering gear cover plate, then unscrew the mounting bolts and remove the power steering gear from the subframe. Take care that the pressure check valve does not fall out of its port as the gear is removed.
23 Using a suitable Allen key, unscrew the clamp bolt securing the flexible coupling to the pinion shaft on the steering gear, and withdraw the coupling.
24 Refer to Section 30, paragraph 11 for details of renewing the Teflon rings.

Refitting

25 Refit the flexible coupling to the pinion shaft on the steering gear, then insert and tighten the new clamp bolt using an Allen key.
26 Locate the power steering gear on the subframe, then insert the mounting bolts and tighten to the specified torque. Where applicable, refit the cover plate, tightening the five bolts to the specified torque.
27 Raise the subframe until it is possible to refit the fluid lines. Support the subframe securely while tightening the union nuts and clamps.
28 Raise the subframe into position, making sure that the alignment holes are in line with the holes in the underbody. At the same time, make sure that the flexible coupling locates correctly on the steering column.

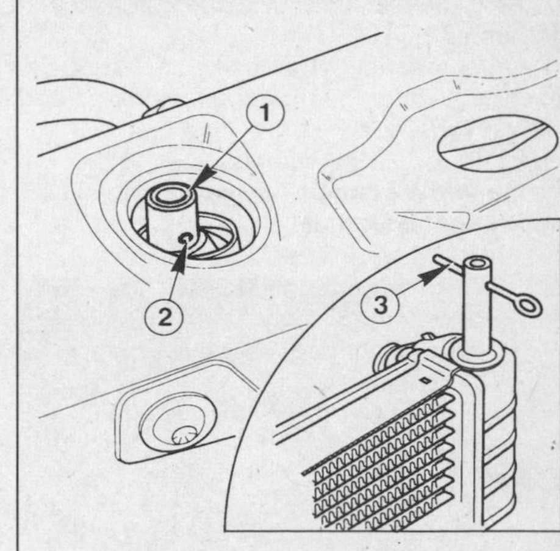

31.8 Method of supporting the radiator in its raised position

1 Radiator upper mounting extension
2 Small hole
3 Pin or split pin inserted through hole

10

29 Use the alignment markings made on removal to refit the subframe in exactly the same position as before - Ford technicians use special aligning tools for this, but if the subframe is refitted accurately, these should not be necessary. When the subframe is correctly aligned, progressively tighten the mounting bolts to the specified torque.

30 Refit and tighten the engine front and rear mounting bolts to the specified torque (see the relevant Part of Chapter 2). On models with automatic transmission, if the rear mounting does not sit centrally in the mounting bracket, loosen the bracket bolts and centre the mounting. Tighten the bracket bolts to the specified torque, then tighten the mounting through-bolt (see the relevant Part of Chapter 2).

31 Working on each side in turn, refit the front suspension lower arm balljoint to the knuckle assembly, and insert the clamp bolt with its head facing forwards. Refit the nut and tighten to the specified torque.

32 Working on each side in turn, refit the anti-roll bar links and tighten the mounting nuts to the specified torque. On models fitted with ABS, don't forget to locate the wheel sensor wiring support brackets beneath the nuts.

33 Refit the track rod end balljoints to the steering knuckles, and tighten the nuts to the specified torque. Check if the split pin holes are aligned, and if necessary turn the nuts to the nearest alignment, making sure that the torque wrench setting is still within the specified range. Insert new split pins, and bend them back to secure.

34 Where applicable, insert and tighten the air conditioning accumulator bolts.

35 Refit the radiator lower mounting brackets and tighten the bolts. Refit the cover under the radiator.

36 Remove the split pins supporting the radiator in its raised position.

37 Refit the exhaust downpipe as described in Chapter 4A.

38 On manual transmission models, reconnect the gearchange linkage and support rods.

39 Refit the front wheels, and lower the vehicle to the ground. Tighten the wheel nuts to the specified torque.

34.2 Disconnect the wiring plug from the power steering fluid pressure switch

40 Working inside the vehicle, reconnect the steering column clamp plate, then insert a new bolt and tighten to the specified torque.

41 Reconnect the battery negative lead.

42 Bleed the power steering hydraulic system as described in Section 33.

43 If on completion, the car pulls to one side, or abnormal tyre wear is noted, have the subframe alignment (and front wheel alignment) checked by a Ford dealer.

32 Power steering gear rubber gaiters - renewal

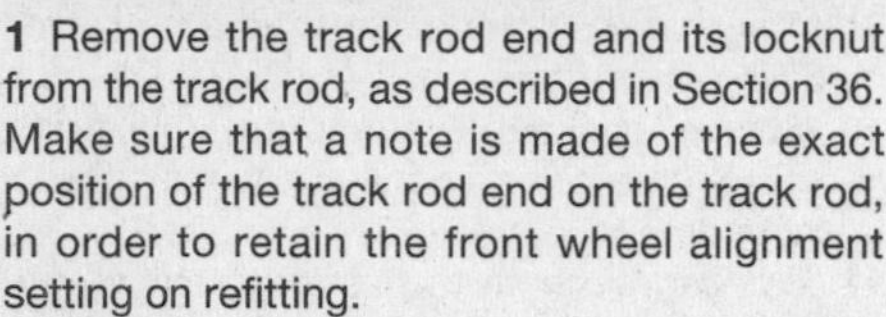

1 Remove the track rod end and its locknut from the track rod, as described in Section 36. Make sure that a note is made of the exact position of the track rod end on the track rod, in order to retain the front wheel alignment setting on refitting.

2 Release the outer retaining clip and inner plastic clamp band, and disconnect the gaiter from the steering gear housing.

3 Disconnect the breather from the gaiter, then slide the gaiter off the track rod.

4 Scrape off all grease from the old gaiter, and apply to the track rod inner joint. Wipe clean the seating areas on the steering gear housing and track rod.

5 Slide the new gaiter onto the track rod and steering gear housing, and reconnect the breather.

6 Fit a new inner plastic clamp band and outer retaining clip.

7 Refit the track rod end as described in Section 36.

8 Have the front wheel alignment checked, and if necessary adjusted, at the earliest opportunity (refer to Section 37).

33 Power steering hydraulic system - bleeding

1 Following any operation in which the power steering fluid lines have been disconnected, the power steering system must be bled, to remove any trapped air.

2 With the front wheels in the straight-ahead position, check the power steering fluid level in the reservoir and, if low, add fresh fluid until it reaches the 'MAX' or 'MAX COLD' mark. Pour the fluid slowly, to prevent air bubbles forming, and use only the specified fluid (refer to "*Weekly checks*" and Chapter 1).

3 Start the engine, and allow it to run at a fast idle. Check the hoses and connections for leaks.

4 Stop the engine, and recheck the fluid level. Add more if necessary, up to the 'MAX' or 'MAX COLD' mark.

5 Start the engine again, allow it to idle, then bleed the system by slowly turning the steering wheel from side to side several times. This should purge the system of all internal air. However, if air remains in the system (indicated by the steering operation being very noisy), leave the vehicle overnight, and repeat the procedure again the next day.

6 If air still remains in the system, it may be necessary to resort to the Ford method of bleeding, which uses a vacuum pump. Turn the steering to the right until it is near the stop, then fit the vacuum pump to the fluid reservoir, and apply 0.15 bars of vacuum. Maintain the vacuum for a minimum of 5 minutes, then repeat the procedure with the steering turned to the left.

7 Keep the fluid level topped-up throughout the bleeding procedure; note that, as the fluid temperature increases, the level will rise.

8 On completion, switch off the engine, and return the front wheels to the straight-ahead position.

34 Power steering pump - removal and refitting

Removal

1 Disconnect the battery negative (earth) lead (refer to Chapter 5A, Section 1).

2 Disconnect the fluid pressure switch wiring plug **(see illustration)**.

Four-cylinder engine models

3 Unscrew and remove the bolt securing the hydraulic fluid line support to the engine lifting bracket on the right-hand side of the engine.

4 Unscrew and remove the bolt securing the hydraulic fluid line support to the pump mounting bracket.

5 Position a suitable container beneath the power steering pump, to catch spilt fluid.

6 Loosen the clip, and disconnect the fluid supply hose from the pump inlet. Plug the hose, to prevent the ingress of dust and dirt.

7 Unscrew the union nut, and disconnect the high-pressure line from the pump. Allow the fluid to drain into the container.

8 Apply the handbrake, then jack up the front of the vehicle and support it on axle stands. Remove the right-hand front wheel.

9 Unbolt and remove the lower drivebelt cover.

10 Using a spanner, rotate the drivebelt tensioner in a clockwise direction to release the belt tension, then slip the drivebelt off the pulleys and remove from the vehicle. Refer to Chapter 1 if necessary.

11 Unscrew and remove the four mounting bolts, and withdraw the power steering pump from its bracket. Access to the bolts on the right-hand side of the engine is gained by turning the pump pulley until a hole lines up with the bolt.

V6 engine models

12 Unscrew and remove the bolt securing the hydraulic fluid line to the engine right-hand mounting.

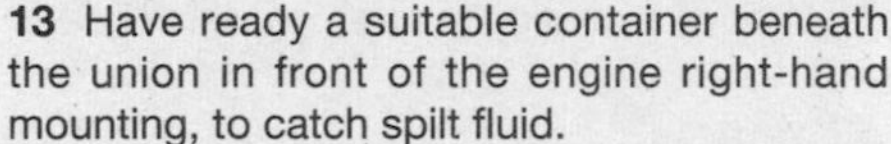
34.17 Removing the upper section of the engine right-hand mounting

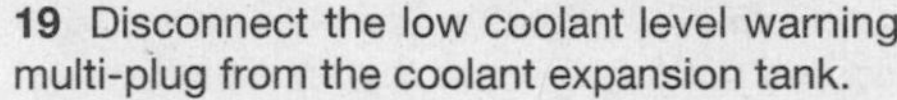
34.21a Remove the two bolts (arrowed) . . .

34.21b . . . and lift out the lower half of the engine mounting

13 Have ready a suitable container beneath the union in front of the engine right-hand mounting, to catch spilt fluid.

14 Disconnect the power steering pressure line joint union in front of the engine right-hand mounting, and let the fluid drain into the container.

15 Disconnect the fluid return hose at the rear of the engine mounting. Plug the hose and the joint union, to prevent further fluid loss or dirt ingress.

16 The right-hand side of the engine must now be supported, while the engine mounting is removed. Ideally, use an engine crane or hoist, or if available, an engine support bar located in the inner wing flanges. Supporting the engine from below is not recommended, as there is a danger of damaging the sump; if this method is chosen, use a large block of wood to spread the load.

17 Unclip the HT lead retainer, then with the engine supported, progressively loosen and remove the six nuts securing the top part of the engine right-hand mounting. Lift the mounting off the studs **(see illustration)**.

18 Refer to Chapter 1 and drain the cooling system. Anticipating a little further loss of coolant, disconnect the hoses from the expansion tank.

19 Disconnect the low coolant level warning multi-plug from the coolant expansion tank.

20 Remove the retaining bolts, and remove the expansion tank from the engine compartment.

21 Unscrew and remove the retaining bolts, and remove the lower half of the engine right-hand mounting from the inner wing **(see illustrations)**.

22 Using a suitable Allen key inserted in the centre of the pulley, hold the steering pump pulley against rotation as the four pulley bolts are loosened **(see illustration)**. Do not remove the bolts at this stage.

23 Apply the handbrake and loosen the right-hand front wheel nuts. Taking care that the engine remains adequately supported, raise the right-hand front corner of the car, and support it on axle stands. Take off the front wheel.

24 Working in the front wheel arch, loosen and remove the screws, and lower the front and rear sections of the auxiliary drivebelt cover for access to the drivebelt.

25 Using a suitable tool, such as a 3/8 inch drive handle, turn the auxiliary drivebelt tensioner clockwise to relieve the tension on the drivebelt. Slip the drivebelt off the power steering pump pulley.

34.22 Loosen the four steering pump pulley bolts

26 Fully loosen and remove the steering pump pulley bolts, and remove the pulley **(see illustration)**.

27 Remove the steering pump hydraulic pipe bracket bolt, and move the bracket aside.

28 Noting their various locations, remove the five nuts and two bolts securing the steering pump retaining plate **(see illustration)**.

29 Unscrew the two steering pump mounting bolts, and remove the pump and retaining plate from the engine **(see illustrations)**.

34.26 Removing the steering pump pulley

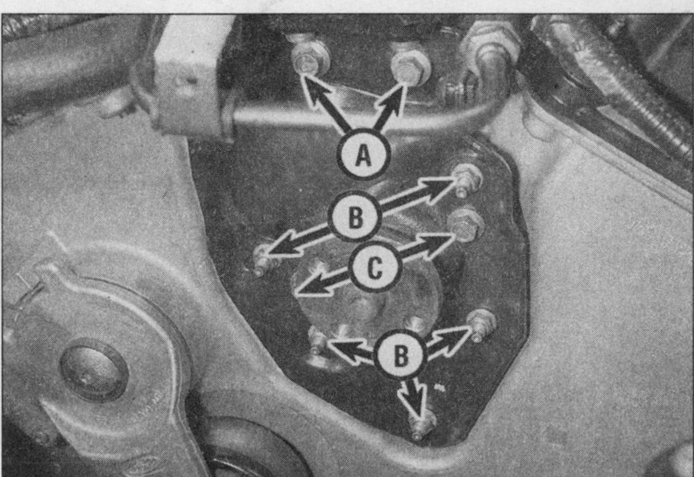

34.28 Steering pump retaining plate bolts (A) and nuts (B) - also shown are the pump mounting bolts (C)

10

34.29a Loosen the steering pump mounting bolts . . .

34.29b . . . support the pump as the bolts are removed . . .

34.29c . . . then withdraw the pump and retaining plate from the engine

Refitting

30 If necessary, the sealing ring on the high-pressure outlet should be renewed, using the same procedure as described in Section 30.

Four-cylinder engine models

31 Locate the power steering pump on the mounting bracket, and secure with the four bolts. Tighten the bolts to the specified torque.
32 Check the condition of the drivebelt before refitting it - if there is any sign of deterioration, it makes sense to fit a new one. Slip the drivebelt over the pulleys, then rotate the drivebelt tensioner in a clockwise direction, and locate the drivebelt around it. Release the tensioner to tension the drivebelt.
33 Refit the lower belt cover.
34 Refit the right-hand front wheel, and lower the vehicle to the ground. Tighten the wheel nuts to the specified torque.
35 Reconnect the high-pressure line to the pump, and tighten the union nut.
36 Reconnect the fluid supply hose to the pump inlet, and tighten the clip.
37 Refit the hydraulic fluid line support to the pump mounting bracket, and tighten the bolt.
38 Refit the hydraulic fluid line support to the engine lifting bracket on the right-hand side of the engine, and tighten the bolt.

V6 engine models

39 Offer the pump and retaining plate into position, and secure with the nuts and bolts. Note the different tightening torques for the various fasteners.
40 Refit the hydraulic pipe bracket, and secure with the bolt.
41 Refit the steering pump pulley, and tighten the four bolts to the specified torque, using an Allen key to hold the pulley against rotation.
42 Check the condition of the drivebelt before refitting it - if there is any sign of deterioration, it makes sense to fit a new one. Slip the drivebelt over the pulleys, then rotate the drivebelt tensioner in a clockwise direction, and locate the drivebelt around it. Release the tensioner to tension the drivebelt.
43 Refit the auxiliary drivebelt covers, then refit the wheel. Lower the car to the ground, again taking care that the engine remains adequately supported. Tighten the wheel nuts to the specified torque.
44 Refit the lower half of the engine right-hand mounting, tightening the bolts to the specified torque (see the relevant Part of Chapter 2).
45 Refit the coolant expansion tank to the inner wing, reconnecting all hoses and the wiring multi-plug securely.
46 Place the top half of the engine mounting into position over the studs, then fit and tighten the six nuts to the specified torque (see the relevant Part of Chapter 2). Clip the HT lead retainer back into position.
47 Once the engine mounting is recon-nected, the support bar or hoist can be removed.
48 Reconnect the fluid return hose and the pressure line joint union, tightening the joint union to the specified torque.
49 Refit the bolt which secures the hydraulic line to the engine mounting, and tighten it securely.
50 Refill the cooling system as described in Chapter 1.

All models

51 Reconnect the battery negative lead.
52 Fill and bleed the power steering hydraulic system as described in Section 33.

35 Power steering fluid cooler - removal and refitting

Removal

1 Disconnect the battery negative (earth) lead (refer to Chapter 5A, Section 1).
2 Apply the handbrake, then jack up the front of the vehicle and support it on axle stands.
3 The fluid hoses to and from the cooler must now be disconnected. The connections at the cooler itself are inaccessible with the unit in place, so trace the hoses back from the cooler, and disconnect them at the front of the subframe. Alternatively, remove the front bumper as described in Chapter 11 for access **(see illustration)**. Have a container ready to catch spilt fluid, and plug the open hose ends quickly, to prevent fluid loss and dirt entry.
4 If a long enough spanner is available, the cooler mounting bolts can be reached from above; take care not to damage the radiator (or the air conditioning condenser). Remove the two mounting bolts, and slide the cooler (and where applicable, its hoses) out of position **(see illustrations)**. Handle the unit carefully, as the cooling fins are easily damaged.

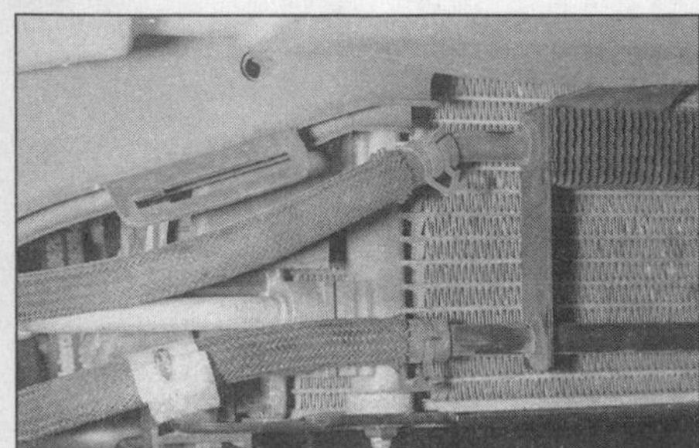
35.3 The fluid cooler hose connections are more easily reached with the front bumper removed

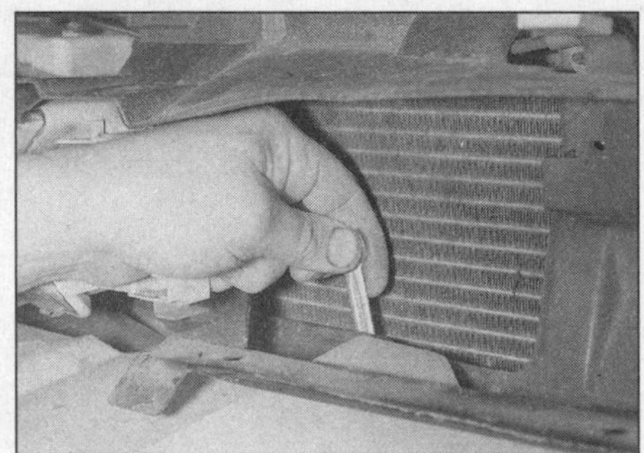
35.4a The cooler mounting bolts may be reached from above

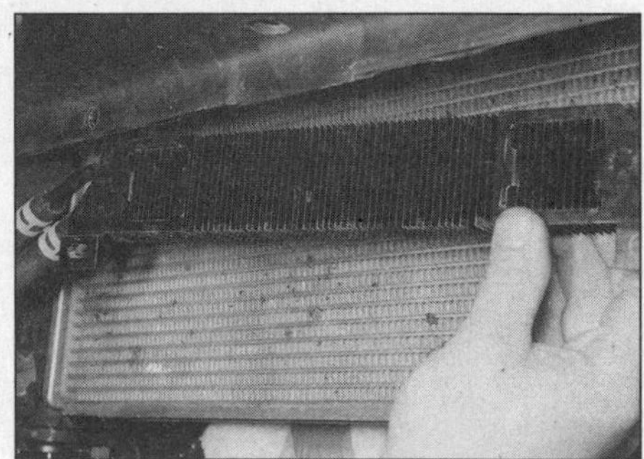
35.4b Removing the power steering fluid cooler from in front of the radiator

Refitting

5 Refitting is a reversal of removal. It may be wise to replace the spring-type hose clips with screw-type items when reconnecting the fluid hoses. On completion, fill and bleed the power steering system as described in Section 33.

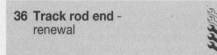

36 Track rod end - renewal

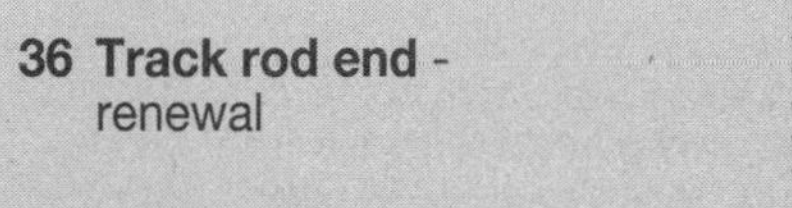

Removal

1 Apply the handbrake and loosen the relevant front wheel nuts. Jack up the front of the vehicle and support it on axle stands. Remove the front roadwheel.

2 Using a suitable spanner, slacken the locknut on the track rod by a quarter-turn. Hold the track rod end stationary with another spanner engaged with the special flats while loosening the locknut **(see illustration)**.

3 Extract the split pin, then unscrew and remove the track rod end balljoint retaining nut.

4 To release the tapered shank of the balljoint from the steering knuckle arm, use a balljoint separator tool **(see illustration)**. If the balljoint is to be re-used, take care not to damage the dust cover when using the separator tool.

5 Count the number of exposed threads visible on the inner section of the track rod, and record this figure.

6 Unscrew the track rod end from the track rod, counting the number of turns necessary to remove it. If necessary, hold the track rod stationary with grips.

Refitting

7 Screw the track rod end onto the track rod by the number of turns noted during removal, until it just contacts the locknut.

8 Engage the shank of the balljoint with the steering knuckle arm, and refit the nut. Tighten the nut to the specified torque. If the balljoint shank turns while the nut is being tightened, press down on the balljoint. The tapered fit of the shank will lock it, and prevent rotation as the nut is tightened.

9 Check that the split pin holes in the nut and balljoint shank are aligned. If necessary turn the nut to the nearest alignment, making sure that the torque wrench setting is still within the specified range. Insert a new split pin, and bend it back to secure.

10 Now tighten the locknut, while holding the track rod end as before.

11 Refit the roadwheel, and lower the vehicle to the ground.

12 Finally check, and if necessary adjust, the front wheel alignment as described in Section 37.

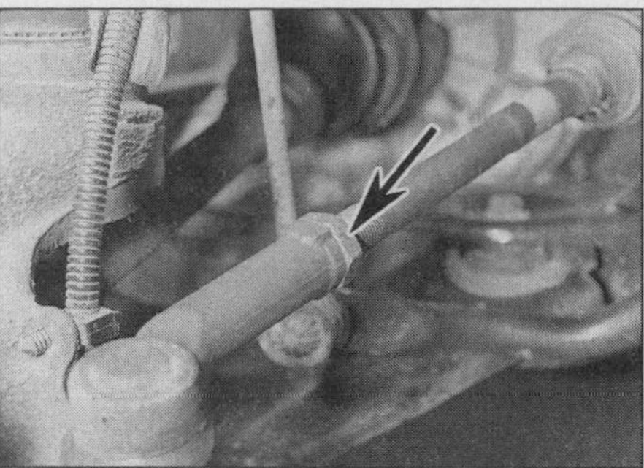

36.2 Track rod end locknut (arrowed)

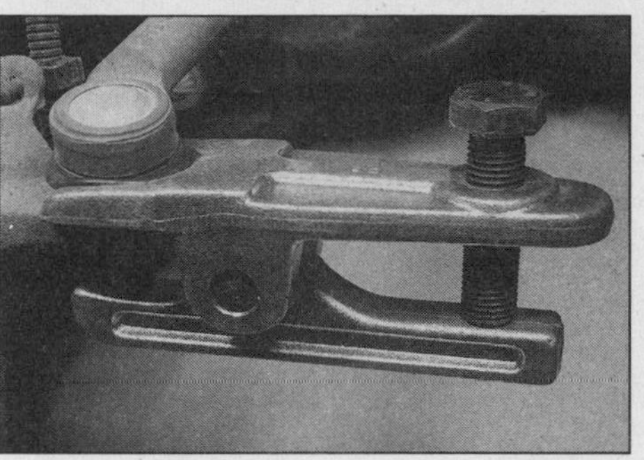

36.4 Using a balljoint separator tool to release the track rod end balljoint

37 Wheel alignment and steering angles - general information

1 Accurate front wheel alignment is essential to provide positive steering, and to prevent excessive tyre wear. Before considering the steering/suspension geometry, check that the tyres are correctly inflated, that the front wheels are not buckled, and that the steering linkage and suspension joints are in good order, without slackness or wear. Alignment of the front subframe is also critical to the front suspension geometry - refer to a Ford dealer for accurate setting-up.

2 Wheel alignment consists of four factors **(see illustration)**:

Camber is the angle at which the front wheels are set from the vertical, when viewed from the front of the vehicle. 'Positive camber' is the amount (in degrees) that the wheels are tilted outward at the top of the vertical.

Castor is the angle between the steering axis and a vertical line, when viewed from each side of the car. 'Positive castor' is when the steering axis is inclined rearward at the top.

Steering axis inclination is the angle (when viewed from the front of the vehicle) between the vertical and an imaginary line drawn through the suspension strut upper mounting and the lower suspension arm balljoint.

Toe setting is the amount by which the distance between the front inside edges of the roadwheels (measured at hub height) differs from the diametrically-opposite distance measured between the rear inside edges of the front roadwheels.

3 With the exception of the toe setting, all other steering angles are set during manufacture, and no adjustment is possible. It can be assumed, therefore, that unless the vehicle has suffered accident damage, all the preset steering angles will be correct. Should there be some doubt about their accuracy, it will be necessary to seek the help of a Ford dealer, as special gauges are needed to check the steering angles.

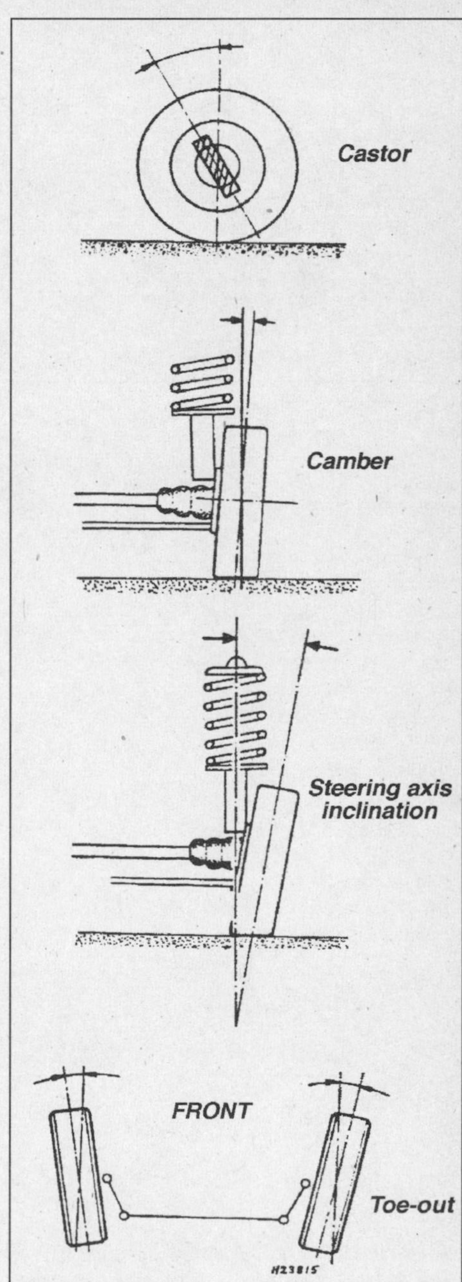

37.2 Wheel alignment and steering angles

4 Two methods are available to the home mechanic for checking the toe setting. One method is to use a gauge to measure the distance between the front and rear inside edges of the roadwheels. The other method is to use a scuff plate, in which each front wheel is rolled across a movable plate which records any deviation, or scuff, of the tyre from the straight-ahead position as it moves across the plate. Relatively-inexpensive equipment of both types is available from accessory outlets.
5 If, after checking the toe setting using whichever method is preferable, it is found that adjustment is necessary, proceed as follows.
6 Turn the steering wheel onto full-left lock, and record the number of exposed threads on the right-hand track rod. Now turn the steering onto full-right lock, and record the number of threads on the left-hand track rod. If there are the same number of threads visible on both sides, then subsequent adjustment can be made equally on both sides. If there are more threads visible on one side than the other, it will be necessary to compensate for this during adjustment. After adjustment, there must be the same number of threads visible on each track rod. This is most important.
7 To alter the toe setting, slacken the locknut on the track rod, and turn the track rod using self-locking pliers to achieve the desired setting. When viewed from the side of the car, turning the rod clockwise will increase the toe-in, turning it anti-clockwise will increase the toe-out. Only turn the track rods by a quarter of a turn each time, and then recheck the setting.
8 After adjustment, tighten the locknuts. Reposition the steering gear rubber gaiters, to remove any twist caused by turning the track rods.
9 The rear wheel toe setting may also be checked and adjusted, but as this additionally requires alignment with the front wheels, it should be left to a Ford dealer or specialist having the required equipment.

Chapter 11
Bodywork and fittings

Contents

Degrees of difficulty

Easy, suitable for novice with little experience 

Fairly easy, suitable for beginner with some experience 

Fairly difficult, suitable for competent DIY mechanic 

Difficult, suitable for experienced DIY mechanic 

Very difficult, suitable for expert DIY or professional

Specifications

Torque wrench settings	**Nm**	**lbf ft**
Bonnet and tailgate hinges	24	18
Boot lid	10	7
Bumper mounting nuts	10	7
Front seat mounting bolts	28	21
Rear seat backrest catch retaining bolts	30	22
Rear seat hinge pins	20	15
Seat belt mounting nuts and bolts	38	28

1 General information

The bodyshell and underframe on all models is of all-steel welded construction, incorporating progressive crumple zones at the front and rear, and a rigid centre safety cell.

The bulkhead behind the engine compartment incorporates crash grooves which determine its energy-absorption characteristics, and special beams to prevent the intrusion of the front wheels into the passenger compartment during a serious accident. All passenger doors incorporate side impact bars.

All sheet metal surfaces which are prone to corrosion are galvanised. The painting process includes a base colour which closely matches the final topcoat, so that any stone damage is not as noticeable.

Automatic seat belts are fitted to all models, and the front seat belt stalks are mounted on automatic tensioners (also known as 'grabbers'). In the event of a serious front impact, the system is triggered and pulls the stalk buckle downwards to tension the seat belt. It is not possible to reset the tensioner once fired, and it must therefore be renewed. On models up to 1996, the system utilises a spring mass sensor and a coil spring to fire the mechanism **(see illustration)**, and the tensioners can in theory operate independently of the air bag. From 1997 onwards, the tensioners are fired by an explosive charge similar to that used in the air bag, and are triggered via the air bag control module.

In the UK, central locking is standard on all models **(see illustration)**. In other countries, it is available on certain models only. Where double-locking is fitted, the lock mechanism is disconnected (when the system is in use) from the interior door handles, making it impossible to open any of the doors or the tailgate/bootlid from inside the vehicle. This means that, even if a thief should break a side window, he will not be able to open the door using the interior handle. Models with the double-locking system are fitted with a control module located beneath the facia on the right-hand side. In the event of a serious accident, a crash sensor unlocks all doors if they were previously locked.

Many of the procedures in this Chapter require the battery to be disconnected. Refer to Chapter 5A, Section 1 first.

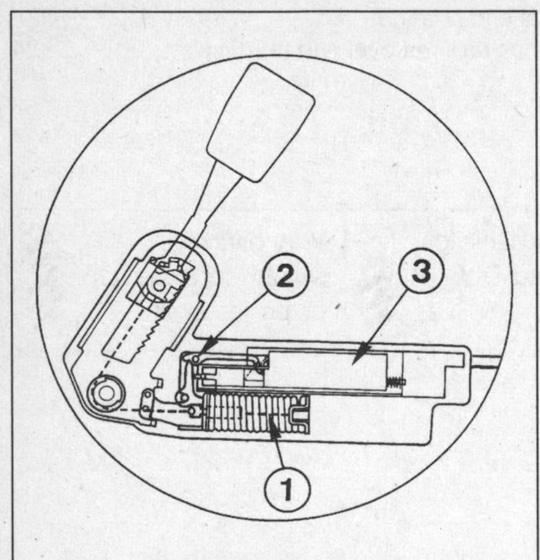

1.4 Seat belt tensioner - models up to 1996

1 Coil spring
3 Spring mass sensor
2 Lever system

2 Maintenance - bodywork and underframe

The general condition of a vehicle's bodywork is the one thing that significantly affects its value. Maintenance is easy, but needs to be regular. Neglect, particularly after minor damage, can lead quickly to further deterioration and costly repair bills. It is important also to keep watch on those parts of the vehicle not immediately visible, for instance the underside, inside all the wheel arches, and the lower part of the engine compartment.

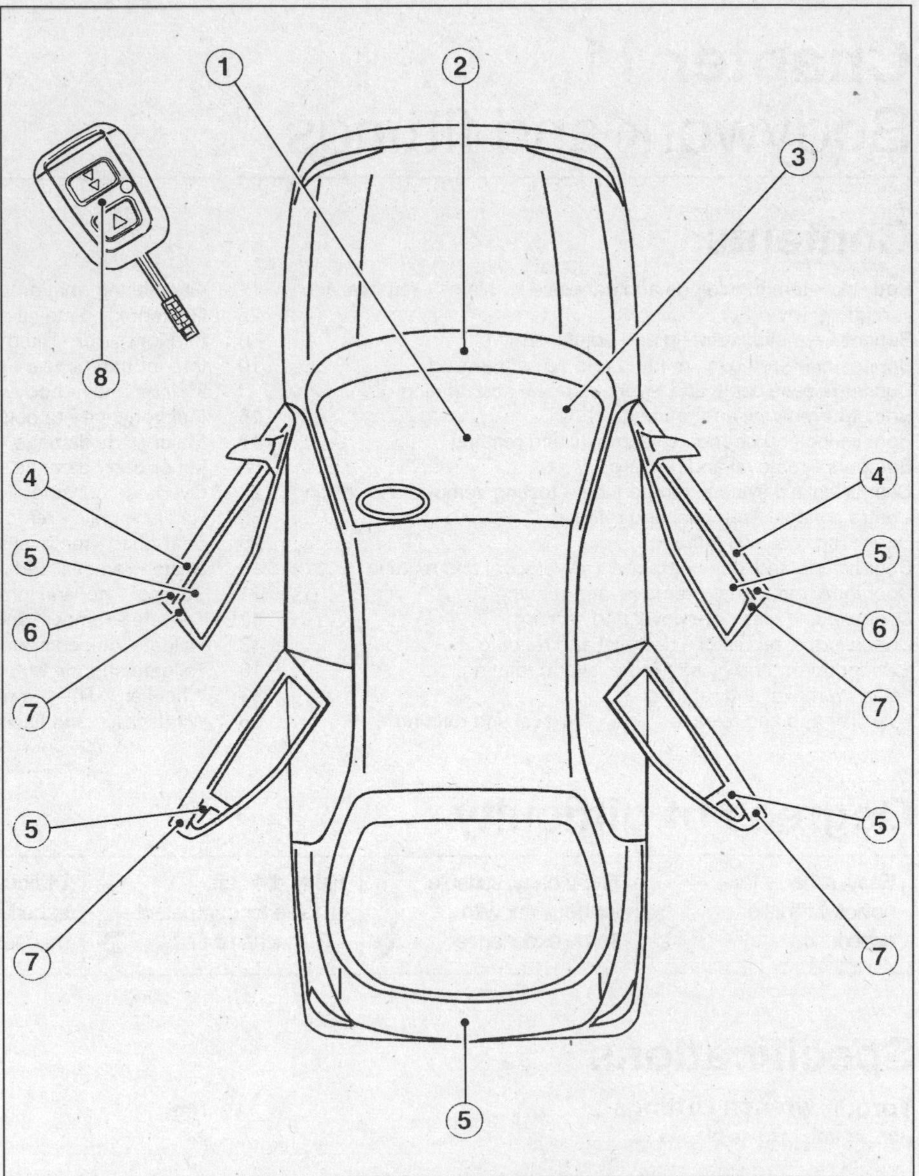

1.5 Central locking component locations

1 Indicator light
2 Buzzer
3 Central locking module
4 Infra-red receiver
5 Lock motor
6 Set/reset switch
7 Ajar switch
8 Infra-red transmitter

The basic maintenance routine for the bodywork is washing - preferably with a lot of water, from a hose. This will remove all the loose solids which may have stuck to the vehicle. It is important to flush these off in such a way as to prevent grit from scratching the finish. The wheel arches and underframe need washing in the same way, to remove any accumulated mud, which will retain moisture and tend to encourage rust. Paradoxically enough, the best time to clean the underframe and wheel arches is in wet weather, when the mud is thoroughly wet and soft. In very wet weather, the underframe is usually cleaned of large accumulations automatically, and this is a good time for inspection.

Periodically, except on vehicles with a wax-based underbody protective coating, it is a good idea to have the whole of the underframe of the vehicle steam-cleaned, engine compartment included, so that a thorough inspection can be carried out to see what minor repairs and renovations are necessary. Steam-cleaning is available at many garages, and is necessary for the removal of the accumulation of oily grime, which sometimes is allowed to become thick in certain areas. If steam-cleaning facilities are not available, there are some excellent grease solvents available which can be brush-applied; the dirt can then be simply hosed off. Note that these methods should not be used on vehicles with wax-based underbody protective coating, or the coating will be removed. Such vehicles should be inspected annually, preferably just prior to Winter, when the underbody should be washed down, and any damage to the wax coating repaired. Ideally, a completely fresh coat should be applied. It would also be worth considering the use of such wax-based protection for injection into door panels, sills, box sections, etc, as an additional safeguard against rust damage, where such protection is not provided by the vehicle manufacturer.

After washing paintwork, wipe off with a chamois leather to give an unspotted clear finish. A coat of clear protective wax polish will give added protection against chemical pollutants in the air. If the paintwork sheen has dulled or oxidised, use a cleaner/polisher combination to restore the brilliance of the shine. This requires a little effort, but such dulling is usually caused because regular washing has been neglected. Care needs to be taken with metallic paintwork, as special non-abrasive cleaner/polisher is required to avoid damage to the finish. Always check that the door and ventilator opening drain holes and pipes are completely clear, so that water can be drained out. Brightwork should be treated in the same way as paintwork. Windscreens and windows can be kept clear of the smeary film which often appears, by the use of proprietary glass cleaner. Never use any form of wax or other body or chromium polish on glass.

3 Maintenance - upholstery and carpets

Mats and carpets should be brushed or vacuum-cleaned regularly, to keep them free of grit. If they are badly stained, remove them from the vehicle for scrubbing or sponging, and make quite sure they are dry before refitting. Seats and interior trim panels can be kept clean by wiping with a damp cloth. If they do become stained (which can be more apparent on light-coloured upholstery), use a little liquid detergent and a soft nail brush to scour the grime out of the grain of the material. Do not forget to keep the headlining clean in the same way as the upholstery. When using liquid cleaners inside the vehicle, do not over-wet the surfaces being cleaned. Excessive damp could get into the seams and padded interior, causing stains, offensive odours or even rot.

Caution: If the inside of the vehicle gets wet accidentally, it is worthwhile taking some trouble to dry it out properly, particularly where carpets are involved. Do not leave oil or electric heaters inside the vehicle for this purpose.

4 Minor body damage - repair

Repairs of minor scratches in bodywork

If the scratch is very superficial, and does not penetrate to the metal of the bodywork, repair is very simple. Lightly rub the area of the scratch with a paintwork renovator, or a very fine cutting paste, to remove loose paint from the scratch, and to clear the surrounding bodywork of wax polish. Rinse the area with clean water.

Apply touch-up paint to the scratch using a fine paint brush; continue to apply fine layers of paint until the surface of the paint in the scratch is level with the surrounding paintwork. Allow the new paint at least two weeks to harden, then blend it into the surrounding paintwork by rubbing the scratch area with a paintwork renovator or a very fine cutting paste. Finally, apply wax polish.

Where the scratch has penetrated right through to the metal of the bodywork, causing the metal to rust, a different repair technique is required. Remove any loose rust from the bottom of the scratch with a penknife, then apply rust-inhibiting paint to prevent the formation of rust in the future. Using a rubber or nylon applicator, fill the scratch with bodystopper paste. If required, this paste can be mixed with cellulose thinners to provide a very thin paste which is ideal for filling narrow scratches. Before the stopper-paste in the scratch hardens, wrap a piece of smooth cotton rag around the top of a finger. Dip the finger in cellulose thinners, and quickly sweep it across the surface of the stopper-paste in the scratch; this will ensure that the surface of the stopper-paste is slightly hollowed. The scratch can now be painted over as described earlier in this Section.

Repairs of dents in bodywork

When deep denting of the vehicle's bodywork has taken place, the first task is to pull the dent out, until the affected bodywork almost attains its original shape. There is little point in trying to restore the original shape completely, as the metal in the damaged area will have stretched on impact, and cannot be reshaped fully to its original contour. It is better to bring the level of the dent up to a point which is about 3 mm below the level of the surrounding bodywork. In cases where the dent is very shallow anyway, it is not worth trying to pull it out at all. If the underside of the dent is accessible, it can be hammered out gently from behind, using a mallet with a wooden or plastic head. Whilst doing this, hold a suitable block of wood firmly against the outside of the panel, to absorb the impact from the hammer blows and thus prevent a large area of the bodywork from being 'belled-out'.

Should the dent be in a section of the bodywork which has a double skin, or some other factor making it inaccessible from behind, a different technique is called for. Drill several small holes through the metal inside the area - particularly in the deeper section. Then screw long self-tapping screws into the holes, just sufficiently for them to gain a good purchase in the metal. Now the dent can be pulled out by pulling on the protruding heads of the screws with a pair of pliers.

The next stage of the repair is the removal of the paint from the damaged area, and from an inch or so of the surrounding 'sound' bodywork. This is accomplished most easily by using a wire brush or abrasive pad on a power drill, although it can be done just as effectively by hand, using sheets of abrasive paper. To complete the preparation for filling, score the surface of the bare metal with a screwdriver or the tang of a file, or alternatively, drill small holes in the affected area. This will provide a really good 'key' for the filler paste.

To complete the repair, see the Section on filling and respraying.

Repairs of rust holes or gashes in bodywork

Remove all paint from the affected area, and from an inch or so of the surrounding 'sound' bodywork, using an abrasive pad or a wire brush on a power drill. If these are not available, a few sheets of abrasive paper will do the job most effectively. With the paint removed, you will be able to judge the severity of the corrosion, and therefore decide whether to renew the whole panel (if this is possible) or to repair the affected area. New body panels are not as expensive as most people think, and it is often quicker and more satisfactory to fit a new panel than to attempt to repair large areas of corrosion.

Remove all fittings from the affected area, except those which will act as a guide to the original shape of the damaged bodywork (eg headlight shells etc). Then, using tin snips or a hacksaw blade, remove all loose metal and any other metal badly affected by corrosion. Hammer the edges of the hole inwards, in order to create a slight depression for the filler paste.

Wire-brush the affected area to remove the powdery rust from the surface of the remaining metal. Paint the affected area with rust-inhibiting paint, if the back of the rusted area is accessible, treat this also.

Before filling can take place, it will be necessary to block the hole in some way. This can be achieved by the use of aluminium or plastic mesh, or aluminium tape.

Aluminium or plastic mesh, or glass-fibre matting, is probably the best material to use for a large hole. Cut a piece to the approximate size and shape of the hole to be filled, then position it in the hole so that its edges are below the level of the surrounding bodywork. It can be retained in position by several blobs of filler paste around its periphery.

Aluminium tape should be used for small or very narrow holes. Pull a piece off the roll, trim it to the approximate size and shape required, then pull off the backing paper (if used) and stick the tape over the hole; it can be overlapped if the thickness of one piece is insufficient. Burnish down the edges of the tape with the handle of a screwdriver or similar, to ensure that the tape is securely attached to the metal underneath.

Bodywork repairs - filling and respraying

Before using this Section, see the Sections on dent, deep scratch, rust holes and gash repairs.

Many types of bodyfiller are available, but generally speaking, those proprietary kits which contain a tin of filler paste and a tube of resin hardener are best for this type of repair. A wide, flexible plastic or nylon applicator will be found invaluable for imparting a smooth and well-contoured finish to the surface of the filler.

Mix up a little filler on a clean piece of card or board - measure the hardener carefully (follow the maker's instructions on the pack), otherwise the filler will set too rapidly or too slowly. Using the applicator, apply the filler paste to the prepared area; draw the applicator across the surface of the filler to achieve the correct contour and to level the surface. As soon as a contour that approximates to the correct one is achieved, stop working the paste - if you carry on too long, the paste will become sticky and begin to 'pick-up' on the applicator. Continue to add thin layers of filler paste at 20-minute intervals, until the level of the filler is just proud of the surrounding bodywork.

Once the filler has hardened, the excess can be removed using a metal plane or file. From then on, progressively-finer grades of abrasive paper should be used, starting with a 40-grade production paper, and finishing with a 400-grade wet-and-dry paper. Always wrap the abrasive paper around a flat rubber, cork, or wooden block - otherwise the surface of the filler will not be completely flat. During the smoothing of the filler surface, the wet-and-dry paper should be periodically rinsed in water. This will ensure that a very smooth finish is imparted to the filler at the final stage.

At this stage, the 'dent' should be surrounded by a ring of bare metal, which in turn should be encircled by the finely 'feathered' edge of the good paintwork. Rinse the repair area with clean water, until all of the dust produced by the rubbing-down operation has gone.

Spray the whole area with a light coat of primer - this will show up any imperfections in the surface of the filler. Repair these imperfections with fresh filler paste or bodystopper, and once more smooth the surface with abrasive paper. Repeat this spray-and-repair procedure until you are satisfied that the surface of the filler, and the feathered edge of the paintwork, are perfect. Clean the repair area with clean water, and allow to dry fully.

If bodystopper is used, it can be mixed with cellulose thinners, to form a really thin paste which is ideal for filling small holes.

The repair area is now ready for final spraying. Paint spraying must be carried out in a warm, dry, windless and dust-free atmosphere. This condition can be created artificially if you have access to a large indoor working area, but if you are forced to work in the open, you will have to pick your day very carefully. If you are working indoors, dousing the floor in the work area with water will help to settle the dust which would otherwise be in the atmosphere. If the repair area is confined to one body panel, mask off the surrounding panels; this will help to minimise the effects of a slight mis-match in paint colours. Bodywork fittings (eg chrome strips, door handles etc) will also need to be masked off. Use genuine masking tape, and several thicknesses of newspaper, for the masking operations.

Before commencing to spray, agitate the aerosol can thoroughly, then spray a test area (an old tin, or similar) until the technique is mastered. Cover the repair area with a thick coat of primer; the thickness should be built up using several thin layers of paint, rather than one thick one. Using 400-grade wet-and-dry paper, rub down the surface of the primer until it is really smooth. While doing this, the work area should be thoroughly doused with water, and the wet-and-dry paper periodically rinsed in water. Allow to dry before spraying on more paint.

Spray on the top coat, again building up the thickness by using several thin layers of paint. Start spraying at one edge of the repair area, and then, using a side-to-side motion, work until the whole repair area and about 2 inches of the surrounding original paintwork is covered. Remove all masking material 10 to 15 minutes after spraying on the final coat of paint.

Allow the new paint at least two weeks to harden, then, using a paintwork renovator, or a very fine cutting paste, blend the edges of the paint into the existing paintwork. Finally, apply wax polish.

Plastic components

With the use of more and more plastic body components by the vehicle manufacturers (eg bumpers. spoilers, and in some cases major body panels), rectification of more serious damage to such items has become a matter of either entrusting repair work to a specialist in this field, or renewing complete components. Repair of such damage by the DIY owner is not really feasible, owing to the cost of the equipment and materials required for effecting such repairs. The basic technique involves making a groove along the line of the crack in the plastic, using a rotary burr in a power drill. The damaged part is then welded back together, using a hot-air gun to heat up and fuse a plastic filler rod into the groove. Any excess plastic is then removed, and the area rubbed down to a smooth finish. It is important that a filler rod of the correct plastic is used, as body components can be made of a variety of different types (eg polycarbonate, ABS, polypropylene).

Damage of a less serious nature (abrasions, minor cracks etc) can be repaired by the DIY owner using a two-part epoxy filler repair material. Once mixed in equal proportions, this is used in similar fashion to the bodywork filler used on metal panels. The filler is usually cured in twenty to thirty minutes, ready for sanding and painting.

If the owner is renewing a complete component himself, or if he has repaired it with epoxy filler, he will be left with the problem of finding a suitable paint for finishing which is compatible with the type of plastic used. At one time, the use of a universal paint was not possible, owing to the complex range of plastics encountered in body component applications. Standard paints, generally speaking, will not bond to plastic or rubber satisfactorily. However, it is now possible to obtain a plastic body parts finishing kit which consists of a pre-primer treatment, a primer and coloured top coat. Full instructions are normally supplied with a kit, but basically, the method of use is to first apply the pre-primer to the component concerned, and allow it to dry for up to 30 minutes. Then the primer is applied, and left to dry for about an hour before finally applying the special-coloured top coat. The result is a correctly-coloured component, where the paint will flex with the plastic or rubber, a property that standard paint does not normally posses.

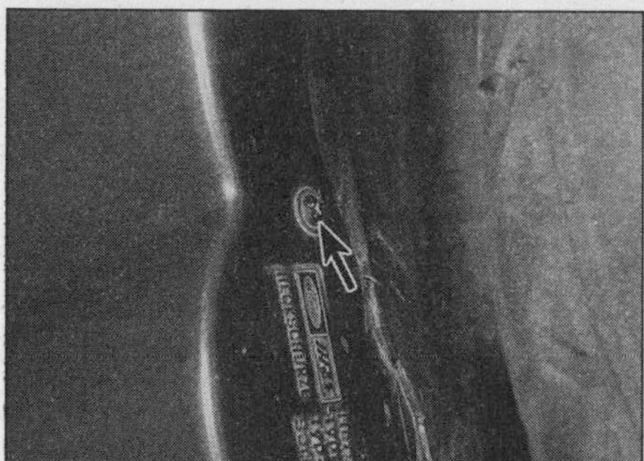
6.4 Screw (arrowed) securing the wheel arch liner to the front bumper

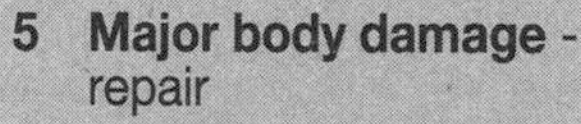

5 Major body damage - repair

Where serious damage has occurred, or large areas need renewal due to neglect, it means that complete new panels will need welding-in; this is best left to professionals. If the damage is due to impact, it will also be necessary to check completely the alignment of the bodyshell; this can only be carried out accurately by a Ford dealer, using special jigs. If the body is left misaligned, it is primarily dangerous, as the car will not handle properly, and secondly, uneven stresses will be imposed on the steering, suspension and possibly transmission, causing abnormal wear or complete failure, particularly to items such as the tyres.

6.6 Remove the three bumper retaining clips (arrowed) below the radiator grille

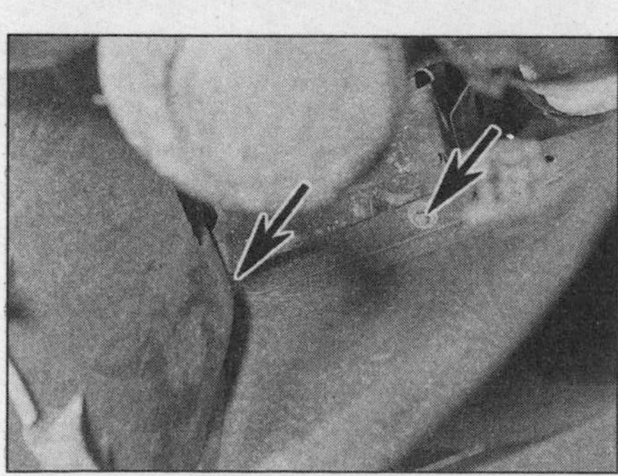
6.11a Remove the two bumper mounting screws (arrowed) from underneath . . .

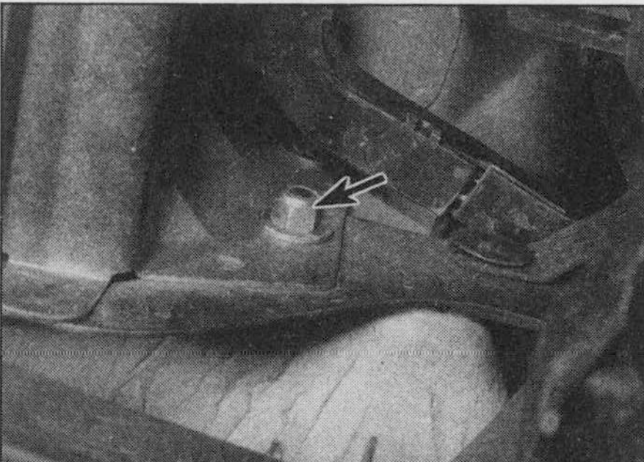
6.5a Front bumper mounting bolt (arrowed)

6 Bumpers - removal and refitting

Removal

Front bumper - models up to 1996

1 Apply the handbrake, jack up the front of the vehicle and support it on axle stands.

2 Where applicable, disconnect the wiring plugs from the front foglights (Chapter 12).

3 Where applicable, disconnect the tubing from the headlight washer pump. Be prepared for loss of fluid as this is done, and have ready a container to catch the spilt fluid.

4 Unscrew the screws securing the wheel arch liners to the front bumper **(see illustration)**.

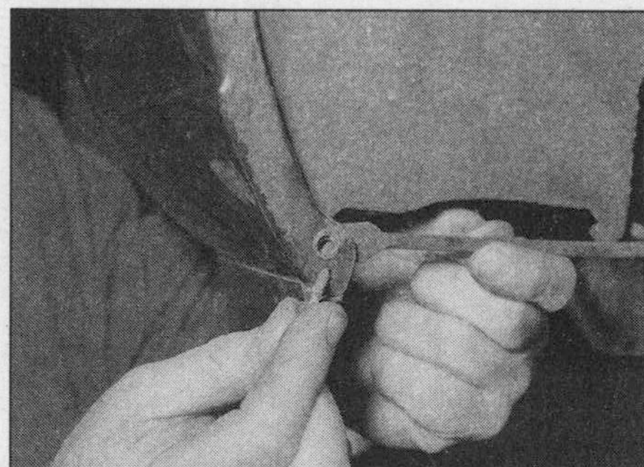
6.10 Remove the bumper stay screw

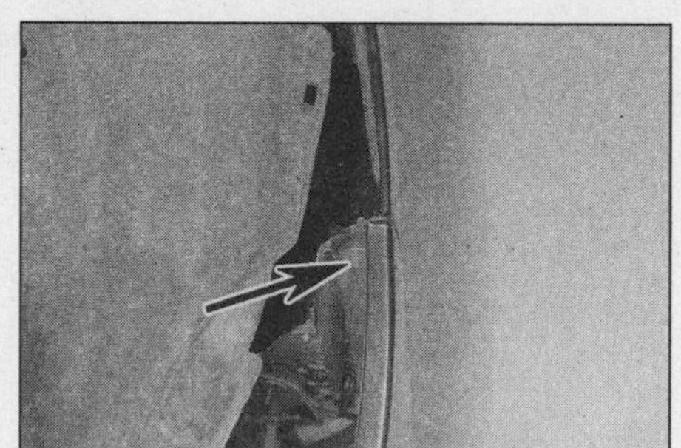
6.11b . . . the rear screw (arrowed) can be reached once the front of the wheel arch liner has been pulled back

6.5b Disconnecting the front bumper from the side guides

5 Unscrew the bumper mounting nuts, and withdraw the bumper forwards from the vehicle, at the same time disconnecting the guides from the side pins **(see illustrations)**. As the bumper is withdrawn, disconnect wiring from the low air temperature sensor, where applicable.

Front bumper - 1997 models onwards

6 Remove the radiator grille as described in Section 7, then prise out and remove the three clips beneath it **(see illustration)**.

7 Apply the handbrake, jack up the front of the vehicle and support it on axle stands. Working under the front of the car, remove the clips and screws securing the radiator lower cover, and remove the cover.

8 Where applicable, disconnect the wiring plugs from the front foglights (see Chapter 12).

9 Where applicable, disconnect the tubing from the headlight washer pump. Be prepared for loss of fluid as this is done, and have ready a container to catch the spilt fluid.

10 At each bumper end, remove the screw from each bumper stay bar **(see illustration)**.

11 Working from underneath, unscrew and remove the two mounting screws each side - if preferred, the rearmost screw can be reached from inside the wheel arch, once the wheel arch liner screws have been removed **(see illustrations)**. Have an assistant ready to support the bumper once the first pair of screws is removed.

12 Withdraw the bumper forwards from the front of the car, and remove it **(see illustration)**.

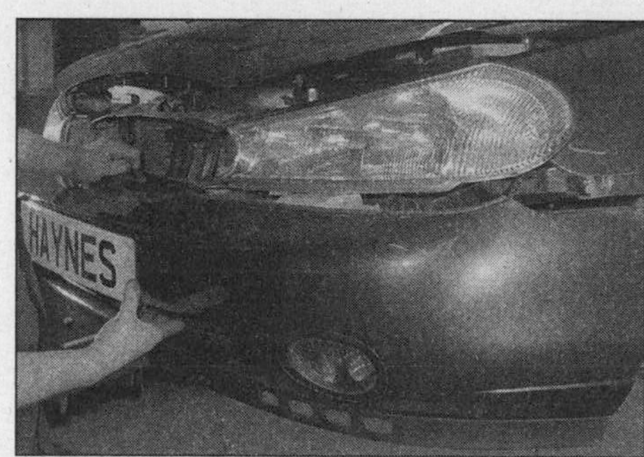

6.12 Removing the front bumper

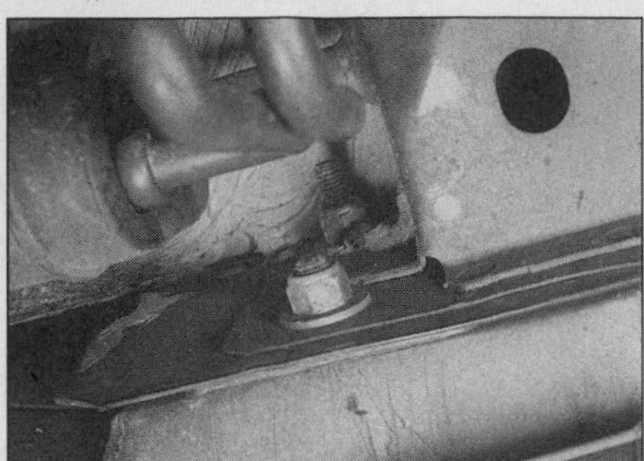
6.16 Rear bumper mounting nuts

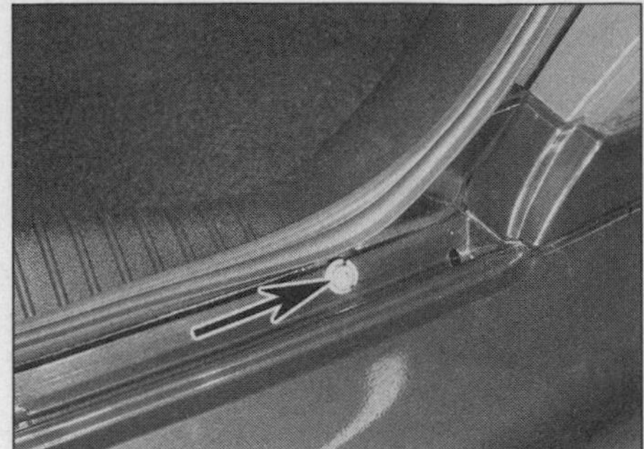
6.17 One of the bumper top edge securing screws (arrowed)

6.19 Removing a bumper-to-wheel arch liner screw

Rear bumper - all models up to 1996

13 Chock the front wheels, jack up the rear of the vehicle and support it on axle stands.

14 Disconnect the rear exhaust mounting rubber, and support the exhaust system on an axle stand.

15 Remove the screws securing the wheel arch liners to the rear bumper.

16 Unscrew the bumper mounting nuts **(see illustration)**, and withdraw the bumper rearwards from the vehicle, at the same time disconnecting the guides from the side pins.

Rear bumper - Saloon and Hatchback models, 1997 onwards

Caution: Wear gloves when handling the rear bumper, as the bottom edge is sharp enough to cause injury.

17 Open the bootlid or tailgate, and remove the two screws securing the top edge of the bumper **(see illustration)**.

18 Chock the front wheels, jack up the rear of the vehicle and support it on axle stands.

19 Remove the screw each side securing the bottom of the bumper end to the wheel arch liner **(see illustration)**.

20 Remove the screws as necessary, and detach the rear edge of the wheel arch liner for access to the bumper upper screw **(see illustration)**.

21 Remove the two screws on the underside of the bumper **(see illustration)**.

22 With the help of an assistant, pull the bumper rearwards to disengage the side pegs.

23 On models with the ultrasonic parking sensor, disconnect the wiring plugs from the sensors as they become accessible.

Rear bumper - Estate models, 1997 onwards

24 Chock the front wheels, jack up the rear of the vehicle and support it on axle stands.

25 Remove the screw each side securing the bottom of the bumper end to the wheel arch liner **(see illustration)**.

26 Remove the screws and clips securing the rear wheel arch liners, and remove the liners **(see illustrations)**.

27 Remove the upper screw each side securing the top of the bumper end to the rear wing **(see illustration)**.

28 Working underneath the rear of the

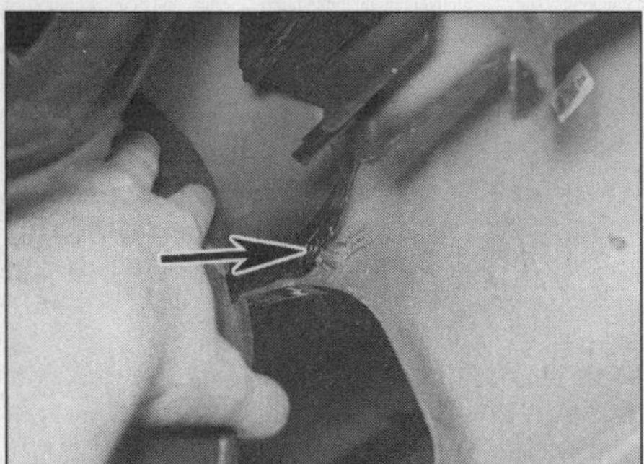
6.20 Bumper-to-wing screw (arrowed) seen from below, with wheel arch liner held aside

6.21 Rear bumper lower securing screws

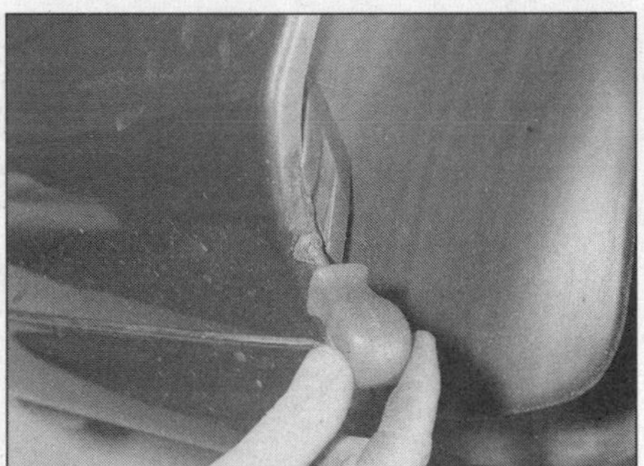
6.25 Remove the bumper-to-wheel arch lower screw

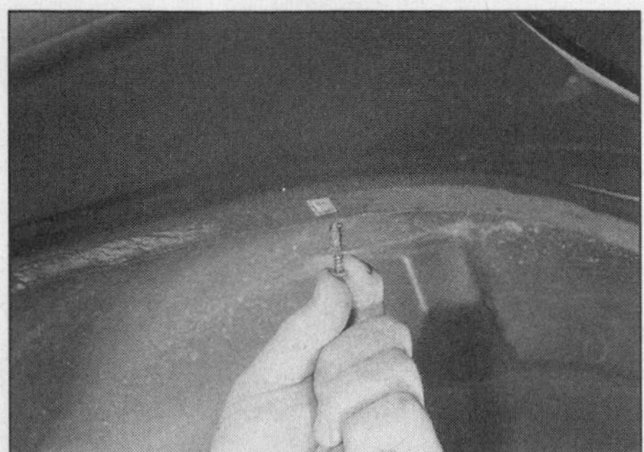
6.26a Remove the screw and clip at the top . . .

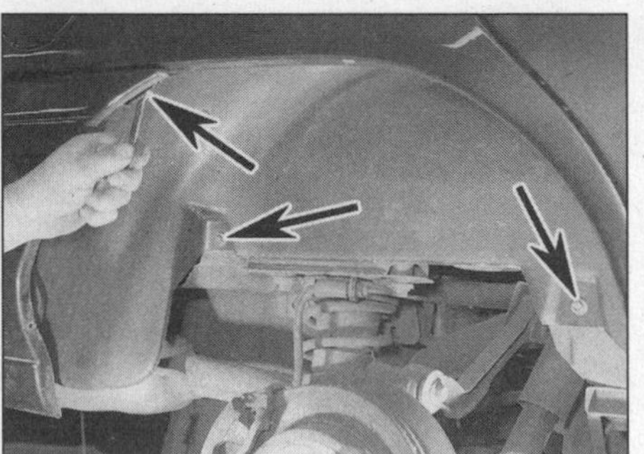
6.26b . . . and the rest of the screws (arrowed) . . .

6.26c . . . and lower the wheel arch liner

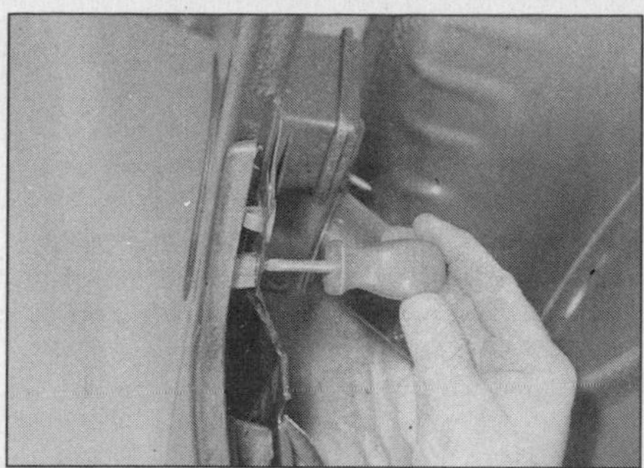

6.27 Remove the upper screw from inside the wheel arch

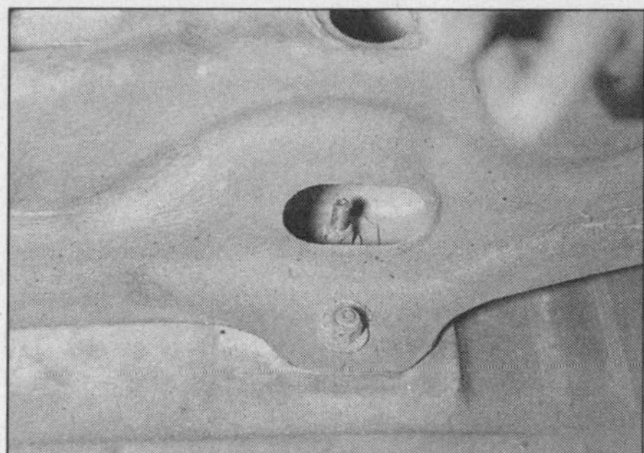

6.28 Two of the rear bumper mounting nuts

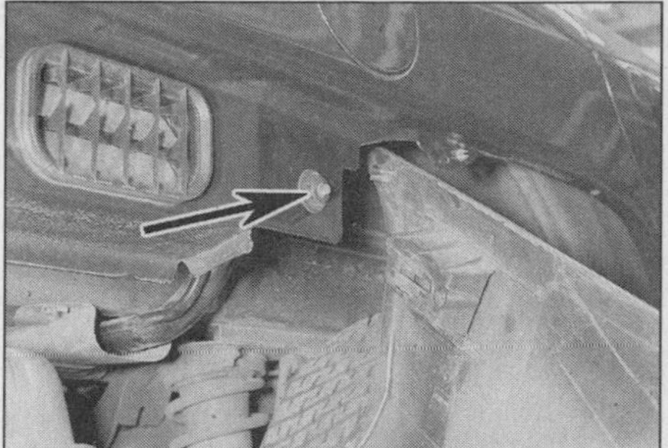

6.29 Slide the bumper off the side locating pegs (one arrowed)

vehicle, remove the two nuts each side securing the bumper to the rear panel **(see illustration)**.

29 With the help of an assistant to support one end of the bumper, slide the bumper to the rear, off the side locating pegs, and remove it **(see illustration)**. On models with the ultrasonic parking sensor, disconnect the wiring plugs from the sensors as they become accessible.

Refitting

Front and rear bumpers - all models

30 Refitting is a reversal of the removal procedure. Make sure that, where applicable, the bumper guides are located correctly.

7 Radiator grille - removal and refitting

Removal

1 Support the bonnet in the open position.

2 On later models, prise out the three securing clips and remove the cover panel around the bonnet lock **(see illustrations)**.

3 Unscrew the two radiator grille upper mounting screws **(see illustrations)**.

4 Release the clips at the base of the grille, and remove the radiator grille from the front panel **(see illustrations)**.

Refitting

5 Refitting is a reversal of the removal procedure.

8 Bonnet - removal, refitting and adjustment

Removal

1 Open the bonnet, and support it in the open position using the stay.

2 Disconnect the battery negative (earth) lead (Chapter 5A, Section 1).

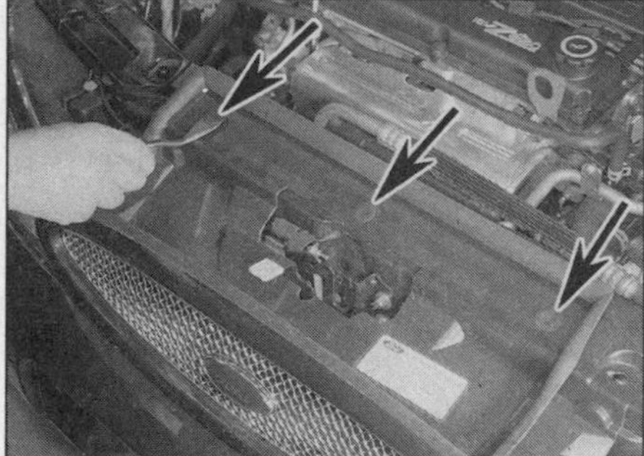

7.2a Using a forked tool if available, prise out the three retaining clips (arrowed) . . .

7.2b . . . and lift away the cover panel, disengaging it from the bonnet release lever

7.3a Removing a radiator grille mounting screw - models up to 1996

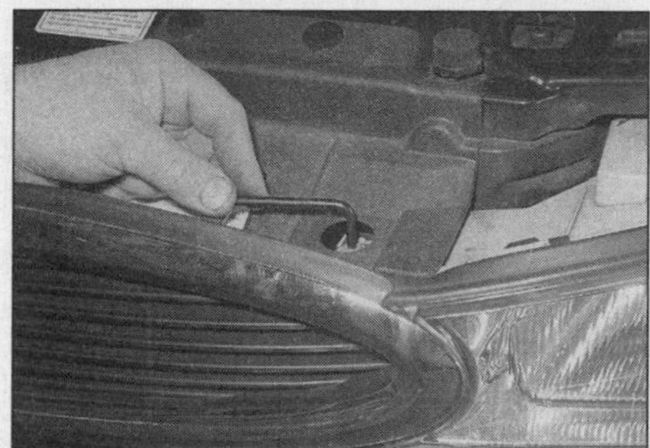

7.3b Radiator grille mounting screw removal - 1997 models onwards

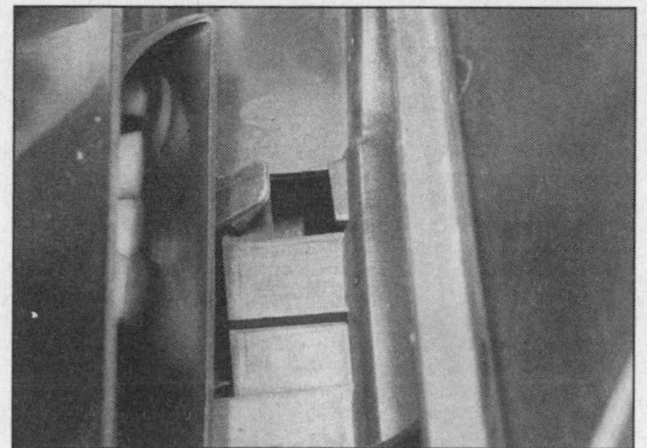

7.4a Unclipping the radiator grille from the front panel - models up to 1996 . . .

7.4b . . . and removing the radiator grille on 1997 and later models

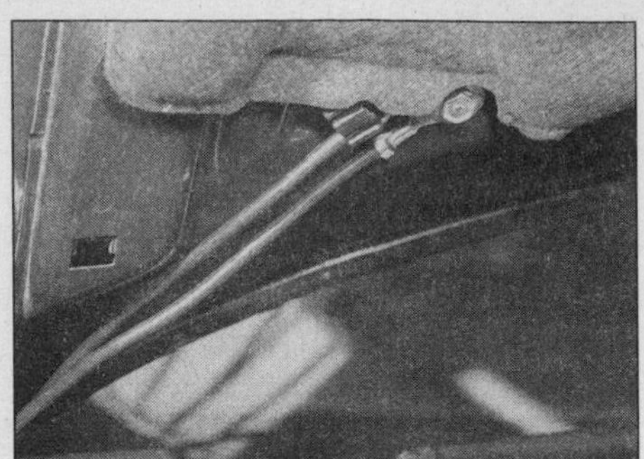

8.5 Earth lead and washer hoses on the underside of the bonnet

8.7 Mark around the bonnet hinges with a soft pencil before removal

8.8 Removing the bonnet

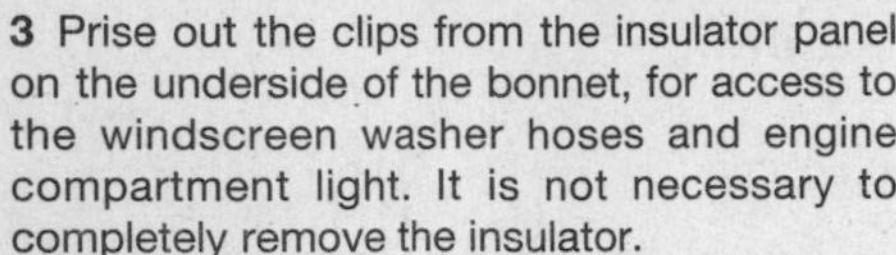

3 Prise out the clips from the insulator panel on the underside of the bonnet, for access to the windscreen washer hoses and engine compartment light. It is not necessary to completely remove the insulator.

4 Disconnect the wiring from the engine compartment light, and unclip the wiring from the bonnet.

5 Unbolt the earth lead from the bonnet **(see illustration)**.

6 Disconnect the windscreen washer hoses from the bottom of the jets, and unclip the hose from the bonnet.

7 To assist in correctly realigning the bonnet when refitting it, mark the outline of the hinges with a soft pencil **(see illustration)**. Loosen the two hinge retaining bolts on each side.

8 With the help of an assistant, unscrew the four bolts, release the stay, and lift the bonnet from the vehicle **(see illustration)**.

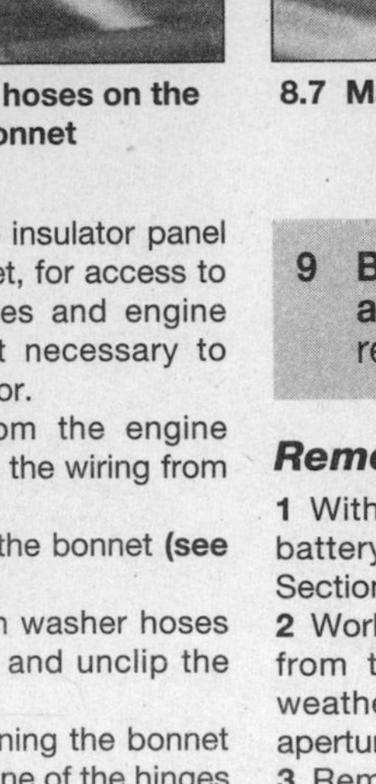

Refitting and adjustment

9 Refitting is a reversal of the removal procedure, noting the following points:

a) Position the bonnet hinges within the outline marks made during removal, but if necessary alter its position to provide a uniform gap all round.

b) Adjust the rear height of the bonnet by repositioning it on the hinges.

*c) Adjust the front height by repositioning the lock (see Section 10) and turning the rubber buffers on the engine compartment front cross panel up or down to support the bonnet **(see illustration)**.*

9 Bonnet release cable and lever - removal and refitting

Removal

1 With the bonnet open, disconnect the battery negative (earth) lead (Chapter 5A, Section 1).

2 Working inside the vehicle, remove the trim from the 'B' pillar, and pull off the door weatherstrips from the bottom of the door apertures.

3 Remove the clips and screws, and withdraw the lower side trim, to give access to the bonnet release lever **(see illustration)**.

4 Release the outer cable from the lever bracket.

5 Unscrew and remove the lever mounting screws, and turn the lever clockwise through a quarter-turn to disconnect it from the cable.

6 Remove the radiator grille (Section 7). Also remove the backing panel from the engine compartment front crossmember.

7 Release the inner and outer cables from the lock.

8 Withdraw the cable from the engine compartment, feeding it through the front crossmember, and removing the grommet from the bulkhead.

Refitting

9 Refitting is a reversal of the removal procedure.

10 Bonnet lock - removal, refitting and adjustment

Removal

1 Remove the radiator grille (Section 7).

2 Release the inner and outer cables from the bonnet lock.

3 Mark the position of the lock on the crossmember, then unscrew the mounting nuts and withdraw the lock **(see illustration)**.

Refitting and adjustment

4 Refitting is a reversal of the removal procedure, starting by positioning the lock as noted before removal.

5 If the front of the bonnet is not level with the front wings, the lock may be moved up or down within the mounting holes. After making an adjustment, raise or lower the rubber buffers to support the bonnet correctly.

11 Door inner trim panel - removal and refitting

Removal

1 Disconnect the battery negative (earth) lead (Chapter 5A, Section 1).

2 Carefully prise out the plastic cover with a small screwdriver. Remove the screw, and

8.9 Buffer for adjustment of the bonnet front height

9.3 Bonnet release lever

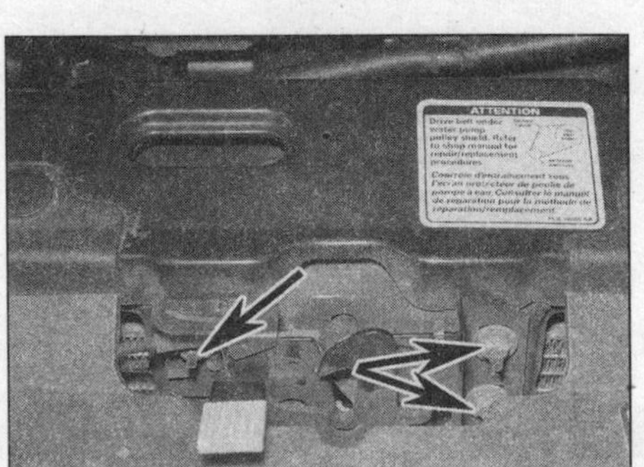

10.3 Bonnet lock mounting nuts (arrowed)

11.2a Prise out the plastic cover . . .

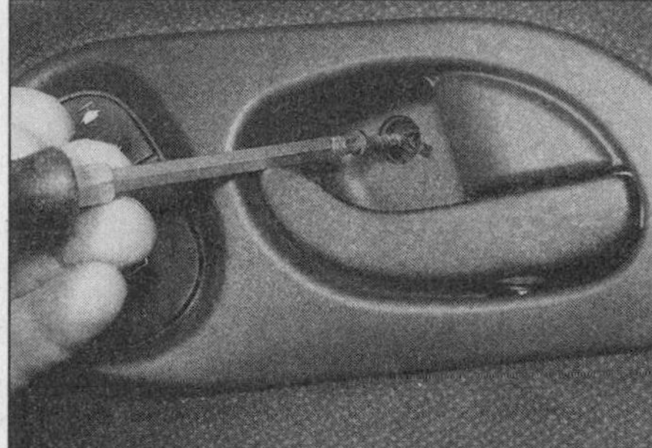

11.2b . . . remove the screw . . .

11.2c . . . and withdraw the bezel from the inner door handle

ease the bezel off the inner door handle **(see illustrations)**.

3 Where applicable, remove the window operating switch and disconnect the multi-plug **(see illustrations)**.

Front door

4 Carefully prise out the cover, remove the screws and withdraw the door pull handle **(see illustrations)**.

5 Prise off the plastic cap, remove the screw, and withdraw the quarter bezel from the front of the window opening **(see illustrations)**.

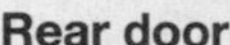

Rear door

6 Prise off the cap, then remove the screw and withdraw the door pull handle **(see illustrations)**.

Front and rear doors

7 On models fitted with manual (ie non-electric) windows, fully shut the window, and note the position of the regulator handle. Release the spring clip by inserting a clean cloth between the handle and the door trim. Using a 'sawing' action, pull the cloth against the open ends of the clip to release it, at the same time pulling the handle from the regulator shaft splines. Withdraw the handle (and where fitted, the spacer) and recover the clip **(see illustrations)**.

11.3a Remove the window operating switch . . .

11.3b . . . and disconnect the multi-plug

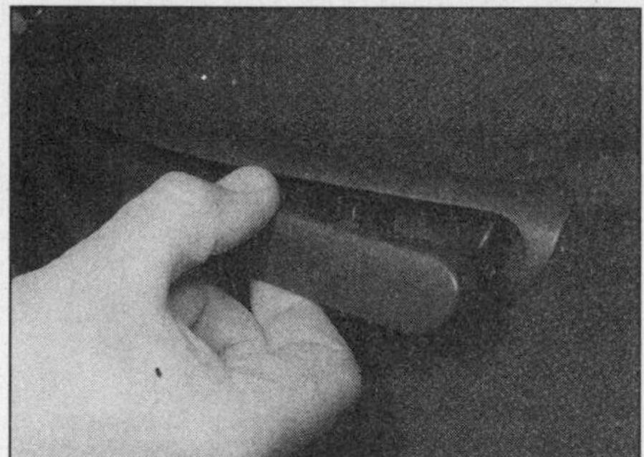

11.4a Remove the cover . . .

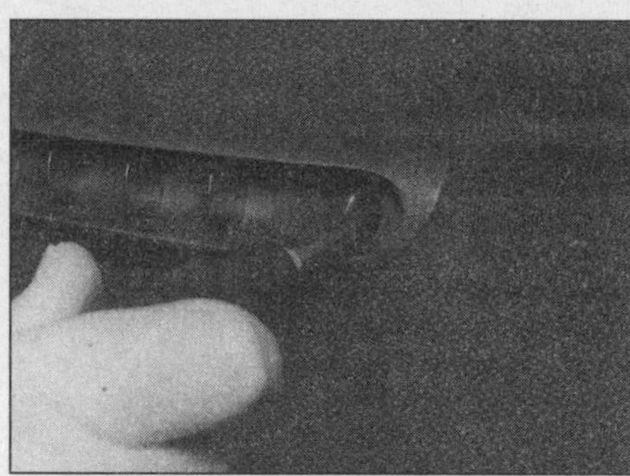

11.4b . . . then remove the screws and withdraw the door pull handle

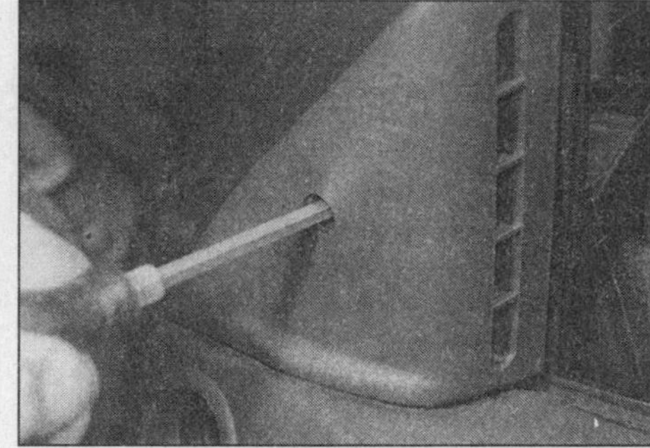

11.5a Remove the plastic cap and the screw . . .

11.5b . . . then withdraw the quarter bezel

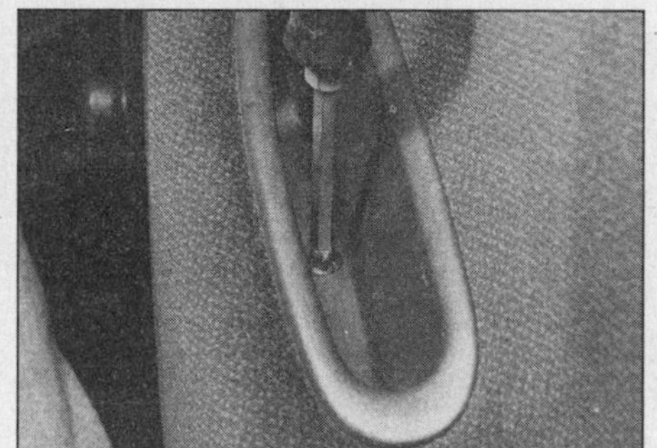

11.6a Remove the screw . . .

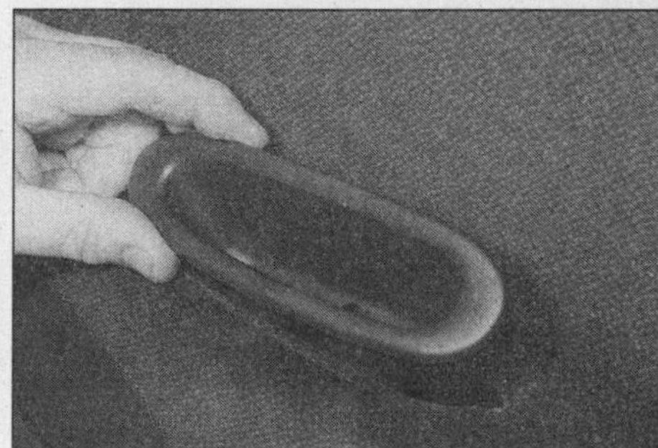

11.6b . . . and withdraw the rear door pull handle

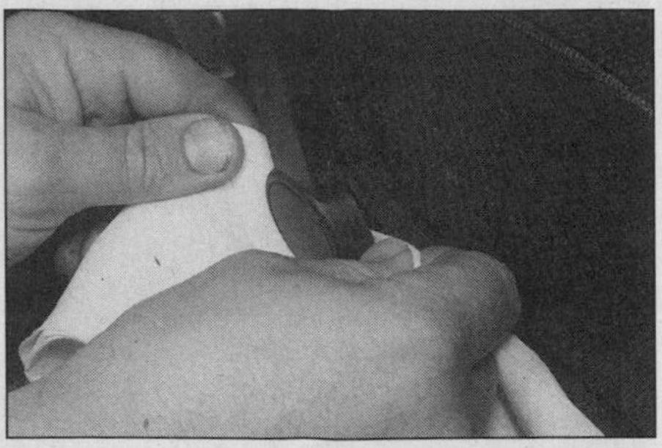

11.7a Using a clean cloth to release the spring clip from the window regulator handle

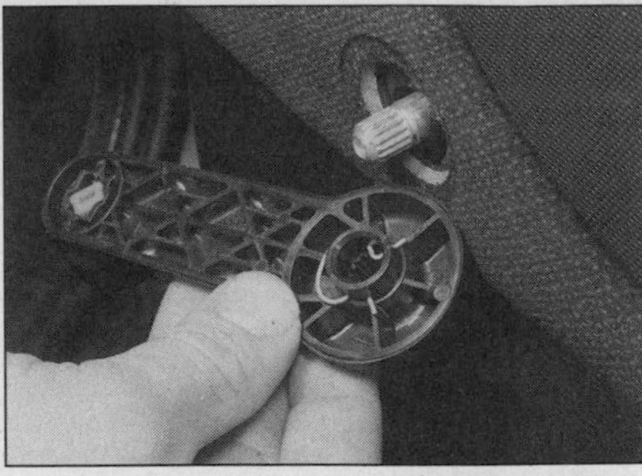

11.7b Withdrawing the window regulator handle

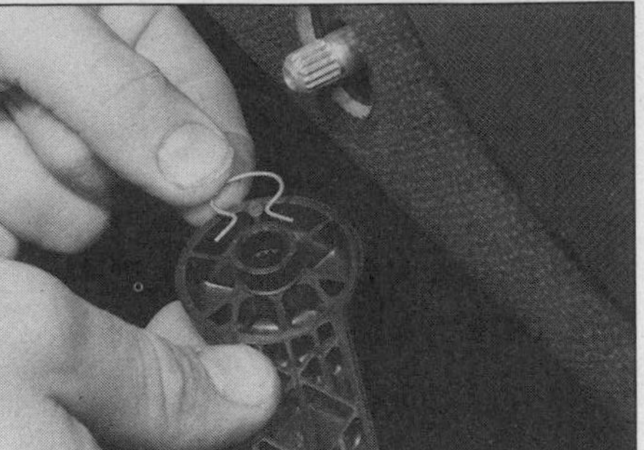

11.7c Recover the spring clip from the window regulator handle

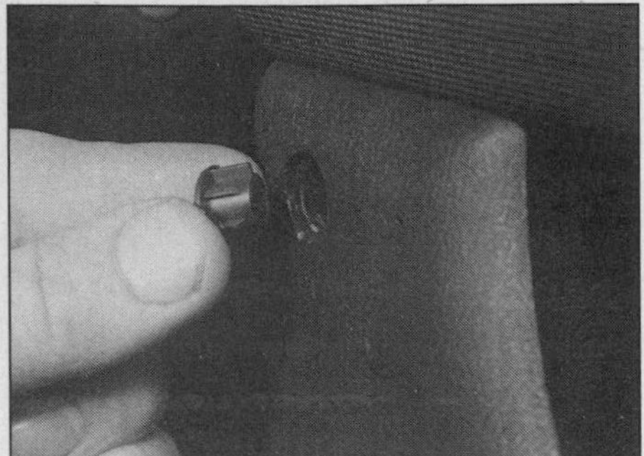

11.8a Prise out the caps . . .

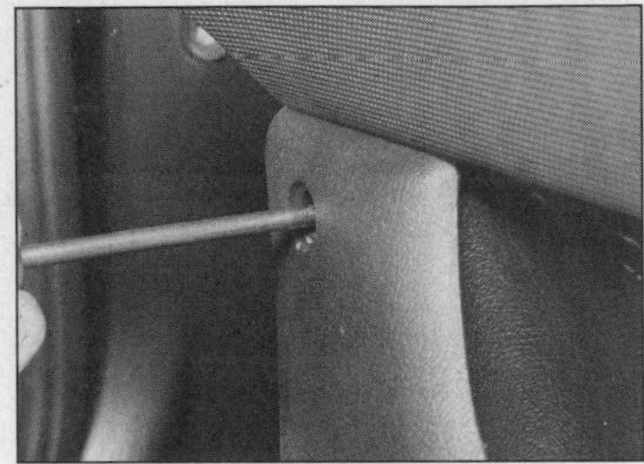

11.8b . . . remove the inner-facing screws . . .

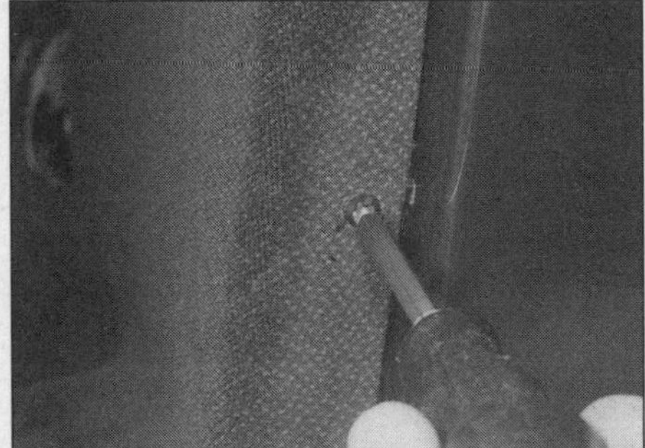

11.8c . . . and the side screws . . .

11.8d . . . then lift off the trim panel

8 Prise the caps from the trim panel retaining screws, then remove the screws and lift off the panel **(see illustrations)**. Where a speaker is attached to the trim panel, disconnect the multi-plug.

9 If necessary, the foam insulation may be removed from the door. First remove the speaker as described in Chapter 12.

10 On models with manual windows, remove the foam spacer from the regulator spindle **(see illustration)**.

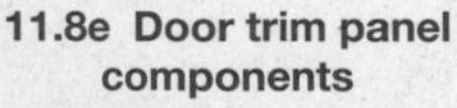

11.8e Door trim panel components

1 Door
2 Foam seal
3 Trim panel
4 Top mounting
5 Centre mounting

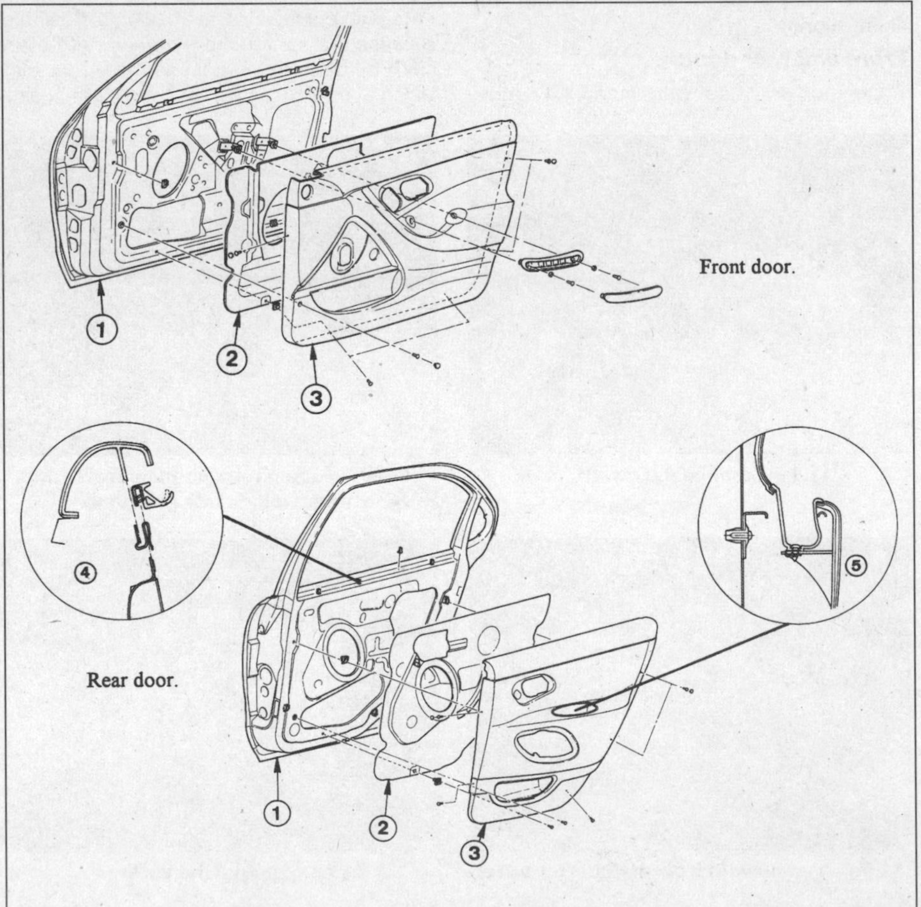

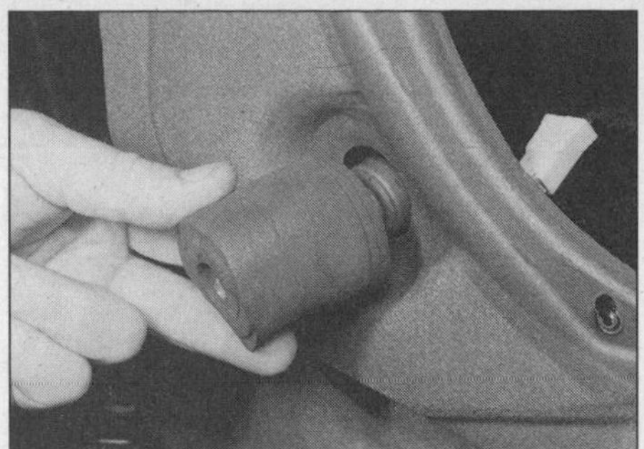
11.10 Removing the foam spacer

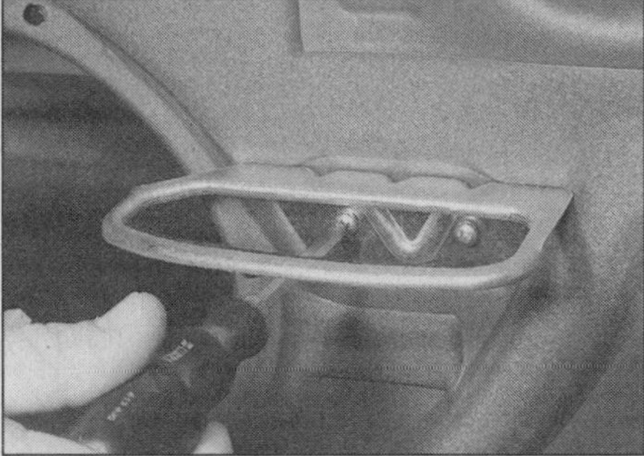
11.11 Removing the door pull bracket from a rear door

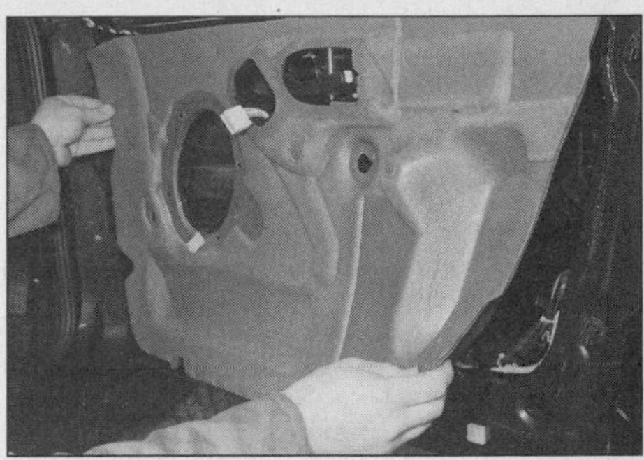
11.12 Removing the foam insulation

11 On the rear door, unscrew the screws and remove the door pull bracket **(see illustration)**.
12 Carefully cut the adhesive with a knife, and remove the foam insulation **(see illustration)**.

Refitting

13 Refitting is a reversal of the removal procedure.

12 Door window glass - removal and refitting

Removal

Front (manual/non-electric)

1 Disconnect the battery negative (earth) lead (Chapter 5A, Section 1).

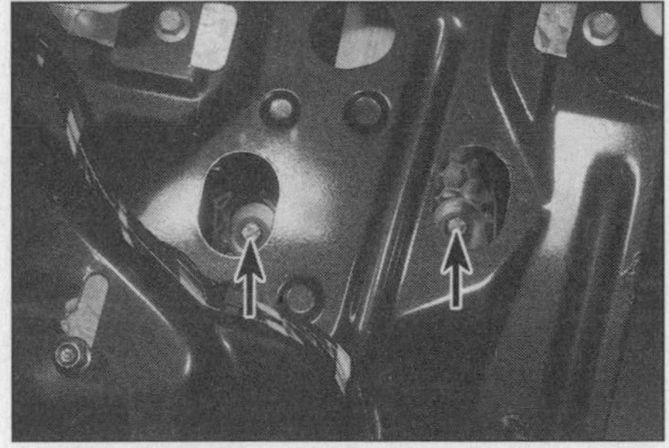
12.12 Window support bracket bolts (arrowed) viewed through the holes in the door inner panel

2 Remove the door inner trim panel (Section 11).
3 Remove the door exterior mirror (Section 16).
4 Temporarily refit the regulator handle on its splines.
5 Lower the window until the glass support bracket is visible through the holes in the door inner panel. Remove the regulator handle.
6 Carefully prise off the weatherstrip from the outside of the door.
7 Support the glass, then unscrew the bolts from the support bracket.
8 Lift the glass from the door while tilting it at the rear, and withdraw it from the outside.

Front (electric)

9 Disconnect the battery negative (earth) lead (Chapter 5A, Section 1).
10 Remove the door inner trim panel (Section 11).
11 Remove the door exterior mirror (Section 16).

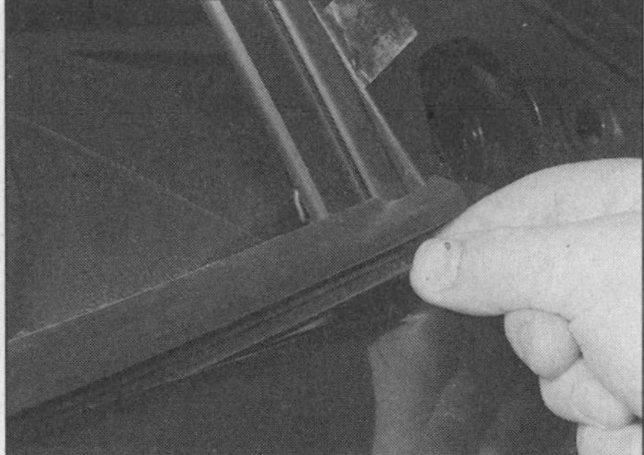
12.13 Removing the weatherstrip from the outside of the door

12 Temporarily reconnect the battery and the window operating switch. Lower the window until the support bracket and bolts are visible through the holes in the door inner panel **(see illustration)**. Disconnect the battery lead and the operating switch again.
13 Carefully prise off the weatherstrip from the outside of the door **(see illustration)**.
14 Support the glass, then unscrew the bolts from the support bracket.
15 Lift the glass from the door while tilting it at the rear, and withdraw it from the outside **(see illustration)**.

Rear (manual/non-electric)

16 Disconnect the battery negative (earth) lead (Chapter 5A, Section 1).
17 Remove the door inner trim panel (Section 11).
18 Temporarily refit the regulator handle on its splines.
19 Lower the window until the glass support bracket and bolts are visible through the holes in the door inner panel. Remove the regulator handle.
20 Support the glass, then unscrew the bolts from the support bracket.
21 Unscrew the screws, and remove the air vent grilles from the rear of the door **(see illustrations)**.
22 Carefully prise off the weatherstrip from the outside of the door.
23 Have an assistant raise the glass from the outside, and hold it near its shut position.
24 Loosen (but do not remove) the three regulator mounting bolts, then slide the top bolts to the right, and push them out. Slide the

12.15 Lifting the glass from the front door

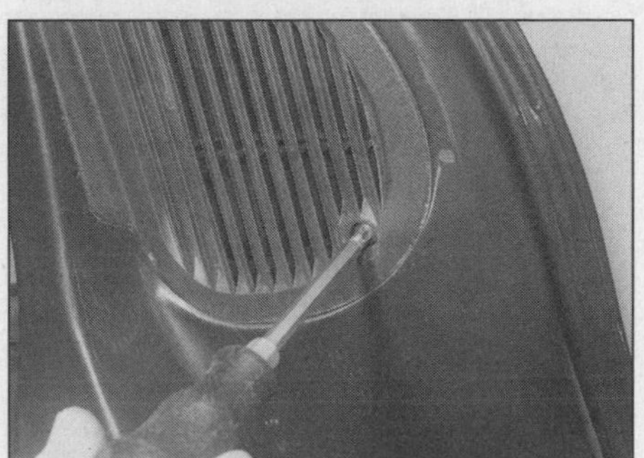
12.21a Unscrew the screws . . .

12.21b . . . and remove the air vent grilles from the rear door

bottom bolt upwards, and push it out. Lower the regulator assembly inside the door.

25 Working inside the door, lower the glass until it is below the regulator position, and move the glass to the outer side of its channels.

26 With the help of an assistant, lift the glass out of the door, and withdraw it from the outside **(see illustration)**.

Rear (electric)

27 The procedure is as just described for manual windows, making allowances for the difference in the regulator mechanism.

Refitting

All doors

28 Refitting is a reversal of the removal procedure, making sure that the glass is correctly located in the support bracket.

13 Door window regulator - removal and refitting

Removal

1 Remove the window glass (Section 12).

2 Loosen (but do not remove) the regulator and manual winder/electric motor mounting bolts **(see illustrations)**.

3 Twist the winder or motor (as applicable) in the bolt slots, and push it inwards.

4 Slide the top bolts to the right, and push them out. Slide the bottom bolt upwards, and push it out.

5 On electric windows, disconnect the wiring multi-plug from the motor **(see illustration)**.

6 Withdraw the window regulator mechanism from inside the door, through the hole in the inner panel **(see illustrations)**.

12.26 Lifting the glass from the rear door

Refitting

7 Refitting is a reversal of the removal procedure.

13.2a Window regulator upper mounting bolts (front door)

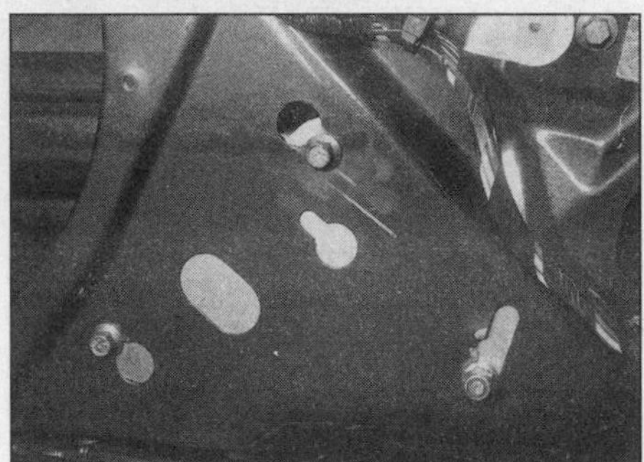

13.2b Electric window motor mounting bolts (front door)

13.2c Window regulator mounting bolts - arrowed (rear door)

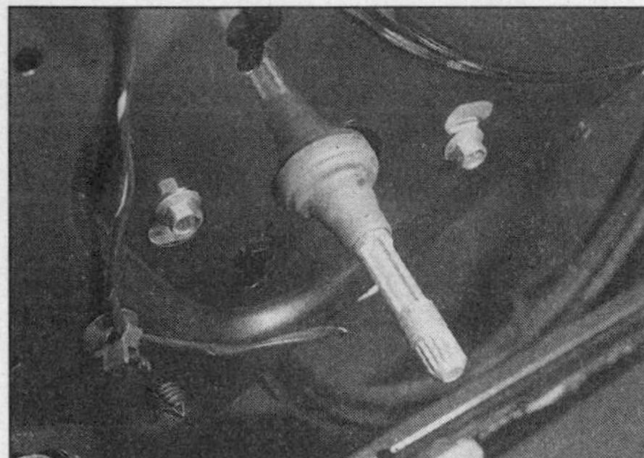

13.2d Manual winder mounting bolts (rear door)

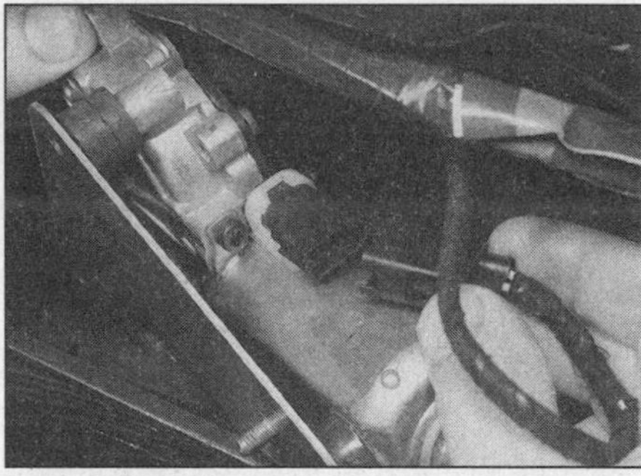

13.5 Disconnecting the wiring multi-plug from an electrically-operated window

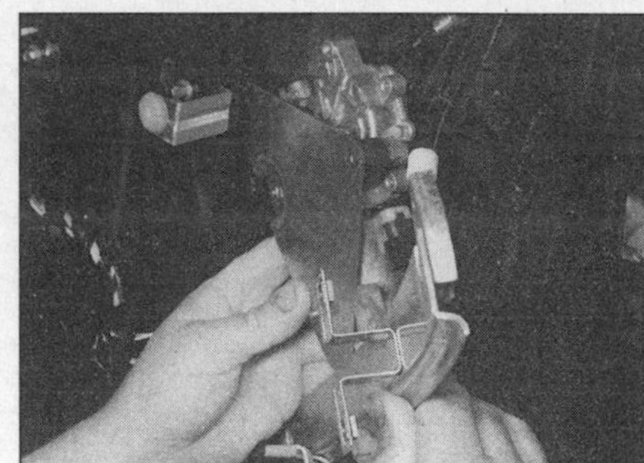

13.6a Removing the window regulator mechanism from the front door

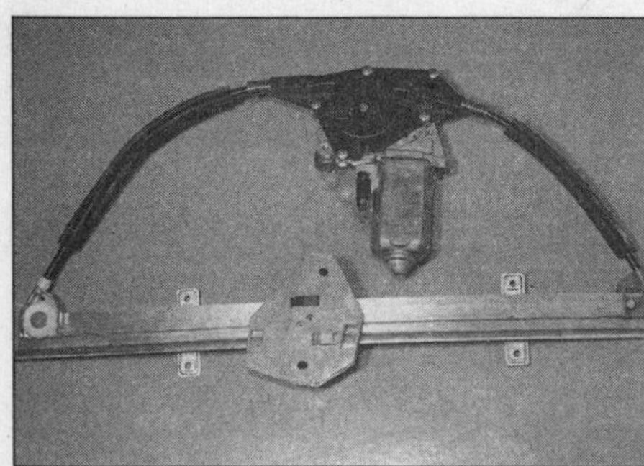

13.6b Front door window regulator removed from the vehicle

13.6c Removing the window regulator mechanism from the rear door

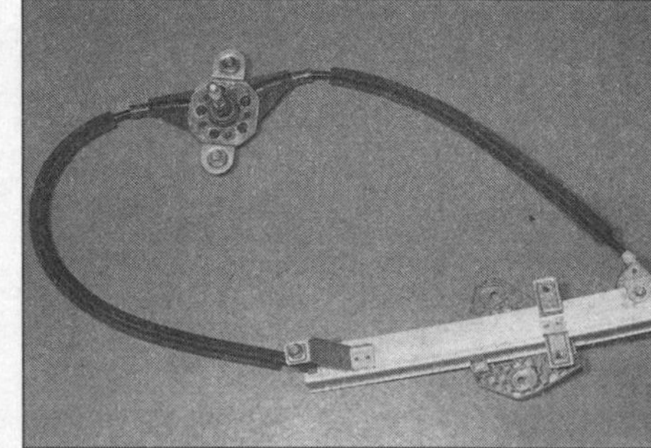

13.6d Rear door window regulator removed from the vehicle

14.3a Remove the two bolts (arrowed) . . .

14.3b . . . followed by the exterior handle bezel

14.4a Unscrew the lock mounting bolts . . .

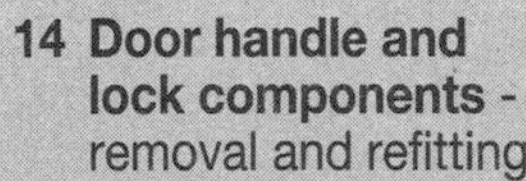

14 Door handle and lock components - removal and refitting

Removal

Front door exterior handle

1 Remove the door inner trim panel (Section 11).

2 Use a knife to cut through the adhesive strip, so that the foam insulator can be peeled back locally for access to the lock. Do not peel back the foam insulator without first cutting through the adhesive strip, otherwise the insulator will be damaged. To ensure a good seal when the insulator is pressed back, do not touch the adhesive strip.

3 Unscrew and remove the two bolts for the exterior handle outer bezel, and remove the bezel **(see illustrations)**.

4 Unscrew and remove the lock mounting bolts on the inner rear edge of the door, and remove the plate. Also remove the additional support screw **(see illustrations)**.

5 Unclip and disconnect the wiring multi-plugs for the central locking and alarm systems **(see illustration)**.

6 Disconnect the wiring multi-plug from the door lock.

7 Disconnect the inner handle illumination light. Undo the screws and remove the inner handle. Disconnect the operating cable from the inner handle, as described later in this Section **(see illustrations)**.

8 Manipulate the lock and handle assembly as necessary, and disconnect the wiring multi-plugs for the alarm sensor and central locking. Withdraw the complete assembly from inside the door **(see illustrations)**.

14.4b . . . and remove the plate

9 To disconnect the handle assembly from the lock bracket, slide the rubber posts inwards, and push out the assembly **(see illustration)**.

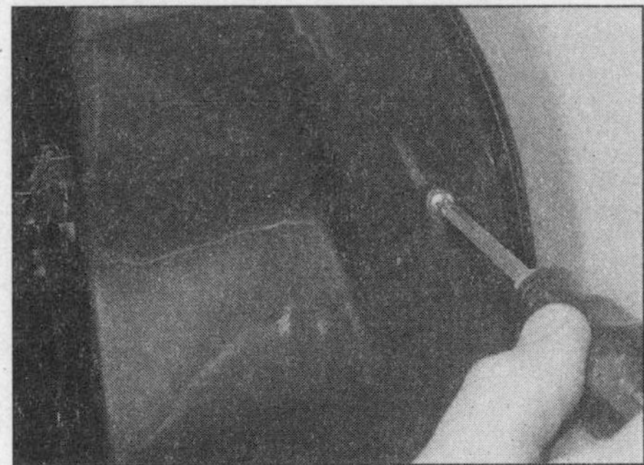
14.4c Removing the additional support screw

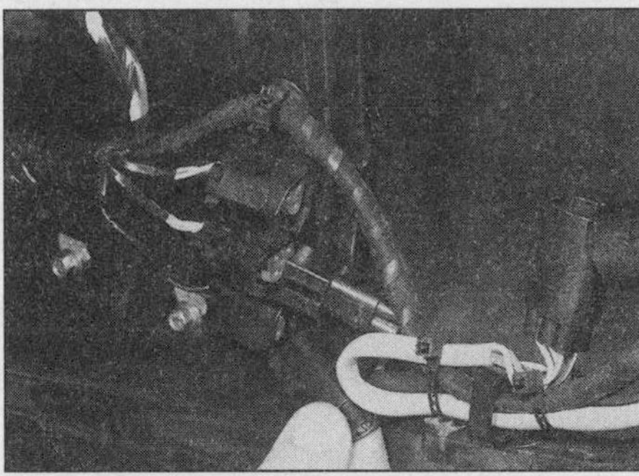
14.5 Disconnecting the central locking and alarm system wiring multi-plugs

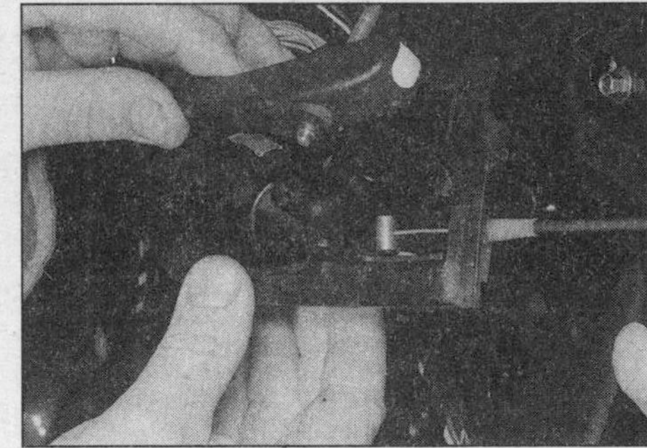
14.7a Removing the inner handle

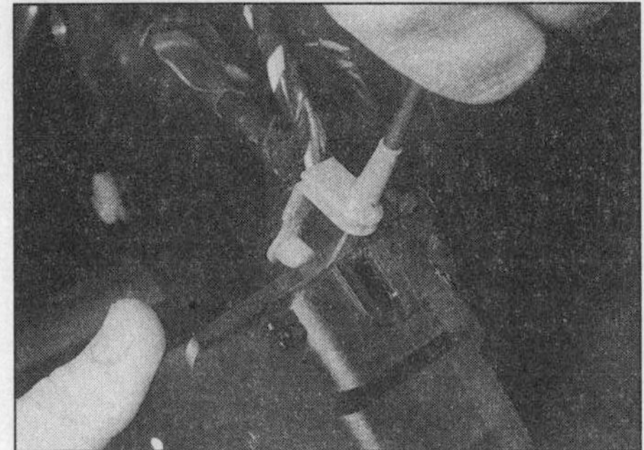
14.7b Disconnecting the operating cable from the inner handle

14.8a Removing the lock and exterior handle assembly from inside the door

14.8b Front door lock and exterior handle assembly removed from the vehicle

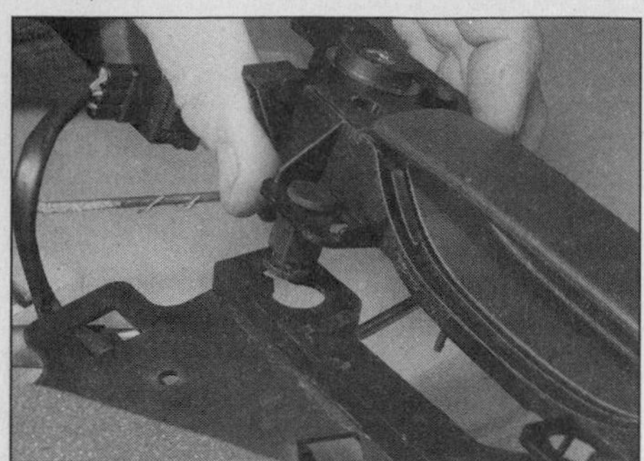
14.9 Disconnecting the handle assembly from the lock bracket

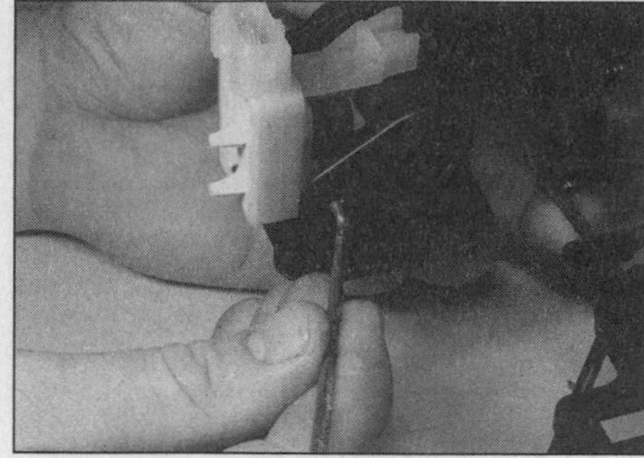
14.10 Pulling out the handle connecting rods

14.11 Removing the central locking 'set-reset' sensor

10 To remove the handle itself, twist the door handle through a quarter-turn, and pull out the connecting rods **(see illustration)**.

11 Remove the alarm sensor and the central locking 'set-reset' sensor **(see illustration)**.

Rear door exterior handle

12 Remove the door inner trim panel (Section 11).

13 Use a knife to cut through the adhesive strip, so that the foam insulator can be peeled back for access to the lock. Do not peel back the foam insulator without first cutting through the adhesive strip. To ensure a good seal when the insulator is pressed back, do not touch the adhesive strip.

14 Prise out the plug from the rear edge of the door, then unscrew the handle mounting nuts **(see illustrations)**.

15 Prise up the clip, and disconnect the operating rod from the lock **(see illustration)**.

16 Withdraw the handle from the outside of the door **(see illustration)**.

Interior handle

17 Remove the door inner trim panel (Section 11).

18 Use a knife to cut through the adhesive strip, so that the foam insulator can be peeled back for access to the lock. Do not peel back the foam insulator without first cutting through the adhesive strip. To ensure a good seal when the insulator is pressed back, do not touch the adhesive strip.

19 Disconnect the interior handle illumination light.

20 Undo the screws and remove the interior handle.

21 To remove the cable, first pull back the plastic outer cable end and blanking piece. Apply light inward pressure to the control lever, with the lever in the locked position, until the inner cable is aligned with the release slot in the bottom of the cable holder.

22 Push down on the cable ferrule, and disconnect the inner cable. Remove the handle assembly.

Lock barrel

23 Remove the exterior handle as described earlier in this Section.

24 Prise out the barrel retaining tab from the handle body, using a small screwdriver **(see illustration)**.

25 Insert the key, turn it so that it engages the barrel, then pull out the barrel **(see illustration)**.

Lock motor - front door

26 Remove the exterior handle as described earlier in this Section.

27 Extract the clip, and pull out the operating rod.

28 Remove the operating rod from the plastic bush, by turning it through a quarter-turn.

29 Release the sensor wiring loom from the clip.

30 Detach the mounting plate from the lock.

31 Release the door-ajar sensor from the clip **(see illustration)**.

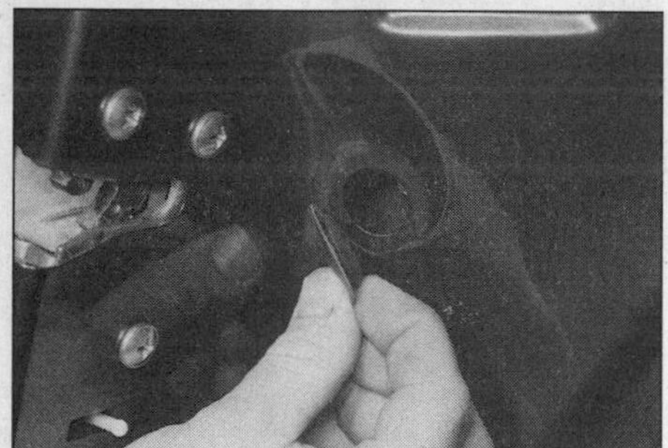
14.14a Prise out the plug . . .

14.14b . . . and unscrew the handle mounting nuts

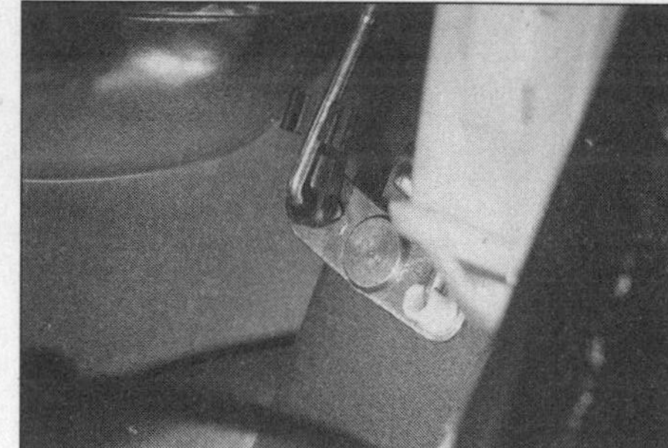
14.15 Disconnect the operating rod from the lock

14.16 Removing the rear door exterior handle

14.24 Prise out the barrel retaining tab . . .

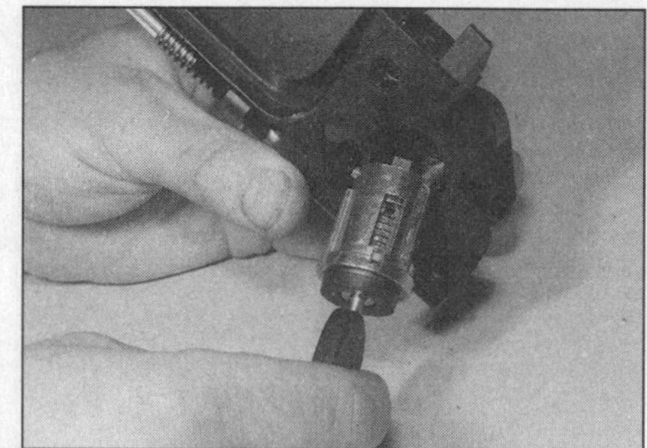
14.25 . . . and pull out the lock barrel

14.31 Unclipping the door-ajar sensor

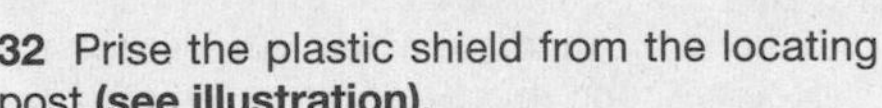

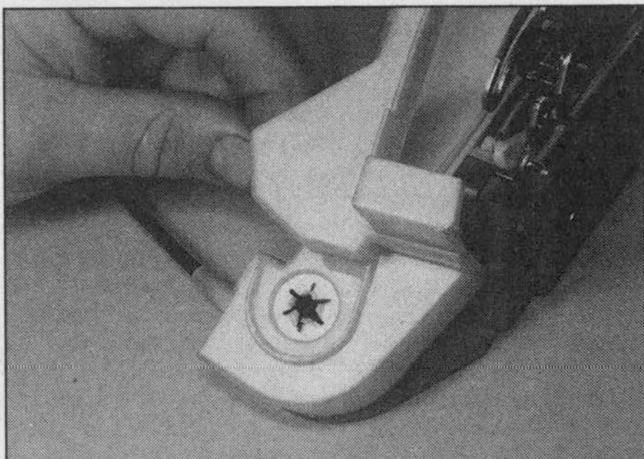

14.32 Removing the plastic shield from the locating post

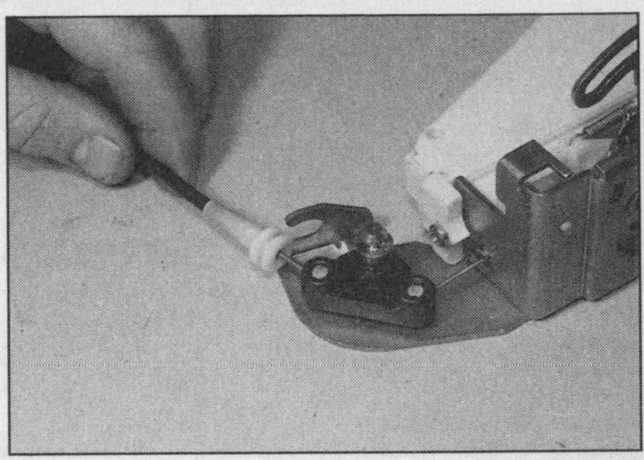

14.33 Slide the outer cable from the lock bracket

32 Prise the plastic shield from the locating post **(see illustration)**.
33 Slide the outer cable from the lock bracket, then turn the inner cable through a quarter-turn to remove it from the bell crank **(see illustration)**.
34 Unscrew the mounting screws and remove the lock motor **(see illustration)**.

Lock motor - rear door

35 Remove the exterior handle as described earlier in this Section.
36 Unscrew and remove the three lock mounting screws.
37 Release the sensor wiring loom from the clip on the door.
38 Disconnect the wiring multi-plug from the door lock.
39 Disconnect the interior handle illumination light.
40 Remove the screws, and remove the interior handle.
41 Remove the lock assembly.
42 Release the door-ajar sensor from the clip.
43 Prise the plastic shield from the locating post.
44 Slide the outer cable from the lock bracket, then turn the inner cable through a quarter-turn to remove it from the bell crank.
45 Unscrew the mounting screws and remove the lock motor.

Striker

46 Using a pencil, mark the position of the striker.
47 Undo the mounting screws using a Torx key, and remove the striker.

Check strap

48 Disconnect the battery negative (earth) lead (Chapter 5A, Section 1).
49 Using a Torx key, unscrew and remove the check strap mounting screw(s). On the front door, there are two screws; on the rear door, there is only one.
50 Prise the rubber grommet from the door aperture, then unscrew the mounting nuts and withdraw the check strap from the door.

Refitting

Handles (exterior and interior)

51 Refitting is a reversal of the removal procedure.

Lock barrel

52 Check that the retaining clip is fitted correctly.
53 Align the grooves on the barrel with the grooves on the body and operating lever, then carefully push the barrel into the handle until it engages the clip.
54 The remaining refitting procedure is a reversal of removal.

Lock motor

55 Refitting is a reversal of the removal procedure.

Striker

56 Refitting is a reversal of the removal procedure, but check that the door lock passes over the striker centrally. If necessary, re-position the striker before fully tightening the mounting screws.

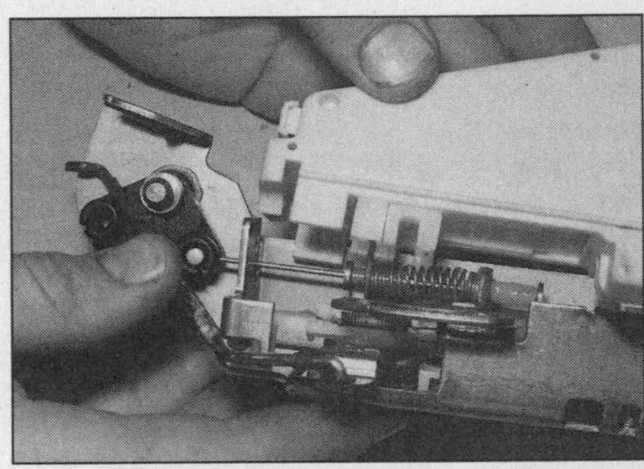

14.34 Removing a lock motor

Check strap

57 Refitting is a reversal of the removal procedure.

15 Door - removal and refitting

Removal

1 Disconnect the battery negative (earth) lead (Chapter 5A, Section 1).
2 Using a Torx key, unscrew and remove the check strap mounting screw(s). On the front door, there are two screws; on the rear door, there is only one **(see illustrations)**.
3 Disconnect the wiring connector(s) by twisting them anti-clockwise. On the front door, there are two connectors; on the rear door, there is only one **(see illustration)**.

15.2a Front door check strap mounting screw removal

15.2b Front door check strap removed

15.3 Disconnecting a door wiring connector

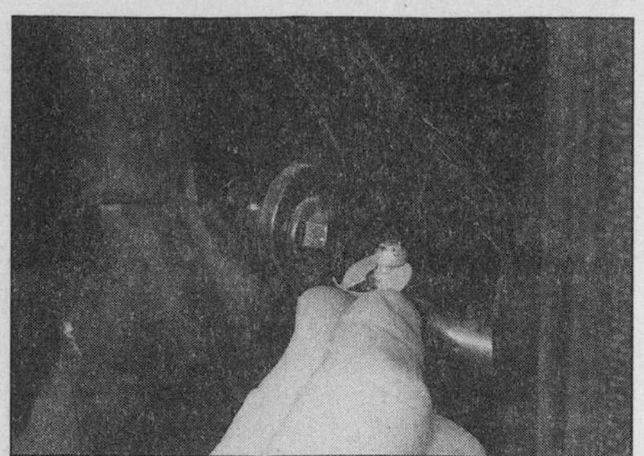
15.4 Extract the small circlips . . .

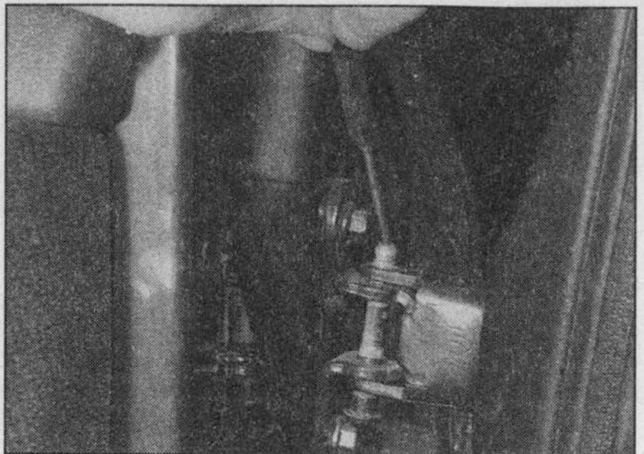
15.5a . . . then drive out the hinge pins . . .

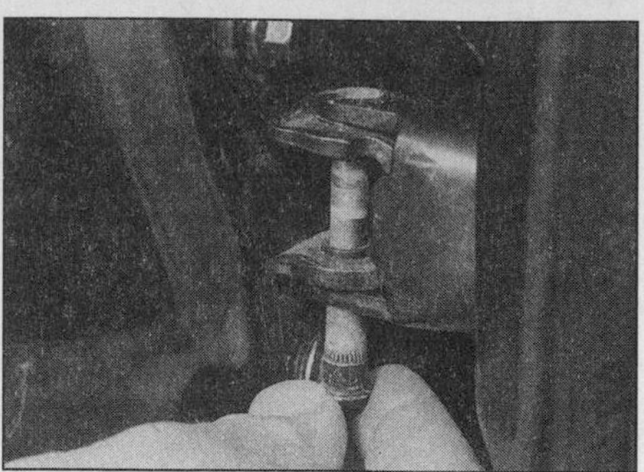
15.5b . . . and remove them

4 Extract the small circlips from the top of the upper and lower hinge pins **(see illustration)**.
5 Have an assistant support the weight of the door, then drive the hinge pins down through the hinges using a small drift **(see illustrations)**.
6 Carefully withdraw the door from the hinges.

Refitting

7 Refitting is a reversal of the removal procedure, but check that the door lock passes over the striker centrally. If necessary, re-position the striker.

16 Exterior mirror and glass - removal and refitting

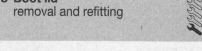

Removal

1 Where electric mirrors are fitted, disconnect the battery negative (earth) lead (Chapter 5A, Section 1).
2 Prise off the cap, unscrew the screw, and remove the quarter bezel from the front of the window opening.
3 On manual mirrors, detach the adjustment lever by removing the two small screws and sliding off the lever.
4 On electric mirrors, disconnect the wiring multi-plug **(see illustration)**.
5 On both types of mirror, use a Torx key to unscrew the mirror mounting screws, then withdraw the mirror from the outside of the door **(see illustrations)**. Recover the gasket.

Refitting

6 Refitting is a reversal of the removal procedure.

17 Interior mirror - removal and refitting

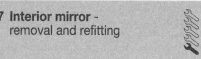

Removal

1 Using a length of strong thin cord or fishing line, break the adhesive bond between the base of the mirror and the glass. Have an assistant support and remove the mirror as it is released.
2 If the original mirror is to be refitted, thoroughly clean its base with methylated spirit and a lint-free cloth. Allow a period of one minute for the spirit to evaporate. Clean the windscreen black patch in a similar manner.

Refitting

3 During the installation of the mirror, it is important that the mirror base, windscreen black patch and the adhesive patch are not touched or contaminated in any way, otherwise poor adhesion will result.
4 Prior to fitting the mirror, the vehicle should ideally have been at an ambient temperature of at least 20°C.
5 With the contact surfaces thoroughly cleaned, remove the protective tape from one side of the adhesive patch, and press it firmly into contact with the mirror base.
6 If fitting the mirror to a new windscreen, the protective tape must also be removed from the windscreen black patch.
7 Using a hairdryer or a hot air gun, warm the mirror base and the adhesive patch for about 30 seconds to a temperature of 50 to 70°C. Peel back the protective tape from the other side of the adhesive patch on the mirror base. Align the mirror base and the windscreen patch, and press the mirror firmly into position. Hold the base of the mirror firmly against the windscreen for a minimum period of two minutes, to ensure full adhesion.
8 Wait at least thirty minutes before adjusting the mirror position.

18 Boot lid - removal and refitting

Removal

1 Disconnect the battery negative (earth) lead (Chapter 5A, Section 1), and open the boot lid.
2 On the right-hand hinge, pull off the trim covering, and release the wiring on the hinge arm. Prise out the grommet to free the wiring **(see illustration)**.
3 Where fitted, remove the trim from inside the boot lid.
4 Disconnect the wiring at the connectors visible through the boot lid inner skin aperture.
5 Attach a length of strong cord to the end of the wires in the aperture, to act as an aid to guiding the wiring through the lid when it is refitted.

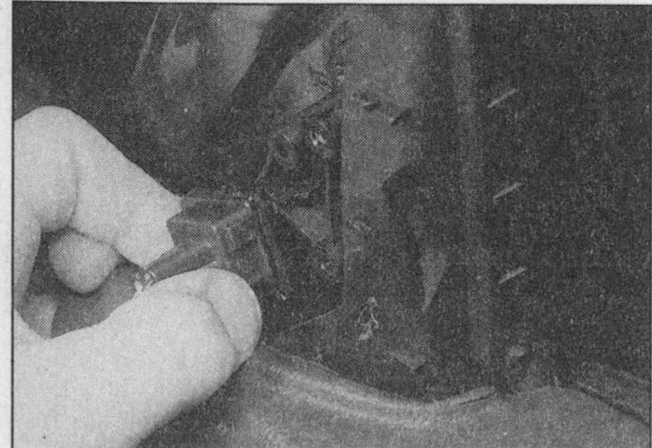
16.4 Disconnecting the wiring multi-plug from an electric exterior mirror

16.5a Unscrew the screws . . .

16.5b . . . and withdraw the mirror

6 Withdraw the wiring loom through the boot lid apertures. Untie the cord, and leave it in the boot lid.
7 Mark the position of the hinge arms with a pencil.
8 Place rags beneath each corner of the boot lid, to prevent damage to the paintwork.
9 With the help of an assistant, unscrew the mounting bolts and lift the boot lid from the car **(see illustration)**.

Refitting

10 Refitting is a reversal of the removal procedure, noting the following points:

a) Check that the boot lid is correctly aligned with the surrounding bodywork, with an equal clearance around its edge.
b) Adjustment is made by loosening the hinge bolts, and moving the boot lid within the elongated mounting holes.
c) Check that the lock enters the striker centrally when the boot lid is closed.

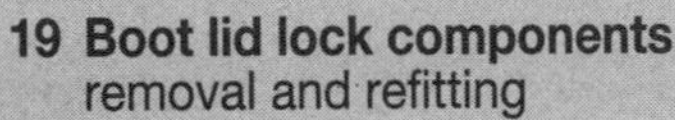

19 Boot lid lock components - removal and refitting

Removal

Lock barrel - models up to 1996

1 Disconnect the battery negative (earth) lead (Chapter 5A, Section 1).
2 With the boot lid open, remove the luggage space trim from the right-hand rear corner.
3 Remove the screws, and prise out the rear light trim cover from the guides.
4 Release the door-ajar sensor from the clip near the lock.
5 Slide the outer cable from the lock bracket. Raise the inner cable until it is aligned with the slot in the barrel lever, and disconnect it.
6 Pull out the lock locating spring clip.
7 Detach the cable mounting bracket from the barrel, and remove the barrel.

Lock barrel - 1997 models onwards

8 Disconnect the battery negative (earth) lead (Chapter 5A, Section 1).
9 With the boot lid open, remove the luggage space trim from the right-hand rear corner.
10 Remove the nuts below the light unit which retain the lock barrel trim panel, and withdraw the panel from the outside **(see illustrations)**.
11 Working from the inside, remove the two nuts which secure the lock barrel housing, then lower the cable mounting bracket and withdraw the barrel and housing from the outside **(see illustrations)**.
12 The lock barrel slides out of the housing for renewal, after removing two small screws **(see illustration)**.

Lock

13 Disconnect the battery negative (earth) lead (Chapter 5A, Section 1).
14 With the boot lid open, prise out the clips, remove the screws, and remove the side and centre trim panels around the lock **(see illustration)**.
15 Release the door-ajar sensor from the clip near the lock, and (where applicable) disconnect the wiring plug for the alarm inhibitor switch. On later models, prise out the wiring harness from the bodywork, and disconnect the multi-plug for the door-ajar sensor **(see illustrations)**.

18.2 Unclip the trim cover, and prise out the wiring grommet

18.9 Boot lid hinge bolts

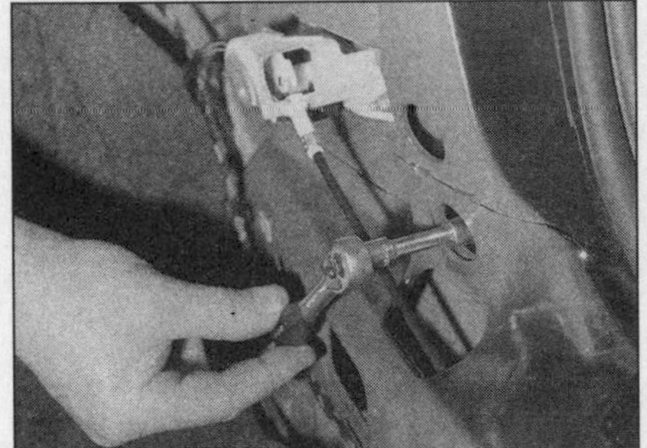

19.10a Remove the lock barrel trim panel mounting nuts from inside . . .

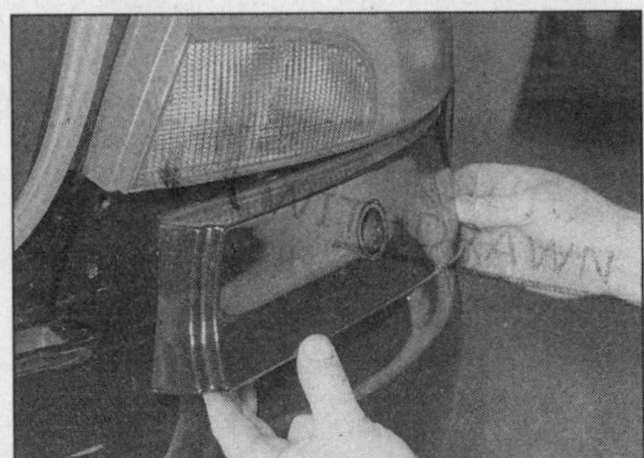

19.10b . . . and withdraw the panel from the outside

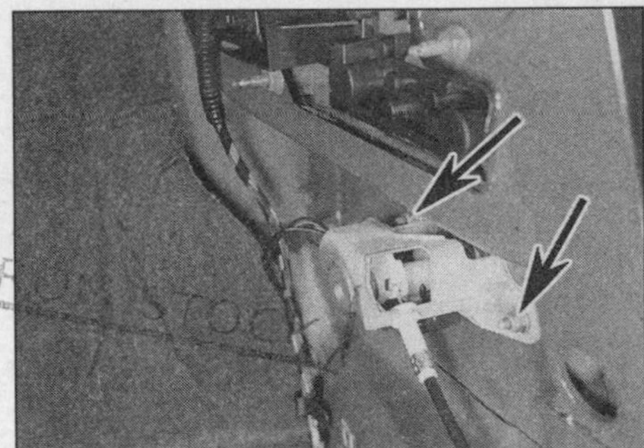

19.11a Remove the two nuts inside . . .

19.11b . . . then withdraw the lock barrel housing from outside

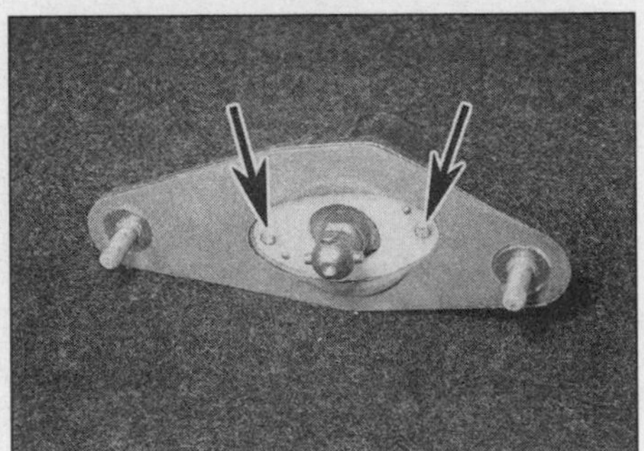

19.12 The lock barrel can be withdrawn after removing two small screws (arrowed)

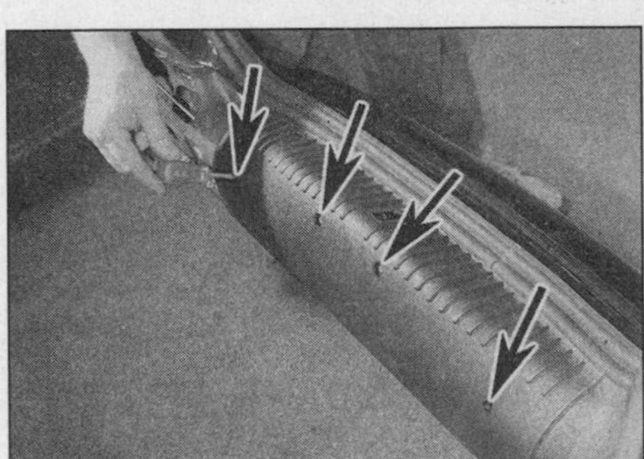

19.14 Remove the screws (arrowed) and lift off the centre trim panel

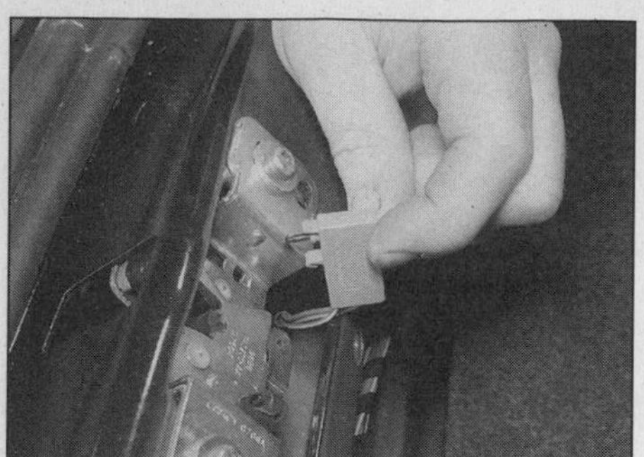

19.15a Unclip the door-ajar sensor/boot light switch from the lock . . .

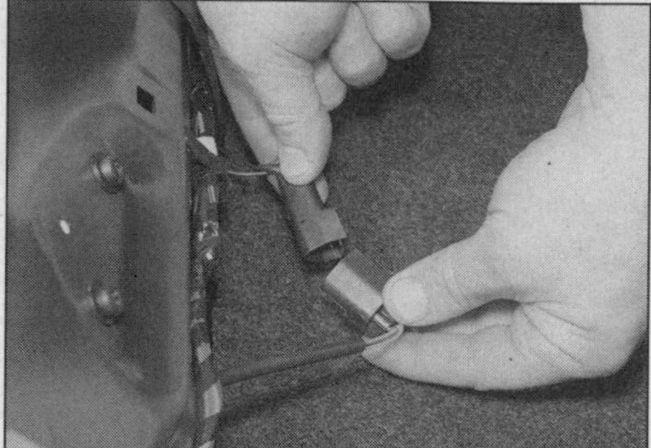

19.15b . . . and disconnect its wiring plug

19.16 Remove the lock securing screws

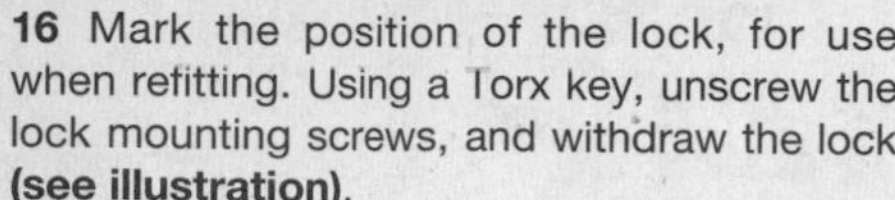

16 Mark the position of the lock, for use when refitting. Using a Torx key, unscrew the lock mounting screws, and withdraw the lock **(see illustration)**.

17 Early models have a cable-operated remote release, as well as the lock operating cable fitted to all models. Disconnect the cable(s) from the lock bracket. Where applicable, prise open the plastic lip, and remove the central locking control rod **(see illustrations)**.

18 Withdraw the lock assembly.

Refitting

Lock barrel and lock

19 Refitting is a reversal of the removal procedure. When refitting the lock, use the alignment marks made on removal to ensure that the lock is positioned accurately.

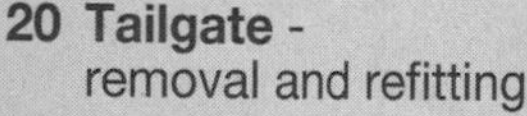

20 Tailgate - removal and refitting

Removal

Hatchback

1 Disconnect the battery negative (earth) lead (Chapter 5A, Section 1). Open the tailgate.

2 The tailgate may be unbolted from the hinges and the hinges left in position, or the hinges may be detached from the roof panel by unscrewing the mounting nuts. In the latter case, carefully pull down the rear edge of the headlining for access to the nuts. Take care not to damage the headlining.

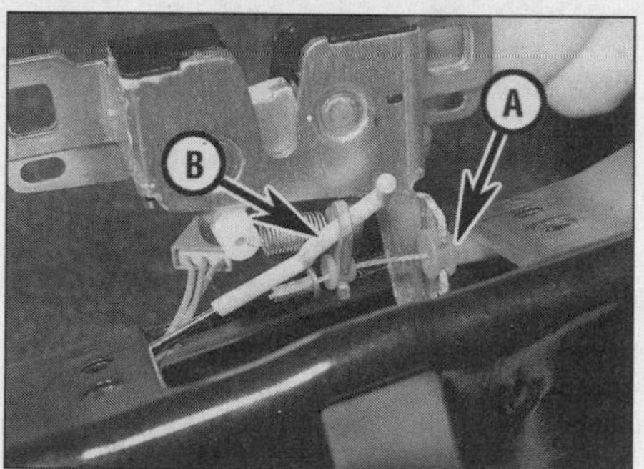

19.17a Lock operating cable (A) and central locking motor rod (B)

3 Remove the parcel shelf left-hand support bracket as follows. Fold the rear seat forwards, and on models up to 1997, disconnect the left-hand seat pull cable from the bracket and clips. Where necessary, pull up the rear seat side bolster (on low-series models, the bolster is retained with a screw), then unscrew the screws and remove the support bracket.

4 Carefully remove the side trim from the left-hand side of the luggage area.

5 Separate the tailgate wiring loom multi-plugs, located on the left-hand side of the luggage compartment, on top of the wheel arch.

6 On models with a high-level rear brake light, remove the two light unit cover screws, and disconnect the bulbholder wiring.

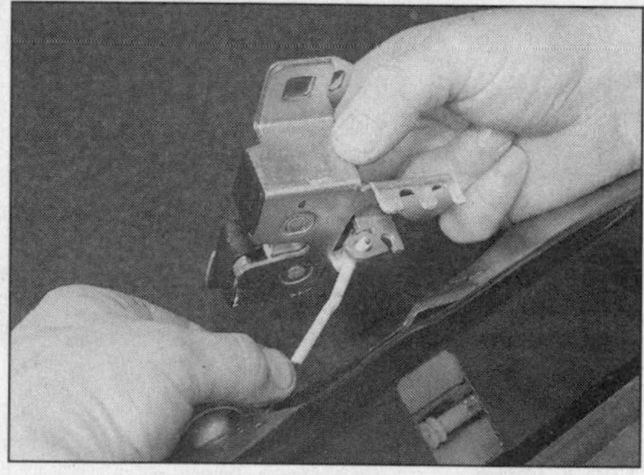

19.17b Disconnect the central locking rod from the lock

7 Unclip and remove the upper trim panel from the inside of the tailgate. Also remove the rear shelf cord plastic post **(see illustrations)**.

8 Prise out the rubber grommet from the top of the tailgate aperture, and pull the wiring loom out through the hole in the body **(see illustration)**.

9 Disconnect the rear window washer tube from the jet.

10 Prise out the rubber grommet from the right-hand side of the tailgate aperture, and pull out the washer tube.

11 Have an assistant support the tailgate in its open position.

12 Using a small screwdriver, prise off the clips securing the struts to the tailgate. Pull the sockets from the ball-studs, and move the struts downwards.

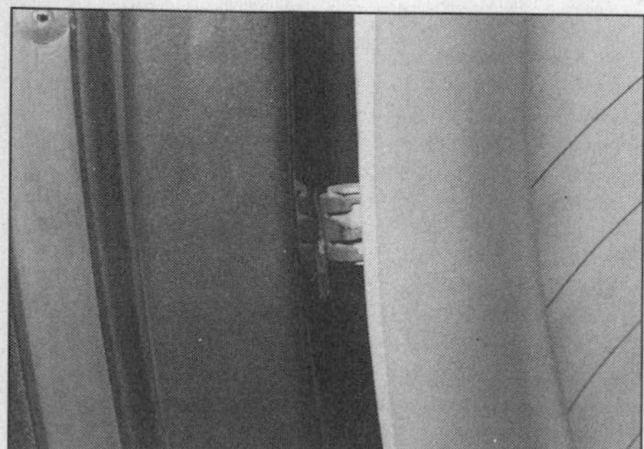

20.7a Unclipping the upper trim panel from the tailgate

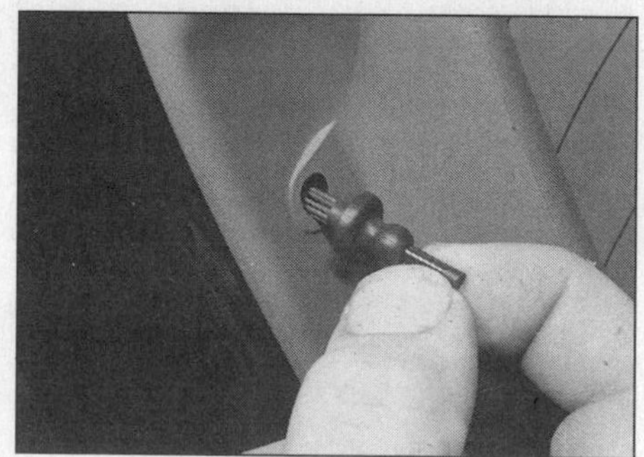

20.7b Shelf cord post removal

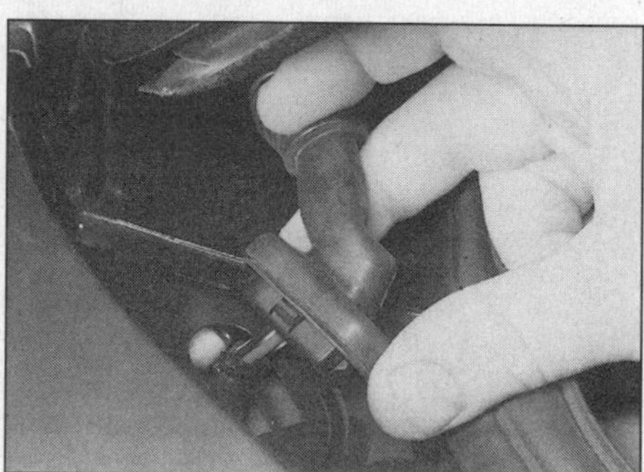

20.8 Removing the wiring loom rubber grommet

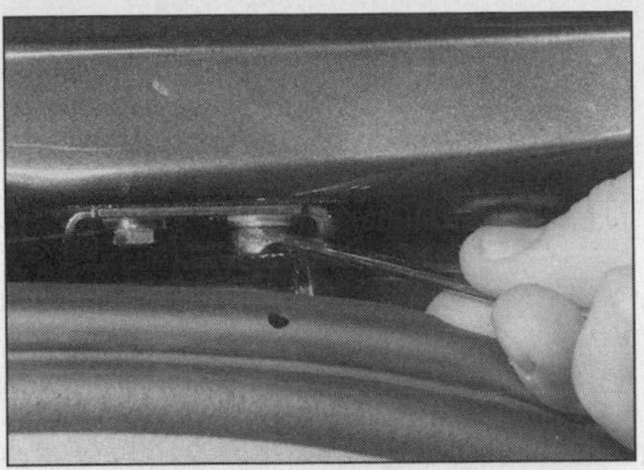
20.13 Unscrewing the bolts securing the tailgate to the hinges

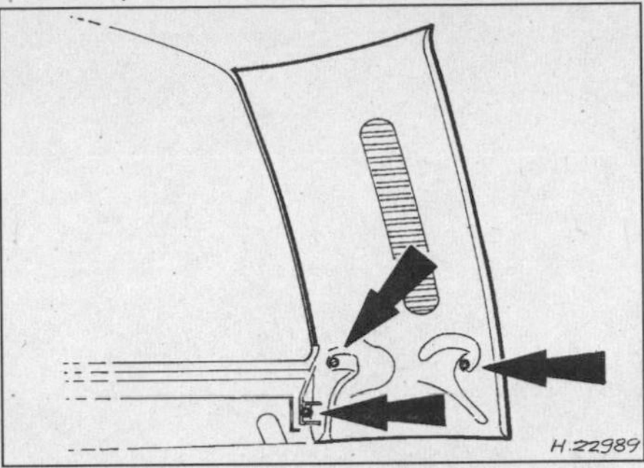

20.17 'D' pillar trim panel retaining screws (arrowed) - Estate models

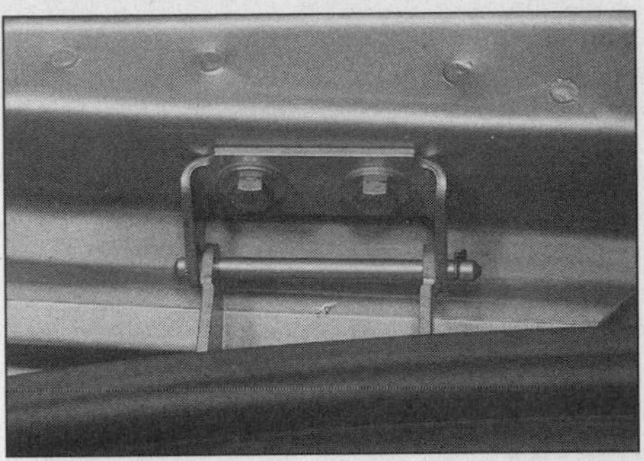
20.26 Tailgate hinge and bolts - Estate models

13 If the headlining has been pulled back, unscrew and remove the hinge nuts from the roof panel. Otherwise, unscrew the bolts securing the tailgate to the hinges **(see illustration).**

14 Withdraw the tailgate from the body aperture, taking care not to damage the paintwork.

Estate

15 Disconnect the battery negative (earth) lead (Chapter 5A, Section 1).

16 The tailgate may be unbolted from the hinges and the hinges left in position, or the hinges may be detached from the rear roof panel by unscrewing the mounting nuts. In the latter case, carefully pull down the rear edge of the headlining for access to the nuts. Take care not to damage the headlining.

17 Unscrew the retaining screws, then unclip the 'D' pillar trim panels from both sides **(see illustration).**

18 Unclip and remove the upper trim panel from inside the tailgate.

19 Carefully remove the side trim from the left-hand side of the luggage area, and separate the tailgate wiring loom multi-plugs in the rear light cluster housing.

20 On models with a high-level rear brake light, remove the two light unit cover screws, and disconnect the bulbholder wiring.

21 Attach a strong fine cord to the end of the wiring loom, to act as an aid to guiding the wiring through the tailgate when it is refitted.

22 Prise the rubber grommet from the top left-hand side of the tailgate aperture, and pull out the wiring loom. Untie the cord, leaving it in position in the 'D' pillar.

23 Disconnect the rear window washer tube from the jet. Pull out the rubber grommet, and remove the tube.

24 Have an assistant support the tailgate in its open position.

25 Using a small screwdriver, prise off the clip securing the struts to the tailgate. Pull the sockets from the ball-studs, and move the struts downwards.

26 Unscrew and remove the hinge nuts from the roof panel, or the hinge bolts from the hinge, as desired **(see illustration).** Withdraw the tailgate from the body aperture, taking care not to damage the paintwork.

Refitting

Hatchback and Estate

27 Refitting is a reversal of the removal procedure, but check that the tailgate is located centrally in the body aperture, and that the striker enters the lock centrally. If necessary, loosen the mounting nuts and re-position the tailgate as required.

21 Tailgate support strut - removal and refitting

Removal

1 Support the tailgate in its open position.

2 Prise off the upper spring clip securing the strut to the tailgate, then pull the socket from the ball-stud **(see illustration).**

3 Similarly prise off the bottom clip, and pull the socket from the ball-stud **(see illustration).** Withdraw the strut.

Refitting

4 Refitting is a reversal of the removal procedure, but make sure that the piston end of the strut is fitted on the body (ie downwards).

22 Tailgate lock components - removal and refitting

Removal

Lock barrel (Hatchback) - models up to 1996

1 Disconnect the battery negative (earth) lead (Chapter 5A, Section 1).

2 With the tailgate open, pull up the weatherstrip for access to the lock. Remove the screws and clips, and remove the trim panel from the rear of the luggage compartment.

3 Unhook the parcel net, then remove the screws and clips, and remove the rear crossmember trim.

4 Remove the screws, and prise out the rear light trim cover from the guides.

5 Release the door-ajar sensor from the clip near the lock.

6 Slide the outer cable from the lock bracket. Raise the inner cable until it is aligned with the slot in the barrel lever, and disconnect it **(see illustration).**

21.2 Prising the spring clip from the upper end of the strut

21.3 Prising the spring clip from the lower end of the strut

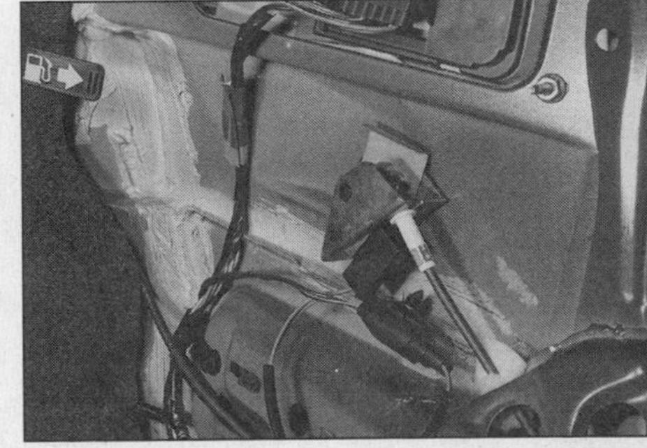
22.6 Tailgate lock barrel and bracket

22.8a Removing the lock barrel . . .

22.8b . . . and cylinder

22.11 Remove the four access plate retaining screws (arrowed)

7 Pull out the lock barrel locating spring clip.

8 Detach the cable mounting bracket from the barrel, and remove the barrel and cylinder **(see illustrations)**.

Lock barrel (Hatchback) - 1997 models onwards

9 Refer to Section 19, paragraphs 8 to 12.

Lock barrel (Estate)

10 Disconnect the battery negative (earth) lead (Chapter 5A, Section 1).

11 Unclip and remove the tailgate trim panel, then undo the four retaining screws and remove the access plate **(see illustration)**.

12 Noting their fitted positions, prise out the central locking and lock operating rods from the lock barrel housing **(see illustration)**.

13 Disconnect the door-ajar sensor wiring plug **(see illustration)**.

14 Prise up the plastic tabs either side, and remove the plastic housing from the lock barrel **(see illustration)**.

15 Working through the aperture in the tailgate inner panel, pull out the lock barrel locating clip **(see illustration)**.

16 Withdraw the lock barrel from the outside of the tailgate **(see illustration)**.

Lock (Hatchback)

17 Disconnect the battery negative (earth) lead (Chapter 5A, Section 1).

18 With the tailgate open, pull up the weatherstrip for access to the lock. Remove the screws and clips, and remove the trim panel from the rear of the luggage compartment.

19 Release the door-ajar sensor from the clip near the lock **(see illustration)**, and disconnect the wiring plug for the alarm inhibitor switch. On later models, prise out the wiring harness from the bodywork, and disconnect the multi-plug for the central locking motor.

20 Mark the position of the lock mounting screws, for use when refitting. Using a Torx key, unscrew the lock mounting screws, and withdraw the lock for access to the cable(s) **(see illustration)**.

21 Early models have a cable-operated remote release, as well as the lock operating cable fitted to all models. Disconnect the cable(s) from the lock bracket **(see illustration)**.

22 Prise open the plastic clip, and remove the central locking control rod.

23 Withdraw the lock assembly.

Lock (Estate)

24 Disconnect the battery negative (earth) lead (Chapter 5A, Section 1).

25 Open the tailgate. Undo the screws and remove the inner trim panel, releasing it from its various retaining clips **(see illustrations)**.

22.12 Central locking and lock operating rods on lock barrel housing

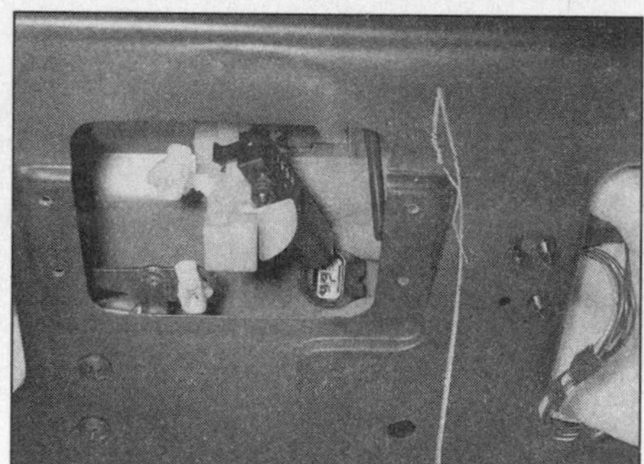
22.13 Disconnect the door-ajar sensor/boot light wiring plug

22.14 Removing the lock barrel housing - note one of the retaining tabs (arrowed)

22.15 Slide out the lock barrel retaining clip . . .

22.16 . . . and withdraw the lock barrel from outside

22.19 Removing the door-ajar sensor from the lock

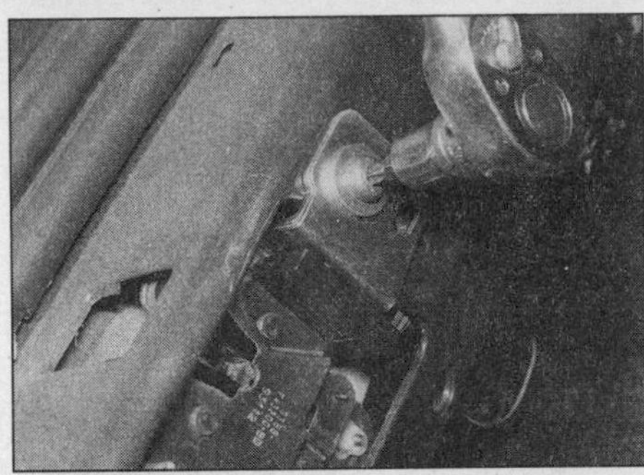
22.20 Removing a lock mounting screw

22.21 Disconnecting the cables from the lock

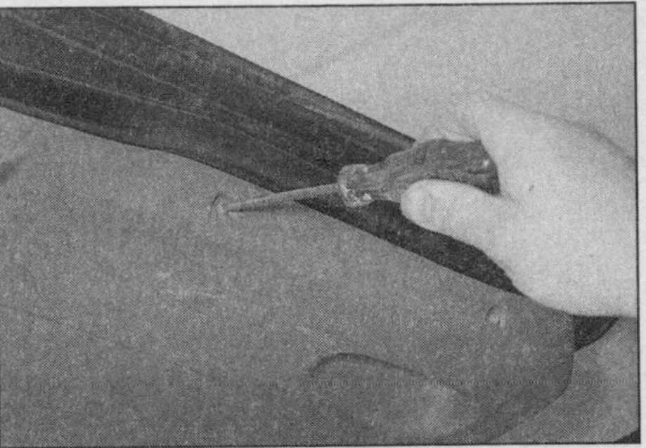
22.25a Remove the trim panel securing screws . . .

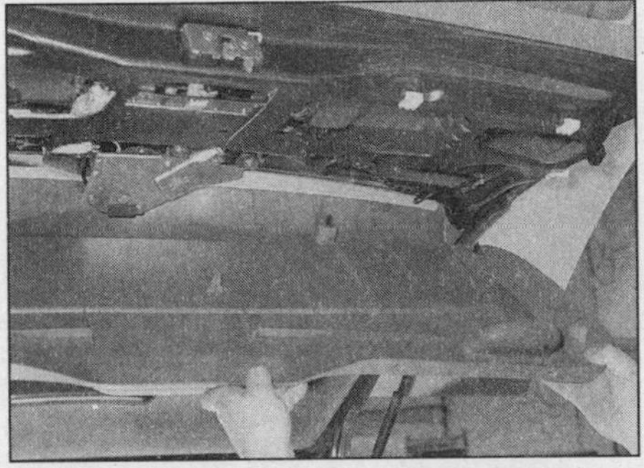
22.25b . . . then release the panel from its retaining clips, and remove it

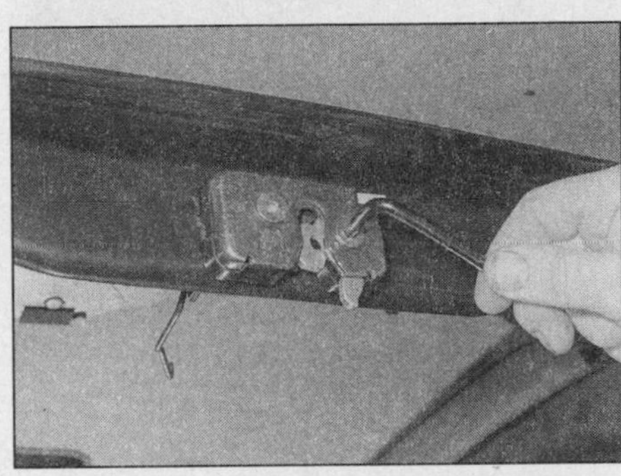
22.27a Unscrew the lock securing screws . . .

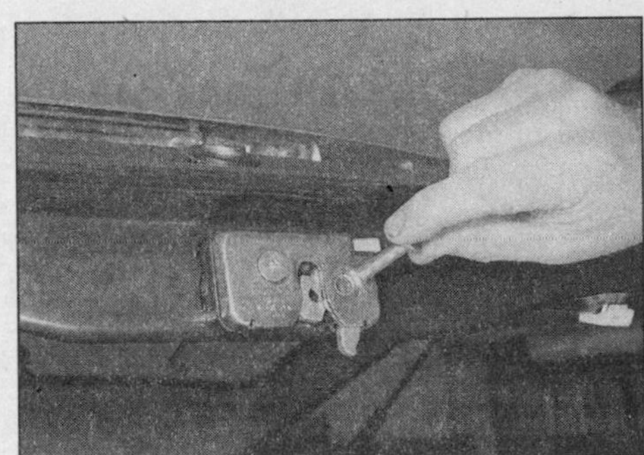
22.27b . . . and withdraw the lock assembly

26 Remove the four retaining screws and take off the access plate, for access to the operating rod(s). Disconnect the rod from the lock barrel, and (where applicable) from the central locking motor, noting their fitted positions (refer to illustration 22.12).

27 Mark the position of the lock mounting screws, for use when refitting. Using a Torx key, unscrew the lock mounting screws, and carefully withdraw the lock **(see illustrations)**.

28 Release the door-ajar sensor from the lock **(see illustration)**.

29 If necessary, the lock striker assembly may be removed by disconnecting the release cable (early models) and unscrewing the mounting bolts **(see illustration)**.

Refitting

Lock barrel and lock - all models

30 Refitting is a reversal of the removal procedure. When refitting the lock, use the alignment marks made on removal to ensure that the lock is positioned accurately.

23 Central locking system components - testing, removal and refitting

Testing

1 The central locking module incorporates a service-test mode, which is activated by operating one of the lock position switches 8 times within 10 seconds. A buzzer will sound, to indicate that the service-test mode is operating, and to indicate that no faults have been found in the system. If a fault has been found, the system should be checked by a Ford dealer or electrical specialist. The central locking module also incorporates the alarm system module.

Removal

Central locking/alarm module

2 To remove the module, first remove the lower right-hand facia panel (right-hand-drive models) or the glovebox (left-hand-drive models).

3 Disconnect the battery negative (earth) lead (Chapter 5A, Section 1).

4 Unscrew the mounting bolts, and remove the module from the bracket beneath the facia.

5 Disconnect the wiring multi-plug, and withdraw the module from inside the vehicle.

6 Note that a different module is used for models without an anti-theft alarm.

Set/reset switch (front doors)

7 This procedure is covered in Section 14, under front door handle removal.

Door-ajar switch/sensor

8 This procedure is covered in the relevant lock removal procedure - refer to Section 14, 19 or 22 as applicable.

Door motors

9 This procedure is covered in Section 14.

Bootlid/tailgate motor

10 Remove the lock as described in Section 19 or 22, as applicable.

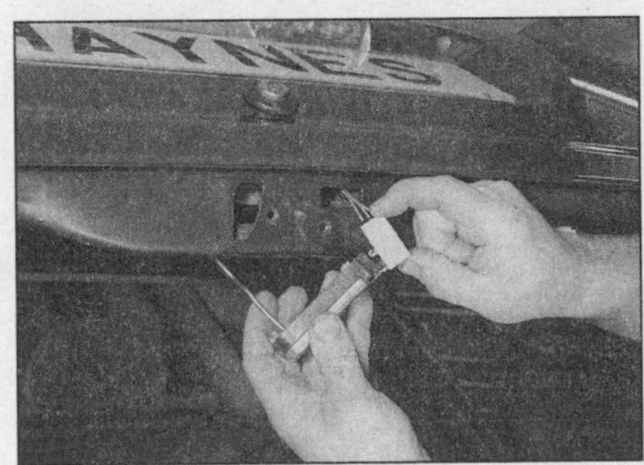
22.28 Unclip the door-ajar sensor/boot light switch from the lock

22.29 Lock striker assembly - early Estate models

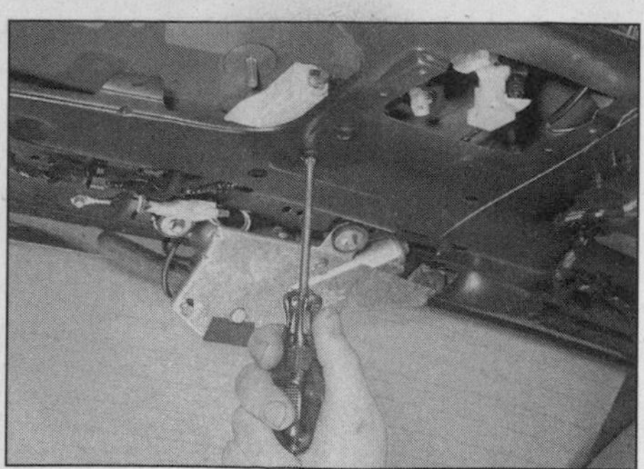

23.11a Remove the two motor securing screws . . .

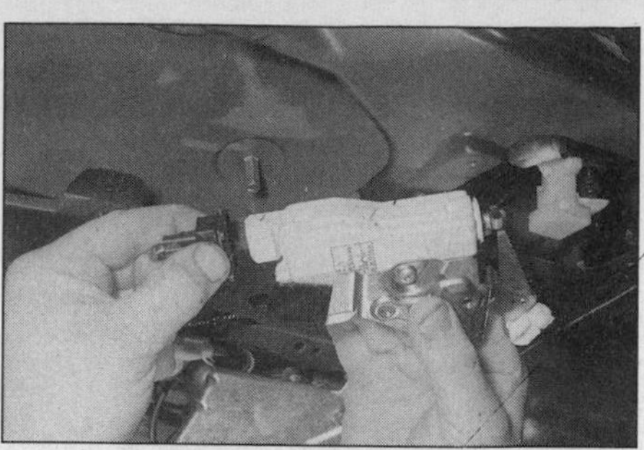

23.11b . . . remove the motor, and disconnect the wiring plug - Estate model shown, others similar

11 Remove the two motor securing screws, then manoeuvre the motor assembly out from the body, disconnecting the wiring plug **(see illustrations)**.

Refitting

12 In all cases, refitting is a reversal of the removal procedure.

24 Windscreen and fixed windows - removal and refitting

1 The windscreen and rear window on all models are bonded in place with special mastic, as are the rear side windows on Estate models. Special tools are required to cut free the old units and fit replacements; special cleaning solutions and primer are also required. It is therefore recommended that this work is entrusted to a Ford dealer or windscreen replacement specialist.

2 Note that the windscreen contributes towards the structural strength of the vehicle as a whole, so it is important that it is fitted correctly.

25 Body side-trim mouldings and adhesive emblems - removal and refitting

Removal

1 Insert a length of strong cord (fishing line is ideal) behind the moulding or emblem concerned. With a sawing action, break the adhesive bond between the moulding or emblem and the panel **(see illustration)**.

2 Thoroughly clean all traces of adhesive from the panel using methylated spirit, and allow the location to dry.

Refitting

3 Peel back the protective paper from the rear face of the new moulding or emblem. Carefully fit it into position on the panel concerned, but take care not to touch the adhesive. When in position, apply hand pressure to the moulding/emblem for a short period, to ensure maximum adhesion to the panel.

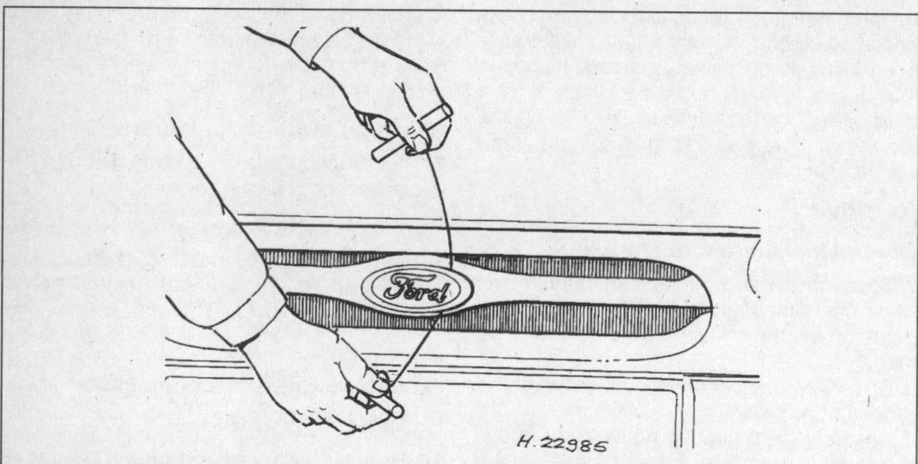

25.1 Using a length of cord to remove the emblem from the radiator grille

26 Sunroof - general information and adjustment

1 The sunroof should operate freely, without sticking or binding, as it is opened and closed. When in the closed position, check that the panel is flush with the surrounding roof panel.

2 If adjustment is required, open the sun blind, but leave the glass panel shut. Unscrew and remove the three lower frame-to-glass panel retaining screws. Slide the lower frame back into the roof.

3 Loosen the central and front securing screws. Adjust the glass roof panel so that it is flush at its front edge with the roof panel, then retighten the securing screws.

4 Pull the lower frame forwards, and insert and tighten its retaining screws to complete.

27 Seats - removal and refitting

Removal

Front seat

1 On models with electrically-operated or heated seats, or with side air bags, disconnect the battery negative lead, and position the lead away from the battery (see Chapter 5A, Section 1).

Warning: Where side air bags are fitted, before proceeding, wait a minimum of 15 minutes, as a precaution against accidental firing of the air bag unit. This period ensures that any stored energy in the back-up capacitor is dissipated.

2 Release the seat belt, and slide the seat fully forwards.

3 Using a Torx key, undo the screws and remove the side and rear mounting trims, then unscrew the rear mounting bolts **(see illustrations)**.

27.3a Unscrew the Torx-headed screws . . .

27.3b . . . and remove the mounting trims for access to the front seat rear mounting bolts

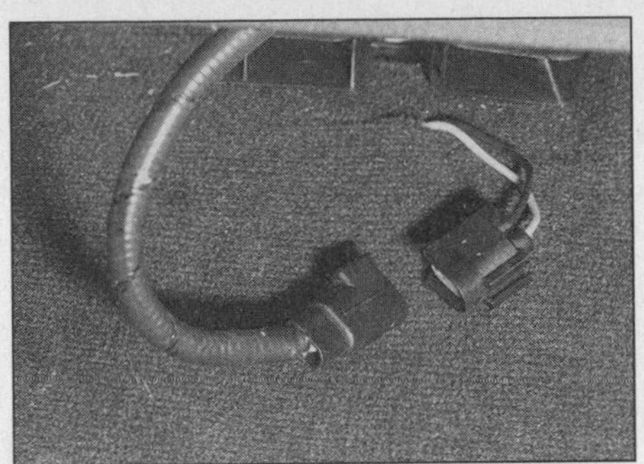

27.5 Disconnecting an electric seat multi-plug

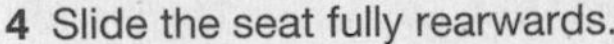

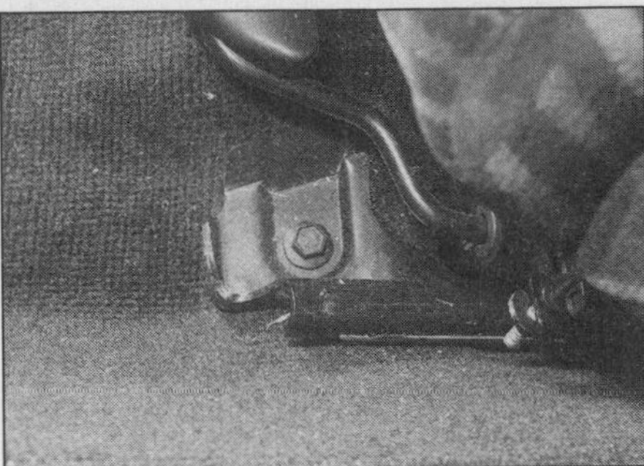

27.7 Front seat front mounting bolt

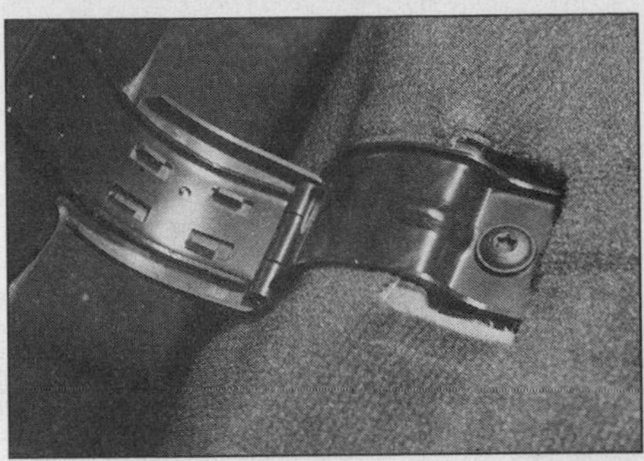

27.8 Rear seat cushion hinge bolt

4 Slide the seat fully rearwards.

5 On models with electrically-operated or heated seats, disconnect the various seat wiring multi-plugs from the seat base, noting their fitted positions **(see illustration)**.

6 Where side air bags are fitted, remove the trim from the seat base to gain access to the air bag wiring plug. Release the retaining clip and disconnect the plug. Note which way round the plug is fitted - it must face the seat base when refitted.

7 Unscrew the front mounting bolts **(see illustration)**, and remove the seat from the vehicle.

Rear seat cushion

8 Fold the rear seat cushion forwards. (Note that, on some models, the seat cushion is held in place by screws which must be removed first.) Using a Torx key, unscrew and remove the mounting bolts from the hinges on each side **(see illustration)**.

9 Withdraw the seat cushion from the vehicle.

Rear seat backrest

10 Fold the rear seat cushion and both backrests forwards.

11 Unclip the backrest rear trims, where fitted, and raise them.

12 Using a Torx key, unscrew the mounting bolts **(see illustration)**.

13 Withdraw the backrest from inside the vehicle.

Rear seat side bolster

14 Fold the rear seat backrest forwards.

15 On low-series models, remove the screw and pull the bolster forwards to disengage the clips. On high-series models, simply pull the bolster upwards to disengage the clips.

Refitting

16 Refitting is a reversal of the removal procedure, but tighten the mounting bolts to the specified torque.

28 Seat belts - removal and refitting

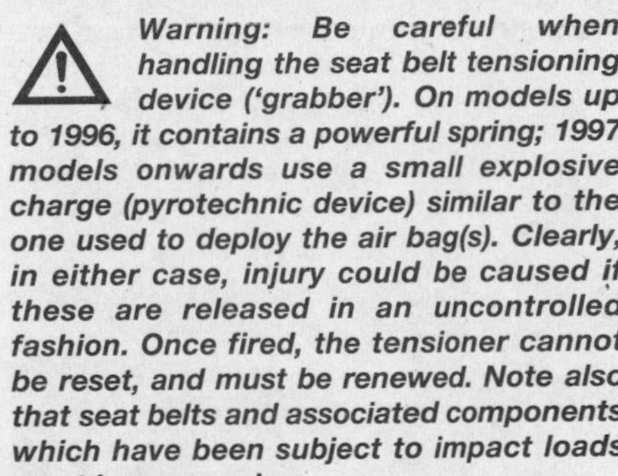

Warning: Be careful when handling the seat belt tensioning device ('grabber'). On models up to 1996, it contains a powerful spring; 1997 models onwards use a small explosive charge (pyrotechnic device) similar to the one used to deploy the air bag(s). Clearly, in either case, injury could be caused if these are released in an uncontrolled fashion. Once fired, the tensioner cannot be reset, and must be renewed. Note also that seat belts and associated components which have been subject to impact loads must be renewed.

Removal

Front seat belt - models up to 1996

Note: *Before removing the seat belt stalk, ask a Ford dealer for one of the special plastic clips used to disarm the tensioner operating cable while it is disconnected.*

27.12 Rear seat backrest mounting bolts

1 Remove the trim from the 'B' pillar and the scuttle.

2 Unscrew the mounting bolts and remove the seat belt reel unit **(see illustration)**.

3 Unscrew the bolt securing the seat belt guide to the 'B' pillar, then unscrew the nut securing the seat belt upper shackle **(see illustrations)**.

4 Where necessary, remove the screws and clips, and take off the seat lower side trim panel for access to the seat belt stalk.

5 Pull down the tensioner inner cable, and slide the end fitting out of the bracket. Twist the outer cable through 90°, and remove it from the bracket. Fit the special plastic clip to the tensioner cable to disarm the tensioner **(see illustration)**.

6 Undo the mounting nut, noting that on the right-hand seat, it has a left-hand thread (ie unscrews clockwise), and remove the stalk

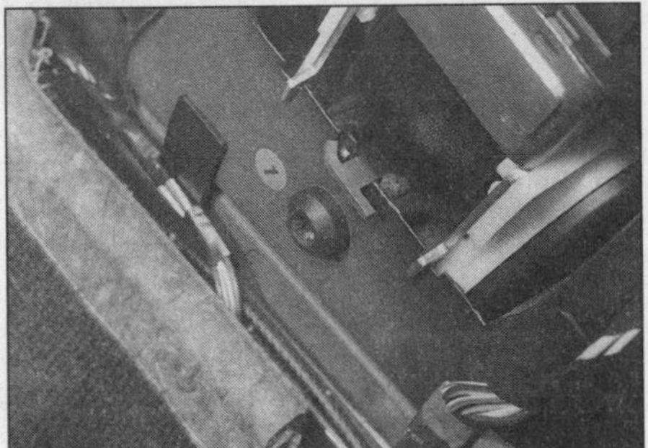

28.2 Front seat belt reel unit lower mounting bolt

28.3a Front seat belt guide and mounting bolt

28.3b Front seat belt shackle and mounting nut

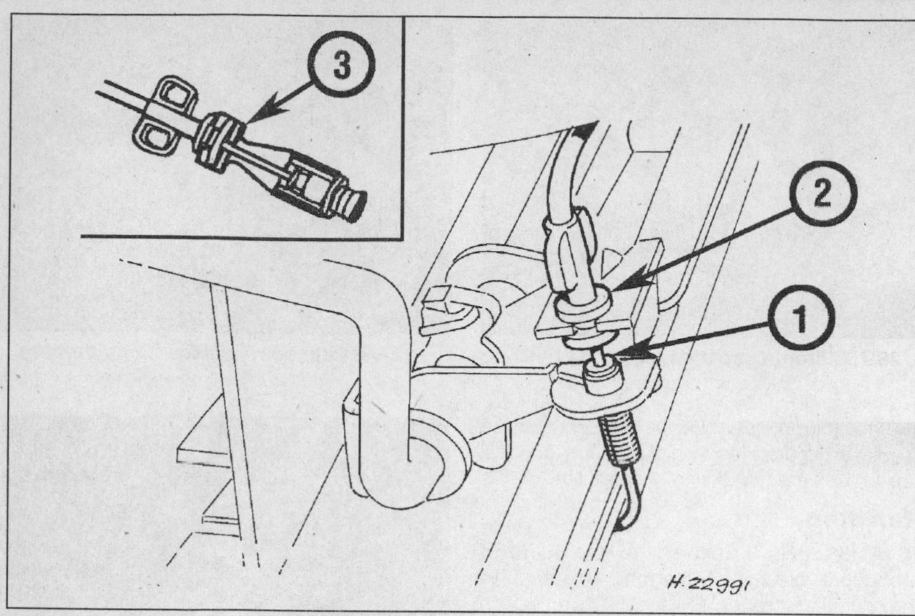

28.5 Front seat belt stalk cable details

1 Inner cable 2 Outer cable 3 Plastic clip

and grabber assembly from the front seat **(see illustration)**.

Warning: There is a potential risk of the grabber firing during (or after) removal, so it should be handled carefully.

7 Remove the recline adjustment knob and trim from the outer side of the front seat, then unscrew the bolt and remove the seat belt end from the seat **(see illustrations)**.

Front seat belt - 1997 models onwards

8 On models with the pyrotechnic type seat belt tensioner, disconnect the battery negative lead, and position the lead away from the battery (see Chapter 5A, Section 1).

Warning: Before proceeding, wait a minimum of 2 minutes, as a precaution against accidental firing of the seat belt tensioner. This period ensures that any stored energy in the back-up capacitor is dissipated.

28.6 Front seat stalk mounting nut

9 Remove the trim from the 'B' pillar and the scuttle.

10 Unscrew the mounting bolt and remove the seat belt reel unit from the pillar.

11 Unscrew the bolt securing the seat belt guide to the 'B' pillar, then unscrew the nut securing the seat belt upper shackle.

12 Where necessary, remove the screws and clips, and take off the seat lower side trim panel for access to the seat belt stalk.

13 Disconnect the wiring plug from the tensioner. Undo the mounting nut, and remove the stalk and grabber assembly from the front seat **(see illustrations)**.

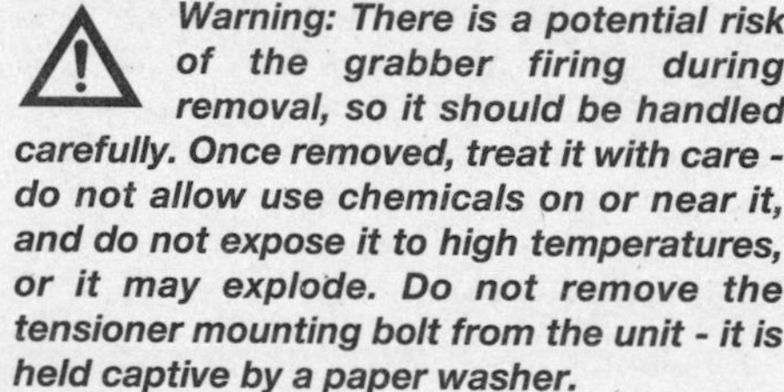

Warning: There is a potential risk of the grabber firing during removal, so it should be handled carefully. Once removed, treat it with care - do not allow use chemicals on or near it, and do not expose it to high temperatures, or it may explode. Do not remove the tensioner mounting bolt from the unit - it is held captive by a paper washer.

14 Remove the recline adjustment knob and trim from the outer side of the front seat, then unscrew the bolt and remove the seat belt end from the seat.

Rear side seat belt

15 Unscrew the screws and remove the trim from the 'C' pillar. It will be necessary to detach the rear seat release cable, and remove the plastic cover from the rear seat lock **(see illustrations)**.

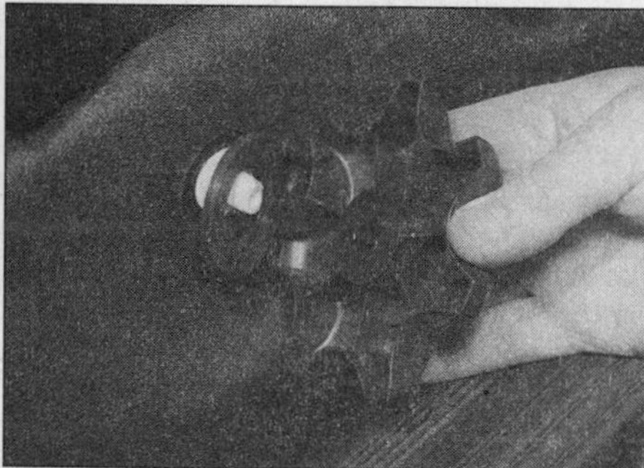

28.7a Remove the recline adjustment knob . . .

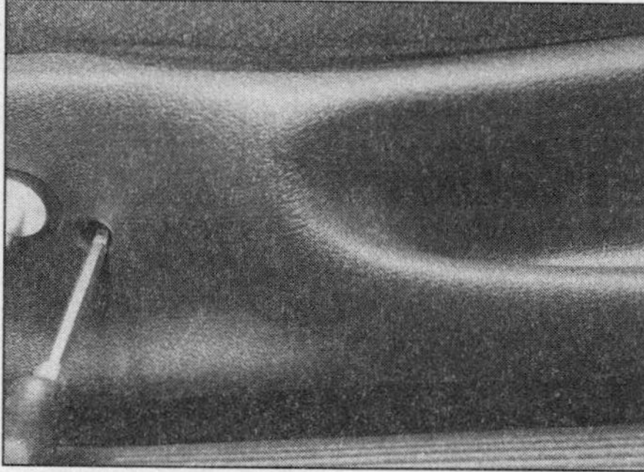

28.7b . . . unscrew the trim retaining screws . . .

28.7c . . . and unscrew the seat belt end retaining bolt

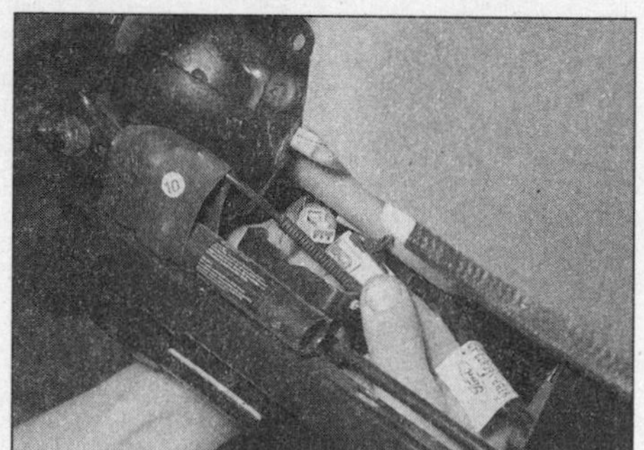

28.13a Disconnect the wiring connector . . .

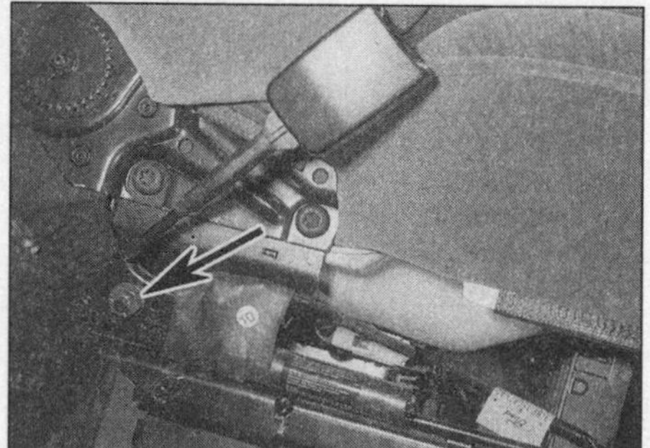

28.13b . . . then unscrew the mounting nut and remove the tensioner assembly

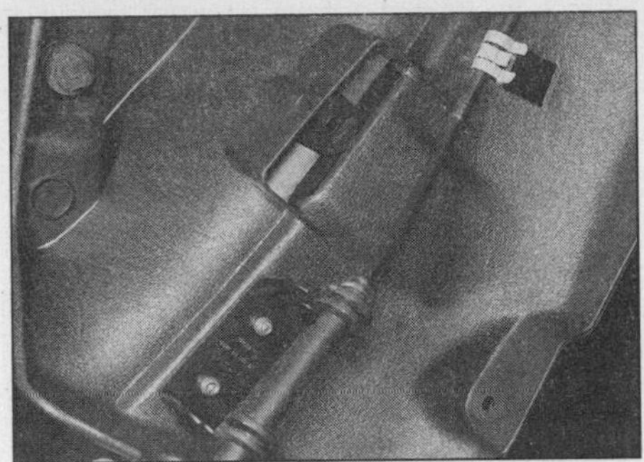
28.15a Detach the rear seat release cable

28.15b Removing the plastic cover from the rear seat lock

28.16a Rear seat belt shackle mounting bolt

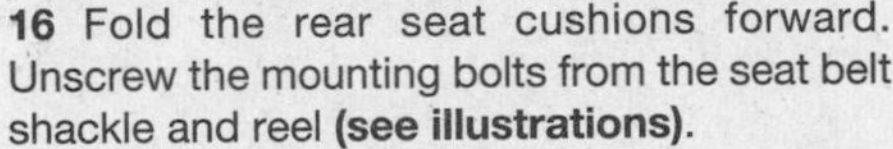

16 Fold the rear seat cushions forward. Unscrew the mounting bolts from the seat belt shackle and reel **(see illustrations)**.

17 Unscrew the mounting bolt securing the seat belt stalk, and withdraw the stalk. Also unscrew the mounting bolt from the lower anchorage, where applicable **(see illustration)**.

Rear centre seat belt

18 The third, centre rear seat belt was offered as an option on 1997 and later models. The belt reel is attached to the base of the seat backrest, but removal requires that the seat fabric be removed, so this operation should be referred to a Ford dealer or competent specialist. The belt stalks can be removed as described in paragraph 17.

Refitting

19 Refitting is a reversal of the removal procedure. Tighten the mounting nuts and bolts to the specified torque.

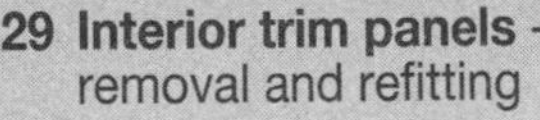

29 Interior trim panels - removal and refitting

Removal

Sun visor

1 Disconnect the wiring for the vanity mirror light, where fitted.

2 Unscrew the mounting screws and remove the visor.

3 Prise up the cover, unscrew the inner

28.16b Rear seat belt reel mounting bolt

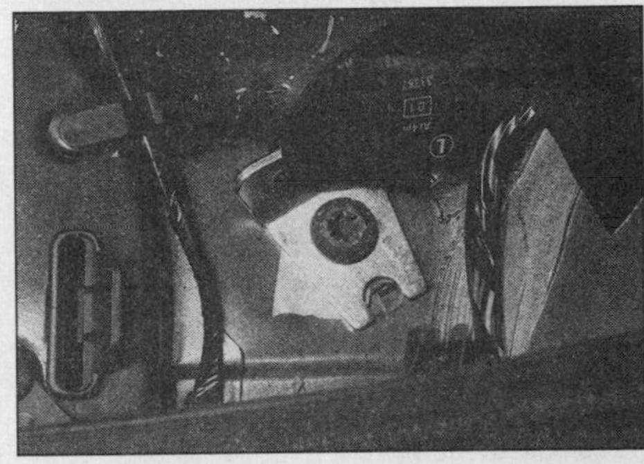
28.17 Rear seat belt lower anchorage

bracket mounting screws, and remove the bracket.

Passenger grab handle

4 Prise up the covers, then unscrew the mounting screws and remove the grab handle.

'A' pillar trim

5 Pull away the door weatherstrip in the area of the trim.

6 Release the alarm and aerial wiring from the upper and middle clips.

7 Carefully press the trim away from the upper and middle clips, and pull the trim upwards. Recover the lower sealing strip.

8 Remove the upper and middle clips from the pillar.

'B' pillar and cowl side trim

9 Pull away the door weatherstrip in the area of the trim.

10 Undo the screws, release the fasteners and remove the lower trim **(see illustrations)**.

11 Carefully separate the lower trim from the upper trim, using a screwdriver if necessary **(see illustration)**.

12 Unscrew the seat belt mounting bolt from under the front seat, remove the remaining trim from the 'B' pillar, and feed the belt through the trim.

'C' pillar trim (Saloon and Hatchback)

13 Pull away the door weatherstrip in the area of the trim.

14 Fold the rear seat cushion forwards.

15 On 1997 and later Hatchback models, prise out the screw covers, and remove the two trim-to-parcel shelf support screws.

16 Pull up the rear seat bolster, and release the upper hook **(see illustrations)**. Note that, on low-series models, the bolster is retained with a screw.

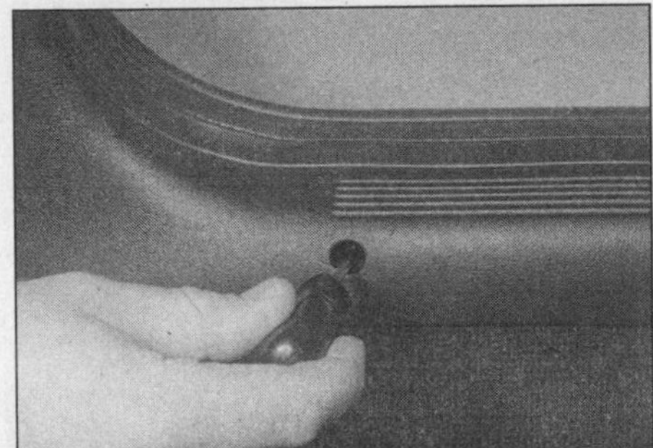
29.10a Removing a middle screw from the lower trim

29.10b Releasing the fasteners from the cowl side trim

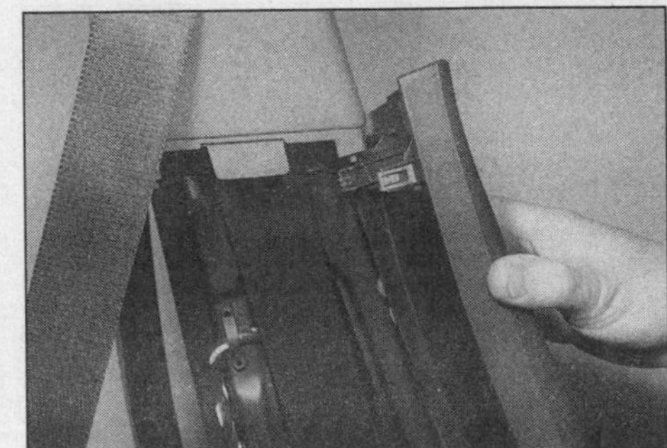
29.11 Separating the 'B' pillar lower and upper trim

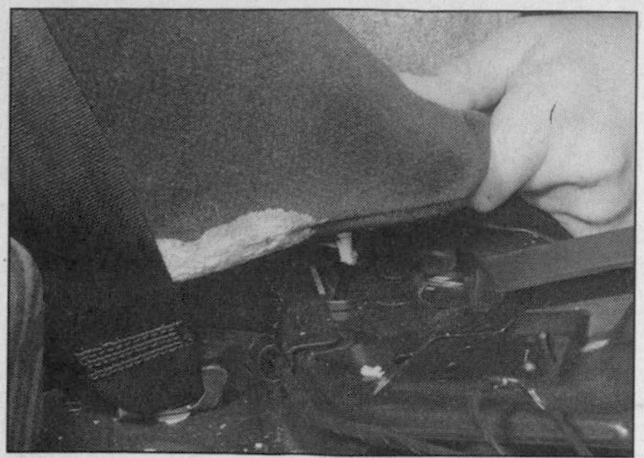
29.16a Pull up the rear seat bolster . . .

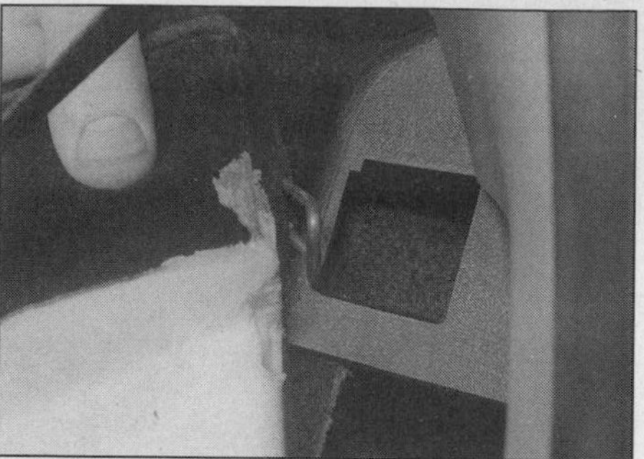
29.16b . . . and release the upper hook

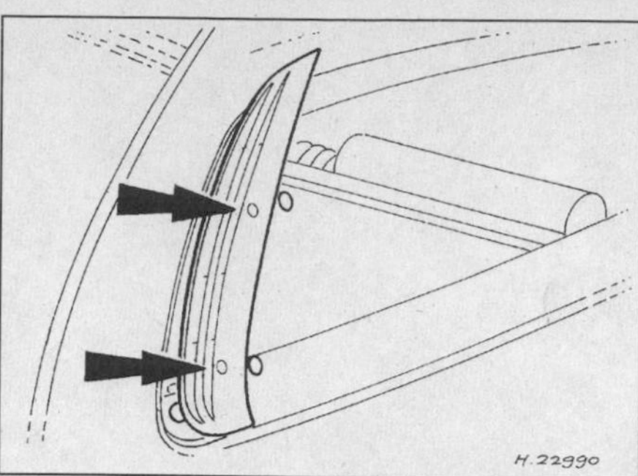

29.19 Screw locations (arrowed) for the 'C' pillar upper trim - Estate models

17 Release the clips and locating tangs, and detach the upper trim. On models equipped with the ultrasonic parking sensor, release the warning light unit from the panel, or disconnect its wiring plug.

18 Remove the rear seat belt lower mounting bolt, then remove the trim, and pass the seat belt through it.

'C' pillar trim (Estate)

19 Prise off the caps, unscrew the screws, and remove the upper trim from the 'C' pillar **(see illustration)**.

20 Unscrew the mounting bolt securing the rear seat belt upper shackle to the 'C' pillar.

21 Unclip and remove the trim.

22 On models equipped with the ultrasonic parking sensor, release the warning light unit from the panel, or disconnect its wiring plug.

'D' pillar trim (Estate)

23 Remove the three mounting screws, then unclip the trim from the 'D' pillar.

Lower facia panel

24 Remove the steering column top and bottom shrouds.

25 Unscrew the mounting screws from the upper corners and above the coin tray position, and withdraw the lower facia panel from the facia **(see illustrations)**. Where applicable, detach the diagnostic plug connector from the panel.

Lower centre panels

26 Release the two screws or clips each side, and withdraw the panels from the front of the centre console **(see illustrations)**.

Refitting

27 Refitting is a reversal of the removal procedure. Where seat belt fastenings have been disturbed, make sure that they are tightened to the specified torque.

30 Centre console - removal and refitting

Removal

1 Disconnect the battery negative (earth) lead (Chapter 5A, Section 1).

2 Pull the ashtray from the facia, and prise off the cigar lighter surround **(see illustrations)**.

Manual transmission models

3 Unscrew the gear lever knob. Prise out the gear lever gaiter, and remove it over the top of the gear lever **(see illustrations)**.

Automatic transmission models

4 Remove the screw on the side of the selector lever which secures the lever knob **(see illustration)**.

29.25a Unscrew the mounting screws from the upper corners . . .

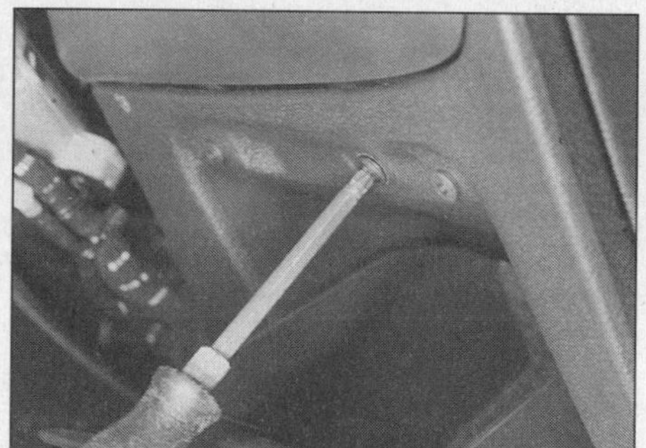
29.25b . . . and above the coin tray position . . .

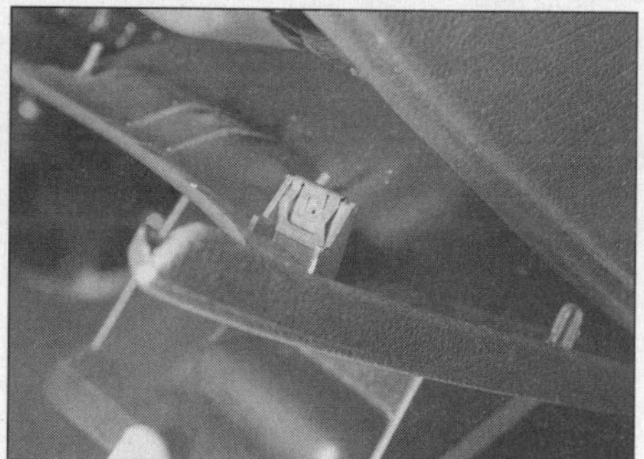
29.25c . . . and withdraw the lower facia panel

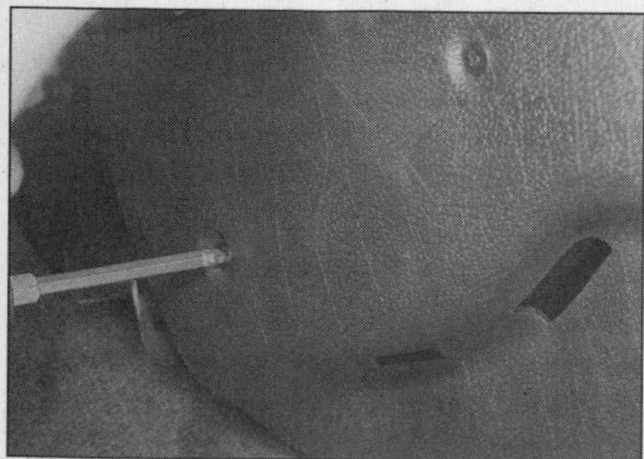
29.26a Unscrew the screws (or release the clips) . . .

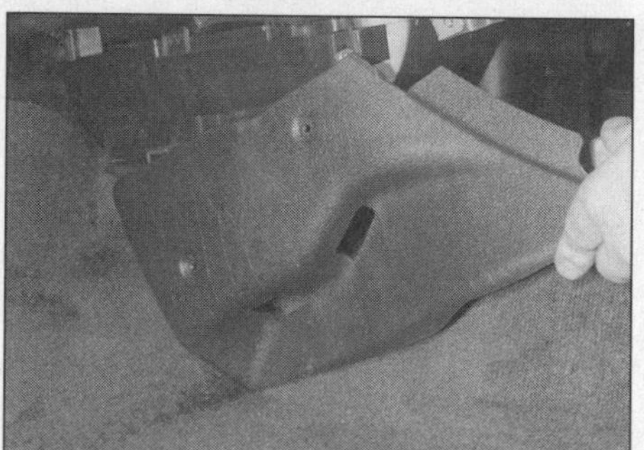
29.26b . . . and remove the lower centre panel

30.2a Remove the ashtray . . .

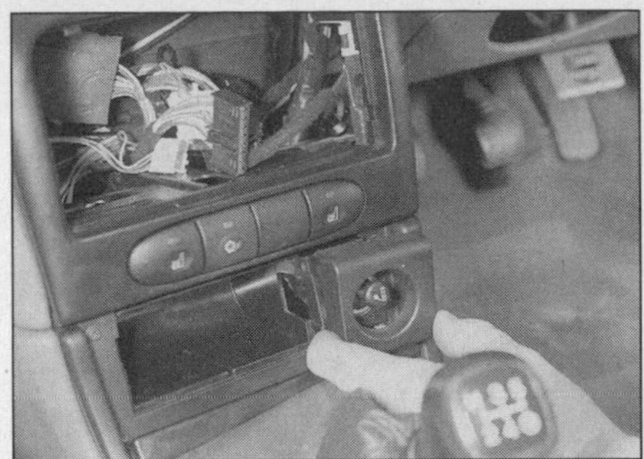
30.2b ... then prise off the cigar lighter surround

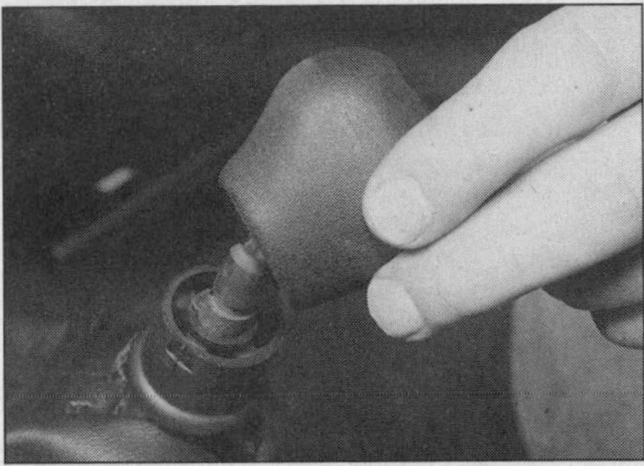
30.3a Gear lever knob removal

30.3b Prising out the gear lever gaiter

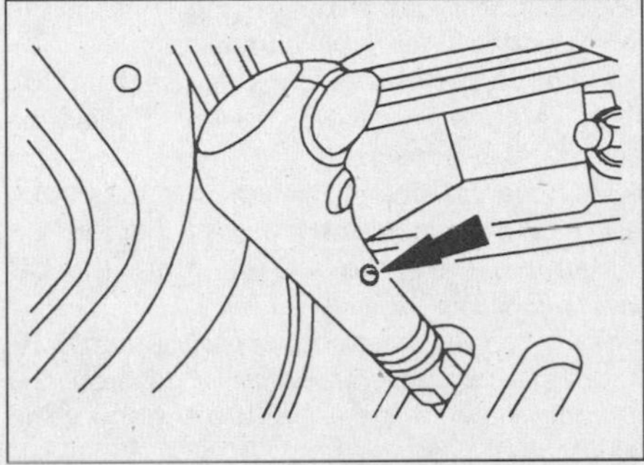
30.4 Selector lever knob retaining screw (arrowed)

30.10a Prise off the plastic caps ...

30.10b ... and unscrew the mounting screws at the front top ...

5 Using a screwdriver, carefully prise out the selector lever panel. Disconnect the wiring multi-plugs, then remove the selector lever knob and panel.

6 Detach and disconnect the wiring plugs inside the centre console. Detach the wiring by cutting the cable-ties as necessary.

All models

7 Remove the adaptive damping switch, when fitted (Chapter 12, Section 4).

8 Where applicable, lift out the rubber mat from the base of the rear storage compartment.

9 Prise out the coin storage tray (if fitted).

10 Prise off the plastic caps (where fitted), then unscrew the centre console mounting screws. These are located on each side, on the front top, and inside the cassette storage box **(see illustrations)**. The screws with the washers go on the side of the console; the front screws are smaller than the others, and black in colour.

11 Fully apply the handbrake lever. On later models, it may be necessary to release the handbrake spring from the ratchet, in order to lift the lever high enough to remove the console.

12 Withdraw the centre console, at the same time passing the gaiter over the handbrake lever **(see illustrations)**.

13 Disconnect the cigar lighter wiring **(see illustration)**.

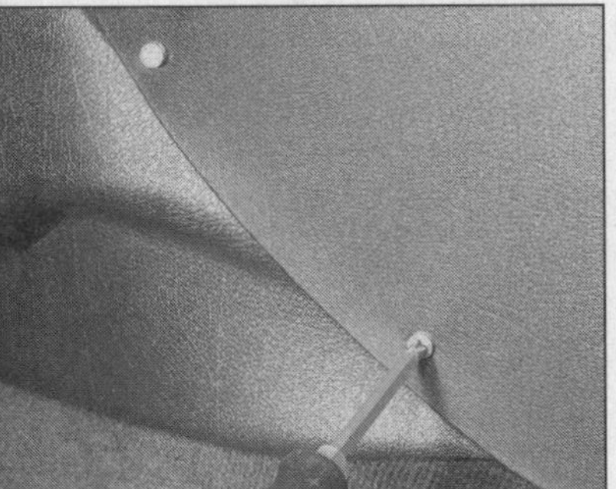
30.10c ... at the sides ...

30.10d ... and inside the cassette storage box

30.12a Withdrawing the front of the console from the facia

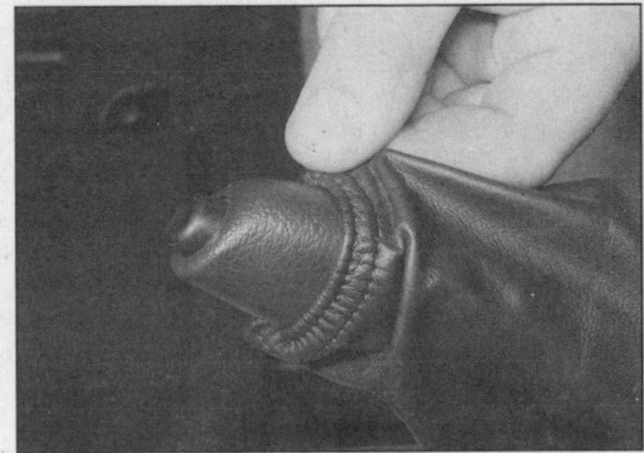
30.12b Passing the gaiter over the handbrake lever

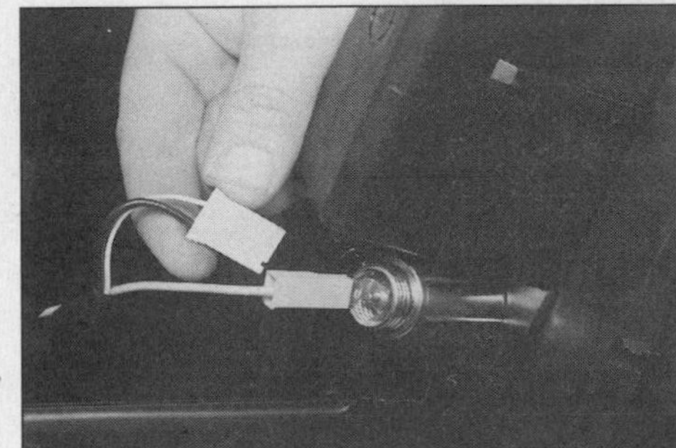
30.13 Disconnecting the cigar lighter wiring

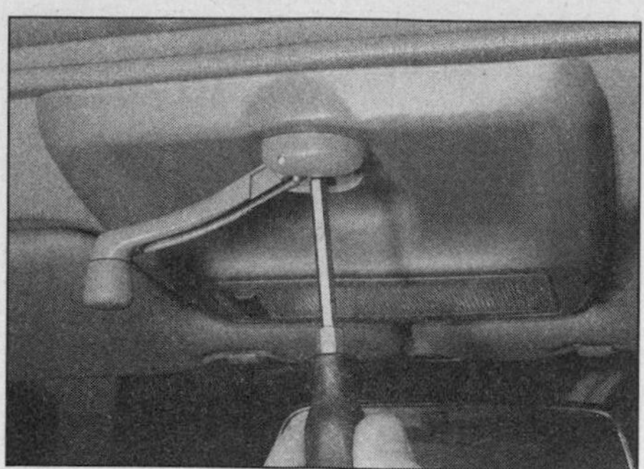

31.3 Removing the sunroof handle securing screw

Refitting

14 Refitting is a reversal of the removal procedure.

31 Overhead console - removal and refitting

Removal

1 Disconnect the battery negative (earth) lead (Chapter 5A, Section 1).

2 On models with an electrically-operated sunroof, remove the sunroof switch (Chapter 12, Section 4).

3 On models with a manual sunroof, remove the sunroof handle, after undoing the securing screw **(see illustration)**.

4 Push the console towards the windscreen, to disengage it from the clips.

Refitting

5 Refitting is a reversal of the removal procedure.

32 Glovebox - removal and refitting

Removal

1 Open the glovebox. Using a screwdriver, carefully press in one side of the glovebox near the hinge, to release it from the plastic clip **(see illustration)**.

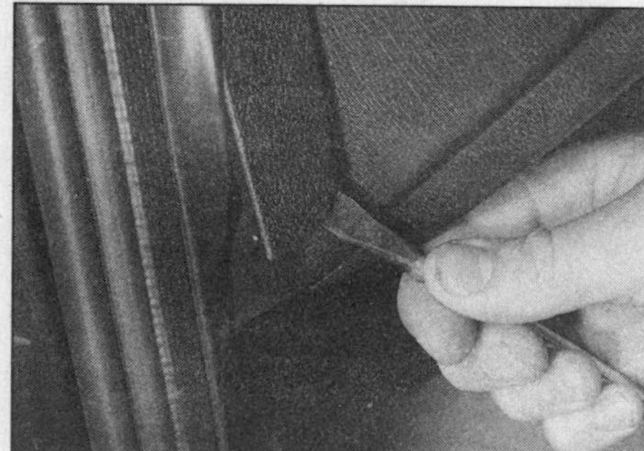

33.18a Prise off the covers . . .

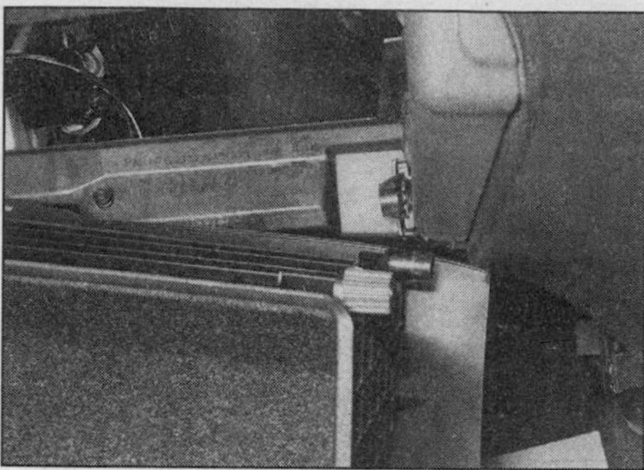

32.1 Glovebox removal

2 Withdraw the glovebox and, where necessary, disconnect the wiring multi-plug for the light.

3 If necessary, the lock may be removed by unscrewing the mounting screws and removing the lock plate and spring **(see illustration)**.

4 To remove the lock barrel, depress the spring tabs.

Refitting

5 Locate the barrel in the lock plate, making sure that the clips are fully engaged.

6 Hold the latch pins together, and engage the right-hand pin of the lock plate.

7 Refit the spring, and engage the left-hand pin of the lock plate.

8 Refit the lock plate, and tighten the screws.

9 Reconnect the wiring multi-plug and refit the glovebox, making sure that it is fully inserted in the plastic clips.

33 Facia - removal and refitting

Removal

1 Disconnect the battery negative (earth) lead (Chapter 5A, Section 1).

2 On models up to 1996, remove the windscreen wiper arms (Chapter 12), then remove the cowl from just in front of the windscreen. The cowl is in two sections, with retaining screws located along its front edge. With the cowl removed, disconnect the speedometer cable by pulling it from the intermediate inner cable extension.

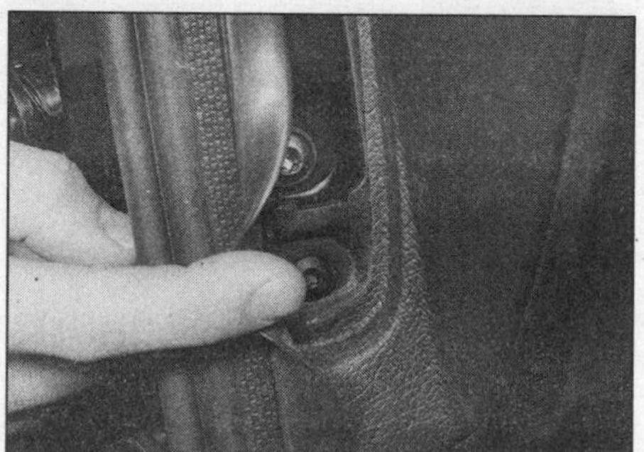

33.18b . . . and pull away the weatherstrip to reveal the facia mounting bolts

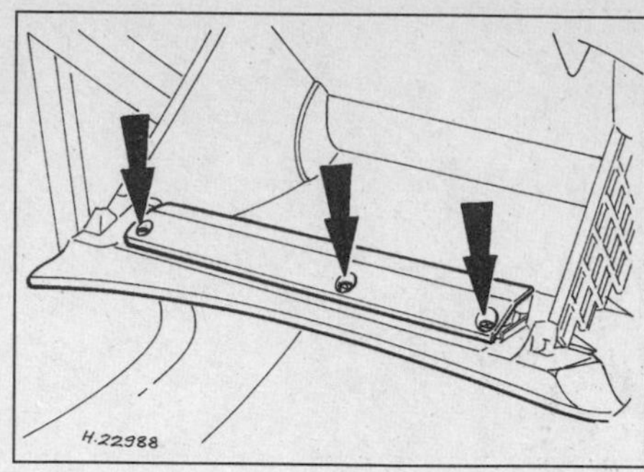

32.3 Glovebox lock mounting screws (arrowed)

3 Remove the centre console (Section 30), then remove the lower centre panels as described in Section 29.

4 Remove the steering column (Chapter 10).

5 Remove the instrument panel (Chapter 12).

6 Remove the radio and (if fitted) the CD player (Chapter 12).

7 Remove the heater control panel (Chapter 3).

8 Using a screwdriver, carefully prise out the headlight switch panel, and disconnect the wiring multi-plugs.

9 Remove the glovebox (Section 32).

10 Where applicable, remove the passenger air bag as described in Chapter 12.

11 Remove the small piece of carpet from under the passenger side of the facia.

12 Remove the side trim panels from the 'A' and 'B' pillars on each side of the vehicle (Section 29). The upper panels on the 'B' pillars can be left in position.

13 At the base of the right-hand 'A' pillar, disconnect the wiring multi-plugs, earth leads and aerial, noting their fitted positions.

14 Identify the position of the wiring multi-plugs on the fusebox, then disconnect them.

15 Disconnect the wiring from the footwell lights, where fitted.

16 On models up to 1996, prise out the speedometer cable rubber grommet at the bulkhead near the pedal bracket, then release the cable from the clips.

17 Remove the screws and withdraw the glovebox side trim, for access to the side facia mounting screw.

18 Open the front doors. Prise off the trim covers, then pull away the door weatherstrip by the side mounting bolt positions on each side **(see illustrations)**.

19 Unscrew the facia side mounting bolts.

20 Unscrew the facia centre mounting bolts **(see illustrations)**.

21 Withdraw the facia from the bulkhead, far enough to be able to reach in behind it.

22 Disconnect the remaining multi-plugs and connections, noting their locations on the various components for correct refitting. It will also be necessary to release some wiring loom holders, clips and plastic ties, and the fresh air vent hoses **(see illustration)**.

23 Withdraw the facia from one side of the vehicle.

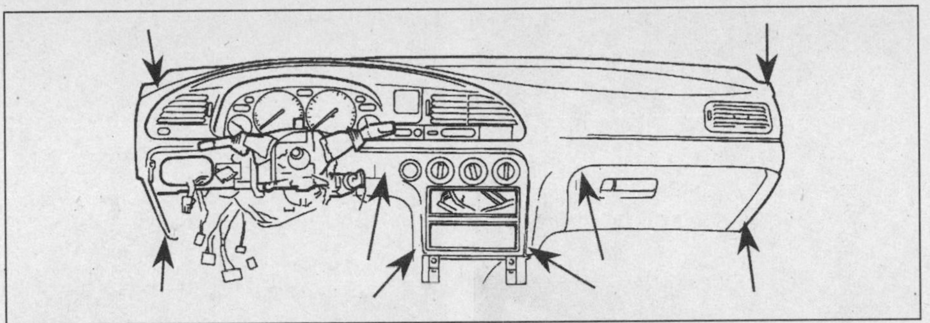

33.20a Facia mounting bolt positions (left-hand-drive shown, right-hand-drive similar)

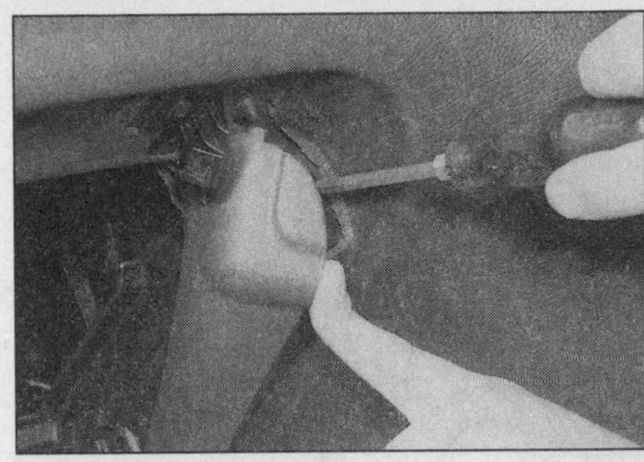

33.20b Facia mounting bolt next to the glovebox

33.20c Facia centre mounting bolt next to the heater panel

33.20d Facia mounting bolt near the heater

33.22 Disconnecting the fresh air hoses

Refitting

24 Refitting is a reversal of the removal procedure. On completion, check the operation of all electrical components.

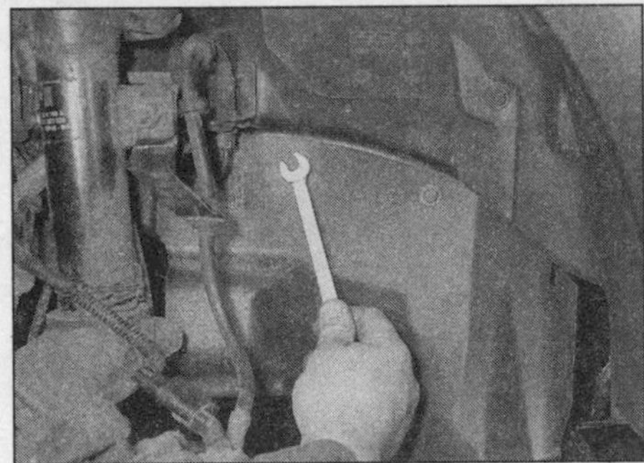

34.2a Remove the auxiliary drivebelt cover panel screws . . .

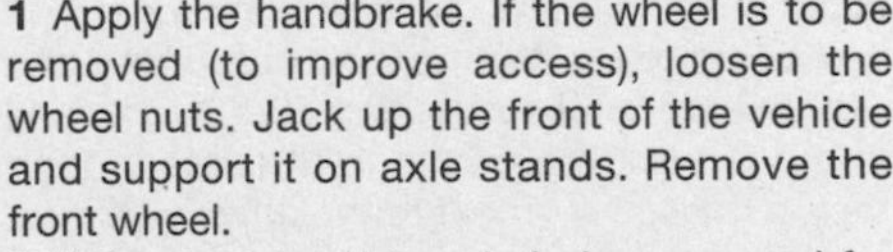

34 Wheel arch liner - removal and refitting

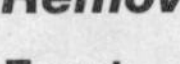

Removal

Front

1 Apply the handbrake. If the wheel is to be removed (to improve access), loosen the wheel nuts. Jack up the front of the vehicle and support it on axle stands. Remove the front wheel.

2 If the right-hand liner is being removed for access to other components, it might be enough to remove the auxiliary drivebelt cover panels from the inner side of the wheel arch, by removing the retaining screws. On some models, there are two panel sections (front and rear) - generally, only the front section need be removed for most work **(see illustrations)**.

3 Prise out the stud clip on the front lower edge of the liner.

4 Unscrew the screws securing the liner to the inner wheel arch panel.

5 Remove the screws and clips securing the liner to the outer edge of the wheel arch and bumper. On later models, disconnect the bumper stay bar from the front of the wheel arch. Withdraw the liner from under the vehicle **(see illustration)**.

Rear

6 Chock the front wheels, and engage 1st gear (or 'P'). If the wheel is to be removed (to improve access), loosen the wheel nuts. Jack up the rear of the vehicle and support it on axle stands. Remove the rear wheel.

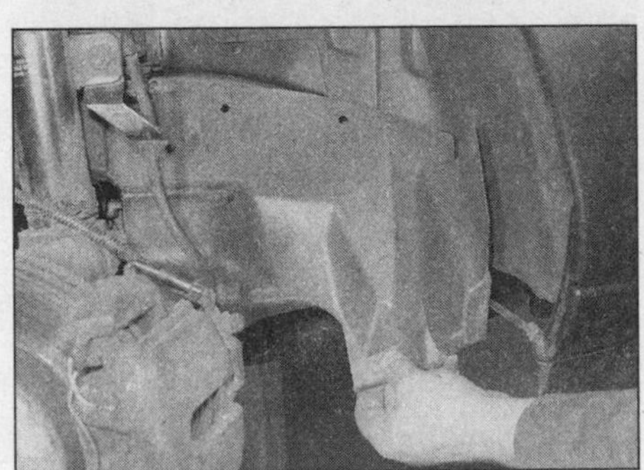

34.2b . . . and remove the panel

34.2c On some models, there is a rear section which can be removed if required

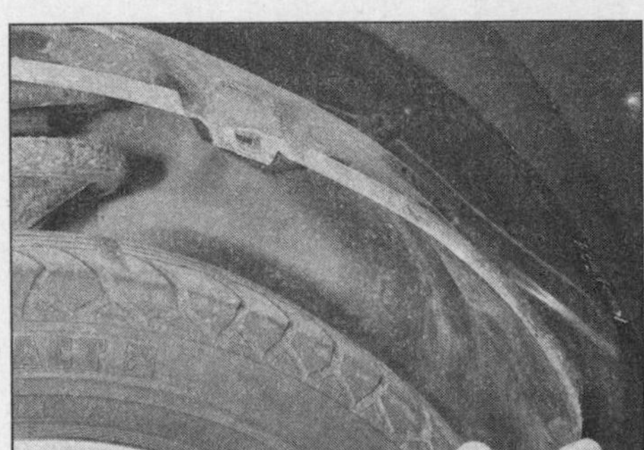

34.5 Removing a front wheel arch liner

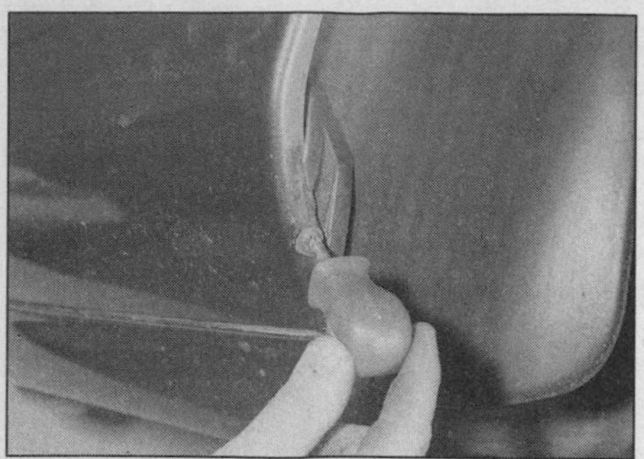

34.7a Remove the screw from the bottom of the liner . . .

7 Remove the screws and clips securing the liner to the outer edge of the wheel arch **(see illustrations)**.

8 Unscrew and remove the screws securing the liner to the inner wheel arch, and withdraw the liner from under the vehicle **(see illustrations)**.

Refitting

9 Refitting is a reversal of the removal procedure. If the wheels were removed, tighten the wheel nuts to the specified torque.

35 Fuel filler flap and release cable - removal and refitting

Removal

Filler flap

1 Working in the luggage compartment, remove the trim clips and fold down the right-hand side trim panel. As the panel is lowered, feed the emergency release cable through.

2 Unclip and remove the emergency filler flap release rod from the flap and the catch.

3 Prise the spring clip off the lock, then working from outside, twist the catch anti-clockwise and withdraw it **(see illustration)**.

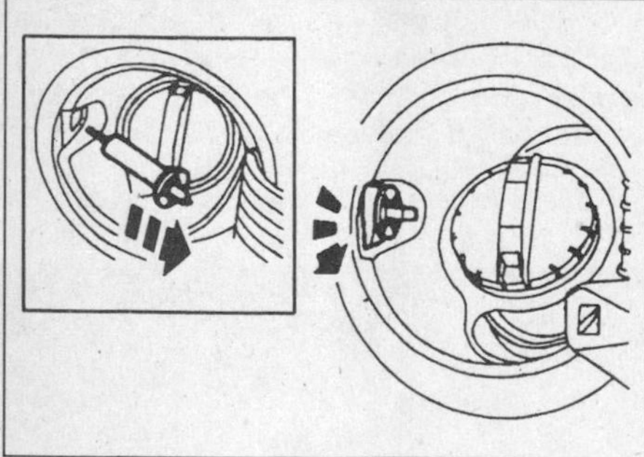

35.3 Twist the fuel filler flap catch anti-clockwise, and withdraw it

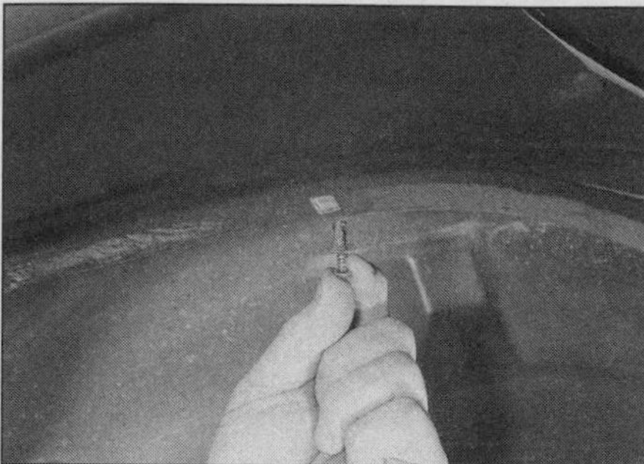

34.7b . . . and the screw and clip from the top

4 Completely remove the fuel filler cap. Remove the retaining screw to the rear of the filler neck, then carefully twist the filler flap housing approximately 30° anti-clockwise and pull it from the aperture in the rear wing **(see illustration)**.

5 If required, the filler flap hinge locating pegs can be prised out of the housing - take care, as both the flap and housing are made of plastic.

Release cable

Note: *If the release cable does not operate the flap, an emergency filler flap release cable is provided in the luggage compartment. Note that an inoperative cable may not have broken, but simply have come detached from the operating lever next to the driver's seat, as a result of the cable stretching in use.*

6 Remove the luggage compartment right-hand side trim panel as described in paragraph 1.

7 Detach the release cable from the filler flap operating linkage **(see illustration)**, then tie a piece of string to the cable end fitting.

8 Moving to the front of the car, unclip the trim panels (refer to Section 29 if necessary) and pull back the carpet in the area around the operating lever next to the driver's seat.

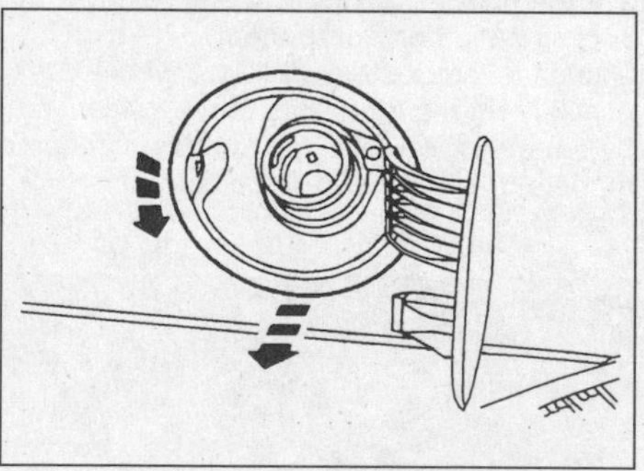

35.4 Carefully twist the flap housing anti-clockwise to remove

34.8a Remove the liner-to-wheel arch screws (arrowed) . . .

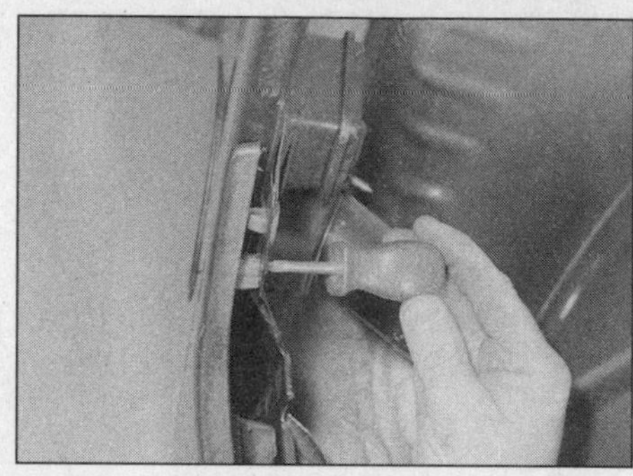

34.8b . . . and remove the liner from the wheel arch

9 Unclip the cable end fitting from the operating lever, and unclip the cable outer from the floor. Gradually pull the cable through into the passenger compartment (it may be necessary to loosen further trim and carpeting to allow passage of the cable), then untie the string from the cable.

10 When fitting the new cable, use the string to pull the cable through and into the correct position.

Refitting

11 Refitting is a reversal of removal.

35.7 Detach the cable end fitting and cable outer (arrowed) from the operating linkage

Chapter 12
Body electrical system

Contents

Degrees of difficulty

Easy, suitable for novice with little experience 	**Fairly easy,** suitable for beginner with some experience 	**Fairly difficult,** suitable for competent DIY mechanic	**Difficult,** suitable for experienced DIY mechanic 	**Very difficult,** suitable for expert DIY or professional

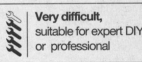

Specifications

Fuses

Refer to the wiring diagrams at the end of this Chapter

Note: *Fuse ratings and circuits are liable to change from year to year. Consult the handbook supplied with the vehicle, or consult a Ford dealer, for the latest information.*

Relays (auxiliary fusebox in engine compartment)

Relay	Colour	Circuit(s) protected
R1	Green	Daytime running lights (left-hand-drive, but not all countries) or dim-dip lights (early UK models)
R2	Black	Radiator electric cooling fan (high speed)
R3	Blue	Air conditioning cut-out
R4	Yellow	Windscreen heater time delay
R5	Dark green	Radiator electric cooling fan (low speed)
R6	Yellow	Starter solenoid
R7	Brown	Horns
R8	Brown	Fuel pump
R9	White	Dipped beam headlights
R10	White	Main beam headlights
R11	Brown	ECU power supply

Relays (main fusebox in passenger compartment)

Relay	Colour	Circuit(s) protected
R12	White	Interior, courtesy and footwell lights
R13	Yellow	Heated rear window
R14	Yellow	Heater blower
R15	Green	Windscreen wiper motor
R16	Black	Ignition

Auxiliary relays (not in the fuseboxes)

Relay	Colour	Location	Circuit(s) protected
R18	Black	Driver's door	'One-touch down' driver's window relay
R19	Blue	Fusebox bracket below instrument panel	Cruise control cut-off
R20	Blue	Bulb module bracket	Headlight washer system
R21	Orange	Bulb module bracket	Rear screen wiper interval
R22	White	Interface module bracket	Foglights (left-hand-drive only)
R23	Black	Steering column	Direction indicators
R24	White	Door lock module bracket	Anti-theft alarm (left-hand side)
R25	White	Door lock module bracket	Anti-theft alarm (right-hand side)
R26	Black	Fusebox bracket below instrument panel	Heated seats
R27	-	Fusebox bracket below instrument panel	Instrument panel illumination cut-off (Scandinavia)
R30	-	Fusebox bracket below instrument panel	Instrument panel illumination cut-off (Scandinavia)
R34	-	Fusebox bracket below instrument panel	Air conditioning

Bulbs

	Wattage	Type
Direction indicator lights	21	Bayonet
Engine compartment	10	Wedge
Front foglight:		
Models up to 1996	55	H1 Halogen
1997 and later models	55	H3 Halogen
Headlight dipped beam:		
Models up to 1996	55	H1 Halogen
1997 and later models	55	H7LL Halogen
Headlight main beam:		
Models up to 1996	55	H1 Halogen
1997 and later models	55	H7 Halogen
Luggage compartment:		
Models up to 1996	10	Festoon
1997 and later models	10	Bayonet
Interior light	10	Festoon
Number plate lights	5	Festoon
Reading light	5	Wedge
Rear foglight (Hatchback to 1996 and 1997-on Saloon)	21	Bayonet
Rear fog/tail lights (Estate, Saloon to 1996, and 1997-on Hatchback)	21/5	Bayonet
Rear tail light (Saloon and Hatchback)	5	Bayonet
Reversing lights	21	Bayonet
Side repeater lights	5	Wedge
Sidelights	5	Wedge
Stop-lights:		
High-level	5	Wedge
In rear light cluster:		
1997-on Saloon (stop- and tail light)	21/5	Bayonet
All other models	21	Bayonet

Torque wrench settings

	Nm	lbf ft
Horn unit mounting bolt	28	21
Windscreen wiper motor bolts:		
Into old motor (see text)	8	6
Into new motor (see text)	12	9
Wiper arm nuts	25	18

1 General information

Warning: Before carrying out any work on the electrical system, read through the precautions given in 'Safety first!' at the beginning of this manual.

The electrical system is of 12-volt negative earth type. Power for the lights and all electrical accessories is supplied by a lead/acid battery which is charged by the alternator.

This Chapter covers repair and service procedures for the various electrical components not associated with the engine. Information on the battery, alternator, and starter motor can be found in Chapter 5A; the ignition system is covered in Chapter 5B.

All models are fitted with a driver's air bag, which is designed to prevent serious chest and head injuries to the driver during an accident. A similar bag for the front seat passenger is also available. The sensor and electronic unit for the air bag is located next to the steering column inside the vehicle, and contains a back-up capacitor, crash sensor, decelerometer, safety sensor, integrated circuit and microprocessor. The air bag is inflated by a gas generator, which forces the bag out of the module cover in the centre of the steering wheel. A 'clock spring' ensures that a good electrical connection is maintained with the air bag at all times - as the steering wheel is turned in each direction, the spring winds and unwinds **(see illustration)**.

Later models equipped with both driver's and passenger's air bags can also be specified with side air bags, which are built into the sides of the front seats. The intention of the side air bags is principally to offer greater passenger protection in a side impact. Although the side air bags are linked to the 'front' air bags, a separate sensor for the side air bags (below the driver's side carpet) is used to detect lateral movement.

All UK models are fitted with an alarm system incorporating a movement sensor and ignition immobiliser. On Saloon and Hatchback models, the alarm system horn is located on the left-hand side of the luggage compartment, but on Estate models, it is on the right-hand side.

Some models are fitted with a headlight levelling system, which is controlled by a knob on the facia. On position '0', the headlights are in their base position, and on position '5', the headlights are in their maximum inclined angle.

It should be noted that, when portions of the electrical system are serviced, the lead should be disconnected from the battery negative terminal, to prevent electrical shorts and fires.

Caution: When disconnecting the battery for work described in the following Sections, refer to Chapter 5A, Section 1.

2 Electrical fault finding - general information

Note: *Refer to the precautions given in "Safety first!" and in Section 1 of this Chapter before starting work. The following tests relate to testing of the main electrical circuits, and should not be used to test delicate electronic circuits (such as engine management systems, anti-lock braking systems, etc), particularly where an electronic control module is used. Also refer to the precautions given in Chapter 5A, Section 1.*

General

1 A typical electrical circuit consists of an electrical component, any switches, relays, motors, fuses, fusible links or circuit breakers related to that component, and the wiring and connectors which link the component to both the battery and the chassis. To help to pinpoint a problem in an electrical circuit, wiring diagrams are included at the end of this Chapter.

2 Before attempting to diagnose an electrical fault, first study the appropriate wiring diagram, to obtain a complete understanding of the components included in the particular circuit concerned. The possible sources of a fault can be narrowed down by noting if other components related to the circuit are operating properly. If several components or circuits fail at one time, the problem is likely to be related to a shared fuse or earth connection.

3 Electrical problems usually stem from simple causes, such as loose or corroded connections, a faulty earth connection, a blown fuse, a melted fusible link, or a faulty relay (refer to Section 3 for details of testing relays). Visually inspect the condition of all fuses, wires and connections in a problem circuit before testing the components. Use the wiring diagrams to determine which terminal connections will need to be checked in order to pinpoint the trouble-spot.

4 The basic tools required for electrical fault-finding include a circuit tester or voltmeter (a 12-volt bulb with a set of test leads can also

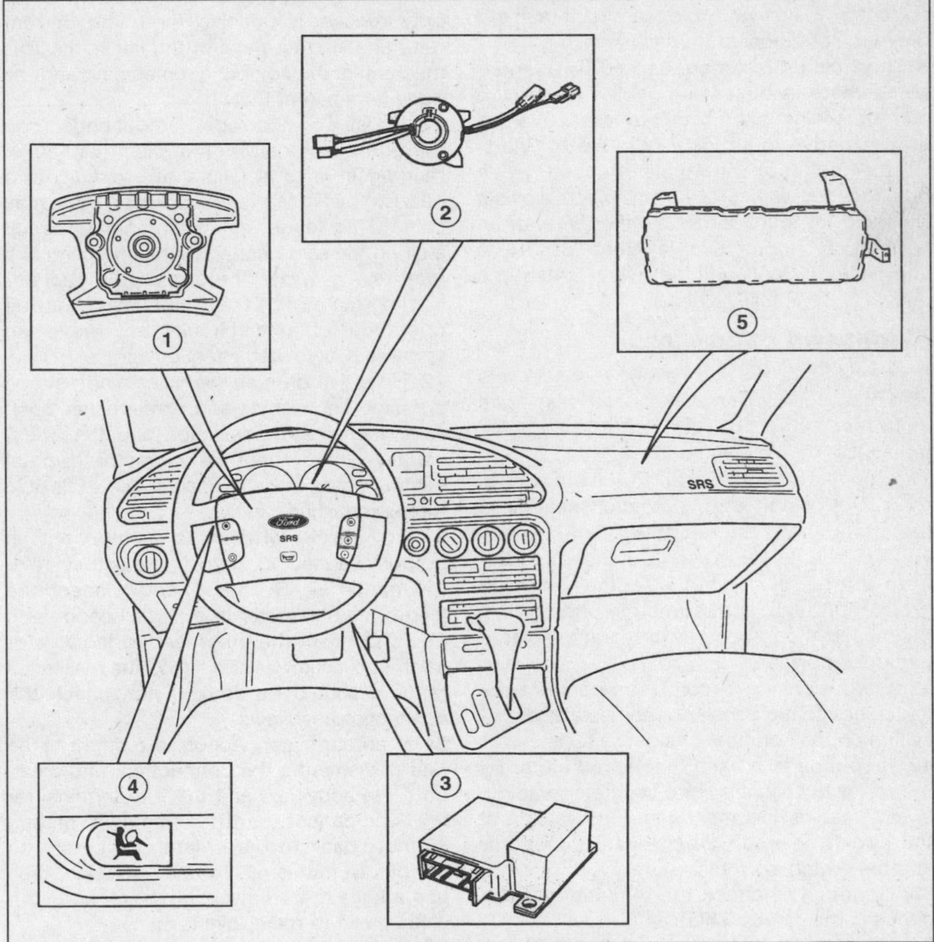

1.3 Air bag system components

1 Air bag module (driver's)
2 Clock spring
3 Diagnostic and sensor unit
4 Air bag indicator light
5 Air bag module (passenger's)

be used for certain tests); an ohmmeter (to measure resistance and check for continuity); a battery and set of test leads; and a jumper wire, preferably with a circuit breaker or fuse incorporated, which can be used to bypass suspect wires or electrical components. Before attempting to locate a problem with test instruments, use the wiring diagram to determine where to make the connections.

5 To find the source of an intermittent wiring fault (usually due to a poor or dirty connection, or damaged wiring insulation), a 'wiggle' test can be performed on the wiring. This involves wiggling the wiring by hand to see if the fault occurs as the wiring is moved. It should be possible to narrow down the source of the fault to a particular section of wiring. This method of testing can be used in conjunction with any of the tests described in the following sub-Sections.

6 Apart from problems due to poor connections, two basic types of fault can occur in an electrical circuit - open-circuit, or short-circuit.

7 Open-circuit faults are caused by a break somewhere in the circuit, which prevents current from flowing. An open-circuit fault will prevent a component from working.

8 Short-circuit faults are caused by a 'short' somewhere in the circuit, which allows the current flowing in the circuit to 'escape' along an alternative route, usually to earth. Short-circuit faults are normally caused by a breakdown in wiring insulation, which allows a feed wire to touch either another wire, or an earthed component such as the bodyshell. A short-circuit fault will normally cause the relevant circuit fuse to blow.

Finding an open-circuit

9 To check for an open-circuit, connect one lead of a circuit tester or the negative lead of a voltmeter either to the battery negative terminal or to a known good earth.

10 Connect the other lead to a connector in the circuit being tested, preferably nearest to the battery or fuse. At this point, battery voltage should be present, unless the lead from the battery or the fuse itself is faulty (bearing in mind that some circuits are live only when the ignition switch is moved to a particular position).

11 Switch on the circuit, then connect the tester lead to the connector nearest the circuit switch on the component side.

12 If voltage is present (indicated either by the tester bulb lighting or a voltmeter reading, as applicable), this means that the section of the circuit between the relevant connector and the switch is problem-free.

13 Continue to check the remainder of the circuit in the same fashion.

14 When a point is reached at which no voltage is present, the problem must lie between that point and the previous test point with voltage. Most problems can be traced to a broken, corroded or loose connection.

Finding a short-circuit

15 To check for a short-circuit, first disconnect the load(s) from the circuit (loads are the components which draw current from a circuit, such as bulbs, motors, heating elements, etc).

16 Remove the relevant fuse from the circuit, and connect a circuit tester or voltmeter to the fuse connections.

17 Switch on the circuit, bearing in mind that some circuits are live only when the ignition switch is moved to a particular position.

18 If voltage is present (indicated either by the tester bulb lighting or a voltmeter reading, as applicable), this means that there is a short-circuit.

19 If no voltage is present during this test, but the fuse still blows with the load(s) reconnected, this indicates an internal fault in the load(s).

Finding an earth fault

20 The battery negative terminal is connected to 'earth' - the metal of the engine/transmission unit and the vehicle body - and many systems are wired so that they only receive a positive feed, the current returning via the metal of the car body. This means that the component mounting and the body form part of that circuit.

21 Loose or corroded mountings can therefore cause a range of electrical faults, ranging from total failure of a circuit, to a puzzling partial failure. In particular, lights may shine dimly (especially when another circuit sharing the same earth point is in operation), motors (eg wiper motors or the radiator cooling fan motor) may run slowly, and the operation of one circuit may have an apparently-unrelated effect on another.

22 Note that on many vehicles, earth straps are used between certain components, such as the engine/transmission and the body, usually where there is no metal-to-metal contact between components, due to flexible rubber mountings, etc.

23 To check whether a component is properly earthed, disconnect the battery (refer to Chapter 5A, Section 1) and connect one lead of an ohmmeter to a known good earth point. Connect the other lead to the wire or earth connection being tested. The resistance reading should be zero; if not, check the connection as follows.

24 If an earth connection is thought to be faulty, dismantle the connection, and clean both the bodyshell and the wire terminal (or the component earth connection mating surface) back to bare metal. Be careful to remove all traces of dirt and corrosion, then use a knife to trim away any paint, so that a clean metal-to-metal joint is made.

25 On reassembly, tighten the joint fasteners securely; if a wire terminal is being refitted, use serrated washers between the terminal and the bodyshell, to ensure a clean and secure connection.

26 When the connection is remade, prevent the onset of corrosion in the future by applying a coat of petroleum jelly or silicone-based grease, or by spraying on (at regular intervals) a proprietary water-dispersant lubricant.

3 Fuses, relays and timer module - testing and renewal

Note: *It is important to note that the ignition switch and the appropriate electrical circuit must always be switched off before any of the fuses (or relays) are removed and renewed. In the event of the fuse/relay unit having to be removed, the battery earth lead must be disconnected. When reconnecting the battery, reference should be made to Chapter 5A.*

1 Fuses are designed to break a circuit when a predetermined current is reached, in order to protect components and wiring which could be damaged by excessive current flow. Any excessive current flow will be due to a fault in the circuit, usually a short-circuit (see Section 2). The main fusebox, which also carries some relays, is located inside the vehicle below the facia panel on the passenger's side, and is accessed by a lever behind the glovebox **(see illustration)**.

2 A central timer module is located on the bottom of the main fusebox. This module contains the time control elements for the heated rear window, interior lights and intermittent wiper operation. The module also activates a warning buzzer/chime when the vehicle is left with the lights switched on, or if a vehicle fitted with automatic transmission is not parked with the selector in position 'P'.

3 The auxiliary fusebox is located in the engine compartment, next to the battery, and is accessed by unclipping and removing the cover. The auxiliary fusebox also contains some relays **(see illustration)**. Each circuit is identified by numbers on the main fusebox and on the inside of the auxiliary fusebox cover. Reference to the wiring diagrams at the end of this Chapter will indicate the circuits protected by each fuse. Plastic tweezers are attached to the main fusebox and to the inside face of the auxiliary fuse and block cover, to remove and fit the fuses and relays.

4 To remove a fuse, use the tweezers provided to pull it out of the holder. Slide the fuse sideways from the tweezers. The wire within the fuse is clearly visible, and it will be broken if the fuse is blown **(see illustration)**.

5 Always renew a fuse with one of an identical rating. Never substitute a fuse of a higher rating, or make temporary repairs using wire or metal foil; more serious damage, or even fire, could result. The fuse rating is stamped on top of the fuse. Never renew a fuse more than once without tracing the source of the trouble.

6 Spare fuses of various current ratings are provided in the cover of the auxiliary fusebox.

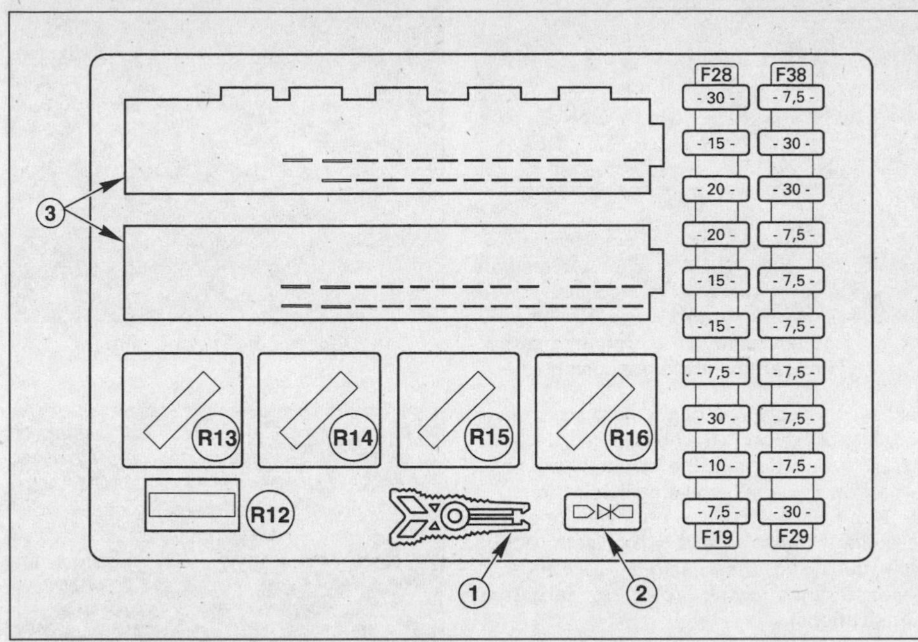

3.1 Main fusebox layout - typical

1 Fuse/relay removal tweezers
2 Diode
3 Multi-plug connections

Note that if the vehicle is to be laid up for a long period, fuse 34 in the main fusebox should be removed, to prevent the ancillary electrical components from discharging the battery.

7 Relays are electrically-operated switches, which are used in certain circuits. The various relays can be removed from their respective locations by carefully pulling them from the sockets. Each relay in the fuseboxes has a plastic bar on its upper surface to enable the use of the tweezers. The locations and functions of the various relays are given in the Specifications **(see illustration)**.

8 If a component controlled by a relay becomes inoperative and the relay is suspect, listen to the relay as the circuit is operated. If the relay is functioning, it should be possible to hear it click as it is energised. If the relay proves satisfactory, the fault lies with the components or wiring of the system. If the relay is not being energised, then either the relay is not receiving a switching voltage, or the relay itself is faulty. (Do not overlook the relay socket terminals when tracing faults.) Testing is by the substitution of a known good unit, but be careful; while some relays are identical in appearance and in operation, others look similar, but perform different functions.

9 The central timer module located on the bottom of the main fusebox incorporates its own self-diagnosis function. Note that diagnosis cannot take place if the heated rear window is defective.

10 To activate the system, press the heated rear window button while the ignition is being switched on, then release the button. Operate the light switch, washer pump switch and all of the door switches one after the other, and check that the buzzer confirms that the input signals are correct.

11 Now move the wiper lever to the intermittent wipe position, and check the output signals by operating the same switches.

12 The self-diagnosis function is turned off by switching the ignition off and on again.

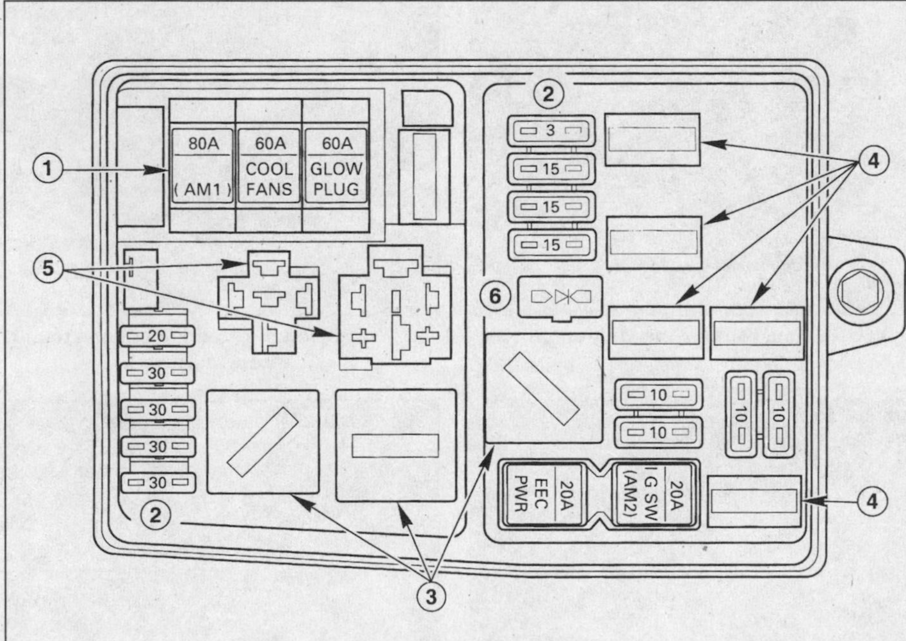

3.3 Auxiliary fusebox layout - typical

1 Fuses 1 to 3
2 Fuses 4 to 8, 11 to 14
3 Relays R2, R5 and R6
4 Relays R7 to R11
5 Relay sockets for relays R1 and R4
6 Diode

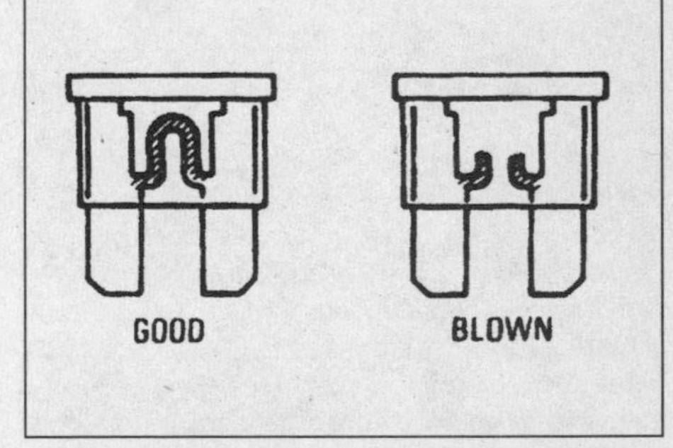

3.4 The fuses can be checked visually to determine if they are blown

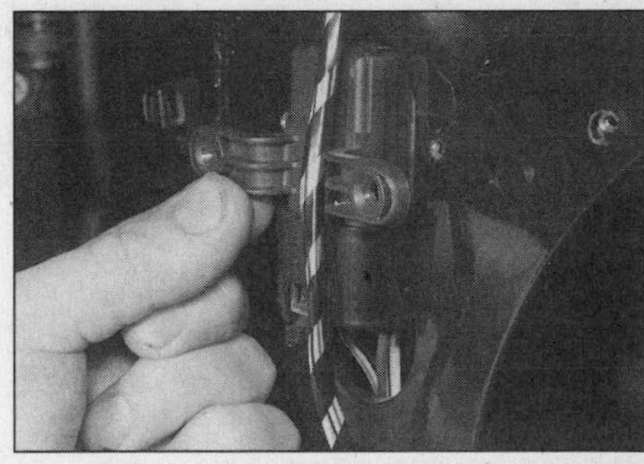

3.7 "One-touch down" window relay in the driver's door

4.3a On models with the PATS immobiliser, disconnect the wiring plug . . .

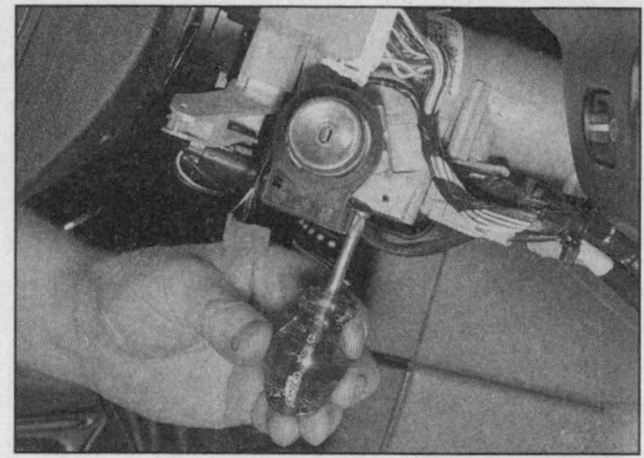

4.3b . . . then remove the mounting screw and remove the transceiver

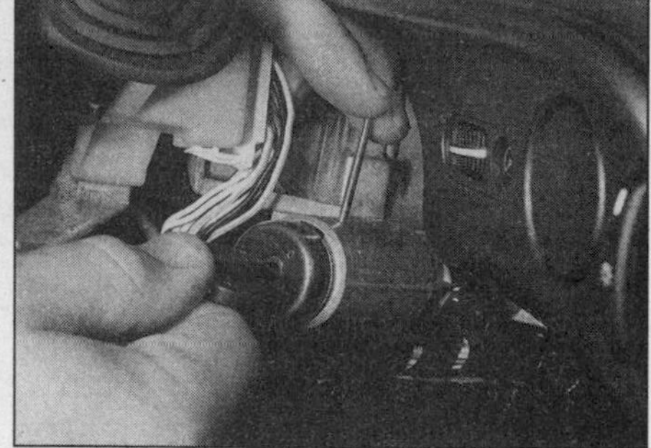

4.4a Depress the locking plunger . . .

4 Switches - removal and refitting

Removal

Ignition switch and lock barrel

1 Disconnect the battery negative (earth) lead (refer to Chapter 5A, Section 1).

2 Remove the securing screws (two above, three below) and take off the steering column upper and lower shrouds.

3 On models with the PATS ('Safeguard') immobiliser, remove the immobiliser transceiver from the ignition switch by disconnecting the wiring plug and removing the mounting screw **(see illustrations)**.

4 Insert the ignition key, and turn it to the

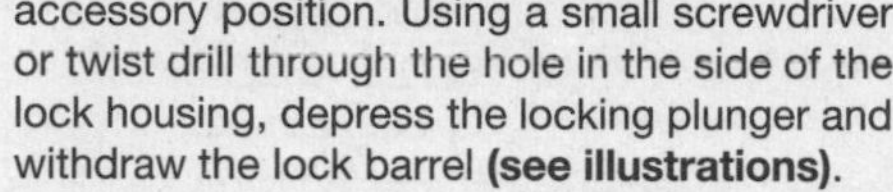

accessory position. Using a small screwdriver or twist drill through the hole in the side of the lock housing, depress the locking plunger and withdraw the lock barrel **(see illustrations)**.

5 The switch may be removed from the steering column assembly by disconnecting the multi-plug, then using a screwdriver to release the switch retaining tab **(see illustrations)**.

Windscreen wiper multi-function switch

6 Disconnect the battery negative (earth) lead (refer to Chapter 5A, Section 1).

7 Remove the two securing screws and take off the steering column upper shroud **(see illustration)**.

8 Disconnect the switch multi-plug, then depress the plastic tab with a screwdriver, and lift the switch assembly from the steering column **(see illustrations)**.

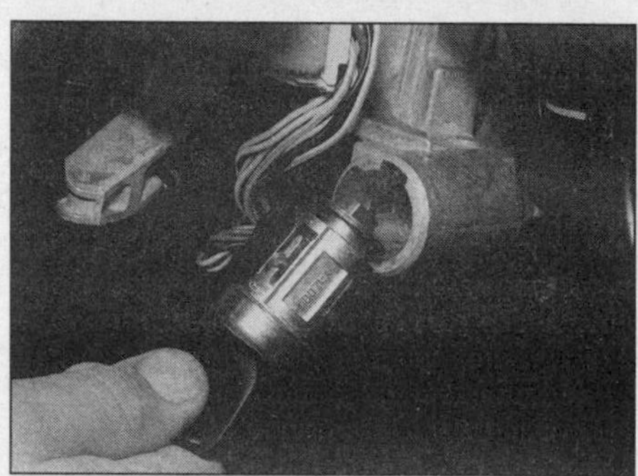

4.4b . . . and withdraw the ignition lock barrel

Main light, auxiliary foglight and rear foglight combination switch

Note: *From July 1994, a revised main light switch was introduced; this was fitted as*

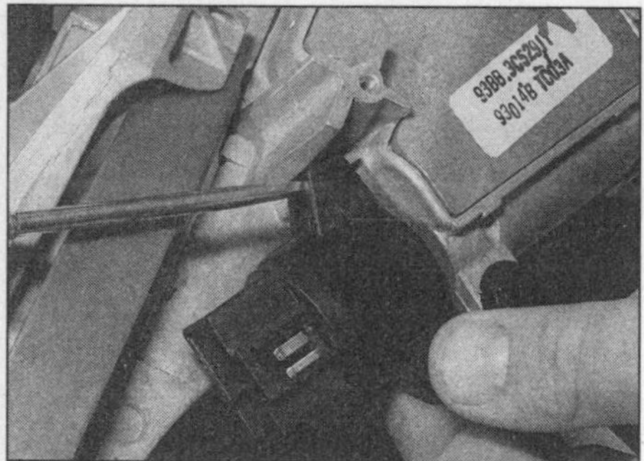

4.5a Release the retaining tab . . .

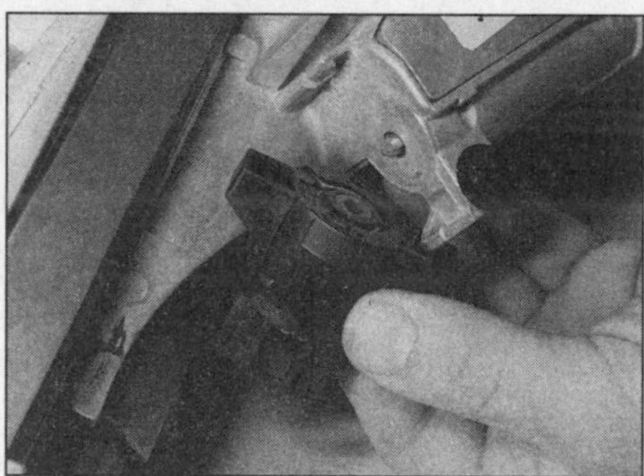

4.5b . . . and remove the ignition switch

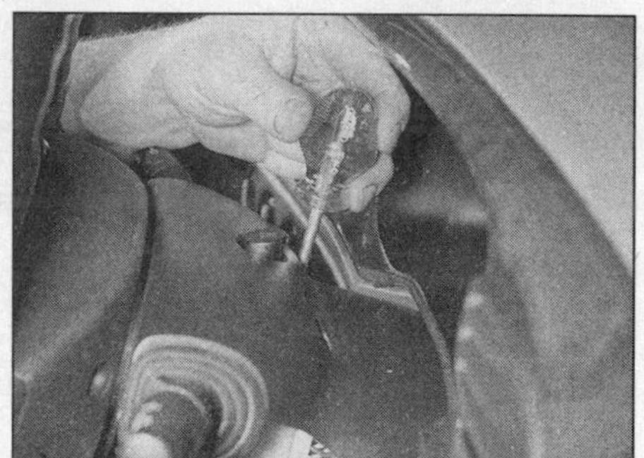

4.7 Removing the steering column upper shroud screws

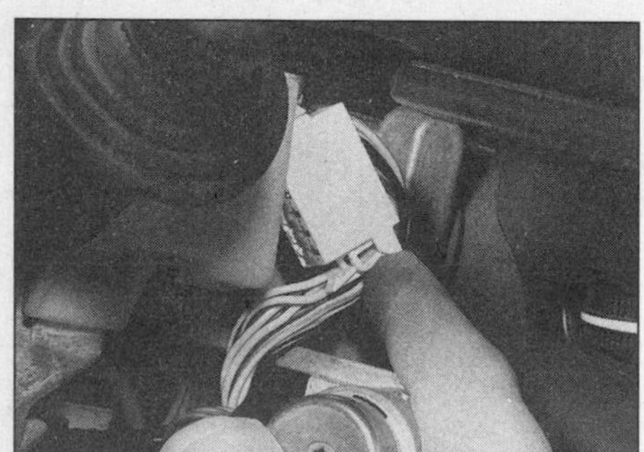

4.8a Disconnect the multi-plug . . .

4.8b . . . then depress the plastic tab with a screwdriver . . .

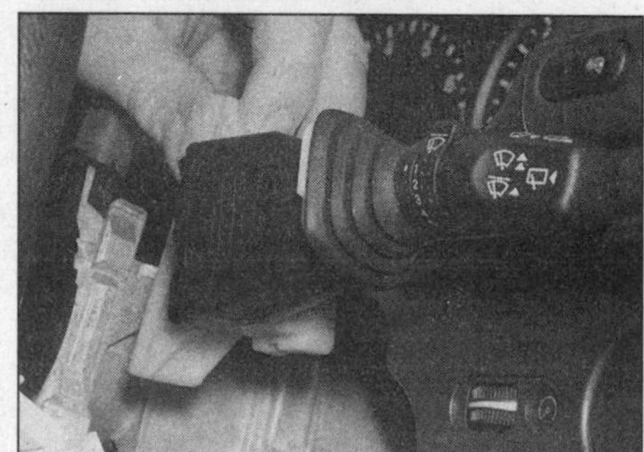

4.8c . . . and remove the windscreen wiper switch

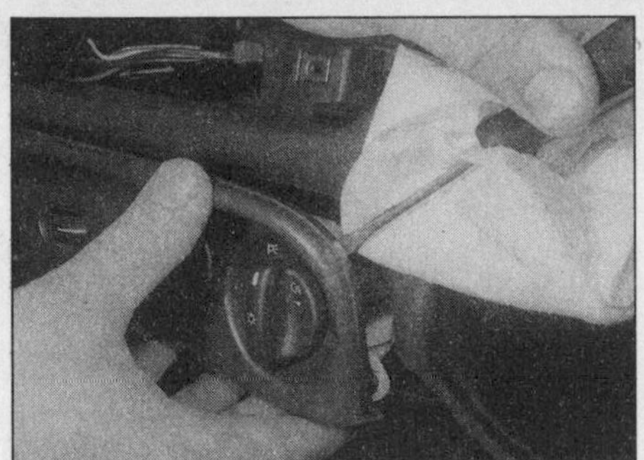
4.10 Prising out the light switch

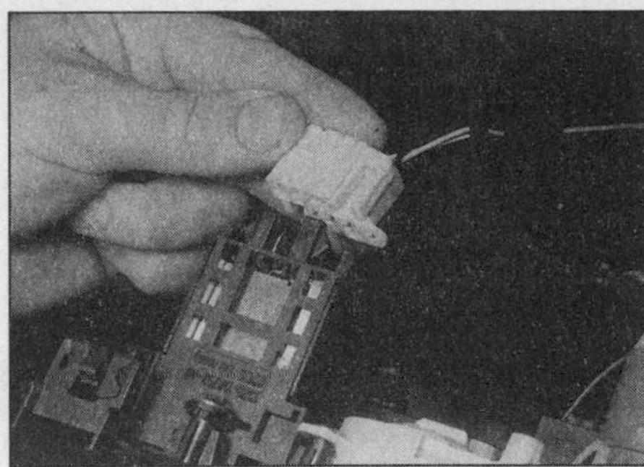
4.11 Disconnecting the multi-plugs from the light switch and rheostat

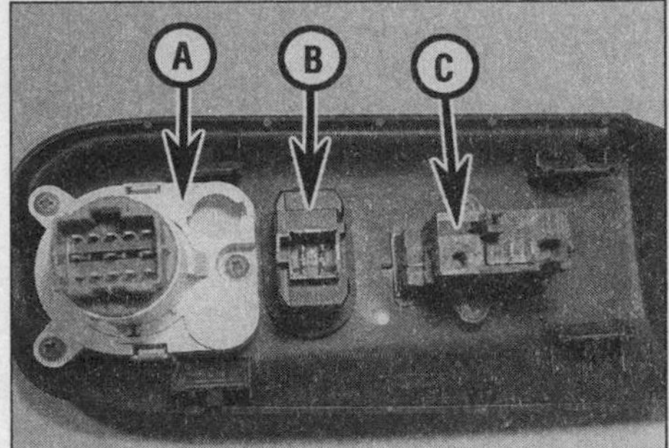

4.12 Light switch panel rear view, showing main light switch (A), headlight aim control (B) and lighting rheostat (C)

standard in production. If the revised switch is to be fitted to a pre-July 1994 model, an adapter lead will also be required to prevent electrical damage occurring. Refer to your Ford dealer for further information.

9 Disconnect the battery negative (earth) lead (refer to Chapter 5A, Section 1).

10 Carefully prise the switch panel from the facia, using a screwdriver against a cloth pad to prevent damage to the facia **(see illustration)**.

11 Disconnect the multi-plugs and withdraw the switch panel **(see illustration)**.

12 Unscrew the mounting screws, and remove the switch from the panel **(see illustration)**.

13 Pull off the switch control knob, and remove the blanking plug and retainer.

14 Depress the plastic tabs, and remove the front cover and switch.

Instrument light rheostat

15 Disconnect the battery negative (earth) lead (refer to Chapter 5A, Section 1).

16 Carefully prise the light switch panel from the facia, using a screwdriver against a cloth pad to prevent damage to the facia.

17 Disconnect the multi-plug from the rear of the switch, then remove the screws and withdraw the instrument light rheostat from the panel.

Headlight aim adjustment control

18 Disconnect the battery negative (earth) lead (refer to Chapter 5A, Section 1).

19 Carefully prise the light switch panel from the facia, using a screwdriver against a cloth pad to prevent damage to the facia.

20 Disconnect the multi-plug from the rear of the control, then prise the control from the panel.

Door mirror control switch

21 Disconnect the battery negative (earth) lead (refer to Chapter 5A, Section 1).

22 Carefully prise the switch from the facia, using a screwdriver against a cloth pad to prevent damage to the facia.

23 Disconnect the multi-plug and withdraw the switch **(see illustration)**.

Direction indicator, dipped beam and hazard flasher multi-function switch

24 Disconnect the battery negative (earth) lead (refer to Chapter 5A, Section 1).

25 Remove the two screws and take off the steering column upper shroud.

26 Depress the retaining lug and withdraw the switch assembly, then disconnect the multi-plug **(see illustration)**.

27 With the switch assembly removed, pull out the direction indicator relay (flasher unit) if required.

Horn switch (steering wheel with air bag)

28 Remove the air bag unit from the steering wheel as described in Section 28.

29 On models with cruise control, remove the switch components as described in Section 21.

30 Disconnect the wiring connector, then (where applicable) remove the two securing screws and carefully prise out the switch assembly.

Horn switch (steering wheel without air bag)

31 Disconnect the battery negative (earth) lead (refer to Chapter 5A, Section 1).

32 Carefully pull off the padded centre of the steering wheel.

33 Disconnect the wiring connector, then carefully prise out the switch assembly.

Radio remote control switch

34 Disconnect the battery negative (earth) lead (refer to Chapter 5A, Section 1).

35 Remove the two screws and take off the steering column upper shroud.

36 Depress the retaining lug and withdraw the switch assembly, then disconnect the multi-plug.

Cruise control switches

37 Refer to Section 21.

Electrically-operated window switch (single)

38 Disconnect the battery negative (earth) lead (refer to Chapter 5A, Section 1).

39 Carefully prise out the switch from the door inner trim panel, using a cloth pad to prevent damage to the trim **(see illustration)**.

40 Disconnect the multi-plug and remove the switch **(see illustration)**.

4.23 Removing the mirror control switch

4.26 Removing the direction indicator multi-function switch and flasher unit

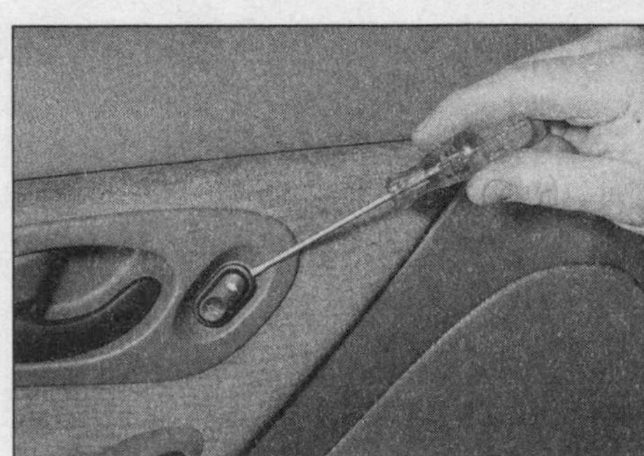
4.39 Prise the switch from the panel . . .

4.40 . . . and disconnect the wiring plug to remove the switch

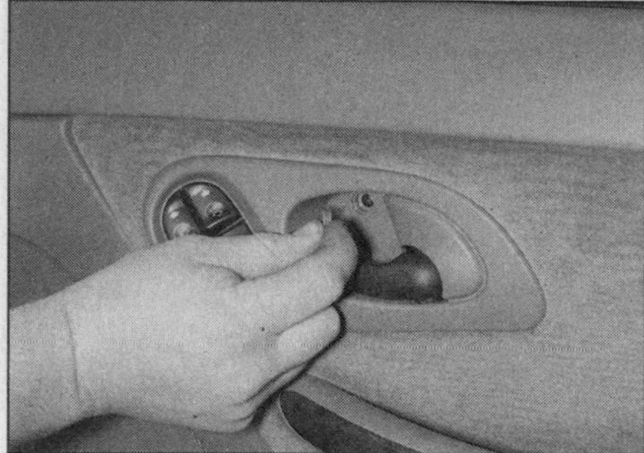
4.42a Prise off the trim cap . . .

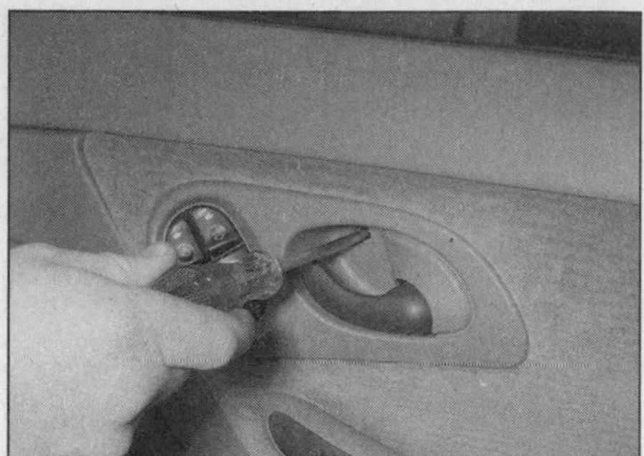
4.42b . . . and remove the screw beneath

Electrically-operated window switch (multiple) and isolator

41 Disconnect the battery negative (earth) lead (refer to Chapter 5A, Section 1).

42 Prise the blanking cap from inside the inner door handle cavity, and remove the screw **(see illustrations)**.

43 Hold the inner door handle in its open position, then remove the bezel and withdraw it over the handle **(see illustration)**.

44 Depress the retaining lug and remove the switch assembly, then disconnect the multi-plug **(see illustrations)**.

Electrically-operated sunroof switch

45 Disconnect the battery negative (earth) lead (refer to Chapter 5A, Section 1).

46 Carefully prise out the switch with a screwdriver, using a cloth pad to prevent damage to the trim.

47 Disconnect the multi-plug and remove the switch.

Handbrake-on warning switch

48 Disconnect the battery negative (earth) lead (refer to Chapter 5A, Section 1).

49 Remove the centre console as described in Chapter 11.

50 Disconnect the multi-plug **(see illustration)**, then remove the screw and withdraw the switch from the handbrake lever mounting bracket.

'Economy/Sport' mode switch (automatic transmission models)

51 Disconnect the battery negative (earth) lead (refer to Chapter 5A, Section 1).

52 Select position 'N', then prise out the selector indicator panel, using a cloth pad to prevent damage to the surrounding trim.

53 Push the switch out of the panel, and disconnect the multi-plug.

Heated windscreen switch and heated rear window switch - models up to 1996

54 Disconnect the battery negative (earth) lead (refer to Chapter 5A, Section 1).

55 Carefully prise out the switch, using a cloth pad to prevent damage to the trim **(see illustration)**.

56 Disconnect the multi-plug and remove the switch **(see illustration)**.

Heated windscreen switch and heated rear window switch - 1997 models onwards

57 Disconnect the battery negative (earth) lead (refer to Chapter 5A, Section 1).

58 Carefully prise the main lighting switch panel from the facia, using a screwdriver against a cloth pad to prevent damage to the facia. If necessary for access, disconnect the wiring plugs from the rear of the switches.

4.43 Withdraw the bezel over the door handle

4.44a Remove the switch assembly . . .

4.44b . . . and disconnect the wiring plugs

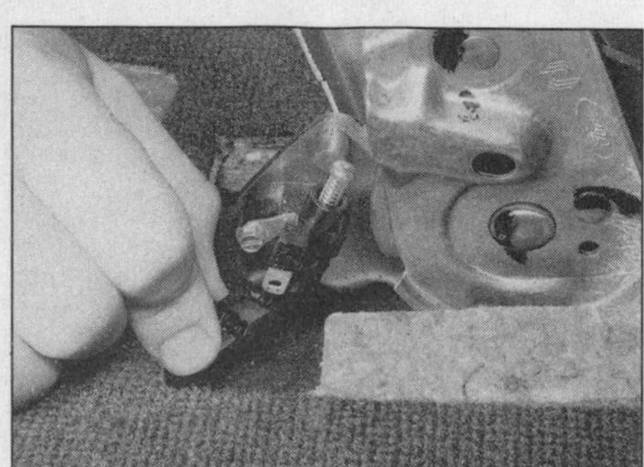
4.50 Disconnecting the multi-plug from the handbrake lever

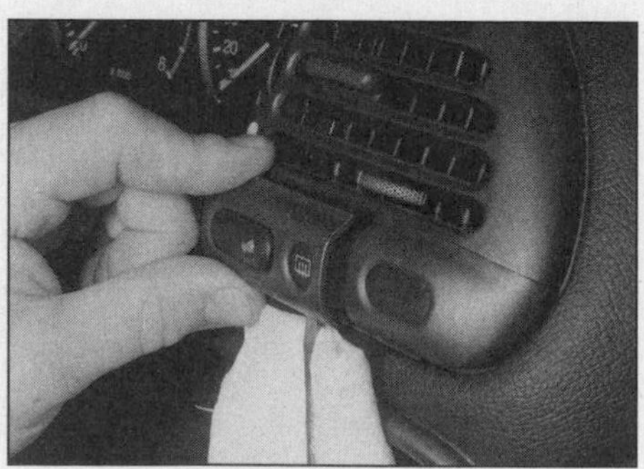
4.55 Prising out the heated rear window switch

4.56 Disconnecting the multi-plug from the heated rear window switch

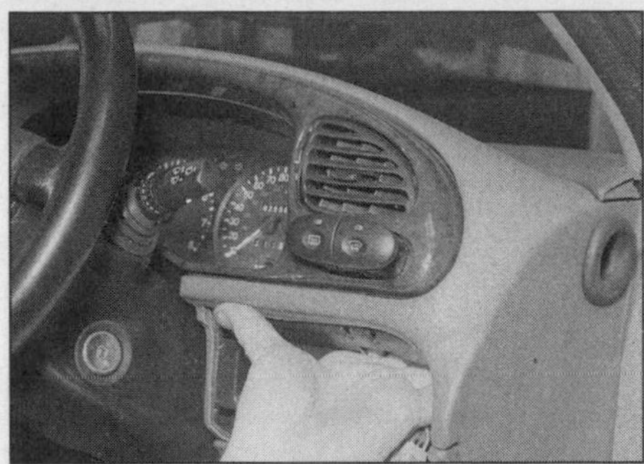

4.59 Reach in through the aperture and push the switches out from behind

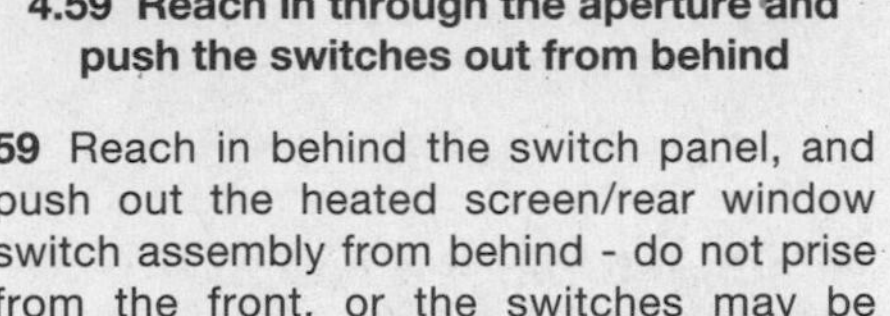

4.60 Disconnect the switch wiring plugs

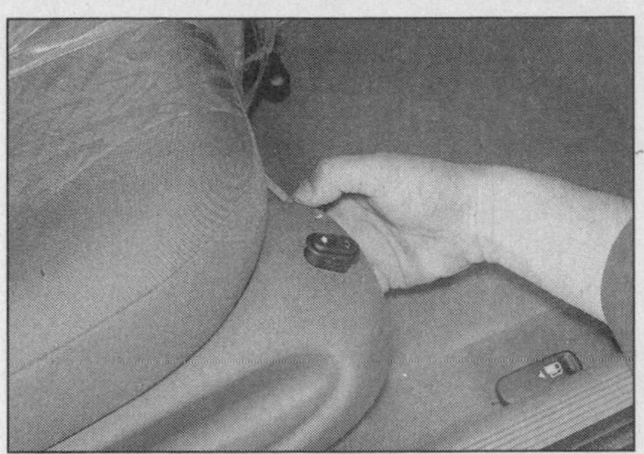

4.62 Push out the switch from below . . .

59 Reach in behind the switch panel, and push out the heated screen/rear window switch assembly from behind - do not prise from the front, or the switches may be damaged **(see illustration)**.

60 Disconnect the multi-plugs and remove the switch assembly **(see illustration)**.

Seat height adjustment switch (single switch)

61 Disconnect the battery negative (earth) lead (refer to Chapter 5A, Section 1).

62 Push the switch out from below **(see illustration)**.

63 Disconnect the multi-plug and remove the switch **(see illustration)**.

Seat adjustment switches (two-part switch)

64 Remove the seat as described in Chapter 11.

65 Pull off the switch control knobs, noting their fitted position and orientation **(see illustration)**.

66 Working from below the seat, unscrew and remove the two switch securing screws, and withdraw the switch **(see illustrations)**.

67 Trace the switch wiring back to the connector plug, and disconnect the plug.

Heated seat switch - models up to 1996

68 Refer to paragraphs 45 to 47.

Heated seat switch - 1997 models onwards

69 Disconnect the battery negative (earth) lead (refer to Chapter 5A, Section 1).

70 Remove the radio/cassette unit as described in Section 23.

71 Reach in through the radio aperture, and push the switch out from behind.

72 Disconnect the multi-plug and remove the switch.

Traction control (TCS) switch - models up to 1996

73 Refer to paragraphs 45 to 47.

Traction control (TCS) switch - 1997 models onwards

74 Disconnect the battery negative (earth) lead (refer to Chapter 5A, Section 1).

75 Remove the radio/cassette unit as described in Section 23.

76 Reach in through the radio aperture, and push the switch out from behind **(see illustration)**.

77 Disconnect the multi-plug and remove the switch **(see illustration)**.

Adaptive damping switch

78 Refer to paragraphs 45 to 47.

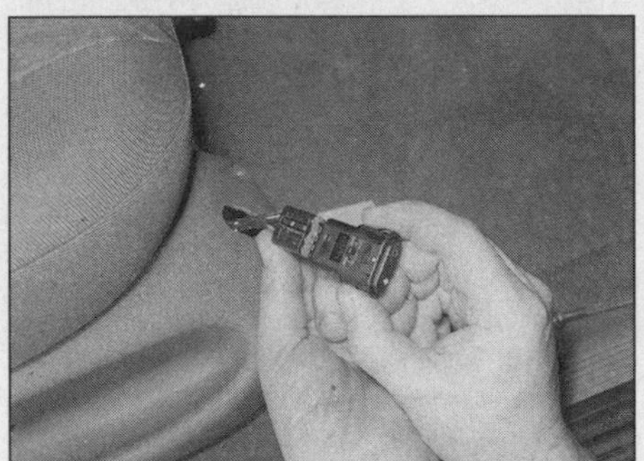

4.63 . . . and disconnect the switch multi-plug

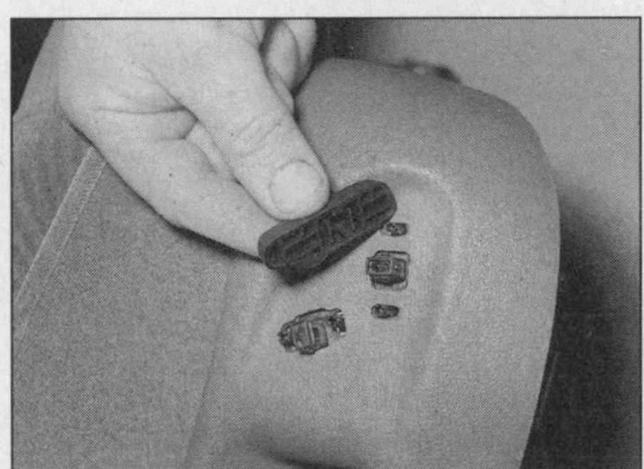

4.65 Pull off the switch control knobs

4.66a Working from below, remove the switch securing screws (arrowed) . . .

4.66b . . . then withdraw the switch from the seat and disconnect the wiring

4.76 Reach in through the radio aperture and push out the switch . . .

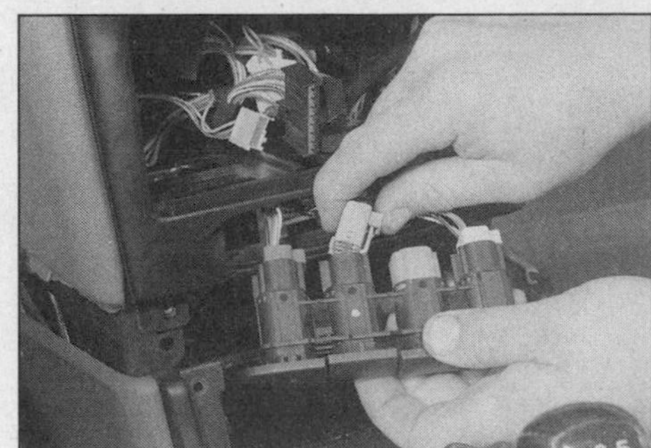

4.77 . . . then disconnect its wiring plug

4.79a Unscrew the cross-head screw . . .

4.79b . . . and pull out the courtesy light switch

4.82 Removing the boot light switch - Estate shown, others similar

Courtesy light door switch

79 Open the door, then unscrew the cross-head screw and carefully pull the switch from the pillar **(see illustrations)**. Take care not to force the wire from the switch terminal, otherwise it will be difficult to retrieve it from the pillar.

80 Disconnect the wire, and tie it in a loose knot to prevent it dropping back into the pillar.

Boot light switch

81 Removing the switch will in most cases entail partially removing the lock components to gain access to the switch and its wiring plug - refer to the relevant Sections of Chapter 11 for lock removal details.

82 The switch unclips from the lock body **(see illustration)**, and once the wiring plug has been disconnected, can be withdrawn from the lock.

Fuel cut-off switch

83 Refer to Chapter 4A.

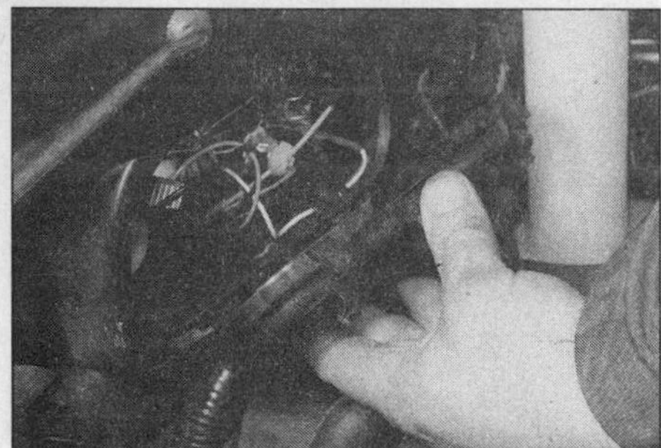

5.2 Removing the cover from the rear of the headlight

Refitting

84 Refitting of all switches is a reversal of the removal procedure.

5 Bulbs (exterior lights) - renewal

1 Whenever a bulb is renewed, note the following points:

a) Switch off all exterior lights, and disconnect the battery negative lead before starting work (see Chapter 5A, Section 1).

b) Remember that if the light has just been in use, the bulb may be extremely hot.

c) Always check the bulb contacts and holder, ensuring that there is clean metal-to-metal contact between the bulb and its live(s) and earth. Clean off any corrosion or dirt before fitting a new bulb.

d) Wherever bayonet-type bulbs are fitted, ensure that the live contact(s) bear firmly against the bulb contact.

e) Always ensure that the new bulb is of the correct rating and that it is completely clean before fitting it; this applies particularly to headlight/foglight bulbs.

f) Do not touch the glass of halogen-type bulbs (headlights, front foglights) with the fingers, as this may lead to rapid blackening and failure of the new bulb; if the glass is accidentally touched, clean it with methylated spirit.

g) If replacing the bulb does not cure the problem, check the relevant fuse and relay with reference to the Specifications, and to the wiring diagrams at the end of this Chapter.

Headlight (dipped beam) - models up to 1996

2 Working under the bonnet, depress the plastic clips and remove the cover from the rear of the headlight unit **(see illustration)**.

3 Release the spring clip and withdraw the bulb, then disconnect the wiring plug **(see illustrations)**.

4 Fit the new bulb using a reversal of the removal procedure. Do not touch the glass of the new headlight bulb with bare fingers. If the glass is accidentally touched, clean it with methylated spirit. Have the headlight beam alignment checked as described later in this Chapter.

Headlight (dipped beam) - 1997 models onwards

Note: *If the right-hand dipped beam has failed, it could be due to the dipped beam relay in the engine compartment fusebox having worked loose. Check that the relay is securely pushed into its socket before assuming the bulb has blown.*

5 Depending on model, and on which headlight is being worked on, it may be necessary to remove the headlight unit as described in Section 7, in order that the headlight rear cover can be removed.

6 At the rear of the headlight, lift up the spring clip and fold down the rear cover for access to the bulb **(see illustration)**.

7 Disconnect the wiring plug from the rear of the bulb **(see illustration)**.

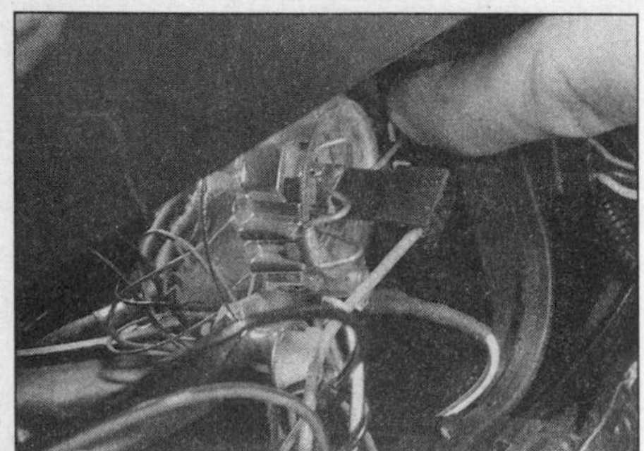

5.3a Release the spring clip . . .

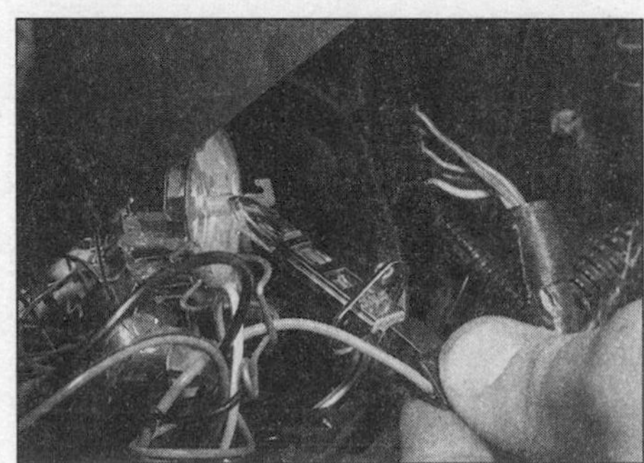

5.3b . . . and withdraw the headlight bulb

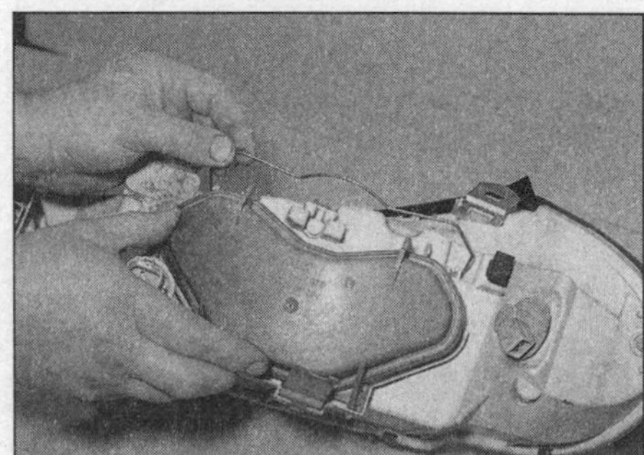

5.6 Release the wire clip, and remove the headlight rear cover

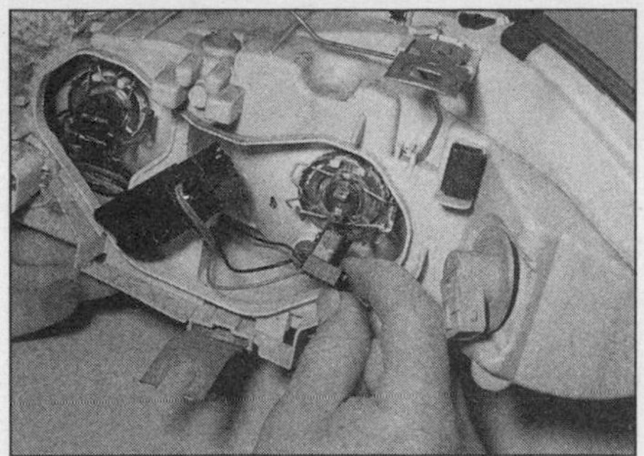
5.7 Disconnect the wiring plug from the bulb

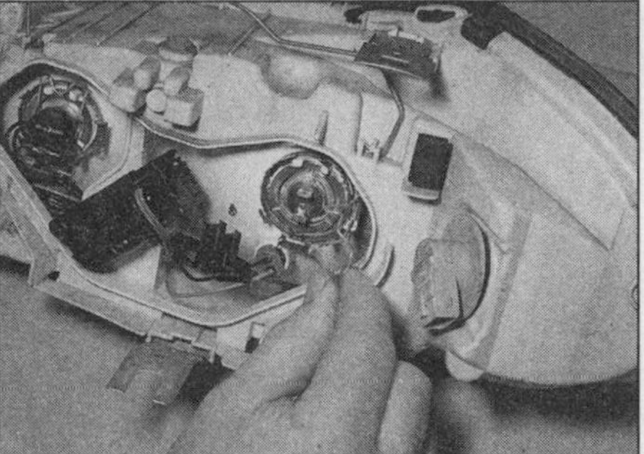
5.8a Release the bulb retaining clip, pivot it aside . . .

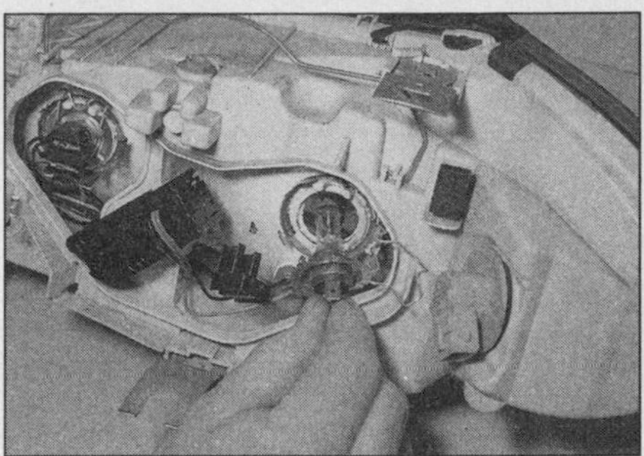
5.8b . . . and withdraw the bulb

8 Release the wire clip securing the bulb, and remove the bulb. Note how the tabs fit in the slots on the rear of the headlight **(see illustrations)**.

9 Fit the new bulb using a reversal of the removal procedure. Have the headlight beam alignment checked as described later in this Chapter.

Headlight (main beam) - models up to 1996

10 Working under the bonnet, depress the plastic clips and remove the cover from the rear of the headlight unit.

11 Turn the bulbholder anti-clockwise, and remove it from the rear of the headlight unit **(see illustration)**.

12 Pull out the bulb and disconnect the wiring plug **(see illustration)**.

13 Fit the new bulb using a reversal of the removal procedure, making sure that the bulbholder is correctly located in the headlight unit. Have the headlight beam alignment checked as described later in this Chapter.

Headlight (main beam) - 1997 models onwards

14 Refer to paragraphs 5 to 9 inclusive **(see illustration)**.

Front sidelight - models up to 1996

15 Working under the bonnet, depress the plastic clips and remove the cover from the rear of the headlight unit.

16 Pull the bulbholder from the rear of the headlight unit, and pull the wedge-type bulb from the bulbholder **(see illustrations)**.

17 Fit the new bulb using a reversal of the removal procedure.

Front sidelight - 1997 models onwards

18 The procedure is as described for models up to 1996, except that it may be necessary to remove the headlight unit as described in Section 7, in order that the headlight rear cover can be removed **(see illustrations)**.

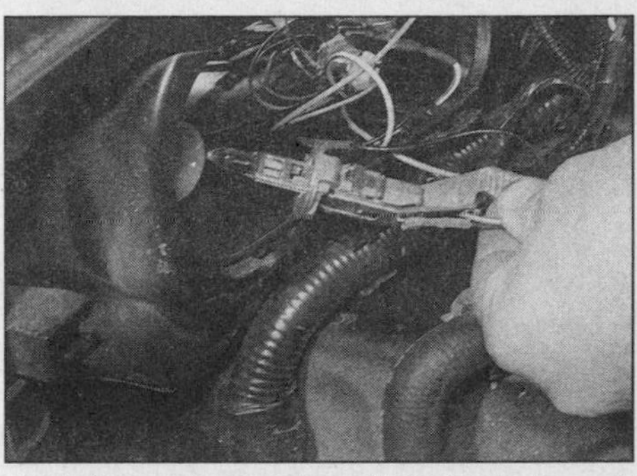
5.11 Removing the headlight (main beam) bulbholder

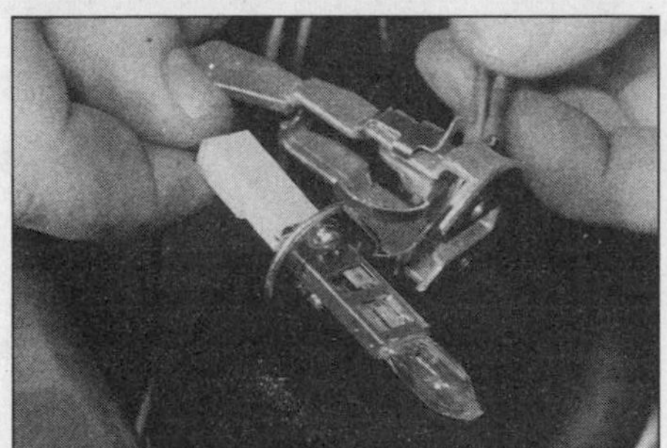
5.12 Removing the headlight (main beam) bulb from the bulbholder

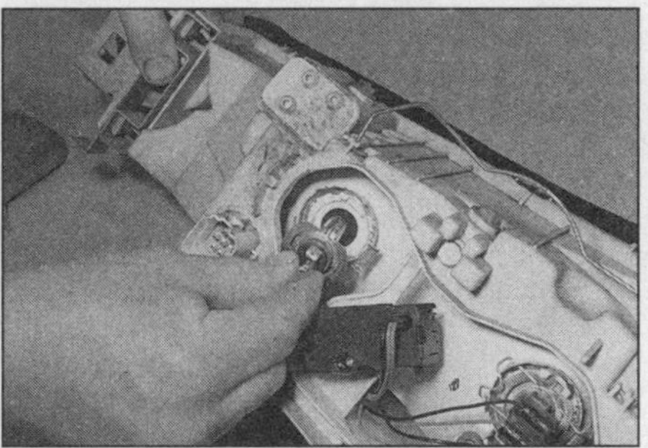
5.14 Removing the headlight main beam bulb

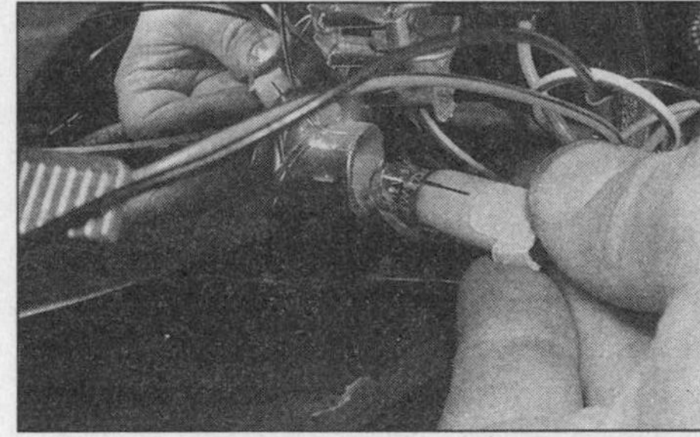
5.16a Remove the front sidelight bulbholder from the rear of the headlight unit . . .

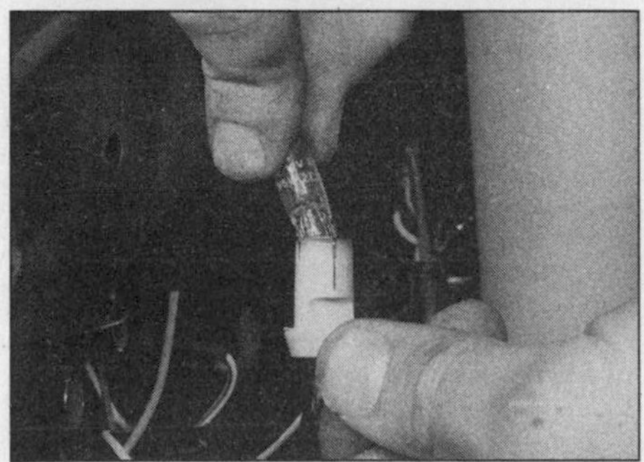
5.16b . . . and pull out the wedge-type bulb

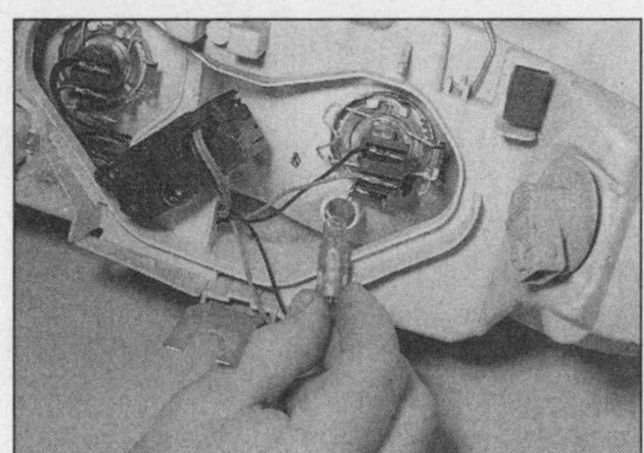
5.18a Pull out the bulbholder . . .

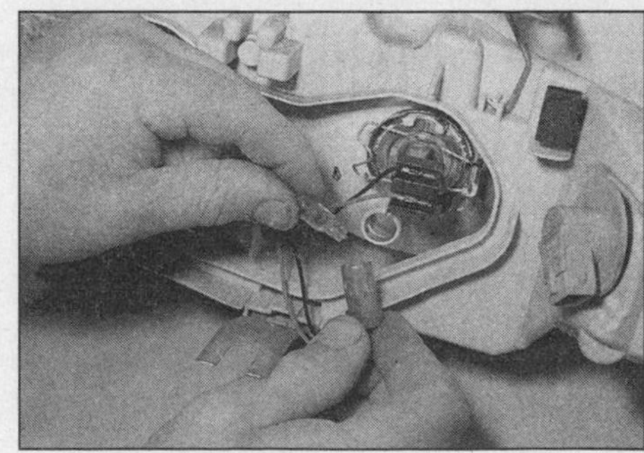
5.18b . . . then pull the bulb from the holder

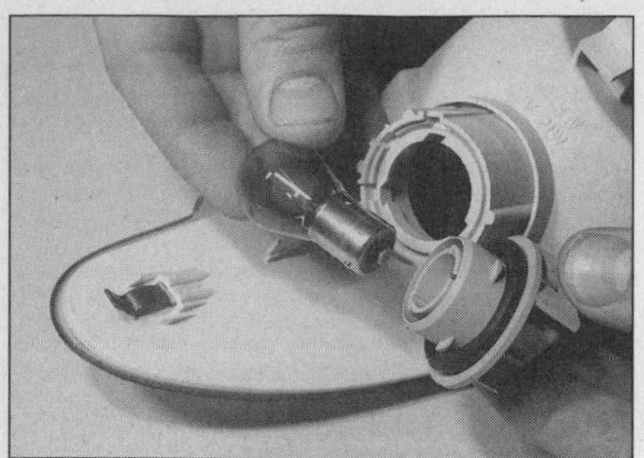

5.22 Removing the front direction indicator bulb

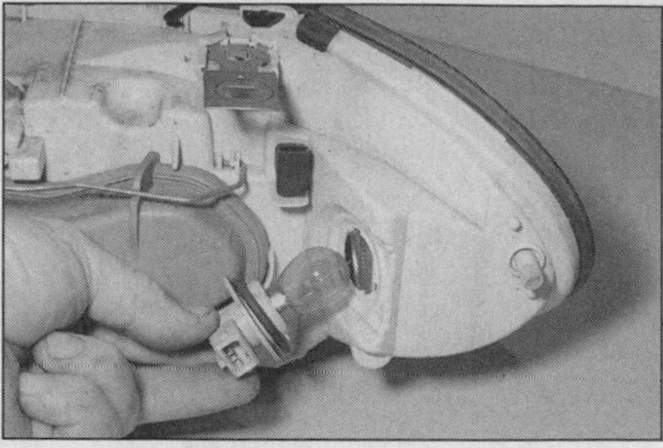

5.25 Removing the direction indicator bulbholder from the rear of the headlight unit

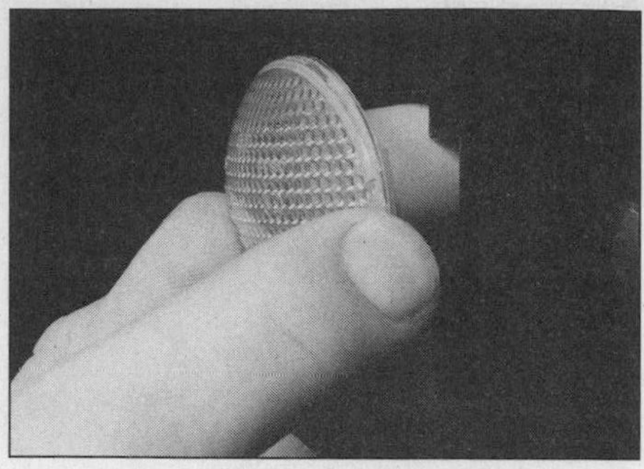

5.28 Removing the side repeater from the front wing

Front direction indicator - models up to 1996

19 Open the bonnet. Loosen (but do not remove) the screw located above the front direction indicator.

20 Withdraw the front direction indicator light unit.

21 Rotate the bulbholder anti-clockwise, and withdraw it from the light unit.

22 Twist the bulb anti-clockwise, and remove it from the bulbholder **(see illustration)**.

23 Fit the new bulb using a reversal of the removal procedure, but before refitting the light unit, first insert the holding spring in its bore.

Front direction indicator - 1997 models onwards

24 The front direction indicator bulbholder is mounted in the rear of the headlight unit. Depending on model, and on which light is being worked on, it may be necessary to remove the headlight unit as described in Section 7, to improve access.

25 The procedure for bulb renewal is as described in paragraphs 21 and 22 **(see illustration)**.

26 Refitting is a reversal of removal.

Side repeaters

27 The side repeater light is held in position by spring pressure.

28 Depending on how the light unit was previously fitted, press it either forwards or rearwards, and remove it from the front wing **(see illustration)**.

29 Turn the bulbholder anti-clockwise, and disconnect it from the housing **(see illustration)**.

30 Pull the wedge-type bulb from the holder **(see illustration)**.

31 Fit the new bulb using a reversal of the removal procedure.

Front foglight - models up to 1996

32 Unscrew the cross-head screws securing the front foglight unit to the valance, and withdraw the light unit.

33 Prise open the plastic clips and remove the rear cover from the light unit.

34 Release the spring clips and withdraw the bulb, then pull off the wiring connector.

35 Fit the new bulb using a reversal of the removal procedure.

Front foglight - 1997 models onwards

36 Using a suitable flat-bladed screwdriver in the recess at the bottom of the light, prise out the light surround trim **(see illustration)**.

37 Unscrew the two cross-head screws, then press the side locking clip outwards and withdraw the light unit forwards. Disconnect the square wiring plug from the rear of the unit **(see illustrations)**.

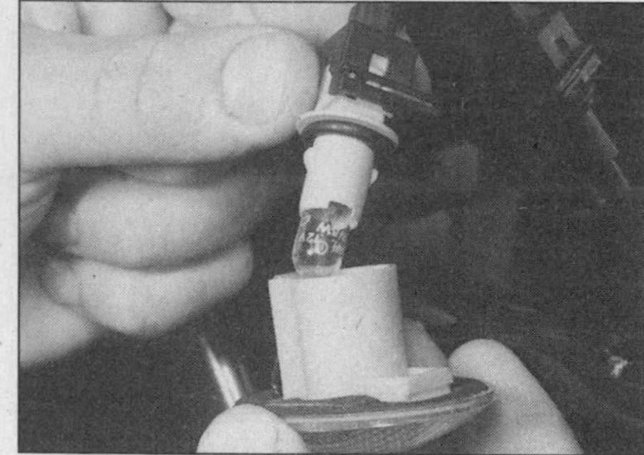

5.29 Removing the bulbholder from the side repeater lens/bulbholder

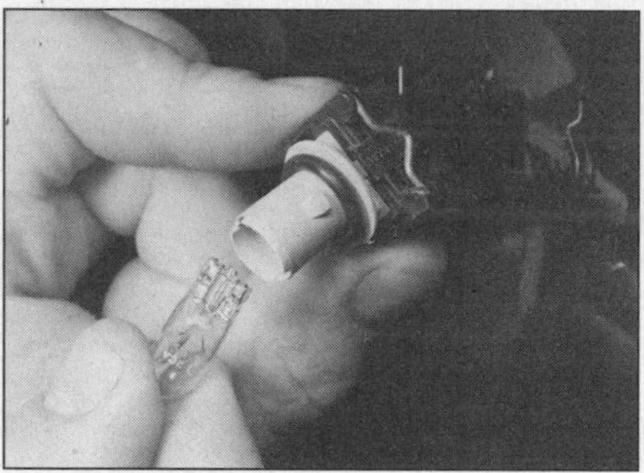

5.30 Removing the wedge-type bulb from the side repeater bulbholder

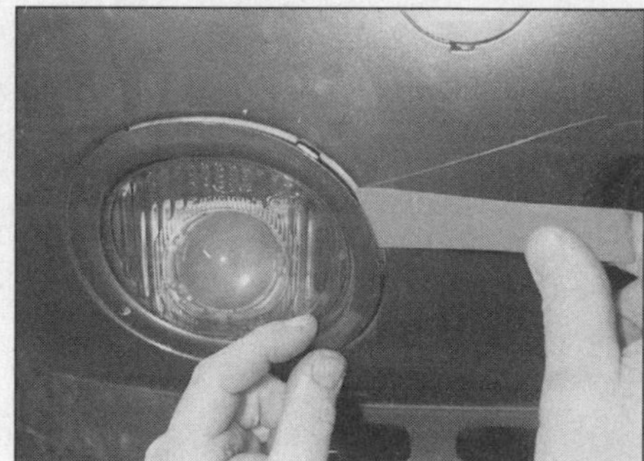

5.36 Prise out the foglight surround trim

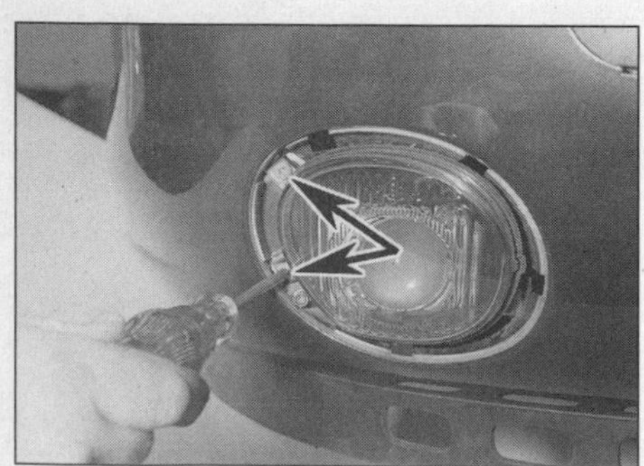

5.37a Undo the retaining screws (arrowed) . . .

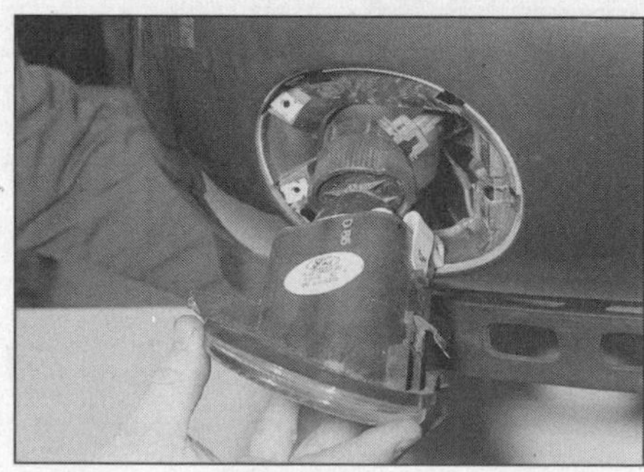

5.37b . . . withdraw the light unit . . .

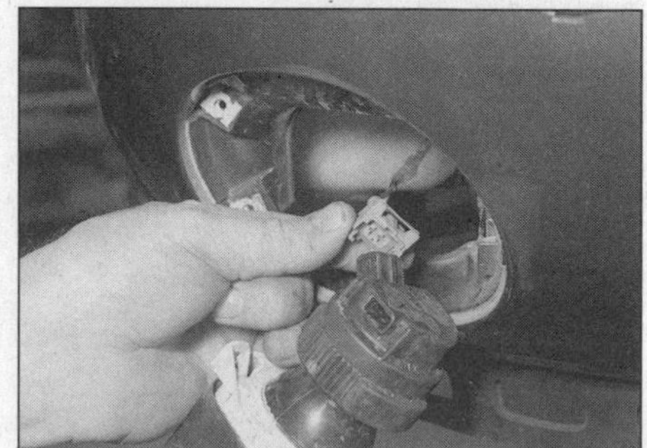

5.37c . . . and disconnect the wiring plug

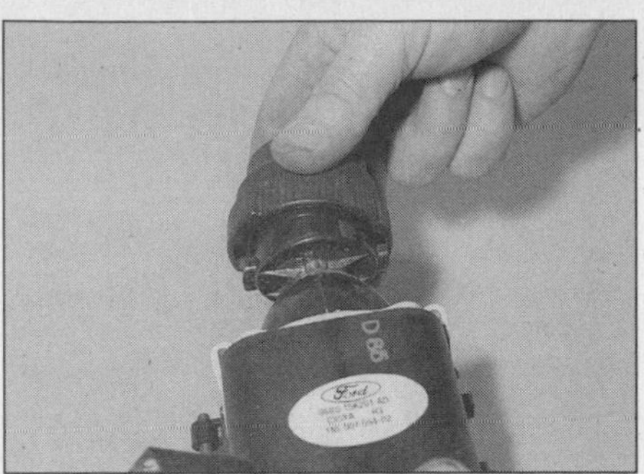
5.38a Twist off the light unit rear cover . . .

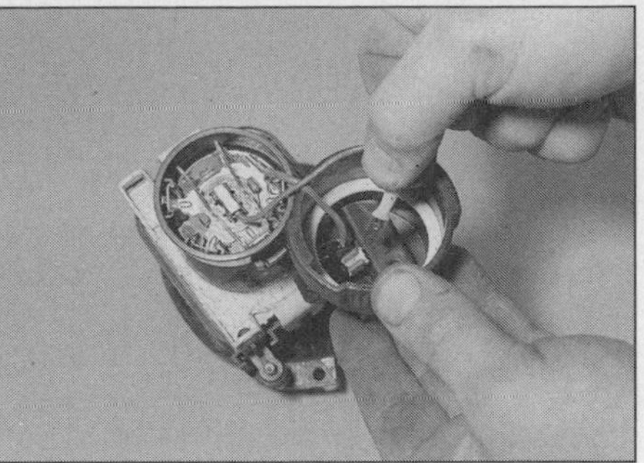
5.38b . . . and disconnect the bulb wiring spade connector

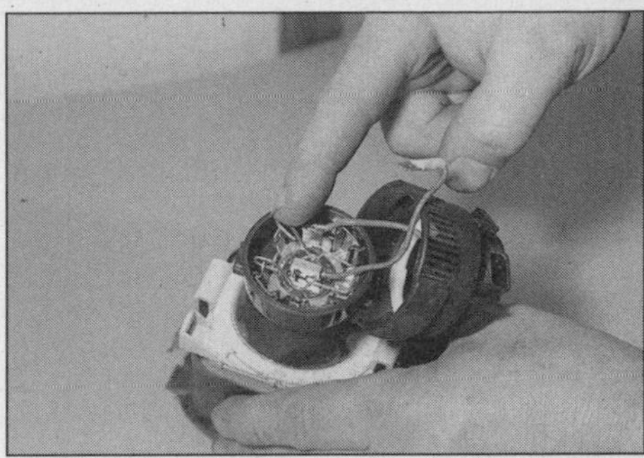
5.39a Release the bulb retaining clip . . .

38 Twist off the rear cover from the light unit, and disconnect the wiring from the rear cover **(see illustrations)**.

39 Release the legs of the wire clip, and take out the bulb, noting its direction of fitting **(see illustrations)**.

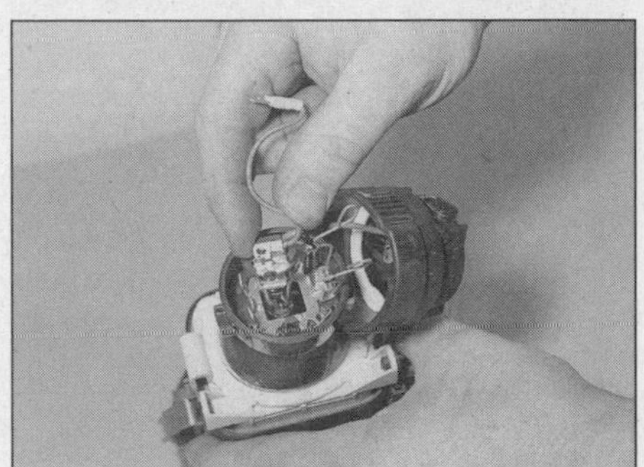
5.39b . . . and withdraw the bulb

40 Fit the new bulb using a reversal of the removal procedure.

Rear light cluster

41 With the tailgate or bootlid open, flip open the trim cover to reveal the bulbholder in the rear corner of the luggage compartment - the trim cover is secured by a number of turn-fasteners. On Estate models, pull back the weatherstrip and release the trim cover clips **(see illustrations)**.

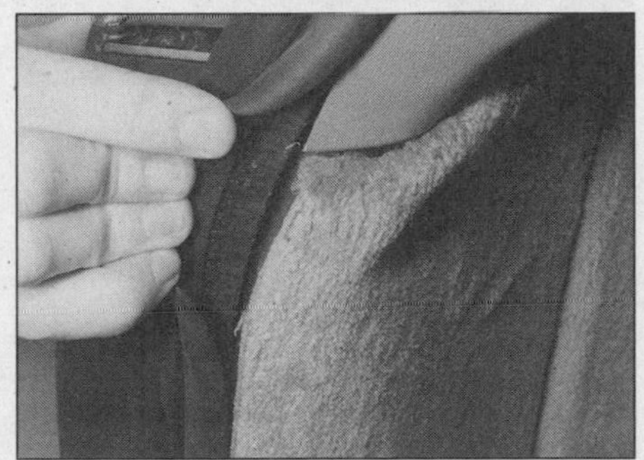
5.41a Pull back the weatherstrip . . .

42 Press the two plastic locking tabs together, and withdraw the rear light cluster bulbholder **(see illustrations)**.

43 Depress and twist the appropriate bulb to remove it from the bulbholder **(see illustration)**.

44 Fit the new bulb using a reversal of the removal procedure. Make sure that the rear light cluster is fully inserted.

Number plate light

45 Remove the cross-head screws from the number plate light, and remove the light unit **(see illustration)**.

5.41b . . . and unclip the trim cover

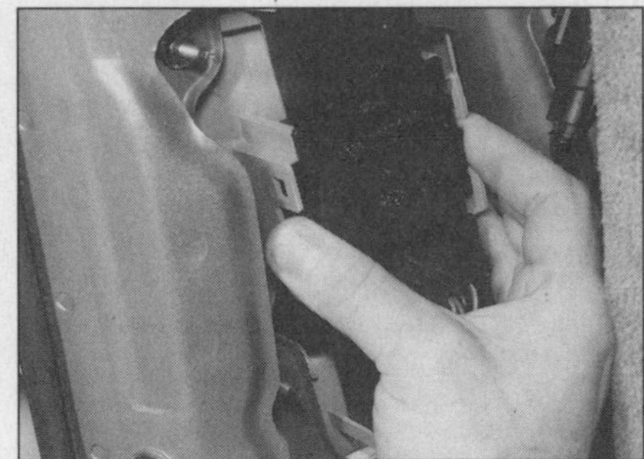
5.42a Pressing the two plastic locking tabs together (Estate)

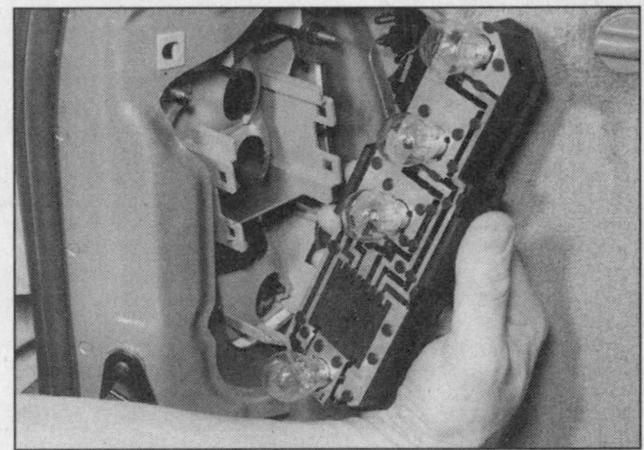
5.42b Removing the rear light cluster (Estate)

5.42c Removing the rear light cluster (Saloon)

5.43 Removing a bulb from the rear light cluster bulbholder

5.45 Remove the cross-head screws . . .

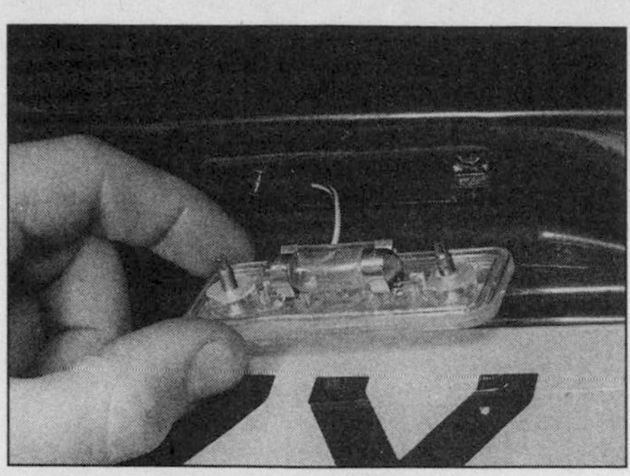
5.46 . . . for access to the festoon-type bulb

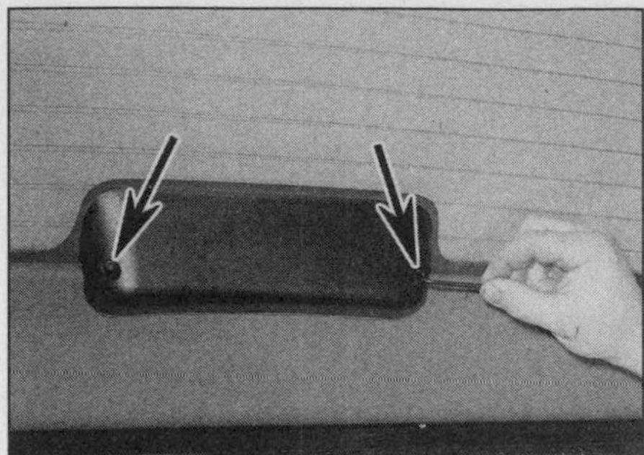
5.48 Remove the two light unit screws (arrowed) . . .

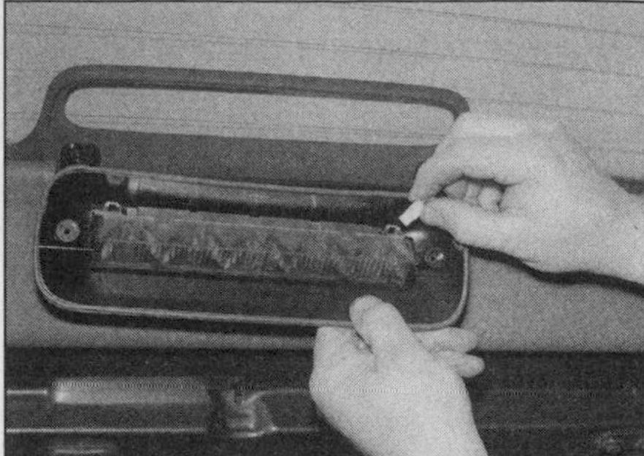
5.49 . . . then lower the light unit and disconnect the wiring plug

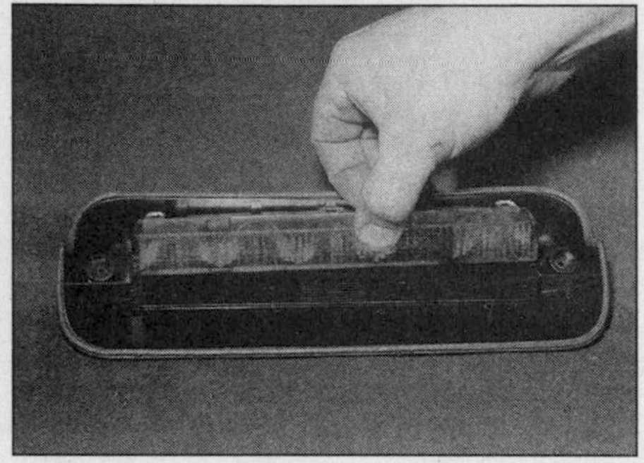
5.50a Slide the light out of the housing . . .

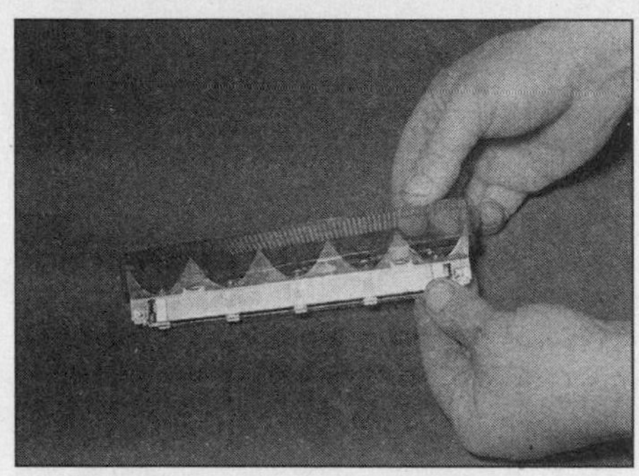
5.50b . . . and unclip the cover from the lens/bulbholder

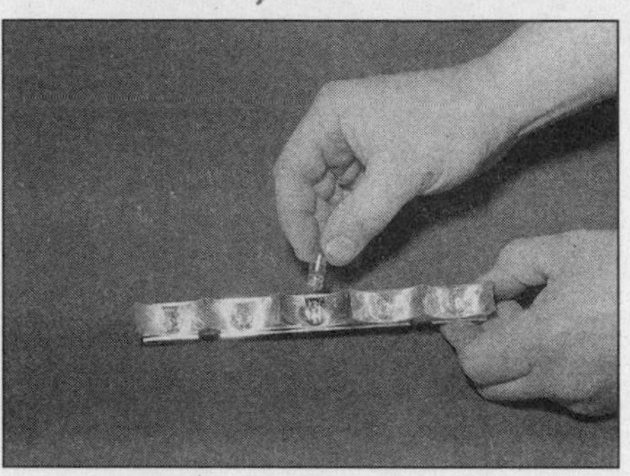
5.51 Pull out the relevant wedge-type bulb

46 Release the festoon-type bulb from the contact springs **(see illustration)**.

47 Fit the new bulb using a reversal of the removal procedure. Make sure that the tension of the contact springs is sufficient to hold the bulb firmly.

High-level stop-light

48 Where applicable, open the tailgate. Remove the two light unit securing screws **(see illustration)**.

49 Lower the light unit from the rear glass, and disconnect the wiring plug **(see illustration)**.

50 Slide the light out of the housing, taking note of its fitted orientation, then unclip the red cover from the lens and bulbholder **(see illustrations)**.

51 Pull out the relevant wedge-type bulb from the holder **(see illustration)**.

52 Fit the new bulb, and refit the light unit using a reversal of the removal procedure.

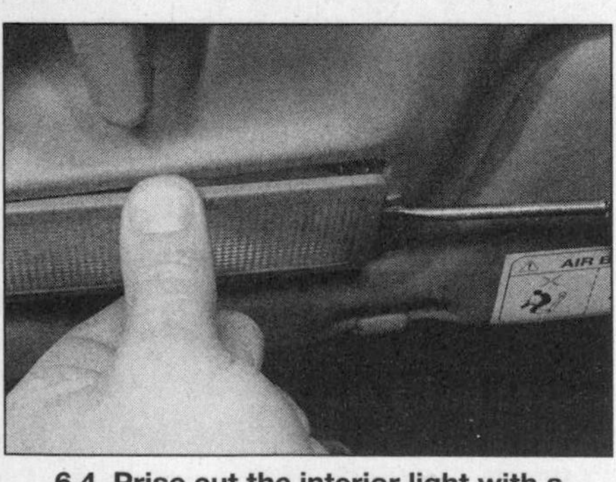
6.4 Prise out the interior light with a screwdriver

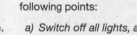

6 Bulbs (interior lights) - renewal

1 Whenever a bulb is renewed, note the following points:

a) Switch off all lights, and disconnect the battery negative lead before starting work (see Chapter 5A, Section 1).
b) Remember that if the light has just been in use, the bulb may be extremely hot.
c) Always check the bulb contacts and holder, ensuring that there is clean metal-to-metal contact between the bulb and its live(s) and earth. Clean off any corrosion or dirt before fitting a new bulb.
d) Wherever bayonet-type bulbs are fitted, ensure that the live contact(s) bear firmly against the bulb contact.
e) Always ensure that the new bulb is of the correct rating and that it is completely clean before fitting it.

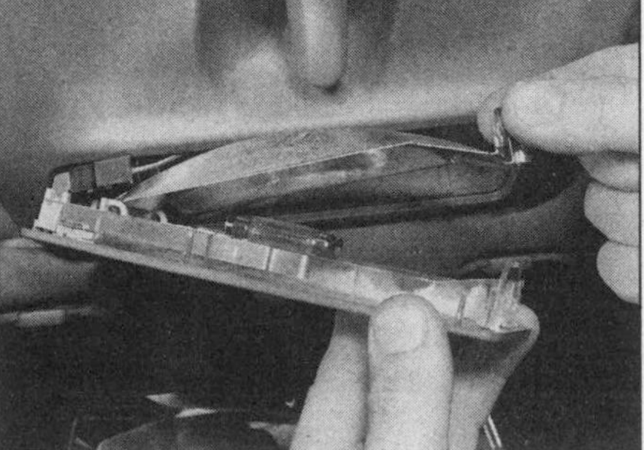
6.5 Lifting the reflector from the interior light

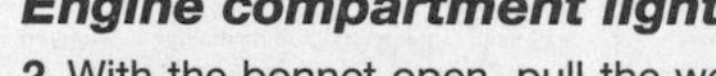

Engine compartment light

2 With the bonnet open, pull the wedge-type bulb from the bulbholder.

3 Fit the new bulb using a reversal of the removal procedure.

Interior light

4 Ensure that the interior light is switched off by locating the switch in its middle position. Using a small screwdriver, carefully prise out the light or bulb cover, as applicable **(see illustration)**.

5 Lift up the reflector, then release the festoon-type bulb from the contact springs **(see illustration)**.

6 Fit the new bulb using a reversal of the removal procedure. Make sure that the tension of the contact springs is sufficient to hold the bulb firmly.

Map reading light

7 With the reading light switched off, prise out the interior light using a small screwdriver.

8 Swivel the contact plate upwards, and remove the bulb **(see illustrations)**.

9 Fit the new bulb using a reversal of the removal procedure. Make sure that the tension of the contact springs is sufficient to hold the bulb firmly.

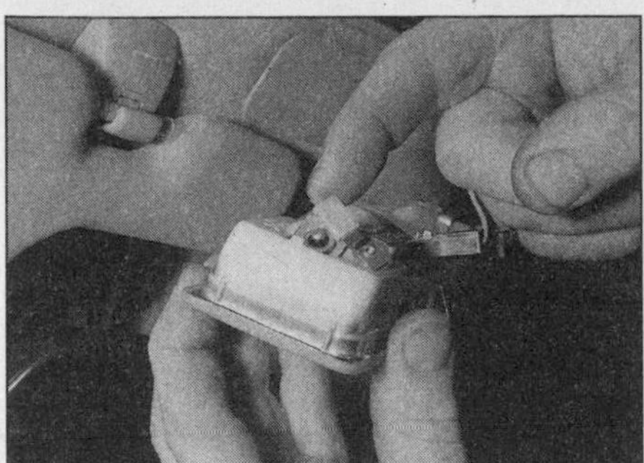

6.8a Swivel the contact plate upwards . . .

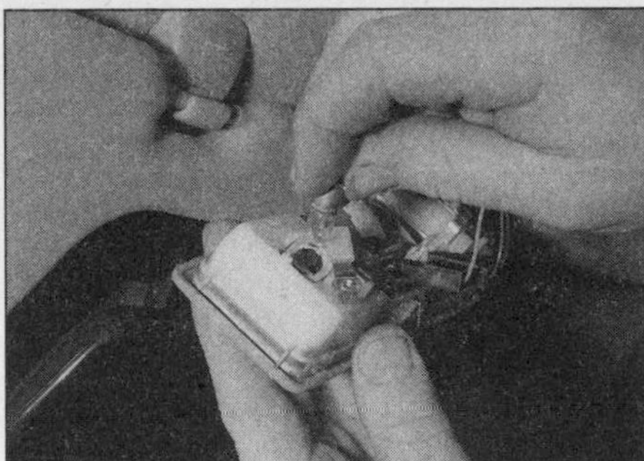

6.8b . . . and remove the reading light bulb

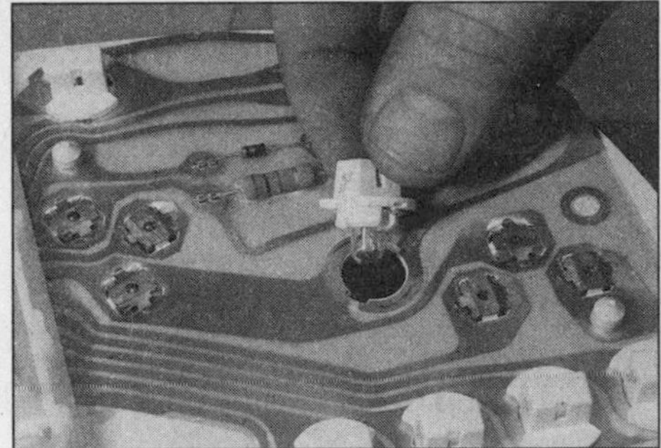

6.11 Removing a bulb from the rear of the instrument panel

Instrument panel illumination and warning lights

10 Remove the instrument panel as described in Section 10.

11 Twist the bulbholder anti-clockwise to remove it **(see illustration)**.

12 Fit the new bulbholder using a reversal of the removal procedure.

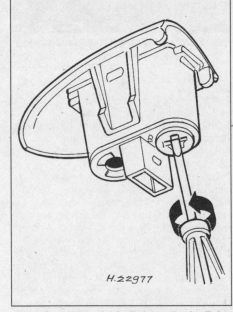

6.14 Removing the bulb from the foglight warning indicator

Foglight warning indicator (models up to 1996)

13 Using a screwdriver, prise out the indicator from the facia, and disconnect the multi-plug.

14 Twist the bulbholder anti-clockwise with the screwdriver, and remove it **(see illustration)**.

15 Fit the new bulb using a reversal of the removal procedure.

Hazard warning light

16 Pull the cover directly up from the switch, then remove the bulb **(see illustrations)**.

17 Fit the new bulb using a reversal of the removal procedure.

Glovebox light

18 Open the glovebox, then pull out the wedge-type bulb from the light located under the upper edge.

Main light switch illumination

19 Carefully prise the switch panel from the facia, using a screwdriver against a cloth pad to prevent damage to the facia.

20 Disconnect the multi-plugs as necessary, and withdraw the switch panel

21 Twist the bulbholder to release it from the light switch, and pull out the wedge-type bulb **(see illustration)**.

22 Fit the new bulb using a reversal of the removal procedure.

Heater fan switch illumination

23 Pull off the switch knob, then depress and twist the bulb to remove it.

Automatic transmission selector panel illumination

24 Disconnect the battery negative (earth) lead (refer to Chapter 5A, Section 1).

25 Remove the ashtray.

26 Select position 'N', then prise out the panel from the centre console.

27 Disconnect the multi-plug from the overdrive control switch.

28 Disconnect the bulbholder and pull out the wedge-type bulb.

29 Fit the new bulb using a reversal of the removal procedure.

Interior door handle illumination

30 Disconnect the battery negative (earth) lead (refer to Chapter 5A, Section 1).

31 Remove the door interior trim panel as described in Chapter 11.

32 Using a knife, cut free the foam watershield for access to the rear of the interior door handle.

33 Pull out the bulbholder and remove the bulb.

34 Fit the new bulb using a reversal of the removal procedure.

Clock illumination

Note: *On later models, the clock illumination bulb is not readily renewable. The clock may have to be removed and taken to a Ford dealer or automotive electrician for bulb renewal.*

35 Disconnect the battery negative (earth) lead (refer to Chapter 5A, Section 1).

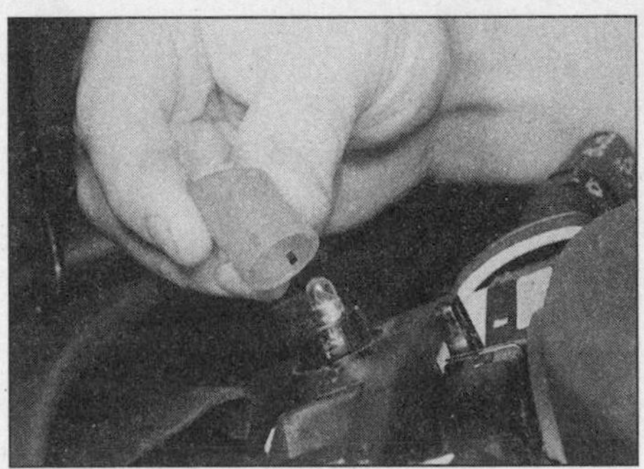

6.16a Pull off the hazard warning light cover . . .

6.16b . . . and remove the bulb

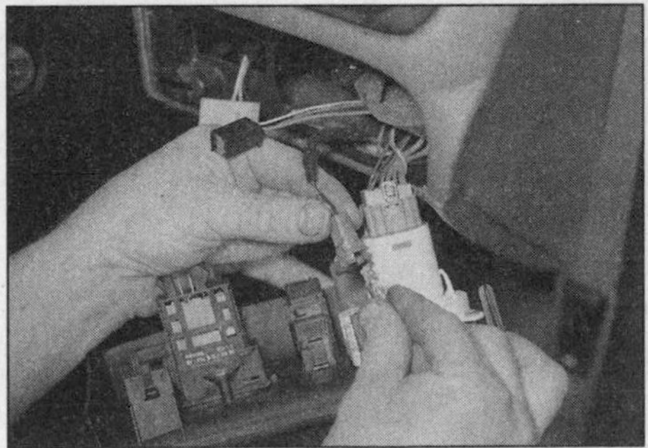

6.21 Removing the main light switch illumination bulb

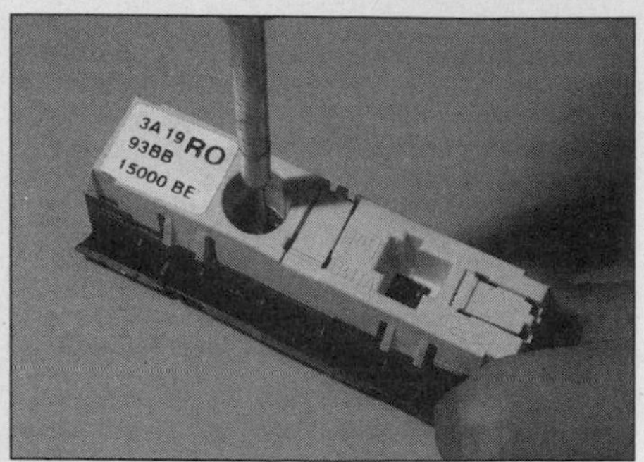

6.37a Twist the bulbholder anti-clockwise . . .

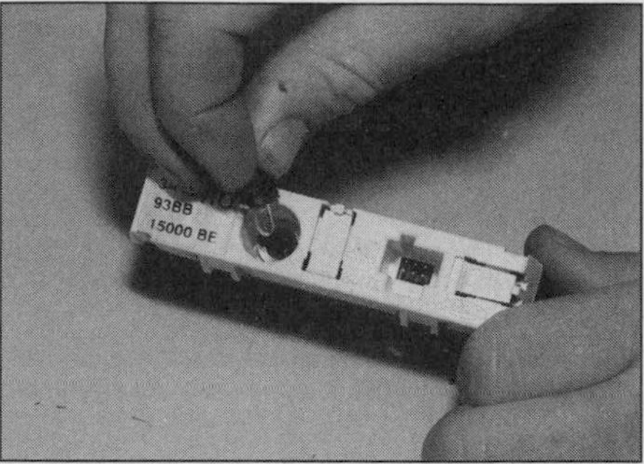

6.37b . . . and remove it from the rear of the clock - early model shown

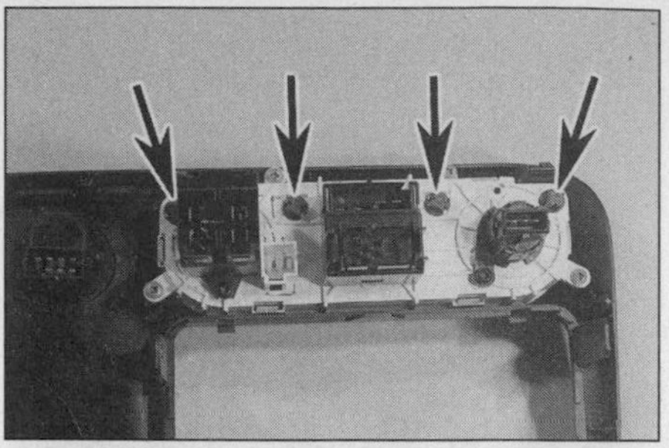

6.39 Heater control panel removed, showing illumination bulbholders (arrowed)

36 Remove the clock as described in Section 13.

37 Twist the bulbholder anti-clockwise using a screwdriver, then remove the bulbholder from the rear of the clock **(see illustrations)**.

38 Fit the new bulb using a reversal of the removal procedure.

Heater control illumination

39 Remove the heater control panel (Chapter 3), then twist the bulbholder anti-clockwise and remove the bulb from the rear of the panel **(see illustration)**.

Luggage compartment light

40 With the light switched off (disconnect the battery negative lead), prise out the light using a small screwdriver.

41 On models up to 1996, hinge back the contact plate, and release the festoon-type bulb from the contact springs.

42 On 1997 and later models, twist the bulb anti-clockwise to remove it.

43 Fit the new bulb using a reversal of the removal procedure. On models with a festoon-type bulb, make sure that the tension of the contact springs is sufficient to hold the bulb firmly.

Footwell illumination light

44 Disconnect the battery negative (earth) lead (refer to Chapter 5A, Section 1).

45 Remove the screws securing the driver's side lower facia panel, and remove the panel for access to the bulb **(see illustration)**.

46 Pull the bulb out of its holder to remove.

47 Fit the new bulb using a reversal of the removal procedure.

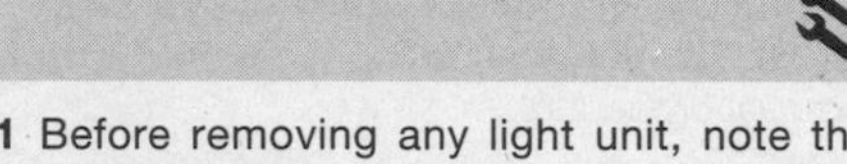

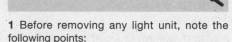

7 Exterior light units - removal and refitting

1 Before removing any light unit, note the following points:

a) Ensure that the light is switched off, and disconnect the battery negative lead before starting work (see Chapter 5A, Section 1).

b) Remember that if the light has just been in use, the bulb and lens may be extremely hot.

Headlight unit - models up to 1996

Note: *From December 1995, certain Mondeos had more powerful headlight units (with H7 bulbs) fitted in production, and the wiring loom was modified. To fit a later light unit to an earlier car, an adaptor lead must also be obtained from your Ford dealer; in this case, find and quote the engine wiring loom part number, which appears on the battery positive lead.*

2 With the bonnet supported in its open position, loosen (but do not remove) the screw located above the front direction indicator.

3 Withdraw the front direction indicator unit forwards, and disconnect the wiring multi-plug. Place the unit to one side.

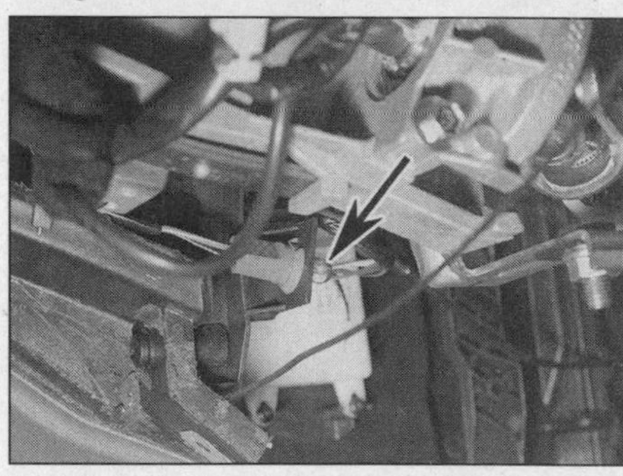

6.45 Driver's footwell illumination bulb (arrowed)

4 Disconnect the wiring multi-plug for the headlight unit **(see illustration)**.

5 Remove the radiator grille as described in Chapter 11.

6 Remove the front bumper as described in Chapter 11.

7 The headlights fitted from new are a single unit, joined by a plastic back-piece running across the front of the vehicle. However, if it is required to renew a headlight unit on one side only, the back-piece must first be removed complete, then cut in half on the bench.

8 Unscrew the mounting bolts from each side of the headlight unit, and withdraw the unit from the front of the vehicle. Use a hacksaw to cut through the centre of the headlight unit (ie between the two headlights), and obtain a connecting kit from a Ford dealer to attach the new unit **(see illustrations)**.

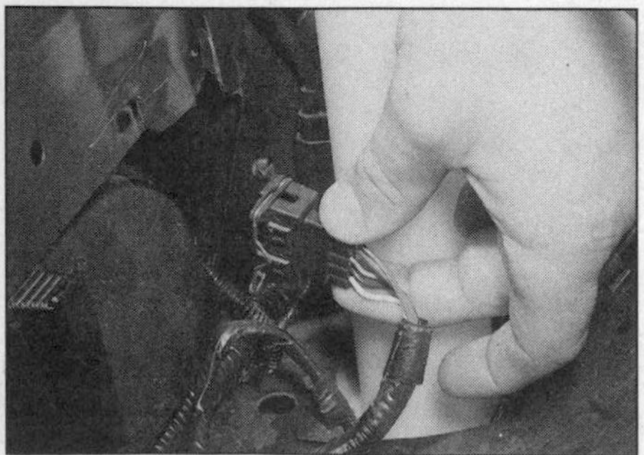

7.4 Disconnecting the headlight unit wiring multi-plug

7.8a Unscrew the outer mounting screws . . .

7.8b . . . and inner mounting screws . . .

7.8c . . . and withdraw the headlight unit assembly

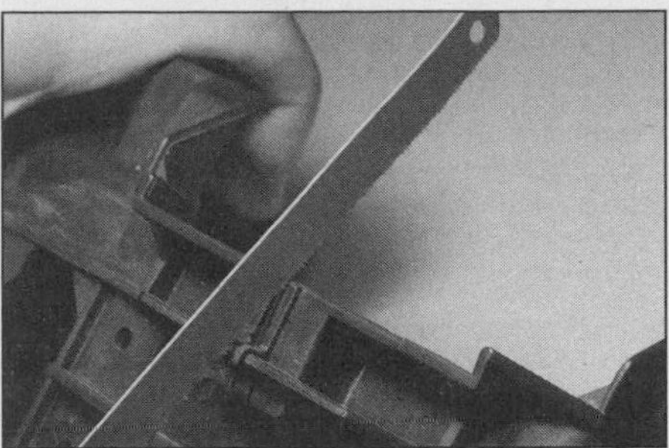

7.8d Using a hacksaw to cut through the middle of the headlight back-piece, in order to fit a new unit

7.9a Release the clips . . .

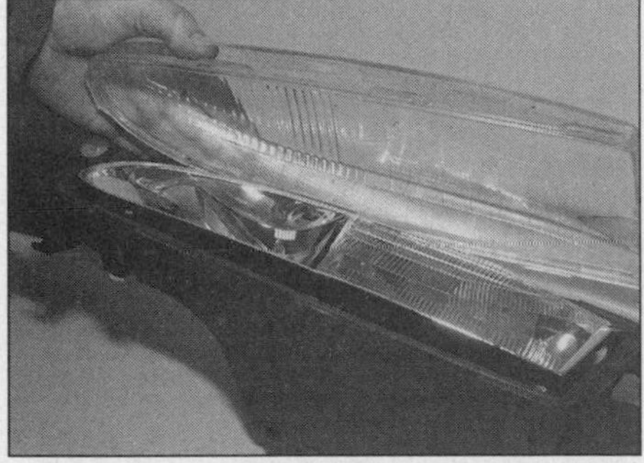

7.9b . . . and remove the headlight lens

7.12a Remove the inner screw (arrowed) . . .

7.12b . . . and the upper screw (arrowed) on the cross panel

9 If necessary, the lens may be removed separately by releasing the clips. To remove the diffuser, release the clips, then remove the rubber seal **(see illustrations)**.

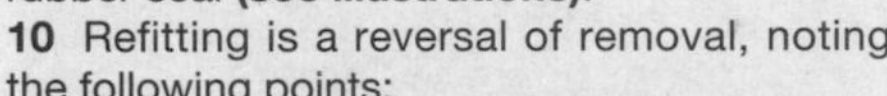

10 Refitting is a reversal of removal, noting the following points:

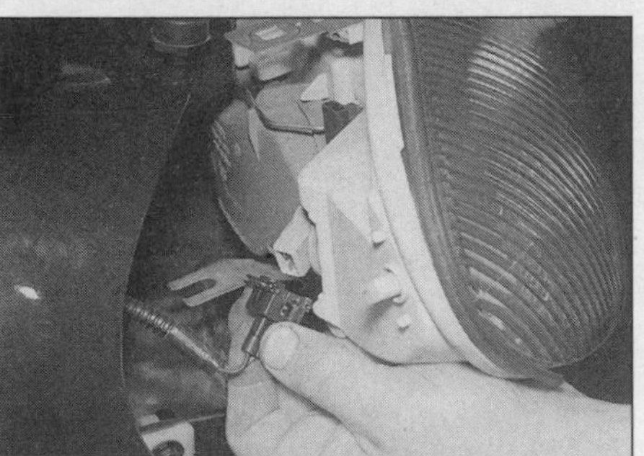

7.14a Withdraw the headlight . . .

a) When refitting the rubber seal on the headlight unit, note that it has a tapered seat.

b) Have the beam alignment checked as described in the next Section.

Headlight unit - 1997 models onwards

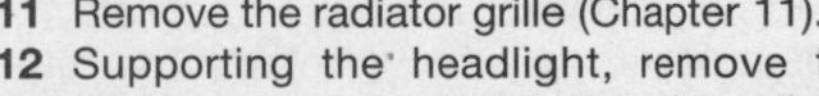

11 Remove the radiator grille (Chapter 11).

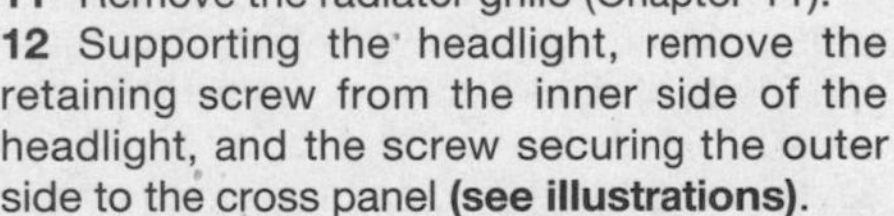

12 Supporting the headlight, remove the retaining screw from the inner side of the headlight, and the screw securing the outer side to the cross panel **(see illustrations)**.

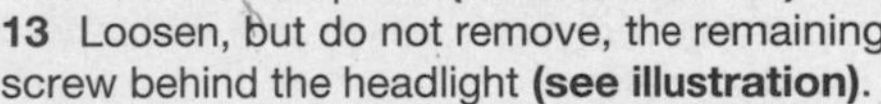

13 Loosen, but do not remove, the remaining screw behind the headlight **(see illustration)**.

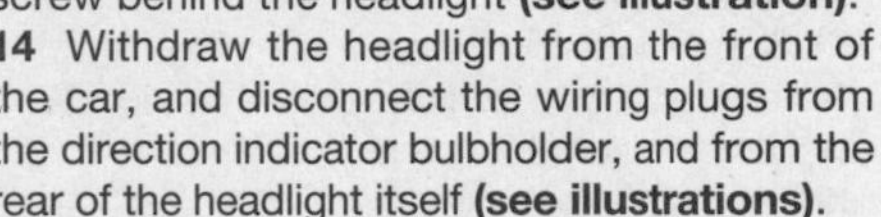

14 Withdraw the headlight from the front of the car, and disconnect the wiring plugs from the direction indicator bulbholder, and from the rear of the headlight itself **(see illustrations)**.

15 Refitting is a reversal of removal. Have the beam alignment checked as described in the next Section.

7.13 Loosen, but do not remove, the screw behind the headlight

Front direction indicator - models up to 1996

16 With the bonnet supported in its open position, loosen (but do not remove) the screw located above the front direction indicator **(see illustration)**.

7.14b . . . and disconnect the wiring plug from the direction indicator . . .

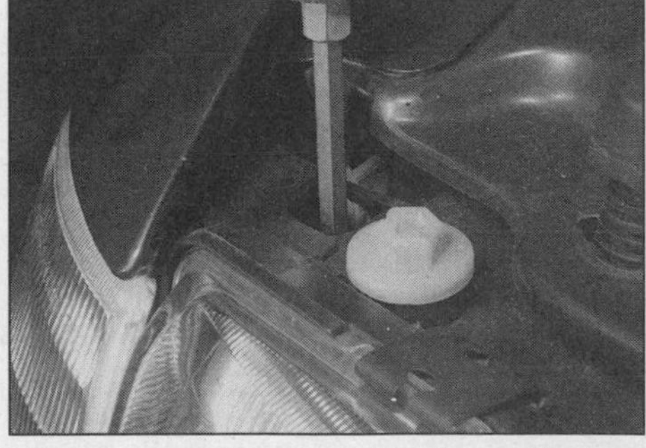

7.14c . . . and from the rear of the headlight

7.16 Loosen the front direction indicator retaining screw

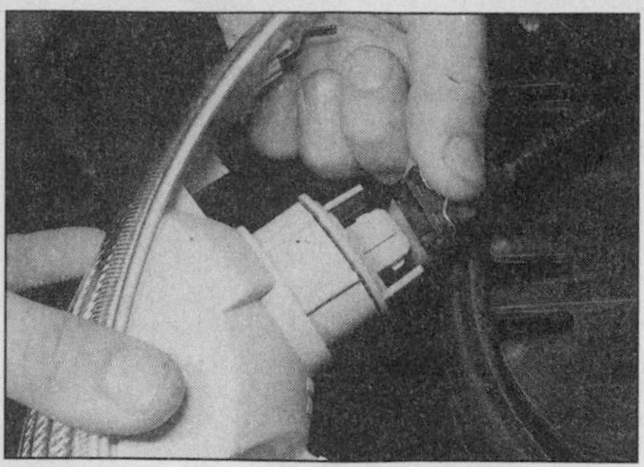
7.18 Disconnecting the wiring plug from the indicator bulbholder

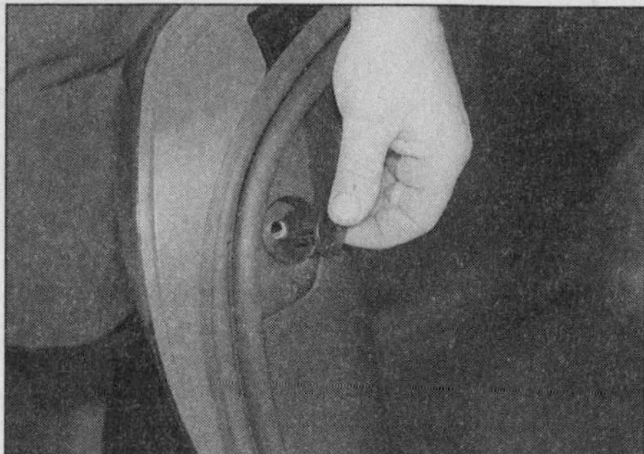
7.30a Turn and remove the fasteners . . .

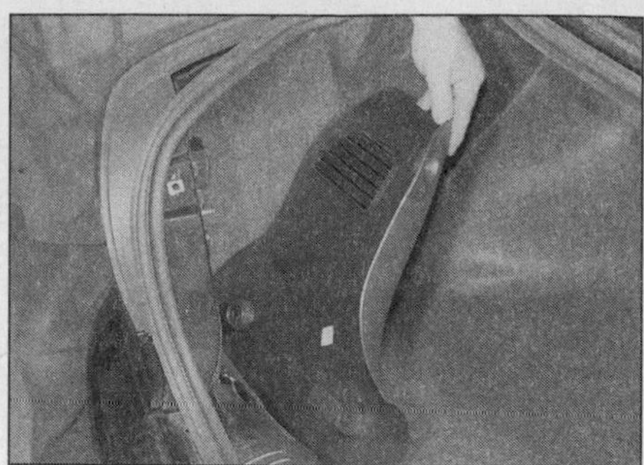
7.30b . . . and remove the trim cover from behind the light unit

17 Withdraw the front direction indicator light unit.

18 Rotate the bulbholder anti-clockwise, and withdraw it from the light unit. Alternatively, the wiring plug can be disconnected from the bulbholder, leaving the bulb in position **(see illustration)**. Remove the light unit.

19 Refitting is a reversal of removal.

Front direction indicator - 1997 models onwards

20 On these models, the front direction indicator is incorporated into the headlight unit, and is not available separately.

Front foglight - models up to 1996

21 Unscrew the cross-head screws securing the front foglight unit to the valance, and withdraw the light unit from the valance.

22 Prise open the plastic clips, and remove the rear cover from the light unit.

23 Release the spring clips and withdraw the bulb, then pull off the wiring connector. Remove the foglight unit.

24 Refitting is a reversal of removal. Have the beam alignment checked as described in the next Section.

Front foglight - 1997 models onwards

25 To improve access to the rear of the light unit, remove the screws and clips, and lower the radiator lower cover.

26 Removal of the foglight is covered in Section 5, paragraphs 36 and 37.

27 Refitting is a reversal of removal. Have the beam alignment checked as described in the next Section.

Rear light cluster

28 With the tailgate or bootlid open, unhook the parcel net (where fitted) from the rear of the luggage compartment.

29 On Saloon and Hatchback models up to 1996, remove the screws, release the clips, and remove the trim panel from the rear cross panel.

30 Release the turn-fasteners, and remove the trim cover from the rear of the light unit **(see illustrations)**.

31 Disconnect the wiring multi-plug from the bulbholder. If a new light unit is being fitted, unclip the bulbholder from the rear of the light unit **(see illustrations)**.

32 Support the light unit, then unscrew the mounting nuts, and withdraw the light unit from the outside of the vehicle **(see illustrations)**.

33 Refitting is a reversal of removal. On models up to 1996, check the condition of the sealer on the body panel, and if necessary renew it.

Rear number plate light assembly

34 Remove both number plate light bulbs as described in Section 5.

35 With the tailgate or bootlid open, remove the screws and withdraw the inner trim panel, releasing it from its various clips.

36 Unscrew the nuts, and remove the outer cover and number plate base from the tailgate.

37 Disconnect the multi-plug and remove the light assembly.

38 Refitting is a reversal of removal.

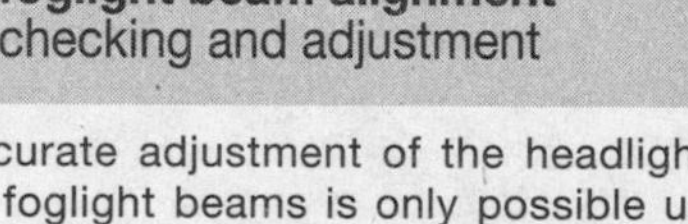

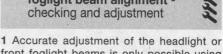

8 Headlight and front foglight beam alignment - checking and adjustment

1 Accurate adjustment of the headlight or front foglight beams is only possible using optical beam-setting equipment. This work should therefore be carried out by a Ford dealer, or other service station with the necessary facilities.

2 Temporary adjustment can be made after renewal of a bulb or light unit, or as an emergency measure if the alignment is incorrect following accident damage.

3 To adjust the headlight aim, turn the adjustment screws on the top of the headlight unit to make the adjustment **(see illustration)**.

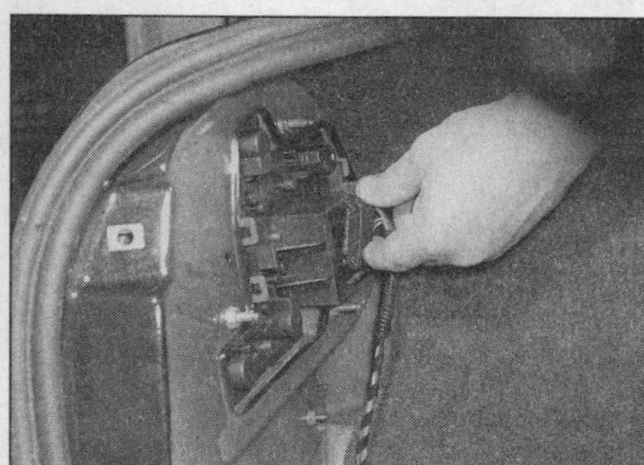
7.31a Disconnect the wiring plug from the bulbholder . . .

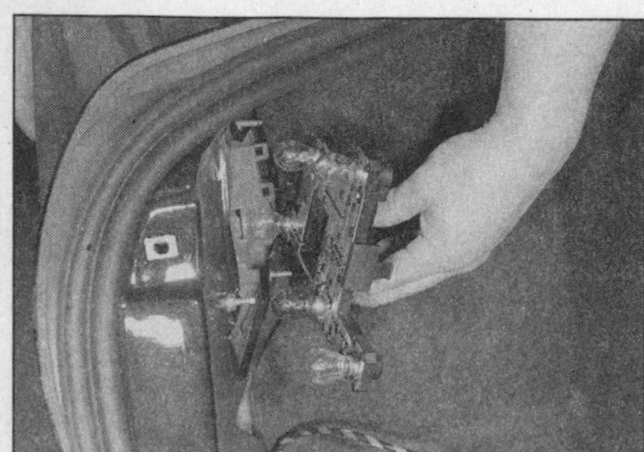
7.31b . . . and if required, unclip the bulbholder from the light unit

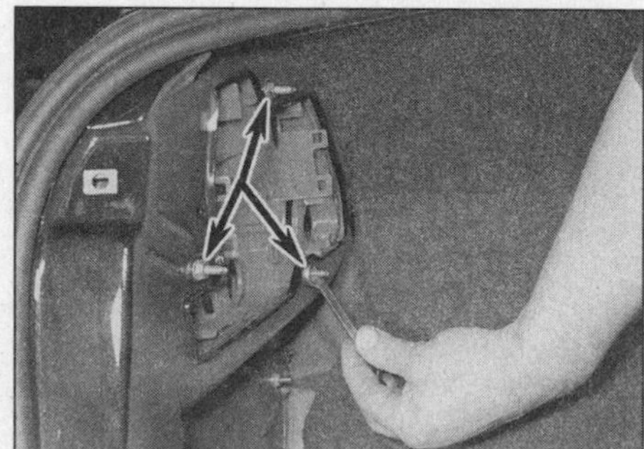
7.32a Depending on model, there will be either three or four mounting nuts (arrowed)

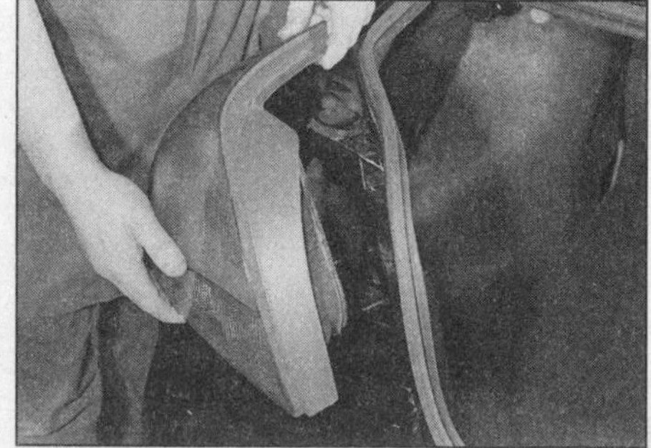
7.32b Removing the rear light cluster (1997-on Saloon shown)

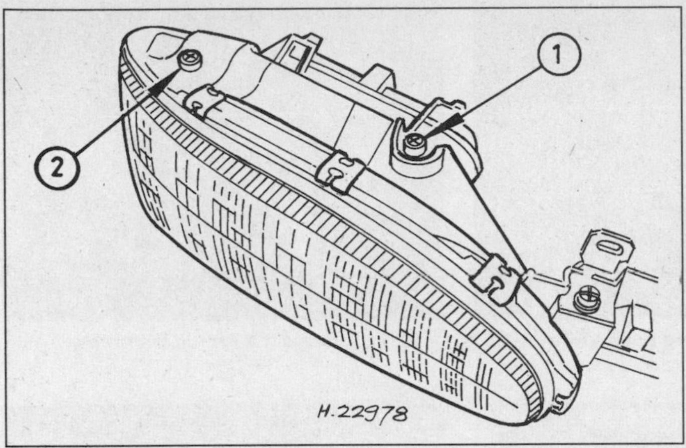

8.3 Headlight beam setting adjustment screws - typical

1 Vertical alignment screw *2 Horizontal alignment screw*

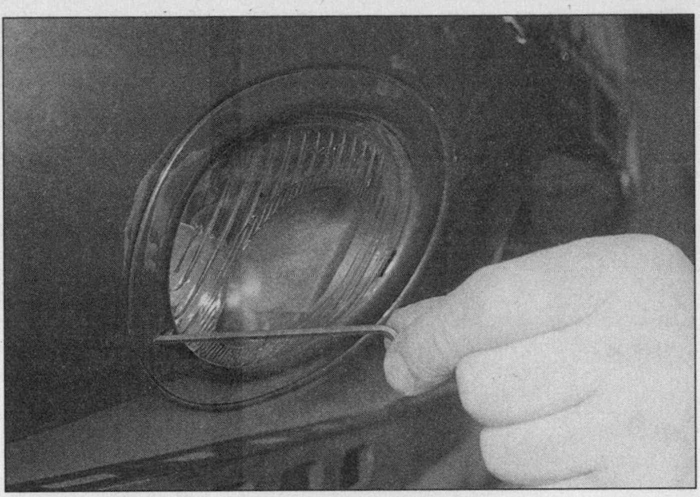

8.4 Adjusting the front foglight beam

4 Adjustment of the front foglight beam is carried out using the small Allen screw visible through the surround trim **(see illustration)**.

5 Before making any adjustments to the settings, it is important that the tyre pressures are correct, and that the vehicle is standing on level ground.

6 Bounce the front of the vehicle a few times to settle the suspension. Ideally, somebody of average size should sit in the driver's seat during the adjustment, and the vehicle should have a full tank of fuel.

7 Where a vehicle is fitted with a headlight beam levelling system, set the switch to the '0' position before making any adjustments.

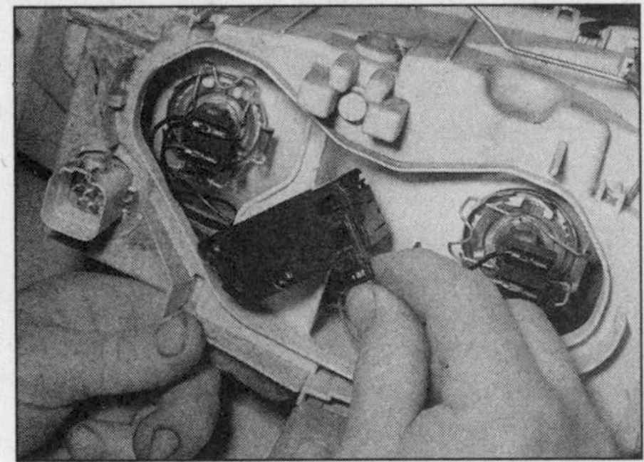

9.3 Disconnect the motor wiring plug

8 Whenever temporary adjustments are made, the settings must be checked and if necessary reset by a Ford dealer or other qualified person as soon as possible.

9 Headlight levelling motor - removal and refitting

Removal

1 Make sure the beam adjustment switch is in the '0' position.

2 Remove the headlight unit as described in Section 7, then remove the rear cover.

3 Disconnect the wiring multi-plug from the motor **(see illustration)**.

Models up to 1996

4 Rotate the motor upwards approximately 60°, then pull it forwards slightly.

5 Disconnect the adjustment spindle by pressing the ball coupling to one side, away from the socket on the reflector.

1997 and later models

6 Unscrew the motor securing screws from the rear of the headlight, and separate the operating linkage balljoint fitting **(see illustrations)**.

All models

7 Withdraw the motor from the headlight unit.

Refitting

8 Refitting is a reversal of the removal procedure, noting the following points:

a) Make sure the beam adjustment switch is still in the '0' position.
b) Refit the motor, then engage the adjuster.
c) On completion, test the operation of the system, and have the beam alignment checked as described in Section 8.

10 Instrument panel - removal and refitting

Removal

1 Disconnect the battery negative (earth) lead (refer to Chapter 5A, Section 1).

2 Remove the clock as described in Section 13.

3 Remove the heated rear window and heated windscreen switches, as applicable, as described in Section 4.

4 On models up to 1996, where fitted, remove the display indicator for the foglights **(see illustration)**.

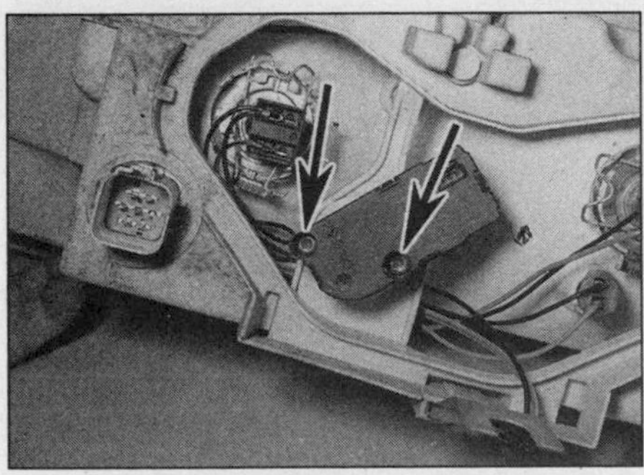

9.6a Remove the motor screws (arrowed) . . .

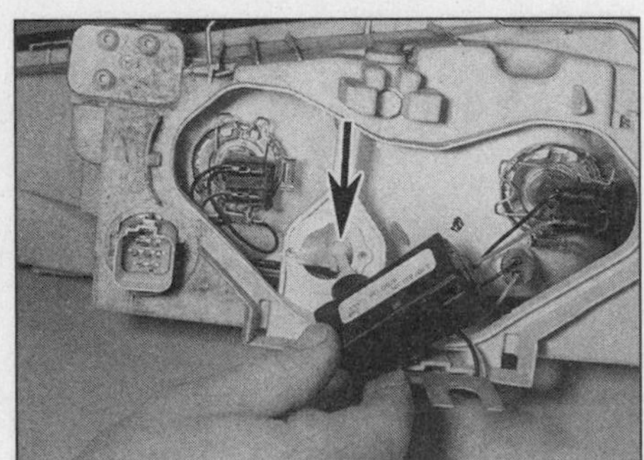

9.6b . . . then separate the motor linkage balljoint (arrowed)

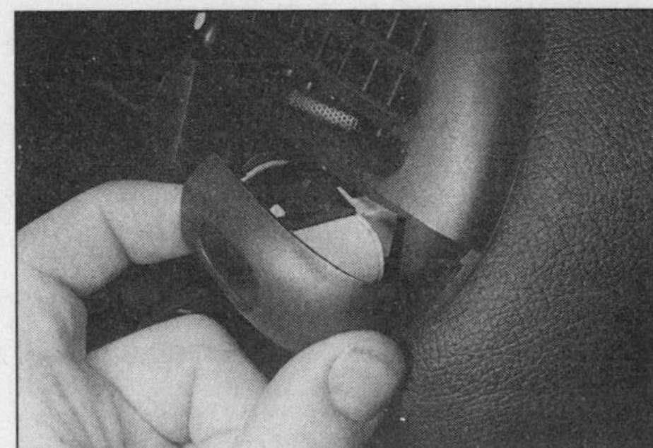

10.4 Removing the foglight warning indicator

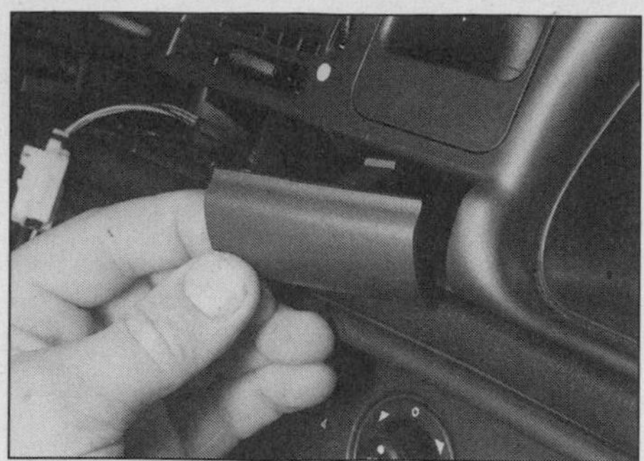

10.5 Removing a switch blanking cover

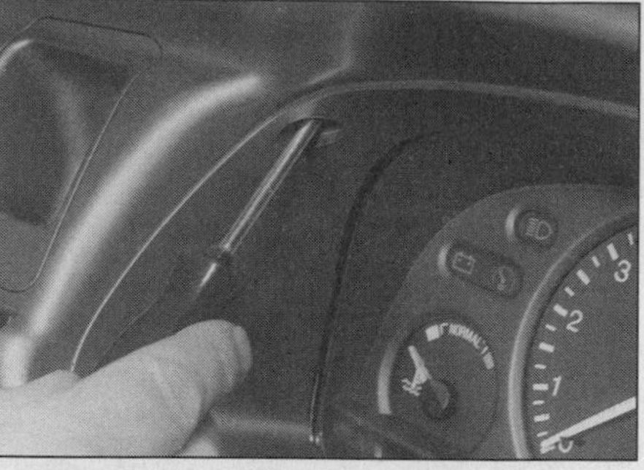

10.6a With the blanking covers removed, unscrew the concealed screws . . .

10.6b . . . and the remaining screws . . .

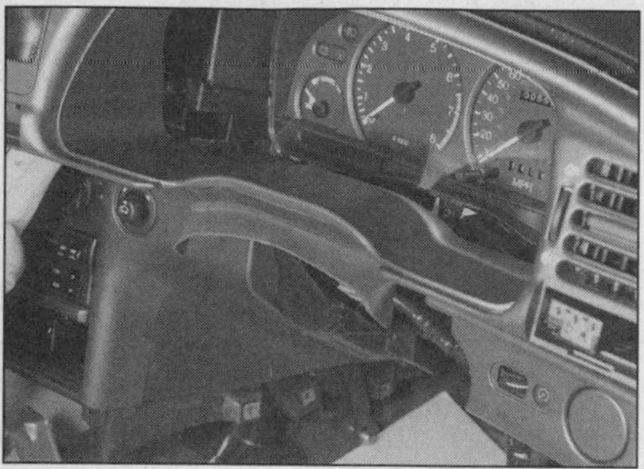

10.6c . . . and lift out the instrument panel surround

10.8 Three of the instrument panel mounting screws (arrowed)

10.9 Disconnecting the multi-plugs from the rear of the instrument panel

5 Where applicable on models up to 1996, remove any blanking covers from the unused switch positions **(see illustration)**.

6 Prise out the blanking covers, then unscrew the retaining screws and remove the instrument panel surround **(see illustrations)**.

7 On 1997 and later models with air conditioning, as the surround is withdrawn, remove the O-ring from the cabin temperature sensor, and detach the sensor from the surround.

8 Unscrew the mounting screws, and withdraw the instrument panel a little way from the facia **(see illustration)**.

9 Disconnect the multi-plugs from the rear of the instrument panel **(see illustration)**.

10 Withdraw the instrument panel from the facia. On models up to 1996, release the speedometer intermediate cable as the panel is withdrawn.

Refitting

11 Refitting is a reversal of the removal procedure.

11 Instrument panel components - removal and refitting

Removal

1 Remove the warning light and illumination bulbs by twisting them anti-clockwise **(see illustration)**.

2 Carefully prise off the glass and bezel from the front of the instrument panel, noting the positions of the retaining lugs **(see illustration)**.

3 Note the positions of the diffusers, then remove them from the instrument panel.

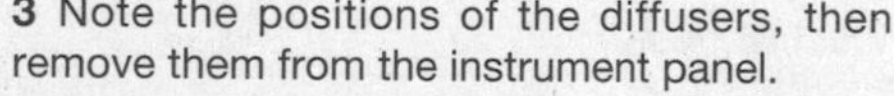

4 To remove the speedometer head, unscrew the Torx mounting screws and withdraw the head from the housing.

5 To remove the tachometer, unscrew the single Torx screw and withdraw it from the housing.

6 Similarly remove the fuel gauge and temperature gauge by unscrewing the single screws.

7 Remove all the pin contacts.

8 Using a small punch, push in the main multi-plugs securing pins, and remove the multi-plugs. The connectors for each gauge should be pressed back through the panel as far as possible without actually removing them.

9 Carefully lift the printed circuit from the location dowels on the housing, taking care not to damage it.

Refitting

10 Refitting is a reversal of the removal procedure.

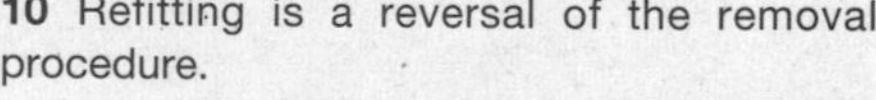

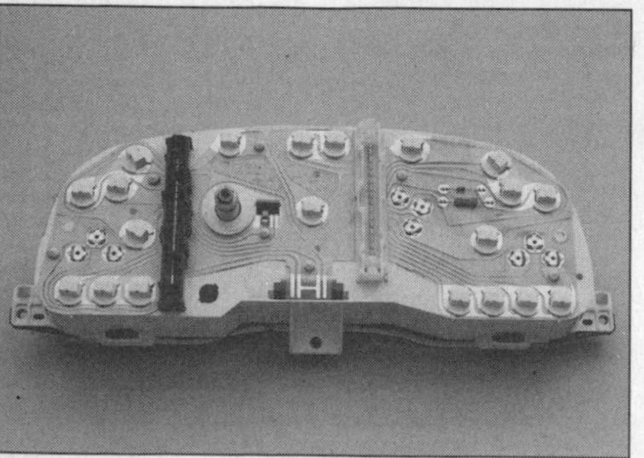

11.1 Rear view of the instrument panel, showing bulbholders

11.2 Bezel retaining lug on the instrument panel

12 Speedometer drive cable (models up to 1996) - removal and refitting

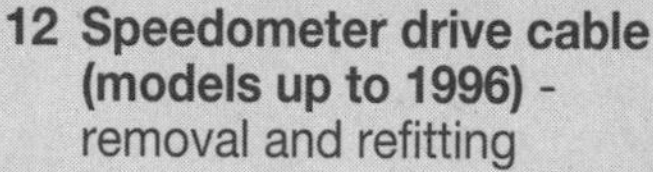

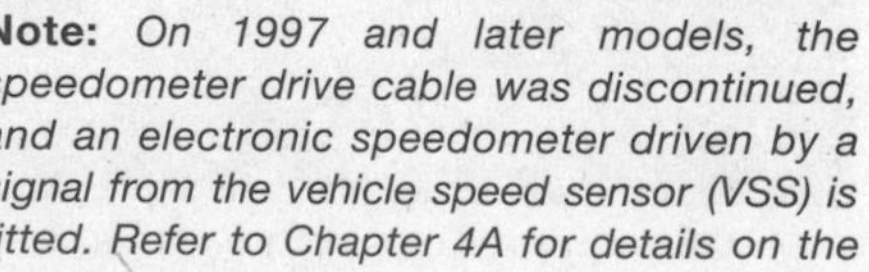

Note: *On 1997 and later models, the speedometer drive cable was discontinued, and an electronic speedometer driven by a signal from the vehicle speed sensor (VSS) is fitted. Refer to Chapter 4A for details on the vehicle speed sensor.*

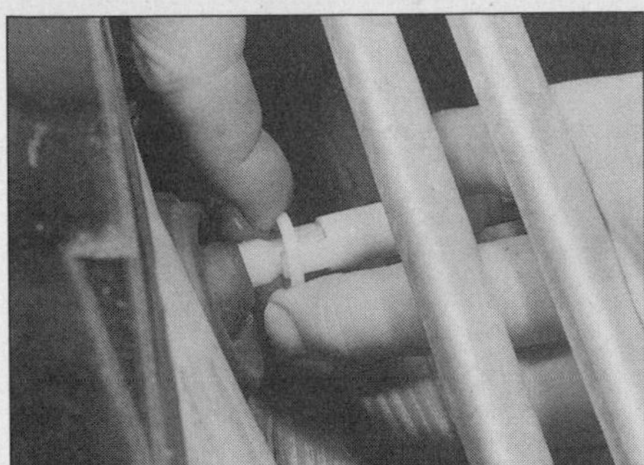

12.7a Squeeze the collar . . .

12.7b . . . and disconnect the speedometer main cable from the intermediate cable

12.9a Unscrew the cable nut . . .

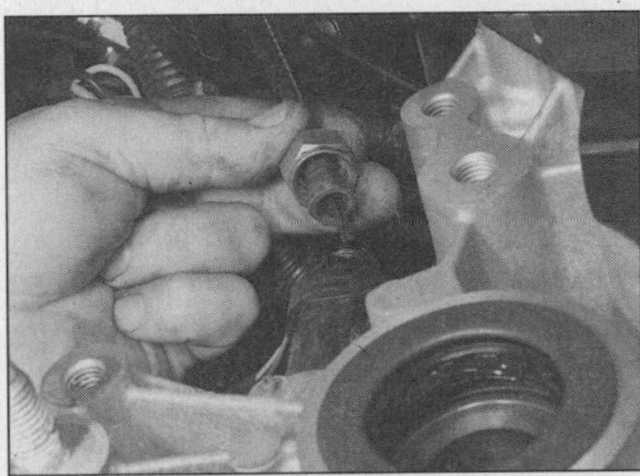

12.9b . . . and disconnect the speedometer cable from the vehicle speed sensor

Removal

1 Remove the windscreen wiper arms as described in Section 15.

2 With the bonnet closed, release the grille panel upper edge from just in front of the windscreen, by prising off the caps and unscrewing the upper retaining screws.

3 Open the bonnet, and support with the stay.

4 Pull off the sealing strip from the cross panel at the rear of the engine compartment.

5 Unscrew the lower screws, and remove the grille panel halves from in front of the windscreen, withdrawing first one side and then the other.

6 Disconnect the battery negative (earth) lead (refer to Chapter 5A, Section 1).

7 Reach in behind the bulkhead. Squeeze the collar on the upper end of the speedometer cable, where it is attached to the intermediate cable from the rear of the speedometer head. Disconnect the cable, and withdraw it from the bulkhead inner panel, together with the rubber grommet **(see illustrations)**.

8 Apply the handbrake, jack up the front of the vehicle and support it on axle stands.

9 Unscrew the nut and disconnect the speedometer cable from the vehicle speed sensor on the transmission, then withdraw the cable from within the engine compartment **(see illustrations)**. Use two spanners to loosen the nut - one to counterhold the sensor, and the other to unscrew the cable nut.

Refitting

10 Refitting is a reversal of the removal procedure.

13 Clock - removal and refitting

Removal

1 Disconnect the battery negative (earth) lead (refer to Chapter 5A, Section 1).

2 Using a small screwdriver, prise the clock out of the facia **(see illustration)**, starting at the lower left corner. To prevent damage to the facia, place a cloth pad beneath the screwdriver.

3 Disconnect the multi-plug(s) from the rear of the clock, and withdraw the clock **(see illustration)**.

4 On some models, the bulb can be removed by twisting it anti-clockwise; on others, the clock should be taken to a Ford dealer or automotive electrical specialist for bulb renewal.

Refitting

5 Refitting is a reversal of the removal procedure. Reset the clock on completion.

14 Horn - removal and refitting

Removal

1 Apply the handbrake, jack up the front of the vehicle and support it on axle stands.

2 Unscrew the bolts, and release the clips securing the radiator lower cover to the front of the vehicle.

3 Disconnect the wiring from the horn terminal.

4 Unscrew the mounting bolt, and withdraw the horn with its mounting bracket from under the vehicle **(see illustration)**.

Refitting

5 Refitting is a reversal of the removal procedure. Tighten the horn unit mounting bolt to the specified torque.

13.2 Prising the clock out of the facia - early model shown, others similar

13.3 Disconnecting the multi-plug from the rear of the clock

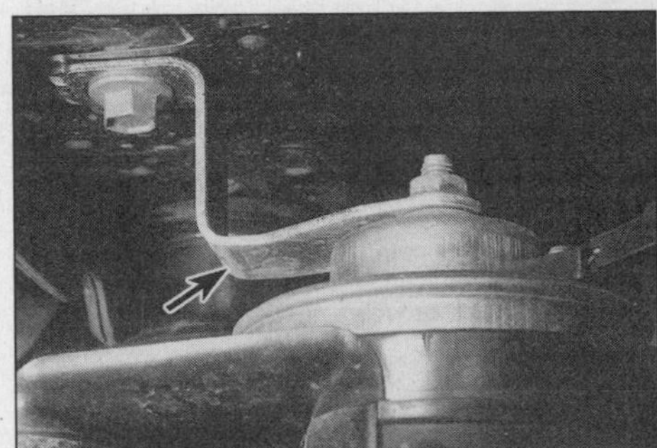

14.4 Horn and mounting bracket (arrowed)

15 Wiper arms - removal and refitting

Removal

1 Disconnect the battery negative (earth) lead (refer to Chapter 5A, Section 1). If the windscreen wiper arms are to be removed, close the bonnet.

2 With the wiper(s) 'parked' (ie in the normal at-rest position), mark the positions of the blade(s) on the screen, using a wax crayon or strips of masking tape.

3 Lift up the plastic cap from the bottom of the wiper arm, and loosen the nut one or two turns **(see illustration).**

4 Lift the wiper arm, and release it from the taper on the spindle by moving it to one side.

5 Completely remove the nut, and withdraw the wiper arm from the spindle **(see illustration).**

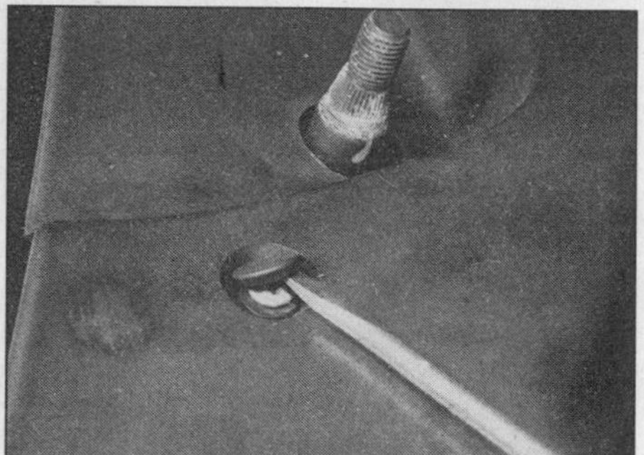

16.3a Prise off the cap . . .

15.3 Loosening the wiper arm retaining nut

Refitting

6 Refitting is a reversal of the removal procedure. Make sure that the arm is fitted in the previously-noted position before tightening its nut to the specified torque.

16 Windscreen wiper motor and linkage - removal and refitting

Removal

1 Disconnect the battery negative (earth) lead (refer to Chapter 5A, Section 1).

2 Remove the wiper arms as described in Section 15.

3 With the bonnet closed, release the grille panel upper edge from just in front of the windscreen, by prising off the caps and

15.5 Removing the wiper arm from the spindle

unscrewing the upper retaining screws **(see illustrations).**

4 Open the bonnet, and support it with the stay.

5 Pull off the bonnet sealing strip from the cross panel at the rear of the engine compartment **(see illustration).**

6 Unscrew the lower screws, and remove the grille panel halves from in front of the windscreen, withdrawing one side then the other side **(see illustrations).**

7 Unscrew the mounting bolts securing the wiper motor and linkage to the bulkhead **(see illustration).** On right-hand-drive models, the linkage is on the right-hand side of the bulkhead; on left-hand-drive models, it is on the left-hand side.

8 Disconnect the wiper motor multi-plug.

9 Withdraw the wiper motor, complete with the linkage, from the bulkhead **(see illustration).**

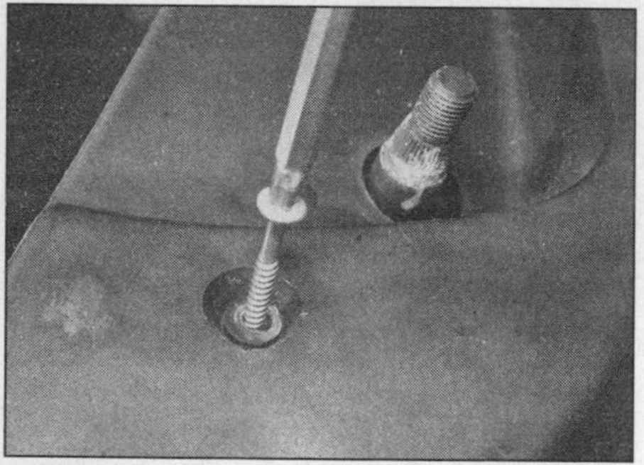

16.3b . . . and remove the upper retaining screws

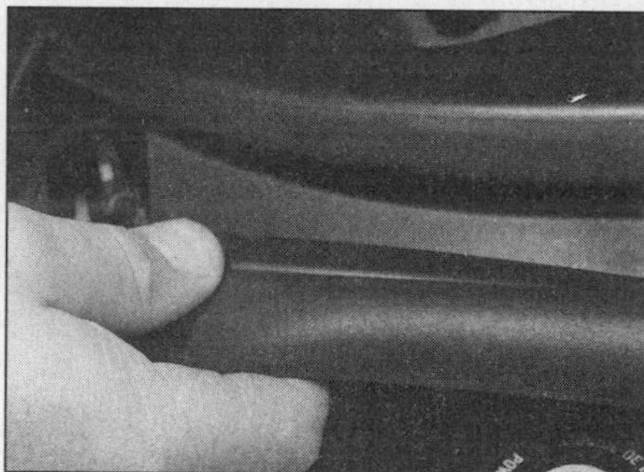

16.5 Removing the bonnet sealing strip

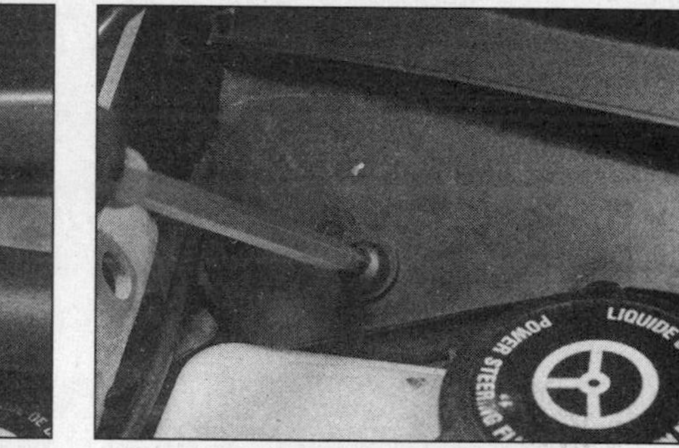

16.6a Unscrew the lower screws . . .

16.6b . . . and remove the grille panel from in front of the windscreen

16.7 Wiper motor mounting bolt locations (right-hand-drive)

16.9 Removing the wiper motor and linkage

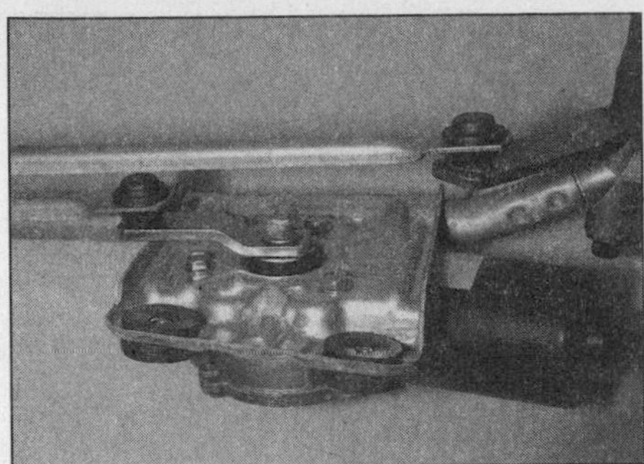

16.10 Wiper motor arm and mounting plate located on the motor

10 Mark the position of the motor arm on the mounting plate, then unscrew the centre nut **(see illustration)**.

11 Unscrew the motor mounting bolts, and separate the motor from the linkage assembly.

Refitting

12 Refitting is a reversal of the removal procedure, noting the following points:

a) There are two tightening torques for the motor mounting bolts - the lower one for bolts that are being re-inserted into an old motor, and the higher ones for bolts that are being inserted into a new motor.

b) Make sure that the wiper motor is in its 'parked' position before fitting the motor arm, and check that the wiper linkage is in line with the motor arm.

17 Tailgate wiper motor assembly - removal and refitting

Removal

1 Disconnect the battery negative (earth) lead (refer to Chapter 5A, Section 1).

2 Remove the tailgate wiper arm as described in Section 15.

3 Remove the tailgate inner trim panel by unscrewing the retaining screws.

4 Release the wiper motor multi-plug from the clip, then disconnect it **(see illustration)**.

5 Disconnect the wiper motor earth lead.

6 Unscrew the mounting bolts, and remove the wiper motor from inside the tailgate **(see illustrations)**.

7 Unbolt and remove the mounting plate. If necessary, remove the mounting rubbers for renewal **(see illustrations)**.

Refitting

8 Refitting is a reversal of the removal procedure. Make sure that the wiper motor is in its 'parked' position before fitting the wiper arm.

18 Trip computer module - removal and refitting

The trip computer is incorporated in the clock. Refer to Section 13.

19 Auxiliary warning system - general information and component renewal

1 Most models are fitted with an auxiliary warning system, which monitors brake lights, sidelights, dipped beam and tail lights, external temperature, door/tailgate/bootlid opening, brake pad wear, and coolant and washer levels. Some models have an engine oil level sensor as part of the system, which works in conjunction with the oil pressure warning light on the instrument panel.

2 The auxiliary warning system module and graphic warning display are combined into one unit.

Service interval reminder

3 The system also includes a service interval reminder warning light, which is illuminated if the specified mileage (or time) since the last service has been reached.

4 To reset the service interval system and turn off the light, on models up to 1996, a switch inside the glovebox must be depressed for a minimum of 4 seconds with the ignition switched on. On 1997 and later models, the switch is behind the arrow-shaped symbol in the display panel, and is depressed using a thin probe, again for 4 seconds with the ignition switched on (see Chapter 1, Section 1). In either case, this should be carried out by a Ford dealer if the vehicle is still in the warranty period.

Component renewal

5 The following paragraphs describe brief removal procedures for the auxiliary warning system components. Disconnect the battery negative (earth) lead before commencing work (refer to Chapter 5A, Section 1). Refitting procedures are a reversal of removal.

Display module

6 Remove the instrument panel surround, referring to Section 10.

7 Unscrew the mounting screws, disconnect the multi-plugs and remove the assembly.

Display module warning bulb

8 Remove the display module as described above.

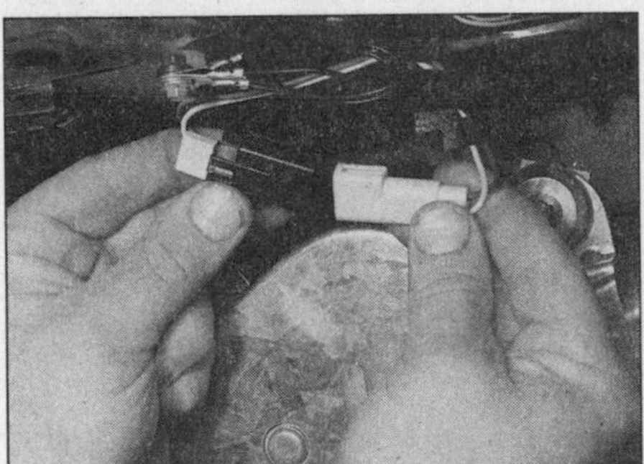

17.4 Disconnecting the tailgate wiper motor multi-plug

17.6a Unscrew the mounting bolts . . .

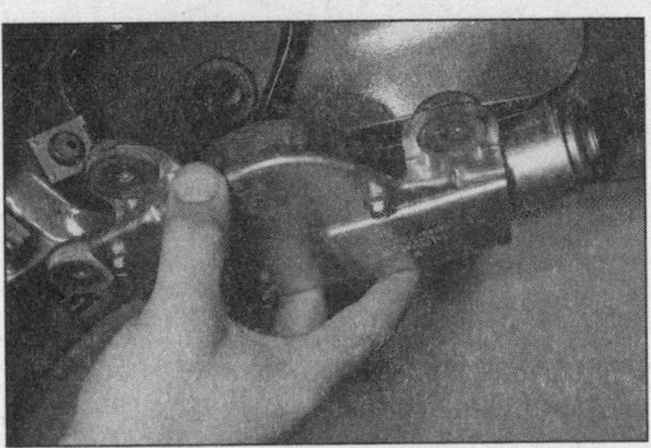

17.6b . . . and remove the tailgate wiper motor assembly (Hatchback shown - Estate similar)

17.7a Tailgate wiper motor assembly and mounting plate

17.7b A mounting rubber removed from the mounting plate

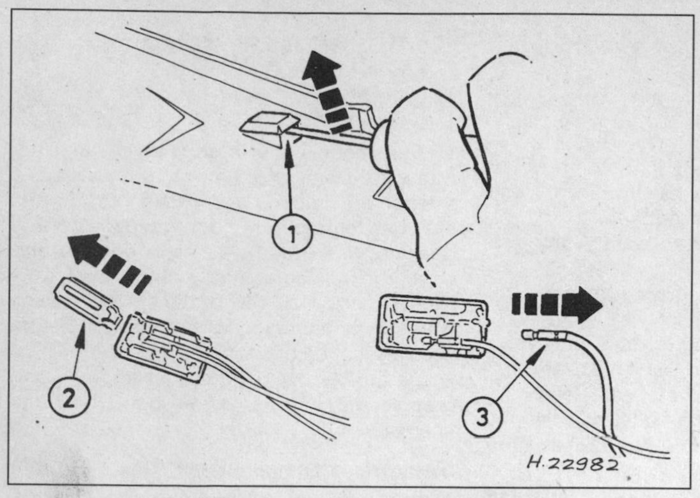

19.14 Service indicator switch removal

1 Lever out the switch
2 Cover
3 Wiring

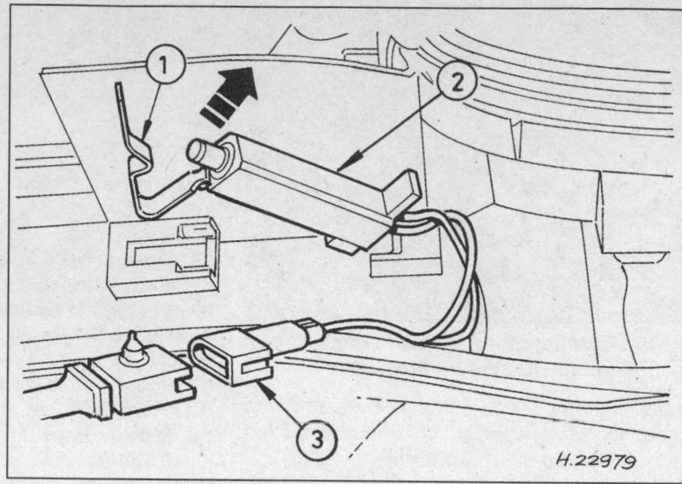

19.16 Low air temperature sender unit removal

1 Clip
2 Sender unit
3 Multi-plug

9 Prise off the cover, and pull out the relevant bulb and bulbholder.

Bulb failure module

10 Remove the lower facia panel from under the steering wheel.
11 Unclip the bulb failure module and disconnect the multi-plug.

Service indicator reset switch - models up to 1996

12 Remove the glove compartment lid as described in Chapter 11, Section 32.
13 Carefully lever out the switch using a small screwdriver.
14 Remove the rear cover and disconnect the wiring **(see illustration)**.

Low air temperature warning sender unit

15 Remove the front bumper.
16 Unclip the sender unit and disconnect the multi-plug **(see illustration)**.

Engine oil level sensor

17 Apply the handbrake, jack up the front of the vehicle and support it on axle stands.
18 Place a container beneath the oil level sensor in the sump, to catch any spilt oil.
19 Unscrew the screws and remove the cover from the sensor.
20 Disconnect the multi-plug.
21 Unscrew and remove the sensor, and remove the seal **(see illustration)**.
22 After refitting the sensor, top-up the engine oil as described in "*Weekly checks*".

Door ajar sensor

23 Remove the door lock as described in Chapter 11, Section 14.
24 Unclip the sensor and disconnect the multi-plug.

Low coolant warning switch

25 Refer to Chapter 3, Section 6.

Low washer fluid switch

26 Disconnect the multi-plug from the washer fluid reservoir.
27 Drain or syphon out the fluid from the reservoir.
28 Using a screwdriver, lever out the switch from the reservoir **(see illustration)**.
29 After refitting the switch, refill the reservoir with reference to "*Weekly checks*".

Brake pad wear sensors

30 The sensor wires are built into the brake pad friction material. When the friction material wears down sufficiently that pad renewal is required, the sensor wire is exposed, and makes contact with the brake disc. This completes the warning light circuit, and the warning light will come on. Note that, if the sensor wire insulation is damaged, this might result in the warning light giving a false indication of pad wear.

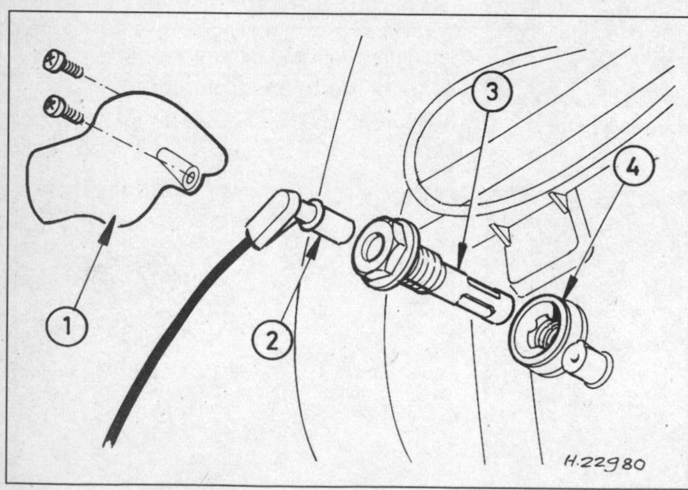

19.21 Engine oil level sensor removal

1 Cover
2 Multi-plug
3 Sensor
4 Seal

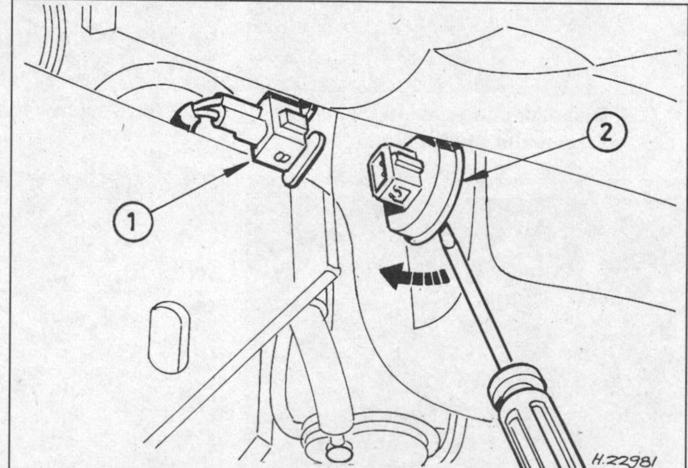

19.28 Removing the low washer fluid switch (2)

1 Multi-plug

20.5a Disconnecting a movement sensor multi-plug

20.5b Removing a movement sensor

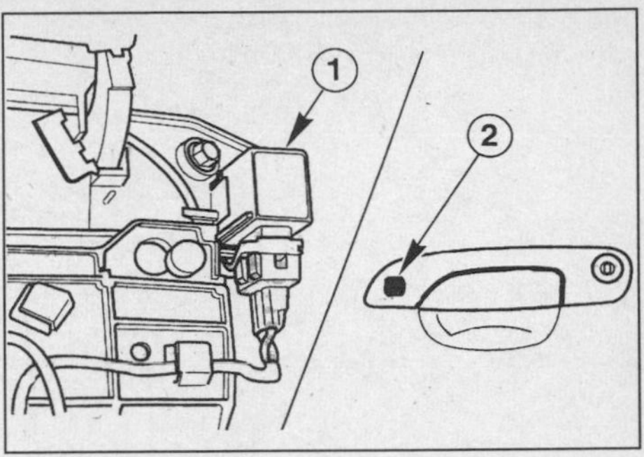

20.8 Infra-red receiver location on the door handle

1 Receiver
2 Infra-red eye on the door handle

20 Anti-theft alarm system - general information

1 All UK models are fitted with a perimetric anti-theft alarm system, incorporating an ignition immobiliser. The system protects all doors, including the bonnet and bootlid/tailgate, and is activated when the vehicle is locked. A volumetric alarm, which protects the interior with ultrasonic detection, is available as an option - on later Estate models with this feature, additional glass breakage detection is incorporated into the rear glass.

2 The system includes a start inhibitor circuit, which makes it impossible to start the engine with the system armed. On later models with the passive anti-theft system (or PATS), the immobiliser is deactivated by a transponder chip built into the ignition key. The PATS (or 'Safeguard') circuit is separate from the alarm, meaning that the car is immobilised even if the alarm is not set.

20.9a Alarm system horn location on Hatchback and Saloon models . . .

20.9b . . . and on Estate models (arrowed)

3 On later models, the radio/cassette unit is incorporated into the alarm system - if an attempt is made to remove the unit while the alarm is active, the alarm will sound.

4 The PATS transceiver unit is fitted around the ignition switch, and it 'reads' the code from a microchip in the ignition key. This means that any replacement or duplicate keys must be obtained through a Ford dealer - any cut locally will not contain the microchip, and will therefore not disarm the immobiliser.

5 The movement sensors on the volumetric system consist of two ultrasonic units, located in the 'B' pillars, incorporating transmitters and receivers **(see illustrations)**. The receivers check that the echo frequency matches the original frequency. If there is any significant difference, the system triggers the alarm.

6 The alarm module is incorporated into the central locking module, on a bracket beneath the right-hand side of the facia, together with the PATS module on later models. The set and reset switches are located in a housing by the lock barrel holder in the front doors.

7 To allow temporary opening of the tailgate or bootlid, an inhibit switch is fitted to the lock. This suppresses the alarm system until the tailgate or bootlid is closed again.

8 Where remote central locking is fitted, an infra-red receiver is located on the exterior door handle **(see illustration)**. Note that excessive heat can destroy this receiver; therefore, it should be covered with aluminium tape if (for instance) a paint-drying heat process is to be used.

9 The alarm system is fitted with its own horn. On Hatchback and Saloon models, it is located on the left-hand side of the luggage compartment; on Estate models, it is located on the right-hand side of the luggage compartment **(see illustrations)**.

10 The alarm system incorporates a self-test function, which can be activated by operating the bonnet switch or one of the lock position switches eight times within 10 seconds. During the check, the horn or buzzer issues acoustic signals which should occur every time a door, bonnet or tailgate is opened. If the doors are double-locked, the signal will occur when something is moved within the passenger compartment. A more comprehensive test can be made using the Ford FDS 2000 diagnostic tester.

11 The door lock switches associated with the alarm system are located behind the door trim panels **(see illustration)**.

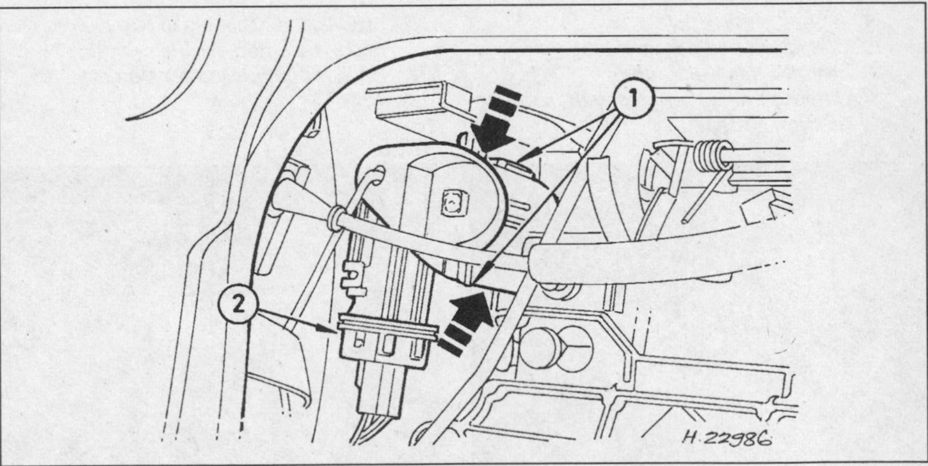

20.11 Alarm system door lock switch removal

1 Clips (arrowed)
2 Multi-plug

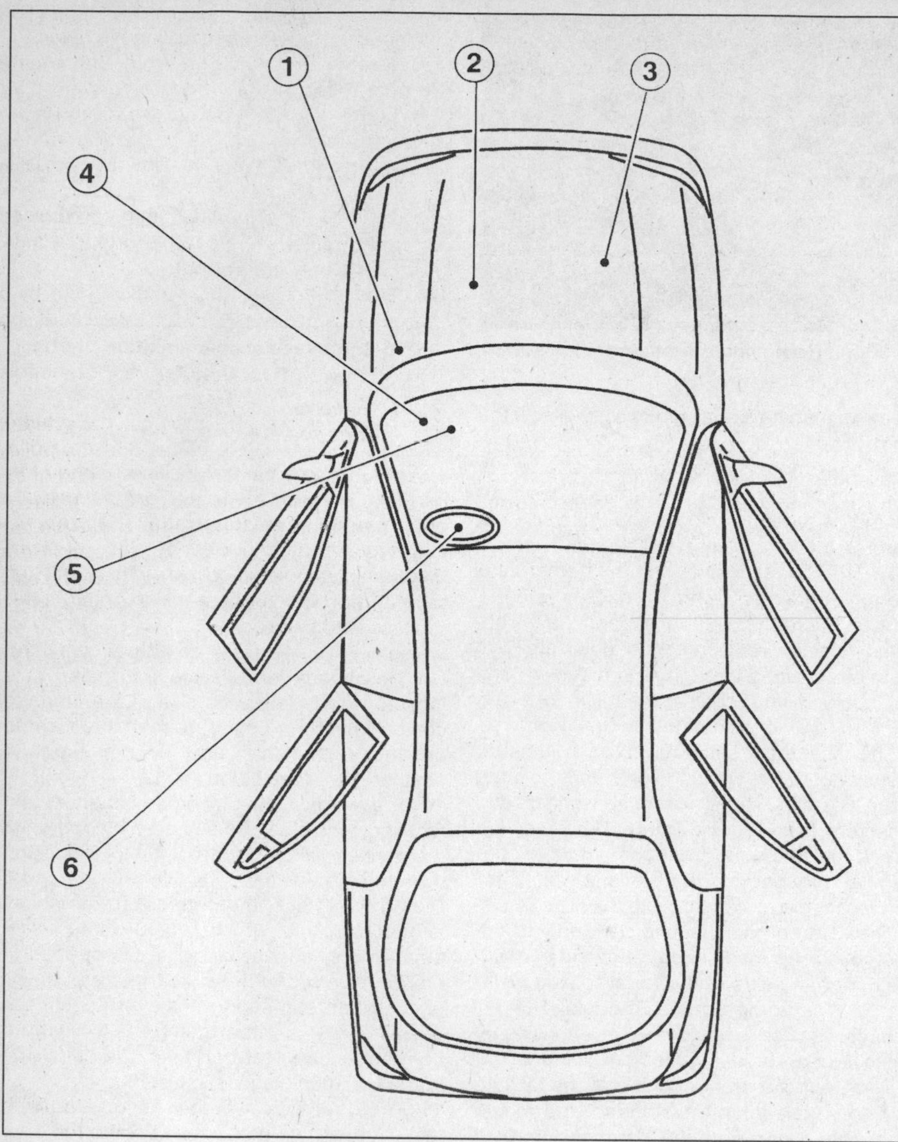

21.2 Cruise control component location - left-hand drive model shown

1 *Speed control unit*
2 *Vehicle speed sensor (VSS)*
3 *Throttle valve actuator*
4 *Interrupt relay (vehicles with traction control system only)*
5 *Stop-light switch, brake and clutch pedal- operated disable switches*
6 *Driver's controls (buttons on steering wheel)*

21 Cruise control system - general information, component renewal

1 Cruise control is available as an option on some models.

2 The cruise control system components are shown in the accompanying illustration **(see illustration)**. The system is active at road speeds between 25 mph and 125 mph.

3 The system comprises an electronic speed control unit with integral actuator and switches mounted in the engine compartment with a control cable connected to the throttle valve actuator, driver-operated switches, brake and clutch pedal switches, an indicator light, and the vehicle speed sensor.

4 The driver-operated switches are mounted on the steering wheel, and allow the driver to control the various functions.

5 The vehicle speed sensor is mounted on the transmission, and generates pulses which are fed to the speed control unit. On early models, the speedometer drive cable is attached to the vehicle speed sensor - on later models, an electronic speedometer uses the speed sensor signal directly.

6 The stop-light switch, brake pedal switch and (when applicable) clutch pedal switch are used to disable the cruise control system. The stop-light switch is activated when the brake pedal is applied gently, and the brake pedal switch is activated when the brake pedal is applied forcibly.

7 An indicator light on the instrument panel is illuminated when the system is in operation.

8 The following paragraphs describe brief removal procedures for the cruise control system components. The battery negative (earth) lead should be disconnected before commencing work (refer to Chapter 5A, Section 1). Refitting is a reversal of removal.

Steering wheel switches

9 Remove the air bag unit from the steering wheel as described in Section 28.

10 Disconnect the wiring plugs, noting the location of each plug and how the wiring is routed for refitting **(see illustrations)**.

11 Remove the two screws each side securing the operating switches, and remove

21.10a Disconnect the spade connectors . . .

21.10b . . . including the earth wire from the contact plate . . .

21.10c . . . and the main multi-plug connector

21.11 Remove the switch securing screws (arrowed), and take out the switch

them as required from the steering wheel **(see illustration)**.

12 If required (for access to the horn switch, for example), the switch contact plates and springs can be removed, after unscrewing the two retaining screws each side.

Brake and clutch pedal switches

13 Remove the lower facia panel from under the steering column.

14 Disconnect the multi-plugs from the clutch switch, brake pedal switch and stop-light switch **(see illustration)**.

15 To remove the clutch and brake pedal switches, twist them anti-clockwise. To remove the stop-light switch, twist it clockwise **(see illustration)**.

16 Refitting is the reverse of removal. To ensure correct operation of the brake pedal switches, reset the switch by fully extending its plunger **(see illustration)**. Depress the pedal until the distance between it and the mounting bracket is as shown for the stop-light switch in Chapter 9. Hold the pedal in this position, clip the switch securely into position and gently raise the pedal to the at-rest position. This will automatically set the position of the switch.

Speed control actuator

17 On four-cylinder engine models, remove the air cleaner as described in Chapter 4A.

18 Disconnect the actuator cable from the throttle linkage on the throttle housing, by releasing the inner cable end fitting from the segment and unclipping the outer cable from the bracket.

19 On models with the V6 engine, disconnect the air temperature sensor wiring plug from the air cleaner top cover.

20 Disconnect the actuator multi-plug, then unscrew the actuator mounting bolt, and slide the actuator out of the mounting pin holes.

21 Remove the actuator from the engine compartment. On models with air conditioning, it may be necessary to unclip and lift up the right-hand section of the windscreen cowl panel, to allow the actuator to be removed.

22 Depress the actuating cable cap locking arm, and remove the cap by turning it anti-clockwise **(see illustration)**.

23 Gently raise the cable retaining lug by a maximum of 0.5 mm, and push the cable end out of the slot in the pulley.

24 When refitting, make sure that the cable end locks into the slot in the pulley.

25 To locate the cable cap onto the actuator pulley, keep the cable taut and in the pulley groove, and pull the throttle linkage end of the cable to draw the cable cap onto the pulley.

26 To refit the cable cap, keep the cable taut and the pulley still, then refit the cable cap tabs into the actuator slots; turn the cap clockwise until the locking arm locates on the locking stop. **Note:** *Incorrect assembly of the cable onto the pulley may result in a high idle speed. Check that the throttle lever is in its idle position after refitting the actuator.*

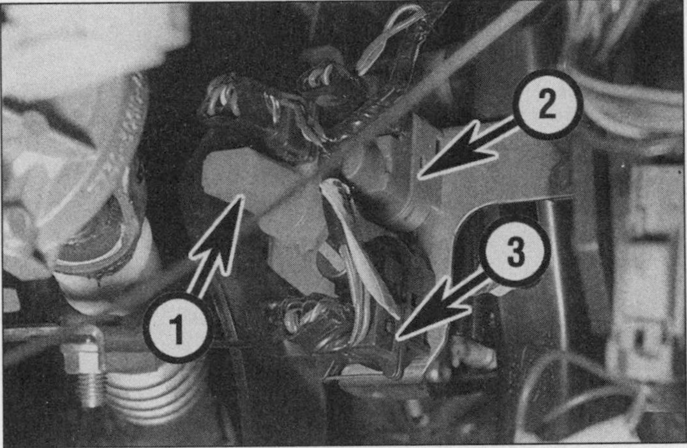

21.14 Cruise control switches on the pedal bracket

1 Clutch pedal position switch
2 Brake pedal de-activator switch
3 Stop-light switch

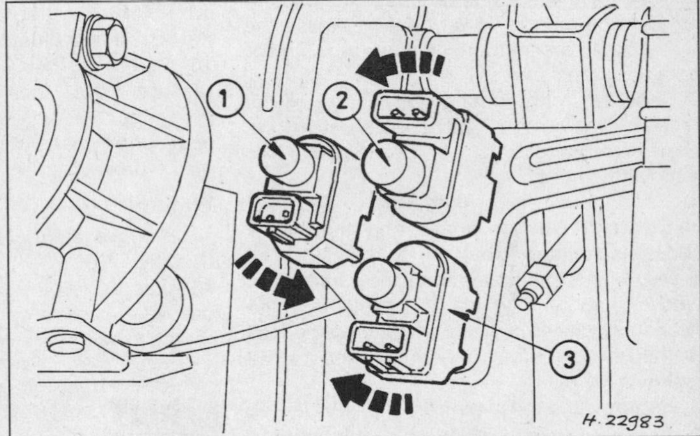

21.15 Removal of the cruise control switches

1 Clutch switch
2 Brake pedal switch
3 Stop-light switch

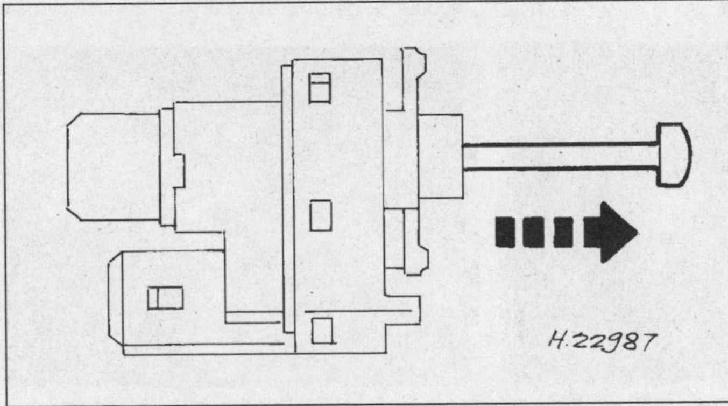

21.16 Resetting the brake pedal and stop-light switches

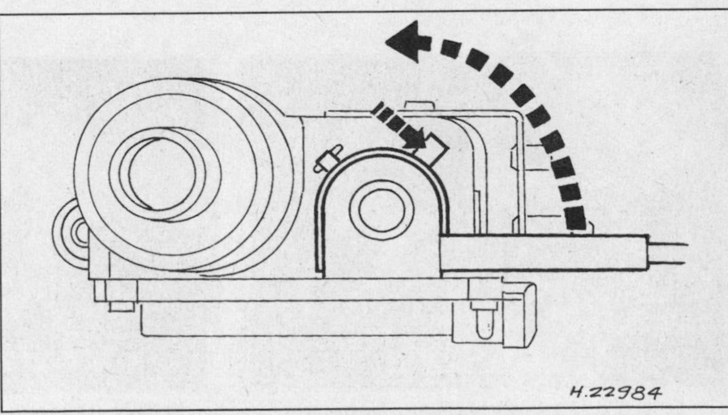

21.22 Removing the actuator cable locking arm

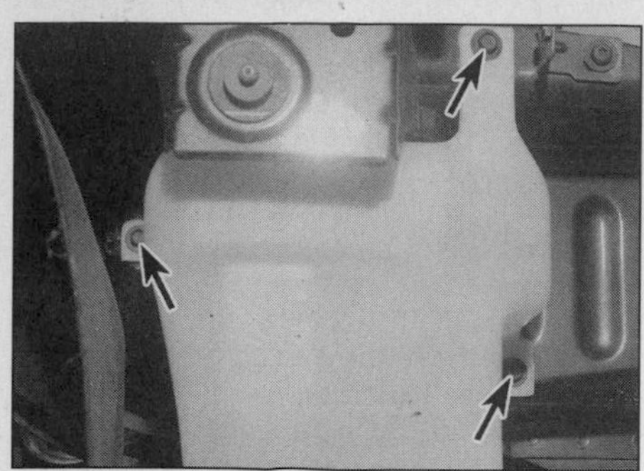

22.3 Washer reservoir mounting bolts (arrowed)

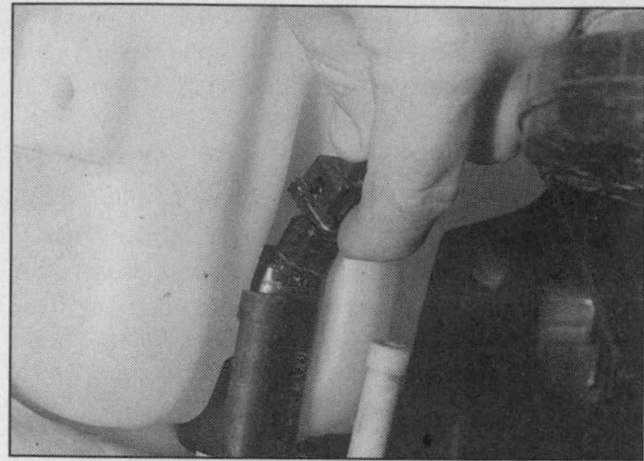

22.4 Disconnecting the washer pump and level sensor multi-plugs

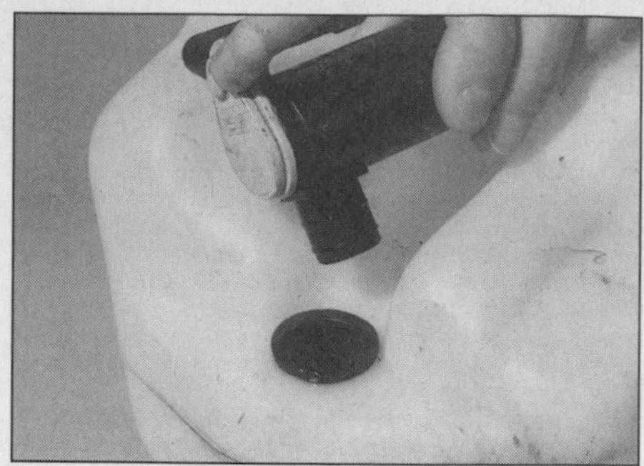

22.7 Pulling the windscreen washer pump from the reservoir

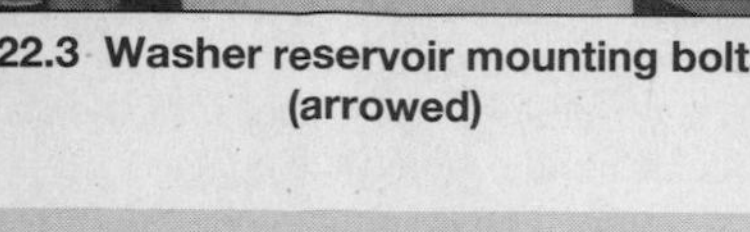

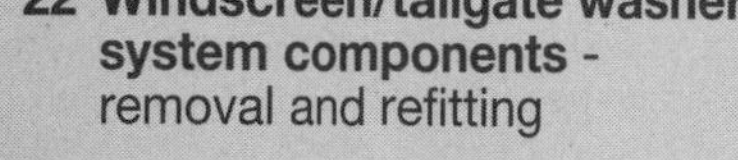

22 Windscreen/tailgate washer system components - removal and refitting

Removal

Washer reservoir and pump

1 Apply the handbrake and loosen the right-hand front wheel nuts. Jack up the front of the car and support on axle stands. Remove the front wheel.

2 Unscrew the bolts, and release the clips to remove the radiator lower cover. Release the wheel arch liner fasteners as necessary for access to the reservoir.

3 Unscrew the mounting bolts, and pull the reservoir forwards slightly **(see illustration)**. For better access, it may be necessary to remove the front bumper.

4 Disconnect the multi-plugs for the windscreen washer pump and fluid level sensor **(see illustration)**.

5 Disconnect the hoses from the windscreen washer pump and (where applicable) from the headlight washer pump. Anticipate some loss of fluid by placing a container beneath the reservoir.

6 Withdraw the reservoir from the vehicle.

7 Pull the level sensor, the windscreen washer pump, and (where applicable) the headlight washer pump, from the reservoir **(see illustration)**.

8 Remove the rubber seals.

Washer nozzle (windscreen)

9 With the bonnet supported in its open position, carefully disconnect the washer tube from the bottom of the nozzle.

10 Using a screwdriver and working from under the bonnet, carefully prise out the nozzle. Where necessary, disconnect the wiring for the nozzle heater.

Washer nozzle (rear window)

11 With the tailgate open, carefully pull off the inner trim panel from the top of the tailgate.

12 Pull the washer tube from the bottom of the nozzle **(see illustration)**.

13 Carefully prise the nozzle out of the tailgate glass, then prise out the rubber grommet **(see illustrations)**. Where necessary, disconnect the wiring for the nozzle heater.

Washer nozzle (headlight)

14 Remove the front bumper as described in Chapter 11.

15 Disconnect the washer tube from the base of the nozzle.

To make disconnecting the washer tubes easier, gently heat the tube where it connects to the nozzle, using a hot-air gun or hairdryer. This will soften the tube, making it easier to prise off the tube.

16 Pull off the nozzle retaining clip and withdraw the nozzle from the bumper.

Refitting

17 Refitting is a reversal of the removal procedure, noting the following points:

a) In the case of the screen washer nozzles, press them in until they are fully engaged.

b) The rear window washer nozzle must rest against the rubber seal.

c) After refitting the headlight washer nozzle, refit the front bumper as described in Chapter 11.

23 Radio/cassette player - removal and refitting

Note: *Special tools are required to remove the radio.*

1 If a Ford 'Keycode' unit is fitted, and the unit and/or the battery is disconnected, the unit will not function again on reconnection until the correct security code is entered. Details of this procedure are given in the 'Ford Audio Systems Operating Guide' supplied with the vehicle when new, with the code itself being given in a 'Radio Passport' and/or a 'Keycode Label' at the same time.

2 For obvious security reasons, the re-coding procedure is not given in this manual - if you do not have the code or details of the correct procedure, but can supply proof of ownership and a legitimate reason for wanting this

22.12 Pull the washer tube from the bottom of the nozzle

22.13a Remove the nozzle from the tailgate glass . . .

22.13b . . . and prise out the rubber grommet

23.6a Using the special U-shaped rods to remove the radio - early type . . .

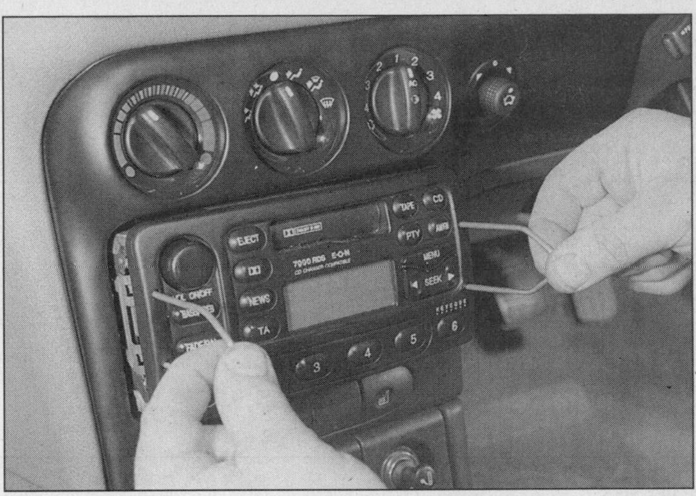

23.6b . . . and later "large bezel" type unit

information, the vehicle's selling dealer may be able to help.

3 Note that these units will allow only ten attempts at entering the code - any further attempts will render the unit permanently inoperative until it has been reprogrammed by Ford themselves. At first, three consecutive attempts are allowed; if all three are incorrect, a 30-minute delay is required before another attempt can be made. Each of any subsequent attempts (up to the maximum of ten) can be made only after a similar delay.

Removal

4 Disconnect the battery negative (earth) lead.

5 Where fitted, prise the cover/surround from the front of the radio/cassette player. Note that the cover is not fitted to all models.

6 On models without the satellite navigation system, in order to release the radio retaining clips, two U-shaped rods must be inserted into the special holes on each side of the radio **(see illustrations)**. If possible, it is preferable to obtain purpose-made rods from an audio specialist, as these have cut-outs which snap firmly into the clips so that the radio can be pulled out.

7 On models with the satellite navigation system, two special removal keys are required to remove the audio unit - these are handed, left and right, and are unlikely to be available anywhere other than from a Ford dealer.

8 Pull the unit squarely from its aperture, or it may jam. If the unit proves difficult to withdraw, remove the cassette tray (or where applicable, the CD player) from beneath the unit, then reach through the aperture and ease it out from behind.

9 With the radio partly withdrawn, disconnect the feed, earth, aerial and speaker leads **(see illustrations)**. Where applicable, also detach and remove the plastic support bracket from the rear of the unit.

Refitting

10 Refitting is a reversal of removal. With the leads reconnected to the rear of the unit, press it into position until the retaining clips are felt to engage. Reactivate the unit by entering the correct code in accordance with the maker's instructions.

24 Radio/cassette player power amplifier - removal and refitting

Removal

1 Disconnect the battery negative (earth) lead. See Chapter 5A, Section 1.

2 Unscrew the screws and remove the lower facia panel.

3 The radio/cassette player power amplifier is located beneath the facia.

4 Unscrew the cross-head screws, disconnect the wiring and remove the amplifier.

Refitting

5 Refitting is a reversal of the removal procedure.

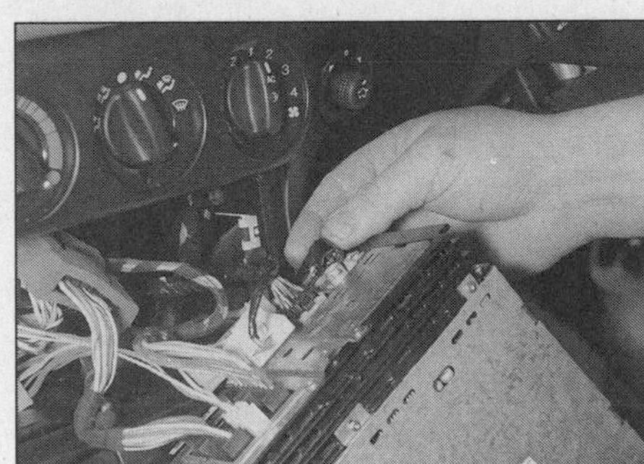

23.9a Disconnect the aerial lead . . .

25 Compact disc player - removal and refitting

1 A compact disc (CD) player is available as an optional extra on most models. On some models, an autochanger version is available, which can hold a number of discs at a time.

Removal

2 The battery negative (earth) lead should be disconnected before commencing work.

CD player, or autochanger control unit

3 The procedure is identical to that for the radio/cassette player described in Section 23.

CD player autochanger - models up to 1996

4 On models up to 1996, the CD player autochanger unit is mounted on the right-hand side of the luggage compartment. The wiring loom passes up the 'C' pillar, across to the left-hand side 'A' pillar, then to the centre console area.

5 Remove the trim cover from the autochanger unit.

6 Unscrew the mounting screws, and remove the autochanger unit from its mounting bracket.

23.9b . . . and the remaining wiring plugs, noting their locations

25.10a Remove the mounting bolts each side (arrowed) . . .

7 Disconnect the multi-plug and remove the unit from the luggage compartment.

CD player autochanger - 1997 models onwards

8 The CD autochanger unit is mounted in a bracket below the front passenger's seat.

9 Refer to Chapter 11 and remove the front passenger's seat.

10 Remove the unit mounting bolts either side, and disconnect the wiring plug **(see illustrations)**. Slide the player out of the brackets below the seat, and remove it from the car.

Refitting

11 Refitting is a reversal of the removal procedure.

26 Speakers - removal and refitting

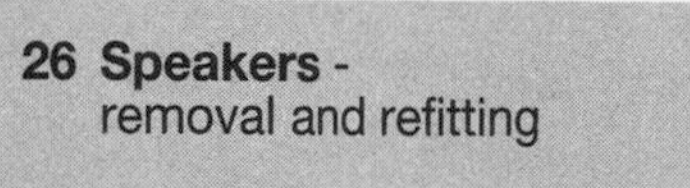

Note: *If the speakers work intermittently, this can be due to the wiring multi-plug overheating - a revised plug is available from your Ford dealer.*

Removal

1 Remove the door trim panel as described in Chapter 11.

2 Unscrew the cross-head screws, and withdraw the speaker from the door inner panel.

3 Disconnect the wiring and remove the speaker.

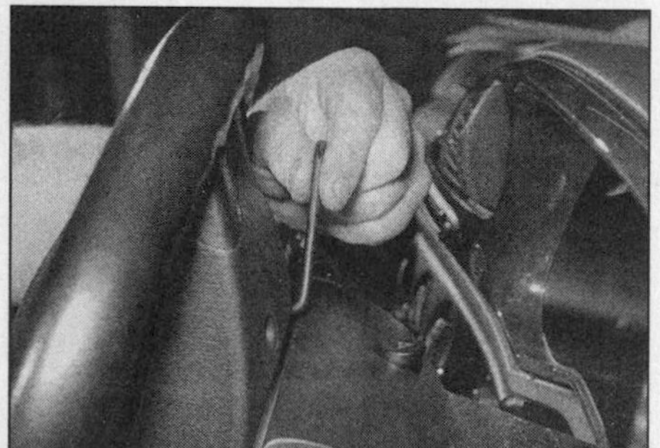

28.3 Unscrewing an air bag mounting bolt

25.10b . . . then disconnect the wiring plug and remove the unit

Refitting

4 Refitting is a reversal of the removal procedure.

27 Radio aerial - removal and refitting

Removal

1 If just the aerial mast is to be removed, this can be unscrewed from the base, from outside.

2 To remove the aerial base, prise out the trim cover from the headlining immediately below the base of the aerial **(see illustration)**.

3 Unscrew the cross-head or Torx screw from the base of the aerial **(see illustration)**, disconnect the wiring, and remove the base and gasket from outside.

Refitting

4 Refitting is a reversal of the removal procedure.

28 Air bag units - removal and refitting

Warning: Handle any air bag unit with extreme care, as a precaution against personal injury, and always hold it with the cover facing away from the body. If in doubt concerning any proposed work involving an air bag unit or its control circuitry, consult a Ford dealer or other qualified specialist.

28.4 Disconnecting the air bag wiring multi-plug

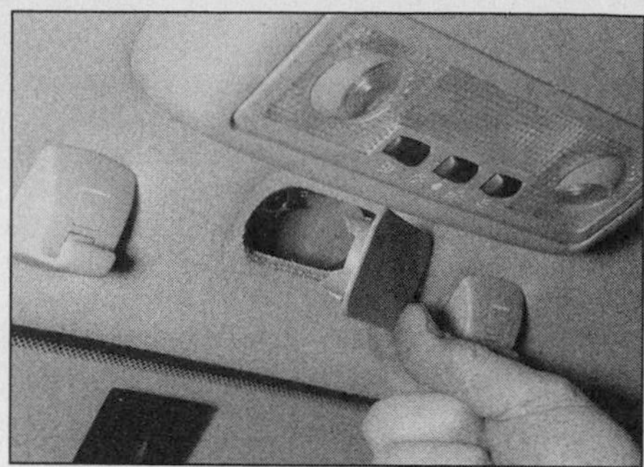

27.2 Remove the trim cover from the headlining . . .

27.3 . . . for access to the aerial mounting screw (arrowed)

Warning: Stand any air bag with the cover uppermost, and do not expose it to heat sources in excess of 100°C.

Warning: Do not attempt to open or repair an air bag unit, or apply any electrical current to it. Do not use any air bag unit which is visibly damaged or which has been tampered with.

Driver's air bag

1 Disconnect the battery negative (earth) lead (refer to Chapter 5A, Section 1).

Warning: Before proceeding, wait a minimum of 15 minutes, as a precaution against accidental firing of the air bag unit. This period ensures that any stored energy in the back-up capacitor is dissipated.

2 Rotate the steering wheel so that one of the air bag mounting bolt holes (at the rear of the steering wheel boss) is visible above the steering column upper shroud.

3 Unscrew and remove the first mounting bolt, then turn the steering wheel through 180° and remove the remaining mounting bolt **(see illustration)**.

4 Carefully withdraw the air bag unit from the steering wheel far enough to disconnect the wiring multi-plug, then remove it from inside the vehicle **(see illustration)**.

5 Refitting is a reversal of the removal procedure.

Passenger's air bag

6 Disconnect the battery negative (earth) lead (refer to Chapter 5A, Section 1).

Warning: Before proceeding, wait a minimum of 15 minutes, as a precaution against accidental firing of the air bag unit. This period ensures that any stored energy in the back-up capacitor is dissipated.

7 Remove the glovebox as described in Chapter 11.

Models up to 1996

8 Remove the three retaining screws and withdraw the closing panel behind the glovebox.

9 Remove the screw securing the inner end of the ventilation duct, and disconnect the duct from the facia end vent.

10 Disconnect the two air bag inflator multi-plugs, noting their locations for refitting.

11 Support the unit, then remove the four air bag unit mounting screws, and remove the unit from the facia.

12 Refitting is a reversal of removal.

1997 and later models

13 Remove the three retaining screws, then release the clip at the right-hand side and withdraw the closing panel behind the glovebox. As the panel is withdrawn, disconnect the bulbholder.

14 Carefully cut the cable-ties securing the wiring harness to the top of the glovebox aperture.

15 Remove the radio/cassette unit as described in Section 23.

16 Working through the radio aperture, remove the screws securing the passenger side ventilation duct for the facia end vent.

17 Detach the ventilation duct from the facia end vent, and remove the duct from the facia.

18 Disconnect the wiring multi-plug from the end of the air bag unit.

19 Support the unit, then remove the four air bag unit mounting screws, and remove the unit from the facia.

20 Refitting is a reversal of removal.

Side air bag

21 The side air bag units are built into the front seats, and their removal requires that the seat fabric be removed. This is not considered to be a DIY operation, and should be referred to a Ford dealer.

29 Air bag control module - removal and refitting

Removal

1 Disconnect the battery negative (earth) lead (refer to Chapter 5A, Section 1).

Warning: Before proceeding, wait a minimum of 15 minutes, as a precaution against accidental firing of the air bag unit. This period ensures that any stored energy in the back-up capacitor is dissipated.

2 On right-hand drive models, remove the driver's side lower facia panel as described in Chapter 11, Section 29. On left-hand-drive models, the facia panel will have to be removed complete for access (see Chapter 11).

3 Disconnect the multi-plug from the module **(see illustration)**, by pressing the two-stage locking handle to the side - the first stage disconnects the multi-plug, and the second releases the connector from the module.

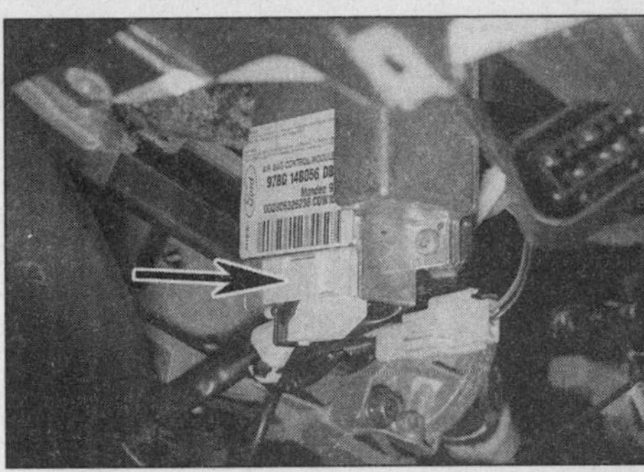

29.3 Air bag control module multi-plug (arrowed)

4 Unscrew the mounting bolts and remove the module from the vehicle.

Refitting

5 Refitting is a reversal of the removal procedure.

30 Air bag clock spring - removal and refitting

Removal

1 Remove the driver's air bag unit as described in Section 28.

2 Disconnect the horn switch multi-plug.

3 If fitted, disconnect the multi-plugs for the cruise control switches.

4 Remove the steering wheel and column shrouds as described in Chapter 10.

5 Disconnect the clock spring wiring plug from the underside of the steering column.

6 Detach the steering column multi-function switches by depressing the plastic retaining tabs with a flat-bladed screwdriver.

7 Using a small screwdriver, release the three retaining tabs, then remove the clock spring from the steering column, feeding the wiring through.

Refitting

8 Refitting is a reversal of the removal procedure, noting the following points:

a) *Make sure that the front wheels are still pointing straight-ahead.*

b) *The clock spring must be fitted in its central position, with the special alignment marks aligned and the TOP mark uppermost. To check for this position, turn the clock spring housing anti-clockwise until it is tight, then turn in the opposite direction by two-and-three-quarter turns.*

31 Parking sensor system - general information

Offered as an option on 1997 and later models, the park reverse aid is an ultrasonic proximity detection system, intended to help avoid rear collisions when reversing.

The system consists of four ultrasonic sensors mounted in the rear bumper, a display/buzzer unit mounted in the 'C' pillar trim panel, and an ECU mounted behind the left-hand side trim panel in the luggage compartment.

The system is only operational when reverse gear is engaged; changing audible and visual signals warn the driver of impending contact as the car reverses towards an object in its path.

The sensors in the bumper can be unclipped and disconnected once the rear bumper is removed as described in Chapter 11.

To remove the display/buzzer unit, remove the 'C' pillar trim panel as described in Chapter 11, Section 29.

The system ECU can be disconnected once the luggage area left-hand trim panel is removed.

32 Satellite navigation system - general information

This system was optional on later models, and uses Global Positioning System (GPS) satellites to track the car against a digital map stored on CD. The system antenna gathers positional information from the satellites. The ABS rear wheel sensors provide the system with data on how far the vehicle has travelled, and a compass is fitted. The CD autochanger is the communication link from the navigation module to the display panel on the radio/cassette unit. The digital map is stored on a CD, which is read by the navigation module. The navigation module is the heart of the system, processing all data received from the antenna, wheel sensors, compass and map CD, and providing instructions which are displayed on the radio/cassette display panel.

Two generations of the system were offered (RNS 1 and 2), and component locations vary according to which system is fitted. Any problems with the system should be referred to a Ford dealer for diagnosis.

33.7 Front seat removed, showing three seat adjustment motors and associated wiring plugs

33.8 Typical seat motor mounting frame bolt (arrowed)

33 Electric seat components - removal and refitting

Heated seats

1 If heated seats are fitted, both driver's and front passenger seats have heating elements built into the seat cushion and backrest.

2 No repairs can be made to the heating elements without dismantling the seat and removing the seat fabric - therefore this work should be left to a Ford dealer or other specialist.

3 The heated seat switches are removed as described in Section 4.

4 For further diagnosis of any problems with the system, refer to Sections 2 and 3, and to the wiring diagrams at the end of this Chapter.

Seat adjustment components

5 Only the driver's seat is equipped with motors, and only the highest specification models have anything other than a height adjustment motor.

6 To gain access to the motors, remove the driver's seat as described in Chapter 11.

7 The motors are bolted to a mounting frame, which in turn is bolted to the seat base. Before removing a motor, trace its wiring back from the motor to its wiring plug, and disconnect it **(see illustration)**.

8 Remove the mounting frame bolts **(see illustration)** or the motor mounting bolts, as applicable, and remove the components from the seat base.

9 Refitting is a reversal of removal. It is worth periodically greasing the worm-drive components and seat runners, to ensure trouble-free operation.

10 The seat adjustment switches are removed as described in Section 4.

11 For further diagnosis of any problems with the system, refer to Sections 2 and 3, and to the wiring diagrams at the end of this Chapter.

Key to symbols

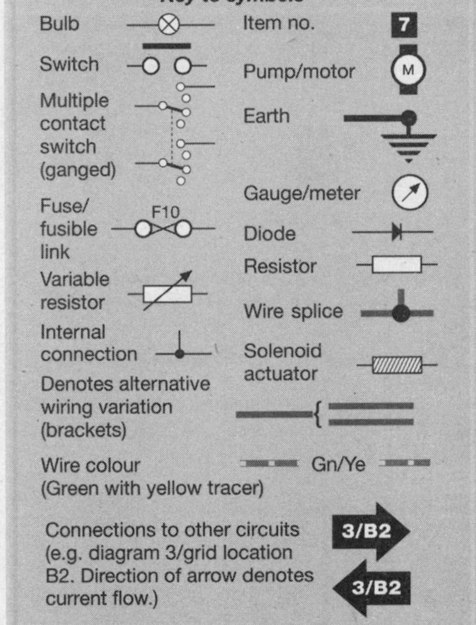
Bulb
Item no.
7
Switch
Pump/motor
M
Multiple contact switch (ganged)
Earth
Gauge/meter
Fuse/ fusible link
F10
Diode
Resistor
Variable resistor
Wire splice
Internal connection
Solenoid actuator
Denotes alternative wiring variation (brackets)
Wire colour (Green with yellow tracer)
Gn/Ye
Connections to other circuits (e.g. diagram 3/grid location B2. Direction of arrow denotes current flow.)
3/B2
3/B2

Earth locations

E1	Behind LH headlight
E2	Front of LH inner sill
E3	Centre of rear panel, luggage comp.
E4	RH rear side of luggage comp.
E5	LH rear side of luggage comp.
E6	RH 'A' pillar
E7	RH 'A' pillar
E8	RH 'A' pillar
E9	LH side of rear panel, luggage comp.
E10	LH side of rear panel, luggage comp.
E11	Behind RH headlight
E12	Behind RH headlight
E13	RH rear engine comp.
E14	RH 'A' pillar
E15	RH 'A' pillar
E16	RH side of dashboard
E17	Behind LH headlight
E18	RH 'A' pillar
E19	RH side of dashboard
E20	In tailgate
E21	LH side of tailgate
E22	RH side of tailgate
E23	RH 'A' pillar
E24	Top of RH 'C' pillar

Fuses in engine fusebox

Fuse	*Rating*	*Circuit protected*
F1	80A	Main power supply
F2	60A	Engine cooling fan
F3	60A	Diesel engine and/or ABS, blower
F4	20A	Daytime running lights and/or ignition
F5	30A	Heated windscreen
F6	30A	Heated windscreen
F7	30A	ABS
F8	30A	Heated seats and/or daytime running lights
F9	20A	Engine management or Diesel cold start solenoid
F10	20A	Ignition switch
F11	3A	ECU memory
F12	15A	Horn and hazard flashers
F13	15A	Oxygen sensor
F14	15A	Fuel pump
F15	10A	RH dipped beam
F16	10A	LH dipped beam
F17	10A	RH main beam
F18	10A	LH main beam

Relays in engine fusebox

Relay	*Colour*	*Circuit controlling*
R1	Green	Running lights or dim/dip
R2	Black	High speed cooling fan relay
R3	Blue	A/C cut out (petrol)
	Brown	A/C (Diesel engine)
R4	Yellow	Windscreen heater time delay
R5	Dk.green	Low speed cooling fan relay (petrol)
	Black	Low speed cooling fan relay (Diesel)
R6	Yellow	Starter solenoid
R7	Brown	Horns
R8	Brown	Fuel pump
R9	White	Dipped beam
R10	White	Main beam
R11	Brown	Power supply or Diesel cold start

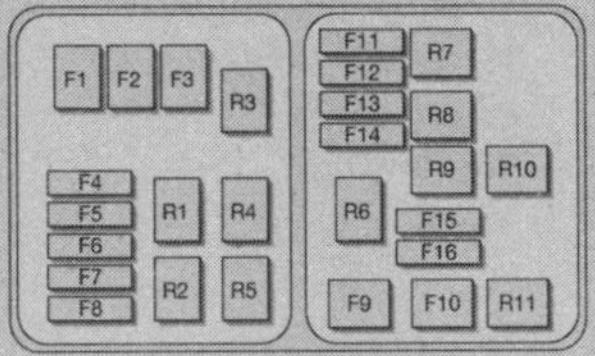
F1
F2
F3
R3
F4
F5
F6
F7
F8
R1
R4
R2
R5
F11
F12
F13
F14
R7
R8
R9
R10
R6
F15
F16
F9
F10
R11

Fuses in passenger fusebox

Fuse	*Rating*	*Circuit protected*
F19	7.5A	Heated rear screen, mirrors
F20	10A	Front/rear wiper
F21	30A	Front electric windows
	40A	Front/rear electric windows
F22	7.5A	ABS module
F23	15A	Reversing lights, park interlock
F24	15A	Brake lights
F25	20A	Central locking/double locking
F26	20A	Fog lights
F27	15A	Cigar lighter
F28	30A	Headlight washer
F29	30A	Heated rear screen
F30	7.5A	Engine management, blower
F31	7.5A	Instrument panel illumination
F32	7.5A	Radio, immobiliser
F33	7.5A	LH side lights
F34	7.5A	Interior lighting
F35	7.5A	RH side lights
F36	30A	Radio
F37	30A	Heater blower
F38	7.5A	Air bags

Relays in passenger fusebox

Relay	*Colour*	*Circuit controlling*
R12	White	Interior lighting
R13	Yellow	Heated rear screen
R14	Yellow	Heater blower
R15	Green	Front wiper motor
R16	Black	Ignition

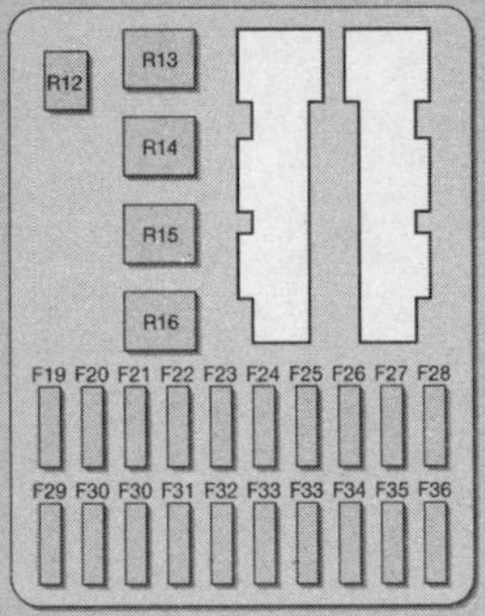
R12
R13
R14
R15
R16
F19 F20 F21 F22 F23 F24 F25 F26 F27 F28
F29 F30 F30 F31 F32 F33 F33 F34 F35 F36

H31333

Diagram 1 : Information for wiring diagrams

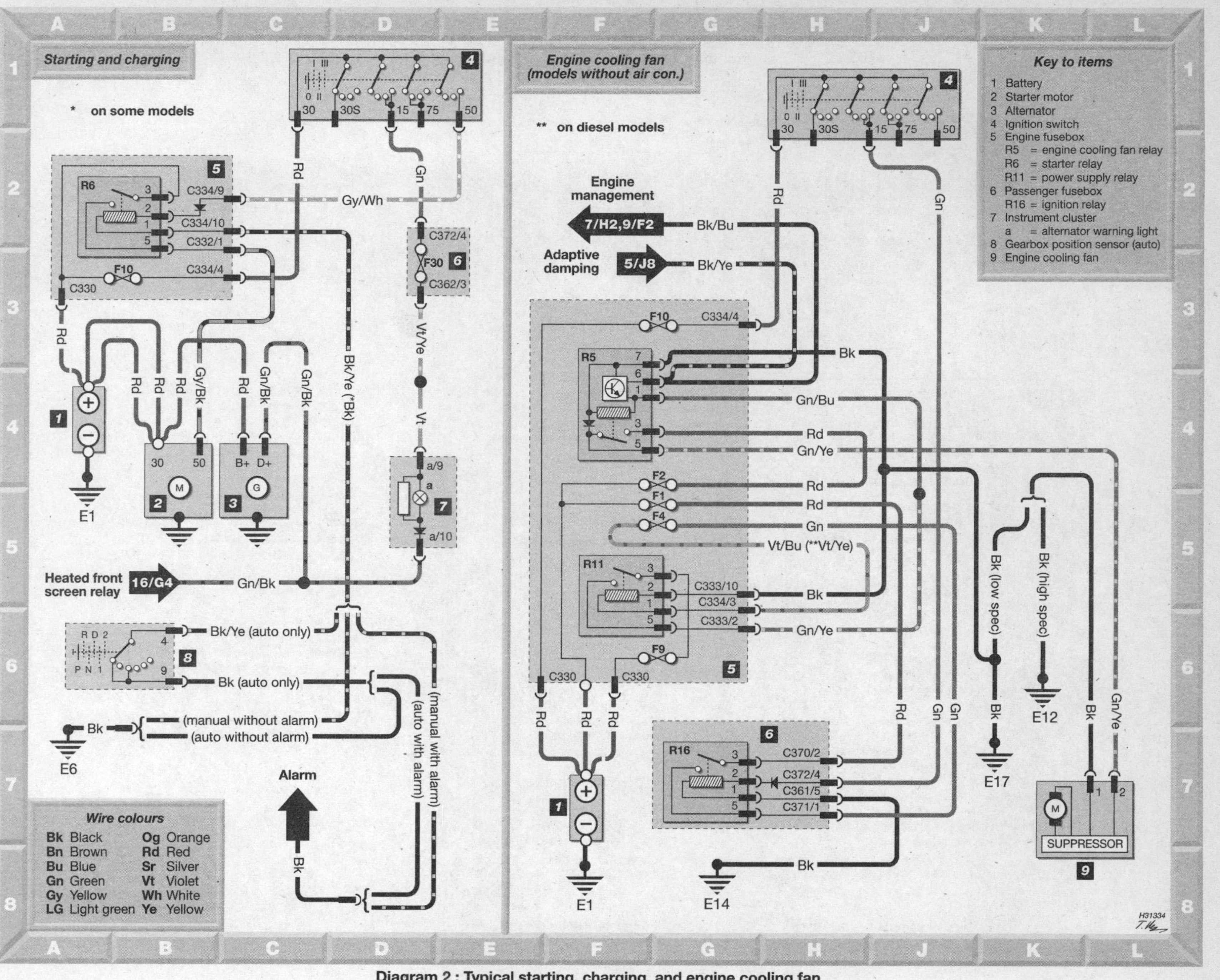

Diagram 2 : Typical starting, charging, and engine cooling fan

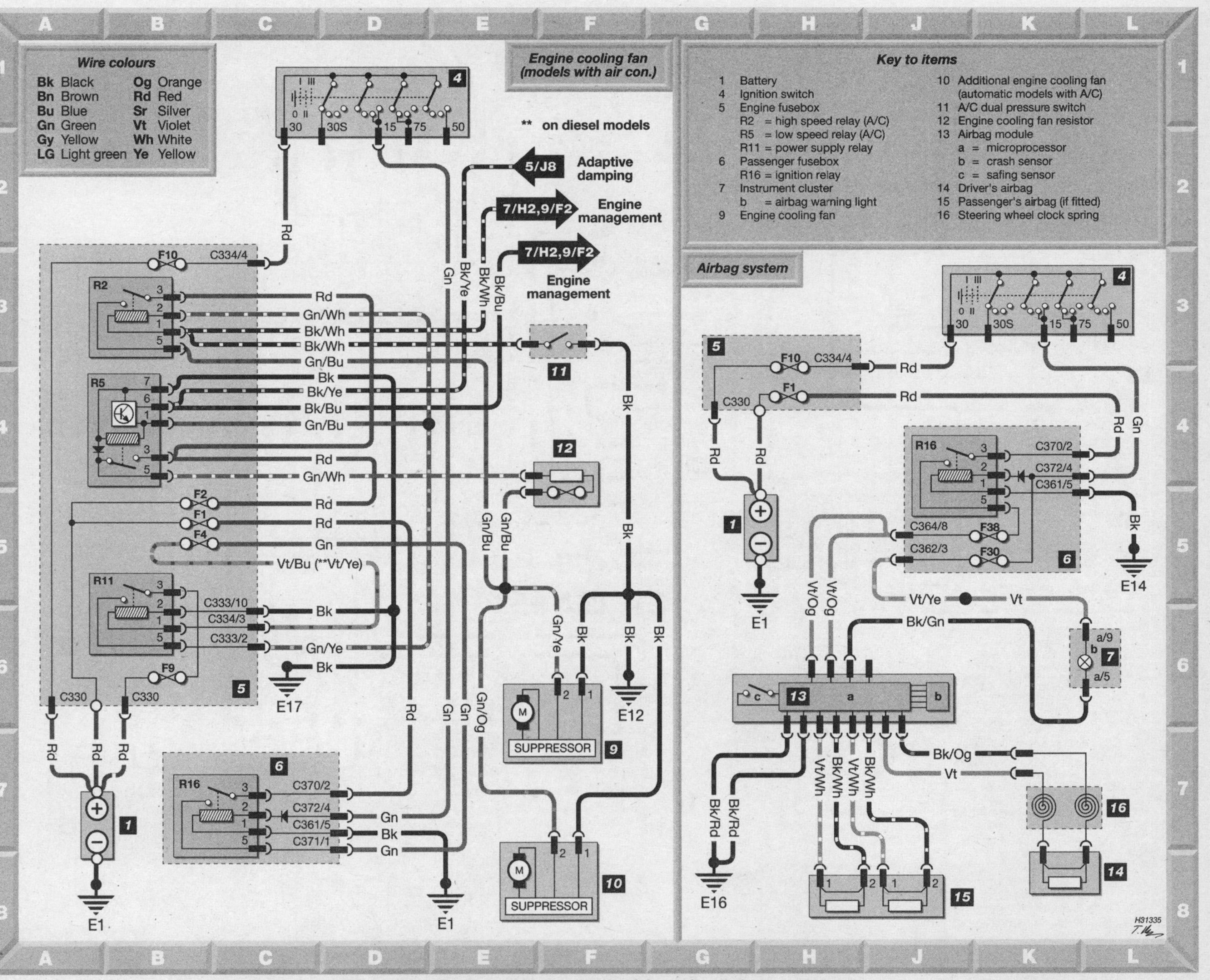

Diagram 3 : Typical engine cooling fan (air con.) and airbag system

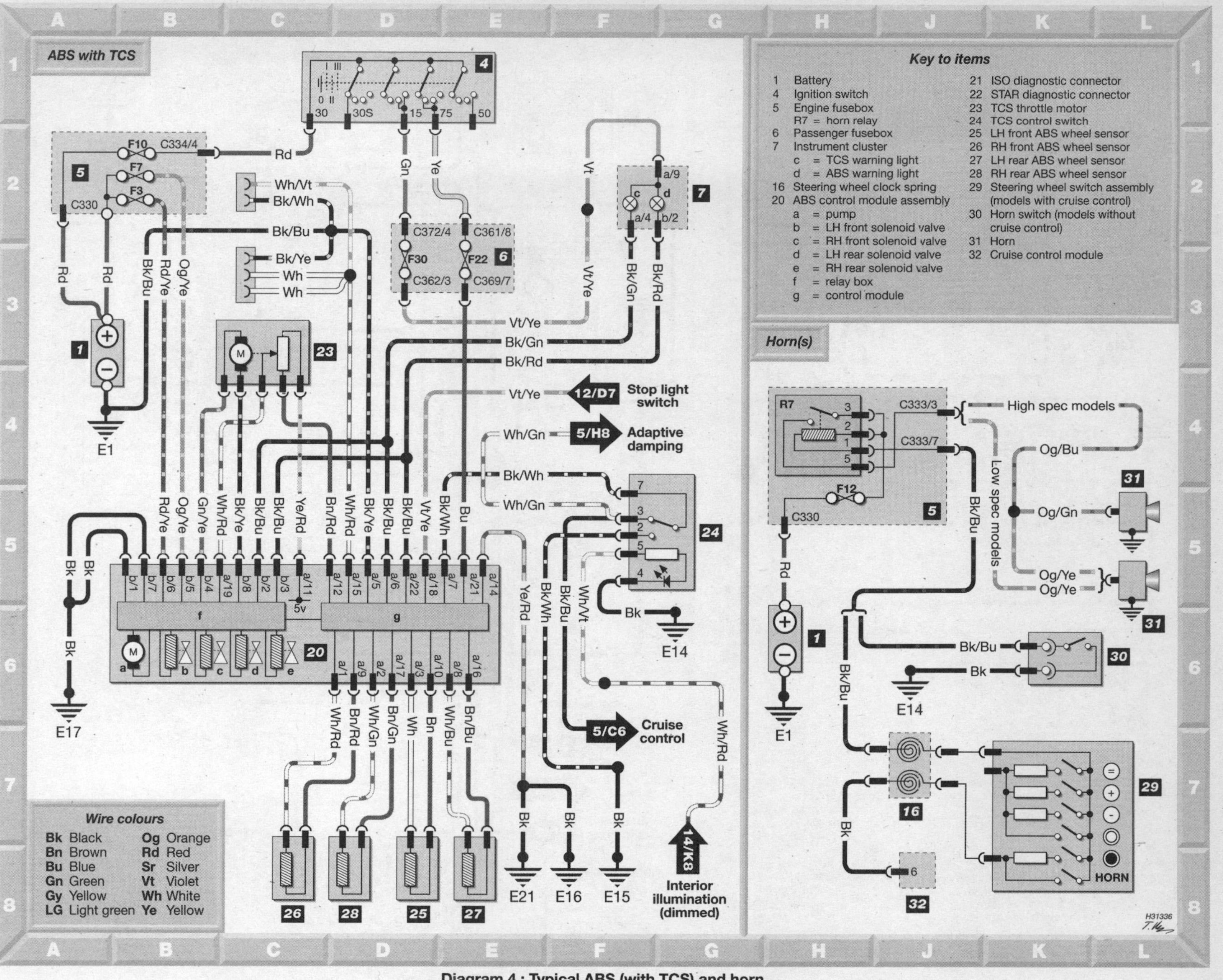

ABS with TCS
Horn(s)
Key to items
1 Battery
4 Ignition switch
5 Engine fusebox
R7 = horn relay
6 Passenger fusebox
7 Instrument cluster
c = TCS warning light
d = ABS warning light
16 Steering wheel clock spring
20 ABS control module assembly
a = pump
b = LH front solenoid valve
c = RH front solenoid valve
d = LH rear solenoid valve
e = RH rear solenoid valve
f = relay box
g = control module
21 ISO diagnostic connector
22 STAR diagnostic connector
23 TCS throttle motor
24 TCS control switch
25 LH front ABS wheel sensor
26 RH front ABS wheel sensor
27 LH rear ABS wheel sensor
28 RH rear ABS wheel sensor
29 Steering wheel switch assembly (models with cruise control)
30 Horn switch (models without cruise control)
31 Horn
32 Cruise control module
Wire colours
Bk Black
Bn Brown
Bu Blue
Gn Green
Gy Yellow
LG Light green
Og Orange
Rd Red
Sr Silver
Vt Violet
Wh White
Ye Yellow
Stop light switch
Adaptive damping
Cruise control
Interior illumination (dimmed)
High spec models
Low spec models
HORN
H31336

Diagram 4 : Typical ABS (with TCS) and horn

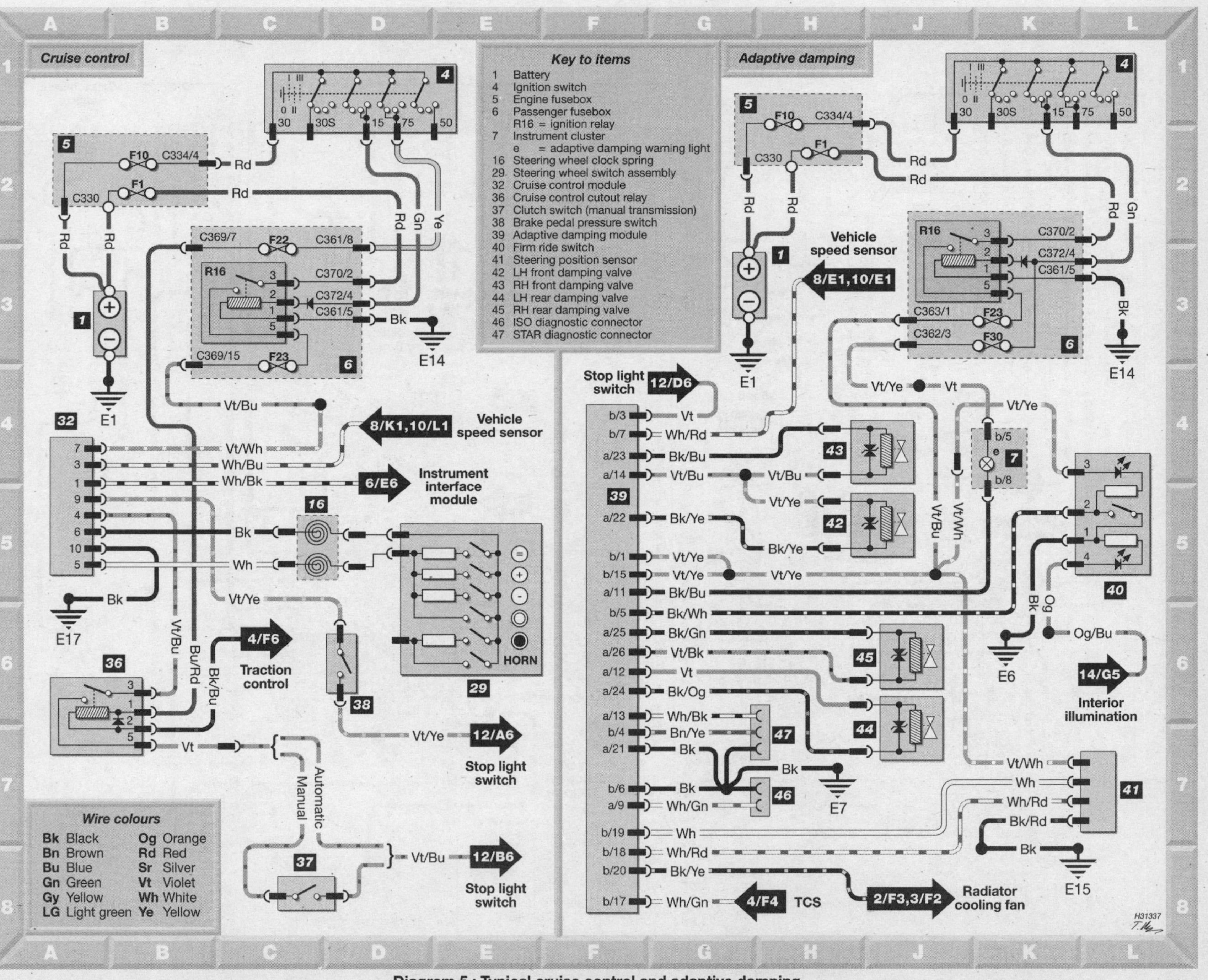

Cruise control
Adaptive damping
Key to items
1 Battery
4 Ignition switch
5 Engine fusebox
6 Passenger fusebox
R16 = ignition relay
7 Instrument cluster
e = adaptive damping warning light
16 Steering wheel clock spring
29 Steering wheel switch assembly
32 Cruise control module
36 Cruise control cutout relay
37 Clutch switch (manual transmission)
38 Brake pedal pressure switch
39 Adaptive damping module
40 Firm ride switch
41 Steering position sensor
42 LH front damping valve
43 RH front damping valve
44 LH rear damping valve
45 RH rear damping valve
46 ISO diagnostic connector
47 STAR diagnostic connector
Wire colours
Bk Black
Bn Brown
Bu Blue
Gn Green
Gy Yellow
LG Light green
Og Orange
Rd Red
Sr Silver
Vt Violet
Wh White
Ye Yellow
Vehicle speed sensor
Instrument interface module
Traction control
Stop light switch
Interior illumination
Radiator cooling fan
TCS
HORN
Automatic
Manual
H31337

Diagram 5 : Typical cruise control and adaptive damping

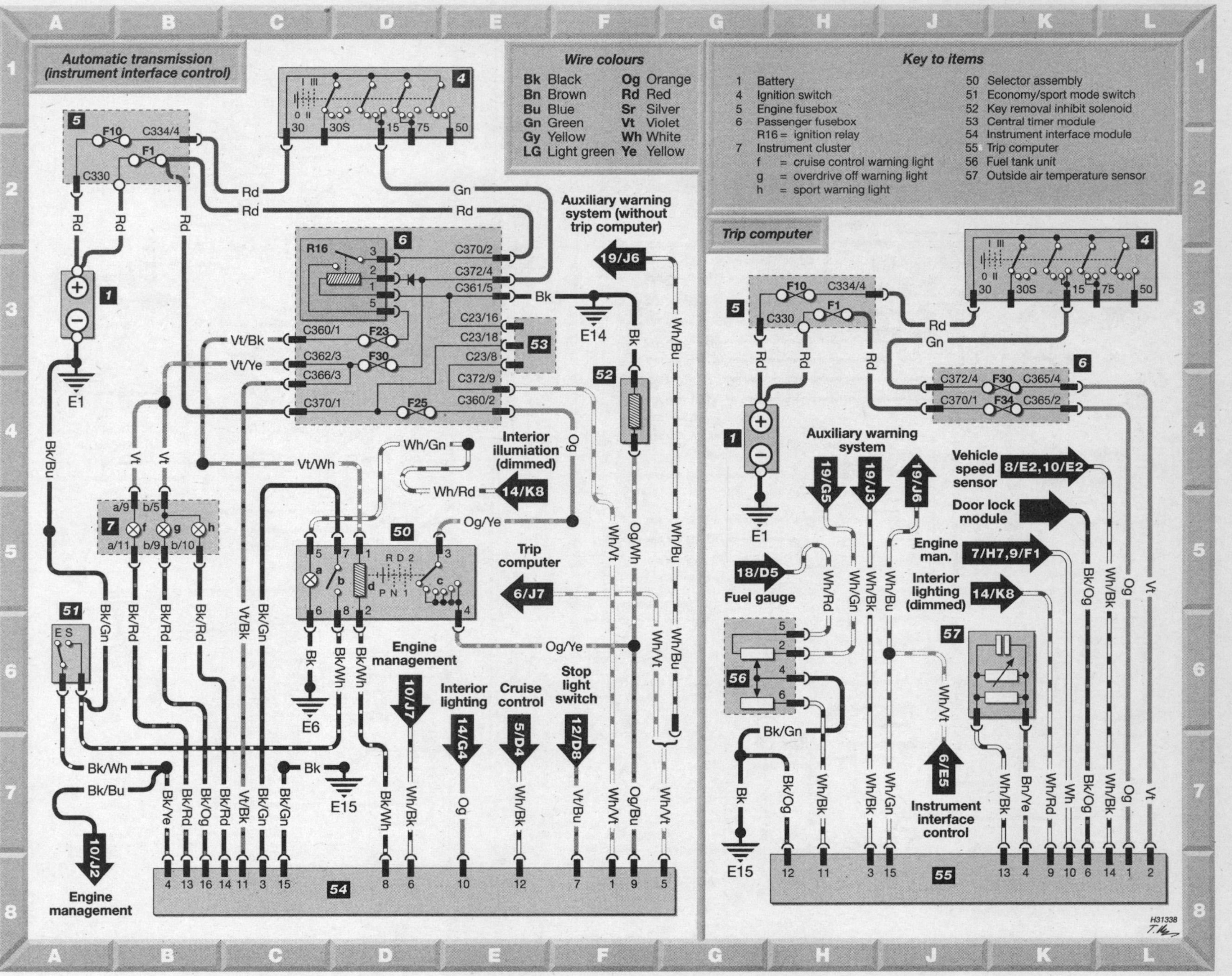
Automatic transmission (instrument interface control)
Wire colours
Bk Black
Bn Brown
Bu Blue
Gn Green
Gy Yellow
LG Light green
Og Orange
Rd Red
Sr Silver
Vt Violet
Wh White
Ye Yellow
Key to items
1 Battery
4 Ignition switch
5 Engine fusebox
6 Passenger fusebox
R16 = ignition relay
7 Instrument cluster
f = cruise control warning light
g = overdrive off warning light
h = sport warning light
50 Selector assembly
51 Economy/sport mode switch
52 Key removal inhibit solenoid
53 Central timer module
54 Instrument interface module
55 Trip computer
56 Fuel tank unit
57 Outside air temperature sensor
Auxiliary warning system (without trip computer)
Interior illumiation (dimmed)
Trip computer
Engine management
Interior lighting
Cruise control
Stop light switch
Trip computer
Auxiliary warning system
Vehicle speed sensor
Door lock module
Engine man.
Interior lighting (dimmed)
Fuel gauge
Instrument interface control
H31338
Diagram 6 : Typical automatic transmission (instrument interface control) and trip computer

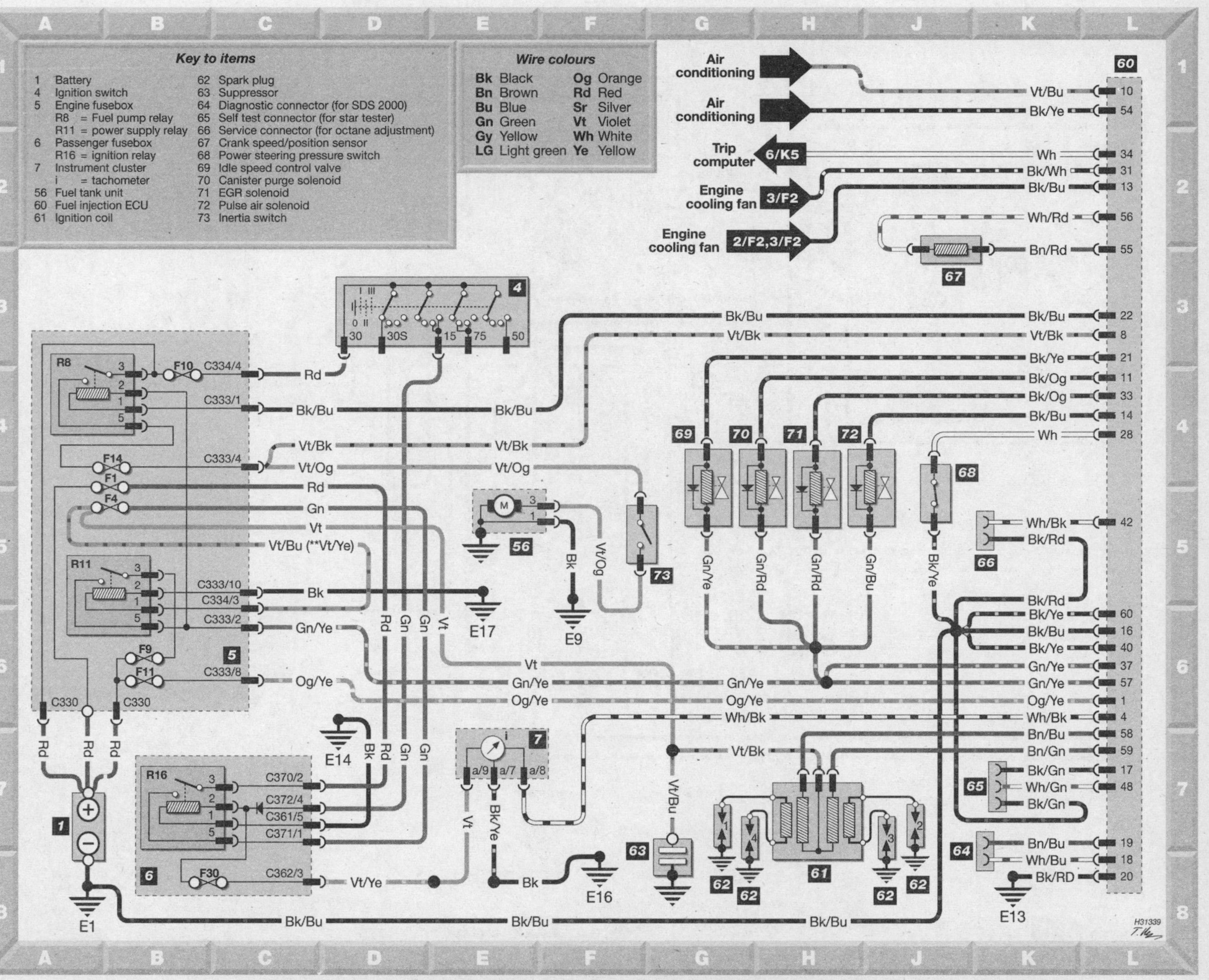

Key to items
1 Battery
4 Ignition switch
5 Engine fusebox
R8 = Fuel pump relay
R11 = power supply relay
6 Passenger fusebox
R16 = ignition relay
7 Instrument cluster
i = tachometer
56 Fuel tank unit
60 Fuel injection ECU
61 Ignition coil
62 Spark plug
63 Suppressor
64 Diagnostic connector (for SDS 2000)
65 Self test connector (for star tester)
66 Service connector (for octane adjustment)
67 Crank speed/position sensor
68 Power steering pressure switch
69 Idle speed control valve
70 Canister purge solenoid
71 EGR solenoid
72 Pulse air solenoid
73 Inertia switch
Wire colours
Bk Black
Bn Brown
Bu Blue
Gn Green
Gy Yellow
LG Light green
Og Orange
Rd Red
Sr Silver
Vt Violet
Wh White
Ye Yellow
Air conditioning
Air conditioning
Trip computer 6/K5
Engine cooling fan 3/F2
Engine cooling fan 2/F2,3/F2
H31339

Diagram 7 : Typical engine management system - models with manual transmission (part of)

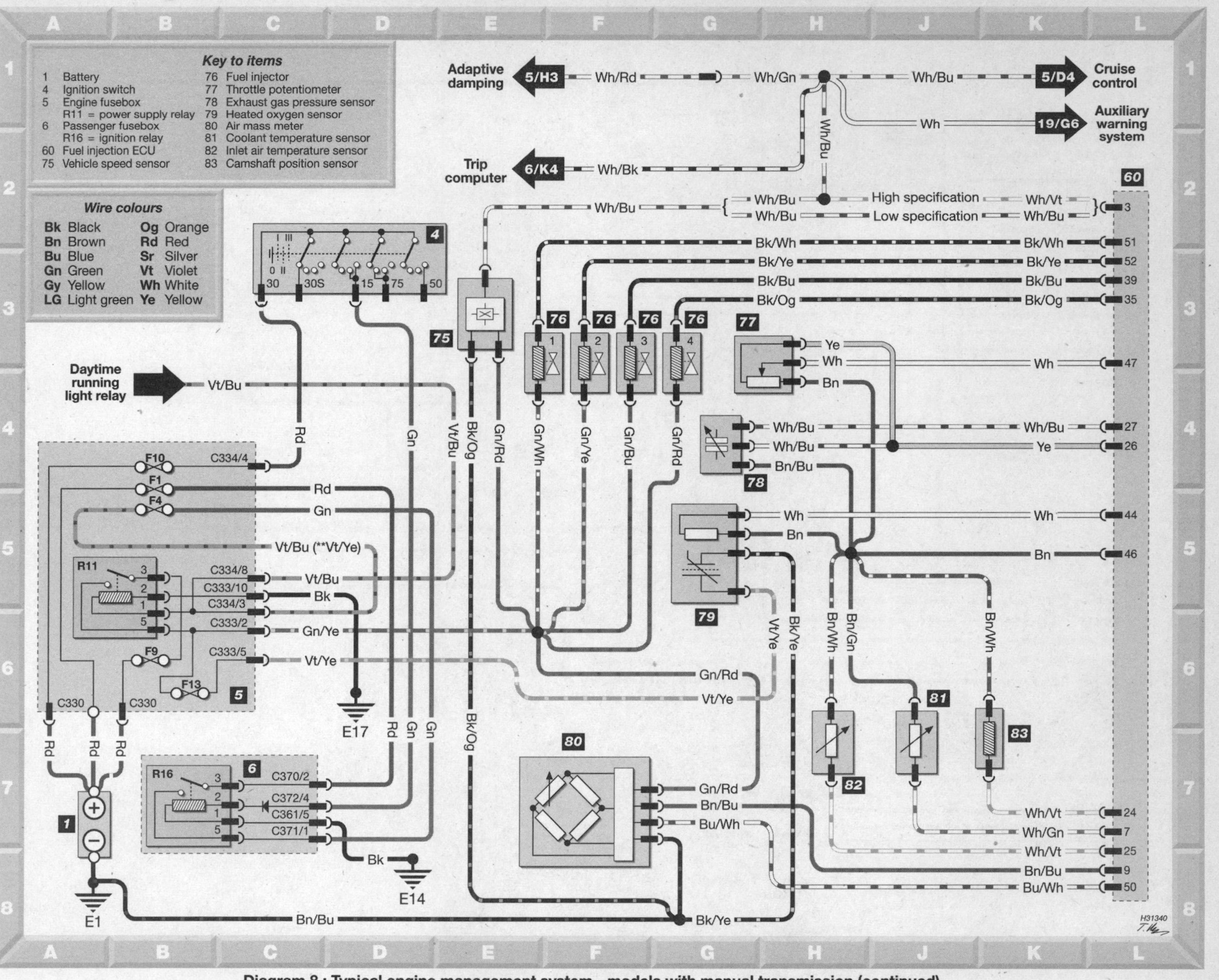

Key to items
1 Battery
4 Ignition switch
5 Engine fusebox
R11 = power supply relay
6 Passenger fusebox
R16 = ignition relay
60 Fuel injection ECU
75 Vehicle speed sensor
76 Fuel injector
77 Throttle potentiometer
78 Exhaust gas pressure sensor
79 Heated oxygen sensor
80 Air mass meter
81 Coolant temperature sensor
82 Inlet air temperature sensor
83 Camshaft position sensor
Wire colours
Bk Black
Bn Brown
Bu Blue
Gn Green
Gy Yellow
LG Light green
Og Orange
Rd Red
Sr Silver
Vt Violet
Wh White
Ye Yellow
Adaptive damping
5/H3
Cruise control
5/D4
Auxiliary warning system
19/G6
Trip computer
6/K4
High specification
Low specification
Daytime running light relay
E1
E14
E17
H31340

Diagram 8 : Typical engine management system - models with manual transmission (continued)

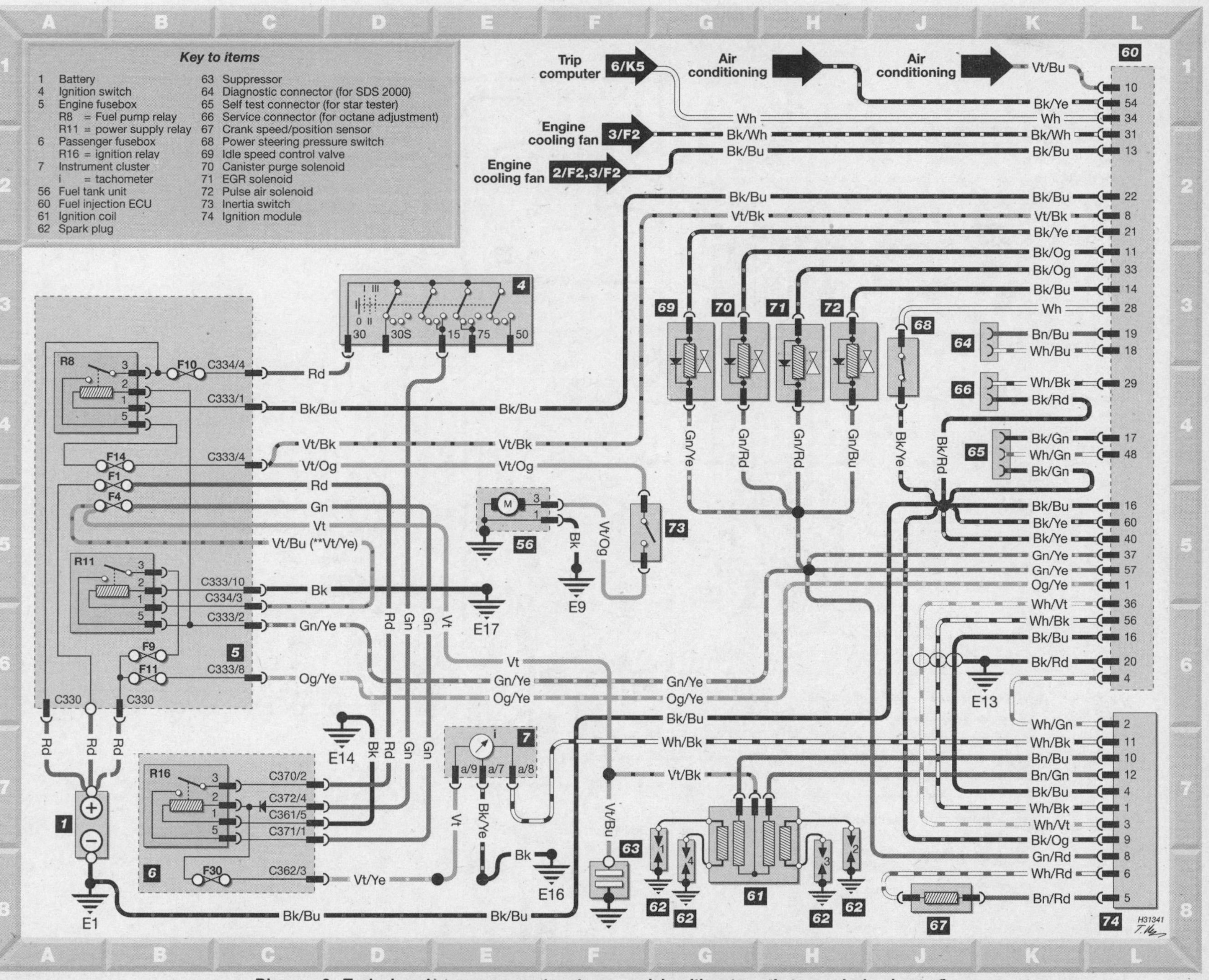

Diagram 9 : Typical engine management system - models with automatic transmission (part of)

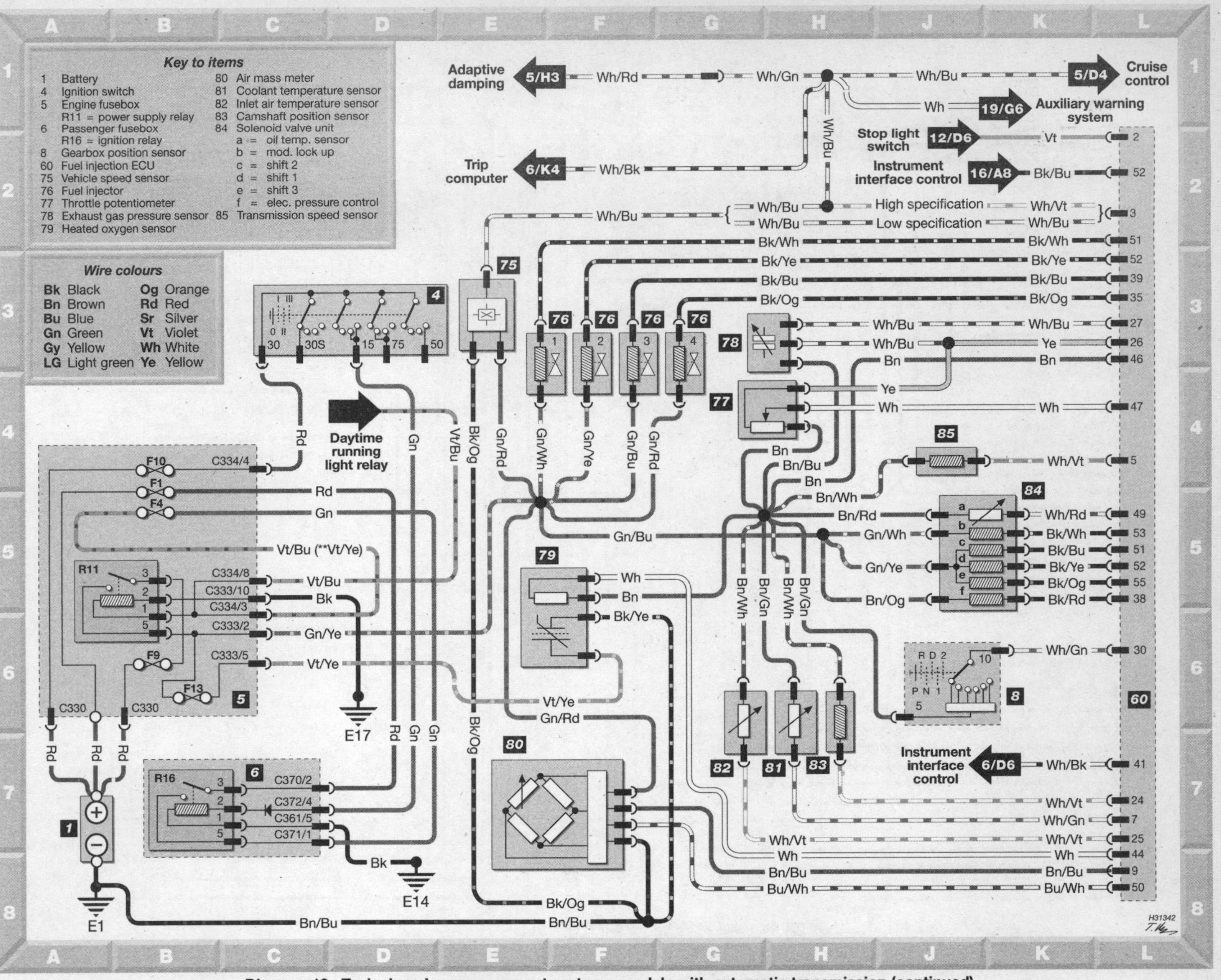
Key to items
1 Battery
4 Ignition switch
5 Engine fusebox
R11 = power supply relay
6 Passenger fusebox
R16 = ignition relay
8 Gearbox position sensor
60 Fuel injection ECU
75 Vehicle speed sensor
76 Fuel injector
77 Throttle potentiometer
78 Exhaust gas pressure sensor
79 Heated oxygen sensor
80 Air mass meter
81 Coolant temperature sensor
82 Inlet air temperature sensor
83 Camshaft position sensor
84 Solenoid valve unit
a = oil temp. sensor
b = mod. lock up
c = shift 2
d = shift 1
e = shift 3
f = elec. pressure control
85 Transmission speed sensor
Wire colours
Bk Black
Bn Brown
Bu Blue
Gn Green
Gy Yellow
LG Light green
Og Orange
Rd Red
Sr Silver
Vt Violet
Wh White
Ye Yellow
Adaptive damping
Cruise control
Auxiliary warning system
Stop light switch
Instrument interface control
Trip computer
High specification
Low specification
Daytime running light relay
Instrument interface control
E1
E14
E17
H31342

Diagram 10 : Typical engine management system - models with automatic transmission (continued)

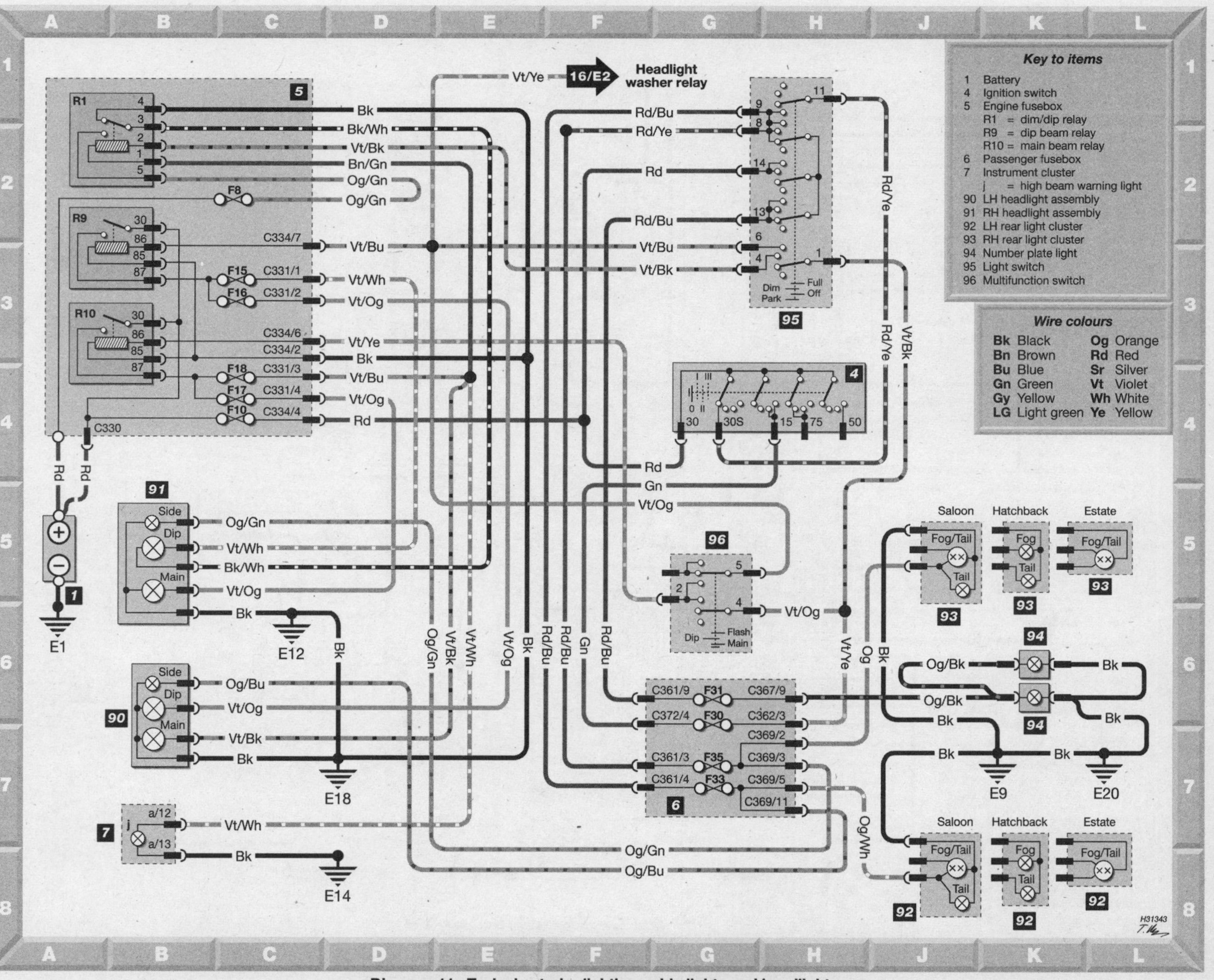

Diagram 11 : Typical exterior lighting - side lights and headlights

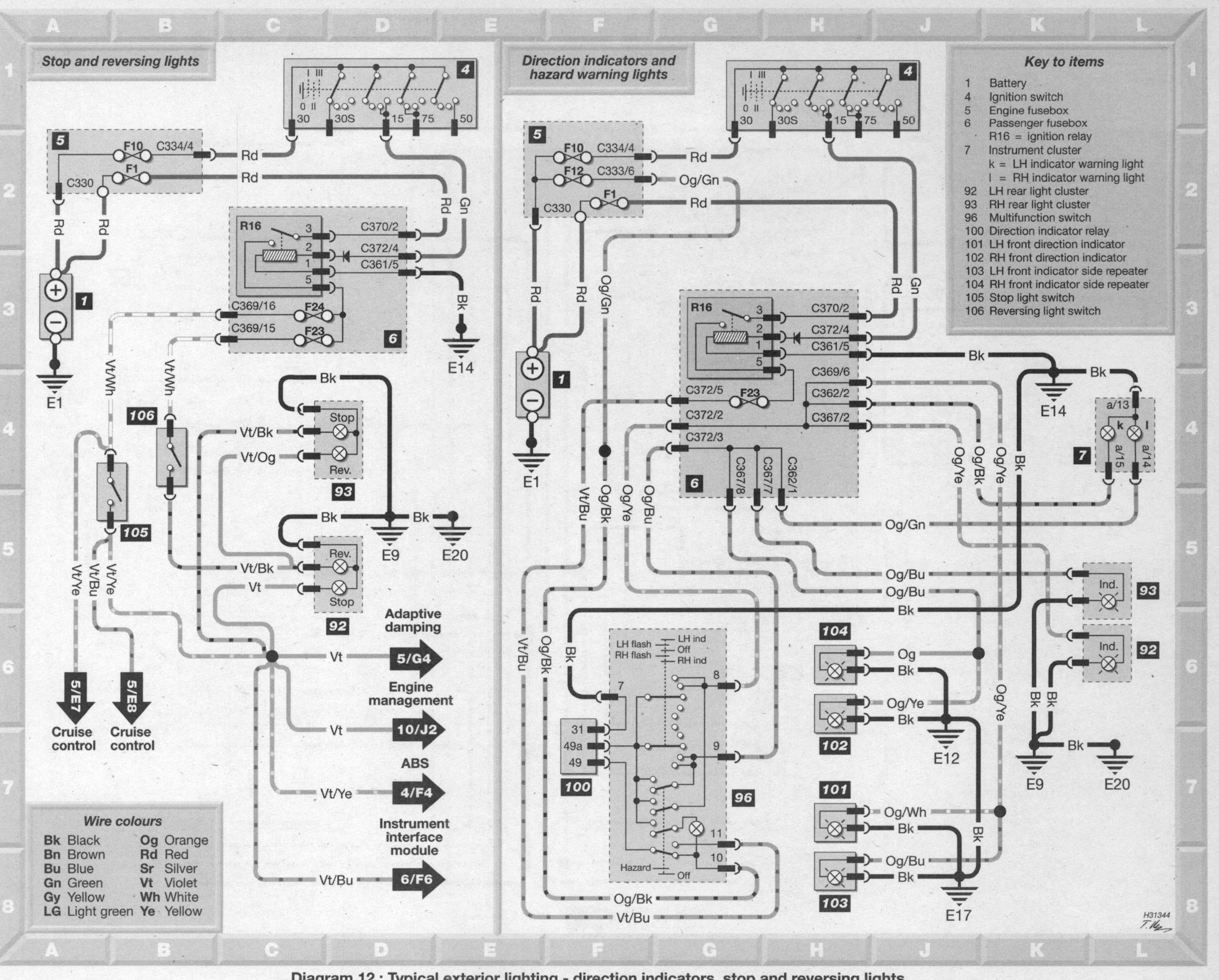

Stop and reversing lights
Direction indicators and hazard warning lights
Key to items
1 Battery
4 Ignition switch
5 Engine fusebox
6 Passenger fusebox
R16 = ignition relay
7 Instrument cluster
k = LH indicator warning light
l = RH indicator warning light
92 LH rear light cluster
93 RH rear light cluster
96 Multifunction switch
100 Direction indicator relay
101 LH front direction indicator
102 RH front direction indicator
103 LH front indicator side repeater
104 RH front indicator side repeater
105 Stop light switch
106 Reversing light switch
Wire colours
Bk Black
Bn Brown
Bu Blue
Gn Green
Gy Yellow
LG Light green
Og Orange
Rd Red
Sr Silver
Vt Violet
Wh White
Ye Yellow
Adaptive damping
Engine management
ABS
Instrument interface module
Cruise control
H31344

Diagram 12 : Typical exterior lighting - direction indicators, stop and reversing lights

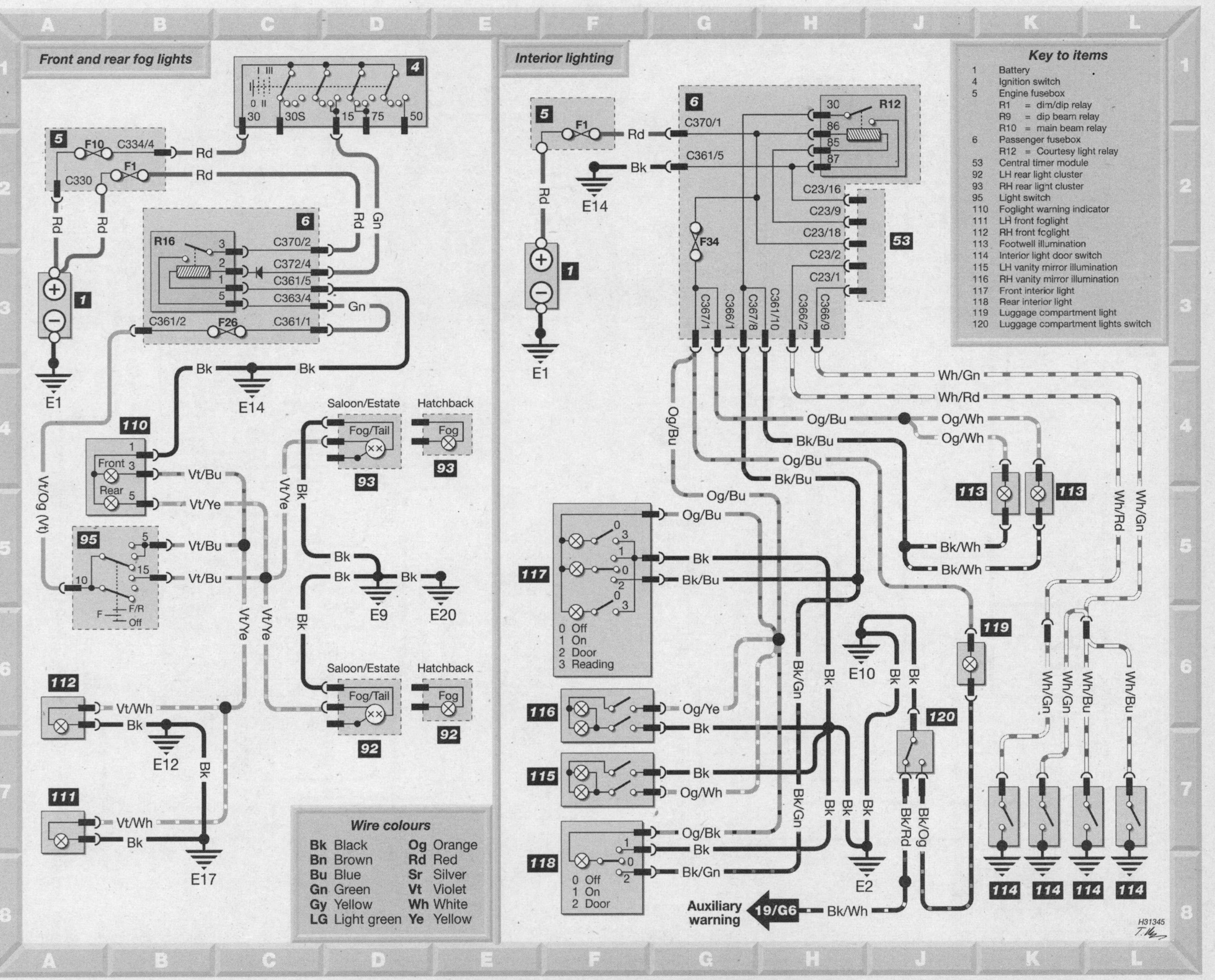

Front and rear fog lights
Interior lighting
Key to items
1 Battery
4 Ignition switch
5 Engine fusebox
R1 = dim/dip relay
R9 = dip beam relay
R10 = main beam relay
6 Passenger fusebox
R12 = Courtesy light relay
53 Central timer module
92 LH rear light cluster
93 RH rear light cluster
95 Light switch
110 Foglight warning indicator
111 LH front foglight
112 RH front foglight
113 Footwell illumination
114 Interior light door switch
115 LH vanity mirror illumination
116 RH vanity mirror illumination
117 Front interior light
118 Rear interior light
119 Luggage compartment light
120 Luggage compartment lights switch
Wire colours
Bk Black
Bn Brown
Bu Blue
Gn Green
Gy Yellow
LG Light green
Og Orange
Rd Red
Sr Silver
Vt Violet
Wh White
Ye Yellow
Saloon/Estate
Hatchback
0 Off
1 On
2 Door
3 Reading
Auxiliary warning
19/G6
H31345

Diagram 13 : Typical exterior lighting - fog lights and interior lighting

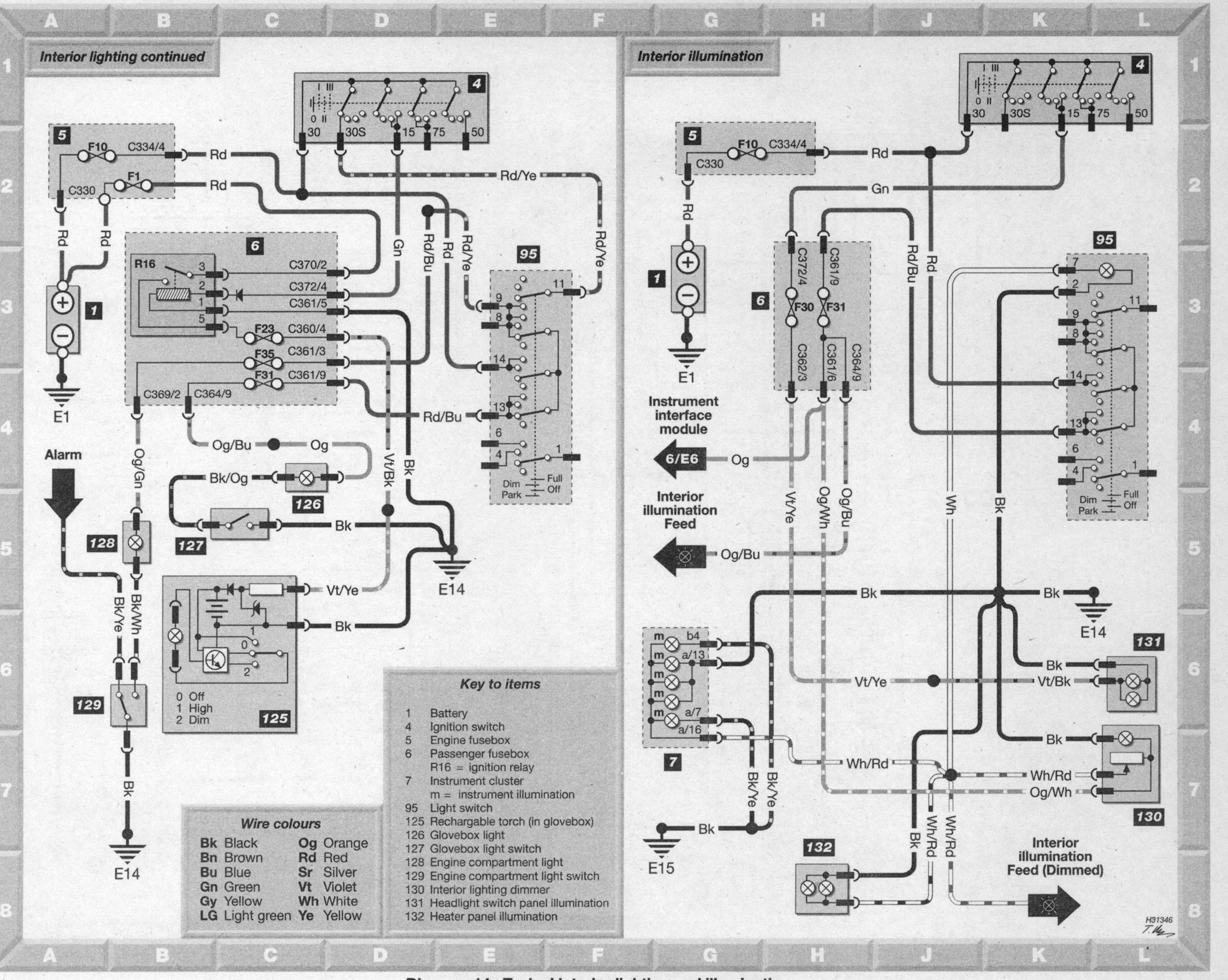

Interior lighting continued
Interior illumination
Alarm
Instrument interface module
Interior illumination Feed
Interior illumination Feed (Dimmed)
0 Off
1 High
2 Dim
Key to items
1 Battery
4 Ignition switch
5 Engine fusebox
6 Passenger fusebox
R16 = ignition relay
7 Instrument cluster
m = instrument illumination
95 Light switch
125 Rechargable torch (in glovebox)
126 Glovebox light
127 Glovebox light switch
128 Engine compartment light
129 Engine compartment light switch
130 Interior lighting dimmer
131 Headlight switch panel illumination
132 Heater panel illumination
Wire colours
Bk Black
Bn Brown
Bu Blue
Gn Green
Gy Yellow
LG Light green
Og Orange
Rd Red
Sr Silver
Vt Violet
Wh White
Ye Yellow
H31346

Diagram 14 : Typical interior lighting and illumination

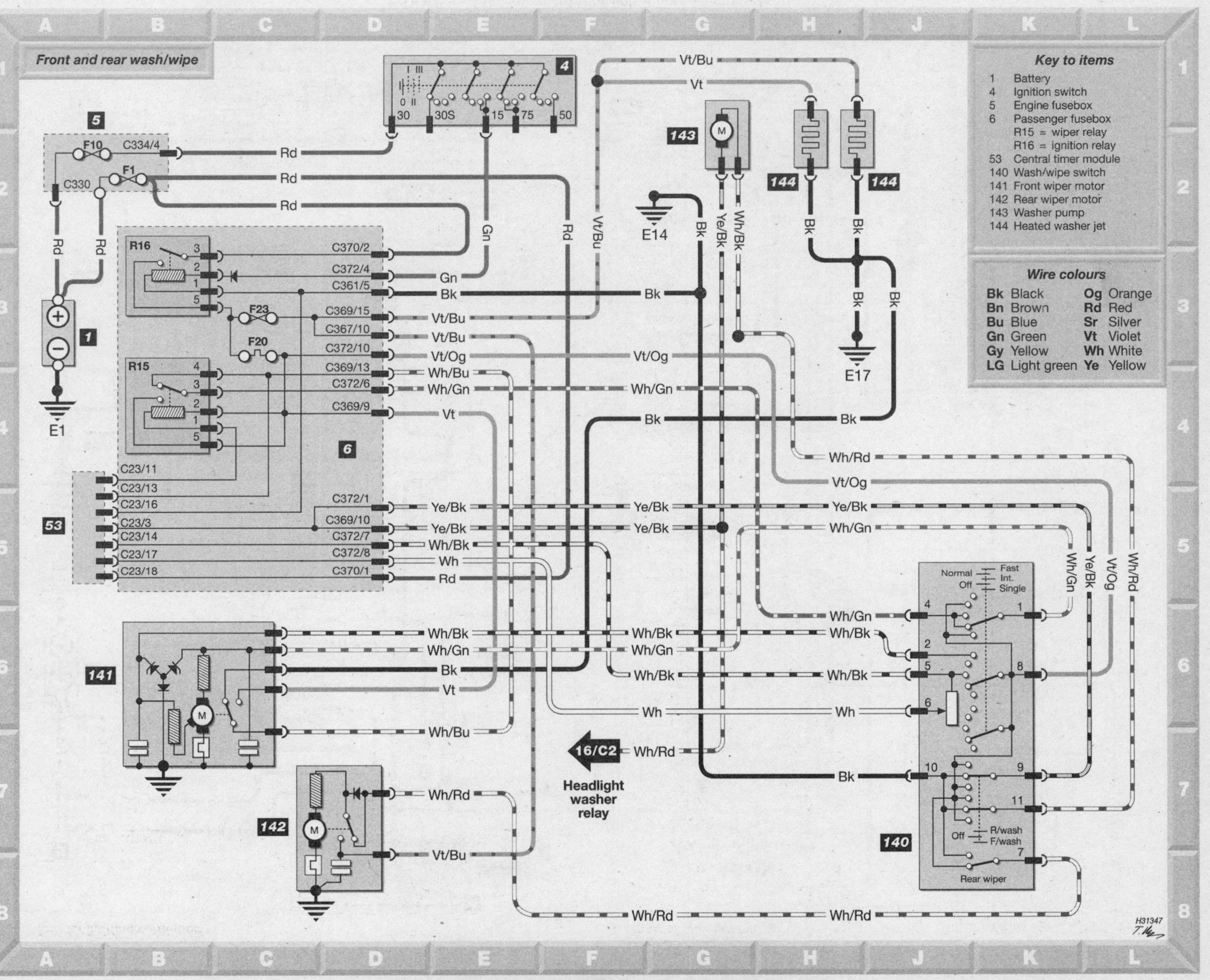

Diagram 15 : Typical Wash/wipe and heated washer jets

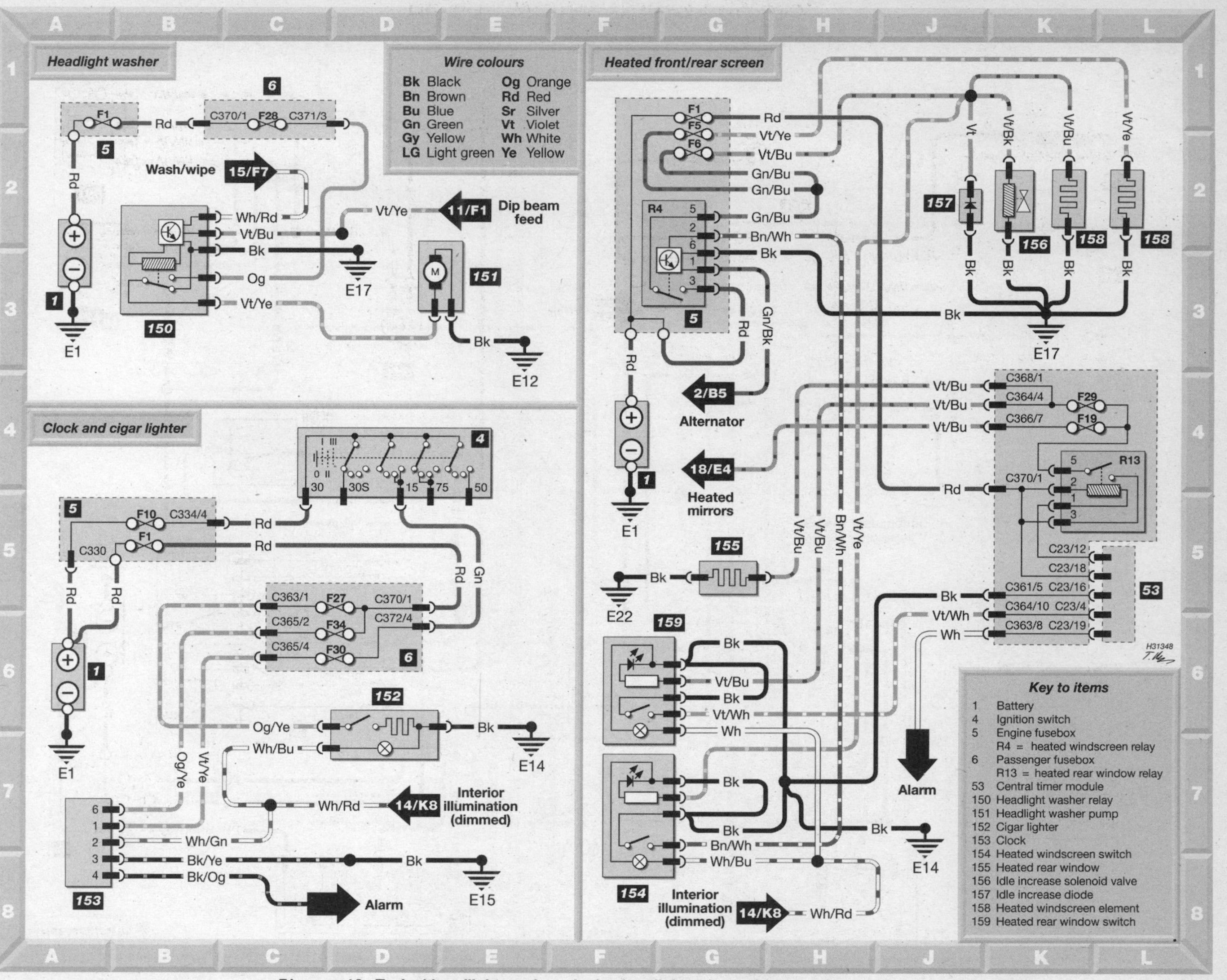

Diagram 16 : Typical headlight washer, clock, cigar lighter, heated front and rear screens

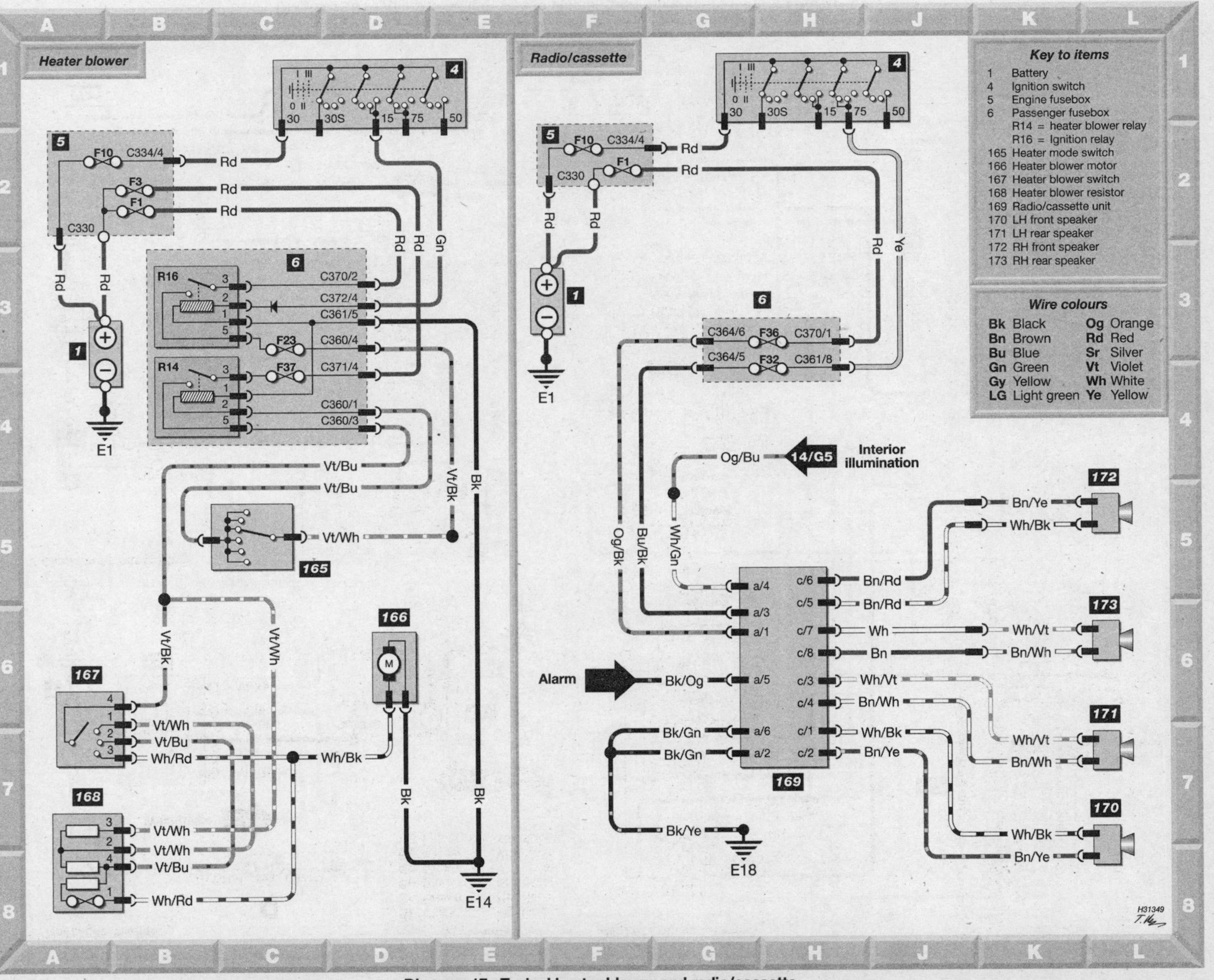

Diagram 17 : Typical heater blower and radio/cassette

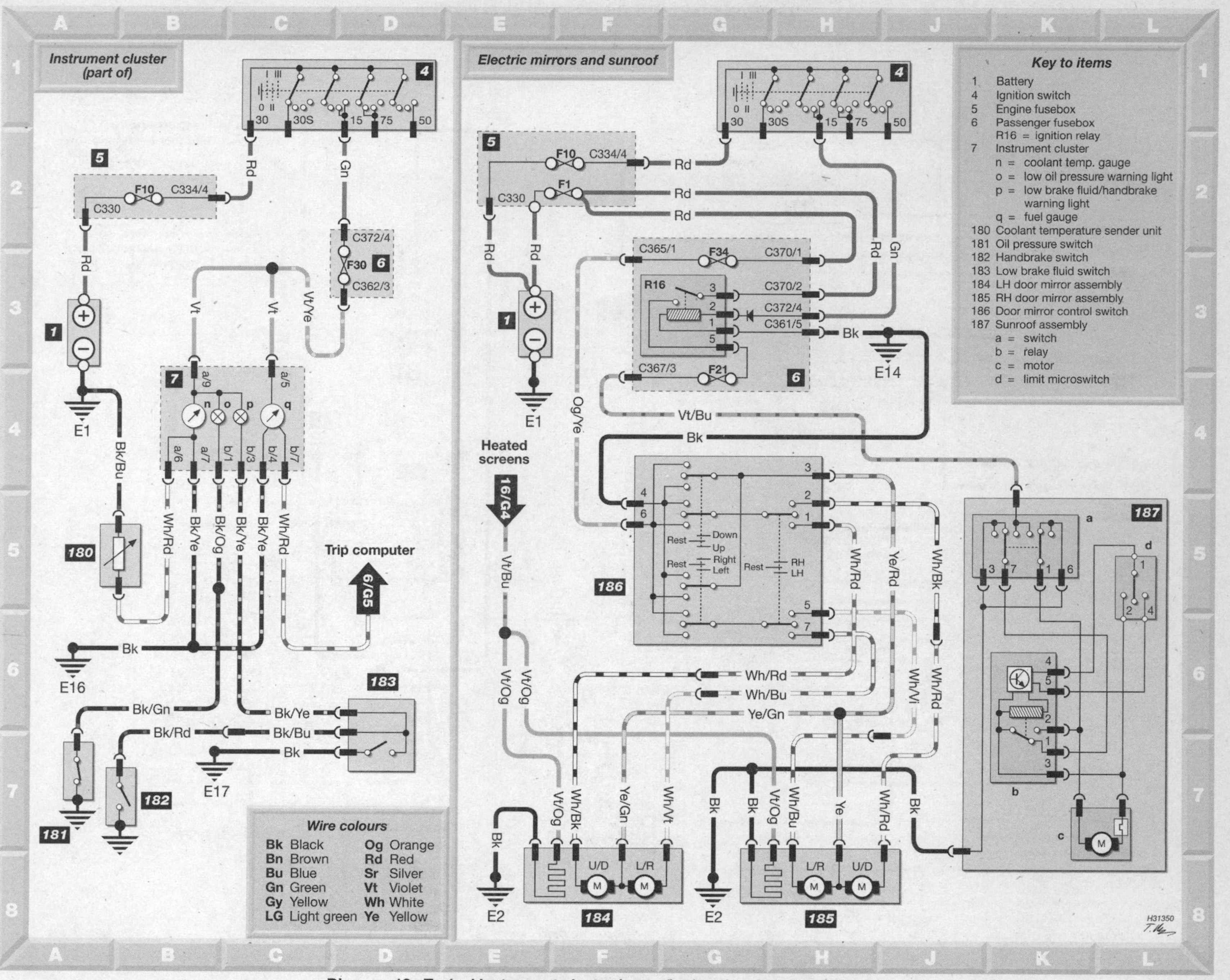

Diagram 18 : Typical instrument cluster (part of), electric mirrors and sunroof

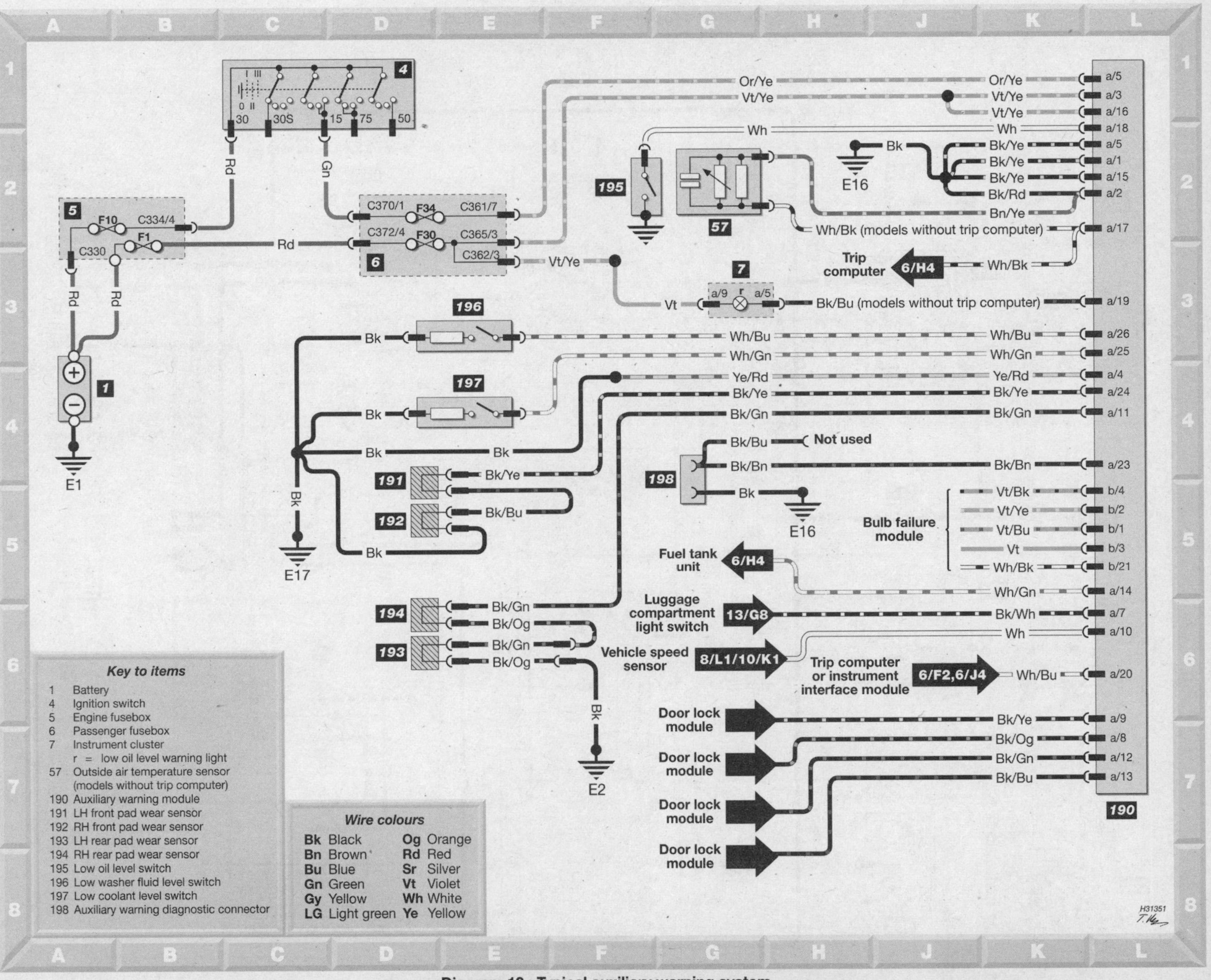
Key to items
1 Battery
4 Ignition switch
5 Engine fusebox
6 Passenger fusebox
7 Instrument cluster
r = low oil level warning light
57 Outside air temperature sensor (models without trip computer)
190 Auxiliary warning module
191 LH front pad wear sensor
192 RH front pad wear sensor
193 LH rear pad wear sensor
194 RH rear pad wear sensor
195 Low oil level switch
196 Low washer fluid level switch
197 Low coolant level switch
198 Auxiliary warning diagnostic connector
Wire colours
Bk Black
Bn Brown
Bu Blue
Gn Green
Gy Yellow
LG Light green
Og Orange
Rd Red
Sr Silver
Vt Violet
Wh White
Ye Yellow
Trip computer
Bulb failure module
Fuel tank unit
Luggage compartment light switch
Vehicle speed sensor
Trip computer or instrument interface module
Door lock module
Not used
Wh/Bk (models without trip computer)
Bk/Bu (models without trip computer)
H31351
Diagram 19 : Typical auxiliary warning system

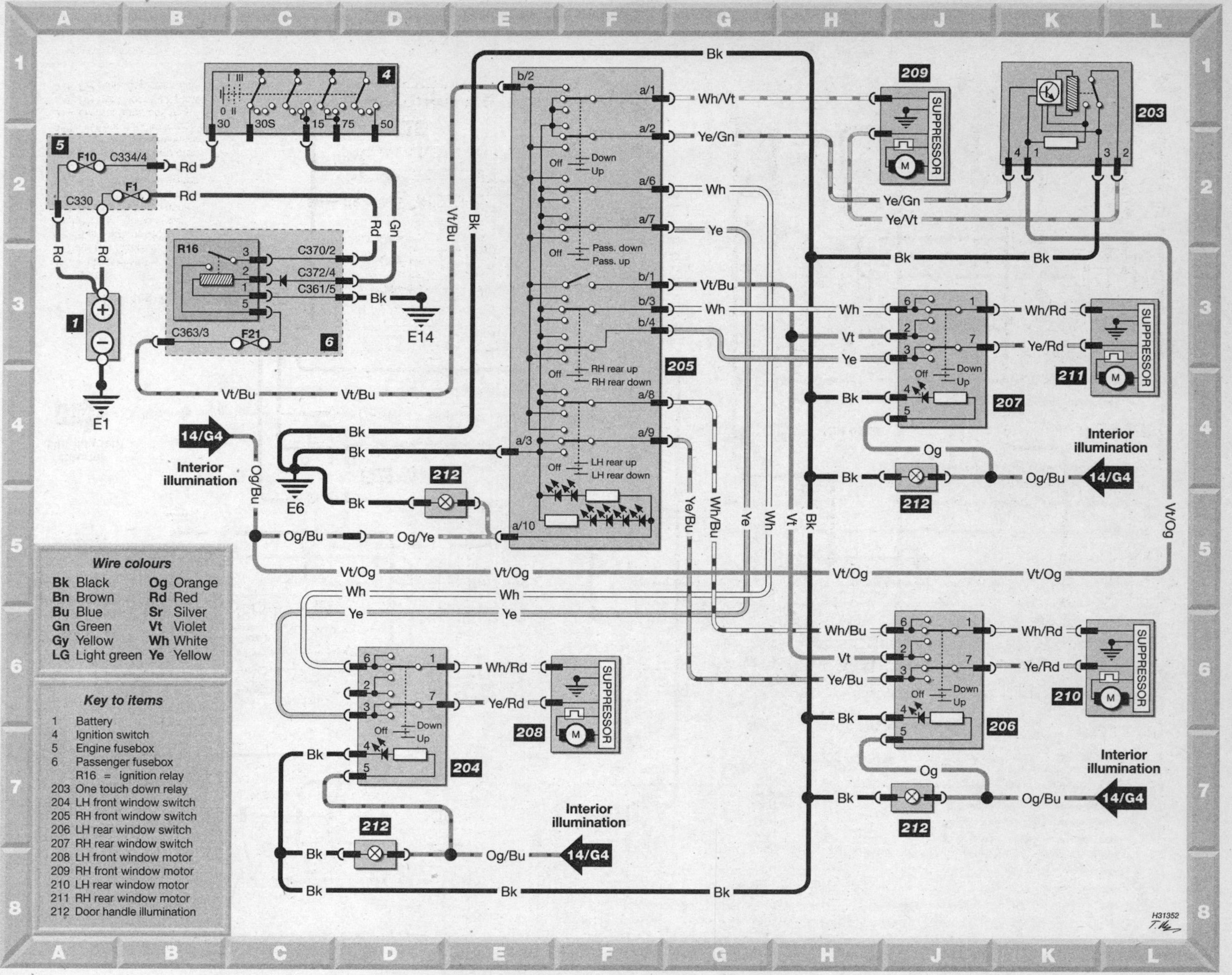

Wire colours
Bk Black
Bn Brown
Bu Blue
Gn Green
Gy Yellow
LG Light green
Og Orange
Rd Red
Sr Silver
Vt Violet
Wh White
Ye Yellow
Key to items
1 Battery
4 Ignition switch
5 Engine fusebox
6 Passenger fusebox
R16 = ignition relay
203 One touch down relay
204 LH front window switch
205 RH front window switch
206 LH rear window switch
207 RH rear window switch
208 LH front window motor
209 RH front window motor
210 LH rear window motor
211 RH rear window motor
212 Door handle illumination
SUPPRESSOR
Interior illumination
14/G4
H31352

Diagram 20 : Typical electric windows (4 windows)

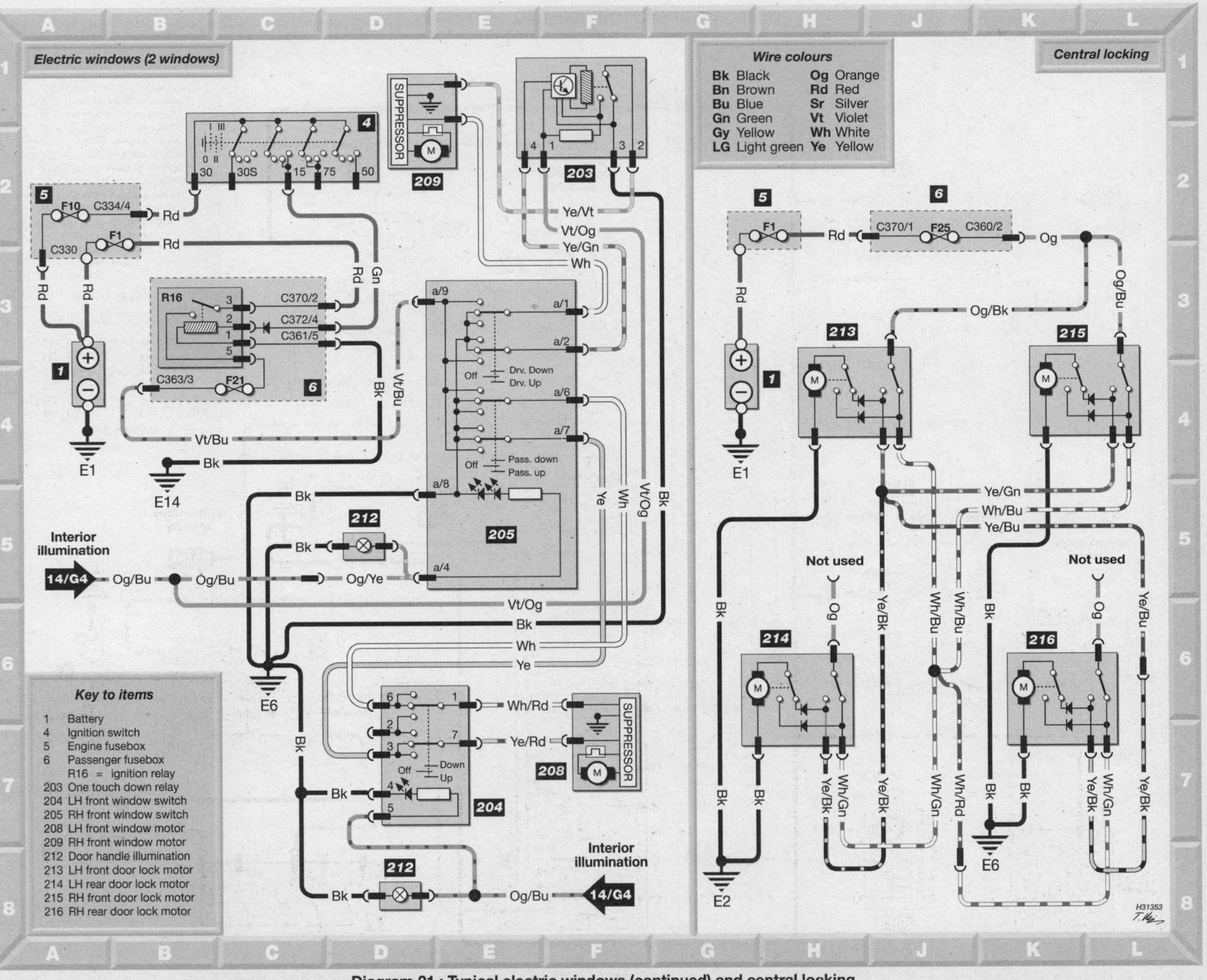

Diagram 21 : Typical electric windows (continued) and central locking

Dimensions and weights

Note: *All figures are approximate, and may vary according to model. Refer to manufacturer's data for exact figures.*

Dimensions

	Up to 1996	1997-on
Overall length:		
Saloon, Hatchback	4481 mm	4556 mm
Estate	4631 mm	4671 mm
Overall width - including mirrors	1925 mm	1925 mm
Overall height - at kerb weight:		
Saloon, Hatchback	1403 to 1435 mm	1327 to 1427 mm
Estate	1416 to 1501 mm	1405 to 1510 mm

Weights

	Up to 1996	1997-on
Kerb weight:		
1.6 Saloon, Hatchback models	1215 to 1250 kg	1293 to 1436 kg
1.6 Estate models	1265 to 1275 kg	1349 to 1499 kg
1.8 Saloon, Hatchback models	1225 to 1260 kg	1295 to 1474 kg
1.8 Estate models	1275 to 1285 kg	1351 to 1550 kg
2.0 Saloon, Hatchback models	1250 to 1310 kg	1317 to 1498 kg
2.0 Estate models	1295 to 1335 kg	1373 to 1562 kg
2.5 Saloon, Hatchback models	1358 to 1377 kg	1388 to 1553 kg
2.5 Estate models	1403 to 1422 kg	1444 to 1616 kg
Maximum roof rack load:		
Estate models with integral roof rack	100 kg	100 kg
All others	75 kg	75 kg
Maximum towing weight	1500 kg	1500 kg
Trailer nose weight limit	75 kg	75 kg

Conversion factors

Length (distance)

Inches (in)	x 25.4	= Millimetres (mm)	x 0.0394	= Inches (in)
Feet (ft)	x 0.305	= Metres (m)	x 3.281	= Feet (ft)
Miles	x 1.609	= Kilometres (km)	x 0.621	= Miles

Volume (capacity)

Cubic inches (cu in; in^3)	x 16.387	= Cubic centimetres (cc; cm^3)	x 0.061	= Cubic inches (cu in; in^3)
Imperial pints (Imp pt)	x 0.568	= Litres (l)	x 1.76	= Imperial pints (Imp pt)
Imperial quarts (Imp qt)	x 1.137	= Litres (l)	x 0.88	= Imperial quarts (Imp qt)
Imperial quarts (Imp qt)	x 1.201	= US quarts (US qt)	x 0.833	= Imperial quarts (Imp qt)
US quarts (US qt)	x 0.946	= Litres (l)	x 1.057	= US quarts (US qt)
Imperial gallons (Imp gal)	x 4.546	= Litres (l)	x 0.22	= Imperial gallons (Imp gal)
Imperial gallons (Imp gal)	x 1.201	= US gallons (US gal)	x 0.833	= Imperial gallons (Imp gal)
US gallons (US gal)	x 3.785	= Litres (l)	x 0.264	= US gallons (US gal)

Mass (weight)

Ounces (oz)	x 28.35	= Grams (g)	x 0.035	= Ounces (oz)
Pounds (lb)	x 0.454	= Kilograms (kg)	x 2.205	= Pounds (lb)

Force

Ounces-force (ozf; oz)	x 0.278	= Newtons (N)	x 3.6	= Ounces-force (ozf; oz)
Pounds-force (lbf; lb)	x 4.448	= Newtons (N)	x 0.225	= Pounds-force (lbf; lb)
Newtons (N)	x 0.1	= Kilograms-force (kgf; kg)	x 9.81	= Newtons (N)

Pressure

Pounds-force per square inch (psi; lbf/in^2; lb/in^2)	x 0.070	= Kilograms-force per square centimetre (kgf/cm^2; kg/cm^2)	x 14.223	= Pounds-force per square inch (psi; lbf/in^2; lb/in^2)
Pounds-force per square inch (psi; lbf/in^2; lb/in^2)	x 0.068	= Atmospheres (atm)	x 14.696	= Pounds-force per square inch (psi; lbf/in^2; lb/in^2)
Pounds-force per square inch (psi; lbf/in^2; lb/in^2)	x 0.069	= Bars	x 14.5	= Pounds-force per square inch (psi; lbf/in^2; lb/in^2)
Pounds-force per square inch (psi; lbf/in^2; lb/in^2)	x 6.895	= Kilopascals (kPa)	x 0.145	= Pounds-force per square inch (psi; lbf/in^2; lb/in^2)
Kilopascals (kPa)	x 0.01	= Kilograms-force per square centimetre (kgf/cm^2; kg/cm^2)	x 98.1	= Kilopascals (kPa)
Millibar (mbar)	x 100	= Pascals (Pa)	x 0.01	= Millibar (mbar)
Millibar (mbar)	x 0.0145	= Pounds-force per square inch (psi; lbf/in^2; lb/in^2)	x 68.947	= Millibar (mbar)
Millibar (mbar)	x 0.75	= Millimetres of mercury (mmHg)	x 1.333	= Millibar (mbar)
Millibar (mbar)	x 0.401	= Inches of water (inH_2O)	x 2.491	= Millibar (mbar)
Millimetres of mercury (mmHg)	x 0.535	= Inches of water (inH_2O)	x 1.868	= Millimetres of mercury (mmHg)
Inches of water (inH_2O)	x 0.036	= Pounds-force per square inch (psi; lbf/in^2; lb/in^2)	x 27.68	= Inches of water (inH_2O)

Torque (moment of force)

Pounds-force inches (lbf in; lb in)	x 1.152	= Kilograms-force centimetre (kgf cm; kg cm)	x 0.868	= Pounds-force inches (lbf in; lb in)
Pounds-force inches (lbf in; lb in)	x 0.113	= Newton metres (Nm)	x 8.85	= Pounds-force inches (lbf in; lb in)
Pounds-force inches (lbf in; lb in)	x 0.083	= Pounds-force feet (lbf ft; lb ft)	x 12	= Pounds-force inches (lbf in; lb in)
Pounds-force feet (lbf ft; lb ft)	x 0.138	= Kilograms-force metres (kgf m; kg m)	x 7.233	= Pounds-force feet (lbf ft; lb ft)
Pounds-force feet (lbf ft; lb ft)	x 1.356	= Newton metres (Nm)	x 0.738	= Pounds-force feet (lbf ft; lb ft)
Newton metres (Nm)	x 0.102	= Kilograms-force metres (kgf m; kg m)	x 9.804	= Newton metres (Nm)

Power

Horsepower (hp)	x 745.7	= Watts (W)	x 0.0013	= Horsepower (hp)

Velocity (speed)

Miles per hour (miles/hr; mph)	x 1.609	= Kilometres per hour (km/hr; kph)	x 0.621	= Miles per hour (miles/hr; mph)

Fuel consumption*

Miles per gallon, Imperial (mpg)	x 0.354	= Kilometres per litre (km/l)	x 2.825	= Miles per gallon, Imperial (mpg)
Miles per gallon, US (mpg)	x 0.425	= Kilometres per litre (km/l)	x 2.352	= Miles per gallon, US (mpg)

Temperature

Degrees Fahrenheit = (°C x 1.8) + 32

Degrees Celsius (Degrees Centigrade; °C) = (°F - 32) x 0.56

** It is common practice to convert from miles per gallon (mpg) to litres/100 kilometres (l/100km), where mpg x l/100 km = 282*

Buying spare parts

Spare parts are available from many sources, including maker's appointed garages, accessory shops, and motor factors. To be sure of obtaining the correct parts, it may sometimes be necessary to quote the vehicle identification number. If possible, it can also be useful to take the old parts along for positive identification. Items such as starter motors and alternators may be available under a service exchange scheme - any parts returned should always be clean.

Our advice regarding spare part sources is as follows.

Officially-appointed garages

This is the best source of parts which are peculiar to your car, and are not otherwise generally available (eg badges, interior trim, certain body panels, etc). It is also the only place at which you should buy parts if the vehicle is still under warranty.

Accessory shops

These are very good places to buy materials and components needed for the maintenance of your car (oil, air and fuel filters, spark plugs, light bulbs, drivebelts, oils and greases, brake pads, touch-up paint, etc). Parts like this sold by a reputable shop are of the same standard as those used by the car manufacturer.

Motor factors

Good factors will stock all the more important components which wear out comparatively quickly and can sometimes supply individual components needed for the overhaul of a larger assembly. They may also handle work such as cylinder block reboring, crankshaft regrinding and balancing, etc.

Tyre and exhaust specialists

These outlets may be independent or members of a local or national chain. They frequently offer competitive prices when compared with a main dealer or local garage, but it will pay to obtain several quotes before making a decision. Also ask what 'extras' may be added to the quote - for instance, fitting a new valve and balancing the wheel are both often charged on top of the price of a new tyre.

Other sources

Beware of parts or materials obtained from market stalls, car boot sales or similar outlets. Such items are not invariably sub-standard, but there is little chance of compensation if they do prove unsatisfactory. In the case of safety-critical components such as brake pads, there is the risk not only of financial loss, but also of an accident causing injury or death.

Second-hand components or assemblies obtained from a car breaker can be a good buy in some circumstances, but this sort of purchase is best made by the experienced DIY mechanic.

Vehicle identification

Modifications are a continuing and unpublicised process in vehicle manufacture, quite apart from major model changes. Spare parts manuals and lists are compiled upon a numerical basis, the individual vehicle identification numbers being essential to correct identification of the component concerned.

When ordering spare parts, always give as much information as possible. Quote the car model, year of manufacture, body and engine numbers as appropriate.

The *vehicle identification plate* is located on the engine compartment front crossmember **(see illustration)**. In addition to many other details, it carries the Vehicle Identification Number, maximum vehicle weight information, and codes for interior trim and body colours.

The *Vehicle Identification Number* is given on the vehicle identification plate. It is also stamped on the engine compartment bulkhead, and into the body, so that it can be seen through the bottom left-hand corner of the windscreen **(see illustrations)**.

The *engine number* on four-cylinder engines is stamped onto the cylinder block/crankcase level with the starter motor, and also on the transmission end of the cylinder head **(see illustration)**. On the V6 engine, the engine number appears at the front of the timing cover **(see illustration)**, and also on the rear left-hand side of the block.

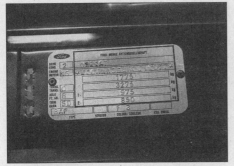

Vehicle identification plate on engine compartment front crossmember

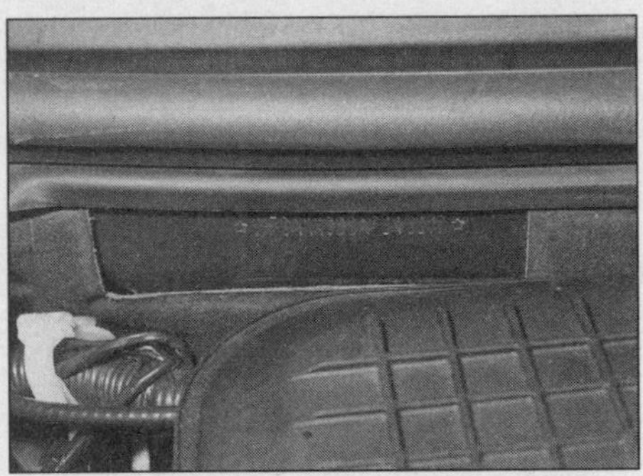

Vehicle identification number on engine compartment bulkhead

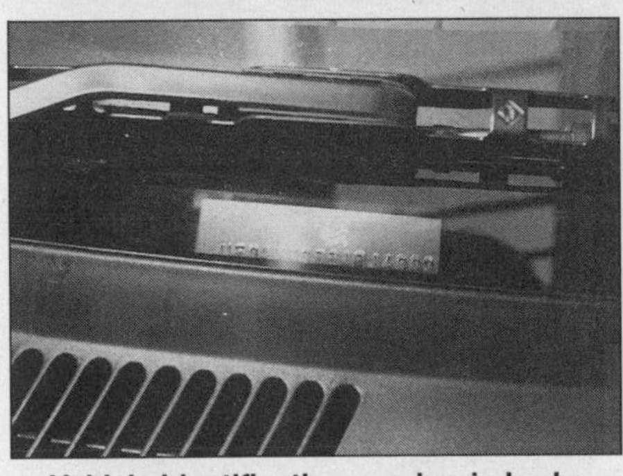

Vehicle identification number in body, visible through bottom left-hand corner of windscreen

Four-cylinder engine number on front of cylinder block/crankcase - seen from below

V6 engine number on the timing cover

General repair procedures

Whenever servicing, repair or overhaul work is carried out on the car or its components, observe the following procedures and instructions. This will assist in carrying out the operation efficiently and to a professional standard of workmanship.

Joint mating faces and gaskets

When separating components at their mating faces, never insert screwdrivers or similar implements into the joint between the faces in order to prise them apart. This can cause severe damage which results in oil leaks, coolant leaks, etc upon reassembly. Separation is usually achieved by tapping along the joint with a soft-faced hammer in order to break the seal. However, note that this method may not be suitable where dowels are used for component location.

Where a gasket is used between the mating faces of two components, a new one must be fitted on reassembly; fit it dry unless otherwise stated in the repair procedure. Make sure that the mating faces are clean and dry, with all traces of old gasket removed. When cleaning a joint face, use a tool which is unlikely to score or damage the face, and remove any burrs or nicks with an oilstone or fine file.

Make sure that tapped holes are cleaned with a pipe cleaner, and keep them free of jointing compound, if this is being used, unless specifically instructed otherwise.

Ensure that all orifices, channels or pipes are clear, and blow through them, preferably using compressed air.

Oil seals

Oil seals can be removed by levering them out with a wide flat-bladed screwdriver or similar implement. Alternatively, a number of self-tapping screws may be screwed into the seal, and these used as a purchase for pliers or some similar device in order to pull the seal free.

Whenever an oil seal is removed from its working location, either individually or as part of an assembly, it should be renewed.

The very fine sealing lip of the seal is easily damaged, and will not seal if the surface it contacts is not completely clean and free from scratches, nicks or grooves. If the original sealing surface of the component cannot be restored, and the manufacturer has not made provision for slight relocation of the seal relative to the sealing surface, the component should be renewed.

Protect the lips of the seal from any surface which may damage them in the course of fitting. Use tape or a conical sleeve where possible. Lubricate the seal lips with oil before fitting and, on dual-lipped seals, fill the space between the lips with grease.

Unless otherwise stated, oil seals must be fitted with their sealing lips toward the lubricant to be sealed.

Use a tubular drift or block of wood of the appropriate size to install the seal and, if the seal housing is shouldered, drive the seal down to the shoulder. If the seal housing is unshouldered, the seal should be fitted with its face flush with the housing top face (unless otherwise instructed).

Screw threads and fastenings

Seized nuts, bolts and screws are quite a common occurrence where corrosion has set in, and the use of penetrating oil or releasing fluid will often overcome this problem if the offending item is soaked for a while before attempting to release it. The use of an impact driver may also provide a means of releasing such stubborn fastening devices, when used in conjunction with the appropriate screwdriver bit or socket. If none of these methods works, it may be necessary to resort to the careful application of heat, or the use of a hacksaw or nut splitter device.

Studs are usually removed by locking two nuts together on the threaded part, and then using a spanner on the lower nut to unscrew the stud. Studs or bolts which have broken off below the surface of the component in which they are mounted can sometimes be removed using a stud extractor. Always ensure that a blind tapped hole is completely free from oil, grease, water or other fluid before installing the bolt or stud. Failure to do this could cause the housing to crack due to the hydraulic action of the bolt or stud as it is screwed in.

When tightening a castellated nut to accept a split pin, tighten the nut to the specified torque, where applicable, and then tighten further to the next split pin hole. Never slacken the nut to align the split pin hole, unless stated in the repair procedure.

When checking or retightening a nut or bolt to a specified torque setting, slacken the nut or bolt by a quarter of a turn, and then retighten to the specified setting. However, this should not be attempted where angular tightening has been used.

For some screw fastenings, notably cylinder head bolts or nuts, torque wrench settings are no longer specified for the latter stages of tightening, "angle-tightening" being called up instead. Typically, a fairly low torque wrench setting will be applied to the bolts/nuts in the correct sequence, followed by one or more stages of tightening through specified angles.

Locknuts, locktabs and washers

Any fastening which will rotate against a component or housing during tightening should always have a washer between it and the relevant component or housing.

Spring or split washers should always be renewed when they are used to lock a critical component such as a big-end bearing retaining bolt or nut. Locktabs which are folded over to retain a nut or bolt should always be renewed.

Self-locking nuts can be re-used in non-critical areas, providing resistance can be felt when the locking portion passes over the bolt or stud thread. However, it should be noted that self-locking stiffnuts tend to lose their effectiveness after long periods of use, and should then be renewed as a matter of course.

Split pins must always be replaced with new ones of the correct size for the hole.

When thread-locking compound is found on the threads of a fastener which is to be re-used, it should be cleaned off with a wire brush and solvent, and fresh compound applied on reassembly.

Special tools

Some repair procedures in this manual entail the use of special tools such as a press, two or three-legged pullers, spring compressors, etc. Wherever possible, suitable readily-available alternatives to the manufacturer's special tools are described, and are shown in use. In some instances, where no alternative is possible, it has been necessary to resort to the use of a manufacturer's tool, and this has been done for reasons of safety as well as the efficient completion of the repair operation. Unless you are highly-skilled and have a thorough understanding of the procedures described, never attempt to bypass the use of any special tool when the procedure described specifies its use. Not only is there a very great risk of personal injury, but expensive damage could be caused to the components involved.

Environmental considerations

When disposing of used engine oil, brake fluid, antifreeze, etc, give due consideration to any detrimental environmental effects. Do not, for instance, pour any of the above liquids down drains into the general sewage system, or onto the ground to soak away. Many local council refuse tips provide a facility for waste oil disposal, as do some garages. If none of these facilities are available, consult your local Environmental Health Department, or the National Rivers Authority, for further advice.

With the universal tightening-up of legislation regarding the emission of environmentally-harmful substances from motor vehicles, most vehicles have tamperproof devices fitted to the main adjustment points of the fuel system. These devices are primarily designed to prevent unqualified persons from adjusting the fuel/air mixture, with the chance of a consequent increase in toxic emissions. If such devices are found during servicing or overhaul, they should, wherever possible, be renewed or refitted in accordance with the manufacturer's requirements or current legislation.

Note: It is antisocial and illegal to dump oil down the drain. To find the location of your local oil recycling bank, call this number free.

The jack supplied with the vehicle tool kit should only be used for changing the roadwheels - see "*Wheel changing*" at the front of this book. When carrying out any other kind of work, raise the vehicle using a hydraulic (or "trolley") jack, and always supplement the jack with axle stands positioned under the vehicle jacking points. If the roadwheels do not have to be removed, consider using wheel ramps - if wished, these can be placed under the wheels once the vehicle has been raised using a hydraulic jack, and the vehicle lowered onto the ramps so that it is effectively resting on its wheels, on the ramps.

When jacking up the vehicle to carry out repair or maintenance tasks, bear in mind the following points:

Do not jack up the vehicle on anything other than firm, level ground. If the area to be used has even a slight slope, take this into account, and be sure to chock the wheels remaining on the ground. Jacking up the vehicle on a soft surface is not advisable, as the vehicle may sink while being worked on. Jacking up on a gravel surface is particularly dangerous, as the jack or axle stands can tilt sufficiently to slip off the jacking point.

Always apply the handbrake, and use wheel chocks on the wheels remaining on the ground. If the handbrake must be released for the work being carried out, engage a gear (or select 'P' on automatic transmissions), and ensure that the wheel chocks are in place before releasing the brake.

Do not jack the vehicle under any other part of the sill, sump, floor pan, or any of the steering or suspension components. With the vehicle raised, an axle stand should be positioned beneath the vehicle jack location point on the sill.

Never work under, around or near a raised vehicle unless it is adequately supported in at least two places with axle stands. Remember - a hydraulic (trolley) jack may 'creep' down in use, and may even lose all hydraulic pressure without warning.

Do not run the engine while the car is raised. If this cannot be avoided, make sure the transmission is not in gear (or that only 'P' or 'N' is selected, on automatic transmissions).

If the front of the vehicle is to be raised, first apply the handbrake, and/or place chocks behind the rear wheels. Either place the jack head under the front jacking points on the door sill, with a block of wood to prevent damage, or use the two front support points shown in the accompanying illustration, and lift the vehicle evenly **(see illustrations)**.

To raise the rear of the vehicle, chock the front wheels and engage a gear (or select 'P'). Use the two rear jacking points on the door sill, with a block of wood to prevent damage **(see illustration)**.

To raise the side of the vehicle, prepare the vehicle as described for front AND rear lifting. Place the jack head under the appropriate point indicated in the accompanying illustration. If a trolley jack or similar is used on the points provided for the vehicle's jack, make up a wooden spacer with a groove cut in it to accept the underbody flange, so that there is no risk of the jack slipping or buckling the flange.

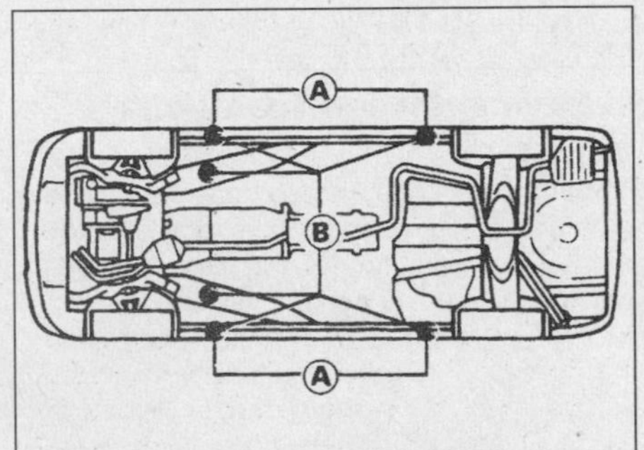

Jacking and supporting points

A Jacking points for vehicle jack in roadside use. May also be used as support points with axle stands

B Jacking points for trolley jack. May be used as additional support points with axle stands

Using the front jacking point and support point (with wooden blocks) to raise the front of the car

Using the rear jacking point to raise the rear of the car

Radio/cassette unit anti-theft system - precaution

If a Ford "Keycode" audio unit is fitted, and the unit and/or the battery is disconnected, the unit will not function again on reconnection until the correct security code is entered. Details of this procedure, which varies according to the unit and model year, are given in the "Ford Audio Systems Operating Guide" supplied with the vehicle when new, with the code itself being given in a "Radio Passport" and/or a "Keycode Label" at the same time. Ensure you have the correct code before you disconnect the battery. For obvious security reasons, the procedure is not given in this manual. If you do not have the code or details of the correct procedure, but can supply proof of ownership and a legitimate reason for wanting this information, the vehicle's selling dealer may be able to help.

Introduction

A selection of good tools is a fundamental requirement for anyone contemplating the maintenance and repair of a motor vehicle. For the owner who does not possess any, their purchase will prove a considerable expense, offsetting some of the savings made by doing-it-yourself. However, provided that the tools purchased meet the relevant national safety standards and are of good quality, they will last for many years and prove an extremely worthwhile investment.

To help the average owner to decide which tools are needed to carry out the various tasks detailed in this manual, we have compiled three lists of tools under the following headings: *Maintenance and minor repair, Repair and overhaul*, and *Special*. Newcomers to practical mechanics should start off with the *Maintenance and minor repair* tool kit, and confine themselves to the simpler jobs around the vehicle. Then, as confidence and experience grow, more difficult tasks can be undertaken, with extra tools being purchased as, and when, they are needed. In this way, a *Maintenance and minor repair* tool kit can be built up into a *Repair and overhaul* tool kit over a considerable period of time, without any major cash outlays. The experienced do-it-yourselfer will have a tool kit good enough for most repair and overhaul procedures, and will add tools from the *Special* category when it is felt that the expense is justified by the amount of use to which these tools will be put.

Maintenance and minor repair tool kit

The tools given in this list should be considered as a minimum requirement if routine maintenance, servicing and minor repair operations are to be undertaken. We recommend the purchase of combination spanners (ring one end, open-ended the other); although more expensive than open-ended ones, they do give the advantages of both types of spanner.

- ☐ *Combination spanners:*
  Metric - 8 to 19 mm inclusive
- ☐ *Adjustable spanner - 35 mm jaw (approx.)*
- ☐ *Spark plug spanner (with rubber insert) - petrol models*
- ☐ *Spark plug gap adjustment tool - petrol models*
- ☐ *Set of feeler gauges*
- ☐ *Brake bleed nipple spanner*
- ☐ *Screwdrivers:*
  Flat blade - 100 mm long x 6 mm dia
  Cross blade - 100 mm long x 6 mm dia
  Torx - various sizes (not all vehicles)
- ☐ *Combination pliers*
- ☐ *Hacksaw (junior)*
- ☐ *Tyre pump*
- ☐ *Tyre pressure gauge*
- ☐ *Oil can*
- ☐ *Oil filter removal tool*
- ☐ *Fine emery cloth*
- ☐ *Wire brush (small)*
- ☐ *Funnel (medium size)*
- ☐ *Sump drain plug key (not all vehicles)*

Repair and overhaul tool kit

These tools are virtually essential for anyone undertaking any major repairs to a motor vehicle, and are additional to those given in the *Maintenance and minor repair* list. Included in this list is a comprehensive set of sockets. Although these are expensive, they will be found invaluable as they are so versatile - particularly if various drives are included in the set. We recommend the half-inch square-drive type, as this can be used with most proprietary torque wrenches.

The tools in this list will sometimes need to be supplemented by tools from the *Special* list:

- ☐ *Sockets (or box spanners) to cover range in previous list (including Torx sockets)*
- ☐ *Reversible ratchet drive (for use with sockets)*
- ☐ *Extension piece, 250 mm (for use with sockets)*
- ☐ *Universal joint (for use with sockets)*
- ☐ *Flexible handle or sliding T "breaker bar" (for use with sockets)*
- ☐ *Torque wrench (for use with sockets)*
- ☐ *Self-locking grips*
- ☐ *Ball pein hammer*
- ☐ *Soft-faced mallet (plastic or rubber)*
- ☐ *Screwdrivers:*
  Flat blade - long & sturdy, short (chubby), and narrow (electrician's) types
  Cross blade – long & sturdy, and short (chubby) types
- ☐ *Pliers:*
  Long-nosed
  Side cutters (electrician's)
  Circlip (internal and external)
- ☐ *Cold chisel - 25 mm*
- ☐ *Scriber*
- ☐ *Scraper*
- ☐ *Centre-punch*
- ☐ *Pin punch*
- ☐ *Hacksaw*
- ☐ *Brake hose clamp*
- ☐ *Brake/clutch bleeding kit*
- ☐ *Selection of twist drills*
- ☐ *Steel rule/straight-edge*
- ☐ *Allen keys (inc. splined/Torx type)*
- ☐ *Selection of files*
- ☐ *Wire brush*
- ☐ *Axle stands*
- ☐ *Jack (strong trolley or hydraulic type)*
- ☐ *Light with extension lead*
- ☐ *Universal electrical multi-meter*

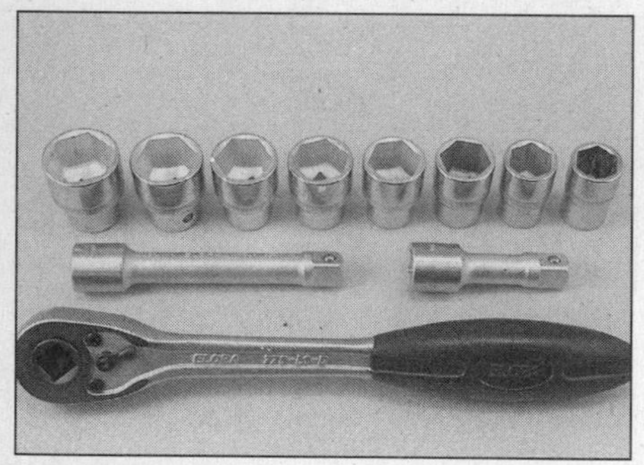

Sockets and reversible ratchet drive

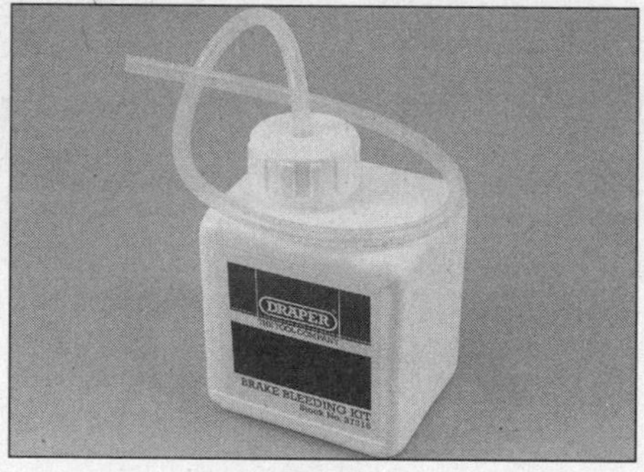

Brake bleeding kit

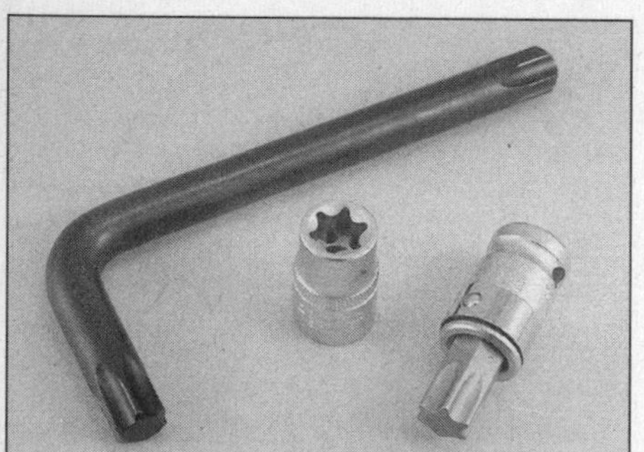

Torx key, socket and bit

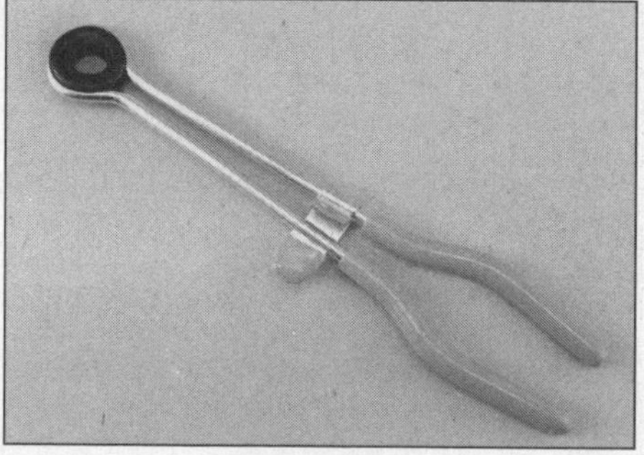

Hose clamp

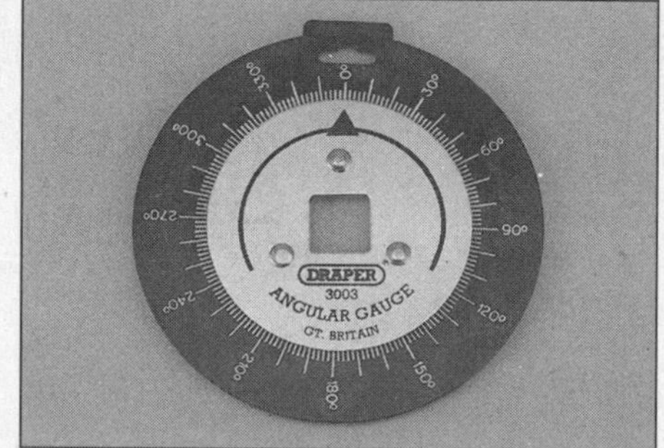

Angular-tightening gauge

Special tools

The tools in this list are those which are not used regularly, are expensive to buy, or which need to be used in accordance with their manufacturers' instructions. Unless relatively difficult mechanical jobs are undertaken frequently, it will not be economic to buy many of these tools. Where this is the case, you could consider clubbing together with friends (or joining a motorists' club) to make a joint purchase, or borrowing the tools against a deposit from a local garage or tool hire specialist. It is worth noting that many of the larger DIY superstores now carry a large range of special tools for hire at modest rates.

The following list contains only those tools and instruments freely available to the public, and not those special tools produced by the vehicle manufacturer specifically for its dealer network. You will find occasional references to these manufacturers' special tools in the text of this manual. Generally, an alternative method of doing the job without the vehicle manufacturers' special tool is given. However, sometimes there is no alternative to using them. Where this is the case and the relevant tool cannot be bought or borrowed, you will have to entrust the work to a dealer.

- ☐ *Angular-tightening gauge*
- ☐ *Valve spring compressor*
- ☐ *Valve grinding tool*
- ☐ *Piston ring compressor*
- ☐ *Piston ring removal/installation tool*
- ☐ *Cylinder bore hone*
- ☐ *Balljoint separator*
- ☐ *Coil spring compressors (where applicable)*
- ☐ *Two/three-legged hub and bearing puller*
- ☐ *Impact screwdriver*
- ☐ *Micrometer and/or vernier calipers*
- ☐ *Dial gauge*
- ☐ *Stroboscopic timing light*
- ☐ *Dwell angle meter/tachometer*
- ☐ *Fault code reader*
- ☐ *Cylinder compression gauge*
- ☐ *Hand-operated vacuum pump and gauge*
- ☐ *Clutch plate alignment set*
- ☐ *Brake shoe steady spring cup removal tool*
- ☐ *Bush and bearing removal/installation set*
- ☐ *Stud extractors*
- ☐ *Tap and die set*
- ☐ *Lifting tackle*
- ☐ *Trolley jack*

Buying tools

Reputable motor accessory shops and superstores often offer excellent quality tools at discount prices, so it pays to shop around.

Remember, you don't have to buy the most expensive items on the shelf, but it is always advisable to steer clear of the very cheap tools. Beware of 'bargains' offered on market stalls or at car boot sales. There are plenty of good tools around at reasonable prices, but always aim to purchase items which meet the relevant national safety standards. If in doubt, ask the proprietor or manager of the shop for advice before making a purchase.

Care and maintenance of tools

Having purchased a reasonable tool kit, it is necessary to keep the tools in a clean and serviceable condition. After use, always wipe off any dirt, grease and metal particles using a clean, dry cloth, before putting the tools away. Never leave them lying around after they have been used. A simple tool rack on the garage or workshop wall for items such as screwdrivers and pliers is a good idea. Store all normal spanners and sockets in a metal box. Any measuring instruments, gauges, meters, etc, must be carefully stored where they cannot be damaged or become rusty.

Take a little care when tools are used. Hammer heads inevitably become marked, and screwdrivers lose the keen edge on their blades from time to time. A little timely attention with emery cloth or a file will soon restore items like this to a good finish.

Working facilities

Not to be forgotten when discussing tools is the workshop itself. If anything more than routine maintenance is to be carried out, a suitable working area becomes essential.

It is appreciated that many an owner-mechanic is forced by circumstances to remove an engine or similar item without the benefit of a garage or workshop. Having done this, any repairs should always be done under the cover of a roof.

Wherever possible, any dismantling should be done on a clean, flat workbench or table at a suitable working height.

Any workbench needs a vice; one with a jaw opening of 100 mm is suitable for most jobs. As mentioned previously, some clean dry storage space is also required for tools, as well as for any lubricants, cleaning fluids, touch-up paints etc, which become necessary.

Another item which may be required, and which has a much more general usage, is an electric drill with a chuck capacity of at least 8 mm. This, together with a good range of twist drills, is virtually essential for fitting accessories.

Last, but not least, always keep a supply of old newspapers and clean, lint-free rags available, and try to keep any working area as clean as possible.

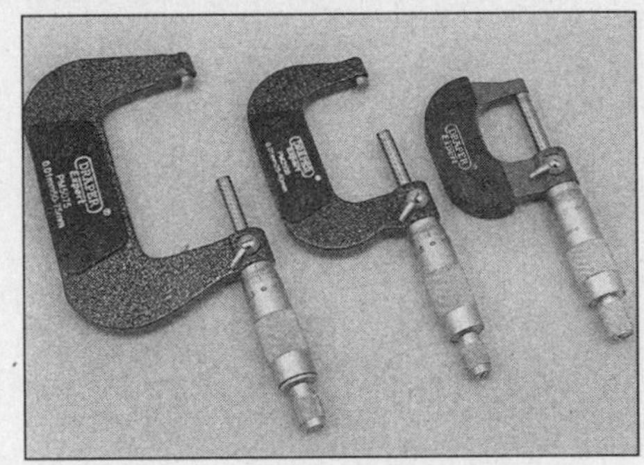

Micrometers

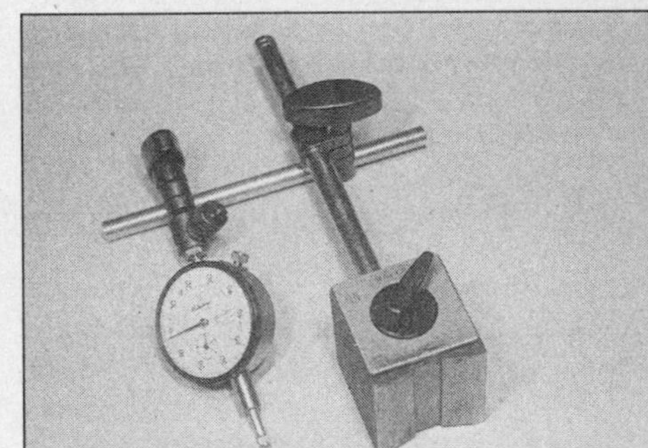

Dial test indicator ("dial gauge")

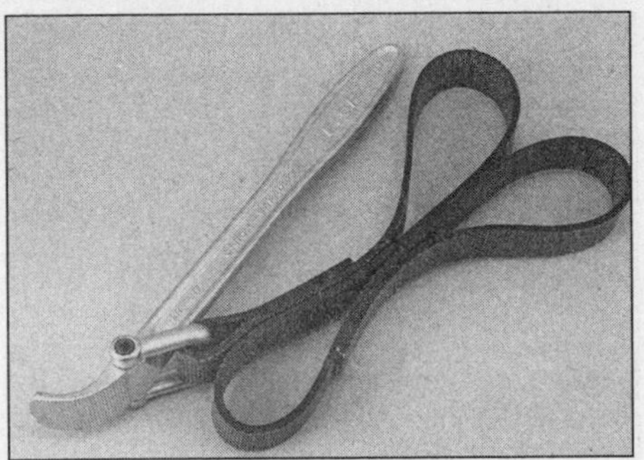

Strap wrench

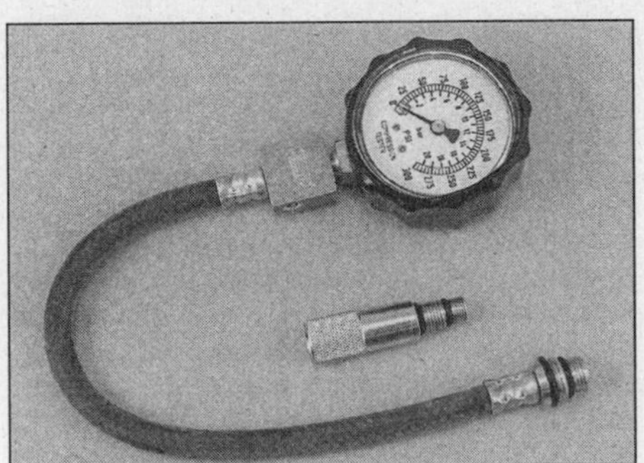

Compression tester

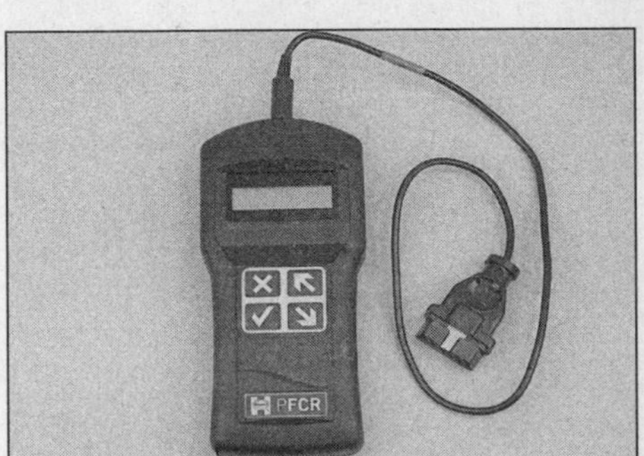

Fault code reader

MOT test checks

This is a guide to getting your vehicle through the MOT test. Obviously it will not be possible to examine the vehicle to the same standard as the professional MOT tester. However, working through the following checks will enable you to identify any problem areas before submitting the vehicle for the test.

Where a testable component is in borderline condition, the tester has discretion in deciding whether to pass or fail it. The basis of such discretion is whether the tester would be happy for a close relative or friend to use the vehicle with the component in that condition. If the vehicle presented is clean and evidently well cared for, the tester may be more inclined to pass a borderline component than if the vehicle is scruffy and apparently neglected.

It has only been possible to summarise the test requirements here, based on the regulations in force at the time of printing. Test standards are becoming increasingly stringent, although there are some exemptions for older vehicles. For full details obtain a copy of the Haynes publication Pass the MOT! (available from stockists of Haynes manuals).

An assistant will be needed to help carry out some of these checks.

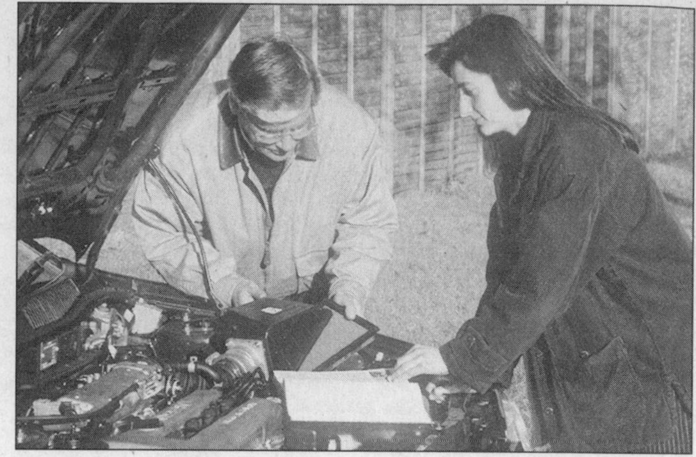

The checks have been sub-divided into four categories, as follows:

1 Checks carried out **FROM THE DRIVER'S SEAT**

2 Checks carried out **WITH THE VEHICLE ON THE GROUND**

3 Checks carried out **WITH THE VEHICLE RAISED AND THE WHEELS FREE TO TURN**

4 Checks carried out on **YOUR VEHICLE'S EXHAUST EMISSION SYSTEM**

1 Checks carried out FROM THE DRIVER'S SEAT

Handbrake

☐ Test the operation of the handbrake. Excessive travel (too many clicks) indicates incorrect brake or cable adjustment.

☐ Check that the handbrake cannot be released by tapping the lever sideways. Check the security of the lever mountings.

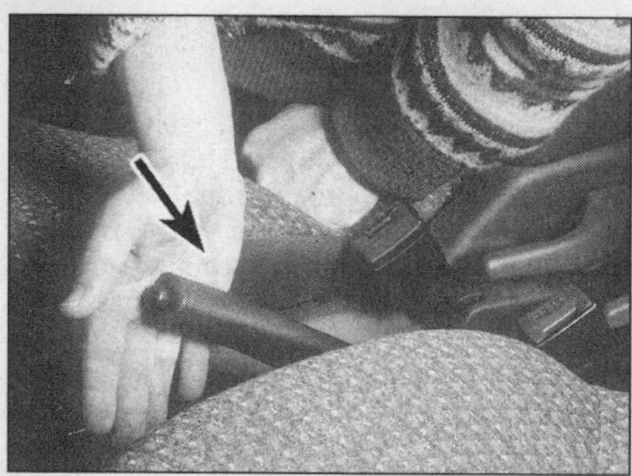

Footbrake

☐ Depress the brake pedal and check that it does not creep down to the floor, indicating a master cylinder fault. Release the pedal, wait a few seconds, then depress it again. If the pedal travels nearly to the floor before firm resistance is felt, brake adjustment or repair is necessary. If the pedal feels spongy, there is air in the hydraulic system which must be removed by bleeding.

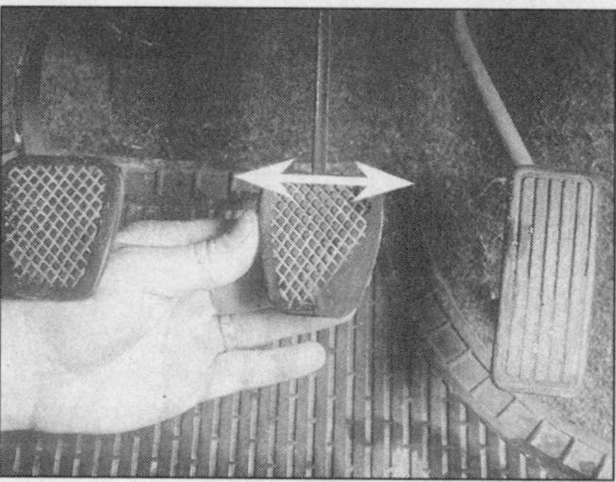

☐ Check that the brake pedal is secure and in good condition. Check also for signs of fluid leaks on the pedal, floor or carpets, which would indicate failed seals in the brake master cylinder.

☐ Check the servo unit (when applicable) by operating the brake pedal several times, then keeping the pedal depressed and starting the engine. As the engine starts, the pedal will move down slightly. If not, the vacuum hose or the servo itself may be faulty.

Steering wheel and column

☐ Examine the steering wheel for fractures or looseness of the hub, spokes or rim.

☐ Move the steering wheel from side to side and then up and down. Check that the steering wheel is not loose on the column, indicating wear or a loose retaining nut. Continue moving the steering wheel as before, but also turn it slightly from left to right.

☐ Check that the steering wheel is not loose on the column, and that there is no abnormal movement of the steering wheel, indicating wear in the column support bearings or couplings.

Windscreen and mirrors

☐ The windscreen must be free of cracks or other significant damage within the driver's field of view. (Small stone chips are acceptable.) Rear view mirrors must be secure, intact, and capable of being adjusted.

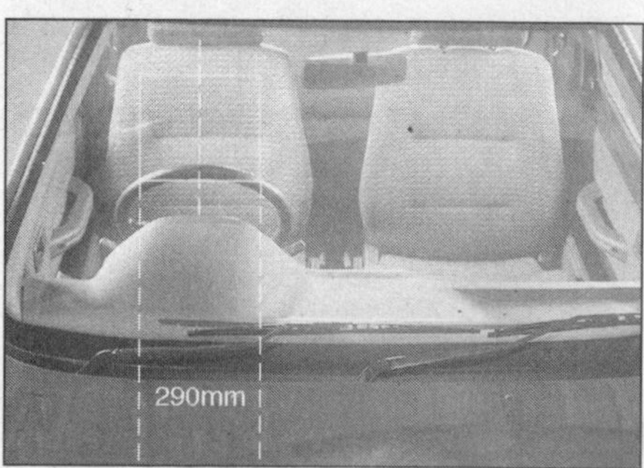

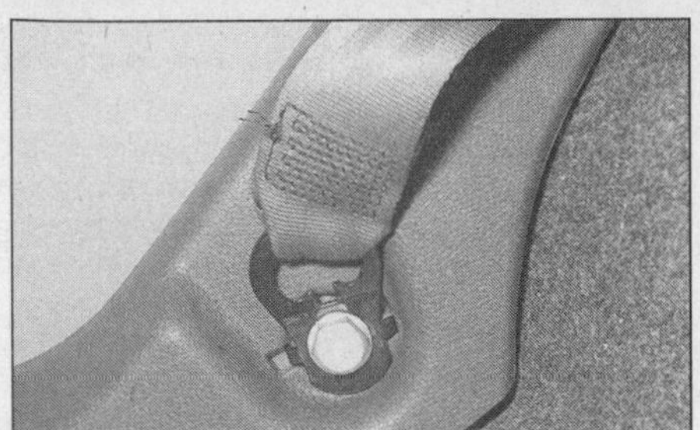

Seat belts and seats

Note: *The following checks are applicable to all seat belts, front and rear.*

☐ Examine the webbing of all the belts (including rear belts if fitted) for cuts, serious fraying or deterioration. Fasten and unfasten each belt to check the buckles. If applicable, check the retracting mechanism. Check the security of all seat belt mountings accessible from inside the vehicle.

☐ The front seats themselves must be securely attached and the backrests must lock in the upright position.

Doors

☐ Both front doors must be able to be opened and closed from outside and inside, and must latch securely when closed.

2 Checks carried out WITH THE VEHICLE ON THE GROUND

Vehicle identification

☐ Number plates must be in good condition, secure and legible, with letters and numbers correctly spaced – spacing at (A) should be twice that at (B).

☐ The VIN plate and/or homologation plate must be legible.

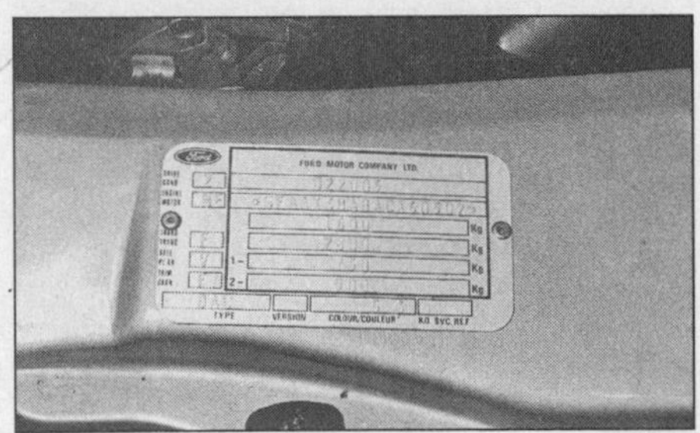

Electrical equipment

☐ Switch on the ignition and check the operation of the horn.

☐ Check the windscreen washers and wipers, examining the wiper blades; renew damaged or perished blades. Also check the operation of the stop-lights.

☐ Check the operation of the sidelights and number plate lights. The lenses and reflectors must be secure, clean and undamaged.

☐ Check the operation and alignment of the headlights. The headlight reflectors must not be tarnished and the lenses must be undamaged.

☐ Switch on the ignition and check the operation of the direction indicators (including the instrument panel tell-tale) and the hazard warning lights. Operation of the sidelights and stop-lights must not affect the indicators - if it does, the cause is usually a bad earth at the rear light cluster.

☐ Check the operation of the rear foglight(s), including the warning light on the instrument panel or in the switch.

Footbrake

☐ Examine the master cylinder, brake pipes and servo unit for leaks, loose mountings, corrosion or other damage.

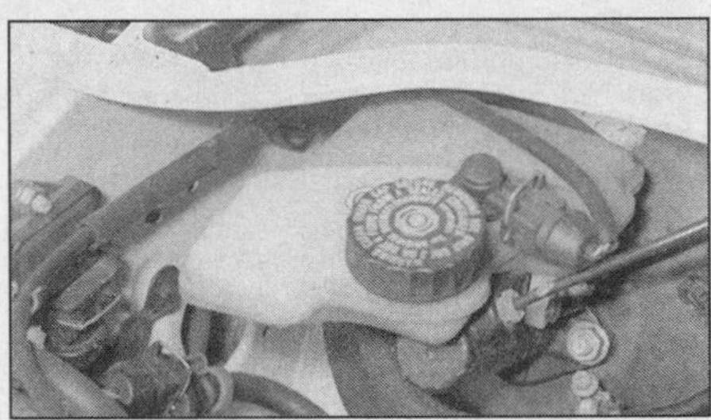

☐ The fluid reservoir must be secure and the fluid level must be between the upper (**A**) and lower (**B**) markings.

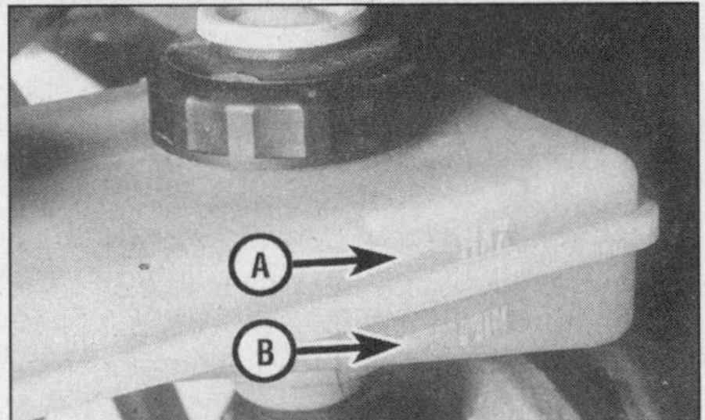

☐ Inspect both front brake flexible hoses for cracks or deterioration of the rubber. Turn the steering from lock to lock, and ensure that the hoses do not contact the wheel, tyre, or any part of the steering or suspension mechanism. With the brake pedal firmly depressed, check the hoses for bulges or leaks under pressure.

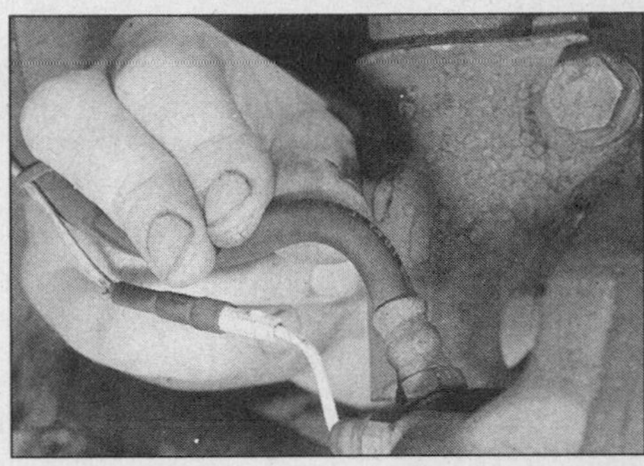

Steering and suspension

☐ Have your assistant turn the steering wheel from side to side slightly, up to the point where the steering gear just begins to transmit this movement to the roadwheels. Check for excessive free play between the steering wheel and the steering gear, indicating wear or insecurity of the steering column joints, the column-to-steering gear coupling, or the steering gear itself.

☐ Have your assistant turn the steering wheel more vigorously in each direction, so that the roadwheels just begin to turn. As this is done, examine all the steering joints, linkages, fittings and attachments. Renew any component that shows signs of wear or damage. On vehicles with power steering, check the security and condition of the steering pump, drivebelt and hoses.

☐ Check that the vehicle is standing level, and at approximately the correct ride height.

Shock absorbers

☐ Depress each corner of the vehicle in turn, then release it. The vehicle should rise and then settle in its normal position. If the vehicle continues to rise and fall, the shock absorber is defective. A shock absorber which has seized will also cause the vehicle to fail.

Exhaust system

□ Start the engine. With your assistant holding a rag over the tailpipe, check the entire system for leaks. Repair or renew leaking sections.

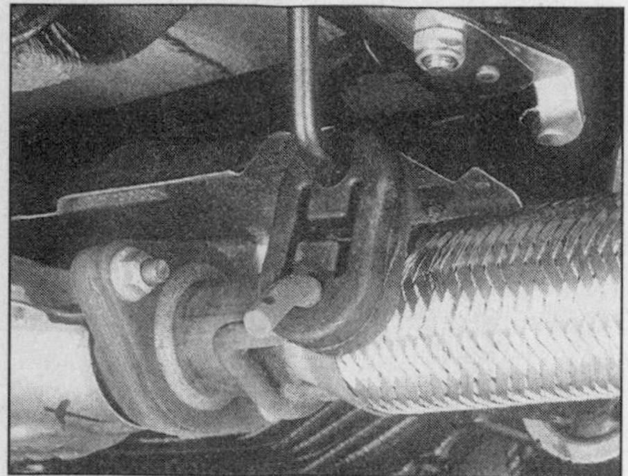

3 Checks carried out WITH THE VEHICLE RAISED AND THE WHEELS FREE TO TURN

Jack up the front and rear of the vehicle, and securely support it on axle stands. Position the stands clear of the suspension assemblies. Ensure that the wheels are clear of the ground and that the steering can be turned from lock to lock.

Steering mechanism

□ Have your assistant turn the steering from lock to lock. Check that the steering turns smoothly, and that no part of the steering mechanism, including a wheel or tyre, fouls any brake hose or pipe or any part of the body structure.

□ Examine the steering rack rubber gaiters for damage or insecurity of the retaining clips. If power steering is fitted, check for signs of damage or leakage of the fluid hoses, pipes or connections. Also check for excessive stiffness or binding of the steering, a missing split pin or locking device, or severe corrosion of the body structure within 30 cm of any steering component attachment point.

Front and rear suspension and wheel bearings

□ Starting at the front right-hand side, grasp the roadwheel at the 3 o'clock and 9 o'clock positions and shake it vigorously. Check for free play or insecurity at the wheel bearings, suspension balljoints, or suspension mountings, pivots and attachments.

□ Now grasp the wheel at the 12 o'clock and 6 o'clock positions and repeat the previous inspection. Spin the wheel, and check for roughness or tightness of the front wheel bearing.

□ If excess free play is suspected at a component pivot point, this can be confirmed by using a large screwdriver or similar tool and levering between the mounting and the component attachment. This will confirm whether the wear is in the pivot bush, its retaining bolt, or in the mounting itself (the bolt holes can often become elongated).

□ Carry out all the above checks at the other front wheel, and then at both rear wheels.

Springs and shock absorbers

□ Examine the suspension struts (when applicable) for serious fluid leakage, corrosion, or damage to the casing. Also check the security of the mounting points.

□ If coil springs are fitted, check that the spring ends locate in their seats, and that the spring is not corroded, cracked or broken.

□ If leaf springs are fitted, check that all leaves are intact, that the axle is securely attached to each spring, and that there is no deterioration of the spring eye mountings, bushes, and shackles.

□ The same general checks apply to vehicles fitted with other suspension types, such as torsion bars, hydraulic displacer units, etc. Ensure that all mountings and attachments are secure, that there are no signs of excessive wear, corrosion or damage, and (on hydraulic types) that there are no fluid leaks or damaged pipes.

□ Inspect the shock absorbers for signs of serious fluid leakage. Check for wear of the mounting bushes or attachments, or damage to the body of the unit.

Driveshafts (fwd vehicles only)

□ Rotate each front wheel in turn and inspect the constant velocity joint gaiters for splits or damage. Also check that each driveshaft is straight and undamaged.

Braking system

□ If possible without dismantling, check brake pad wear and disc condition. Ensure that the friction lining material has not worn excessively, (A) and that the discs are not fractured, pitted, scored or badly worn (B).

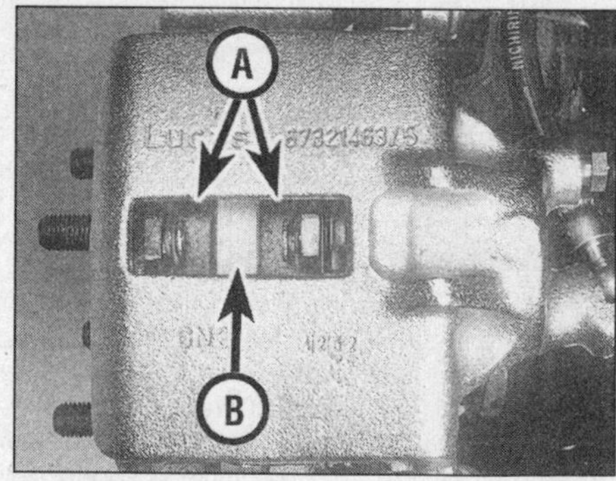

□ Examine all the rigid brake pipes underneath the vehicle, and the flexible hose(s) at the rear. Look for corrosion, chafing or insecurity of the pipes, and for signs of bulging under pressure, chafing, splits or deterioration of the flexible hoses.

□ Look for signs of fluid leaks at the brake calipers or on the brake backplates. Repair or renew leaking components.

□ Slowly spin each wheel, while your assistant depresses and releases the footbrake. Ensure that each brake is operating and does not bind when the pedal is released.

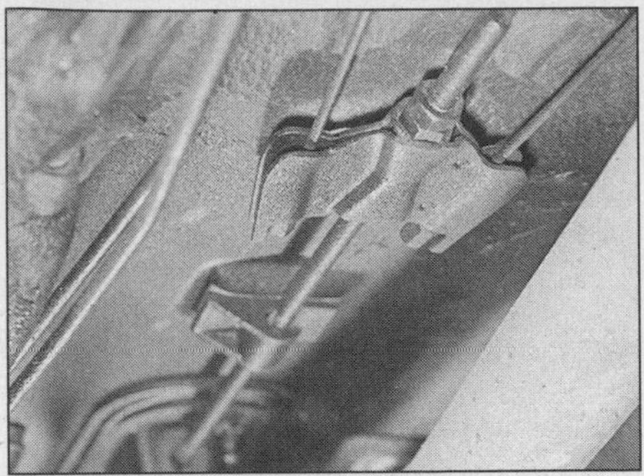

☐ Examine the handbrake mechanism, checking for frayed or broken cables, excessive corrosion, or wear or insecurity of the linkage. Check that the mechanism works on each relevant wheel, and releases fully, without binding.

☐ It is not possible to test brake efficiency without special equipment, but a road test can be carried out later to check that the vehicle pulls up in a straight line.

Fuel and exhaust systems

☐ Inspect the fuel tank (including the filler cap), fuel pipes, hoses and unions. All components must be secure and free from leaks.

☐ Examine the exhaust system over its entire length, checking for any damaged, broken or missing mountings, security of the retaining clamps and rust or corrosion.

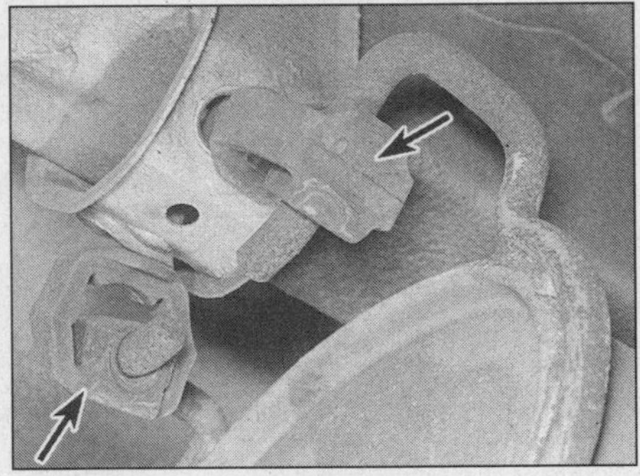

Wheels and tyres

☐ Examine the sidewalls and tread area of each tyre in turn. Check for cuts, tears, lumps, bulges, separation of the tread, and exposure of the ply or cord due to wear or damage. Check that the tyre bead is correctly seated on the wheel rim, that the valve is sound and

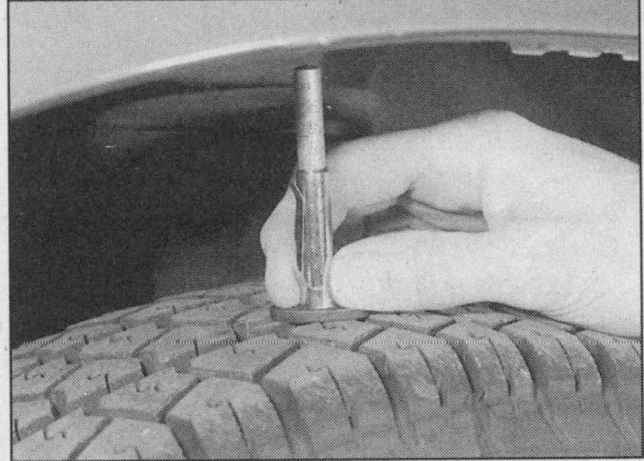

properly seated, and that the wheel is not distorted or damaged.

☐ Check that the tyres are of the correct size for the vehicle, that they are of the same size and type on each axle, and that the pressures are correct.

☐ Check the tyre tread depth. The legal minimum at the time of writing is 1.6 mm over at least three-quarters of the tread width. Abnormal tread wear may indicate incorrect front wheel alignment.

Body corrosion

☐ Check the condition of the entire vehicle structure for signs of corrosion in load-bearing areas. (These include chassis box sections, side sills, cross-members, pillars, and all suspension, steering, braking system and seat belt mountings and anchorages.) Any corrosion which has seriously reduced the thickness of a load-bearing area is likely to cause the vehicle to fail. In this case professional repairs are likely to be needed.

☐ Damage or corrosion which causes sharp or otherwise dangerous edges to be exposed will also cause the vehicle to fail.

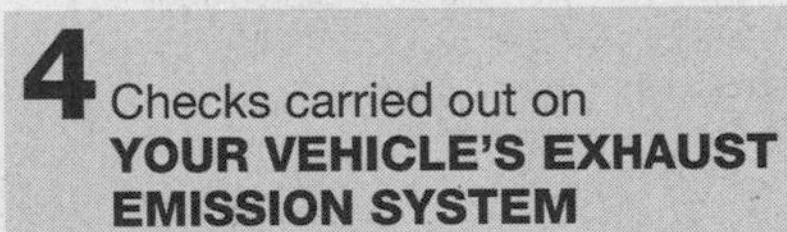

4 Checks carried out on **YOUR VEHICLE'S EXHAUST EMISSION SYSTEM**

Petrol models

☐ Have the engine at normal operating temperature, and make sure that it is in good tune (ignition system in good order, air filter element clean, etc).

☐ Before any measurements are carried out, raise the engine speed to around 2500 rpm, and hold it at this speed for 20 seconds. Allow the engine speed to return to idle, and watch for smoke emissions from the exhaust tailpipe. If the idle speed is obviously much too high, or if dense blue or clearly-visible black smoke comes from the tailpipe for more than 5 seconds, the vehicle will fail. As a rule of thumb, blue smoke signifies oil being burnt (engine wear) while black smoke signifies unburnt fuel (dirty air cleaner element, or other carburettor or fuel system fault).

☐ An exhaust gas analyser capable of measuring carbon monoxide (CO) and hydrocarbons (HC) is now needed. If such an instrument cannot be hired or borrowed, a local garage may agree to perform the check for a small fee.

CO emissions (mixture)

☐ At the time of writing, the maximum CO level at idle is 3.5% for vehicles first used after August 1986 and 4.5% for older vehicles. From January 1996 a much tighter limit (around 0.5%) applies to catalyst-equipped vehicles first used from August 1992. If the CO level cannot be reduced far enough to pass the test (and the fuel and ignition systems are otherwise in good condition) then the carburettor is badly worn, or there is some problem in the fuel injection system or catalytic converter (as applicable).

HC emissions

☐ With the CO emissions within limits, HC emissions must be no more than 1200 ppm (parts per million). If the vehicle fails this test at idle, it can be re-tested at around 2000 rpm; if the HC level is then 1200 ppm or less, this counts as a pass.

☐ Excessive HC emissions can be caused by oil being burnt, but they are more likely to be due to unburnt fuel.

Diesel models

☐ The only emission test applicable to Diesel engines is the measuring of exhaust smoke density. The test involves accelerating the engine several times to its maximum unloaded speed.

Note: *It is of the utmost importance that the engine timing belt is in good condition before the test is carried out.*

☐ Excessive smoke can be caused by a dirty air cleaner element. Otherwise, professional advice may be needed to find the cause.

Introduction

The vehicle owner who does his or her own maintenance according to the recommended service schedules should not have to use this section of the manual very often. Modern component reliability is such that, provided those items subject to wear or deterioration are inspected or renewed at the specified intervals, sudden failure is comparatively rare. Faults do not usually just happen as a result of sudden failure, but develop over a period of time. Major mechanical failures in particular are usually preceded by characteristic symptoms over hundreds or even thousands of miles. Those components which do occasionally fail without warning are often small and easily carried in the vehicle.

With any fault-finding, the first step is to decide where to begin investigations. Sometimes this is obvious, but on other occasions, a little detective work will be necessary. The owner who makes half a dozen haphazard adjustments or replacements may be successful in curing a fault (or its symptoms), but will be none the wiser if the fault recurs, and ultimately may have spent more time and money than was necessary. A calm and logical approach will be found to be more satisfactory in the long run. Always take into account any warning signs or abnormalities that may have been noticed in the period preceding the fault - power loss, high or low gauge readings, unusual smells, etc - and remember that failure of components such as fuses or spark plugs may only be pointers to some underlying fault.

These pages provide an easy-reference guide to the more common problems which may occur during the vehicle's life. These problems and their possible causes are grouped under headings such as Engine, Cooling system, etc. The Chapter and/or Section which deals with the problem is also shown in brackets. Whatever the fault, certain basic principles apply. These are as follows:

Verify the fault. This is simply a matter of being sure you know exactly what the symptoms are before starting work. This is particularly important if you are investigating a fault for someone else, who may not have described it very accurately.

Don't overlook the obvious. For example, if it won't start, is there fuel in the tank? (Don't take anyone else's word on this particular point, and don't trust the fuel gauge either!) If an electrical fault is indicated, look for loose or broken wires before digging out the test gear.

Cure the disease, not the symptom. Substituting a flat battery with a fully-charged one will get you off the hard shoulder, but if the underlying cause is not attended to, the new battery will go the same way. Similarly, changing oil-fouled spark plugs (petrol models) for a new set will get you moving again, but remember that the reason for the fouling (if it wasn't simply an incorrect grade of plug) will have to be established and corrected.

Don't take anything for granted. Particularly, don't forget that a "new" component may itself be defective (especially if it's been rattling around in the boot for months), and don't leave components out of a fault diagnosis sequence just because they are new or recently-fitted. When you do finally diagnose a difficult fault, you'll probably realise that all the evidence was there from the start.

1 Engine

Engine fails to rotate when attempting to start

- ☐ Battery terminal connections loose or corroded ("*Weekly checks*").
- ☐ Battery discharged or faulty (Chapter 5A).
- ☐ Broken, loose or disconnected wiring in the starting circuit (Chapter 5A).
- ☐ Automatic transmission not in "P" or "N" (Chapter 7B).
- ☐ Defective starter solenoid or switch (Chapter 5A).
- ☐ Defective starter motor (Chapter 5A).
- ☐ Starter pinion or flywheel ring gear teeth loose or broken (Chapter 2 or 5A).
- ☐ Engine earth strap broken or disconnected (Chapter 5A).

Engine rotates, but will not start

- ☐ Fuel tank empty.
- ☐ Battery discharged (engine rotates slowly) (Chapter 5A).
- ☐ Battery terminal connections loose or corroded ("*Weekly checks*").
- ☐ Alarm or immobiliser fault (Chapter 12).
- ☐ Ignition components damp or damaged (Chapter 1 or 5B).
- ☐ Fuel cut-off switch activated (Chapter 4A).
- ☐ Engine filled with higher-viscosity oil than recommended ("*Weekly checks*").
- ☐ Ignition timing incorrect (Chapter 5B).
- ☐ Broken, loose or disconnected wiring in the ignition circuit (Chapter 5B).
- ☐ Worn, faulty or incorrectly-gapped spark plugs (Chapter 1).
- ☐ Fuel injection system fault (Chapter 4A).
- ☐ Major mechanical failure (eg camshaft drive) (Chapter 2).

Engine difficult to start when cold

- ☐ Battery discharged (Chapter 5A).
- ☐ Ignition timing incorrect (Chapter 5B).
- ☐ Battery terminal connections loose or corroded ("*Weekly checks*").
- ☐ Worn, faulty or incorrectly-gapped spark plugs (Chapter 1).
- ☐ Engine filled with higher-viscosity oil than recommended ("*Weekly checks*").
- ☐ Fuel injection system fault (Chapter 4A).
- ☐ Other ignition system fault (Chapter 5B).
- ☐ Low cylinder compressions (Chapter 2A or 2B).

Engine difficult to start when hot

- ☐ Air filter element dirty or clogged (Chapter 1).
- ☐ Fuel injection system fault (Chapter 4A).
- ☐ Low cylinder compressions (Chapter 2A or 2B).
- ☐ Ignition timing incorrect (Chapter 5B).

Starter motor noisy or excessively-rough in engagement

- ☐ Starter pinion or flywheel ring gear teeth loose or broken (Chapter 2 or 5A).
- ☐ Starter motor mounting bolts loose or missing (Chapter 5A).
- ☐ Starter motor internal components worn or damaged (Chapter 5A).

Engine starts, but stops immediately

- ☐ Loose or faulty electrical connections in the ignition circuit (Chapter 5B).
- ☐ Vacuum leak at the inlet manifold (Chapter 4A or 4B).
- ☐ Blocked injector/fuel injection system fault (Chapter 4A or 4B).

Engine idles erratically

- ☐ Air filter element clogged (Chapter 1).
- ☐ Vacuum leak at the inlet manifold or associated hoses (Chapter 4A or 4B).
- ☐ Worn, faulty or incorrectly-gapped spark plugs (Chapter 1).
- ☐ Uneven or low cylinder compressions (Chapter 2A or 2B).
- ☐ Camshaft lobes worn (Chapter 2A or 2B).
- ☐ Timing belt or chains incorrectly tensioned (Chapter 2A or 2B).
- ☐ Blocked injector/fuel injection system fault (Chapter 4A or 4B).

Engine misfires at idle speed

- ☐ Worn, faulty or incorrectly-gapped spark plugs (Chapter 1).
- ☐ Faulty spark plug HT leads (Chapter 5B).
- ☐ Vacuum leak at the inlet manifold or associated hoses (Chapter 4A or 4B).
- ☐ Blocked injector/fuel injection system fault (Chapter 4A or 4B).
- ☐ Uneven or low cylinder compressions (Chapter 2A or 2B).
- ☐ Disconnected, leaking, or perished crankcase ventilation hoses (Chapter 4B).

Engine misfires throughout the driving speed range

- ☐ Fuel filter choked (Chapter 1).
- ☐ Fuel pump faulty, or delivery pressure low (Chapter 4A).
- ☐ Fuel tank vent blocked, or fuel pipes restricted (Chapter 4A or 4B).
- ☐ Vacuum leak at the inlet manifold or associated hoses (Chapter 4A or 4B).
- ☐ Worn, faulty or incorrectly-gapped spark plugs (Chapter 1).
- ☐ Faulty spark plug HT leads (Chapter 5B).
- ☐ Faulty ignition coil (Chapter 5B).
- ☐ Uneven or low cylinder compressions (Chapter 2A or 2B).
- ☐ Blocked injector/fuel injection system fault (Chapter 4A or 4B).

Engine hesitates on acceleration

- ☐ Worn, faulty or incorrectly-gapped spark plugs (Chapter 1).
- ☐ Vacuum leak at the inlet manifold or associated hoses (Chapter 4A or 4B).
- ☐ Blocked injector/fuel injection system fault (Chapter 4A or 4B).

Engine stalls

- ☐ Vacuum leak at the inlet manifold or associated hoses (Chapter 4A or 4B).
- ☐ Fuel filter choked (Chapter 1).
- ☐ Fuel pump faulty, or delivery pressure low (Chapter 4A).
- ☐ Fuel tank vent blocked, or fuel pipes restricted (Chapter 4A or 4B).
- ☐ Blocked injector/fuel injection system fault (Chapter 4A or 4B).

1 Engine (continued)

Engine lacks power

- ☐ Timing belt or chains incorrectly fitted or tensioned (Chapter 2A or 2B).
- ☐ Fuel filter choked (Chapter 1).
- ☐ Ignition timing incorrect (Chapter 5B).
- ☐ Fuel pump faulty, or delivery pressure low (Chapter 4A).
- ☐ Uneven or low cylinder compressions (Chapter 2A or 2B).
- ☐ Worn, faulty or incorrectly-gapped spark plugs (Chapter 1).
- ☐ Vacuum leak at the inlet manifold or associated hoses (Chapter 4A or 4B).
- ☐ Blocked injector/fuel injection system fault (Chapter 4A or 4B).
- ☐ Brakes binding (Chapter 1 or 9).
- ☐ Clutch slipping (Chapter 6).

Engine backfires

- ☐ Timing belt or chains incorrectly fitted or tensioned (Chapter 2A or 2B).
- ☐ Vacuum leak at the inlet manifold or associated hoses (Chapter 4A or 4B).
- ☐ Blocked injector/fuel injection system fault (Chapter 4A or 4B).
- ☐ Ignition timing incorrect (Chapter 5B).

Oil pressure warning light illuminated with engine running

- ☐ Low oil level, or incorrect oil grade ("*Weekly checks*").
- ☐ Worn engine bearings and/or oil pump (Chapter 2C).
- ☐ High engine operating temperature (Chapter 3).
- ☐ Oil pressure relief valve defective (Chapter 2A or 2B).
- ☐ Oil pick-up strainer clogged (Chapter 2A or 2B).

Engine runs-on after switching off

- ☐ Excessive carbon build-up in engine - overhaul required (Chapter 2C).
- ☐ High engine operating temperature (Chapter 3).
- ☐ Fuel injection system fault (Chapter 4A or 4B).

Engine noises

Pre-ignition (pinking) or knocking during acceleration or under load

- ☐ Ignition timing incorrect/ignition system fault (Chapter 5B).
- ☐ Incorrect grade of spark plugs (Chapter 1).
- ☐ Incorrect grade of fuel (Chapter 4A).
- ☐ Vacuum leak at the throttle body, inlet manifold or associated hoses (Chapter 4A or 4B).
- ☐ Excessive carbon build-up in engine - overhaul required (Chapter 2C).
- ☐ Blocked injector/fuel injection system fault (Chapter 4A).

Whistling or wheezing noises

- ☐ Leaking inlet manifold gasket (Chapter 4A).
- ☐ Leaking exhaust manifold gasket or pipe-to-manifold joint (Chapter 4A).
- ☐ Leaking vacuum hose (Chapter 4, 5B or 9).
- ☐ Blowing cylinder head gasket (Chapter 2A or 2B).

Tapping or rattling noises

- ☐ Worn hydraulic tappet or camshaft (Chapter 2A or 2B).
- ☐ Ancillary component fault (water pump, alternator, etc) (Chapter 3, 5A, etc).

Knocking or thumping noises

- ☐ Worn big-end bearings (regular heavy knocking, perhaps less under load) (Chapter 2C).
- ☐ Worn main bearings (rumbling and knocking, perhaps worsening under load) (Chapter 2C).
- ☐ Piston slap (most noticeable when cold) - engine worn (Chapter 2C).
- ☐ Ancillary component fault (water pump, alternator, etc) (Chapter 3, 5A, etc).

2 Cooling system

Overheating

- ☐ Insufficient coolant in system ("*Weekly checks*").
- ☐ Auxiliary drivebelt broken or drivebelt tensioner faulty (Chapter 1).
- ☐ Thermostat faulty (Chapter 3).
- ☐ Radiator core blocked, or grille restricted (Chapter 3).
- ☐ Electric cooling fan or thermoswitch faulty (Chapter 3).
- ☐ Pressure cap faulty (Chapter 3).
- ☐ Ignition timing incorrect/ignition system fault (Chapter 5B).
- ☐ Inaccurate temperature gauge sender unit (Chapter 3).
- ☐ Airlock in cooling system (Chapter 1).

Overcooling

- ☐ Thermostat faulty (Chapter 3).
- ☐ Inaccurate temperature gauge sender unit (Chapter 3).

External coolant leakage

- ☐ Deteriorated or damaged hoses or hose clips (Chapter 1).
- ☐ Radiator core or heater matrix leaking (Chapter 3).
- ☐ Pressure cap faulty (Chapter 3).
- ☐ Water pump seal leaking (Chapter 3).
- ☐ Boiling due to overheating (Chapter 3).
- ☐ Core plug leaking (Chapter 2C).

Internal coolant leakage

- ☐ Leaking cylinder head gasket (Chapter 2A or 2B).
- ☐ Cracked cylinder head or cylinder bore (Chapter 2A, 2B or 2C).

Corrosion

- ☐ Infrequent draining and flushing (Chapter 1).
- ☐ Incorrect coolant mixture or inappropriate coolant type ("*Weekly checks*").

3 Fuel and exhaust systems

Excessive fuel consumption

- ☐ Air filter element dirty or clogged (Chapter 1).
- ☐ Fuel injection system fault (Chapter 4A).
- ☐ Ignition timing incorrect/ignition system fault (Chapter 5B).
- ☐ Tyres under-inflated ("*Weekly checks*").
- ☐ Brakes binding (Chapter 1 or 9).

Fuel leakage and/or fuel odour

- ☐ Damaged or corroded fuel tank, pipes or connections (Chapter 4A or 4B).

Excessive noise or fumes from exhaust system

- ☐ Leaking exhaust system or manifold joints (Chapter 1 or 4A).
- ☐ Leaking, corroded or damaged silencers or pipe (Chapter 1 or 4A).
- ☐ Broken mountings causing body or suspension contact (Chapter 1 or 4A).

4 Clutch

Pedal travels to floor - no pressure or very little resistance

- ☐ Broken clutch cable - cable-operated clutch (Chapter 6).
- ☐ Clutch out of adjustment (Chapter 6).
- ☐ Clutch master cylinder failure - hydraulic clutch (Chapter 6).
- ☐ Clutch fluid leak - hydraulic clutch (Chapter 6).
- ☐ Broken clutch release bearing or fork, as applicable (Chapter 6).
- ☐ Broken diaphragm spring in clutch pressure plate (Chapter 6).

Clutch fails to disengage (unable to select gears)

- ☐ Clutch out of adjustment (Chapter 6).
- ☐ Air in clutch hydraulic system - bleeding required - hydraulic clutch (Chapter 6).
- ☐ Clutch master or slave cylinder fault - hydraulic clutch (Chapter 6).
- ☐ Clutch disc sticking on gearbox input shaft splines (Chapter 6).
- ☐ Clutch disc sticking to flywheel or pressure plate (Chapter 6).
- ☐ Faulty pressure plate assembly (Chapter 6).
- ☐ Clutch release mechanism worn or incorrectly assembled - cable-operated clutch (Chapter 6).

Clutch slips (engine speed increases, with no increase in vehicle speed)

- ☐ Clutch out of adjustment (Chapter 6).
- ☐ Clutch disc linings excessively worn (Chapter 6).
- ☐ Clutch disc linings contaminated with oil or grease (Chapter 6).
- ☐ Faulty pressure plate or weak diaphragm spring (Chapter 6).

Judder as clutch is engaged

- ☐ Clutch disc linings contaminated with oil or grease (Chapter 6).
- ☐ Clutch disc linings excessively worn (Chapter 6).
- ☐ Clutch cable sticking or frayed - cable-operated clutch (Chapter 6).
- ☐ Faulty or distorted pressure plate or diaphragm spring (Chapter 6).
- ☐ Worn or loose engine or gearbox mountings (Chapter 2A or 2B).
- ☐ Clutch disc hub or gearbox input shaft splines worn (Chapter 6).

Noise when depressing or releasing clutch pedal

- ☐ Worn clutch release bearing (Chapter 6).
- ☐ Worn or dry clutch pedal bushes (Chapter 6).
- ☐ Clutch cable sticking or frayed - cable-operated clutch (Chapter 6).
- ☐ Clutch master cylinder fault - hydraulic clutch (Chapter 6).
- ☐ Faulty pressure plate assembly (Chapter 6).
- ☐ Pressure plate diaphragm spring broken (Chapter 6).
- ☐ Broken clutch disc cushioning springs (Chapter 6).

5 Manual transmission

Noisy in neutral with engine running

- ☐ Input shaft bearings worn (noise apparent with clutch pedal released, but not when depressed) (Chapter 7A).*
- ☐ Clutch release bearing worn (noise apparent with clutch pedal depressed, possibly less when released) (Chapter 6).

Noisy in one particular gear

- ☐ Worn, damaged or chipped gear teeth (Chapter 7A).*

Difficulty engaging gears

- ☐ Clutch fault (Chapter 6).
- ☐ Worn or damaged gearchange linkage (Chapter 7A).
- ☐ Incorrectly-adjusted gearchange linkage (Chapter 7A).
- ☐ Worn synchroniser units (Chapter 7A).*

Jumps out of gear

- ☐ Worn or damaged gearchange linkage (Chapter 7A).
- ☐ Incorrectly-adjusted gearchange linkage (Chapter 7A).
- ☐ Worn synchroniser units (Chapter 7A).*
- ☐ Worn selector forks (Chapter 7A).*

Vibration

- ☐ Lack of oil (Chapter 1).
- ☐ Worn bearings (Chapter 7A).*

Lubricant leaks

- ☐ Leaking differential output oil seal (Chapter 7A).
- ☐ Leaking housing joint (Chapter 7A).*
- ☐ Leaking input shaft oil seal (Chapter 7A).*

**Although the corrective action necessary to remedy the symptoms described is beyond the scope of the home mechanic, the above information should be helpful in isolating the cause of the condition, so that the owner can communicate clearly with a professional mechanic.*

6 Automatic transmission

Note: *Due to the complexity of the automatic transmission, it is difficult for the home mechanic to properly diagnose and service this unit. For problems other than the following, the vehicle should be taken to a dealer service department or automatic transmission specialist. Do not be too hasty in removing the transmission if a fault is suspected, as most of the testing is carried out with the unit still fitted.*

Fluid leakage

- ☐ Automatic transmission fluid is usually dark in colour. Fluid leaks should not be confused with engine oil, which can easily be blown onto the transmission by airflow.
- ☐ To determine the source of a leak, first remove all built-up dirt and grime from the transmission housing and surrounding areas using a degreasing agent, or by steam-cleaning. Drive the vehicle at low speed, so airflow will not blow the leak far from its source. Raise and support the vehicle, and determine where the leak is coming from.

General gear selection problems

- ☐ Chapter 7B deals with checking and adjusting the selector cable on automatic transmissions. The following are common problems which may be caused by a poorly-adjusted cable:
  - a) *Engine starting in gears other than Park or Neutral.*
  - b) *Indicator panel indicating a gear other than the one actually being used.*
  - c) *Vehicle moves when in Park or Neutral.*
  - d) *Poor gear shift quality or erratic gear changes.*
- ☐ Refer to Chapter 7B for the selector cable adjustment procedure.

Transmission will not downshift (kickdown) with accelerator pedal fully depressed

- ☐ Low transmission fluid level (Chapter 1).
- ☐ Incorrect selector cable adjustment (Chapter 7B).

6 Automatic transmission (continued)

Engine will not start in any gear, or starts in gears other than Park or Neutral

☐ Incorrect selector cable adjustment (Chapter 7B).

Transmission slips, shifts roughly, is noisy, or has no drive in forward or reverse gears

☐ There are many probable causes for the above problems, but unless there is a very obvious reason (such as a loose or corroded wiring plug connection on or near the transmission), the car should be taken to a Ford dealer for the fault to be diagnosed. The transmission control unit incorporates a self-diagnosis facility, and any fault codes can quickly be read and interpreted by a Ford dealer with the proper diagnostic equipment.

7 Driveshafts

Clicking or knocking noise on turns (at slow speed on full-lock)

☐ Lack of constant velocity joint lubricant, possibly due to damaged gaiter (Chapter 8).
☐ Worn outer constant velocity joint (Chapter 8).

Vibration when accelerating or decelerating

☐ Worn inner constant velocity joint (Chapter 8).
☐ Bent or distorted driveshaft (Chapter 8).

8 Braking system

Note: *Before assuming that a brake problem exists, make sure that the tyres are in good condition and correctly inflated, that the front wheel alignment is correct, the front wheels are balanced, and that the vehicle is not loaded with weight in an unequal manner. The alignment of the front subframe is also important - if the vehicle pulls to one side, it may be worth having the subframe alignment checked and adjusted by a Ford dealer, in addition to the more usual checks. Apart from checking the condition of all wiring and hose connections, any faults occurring on the anti-lock braking system should be referred to a Ford dealer for diagnosis.*

Vehicle pulls to one side under braking

☐ Worn, defective, damaged or contaminated brake pads/shoes on one side (Chapter 1 or 9).
☐ Seized or partially-seized front brake caliper/wheel cylinder piston (Chapter 1 or 9).
☐ A mixture of brake pad/shoe lining materials fitted between sides (Chapter 1 or 9).
☐ Brake caliper or backplate mounting bolts loose (Chapter 9).
☐ Worn or damaged steering or suspension components (Chapter 1 or 10).

Noise (grinding or high-pitched squeal) when brakes applied

☐ Brake pad or shoe friction lining material worn down to metal backing (Chapter 1 or 9).
☐ Excessive corrosion of brake disc or drum. may be apparent after the vehicle has been standing for some time (Chapter 1 or 9).
☐ Foreign object (stone chipping, etc) trapped between brake disc and shield (Chapter 1 or 9).

Excessive brake pedal travel

☐ Inoperative rear brake self-adjust mechanism - drum brakes (Chapter 1 or 9).
☐ Faulty master cylinder (Chapter 9).
☐ Air in hydraulic system - bleeding required (Chapter 9).
☐ Brake fluid contaminated - change fluid (Chapter 1).
☐ Faulty vacuum servo unit (Chapter 9).

Brake pedal feels spongy when depressed

☐ Air in hydraulic system - bleeding required (Chapter 9).
☐ Brake fluid contaminated - change fluid (Chapter 1).
☐ Deteriorated flexible rubber brake hoses (Chapter 1 or 9).
☐ ☐aster cylinder mounting nuts loose (Chapter 9).
☐ Faulty master cylinder (Chapter 9).

Excessive brake pedal effort required to stop vehicle

☐ Faulty vacuum servo unit (Chapter 9).
☐ Disconnected, damaged or insecure brake servo vacuum hose (Chapter 9).
☐ Primary or secondary hydraulic circuit failure (Chapter 9).
☐ Seized brake caliper or wheel cylinder piston(s) (Chapter 9).
☐ Brake pads or brake shoes incorrectly fitted (Chapter 1 or 9).
☐ Incorrect grade of brake pads or brake shoes fitted (Chapter 1 or 9).
☐ Brake pads or brake shoe linings contaminated (Chapter 1 or 9).

Judder felt through brake pedal or steering wheel when braking

☐ Excessive run-out or distortion of discs/drums (Chapter 9).
☐ Brake pad or brake shoe linings worn (Chapter 1 or 9).
☐ Brake caliper or brake backplate mounting bolts loose (Chapter 9).
☐ Wear in suspension or steering components or mountings (Chapter 1 or 10).
☐ Vibration through pedal - Anti-lock Braking System (ABS) in operation - no fault (models with ABS).

Brakes binding

☐ Seized brake caliper or wheel cylinder piston(s) (Chapter 9).
☐ Incorrectly-adjusted handbrake mechanism (Chapter 9).
☐ Faulty master cylinder (Chapter 9).

Rear wheels locking under normal braking

☐ Rear brake shoe linings contaminated (Chapter 1 or 9).
☐ Faulty brake pressure regulator (Chapter 9).

9 Suspension and steering

Note: *Before diagnosing suspension or steering faults, be sure that the trouble is not due to incorrect tyre pressures, mixtures of tyre types, worn tyres, or binding brakes. The alignment of the front subframe is also important - if the vehicle pulls to one side or exhibits abnormal front tyre wear, it may be worth having the subframe alignment checked and adjusted by a Ford dealer, in addition to the more usual checks.*

Vehicle pulls to one side

- ☐ Defective or worn tyre ("*Weekly checks*").
- ☐ Tyre pressure low on one side of the car ("*Weekly checks*").
- ☐ Excessive wear in suspension or steering components (Chapter 1 or 10).
- ☐ Incorrect front wheel alignment (Chapter 10).
- ☐ Front subframe out of alignment - see note above.
- ☐ Accident damage to steering or suspension components (Chapter 1).

Wheel wobble and vibration

- ☐ Front roadwheels out of balance (vibration felt mainly through the steering wheel) ("*Weekly checks*" and Chapter 1).
- ☐ Rear roadwheels out of balance (vibration felt throughout the vehicle) ("*Weekly checks*" and Chapter 1).
- ☐ Roadwheels damaged or distorted ("*Weekly checks*").
- ☐ Faulty, worn or damaged tyre ("*Weekly checks*").
- ☐ Worn steering or suspension joints, bushes or components (Chapter 1 or 10).
- ☐ Wheel bolts loose (Chapter 1).

Excessive pitching and/or rolling around corners, or during braking

- ☐ Defective shock absorbers (Chapter 1 or 10).
- ☐ Broken or weak spring and/or suspension component (Chapter 1 or 10).
- ☐ Worn or damaged anti-roll bar or mountings (Chapter 10).

Wandering or general instability

- ☐ Incorrect front wheel alignment (Chapter 10).
- ☐ Front subframe out of alignment - see note at the start of this Section.
- ☐ Worn steering or suspension joints, bushes or components (Chapter 1 or 10).
- ☐ Roadwheels out of balance ("*Weekly checks*" and Chapter 1).
- ☐ Faulty or damaged tyre ("*Weekly checks*").
- ☐ Wheel bolts loose (Chapter 1).
- ☐ Defective shock absorbers (Chapter 1 or 10).

Excessively-stiff steering

- ☐ Incorrect power steering fluid level ("*Weekly checks*").
- ☐ Lack of steering gear lubricant (Chapter 10).
- ☐ Seized track rod end balljoint or suspension balljoint (Chapter 1 or 10).
- ☐ Broken auxiliary drivebelt or drivebelt tensioner fault - power steering (Chapter 1).
- ☐ Incorrect front wheel alignment (Chapter 10).
- ☐ Steering rack or column bent or damaged (Chapter 10).

Excessive play in steering

- ☐ Worn steering column flexible coupling (Chapter 10).
- ☐ Worn steering track rod end balljoints (Chapter 1 or 10).
- ☐ Worn rack-and-pinion steering gear (Chapter 10).
- ☐ Worn steering or suspension joints, bushes or components (Chapter 1 or 10).

Lack of power assistance

- ☐ Broken or incorrectly-adjusted auxiliary drivebelt (Chapter 1).
- ☐ Incorrect power steering fluid level ("*Weekly checks*").
- ☐ Restriction in power steering fluid hoses (Chapter 1).
- ☐ Faulty power steering pump (Chapter 10).
- ☐ Faulty rack-and-pinion steering gear (Chapter 10).

Noises from power steering system

- ☐ Air in hydraulic system - bleeding required (Chapter 10).
- ☐ Faulty power steering pump (Chapter 10).
- ☐ High-pressure pipes poorly routed (Chapter 10).

Tyre wear excessive

Tyres worn on inside or outside edges

- ☐ Tyres under-inflated (wear on both edges) ("*Weekly checks*").
- ☐ Incorrect camber or castor angles (wear on one edge only) (Chapter 10).
- ☐ Worn steering or suspension joints, bushes or components (Chapter 1 or 10).
- ☐ Front subframe out of alignment - see note at the start of this Section.
- ☐ Excessively-hard cornering.
- ☐ Accident damage.

Tyre treads exhibit feathered edges

- ☐ Incorrect toe setting (Chapter 10).

Tyres worn in centre of tread

- ☐ Tyres over-inflated ("*Weekly checks*").

Tyres worn on inside and outside edges

- ☐ Tyres under-inflated ("*Weekly checks*").

Tyres worn unevenly

- ☐ Tyres/wheels out of balance ("*Weekly checks*" and Chapter 1).
- ☐ Excessive wheel or tyre run-out ("*Weekly checks*").
- ☐ Worn shock absorbers (Chapter 1 or 10).
- ☐ Faulty tyre ("*Weekly checks*").

10 Electrical system

Note: *For problems associated with the starting system, refer to the faults listed under "Engine" earlier in this Section.*

Battery will not hold a charge for more than a few days

- ☐ Battery defective internally (Chapter 5A).
- ☐ Battery terminal connections loose or corroded ("*Weekly checks*").
- ☐ Auxiliary drivebelt worn or incorrectly adjusted (Chapter 1 or 2).
- ☐ Alternator not charging at correct output (Chapter 5A).
- ☐ Alternator or voltage regulator faulty (Chapter 5A).
- ☐ Short-circuit causing continual battery drain (Chapters 5A and 12).

10 Electrical system (continued)

Ignition/no-charge warning light remains illuminated with engine running

- ☐ Auxiliary drivebelt broken, worn, or incorrectly adjusted (Chapter 1).
- ☐ Alternator brushes worn, sticking, or dirty (Chapter 5A).
- ☐ Alternator brush springs weak or broken (Chapter 5A).
- ☐ Internal fault in alternator or voltage regulator (Chapter 5A).
- ☐ Broken, disconnected, or loose wiring in charging circuit (Chapter 5A).

Ignition/no-charge warning light fails to come on

- ☐ Warning light bulb blown (Chapter 12).
- ☐ Broken, disconnected, or loose wiring in warning light circuit (Chapter 12).
- ☐ Alternator faulty (Chapter 5A).

Lights inoperative

- ☐ Bulb blown (Chapter 12).
- ☐ Corrosion of bulb or bulbholder contacts (Chapter 12).
- ☐ Blown fuse (Chapter 12).
- ☐ Faulty relay (Chapter 12).
- ☐ Broken, loose, or disconnected wiring (Chapter 12).
- ☐ Faulty switch (Chapter 12).

Instrument readings inaccurate or erratic

Instrument readings increase with engine speed

- ☐ Faulty voltage stabiliser (Chapter 12).

Fuel or temperature gauges give no reading

- ☐ Faulty gauge sender unit (Chapter 3 or 4A).
- ☐ Wiring open-circuit (Chapter 12).
- ☐ Faulty gauge (Chapter 12).

Fuel or temperature gauges give continuous maximum reading

- ☐ Faulty gauge sender unit (Chapter 3 or 4A).
- ☐ Wiring short-circuit (Chapter 12).
- ☐ Faulty gauge (Chapter 12).

Horn inoperative, or unsatisfactory in operation

Horn operates all the time

- ☐ Horn push either earthed or stuck down (Chapter 12).
- ☐ Horn cable-to-horn push earthed (Chapter 12).

Horn fails to operate

- ☐ Blown fuse (Chapter 12).
- ☐ Cable or cable connections loose, broken or disconnected (Chapter 12).
- ☐ Faulty horn (Chapter 12).

Horn emits intermittent or unsatisfactory sound

- ☐ Cable connections loose (Chapter 12).
- ☐ Horn mountings loose (Chapter 12).
- ☐ Faulty horn (Chapter 12).

Windscreen/tailgate wipers inoperative, or unsatisfactory in operation

Wipers fail to operate, or operate very slowly

- ☐ Wiper blades stuck to screen, or linkage seized or binding ("*Weekly checks*" or Chapter 12).
- ☐ Blown fuse ("*Weekly checks*" or Chapter 12).
- ☐ Cable or cable connections loose, broken or disconnected (Chapter 12).
- ☐ Faulty relay (Chapter 12).
- ☐ Faulty wiper motor (Chapter 12).

Wiper blades sweep over too large or too small an area of the glass

- ☐ Wiper arms incorrectly positioned on spindles (Chapter 12).
- ☐ Excessive wear of wiper linkage (Chapter 12).
- ☐ Wiper motor or linkage mountings loose or insecure (Chapter 12).

Wiper blades fail to clean the glass effectively

- ☐ Wiper blade rubbers worn or perished ("*Weekly checks*").
- ☐ Wiper arm tension springs broken, or arm pivots seized (Chapter 12).
- ☐ Insufficient windscreen washer additive to adequately remove road film ("*Weekly checks*").

Windscreen/tailgate washers inoperative, or unsatisfactory in operation

One or more washer jets inoperative

- ☐ Blocked washer jet.
- ☐ Disconnected, kinked or restricted fluid hose (Chapter 12).
- ☐ Insufficient fluid in washer reservoir ("*Weekly checks*").

Washer pump fails to operate

- ☐ Broken or disconnected wiring or connections (Chapter 12).
- ☐ Blown fuse ("*Weekly checks*" or Chapter 12).
- ☐ Faulty washer switch (Chapter 12).
- ☐ Faulty washer pump (Chapter 12).

Washer pump runs for some time before fluid is emitted from jets

- ☐ Faulty one-way valve in fluid supply hose (Chapter 12).

Electric windows inoperative, or unsatisfactory in operation

Window glass will only move in one direction

- ☐ Faulty switch (Chapter 12).

Window glass slow to move

- ☐ Regulator seized or damaged, or in need of lubrication (Chapter 11).
- ☐ Door internal components or trim fouling regulator (Chapter 11).
- ☐ Faulty motor (Chapter 11).

Window glass fails to move

- ☐ Blown fuse (Chapter 12).
- ☐ Faulty relay (Chapter 12).
- ☐ Broken or disconnected wiring or connections (Chapter 12).
- ☐ Faulty motor (Chapter 11).

Central locking system inoperative, or unsatisfactory in operation

Complete system failure

- ☐ Blown fuse ("*Weekly checks*" or Chapter 12).
- ☐ Faulty relay (Chapter 12).
- ☐ Faulty control module (Chapter 11).
- ☐ Broken or disconnected wiring or connections (Chapter 12).

Latch locks but will not unlock, or unlocks but will not lock

- ☐ Broken or disconnected latch operating rods or levers (Chapter 11).
- ☐ Faulty relay (Chapter 12).
- ☐ Faulty control module (Chapter 11).

One solenoid/motor fails to operate

- ☐ Broken or disconnected wiring or connections (Chapter 12).
- ☐ Faulty operating assembly (Chapter 11).
- ☐ Broken, binding or disconnected latch operating rods or levers (Chapter 11).
- ☐ Fault in door latch (Chapter 11).

A

ABS (Anti-lock brake system) A system, usually electronically controlled, that senses incipient wheel lockup during braking and relieves hydraulic pressure at wheels that are about to skid.

Air bag An inflatable bag hidden in the steering wheel (driver's side) or the dash or glovebox (passenger side). In a head-on collision, the bags inflate, preventing the driver and front passenger from being thrown forward into the steering wheel or windscreen.

Air cleaner A metal or plastic housing, containing a filter element, which removes dust and dirt from the air being drawn into the engine.

Air filter element The actual filter in an air cleaner system, usually manufactured from pleated paper and requiring renewal at regular intervals.

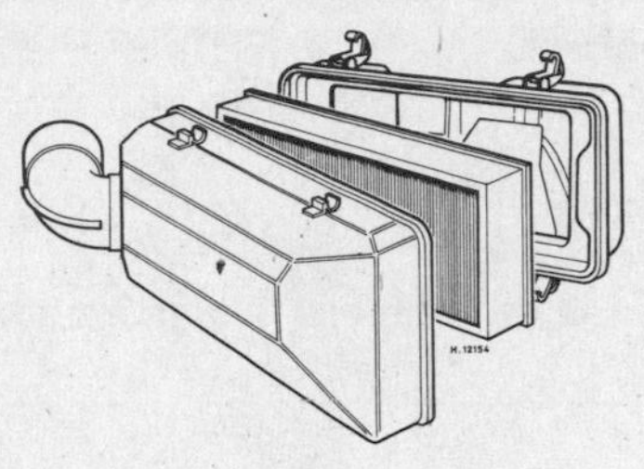

Air filter

Allen key A hexagonal wrench which fits into a recessed hexagonal hole.

Alligator clip A long-nosed spring-loaded metal clip with meshing teeth. Used to make temporary electrical connections.

Alternator A component in the electrical system which converts mechanical energy from a drivebelt into electrical energy to charge the battery and to operate the starting system, ignition system and electrical accessories.

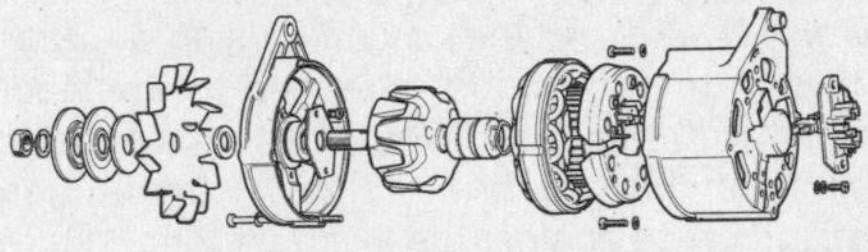

Alternator (exploded view)

Ampere (amp) A unit of measurement for the flow of electric current. One amp is the amount of current produced by one volt acting through a resistance of one ohm.

Anaerobic sealer A substance used to prevent bolts and screws from loosening. Anaerobic means that it does not require oxygen for activation. The Loctite brand is widely used.

Antifreeze A substance (usually ethylene glycol) mixed with water, and added to a vehicle's cooling system, to prevent freezing of the coolant in winter. Antifreeze also contains chemicals to inhibit corrosion and the formation of rust and other deposits that would tend to clog the radiator and coolant passages and reduce cooling efficiency.

Anti-seize compound A coating that reduces the risk of seizing on fasteners that are subjected to high temperatures, such as exhaust manifold bolts and nuts.

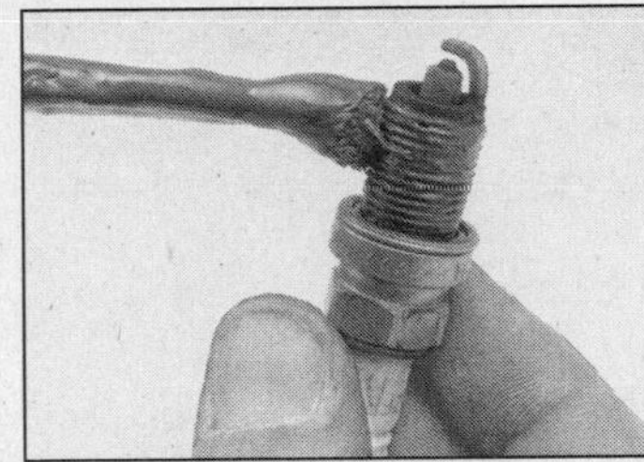

Anti-seize compound

Asbestos A natural fibrous mineral with great heat resistance, commonly used in the composition of brake friction materials. Asbestos is a health hazard and the dust created by brake systems should never be inhaled or ingested.

Axle A shaft on which a wheel revolves, or which revolves with a wheel. Also, a solid beam that connects the two wheels at one end of the vehicle. An axle which also transmits power to the wheels is known as a live axle.

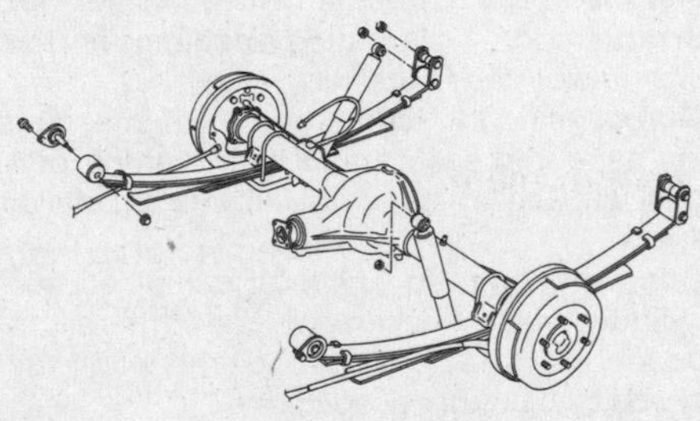

Axle assembly

Axleshaft A single rotating shaft, on either side of the differential, which delivers power from the final drive assembly to the drive wheels. Also called a driveshaft or a halfshaft.

B

Ball bearing An anti-friction bearing consisting of a hardened inner and outer race with hardened steel balls between two races.

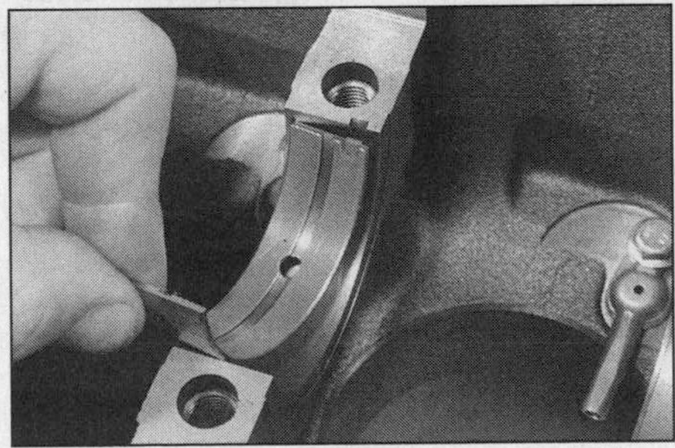

Bearing

Bearing The curved surface on a shaft or in a bore, or the part assembled into either, that permits relative motion between them with minimum wear and friction.

Big-end bearing The bearing in the end of the connecting rod that's attached to the crankshaft.

Bleed nipple A valve on a brake wheel cylinder, caliper or other hydraulic component that is opened to purge the hydraulic system of air. Also called a bleed screw.

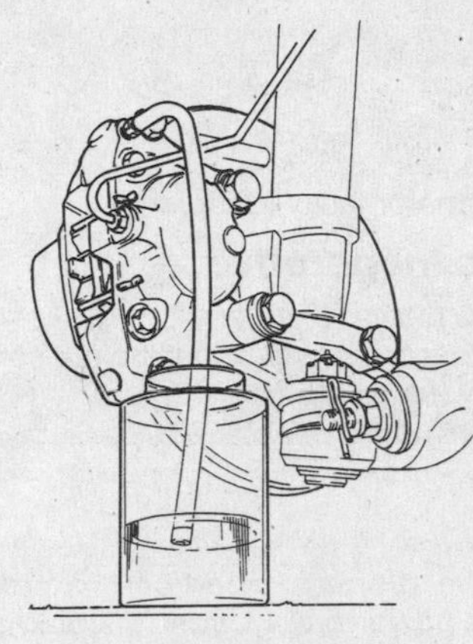

Brake bleeding

Brake bleeding Procedure for removing air from lines of a hydraulic brake system.

Brake disc The component of a disc brake that rotates with the wheels.

Brake drum The component of a drum brake that rotates with the wheels.

Brake linings The friction material which contacts the brake disc or drum to retard the vehicle's speed. The linings are bonded or riveted to the brake pads or shoes.

Brake pads The replaceable friction pads that pinch the brake disc when the brakes are applied. Brake pads consist of a friction material bonded or riveted to a rigid backing plate.

Brake shoe The crescent-shaped carrier to which the brake linings are mounted and which forces the lining against the rotating drum during braking.

Braking systems For more information on braking systems, consult the *Haynes Automotive Brake Manual*.

Breaker bar A long socket wrench handle providing greater leverage.

Bulkhead The insulated partition between the engine and the passenger compartment.

C

Caliper The non-rotating part of a disc-brake assembly that straddles the disc and carries the brake pads. The caliper also contains the hydraulic components that cause the pads to pinch the disc when the brakes are applied. A caliper is also a measuring tool that can be set to measure inside or outside dimensions of an object.

Camshaft A rotating shaft on which a series of cam lobes operate the valve mechanisms. The camshaft may be driven by gears, by sprockets and chain or by sprockets and a belt.

Canister A container in an evaporative emission control system; contains activated charcoal granules to trap vapours from the fuel system.

Canister

Carburettor A device which mixes fuel with air in the proper proportions to provide a desired power output from a spark ignition internal combustion engine.

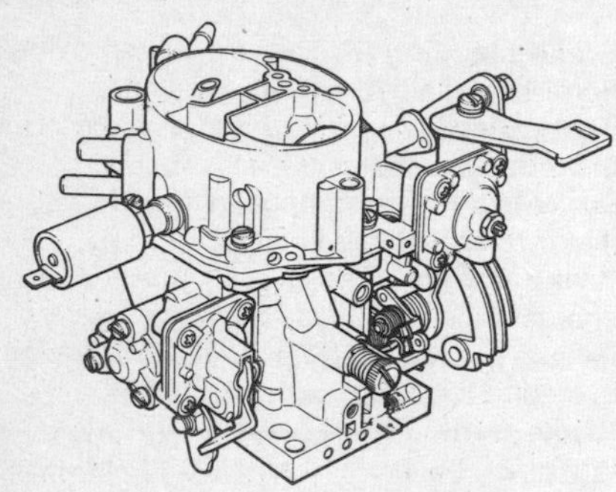

Carburettor

Castellated Resembling the parapets along the top of a castle wall. For example, a castellated balljoint stud nut.

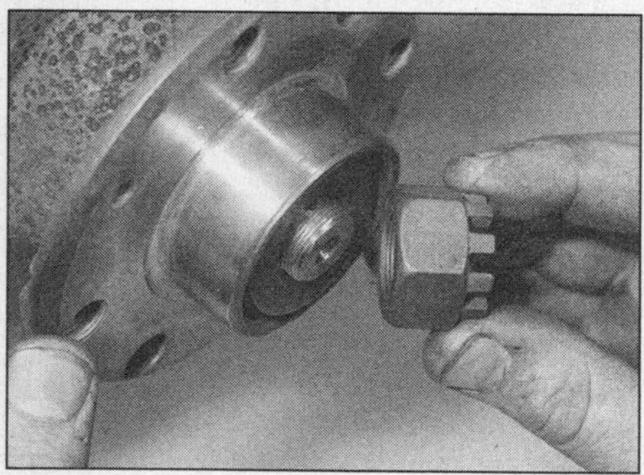

Castellated nut

Castor In wheel alignment, the backward or forward tilt of the steering axis. Castor is positive when the steering axis is inclined rearward at the top.

Catalytic converter A silencer-like device in the exhaust system which converts certain pollutants in the exhaust gases into less harmful substances.

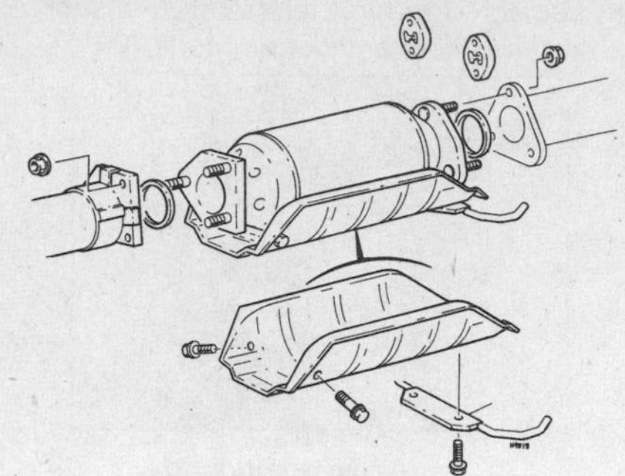

Catalytic converter

Circlip A ring-shaped clip used to prevent endwise movement of cylindrical parts and shafts. An internal circlip is installed in a groove in a housing; an external circlip fits into a groove on the outside of a cylindrical piece such as a shaft.

Clearance The amount of space between two parts. For example, between a piston and a cylinder, between a bearing and a journal, etc.

Coil spring A spiral of elastic steel found in various sizes throughout a vehicle, for example as a springing medium in the suspension and in the valve train.

Compression Reduction in volume, and increase in pressure and temperature, of a gas, caused by squeezing it into a smaller space.

Compression ratio The relationship between cylinder volume when the piston is at top dead centre and cylinder volume when the piston is at bottom dead centre.

Constant velocity (CV) joint A type of universal joint that cancels out vibrations caused by driving power being transmitted through an angle.

Core plug A disc or cup-shaped metal device inserted in a hole in a casting through which core was removed when the casting was formed. Also known as a freeze plug or expansion plug.

Crankcase The lower part of the engine block in which the crankshaft rotates.

Crankshaft The main rotating member, or shaft, running the length of the crankcase, with offset "throws" to which the connecting rods are attached.

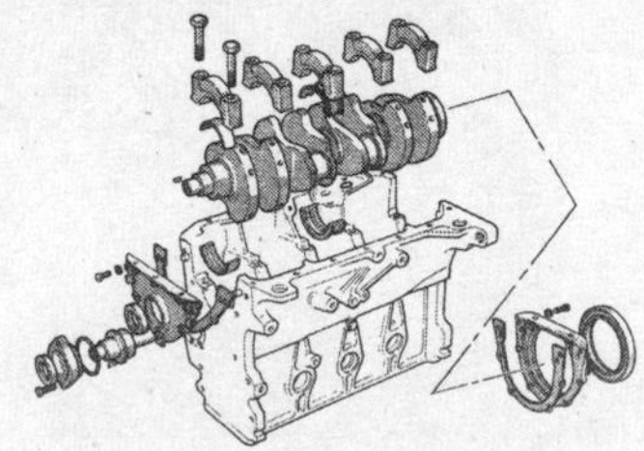

Crankshaft assembly

Crocodile clip See Alligator clip

D

Diagnostic code Code numbers obtained by accessing the diagnostic mode of an engine management computer. This code can be used to determine the area in the system where a malfunction may be located.

Disc brake A brake design incorporating a rotating disc onto which brake pads are squeezed. The resulting friction converts the energy of a moving vehicle into heat.

Double-overhead cam (DOHC) An engine that uses two overhead camshafts, usually one for the intake valves and one for the exhaust valves.

Drivebelt(s) The belt(s) used to drive accessories such as the alternator, water pump, power steering pump, air conditioning compressor, etc. off the crankshaft pulley.

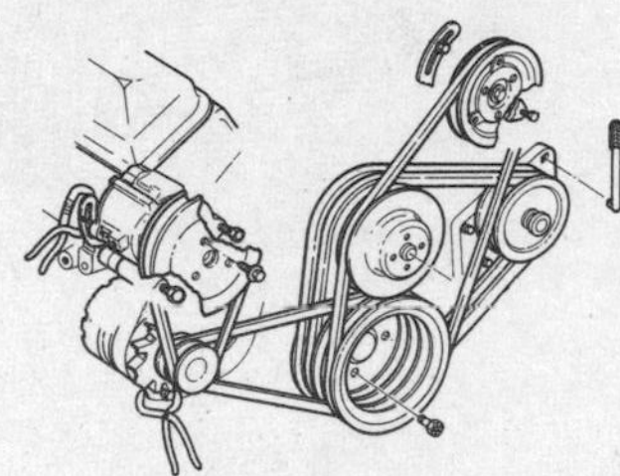

Accessory drivebelts

Driveshaft Any shaft used to transmit motion. Commonly used when referring to the axleshafts on a front wheel drive vehicle.

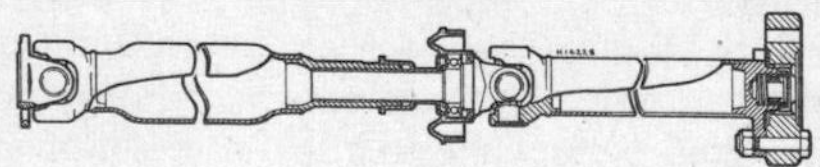

Driveshaft

Drum brake A type of brake using a drum-shaped metal cylinder attached to the inner surface of the wheel. When the brake pedal is pressed, curved brake shoes with friction linings press against the inside of the drum to slow or stop the vehicle.

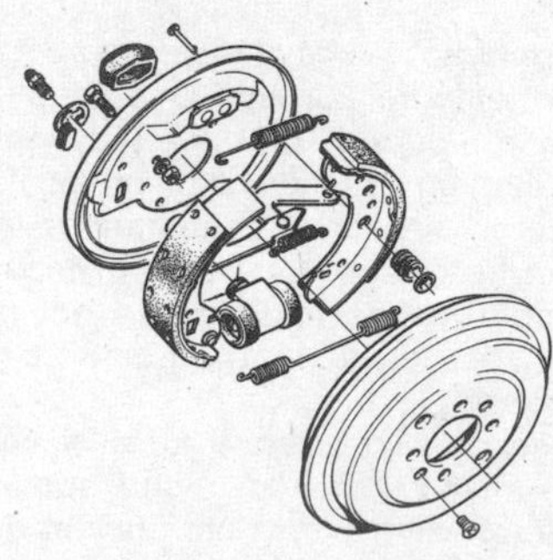

Drum brake assembly

E

EGR valve A valve used to introduce exhaust gases into the intake air stream.

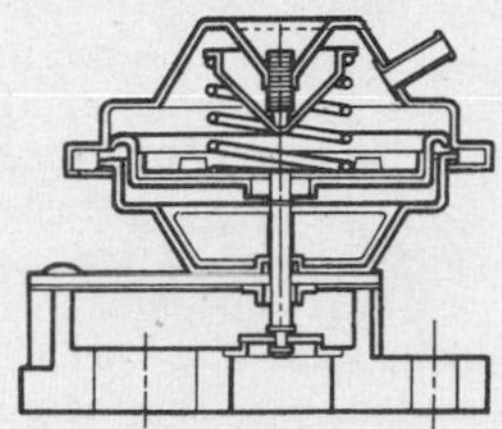

EGR valve

Electronic control unit (ECU) A computer which controls (for instance) ignition and fuel injection systems, or an anti-lock braking system. For more information refer to the *Haynes Automotive Electrical and Electronic Systems Manual.*

Electronic Fuel Injection (EFI) A computer controlled fuel system that distributes fuel through an injector located in each intake port of the engine.

Emergency brake A braking system, independent of the main hydraulic system, that can be used to slow or stop the vehicle if the primary brakes fail, or to hold the vehicle stationary even though the brake pedal isn't depressed. It usually consists of a hand lever that actuates either front or rear brakes mechanically through a series of cables and linkages. Also known as a handbrake or parking brake.

Endfloat The amount of lengthwise movement between two parts. As applied to a crankshaft, the distance that the crankshaft can move forward and back in the cylinder block.

Engine management system (EMS) A computer controlled system which manages the fuel injection and the ignition systems in an integrated fashion.

Exhaust manifold A part with several passages through which exhaust gases leave the engine combustion chambers and enter the exhaust pipe.

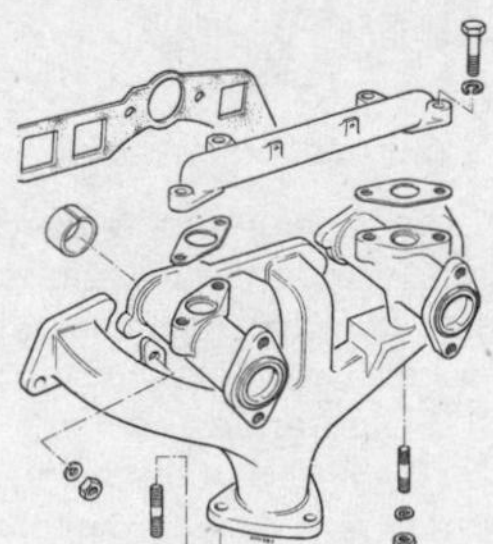

Exhaust manifold

F

Fan clutch A viscous (fluid) drive coupling device which permits variable engine fan speeds in relation to engine speeds.

Feeler blade A thin strip or blade of hardened steel, ground to an exact thickness, used to check or measure clearances between parts.

Feeler blade

Firing order The order in which the engine cylinders fire, or deliver their power strokes, beginning with the number one cylinder.

Flywheel A heavy spinning wheel in which energy is absorbed and stored by means of momentum. On cars, the flywheel is attached to the crankshaft to smooth out firing impulses.

Free play The amount of travel before any action takes place. The "looseness" in a linkage, or an assembly of parts, between the initial application of force and actual movement. For example, the distance the brake pedal moves before the pistons in the master cylinder are actuated.

Fuse An electrical device which protects a circuit against accidental overload. The typical fuse contains a soft piece of metal which is calibrated to melt at a predetermined current flow (expressed as amps) and break the circuit.

Fusible link A circuit protection device consisting of a conductor surrounded by heat-resistant insulation. The conductor is smaller than the wire it protects, so it acts as the weakest link in the circuit. Unlike a blown fuse, a failed fusible link must frequently be cut from the wire for replacement.

G

Gap The distance the spark must travel in jumping from the centre electrode to the side electrode in a spark plug. Also refers to the spacing between the points in a contact breaker assembly in a conventional points-type ignition, or to the distance between the reluctor or rotor and the pickup coil in an electronic ignition.

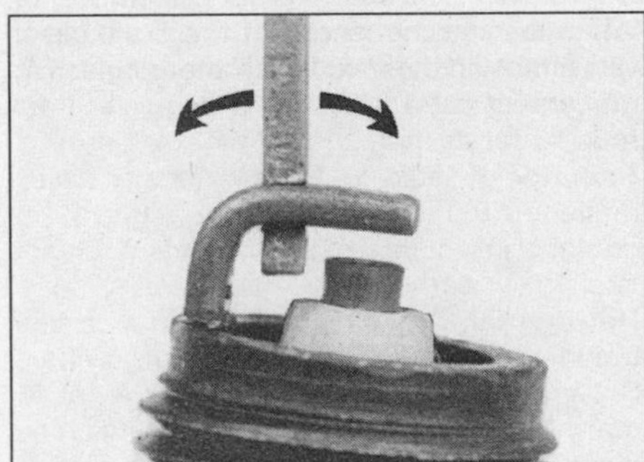

Adjusting spark plug gap

Gasket Any thin, soft material - usually cork, cardboard, asbestos or soft metal - installed between two metal surfaces to ensure a good seal. For instance, the cylinder head gasket seals the joint between the block and the cylinder head.

Gasket

Gauge An instrument panel display used to monitor engine conditions. A gauge with a movable pointer on a dial or a fixed scale is an analogue gauge. A gauge with a numerical readout is called a digital gauge.

H

Halfshaft A rotating shaft that transmits power from the final drive unit to a drive wheel, usually when referring to a live rear axle.

Harmonic balancer A device designed to reduce torsion or twisting vibration in the crankshaft. May be incorporated in the crankshaft pulley. Also known as a vibration damper.

Hone An abrasive tool for correcting small irregularities or differences in diameter in an engine cylinder, brake cylinder, etc.

Hydraulic tappet A tappet that utilises hydraulic pressure from the engine's lubrication system to maintain zero clearance (constant contact with both camshaft and valve stem). Automatically adjusts to variation in valve stem length. Hydraulic tappets also reduce valve noise.

I

Ignition timing The moment at which the spark plug fires, usually expressed in the number of crankshaft degrees before the piston reaches the top of its stroke.

Inlet manifold A tube or housing with passages through which flows the air-fuel mixture (carburettor vehicles and vehicles with throttle body injection) or air only (port fuel-injected vehicles) to the port openings in the cylinder head.

J

Jump start Starting the engine of a vehicle with a discharged or weak battery by attaching jump leads from the weak battery to a charged or helper battery.

L

Load Sensing Proportioning Valve (LSPV) A brake hydraulic system control valve that works like a proportioning valve, but also takes into consideration the amount of weight carried by the rear axle.

Locknut A nut used to lock an adjustment nut, or other threaded component, in place. For example, a locknut is employed to keep the adjusting nut on the rocker arm in position.

Lockwasher A form of washer designed to prevent an attaching nut from working loose.

M

MacPherson strut A type of front suspension system devised by Earle MacPherson at Ford of England. In its original form, a simple lateral link with the anti-roll bar creates the lower control arm. A long strut - an integral coil spring and shock absorber - is mounted between the body and the steering knuckle. Many modern so-called MacPherson strut systems use a conventional lower A-arm and don't rely on the anti-roll bar for location.

Multimeter An electrical test instrument with the capability to measure voltage, current and resistance.

N

NOx Oxides of Nitrogen. A common toxic pollutant emitted by petrol and diesel engines at higher temperatures.

O

Ohm The unit of electrical resistance. One volt applied to a resistance of one ohm will produce a current of one amp.

Ohmmeter An instrument for measuring electrical resistance.

O-ring A type of sealing ring made of a special rubber-like material; in use, the O-ring is compressed into a groove to provide the sealing action.

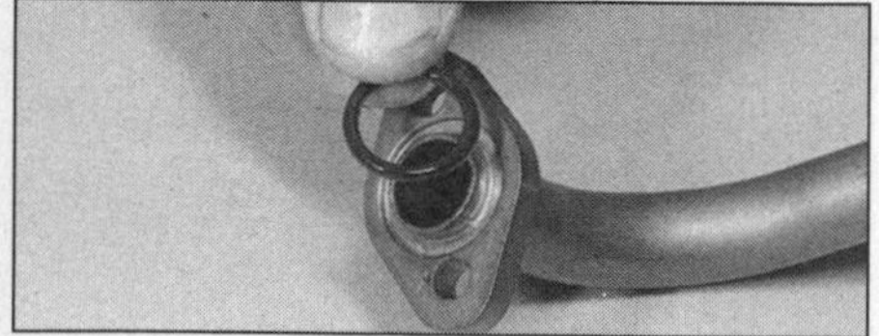

O-ring

Overhead cam (ohc) engine An engine with the camshaft(s) located on top of the cylinder head(s).

Overhead valve (ohv) engine An engine with the valves located in the cylinder head, but with the camshaft located in the engine block.

Oxygen sensor A device installed in the engine exhaust manifold, which senses the oxygen content in the exhaust and converts this information into an electric current. Also called a Lambda sensor.

P

Phillips screw A type of screw head having a cross instead of a slot for a corresponding type of screwdriver.

Plastigage A thin strip of plastic thread, available in different sizes, used for measuring clearances. For example, a strip of Plastigage is laid across a bearing journal. The parts are assembled and dismantled; the width of the crushed strip indicates the clearance between journal and bearing.

Plastigage

Propeller shaft The long hollow tube with universal joints at both ends that carries power from the transmission to the differential on front-engined rear wheel drive vehicles.

Proportioning valve A hydraulic control valve which limits the amount of pressure to the rear brakes during panic stops to prevent wheel lock-up.

R

Rack-and-pinion steering A steering system with a pinion gear on the end of the steering shaft that mates with a rack (think of a geared wheel opened up and laid flat). When the steering wheel is turned, the pinion turns, moving the rack to the left or right. This movement is transmitted through the track rods to the steering arms at the wheels.

Radiator A liquid-to-air heat transfer device designed to reduce the temperature of the coolant in an internal combustion engine cooling system.

Refrigerant Any substance used as a heat transfer agent in an air-conditioning system. R-12 has been the principle refrigerant for many years; recently, however, manufacturers have begun using R-134a, a non-CFC substance that is considered less harmful to the ozone in the upper atmosphere.

Rocker arm A lever arm that rocks on a shaft or pivots on a stud. In an overhead valve engine, the rocker arm converts the upward movement of the pushrod into a downward movement to open a valve.

Rotor In a distributor, the rotating device inside the cap that connects the centre electrode and the outer terminals as it turns, distributing the high voltage from the coil secondary winding to the proper spark plug. Also, that part of an alternator which rotates inside the stator. Also, the rotating assembly of a turbocharger, including the compressor wheel, shaft and turbine wheel.

Runout The amount of wobble (in-and-out movement) of a gear or wheel as it's rotated. The amount a shaft rotates "out-of-true." The out-of-round condition of a rotating part.

S

Sealant A liquid or paste used to prevent leakage at a joint. Sometimes used in conjunction with a gasket.

Sealed beam lamp An older headlight design which integrates the reflector, lens and filaments into a hermetically-sealed one-piece unit. When a filament burns out or the lens cracks, the entire unit is simply replaced.

Serpentine drivebelt A single, long, wide accessory drivebelt that's used on some newer vehicles to drive all the accessories, instead of a series of smaller, shorter belts. Serpentine drivebelts are usually tensioned by an automatic tensioner.

Serpentine drivebelt

Shim Thin spacer, commonly used to adjust the clearance or relative positions between two parts. For example, shims inserted into or under bucket tappets control valve clearances. Clearance is adjusted by changing the thickness of the shim.

Slide hammer A special puller that screws into or hooks onto a component such as a shaft or bearing; a heavy sliding handle on the shaft bottoms against the end of the shaft to knock the component free.

Sprocket A tooth or projection on the periphery of a wheel, shaped to engage with a chain or drivebelt. Commonly used to refer to the sprocket wheel itself.

Starter inhibitor switch On vehicles with an automatic transmission, a switch that prevents starting if the vehicle is not in Neutral or Park.

Strut See MacPherson strut.

T

Tappet A cylindrical component which transmits motion from the cam to the valve stem, either directly or via a pushrod and rocker arm. Also called a cam follower.

Thermostat A heat-controlled valve that regulates the flow of coolant between the cylinder block and the radiator, so maintaining optimum engine operating temperature. A thermostat is also used in some air cleaners in which the temperature is regulated.

Thrust bearing The bearing in the clutch assembly that is moved in to the release levers by clutch pedal action to disengage the clutch. Also referred to as a release bearing.

Timing belt A toothed belt which drives the camshaft. Serious engine damage may result if it breaks in service.

Timing chain A chain which drives the camshaft.

Toe-in The amount the front wheels are closer together at the front than at the rear. On rear wheel drive vehicles, a slight amount of toe-in is usually specified to keep the front wheels running parallel on the road by offsetting other forces that tend to spread the wheels apart.

Toe-out The amount the front wheels are closer together at the rear than at the front. On front wheel drive vehicles, a slight amount of toe-out is usually specified.

Tools For full information on choosing and using tools, refer to the *Haynes Automotive Tools Manual*.

Tracer A stripe of a second colour applied to a wire insulator to distinguish that wire from another one with the same colour insulator.

Tune-up A process of accurate and careful adjustments and parts replacement to obtain the best possible engine performance.

Turbocharger A centrifugal device, driven by exhaust gases, that pressurises the intake air. Normally used to increase the power output from a given engine displacement, but can also be used primarily to reduce exhaust emissions (as on VW's "Umwelt" Diesel engine).

U

Universal joint or U-joint A double-pivoted connection for transmitting power from a driving to a driven shaft through an angle. A U-joint consists of two Y-shaped yokes and a cross-shaped member called the spider.

V

Valve A device through which the flow of liquid, gas, vacuum, or loose material in bulk may be started, stopped, or regulated by a movable part that opens, shuts, or partially obstructs one or more ports or passageways. A valve is also the movable part of such a device.

Valve clearance The clearance between the valve tip (the end of the valve stem) and the rocker arm or tappet. The valve clearance is measured when the valve is closed.

Vernier caliper A precision measuring instrument that measures inside and outside dimensions. Not quite as accurate as a micrometer, but more convenient.

Viscosity The thickness of a liquid or its resistance to flow.

Volt A unit for expressing electrical "pressure" in a circuit. One volt that will produce a current of one ampere through a resistance of one ohm.

W

Welding Various processes used to join metal items by heating the areas to be joined to a molten state and fusing them together. For more information refer to the *Haynes Automotive Welding Manual.*

Wiring diagram A drawing portraying the components and wires in a vehicle's electrical system, using standardised symbols. For more information refer to the *Haynes Automotive Electrical and Electronic Systems Manual.*

Index

Note: *References throughout this index are in the form - "Chapter number" • "Page number"*

D

E

F

G

H

Haynes Manuals – The Complete List

Title	Book No.
ALFA ROMEO	
Alfa Romeo Alfasud/Sprint (74 - 88) up to F	0292
Alfa Romeo Alfetta (73 - 87) up to E	0531
AUDI	
Audi 80 (72 - Feb 79) up to T	0207
Audi 80, 90 (79 - Oct 86) up to D & Coupe (81 - Nov 88) up to F	0605
Audi 80, 90 (Oct 86 - 90) D to H & Coupe (Nov 88 - 90) F to H	1491
Audi 100 (Oct 82 - 90) up to H & 200 (Feb 84 - Oct 89) A to G	0907
Audi 100 & A6 Petrol & Diesel (May 91 - May 97) H to P	3504
Audi A4 (95 - Feb 00) M to V	3575
AUSTIN	
Austin A35 & A40 (56 - 67) *	0118
Austin Allegro 1100, 1300, 1.0, 1.1 & 1.3 (73 - 82)*	0164
Austin Healey 100/6 & 3000 (56 - 68) *	0049
Austin/MG/Rover Maestro 1.3 & 1.6 (83 - May 95) up to M	0922
Austin/MG Metro (80 - May 90) up to G	0718
Austin/Rover Montego 1.3 & 1.6 (84 - 94) A to L	1066
Austin/MG/Rover Montego 2.0 (84 - 95) A to M	1067
Mini (59 - 69) up to H	0527
Mini (69 - Oct 96) up to P	0646
Austin/Rover 2.0 litre Diesel Engine (86 - 93) C to L	1857
BEDFORD	
Bedford CF (69 - 87) up to E	0163
Bedford/Vauxhall Rascal & Suzuki Supercarry (86 - Oct 94) C to M	3015
BMW	
BMW 1500, 1502, 1600, 1602, 2000 & 2002 (59 - 77)*	0240
BMW 316, 320 & 320i (4-cyl) (75 - Feb 83) up to Y	0276
BMW 320, 320i, 323i & 325i (6-cyl) (Oct 77 - Sept 87) up to E	0815
BMW 3-Series (Apr 91 - 96) H to N	3210
BMW 3- & 5-Series (sohc) (81 - 91) up to J	1948
BMW 520i & 525e (Oct 81 - June 88) up to E	1560
BMW 525, 528 & 528i (73 - Sept 81) up to X	0632
CITROËN	
Citroën 2CV, Ami & Dyane (67 - 90) up to H	0196
Citroën AX Petrol & Diesel (87 - 97) D to P	3014
Citroën BX (83 - 94) A to L	0908
Citroën C15 Van Petrol & Diesel (89 - Oct 98) F to S	3509
Citroën CX (75 - 88) up to F	0528
Citroën Saxo Petrol & Diesel (96 - 01) N to X	3506
Citroën Visa (79 - 88) up to F	0620
Citroën Xantia Petrol & Diesel (93 - 98) K to S	3082
Citroën XM Petrol & Diesel (89 - 00) G to X	3451
Citroën Xsara Petrol & Diesel (97 - Sept 00) R to W	3751
Citroën ZX Diesel (91 - 98) J to S	1922
Citroën ZX Petrol (91 - 98) H to S	1881
Citroën 1.7 & 1.9 litre Diesel Engine (84 - 96) A to N	1379
FIAT	
Fiat 126 (73 - 87) *	0305
Fiat 500 (57 - 73) up to M	0090
Fiat Bravo & Brava (95 - 00) N to W	3572
Fiat Cinquecento (93 - 98) K to R	3501
Fiat Panda (81 - 95) up to M	0793
Fiat Punto Petrol & Diesel (94 - Oct 99) L to V	3251
Fiat Regata (84 - 88) A to F	1167
Fiat Tipo (88 - 91) E to J	1625
Fiat Uno (83 - 95) up to M	0923
Fiat X1/9 (74 - 89) up to G	0273
FORD	
Ford Anglia (59 - 68) *	0001
Ford Capri II (& III) 1.6 & 2.0 (74 - 87) up to E	0283
Ford Capri II (& III) 2.8 & 3.0 (74 - 87) up to E	1309
Ford Cortina Mk III 1300 & 1600 (70 - 76) *	0070
Ford Cortina Mk IV (& V) 1.6 & 2.0 (76 - 83) *	0343
Ford Cortina Mk IV (& V) 2.3 V6 (77 - 83) *	0426
Ford Escort Mk I 1100 & 1300 (68 - 74) *	0171
Ford Escort Mk I Mexico, RS 1600 & RS 2000 (70 - 74)*	0139
Ford Escort Mk II Mexico, RS 1800 & RS 2000 (75 - 80)*	0735
Ford Escort (75 - Aug 80) *	0280
Ford Escort (Sept 80 - Sept 90) up to H	0686
Ford Escort & Orion (Sept 90 - 00) H to X	1737
Ford Fiesta (76 - Aug 83) up to Y	0334
Ford Fiesta (Aug 83 - Feb 89) A to F	1030
Ford Fiesta (Feb 89 - Oct 95) F to N	1595
Ford Fiesta (Oct 95 - 01) N-reg. onwards	3397
Ford Focus (98 - 01) S to Y	3759
Ford Granada (Sept 77 - Feb 85) up to B	0481
Ford Granada & Scorpio (Mar 85 - 94) B to M	1245
Ford Ka (96 - 02) P-reg. onwards	3570
Ford Mondeo Petrol (93 - 99) K to T	1923
Ford Mondeo Diesel (93 - 96) L to N	3465
Ford Orion (83 - Sept 90) up to H	1009
Ford Sierra 4 cyl. (82 - 93) up to K	0903
Ford Sierra V6 (82 - 91) up to J	0904
Ford Transit Petrol (Mk 2) (78 - Jan 86) up to C	0719
Ford Transit Petrol (Mk 3) (Feb 86 - 89) C to G	1468
Ford Transit Diesel (Feb 86 - 99) C to T	3019
Ford 1.6 & 1.8 litre Diesel Engine (84 - 96) A to N	1172
Ford 2.1, 2.3 & 2.5 litre Diesel Engine (77 - 90) up to H	1606
FREIGHT ROVER	
Freight Rover Sherpa (74 - 87) up to E	0463
HILLMAN	
Hillman Avenger (70 - 82) up to Y	0037
Hillman Imp (63 - 76) *	0022
HONDA	
Honda Accord (76 - Feb 84) up to A	0351
Honda Civic (Feb 84 - Oct 87) A to E	1226
Honda Civic (Nov 91 - 96) J to N	3199
HYUNDAI	
Hyundai Pony (85 - 94) C to M	3398
JAGUAR	
Jaguar E Type (61 - 72) up to L	0140
Jaguar MkI & II, 240 & 340 (55 - 69) *	0098
Jaguar XJ6, XJ & Sovereign; Daimler Sovereign (68 - Oct 86) up to D	0242
Jaguar XJ6 & Sovereign (Oct 86 - Sept 94) D to M	3261
Jaguar XJ12, XJS & Sovereign; Daimler Double Six (72 - 88) up to F	0478
JEEP	
Jeep Cherokee Petrol (93 - 96) K to N	1943
LADA	
Lada 1200, 1300, 1500 & 1600 (74 - 91) up to J	0413
Lada Samara (87 - 91) D to J	1610
LAND ROVER	
Land Rover 90, 110 & Defender Diesel (83 - 95) up to N	3017
Land Rover Discovery Petrol & Diesel (89 - 98) G to S	3016
Land Rover Series IIA & III Diesel (58 - 85) up to C	0529
Land Rover Series II, IIA & III Petrol (58 - 85) up to C	0314
MAZDA	
Mazda 323 (Mar 81 - Oct 89) up to G	1608
Mazda 323 (Oct 89 - 98) G to R	3455
Mazda 626 (May 83 - Sept 87) up to E	0929
Mazda B-1600, B-1800 & B-2000 Pick-up (72 - 88) up to F	0267
Mazda RX-7 (79 - 85) *	0460
MERCEDES-BENZ	
Mercedes-Benz 190, 190E & 190D Petrol & Diesel (83 - 93) A to L	3450
Mercedes-Benz 200, 240, 300 Diesel (Oct 76 - 85) up to C	1114
Mercedes-Benz 250 & 280 (68 - 72) up to L	0346
Mercedes-Benz 250 & 280 (123 Series) (Oct 76 - 84) up to B	0677
Mercedes-Benz 124 Series (85 - Aug 93) C to K	3253
Mercedes-Benz C-Class Petrol & Diesel (93 - Aug 00) L to W	3511
MG	
MGA (55 - 62) *	0475
MGB (62 - 80) up to W	0111
MG Midget & AH Sprite (58 - 80) up to W	0265
MITSUBISHI	
Mitsubishi Shogun & L200 Pick-Ups (83 - 94) up to M	1944
MORRIS	
Morris Ital 1.3 (80 - 84) up to B	0705
Morris Minor 1000 (56 - 71) up to K	0024
NISSAN	
Nissan Bluebird (May 84 - Mar 86) A to C	1223
Nissan Bluebird (Mar 86 - 90) C to H	1473
Nissan Cherry (Sept 82 - 86) up to D	1031
Nissan Micra (83 - Jan 93) up to K	0931
Nissan Micra (93 - 99) K to T	3254
Nissan Primera (90 - Aug 99) H to T	1851
Nissan Stanza (82 - 86) up to D	0824
Nissan Sunny (May 82 - Oct 86) up to D	0895
Nissan Sunny (Oct 86 - Mar 91) D to H	1378
Nissan Sunny (Apr 91 - 95) H to N	3219
OPEL	
Opel Ascona & Manta (B Series) (Sept 75 - 88) up to F	0316
Opel Ascona (81 - 88) *(Not available in UK see Vauxhall Cavalier 0812)*	3215
Opel Astra (Oct 91 - Feb 98) *(Not available in UK see Vauxhall Astra 1832)*	3156
Opel Astra & Zafira Diesel (Feb 98 - Sept 00) *(See Astra & Zafira Diesel Book No. 3797)*	
Opel Astra & Zafira Petrol (Feb 98 - Sept 00) *(See Vauxhall/Opel Astra & Zafira Petrol Book No. 3758)*	
Opel Calibra (90 - 98) *(See Vauxhall/Opel Calibra Book No. 3502)*	
Opel Corsa (83 - Mar 93) *(Not available in UK see Vauxhall Nova 0909)*	3160
Opel Corsa (Mar 93 - 97) *(Not available in UK see Vauxhall Corsa 1985)*	3159
Opel Frontera Petrol & Diesel (91 - 98) *(See Vauxhall/Opel Frontera Book No. 3454)*	
Opel Kadett (Nov 79 - Oct 84) up to B	0634
Opel Kadett (Oct 84 - Oct 91) *(Not available in UK see Vauxhall Astra & Belmont 1136)*	3196
Opel Omega & Senator (86 - 94) *(Not available in UK see Vauxhall Carlton & Senator 1469)*	3157
Opel Omega (94 - 99) *(See Vauxhall/Opel Omega Book No. 3510)*	
Opel Rekord (Feb 78 - Oct 86) up to D	0543
Opel Vectra (Oct 88 - Oct 95) *(Not available in UK see Vauxhall Cavalier 1570)*	3158
Opel Vectra Petrol & Diesel (95 - 98) *(Not available in UK see Vauxhall Vectra 3396)*	3523
PEUGEOT	
Peugeot 106 Petrol & Diesel (91 - 01) J to X	1882
Peugeot 205 Petrol (83 - 97) A to P	0932
Peugeot 206 Petrol and Diesel (98 - 01) S to X	3757
Peugeot 305 (78 - 89) up to G	0538

* Classic reprint

Title	Book No.
Peugeot 306 Petrol & Diesel (93 - 99) K to T	**3073**
Peugeot 309 (86 - 93) C to K	**1266**
Peugeot 405 Petrol (88 - 97) E to P	**1559**
Peugeot 405 Diesel (88 - 97) E to P	**3198**
Peugeot 406 Petrol & Diesel (96 - 97) N to R	**3394**
Peugeot 505 (79 - 89) up to G	**0762**
Peugeot 1.7/1.8 & 1.9 litre Diesel Engine (82 - 96) up to N	**0950**
Peugeot 2.0, 2.1, 2.3 & 2.5 litre Diesel Engines (74 - 90) up to H	**1607**
PORSCHE	
Porsche 911 (65 - 85) up to C	**0264**
Porsche 924 & 924 Turbo (76 - 85) up to C	**0397**
PROTON	
Proton (89 - 97) F to P	**3255**
RANGE ROVER	
Range Rover V8 (70 - Oct 92) up to K	**0606**
RELIANT	
Reliant Robin & Kitten (73 - 83) up to A	**0436**
RENAULT	
Renault 4 (61 - 86) *	**0072**
Renault 5 (Feb 85 - 96) B to N	**1219**
Renault 9 & 11 (82 - 89) up to F	**0822**
Renault 18 (79 - 86) up to D	**0598**
Renault 19 Petrol (89 - 94) F to M	**1646**
Renault 19 Diesel (89 - 96) F to N	**1946**
Renault 21 (86 - 94) C to M	**1397**
Renault 25 (84 - 92) B to K	**1228**
Renault Clio Petrol (91 - May 98) H to R	**1853**
Renault Clio Diesel (91 - June 96) H to N	**3031**
Renault Clio Petrol & Diesel (May 98 - May 01) R to Y	**3906**
Renault Espace Petrol & Diesel (85 - 96) C to N	**3197**
Renault Fuego (80 - 86) *	**0764**
Renault Laguna Petrol & Diesel (94 - 00) L to W	**3252**
Renault Mégane & Scénic Petrol & Diesel (96 - 98) N to R	**3395**
Renault Mégane & Scénic (Apr 99 - 02) T-reg onwards	**3916**
ROVER	
Rover 213 & 216 (84 - 89) A to G	**1116**
Rover 214 & 414 (89 - 96) G to N	**1689**
Rover 216 & 416 (89 - 96) G to N	**1830**
Rover 211, 214, 216, 218 & 220 Petrol & Diesel (Dec 95 - 98) N to R	**3399**
Rover 414, 416 & 420 Petrol & Diesel (May 95 - 98) M to R	**3453**
Rover 618, 620 & 623 (93 - 97) K to P	**3257**
Rover 820, 825 & 827 (86 - 95) D to N	**1380**
Rover 3500 (76 - 87) up to E	**0365**
Rover Metro, 111 & 114 (May 90 - 98) G to S	**1711**
SAAB	
Saab 90, 99 & 900 (79 - Oct 93) up to L	**0765**
Saab 95 & 96 (66 - 76) *	**0198**
Saab 99 (69 - 79) *	**0247**
Saab 900 (Oct 93 - 98) L to R	**3512**
Saab 9000 (4-cyl) (85 - 98) C to S	**1686**
SEAT	
Seat Ibiza & Cordoba Petrol & Diesel (Oct 93 - Oct 99) L to V	**3571**
at Ibiza & Malaga (85 - 92) B to K	**1609**
ODA	
Estelle (77 - 89) up to G	**0604**
orit (89 - 96) F to N	**1801**
Petrol & Diesel (95 - 01) M to X	**3505**

Title	Book No.
SUBARU	
Subaru 1600 & 1800 (Nov 79 - 90) up to H	**0995**
SUNBEAM	
Sunbeam Alpine, Rapier & H120 (67 - 76) *	**0051**
SUZUKI	
Suzuki SJ Series, Samurai & Vitara (4-cyl) (82 - 97) up to P	**1942**
Suzuki Supercarry & Bedford/Vauxhall Rascal (86 - Oct 94) C to M	**3015**
TALBOT	
Talbot Alpine, Solara, Minx & Rapier (75 - 86) up to D	**0337**
Talbot Horizon (78 - 86) up to D	**0473**
Talbot Samba (82 - 86) up to D	**0823**
TOYOTA	
Toyota Carina E (May 92 - 97) J to P	**3256**
Toyota Corolla (Sept 83 - Sept 87) A to E	**1024**
Toyota Corolla (80 - 85) up to C	**0683**
Toyota Corolla (Sept 87 - Aug 92) E to K	**1683**
Toyota Corolla (Aug 92 - 97) K to P	**3259**
Toyota Hi-Ace & Hi-Lux (69 - Oct 83) up to A	**0304**
TRIUMPH	
Triumph Acclaim (81 - 84) *	**0792**
Triumph GT6 & Vitesse (62 - 74) *	**0112**
Triumph Herald (59 - 71) *	**0010**
Triumph Spitfire (62 - 81) up to X	**0113**
Triumph Stag (70 - 78) up to T	**0441**
Triumph TR2, TR3, TR3A, TR4 & TR4A (52 - 67)*	**0028**
Triumph TR5 & 6 (67 - 75) *	**0031**
Triumph TR7 (75 - 82) *	**0322**
VAUXHALL	
Vauxhall Astra (80 - Oct 84) up to B	**0635**
Vauxhall Astra & Belmont (Oct 84 - Oct 91) B to J	**1136**
Vauxhall Astra (Oct 91 - Feb 98) J to R	**1832**
Vauxhall/Opel Astra & Zafira Diesel (Feb 98 - Sept 00) R to W	**3797**
Vauxhall/Opel Astra & Zafira Petrol (Feb 98 - Sept 00) R to W	**3758**
Vauxhall/Opel Calibra (90 - 98) G to S	**3502**
Vauxhall Carlton (Oct 78 - Oct 86) up to D	**0480**
Vauxhall Carlton & Senator (Nov 86 - 94) D to L	**1469**
Vauxhall Cavalier 1300 (77 - July 81) *	**0461**
Vauxhall Cavalier 1600, 1900 & 2000 (75 - July 81) up to W	**0315**
Vauxhall Cavalier (81 - Oct 88) up to F	**0812**
Vauxhall Cavalier (Oct 88 - 95) F to N	**1570**
Vauxhall Chevette (75 - 84) up to B	**0285**
Vauxhall Corsa (Mar 93 - 97) K to R	**1985**
Vauxhall/Opel Corsa (Apr 97 - Oct 00) P to X	**3921**
Vauxhall/Opel Frontera Petrol & Diesel (91 - Sept 98) J to S	**3454**
Vauxhall Nova (83 - 93) up to K	**0909**
Vauxhall/Opel Omega (94 - 99) L to T	**3510**
Vauxhall Vectra Petrol & Diesel (95 - 98) N to R	**3396**
Vauxhall/Opel 1.5, 1.6 & 1.7 litre Diesel Engine (82 - 96) up to N	**1222**
VOLKSWAGEN	
Volkswagen 411 & 412 (68 - 75) *	**0091**
Volkswagen Beetle 1200 (54 - 77) up to S	**0036**
Volkswagen Beetle 1300 & 1500 (65 - 75) up to P	**0039**
Volkswagen Beetle 1302 & 1302S (70 - 72) up to L	**0110**
Volkswagen Beetle 1303, 1303S & GT (72 - 75) up to P	**0159**
Volkswagen Beetle Petrol & Diesel (Apr 99 - 01) T reg onwards	**3798**
Volkswagen Golf & Bora Petrol & Diesel (April 98 - 00) R to X	**3727**

Title	Book No.
Volkswagen Golf & Jetta Mk 1 1.1 & 1.3 (74 - 84) up to A	**0716**
Volkswagen Golf, Jetta & Scirocco Mk 1 1.5, 1.6 & 1.8 (74 - 84) up to A	**0726**
Volkswagen Golf & Jetta Mk 1 Diesel (78 - 84) up to A	**0451**
Volkswagen Golf & Jetta Mk 2 (Mar 84 - Feb 92) A to J	**1081**
Volkswagen Golf & Vento Petrol & Diesel (Feb 92 - 96) J to N	**3097**
Volkswagen LT vans & light trucks (76 - 87) up to E	**0637**
Volkswagen Passat & Santana (Sept 81 - May 88) up to E	**0814**
Volkswagen Passat Petrol & Diesel (May 88 - 96) E to P	**3498**
Volkswagen Passat 4-cyl Petrol & Diesel (Dec 96 - Nov 00) P to X	**3917**
Volkswagen Polo & Derby (76 - Jan 82) up to X	**0335**
Volkswagen Polo (82 - Oct 90) up to H	**0813**
Volkswagen Polo (Nov 90 - Aug 94) H to L	**3245**
Volkswagen Polo Hatchback Petrol & Diesel (94 - 99) M to S	**3500**
Volkswagen Scirocco (82 - 90) up to H	**1224**
Volkswagen Transporter 1600 (68 - 79) up to V	**0082**
Volkswagen Transporter 1700, 1800 & 2000 (72 - 79) up to V	**0226**
Volkswagen Transporter (air-cooled) (79 - 82) up to Y	**0638**
Volkswagen Transporter (water-cooled) (82 - 90) up to H	**3452**
Volkswagen Type 3 (63 - 73) *	**0084**
VOLVO	
Volvo 120 & 130 Series (& P1800) (61 - 73) *	**0203**
Volvo 142, 144 & 145 (66 - 74) up to N	**0129**
Volvo 240 Series (74 - 93) up to K	**0270**
Volvo 262, 264 & 260/265 (75 - 85) *	**0400**
Volvo 340, 343, 345 & 360 (76 - 91) up to J	**0715**
Volvo 440, 460 & 480 (87 - 97) D to P	**1691**
Volvo 740 & 760 (82 - 91) up to J	**1258**
Volvo 850 (92 - 96) J to P	**3260**
Volvo 940 (90 - 96) H to N	**3249**
Volvo S40 & V40 (96 - 99) N to V	**3569**
Volvo S70, V70 & C70 (96 - 99) P to V	**3573**
AUTOMOTIVE TECHBOOKS	
Automotive Air Conditioning Systems	**3740**
Automotive Brake Manual	**3050**
Automotive Carburettor Manual	**3288**
Automotive Diagnostic Fault Codes Manual	**3472**
Automotive Diesel Engine Service Guide	**3286**
Automotive Electrical and Electronic Systems Manual	**3049**
Automotive Engine Management and Fuel Injection Systems Manual	**3344**
Automotive Gearbox Overhaul Manual	**3473**
Automotive Service Summaries Manual	**3475**
Automotive Timing Belts Manual – Austin/Rover	**3549**
Automotive Timing Belts Manual – Ford	**3474**
Automotive Timing Belts Manual – Peugeot/Citroën	**3568**
Automotive Timing Belts Manual – Vauxhall/Opel	**3577**
Automotive Welding Manual	**30**
In-Car Entertainment Manual (3rd Edition)	**3**

* Classic r

ucts featured on this page are available through most motor accessory shops, cycle shops and book stores. Our policy of continuo development means that titles are being constantly added to the range. For up-to-date information on our complete list of titles, +44 1963 442030 • (USA) +1 805 498 6703 • (France) +33 1 47 78 50 50 • (Sweden) +46 18 124016 • (Australia) +61 3 97

Preserving Our Motoring Heritage

< *The Model J Duesenberg Derham Tourster. Only eight of these magnificent cars were ever built – this is the only example to be found outside the United States of America*

Almost every car you've ever loved, loathed or desired is gathered under one roof at the Haynes Motor Museum. Over 300 immaculately presented cars and motorbikes represent every aspect of our motoring heritage, from elegant reminders of bygone days, such as the superb Model J Duesenberg to curiosities like the bug-eyed BMW Isetta. There are also many old friends and flames. Perhaps you remember the 1959 Ford Popular that you did your courting in? The magnificent 'Red Collection' is a spectacle of classic sports cars including AC, Alfa Romeo, Austin Healey, Ferrari, Lamborghini, Maserati, MG, Riley, Porsche and Triumph.

A Perfect Day Out

Each and every vehicle at the Haynes Motor Museum has played its part in the history and culture of Motoring. Today, they make a wonderful spectacle and a great day out for all the family. Bring the kids, bring Mum and Dad, but above all bring your camera to capture those golden memories for ever. You will also find an impressive array of motoring memorabilia, a comfortable 70 seat video cinema and one of the most extensive transport book shops in Britain. The Pit Stop Cafe serves everything from a cup of tea to wholesome, home-made meals or, if you prefer, you can enjoy the large picnic area nestled in the beautiful rural surroundings of Somerset.

> *John Haynes O.B.E., Founder and Chairman of the museum at the wheel of a Haynes Light 12.*

< *Graham Hill's Lola Cosworth Formula 1 car next to a 1934 Riley Sports.*

MOTOR MUSEUM
A359 CASTLE CARY
A303 ANDOVER
SPARKFORD
A303 EXETER TO M5 J 25 TAUNTON
A359 YEOVIL
HAYNES PUBLISHING
OLD A303
NOT TO SCALE

is situated on the A359 Yeovil to Frome road at Sparkford, just off the A303 in Somerset. It is about 40 miles south of Bristol, and 25 minutes drive from the M5 intersection at Taunton.

30am - 5.30pm (10.00am - 4.00pm Winter) 7 days a week, *except Christmas Day, Boxing Day and New Years Day*

Special rates available for schools, coach parties and outings Charitable Trust No. 292048